Handbook of ICC Arbitration

Commentary, Precedents, Materials

Handbook of ICC Arbitration

Commentary, Precedents, Materials

Third Edition

Thomas H. Webster
Michael W. Bühler

SWEET & MAXWELL

THOMSON REUTERS

First edition 2005
Second edition 2008

Published in 2014 by Sweet & Maxwell, 100 Avenue Road, London, NW3 3PF
part of Thomson Reuters (Professional) UK Limited
(Registered in England & Wales, Company No 1679046.
Registered Office and address for service:
Aldgate House, 33 Aldgate High Street, London EC3N 1DL)
For further information on our products and services, visit
www.sweetandmaxwell.co.uk

Typeset by LBJ Typesetting Ltd of Kingsclere
Printed and bound by CPI Group (UK) Ltd, Croydon, CR0 4YY

No natural forests were destroyed to make this product; only farmed timber was used and replanted.

A CIP catalogue record for this book is available from the British Library

ISBN 978-0-414-04463-0

To Birgit and our boys Kevin,
Andreas and Anthony

To Federica and our girls
Stella and Chiara Bühler

PREFACE

One of the main focuses of this third edition is the new ICC Rules that have now been in force for two years. As discussed in the Introduction, the new ICC Rules have a number of significant provisions relating to issues of multiparty and multicontract arbitration (arts 7–10), case management (art.24 and App.IV) and emergency arbitration provisions (art.29 and App.V). The Rules now consist of 41 articles and five appendices. In addition, the ICC has issued numerous ancillary documents relating to ICC arbitration, most of which are provided in Part II and Part III of this book. These ancillary documents relate to issues such as how the proceedings should be conducted, to reimbursement of Tribunal expenses, to use of Secretaries of the Tribunal and include a checklist for ICC Awards. All of this material is relevant to how an ICC arbitration is to be conducted under the Rules and is therefore discussed in this Handbook.

In addition, the manner in which the ICC Court administers ICC arbitration is an important element and this Handbook seeks to promote that transparency by dealing in detail with the procedure and the decisions rendered by the ICC Court. As regards the procedure, Annex I to Part I describes the ICC Court's Plenary and Committee Sessions. As regards the substance of the ICC Court's decisions, the Handbook reflects years of experience on the Court deciding these types of issues. In this respect, it is of particular interest to review how the ICC Court confirms and selects arbitrators and how it deals with challenges and the nature of the scrutiny of Awards.

However, approaching ICC arbitration is much more complex, whether as counsel or arbitrator. The complexity is reflected in procedural orders and Awards issued by Tribunals. It is also reflected in the case law of the courts, whether the courts of the place of arbitration or the case of the place of enforcement. In scrutinising awards, the ICC Court "considers to the extent practicable, the requirements of the mandatory law at the place of arbitration" (art.6, App.II to the Rules) and the ICC Court and the Tribunal shall "make every effort to make sure that the award is enforceable at law" (art.41).

A key element of this Handbook is analysing how Tribunals seek to meet these requirements and how the state courts interpret legal requirements at the place of arbitration or the place of enforcement with respect to arbitration in general. As with the prior editions, this third edition focuses on the law applicable in the places where most ICC arbitrations take place: France, Switzerland, England, the United States and the UNCITRAL Model law countries. The latter category is expanding and becoming more important. The Handbook reflects and provides an English translation of the new French arbitration law. It discusses issues including how the state courts view ICC court decisions on challenges and on the obligations not dealt with in the ICC Rules, such as the collegiality amongst arbitrators. The Handbook also examines issues such as non-signatories and the differing treatment of the same Award in *Dallah Real Estate* in the UK Supreme Court[1] and the Paris Court of Appeal.[2] Another issue is whether it is for the Tribunal or the state court to interpret the scope of the arbitration clause and the US Supreme Court case of *Oxford Health Plans v Sutter* and, for England, once again *Dallah Real Estate*. The issue of enforcement of annulled awards has proceeded beyond the *Hilmarton* cases and is now the subject of cases such as *Termorio*[3] and *COMMISA*[4] in the United States and *Yukos Capital* in the UK.[5] In what may be a significant change of direction, the French Supreme Court has limited the scope of waivers of sovereign immunity in *NML v Argentina*.[6]

In addition to the ICC's internal material relating to arbitration, various other entities, such as the International Bar Association (IBA) and the International Law Association (ILA) have produced guidelines or recommendations that continue to be discussed and used in international arbitration. The IBA Rules on the Taking of Evidence in International Arbitration as revised in 2010 have become a standard point of reference for arbitration procedure. The IBA Guidelines on Conflict of Interest continue to provide a point of reference and a subject of debate. The new IBA Guidelines on Party Representation in International Arbitration have now been adopted and will presumably also be used as a point of reference. The ILA recommendations seek to grapple with issues of parallel proceedings, res judicata and the ascertaining of applicable law and also provide a point of reference in those areas. The trend – despite the hesitation of some practitioners – is to seek to ensure that there are objective points of reference to decide issues in international arbitration rather than leaving matters to the discretion of the Tribunals.

The reception of the first and second editions of this book have been very gratifying. Without limiting any responsibility for any shortcomings in this third edition, it is appropriate to thank various persons. This edition, like the prior editions reflects the value of discussion of the various legal issues under both the 1998 Rules and the current rules with the ICC Court members and the members of the Secretariat. In addition, the Handbook refers to and relies on the considerable work that has been carried out by the ICC ADR Commission with respect not only to the Rules themselves but also with respect to issues such as controlling time and costs. We would like to thank Jennifer Sharman-Koh, who assisted with the second edition, returned and contributed extensively to this edition. Andreas Webster carried out research for the book in an effort to reflect the latest developments, particularly with respect to US law. We also very much appreciate the enthusiastic and effective assistance from the entire team at Thomson Reuters.

London, January 2013

Tom Webster
Michael Bühler

[1] *Dallah Real Estate* [2010] UKSC 46.
[2] *Dallah Real Estate*, Paris Court of Appeal, February 7, 2011.
[3] See (2007) ASA Bull Vol.25 No.3, p.643.
[4] *COMMISA* 2013 WL 4517225 (SDNY August 27, 2013).
[5] *Yukos Capital* [2012] EWCA 855.
[6] *NML v Argentina* Cass 1iere March 28, 2013 (No.395); see also the other two decisions of that date Nos 394 and 396.

TABLE OF CONTENTS

II—Models, Precedents and Examples

ABBREVIATIONS

ABA	American Bar Association
Am Rev Int'l Arb	The American Review of International Arbitration
Arb Int	Arbitration International
ASA Bull	Swiss Arbitration Association Bulletin
CA	Cour d'appel (Court of Appeal)
Cass Civ le	Cour de cassation lère Chambre Civile (French Supreme Court)
Code of Ethics for Arbitrators	Code of Ethics for Arbitrators in Commercial Disputes (2004) (adopted by the AAA and ABA in 2004)
Colum J Transnat'l L	Columbia Journal of Transnational Law
England	England and Wales
Handbook Commercial Arbitration	ICCA Handbook on International Commercial Arbitration
JDI	Journal de droit international (Clunet)
EU	European Union
IntlALR	International Arbitration Law Review
Int'l Am L R	International American Law Review
Int'l Comp Law Quart	International and Comparative Law Quarterly
IBA	International Bar Association
IBA Guidelines on Conflict of Interest	IBA Guidelines on Conflict of Interest in International Arbitration (2004)
IBA Rules of Evidence	IBA Rules on Taking of Evidence in International Commercial Arbitration (1999)
ICC	International Chamber of Commerce
ICCA	International Council for Commercial Arbitration
ICC Court	ICC International Court of Arbitration
ICC ICArb Bull	ICC International Court of Arbitration Bulletin
ICC Rules	ICC Rules of Arbitration (1998)
ILM	International Legal Materials

Internal Rules	International Rules of the ICC Court (Appendix II to the Rules)
J Chart Inst Arb	Journal of the Chartered Institute of Arbitrators
J Int'l Arb	Journal of International Arbitration
Mealey's IAR	Mealey's International Arbitration Report
NCPC	French New Code of Civil Procedure
New York Convention	United Nations Convention on the Recognition and Enforcement of Foreign Arbitral Awards (1958)
PILA	Swiss Private International Law Act
Rev Arb	Revue de l'arbitrage
RDAI/IBLJ	Revue de droit des affaires internationales International Business Law Journal
Rev Crit DIP	Revue critique de Droit International Privé
s.	Section
SAR or SIAR	Stockholm Arbitration Report or Stockholm International Arbitration Report
Secretariat	Secretariat of the Court
Statutes	Statutes of the ICC Court (Appendix 1 to the Rules)
TGI	Tribunal de Grande Instance (French Court of First Instance)
Tribunal	Arbitral Tribunal
UNCITRAL Model Law	UNCITRAL Model Law on International Commercial Arbitration (1985) as amended in 2006
UNCITRAL Notes	UNCITRAL Notes on Organising Arbitral Proceedings (1996)
UNCITRAL Rules	UNCITRAL Arbitration Rules (1976)
UNIDROIT Principles	UNIDROIT Principles of International Commercial Contracts (2004)
YBCA	Yearbook of Commercial Arbitration

TABLE OF CASES

Australia

Belgium

Canada

European Court of Justice

France

Holland

Hong Kong

India

Italy

Lebanon

Philippines

Singapore

South Africa

Sweden

Switzerland

Tunisia

United Kingdom

United States of America

TABLE OF AWARDS

ICC Awards and Decisions

Iran_US Award

SCC Awards

UNCITRAL Awards

Other

TABLE OF CONVENTIONS, MODEL LAWS AND RULES

TABLE OF NATIONAL LEGISLATION

INTRODUCTION

The Third Edition—The 2012 Rules

As we noted in the prior editions, for parties, legal counsel and arbitrators involved in ICC arbitration, an initial review of the Rules is deceptively simple. The Rules are set out in a short pocket-sized booklet in plain language. This simplicity, coupled with the flexibility provided for in the Rules, helps explain the success of ICC arbitration, which can be adequately adapted to almost every situation. This simplicity sometimes also gives rise to complication, when the parties, and the arbitrators, are seeking to apply these Rules to a concrete set of facts. In most instances, the issues in an ICC arbitration are at some intermediate point on this continuum between simplicity and complexity. As was stated in the first and second editions, this Handbook is aimed at dealing in direct terms with the basic issues in ICC arbitration while providing the essential tools to understand and resolve the most complex issues in preparing and handling all aspects of an ICC arbitration. **0–1**

0–2 This Handbook deals with the Rules as revised effective January 1, 2012. That, in itself, is an occasion for a new edition with particular emphasis on the new provisions of the Rules. The 2012 Rules have seen an increase of the number of articles from 35 to 41 and two new appendices were added.[1] The Handbook deals with key areas of change, such as multiparty disputes (arts 7–10); case management (arts 22 and 24), and emergency arbitrator proceedings (art.29).[2]

0–3 Although the articles relating to these provisions are new, the issues they deal with, for the most part, are not. Multiparty disputes have existed for a long time, and led to various attempts by the ICC Court to deal with them under the prior Rules. Case management is a more formalised, and, for some, a more fashionable term for the type of procedural organisation that takes place in conjunction with the signing of the Terms of Reference, and the establishment of a procedural timetable. The provision for the Emergency Arbitrator was inspired by the Pre-Arbitral Referee Rules, which as such were never part of the ICC Rules of arbitration.

0–4 However, in discussing and drafting the specific Rules dealing with these situations the members of the ICC Commission on Arbitration and of the ICC Court, its National Committees and its Secretariat had an opportunity to consider them afresh. No *travaux préparatoires* as such for the Rules have been published.[3] The ICC created the ICC Commission Task Force on Revision of the ICC Rules of Arbitration ("Task Force"), and of a Drafting Sub-Committee[4] for the drafting of these provisions. This Handbook deals with those changes from the perspective of the genesis of the new Rules. However, it does so based in particular on the practice of arbitrators, counsel and the ICC Court with respect to those issues both under the prior Rules and in the initial application of the new Rules.[5]

0–5 To understand the approach taken by the Drafting Sub-Committee, one should note the Mandate for the Task Force which was as follows:

[1] App.IV (Case Management Techniques) and App.V (Emergency Arbitrator Rules). Although the 2012 Rules are now published together in a booklet with the ICC's 2011 ADR Rules, the third edition of this Handbook limits its comments to the 2012 Rules and its five Appendices.

[2] As to the reasons that prompted the change of the Rules, see, e.g. Tercier, "ICC Rules of Arbitration: A Decade of Use", ICC ICArb Bull. 2008 Vol.19 No.1, pp.47, 49 and Steindl, "The Arbitrator and the Arbitration Procedure: The 2012 ICC Arbitration Rules – Origin, Development and Practicability" in Christian Klausegger, Peter Klein, et al. (eds), Aus YB Int. Arb 2012, Ch.2 pp.151–152 ; Nathalie Voser, "Overview of the Most Important Changes in the Revised ICC Arbitration Rules", ASA Bull 2011, Vol.29 No.4 pp.784–786 ; Karin Calvo Goller, "The 2012 ICC Rules of Arbitration – An Accelerated Procedure and Substantial Changes", J Int'l Arb, 2012 Vol.29 No.3 p.324.

[3] Working Papers for the ICC Arbitration Commission were prepared. However, although these are of course available to the authors, they have not been published by the ICC. Unlike the *travaux préparatoires* for the UNCITRAL Arbitration Rules, there were no detailed minutes including reasons for each change at each session of the ICC Arbitration Commission.

[4] The Task Force and Drafting Sub-Committee were chaired by Peter Wolrich, with Michael W. Bühler and L. William Craig as co-chairs (2008–2011).

[5] As an ICC Court member, Thomas Webster was involved in the initial application of the Rules by the ICC Court.

- to study all suggestions received from National Committees, members of the ICC, users of the ICC rules of arbitration, Court members and members of the Secretariat;
- to determine if amendments to the ICC rules of arbitration are useful or necessary;
- to make any recommendations for the amendment of the ICC rules of arbitration that the Task Force deems to be useful or necessary.[6]

Therefore, the focus in revising the Rules was on making any necessary changes to the 1998 ICC Rules that were thought useful or necessary. As mentioned, the majority of the articles in the 2012 Rules are not new and, at most, have been subject to some drafting or purely linguistic changes. With respect to those articles in particular, there is an even stronger justification for relying on the past practice of arbitrators and the ICC Court. That practice continues to evolve and therefore various aspects of the commentary in this third edition have evolved from the prior editions. **0–6**

Likewise, the new 2012 Rules are not a static image of the ICC Court's practice prior to these Rules coming in force. They reflect practice as of that date and an attempt to improve certain provisions. The changed, and sometimes truly new provisions of the 2012 Rules had to be tested in practice. The ICC Court together with its Secretariat as well as the Tribunals themselves are to ensure through an evolving practice that the 2012 Rules can be applied in the best possible way for its users. In the two years since the 2012 Rules have been in force, certain practices can be discerned. Others will undoubtedly be forthcoming. **0–7**

As in the previous edition, this third edition seeks to provide an objective view of practices with respect to ICC arbitration. ICC arbitration is one form of administered arbitration, and it has its differences. While some of those differences reflect undoubted strengths, others are not universally appreciated. For example, most view that scrutiny by the ICC Court of draft Awards is a valuable aspect of ICC arbitration. However, that process has a price in the time that it takes for the Secretariat to prepare the file for review by the ICC Court and the review by the ICC Court itself. As a result, the discussion on art.33 focuses not simply on the nature and extent of that review (and how it is in fact carried out) but also on the usual time frame that is required for the review. **0–8**

Steps in a dispute subject to ICC Arbitration

The Rules deal with a dispute between the filing of the Request for Arbitration (Request) and the rendering of a Final Award (with any addendum). However, almost every dispute subject to ICC arbitration is more complex. Most ICC arbitrations originate with a contract. The disputes with respect to those contracts end with the final enforcement (or not) of the Award—and in some instances with the enforcement (or failure to enforce) of a second Final Award. Therefore, in **0–9**

[6] See Working Paper for the Commission Meeting of May 4–5, 2010 for example, p.2.

analysing ICC arbitration, one has to refer to proceedings prior to, after and parallel to the ICC arbitration itself.

0–10 Prior to the Request for Arbitration, the parties usually consider settling their dispute, by direct negotiation, mediation or other forms of dispute resolution. Parties also consider issues such as documentary collection and organisation and the strategy and preparation for requests for interim measures. As the proceedings progress, the possibility of parallel proceedings may also arise, before either state courts or other Tribunals. Those may relate for example to attempts to procure evidence or to attempts to remove arbitrators. In addition, the rendering of the Award is a major step but not always the final step in the dispute. It is commonplace to seek to annul Awards and to seek to object to enforcement of Awards. The grounds for both have generally become more limited, but should not be ignored when considering the procedure as a whole. All of these factors require that the parties and arbitrators have some degree of familiarity with respect to laws and practices that go beyond the ICC Rules themselves. Therefore, one of the major aspects of this approach is to focus on court decisions and international practices that may affect an ICC arbitration.

0–11 As counsel, the main focus of lawyers is of course on the ICC arbitration itself. But the client does not focus on the ICC arbitration only. A client will focus on the results that can be obtained in all settings and as against all relevant parties. Those results may be procedural rights or adjudication of other or related disputes. And therefore to properly advise a client with respect to an ICC arbitration a certain peripheral vision of other potential issues is required. As arbitrators, once the Tribunal is constituted under the Rules they have their specific set of rights, duties and obligations. But arbitrators are generally concerned about the law of the place of arbitration and the effects that that law may have on their role as arbitrators. Arbitrators are also concerned about the efficacy of any Award that is rendered and therefore consider the issues of annulment and enforcement of the Awards. In addition, arbitrators are concerned, and correctly so, about the manner in which deliberations take place amongst them. These are all issues that go beyond the Rules themselves and that are addressed in this Handbook.

Overall approach and principles

0–12 As regards the ICC proceedings themselves, this third edition seeks to build the approach in the first and second editions to focus on how arbitrators and the ICC Court decide issues that are submitted to them and how the Secretariat handles the administrative aspects of ICC arbitrations. The first aspect relates to and is based on work by Tribunals in ICC arbitrations. This is based on participation in, and review of, a wide variety of arbitral proceedings to reflect the best practices of leading arbitrators in this Handbook. A second aspect is a detailed discussion of the breakdown in matters handled by the ICC Court at its sessions with practical illustrations of the type of material considered and examples of decisions rendered in each context. In the second edition, we summarised in Annex 1 how the ICC Court conducted its plenary and committee sessions. Since we published the second edition in 2008, the ICC Court has decided to publicise how it works with mock ICC Court sessions. This is a very welcome development despite the limitations that a mock session always entails. Another aspect of the third edition of this Handbook is to reflect the further development in international norms that are used in international arbitration. For example, the IBA's Rules on the Taking of Evidence in International Arbitration as revised in 2010 (the "IBA Rules of Evidence")[7] have become virtually a standard reference of international arbitrations, albeit with some exceptions. In the authors' view, the IBA Guidelines on Conflict of Interest in International Arbitration (the "IBA Conflicts Guidelines")[8] have not met with quite the same success and are currently under review. Most recently, the IBA has published the IBA Guidelines on Party Representation in International Arbitration.[9]

This edition also deals with the law and practices prevailing at both the place of arbitration, as well as the place or places of probable enforcement. The place of arbitration is important because this is where either party to the arbitration can bring an annulment action against the Award. The standards to be observed at the place of arbitration, as applied by the national courts, should therefore never be ignored by counsel or the arbitrators. With regard to places of enforcement, the key requirements are those set out in the New York Convention, as it is applicable to enforcement of arbitral Awards in 149 countries.[10] However, counsel and the arbitrators should be aware that, even in New York Convention countries, the standards applied by the courts, for instance to the binding effect of an arbitration clause to a non-signatory, may be different. Therefore, an Award that may be enforceable in one country may not be enforceable in another due to the particularities of national case law. As the former President of the ICC Court has said: **0–13**

> "Equally obvious is the need to better integrate arbitration within national legal systems. Sadly, national courts sometimes undermine the efficiency of arbitration through undue intervention in the proceedings (injunctions), highly restrictive case law when it comes to setting aside Awards, and laying down excessive requirements for their enforcement even with the context of the New York Convention."[11]

Unlike counsel to the parties, a Tribunal will not necessarily know the probable places of enforcement; although the country where the Respondent is incorporated or has its headquarters will often be the most likely, although not the only possible, place of enforcement of the Award. Major banking centres, such as New York, London and Frankfurt are also places of enforcement. Moreover, a Tribunal will be influenced by the arguments advanced by the parties and a party should hesitate to advance a position, which if adopted by the Tribunal in the Award, would create issues as to enforcement at the likely place of enforcement. **0–14**

Once an Award is rendered against the Respondent who decides voluntarily not to honour it, there always are at least two options. First, the Respondent can file an application for annulment action at the place of arbitration. Secondly, the **0–15**

[7] See Pt III, App.10.
[8] See Pt III, App.11.
[9] See Pt III, App.12.
[10] See http://www.uncitral.org [accessed November 12, 2013].
[11] Tercier, "Emerging trends in ICC arbitration and the Institution's vision for the future" in Global Arbitration Review 2007, at p.2.

Respondent can wait until a request for recognition and enforcement of the Award is filed by the Claimant, usually in the country in which the Respondent is incorporated. The choice between these two options will in part depend on the Respondent's analysis of the arbitration law as applied by the courts in these two jurisdictions, and whether the Award will be seen in compliance therewith.[12]

0–16 It would go far beyond the scope of this Handbook, and the expertise of its authors, to attempt to give a comprehensive overview of the law and practice of international arbitration in all arbitration venues. Instead, the authors have sought to give an overview of certain basic principles and cases for arbitrations held at major centres of ICC arbitration, the United States, France, Switzerland and England, as well as providing some reference to the UNCITRAL Model Law. The goal is to provide the reader with basic indications of what is to be expected when arbitrating in these jurisdictions. Wherever possible, references are provided to some of the important cases decided by the courts in the countries of these venues. These basic indications cannot be exhaustive and are of course no substitute for review of the local authorities in detail with an experienced local practitioner. However, these indications are intended to provide a bridge to enable the international practitioner to understand the issues that arise in the various jurisdictions.

0–17 The overall approach of this Handbook in presenting the basic features of ICC arbitration has been integrated in four building blocks:

- The first block, which is set out immediately below, is a description of ten basic principles underlying ICC arbitration. These principles are points of reference to resolve the various types of problems that occur in an ICC arbitration.

  The ten principles are:

  (i) ICC Arbitration is an Administered and Supervised Arbitration;
  (ii) ICC Arbitration is aimed Primarily at Resolving Business Disputes;
  (iii) ICC Arbitration is aimed Primarily at Resolving International Disputes;
  (iv) ICC Arbitration is based on the Free Choice of Arbitrators by the Parties and the Arbitrators' Impartiality and Independence of the Parties;
  (v) the ICC Rules provide a Flexible Framework and not a Procedural Code of Arbitration;
  (vi) the ICC Rules are based Largely on Party Autonomy;
  (vii) ICC Arbitrations are to be conducted in a Cost Efficient and Fair Manner;
  (viii) ICC Arbitration is linked to the Law of the Place of Arbitration;
  (ix) ICC Awards should meet the New York Convention Requirements; and
  (x) ICC Arbitration continues to evolve, even under the 2012 Rules.

- The second block consists of a commentary on an article-by-article basis of the Rules by reference to relevant case law, arbitral Awards, whether published or not and internationally accepted guidelines, also known as "soft"

[12] Delaume, "Reflections on the Effectiveness of International Arbitral Awards" (1995) J Int'l Arb Vol.12 No.1, at pp.5–8.

law. Annex 1 to this commentary (Pt I) is a brief description of the functioning of the ICC Court at its monthly Plenary Session and its weekly Committee Sessions. Annex 1 provides a description of the matters addressed at those sessions, the documents relied upon and the proceedings of the sessions themselves.

- The third building block is to set out certain precedents for ICC arbitrations as a sort of "site visit" of an ICC arbitration. These precedents are intended to reflect what happens in certain specific types of arbitrations. They are not models: in each case the lawyers involved will craft their own solutions to the issues dealt with. Instead, these precedents are intended to be an illustration of what has been used in ICC arbitration so that the reader is not taken by surprise. However, in analysing these precedents and the Rules themselves, the starting point should be the basic principles.
- The fourth building block is a set of materials relating to international arbitration and ICC arbitration in particular. These materials include five Appendices to the Rules and various guidelines used in international arbitration, excerpts from national laws of major centres of arbitration, the UNCITRAL Model Law (as amended) and the New York Convention.

Principle 1: ICC arbitration is an administered and supervised arbitration

By choosing ICC arbitration, parties are opting for an institutional arbitration **0–18** that is administered by the ICC. The focus of this Handbook is dealing with an ICC arbitration and not on deciding whether ICC arbitration is suitable for specific cases. However, some basic points should be noted. First, parties have a choice between institutional and ad hoc arbitration, under the UNCITRAL Rules for example.[13] Secondly, as regards the type of arbitral institutions, parties have the choice amongst a number of institutions in addition to the ICC, such as the London Court of International Arbitration (LCIA) and the Swiss Chambers of Arbitration. The choice of an arbitral institution will depend on the arbitration rules, the perception of how they are administered and the place of arbitration. The cost and method of functioning under the various institutions differs and therefore will be a factor in deciding which to prefer. However, one of the goals of the ICC, as discussed in this Handbook, is to provide for detailed, consistent and to a very large extent transparent administrative practice with respect to international commercial arbitrations conducted around the world.

The administration of each arbitration is carried out under the overall responsi- **0–19** bility of the ICC Court and its Secretariat. Therefore, the Rules have to be read taking into account the role of the ICC Court, which is organised pursuant to the provisions in App.I of the Rules.

The administration of an ICC arbitration is discussed in detail under art.1. The **0–20** basic point is that an ICC arbitration is a highly developed form of administered arbitration that is widely recognised as a leading form of institutional

[13] See for example an article by article commentary of the latter, Webster, *Handbook of UNCITRAL Arbitration* (Sweet & Maxwell 2010).

international arbitration.[14] In one form or the other, the ICC Court and the Secretariat follow every aspect of the procedure, beginning with the notification of the Request for Arbitration, followed by the constitution of the Tribunal and ending with the scrutiny of the Award and its notification to the parties. The ICC Court intervenes where necessary in an arbitration with decisions on various issues that in effect insulate in some instances the arbitration to a certain extent from national court procedures. The ICC Court, and not the Tribunal, sets the fees for the arbitrators. In doing so the Court takes into account its detailed knowledge of the procedure and the efficiency and rapidity with which the Tribunal has to conduct the arbitration. As discussed in art.37(2), in doing so the Court takes into account, amongst other things, the complexity of the matter, the amount in dispute and the number of arbitrators.

0–21 Even for experienced practitioners, whether acting as counsel or arbitrator, the administrative role of the ICC is important. Many practitioners are familiar with the ICC Court's structure, although they are perhaps not as well versed in the actual mechanics of the ICC Court's decision-making process. For other practitioners, ICC arbitration is more novel. In either case, it is important to keep in mind what information is provided to the ICC Court; how the ICC Court reaches its decisions; and the consequences of those decisions in an actual case. The second edition of this Handbook sought to further demystify the decision-making process of the ICC Court, in the hope that further transparency will lead to a better understanding of the entire process and enhance the acceptability of the ICC Court's decision, which its Secretariat communicates to the parties. As noted above, since the second edition was published, the ICC Court has indeed opened up as to the internal court procedures.

0–22 The ICC Court is not a court in the normal judicial sense. It is a body composed of persons (mainly lawyers) nominated by the National Committees or Groups of the International Chamber of Commerce ("ICC") who decide, on an administrative basis, matters that fall under its competence under the Rules. The ICC Court is in fact an independent but constituent part of the ICC, and does not have its own legal personality. The role of the ICC Court is determined by the ICC Rules. The ICC Court is represented by its President and Vice Presidents who are authorised to take certain decisions pursuant to art.1(3). However, as discussed in more detail in art.1 and in Annex 1, the ICC Court reaches most of its decisions either at Plenary Sessions attended by all available members of the ICC Court or at Committee Sessions attended by the President or a Vice President of the ICC Court and two other members of the ICC Court in the presence of the Secretary General, the General Counsel and a representative of each team of the Secretariat (normally the Counsel). There are generally 12 plenary and approximately 50 committee sessions of the ICC Court each year.

0–23 For practitioners, it is important to understand whether a matter is generally dealt with in a Plenary Session or in a Committee Session and how matters are dealt with in those sessions. Basically, in a Plenary Session, a matter is reviewed

[14] See Mistelis, "The International Arbitration—Corporate Attitudes and Practices—12 Perceptions Tested: Myths, Data and Analysis Research Report", op. cit., at p.562, indicating that the ICC was preferred by 42 per cent of the persons responding to the questionnaire.

by the ICC Court as a whole (i.e. all members in attendance), based on the report of a rapporteur. In a Committee Session, a matter is reviewed as one of a great number of matters by three members of the ICC Court. Therefore, the basic difference relates to the body that will review the decision, and the frequency of its sessions. The Plenary Session takes place once a month, the Committee Session every week. This is one of the subjects dealt with in the discussion of art.1 and in Annex 1 Pt I. The commentary in art.1 and Annex 1 Pt I has been prepared based on the authors' experience as Court members at the Plenary and Committee Sessions of the ICC Court.[15] As such it represents their personal appreciation and views and not the views of the ICC Court as such. Moreover, since one of the hallmarks of ICC arbitration is flexibility, there is bound to be evolution in the practice of the ICC Court over time, and there has been a tendency under the current President to have more matters handled by a Committee rather than in a Plenary Session.

The ICC Court has a permanent Secretary General and Secretariat, which is based mainly in Paris at the ICC's headquarters with additional staff in Hong Kong and in New York.[16] The Secretariat's role is to administer ICC arbitrations. This includes preparing the material for the ICC Court sessions and implementing the decisions of the ICC Court. Members of the Secretariat attend Court sessions and, although they have no role in the actual decision, they influence it with varying degrees. It is the Secretariat that will in many cases prepare a proposal for a matter that goes before the Court; it does so by referring to the current practice of the Court, as well as what the past practice of the Court has been with respect to certain types of decisions. The decisions of the ICC Court are always notified to the parties through the Secretariat. The Secretariat's role is not simply to administer incoming and pending ICC arbitration cases,[17] but to provide general assistance, if necessary, to ensure that the parties understand how an ICC arbitration is administered. If a party has a question relating to the ICC's administration of an arbitration, it can approach the Secretariat for general information. **0–24**

Principle 2: ICC arbitration is aimed primarily at resolving business disputes

The ICC was created after World War I to further the interests of international commerce. ICC arbitration was set up to provide a dispute resolution for international business disputes in particular. Until the most recent version of the Rules, there was a reference to business disputes in the rules themselves. That has been abandoned in the 2012 Rules, but the focus of the Rules is nevertheless on resolving business disputes in the broadest terms rather than consumer disputes, for example. **0–25**

The ICC's approach has always been to have one set of rules for various types of disputes rather than by industry sectors. **0–26**

[15] Covering the combined period from January 1997 to June 2012.
[16] http://www.iccwbo.org [accessed November 12, 2013].
[17] At the end of 2012, over 1476 cases were pending at the ICC Court, see (2013) ICC ICArb Bull Vol.24 No.1, p.5.

0–27 In 2012, the following principal economic sectors in the cases submitted to ICC arbitrations were[18]:

Sector:	2012 (in %)
Construction and engineering (part of the goods contracts)	17
Energy	15
Information technology	8
Finance and insurance	8
General trade	6
Industrial equipment and services	6

0–28 In 2002 and 2012, 9.4 per cent and 9.9 per cent respectively of the cases registered with the ICC involved a state or a parastatal entity as one or more of the parties.[19] Most of these entities were from Central and East Europe (approximately 13 per cent in 2002 and 18.8 per cent in 2012), Asia (14.6 per cent in 2002, 28.2 per cent in 2012), Africa (21.2 per cent in 2002, 25.9 per cent in 2012) and the Americas (4.6 per cent in 2002 and 27.1 per cent in 2012, all from Latin America and Caribbean). One can notice that the caseload from Asia has significantly increased in 10 years.

0–29 Most of these disputes involving states or state entities concern business disputes, often in relation to infrastructure projects such as the construction of a road, airport or presidential palace, the revamping of a cement factory or power plant, the rehabilitation of a dam, the purchase of defense material, or similar projects.

0–30 The ICC Court is, however, also a possible forum for investment disputes under bilateral investment treaties (or BITs). These treaties often provide the foreign investor with a right to submit certain types of disputes relating to the investment to a local court or to arbitration under arbitration rules of the International Center for the Settlement of Investment Disputes ("ICSID"), under the UNCITRAL Arbitration Rules or under rules of other arbitration institutions, such as the ICC. One particularity of BITs is that the investor is sometimes only required to opt for arbitration and select the type of arbitration once the dispute has arisen.[20]

0–31 ICC arbitration has not traditionally been used in inheritance disputes and/or family law matters in general or disputes arising out of trusts. Many of those disputes are subject to limitations on arbitrability in any event. However, work has been done to increase the use of international arbitration for trust disputes, which frequently have a family element.[21]

[18] (2013) ICArb Bull Vol.24, No.1 p.13.

[19] (2003) ICC ICArb Bull Vol.14 No.1, p.11; (2013) ICC ICArb Bull. Vol.24 No.1, p.10. Between 2002 and 2011 the percentage of ICC cases involving a state or a parastatal entity remained stable, fluctuating between 9 per cent and 11 per cent, with a peak at 13.1 per cent in 2005. The 2012 percentage confirms this pattern.

[20] See Reed, Paulson & Blackaby, *Guide to ICSID Arbitration* (Kluwer, 2004), p.58 ; Schreuer, "Article 25 [Jurisdiction]" in *The ICSID Convention: A Commentary*, 2nd edn (Cambridge UP, 2010), para.23 at p.97; and Webster, *Handbook of Investment Arbitration* (Thomson/Sweet & Maxwell,2012), para.25-1 et seq.

[21] See the work of the ICC Commission of Arbitration on Trusts which published a clause for trusts disputes in its Report (2008) ICC ICArb Bull Vol.19 No.2, p.9. Chistopher P. Koch, "A tale of two

Any kind of business dispute may be submitted although no threshold amount exists for doing so, it is recognised that the ICC arbitration system is not well suited for "small claims disputes".[22] In response to the parties' need in this respect, the ICC published in March 2003 its Guideline for Arbitrating Small Claims under the ICC Rules of Arbitration. The Guidelines, which were elaborated as a list of suggestions, are intended to assist the parties who seek to rationalise or to reduce the cost and time of arbitrating small claims.[23] During the revision of the current Rules, it was debated whether a special regime for small claims disputes should be introduced into the Rules. This idea was not pursued, but certain measures were adopted which should prove beneficial also for the conduct of small claims disputes.[24] **0–32**

Disputes involving sums of all sizes are referred to the ICC. The breakdown for 2012 appears to be similar to previous years if one takes again 2002 as the reference year with a concentration of cases in the middle of the range.[25] The fall during the past decade of the US Dollar against hard currencies such as the Euro, has led to an increase of amounts in dispute by virtue of the exchange rate ratio: **0–33**

cities! – Arbitrating trust disputes and the ICC's arbitration clause for trust disputes", YB Int. Arb. 2012 Roth/Geistlinger Vol.2 pp.180–207.

22 One example occurred with the insertion of an ICC arbitration clause in a consumer sales contract for a Gateway computer. In *Brower v Gateway 2000, Inc* (1998) New York Supreme Court, Appellate Division, First Department 676 N.Y.S.2d 569, the court focused on the ICC fee structure and noted that the amount at issue in the case was less than the filing fee and that the clause could be enforced through a less costly system. The court rejected the enforceability of an ICC arbitration clause based on unconscionability ("With respect to the substantive element, which entails an examination of the substance of the agreement in order to determine whether the terms unreasonably favor one party . . . the excessive cost factor that is necessarily entailed in arbitrating before the ICC is unreasonable and surely serves to deter the individual consumer from invoking the process. Barred from resorting to the courts by the arbitration clause in the first instance, the designation of a financially prohibitive forum effectively bars consumers from this forum as well; consumers are thus left with no forum at all in which to resolve a dispute."), (1999) YBCA Vol.XXIVa p.343. The Federal Court in Kansas also leaned to this conclusion although it ruled the issue moot; see *Klocek v Gateway, Inc* (2000) 104 F.Supp. 2d 1332. In the European Union, Council Directive 93/13, which has been implemented in the Member States, lists as one of the possible provisions that may be unfair "excluding or hindering the consumer's right to take legal action or exercise any other legal remedy, particularly by requiring the consumer to take disputes exclusively to arbitration not covered by legal provisions, unduly restricting the evidence available to him or imposing on him a burden of proof which, according to the applicable law, should lie with another party to the contract". Thus the result in the EU may well be the same as that in the United States.

23 (2003) ICC ICArb Bull Vol.14 No.1, p.29; see also http://www.iccwbo.org [accessed November 12, 2013].

24 For a further discussion of this issue and the solution adopted under the 2012 Rules see the discussion under art.22 below. Interestingly, the revised CEPANI Rules, which came into force on January 1, 2013, provide for special rules where the amount in dispute does not exceed €25,000. This may make sense in the context of an arbitration institution that seeks to capture a domestic market, but such figure, and even a much higher threshold would be quite meaningless for ICC arbitration. It is extremely rare that the ICC Court would receive a request for arbitration for an amount below $30,000.

25 (2003) ICC ICArb Bull Vol.14 No.1, p.15.

Amounts in dispute (US dollars)		2002 (in%)	2012 (in %)
≤50,000		4.9	1.1
>50,000	≤200,000	7.6	4.7
>200,000	≤500,000	11.1	8
>500,000	<1 million	10.1	11.1
>1 million	<10 million	32.2	36.1
>10 million	≤50 million	16.2	19.3
>50 million	<100 million	2.7	5.6
>500 million			1.7
Not quantified		11.5	6.1

0–34 In 2002, 3.5 per cent of the cases involved amounts between 100 million and 1 billion dollars and 0.2 per cent involved amounts superior to 1 billion dollars. In 2012, 6.3 per cent of the cases involved amounts between 100 and 500 million dollars and 1.7 per cent involved amounts superior to 500 million dollars.

0–35 The Rules are not designed to cover consumer disputes. Indeed, the costs of ICC arbitration are such that an ICC arbitration clause may be struck down in the consumer area.[26] In addition, in some countries there are limitations on the arbitrability of consumer disputes.

Principle 3: ICC arbitration is aimed primarily at resolving international disputes

0–36 ICC arbitration was designed for business disputes of an international nature. The ICC, of which the ICC Court is an integral part, is and represents the world's business organisation (http://www.iccwbo.org [accessed November 12, 2013]). One of the attractions of international arbitration in general and of ICC arbitration in particular is the availability of a neutral forum for resolution of disputes involving persons or companies from different countries. However, there is no requirement that the parties be from different countries and, for various reasons, entities in the same country may opt for ICC arbitration. Nevertheless, the term "international" may be of significance in an ICC arbitration due to the differing consequences under national law if an arbitration is international or not.[27]

0–37 Having recourse to arbitration to decide upon the merits of a dispute means excluding the jurisdiction of the state courts. In some instances, private parties may fear that they will not be treated fairly in the courts of their own countries, in particular when the state or a state entity is a party to the dispute. In these instances, it has been observed more than once that parties from the same country would agree to ICC arbitration rather than to the jurisdiction of their own courts, even though the transaction is governed by the law of their country and handled in the language of that country, as would be any ensuing arbitration.

0–38 In 2012, the parties to ICC arbitration originated from 137 countries, which compares well with the 149 countries that have ratified the New York Convention

[26] See *Gateway* case, para.0–32 n.22.

[27] Under French law, for example, there is a distinction between international and domestic arbitration, see art.1504 of the French CCP.

at the end of 2012.[28] The breakdown by country of the most frequent nationalities in 2012, as published by the ICC, is as follows:[29]

Country of origin	Number of parties	As percentage of total number of parties in all 2012 filings
USA	145	7.12%
Germany	132	6.48%
France	124	6.09%
Brazil	82	4.03%
India	81	3.98%
Spain	73	3.59%
Italy	71	3.49%
Switzerland	59	2.90%
United Arab Emirates	59	2.90%
China (incl. SARs Hong Kong & Macau)	55	2.70%
Netherlands	54	2.65%
Romania	50	2.46%

Principle 4: ICC arbitration is based on the free choice of arbitrators by the parties and the arbitrators' impartiality and independence of the parties

In most cases, the parties nominate the co-arbitrators. The parties can nominate the co-arbitrators they wish, provided that the co-arbitrator is impartial and independent of the parties within the meaning of art.11(1) and applicable law and is capable of meeting the requirements of the Rules. The parties or the co-arbitrators may agree on the president of the Tribunal. If they fail to agree, the ICC Court appoints the president.[30] As with co-arbitrators, the president needs to be and remain impartial, as well as independent of the parties and otherwise meet the requirements of the Rules. The ICC Court does not generally impose either the co-arbitrators or the president and, even when the ICC Court designates a president, it is not from one of its members or from an approved list. **0–39**

As is discussed in detail under art.11, all members of an ICC Tribunal must be impartial and independent of the parties. The issue of what is meant by these requirements remains one of the thorniest issues in ICC arbitration. The ICC Court has considerable experience in assessing what is required under art.11 particularly within the context of challenges under art.14. However, the ICC Court does not provide reasons for its decisions on challenges, let alone publish them.[31] In addition, even though ICC Court decisions are often accepted by the **0–40**

[28] The latest countries to ratify the New York Convention were Tajikistan (14/08/2012), Sao Tome and Principe (20/11/2012), Myanmar (16/04/2013), http://www.uncitral.org [accessed November 12, 2013].

[29] (2003) ICC ICArb Bull Vol.14 No.1, p.10; (2013) ICC ICArb Bull Vol.24 No.1, pp.9-10. [AG]

[30] In ICC Arbitration, the rule is the appointment by the ICC Court, unless the Parties have agreed otherwise, see art.13(5).

[31] One of the problems is that various members of the ICC Court may uphold or reject a challenge for different reasons. The ICC Court may publish in the future case notes, in addition to the general reviews made in the ICC Court's Bulletin. See for example, Fry & Greenberg, "The Arbitral

parties, in most jurisdictions, in the case of an unsuccessful challenge, the challenging party also has the options of either bringing state court proceedings to challenge the arbitrator or of seeking to annul the Award based on the same grounds as the challenge. Moreover, whatever the decision may be, if a party has reservations about the independence of an arbitrator, it can and often does affect the arbitral proceedings as well as the party's attitude towards acceptance of the Award.

0–41 To deal with this myriad of possibilities, in 2004 a working group of the IBA published the IBA Conflicts Guidelines. These guidelines deal in particular with the fundamental issue of when arbitrators should make disclosure and when they have conflicts of interest. Although prepared by an impressive group of practitioners, the guidelines are—as they say—a starting point in the process of developing overall guidelines for international arbitration. In a number of respects, the IBA Conflicts Guidelines may go beyond the requirements of relevant law and therefore may be more of an indication of "best practices" rather than a true guideline as to the legal principles. Parties refer to the IBA Conflicts Guidelines when they make challenges, although there has been reticence to place too much weight on them due to the fact that the factual situations are so different in individual cases. Arbitrators refer to the IBA Conflicts Guidelines as well, in particular when they have to consider whether a disclosure should be made when accepting an arbitral appointment. The IBA is currently working on revising the IBA Conflicts Guidelines.

0–42 For arbitrations in the United States, the AAA/ABA Code of Ethics for Arbitrators of 2004 provides similar guidelines. Unlike the IBA Conflict Guidelines, the AAA/ABA rules are arguably based in part on specific case law rather than on a blend of international principles.

Principle 5: ICC Rules provide a flexible framework, not a procedural code for arbitration

0–43 The Rules do not provide a procedural code for ICC arbitration. ICC arbitration does not involve one procedure, but, within a framework, a range of procedures based on several basic principles.[32] Therefore, the approach of this Handbook is to seek to insert the interpretation of the Rules in their procedural and substantive context as reflected in actual practice in specific situations.

0–44 The need for flexibility in an ICC arbitration has to be balanced against the concern that parties have the procedure of the arbitration correspond to what they could reasonably expect in the international context. Flexibility should

Tribunal: Application of Articles 7–12 of the ICC Rules in the Recent Cases" (2009) ICArb Bull Vol.20 No 2, p.12.; Whitesell, "Independence of ICC Arbitration: ICC Court Practice concerning the Appointment, Confirmation, Challenge and Replacement of Arbitrators" in Independence of Arbitrators, (2007) ICArb Bull Special Supplement, p.7.

32 Jolivet, "L'intérêt de recourir 'a une institution d'arbitrage. L'exemple de la Cour internationale d'arbitrage de la CCI" in Liber Amicorum in honour of Robert Briner, op. cit., p.413, at pp.418–419; Whitesell, "The 1998 ICC Rules of Arbitration Today" in Liber Amicorum in honour of Robert Briner, op. cit., p.919, discussing the most significant modifications of the ICC Rules and emphasising the necessary need for flexibility in cases like fast-track arbitration (art.32), at p.924; Tercier, "ICC Rules of Arbitration: A Decade of Use," (2008) ICC Bull. Vol.19 No.1, pp.33–50.

not result in unpredictable or arbitrary procedures. As a result, over the years various practical guidelines have been developed for international arbitration by bodies such as UNCITRAL and the International Bar Association. These guidelines are not automatically applicable in an ICC arbitration and in most arbitrations are not expressly adopted by the parties or the Tribunal. Nor are these guidelines used solely with respect to ICC arbitration. However, the guidelines provide helpful objective criteria that are also relevant to ICC arbitrations. In a sense, they provide a link between the general framework of the Rules and the specifics of individual procedural orders and, as a result, are referred to extensively in this book.

The IBA Rules on the Taking of Evidence provide very helpful guidelines as to **0–45**
the issue of documentary production and witness and expert testimony.[33] In addition to the IBA Rules of Evidence themselves, the working group that prepared them provided a very helpful commentary on the rules. The IBA Rules of Evidence have been criticised and many practitioners do not apply them as such, but in procedural discussions they are often viewed as a sensible point of departure and an excellent way in which to avoid a debate between national procedural preferences.

Principle 6: ICC Rules are based largely on party autonomy

One of the fundamental principles that forms the basis and runs through most **0–46**
aspects of modern international arbitration is party autonomy. The parties can agree on many aspects of the procedure in an ICC arbitration, provided that it retains the essential characteristics of the ICC Rules. Party autonomy has to be seen, however, in the light of the fact that parties tend not to agree on procedural as well as substantive matters as a dispute arises and progresses.

This principle of party autonomy and party control has to be contrasted with the **0–47**
reality, which is the shift in authority to the Tribunal.[34] The process could be described as follows:

There are four stages during the life of an ICC arbitration: during the First **0–48**
Stage, party autonomy is virtually total. The parties agree on arbitration. The parties may decide on the place of arbitration, the language of the proceedings, the procedure to be followed (including the number of arbitrators) and the applicable law.

During the Second Stage, while the parties maintain a certain degree of **0–49**
autonomy when acting separately, there is also the beginning of a shift to the control by the Tribunal. However, despite this shift, if the parties agree on a specific matter, that agreement will generally prevail. This position is reflected in

[33] Pt III, App.10.

[34] Gabriel, "Chemin du droit et droit chemin—Libres propos sur l'arbitrage commercial international" in Liber Amicorum in honour of Robert Briner, op. cit., p.297, para.5 at p.299 ("The parties are necessarily free to rely on their contractual freedom. In case of the absence of an agreement, they must be aware that the back-up mechanism provided by the Rules (choice by the arbitral tribunal or the Court, as the case may be) avoids certainly deadlock situations but introduces an element of uncertainty that is excluded when there is a direct choice made by the parties.") (Authors' translation).

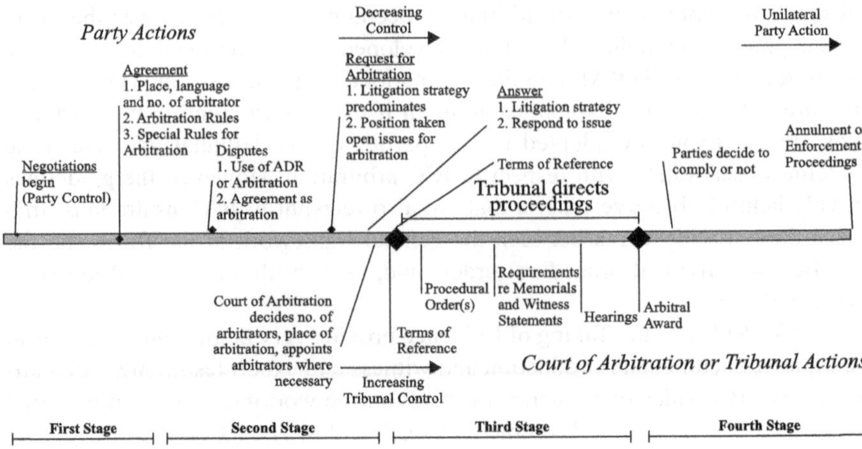

numerous occasions in the Rules where there is reference to the Tribunal having the power to decide an issue if the parties have not otherwise agreed.[35]

0–50 During the Third Stage, party autonomy generally prevails but the Tribunal tends to direct the proceedings because the parties are either unable to agree on the procedure or because they simply prefer to let the Tribunal direct the proceedings.

0–51 During the Fourth Stage, the parties in a sense recover their freedom of action but within a new legal framework: that of the arbitral Award.

Principle 7: ICC arbitrations are to be conducted in a cost efficient and fair manner

0–52 Arbitration under the ICC Rules is a private form of rendering justice in accordance with applicable law. Rendering justice imposes a particular obligation on Tribunals in particular, although it is also the guiding principle with respect to the ICC Court. A fundamental attraction of international arbitration is that it is more neutral as between persons from various countries. It is also intended to be neutral as to the relative position of the parties and of their counsel.

0–53 The concern with this fundamental issue of fairness has become particularly acute in investment arbitration. Nevertheless, it is also a major issue in international commercial arbitration. Various courts, such as the French courts, have not hesitated to set aside Awards where they have decided that these principles have not been respected, whether due to the economic interests of the arbitrators or the failure to respect collegiality among arbitrators. In all likelihood, this type of review will continue and if anything increase.

0–54 Fairness is required on the substantive and procedural level, and it is perhaps easiest to police when there is a failure to respect basic procedural requirements. These procedural requirements are set out in particular in art.22 (Conduct of the

[35] See for example arts 19 (rules governing the proceedings), 20 (regarding the language of the arbitration) and 21 (regarding the applicable rules of law) and 22 (conduct of the procedure) and 25 (establishing the facts of the case).

Arbitration), art.24 (Case Management Conference and Procedural Timetable) and art.27 (Closing of Proceedings and Date for Submission of Draft Awards).

However, one of the other basic attractions of arbitration is that the procedure is intended to be cost-effective. Therefore, procedural fairness does not require acceptance of all requests by the parties. It requires, in the words of art.22(4), the Tribunal to "act fairly and impartially and ensure that each party has a reasonable opportunity to present its case". **0–55**

Principle 8: ICC Arbitration is linked to the law of the place of arbitration

ICC arbitration is international and the role of the ICC Court makes it more international. However, ICC arbitration does not exist in a vacuum. Neither the ICC Court nor an ICC Tribunal has the imperium of a state court. **0–56**

One of the basic relationships in international arbitration is between the Tribunal and the courts of the place of arbitration, which are referred to in France as the "*juges d'appui*" (the "supporting judges").[36] The role of the place of arbitration has changed over time.[37] However, it is, to use the words of the US court interpreting the New York Convention, the primary jurisdiction with respect to arbitration. To properly conduct an ICC arbitration, one has to generally meet the requirements of the law of the place of arbitration.[38] That law is usually relevant for: (i) establishing the minimum procedural requirements of the arbitration; (ii) providing the forum in which to challenge arbitrators; (iii) criteria as to annulment of arbitral Awards; and (iv) criteria for remand of a decision to the arbitrators, which is possible in certain jurisdictions, such as the United States and England, and now expressly contemplated under art.35(4) of the 2012 Rules. In addition, the plan of arbitration may influence or determine the law applicable to the arbitration agreement. **0–57**

The trend has been to reduce the role of the law of the place of arbitration as regards the detail of the procedure. An ICC Tribunal sitting in Paris will not generally refer to the French Code of Civil Procedure any more than an ICC Tribunal sitting in New York will refer to the Federal Code of Civil Procedure. Indeed, the language of many of the arbitration laws is so general as to provide little indication as to any special requirements in a place of arbitration. Nevertheless, the case law of the national courts must be kept in mind in interpreting the legal requirements with respect to arbitration. Refusing certain procedural steps may be interpreted differently depending on whether the place of arbitration is in Paris or New York, for example. If there is a serious dispute with respect to arbitral proceedings, the relevant cases are usually those of the place of arbitration. **0–58**

[36] See arts1459 and 1460 of the French Code of Civil Procedure (as of January 13, 2011).

[37] A number of years ago there was reference of the law of the place of arbitration as the law of the procedure. However, it is submitted that this is no longer the general approach. The national court procedure of the law of the place of arbitration is seldom of great importance in and of itself. See Pinsolle and Kreindler, "Les limites du rôle de la volonté des parties dans la conduite de l'instance arbitrale" (2003) Rev Arb No.1, p.41. ("An old idea consisted of linking to the procedure of the law of the state of the place of arbitration. This idea is now very largely abandoned (since the 1975 revision of the ICC Rules) and the law of the place of arbitration is only relevant in relation to eventual annulment proceedings in cases where the manner of conducting the proceedings would be in breach of fundamental ideas of the place of arbitration, in particular with regard to the procedural ordre public . . ."). (Authors' translation)

[38] For an exceptional case, see ICC case No.10623 (2001) (Final Award) at para.34 n.28.

0–59 Although the link between arbitration and the courts of the place of arbitration is very real, one should not neglect the development of the principle of the independence of the resulting arbitral Awards from the national law of the place of arbitration. This doctrine was developed in France and has been endorsed once again by the French Supreme Court in the *Putrabali* case.[39] The result is that French courts examine whether to enforce international arbitral Awards whether or not they have been annulled at the place of arbitration. However, this presupposes that an Award has been rendered. Moreover, for the time being at any rate, it would appear that the doctrine of the independence of international arbitration Awards has not been widely accepted outside of France.[40]

0–60 ICC arbitration can take place in virtually any country in the world. As discussed under art.18, ICC arbitrations tend to be held in certain countries. In fact in over 80 per cent of the ICC arbitrations in 2012, the place of arbitration was in France, Switzerland, England,[41] the United States,[42] or a country where the UNCITRAL Model Law has been adopted.[43]

Rank	Countries in 2002	2002	Countries in 2012	2012
1	Switzerland	111	Switzerland	122
2	France	88	France	101
3	United Kingdom	53	United Kingdom	71
4	United States	50	United States	41
5	Germany	16	Singapore	36
6	Singapore	14	Germany	19
7	Netherlands	13	Brazil	15
8	Austria and Turkey	10	Austria	13
9	Greece	8	China and Mexico	12
10	Italy	7	India	11

39 Cass. 1ère ch. civ., June 29, 2007, No.05-18.053 and No.06-13.293.

40 Although it has been advanced by some learned authors in the field, see Fouchard, "La partie internationale de l'annulation de la sentence arbitrale dans son pays d'origine" (1997) Rev. Arb. p.329; Paulsson, "Enforcing Arbitral Awards Notwithstanding a Local Standard Annulment (LSA)" (1998) ICC Bull. Vol.9 No.1, p.14; Gaillard, "L'exécution des sentences annulées dans leur pays d'origine" (1998) JDI, p.645 and "The Enforcement of Awards set Aside in the Country of Origins", (1999) ICSID Review No.14, p.16. See also Elvira R. Gadelshina, Khrenov & Partners "Ciments Français: Russian Putrabali No More", and Case No.A27-781/11, *Judge Elena Nikolaevna Mikhalenko*, decision available at http://kad.arbitr.ru/data/pdf/ebeeab0f-98d9-4b3b-ba28-d4e99240e21d/A27-781-2011_20110720_Opredelenie.pdf [accessed November 12, 2013].

41 The English Arbitration Act of 1996 is applicable in England, Wales and Northern Ireland. Scotland adopted the UNCITRAL Model Law. For ease of reference we refer to the English Arbitration Act of 1996 and to an arbitration in England under that Act.

42 The US system is a federal system with both federal and state courts and federal and state arbitration acts. Almost all ICC arbitrations are subject to the Federal Arbitration Act and are decided by the US federal rather than the state courts. However, the US federal system is divided into 12 circuits with each having a Court of Appeals. The case law in each circuit may evolve somewhat differently (until any difference is resolved by the US Supreme Court). The most important circuits are the 2nd Circuit (including New York), the 5th Circuit (including Texas), the 7th Circuit (including Chicago) and the 9th Circuit (including California).

43 In 2012, 35 per cent of places of arbitration (i.e. 266 arbitrations in total) were located in 29 different countries which have enacted legislation based on the UNCITRAL Model Law, ranging from Austria to Turkey. See (2013) ICC ICArb Bull Vol.24 No.1, p.14.

Each model law country may and many do add additional provisions or modify the law to a certain extent but this is usually done without materially changing the overall approach. 0–61

The approach with respect to procedural issues is therefore to focus not simply on the ICC Rules, but on the law and the case law in these countries, which are referred to as "major centres of arbitration". In making these references, we have sought to rely on the language of the statute and the case law from each country to seek to communicate the flavour of the decisions. 0–62

Principle 9: ICC Awards should meet the requirements of the New York Convention

The object of any ICC arbitration proceeding is to obtain an Award that can be enforced to ensure that the winning party has the benefit of the Award. If the primary national jurisdiction is the place of arbitration, the secondary jurisdiction is the place of enforcement. The place of arbitration is frequently a neutral jurisdiction, but the place of enforcement is normally not. The place of enforcement is usually the place where the losing party has its headquarters or significant operations. To be enforceable, an ICC Award should meet the requirements of the secondary jurisdiction as well as those of the primary jurisdiction. 0–63

For some commentators, it cannot reasonably be expected that the arbitrators keep in mind the secondary as well as the primary jurisdiction. This seems to be underestimating arbitrators or overestimating these requirements, or both. It should also be noted that counsel to the parties would normally seek to direct the arbitrators' attention to any specific points that need to be considered at the place of arbitration or in the Respondent's country, which is often the most likely place of enforcement of the Award. In any event, the New York Convention sets out basic principles that can be kept in mind by any arbitrator in handling a matter. Moreover, whether the arbitrators have these factors in mind or not, the parties will. Therefore, the reality of ICC arbitration is linked to enforcement of the Award and that enforcement is frequently based on the New York Convention.[44] 0–64

Principle 10: ICC arbitration continues to evolve even under the 2012 Rules

The principle of flexibility in ICC arbitration leaves room for a continued evolution in the procedure. This evolution is reflected in various areas, and in particular in presentation of evidence and evidence-taking itself. 0–65

For example, written witness statements, followed at the hearing by limited direct examination, and thereafter cross-examination, of the witness has become common in ICC arbitration, although the ICC Rules are mostly silent on how to take testimonial evidence.[45] This practice has become prevalent whatever the origin of the parties, their counsel and the arbitrators. Witness statements have 0–66

[44] Article VII(1) of the New York Convention permits parties to rely on more favorable provisions of national law. As discussed at para.0–59, French law regarding enforcement of foreign arbitral Awards is in several respects more favorable than that of the New York Convention.

[45] In App.IV to the 2012 Rules (Case Management Techniques) there exists now at least a reference to "written and oral" witness evidence.

been embraced in ICC arbitration but there are limits as to their usefulness. For example, in cases where the cross-examination demonstrates that the witness is not familiar with the contents of the witness statement, it is questionable whether the witness statement can be given much weight on the areas of weakness. In addition, there is an issue as to the completeness of witness statements and where witnesses spontaneously or not seek to add material factual examinations when under cross-examination. Therefore, although witness statements are cost-effective in giving advance notice of the evidence and reducing hearing time, there is an ongoing issue as to whether a greater element of direct testimony should be introduced.

0–67 As regards the presentation of evidence, it has become commonplace for more and more parties to present all their exhibits in electronic format as well. With these types of presentations, the parties are also in the position to submit very helpful audiovisual aids, such as a movie describing the facilities that are the subject of the arbitration. The electronic presentation of the evidence also makes it easier to organise documents in chronological or exhibit order and to make the documents transportable and accessible.

0–68 With regard to evidence taking, the practice with experts is evolving. The long-standing practice of having the expert present when an opposing expert is testifying has evolved in some instances to questioning the experts together. Similarly, there is some use of factual witness panels that in some cases amounts virtually to a "confrontation" of factual witnesses.

0–69 An area that is currently evolving is with respect to provisional measures discussed under art.28 and with respect to Emergency Arbitrators under art.29. Article 29 is an entirely new provision in the Rules and is applicable only to arbitration agreements concluded after January 1, 2012 (and even then only when its provisions have not been excluded by the parties). The Emergency Arbitrator is entitled to make a broad range of orders. However, there is no provision for ex parte proceedings and no limitation on the rights of a party to go to a competent court, for example.

0–70 Finally, the ICC Court has planned for a number of years to introduce online filing and notification of Requests for arbitration and other relevant documents. The ICC Netcase system, launched in 2005, was generally viewed as helpful by those who made use of it, but it was essentially a parallel electronic system and not a filing system. Once the ICC is technically in a position to offer an online platform for filings, it may have to modify and supplement art.3 of the 2012 Rules, which deal with notifications and communications.[46]

[46] Article 7 of App.I of the 2012 Rules was changed so as to allow the ICC Court to modify or supplement art.3 without the approval of the ICC Commission on Arbitration.

Arbitration Rules

CHAPTER 1

INTRODUCTORY PROVISIONS

Article 1 International Court of Arbitration

1 The International Court of Arbitration (the "Court") of the International Chamber of Commerce (the "ICC") is the independent arbitration body of the ICC. The statutes of the Court are set forth in Appendix I.

2 The Court does not itself resolve disputes. It administers the resolution of disputes by arbitral tribunals, in accordance with the Rules of Arbitration of the ICC (the "Rules"). The Court is the only body authorized to administer arbitrations under the Rules, including the scrutiny and approval of awards rendered in accordance with the Rules. It draws up its own internal rules, which are set forth in Appendix II (the "Internal Rules").

3 The President of the Court (the "President") or, in the President's absence or otherwise at the President's request, one of its Vice-Presidents shall have the power to take urgent decisions on behalf of the Court, provided that any such decision is reported to the Court at its next session.

4 As provided for in the Internal Rules, the Court may delegate to one or more committees composed of its members the power to take certain decisions, provided that any such decision is reported to the Court at its next session.

5 The Court is assisted in its work by the Secretariat of the Court (the "Secretariat") under the direction of its Secretary General (the "Secretary General").[1]

[1] Article 1 corresponds to art.1 of the 1998 ICC Rules. Article 1(1) has been changed by deleting reference to how members of the ICC Court are appointed (dealt with in App. II) and to reference to international arbitration disputes.

Introductory remarks

1–1 Article 1 sets out the basic principles with respect to the ICC Court and ICC Arbitration. As described in the Introduction, ICC arbitration is a form of administered and supervised arbitration, which can take place virtually anywhere in the world. However, like any other commercial arbitration, it is anchored in a national and international framework. Schematically, ICC arbitration can be described as follows[2]:

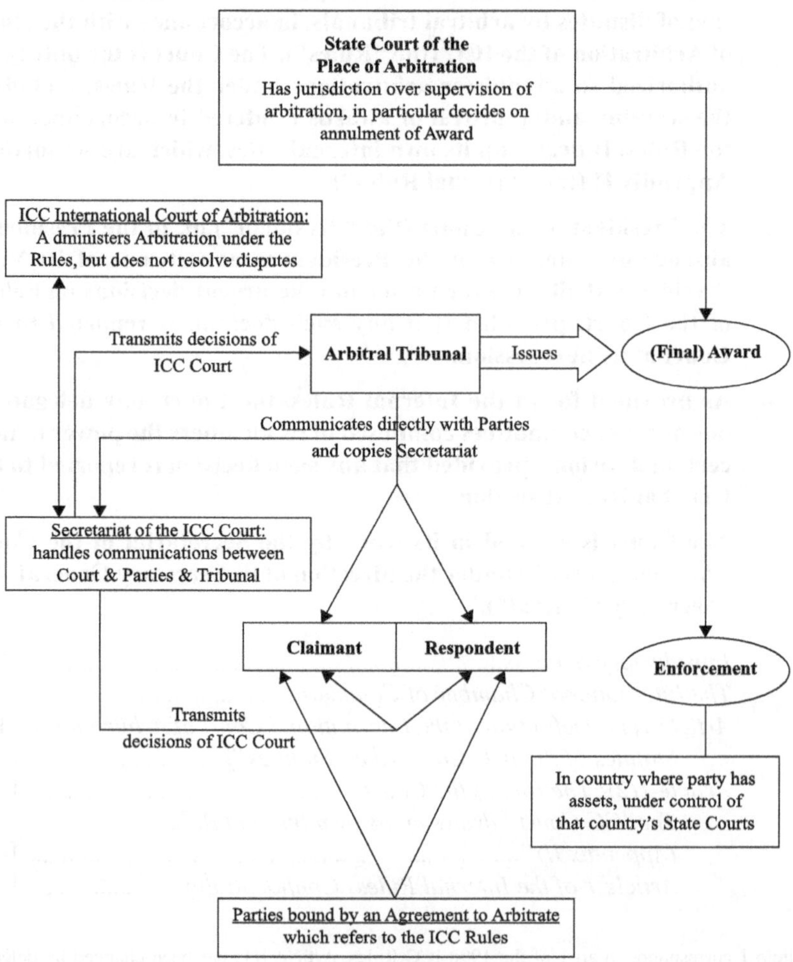

[2] As noted in the Introduction, an ICC arbitration, like any arbitration, is subject to the law of the place of the arbitration, and, in case of enforcement proceedings, the law of the place of enforcement.

The diagram is intended to reflect various interrelated aspects of ICC arbitration. The issue is effective dispute resolution and a dispute is not effectively resolved by arbitration until a final Award has been rendered and that Award has been satisfied. The Rules are essential to that procedure but they are only part of it. As discussed in more detail under art.34, the New York Convention[3] is the basis for international enforcement of foreign Awards. Therefore, in the interest of effectiveness, it is desirable to interpret the requirements of the Rules in the light of the requirements of that Convention.[4] **1–2**

The administration and supervision of the arbitral process by the ICC Court and its Secretariat is generally subject to the overall and ultimate control of the national courts at the place of arbitration. As discussed under arts 18 and 34, in many countries national courts tend to be supportive of international arbitration. However, there are differences in treatment of arbitration by the courts of various places of arbitration and, in what would appear to be very exceptional circumstances Tribunals have decided to disregard the decisions of the national courts of the place of arbitration.[5] **1–3**

The International Chamber of Commerce

Article 1 sets out basic elements relating to this form of arbitration that are used throughout the Rules and this book and therefore are discussed in detail below. **1–4**

The "ICC" is the International Chamber of Commerce. The ICC is a private non-governmental organisation established, in 1919, as a non-profit association under French law. The ICC is made up of National Committees from 90 countries and national trade organisations, industrial companies and associations from various areas or countries that are referred to as "Groups" but which fulfill the same role. The National Committees and Groups of the ICC are themselves generally non-governmental organisations.[6] In some instances, they are associated with the local chambers of commerce. The purpose of the ICC is to promote open international trade and investment around the world. The ICC is not solely or even principally devoted to arbitration. The ICC's constitution and a description of its functions can be found at its website http://www.iccwbo.org [accessed November 12, 2013]. **1–5**

The ICC's funding comes from membership fees, the sale of various publications[7] and organisation of seminars,[8] the administrative fees for ICC arbitrations[9] and the interest on the cash deposits made by parties involved in ICC arbitrations. The ICC's costs include in particular the costs related to the Court and its Secretariat. **1–6**

[3] Pt III App.4.
[4] See also art.41.
[5] See the discussion under art.18.
[6] A list of ICC National Committees and groups can be found at http://www.iccwbo.org/worldwide-membership/national-committees/ [accessed November 12, 2013].
[7] See http://www.iccbooks.com [accessed November 12, 2013].
[8] The ICC Institute of World Business Law organises seminars throughout the year via ICC Events; see http://www.iccwbo.org [accessed November 12, 2013].
[9] The ICC's administrative fees are discussed in connection with arts 36 and 37.

Article 1(1): "The International Court of Arbitration (the "Court") of the International Chamber of Commerce (the "ICC") is the independent arbitration body of the ICC. The statutes of the Court are set forth in Appendix I."

1–7 The International Court of Arbitration, or the "ICC Court", created in 1923, is the body that ensures the application of the Rules as provided for in art.1(2). Set out in Pt III are the Statutes of the Court (App.I to the Rules) as well as its Internal Rules (App.II to the Rules) that are discussed under art.1(2).

1–8 Article 1(1) refers to the ICC Court as the "independent arbitration body" of the ICC. As noted above, the ICC is a French not-for-profit association. The ICC Court is not a separate legal entity from the ICC, but is part of it from a legal point of view. Therefore, it is the ICC that is responsible for the actions of the Court. The scope of this liability is discussed under art.39. The French Supreme Court has held that there is a contractual relationship between the parties and the ICC with respect to the organisation of arbitration.[10]

1–9 Despite the fact that the ICC Court is not a legal entity separate from the ICC, it is independent of other parts of the ICC, in particular the President and Secretary General of the ICC, with respect to the functions that it exercises. The decisions of the ICC Court are taken by members of the ICC Court and not by any other persons at the ICC. The Rules have been amended to specifically refer to that independence.

Statutes of the ICC Court (the "Statutes")

1–10 The Statutes are set out in App.I to the Rules and are reproduced in Pt III of this book. They deal with:

Article 1: Function (see paras 1–16 et seq. below).

Article 2: Composition of the ICC Court (see paras 1–11f below).

Article 3: Appointment (see paras 1–11 et seq. below).

Article 4: Plenary Session of the ICC Court (see para.1–69ff below).

Article 5: Committees (see paras 1–71 et seq. below).

Article 6: Confidentiality (see paras 1–37 et seq. below).

Article 7: Modification of the Rules of Arbitration.

[10] Cass Civ. 1re, February 20, 2001, *Société Cubic Defense Systems Inc v Chambre de commerce internationale* (2001) Rev Arb No.3 p.511, note Clay; Paris, September 15, 1998, *Société Cubic Defense Systems Inc v Chambre de commerce internationale* (1999) Rev Arb No.1 p.103, note Lalive; TGI Paris, May 21, 1997, *Société Cubic Defense v Chambre de commerce internationale* (1997) Rev Arb No.3 p.417. See also, Paris TGI, October 10, 2007, *Société SNF v Chambre de Commerce Internationale* (2007) Rev Arb No.4 p.847, note Jarrosson, and (2007) Dalloz No.41 p.2916, note Clay; see also Fouchard, "Les institutions permanentes d'arbitrage devant le juge étatique (a'propos d'une jurisprudence récente)" (1987) Rev Arb No.2, p.281; TGI Paris, December 16, 2004, *M. Marcel Taffin v Cour internationale d'arbitrage de la Chambre de Commerce Internationale & Société Goather Versicherungsbank VVag*, unreported. Paris TGI, January 01, 2009, *Société SNF v Chambre de Commerce Internationale*, (2009). See Jolivet, "*La Responsabilité des centres d'arbitrage et leur assurance*", Revue générale du droit des assurances 2012 Vol.1. p.216.

The President of the ICC Court is elected by the ICC World Council upon recommendation of the Executive Board of the ICC (Statutes art.3(1)). He or she is an independent consultant to the ICC (and not an employee) paid an annual consulting fee. The ICC Council upon proposal of the National Committees or Groups appoints the members of the ICC Court with one member for each Committee or Group (Statutes art.3(3)). The ICC World Council appoints the Vice-Presidents of the ICC Court who may but need not otherwise be members of the ICC Court (Statutes art.3(2)). In practice the Vice-Presidents are not otherwise members of the Court and are appointed upon proposal of the President. The members of the ICC Court are independent from the National Committee or Group that proposed them (Statutes art.1(3)). The members of the ICC Court are generally appointed for a term of three years (Statutes art.3(5)). The National Committee or Group can propose that the term be renewed. If a member of the ICC Court resigns or is unable to carry out his functions, he or she may be replaced by another member nominated by the same National Committee or Group for the remaining period of appointment of the original member (Statutes art.3(5)). The ICC Court also has alternate members for several countries. Alternate members are appointed by the ICC Council upon proposal of the President of the ICC Court (Statutes art.3(4)). **1–11**

A list of the members and alternate members of the ICC Court can be found on the ICC's website. At the end of mid-2013, there were 137 members of the ICC Court, 87 regular, 32 alternate members and 17 vice-presidents. As is reflected in that list, the members of the ICC Court come from many countries, and represent 88 different nationalities. Therefore, the legal and linguistic backgrounds of the ICC Court's members are extremely varied. **1–12**

The members of the ICC Court are frequently lawyers in private practice or employees of companies with an interest in international arbitration. They are paid a nominal amount per diem for each day of meetings and are not reimbursed for their expenses.[11] **1–13**

Although not referred to in the ICC Rules (or the appendices), the ICC Court has what is referred to as the "Bureau", which is composed of the President and Vice-Presidents of the Court, the Secretary General, Deputy Secretary General and General Counsel. The Bureau is an informal consultative body of the Court that is intended to provide a forum for discussion. The Bureau does not publish reports or findings. However, its discussions influence the approach of the ICC Court and publications by the Secretariat. **1–14**

In addition, the ICC has recently created a Governing Board for the ICC Court to advise the ICC and the Court on all matters concerning the organisation and functioning of the ICC Court. The Governing Board was set up in particular to advise with respect to the development of ICC arbitration. As such it is intended to be a body advising on policy in general rather than on specific arbitrations. **1–15**

[11] The President of the ICC Court has the status of a consultant to the ICC, and receives a substantial annual consultant's fee, plus reimbursement of expenses. The expenses of the Vice-Presidents of the ICC Court are treated differently by the ICC as far as their expenses are concerned, due to their respective roles.

Article 1(2): "The Court does not itself resolve disputes. It administers the resolution of disputes by arbitral tribunals, in accordance with the Rules of Arbitration of the ICC (the "Rules"). The Court is the only body authorized to administer arbitrations under the Rules, including the scrutiny and approval of awards rendered in accordance with the Rules. It draws up its own internal rules, which are set forth in Appendix II (the "Internal Rules")."

1–16 Article 1(2) refers to the limited and administrative role that the ICC Court plays under the Rules. In the *Cubic* case,[12] the French Supreme Court noted that the Rules maintain a distinction between the function of organising the arbitration and the "judicial function".

1–17 The ICC Court does not settle disputes itself. It has an administrative function with respect to the Rules. The Tribunal decides the actual procedure for an ICC arbitration and decides the merits of the disputes. The ICC Court's role is to organise and supervise the framework for arbitration under the Rules for business disputes as discussed below. The ICC Court is the entity that seeks to ensure that the procedural safeguards provided for in the Rules are correctly observed. It issues administrative decisions in this respect in accordance with the Rules. The ICC Court does not seek to ensure a uniform application of the Rules and generally leaves it to the Tribunal to interpret the Rules.

1–18 Under art.1(2), the ICC Court is to administer resolution of disputes by Tribunals in accordance with the Rules. Therefore, both the ICC Court and Tribunals are to apply the Rules. In certain areas, the ICC Court has sole responsibility for applying the Rules (prior to constitution of the Tribunal, for example or with respect to decisions on challenges). In other areas, it is the Tribunal that has the basic responsibility for the application of the Rules (such as with respect to conducting the hearings). The ICC Court can only intervene in the areas that are within the domain of the Tribunal where the Rules so provide (such as by appointing or removing an arbitrator under arts 13, 14 and 15).

1–19 The amendments in the new Rules were intended to focus on the ICC Court's administrative role and to avoid the implication that the ICC Court was responsible for ensuring that the Rules were properly applied by Tribunals.

1–20 Article 1(2) also provides that the ICC Court is the only body authorised to administer arbitrations under the Rules. This provision was inserted in the most recent version of the Rules because in some instances, parties had sought to have arbitrations under the ICC Rules without the involvement of the ICC Court. This is not possible under the Rules. As noted in art.1(2), the ICC Court is in particular the sole entity authorised to scrutinise and approve ICC Awards.

1–21 These provisions raise two related issues. The first issue is to what extent the parties are permitted to adapt the ICC Rules and to still be entitled to conduct an ICC arbitration. The second issue is what the legal effect is of an agreement that purports to have an ICC arbitration but without the involvement of the ICC Court.

1–22 As regards the extent to which modifications are possible to the Rules, the basic principle is that the Rules provide the overall framework for an ICC arbitration. The standard ICC arbitration clause set out is straightforward:

[12] See para.1–8 n.10.

> "All disputes arising out of or in connection with the present contract shall be finally settled under the Rules of Arbitration of the International Chamber of Commerce by one or more arbitrators appointed in accordance with the said Rules."[13]

As noted by the ICC in connection with the standard arbitration clauses, the parties may wish to set out as well the law governing the contract, the number of arbitrators, the place of arbitration and the language of the arbitration. The parties may also wish to take into account the national laws applicable at the place of arbitration or at the place of probable enforcement, the potential participation of more than two parties and the use of other dispute resolution mechanisms such as ICC Pre-arbitral Referee Procedure, ICC Amicable Dispute Resolution (ADR), ICC Expertise and ICC Dispute Boards. **1–23**

As discussed under art.18, most arbitration clauses establish the place of arbitration. Many clauses refer to the language of the arbitration if that is not clear from the context. Arbitration clauses frequently specify the applicable law. **1–24**

Parties are permitted to agree on additional provisions with respect to the arbitration and do so, in particular in the more complex transactions. There is nothing wrong with these provisions that supplement the Rules provided that the parties give careful thought to the consequences of those changes in each specific case. **1–25**

A somewhat different issue arises where the arbitration clause purports to modify a provision of the Rules itself. Article 1(1) states that part of the ICC Court's function is to provide for arbitration "in accordance with the Rules". This proviso applies to both the ICC Court and to the parties. The ICC Court cannot intervene in matters that go beyond its function defined in art.1. For instance, the ICC Court could not act as an adjudicator or a mediator in a given dispute.[14] Nevertheless, it would be possible for parties to agree that certain more limited decisions could be taken by the ICC Court. For example, although art.20 provides that, in the absence of an agreement of the parties, the Tribunal shall decide the language(s) of arbitration, the parties could agree to have the ICC Court decide that issue. **1–26**

Article 1(1) restricts the freedom of the parties to depart unilaterally from the arbitral system contained in the Rules. Based on art.1(1), the ICC Court may decline to administer a given case where parties seek to deviate significantly from the Rules. This issue is often referred to under the somewhat misleading reference to "mandatory" and "non-mandatory" provisions in the Rules. **1–27**

By issuing the Rules, the ICC makes an offer to parties to agree upon the use, in case of disputes, of its arbitration services, as embodied in its Rules.[15] To the extent that the Rules specifically give the power to the parties to agree on certain **1–28**

[13] For arbitration clauses agreed to after January 1, 2012, if the parties wish to exclude the emergency arbitrator provisions, the standard ICC clause is as follows: "All disputes arising out of or in connection with the present contract shall be finally settled under the Rules of Arbitration of the International Chamber of Commerce by one or more arbitrators appointed in accordance with the said Rules. The Emergency Arbitrator Provisions shall not apply."

[14] The ICC does provide for alternative dispute resolution. See http://www.iccwbo.org/index-adr.asp. However, that is a procedure distinct from the arbitration procedure.

[15] Fouchard, "Final Report on the Status of the Arbitrator" (1996) ICC ICArb Bull Vol.7 No.1, p.27; see also the discussion under art.6(1).

matters that may arise in the course of an ICC arbitration, such as the number of arbitrators, the method of their selection, or the place of arbitration, the ICC Court is obviously bound by such agreement.

1–29 In all other cases, it would seem that parties cannot impose unilaterally any deviation from the Rules without the acceptance of the ICC Court. It then becomes a policy question for the ICC Court whether or not to accept such change. The ICC has its reputation to protect regarding both how satisfactorily the arbitration procedure is conducted, and the enforceability of Awards rendered under its auspices.

1–30 The general policy of the ICC Court is not to accept modifications to its Rules that would eliminate or significantly alter the provisions relating to matters such as the following:

—the establishment of the Terms of Reference;
—the fixing of arbitrators' fees by the ICC Court;
—the scrutiny and approval of draft Awards by the ICC Court.

Those matters are viewed as being the cornerstones of ICC arbitration, and the corresponding rules are often referred to as being of "mandatory" nature.

1–31 There are many cases where the ICC Court has accepted a modification of its Rules, so long as they were considered compatible with the ICC arbitral system as such. In practice, the ICC Court decides upon the admissibility of deviations/variations from the Rules on a case-by-case basis. Thus, the drafters of ICC arbitration clauses and agreements must be aware that they depart from the Rules at their own risk, and that the ICC Court is not obliged to agree.

1–32 The ICC Court has accepted, for example, arbitration clauses that provided that the arbitrators determine the place of arbitration, rather than the ICC Court itself. This is despite the fact that, under art.18, the choice of the place of arbitration is generally the responsibility of the Court in the absence of an agreement between the parties.

1–33 In other cases, for example where parties have provided in their arbitration clause a short time limit for the arbitrators to render the final Award, the ICC Court would normally explain to the parties the difficulty of implementing such a time limit, and seek to ensure that the parties agree that the ICC Court may extend this time limit (see art.30).[16]

1–34 As regards cases where parties have entered into an agreement adopting the Rules but to be administered by a body other than the ICC Court, the effect of that

[16] Article 38 allows the parties to shorten the time limits provided in the Rules. The issue is therefore when a proposed shortening of the time limits could give rise either to concerns about due process or that the Tribunal would not have adequate time to conduct the proceedings and render the Award. In a recent case, the three-month time limit for rendering the Award was extended by the ICC Court, but the Tribunal conducted the proceedings on an expedited basis. The Terms of Reference were signed within five weeks of transmission of the file to the Tribunal and the Award was rendered four months after the signing of the Terms of Reference. In some instances, the agreement of the parties may not be enough. In one ICC Case No.17489, the arbitration clause provided that the Award was to be issued within six months after the signing of the Terms of Reference. The government Respondent offered to extend that period. The Claimant rejected this offer on the basis that the Award might be attacked in the local courts of the Respondent due to the extension. The Tribunal managed to issue a unanimous Award, which was complied with by the parties, within the six-month period.

agreement will depend on applicable law. The ICC is naturally opposed to parties agreeing to an arbitration under the Rules but providing for decisions by a body other than the ICC Court.[17] However, parties and courts are not necessarily bound by the restriction in the second sentence of art.1(2). In a recent case in Singapore under the current Rules, the court upheld a provision calling for an arbitration under the Rules but without the involvement of the ICC Court. The Court held as follows[18]:

> "10 Where the words 'Arbitration Committee' used in the arbitration clause do not refer to any particular arbitral institution, it was in my view, unnecessary to limit the options of the parties in resolving the dispute. Although Art 1(2) of the ICC Rules claims for the International Court of Arbitration the sole authority to administer ICC arbitrations, the power of the rules to bind emanates from the consent of the parties. Art 1(2) cannot curtail the freedom of the parties to agree to be bound by the result of an arbitration administered by a different arbitral institution applying the ICC Rules, neither can it curtail the power of the court to give an interpretation to a pathological arbitration clause, where that clause uses language which admits the possibility of different arbitral institutions, which provides a wider range of solutions to the parties.
> 11 I must emphasise, however, that leaving open this possibility of a hybrid arbitration as part of a range of solutions to resolve the problems created by the pathological arbitration clause is in no way a judicial endorsement of a hybrid arbitration. I had noted the inconvenience associated with a hybrid arbitration"

As noted by the court in the above case (and as illustrated by the decision in which the court sought the parties' agreement to another arbitral institution), in many if not most instances, those arbitration clauses create serious issues due to the complex nature of the duties of the ICC Court. For example, the ICC Court has a duty in scrutinising draft Awards that may be difficult to entrust to one person or to a body other than the ICC Court itself. Therefore, although the decision in *HKL* is logical from the point of view of the agreement between the parties itself, it is of course preferable if parties do not wish to have the ICC Court involved for the parties to agree on the application of an entirely different set of arbitration rules, such as the UNCITRAL Arbitration Rules and to provide for the appointing authority rather than to seek to adapt the ICC Rules.[19] **1–35**

[17] *HKL Group Co Ltd v Rizq International Holdings Pte Ltd* [2013] SGHCR 5. The arbitration clause provided that: "Any dispute shall be settled by amicable negotiation between two Parties. In case both Parties fail to reach amicable agreement, all dispute out of in connection with the contract shall be settled by the Arbitration Committee at Singapore under the rules of The International Chamber of Commerce of which awards shall be final and binding both parties. Arbitration fee and other related charge shall be borne by the losing Party unless otherwise agreed".

[18] *HKL Group Co Ltd v Rizq International Holdings Pte Ltd* [2013] SGHCR 5.

[19] For example, it is possible to designate the ICC Court as an appointing authority under the UNCITRAL Arbitration Rules. For a discussion of the ICC Court and other entities acting as appointing authorities under the UNCITRAL Arbitration Rules, see Webster, *Handbook of UNCITRAL Arbitration* (Thomson/Sweet & Maxwell, 2010).

The ICC Court "draws up its own Internal Rules (Appendix II)"

1–36 The Internal Rules are included in App.II to the Rules and are reproduced in Pt III of this book. They deal with:

Article 1: Confidential Character of the Work of the ICC Court (see paras 1–37 et seq. below).

Article 2: Participation of Members of the ICC Court in ICC Arbitration (see paras 1–46 et seq. below).

Article 3: Relations between the Members of the ICC Court and ICC National Committees (see paras 1–56 et seq. below).

Article 4: Committee of the ICC Court (discussed at paras 1–69 et seq. below).

Article 5: ICC Court Secretariat (discussed at paras 1–84 et seq. below).

Article 6: Scrutiny of Arbitral Awards (discussed under art.33).

Article 1 of the Internal Rules: Confidentiality

1–37 Article 6 of the Statutes of the Court provide for the confidentiality of proceedings of the ICC Court. Articles 1(1)–(3) of the ICC Court's Internal Rules provide that:

> "1. For the purposes of this Appendix, members of the Court include the President and Vice-Presidents of the Court.
> 2. The sessions of the Court, whether plenary or those of a Committee of the Court, are open only to its members and to the Secretariat.
> 3. However, in exceptional circumstances, the President of the Court may invite other persons to attend. Such persons must respect the confidential nature of the work of the Court."

This Article of the ICC Court's Internal Rules deals only with confidentiality of the proceedings of the ICC Court and not with the issue of confidentiality in ICC arbitrations generally, which is discussed under art.22(3).

1–38 Sessions of the ICC Court are confidential. Persons who are not members of the ICC Court are generally not permitted to attend its sessions without the consent of the President and, if they do attend sessions, they must agree to respect the confidentiality of the proceedings.

1–39 Parties (and their lawyers) are not permitted to attend sessions of the ICC Court. The authors are aware of no circumstance in which this has been waived. Therefore, in seeking a decision of the ICC Court, lawyers should be conscious of the fact that they will not have an opportunity to make an oral presentation to the ICC Court. The ICC Court usually ensures that parties have an opportunity to make written submissions with respect to procedural matters that the ICC Court is called upon to decide with respect to a particular arbitration. The counsel in charge of a file within the Secretariat regularly makes an oral and written submission to the ICC Court, and will answer questions of its members. The Secretariat sets out the positions of both parties and the Tribunal if need be. Counsel of the parties are free to speak directly with the Secretariat, if they feel that an oral explanation may assist the Secretariat in better understanding a party's position, but the Secretariat should ensure that any substantive point raised is presented to the other party as well.[20]

Article 1(4) of the Internal Rules provides that: **1–40**

> "The documents submitted to the Court, or drawn up by it in the course of its proceedings, are communicated only to the members of the Court and to the Secretariat and to persons authorised by the President to attend Court sessions."

The documents to be submitted to the ICC Court are generally prepared and organised by the Secretariat. The documents selected by the Secretariat for submission will depend on the issue before the ICC Court. Certainly, the correspondence from the parties relevant to the issue would be submitted together with extracts of other relevant material. Set out in Annex 1 Pt I ("The ICC Court's sessions in a Nutshell") is a list of issues discussed and dealt with at Plenary and Committee sessions of the ICC Court. **1–41**

The parties to the proceedings will not know what has been submitted to the ICC Court with respect to the decision sought, although it is safe to assume that all relevant correspondence between the parties and the Secretariat is usually submitted to the ICC Court. This aspect of confidentiality, as with the confidentiality of the sessions themselves, reflects the administrative nature of the ICC Court's role. **1–42**

Article 1(5) of the Internal Rules provides that: **1–43**

> "[t]he President or the Secretary General of the Court may authorise researchers undertaking work of a scientific nature on international trade law to acquaint themselves with Awards and other documents of general interest, with the exception of memoranda, notes, statements and documents remitted by the parties within the framework of arbitration proceedings."

Article 1(6) of the Internal Rules provides that such authorisation "shall not be given unless the beneficiary has undertaken to respect the confidential nature of the documents made available . . .".[21]

[20] If a party raises a substantive point with the Secretariat, the Secretariat usually invites the party to set out the comment in a letter copied to the other side. The parties' correspondence with the Secretariat usually forms part of the file submitted to the ICC Court.

[21] Jolivet, "Access to information and Awards" (2006) Arb Int Vol.22 No.2, p.265, at pp.273–274 rightly points out: "A distinction should be drawn between the information that is aimed at being communicated without specific control, such as promotional brochures . . . and information that is communicated under the condition that it will be controlled. Control can be exercised on the communication itself or the use of the information. The latter situation is, for example, encountered when arbitral institutions grant access to arbitral decisions for research of an academic nature. Once the information has been processed by the researcher in a doctoral thesis, a book or an article, the institution will check that the information chosen and the reference thereto do not contravene its confidentiality policy and are not likely to be detrimental to its image. Such considerations will affect the way in which the information is provided . . . As arbitration develops and becomes the normal dispute resolution mechanism for international commercial disputes, journalists are becoming increasingly interested in certain types of information such as the amount in dispute, the names of the parties and their in-house representatives in the case of legal entities, the names of their

1–44 The ICC Court's desire for confidentiality has to be balanced against the need for potential users of ICC arbitration to understand how the ICC Court and ICC arbitration function. The issue of confidentiality with respect to arbitration extends beyond the issue of confidentiality of the proceedings of the ICC Court but there is considerable overlap. As regards the proceedings of the ICC Court, the ICC and the members of the Secretariat publish articles regarding types of decisions and trends but without identifying the parties involved.[22] This approach has also been adopted by the authors who have sought to reflect their experience as members of the ICC Court, arbitrators and counsel with respect to its procedures and as regards the trends regarding certain decisions.

1–45 As regards the proceedings of Tribunals, the ICC has permitted publication of extracts of Awards and procedural orders that do not identify the parties (or frequently, the arbitrators).[23] Therefore, there is resource material on ICC procedural orders and Awards that is published by and under the control of the ICC,[24] but that material is less extensive than corresponding material for many national courts. Perhaps more importantly, although there are trends and tendencies in international arbitration, particularly concerning the procedural aspects, there is little opportunity to see how specific arbitrators have in fact decided cases, unless of course the cases are the subject of court proceedings relating to enforcement, annulment or challenge of arbitrators, for example.

Article 2 of the Internal Rules: Participation of Members of the ICC Court in ICC Arbitration

1–46 Article 2(1) of the Internal Rules provides that "[t]he President and the members of the Secretariat of the Court may not act as arbitrators or as counsel in cases submitted to ICC arbitration".

1–47 This rule is intended to reflect the fact that the members of the Secretariat are in effect full-time employees of the ICC with access to its records. They are therefore in a privileged position with respect to ICC arbitrations. The authority and the neutrality of the President of the ICC Court is to be protected by excluding him or her from any role as counsel or arbitrator in an ICC arbitration. As a result of this provision, in an ICC arbitration, there is no danger that the opposing party will

counsel. For such persons, access to information is very rarely prompted by the desire to understand the legal issues at stake and the legal reasoning of the parties".

[22] See for example Jolivet, "Chronique de jurisprudence arbitrale de la Chambre de commerce internationale (CCI): l'incompétence de l'arbitre" (2006) Les Cahiers de l'Arbitrage 2006/1, p.38; Whitesell and Silva Romero, "Multiparty and Multicontract Arbitration: Recent ICC Experience" (2003) ICC ICArb Bull, Special Supplement, p.7.

[23] For research purposes and abstracts, see, for example, Arnaldez, Derains & Hascher, *Collection of ICC Arbitral Awards 1996–2000*, Vol.IV (ICC Publishing/Kluwer, 2003); Arnaldez, Derains & Hascher, *Collection of ICC Arbitral Awards 1991–1995*, Vol.III (ICC Publishing/Kluwer, 1997); Jarvin, Derains & Arnaldez, *Collection of ICC Arbitral Awards 1986–1990*, Vol.II (ICC Publishing/Kluwer, 1994); Jarvin & Derains, *Collection of ICC Arbitral Awards 1974–1985*, Vol.1 (ICC Publishing/Kluwer, 1990); Hascher, *Collection of Procedural Decisions in ICC Arbitration 1993–1996* (ICC Publishing/Kluwer, 1997); see also *ICC Bulletin, ICCA Congress Series, Yearbook of Commercial Arbitration, Clunet.*

[24] There seem to be no basis or good reason preventing practitioners from citing publications from extracts of unpublished ICC Awards in which they were involved, as long as they do not disclose the names of the parties.

hire such a person as counsel or that they will nominate them as an arbitrator in the proceedings.

Article 2(2) of the Internal Rules provides that "[t]he Court shall not appoint Vice-Presidents or members of the Court as arbitrators. They may, however, be proposed for such duties by one or more of the parties, or, pursuant to any other procedure agreed upon by the parties, subject to confirmation". **1–48**

The ICC Court appoints the president of the Tribunal or the sole arbitrator where the parties are unable to agree on the choice of such person, or in some instances to appoint co-arbitrators where there is multi- party arbitration or a party fails to appoint a co-arbitrator under art.12. Article 2(2) of the Internal Rules prohibits the ICC Court from appointing one of its own members in such circumstances, as the ICC Court's role is to assist arbitration, but not to propose its own members as arbitrators. **1–49**

The members of the ICC Court, who are not employees of the ICC, are practitioners who are paid a nominal amount for their activities with respect to the ICC Court.[25] The ICC Court members are frequently active in international arbitration, as counsel or arbitrators, or both. Nothing in the Rules prevents them from acting in ICC arbitrations as counsel to parties in ICC arbitrations or from accepting appointments when proposed as arbitrators by one or both of the parties.[26] As a result, in some ICC arbitrations a member or alternate member of the ICC Court acts as an arbitrator or counsel. **1–50**

Article 2(3) provides that "[w]hen the President, a Vice-President or a member of the Court or of the Secretariat is involved in any capacity whatsoever in proceedings pending before the Court, such person must inform the Secretary General of the Court upon becoming aware of such involvement". **1–51**

This provision imposes a broad requirement of giving notice of involvement "in any capacity whatsoever" of the persons referred to. As noted above, the President of the ICC Court or a member of the Secretariat cannot be involved as counsel or as an arbitrator in an ICC proceeding. However, they can be involved in other capacities (as factual witnesses for example) and if so, the Secretary General of the ICC Court must be informed. This involvement would include participation as a secretary to the Tribunal, participation as a witness or expert or special personal links with the parties to the case or their counsel but professional relationships would not generally fall within this requirement. In the former cases, the President of the ICC Court or member of the Secretariat would be excused from the case. **1–52**

As noted above, the Vice-Presidents or members of the ICC Court can participate as either counsel or arbitrators in ICC arbitrations and the Secretariat must be given notice of such involvement. The obligation to inform the Secretary General of the ICC Court extends beyond that type of involvement such as acting as a witness or of course being a party to the arbitration. In addition, many of the members of the ICC Court are partners in law firms and the involvement of a law firm in an ICC arbitration or of another lawyer from the law firm as arbitrator or **1–53**

[25] They receive a per diem per attendance of a Court's session. In 2007, it was US$100.

[26] They cannot, however, be proposed by their National Committees to act as arbitrators in ICC arbitration.

counsel in an ICC arbitration would give rise to a duty of disclosure under art.2(3) of the Internal Rules.[27]

1–54 The consequences of such participation are set out in arts 2(4) and (5) of the Internal Rules: "4. Such person [involved in an arbitration] must be absent from the Court session whenever the matter is considered by the Court and shall not participate in the discussions or in the decisions of the Court" and "5. Such person will not receive any material documentation or information pertaining to such proceedings".

1–55 Given the basic principle of confidentiality with respect to the ICC Court's proceedings, these provisions are important to ensure that all parties are treated with equality and fairness. In practice, the Secretariat will ensure that the members of the ICC Court involved in a matter will not receive any documents relating to a matter in which they may have an interest and ICC Court members pay scrupulous attention to leaving the room when matters in which they are involved are about to be discussed.

Article 3 of Internal Rules: Relations between the Members of the ICC Court and the ICC National Committees and Groups

1–56 Article 3(1) of the Internal Rules provides that "[b]y virtue of their capacity, the members of the Court are independent of the ICC National Committees and Groups which proposed them for appointment by the ICC World Council".

1–57 Article 3(2) of the Internal Rules specifies that the obligation of confidentiality extends to relations between the members of the ICC Court and their National Committee and Groups. It states that:

> "Furthermore, they must regard as confidential, *vis-à-vis* the said National Committees and Groups, any information concerning individual cases with which they have become acquainted in their capacity as members of the Court, except when they have been requested by the President of the Court or by its Secretary General to communicate specific information to their respective National Committees or Groups."

1–58 Once appointed to the ICC Court, the members owe a duty to the ICC Court and not to their National Committee. The members of the ICC Court do not act as representatives of their National Committee. This relationship is therefore fundamentally different than the relationship of members of the ICC Council to their National Committee or the members of the ICC Commission on Arbitration and their National Committee. In both these instances, the members act as representatives of the National Committee, while that is not the case for the members of the ICC Court.

Article 1(3): "The President of the Court (the "President") or, in the President's absence or otherwise at the President's request, one of its

[27] See Cass Civ 2e, March 31, 1978, *Société Métal Profil v Société Intercraft*, (1979) Rev Arb No.4 p.457, note Fouchard.

Vice-Presidents shall have the power to take urgent decisions on behalf of the Court, provided that any such decision is reported to the Court at its next session."

Article 3(1) of the Statutes provides that "[t]he President is elected by the ICC World Council upon the recommendation of the Executive Board of the ICC". Since January 2009, the President of the ICC Court has been Mr John Beechey, an English solicitor. Prior to Mr Beechey the President was Professor Pierre Tercier from Switzerland who in turn succeeded Dr Robert Briner, another Swiss lawyer.[28] **1–59**

Article 3(2) of the Statutes provides that "[t]he ICC World Council appoints the Vice-Presidents of the Court from among the members of the Court or otherwise". Currently, there are 17 Vice-Presidents who are from around the world. The Vice-Presidents are not employees of the ICC, and unlike the President, they have no office at their disposal at the ICC headquarters in Paris. **1–60**

The President of the ICC Court is in charge of the overall functioning of the Court and, as discussed below, and generally presides over Plenary Sessions and often presides over Committee Sessions of the ICC Court. Article 1(3) provides that the President (or in his absence a Vice-President) is entitled to take "urgent decisions" on behalf of the ICC Court. **1–61**

There are no express restrictions in the Rules upon the ability of the President of the ICC Court (or in his absence, a Vice-President) to render on behalf of the ICC Court an urgent decision. One of the most common decisions is to replace members for Committee sessions.[29] Other matters as to which the President may take urgent decisions include approval of Awards (whether partial, final and/or revised final Awards),[30] approval of a correction to an Award, approval of advances on fees in exceptional circumstances, and fixing the costs of arbitration, nomination of a sole arbitrator or president of the Tribunal where there has been some delay, extending of the time for a party to nominate a co-arbitrator, appointing a replacement for an arbitrator who has been removed by the ICC Court where hearings are to take place shortly. There must be a good reason for the urgency that justifies that exceptionally the matter not be submitted for consideration by the entire ICC Court, or one of its (three-member) Committees, but simply be decided by the President of the ICC Court. **1–62**

In one case where the President of the ICC Court approved an interim Award, the urgency resulted from the fact that the Award had to be notified to the parties immediately so as to allow them to prepare for an upcoming hearing that had been **1–63**

[28] The two prior Chairmen were both from France. Mr *Michel Gaudet*, a jurist, was the first director of legal affairs of the European Commission and thereafter president of the European Insurers Committee. Mr *Alain Plantey* was a former member of the French Conseil d'Etat (French Supreme Administrative Court) and a French Ambassador.

[29] As a general matter, the ICC Court designates Committee members for each Committee session at the Plenary Session in accordance with art.4(3) of the Court's Internal Rules (App.II). It may be necessary to replace a member for example where a Court member residing abroad is unable to travel to Paris to attend a Committee session for which he or she has been designated. This is specifically provided for in art.9(2) of the Internal Regulations of the Court.

[30] This could be necessary to permit a filing for a state court or, where the Tribunal had calculated interest to a certain date and delay would have necessitated further complex calculations. In another ICC case, it was considered necessary with respect to an agreed Award where the parties considered it essential to carry out the terms of the settlement promptly.

scheduled for quite some time by the Tribunal. In another case, the parties had agreed on a "fast-track" arbitration procedure, according to which the Award was to be notified within six weeks after the hearing. The existence of urgency was also accepted where a Respondent had filed for bankruptcy, and where the Claimant was required to declare its claims before a certain date by producing the Award. In another case, an Award had to be made before a certain date, otherwise the assets held in custody by a third party would have been released.

1–64 The decision of the President (or Vice-President) is to be reported to the ICC Court "at its next session", i.e. at the next monthly Plenary Session of the Court. This report is only for purposes of information, not for ratification or for revision.

1–65 However, it may be assumed that the President will make use of its prerogative only in truly urgent cases such as fast-track arbitrations, in order not to reduce the breadth of the decision-making power normally reserved to, and to be exercised by the ICC Court alone. In addition, in truly complex and sensitive matters, however urgent they may be, the President would tend to seek informally the views of other members of the ICC Court, in particular the Vice-Presidents, prior to rendering his decision.

1–66 The Vice-Presidents have duties delegated to them by the President of the ICC Court. These duties include in particular presiding over Committee or Plenary Sessions of the Court.

1–67 The role of the President includes ensuring that the ICC Court functions effectively. The President has the ultimate responsibility for the ICC Court. The Statutes provide that the President is to preside over Plenary Sessions of the ICC Court, and the President has the casting (i.e. tie-breaking) vote (App.I Art.4). Also, it is upon the President's proposal that alternate members may be appointed by the Council (App.I Art.3). The Internal Rules specifically require also that it is only upon the President's invitation that outside persons may attend sessions of the ICC Court and upon the President's authorisation (and also the Secretary General's) that certain persons can have limited access to ICC Court documentation and Awards. The President frequently also chairs the Committee Sessions of the ICC Court. In these tasks, the President may and often does designate one of the Vice-Presidents to act on his behalf in his absence.

1–68 The President of the ICC Court has to assume many other more informal, albeit important, functions. The President regularly attends outside arbitration events. The President of the ICC Court travels frequently to foreign countries to meet the respective National Committees, members of the judiciary, members of government, in particular the Minister of Justice, and representatives of the business community. International arbitration has expanded significantly in recent years and this expansion has been rendered possible in part through the support provided by national courts and institutions. It is important therefore not only that the President be in a position to explain and represent ICC arbitration but that he also receives comments from national courts and users of arbitration as to positive and negative aspects of international arbitration. The President of the ICC Court will often be accompanied by the ICC Court's Secretary General, or other members of the Secretariat.

Article 1(4): "As provided for in the Internal Rules, the Court may delegate to one or more committees composed of its members the power to take certain decisions, provided that any such decision is reported to the Court at its next session."

Article 1(4) was drafted based on the assumption that the ICC Court is a collegial body and that, as a general rule it functions as a whole in Plenary Sessions. **1–69**

Article 4 of the Statutes provides that "[t]he Plenary Sessions of the Court are presided over by the President or, in his absence, by one of the Vice-Presidents designated by him. The deliberations shall be valid when at least six members are present. Decisions are taken by a majority vote, the President having a casting vote in the event of a tie". **1–70**

Article 5 of the Statutes provides that "[t]he Court may set up one or more Committees and establish the functions and organisation of such Committees". **1–71**

The ICC Court holds Plenary Sessions on a monthly basis, normally on the last Thursday (afternoon) of the month. The members and alternate members are free to attend any Plenary Session of the ICC Court. Alternate members have the same standing as the members of the ICC Court. Frequently, both a member and an alternate member from the same country attend the Plenary Session of the ICC Court, although this was probably not the original intention when provision was made for alternate members of the ICC Court. Between 20 and 30 members of the ICC Court frequently attend its Plenary Sessions. **1–72**

For decisions that require particular consideration, a member of the ICC Court, selected by the Secretariat, will act as special "rapporteur" and prepare and present a report to the Plenary Session regarding the issue. These reports are based on a review of the relevant submissions of the parties and the applicable legal principles and law, including the Rules. **1–73**

Many decisions of the ICC Court need not be dealt with in Plenary Session. Therefore, art.4(1) of the Internal Rules establishes a Committee. Articles 4(2) and (3) of the Internal Rules provide that: **1–74**

> "2. The members of the Committee consist of a President and at least two other members. The President of the Court acts as the President of the Committee. In the President's absence or otherwise at the President's request, the President may designate a Vice-President of the Court or, in exceptional circumstances, another member of the Court as President of the Committee.
> 3. The other two members of the Committee are appointed by the Court from among the Vice-Chairmen or the other members of the Court. At each Plenary Session the Court appoints the members who are to attend the meetings of the Committee to be held before the next Plenary Session."

The members of the Committee are established on an ad hoc basis by the President of the ICC Court and proposed to the Plenary Session. Therefore the members of the Committee will generally change with each Plenary Session of the ICC Court. The members of the Committees tend to be from among the very active members of the ICC Court. The Committee meets when convened by its **1–75**

President, which can in some instances be on short notice. In general there are four Committee meetings a month, usually on Thursday morning. In addition there are Committees in some instances to review matters in Spanish or German, for example.

1–76 The key restrictions on the work of the Committee are set out in art.4(5) of the Internal Rules:

> "a) The Court shall determine the decisions that may be taken by the Committee.
> b) The decisions of the Committee are taken unanimously.
> c) When the Committee cannot reach a decision or deems it preferable to abstain, it transfers the case to the next Plenary Session, making any suggestions it deems appropriate.
> d) The Committee's decisions are brought to the notice of the Court at its next Plenary Session."

1–77 Annex 1 Pt I, contains a description of Plenary and Committee Sessions and the matters dealt with at each. All matters arising under the Rules may be delegated to a Committee. However, most challenges of arbitrators and decisions to remove arbitrators are dealt with in a Plenary Session. In addition, approval of draft Awards involving a dissenting opinion are generally reserved to the Plenary Session. The scrutiny of draft Awards raising particularly difficult or sensitive issues, or being of particular importance because of the identities of the parties (e.g. a sovereign state) or the amounts involved, are also normally decided in a Plenary Session of the ICC Court rather than by a Committee.

1–78 A Committee Session lasts generally two to three hours. In 2012, the ICC issued 491 Awards. In many Committee Sessions eight to ten Awards are scrutinised and dozens of decisions are rendered on various procedural issues. Therefore, during the Committee sessions there is a premium on dealing with each decision in a time effective manner. Committees are required to act unanimously. If the Committee members do not agree, the matter is dealt with in the next Plenary Session. If the Committee does agree, then the matter is generally final in the absence of demonstration by a party that new elements have emerged, which might alter the ICC Court's decision.[31] Committees report on their decisions to the ICC Court but the decisions of the Committees are not subject to ratification or review by the ICC Court in a Plenary Session. Decisions by a Committee are deemed to be decisions of the entire ICC Court.

1–79 Some parties feel in certain cases that a matter should be examined at the Plenary Session, not just by a Committee, or, once a Committee has taken a decision, that the matter should be reviewed at a Plenary Session. A Committee has discretion whether or not a matter should be submitted for decision by the Plenary

[31] Kirby, "The ICC Court: A Behind-the-Scenes Look" (2005) ICC ICArb Bull Vol.16 No.2, p.9 explaining the ICC Court, the Secretariat and the key functions of the ICC Court; Grigera Nao´n, "The Role of the Secretariat of the International Court of Arbitration" (1997) ICC ICArb Bull, Special Supplement, p.18; Philippe-Gazon, "The Role of the ICC International Court of Arbitration" (1997) RDAI/IBLJ No.4, p.443; Kuckenburg "Die Rolle des Sekretariats des Internationalen Schiedsgerichtshofes in ICC-Schiedsverfahren" *in Festschrift für Ottoarndt Glossner zum 70. Geburtstag* (Verlag Recht und Wirtschaft GmbH, 1994), p.177.

Session. In general, once the ICC Court has taken a decision at a Plenary or Committee Session, it will not revisit it. Indeed, a party is usually not aware of whether a decision has been taken by a Committee or the ICC Court in a Plenary Session.

The Rules provide that the ICC Court is to take decisions in a number of situations. It is the ICC Court that decides whether there is a prima facie case that jurisdiction may exist under art.6, for example. It is the ICC Court that deals with challenges to arbitrators under art.14. It is the ICC Court that scrutinises draft Awards under art.33. These decisions are all administrative in nature, as has been confirmed by the French Supreme Court in the *Cubic* case.[32] Because the decisions are administrative of a private body, the ICC Court is not required to provide reasons for its decisions. **1–80**

However, because the ICC Court's decisions are administrative in nature, the national courts may well have jurisdiction over the issues that gave rise to the decisions in the first place. For example, the national courts will review the issue of jurisdiction, issues relating to challenges to arbitrators and the validity of the Award. In reviewing those decisions of the ICC Court, the state court will generally have to approach the matter in a de novo fashion. The state court will not have the benefit of the reasons from the ICC Court for the decision.[33] **1–81**

If a party is dissatisfied with the ICC Court's decisions, it is very difficult to have the decision reconsidered by the ICC Court. The ICC Court will only reconsider a decision if relevant new information is brought to its attention that could not have been made available before. In any event, the ICC will not reconsider a decision regarding arbitrators under art.11(4), as those decisions are final. Therefore, the only recourse for a party before the ICC is generally to make a new application based on new facts. **1–82**

Parties can, in some instances, seek to have recourse to the national courts against the ICC. The ICC is a French non-profit association subject to the provisions of art.40 regarding limitation of liability. Generally one would expect that proceedings would be brought before the French courts as the ICC is a French non-profit organisation.[34] Under French law, it is clear that the ICC's obligation is to ensure the organisation of the arbitration and that the French courts will look to the arbitrators to decide the issues on the merits and to the courts of the place of arbitration to reach any judicial decisions required with respect to the arbitration (such as the validity of a challenge). The French courts and United States courts will not interfere with the ICC Court's decisions, as long as they are the result of the exercise by the ICC Court of its discretion in applying the Rules. Most of the **1–83**

[32] See the discussion at para.1–8 n.10.

[33] For many practitioners, it would be preferable for the parties to accept the decisions of the ICC Court. However, as international arbitration expands, the tendency has arguably increased to see whatever recourse is available. Therefore, the first step of many parties upon receipt of an ICC decision is often to consider whether they have recourse, in particular before the courts of the place of arbitration. See the discussion under art.34.

[34] Recently, however, proceedings were bought against the ICC in New York. The proceedings were dismissed on grounds of immunity. See *Global Mining LLC v Peter Robinson and the ICC*, 2008 WL 336821 (SDNY 2008); Neilson "When Is An Arbitration Not An Arbitration?—Global Gold And The Problem Of Institutional Veto" (2008) Mealey's IAR Vol.23 No.3, p.26.

ICC Court's decisions in applying its Rules will therefore never become the subject of review by a court or by the Arbitral Tribunal.

Article 1(5): "The Court is assisted in its work by the Secretariat of the Court (the "Secretariat") under the direction of its Secretary General (the "Secretary General")."

1–84 As stated in the new Rules, the Court is assisted by the Secretariat. The Secretariat consists of a Secretary General, a Deputy Secretary General, and a General Counsel. The Secretariat is also assisted by the ICC's General Counsel. The Secretariat is based at the ICC headquarters in Paris with a branch office in Hong Kong (since 2009)[35] and an office that has been opened in New York in 2013.

1–85 The Secretary General of the ICC Court (who is often confused with, but is different from, the Secretary General of the ICC), is the head of the Secretariat of the ICC Court. The current Secretary General is an Italian national. In the last 20 years, four Secretaries General were from the United States, New Zealand and one from Argentina. The Secretary General is assisted by a Deputy Secretary General, currently, a Managing Counsel who is American and a General Counsel, a French jurist.

1–86 In 2012, the Secretariat of the ICC Court had over 80 full-time employees. The Secretariat's employees included over 35 lawyers of over 30 different countries of whom eight are Counsel. The staff speaks numerous languages, including English, French, German, Italian, Spanish, Russian, Mandarin, Polish, Arabic, and Romanian. The Secretariat handles day-to-day administration of the approximately 1,600 cases pending with the ICC Court. Each Counsel heads a team, composed of three Deputy counsel who administer, under the Counsel's supervision, the pending cases, and two secretaries. The Counsels are of different nationalities and are fluent in at least two languages. They report directly to the Secretary General. The Counsel prepare the documents for submission to the ICC Court and attend sessions of the ICC Court where they report on the status of the cases, and answer questions that members of the ICC Court may have with respect to particular cases.

1–87 In preparing a matter for a decision by the ICC Court at a Plenary Session, the Secretariat will provide an overview of the case but there will generally be a report by a member of the ICC Court who will act as rapporteur. In these cases, it is the rapporteur who makes any recommendation to the ICC Court and not the Secretariat. The Secretariat will provide case information to the ICC Court and any background information that may be required by the rapporteur.

1–88 In preparing a matter for a decision by the ICC Court at a Committee Session, the Secretariat will set out in an agenda and may include a proposal for the decision to be taken by the ICC Court. Internally, the Secretariat has its own weekly meetings to agree on recommendations to be made to the ICC Court at its Committee Sessions. In complex or important matters, the team dealing with the

[35] "ICC Arbitration News: Secretariat's Hong Kong office opens to great acclaim" (2009) ICC ICArb Bull Vol.19 No.2, pp.5–6.

case will prepare a report and distribute it to the other teams for discussion at the weekly meeting. The recommendation is then discussed at the weekly meeting and a report prepared for the ICC court. The proposal prepared by the team and the discussion at the weekly meeting is not disclosed to the parties. The discussion is referred to orally in many instances in discussing the case at the ICC Court session. The advantage of this procedure is to harmonise the practices between the teams. The disadvantage is that this procedure takes time and therefore can result in delay.

In many instances, the ICC Court will adopt the Secretariat's proposal, after having received further clarification or an explanation for the rationale of the Secretariat's proposal if necessary. The Secretariat will try to anticipate the ICC Court's decision based on past practice. If the ICC Court agrees with the Secretariat's proposal, it will endorse it; if not, it will modify or change it as it deems fit. In that way, the members of the ICC Court benefit from the institutional experience of the ICC Secretariat in dealing with issues under the Rules. **1–89**

The ICC Court's Secretariat is based at the ICC's headquarters in Paris with offices in Hong Kong and, most recently, in New York.[36] Requests for Arbitration may be filed at any of these offices. Parties to an ICC arbitration may conduct their arbitration in any other place on the globe and under any legal system.[37] **1–90**

The ICC Court administers the Rules as applied to each arbitration through the Secretariat in accordance with art.2 of the Statutes. It is the Secretariat that receives the Request, the Answer and any Reply to the counterclaim and that generally corresponds with the parties with respect to the Rules. **1–91**

For lawyers and arbitrators, the key interaction with the ICC Court will be with the Secretariat. Of course, once the Tribunal has been constituted, the parties will correspond with the Tribunal and vice versa (with a copy to the Secretariat). However, requests to the ICC Court will be handled by the Secretariat and will be presented to the ICC Court by the Secretariat. In addition, the Secretariat interacts with the members of the Tribunal with respect to the administration of the arbitration, for example, with respect to the Terms of Reference, the payment of advances on fees and the review of the draft Award. **1–92**

To prepare for Plenary or Committee sessions, the Secretariat will prepare a set of documents relating to the arbitration for review by the members of the ICC Court. Some of these documents are prepared by all parties, in particular the Terms of Reference. With respect to other matters, such as challenges to arbitrators, the Secretariat will have to select the relevant documents. Usually, this poses no problem as the correspondence relating to a specific issue that is to be submitted to the ICC Court is clearly identified. If a party believes that specific prior letters or documents are relevant to an issue, it would be appropriate to highlight that fact in correspondence with the Secretariat (copied to the other party). **1–93**

Article 5 of the Internal Rules expressly provides that "[t]he Secretariat may, with the approval of the Court, issue notes and other documents for the **1–94**

[36] The ICC Court has teams located in Hong Kong and, more recently, in New York.

[37] The fact that the Secretariat is located mainly in France does not affect the law applicable to the arbitration. As discussed with regard to art.18, the key legal systems with respect to any arbitration are the law of the arbitration agreement and the law of the place of arbitration and depending on the circumstances, various other legal systems may be relevant. See the discussion of arts 18 and 34.

information of the parties and the arbitrators, or as necessary for the proper conduct of the arbitral proceedings". The Secretariat has issued a number of general notes relating to various issues such as expenses and the appointment of administrative secretaries.[38]

1–95 The Secretariat may also provide information to parties with respect to specific arbitrations. This reflects the fact that arbitrations are different and in many cases the parties or the arbitrators may seek some information or guidance usually informally from the Secretariat. The Counsel at the Secretariat handling a case will remain neutral with respect to all matters relating to the arbitration (and should not permit what are in effect ex parte submissions by counsel with respect to issues to be decided by the ICC Court). However, that does not prevent the communication of information relating to the status of the proceedings. Certainly, if counsel to a party does not understand a communication from the Secretariat, it may be helpful to call the Secretariat to have the matter clarified.

1–96 Parties with concerns about arbitration, and in particular regarding the timing of the issue of Awards, frequently contact the counsel in charge of the case to check on the status. This can have a salutary effect as the Secretariat can remind the Tribunal of the importance of issuing the Award. Parties also contact the President of the Court or the Secretary General with respect to issues relating to arbitrations or in some instances the administration of cases. However, such approaches should be infrequent. The ICC Secretariat administers over 1,600 cases and the President or Secretary General would have to go back to the counsel to find out the details of any particular case.[39]

1–97 In the course of arbitration proceedings, the Secretariat may receive a large number of submissions, documents and correspondence. It is not practicable for the ICC to keep these documents in their entirety once the arbitration proceedings have come to an end. Therefore, normally, when the final Award is communicated to the parties, or when the file is being closed for other reasons, the Secretariat will invite the parties to indicate within a fixed time limit whether they wish any documents that they have submitted to the ICC in the course of the arbitration to be returned to them. If so, the documents will be returned at the expense of the party requesting them (art.1(7) of the Internal Rules). In the absence of such request, the ICC will not send the often voluminous briefs and exhibit volumes to its external archives, but rather will simply have them destroyed.

1–98 In accordance with art.1(6) of the Internal Rules, "[t]he Secretariat will in each case submitted to arbitration under the Rules retain in the archives of the Court all Awards, Terms of Reference, and decisions of the Court, as well as copies of the pertinent correspondence of the Secretariat". In addition, the Secretariat will issue

[38] See, for example, the ICC Notes set out in Pt II relating to Personal and Arbitral Tribunal Expenses (Document 12.1), Administrative Secretaries (Document 12.3); the Correction and Interpretation of Arbitral Awards and the Administration of VAT, Charges and Imposts Applicable to Arbitrators' Fees.

[39] Fry, Greenberg and Mazza, refer to this possibility if parties wish to "raise particularly sensitive concerns or concerns about the team in charge of the case", The Secretariat Guide to ICC Arbitration (ICC Publication 725). Nevertheless, this should not be viewed as an invitation to raise substantive concerns about decisions of a Tribunal. That is generally the province of the Tribunal and not the ICC Court or Secretariat. As regards complaints about the team in charge, the main legitimate one will be in the team's ability to deal with issues to be handled by the Secretariat in a timely fashion.

certified copies of an ICC Award and Terms of Reference which may be necessary for enforcement purposes or otherwise.[40]

After an arbitration has been completed, the Secretariat will invite feedback from the parties as to the conduct of the arbitration. In addition, the parties have the possibility of contacting the Secretariat to express their views as to particular aspects of the arbitration of which they approved or disapproved. Comments on the substantive issues are less likely to have an impact, as the substantive issues are decided by the Tribunal and there is a tendency for the party who is unsuccessful in whole or in part to be disappointed with that aspect. However, comments as regards the Tribunal's conduct of the proceedings will be of interest to the Secretariat and the ICC Court, as the goal is to ensure that ICC arbitrations are conducted in a cost and time effective manner. **1–99**

[40] See the discussion under art.34.

Article 2 Definitions

In the Rules:

(i) "arbitral tribunal" includes one or more arbitrators;

(ii) "claimant" includes one or more claimants, "respondent" includes one or more respondents, and "additional party" includes one or more additional parties;

(iii) "party" or "parties" include claimants, respondents or additional parties;

(iv) "claim" or "claims" include any claim by any party against any other party;

(v) "award" includes, *inter alia*, an interim, partial or final award.[1]

Introductory remarks

2–1 Article 2 deals with terms that are widely used in ICC arbitration. The terms are defined in an inclusive fashion to retain flexibility. The main change from the 1998 Rules has been to add reference to additional parties and claims.[2] The purpose was to formally adapt the Rules to the fact that many ICC arbitrations are multiparty arbitrations in nature.

"arbitral tribunal"

2–2 The definition of "arbitral tribunal" includes one or more arbitrators. Thus, the Rules do not preclude the possibility for the parties from agreeing on the number of arbitrators other than one or three, although this is rather rare in practice. In practice, an "arbitral tribunal" is often referred to simply as the "Tribunal" as it is in this commentary. The members of the Tribunal are known as the arbitrators. If there is only one arbitrator, he or she is called the sole arbitrator. Many laws on arbitration refer to the arbitrator(s) rather than to the Arbitral Tribunal.

2–3 Under the Rules, all the members of the Tribunal have, in principle, the same status and the same rights and obligations. The Rules do not contemplate a differ-

[1] Article 2 corresponds to art.2 of the 1998 ICC Rules. Part (iii) and (iv) were added in the 2012 rules.

[2] In addition, the defined terms are no longer capitalised. The authors have retained capitalisation of certain terms as this is in accordance with international arbitration practice.

entiation among the arbitrators with the notable exception of art.31(1).[3] The third arbitrator, known in the Rules as the President,[4] enjoys certain prerogatives, and normally receives a higher fee than the one of his two colleagues known as the co-arbitrators, as will be further discussed below.[5] Although the term co-arbitrator is not used in the Rules, it is used in this book to denote the arbitrator nominated by (or on behalf of) one or more of the parties or as the non-presiding arbitrators if the ICC appoints all three arbitrators.

Several articles of the Rules deal with the rights and duties of the arbitrators, but the Rules do not contain a catalogue of those rights and duties. The rights and duties of the arbitrators are personal and cannot be delegated, except for some administrative tasks within certain limits. **2–4**

The arbitrator's duties: Article 11(5) contains a general provision pursuant to which every arbitrator, who accepts to serve as such under the Rules, undertakes to carry out his responsibilities in accordance with the Rules. Article 11(1) requires that arbitrators must be and remain impartial and independent of the parties involved in the arbitration. Article 11(2) requires a signed statement of availability, impartiality and independence from the arbitrator and obliges him to disclose certain facts or circumstances to the Secretariat. The obligation of disclosure continues during the arbitration in accordance with art.11(3). Pursuant to art.23(2), the Tribunal is required to establish Terms of Reference, and to have them signed within two months of receipt of the file in the absence of an extension. Once the parties have also signed the Terms of Reference, art.23(2) provides that the Tribunal is to transmit them to the ICC Court. The Tribunal is further obliged to convene a case management conference and to establish a procedural timetable in accordance with art.24. **2–5**

Article 22 sets out the requirements for the conduct of the arbitration, and in particular the obligation that the Tribunal "make every effort to conduct the arbitration in an expeditious and cost-effective manner" and the overriding duty to "act fairly and impartially and ensure that each party has a reasonable opportunity to present its case". Article 25(1) requires the Tribunal to proceed "within as short a time as possible" to establish the facts of the case. The Tribunal must also hear the parties, unless none of the parties requests a hearing (arts 25(2) and (6)). Finally, the Tribunal must render a (final) Award in accordance with arts 30 and 31 and must submit the draft Award to the ICC Court for scrutiny and approval (art.33). In the final Award, the Tribunal must decide upon the costs of arbitration, as provided for in art.37(4). **2–6**

In addition to the specific duties of the Tribunal under the Rules, the Tribunal is also subject to duties imposed by applicable law, and in particular the law of the place of arbitration. The duties—and the consequence of the breach of the duties—vary to some extent from country to country and, prior to accepting any appointment, a potential arbitrator is well advised to review the local arbitration law in this respect. However, certain duties are common in most jurisdictions as for **2–7**

[3] Article 31(1) provides for Awards made by the president if there is no majority decision of the Tribunal. See the discussion at para.2–11.

[4] Sometimes referred to as the "president" or "chair" of the Tribunal.

[5] See discussion under art.31.

example, the duty of confidentiality with respect to the arbitral proceedings, including the deliberations of the Tribunal with respect thereto. A Tribunal is a collegial body and there is an obligation to function as such and to permit all members of the Tribunal to participate in the proceedings.

2–8 *The arbitrator's rights*: The Rules also refer at various places to an arbitrator's rights. Article 18(2) permits the Tribunal to hold hearings at any location it considers appropriate in the absence of an agreement to the contrary of the parties. The Tribunal may deliberate where it considers it appropriate in accordance with art.18(3). Article 19 confirms the Tribunal's right to settle on the procedural rules of the proceedings for the arbitration, unless the parties have agreed themselves on the rules of proceedings. Article 25(1) provides the Tribunal with the right to establish the facts of the case "by all appropriate means". More specifically, the Tribunal may hear witnesses (art.25(3)), appoint experts (art.25(4)) and summon the parties to provide additional evidence. The Tribunal may also order interim measures pursuant to art.28(1).

2–9 Absent an agreement of the parties, the Tribunal has also the right to determine the language of the arbitration (art.20) as well as the applicable law to the merits of the dispute (art.21(1)). The Tribunal may render interim and partial Awards, as follows from the definition of the Award in art.2(v), and may, at its own initiative and within certain limits, correct the Award (art.35(1)). As regards the decision on costs, other than those fixed by the Court, the Tribunal may take them at any time during the proceedings in accordance with art.37(3).

2–10 ICC arbitrators are entitled to remuneration for their services in accordance with the Rules, and reimbursement of their expenses in accordance with the Rules and the Secretariat's guidelines.[6]

2–11 *The role of the President of the Tribunal*: Although the role of the president of a Tribunal is predominant in practice as regards organisational and procedural matters,[7] the Rules generally do not differentiate the president's role from the one of his fellow arbitrators. The Tribunal is a collegial body and decisions are normally made by the whole Tribunal. Under art.26(3), the Tribunal shall be in full charge of the hearings, although it is usually the president who maintains that control. Provision is usually made in the Terms of Reference for procedural orders to be signed by the president alone, although the orders have been adopted by the Tribunal in its entirety. One of the most important and striking provisions of the Rules is contained in art.31(1), which gives the president of the Tribunal the right to decide alone, when no majority can be obtained. In the ICC Court's practice, the president's fee will normally be higher than the one of the co-arbitrators, although the Rules do not specifically state so.[8] Since the president usually provides the leadership for the Tribunal, he/she has a particular duty to ensure that

[6] See the discussion under art.37.

[7] See, for example, Briner, "The Role of the Chairman" in *The Leading Arbitrators' Guide to International Arbitration* (Juris Publishing/Staempfli Publishers, 2004), p.49 addressing the main questions of the powers of the president when decisions are to be taken, be they procedural orders or Awards; Reymond, "Le président du tribunal arbitral", in *Etudes offertes à Pierre Bellet* (Litec, 1991), p.467.

[8] See the discussion under art.37(2) regarding the fixing of the arbitrators' fees by the ICC Court.

the principle of collegiality is respected with respect to the Tribunal's deliberations.

The term "arbitral tribunal" does not include the secretary of the Tribunal, if a secretary has been appointed. The duty of a secretary appointed by a sole arbitrator or by the president of the Tribunal is to assist with respect to the organisational aspects of the arbitration. **2–12**

"claimant," "respondent," "additional party" and "parties"

The definitions of "Claimant" and "Respondent" reflect the fact that ICC arbitration can be multiparty as is discussed under art.12. The words "Claimant" and "Respondent" are the substitute words for plaintiff and defendant, as the parties are typically referred to in court litigation. The Claimant and Respondent can be physical or legal persons. When a consortium or joint venture, which has no legal personality, consists of two members or more, all members may, and sometimes must be, parties to the arbitration, either as Claimants or Respondents.[9] **2–13**

The reference to "additional party" is intended to cover parties who are neither Claimants nor Respondents. This terminology was adopted to avoid the complication in alternative terms, such as Respondent to a counterclaim or Respondent to a cross claim or instances where such descriptions may be inappropriate. The scope for additional parties is discussed under art.7. **2–14**

"claim" and "claims"

A claim is the allegation made against the other party and is referred to in particular in art.4(3) and art.23(4). The purpose of the definition is to ensure that in those subsequent references all claims of any type among the parties to the arbitration are covered. **2–15**

"award"

The definition of "Award" is still the subject of debate. Traditionally, a distinction was drawn between an "interim Award" which resolves an issue relating to jurisdiction for example, and a "partial Award" which decides a substantive issue as far as the Tribunal is concerned in the case, for example, the issue of liability for a claim.[10] **2–16**

[9] The approach as to dealing with joint ventures will usually depend on the law under which the joint venture was created and the underlying law of the members of the joint venture. See the discussion of parties with respect to the Request (under art.4), the Answer (under art.5), and the constitution of the Tribunal in multiple parties cases under art.12. In ICC Case No.18122/ND (unpublished) the Tribunal held that the joint venture did not have legal personality under applicable law and was therefore not a valid party.

[10] See Redfern & Hunter with Blackaby & Partasides, *Law and Practice of International Commercial Arbitration,* 4th edn (Thomson/Sweet & Maxwell, 2004), para.8–05, p.353; Delvolvé, Rouche & Pointon, *op. cit.*, para.302, p.167; Poudret & Besson, *Comparative Law of International Arbitration*, 2nd edn (Thomson/Sweet & Maxwell, 2007), para.731, p.644; Fouchard, Gaillard & Goldman, *On International Commercial Arbitration* (Kluwer, 1999), paras 1348–1366, p.734; Craig, Park & Paulsson, *International Chamber of Commerce Arbitration*, 3rd edn (Oceana/ICC Publishing, 2000), p.358; de Boisséson, *Le droit français de l'arbitrage interne et international* (GLN Joly, 1990), para.784, p.807; Hunter "Final Report on Interim and Partial Awards" (1990), ICC ICArb Bull. Vol.1 No.2, p.26. See also the discussion under art.33.

2–17 Tribunals act by issuing procedural orders or directions and Awards. The Rules do not define what constitutes an "Award" and do not define or deal with what constitutes a procedural order. Indeed, art.25 gives the Tribunal broad leeway to establish the facts of the case without mentioning procedural orders. However, the distinction between Awards and procedural orders is fundamental in ICC arbitration because Awards are subject to scrutiny by the Court pursuant to art.33. In addition, the New York Convention provides for the recognition and enforcement of Awards, but not for procedural orders.

2–18 As discussed under art.31, an Award of whatever nature finally decides an issue in the arbitration. Once that Award has been rendered, that issue is res judicata and is not open to reconsideration by the Tribunal (unless the Award is annulled). The Tribunal has limited rights for a limited period to correct or interpret the Award (art.35). However, as long as that Award has not been annulled, it is a final decision with respect to the subject matter of the Award. A procedural order deals with an issue of procedure that may be reconsidered by a Tribunal prior to the final Award. The distinction between an Award and a procedural order will be discussed below at art.33.

2–19 Whenever a Tribunal corrects or interprets an Award under art.35, it will render a so-called *addendum*, which will form an integral part of the original Award, not a new or additional Award.

2–20 A Tribunal has the right to issue Awards and the procedure with respect to corrections and interpretations is equally applicable to such partial awards.

Article 3 Written Notifications or Communications; Time Limits

1 **All pleadings and other written communications submitted by any party, as well as all documents annexed thereto, shall be supplied in a number of copies sufficient to provide one copy for each party, plus one for each arbitrator, and one for the Secretariat. A copy of any notification or communication from the arbitral tribunal to the parties shall be sent to the Secretariat.**

2 **All notifications or communications from the Secretariat and the arbitral tribunal shall be made to the last address of the party or its representative for whom the same are intended, as notified either by the party in question or by the other party. Such notification or communication may be made by delivery against receipt, registered post, courier, email, or any other means of telecommunication that provides a record of the sending thereof.**

3 **A notification or communication shall be deemed to have been made on the day it was received by the party itself or by its representative, or would have been received if made in accordance with Article 3(2).**

4 **Periods of time specified in or fixed under the Rules shall start to run on the day following the date a notification or communication is deemed to have been made in accordance with Article 3(3). When the day next following such date is an official holiday, or a non-business day in the country where the notification or communication is deemed to have been made, the period of time shall commence on the first following business day. Official holidays and non-business days are included in the calculation of the period of time. If the last day of the relevant period of time granted is an official holiday or a nonbusiness day in the country where the notification or communication is deemed to have been made, the period of time shall expire at the end of the first following business day.**[1]

[1] Article 3 corresponds to art.3 of the 1998 ICC Rules. There have been no substantive changes.

Introductory remarks

3–1 Article 3 is a general provision of the Rules relating to written communications and time limits to be followed by the parties, the Tribunal and the Secretariat. The 2012 Rules make no major changes in this provision, although there is reference to "notifications" in art.3(1) and to email in art.3(2). Usually art.3 will be supplemented by rules that are set out either in the Terms of Reference or in procedural orders. Therefore, art.3 should normally be read in conjunction with those documents once they have been drafted. However, particularly for the Request, the Answer and, where there is a counterclaim filed with the Answer, the Reply to the counterclaim, the basic provisions on communication are those set out in art.3.

3–2 Article 3 does not expressly deal with when the parties should transmit documents directly to the other party and when the transmittal should take place through the Secretariat.

3–3 The Request and the Answer and any Reply to the counterclaim, as well as any Request for Joinder are sent to the Secretariat for transmittal to the other party in accordance with arts 4(5), 5(4) and 7(1). The parties are not expected to exchange these documents directly or to provide copies of them to the other party. However, communications sent by the parties to the Tribunal or the Secretariat after this initial exchange are expected to be copied to the other party to ensure that the other party has an opportunity to take note of them and comment upon them.

Article 3(1): "All pleadings and other written communications submitted by any party, as well as all documents annexed thereto, shall be supplied in a number of copies sufficient to provide one copy for each party, plus one for each arbitrator, and one for the Secretariat. A copy of any notification or communication from the arbitral tribunal to the parties shall be sent to the Secretariat."

3–4 The first sentence of art.3(1) deals with communications made by the parties to the Tribunal and the Secretariat. The last sentence refers to communication by the Tribunal to the parties.

Article 3(1) anticipates the submission of paper copies of pleadings in particular to commence the arbitration. The ICC does not yet have a system for electronic filing of pleadings, although provision has been made in art.7 of App.I (Statutes of the International Court of Arbitration) for expedited amendment of art.3 with the intention of providing such filings.[2] **3–5**

The issue may arise in some arbitrations as to when the arbitration is commenced for purposes of interrupting limitation periods. In particular, there may be an issue as to whether the arbitration is commenced on the date of receipt in electronic format or in hard copy if a party transmits the Request for Arbitration or Request for Joinder in both formats. The issue of whether a limitation period has been interrupted would normally be decided under the law governing the limitation period itself or the contract with the limitation period if the limitation period arises by contract. Article 3(1) as drafted anticipates hard copy filings and receipt by the Secretariat of the hard copies to commence the arbitration. However, filing by email should generally interrupt any limitation period as the underlying purpose is to require a party to manifest its claim within a certain period and that is carried out just as effectively with an electronic version. **3–6**

The number of copies will be based on the number of parties to the arbitration in the Request or the Answer to the Request, as the case may be, or subsequently in the Request for Joinder. Article 3(1) requires that there be one copy for each party, for each arbitrator and for the Secretariat. There is no requirement that a party provide a copy for each law firm involved if a party is represented by more than one law firm, although it may elect to do so as a professional courtesy.[3] **3–7**

Communications between the parties

Article 3(1) does not cover communications between the parties or between their counsel that are not copied to the Tribunal. One of the practical issues that arises in many arbitrations is when the parties should copy the Tribunal on their correspondence with the other party. Another is whether the party is entitled to send copies of the correspondence to the Tribunal. **3–8**

On some occasions, the communications between the parties relate to attempts to agree on procedural issues. There is an ongoing debate about who should or does control the arbitral proceedings. For the authors, the answer depends at the point of time in the proceedings.[4] However, the basic point is that Tribunals welcome and expect lawyers to seek to agree on certain aspects of the procedure. Particularly at the outset of the arbitration, the lawyers are much more familiar with the details of the claims and defenses than the Tribunal. As a result, the **3–9**

[2] Article 7 of App.I provides in relevant part that "in order to take into account developments in information technology [the ICC Court] may propose to modify or supplement the provisions of Article 3 of the Rules without laying any such proposal before the Commission". This was intended to cover electronic filings when the Secretariat has developed the facilities for handling them.

[3] Usually, these issues are dealt with in the Terms of Reference or in the initial procedural order.

[4] Kaufmann-Kohler, "Qui contrôle l'arbitrage? Autonomie des parties, pouvoirs des arbitres et principes d'efficacité" in *Liber Amicorum Claude Reymond, Autour de l'arbitrage* (Litec, 2004), p.153; Webster, "Party Control in International Arbitration" (2003) Arb Int Vol.19 No.2, p.119; Werner, "Who controls speed? A few reflections on the relationship between parties and arbitrators in ICC arbitration" in *Liber Amicorum Michel Gaudet, Improving International Arbitration—The need for speed and trust* (ICC, 1999), p.99.

Tribunal may be concerned about becoming entangled in details when it does not understand their real importance in the case.

3–10 Another issue is whether a party is entitled to send to the Tribunal copies of documents exchanged with the other party in seeking to reach an agreement about a procedural or substantive aspect. In national legal systems, the rules and practices are different. In French domestic proceedings, for example, communications between lawyers admitted to the French Bar and practicing as such in France, are confidential unless otherwise indicated. In the United States, communications with a view to settlement of a dispute are generally considered confidential whether or not the document states so. In England and many Commonwealth jurisdictions, the practice is to indicate that a document is sent "without prejudice" if it is not to be disclosed.

3–11 In international arbitration for practical purposes, the most prudent course is to assume that any document exchanged between the parties or their lawyers is not confidential unless it states otherwise. This is in line with the rules for lawyers in the European Union for example.[5]

3–12 If a Tribunal receives a communication that one party maintains should have been treated as confidential, then it will have to reach a decision as to the admissibility and weight to be given to the document. As regards admissibility, the initial issue is which legal system is applicable. Conceivably, the applicable system could be that of the party sending the communication, that of the party receiving the communication, that of the place of arbitration or that of the law governing the underlying contract.[6] Faced with these diverse theoretical possibilities, the approach of some Tribunals is to admit these types of documents but to indicate to the parties that they will be given relatively little weight. In that way, some arbitrators consider that they can avoid the possibility of annulment based on the argument that relevant evidence was excluded while, at the same time, indicating that the evidence will be given little weight. As discussed with respect to art.25, Tribunals are generally not bound by the strict rules of evidence and are entitled to give evidence different weight depending on the circumstances.[7] Many Tribunals will use this discretion to give less weight to documents that one party would have expected to be treated as confidential.

Communications between the parties and the Tribunal

3–13 Article 3(1) covers the basic pleadings, such as the Request, the Answer and the Reply to the counterclaim as well as the Request for Joinder. It also covers the

[5] Article 5.3.1 of the Code of Conduct for Lawyers in the European Union provides for example that "If a lawyer sending a communication to a lawyer in another Member State wishes it to remain confidential or without prejudice he should clearly express his intention when communicating the document".

[6] The sender is of course familiar with the legal principles applicable in its jurisdiction. However, the receiver is not necessarily familiar with those legal principles. Depending on the place of arbitration, it may be that neither counsel is familiar with the confidentiality principles of the place of arbitration. Moreover, given the procedural nature of the issue, arguably the law governing the underlying contract should not be taken into consideration.

[7] See art.9(1) of the IBA Rules on the Taking of Evidence.

subsequent pleadings, which are frequently referred to as memorials or briefs.[8] In addition, it covers the documents submitted with such pleadings, such as the exhibits.

However, the language is even broader as it covers "communications", which would include letters, faxes and emails transmitted by the parties to the Tribunal or to the Secretariat. **3–14**

The better view is that art.3(1) does not cover exchange of documents by disclosure or discovery because such documents are not submitted by a party as part of their case. If the party producing the documents or the party receiving the documents deems it relevant, then presumably the documents will be submitted as exhibits to the submissions. **3–15**

The basic rule is that, assuming there are two parties to the arbitration, a party should submit three sets of documents where there is a Tribunal of one arbitrator and five sets of documents where there is to be a three-person Tribunal. If the number of arbitrators is not set in the arbitration clause itself, it will be decided by the ICC Court in accordance with art.12. Practices vary; however to ensure that they meet the literal requirements of art.3(1), some parties submit five sets of documents even if they are seeking to have the matter settled by a sole arbitrator. If there are more than two parties, an additional copy should be provided for each party. If a party seeks to join an additional party under art.7, there should be a copy of the document for each party including the additional party. **3–16**

All written communications by a party with the Tribunal should be copied to the other party. As a general rule there should be no ex parte communications with an arbitrator by counsel whether written or oral. As stated in the IBA Guidelines on Party Representation in International Arbitration of 2013 (the "IBA Representation Guidelines"): "7. Unless agreed otherwise by the Parties, and subject to the exceptions below, a Party Representative should not engage in any Ex Parte Communications with an Arbitrator concerning the arbitration". (The exception relates to contacts prior to requesting the arbitrator to act as such.)[9] **3–17**

Tribunals generally also try to hold telephone conferences with all parties present rather than speak individually to the parties. However, in some instances the president of the Tribunal or the sole arbitrator discusses an issue such as the timing of submissions with one party and sends a letter to the other party setting out the essence of the conversation. This practice has, however, decreased since it is straightforward to send an email to all parties at the same time. **3–18**

Communications to the Secretariat

Since ICC arbitration is an administered arbitration, the parties and the Tribunal are to submit documents to the Secretariat. The Secretariat will maintain an **3–19**

[8] There is no standard terminology for submissions in ICC arbitration. Tribunals will tend to use the words with which it is most familiar to describe the parties' written pleadings. "Rebuttal", "Rejoinder", "Pre-Hearing Memorial", "Counter-Memorial" are among the many terms one can find in English speaking ICC proceedings.

[9] The IBA Representation Guidelines are only applicable if adopted by the parties. However, they are a useful set of guidelines as to appropriate practices in international arbitration.

overview of the procedural status of the file, but parties should not expect the Secretariat to study their submissions in detail. The Counsels at the Secretariat have a great number of cases to deal with and are not in the position to review each submission as to the substance. In any event, as an administrative body, the reading of the parties' memorial is required by the Secretary only to a limited extent, for instance to verify whether new claims have been added or whether the amount in dispute was increased/decreased significantly. The merits of the dispute are to be dealt with by the Tribunal although the Award is scrutinised by the ICC Court. The documents are copied to the Secretariat so that it has a meaningful overview of the procedure that is taking place and so that one full set be kept until the end of the arbitral proceedings. The Secretariat maintains an internal database with respect to each arbitration, which allows it at a glance to get a full picture of the status of each file.

3–20 Usually, all communications by the parties with the Secretariat are to be copied to the other party. In some instances, parties contact the Secretariat either by telephone or in person to discuss issues of particular concern relating either to the progress of the arbitration or the conduct of an arbitrator. In this respect, the Secretariat can act as a buffer between the parties and the Tribunal, often by simply listening to the grievances of a party. In case of an ex parte communication with one of the parties, the Secretariat will generally only provide information as to what may be considered normal in ICC proceedings (if a party is not familiar with them) or refer the party to the relevant procedure to deal with the issue under the Rules.

Communications by the Tribunal

3–21 Article 3(1) requires that all communications between a party and the Tribunal be copied to the other party and the Secretariat. Article 3(1) does not require the Tribunal to send copies of all documents it sends to the Secretariat to the parties and generally Tribunals do not do so. With regard to certain aspects (such as comments with respect to advances on costs in accordance with art.36(4)), one might expect the Tribunal to make submissions to the Secretariat, although there is more of a tendency to indicate that such submissions may be disclosed to the parties. With respect to other issues, such as challenges to arbitrators pursuant to art.14, any correspondence between the members of the Tribunal and the Secretariat must be copied to the parties under art.14(3).

Communications by the Tribunal with persons other than the parties and the Secretariat

3–22 Article 3 does not cover communications between the arbitrators and persons other than the parties or the Secretariat. Such persons may include experts appointed by the Tribunal, courts or national authorities.

3–23 With respect to experts appointed by the Tribunal itself, the basic principle is that the Tribunal must ensure there is due process as discussed under arts 22 and 25. Therefore, the communications by the Tribunal with the expert should not be of a nature to prevent a party from having a reasonable opportunity to present its case.

With respect to third parties to the arbitration, the basic principle is that arbitration is understood to be confidential, although, as discussed under art.22(3), this concept has received some challenge in the recent past. Therefore, one would not expect the Tribunal to take the initiative in disclosing matters relating to the arbitration to third parties. Where the Tribunal receives a request from a court of competent jurisdiction, the Tribunal may well decide that it should communicate with the court in accordance with its obligation under art.41 to "make every effort to make sure that the Award is enforceable at law". In addition, ICC arbitration and ICC Tribunals do not operate in a vacuum. They are part of a system of dispute resolution that is related to that of national courts. Therefore, a Tribunal may feel a natural obligation to cooperate with national courts or authorities in the interest of justice. In doing so, however, the Tribunal should keep in mind its role vis-à-vis the parties. The parties have agreed to ICC arbitration and as such are entitled to have the proceedings conducted without inappropriate interference. To ensure that the intervention of the third parties is not inappropriate in the eyes of the parties, it is submitted that the best practice is to give the parties an opportunity to comment on the intervention. In addition the Tribunal should provide a copy of such communications unless the circumstances dictate otherwise. **3–24**

Communications within the Tribunal

The Tribunal will have internal communications between its members, frequently by email. As discussed under art.31, these communications are of course confidential and should not be disclosed to the parties, as one of the arbitrator's most basic requirements is that he or she be independent of the parties. Virtually the sole exception in this regard is the dissenting opinion to an Award, which is discussed under art.31. In accordance with the duty of collegiality, communications amongst the members of the Tribunal should generally be made to all of them. **3–25**

Article 3(2): All notifications or communications from the Secretariat and the arbitral tribunal shall be made to the last address of the party or its representative for whom the same are intended, as notified either by the party in question or by the other party. Such notification or communication may be made by delivery against receipt, registered post, courier, email, or any other means of telecommunication that provides a record of the sending thereof.

The address for notifications and communications

The Request sets out the name and address of the Claimant and the Respondent in accordance with art.4(3)(a). The Secretariat then sends a copy of the Request to the Respondent, who replies with its address in accordance with art.5(1)(a). This is also applicable under art.7 with respect to commencement of proceedings against additional parties by a Request for Joinder. **3–26**

The Secretariat generally does not verify the address and does not review the underlying contract to ensure that the Request provides addresses that may be **3–27** required under the underlying contract. It is up to the Claimant to determine in the first instance the address for notification and whether copies have to be provided to any party or any office.[10] As a practical matter, the Secretariat usually refers to the addresses which were agreed between the parties and the Tribunal in the Terms of Reference (art.23(1)(b)). If that address has changed since the signing of the Terms of Reference, or if the name of a party has changed, it is important that such changes be communicated to both the Tribunal and the Secretariat. As discussed under art.23, Terms of Reference will often require language to that effect, making it a duty for the parties to notify any such changes.

3–28 It is important that the addresses be correct, especially if the Respondent may default in the proceedings. Article V(1)(b) of the New York Convention provides, for example, that a court may refuse to enforce an Award where "[t]he party against whom the award is invoked was not given proper notice of the appointment of the arbitrator or of the arbitration proceedings or was otherwise unable to present his case".

3–29 In the European Union, the registered seat of a company should be available from the Companies' Registry or equivalent.[11] In the United States, usually one would expect that the company should be notified at its "head office" which, in many cases, is not in the state of incorporation.[12] In other countries, the situation varies. The Commercial Registry type of system is found in many countries. In countries where the alphabet is not based on Latin, it may be worthwhile to transcribe the foreign name of the company in its original form, followed by the Latin-alphabet word. This may be of assistance at the time of enforcement of the Award if, in the Respondent's country, there may otherwise appear a doubt which company or individual is intended to be subject to the Award.

3–30 If a party is notified at an incorrect address, but fails to object, it will usually be deemed to have waived its right to object under art.39.

3–31 A party may change the address for notification. The general practice is, however, for communications to the parties to be made through their lawyers, once the Request was notified. The reference to "last address" is intended to cover situations where the Respondent cannot be located.

3–32 Article 3 should be read in conjunction with the relevant national law, in particular the law of the place of arbitration. Some national laws have more precise provisions regarding notice. Article 3(1) of the UNCITRAL Model Law for example provides as follows:

> "1. Unless otherwise agreed by the parties: (a) any written communication is deemed to have been received if it is delivered to the addressee personally or if it is delivered at his place of business, habitual residence or mailing address; if none of these can be found after making a reasonable inquiry, a written communication is deemed to have been

[10] Some contracts provide that notifications are to be copied to the in-house or external lawyers, for example.

[11] This is in accordance with arts 2 and 3 of EU Directive 68/151/EEC of March 9, 1968 which has been transposed into the law of the Member States.

[12] Many US companies are incorporated in one state (such as Delaware) and registered to do business in another state, where they maintain their head office.

received if it is sent to the addressee's last- known place of business, habitual residence or mailing address by registered letter or any other means which provides a record of the attempt to deliver it."

Parties should ensure that they comply with the mandatory (or even recommended) provisions with respect to notification under the law of the place of arbitration to avoid an issue arising in this respect in annulment or enforcement proceedings.

The method of transmittal

Article 3(2) permits transmittal by "delivery against receipt". This permits transmittal by hand delivery or by various methods by which the recipient confirms that it has received the transmittal. Therefore, transmittal by registered letter with a return receipt or international courier (where the recipient signs for the package) would be acceptable. To be effective, the sending party must be able to prove receipt. As a result, use of registered letter without a return receipt should be avoided. It is not as clear that a facsimile transmission will necessarily be viewed as "delivery against receipt" as the acknowledgment by the recipient's fax machine is simply a confirmation that the electronic message has been received and not necessarily that it was printed by the recipient fax machine. **3–33**

Article 3(2) also permits any method of transmittal that "provides a record of sending". Registered mail and international courier provide a record of sending (and usually of receipt). However, it is noteworthy—especially if there are time constraints—that transmittal by email or facsimile is possible. The basic distinction between a fax and an email is that the former uses a dedicated line and the latter transmits the data in packets that may be subject to viewing and tampering by third parties. Therefore, in some circumstances it is conceivable that a party will contest not the fact that it received the email but rather the contents. Where the parties are both actively participating in the arbitration, this should not give rise to difficulties. However, if one party is in default, transmittal in a form that provides an exact paper copy of what was sent is usually preferable. **3–34**

With the increased use of .pdf or .tif documents, which are attached to the email, it becomes more difficult to challenge the contents of the transmittal. In any event, it happens once in a while that an email does in fact not reach its recipient. One way of securing email receipt is by the sender to request the recipients to confirm receipt by return email no later than within 24 or 48 hours. If the sender does not receive such receipt message from one of the recipients, he or she may wish to use a more reliable method of transmission. In the authors' practice, the system of seeking confirmation of receipt by return email works well. **3–35**

As stated before, the method of transmittal of documents and communications is usually dealt with in more detail in the Terms of Reference and the procedural orders which are discussed under arts 22 and 25. **3–36**

Format of the communication

Article 3(2) refers to various forms of communication in paper format but also to electronic transmission by email. Parties to ICC arbitrations may also **3–37** agree with the Tribunal to use the ICC NetCase facility either for the main communications or for a supplementary form of communication, although it does not appear that the system is in widespread use. If the parties so agree, then they will be asked to sign an agreement.[13] The question as to whether to use the NetCase facility is best discussed when the parties and the Tribunal are establishing the Terms of Reference. The ICC does not charge for the use of NetCase. Users of NetCase, have secured electronic access to: (i) a summary of the case; (ii) the correspondence relating to the arbitration; (iii) procedural documents (including the Terms of Reference and procedural orders); (iv) the various memorials; and (v) exhibits to the memorials. All of these documents are submitted in pdf format and can be downloaded by the parties. If used as the primary means of communication, the parties and the Tribunal should take into account any mandatory provisions of applicable law regarding the notification of documents. Even where NetCase is in use, generally one would expect the Award to be notified in writing by the Secretariat.

3–38 Generally, one would expect that pleadings and exhibits would be provided in paper format. However, in many cases this format may not be an effective way of transmitting the data and it may be preferable to transmit the data in an electronic format that is searchable (such as in a database format). These aspects are a matter for the Tribunal and the parties to discuss and will often be agreed upon or dealt with as part of the procedure under arts 22 and 25.

3–39 Article 3(2) does not expressly require all recipients to receive the same format of document or even that the same method of transmittal be used. The general rule is that one should ensure that the other side receives documents in the same format as the Tribunal and that the method of transmittal be as rapid.[14]

Language of the communication

3–40 Article 3 does not deal with the language of the notifications or communications. The Tribunal determines the language of the arbitration under art.20. Therefore, before the Tribunal is in place, there may be an issue as to which language should be used.

3–41 If the agreement to arbitrate is contained in an agreement requiring notices to be given in a specific language, it may well be a contractual requirement that all notices and other communications be given in that language. If there is no such requirement but all factors point to use of one language (such as the language of the underlying agreement and the language used by the parties), then notices will

[13] For a description of NetCase, see Philippe (ICC Special Counsel), "New IT facility for ICC arbitration users" (2005) ICC ICArb Vol.16 No.2, p.5 and "NetCase: A New ICC Arbitration Facility" (2004) ICC ICArb Bull, Special Bulletin, p.53; "ICC NetCase: At The Forefront of IT In Arbitration", http://www.iccwbo.org [accessed November 12, 2013]; email:support@iccnetcase.org. More generally, see http://iccnetcase.org.

[14] One issue that may legitimately arise is whether a party is obliged to provide the other side with documents in a searchable format (such as pdf image on text) if it is providing the Tribunal with documents in that format in cases where the other side is not providing documents in the same format. Since there is no easy solution to that issue, some lawyers prefer to avoid it by simply providing the Tribunal with non-searchable formatted documents although they have searchable documents on their system on the assumption that they will be directing the Tribunal to the relevant passages.

often be made in that language. However, until there has been a decision on the language—or the languages—of the arbitration, parties may use the language they consider appropriate and may refrain from translating exhibits that are in a language that the other party (and the arbitrators) are likely to understand anyway.

In its communications with the parties and/or arbitrators, the language of arbi- **3–42**
tration agreed to between the parties or fixed by the Tribunal does not bind the Secretariat. Many members of the Secretariat are fluent in other than the two official working languages of the ICC Court, which are English and French. Therefore the Secretariat will whenever possible, write in the actual language of arbitration, such as German, Italian and Spanish in particular.

An arbitrator addressing solely the Secretariat may use the language he or she **3–43**
deems fit, although most arbitrators would use the language of arbitration also in their dealings with the Secretariat.

Article 3(3): "A notification or communication shall be deemed to have been made on the day it was received by the party itself or by its representative, or would have been received if made in accordance with Article 3(2)."

The first part of art.3(3) focuses on actual receipt by a party "or its representa- **3–44**
tive". The second part focuses on the date on which the party "or its representative" would have received the notice or communication if it had been made in accordance with art.3(2).[15]

The reference to a party's representative is generally meant to cover the lawyer **3–45**
representing the party. It is standard practice in the Request and the Answer to state that communications should be transmitted to the lawyers. In certain circumstances, a party may hold a power of attorney or be an agent for a party. Given the importance of notifications under art.V(1)(b) of the New York Convention, the prudent course is to give notice by having the Request transmitted to the company at its seat or head office as well as to the agent.

The "deemed receipt" provision is intended to cover, in particular, situations **3–46**
where the Respondent has not been located. In some instances, the Respondent or one of the Respondents may no longer exist as a corporate entity, in which case there may be issues under national law both as to service and as to whether the company has to be revived for the proceedings.[16]

The "deemed receipt" provision in art.3(3) refers back to art.3(2) as to the **3–47**
manner in which the communication is to be made. Article 3(2) itself permits electronic and written communications. As a result, there is an issue as to which forms of communication under art.3(2) give rise to "deemed receipt". In deciding that issue, regard should be given to both the national law of the place of arbitration and the probable place of enforcement and the New York Convention.

[15] By way of comparison, art.3(1)(b) of the UNCITRAL Model Law provides that "the communication [in accordance with Art.3(1)(a) of the Model Law] is deemed to have been received on the day it is so delivered". However, this is subject to any other agreement of the parties and the ICC Rules would constitute such an agreement.

[16] This can be the case where the Claimant is seeking to establish a claim against the corporate entity and then to pursue the remedy against its former shareholders or an entity which managed the company which may raise issues as to the proper parties to the arbitration. This is discussed under art.6.

3–48 Article 3(1) of the UNCITRAL Model Law appears to suggest that notifications should be in writing. Indeed, the most prudent course is to provide for notice and calculation of the deemed receipt based notifications in writing rather than notice by electronic means. For example, if a notification is sent with a hard copy by international courier and by email, the more prudent course for the party giving the notice is to calculate the time based on the assumption that the effective date is the date of receipt of the hard copy.

3–49 As regards the date of receipt, there are two issues. The first is when the communication would have been received (in the number of days after transmittal). The second is the effect of local holidays or vacations in the place of receipt. In either case, the most prudent course for planning how to give notice is to assume the maximum normal time for delivery for the recipients to actually receive the notification.

Article 3(4): "Periods of time specified in or fixed under the Rules shall start to run on the day following the date a notification or communication is deemed to have been made in accordance with Article 3(3). When the day next following such date is an official holiday, or a non-business day in the country where the notification or communication is deemed to have been made, the period of time shall commence on the first following business day. Official holidays and non-business days are included in the calculation of the period of time. If the last day of the relevant period of time granted is an official holiday or a non-business day in the country where the notification or communication is deemed to have been made, the period of time shall expire at the end of the first following business day."

Scope and general interpretation of Article 3(4)

3–50 Article 3(4) deals with the calculation of time periods in the Rules and under the Rules. Therefore, it applies to time limits set by the Tribunal as well as to time limits applicable to the Tribunal. Article 3(4) does not apply generally to time periods under the underlying contract, which would be determined in accordance with the law applicable to the underlying contract or that part of the underlying contract.

3–51 For the Tribunal, the key time limits are the time for signing of the Terms of Reference (referred to in art.23(2)) and the time for rendering an Award (referred to in art.30). These time limits are guidelines intended to ensure that the Tribunal proceeds with acceptable speed with the arbitration.

3–52 For the parties, the key time periods prior to the appointment of the Tribunal relate to the 30-day period for filing the Answer or Answer to the Claim for Joinder pursuant to art.5(1) and the 30-day period for filing any Reply to a counterclaim under art.5(6). As noted below, the Secretariat will grant initial extensions for these periods almost as a matter of course.

3–53 After the appointment of the Tribunal, there are various other time limits that are applicable. With respect to the Tribunal itself, one of the key provisions relates to challenges, for which a 30-day period is provided under art.14(2). This period is interpreted and monitored by the ICC Court strictly when faced with a challenge by a party. Requests for correction and/or interpretation of Awards need also to be made within a 30-day time limit under art.35. Requests are filed with the Secretariat but it is for the Tribunal, not the ICC Court to determine whether the time limit was met, when examining the admissibility of requests for correction and/or interpretation.

In the course of the arbitral proceedings, it is for the Tribunal to set the parties' time limits for making their written submissions. It is sometimes a source of frustration to parties that time limits set by the Tribunal may be extended with limited apparent justification in response to requests of the other party. This flexible approach is intended to ensure that parties from different legal backgrounds have a full opportunity of presenting their case. It is also aimed at encouraging participation in the arbitral proceedings. Tribunals are usually quite keen on having the parties participate in the proceedings so that there is less occasion to challenge an Award for breach of due process. **3–54**

The "next business day" rule

The general rule in art.3(4) is that the time period begins to run on the next business day. Therefore, if notice is received on a holiday but the next day is a business day, the period of time will start to run on the next day just as if the notice had been received on a business day. **3–55**

Article 3(4) distinguishes between an "official holiday" and a "non- business day" and a "business day" in the place where the notification or communication is deemed to have been made. **3–56**

For purposes of this section, the relevant place is the place where the notification or communication was received or was deemed to have been received. Therefore, the fact that a day is an official holiday at the place of arbitration or in the country of the sender is not relevant. **3–57**

"Official holidays" are holidays set by law. "Non-business days" are intended to cover days on which office businesses are generally not open for regular business. For example, in the European Union, the United States of America and in many countries in Asia, Saturday and Sunday would generally be viewed as "non-business days". In Saudi Arabia and the Gulf states, Friday would be viewed as a "non-business day". Whether Thursday is a non-business day in certain predominantly Muslim countries would appear to depend on the country and the practices. **3–58**

In the calculation of the 30-day period to file a Reply to the Request, official holidays and non-business days are included within that 30-day period. This is in accordance with practice in many national legal systems. **3–59**

If the last day of a period is an official holiday or a non-business day, then the period of time expires on the next following business day. In either case, the time would expire at midnight of the following business day. **3–60**

CHAPTER 2

COMMENCING THE ARBITRATION

Article 4 Request for Arbitration

1 A party wishing to have recourse to arbitration under the Rules shall submit its Request for Arbitration (the "Request") to the Secretariat at any of the offices specified in the Internal Rules. The Secretariat shall notify the claimant and respondent of the receipt of the Request and the date of such receipt.

2 The date on which the Request is received by the Secretariat shall, for all purposes, be deemed to be the date of the commencement of the arbitration.

3 The Request shall contain the following information:

a) the name in full, description, address and other contact details of each of the parties;
b) the name in full, address and other contact details of any person(s) representing the claimant in the arbitration;
c) a description of the nature and circumstances of the dispute giving rise to the claims and of the basis upon which the claims are made;
d) a statement of the relief sought, together with the amounts of any quantified claims and, to the extent possible, an estimate of the monetary value of any other claims;
e) any relevant agreements and, in particular, the arbitration agreement(s);
f) where claims are made under more than one arbitration agreement, an indication of the arbitration agreement under which each claim is made;
g) all relevant particulars and any observations or proposals concerning the number of arbitrators and their choice in accordance with the provisions of Articles 12 and 13, and any nomination of an arbitrator required thereby; and
h) all relevant particulars and any observations or proposals as to the place of the arbitration, the applicable rules of law and the language of the arbitration.

The claimant may submit such other documents or information with the Request as it considers appropriate or as may contribute to the efficient resolution of the dispute.

4 Together with the Request, the claimant shall:

a) submit the number of copies thereof required by Article 3(1); and

b) make payment of the filing fee required by Appendix III ("Arbitration Costs and Fees") in force on the date the Request is submitted.

In the event that the claimant fails to comply with either of these requirements, the Secretariat may fix a time limit within which the claimant must comply, failing which the file shall be closed without prejudice to the claimant's right to submit the same claims at a later date in another Request.

5 The Secretariat shall transmit a copy of the Request and the documents annexed thereto to the respondent for its Answer to the Request once the Secretariat has sufficient copies of the Request and the required filing fee.[1]

Introductory remarks

Article 4 deals with the commencement of arbitration proceedings. Article 4(1) expressly provides that it is possible to do so by filing with one of the ICC's offices (Paris, Hong Kong or New York), which is a change from the prior Rules. Aside from some minor drafting changes, the provision regarding consolidation in the former art.4(6) has been moved to art.10. As mentioned in the Introduction, in 2012, the ICC received 759 Requests for Arbitration. **4–1**

The Request begins the arbitral proceedings. The first consideration for the parties is whether and when to commence the arbitration. **4–2**

Aside from the limitation issues discussed below under art.4(2), there are sometimes issues for example relating to: (i) the compliance with pre- arbitration procedural requirements; or (ii) the exercise of contractual rights prior to commencement of an arbitration; or (iii) where both parties have claims against one another, a party's preference to appear as Claimant or Respondent. **4–3**

[1] Article 4 corresponds to art.4 of the 1998 ICC Rules. There have been some substantive changes.

Compliance with pre-arbitral procedural requirements

4–4 In some arbitration agreements there is an obligation that the parties either meet and discuss issues or engage in some form of negotiation or mediation prior to commencing an arbitration. The ICC standard arbitration clause contains no such obligation. However, parties are free to adapt the standard clause to suit their needs, and so-called multi-tiered arbitration clauses are the result of such drafting. The effect of these agreements will depend on the terms of the agreements themselves, the law governing these agreements and the law of the place of arbitration.[2] Under the ICC Dispute Board Rules (September 2004) if the parties have agreed to submit their dispute to a Dispute Review Board (or Dispute Adjudication Board), they will normally have to do so, before they can start an ICC arbitration. Once a dispute has arisen, a party may reasonably view the procedures contemplated in the dispute resolution clause prior to arbitration, in the then prevailing circumstances, as a waste of time. Or it may view them as harmful by requiring disclosure of information[3] or causing delay.[4] However, if expressed as a condition precedent to arbitration in the arbitration clause, the clause should be either followed or the party proposing to commence the arbitration should ensure that it is in a position to demonstrate that the condition was no longer applicable due to rejection by the other party or for some other recognised ground.

[2] On multi-tiered dispute resolution clauses and their enforcement, see Jolles, "Consequences of Multi-tier Arbitration Clauses: Issues of Enforcement" (2006) Arbitration Vol.72 No.4, p.329; Jimenez Figueres, "Multi-Tiered Dispute Resolution Clauses in ICC Arbitration" (with extracts of ICC Awards), (2003) ICC ICArb Bull Vol.14 No.1, p.71; "Amicable Means to Resolve Disputes How the ICC ADR Rules work" (2004) J Int'l Arb Vol.21 No.1, p.91; Craig, Park & Paulsson, *op. cit.*, p.587; Jolivet, "Chronique de jurisprudence arbitrale de la Chambre de commerce internationale (CCI): arbitrage CCI et proc´edure ADR", (2001) Cahiers de l'Arbitrage of November 16/17 2001, Pt 2, Nos 320 to 321; Sutton, Gill and Gearing, *Russell on Arbitration*, 23rd edn (Thomson, Sweet & Maxwell 2007), para.2–036, p.48; in *England*, see *Cable & Wireless Plc v IBM United Kingdom Ltd* [2002] EWHC 2059; [2002] 2 All E.R. (Comm) 1041 (October 11, 2002); Mackie, "The Future for ADR Clauses After Cable & Wireless v IBM" (2003) Arb Int Vol.19 No.3, p.345; in *France*, see Cass Civ mixte, February 14, 2003, *Poirév Tripier*,(2003) Arb Int Vol.19 No.3 p.363 and (2003) Rev Arb No.2 p.403, note Jarrosson. See also Paris, March 4, 2004, (2005) Rev Arb No.1 p.151, note Train (a pre-arbitration clause is a contractual clause which binds not only the parties but also the Tribunal). French jurisdictions have opted for the same position in judicial proceedings. See Cass civ 2‘e, April 21, 2005, *Sté Maison girondine v Lonne* (2005) JCP ed G II 10153 p.2063, note Croze (conciliation is a condition precedent to court action); in *Switzerland*, see Swiss Supreme Court, June 6, 2007, *X. Ltd v Y*,, 4A—18/2007, referred to at para.4–5; Swiss Supreme Court, August 17, 1995, *Vekoma v Maran Coal Co* (1996) ASA Bull Vol.14 No.4 p.673, note Schweizer; Friedland, "The Swiss Supreme Court Sets Aside an ICC Award", (1996) J Int'l Arb Vol.13 No.1, p.111; in *Sweden*, see SCC Case 21/1999, SAR 2002:2, p.59. For a discussion in the context of investment arbitration, see Webster, *Handbook of Investment Arbitration* (Thomson/Sweet & Maxwell, 2010), paras 3–20 et seq.

[3] The mediation or alternative procedure usually provides for the confidentiality of documents communicated during the procedure. However, by entering into a mediation, it is virtually inevitable that a party will disclose its approach to the case. Therefore, it can affect requests for documents in the arbitration proceedings themselves (as the requesting party may have confirmation that certain documents exist). In a recent unpublished case (ICC Case No.18701), the requesting party requested production of documents that had been referred to in the mediation indicating that the documents had been referred to in the mediation. Although arguably such a use of information from the mediation was inappropriate, production of some of the documents was ordered.

[4] Some clauses provide a specific cooling off period of sometimes several weeks or even months before recourse to arbitration is authorised.

If the situation is unclear, one would expect that the Tribunal would clarify the position in the Terms of Reference discussed under art.23. The Tribunal may for example either seek confirmation from the parties that the condition has been complied with or adjourn the arbitration to permit the condition to be met (if this is possible under the terms of the arbitration agreement, which may not always be the case). If the Respondent wishes to see this defense dealt with as a jurisdictional objection, the Tribunal may have to address it as such. If the issue with respect to the effect of the mediation agreement is not resolved with the Terms of Reference, the party who alleges that there is a procedural defect as a result, is required to raise the issue promptly under art.39 of the Rules and possibly also under applicable law. In a Swiss case, the Supreme Court noted that the obligation to mediate was an ongoing one that the parties could have invoked during the course of the proceedings. The court held that it was an abuse of right for the party to raise the failure to meet this requirement after the hearings had been terminated.[5] 4–5

Exercising contractual rights prior to commencement of the arbitration

In many franchise and distribution agreements a party has the contractual right to inspect the records of the other party. If a party seeks to exercise those rights prior to the commencement of the arbitration, then a failure to comply by the other party may be the subject of a substantive claim in the arbitral proceedings. If the party does not seek to exercise those rights prior to the arbitration, then there is a danger that the issue will be treated by the Tribunal as a procedural aspect of the arbitration and not as a substantive right. In addition, if parallel court proceedings are required to force compliance with the contractual right, there may be a danger of alienating the Tribunal if these proceedings are brought after the arbitration has been commenced due to the impact on the arbitral proceedings.[6] 4–6

The desire to be Claimant (or, in some instances, Respondent)

Another frequent concern is that many parties prefer to be Claimants rather than Respondents. Where both parties have claims against one another, the commencement of the proceedings may simply be the result of more rapid reaction by one party. Acting as Claimant is less important in defining the parties to the arbitration under the Rules than it was under the 1998 Rules due to the introduction of art.7. 4–7

Article 4(1): "A party wishing to have recourse to arbitration under the Rules shall submit its Request for Arbitration (the "Request") to the Secretariat at any of the offices specified in the Internal Rules. The Secretariat shall notify the claimant and respondent of the receipt of the Request and the date of such receipt."

As discussed under art.2, a party may be a natural or legal person and may include several parties. Affiliated parties may and frequently do bring claims 4–8

[5] Swiss Supreme Court, June 6, 2007, *X. Ltd v Y*, 4A—18/2007, ITA Monthly Report, September 2007, Vol.V Issue 9, contribution by Dr Georg von Segesser, http:// www.kluwerarbitration.com.

[6] See the discussion in Webster, "Obtaining Documents from Adverse Parties in International Arbitration" (2001) Arb Int Vol.17 No.1, p.41 at p.42.

together. In some instances, unaffiliated parties also jointly file Requests for Arbitration, although in such instances the interests of the parties should be identical or closely aligned. By submitting a Request jointly, the parties are electing to be treated together for purposes such as the nomination of arbitrators for example and presumably for the purposes of filings. For affiliated parties, the advantage is to ensure that all relief against the Respondent is available to one of the Claimants. Therefore, even where the Claimants' claims are different, there is a community of interest. If the Claimants are not affiliated and they have different claims, there is a greater potential for subsequent conflict.[7]

4–9 To commence arbitration under the Rules, the Claimant must send the Request to the Secretariat at one of the Secretariat's offices in accordance with art.5 of Ap.II to the Rules. The Secretariat currently has offices in Paris, Hong Kong and New York.[8] Articles 3(1) and 4(4) require that a copy of the Request be submitted for the Secretariat, for each Respondent and for each arbitrator.[9] The Secretariat then opens a file and, in accordance with art.4(5), after receipt of the advance payment of US$3,000, sends a copy of the Request to the Respondent indicating the date of receipt.

4–10 The Secretariat notifies the Respondent at the address provided by the Claimant. Therefore, it is the Claimant's obligation to ensure that this address is the appropriate one in accordance with art.3(2).

4–11 The Secretariat will not notify or provide a copy of the Request to any other person or even confirm the existence of the arbitration to a third party. The existence and nature of the arbitration are confidential as far as the ICC Court and its Secretariat are concerned.[10]

Article 4(2): "The date on which the Request is received by the Secretariat shall, for all purposes, be deemed to be the date of the commencement of the arbitration."

4–12 Article 4(2) provides that it is the date of the receipt by the Secretariat and not the date of receipt by the Respondent that is the date of the commencement of the proceedings.[11] In this respect, ICC arbitration is to be distinguished from *ad hoc*

[7] The alternative is for a Claimant to file a Request for Arbitration against the main Respondent and to join the other party as a Respondent.

[8] Article 4(1) does not preclude transmission of a Request by fax or electronically. However, by making reference to the number of copies in art.3(1) and with the reference to the number of copies in art.4(4), the Rules are indicating that it is expected that hard copies will be provided.

[9] Article 4(1) does not preclude transmission of a Request by fax or electronically. However, by making reference to the number of copies in art.3(1) and with the reference to the number of copies in art.4(4), the Rules are indicating that it is expected that hard copies will be provided.

[10] See art.6 of the Statutes and above para.1–37.

[11] Bühler & Jarvin, "The Arbitration Rules of the International Chamber of Commerce" *in Practitioner's Handbook on International Arbitration* (C.H. Beck Djøf, 2002), No.9, p.143; see also Carbonneau, "Arbitration in the United States" in *Practitioner's Handbook on International Arbitration, op. cit.*, No.95, p.113; Gaillard & Edelstein, "Arbitration in France" in *Practitioner's Handbook on International Arbitration, op. cit.*, No.80, p.660; Karrer& Straub, "Arbitration in Switzerland" in *Practitioner's Handbook on International Arbitration, op. cit.*, No.88, p.1061; Maxwell, "Arbitration in England" in *Practitioner's Handbook on International Arbitration, op. cit.*, No.108, p.615.

arbitrations or the general provision under the UNCITRAL Model Law providing that an arbitration is commenced when the Respondent receives notice.[12]

Therefore, whatever difficulties the Secretariat may have in notifying the Respondent, the date of receipt by the Secretariat will prevail. The date of commencement of the arbitration may be crucial in determining whether the Claimant's claim is timely or whether it is barred due to a limitation period. **4–13**

The Rules do not set out or refer to limitation periods and there is a basic distinction between the approach to limitation periods in common law and civil law countries. In common law countries, the limitation period gives rise to a procedural bar to enforcement. In most civil jurisdiction, the issue of limitations is a matter of substantive law. **4–14**

Therefore, in a civil law context, the law applicable to such periods is usually treated as the law governing the underlying agreement. In the common law system, the law applicable to the procedure (if any) may be deemed relevant, as may the law of the place of arbitration.[13] However, the law of the place of arbitration frequently is viewed as limited to setting the minimum standards for due process rather than as providing any indication of the actual procedure to be followed. Therefore, it would be somewhat incongruous to "import" the local limitations provisions due solely to the place of arbitration.[14] **4–15**

The first attempt to deal with this issue in a broad international context was with the UNCITRAL Convention on the Application of Limitation Periods to the Sale of Goods. However, the number of signatories to that convention is limited and the convention is limited to the sale of goods.[15] Article 10 of the UNIDROIT Principles sets out specific provisions of limitation periods but, unlike certain other provisions in those principles, it is difficult to see these provisions being applied by analogy if the governing law is a national law.[16] **4–16**

A separate issue is whether the court or the Tribunal should decide whether a limitation period is applicable and whether a party may bring court proceedings to **4–17**

[12] Article 21 of the UNCITRAL Model Law provides: "Unless otherwise agreed by the parties, the arbitral proceedings in respect of a particular dispute commence on the date on which a request for that dispute to be referred to arbitration is received by the Respondent".

[13] English law was applied with respect to limitations periods based on the place of arbitration prior to the Foreign Limitations Period Act of 1984 to which reference is made in art.13 of the English Arbitration Act 1996 as amended. See also Sutton, Gill & Gearing, *op. cit.*, para.5–021 and para.8–177. For Switzerland, see Vogt, "Article 181" *in International Arbitration in Switzerland—An Introduction to and a Commentary on Articles 176–194 of the Swiss Private International Law Statute* (Helbing & Lichtenhahn/Kluwer, 2000), p.182.

[14] The situation may be somewhat different, although unintentionally perhaps, where the parties agree that the procedural law of one country will apply to their dispute. See the discussion of the place of arbitration under art.18. In addition, the place of arbitration may affect the law governing the arbitration agreement.

[15] For a description, see Sono, "The Limitation Convention: The Forerunner to Establish UNCITRAL Credibility" (September 2003), http://www.cisg.law.pace.edu/cisg/biblio/sono3.html.

[16] The UNIDROIT Principles are intended to reflect principles that are common in international business. However, with regard to limitation periods, the question is usually not one of interpretation but of application of a set limitation period. The English High Court has been critical of Tribunals applying principles other than those of the applicable law where the application appears to have changed substantive rights in the *Peterson Farms* case (paras 6–99, 21–22, 21, 50). One would expect the approach to be very critical indeed if a limitation period were "imported" into the applicable law.

obtain a declaration that the limitation period prevents the arbitration. This will depend on national law applicable to this aspect of the case.

4–18 The US Supreme Court has held that it is for the Tribunal to decide this issue when the limitation is contained in the contract itself. In *Howsam v Dean Witter Reynolds*,[17] the issue was whether the Claimant had filed a claim within the six-year period provided by the National Association of Securities Dealers (NASD) Code of Arbitration Procedure. The Court held that:

> "we find the applicability of the NASD time limit rule is a matter presumptively for the arbitrator, not for the judge. The time limit rule closely resembles the gateway questions that this Court has found not to be 'questions of arbitrability' . . . Moreover, the NASD arbitrators, comparatively more expert about the meaning of their own rule, are comparatively better able to interpret and apply it."

4–19 The *Howsam* case deals with a contractual limitation period under the NASD Rules and not statutory limitation periods. However, in the international setting, the justification for having such periods decided by the Tribunal and not by national courts would be similar. In most ICC arbitrations, the Tribunals will have different legal backgrounds. Therefore, they will be in a better position to decide on the applicability of a limitation period, including the civil equivalent thereof, than national courts.[18] In Canada, for example, the trial court in Ontario held that the limitation period was a matter for the Tribunal and not for the court.[19]

4–20 Under French law, it appears that not only is the issue of limitations ("*prescription*") a matter for the arbitrator, but, if the arbitrator is authorised to decide *ex aequo et bono* (as is provided as a possibility under art.21), the arbitrator may even set aside the limitation period.[20]

Article 4(3): "The Request shall contain the following information:

> **a) the name in full, description, address and other contact details of each of the parties;**

[17] *Karen Howsam v Dean Witter*, 537 United States Reports 79; 2002 US Lexis 9235 (US Supreme Court 2002); (2004) YBCA Vol.XXIX p.232 (excerpt).

[18] The basic point is that the responsibility for making decisions as to arbitrability under US law depends on the language of the clause and applicable rules. Due to the wording of the Rules there may be less of a carve out under an ICC arbitration than otherwise. See *Stone & Webster Asia Inc v Triplefine International Corp*, 322 F. 3d 115 (2nd Cir. 2003); *Apollo Computer, Inc v Berg*, 886 F.2d 469 (1st Cir. 1989); and *Daiei v United States Shoe Corp*, 755 F. Supp.299 (D. Haw. 1991).

[19] See for example *Amec E & C Services Ltd v Nova Chemicals (Canada) Ltd* (Ont. Sup. Ct. June 20, 2003) applying the UNCITRAL Model Law applicable in Ontario where the Court stated: "if I find that the dispute between the parties in the Application is one that is arguably covered by the arbitration clause, I should make no definitive determination on that issue and should refer that matter to the Arbitral Tribunal for a decision in the first instance. The arbitration clause in the Contract is clearly broad enough to potentially encompass a dispute between the parties as to whether or not the Contract contains a two- year limitation period. Therefore, on the face of it, the matter should be referred to arbitration, unless considerations such as undue delay apply".

[20] Cass Civ 2e, May 31, 2001, *Huon v Consorts Huon*, where the French Supreme Court has set aside a lower court decision deciding not to appoint an arbitrator based on the expiration of a limitation period, (2002) Rev Arb No.3 p.691. See also Paris, November 28, 2002, *Panalpina World Transports Holding AG v Transco* (2003) Rev Arb No.4, p.1359, note Betto.

b) the name in full, address and other contact details of any person(s) representing the claimant in the arbitration;

c) a description of the nature and circumstances of the dispute giving rise to the claims and of the basis upon which the claims are made;

d) a statement of the relief sought, together with the amounts of any quantified claims and, to the extent possible, an estimate of the monetary value of any other claims;

e) any relevant agreements and, in particular, the arbitration agreement(s);

f) where claims are made under more than one arbitration agreement, an indication of the arbitration agreement under which each claim is made;

g) all relevant particulars and any observations or proposals concerning the number of arbitrators and their choice in accordance with the provisions of Articles 12 and 13, and any nomination of an arbitrator required thereby; and

h) all relevant particulars and any observations or proposals as to the place of the arbitration, the applicable rules of law and the language of the arbitration.

The claimant may submit such other documents or information with the Request as it considers appropriate or as may contribute to the efficient resolution of the dispute."

The Rules provide a framework for arbitration and give broad leeway as to how each arbitration is conducted. The Request must set out the basic elements referred to in art.4(3), but the detail and the number of exhibits will vary from case to case and the strategy adopted. The Rules are to be distinguished from the UNCITRAL Rules for example that provide for a "Notice of Arbitration" with the possibility of a Statement of Claim.[21] As an institutional, rather than an ad hoc form of arbitration, it is viewed as important that the ICC Court has from the outset more complete information about the nature of the dispute, since it will take it into consideration when constituting the Tribunal, and fixing the place of arbitration. It is typically only based on the information contained in the Request for Arbitration and the Answer thereto, that the Tribunal will establish the Terms of Reference. That would not be possible if a simple "Notice of Arbitration" was to be filed. **4–21**

In accordance with art.25, the Tribunal will usually provide for at least one and usually two memorials from each side prior to the oral hearings.[22] Therefore, there is no real danger that the facts that the Claimant wishes to set out will not be brought to the attention of the Tribunal in the Request. The issue is when and how those facts will be brought to the Tribunal's attention within the limits provided by the Rules. **4–22**

[21] As discussed in Webster, *Handbook of UNCITRAL Arbitration* (Thomson/Sweet & Maxwell, 2010, paras 3–3 et seq.) The UNCITRAL Rules are based on a two stage procedure with a notice of arbitration and statement of claim.

[22] This may be true for each phase of the arbitration proceedings, depending on how it was decided to structure them. Hearings on a preliminary issue, including on jurisdiction may in some cases give place to only one round of memorials.

4–23 The nature of the dispute will usually affect the types of Request that is filed. For example, where there are multiple agreements and multiple parties, the Request may well have to be complex.

4–24 A Claimant usually submits a detailed Request with substantial supporting documents for specific procedural reasons. A detailed Request provides the Tribunal with a reasoned argument with the Claimant's version of the facts, and that will be the first version that the Tribunal will read (although it will read the Answer immediately thereafter). By filing a detailed Request, the Claimant is indicating that it can proceed promptly with the arbitration, which can put pressure on a Respondent. In addition, a detailed request setting out the complexity of the matter is an effective manner of showing the ICC Court that a Tribunal of three arbitrators (rather than having a sole arbitrator) may be more appropriate. For the selection of the president of the Tribunal, the Request (and/or the Respondent's Answer) may also be of assistance in indicating in particular the complexity of the case. A lack of precision and detail in the Request may make it more difficult for the ICC Court to take the appropriate decisions when setting in motion the arbitration. Finally, a detailed Request is a method of forcing, or attempting to force, the Respondent to file a detailed response.

4–25 A Claimant may choose to submit a less detailed Request, when the key point is to commence the proceedings.[23] This can be the case if there is a potential problem with a limitation period or where negotiations between the parties have broken down and the Claimant wishes to indicate that the matter will proceed to arbitration in the absence of an agreement. The Claimant may also submit a less detailed Request where it is certain of the claim, but less confident of the details or the calculation of damages. A Claimant may also file a general request to see the type of response that it receives in the Reply. In addition, in complex construction, oil and gas or telecommunication disputes, the Claimant may decide that the matter will have to be the subject of detailed submissions later in any event and limit itself to outlining the basic elements and framework for the claim in the Request.

4–26 In deciding which approach to adopt, the Claimant should keep in mind that there will be supplemental memorials and filings. However, the basic documents for the establishment of the Terms of Reference and the initial procedural order are the Request, the Answer and the Reply to the Counterclaim, if any. In deciding whether the minimum requirements are met, one of the issues that may be expected to be is whether the Respondent was made aware in a general fashion of the claims being made against it. As a result, in most cases, where the Claimant has sought to comply with the list of required elements in art.4(3) there should be very little risk of the brevity of the Request causing a procedural issue in annulment or enforcement proceedings.[24] A more serious issue may arise with respect to

[23] See generally Bennett, *Arbitration: Essential concepts* (ALM Publishing, 2002), pp.94–96; Born, *International Commercial Arbitration—Commentary and Materials*, 2nd edn (Transnational Publishers/Kluwer, 2001), pp.451–453.

[24] See Hoge Raad (Dutch Supreme Court), January 17, 2003, *International Military Services Ltd v Ministry of Defence and Support for Armed Forces of the Islamic Republic of Iran and Islamic Republic of Iran*, NJ 2004, 384, Tijdschrift voor Arbitrage, p.143, note Asser; Les Cahiers de l'Arbitrage No.2004/2 p.61, note Ingen-Housz (the Dutch Supreme Court dismissed Respondent's challenge of the Award considering that the description of the claims in the Request for Arbitration was sufficiently clear to allow the preparation of its defense).

whether a Request covers a specific claim if there is a limitations argument that is made with respect to the claim.

The Secretariat reviews the material received from a Claimant to check the names of the parties and the existence of an ICC arbitration agreement between the parties named in the Request. However, the Secretariat does not review the Request to determine whether the Claimant has met each requirement of the Rules. That will be a matter for the Tribunal, if challenged by the Respondent. **4–27**

There is no provision of the Rules relating to amendments to the Request. It is not unheard of for a Request to be amended prior to the filing of an Answer. However, the need for an amendment in ICC arbitration is not the same as in many state court proceedings. Under art.23(1), for example, the Terms of Reference are prepared taking into account the parties' "most recent submissions", which may take the form of submissions by letters or email to the Tribunal. After the Terms of Reference have been established the parties will have the opportunity to make further submissions and these can also result in changes to the elements outlined by the Request. Therefore, subject to art. 8, there is no need in such circumstances to file an "Amended" or "Re-amended" Request, although the further submissions must fall within what is permitted by the Terms of Reference and, with regard to new claims, by art.23(4). **4–28**

Prior to the establishment of the Terms of Reference, the Claimant may consider amending the Request for Arbitration if the Claimant wishes to add another Claimant (that may be an affiliate, for example). If the Claimant wishes to amend its Request to add another Respondent, it may be faced with the argument that this should be done under art.7(1) and that the Claimant should file a Request for Joinder instead. **4–29**

The amendment of the Request is especially useful when a misapprehension of the Respondent's corporate identity has been made by Claimant. In a recent ICC case, the Claimant wrongly filed the Request against a company which had never signed nor participated in the performance of the contracts which were the subject of the dispute. However, that company was part of a group of companies and another company in that group had signed the contracts. The original Respondent suggested the second company be substituted. The Claimant agreed and filed an amended Request. **4–30**

In a recent Award, an ICC Tribunal confirmed the need for the Claimant to identify and name the proper party, over which it wishes the Tribunal to exercise jurisdiction. The Respondent was the holding company of several companies that were the results of mergers and acquisitions with various name changes. After the Respondent challenged the Tribunal's jurisdiction,[25] the Claimant argued that the Respondent had a duty to alert it in advance that it had incorrectly named the parent company in its draft Request for Arbitration, which it had provided a month prior to filing the Request for Arbitration. The sole arbitrator, a French lawyer, found: **4–31**

[25] Since the contract on which the Claimant relied contained an ICC arbitration clause, the ICC Court took an art.6(2) decision and thus allowed the case to move forward. See the discussion under art.6(4) on the ICC Court's prima facie decisions.

> "While Claimant might have appreciated receiving notice from Respondent prior to the filing of this arbitration that the latter could not be subject to jurisdiction, Respondent had no duty to do so. Respondent was only required to raise lack of jurisdiction as a defence in accordance with the rules of the arbitral proceeding and did so at the first opportunity provided under the Rules, i.e. in its Answer."[26]

The Tribunal declined jurisdiction over the Respondent, the parent company of the group which "had no involvement whatsoever in the conclusion, performance or termination of the [. . .] contract".[27] The Tribunal added that the mere participation of the various group entities in their negotiations with the Claimant regarding its claims arising out of the termination of the contract "cannot form a basis for an express or implied consent to arbitral jurisdiction. [. . .] it would be contrary to common sense and singularly inappropriate to hold that the mere willingness of a party to participate in settlement negotiations results in an admission of liability, waiver of defences, or other forfeiture of its rights".[28]

Article 4(3): "The Request shall contain the following information:

> **a) the name in full, description, address and other contact details of each of the parties;"**

4–32 Article 4(3)(a) requires proper identification of the parties in the Request. The description of the parties is usually brief and is aimed at identifying the parties and their roles. For example, it is fairly common to describe the activity of the parties and their relative importance as well as indicating their origin. If a party is part of a well-known group of companies, it may be of interest to indicate so. To the extent a party has a homepage on the internet, it may also provide it, in order to allow the Tribunal to gain better familiarity with the parties. Frequently arbitrators live in different countries. Therefore, they may not be familiar with entities that are well known in other countries.

4–33 Whether or not the parties named in the Request are also the proper parties to the arbitration is discussed under art.6. However, there is a basic distinction between court proceedings and arbitration in this respect. In court proceedings one may tend to name as a party to the litigation the company or other entity that signed the relevant contract and any other parties against whom a Claimant may consider that it has a claim. In arbitration, the proper party is only the party to an arbitration agreement with the Claimant. It is generally not possible to require parties who have not agreed to the arbitration clause to submit to arbitration. If such parties are added, they may object to jurisdiction during the proceedings or if there is an attempt to enforce the Award, in enforcement proceedings.

4–34 The initial question for any Claimant is whether he can force a Respondent to arbitrate a dispute. Article II of the New York Convention requires the courts of Member States to refer parties to arbitration if there is an arbitration agreement

[26] ICC case no.13645 (Final Award) (2006), (presently unreported, at para.82).

[27] ICC case no.13645 (Final Award) (2006), (presently unreported, at para.80).

[28] ICC case no.13645 (Final Award) (2006), (presently unreported, at para.81).

within the meaning of that article.[29] National legal systems generally either incorporate the New York Convention or have similar requirements, although some do not require that the arbitration agreement be in writing. As discussed elsewhere, UNCITRAL adopted a recommendation on July 6, 2006 that art.II(2) not be interpreted to be exhaustive.[30] If there is no authority for extending the arbitration agreement to a particular party, then the Claimant may be faced with national court proceedings as well as an application by the non-signatory under art.6. A secondary question is whether, as a result of adding parties, the dispute may end up being considered a multiparty dispute with the selection of arbitrators governed by art.12.

Aside from whether the Claimant decides that one or more Respondents are covered by the arbitration agreement, the Claimant may consider that the non-signatory may accept the arbitration agreement. This can arise where the dispute is between a Claimant and several companies within a group. In such a case, rather than having separate arbitral or court proceedings, the Respondents may prefer to have the matter addressed by one Tribunal. Nevertheless, by adding the non-signatory in such a case, the Claimant is, in essence, seeking to broaden the arbitration agreement and taking the risk that there will be an objection by the non-signatory. **4–35**

During the period from 2007–2011, 70 per cent of the Requests were filed by one Claimant against one Respondent. There were multiple Claimants in 13 per cent of the Requests and multiple Respondents in 22 per cent of the Requests.[31] In 2012, almost one third of the cases involved either more than one Claimant or more than one Respondent or both.[32] **4–36**

Article 4(3)(b): "the name in full, address and other contact details of any person(s) representing the claimant in the arbitration;"

This new provision is intended to reflect the fact that most parties are represented by lawyers in ICC arbitrations. Frequently, parties are represented by co-counsel. Although not binding unless accepted by the parties, the IBA Guidelines on Party Representation in International Arbitration provide as follows: **4–37**

> "4. Party Representatives should identify themselves to the other Party or Parties and the Arbitral Tribunal at the earliest opportunity. A Party

[29] Article II of the New York Convention: "1. Each Contracting State shall recognize an agreement in writing under which the parties undertake to submit to arbitration all or any differences which have arisen or which may arise between them in respect of a defined legal relationship, whether contractual or not, concerning a subject matter capable of settlement by arbitration. 2. The term 'agreement in writing' shall include an arbitral clause in a contract or an arbitration agreement, signed by the parties or contained in an exchange of letters or telegrams. 3. The court of a Contracting State, when seized of an action in a matter in respect of which the parties have made an agreement within the meaning of this article, at the request of one of the parties, refer the parties to arbitration, unless it finds that the said agreement is null and void, inoperative or incapable of being performed".

[30] For a discussion see Webster, *Handbook of UNCITRAL Arbitration* (Thomson/Sweet & Maxwell, 2010) paras 1–8 et seq.

[31] Fry, Greenberg & Mazza, op. cit., para. 3–94.

[32] 2013 ICArb Bull. vol 24, No.1, p.9.

should promptly inform the Arbitral Tribunal and the other Party or Parties of any change in such representation."

4–38 Therefore, to the extent that a lawyer is representing a party in an ICC arbitration, that lawyer should be identified in the Request or the Answer, as the case may be. This facilitates communications but also ensures transparency as to the representation.

Article 4(3)(c): "a description of the nature and circumstances of the dispute giving rise to the claims and of the basis upon which the claims are made;"

4–39 The Rules have been amended to add reference to the the basis upon which the claims are made. This reinforces the substantive requirements for the Request and focuses on the legal basis for the claims.

4–40 The main circumstance giving rise to any arbitration is usually the contract in which the arbitration agreement is found. In drafting a description of the dispute, the events that led to that contract, what happened during the term of that contract and the events that gave rise to the dispute will be set out to help to understand the Claimant's allegations and in support of the claims pursued in the arbitration.

4–41 As discussed above, the detail in which these circumstances are dealt with will vary with the individual case. It is important to provide the factual chain that leads not only to the dispute but also to the claim and therefore also to the amount of damages. Unlike some national pleadings, the Request should set out the basic elements of the Claimant's legal case and not be limited to facts.

4–42 The Request will also indicate the bases or the alternative bases for the claims. For example, if the Claimant is maintaining that the dispute is both contractual and quasi contractual or in tort, then one would expect that to be set out in the Request so that the Tribunal knows whether it is being called upon to decide a claim going beyond a contractual claim.

Article 4(3)(d): "a statement of the relief sought, together with the amounts of any quantified claims and, to the extent possible, an estimate of the monetary value of any other claims;"

4–43 The Rules have introduced in this paragraph reference to the amounts of any quantified claims and to the monetary value of other claims. This is part of an attempt to ensure that, to the extent possible, the ICC Court knows the amount in dispute.

4–44 The basic relief most normally sought in international arbitration is monetary damages. Parties may seek other relief such as specific performance or a declaration of rights. Under the common law systems, the normal remedy in court cases is monetary damages and specific performance is an exceptional remedy.[33] In

[33] See for example *Restatement (Second) of Contracts*, para.359(1) (1981): "Specific performance or an injunction will not be ordered if damages would be adequate to protect the expectation interest of the injured party".

civil law systems, theoretically at least the situation is reversed, with specific performance being the normal remedy.[34]

For practical reasons, monetary damages or a declaration are more frequently requested and granted in international arbitration. Courts grant injunctions on the basis that parties can always return to the court for enforcement or modification of the injunction. The judge may not be the same person who granted the injunction but the court as an entity remains. Arbitral Tribunals are transient in nature. Therefore, they are generally not in a position to supervise an injunction. In fact, enforcement of an injunction will depend on the cooperation of a national court. This may not be problematic in many countries where the New York Convention applies. It may be more problematic in other countries or where it is not entirely clear in which jurisdiction the injunction would be enforced. **4–45**

The Request sets out the basic relief sought. That request for relief may be modified up to the Terms of Reference and even thereafter subject to the provisions of art.23(4). Nevertheless, it is a basic principle that a Tribunal cannot award relief that has not been sought. For example, if a party does not seek interest on amounts due or if the date as of which the party seeks interest is set out in the Request for relief or elsewhere, the Tribunal can generally not, under the applicable law, go beyond the relief requested by the party to award interest that has not been sought or for a period for which interest has not been sought. A more complex issue may arise with respect to a Tribunal's attempt to craft a solution to an arbitration to meet its understanding of the relief that the party should be seeking.[35] If a party has in some form or another requested the relief, it should be possible to grant it and the Request should be drafted with this in mind. **4–46**

Article 4(3)(d) refers to an the amount of any quantified claims and an indication "to the extent possible" of an estimate of the monetary value of any other claims. This provision requires the Claimant to state the amount of quantified claims. Those claims may have been quantified in the context of a notification of the claim under the relevant agreement, for example. However, in many instances, the claims will not have been quantified at this stage of the proceedings, and any change in quantification will often be the subject of criticism by the other side. In such cases, the Claimant is only required to provide an estimate of the monetary value to the extent possible. If a Claimant does not provide an estimate of the monetary value, the ICC Court will have to calculate the advance on fees based on an overall impression as to the amount in dispute. However, the parties may object subsequent to the decision and provide additional information for reconsideration of the amount of the advance. **4–47**

Perhaps one of the most salutary effects of this use of the amount in dispute is that the parties generally seek to make claims that are reasonable in amount. Neither party wishes to pay the advance on costs based on a farfetched or **4–48**

[34] Elder, "The Case Against Arbitral Awards of Specific Performance in Transnational Commercial Disputes" (1997) Arb Int Vol.13 No.1, p.1.

[35] For example, art.33 of the UNCITRAL Model Law provides that an Award may be annulled if it "contains decisions on matters beyond the scope of the submission to arbitration". Article 36 of the UNCITRAL Model Law provides for objection to enforcement on the same grounds. As a result, if a party has not requested relief, there is an issue as to whether that matter has in fact been part of the submission to arbitration.

frivolous claim. Therefore the tendency of the Claimant is to either set the amount at a reasonable figure or to state that the damages "are subject to further verification but in any event no less than . . ." or simply to state that the damages will be set out in a later submission. The authors do not believe it is common or appropriate to provide an estimate as to possible damages in the Request if the material is not available to ensure that that estimate is reliable.[36]

4–49 Article 4(3)(d) anticipates that it may not be possible to establish the amount of the damage claim prior to the filing of the Request. In some cases Claimants do not set out the amount claimed to reduce the amount of the advance on costs that is fixed by the ICC Court on the amount in dispute. In the latter case, the Claimant will have to indicate the amount of the claim at some point in the proceedings. Usually, this will be in the Terms of Reference or with its first subsequent filing. At that time, the Secretariat will usually ask the ICC Court to seek a further advance on costs from the parties. ICC arbitration is a system for resolving commercial disputes and it has its costs that are to be borne by the parties in accordance with the Rules based on the amount in dispute, whenever an amount may be identified.

4–50 Article 4(3)(d) does not require the amount of the claim be quantified in any particular currency, although the advance on costs is in US dollars. Usually, one would expect that the estimate of damages would be in the currency used by the parties for the underlying contract. If more than one currency is used, then the Claimant may have the possibility of formulating the claim in one or more currencies. The appropriate currency will generally depend on the applicable law. Article 7.4.12 of the UNIDROIT Principles provides that "[d]amages are to be assessed either in the currency in which the monetary obligation was expressed or in the currency in which the harm was suffered, whichever is more appropriate". Therefore, for a Swiss distributor who purchases products in dollars, the damages may be calculated under that rule either in dollars or in Swiss francs, depending on which currency is more appropriate.

Article 4(3)(e): "any relevant agreements and, in particular, the arbitration agreement(s);"

4–51 As discussed below, art.4(3)(e) expressly refers to arbitration agreements in the plural, which is a reflection of the overall approach under the Rules of contemplating that there may be one arbitration that deals with disputes under several arbitration agreements, subject to the provisions of art.6 and art.9.

4–52 Usually the arbitration agreement (or the arbitration clause from the overall contract) is set out in the Request and the main overall contract is exhibited to the

[36] There is a natural difference of opinion between the Secretariat (which would like to have quantification of claims early in the proceedings) and counsel (who wish to avoid the risk that quantification is inaccurate). It may be inappropriate for Parties to provide an estimate of the value of declaratory relief or specific performance, as this will frequently be difficult to ascertain at this stage. For what appears to be a contrary view see Fry, Greenberg & Mazza, op. cit. para.3–97.

Request. If the arbitration agreement consists of an exchange of letters or emails, those documents should also be attached. It is important that the ICC Court and the Tribunal have a clear idea from the outset of all documentation based on which a Claimant is maintaining that there is an arbitration agreement with respect to each Respondent to the proceedings.

Article 4(3)(f): "where claims are made under more than one arbitration agreement, an indication of the arbitration agreement under which each claim is made;"

The Rules anticipate that a Claimant may bring proceedings under several contracts, subject to the provisions of arts 6 and 9. The Rules thus provide formally for a situation that arises where parties have several contracts with several different arbitration agreements and the Claimant seeks to have the issues heard together. **4–53**

Article 4(3)(f) requires the Claimant to indicate the arbitration agreement under which each claim is made. A factual issue may give rise to a contractual claim under several contracts each with different arbitration agreements. It may also give rise to an extra contractual claim arising under one or more contracts. Therefore, there is the possibility for claims being made under or with respect to claims under several contracts or for claims to be made in the alternative under several contracts. A basic element for art.4(3)(f) is to provide with reasonable clarity the link between the claim and the arbitration agreement in particular to deal with any issues that may arise under art.6. **4–54**

Article 4(3)(g): "all relevant particulars and any observations or proposals concerning the number of arbitrators and their choice in accordance with the provisions of Articles 12 and 13, and any nomination of an arbitrator required thereby; and"

The Rules require disclosure of particulars concerning the number of arbitrators and their choice and have been amended to invite observations or proposals from the Claimant in this respect. **4–55**

If the arbitration agreement provides for three arbitrators, then the Claimant should nominate an arbitrator in the Request in accordance with the provisions of art.12. If the arbitration agreement provides for one arbitrator, then the Claimant should not propose any person as sole arbitrator in the Request, unless the Claimant has the Respondent's prior agreement on the person to be sole arbitrator. Otherwise, it is highly unlikely that the person proposed by the Claimant will be selected as the sole arbitrator.[37] **4–56**

The standard ICC arbitration clause does not set the number of arbitrators. In the absence of an agreement between the parties, the number will be set by the ICC Court in accordance with art.12. In reaching that decision, the ICC Court will rely in particular on the submissions of the parties in the Request and the Answer. **4–57**

[37] Of course, the Respondent may accept the Claimant's proposal but most Respondents instinctively reject the Claimant's first proposal for a sole arbitrator. For a general discussion of appointment of arbitrators, see Webster, "Selection of Arbitrators in a Nutshell" (2002) J Int'l Arb Vol.19 No.3, p.261.

As a result, it is important to outline in the Request each of the elements relied upon by the Claimant to justify its preference for either one arbitrator or three arbitrators and as to any other qualifications of the arbitrator. As discussed under art.12, the main issues are usually the amount in dispute and the complexity of the dispute.[38] If the Claimant has expressed its preference for three arbitrators without nominating an arbitrator in the Request, it will be usually requested by the Secretariat to proceed with such a nomination within 15 days in order to accelerate the constitution of the Tribunal. The failure by a Claimant to nominate an arbitrator is not viewed as invalidating the Request, as art.12(4) provides that the ICC Court will nominate the arbitrator in such a case.[39]

Article 4(3)(h): "all relevant particulars and any observations or proposals as to the place of the arbitration, the applicable rules of law and the language of the arbitration."

4–58 The Rules require the Claimant to provide all relevant particulars and any observations and proposals on three basic elements of the arbitration that may be the subject of an agreement between the parties and which are dealt with elsewhere in the Rules: the place of arbitration (art.18), the applicable rules of law (art.21) and the language of arbitration (art.20).

4–59 The ICC recommends that the parties to an arbitration clause consider setting the place of arbitration. As discussed under art.18, the courts of the place of arbitration generally have the authority to annul any Award for failure to meet mandatory requirements of that jurisdiction. While the place of arbitration generally is not taken to indicate a procedural preference of the parties, it does designate the national courts with overall jurisdiction over many aspects of the arbitral proceedings and may be relevant to determining the law applicable to the arbitration agreement.

4–60 If the parties do not agree on the place of arbitration, it will be set by the ICC Court based on the factors referred to under art.18.[40] Consequently, it is important in such a case to set out the relevant factors referred to in that Article pointing to any particular place of arbitration in the Request.

4–61 If not agreed by the parties, the Tribunal decides upon the applicable rules of law pursuant to art.21.[41] The ICC Court does not decide upon the applicable rules of law. As a result, the comments on this point in the Request are preliminary in nature and may be subject to substantial briefing later. The comments on the applicable law may well be considered relevant in choosing a president of the Tribunal, and in any event will be useful in preparation of the Terms of Reference. The law applicable on the merits of the dispute may be the first issue to be determined by the Tribunal.

4–62 The Tribunal determines the language or languages of the arbitration under art.20. If the arbitration agreement sets out the language of the arbitration, the

[38] See para.12–16 et seq.

[39] In a number of cases, parties from countries that are not used to ICC arbitration fail to nominate an arbitrator either because they do not realise that the nominee need not be on any list of approved arbitrators, which is of course not the case. The parties are free to nominate as arbitrators individuals who meet the requirements of the Rules and in particular art.11.

[40] See para.18–16 et seq.

[41] See para.21–4 et seq.

Claimant should file the Request in that language to face the possible objection that the Request is not valid to commence the arbitration. If the exhibits to the Request are not in the language of the arbitration, then an objection may be made to their admission until they have been translated. However, this should not affect the validity of the Request itself, as a Request generally does not have to be supported by exhibits other than the Contract containing the arbitration agreement.

If the arbitration agreement does not specify a language for the arbitration, it would be understandable if the Claimant submitted the Request in the language of the arbitration agreement and/or the language in which the parties corresponded, as these are usually highly relevant factors in determining the language to be used in the proceedings. If not set out in the arbitration clause itself, in the absence of an agreement between the parties, the Tribunal will decide the language or languages of the arbitration in accordance with art.20.[42] In that case, the Request should set out as many relevant factors relating to this choice as possible. In some cases, the language of the arbitration will also be important in setting the requirements for the president of the Tribunal. As a result, if the language is one which is not commonly used in international arbitration, the parties should consider whether maintaining that language will limit the potential candidates either as co-arbitrators or as chairmen. **4–63**

As mentioned above, the members of the Secretariat have broad language capabilities. If a Request is received in a language other than one that can be handled by the Secretariat, then the Secretariat will have a translation prepared. If a Claimant submits a Request in a language with which the Secretariat or the other party is unfamiliar, the Claimant should be prepared for a delay in notification of the Request and for additional time periods being accorded to the Respondent to prepare a response. The Secretariat is however free to use the language it considers appropriate in its correspondence with the parties and to request that the parties correspond with the staff in a language that it understands for a good administration of the case. **4–64**

Article 4(3): [. . .] The claimant may submit such other documents or information with the Request as it considers appropriate or as may contribute to the efficient resolution of the dispute.

The last sentence of art.4(3) was added to the Rules to provide flexibility with respect to the documents to be submitted with the Request. One of the issues is the extent to which the documentary support should be provided with the Request. Unlike in some national systems, it is not necessary or even usual to provide a reference to the evidence that will be submitted to support each allegation of fact. Most Tribunals will assume that the evidence will be provided in due course. However, the key documents are usually submitted with the Request, and, as noted below, the key documents include the contract and the arbitration agreement pursuant to which the Request has been filed. **4–65**

42 See paras.20–17 et seq.

4–66 For example, in a dispute with respect to termination of a distribution agreement, one would usually expect to have attached to the Request the full distribution agreement (but not necessarily with all its exhibits), any notice of default, the notice of termination and any rejection of the notice of termination.

4–67 For a dispute relating to a distribution agreement in the luxury goods sector, for example, submitting the contract with all or some of the most relevant annexes may provide the ICC Court and the Tribunal with an overview of the contractual relationship, the products covered and information relating to minimum quantities. In other sectors, such as construction or mechanical engineering, the main agreement may be provided without technical annexes. Given the technical nature of these documents (and their size), the technical annexes may be furnished with subsequent memorials, when their relevance will also be discussed. In each case, parties will have to use their judgment as they deem fit. There exist no rigid rules in that respect.

Article 4(4): "Together with the Request, the claimant shall:

a) submit the number of copies thereof required by Article 3(1); and

b) make payment of the filing fee required by Appendix III ("Arbitration Costs and Fees") in force on the date the Request is submitted.

In the event that the claimant fails to comply with either of these requirements, the Secretariat may fix a time limit within which the claimant must comply, failing which the file shall be closed without prejudice to the claimant's right to submit the same claims at a later date in another Request."

4–68 As discussed under art.3(1) above, if there is to be a Tribunal with three arbitrators, five copies of the Request should be submitted (if there are two parties).[43] If there is to be a sole arbitrator, three copies of the Request suffice (assuming that there are two parties).

4–69 The Rules have been amended to refer to a filing fee rather than an advance on administrative expenses. The current filing fee is US$3,000 (art.1 App.III to the Rules). This is the filing fee for the Secretariat to open the file. It is not refundable, but will be credited to the advance on costs subsequently fixed on the basis of art.36, as is expressly provided for in art.1 of App.III.

4–70 If either of these requirements, whether as to the number of copies of the Request or as to the filing fee is not met, the Secretariat may close the file. It will normally do so after having given the Claimant the opportunity to fulfil whatever formal requirements may have been missing, such as the payment of the US$3,000 filing fee. If the file is closed, the Claimant may resubmit the same claims in another Request. However, these claims would be part of a new arbitration. Therefore, the Claimant may be faced with limitations issues on submitting the new Request, as the commencement date for the new arbitration would be the date on which the Secretariat receives the new Request.

[43] See para.3–7.

Although art.4(4) requires the Claimant to submit the filing fee together with the Request, arts 4(1) and (2) appear to indicate that the arbitration is commenced on the date on which the Request itself is received. The reference in art.4(4) to the possibility of closing the file if the filing fee is not received reinforces this impression. The payment is usually made by bank transfer to the bank account indicated on the ICC website. However, it may also be made by cheque, bank transfer or even in cash. At the Claimant's request, the Secretariat will issue an invoice for the US$3,000 filing fee. As a general practice of the Secretariat, the payment by a party is considered to have been made when it is in fact received on the ICC bank account in the case of a bank transfer, and on the date of receipt of the corresponding check or cash by the Secretariat. **4–71**

Article 4 does not require that the person filing the Request on behalf of the Claimant (usually its legal counsel) provide the Secretariat with a power of attorney. The Secretariat or the Tribunal may decide to request the parties to submit a proof of authority at any time after the commencement of the arbitration under art.17. Therefore, the arbitration is deemed commenced prior to receipt of the power of attorney, subject of course to a subsequent finding that the legal representative was not authorised to represent the party. **4–72**

Article 4(5): "The Secretariat shall transmit a copy of the Request and the documents annexed thereto to the respondent for its Answer to the Request once the Secretariat has sufficient copies of the Request and the required filing fee."

The Secretariat acknowledges receipt of the Request, assigns it a case number and assigns it to one of the Secretariat's teams based in particular on the office at which the Request was registered and the areas and languages involved. If the filing fee has not been received, the Secretariat will state that it will notify the Request on receipt of the filing fee. Therefore, it is possible that the Secretariat will refrain from forwarding the Request for several days or even weeks while it seeks to obtain the advance payment from the Claimant. **4–73**

The Secretariat transmits the Request to the Respondent. The Claimant is not required to transmit a copy of the Request directly to the Respondent and generally does not do so. If the Claimant does so, it serves only to provide advance notice of the Request (which may be relevant if the Respondent seeks one or more extensions to file its Answer). **4–74**

Article 4(5) does not specify how the Secretariat transmits the Request and the documents submitted to it to the Respondent, although the reference to "sufficient copies" would suggest that the Secretariat does not transmit the Request for arbitration electronically, but rather by forwarding a hard copy thereof. The Secretariat usually sends the Request and other documents to the Respondent by international courier or messenger service. This permits rapid transmission, tracking possibilities and proof of receipt. **4–75**

In some countries, the Secretariat may have difficulty using an international courier and may resort to various other means, including giving notice by registered mail against return receipt, fax or email. The Secretariat will contact the **4–76**

Claimant if there are issues as to the delivery of the Request and related documents to seek to circumvent any problems.

4–77 When it transmits the Request to the Respondent, the Secretariat will enclose a copy of the Rules, inform the Respondent of its obligation to file an Answer within 30 days after receipt of the Request and invite the Respondent to copy the Claimant on any correspondence.

Article 5 Answer to the Request; Counterclaims

1 Within 30 days from the receipt of the Request from the Secretariat, the respondent shall submit an Answer (the "Answer") which shall contain the following information:

a) its name in full, description, address and other contact details;
b) the name in full, address and other contact details of any person(s) representing the respondent in the arbitration;
c) its comments as to the nature and circumstances of the dispute giving rise to the claims and the basis upon which the claims are made;
d) its response to the relief sought;
e) any observations or proposals concerning the number of arbitrators and their choice in light of the claimant's proposals and in accordance with the provisions of Articles 12 and 13, and any nomination of an arbitrator required thereby; and
f) any observations or proposals as to the place of the arbitration, the applicable rules of law and the language of the arbitration.

The respondent may submit such other documents or information with the Answer as it considers appropriate or as may contribute to the efficient resolution of the dispute.

2 The Secretariat may grant the respondent an extension of the time for submitting the Answer, provided the application for such an extension contains the respondent's observations or proposals concerning the number of arbitrators and their choice and, where required by Articles 12 and 13, the nomination of an arbitrator. If the respondent fails to do so, the Court shall proceed in accordance with the Rules.

3 The Answer shall be submitted to the Secretariat in the number of copies specified by Article 3(1).

4 The Secretariat shall communicate the Answer and the documents annexed thereto to all other parties.

5 Any counterclaims made by the respondent shall be submitted with the Answer and shall provide:

a) a description of the nature and circumstances of the dispute giving rise to the counterclaims and of the basis upon which the counterclaims are made;
b) a statement of the relief sought together with the amounts of any quantified counterclaims and, to the extent possible, an estimate of the monetary value of any other counterclaims;
c) any relevant agreements and, in particular, the arbitration agreement(s); and

d) where counterclaims are made under more than one arbitration agreement, an indication of the arbitration agreement under which each counterclaim is made.

The respondent may submit such other documents or information with the counterclaims as it considers appropriate or as may contribute to the efficient resolution of the dispute.

6 The claimant shall submit a reply to any counterclaim within 30 days from the date of receipt of the counterclaims communicated by the Secretariat. Prior to the transmission of the file to the arbitral tribunal, the Secretariat may grant the claimant an extension of time for submitting the reply.[1]

Introductory remarks

5–01 Article 5 of the Rules has been amended in corresponding fashion to art.4. Therefore, many of the comments set out in art.4 are equally applicable to art.5. In addition, due to art.7 regarding additional parties, there are consequential changes with respect to claims against additional parties.

5–02 The Answer is the first written submission of the Respondent in reply to the Request and it is a key element in preparation of the Terms of Reference pursuant to art.23. The Answer may not be necessarily the first time that the Respondent acknowledges receipt of the Request. Often, the Respondent will have solicited from the Secretariat an extension of time to file the Answer. In doing so, the

[1] Article 5 corresponds to art.5 of the 1998 ICC Rules. There have been substantive changes as mentioned under art.5(1)(b) and (c).

Respondent will at a minimum acknowledge receipt of the Request, as will be discussed below under art.5(2).

The preliminary issues for the Respondent include whether: (i) there is a valid arbitration clause; (ii) all pre-arbitration procedures have been complied with; and (iii) that notice has been given to the Respondent in accordance with the contractual or legal requirements. **5–03**

The first issue for the Respondent upon receipt of the Request is to decide whether to file an Answer. The second issue for the Respondent is what procedurally the Respondent must and should file with its Answer. The third issue is when to file the Answer. The fourth issue is whether to file a counterclaim or a Request for Joinder at the same time. **5–04**

Existence and validity of the arbitration agreement

If the Respondent is of the opinion that the arbitration agreement is invalid or that it is not a party to it, the Respondent will normally raise the issue in its Answer. Under the Rules, the Respondent is not required to raise a jurisdictional objection in the Answer. Nevertheless, if the Respondent files its Answer without raising a jurisdictional objection, it may risk being found to have waived its right to object to jurisdiction under the applicable law.[2] **5–05**

The objections that can be raised with respect to the validity of the arbitration clause agreement are discussed under art.6. For the purpose of the Answer, it is important to provide as much detail as possible if the Respondent wishes to seek to have the ICC Court hold that prima facie there is no reasonable basis for deciding that an ICC arbitration clause may exist. **5–06**

It is of course possible for the Respondent to simply ignore the Request if the Respondent believes that the arbitration agreement is not applicable. However, the silence of the Respondent will not affect the validity of the arbitration or the jurisdiction of the Tribunal. If the Respondent opts not to respond, the ICC Court retains the right to decide on prima facie jurisdiction in accordance with art.6(4). Therefore, by failing to file an Answer, the Respondent merely deprives itself of the opportunity to provide the ICC Court with reasons to decide not to put the arbitration into motion under art.6. Nor will the Respondent be providing the Tribunal with reasons to hold that the Tribunal does not have jurisdiction unless, at some point in the proceedings, the Respondent makes a filing in that respect.[3] In addition, the Respondent will lose the possibility to submit comments on the place of arbitration to be fixed by the ICC Court when it was not agreed between the parties. Finally, if a Respondent does not file an Answer, the Respondent will **5–07**

[2] See for example art.186(2) of the Swiss PILA which provides that any objection to the jurisdiction must be raised prior to any defence on the merits. Article 16(2) of the UNCITRAL Model Law provides that: "A plea that the arbitral tribunal does not have jurisdiction shall be raised not later than the submission of the statement of defence".

[3] As discussed under art.23, the Terms of Reference are intended to take into account "the most recent submissions" of the parties. Therefore, parties can and do make submissions after the Request, Answer and any Reply have been filed.

be depriving itself of the opportunity to comment on the number of arbitrators and, will usually eventually waive its right to nominate an arbitrator.[4]

5–08 If the Respondent fails to file an Answer, it still may have the opportunity of contesting the arbitral Awards in many jurisdictions under art.V(1) of the New York Convention based on invalidity of the arbitration agreement or the lack of jurisdiction of the Tribunal and the national court would generally consider the matter de novo. However, the Respondent would be opposing both the position of the other party and the Tribunal and not just the position of the other party. Therefore, the more usual course is for a party objecting to jurisdiction to file an Answer focused on jurisdiction.[5]

5–09 In some cases, a Respondent objecting to jurisdiction will also consider bringing court proceedings with regard to the dispute. The Claimant would then be expected to object to the court proceedings based on the arbitration agreement invoking, if applicable under national law, art.2 of the New York Convention. That provision states that "[t]he court of a Contracting State, when seized of an action in a matter in respect of which the parties have made an agreement within the meaning of this article, shall at the request of one of the parties, refer the parties to arbitration, unless it finds that the said agreement is null and void, inoperative or incapable of being performed". This has been adopted (and interpreted) in various fashions under national law.[6] However, it is important to note that concurrent court proceedings do not generally require or result in a stay of the arbitral proceedings.[7]

5–10 In the United States, it is generally possible to seek to stay arbitration proceedings on the basis that the arbitration clause is non-existent or not applicable or that the matter is not subject to arbitration or is not arbitrable.

5–11 However, the prevailing authority is that this is limited in the case of an ICC arbitration as, in ICC arbitration, questions of arbitral jurisdiction and arbitrability are to be decided on a prima facie basis by the ICC Court and substantively by the Tribunal.[8] Therefore, while a Respondent may initiate parallel court proceedings in the United States, it may then be faced with two sets of proceedings and it

[4] Respondents who do not file often default with respect to the proceedings as a whole. If the arbitration clause provides for three arbitrators or if the ICC Court decides that the Tribunal should consist of three arbitrators, the Claimant will generally nominate one arbitrator. Defaulting Respondents generally do not nominate an arbitrator and the ICC will generally have the National Committee of the defaulting Respondent propose an arbitrator, whom frequently the Respondent will not know.

[5] Dallah Real Estate v. Ministry of Religious Affairs of Pakistan [2010] UKSC 46, Para 30–1, (per Lord Mance, Para. 104 (per Lord Collins).

[6] Article 8 of the UNCITRAL Model Law provides for example that "(1) A court before which an action is brought in a matter which is the subject of an arbitration agreement shall, if a party so requests not later than when submitting his first statement on the substance of the dispute, refer the parties to arbitration unless it finds that the agreement is null and void, inoperative or incapable of being performed".

[7] The UNCITRAL Model Law permits the arbitration to continue as does s.32(4) of the English Arbitration Act of 1996.

[8] See *The Shaw Group Inc and Stone & Webster Asia v Triplefine International*: "Because the arbitration agreement at issue in this case provides for all disputes between the parties to be referred to the International Chamber of Commerce ('ICC'), and because the rules of that organization expressly provide for the International Court of Arbitration ('ICA') to resolve in the first instance any disputes about its own jurisdiction, we conclude that the arbitrability of Triplefine's contract claim for attorneys' fees and costs was a question for the arbitrator rather than the court. Accordingly, we vacate the district court's injunction".

may be held liable for the costs of the national proceedings if it loses on the jurisdictional issue.[9]

Another approach adopted by some Respondents if they object to jurisdiction is to refuse to pay the Respondent's share of the advance on costs. Thus, as discussed under art.36, the Claimant may be forced to pay the entire amount of the advance on costs for the claim, at least until the decision on jurisdiction was taken by the Tribunal.[10] **5–12**

Compliance with pre-arbitral procedure

If the Respondent wishes to maintain that any applicable pre-arbitral procedure has not been complied with, then it should raise the issue in the Answer if it wishes to rely on it. Otherwise the Respondent may risk finding that the right to raise it has been waived. On many occasions, the failure to comply with a pre-arbitral procedure is not raised by the Respondent on the basis that there is no reasonable prospect that the pre-arbitral procedure will result in a settlement. In any event, the Tribunal may seek to deal with this type of issue when drafting the Terms of Reference by recording the fact that compliance with such procedure had been made or waived. In doing so, the Tribunal (and the lawyers) should consider the *Poiré* case. In that case, the French Supreme Court held that a contractual clause that provides for the settlement of disputes by conciliation precludes any recourse to judicial redress before the completion of the conciliation process.[11] **5–13**

For example, in an ICC case,[12] a Tribunal sitting in Switzerland and applying Tunisian law held that the Request for Arbitration was inadmissible prior to the completion of the pre-arbitral phase as foreseen in the arbitration agreement. The Tribunal refused to suspend the arbitration procedure pending the completion of the pre-arbitral phase since this had not been provided for by the parties in the arbitration agreement and decided that there was no jurisdiction to hear the case, as the Request was filed prematurely. **5–14**

Notice in accordance with contractual requirements

The failure to meet these requirements may be relevant if there is a statute of limitations issue in which case the Respondent may wish to argue that the arbitration has not been validly commenced in accordance with the Rules. Otherwise, the fact that notice has been given at an improper address or was not copied as required under the contract usually gives rise at most to an issue of whether the Respondent should have further time to prepare its Answer. **5–15**

[9] For a discussion of the costs of ancillary proceedings, see para.37–16. However, in the United States, the losing party is generally not liable for the costs of the successful party.

[10] If the parties have signed an agreement with an ICC arbitration clause, then the Tribunal in first instance is to decide on its jurisdiction in accordance with art.6(5). By agreeing to the Rules, the parties have agreed to pay the advance on costs in accordance with art.36(2). Therefore, failure by the Respondent to pay its share of the advance on costs would appear to be a breach of its obligations under the Rules. However, where the claim is that the Respondent is not even a party to the arbitration clause, then it is difficult to see the basis for the claim that the Respondent should pay its share of the advance on fees.

[11] See para.4–4 n.2.

[12] ICC case No.12739 (2004), unreported.

Contents of the Answer

5–16 Article 5(1) enumerates the basic requirements of an Answer. An example of an Answer in the context of a dispute relating to a distribution agreement is provided in Pt II of this book.

Article 5(1)(a): "[Respondent's] name in full, description, address and other contact details;

5–17 Article 5(1)(a) requires the Respondent to set out its corporate name in full usually with a brief description of its activities and the address to which notifications should be provided. Article 5(1)(a) does not mention the Respondent's comments on the Claimant. Nevertheless, one would expect a brief description of the Claimant by the Respondent if it disagrees with the description provided by the Claimant itself.

Article 5(1)(b): "the name in full, address and other contact details of any person(s) representing the respondent in the arbitration;"

5–18 As noted with respect to art.4(1)(b), this new provision is intended to reflect the fact that most parties are represented by lawyers in ICC arbitrations. Frequently, parties are represented by co-counsel. Although not binding unless accepted by the parties, the IBA Guidelines on Party Representation in International Arbitration provide as follows:

> "4. Party Representatives should identify themselves to the other Party or Parties and the Arbitral Tribunal at the earliest opportunity. A Party should promptly inform the Arbitral Tribunal and the other Party or Parties of any change in such representation."

5–19 Therefore, to the extent that a lawyer is representing a party in an ICC arbitration, that lawyer should be identified in the Request or the Answer, as the case may be. This facilitates communications but also ensures transparency as to the representation.

5–20 In addition, where the Claimant has nominated an arbitrator in its request, there may be an issue as to whether counsel for the Respondent may represent it. As stated in the IBA Guidelines on Party Representation in International Arbitration:

> "5. Once the Arbitral Tribunal has been constituted, a person should not accept representation of a Party in the arbitration when a relationship exists between the person and an Arbitrator that would create a conflict of interest, unless none of the Parties objects after proper disclosure."

5–21 This provision, which is only applicable if the parties so agree, suggests that, even where a Claimant has nominated an arbitrator, a Respondent should not hire counsel that would cause a conflict with that nomination. If retaining certain counsel causes a conflict, the Respondent may be deemed to have waived any objection that it could have arising from the counsel that it designates.

Article 5(1)(c): "[Respondent's] comments as to the nature and circumstances of the dispute giving rise to the claims and the basis upon which the claims are made;"

The Rules have been amended to add reference to the the basis upon which the claims are made. This reinforces the substantive requirements for the Answer and focuses on the legal basis for the claims. Oddly enough, art.5(1)(c) does not refer to basis on which the defences to the claims are made, although it was presumably intended to refer not just to claims but also to defences. **5–22**

The Answer does not require the Respondent to provide a detailed description of the nature and circumstances relating to the dispute. The Respondent may limit the Answer to commenting on the aspects mentioned by the Claimant. However, that approach is not often adopted as the Respondent usually wishes to set out its version of the relevant facts. **5–23**

The Respondent usually sets out in the Answer its version of the circumstances giving rise to the dispute in narrative form (in numbered paragraphs) that is understandable as a self-standing document. In ICC arbitration, one would not expect a Respondent to respond paragraph-by-paragraph limiting itself to denials as in some national pleadings. At some point in the Answer, either at the beginning or at the end, the Respondent usually records that, except where it expressly accepts an allegation made by the Claimant, the Respondent contests it. **5–24**

If the Respondent is objecting to jurisdiction, the Answer should contain an objection to jurisdiction. In such a case, one would expect the Answer to concentrate on the circumstances relating to the position on jurisdiction. In some cases, a Respondent may limit itself to the points on jurisdiction and not respond as to the circumstances relating to the merits. In other cases, the Respondent may object first to jurisdiction and, on an alternative basis, include as well its arguments on the merits of the dispute. **5–25**

As regards the circumstances themselves, as noted with respect to the Request, the main circumstance giving rise to any arbitration is the agreement in which the arbitration agreement is found. The description should include the events that led to that agreement, what happened during the term of that agreement and the events that gave rise to the dispute. It is important to provide the factual chain that leads not only to the dispute but also to rebut the claim and the amount of damages. **5–26**

Article 5(1)(d): "[Respondent's] response to the relief sought;"

The Respondent usually sets out in the Answer a point-by-point denial of the request for damages or injunctive relief and a request for reimbursement of the Respondent's arbitration costs, including legal fees and expenses. If the Claimant has sought to quantify the value of claims for declaration or for specific performance, the Respondent may wish to comment on these amounts to the extent that it is able to do so with the information available. **5–27**

Article 5(1)(e): "any observations or proposals concerning the number of arbitrators and their choice in light of the claimant's proposals and in

accordance with the provisions of Articles 12 and 13, and any nomination of an arbitrator required thereby;"

5–28 As with the Request, the Rules require disclosure of particulars concerning the number of arbitrators and their choice and have been amended to invite observations or proposals from the Claimant in this respect.

5–29 If the arbitration agreement provides for three arbitrators, the Respondent should nominate an arbitrator in the Answer in accordance with the provisions of art.12. If the arbitration agreement provides for one arbitrator, then the Respondent should not propose any person as sole arbitrator in the Answer, unless the parties have agreed on the person to be sole arbitrator. Otherwise, it is highly unlikely that the person proposed by the Respondent will be selected as the sole arbitrator.[13]

5–30 An issue may arise where the Claimant has failed to nominate a co-arbitrator in the Request or the Claimant has nominated a person who is, in the view of the Respondent, not independent of the Claimant. In these cases, a Respondent may refrain from nominating an arbitrator on the basis that it is for the Claimant to nominate an arbitrator first. If the Respondent fails to nominate an arbitrator, the Secretariat will almost invariably contact the Respondent prior to setting in motion the procedure for designating an arbitrator for the Respondent. Therefore, in these cases, there will usually be no sanction for the Respondent's failure to nominate an arbitrator in the Answer.

5–31 As noted under art.4, the standard ICC arbitration clause does not set the number of arbitrators. If this type of provision is applicable and the Claimant has made a suggestion as to whether there should be a sole arbitrator or the three-person Tribunal, the Respondent should carefully consider whether this proposal is acceptable. In the absence of an agreement between the parties, the number will be set by the ICC Court in accordance with art.12(2). The particulars referred to in art.5(1)(d) are very important when there is an issue of whether there should be one or three arbitrators. In that case, the particulars should seek to address each of the points discussed under art.12 and in particular, the amount in dispute and the complexity of the dispute.[14]

Article 5(1)(f): "any observations or proposals as to the place of the arbitration, the applicable rules of law and the language of the arbitration."

5–32 The Rules require the Claimant to provide all relevant particulars and any observations and proposals on three basic elements of the arbitration that may be the subject of an agreement between the parties and which are dealt with elsewhere in the Rules Those three elements are the place of arbitration (art.18), the applicable rules of law (art.21) and the language of arbitration (art.20).

5–33 The ICC recommends that the parties to an arbitration clause consider setting the place of arbitration. As discussed under art.18, the place of arbitration is of particular importance as the courts of the place of arbitration generally have the authority to annul any Award for failure to meet mandatory requirements of that jurisdiction.

13 See para.4–56.

14 See para.12–19 et seq.

If the place of arbitration is not set in the arbitration clause itself, the Claimant will usually have made comments in accordance with art.4(3)(h). In considering whether to accept that proposal, the Respondent should consider the factors set out in art.18. **5–34**

If the parties do not agree on the place of arbitration, it will be fixed by the ICC Court based on the factors referred to under art.18. Therefore, as for the Claimant in the Request, it is in such a case as important for the Respondent to set out in the Answer the relevant factors referred to in that Article.[15] **5–35**

In a similar vein, with respect to art.21, the Claimant will have made comments on the applicable rules of law.[16] The Respondent may wish to accept such rules, in particular to streamline the procedure. If the parties do not agree, the applicable rules of law are decided upon by the Tribunal pursuant to art.21 and not by the ICC Court. As a result, the comments on this point are preliminary in nature and may be subject to substantial briefing later. However, the comments in this respect may be considered relevant in choosing a chairman of the Tribunal and in any event will be useful in preparation of the Terms of Reference pursuant to art.23. **5–36**

As regards art.20, if not set out in the arbitration clause itself, the Claimant will presumably have made comments as to the language of the arbitration.[17] In deciding whether to accept such a proposal and in making its comments, the Respondent should keep in mind the factors referred to in art.20.[18] In some cases, the probable language of the arbitration may be important in setting the requirements for the members of the Tribunal although the Tribunal decides the language of the arbitration pursuant to art.20 if there is no agreement between the parties. **5–37**

Since the Tribunal decides upon the language of the arbitration, there may be some uncertainty as to the language of the arbitration for purposes of the Answer until the matter is decided by the Tribunal. Usually, one would expect the Respondent to file the Answer in the language of either the underlying agreement or the correspondence between the parties. **5–38**

The members of the Secretariat have broad language capabilities. If an Answer is received in a language other than those that can be handled by the Secretariat, then the Secretariat will have a translation prepared, as it would in a similar situation do for the Request.[19] **5–39**

Article 5(1): "[. . .] The respondent may submit such other documents or information with the Answer as it considers appropriate or as may contribute to the efficient resolution of the dispute."

As with the Request, one of the issues for the Answer is the extent to which documentary support should be provided with the Answer. It is not necessary or usual to provide a reference to the evidence that will be submitted to support each **5–40**

[15] See para.4–58 et seq.
[16] See para.4–61.
[17] See para.4–62 et seq.
[18] See paras 20–17 et seq.
[19] See para.4–64.

allegation of fact. Most Tribunals will assume that the evidence will be provided in due course. Key documents are often submitted with the Answer, if they were not included in the Request.[20]

5–41 For example, in a dispute with respect to termination of a distribution agreement, one would expect to have attached to the Answer the letters that led to the termination, such as notification that the distributor had failed to purchase the minimum requirements or to make payments in a timely fashion.

Article 5(2): "The Secretariat may grant the respondent an extension of the time for submitting the Answer, provided the application for such an extension contains the respondent's observations or proposals concerning the number of arbitrators and their choice and, where required by Articles 12 and 13, the nomination of an arbitrator. If the respondent fails to do so, the Court shall proceed in accordance with the Rules."

Timing of the Answer

5–42 Article 5(1) provides a time limit of 30 days from the Respondent's receipt of the Request for the Respondent to file the Answer. Article 5(2) permits the Secretariat to grant extensions provided that the Respondent makes such request and provides comments on the number of arbitrators or, where required, the nomination of an arbitrator.

5–43 The extension is granted by the Secretariat and not by the ICC Court. This reflects the fact that extensions for filing of an Answer are granted as a matter of routine as long as such extensions will not delay the constitution of the Tribunal and thus have no impact on the duration of the arbitration proceedings. The usual justification for this approach is that the Claimant has had time to prepare its case and the Respondent has not. In reasonably complicated arbitrations, the time for preparation of a Request would probably far exceed 30 days, which is why an extension is generally granted for the Answer even if it is clear that both sides have been preparing for the dispute. The Secretariat's concern is that, even in such cases, it would be unfair to permit the Claimant to dictate the schedule.[21] This is even more so the case when the Request and the documents filed with it are in a language with which the Respondent is not readily familiar.

5–44 The usual extension would be 30 days. The Secretariat may at the Respondent's request grant longer extensions or even several extensions depending on the circumstances of the case and the Claimant's position with regard to such extensions. Prior to granting extensions for periods greater than 30 days, the Secretariat generally asks for the comments of the Claimant with respect to the extension.

5–45 In requesting an extension, the Respondent should provide the Secretariat with detail in writing as to the grounds for an extension, particularly if it is sought for a period of more than 30 days. In any event, in requesting the extension, the

[20] See para.4–65.

[21] There is a concern about equal treatment of the parties if an extension is not granted to file the Answer. However, this concern is tempered by the fact that the parties have accepted the Rules which provide for a 30-day period for filing an Answer and the Answer is far from being the last submission in the case.

Respondent is required under art.5(2) to provide the comments referred to above with respect to the number of arbitrators, and if appropriate, to appoint an arbitrator. The appointment of an arbitrator is generally viewed as required where the arbitration clause expressly provides for three arbitrators or where the Respondent agrees that there should be three arbitrators.[22] The Respondent's request for an extension should be copied to the Claimant who, depending on the circumstances, may either consent or not object to the extension.

The Respondent may object to appointing an arbitrator where, in the Respondent's view, the Claimant has failed to meet its obligation to nominate an arbitrator in accordance with art.4(3)(e) of the Rules. This may arise, for example, where the Claimant has nominated an arbitrator who does not meet the requirements of art.11 due to some close relationship with the Claimant. Since the general principle is that the Claimant should nominate its arbitrator first, the Respondent may take the position that, by nominating a person who cannot reasonably be confirmed by the ICC Court as arbitrator, the Claimant will have the opportunity to nominate another arbitrator once the ICC Court has failed to confirm the original nominee. If the Respondent takes this position, the Secretariat may seek to have a decision on confirmation of the Claimant's nominee made rapidly to resolve the issue. However, the ICC Court will be reluctant to appoint an arbitrator for the Respondent without putting the Respondent on notice that this will occur if it fails to nominate an arbitrator within a specific time limit. **5–46**

Although drafted as an obligation in the Rules, a failure by the Respondent to comment on the number of arbitrators when requesting the extension does deny the Respondent a later opportunity to comment. In practice, any such comments will generally be taken into consideration so long as they are made at some time prior to a decision on this issue by the ICC Court. **5–47**

If the Respondent wishes to reserve the right to make a jurisdictional objection, it should refer to this reservation when requesting an extension for filing the Answer and commenting upon the number of arbitrators. For example, the Respondent could state expressly that the nomination of the arbitrator is made without prejudice to the Respondent's right to raise jurisdictional pleas in the Answer. **5–48**

Article 5(3): "The Answer shall be submitted to the Secretariat in the number of copies specified by Article 3(1)."

Article 5(3) requires the Respondent to transmit the Answer and supporting documents with the Secretariat in the number specified under art.3(1) (either three copies if there is a sole arbitrator or five copies if the Tribunal consists of three members and there is only one Claimant and one Respondent). **5–49**

Article 5(4): "The Secretariat shall communicate the Answer and the documents annexed thereto to all other parties."

[22] Article 12(4) only requires the appointment of an arbitrator in the Answer but this should be read in conjunction with art.5(2) which requires the appointment where it is clear that there are to be three arbitrators.

5–50 Article 5(4) has been amended to reflect the fact that the Answer may be delivered to additional parties as well as the Claimant if such additional parties have been added pursuant to art.7.

5–51 This is not simply an obligation of notification in many circumstances. If the Respondent is making claims against additional parties then it must ensure, in accordance with art.8(2) that the information specified in art.4(3)(c), (d), (e) and (f) is provided with respect to that other party. In substance, the claim against the third parties has to meet the same requirements as for counterclaims against the Claimant as discussed under art.5(5).

5–52 The Secretariat will communicate the Answer to the other parties even if it is filed after the deadline. The Secretariat has a strong preference for having all parties participate in the proceedings. The Claimant may of course raise the issue that the Answer has been filed after the deadline with the Tribunal, although a filing after the deadline will normally not preclude a Respondent from making further submissions and will not make its Answer inadmissible. Tribunals are therefore unlikely to ever exclude an Answer because it has been filed late, in particular when the Answer was filed before the Tribunal was even in place.

5–53 The Secretariat then communicates the Answer and the supporting documents related thereto to the Claimant in accordance with art.5(4). The Secretariat thereafter invites the parties to communicate directly, by having each side copy to the other any communication addressed to the ICC Court.

Article 5(5): "Any counterclaims made by the respondent shall be submitted with the Answer and shall provide:

a) a description of the nature and circumstances of the dispute giving rise to the counterclaims and of the basis upon which the counterclaims are made;

b) a statement of the relief sought together with the amounts of any quantified counterclaims and, to the extent possible, an estimate of the monetary value of any other counterclaims;

c) any relevant agreements and, in particular, the arbitration agreement(s); and

d) where counterclaims are made under more than one arbitration agreement, an indication of the arbitration agreement under which each counterclaim is made.

The respondent may submit such other documents or information with the counterclaims as it considers appropriate or as may contribute to the efficient resolution of the dispute.

Contents of the counterclaim

5–54 The same principles as regards the description of the circumstances of the dispute and the nature of the relief sought set out in art.4 with respect to claims are applicable to a counterclaim. The introduction of a counterclaim will cause the amount of the advance on costs to increase, as it increases the amount in dispute and the Respondent should be prepared to meet the additional advance on costs with respect to the counterclaim.[23]

Article 5(5) states that any counterclaims "shall be filed" with the Answer. However, this language has to be read with the practice relating to the drafting of the Terms of Reference under art.23 and for new claims under art.23(4). If the Respondent makes counterclaims prior to the drafting of the Terms of Reference, then they have to be included in the Terms of Reference. If the Respondent makes counterclaims after the Terms of Reference have been signed, such new claims may be added subject to the provisions of art.23. **5–55**

In some cases, the Respondent will file a claim for set-off. Some practitioners maintain that this is different from a counterclaim based on the characterisation of the set-off claims under the applicable law. However, the distinction is difficult to see. Under most legal systems, to establish a set-off, a party must demonstrate that it has a claim in a certain amount and that the claim arose in a context where the party is entitled to set it off against a corresponding claim of the other party. **5–56**

If this is the situation, the first step for a set-off is to demonstrate that the Respondent has a claim, which is in essence a counterclaim. The second step is to demonstrate that the claims in the Request and this counterclaim are sufficiently connected to provide a basis for a set-off.[24] **5–57**

Counterclaims based on a different contract between the same parties

If the parties have entered into several contracts and the Respondent wishes to make a claim under another contract, then it may do so provided that it provides a copy of the relevant agreement and in particular arbitration agreement on which the counterclaim is based and that it identifies the agreement under which each counterclaim is made. **5–58**

Documents to be submitted with respect to the counterclaim

The concerns discussed under art.4(4) (last sentence) are equally applicable with respect to the documentation regarding counterclaims. **5–59**

Article 5(6): "The claimant shall submit a reply to any counterclaim within 30 days from the date of receipt of the counterclaims communicated by the Secretariat. Prior to the transmission of the file to the arbitral tribunal, the Secretariat may grant the claimant an extension of time for submitting the reply."

The Reply to the counterclaim is analogous to the Answer and the same principles should be applied in preparing it. Here again, upon the Claimant's request, **5–60**

[23] For a discussion of the issue of separate advances for the claim and counterclaim, see para.36–33 et seq.

[24] See art.36(7) as regards the possible impact of the set-off claim on the amount of the advance on costs.

the Secretariat may extend the time limit for filing the Reply to the counterclaim. If the Tribunal has already been fully constituted, the Secretariat may provide it with the file and have the Tribunal deal directly with an extension of time to file the Reply to the counterclaim.

5–61 Article 5(6) provides for the last of the pleadings as such under arts 4 and 5 with respect to the claims and counterclaims, although there may be further pleadings with respect to a Request for Joinder under art.7. However, as discussed under art.23, the Terms of Reference are prepared based on the most recent submissions of the parties. Therefore, additional comments may be made prior to the Terms of Reference. In addition, the parties generally have broad leeway to comment on the claims and arguments of the other parties in the further written submissions made during the course of the arbitral proceedings in accordance with arts 22 and 25. The authors have never encountered a case where the Tribunal has proceeded directly to the final hearings based solely on the documents filed in accordance with arts 4 and 5 of the Rules.

Article 6 Effect of the Arbitration Agreement

1 Where the parties have agreed to submit to arbitration under the Rules, they shall be deemed to have submitted ipso facto to the Rules in effect on the date of commencement of the arbitration, unless they have agreed to submit to the Rules in effect on the date of their arbitration agreement.

2 By agreeing to arbitration under the Rules, the parties have accepted that the arbitration shall be administered by the Court.

3 If any party against which a claim has been made does not submit an Answer, or raises one or more pleas concerning the existence, validity or scope of the arbitration agreement or concerning whether all of the claims made in the arbitration may be determined together in a single arbitration, the arbitration shall proceed and any question of jurisdiction or of whether the claims may be determined together in that arbitration shall be decided directly by the arbitral tribunal, unless the Secretary General refers the matter to the Court for its decision pursuant to Article 6(4).

4 In all cases referred to the Court under Article 6(3), the Court shall decide whether and to what extent the arbitration shall proceed. The arbitration shall proceed if and to the extent that the Court is prima facie satisfied that an arbitration agreement under the Rules may exist. In particular:

(i) where there are more than two parties to the arbitration, the arbitration shall proceed between those of the parties, including any additional parties joined pursuant to Article 7, with respect to which the Court is prima facie satisfied that an arbitration agreement under the Rules that binds them all may exist; and

(ii) where claims pursuant to Article 9 are made under more than one arbitration agreement, the arbitration shall proceed as to those claims with respect to which the Court is prima facie satisfied (a) that the arbitration agreements under which those claims are made may be compatible, and (b) that all parties to the arbitration may have agreed that those claims can be determined together in a single arbitration.

The Court's decision pursuant to Article 6(4) is without prejudice to the admissibility or merits of any party's plea or pleas.

5 In all matters decided by the Court under Article 6(4), any decision as to the jurisdiction of the arbitral tribunal, except as to parties or claims with respect to which the Court decides that the arbitration cannot proceed, shall then be taken by the arbitral tribunal itself.

6 Where the parties are notified of the Court's decision pursuant to Article 6(4) that the arbitration cannot proceed in respect of some or all of them, any party retains the right to ask any court having jurisdiction whether or not, and in respect of which of them, there is a binding arbitration agreement.

7 Where the Court has decided pursuant to Article 6(4) that the arbitration cannot proceed in respect of any of the claims, such decision shall not prevent a party from reintroducing the same claim at a later date in other proceedings.

8 If any of the parties refuses or fails to take part in the arbitration or any stage thereof, the arbitration shall proceed notwithstanding such refusal or failure.

9 Unless otherwise agreed, the arbitral tribunal shall not cease to have jurisdiction by reason of any allegation that the contract is non-existent or null and void, provided that the arbitral tribunal upholds the validity of the arbitration agreement. The arbitral tribunal shall continue to have jurisdiction to determine the parties' respective rights and to decide their claims and pleas even though the contract itself may be non-existent or null and void.[1]

[1] Article 6 corresponds to art.6 of the 1998 Rules. There are a number of substantive and drafting changes that are discussed in the commentary.

Introductory remarks

Article 6 refers to the bedrock for ICC arbitration: the arbitration agreement incorporating reference to the ICC Rules. Article 6(9), discussed below, sets out the basic principle of the autonomy of the arbitration agreement. Article 6 does not (and probably could not) deal otherwise with the detail of the arbitration agreement as the validity of that agreement depends on various national laws. **6–1**

The ICC Court and the Tribunal interpret the arbitration agreement. Under the New York Convention, the UNCITRAL Model Law and the national law of countries such as France, England, Germany and Switzerland, the final decision on jurisdiction generally is viewed as belonging ultimately to the national courts. As discussed below, under US law certain limited issues of arbitrability are decided by the Courts but issues relating to the scope of the arbitration agreement are decided by the arbitrator. Arbitration is an exclusion (or derogation) of the jurisdiction of the national courts. Consequently, the national courts maintain the ultimate control to decide whether the parties have validly decided to derogate the court's jurisdiction by entering into an arbitration agreement. In rendering their decisions on those issues, the national courts review jurisdictional issues de novo, although they often do so by reviewing the Tribunal's analysis, to which they may give weight. In this respect, the jurisdictional issues are to be distinguished from most other issues on the merits. With regards to non-jurisdictional issues, most national courts seek to avoid re-opening substantive issues. That is not the case with jurisdictional issues. **6–2**

6–3 As discussed beginning at para.6–137 below, for the arbitration agreement to be valid, the parties must have legal capacity and must have validly entered into the arbitration agreement and the subject matter of the arbitration agreement must be arbitrable under the applicable law. These are matters that a Tribunal will have to decide, but generally under the ultimate control of the national courts.

6–4 The following discussion deals with which law governs the arbitration agreement. The discussion under arts 6(5) and 6(9) deal with further issues. Those include the formal requirements of the arbitration agreement; determining whether the reference is to arbitration under the Rules; and non-signatories of the arbitration agreement (discussed under art.6(5)). Other issues, relating to the capacity of the parties and arbitrability are also discussed under art.6(5).

The law governing the arbitration agreement

6–5 There are two basic types of arbitration agreements. The first, and by far the most frequent, are in effect arbitration agreements or *clauses compromissoires*, which are part of and often incorporated into a broader agreement, the main contract. The second are agreements to arbitrate that are separate documents, analogous to the submission agreement or *compromis*.[2] As discussed under art.6(9), arbitration agreements are viewed as autonomous agreements even if contained in an overall contract.

6–6 Where the arbitration agreement is part of a contract, the latter may or may not contain a governing law clause. If there is a governing law, in most cases, it will not be restricted to any particular provisions of the entire contract, unless otherwise stipulated by the parties. In the absence of such a stipulation, there has been a tendency to assume that the choice of law made by the parties is equally applicable to the arbitration agreement, although there is some support for the law of the place of arbitration.[3] If there is no governing law clause in the contract, then the applicable conflicts of law principles will be used to determine the applicable law. Usually, those principles would be expected to result in determination of an applicable law for the whole contract. As discussed below, this tendency is subject to developments with respect to English, American and French law in particular.

6–7 The threshold issue with respect to an arbitration agreement is the law, if any, that governs its validity and interpretation. Many practitioners, in particular domestic litigators, may find it surprising that there is no clear answer to this question.[4] Article 1(2)(d) of the Rome Convention specifically excludes arbitration agreements from its scope.[5] The authorities are split between the

[2] See the distinction in option of art.7(1) of the UNCITRAL Model Law.

[3] Lew, "The Applicable Law to the Form and Substance of the Arbitration Clause" (1999) *ICCA Congress Series No.14*, p.114. See also Sutton, Gill & Gearing, *op. cit.*, paras 2–094–2–098, pp.82–84; Poudret & Besson, *op. cit.*, p.259.

[4] See the nine different approaches mentioned in Lew, Mistelis & Kröll, *Comparative International Commercial Arbitration* (Kluwer, 2003), para.6–26, p.108.

[5] The reasons are based in the differing approaches to arbitration clauses discussed below. The Giulano Lagarde Text on the Rome Convention (*http://www.rome-convention.org* [accessed November 18, 2013]) pointed out that: "the United Kingdom delegation, had proposed that these should not be excluded from the Convention. It was emphasized that an arbitration agreement does

governing law of the underlying contract, the law of the place of arbitration and a form of transnational law.

English law

For instance, the English view is that an arbitration agreement is autonomous and the law governing it may be independent of the law otherwise governing the contract in some instances. While the arbitration agreement is autonomous, it is generally subject to national law. The issue was discussed as follows in *Sulamérica*: **6–8**

> "56. Accordingly, (i) there are a number of cases which support the contention that it is rare for the law of the arbitration to be that of the seat of the arbitration rather than that of the chosen contractual law, as the arbitration clause is part of the contract, but (ii) the most recent authority is a decision of this court which contains clear dicta (albeit obiter) to the opposite effect, on the basis that the arbitration clause is severable from the rest of the contract and plainly has a very close connection with the law of the seat of the arbitration.
>
> 57. Faced with this rather unsatisfactory tension between the approach in the earlier cases and the approach in C v D [2008] 1 All ER (Comm) 1001, it seems to me that, at any rate in this court, we could take one of two courses. The first would be to follow the approach in the most recent case, given that it was a decision of this court, namely C v D [2008] 1 All ER (Comm) 1001. The alternative course would be to accept that there are sound reasons to support either conclusion as a matter of principle. Whichever course is adopted, it is necessary to consider whether there is anything in the other provisions of the contract or the surrounding circumstances which assist in resolving the conundrum.
>
> [. . .]
>
> 61. On the other hand, the fact that, if Brazilian, rather than English, law applies to the arbitration agreement, it may very well not be possible to give effect to the apparently mandatory and plainly unqualified provision for arbitration in condition 12 unless the insured was prepared to have an

not differ from other agreements as regards the contractual aspects, and that certain international Conventions do not regulate the law applicable to arbitration agreements, while others are inadequate in this respect. [. . .] Other delegations, notably the German and French delegations, opposed the United Kingdom proposal, emphasizing particularly that any increase in the number of conventions in this area should be avoided, that severability is accepted in principle in the draft and the arbitration clause is independent, that the concept of 'closest ties' is difficult to apply to arbitration agreements, that procedural and contractual aspects are difficult to separate, that the matter is complex and the experts' proposals show great divergences; that since procedural matters and those relating to the question whether a dispute was arbitrable would in any case be excluded, the only matter to be regulated would be consent; that the International Chamber of Commerce–which, as everyone knows, has great experience in this matter–has not felt the need for further regulation. [. . .] The Group [. . .]. excluded arbitration agreements from the scope of the uniform rules, subject to returning to an examination of these problems and of agreements on the choice of court once the Convention has been finally drawn up".

issue referred to arbitration, is a pretty strong argument for English law applying. All the more so if one bears in mind that the question is to be determined by reference to the apparent intention of the parties as gathered from the terms of the contract. In addition, as Toulson J said in XL Insurance Ltd [2011] 1 All ER (Comm) 530, the fact that certain provisions of the 1996 Act will, on any view, govern the arbitration agreement tends to support the respondents' case that English law applies."

6–9 As noted by the English Court of Appeal itself, this approach represents a change. The basic approach that the Court should try to interpret the provisions of the contract to be effective is understandable. However, the reference to the law of the place of arbitration gives the choice of the place of arbitration an increased, and, some would say, new, significance under English law. In addition, in this case, under the law of the place of arbitration (England) the contract was enforceable. If the law of the place of arbitration had been in a jurisdiction that did not permit arbitration of insurance contracts, the result would presumably have been different.

6–10 The test has been applied in *Arsanovia Ltd, Burley Holdings Ltd and Unitech Ltd v Cruz City 1 Mauritius Holdings* to the effect that the place of arbitration is a factor in deciding the law applicable to the arbitration agreement. However, in that instance, the factor was displaced by reference in the arbitration agreement itself to certain provisions of Indian law. Therefore, the court held that Indian law governed the arbitration agreement.[6]

US Law

6–11 Under American law, each state has its own system of law. In *American Express v Italian Colors Restaurant* (US Supreme Court June 20, 2013) the US Supreme Court was called upon to interpret an arbitration clause that expressly prohibited class action arbitration. The Supreme Court held that the exclusion was effective noting that arbitration clauses should be rigorously enforced in accordance with their terms.[7] The Federal Arbitration Act is generally applicable to international

[6] *Arsanovia Ltd, Burley Holdings Ltd and Unitech Ltd v Cruz City 1 Mauritius Holdings* [2012] EWHC 3702 (Comm). See the discussion in DLA Piper, News and Insights, March 27, 2013; and Allen & Overy, "Determining the governing law of an arbitration clause", March 5, 2013.

[7] 570 US_2013 at p. 3 Congress enacted the FAA in response to widespread judicial hostility to arbitration. See AT&T Mobility v Conception, 563 U.S. 321 (2011) (slip op., at 4). As relevant here, the Act provides: "A written provision in any maritime transaction or contract evidencing a transaction involving commerce to settle by arbitration a controversy thereafter arising out of such contract or transaction [. . .] shall be valid, irrevocable, and enforceable, save upon such grounds as exist at law or in equity for the revocation of any contract." 9 U. S. C. §2. This text reflects the overarching principle that arbitration is a matter of contract. See Rent-A-Center, West, Inc v Jackson, 130 S. Ct. 665 (2010) (slip op., at 3). And consistent with that text, courts must "rigorously enforce" arbitration agreements according to their terms, Dean Witter Reynolds Inc v Byrd, 470 U. S. 213, 221 (1985), including terms that "specify with whom[the parties] choose to arbitrate their disputes," Stolt-Nielsen, infra, at 683, and "the rules under which that arbitration will be conducted," Volt Information Sciences, Inc v Board of Trustees of Leland Stanford Junior Univ, 489 U. S. 468, 479 (1989). That holds true for claims that allege a violation of a federal statute, unless the FAA's mandate has been " 'overridden by a contrary congressional command.' " CompuCredit Corp v Greenwood, 132 S. Ct. 665 (2012) (slip op., at 2–3) (quoting Shearson/American Express Inc v McMahon, 482 U. S. 220, 226." "(1987)). However, the issue is the scope of the arbitration clause. For a case upholding class action arbitration see *Oxford Health Plans v. Sutter* discussed at para. 6.51.

arbitrations in the United States, and the Federal Arbitration Act comports with it a strong policy in favour of arbitration. In addition, US law evolves around the concept of arbitrability.

Until the *Preston v Ferrer* decision referred to below, it was generally thought that the law applicable to the arbitration clause was the state law that was applicable to the underlying contract, subject to the overriding provisions of the Federal Arbitration Act. In *Preston v Ferrer*,[8] the talent agency contract expressly provided for the application of California law to the contract itself. California law gave exclusive jurisdiction to the California Labor Commissioner. The US Supreme Court held that the arbitrator was to decide whether the claim was arbitrable stating in part: **6–12**

> "Preston and Ferrer's contract, as noted, provides for arbitration in accordance with the AAA rules. App. 18. One of those rules states that '[t]he arbitrator shall have the power to determine the existence or validity of a contract of which an arbitration clause forms a part.' AAA, Commercial Arbitration Rules ¶R–7(b) (2007). ... The incorporation of the AAA rules, and in particular Rule 7(b), weighs against inferring from the choice-of-law clause an understanding shared by Ferrer and Preston that their disputes would be heard, in the first instance, by the Labor Commission [as provided for by California law]. Following the guide Mastrobuono provides, the 'best way to harmonize' the parties' adoption of the AAA rules and their selection of California law is to read the latter to encompass prescriptions governing the substantive rights and obligations of the parties, but not the State's 'special rules limiting the authority of arbitrators'."

Therefore, in *Preston*, the state law governing the Contract governed the "substantive rights and obligations of the parties" but not the "special rules limiting the authority of arbitrators". As a result, given the broad institutional arbitration clause, it was for the arbitrator to decide whether the arbitrator had jurisdiction notwithstanding the California law providing that the California Labor Commissioner had jurisdiction. This procedural precedence of the Federal Arbitration Act is, however, not its only effect. **6–13**

The Federal Arbitration Act also includes a broad policy favouring arbitration, an arbitration clause is to be interpreted in accordance with state contract law. However, this interpretation of the state contract law is to be carried out within the overall federal framework in favour of arbitration.[9] In the United States, contracts are generally governed by the contract law of a given state. For almost all US states contract law is based on common law. State law governs whether there is an agreement to arbitrate and the scope of that agreement. US federal law is in favour of arbitration and basically prohibits state law from singling out arbitration agreements for special forms of contract requirements. Therefore, if the parties sign a distribution contract providing for ICC arbitration, then under those legal systems, **6–14**

[8] *Preston v Ferrer*, 552 U.S. 346 (2008).

[9] See Carbonneau, "Arbitration in the United States" in *Practitioner's Handbook on International Arbitration, op. cit.*

the law governing the arbitration provision in that contract would be the same as that of the rest of the contract unless, of course, the contract stated otherwise.

6–15 The effect of this decision is that Federal law, and in particular the Federal Arbitration Act, pre-empts US state law with respect to issues relating to arbitration issues. The Federal Arbitration Act is applicable to international arbitrations in the United States. *Preston v Ferrer* deals with arbitrability (which was the case for example in *Sulamérica*). As regards the interpretation of the scope of the arbitration clause itself, the Federal Arbitration Act supports a broad and effective treatment of arbitration clauses. However, the issue is always the scope of the parties' agreement to arbitration. *American Express Co. v. Italian Colors Restaurant* 133S Ct. 2304 (2013) (contractual waiver of class arbitration upheld).

Swiss law

6–16 In Switzerland, art.178(2) of the Swiss PILA provides that an arbitration agreement is valid as to substance if valid under either the law chosen by the parties, the law applicable to the overall agreement, or under Swiss law as the law of the place of arbitration.[10] In effect, this provision provides for alternative laws to be applicable to the arbitration clause, although it does not express itself as a choice of law provision.

French law

6–17 Under French law, the agreement to arbitrate is totally autonomous and may be reviewed without reference to a national legal system. In the *Dalico* case, the issue was whether an arbitral Award should be annulled for failing to apply Libyan law to the arbitration clause. The law governing the underlying contract was Libyan. The French Supreme Court upheld the decision by stating:

> "by virtue of a substantive rule of international arbitration, the submission to arbitration is legally independent of the main contract in which it is contained directly or by reference and its existence and effectiveness are analyzed subject to the mandatory rules of French law and public international order, according to the common intent of the parties, without it being necessary to refer to a national law."[11] (Authors' translation)

6–18 In the first edition, the authors noted that the transnational approach may be difficult to reconcile with the lawyers' need to advise a client on entering into the

[10] See for example Poudret & Besson, *op. cit.*, para.300, p.259; Wenger, "Article 178" in *International Arbitration in Switzerland–An Introduction to and a Commentary on Arts 176–194 of the Swiss Private International Law Statute, op. cit.*, para.22, p.490; Abdulla, "The Arbitration Agreement" in *International Arbitration in Switzerland–A Practitioner's Handbook, op. cit.*, pp.17–18; see also Müller, *International Arbitration–A Guide to the Complete Swiss Case Law (Unreported and Reported)* (Thomson/Schulthess, 2004), p.33.

[11] Cass Civ 1re, December 20, 1993, *Municipalité de Khoms El Mergeb v société Dalico* (1994) Rev Arb No.1 p.118, note Gaudemet-Talon; see also Paris, December 1994, *Société V 2000 v société Projects XJ 220 ITD et autre*, (1996) Rev Arb No.2 p.245; Cass Civ 1re, March 30, 2004, *Société Uni-Kod v Société Ouralkali* (2005) Rev Arb No.4 p.959, note Seraglini; see also ICC case No.8910 (1998) in Truong, *Les différends liés à la rupture des contrats internationaux de distribution dans les sentences arbitrales CCI* (Litec, 2002), para.93, p.97.

basic agreement with the arbitration provision. In larger contracts, parties carefully cover their legal situation with opinions on the national law governing the contract. For a Tribunal, or a national court, to decide that the express choice of law clause in the contract does not cover the arbitration provision creates uncertainty.[12] Nevertheless, the French transnational approach does prevent nullifying certain agreements based on a prohibition on local law and is squarely based on the common intent of the parties.[13] It is also in accordance with the pro-arbitration trend in courts in the major centers of arbitration, a trend that has been reinforced particularly in England for example.[14] Therefore, the authors believe that, as in other areas of arbitration law, the French approach could well have further influence elsewhere, particularly given the trend in national courts to cite jurisdictions from other national courts relating to international arbitration. Despite these trends, for the practitioner, it is important to adapt the argument and the solution as regards the governing law of the arbitration agreement to the interpretation given particularly by the national courts of the place of arbitration, and for the time being, the approaches remain distinct.

Given this evolution, several basic points should be noted. First, the place of arbitration is important to the issue of determination of the law applicable to the validity of the arbitration clause. Secondly, there is a strong and continuing support for favouring arbitration clauses. The most justifiable grounds for that approach is an attempt to give effect to an arbitration clause agreed to by the parties. Thirdly, this liberal approach to the interpretation of arbitration clauses may well give rise to issues as to enforceability of the Awards. Fourthly, there is an issue—highlighted by the American cases—of whether it should be the courts or the Tribunal that should determine the scope of the arbitration agreement. **6–19**

Article 6(1): "Where the parties have agreed to submit to arbitration under the Rules, they shall be deemed to have submitted *ipso facto* to the Rules in effect on the date of commencement of the arbitration, unless they have agreed to submit to the Rules in effect on the date of their arbitration agreement."

[12] For example, if there is a contract providing a commitment to purchase a minimum quantity of products each year, the parties will wish to be certain as to which companies in a group are liable for that obligation. Provided that one legal system is clearly applicable, the agreement can be drafted to create a certain degree of legal certainty. If it is not clear if or whether a legal system will govern the arbitration clause, it will be less clear as to whether an answer can be given with respect to liability.

[13] The reference to the common intention of the parties is of course fundamental. However, there is an issue of whether this approach is not adopted due to concern about countries frustrating arbitration clauses to escape liability. This would be analogous to the issue of the intervention of state courts with respect to arbitration involving state entities dealt with under art.35.

[14] As Lord Hoffman stated in *Premium Nafta Products* (20th Defendant) & Others v Fili Shipping Co Ltd & Others [2007] UKHL 40; [2007] 4 All E.R. 951; [2007] 2 All E.R. (Comm) 1053; [2007] Bus L.R. 1719; [2008] 1 Lloyd's Rep. 254: "13. In my opinion the construction of an arbitration clause should start from the assumption that the parties, as rational businessmen, are likely to have intended any dispute arising out of the relationship into which they have entered or purported to enter to be decided by the same tribunal". It is submitted that this common sense approach as to the scope of an agreement is similar to that adopted by the French Supreme Court to determine whether there is a valid arbitration clause, which is based on the common intention of the parties. See also the judgment of Longmore J. in the Court of Appeal (cited at para.6–79).

6–20 Assuming that there is an agreement to arbitrate under the ICC Rules (which is discussed under arts 6(3) and 6(4)), the issue may arise which version of Rules should apply. Article 6(1) establishes the presumption that the applicable rules are the current Rules unless the parties have agreed on the rules as of the date of the arbitration agreement. Article 6 of the 1998 Rules had a similar provision. The 1988 ICC arbitration rules did not contain such a provision.

6–21 The issue is a practical and theoretical one. Agreements to arbitrate do not usually result in arbitration soon after they are signed. However, most arbitrations occur within 5–10 years after the date of signature. Therefore, the majority of new disputes are now under contracts that have been signed since 1998, although a significant number still predates the 1998 version of the Rules. In addition, in some clauses there is an express reference to a prior version of the Rules, which should be enforced whether or not the version of the ICC Rules is that in force on the date of the arbitration agreement or not. The key issue is the parties' agreement to arbitrate and if the parties have agreed on a specific set of ICC Rules, they form part of their agreement.[15]

6–22 Practically, the solution of art.6(1), providing for reference to the most recent Rules is very sound. The Rules were revised to deal with various problems with the prior Rules. The ICC Court, its Secretariat and arbitrators prefer dealing with the current set of rules especially given the time lapse between 1998 and 2013.

6–23 On a more abstract level, the solution in art.6(1) requires a leap of faith for arbitration agreements entered into prior to 1998. The 1988 version of the ICC Rules did not provide for automatic reference to the most recent Rules. Therefore, it could be argued that when the parties accepted the prior ICC Rules they could have had no indication that the amended rules may be applied. However, this more abstract issue raises more of a theoretical than a practical issue, as the differences between the 1998 and 2012 ICC Rules are not such as to generally create a major issue in this respect except with respect to the Emergency Arbitrator provisions of art.29 and the Rules provide that art.29 is only applicable to arbitration agreements entered into after January 1, 2012 or if the parties have expressly agreed that art.29 is applicable. In order to avoid any potential problem, when the contract and the arbitration agreement were signed prior to the 1998 Rules, the Secretariat usually draws the parties' attention to this point and the possibility for them to expressly opt for the new Rules. The decision of the parties can thus occur at the beginning of the proceedings, and many Tribunals will suggest to the parties, in the draft Terms of Reference, language to that effect. There is in fact rarely something to be gained from arbitrating a case under Rules that have been superseded by newer and better Rules. It is for the parties, however, to make the ultimate decision.

Article 6(2): "By agreeing to arbitration under the Rules, the parties have accepted that the arbitration shall be administered by the Court."

[15] The ICC Court generally will administer the arbitration in accordance with the version of the ICC Rules chosen by the parties and the Tribunal is left to deal with the issue of the validity: See, Fry, Mazza and Greenberg, *op.cit.*, para.3–189.

Article 6(2) is a new provision of the Rules. It is designed to reinforce the parties' agreement to have the Court administer the arbitration. Various provisions of the Rules set out how and under what conditions the Court will administer ICC arbitrations. In particular, the Court has a central role with respect to the commencement of the arbitration, ensuring that the costs with respect to it are covered, with respect to constitution of the Tribunal and scrutiny and issue of the Award. Under the Rules, the parties are not free to decide that the arbitration should not be one administered by the Court. If they do so, then it is not an ICC arbitration. **6–24**

As discussed under art.1, that does not mean that an arbitration agreement referring to the ICC Rules but excluding the ICC Court is necessarily invalid. That is a matter to be resolved under the law governing the arbitration agreement. And the Singapore courts, albeit with some reluctance, have upheld such a clause.[16] **6–25**

Article 6(3): "If any party against which a claim has been made does not submit an Answer, or raises one or more pleas concerning the existence, validity or scope of the arbitration agreement or concerning whether all of the claims made in the arbitration may be determined together in a single arbitration, the arbitration shall proceed and any question of jurisdiction or of whether the claims may be determined together in that arbitration shall be decided directly by the arbitral tribunal, unless the Secretary General refers the matter to the Court for its decision pursuant to Article 6(4)."

Article 6(3) provides that the Secretary General may refer a matter to the Court for a decision as to whether the arbitration should proceed if: (i) a party does not submit an Answer; or (ii) a party raises one or more pleas concerning the existence, validity or scope of the arbitration agreement; or (iii) concerning whether all of the claims made in the arbitration may be determined together in a single arbitration. **6–26**

If the parties do submit answers and no party raises such a jurisdictional objection nor asks that the claims proceed in separate arbitrations, then art.6(3) and the reference to art.6(4) are not applicable by their terms. In such circumstances, the Secretary General under the Rules has no authority to refer the matter to the ICC Court. **6–27**

Article 6(3) refers to the failure to submit an Answer. If an Answer is submitted but not within the period provided for in art.5 and it is accepted as an Answer by the ICC, then an Answer will have been filed within art.6(3). If the Secretary General has received an Answer in either case prior to deciding whether or not to refer the matter to the ICC Court, the Secretary General should take that Answer into account. **6–28**

Where the Respondent fails to file an Answer

If the Respondent does not file an Answer to the Request for Arbitration, the Secretariat may raise the issue of the "existence, validity or scope of the arbitration agreement" on its own initiative or may in effect respond to the issue due to submissions of the Claimant. In its Request, the Claimant may deal with **6–29**

[16] HKL Group Co Ltd v Rizq International Holdings Pte Ltd [2013] SGHCR 5 and para.1–34.

a jurisdictional issue with the objective of either seeking the Respondent's agreement or an initial decision from the ICC Court (as to the prima facie case) and a partial or interim Award from the Tribunal on this issue. The Claimant's interest in this approach would be to have a decision on jurisdiction by the Tribunal prior to incurring the expense of setting out its entire case on the merits.

6–30 If the Respondent does not file an Answer, the issue therefore may be clearly part of the Request in any event. Even if the Request does not directly raise the issue, the Secretariat may, in its review of the Request, note that there is a prima facie jurisdictional issue and raise the matter with the ICC Court. Prior to referring the matter to the ICC Court, the Secretariat would and should send a letter to the Claimant (with a copy to the Respondent) raising the jurisdictional issue. The Claimant would then be expected to respond and the Secretariat would submit that response, together with its comments to the Court for its review and decision.

Where the Respondent does file an Answer

6–31 In a more typical case, the Respondent will have filed an Answer raising the jurisdictional issue. There is no set procedure in the Rules for making submissions on this point. However, if an Answer raises a jurisdictional issue, the Secretariat will almost invariably and should provide the Claimant with an opportunity to respond and, where appropriate, provide a limited time period for the Respondent to file a rejoinder. In some cases, a substantial exchange of correspondence with the Secretariat may take place before the Secretary General decides whether or not to submit the matter to the ICC Court for a decision pursuant to art.6(4).

6–32 Unlike with the Request and Answer, the further correspondence on the jurisdictional issue will often contain factual clarifications and possibly additional evidence, as well as legal argument and authorities to support the respective arguments of the parties. As discussed below, although the ICC Court is rendering an administrative decision, the potential consequences of an administrative decision against jurisdiction are very serious for the Claimant.

6–33 Article 6(3) does not state when the Secretary General should refer the matter to the Court. However, art.6(3) represents a shift from the prior rules. Under the new Rules, the general rule is that matters are referred to the Tribunal unless the Secretary General decides to refer matters to the Court for a prima facie ruling on jurisdiction. The main purpose of that change was to streamline Court proceedings and expedite matters. It was intended to permit the Secretary General to decide not to submit a matter to the Court despite the request from a party to do so.[17] To make that decision, the Secretary General must determine that the party objecting to jurisdiction does not have a reasonable possibility of obtaining a ruling in its favour from the ICC Court.

[17] Fry, Mazza and Greenberg, *op. cit.*, state at para. 3–198 that in 2011 42% of the new cases required an art.6(2) decision under the 1998 Rules but in only 4% of those cases the Court decided that the arbitration should not proceed at all but in an additional 5% of the cases there was a partially negative decision (*op. cit.*, para.3–218). Therefore in 9% of the cases the arbitration was at least partially reconfigured as a result of art.6(2) of the 1998 Rules, which is not immaterial for a gatekeeper rule.

The Secretary General should be able to determine in particular whether an additional party has been joined either prior to the confirmation or appointment of an arbitrator under art.7(1) and if not, whether the consent of all parties has been obtained. The Secretary General should be able to determine whether, in the case of multiple contracts, they are all made in accordance with art.9 of the Rules. Therefore, in such cases, the Secretary General may decide that an objection to jurisdiction is manifestly unfounded and decide not to refer the matter to the ICC Court. 6–34

Internally, the team at the Secretariat will review the submissions in accordance with instructions of the Secretary General. In a straightforward case, where there is one contract, apparently signed by all parties, providing on its face for ICC arbitration the matter will be referred to the Tribunal. In other cases, there will be a more detailed review by the Secretary General. If, there is an objection to jurisdiction by a party and there is a decision not to refer the matter to the ICC Court, it is a decision of the Secretary General and not a decision of the ICC Court and should be notified to the parties as such.[18] 6–35

Although introduced to streamline proceedings, it is not clear how often the Secretary General has declined to refer a matter to the ICC Court when requested to do so by a party. 6–36

There is no time limit for the Secretary General to take a decision under art.6(4). However, since the purpose of the provision is to streamline procedures, one would expect that this would be handled promptly after the parties have been given an opportunity if appropriate for further comment. 6–37

Another issue under art.6(3), particularly in the light of US law is the effect of the statement that "any question of jurisdiction [. . .] shall be decided directly by the arbitral tribunal". Under US law, this would appear to be attribution of the issue of arbitrability to the Tribunal rather than to the Courts at first instance.[19] 6–38

Article 6(4): "In all cases referred to the Court under Article 6(3), the Court shall decide whether and to what extent the arbitration shall proceed. The arbitration shall proceed if and to the extent that the Court is prima facie satisfied that an arbitration agreement under the Rules may exist. In particular:

(i) where there are more than two parties to the arbitration, the arbitration shall proceed between those of the parties, including any additional parties joined pursuant to Article 7, with respect to which the Court is prima facie satisfied that an arbitration agreement under the Rules that binds them all may exist; and

(ii) where claims pursuant to Article 9 are made under more than one arbitration agreement, the arbitration shall proceed as to those

[18] Fry, Greenberg and Mazza, *op. cit.* para.3–207 state that in straightforward cases, the team refers the matter to Tribunal and communicates the information to the Secretary General for his information. Since art.6(3) does not require the Secretary General to make a decision not to refer the matter to ICC Court, this is consistent with the ICC Rules.

[19] See for example *Oracle America, Inc v Myriad Group AG* No.11-17186 (USCA 9th Cir. July 26, 2013) (art. 23(3) of the UNCITRAL Arbitration Rules held to be delegation of authority to decide arbitrability to the arbitral panel). Under US law, arbitrability relates to the right to submit a dispute to arbitration and to the scope of the arbitration clause itself. As discussed below, the US Courts defer to the Tribunal on the interpretation of the latter.

> **claims with respect to which the Court is prima facie satisfied (a) that the arbitration agreements under which those claims are made may be compatible, and (b) that all parties to the arbitration may have agreed that those claims can be determined together in a single arbitration.**

The Court's decision pursuant to Article 6(4) is without prejudice to the admissibility or merits of any party's plea or pleas."

Procedural aspects

6–39 The first sentence of art.6(4) limits the ICC Court's role to cases referred to it by the Secretary General and highlights the issue of whether and to what extent the arbitration should proceed. The second sentence refers to the fact that the arbitration shall proceed if the ICC Court is prima facie satisfied that an arbitration agreement may exist under the Rules. The third sentence sets out specific rules for multiparty arbitration (under art.7) or under more than one arbitration agreement (art.9) and sets out the criteria for those cases.

6–40 Article 6(4) deals in particular with a decision of the ICC Court as to whether prima facie there may be an agreement to arbitrate under the Rules or under arts 7 or 9, as the case may be. The ICC Court's decision implies there may be an arguable case for jurisdiction. If so, the decision on jurisdiction will be taken by the Tribunal since the decision of the ICC Court is administrative in nature and not binding upon the Tribunal. It is for the Tribunal, not the ICC Court to decide the dispute, and that includes the issue of arbitral jurisdiction. While a Claimant will always try to seek comfort from an affirmative art.6(4) decision of the ICC Court, it would be wrong for a Tribunal to take the ICC Court's prima facie decision as indicative for its arbitral jurisdiction. It is not, since the analysis of the ICC Court and that of a Tribunal are carried out at two different levels.[20]

6–41 An art.6(4) decision is based generally on the ICC Court's review of the arguments and evidence relating to the matter on a prima facie basis. Therefore, a party should not anticipate that the ICC Court will raise arguments of its own initiative and should present them so that the Secretariat can forward them in succinct form for the ICC Court. With respect to the evidence, usually one would expect basic documentary evidence (such as a copy of a signed agreement or exchange of emails). However, in other instances, there may be a witness statement. This could be particularly important if there is an allegation of an oral agreement or understanding.

6–42 As a general rule, the ICC Court will be seeking to determine whether the Tribunal may decide that it has jurisdiction. Therefore, in doing so, the ICC Court will consider the various issues that are discussed in particular under art.6(5) and (9) below. Since the issue of jurisdiction is subject to the law of the arbitration agreement, the issue for the ICC Court will be to determine whether, under the relevant law, the Tribunal may decide it has jurisdiction. Therefore, an arbitration clause subject to French (or transnational) law may well be considered differently

[20] Philippe, "Les pouvoirs de l'arbitre et de la Cour d'arbitrage de la CCI relatifs à leur compétence" (2006) Rev Arb No.3, p.591.

from that subject to English law, for example. As a result, the arguments should specifically address the cases under applicable law.

Article 6 has been amended to deal with multiparty arbitration under art.7 and arbitration involving multiple arbitration agreements under art.9. The particular aspects relating to each type of situation are discussed below. 6–43

As discussed in Annex 1 Pt I, the decisions by the ICC Court with respect to art.6(4) matters are invariably dealt with at Committee Sessions of the ICC Court, unless exceptional circumstances of the case require its submission to the Plenary Sessions. Therefore, the review is generally carried out by three members of the ICC Court. 6–44

Multiparty claims

Article 6(4) "(i) where there are more than two parties to the arbitration, the arbitration shall proceed between those of the parties, including any additional parties joined pursuant to Article 7, with respect to which the Court is prima facie satisfied that an arbitration agreement under the Rules that binds them all may exist;"

Clause (i) deals with multiparty arbitrations. These may arise because of multiple Claimants, multiple Respondents, multiple Claimants and Respondents, or additional parties. With respect to each Claimant or Respondent, as the case may be the issue is whether there is a prima facie case that an arbitration agreement under the Rules may exist. That depends usually on an interpretation on the terms of the arbitration agreement and the various principles that are discussed in particular under art.6(9). 6–45

With respect to additional parties, the preliminary issue is whether the Request for Joinder is timely in that it is made prior to the confirmation or appointment of any arbitrator or with the consent of all parties, including the additional party. This determination should be made initially by the Secretary General prior to referring the matter to the ICC Court. However, if there is uncertainty in this respect, the Secretary General may refer the matter to the ICC Court. 6–46

The second issue is whether there is a prima facie case that an arbitration agreement binding that additional party and the other parties may exist under the ICC Rules in accordance with the factors discussed under art.6(5). As discussed above, this threshold is not particularly high, as the basic test is whether this is an issue that the Tribunal should adjudicate or not or whether an administrative decision suffices. This would involve the same considerations as for bipartite arbitration with the added factor that there may be special considerations with respect to one or more parties. For example, if there are pending proceedings between the additional party and a party in another forum, this may be a factor, although a factor to be decided by the Tribunal. 6–47

Multiple Arbitration Agreements

Article 6(4): "(ii) where claims pursuant to Article 9 are made under more than one arbitration agreement, the arbitration shall proceed as to those

claims with respect to which the Court is prima facie satisfied (a) that the arbitration agreements under which those claims are made may be compatible, and (b) that all parties to the arbitration may have agreed that those claims can be determined together in a single arbitration."

6–48 The basic provision for arbitration under multiple contracts is set out in art.9. However, the actual criteria for when the claims may be brought together with respect to multiple arbitration agreements are set out in art.6(4)(ii). At the outset there is an issue as to whether there is more than one arbitration agreement. If there is incorporation in one contract of an arbitration agreement in another contract, there is one arbitration agreement. If there is incorporation in one contract of an arbitration agreement from another contract with modifications, then what the parties have agreed to is another arbitration agreement. If the same parties have several parallel agreements with identical arbitration clauses, then there is a basis for inferring that there is one arbitration agreement and therefore art.6(4)(ii) would not be applicable. However, that may not always be the case, if the transactions are completely separate for example.

6–49 The first criteria is that the arbitrations agreements "may be compatible". Since the ICC Court is only to take a prima facie decision, the only issue is whether the arbitration clauses "may" be considered compatible by a Tribunal. The focus on the arbitration agreement means that the fact that the governing law of the underlying contract is different may well be irrelevant. Similarly, if the arbitration agreement is in a different language or has different terminology in the absence of other distinctions, there may be no incompatibility. If the governing law of the arbitration agreements is different, that may be more problematic, although not necessarily fatal. A Tribunal may interpret two different arbitration agreements in one Award. If the place of arbitration is different under the arbitration agreements, then the arbitration agreements are not compatible. One cannot render one Award that is subject to annulment in two different jurisdictions.[21] If the arbitration agreements provide for arbitration under different arbitration rules, then they are also inconsistent. A more difficult issue is where the time limits in the arbitration agreements are different.

6–50 Another issue is whether the ICC Court should exercise its rights under the Rules to make provisions compatible. For example, if one arbitration agreement provides for a place of arbitration and the other does not, the ICC Court could decide that the place of arbitration with respect to the second arbitration should be that of the first arbitration agreement. Or, if one arbitration agreement states that there are to be three arbitrators and another does not specify the number of arbitrators, then the ICC Court could decide that there should be three arbitrators in each case. In both these cases, the basic issue is whether, under a proper construction of the arbitration agreement, the parties intended to give the ICC Court the role of basically conforming the arbitration agreements to render them compatible. On

[21] See Paris, November 16, 2006, *La société Empresa de Telecommunicaciones de Cuba SA v 1. La Telefonica Antillana 2. SNC Banco Nacional de Comercio Exterior* (2006) Les Cahiers de l'Arbitrage 2006/3 p.65. The treatment of the French and UK courts in the *Hilmarton* (para. 34–46ff) and *Dallah* (para. 6–88f) cases shows the potential for disruption. One could have an even more difficult situation where the Award would be annulled in one jurisdiction and not the other.

balance, the ICC Court should have the right to so act, if there is a legitimate interest in having the arbitrations heard together, for example to avoid potential inconsistency in results.

The second criteria relates to whether all parties may have agreed that the matters be dealt with together in a single arbitration. This is the issue dealt with in *Oxford Health Plans LLC v Sutter*[22] where the issue was whether the following clause permitted class arbitration: 6–51

> "No civil action concerning any dispute arising under this Agreement shall be instituted before any court, and all such disputes shall be submitted to final and binding arbitration in New Jersey, pursuant to the rules of the American Arbitration Association with one arbitrator."

The arbitrator held that this clause permitted class action arbitration. The US Supreme Court did not necessarily agree or disagree with the interpretation but held that the courts had no authority to review it. Therefore, in this instance, for example, an arbitration clause that made no mention of class action arbitration was held (by the arbitrator) to permit it. It is not clear how Tribunals would decide such an issue in the abstract. However, for the purposes of art.6(4), a party claiming that there was agreement to class action arbitration would clearly have a prima facie case. 6–52

On a more general level, there is an issue of whether the criteria under art.6(4) with respect to arbitration under more than one arbitration agreement should be interpreted in the light of the requirements for joinder under art.10, and in particular art.10(c) The basic issue is of course the same, in that it is whether various claims should be heard in the same arbitration. However, there is no cross reference to art.10 in art.6(4), and it is not clear that the requirement in art.10(c) that the arbitration be between the same parties should be applicable. 6–53

As mentioned above, art.6(4) deals with whether there is a prima facie case for jurisdiction with respect to arbitrations involving multiple parties or multiple arbitration agreements shall be decided under art.6(5). Therefore, these issues, if in dispute must be addressed in the Award and may be subject to judicial review. 6–54

Article 6(4): [...]"The Court's decision pursuant to Article 6(4) is without prejudice to the admissibility or merits of any party's plea or pleas."

If the ICC Court accepts that there may be an ICC arbitration agreement and decides that the arbitration can proceed in accordance with art.6(4), it will put the arbitration into motion. As a result, the Tribunal will be constituted and the ICC Court will fix, where necessary, the place of arbitration and set the amount of the advance to cover the costs of arbitration. As discussed under art.6(5), the decision of the ICC Court that the arbitration may proceed under art.6(4) does not change the fact that it is for the Tribunal to decide whether it has jurisdiction. Therefore, it is for the Tribunal to decide whether the claims are admissible. 6–55

[22] *Oxford Health Plans LLC v Sutter*, 133 S. Ct. 2064 (2013).

Article 6(5): "In all matters decided by the Court under Article 6(4), any decision as to the jurisdiction of the arbitral tribunal, except as to parties or claims with respect to which the Court decides that the arbitration cannot proceed, shall then be taken by the arbitral tribunal itself."

6–56 Article 6(5) provides that any decision as to jurisdiction shall be taken by the Tribunal. Article 6(5) does not specify whether or not such a decision should take the form of an Award or procedural order. As discussed under art.34, if the Tribunal finally decides an issue, then it is rendering an Award. Although it is possible that the Tribunal decide an issue of jurisdiction in a procedural order on a preliminary basis (that is reserving the right to modify it), then it presumably would have to expressly say so or the procedural order might be re-interpreted as an Award subject to scrutiny under art.33. It is submitted that a Tribunal does not have the right to finally determine an issue as to jurisdiction without issuing an Award which in turn is subject to scrutiny of the ICC Court.

6–57 Pursuant to art.31(2), an Award must be reasoned. Those reasons must include reasons as to jurisdiction. Therefore, the Tribunal will set out in the Award the arbitration clause, any arguments with respect to jurisdiction raised by the parties, any issues as to jurisdiction that may occur to the Tribunal (and that have been raised with the parties) and the Tribunal's discussion and decision on jurisdiction. The Secretary General's decision under art.6(3) or the ICC Court's decision under art.6(4) that the arbitration may proceed are procedural elements that are referred to in the Award but they do not provide the reasons for holding that the Tribunal has jurisdiction. That is a matter that must be decided by the Tribunal as is expressly provided for in art.6(5).

6–58 The ICC Court has an administrative function and therefore cannot adjudicate issues, such as issues with respect to jurisdiction. Those issues are to be decided by the Tribunal. However, the Tribunal cannot exceed its jurisdiction under the relevant arbitration agreement and cannot deal with matters that the Court has decided shall not proceed. However, by agreeing to ICC arbitration, the parties are agreeing to the Rules and therefore agreeing to the criteria in the Rules, such as those set out in art.6(4)(i) and (ii). As a result, the Tribunal should interpret those principles as well as applicable law where they may arise in the light of applicable law.

6–59 Article 6(5) anticipates that, in some cases, some claims against a party may proceed and that the Court will decide that other claims shall not proceed. If a party is and is to remain a party to the arbitration, then the issue is whether these claims may subsequently be added under art.23(4) of the Rules for example, if the party making the claim provided further evidence of an arbitration agreement with respect to the claim.

6–60 A strict reading of art.6(5) would make the addition of such claims impossible. That reading is reinforced by art.6(7). The remit of the Tribunal has been limited by the decision of the Court and there is no provision for changing that remit. The only provision is for bringing the proceedings in court proceedings (in accordance with art.6(6) or in subsequent arbitration proceedings (in accordance with art.6(7)). However, that could in some instances be contrary to the basic objective of the Rules which is to ensure cost and time effective adjudication.

In most cases, the issue of whether the Tribunal has jurisdiction is to be decided by the Tribunal. This raises issues of national law as well as of arbitration practice. As mentioned elsewhere, these issues are matters that should be considered with experts under the national legal systems. However, the ICC Court when it is considering whether there is a prima facie case that there may be jurisdiction, and Tribunals and parties are routinely faced with these issues and therefore set out below is a discussion of the principles that are applicable with respect thereto. **6–61**

Formal elements of the agreement to arbitrate

The Rules themselves do not place any formal requirements on an arbitration agreement. The issue is therefore whether there are national or international requirements as to form with respect to arbitration agreements. The requirements may be imposed in different ways, whether as the law applicable to the arbitration agreement itself, the law of the place of arbitration or the law governing one of the parties to the arbitration agreement. Most legal systems do not require that the arbitration agreement be in a document signed by the parties. It is sufficient that the agreement be in writing (even if not signed). This is consistent with the New York Convention, which applies to "agreements in writing" of which art.II 2 of the Convention defines that term to include "an arbitral clause in a contract or an arbitration agreement, signed by the parties or contained in an exchange of letters or telegrams". The laws of major centers of arbitration do not require a signed arbitration agreement, although they generally provide for some form of written documentation.[23] **6–62**

An arbitration agreement would usually be in writing (whether signed or not), although art.6(1) does not require it to be in writing.[24] However, there are **6–63**

[23] For the *United States*, s.2 of the Federal Arbitration Act provides: "A written provision in any maritime transaction or a contract evidencing a transaction involving commerce to settle by arbitration a controversy thereafter arising out of such contract or transaction, or the refusal to perform the whole or any part thereof, or an agreement in writing to submit to arbitration an existing controversy arising out of such a contract, transaction, or refusal, shall be valid, irrevocable, and enforceable, save upon such grounds as exist at law or in equity for the revocation of any contract". In England, s.5 of the Arbitration Act 1996 states: "Agreements to be in writing. 5.–(1) The provisions of this Part apply only where the arbitration agreement is in writing, and any other agreement between the parties as to any matter is effective for the purposes of this Part only if in writing. The expressions 'agreement', 'agree' and 'agreed' shall be construed accordingly. (2) There is an agreement in writing- (a) if the agreement is made in writing (whether or not it is signed by the parties), (b) if the agreement is made by exchange of communications in writing, or (c) if the agreement is evidenced in writing. (3) Where parties agree otherwise than in writing by reference to terms which are in writing, they make an agreement in writing. (4) An agreement is evidenced in writing if an agreement made otherwise than in writing is recorded by one of the parties, or by a third party, with the authority of the parties to the agreement. (5) An exchange of written submissions in arbitral or legal proceedings in which the existence of an agreement otherwise than in writing is alleged by one party against another party and not denied by the other party in his response constitutes as between those parties an agreement in writing to the effect alleged. (6) References in this Part to anything being written or in writing include its being recorded by any means". In Switzerland, art.178(1) of the Swiss PILA provides: "The Arbitration agreement must be if made in writing by telegram, telex, telecopier or any other means of communication which permits it to be evidenced by a text" (See Pt III App.7). French law does not impose such requirement, and the issue is rather whether the party was informed of the arbitration clause prior to final acceptance. See Cass civ 1re, November 21, 2006, *Société Deher Frères v société Groupama*, No.05-21818, at *http://www.legifrance.gouv.fr*.

[24] On the formal requirements, see for example for Switzerland, Karrer and Straub, "I. Switzerland" in *Practitioner's Handbook on International Arbitration, op. cit.*, para.13, p.1049; Blessing, "The

examples where unsigned written agreements have been enforced.[25] Option of art.7 of the UNCITRAL Model Law (Pt III App.5) expressly permits arbitration agreements concluded orally if they are recorded "in any form" and deals with electronic agreements.[26] In addition, there is a related issue of whether a party is bound by an arbitration agreement that is in writing but which that party has not signed. This is discussed below with respect to "non-signatories".

Whether the arbitration is to be under the ICC Rules

6–64 For an arbitration to be an arbitration under the Rules, the arbitration agreement must refer in some fashion to arbitration pursuant to the ICC Rules. With the ICC arbitration model clause, there is, of course, no issue as there is express reference to the Rules. However, in many instances parties have agreed on clauses that provide no clear reference to ICC arbitration let alone to the ICC Rules. In fact, the examples of arbitration clauses that have given rise to issues of interpretation are legion.[27] The approach adopted below, is to set out a step-by-step analysis of the issues that arise in the analysis of an arbitration clause to determine whether it does provide for arbitration under the Rules.

Arbitration Agreement–Its Multifold Critical Aspects" in *ASA Special Series no 8*, Basel 1994, paras 8 et seq.; for the United States, see Carbonneau, "United States" in *Practitioner's Handbook on International Arbitration, op. cit.*, para.17, p.1092; for England, see Maxwell, "England", in *Practitioner's Handbook on International Arbitration, op. cit.*, paras 19–20, p.597.

[25] Oral arbitration agreements may be enforced in France. See Paris, June 8, 1995, *SARL Centro Stoccaggio Grani v Société Granit* (1997) Rev Arb No.1 p.89 (an unsigned agreement with an arbitration clause binds the parties to arbitration).

[26] The UNCITRAL Model Law provides for two options, a detailed option (Option 1) and a short option (Option 2). Option 1 provides that:

"2. The arbitration agreement shall be in writing.

3. An arbitration agreement is in writing if its content is recorded in any form, whether or not the arbitration agreement or contract has been concluded orally, by conduct, or by other means.

4. The requirement that an arbitration agreement be in writing is met by an electronic communication if the information contained therein is accessible so as to be useable for subsequent reference; "electronic communication" means any communication that the parties make by means of data messages; "data messages" means information generated, sent, received or stored by electronic, magnetic, optical or similar means, including, but not limited to, electronic data interchange (EDI), electronic mail, telegram, telex or telecopy.

5. Furthermore, an arbitration agreement is in writing if it is contained in an exchange of statements of claim and defence in which the existence of an agreement is alleged by one party and not denied by the other.

6. The reference in a contract to a document containing an arbitration clause constitutes an arbitration agreement in writing, provided that the reference is such as to make that clause part of the contract." See in this respect, Degos, "La CNUDCI abandonne l'exigence d'écrit pour la convention d'arbitrage" (2007) Les Cahiers de l'Arbitrage No.2007/1, p.5; Jacobs, "Requirement Of Writing And Of Signatures Under the UNCITRAL Model Law And the New York Convention" (2006) Mealey's IAR Vol.21 No.11, p.46.

[27] See, for example, Sherman and Bennett, "Avoiding 'Pathological' Arbitration Clauses", *Practical Lawyer*, August 2006, p.43; Eisemann, "La clause d'arbitrage pathologique" in *Arbitrage commercial–Essais in memoriam Eugenio Minoli*, Colloria die Studi sull' Arbitrator (AIA, 1974), p.129; Gélinas, "Arbitration Clauses: Achieving Effectiveness" (1999) *ICCA Congress Series No.9*, p.47; Davis, "Pathological Clauses: Frédéric Eisemann's Still Vital Criteria" (1991) Arb Int Vol.7, No.4, p.365; Scalbert and Malville, "Les clauses compromissoires pathologiques" (1988) Rev Arb No.1, p.117; Maleville, "Pathologies des clauses compromissoires 'Pathological' arbitration clauses" (2000) RDAI/IBLJ No.1, p.61.

The first issue is to determine how to interpret the arbitration agreement. This will depend on the legal system governing the agreement. If the arbitration agreement is contained in an overall agreement subject to a specific national law, in many jurisdictions that national law would be applied to interpret it. However, as noted above this is not entirely clear and there may be reference to the law of the place of arbitration or transnational law. 6–65

The national legal systems vary. A useful indication of the approach to be taken in this respect, and of the importance in most systems of the "common intent principle", is provided by art.4.1 of the UNIDROIT Principles which states: 6–66

> "(1) A contract shall be interpreted according to the common intention of the parties.
>
> (2) If such an intention cannot be established, the contract shall be interpreted according to the meaning that reasonable persons of the same kind as the parties would give to it in the same circumstances."

The second issue is to determine the material that should be reviewed to establish the common intent of the parties. In particular, in many common law countries there are limits to the use of extraneous documents in the interpretation of the agreement. In addition, in countries such as England, reference to conduct of the parties after the signing of the agreement is, subject to limited exceptions, excluded. In addition, frequently in common law countries, documents dated or actions of the parties after the signing of the agreement are not considered relevant to the interpretation of the agreement. In other legal systems, extraneous documents are viewed as helpful and conduct of the parties after the date of the agreement is considered relevant to the interpretation of the agreement.[28] The issue for a Tribunal constituted under the Rules is to determine which system is applicable so that the agreement can be properly analysed. 6–67

The third issue is whether, despite ambiguity in the language, the parties agreed on arbitration and, in particular, international arbitration. The parties are usually from different countries and perhaps different legal systems. If the language in the agreement is clear in showing that there was an attempt to opt out of national legal systems in favour of international arbitration, that should be given considerable if not decisive weight in the interpretation of the clause. 6–68

The fourth issue is whether the arbitration was intended to be an administered arbitration or an ad hoc arbitration. If parties wished to have an administered rather than ad hoc arbitration, then they sought to have some arbitration institution to have control over the arbitral proceedings. This is significant as it reinforces the international aspect. In ICC arbitration, for example, it is the ICC that decides challenges to arbitrators, at least at first instance. 6–69

[28] The UNIDROIT Principles (art.4.3) in this respect are quite different from those in the common law: "In applying Articles 4.1 and 4.2, regard shall be had to all the circumstances, including:
(a) preliminary negotiations between the parties;
(b) practices which the parties have established between themselves;
(c) the conduct of the parties subsequent to the conclusion of the contract;
(d) the nature and purpose of the contract;
(e) the meaning commonly given to terms and expressions in the trade concerned;
(f) usages."

6–70 The fifth issue is whether the administrative body was intended to be the ICC. In this respect one of the most frequent sources of potential confusion is the distinction between the institution and the place of arbitration. References to arbitration under "the rules of the International Chamber of Commerce in Geneva" are, for example, usually interpreted as a reference to the Rules with Geneva as the place of arbitration.[29]

6–71 If, after having analysed these factors, the Claimant determines that it has a reasonable chance of success, then it will file the Request for Arbitration with the ICC. At that point, the Respondent has a choice. If, whatever the weaknesses are in the arbitration clause, the Respondent wishes to have the dispute resolved, it can simply accept the ICC arbitration. If, however, the Respondent believes that there was clearly no agreement to arbitrate or no agreement to arbitrate under the Rules, it may object to the arbitration before the ICC Court, the Tribunal, and possibly even the national courts at the place of arbitration and/or of enforcement of the Award.

6–72 If the Respondent's jurisdictional argument is successful, then possibly there will be national court proceedings somewhere, although not necessarily in the Respondent's home country. Generally, the dispute will not simply disappear. If the Respondent's jurisdictional argument is unsuccessful, then the Claimant will not only score an initial success, but will also tend to try to categorise the Respondent as seeking to avoid dealing with the merits of the dispute. That attempt will usually be of no effect if the issues as to the interpretation of the agreement to arbitrate are substantive. However, if the arguments on jurisdiction were flimsy, then a Tribunal may well tend to view the objection as procedurally motivated.

Scope of the arbitration agreement

6–73 In most cases, the agreement to arbitrate and the subject matter are reasonably clear. The parties intend to submit any dispute arising out of a particular contract for adjudication by arbitration.

6–74 Sometimes arbitration clauses contain language that can limit the scope of their application. If, for instance, only disputes regarding the interpretation of the contract are mentioned in the arbitration clause, the question may arise whether the Tribunal has also jurisdiction to deal with other claims regarding the performance of the contract, such as tort claims.[30] In other instances, the issue is whether the arbitration agreement covers claims in tort.

[29] See ICC case No.2626 (1977), *Collection of ICC Arbitral Awards 1974–1985, Vol.I, op. cit.*, p.316, note Jarvin and Derains; see also ICC case No.10671 (2000) (Interim Award), (2001) ASA Bull Vol.19, No.2, p.276 ("Rules of Conciliation and Arbitration of the International Chamber of Commerce of Genève"); ICC case No.7895 (1994) ("Rules of concilliation (sic) and arbitration of the Chambre de Commerce Internationale de Paris"), ICC case No.9772 (1999) ("Règles de l'Association Internationale de l'arbitrage") in Truong, *op. cit.*, p.44; ICC case No.10422 (2001), (2003) JDI p.1142, note Jolivet and Truong, *op. cit.*, para.51, p.49: "Le présent contrat, comme toutes ses dispositions, seront régies par la 'CHAMBRE DE COMMERCE INTERNATIONALE' ou à son défaut par une législation neutre définie d'un commun accord entre les parties, mais qui en aucun cas ne pourront être les Tribunaux de justice des pays respectifs des parties contractantes".

[30] For a general discussion, see Fouchard, Gaillard & Goldman, *op. cit.*, para.524, p.306; for *England*, see Sutton, Gill & Gearing, *op. cit.*, para.2–075, p.74; Maxwell, "England" in *Practitioner's Handbook on International Arbitration, op. cit.*, para.17, p.596; for *France*, see Gaillard, "La jurisprudence de la Cour de cassation en matière d'arbitrage international" (2007) Rev.Arb.No.4, p.697; Gaillard & Edelstein, "France" in *Practitioner's Handbook on International Arbitration, op. cit.*,

As mentioned at para 6-52 with respect to *Oxford Health Plans* v *Sutter*, the US courts defer to arbitrators provided they are interpreting the scope of the arbitration clause pursuant to arbitration rules granting the arbitrator this role. As to how arbitrators should interpret of the arbitration clause, in the *Louis Dreyfus* case,[31] the US Court of Appeals for the Second Circuit suggested a three-part analysis of whether collateral matters are within the scope of an arbitration clause, as follows: **6–75**

> "To determine whether a particular dispute falls within the scope of an agreement's arbitration clause, a court should undertake a three-part inquiry. First, recognizing there is some range in the breadth of arbitration clauses, a court should classify the particular clause as either broad or narrow [. . .] Next, if reviewing a narrow clause, the court must determine whether the dispute is over an issue that 'is on its face within the purview of the clause', or over a collateral issue that is somehow connected to the main agreement that contains the arbitration clause [. . .] Where the arbitration clause is narrow, a collateral matter will generally be ruled beyond its purview [. . .] Where the arbitration clause is broad, 'there arises a presumption of arbitrability' and arbitration of even a collateral matter will be ordered if the claim alleged 'implicates issues of contract construction or the parties' rights and obligations under it." (citations deleted)

In the case of an arbitration under the ICC Rules, it is for the arbitrator to determine the scope of the arbitration clause as discussed with respect to *Oxford Health Plans* under paras 6–51 et seq. Therefore, the issue of whether the arbitration clause covers tort claims will depend on the terms of the arbitration agreement and the Tribunal's interpretation of that agreement as reflecting the intention of the parties. The issue is basically one of contract interpretation. However, in cases where the scope of the arbitration agreement is left to the courts, the US courts have consistently upheld a broad interpretation of the scope of arbitration agreements rationae materiae provided that the Tribunal is not simply imposing its own policy.[32] Therefore, a Tribunal would be equally permitted, as the sole arbitrator did in the Award subject to *Oxford Health Plans,* to give a broad interpretation to an arbitration clause. **6–76**

para.28, p.651; for *Switzerland*, see Poudret & Besson, *op. cit.*, para.307, p.266. ATF 116 Ia 56, JT 1990 I 563; see also ICC case No.14046 (Final Award) (2007), unreported ("Pursuant to Swiss case law, when the existence of an arbitration clause is established, as it is the case here, there is no ground for a restrictive interpretation. Quite to the contrary, one has to consider that the parties want that the arbitral tribunal be vested with a general jurisdiction, and, in case of doubt, that they did not intend to refer to arbitration only their disputes relating to the implementation of their respective obligations, but also the ones concerning the validity of the arbitration agreement that embodies such obligations. The formal validity of the arbitration agreement at stake having been ascertained by this Tribunal, there is no doubt therefore that this agreement contends the arbitral's jurisdiction on all and any disputes arising out of the implementation of the agreement in dispute. [. . .] As regards the arbitrability of the dispute, an issue which also relates to the validity as to substance of the arbitration agreement, the Arbitral Tribunal examines the issue *in concreto* below (chapter IV.2) to conclude that the dispute at hand is arbitrable. [. . .]. .").

31 *Louis Dreyfus Negoce v Blystad Shipping*, 252 F.3d 218, (2D CIR., 2001). (cert, denied)

32 See *Stolt–Nielsen S.A. v. AnimalFeeds International Corp.* 559 U.S. 662, at 666–7 (Vacating the Award, the Supreme Court stated: "In sum, instead of identifying and applying a rule of decision derived from the FAA or either maritime or New York law, the arbitration panel imposed its own policy choice and thus exceeded its powers.").

6–77 The American authorities are in line with a practical approach to arbitration. If the parties have clearly agreed on arbitration with a broadly worded clause, then the natural tendency is to assume that they intended to have all related disputes resolved in one forum and therefore by arbitration.

6–78 This approach has been adopted in a particularly trenchant fashion by the English Court of Appeal in the *Fiona Trust* case[33] where it was argued that the tribunal had no jurisdiction as the agreement, of which the arbitration clause formed part, had been induced by bribery. In that case the Court said in particular after reviewing the case law:

> "17. [. . .] For our part we consider that the time has now come for a line of some sort to be drawn and a fresh start made at any rate for cases arising in an international commercial context. Ordinary business men would be surprised at the nice distinctions drawn in the cases and the time taken up by argument in debating whether a particular case falls within one set of words or another very similar set of words. If business men go to the trouble of agreeing that their disputes be heard in the courts of a particular country or by a tribunal of their choice they do not expect (at any rate when they are making the contract in the first place) that time and expense will be taken in lengthy argument about the nature of particular causes of action and whether any particular cause of action comes within the meaning of the particular phrase they have chosen in their arbitration clause. If any businessman did want to exclude disputes about the validity of a contract, it would be comparatively simple to say so.
>
> 18. As it seems to us any jurisdiction or arbitration clause in an international commercial contract should be liberally construed. The words 'arising out of' should cover 'every dispute except a dispute as to whether there was ever a contract at all', see Mustill and Boyd, Commercial Arbitration, 2nd ed page 120 (the debate, to which we were treated, about whether the authorities there cited support the proposition is, since *Harbour v Kansa*, both technical and sterile). Although in the past the words 'arising under the contract' have sometimes been given a narrower meaning, that should no longer continue to be so.[. . .].
>
> 19. One of the reasons given in the cases for a liberal construction of an arbitration clause is the presumption in favour of one-stop arbitration. It is not to be expected that any commercial man would knowingly create a system which required that the court should first decide whether the contract should be rectified or avoided or rescinded (as the case might be) and then, if the contract is held to be valid, required the arbitrator to resolve the issues that have arisen. This is indeed a powerful reason for a liberal construction [. . .].
>
> 21. We would, therefore, conclude that a dispute whether the contract can be set aside or rescinded for alleged bribery does fall within the arbitration clause on its true construction. The case is different from a

33 [2007] EWCA 20; [2007] Bus. L.R. 686; [2007] 1 All ER. (Comm.) 891.

> dispute 'as to whether there were ever a contract at all', in the Mustill and Boyd sense."

The House of Lords upheld this judgment,[34] in similar terms with Lord Hoffman stated: **6–79**

> "13. In my opinion the construction of an arbitration clause should start from the assumption that the parties, as rational businessmen, are likely to have intended any dispute arising out of the relationship into which they have entered or purported to enter to be decided by the same tribunal. The clause should be construed in accordance with this presumption unless the language makes it clear that certain questions were intended to be excluded from the arbitrator's jurisdiction. As Longmore LJ remarked, at para.17: 'if any businessman did want to exclude disputes about the validity of a contract, it would be comparatively easy to say so.' "

With respect to competition law claims, since the *Mitsubishi* case,[35] it has been established that US antitrust claims are arbitrable and that a broad arbitration clause will cover them. This approach has been followed in numerous other cases in interpreting broad arbitration agreements.[36] The main case in the European Union, is known as *Eco Swiss*.[37] That case established the principle that a Tribunal is required to take into account mandatory principles of EU competition law. It would appear to be a natural corollary of that approach that an arbitration clause should generally be interpreted to cover EU competition law claims.[38] **6–80**

To ensure that all disputes are resolved in one set of proceedings, parties are normally well advised to include in the arbitration clause broad language as to its scope of application. By using the standard arbitration clause recommenced by the ICC, parties will normally avoid such difficulties. There exists ample case law confirming the broad scope of the standard ICC arbitration clause.[39] **6–81**

In other cases, the issue arises whether the arbitration agreement covers only disputes arising out of the very contract in which it is contained, or also other contracts that may contain no arbitration clauses, but that form part of the same transaction. If the transaction is between the same parties, the issue is whether the parties have agreed that the disputes should be submitted to ICC arbitration on the same terms. A related issue is whether the parties intended one arbitration or different arbitrations. For example where parties entered into two related agreements that **6–82**

[34] See the *Premium Nafta Products Ltd* case cited at para.16–18.

[35] See the *Mitsubishi* case, paras 6–158 n.122.

[36] For a discussion in the context of a class action based on the Sherman Act, see *JLM Industries v Stolt-Nielsen SA*, 387 F.3d 163 (2d Cir., 2004).

[37] CJEC, June 1, 1999, C-126/97, *Eco Swiss China Time Ltd v Benetton International* (1999) YBCA Vol.XXIVa, p.629; (1999) Rev Arb No.3, p.631, note Idot.

[38] With reference to the standard ICC arbitration clause, EU competition law claims would appear to arise out of the contract(s) that established the relationship between the parties.

[39] See, for example, ICC case No.8195 (1995) (Partial Award), in Truong, *op. cit.*, para.55, p.52: A Tribunal sitting in Paris and applying Lebanese law, decided that disputes arising out of the "execution" of the distribution contract are not limited to a material performance of the rights and obligations of the parties but also include those arising out of the breach or termination of the contract.

provided for arbitration in different places (Madrid and Paris), the French Court of Appeal held that the ICC Tribunal did not have jurisdiction over both matters.[40]

6–83 If the transaction involves third parties, then there is an added issue as to how the arbitrators are to be appointed so that the parties will have equal treatment.[41] As discussed in more detail below with respect to non-signatories, the key distinction is the approach adopted in jurisdictions like England and the United States, where the scope of the arbitral agreement is basically to be interpreted in accordance with national contract law principles and other countries, such as France, where reference is made to transnational principles.

Non-signatories to the arbitration agreement

6–84 Disputes arise in a contractual context that may involve various companies of the same group or they may relate in part to work done for a subcontractor, for example. As a result, a Claimant may wish to add as a Respondent a subsidiary or an affiliate of the party who signed the agreement to arbitrate or a third party who is somehow linked to the dispute. Similarly, a Respondent may wish to add parties either by way of counterclaim or cross-claim.

6–85 In national court proceedings, it is frequently possible to join to legal proceedings any party who is a "necessary and proper" party to pending proceedings.[42] The national judicial systems seek to thereby avoid a multiplication of litigation and the possibility of inconsistent results. If there is a doubt as to whether a parent and subsidiary should be joined in a lawsuit, usually both will be made parties to it. If an issue may arise with a subcontractor, then frequently the subcontractor can be joined to the proceedings.

6–86 With arbitration, joinder is not possible generally without a contractual nexus of some sort between the parties.[43] By entering into an arbitration agreement, the parties have consented to opting out of at least part of the national procedure. Therefore, the issue is what is sufficient to constitute this contractual nexus and what steps parties can take if the contractual nexus is insufficient.

6–87 Conceptually there are several basic situations. The first is where the non-signatory wishes to be a Claimant either directly or by way of counterclaim. The second is where there is an attempt to make a non-signatory a Respondent. In the *Dow Chemical* case,[44] one company in a group signed an arbitration agreement for ICC arbitration. Another company in the same group was involved in the

[40] See Paris, November 16, 2006, *La société Empresa de Telecommunicaciones de Cuba SA v 1. La Telefonica Antillana 2. SNC Banco Nacional de Comercio Exterior* (2006) Les Cahiers de l'Arbitrage 2006/3 p.65.

[41] For a discussion of the principles, see Hanotiau, "Complex–Multicontract-Multiparty–Arbitrations" (1998) Arb Int Vol.14, No.4, p.369. See also Fouchard, Gaillard & Goldman, *op. cit.*, paras 518–523, pp.301–306; Poudret & Besson, *op. cit.*, paras 308–316, pp.268–273.

[42] For example, the English provision is set out in the Civil Procedure Rules r.19(2) which provides that "[t]he Court may order a person to be added as a new party if (a) it is desirable to add the new party so that the court can resolve all the matters in dispute in the proceedings; or (b) there is an issue involving the new party and an existing party which is connected to the matters in dispute in the proceedings and it is desirable to add the new party so that the court can resolve that issue".

[43] One of the main exceptions to this is where arbitration is rendered possible by international convention. See the discussion of Bilateral Investment Treaties above at para.0–30. See also Paulsson, "Arbitration Without Privity" (1995) ICSID Rev Vol.10, p.232.

[44] ICC case No.4131 (1982) (Interim Award), (1984) YBCA Vol.IX p.131.

negotiation and performance of the overall contract containing the agreement to arbitrate. The Tribunal held that it had jurisdiction over the non-signatory. This doctrine became known as the "group of companies doctrine" and met with some success in ICC arbitration circles.[45] The theoretical underpinnings for the doctrine have been interpreted in different ways. However, several basic points should be noted: (i) The Tribunal in the *Dow Chemical* case was applying French law; however, it drew a distinction between the law on the merits and the law as to the scope of the arbitration clause; (ii) The Tribunal based itself squarely on the intention of the parties; (iii)The Tribunal relied in particular on the participation of the non-signatories in the conclusion, performance and termination of the contracts and linked this to the common intent of the parties; (iv) The Tribunal expressly relied upon usages of trade referred to in the Rules and prior arbitral awards as creating precedent.

As discussed below, the French courts have developed theories of alter ego and chain of contracts that have the effect of bringing in non-signatories to an arbitration through contract and corporate law theories that differ from those in the group of companies doctrine. Therefore, to that extent, the doctrine may be considered obsolete. However, the area is not without its difficulties due to the *Dallah* case which resulted in both decisions of the UK Supreme Court and the French Court of Appeal. **6–88**

The facts were as follows. On July 24, 1995, the Claimant a Saudi company (Dallah) signed a Memorandum of Understanding with the Government of Pakistan for the construction of a project for pilgrims in Mecca. On September 10, 1996, Dallah signed a contract to carry out the project with a trust that had been created by Presidential decree. The contract did not have a governing law provision. It provided for ICC arbitration in Paris. The Presidential decree was of limited duration and therefore the trust ceased to exist in late 1996. In 1998, as a result of difficulties, Dallah brought an ICC arbitration in Paris against the Government of Pakistan. The ICC Tribunal rendered three awards, holding that the Government of Pakistan was a party to the arbitration agreement and liable for damages. **6–89**

As discussed below, applying French law, the UK Supreme Court held that the Government of Pakistan was not subject to the arbitration clause in question. Three months later, the Paris Court of Appeal held that the Government of Pakistan was subject to the arbitration clause. The method by which the UK and French courts reached opposite conclusions on the same Award are briefly discussed below as part of a discussion of the treatment of non-signatories in major centres of arbitration.[46] **6–90**

The United States

The approach in the United States with respect to whether non-signatories are bound by an arbitration agreement may vary somewhat from district to district. Therefore, the references below should be read also by reference to similar **6–91**

[45] On the application of the doctrine to arbitration involving a state party, see for further discussions, Henry, "The Group of Companies Doctrine Applied to Arbitration Involving a State" (2006) RDAI/IBLJ No.3, p.297.

[46] For an overall discussion of the issue prior to the *Dallah* case, see Park, *Non-signatories and International Contracts: An arbitrator's dilemma, Multiple Parties in International Arbitration* (Oxford 2009).

decisions in the relevant district.[47] In addition, in *Sarhank Group v Oracle Corporation* (404 F.3d 657) the Second Circuit Court of Appeals held that to enforce an award rendered under foreign law, a non signatory would only be bound if its law requirements to bind non signatories were met.

6–92 In *EI Dupont de Nemours and Co v Rhone Poulenc Fiber and Resins Intermediates, SAS* (269 F.3d 187 (3d Cir. October 15, 2001), the court analysed the issue of non-signatories in the context of an arbitration under the rules of the Singapore International Arbitration Centre in the following terms:

> "The thrust of this appeal is whether the District Court erred in its refusal to compel arbitration. There is no dispute that the Agreement contained a valid and enforceable arbitration clause which required all disputes arising out of the Agreement between the parties be submitted to binding arbitration in Singapore. The only question is whether DuPont, a non-signatory to that Agreement, is bound by that arbitration clause. Similarly, there is no dispute that a non-signatory cannot be bound to arbitrate unless it is bound 'under traditional principles of contract and agency law' to be akin to a signatory of the underlying agreement. *Bel-Ray Co., Inc. v. Chemsite (Pty) Ltd.*, Appellants appeal from the District Court's conclusion that Dupont was not bound to arbitrate because it was not (a) an intended third party beneficiary of the Agreement, (b) the disclosed principal of its agent, DPC, a party to the Agreement, or (c) equitably estopped from avoiding arbitration. We review the District Court's conclusions de novo." (citation deleted)

6–93 The Third Circuit Court of Appeals then went on to analyse each of these headings to find that Dupont was not bound by the agreement to arbitrate.

6–94 In *General Electric Co v Deutz AG*,[48] Deutz AG had signed the agreement, agreeing to be bound by specific provisions of that agreement. Those provisions did not include the arbitration clause that provided for ICC arbitration. The District Court decided that the scope of the arbitration agreement was ambiguous and left the matter to the jury. The jury held that there was no arbitration agreement. Deutz AG argued that this decision was clearly wrong based on the evidence (the only way to overturn the jury's finding). The Court of Appeals upheld the jury's finding and commented as follows:

> "although not controlling on us or the District Court, it is interesting that the ICC Panel, applying Swiss law, also held that Deutz was not entitled to arbitration. Focusing first on the provisions listed in Deutz's signature block and the fact that the article establishing arbitration procedures did not mention Deutz, the Panel found the

[47] See Born, *op. cit.*, p.668; Carbonneau, *op. cit.*, p.477; see also Cambria and Yates, "Arbitration v Litigation: Nonsignatories, Parallel Proceedings", New York Law Journal, April 24, 2006; McSherry, Jr., "Arbitrating By And Against Parties Who have not Signed An Arbitration Agreement" (August 2005) The Metropolitan Corporate Counsel; Robert B. Davidson, "Arbitrability and the Non-Signatory", New York Law Journal, June 20, 2005. See also, *Regent Seven Seas Cruises Inc v Rolls Royce Plc*, No.06-22347-CIV; and *Alstom Power Conversion v Radisson Seven Seas (France) SNC*, No.06-22539, SD Fla, (2007) Mealey's IAR Vol.22 No.3 pp.7–8.

[48] *General Electric Co v Deutz AG*, 270 F.3d 144 (3d Cir., 2001); (2002) YBCA Vol.XXVII, p.795.

> contract ambiguous. Swiss law required the Panel to look to the parties' pre-contract history and other relevant circumstances. After considering Deutz's active participation in the negotiations, its refusal to add a reference to Article 7 in the signature block in spite of the attention this portion of the contract received during the final two weeks of negotiations, and the fact that all parties were assisted by lawyers, the Panel held that there was no arbitration agreement between Deutz and General Electric. It also observed that the outcome would not have been different had it adhered to one of the other possibly applicable national laws."

In *International Paper Co v Schwabedissen Maschinen & Anlagen GmbH*,[49] the issue was enforcing an agreement to arbitrate under the Rules. The Court set out the issue (and its conclusion) as follows: **6–95**

> "A buyer became dissatisfied with an industrial saw and brought suit against the manufacturer of the saw on the basis of a contract between the distributor and the manufacturer. The question presented to us is whether an arbitration clause in the distributor-manufacturer contract requires the buyer, a non-signatory to that contract, to arbitrate its claims against the manufacturer. The district court held that it did. Concluding that the buyer cannot sue to enforce the guarantees and warranties of the distributor-manufacturer contract without complying with its arbitration provision, we affirm."

The Court discussed the principles which led it to require International Paper Company (the buyer) to arbitrate the dispute in the following terms: **6–96**

> "Well-established common law principles dictate that in an appropriate case a non-signatory can enforce, or be bound by, an arbitration provision within a contract executed by other parties [. . .]. We further explained that '[t]he same result has been reached under a theory of equitable estoppel. [. . .] Moreover, the Second Circuit recently noted that it had recognized that five theories 'aris[ing] out of common law principles of contract and agency law' could provide a basis 'for binding non-signatories to arbitration agreements: 1) incorporation by references; 2) assumption; 3) agency; 4) veil piercing/alter ego; and 5) estoppel.' *Thomson-CSF, S.A. v American Arbitration Ass'n*, 64 F.3d 773, 776 (2d Cir. 1995) (citing cases) [. . .] We believe that the doctrine of equitable estoppel applies here. Equitable estoppel precludes a party from asserting rights 'he otherwise would have had against another' when his own conduct renders assertion of those rights contrary to equity. [. . .] In the arbitration context, the doctrine recognizes that a party may be estopped from asserting that the lack of his signature on a written contract precludes enforcement of the contract's arbitration clause when he has consistently maintained that other provisions of the same contract should be enforced to benefit him [. . .] Applying these

[49] *International Paper Co v Schwabedissen Maschinen & Anlagen GmbH*, 206 F.3d 411 (4th Cir., 2000).

> principles here we can only conclude that International Paper is estopped from refusing to arbitrate its dispute with Schwabedissen. The Wood-Schwabedissen contract provides part of the factual foundation for every claim asserted by International Paper against Schwabedissen. In its amended complaint, International Paper alleges that Schwabedissen failed to honor the warranties in the Wood-Schwabedissen contract, and it seeks damages, revocation, and rejection 'in accordance with' that contract. International Paper's entire case hinges on its asserted rights under the Wood-Schwabedissen contract; it cannot seek to enforce those contractual rights and avoid the contract's requirement that 'any dispute arising out of' the contract be arbitrated. The district court did not err in so holding." (certain citations omitted).

6–97 In *Regent Seven Seas*,[50] the non-signatories sought to compel a party to arbitrate an agreement on various grounds including estoppel. However, after following the analysis similar to that set out above, the court noted that the claimant in the court proceedings had carefully phrased the state pleadings to avoid relying on the underlying contract with the arbitration agreement. In addition, the court noted that the non-signatories were not parties to the underlying contract with the arbitration agreement. As a result, the claimant was permitted to continue the court proceedings.

6–98 In a recent New York Court of Appeals case, the court reviewed the principles of estoppel stating that: "Under the direct benefits theory of estoppel, a nonsignatory may be compelled to arbitrate where the nonsignatory 'knowingly exploits' the benefits of an agreement containing an arbitration clause and receives benefits flowing directly from the agreement . . .". The court reviewed the cases on direct and indirect benefits and held that the fact that a nonsignatory could not be compelled to arbitrate where the profits from the agreement went to a third party, although the third party was involved at the instigation of the nonsignatory.[51]

England

6–99 In England, in the *Peterson Farms* case, the High Court has rejected the group of companies doctrine and several aspects of the approach taken by the Tribunal in the *Dow Chemical* case.[52] The case concerned annulment proceedings brought in England as the place of arbitration with respect to an ICC Award. The governing law of the underlying contract was the law of Arkansas, but the Tribunal held that the law applicable to the agreement to arbitrate was distinct and depended on the common intent of the parties.

6–100 The Court noted that:

> "The tribunal decided that it had jurisdiction on two bases: i) First, and primarily, by application of what has come to be known as 'the group of companies doctrine'. The 'doctrine' finds its origin in the interim award of an ICC tribunal dated 23 September 1982 in case No 4131 in which

[50] *Regent Seven Seas Cruises, Inc v Rolls Royce*, PLC S.D.Fla., 2007. Slip Copy, 2007 WL 601992 (S.D.Fla.), 20 Fla. L. Weekly Fed. D 535.

[51] *In the matter of Samuel Belzberg* (NY CA October 17, 2013).

[52] See the *Peterson Farms* case, para.4–16 n.16; see also Redfern & Hunter with Blackaby & Partasides, *op. cit.*, para.3–32, p.149.

> the Claimants were a number of companies in the *Dow Chemical*; and ii) Second, on the basis that C&M entered into the Agreement as agent for the other entities in the group who were thus parties to the Agreement and the arbitration clause contained in it."

The Court rejected categorically the Tribunal's approach with respect to the governing law of the arbitration agreement. The Court held that that law was the law of Arkansas, as was the remainder of the contract of which it was part. In so doing, the Court noted: **6–101**

> "There was, therefore, no basis for the tribunal to apply any other law whether supposedly derived from 'the common intent of the parties' or not. The common intent was indeed expressed in the Agreement: that is both English and Arkansas law (paragraph 17 of Mr. Hollingsworth's statement). The 'law' the tribunal derived from its approach was not the proper law of the Agreement nor even the law of the chosen place of the arbitration but, in effect, the group of companies doctrine itself."

The Court went on to state: "In the context of the group of companies doctrine the agreement was that Arkansas law was the same as English law. As I have already said, English law treats the issue as one subject to the chosen proper law of the Agreement and that excludes the doctrine which forms no part of English law." The Court then rejected the agency argument[53] and the estoppel argument.[54] **6–102**

As mentioned above, in *Dallah*, the UK Supreme Court dealt with the enforcement in the United Kingdom of an ICC arbitration award rendered in Paris against the Government of Pakistan. The Government of Pakistan had not signed the arbitration agreement. The UK Supreme Court held that the applicable law was French law as the law of the place of arbitration, analysed the common intention of the parties and concluded that the Government of Pakistan should not be considered as a party to the arbitration agreement.[55] Since the Paris Court of Appeal, applying French law, came to the opposite conclusion, one is left with the impression that it is more difficult to extend an arbitration agreement to a non-signatory under English law than under French law. It is submitted that this is based not solely on legal traditions but on the method of interpreting the common intention of the parties. Moreover, it is, as noted above, subject to exceptions based on traditional legal concepts. For example, the English Courts held **6–103**

[53] The Court noted with respect to agency: "The principles of the law of agency in Arkansas law are also in substance the same as those of English law. The questions whether there is a relationship of principal and agent and whether an agent acted as such are questions of fact. Unsurprisingly, as agency was not alleged or addressed in the evidence before the tribunal, there was no evidence to establish either fact. Indeed the evidence and commercial reality was to the contrary and there is no further evidence on the matter before me".

[54] In this respect, the Court noted: "There was no evidence before the tribunal and there is no evidence before me to establish an estoppel. Further the conclusions I have already reached that the Agreement clearly names the parties to it and that C&M was not acting as an agent in making it are themselves inconsistent with a case that Peterson represented that the Agreement was made with other group entities or that such entities or C&M relied on any representation or suffered any detriment in doing so". The Privy Council annulled an AAA Award joining a non-signatory on the basis that there was no evidence of consent to arbitration. See *Bay Hotel & Resort Ltd and Zurich Indemnity of Canada v Cavalier Construction Co Ltd* UKPC 34 (June 16, 2001).

[55] [2010] UKSC 46.

non-signatory states bound by an arbitration agreement where they were claiming under or with respect to an insurance policy with an arbitration clause.[56]

France

6–104 The Paris Court of Appeal upheld the extension of a contract to the French distributor in a contract between a purchaser and the manufacturer in the *Jaguar* case in the following terms:

> "Whereas Jaguar France, the rights of which have been assumed by the company V2000 which Mr. Philippe Renault claims is his contracting party, has a direct interest in the litigation; although it was not a signatory, it was aware of the contract in dispute and in particular the submission to arbitration of which it claims the benefit and undertook to have the contract translated;
>
> Whereas international arbitration, the effects of the submission agreement extend to the parties directly involved in the performance of the contract provided that their situation and their activities create the presumption that they knew of the existence and the extent of the contract in order that the arbitrator may be seized of all of the economic and legal aspects of the disputes and that in application of this rule, the claim of Jaguar France must be accepted."[57] (Authors' translation).

6–105 The French Supreme Court has broadened its approach with what could be referred to as the "chain of contracts" doctrine in the *ABS* case.[58] The Court described the facts as follows:

> "Considering that, according to the appealed decision (Paris, 3 November 2004), that the French company Alcatel business systems (ABS), a mobile terminal and portable cellular phones manufacturer, and the Belgian company Alcatel micro electronics (AME), both part of the same group, collaborated on the production of a new electronic chip; that AME and the American company Amkor technology Inc (Amkor) entered into an agreement related to the sale of electronic components which contained an arbitration clause referring to the American arbitration association (AAA) of Philadelphia ; that Amkor and the Korean company Anam semiconductor Inc (Anam), which manufactures components, had entered into a [foundry] agreement which contained an arbitration clause referring to the American arbitration association (AAA) of Santa Clara in California; that the chips manufactured by Anam were directly delivered to AME which then 'encapsulated' them and delivered them to ABS; that, following

[56] *The London Steam-Ship Owners' Mutual Insurance Association Ltd v The Kingdom of Spain* [2013] EWHC 3188 (Comm).

[57] Paris Court of Appeals December 7, 1994, (1996) Rev Arb 245, note Jarosson, Cass Civ 1re, May 21, 1997, (1997) Rev Arb. 537; however, the French Supreme Court seems to have taken a more traditional approach. See Cass Civ 1re, June 11, 1991, *Orri v Société des Lubrifiants Elf Aquitaine* (1992) Rev Arb No.1 p.73 (extension of arbitration agreement to an individual based on the argument that it was in essence his alter ego). See Delvolvé, Rouche & Pointon, *op. cit.*, para.126, p.69.

[58] Cass 1re Civ March 27, 2007 (2007) Rev Arb 785, note Al Ahdab.

> problems, ABS and its insurers AGF, which partially indemnified them, brought proceedings before a commercial court for damages against Amkor and its two French subsidiaries, namely Amkor technology euroservices and Amkor Wafer fabrication services, and Anam; that the defendants referred to the arbitration clause and stated that this matter was outside the jurisdiction of national courts." (Authors' translation)

The Court then held that the arbitration clause was passed through with the contracts in the following terms:

> "But considering that in a chain of contracts under which property passes, the arbitration clause is transferred automatically as accessory to the right of action, which is itself accessory of the substantial right transferred, without any consequence as to the homogenous or heterogeneous character of this chain; that the decision states that firstly the litigious electronic component was manufactured and sold by Anam to Amkor which then sold it to AME; further that AME encapsulated the product which, according to the expert witness, remained dissociable, and delivered it to ABS which in turn integrated it into its mobile phones; that consequently, *the court of appeal rightly decided that that there was a chain of contracts under which property passes and correctly deduced that the arbitration clause contained in the agreement between Amkor and AME and to which Anam had adhered, was binding for ABS since this provision is transmitted as an accessory to the right of action, itself accessory to the substantial right transferred*; and for this reason, the court of appeal has legally founded its decision;" (Authors' translation) (emphasis added)

In the *Dallah* case mentioned above, the Claimant, Dallah, sought to enforce the ICC Award rendered in France before the French courts. In a decision dated February 7, 2011, the Paris Court of Appeal upheld the enforcement of the Award based on the alter ego principle. In so doing, the Paris Court of Appeal stated that the involvement of the Ministry of Religious Affairs of the Government of Pakistan in pre-contractual negotiations confirmed that the creation of the trust was a pure formality and the Ministry of Religious Affairs of the Government of Pakistan "as the real Pakistani party during the economic operation". Although literally this could be interpreted as ignoring the form, it is important to note that the Government of Pakistan originally signed the Memorandum of Understanding and was responsible for creating the trust (which ceased to exist). Therefore, the trust could be viewed as the alter ego of the Government of Pakistan.[59] **6–106**

Switzerland

In the *Westland Helicopters* case, an ICC Tribunal held that countries that were shareholders in an entity were bound by the arbitration clause signed by that **6–107**

[59] See the discussion in the Blog of Me. Edouard Bertrand (http://avocats.fr/space/edouard.bertrand/content/6-11-dallah—-l-emergence-de-la-theorie-de-l-alter-ego-en-droit-francais—the-emergence-of-the-alter-ego-doctrine-in-french-law_4AA7332E-BA2B-4F59-B921-CA2997051BF2) last consulted on 13 November 2013.

entity. The Award was annulled since the Swiss Federal Tribunal held that the countries were not bound as they had not signed the arbitration agreement, the entity was separate from the countries, and there was no indication in the entity's statutes that the countries were to be bound by the clause.[60]

6–108 However, Swiss law has evolved since the *Westland* case as is reflected in a 2003 case, where Y, X and Z had signed an agreement with an arbitration clause.[61] The issue was whether a third party, A, was a proper party to the arbitration. A was a majority shareholder of one of the parties and was involved in the performance of the contract. The Federal Court noted that certain commentators applied a literal approach limiting the arbitration clause to the signatories. However, the court distinguished between the existence of a valid arbitration agreement (which must meet the requirements of art.178 (1) of the Swiss PILA) and the extension of a clause meeting those formal requirements to an additional party. The court held that A was subject to the clause due to his involvement in the contract and his management of one of the corporate signatories of the contract. It is noteworthy that the Swiss court upheld the Tribunal's interpretation of Lebanese law and through that law the reliance on French case law to support this argument. In part, this was based on art.17 of the Rules. As a result, the Swiss court did not adopt the French approach as its own, but confirmed that the result would have been the same under Swiss law.

6–109 In *X Ltd v Y & Z SpA*,[62] the Swiss Federal Tribunal upheld an ICC Award holding that the Tribunal had no jurisdiction against a guarantor summarising the situation and then concluding as follows:

> "Pursuant to the principle according to which a contract can only bind the entities which have signed it, the arbitration agreement contained in a contract only binds the signatory to that contract. However, in certain circumstances, such as the transfer of debts, the take-over of debts (whether simple or cumulative) or the transfer of a contractual obligation, the federal Tribunal allows, and has done so for some time, that an arbitration agreement bind persons that have neither signed it nor are mentioned in it (ATF 129 III 727 consid. 5.3.1 p. 735 and the cases quoted). Also, the third party, who interferes in the execution of a contract which contains an arbitration clause, shall be deemed to have adhered to it by its determining actions (ATF 129 III 727 consid. 5.3.2 p. 737; case 4P.48/2005 of 20 September 2005, consid. 3.4.1).
>
> The take-over of external debt causes the transfer of accessory rights, from the debtor to the person taking over the debts, within the meaning of art. 178 al. 1 CO,.[63]

[60] Swiss Supreme Court, July 19, 1988, *Westland Helicopters v AOI* (1991) YBCA Vol.XVI, p.174; (1989) ASA Bull Vol.7 p.63.

[61] Swiss Supreme Court, October 16, 2003, *X. S.A.L, Y S.A.L and A v Z. Sarl*, case No. 4P.115/2003 ATF 129 III 727.

[62] BGE 134 III 565 (4A_128/2008 of August 19, 2008) For unofficial translations and a regular update of Swiss decisions see: http://www.swissarbitrationdecisions.com (last consulted on November 3, 2013).

[63] See also the decision of the Swiss Federal Tribunal of March 8, 2012 (4A_627/2011) annulling a TAS Tribunal Award extending the jurisdiction clause to non signatory hockey clubs on the basis that the relevant agreement neither expressly or implicitly referred to the right of non signatories to claim rights.

> [. . .]
>
> In order to have jurisdiction, the contract of guarantee must include an arbitration clause specifically to that effect, contain sufficient reference to the arbitration clause contained in the main contract or, failing this, the guarantor must, either expressly or by determining actions, which the creditor could interpret in good faith, pursuant to the principle of trust, show its intention to be bound by the arbitration agreement contained in the contract."

Dealing with non-signatories

The approach to non-signatories is coloured, if not dictated, by the national legal system that is applicable to the arbitration agreement, to annulment proceedings and to enforcement. On the facts of many of the cases, the results may well have been similar in the various legal systems. However, the issue for the practitioner is how to argue and decide them in the specific context of an individual arbitration. **6–110**

In an article written before the *Dallah* decisions,[64] a leading authority noted that there were five common scenarios regarding non-signatories stating (with footnotes deleted): **6–111**

> "At least live common scenarios are often present in cases where an arbitrator's analysis leads to joinder of a non-signatory. These might be listed as follows:
>
> (1) non-signatory participation in contract formation;" sometimes linked to confusion created by mention of the non-signatory in contract documents.
> (2) a single contract scheme constituted by multiple documents.
> (3) implied or express acceptance of the arbitration agreement by the non-signatory, whether in the particular arbitration itself or in another forum;
> (4) absence of the signatory corporate personality and
> (5) fraud or fraud-like abuse of the corporate form.
>
> The first three elements relate principally of implied consent, while the last two address the corporate veil."[65]

In this area, the most prudent course is to adopt an approach that is suited in particular to the place of arbitration, as the courts of the place of arbitration deal with the annulment of the Awards. However, the issue is also relevant to enforcement, and the approach may be different from that at the place of arbitration. The English and American cases give strong indication that any attempt to extend a contract to **6–112**

[64] Park, *Non-signatories and International Contracts: Dilemma of the Arbitrator* (Oxford, 2009), p.3-10.

[65] The author then provides in an annex a list of Awards applying the various principles, some of which have been published in full or in extract form. That is very instructive for arbitrators and counsel acting before arbitrators. However, it is submitted that the key issue for enforceability is the court cases and not the Awards which are not always complete, the authors of which are often not identified and which are not frequently cited as authority in state courts.

non-signatories should be grounded on national legal concepts that are applicable to the arbitration, usually by reference to the law governing the underlying agreement. The French cases render reliance on a transnational approach possible. However, they do so in most instances based on an understanding of the "common intent of the parties", which is found in many national legal systems and is reflected in art.4.1 of the UNIDROIT Principles.[66] For the Tribunal, it is important to focus on the evidence before it, in particular with a mind to the courts that may be involved in interpreting it. The English and American concepts, and particularly the concepts of estoppel and agency, have to be based on the evidence. If there is a lack of evidence on these points, then because the national court has the last word on jurisdictional issues, there may be no basis for upholding the Tribunal's findings.

Article 6(6): "Where the parties are notified of the Court's decision pursuant to Article 6(4) that the arbitration cannot proceed in respect of some or all of them, any party retains the right to ask any court having jurisdiction whether or not, and in respect of which of them, there is a binding arbitration agreement."

6–113 There are four possible ICC Court decisions under art.6(4): (i) that the arbitration shall proceed for all claims against all parties; (ii) that the arbitration shall not proceed with respect to any claims or parties; (iii) that the arbitration shall proceed against some but not all parties but with respect to all claims against those parties; (iv) that the arbitration shall proceed against some parties with respect to some claims. In situations (ii) to (iv), there are some claims that will not proceed against some parties. In such cases which amounted to approximately 9 per cent of the cases in 2011,[67] art.6(6) expressly provides that recourse may be had to a court having jurisdiction to determine whether there is a binding arbitration agreement.

6–114 It is relatively rare that the ICC Court decides that prima facie there is no basis on which there may be an ICC arbitration agreement. Since the basic standard is whether the Claimant has an arguable case that there *may* be an agreement for ICC arbitration, usually the ICC Court will leave the matter to the Tribunal. If the ICC Court decides that the arbitration should not proceed, it will not provide reasons for that decision, although art.6, unlike art.11(4), does not state expressly that the reasons for the Court's decisions shall not be communicated to the parties. As noted above, the decisions of the ICC Court are administrative rather than judicial and therefore no reasons are provided.

6–115 If the ICC Court decides that the arbitration should not proceed, the Claimant's sole other avenue of recourse may be to national courts and perhaps to the national courts of the Respondent's place of incorporation. If the Claimant has no confidence in those national courts, the effect of the Court's decision may be to render all practical forms of recourse ineffective. If the Claimant finds new facts and arguments, it may also seek a reconsideration of the ICC Court's decision. However, the ICC Court rarely amends its initial decision, and will generally only do so if material new elements are presented by the parties that were not known to

[66] Article 17(2) also provides: "In all cases the Arbitral Tribunal shall take account of the provisions of the contract and the relevant trade usages". However, although relied upon in *Dow Chemical*, the other cases on non-signatories do not appear to emphasise either aspect of art.17(2).

[67] Fry, Greenberg and Mazza, *op.cit.*, para. 3–218.

the ICC Court at the time it took its decision. New material elements will often be new information for the ICC Court that may lead it to a different conclusion.

Article 6(6) is intended to permit parties to seek a final adjudication of the jurisdictional issue by the Courts. If a binding court order is issued that there is a binding arbitration agreement, then the matter would be res judicata as between the parties and the party asserting the validity of the agreement could bring subsequent proceedings. This is confirmation that the ICC Court decision is an administrative one and is not intended to be final. It is an express acknowledgment that the issue of arbitrability as used in a US context is not intended to be decided by the ICC Court, although, as discussed above, it is intended to be decided by a Tribunal in an ICC arbitration. **6–116**

The possible use of this provision is found in a US case where the ICC Court rendered a partially negative decision with respect to a Respondent. The Claimant then sued the ICC Court in New York to overturn the Article.6(2) decision under the 1998 Rules. After that decision failed, the Claimant brought successful default proceedings in New York to order the Respondent to be joined in the arbitration. The ICC Court then reconsidered its position and ordered the Respondent to be joined.[68] **6–117**

Article 6(7): "Where the Court has decided pursuant to Article 6(4) that the arbitration cannot proceed in respect of any of the claims, such decision shall not prevent a party from reintroducing the same claim at a later date in other proceedings."

Article 6(7) refers to "any of the claims", which should be understood to be any claims against any party. Therefore, if in the context of a particular arbitration, the ICC Court decides that either the matter should not proceed against a particular party ("X") or with respect to a particular claim ("1"), then the party seeking to advance the claim against X or claim 1 can bring the same claim in subsequent ICC or other proceedings depending on the nature of the arbitration clause. However, any such claim would be brought at a subsequent date and therefore may be subject to other limitations arguments for example. **6–118**

Article 6(8): "If any of the parties refuses or fails to take part in the arbitration or any stage thereof, the arbitration shall proceed notwithstanding such refusal or failure."

The failure of a party to participate in an arbitration has no direct effect on the jurisdiction of the Tribunal, and more generally on the arbitration proceedings. Article 6(3) thus confirms the power of the Tribunal to proceed with the arbitration with a defaulting party. It is complemented in this respect by arts 8 and 10 on the constitution of the Tribunal and art.23[69] which provides that the failure of a party to sign the Terms of Reference does not prevent them from entering into force after approval by the ICC Court. **6–119**

The more complex issue, which is discussed under art.25, is how the Tribunal should proceed if a party fails to participate or refuses to participate. The main **6–120**

[68] Fry, Greenberg and Mazza, op.cit., para. 3–273. *Global Mining LLC v Robinson*, 533 F.Supp. 2d 442 (2008 SDNY).

[69] See para.23–72.

point in this respect is that arbitral proceedings do not provide for default Awards. Therefore, even if a party fails to take part in the arbitral procedure, the Tribunal must proceed to determine the facts of the case and give a reasonable opportunity to the defaulting party to participate or to present its case.[70]

Article 6(9): "Unless otherwise agreed, the arbitral tribunal shall not cease to have jurisdiction by reason of any allegation that the contract is non-existent or null and void, provided that the arbitral tribunal upholds the validity of the arbitration agreement. The arbitral tribunal shall continue to have jurisdiction to determine the parties' respective rights and to decide their claims and pleas even though the contract itself may be non-existent or null and void."

In General

6–121 Article 6(4) deals broadly with the principle of autonomy or separability of the arbitration agreement with two separate issues: the autonomous nature of the arbitration agreement and the power of arbitrators to rule on their own jurisdiction ("*Kompetenz-Kompetenz*").[71] Article 6(4) is based on the underlying assumption that the Tribunal may uphold the validity of the arbitration agreement although the underlying contract is null and void. In reaching that decision, the Tribunal may have to deal with the capacity of the parties to enter into an agreement, as further discussed below beginning at para.6–139. Further, although the Tribunal may consider an arbitration agreement to be valid, it may find that the dispute submitted to it is not arbitrable. Arbitrability will therefore be briefly discussed below at para.6–145.

6–122 The basic principle is that the arbitration agreement, even if contained in another broader contract, is an autonomous agreement separate from the main contract in which it is contained. The arbitration agreement is not in any way dependent on the broader agreement. For example, art.16(1) of the UNCITRAL Model Law states:

> "The arbitral tribunal may rule on its own jurisdiction, including any objections with respect to the existence or validity of the arbitration agreement. For that purpose, an arbitration clause, which forms part of a contract, shall be treated as an agreement independent of the other terms of the contract. A decision by the arbitral tribunal that the contract is null and void shall not entail *ipso jure* the invalidity of the arbitration clause."

6–123 Article 6(9) deals with both the procedure and the substance. The first sentence confirms that the Tribunal has authority notwithstanding a claim that the broader contract of which the arbitration agreement is a part is either void or non-existent. It is also accepted that the Tribunal continues to have jurisdiction even if there is a claim that the arbitration agreement itself is void or non-existent provided that, in the end, it upholds the validity of the arbitration agreement.[72]

[70] See paras 23–14, 23–76, 24–13.

[71] See Park, "The Arbitrator's Jurisdiction to Determine Jurisdiction" (2007) *ICCA Congress Series No.13*, pp.55 at 153.

[72] Cass civ 1re, March 13, 2007, *Société Chefaro International BV v Consorts X.*, case No.406, 04-10.970, *http://www.courdecassation.fr/jurisprudence* [accessed November 18, 2013] ; (2007) Rev Arb no.2, p.346 (the mandatory character of art.1504 of the French NCPC which provided for

To uphold the validity of the arbitration agreement, the Tribunal will have to resolve any issues as to the capacity and identity of the parties and the arbitrability of the dispute discussed below.[73] As noted above, the decision of the Tribunal as to jurisdiction under the arbitration agreement is generally subject to review by the national courts of the place of arbitration and/or the place of enforcement of the Award. Therefore, the decision of the Tribunal on such matters is final within the arbitration, but interim within the context of the overall proceedings. **6–124**

Even if the arbitration agreement is valid, the underlying agreement or contract may be held to be invalid. For example, the Tribunal may hold a contract invalid for failure to set a fixed or determinable price. That type of decision would generally be within the purview of the arbitrators alone subject to principles of public policy. Often, when a contract has been terminated, the invalidity of the arbitration agreement is also invoked. In an ICC case, the Tribunal dealt with this point in a rather "classic" fashion: **6–125**

> "The Tribunal also considered [Respondent's] argument, apparently raised in the Guatemalan proceedings that the arbitration clauses did not survive [Claimant's] termination of the Agreements. We cannot accept that argument, however, because it contradicts the well-established doctrine of severability, which provides that an arbitration agreement forming part of another agreement (as in this case) should not be regarded as invalid, non-existent or ineffective because the other agreement has been terminated; rather the arbitration clause is to be treated as a distinct and independent agreement for that purpose (see, for example, article 16(1) of the UNCITRAL Model Law on International Commercial Arbitration adopted on 21 June 1985). This doctrine is embodied in the ICC Rules of Arbitration, art.6(4) [now art.6(9)], which provides expressly that the Tribunal shall continue to have jurisdiction to determine the respective rights of the parties and to adjudicate on their claims and pleas even though the contract itself may be non-existent or null and void."[74]

Usually, one would expect to have jurisdictional issues dealt with first by the Tribunal and then by the national court.[75] There has been a suggestion by one author that this should be part of the negative rule of *Kompetenz-Kompetenz*. That is the national courts should generally refrain from deciding jurisdictional issues until the arbitral tribunal has rendered its decision on the point.[76] The French **6–126**

the different grounds of a challenge of the Award in an international arbitration, could not be eluded by the parties which had foreseen the possibility to make an "appeal" against the Award in the arbitration agreement. In consideration of its autonomy, the arbitration agreement remained valid except the reference to the appeal of the Award which was considered as non-existent, i.e. inapplicable under French law). See also Ortcheidt, "Un nouvel exemple de l'effacement du droit commun des contrats en ce qui concerne les conventions d'arbitrage international" (2007) JCP (E) No.1602 p.23.

73 See paras 6–139 et seq and 6–145 et seq.

74 ICC case No.11761 (2003) (final Award), unreported (arbitration between a US and a Guatemalan party, place of arbitration Paris, p.43).

75 For example a party may seek to annul an interim Award on jurisdiction. See also the discussion at para.22–33 et seq on anti-suit or anti-arbitration injunctions.

76 Gaillard, "L'effet négatif de la compétence-compétence", *op. cit.* para.22–33 et seq. See also Figueroa Valdés, "The Principle Of Kompetenz-Kompetenz In International Commercial Arbitration" (2007) Mealey's IAR Vol.22 No.5 p.29.

Courts, for example, refuse to take jurisdiction in a dispute involving an arbitration agreement so as to allow the Tribunal to proceed with the case unless the arbitration agreement is manifestly null and void[77] or manifestly inapplicable.[78] In some instances, a party may seek to cut short the proceedings by obtaining a court ruling as to jurisdiction. The German Supreme Court has confirmed that under the 1998 German Arbitration Act, a Tribunal had the power to decide upon its own jurisdiction. However, the court held that the ultimate power to decide the Tribunal's jurisdiction was for the courts. The court further held that, where a party challenges the validity of an arbitration agreement, the courts did not have to wait for a determination by the Tribunal, but could decide immediately upon the validity of the arbitration agreement.[79] In other countries, the Respondent in the arbitral proceedings may seek a stay or injunction to prevent the arbitration from proceeding or the Claimant may seek an injunction to enforce the arbitration clause (and thereby may have to decide upon its validity) and to enjoin parallel national proceedings.[80]

6–127 If a party applies to a national court for a ruling on a jurisdictional issue, the general rule is that the Tribunal will continue to have jurisdiction to proceed with the arbitration notwithstanding the national proceedings. This is reflected, for example in the UNCITRAL Model Law.[81] The English Arbitration Act of 1996 adopts this approach with a twist. In s.31 of the Act, the law expressly permits (but does not require) a Tribunal to stay proceedings pending jurisdictional proceedings under s.32 of the Act. That section limits jurisdictional applications to the court without either the consent of the parties or of the Tribunal.[82] Therefore,

[77] Cass Civ 1re, July 11, 2006, *Société National Broadcasting v Bernadaux*, Juris-data No.2006/0334549, (2006) JCP (G) 2006.II.10182, note Callé; Cass Civ 1re, *Copropriété maritime Jules Verne et autre v American Bureau of Shipping et autre (ABS)*, (2006) Rev Arb No.4 p.944, note Gaillard; Cass Civ 1re, June 28, 1989, *Eurodif v République islamique d'Iran*, (1989) Rev Arb No.4 p.653, note Fouchard.

[78] Cass Civ 1re, February 20, 2007, *Société UOP nv v société BP France SA et al*, (2007) Rev Arb 2007 No.4 p.775, note Train (the arbitration agreement providing for two arbitration institutions is not necessarily inapplicable); see also Kaplan, "Simultaneous Choice of Two Arbitration Institutions Not (Immediately) Fatal", Arbitration–France, July 12, 2007, *http://www.internationallawoffice.com* [accessed November 18, 2013]; Cass Civ 1re, July 11, 2006, *SA PT Andhika Lines et al v SA Axa corporate solutions assurance et al* (2007) JDI No.1 p.146, note Sana-Cahillé de Néré, (2007) Rev. Crit. DIP No.1 p.96, note Jault-Seseke. More generally, see Cachard, "Le contrôle de la nullité ou de l'inapplicabilité manifeste de la clause compromissoire" (2006) Rev Arb No.4, p.893; Clay, "Panorama–Arbitrage et modes alternatifs de règlement des litiges" (2006) Dalloz No.44, p.3026, at pp.3028-3029; Loquin, "Chroniques–Tribunaux de commerce et arbitrage" (2006) RTD com No.4, p.760, at p.764; Kaplan, "Supreme Court Steers the Tag Heuer Into International Waters", Arbitration–France, July 20, 2006, *http://www.internationallawoffice.com* [accessed November 18, 2013].

[79] Bundesgerichtshof, January 15, 2005, NJW 16/2005 p.1125.

[80] See *Borden Inc v Meiji Milk Products Co Ltd*, 919 F.2d, 822–829 (2d Cir. 1990) (injunction to enforce arbitration agreement consistent with the New York Convention).

[81] Article 16(3) of the UNCITRAL Model Law.

[82] English Arbitration Act 1996 s.32 provides:

"(1) The court may, on the application of a party to arbitral proceedings (upon notice to the other parties), determine any question as to the substantive jurisdiction of the tribunal. A party may lose the right to object (see section 73).

(2) An application under this section shall not be considered unless–
(a) it is made with the agreement in writing of all the other parties to the proceedings, or
(b) it is made with the permission of the tribunal and the court is satisfied
(i) that the determination of the question is likely to produce substantial savings in costs,
(ii) that the application was made without delay, and
(iii) that there is good reason why the matter should be decided by the court."

in England, it is the Tribunal that decides whether the court should hear the matter at the outset.[83] In France, the courts are only entitled to hear an issue of jurisdiction if the arbitration clause is "manifestly inapplicable" and that term is interpreted restrictively. Following the *Fomento* case,[84] Swiss arbitration law was modified to provide that the Tribunal is entitled to decide upon its own jurisdiction notwithstanding pending state proceedings.[85] The situation in the United States is different as is discussed beginning of para.6–130.

In countries other than the United States, for both parties and the Tribunal, there may be an issue of whether the proceedings should proceed either with respect to jurisdiction or with respect to the merits in the face of a jurisdictional challenge. Practices of Tribunals vary with the circumstances. The relevant circumstances would include the relative strength or weakness of the arbitration agreement and the attack on it; the importance of a rapid decision for one or both the parties and the court which has been seized of the jurisdictional issue and the timing of the court proceedings. The fact that the national laws generally emphasise the role of Tribunals in deciding on their own jurisdiction is a significant factor in encouraging Tribunals to proceed to hear the jurisdictional part of an arbitration. **6–128**

If the Tribunal decides the jurisdictional issue and issues a partial Award, in most countries a party may seek to annul that Award. Article 16(3) of the UNCITRAL Model Law expressly provides for the possibility of continuing the proceedings in such circumstances.[86] Pending those annulment proceedings, the Tribunal may generally proceed with the merits. Whether the Tribunal does proceed on the merits should depend in first instance on the parties. If the parties agree that the national courts should first decide the jurisdictional issue, then the matter should be left to the national courts. More frequently, however, the parties do not agree and the party asserting that the Tribunal has jurisdiction wishes to proceed. Since the basic principle is that it is for the Tribunal to decide the jurisdictional issue in first instance, many Tribunals do proceed to hear the merits notwithstanding a jurisdictional challenge before the courts. **6–129**

The United States

In the United States the prevailing view is that an arbitration may be stayed pending resolution of certain "threshold issues" with respect to jurisdiction. **6–130**

[83] The factors cited above show a certain realism and practicality with respect to the jurisdictional issue. In fact, if the arbitration agreement presents difficult issues and the proceedings would be expensive then the Tribunal can refer the matter to the court without rendering a decision on jurisdiction.

[84] See also the discussion at para.22–25f.

[85] Article 186(1) of the Swiss PILA was amended to include 1 bis and now reads as follows: "The arbitral tribunal shall itself decide on its jurisdiction. 1 bis. It shall decide on its jurisdiction notwithstanding an action on the same matter between the same parties already pending before a State Court or another arbitral tribunal, unless there are serious reasons to stay the proceedings". See Pt III App.7.

[86] Article 16(3) of the UNCITRAL Model Law provides: "(3) The arbitral tribunal may rule on a plea referred to in paragraph (2) of this article [regarding jurisdiction] either as a preliminary question or in an award on the merits. If the arbitral tribunal rules as a preliminary question that it has jurisdiction, any party may request, within thirty days after having received notice of that ruling, the court specified in article 6 to decide the matter, which decision shall be subject to no appeal; while such a request is pending, the arbitral tribunal may continue the arbitral proceedings and make an award".

Although the New York Convention is applicable in the United States, the case law appears to have been influenced by art.4 of the Federal Arbitration Act, which provides in part that "The court shall hear the parties, and upon being satisfied that the making of the agreement for arbitration or the failure to comply therewith is not in issue, the court shall make an order directing the parties to proceed to arbitration in accordance with the terms of the agreement".

6–131 The reference to the "making of the agreement for arbitration" has resulted in a distinction being drawn between the issue of the scope of the arbitration clause (which is left to the Tribunal in first instance) and "threshold questions" relating to the existence of an arbitration agreement, whether a party is bound by it or whether the subject matter is arbitrable.

6–132 This principle is set out in various US Supreme Court cases and was applied in the context of an ICC arbitration in *Microchip Tech Inc v US Philips Corp*.[87] In that case, the issue was whether a party was bound by an arbitration agreement as a successor to the signatory. The Court of Appeals for the Federal Circuit held that "[i]n *John Wiley & Sons, Inc. v Livingston*, 376 U.S. 543 (1964), the Supreme Court held that the question of whether a party is bound by an agreement containing an arbitration provision is a 'threshold question' for the court to decide". In addition, the court held that the issue of whether the agreement had expired was also a "threshold issue" stating: "Just as the question of whether an agreement to arbitrate exists between the parties is for judicial resolution, we conclude that under the Supreme Court's precedent the question of whether an arbitration agreement has expired is for the court to decide, even if this requires interpretation of the language of the agreement". Therefore, the Federal Circuit upheld the lower court's refusal to order the parties to arbitrate. The Second Circuit came to the opposite conclusion in *Contec Corp v Remote Solution Co*, 398 F.3d 205 (2d Cir. 2005). The Second Circuit distinguished *Microchip Tech* based on the fact that the non-signatory was seeking to enforce the arbitration agreement against a signatory. However, it acknowledged that this distinction was viewed as irrelevant in *Microchip Tech.* The decision in *Contec* has itself been distinguished in some US cases. As a result there is a split between the US Courts of Appeals in different Circuits and it is important to review the case law of the relevant Circuit with respect to this issue.

6–133 "Threshold issues" generally include issues that relate to whether the parties are bound by an arbitration agreement and whether issues are arbitrable. US courts generally decide such issues as well. However, parties may agree that the issue of arbitrability is to be decided by the Tribunal in their arbitration agreement or by accepting specific rules of arbitration. In *Shaw Group Inc, Stone and Webstar Inc Stone & Webster Asia Inc v Triplefine International Corp*,[88] the US Second Circuit

[87] *Microchip Tech Inc v US Philips Corp*, 367 F.3d 1350 (Fed. Cir., 2004).

[88] *Shaw Group Inc, Stone and Webstar Inc Stone & Webster Asia Inc v Triplefine International Corp*, 322 F.3d 115 (2d Cir., 2003). The arbitration clause provided: "All disputes between you [Triplefine] and us [Stone & Webster] concerning or arising out of this Agreement shall be referred to arbitration to the International Chamber of Commerce, New York, New York, in accordance with the rules and procedures of International Arbitration. This Agreement and the rights and obligations of the parties shall be construed in accordance with and governed by the laws of New York".

Court of Appeals held that it was for an ICC Tribunal to decide arbitrability, in the following terms:

> "In sum, because the parties' arbitration agreement is broadly worded to require the submission of 'all disputes' concerning the Representation Agreement to arbitration, and because it provides for arbitration to be conducted under the rules of the ICC, which assign the arbitrator initial responsibility to determine issues of arbitrability, we conclude that the agreement clearly and unmistakably evidences the parties' intent to arbitrate questions of arbitrability. We hold that Triplefine should not have been enjoined from pursuing its amended arbitration claim for breach of contract against Stone & Webster. Rather, the district court should have deferred to the arbitrator on the parties' dispute about the arbitrability of that claim."

In 2006, the US Supreme Court rendered the decision of *Buckeye Check Cashing v Cardegna*.[89] In that decision, the court held that issues as to the validity of the overall contract as well as to the validity of the arbitration agreement are to be left to the arbitrator in the first instance, whether or not the argument was that the contract was void or voidable. The US Supreme Court left undecided whether the issues of assent should be left to the arbitrators as well, thus leaving open a possible change in approach with regard to "threshold issues". In 2008 the US Supreme Court rendered the *Preston* decision which confirmed its approach in the *Buckeye* case, in the context of administration proceedings. As a result the scope for threshold issues has been reduced.[90] **6–134**

In *Oxford Health Plans LLC v Sutter*, the US Supreme Court was called upon to deal with whether an arbitration clause permitted class action arbitration. The arbitrator had held that it did. The US Supreme Court held that it was not for the courts to reconsider the arbitrator's interpretation of the arbitration clause. Provided that the arbitrator was construing the arbitration clause he was not exceeding his jurisdiction. Therefore, the potential for US court review of even the interpretation of the jurisdictional clause is limited.[91] **6–135**

A particularity with respect to "threshold issues" under US arbitration law is that, if they are to be subject to a decision of the courts, they are subject to a jury trial.[92] For the non-American practitioner, the time required for these proceedings, **6–136**

[89] *Buckeye Check Cashing v Cardegna*, 126 S.Ct. 1204 (2006); (2006) ASA Bull Vol.24 No.2 p.374; Sheppard, "The Moth, the Light and the United States' Severability Doctrine. The Decision of the Supreme Court in *Buckeye Cashing, Inc v Cardegna*" (2006) J Int'l Arb Vol.23 No.5, p.49.

[90] *Preston v Ferrer*, No.06-1463.

[91] *Oxford Health Plans LLC v Sutter*, 133 S.Ct. 2064. The Court stated (footnotes deleted): "In sum, Oxford chose arbitration, and it must now live with that choice. Oxford agreed with Sutter that an arbitrator should determine what their contract meant, including whether its terms approved class arbitration. The arbitrator did what the parties requested: He provided an interpretation of the contract resolving that disputed issue. His interpretation went against Oxford, maybe mistakenly. But still, Oxford does not get to rerun the matter in a court. Under §10(a)(4), the question for a judge is not whether the arbitrator construed the parties' contract correctly, but whether he construed it at all. Because he did, and therefore did not 'exceed his powers,' we cannot give Oxford the relief it wants. We accordingly affirm the judgment of the Court of Appeals".

[92] Article 4 of the US Federal Arbitration Act provides in its relevant part: "A party aggrieved by the alleged failure, neglect, or refusal of another to arbitrate under a written agreement for arbitration

as well as the role of the jury in deciding the factual issues, is often a matter of concern.[93] Finally, as with most US proceedings, the "threshold issues" may be the subject of documentary and deposition discovery. The discovery should relate to the "threshold issue" to be decided by the court. However, despite the sensitivity of most US courts as to the permissible scope of that discovery, it may result in the disclosure of information that would not normally be the subject of disclosure in international arbitration.

Capacity and Arbitrability

6–137 Articles 1(1) and 6 presuppose that the parties have entered into a valid and binding agreement to arbitrate disputes under the Rules. To be valid and binding, the parties must have had the capacity to enter into the agreement and the subject matter must be arbitrable under the relevant national law. This is also reflected in art.V of the New York Convention. This Article permits the courts of signatory states to refuse to enforce an Award if "the parties to the agreement referred to in Article II [of the Convention] were, under the law applicable to them, under some incapacity, or the said agreement is not valid under the law to which the parties have subjected it or, failing any indication thereon, under the law of the country where the award was made".

6–138 Article V of the New York Convention raises three issues: capacity of the parties, arbitrability under the law governing the arbitration and arbitrability under the law of the place of arbitration (i.e. the place where the Award is made).

Capacity of the parties

6–139 The issue of the capacity of the parties relates strictly speaking to whether it is possible in accordance with applicable law for the party to agree to arbitration. In many cases there is a related issue of whether the person who actually signed the agreement to arbitrate was authorised to do so.

may petition any United States district court which, save for such agreement, would have jurisdiction under Title 28, in a civil action or in admiralty of the subject matter of a suit arising out of the controversy between the parties, for an order directing that such arbitration proceed in the manner provided for in such agreement. [. . .] The court shall hear the parties, and upon being satisfied that the making of the agreement for arbitration or the failure to comply therewith is not in issue, the court shall make an order directing the parties to proceed to arbitration in accordance with the terms of the agreement. The hearing and proceedings, under such agreement, shall be within the district in which the petition for an order directing such arbitration is filed. If the making of the arbitration agreement or the failure, neglect, or refusal to perform the same be in issue, the court shall proceed summarily to the trial thereof. If no jury trial be demanded by the party alleged to be in default, or if the matter in dispute is within admiralty jurisdiction, the court shall hear and determine such issue. Where such an issue is raised, the party alleged to be in default may, except in cases of admiralty, on or before the return day of the notice of application, demand a jury trial of such issue, and upon such demand the court shall make an order referring the issue or issues to a jury in the manner provided by the Federal Rules of Civil Procedure, or may specially call a jury for that purpose. If the jury finds that no agreement in writing for arbitration was made or that there is no default in proceeding thereunder, the proceeding shall be dismissed. If the jury finds that an agreement for arbitration was made in writing and that there is a default in proceeding thereunder, the court shall make an order summarily directing the parties to proceed with the arbitration in accordance with the terms thereof".

[93] For example, the issue of whether a parent company was bound by an arbitration clause was decided by the jury in the case under appeal in *General Electric Co v Deutz AG*, see above para.6–94.

The capacity of individuals is generally subject to the law of their domicile or residence or in some instances the law of the place where the contract was concluded.[94] In common law countries, there is generally no restriction as to the capacity of individuals to agree to arbitration (although, as discussed below, certain matters are not arbitrable). In civil law countries, a distinction is sometimes drawn between the capacity of merchants to agree to arbitration and the capacity of non-merchants. However, in the context of international arbitration, this distinction appears to have less force.[95] **6–140**

The capacity of corporate entities is generally subject to the law of their place of incorporation. In some jurisdictions, such as Delaware, corporations are expressly authorised to accept arbitration.[96] In other jurisdictions, it is implied from the general corporate powers. **6–141**

As regards the proper signatories, in the European Union, the legal representatives of a company can be found in the Commercial or Companies Registry. The Commercial Registry also indicates whether one or two signatures are required to bind the company.[97] In the United States, the general rule is that companies are managed by or under the direction of a board of directors.[98] The by-laws generally provide for various officers, including a president. Usually, authority to represent a US corporation is proven by submitting an officer's certificate attaching the resolution electing the officer and confirming the authority of the officer under the by-laws. Often, specific transactions including those subject to arbitration are the subject of board resolutions and opinions of outside law firms when they are entered into. **6–142**

The capacity of government entities is generally subject to the law of their country of origin as is the procedure for approving the appropriate signatory. However, this is subject to an important caveat where a government entity has specifically agreed to ICC arbitration and then seeks to avoid it by relying on its **6–143**

[94] The EU Treaty of Rome on applicable law is not applicable as such to arbitration agreements. However, art.11 of the Treaty reflects a more general principle by stating: "In a contract concluded between persons who are in the same country, a natural person who would have capacity under the law of that country may invoke his incapacity resulting from another law only if the other party to the contract was aware of this incapacity at the time of the conclusion of the contract or was not aware thereof as a result of negligence". This provision avoids the concept of domicile and residence and focuses solely on the place where the contract is entered into.

[95] Under French law, in international arbitration, the distinction is not relevant. However, art.2061 of the French Civil Code as amended by the law of May 15, 2001, provides that "subject to specific legislative provisions, arbitration clauses are valid in contracts entered into by reason of a professional activity". As noted by Mourre, "L'impact de la réforme de la clause compromissoire sur les litiges relatifs aux sociétés" in *Les Cahiers de l'Arbitrage, Volume II, op. cit.*, p.125, this text is particular not only in generally permitting arbitration clauses but also in that art.2061 bases the validity of the clause on the nature of the activity for which it was entered into and not the professional qualification of the contracting parties (whether "commerçants" or not). Therefore, even in French domestic law, the distinction seems to be disappearing.

[96] Delaware General Corporation Law, Title 8, Subchapter II, p.122.

[97] This was required by EU Directive 68/151, the First Directive of March 9, 1968, as amended.

[98] In the United States, companies are referred to as corporations and are incorporated under state corporation law statutes. Section 141 of the Delaware General Corporation Law provides for example that "The business and affairs of every corporation organized under this chapter shall be managed by or under the direction of a board of directors, except as may be otherwise provided in this chapter or in its certificate of incorporation". The board of directors elects the President and the other officers of the corporation.

national legislation. Some authors maintain that it is contrary to good faith to permit the government entity to invoke such an argument. In essence, by entering into and participating in the performance of a contract with an arbitration clause, the government entity is implicitly representing that it has the capacity to agree to the clause. Therefore, to argue to the contrary in arbitral proceedings, may well be contrary to basic principles of good faith.[99] In 2006, the English Court of Appeal dismissed the appeal of the Government of Lithuania against a decision that a Danish Arbitration Award could be enforced against it in the English Court and based its argument on amenability rather than good faith. It held, in particular, that "if a State has agreed to submit to arbitration, it has rendered itself amenable to such process as may be necessary to render the arbitration effective".[100] In making this analysis, however, one should not lose sight of the fact that the public and quasi-public entities come largely from certain parts of the world and therefore there is sometimes a concern that this approach reflects a bias to countries whose public and quasi-public entities do not use ICC (or other international) arbitration.[101] National courts in some countries have a similar tendency, albeit not based on good faith. For example, the French Supreme Court has held that legal incapacity of French state-owned entities to submit to arbitration is inapplicable in the context of international contracts.[102] In Switzerland, art.177(2) of the Swiss PILA

[99] UNCITRAL Final Award, May 4, 1999, *Himpurna California Energy Ltd v t PT (Persero) Perusahaan Listruik Negara* (2000) YBCA Vol.XXV p.11; (1999) Mealey's IAR Vol.144 $EO 12: "PLN [the government entity] requested that even if the arbitral tribunal did not uphold its defenses to the claims of contractual breach, PLN would be entitled to have the ESC [relevant] agreement declared invalid due to non-compliance with mandatory provisions of Indonesian law. PLN's arguments here are unattractive. They amount to saying that the Indonesian officials, acting with actual or at least apparent, authority entered into agreements with a foreign investor that were illegal or otherwise invalid as a matter of Indonesian law. Precedents in the field of international arbitration show that such arguments are most often raised by States or State entities in the wake of important economic or political events which have resulted in major policy changes, and indeed replacement of high officials. The fact that new directions are pursued in such a context is natural enough, and do not per se rule out arguments of illegality or other invalidity. On the other hand, they must be treated with great circumspection. It is contrary to all experience that a State-owned institution [. . .], whose director is appointed directly by the Head of State, engages in activities contrary to the mandatory laws of that country".

[100] *Svenska Petroleum Exploration AB v (1) Government of the Republic of Lithuania (2) Ab Geonafta* [2006] EWCA Civ 1529. With respect to sovereign immunity in general see *NML Capital Ltd v Argentina* [2011] UKSC 31 (July 6, 2011).

[101] In 2012, 75 new cases, i.e. 9.9 per cent of all new cases involved a State or a State-Entity, with a total number of 85 cases involving States or State-Entities. A sharp increase of Latin Amercian States and State-Entities ICC arbitration has been observed,(2013) ICC ICArb Bull Vol.24 No.1, p.10.

[102] Cass Civ 1re, May 2, 1966, *Trésor Public v Galakis* (1966) JDI p.648, note Level; (1967) Rev crit DIP p.553, note Goldman; (1966) Dalloz p.575, note Robert; See also Battifol, "Arbitration Clauses Concluded between French Government-Owned Enterprises and Foreign Private Parties" (1968) 7 Colum J. Transnat'l L 32; see also examples in Tunisian case law, TGI Tunis, March 22, 1976, *Société Tunisienne d'Electricité et de gaz (STEG) v Société Entrepose*, (1978) YBCA Vol.III p.283; (1976) Rev Arb No.4 p.268; Court of First Instance (October 17, 1987) and Court of Appeal of Tunis (February 1, 1988), *BEG-GTAF v State of Tunisia*, (1988) Rev Arb No.4 p.732, note Mechri; more generally, see Annacker and Greig, "State Immunity and Arbitration" (2004) ICC ICArb Bull Vol.15 No.2, p.70; Silva Romero, "The Dialectic of International Arbitration Involving State Parties, Observations on the Applicable Law in State Contract Arbitration" (2004) ICC ICArb Bull Vol.15 No.2, p.79; Leboulanger, "Some Issues in ICC Awards relating to State Contracts" (2004) ICC ICArb Bull Vol.15 No.2, p.93; Extracts from ICC Arbitral Awards relating to State Contracts (2004) ICC ICArb Bull Vol.15 No.2, p.102 (especially Partial Award No.6474 (1992) and Final Award No.10157 (2000) regarding the capacity of a State to submit disputes to

provides that "[a] State, or an enterprise held by, or an organisation controlled by a State, which is party to an arbitration agreement, cannot invoke its own law in order to contest its capacity to arbitrate or the arbitrability of a dispute covered by the arbitration agreement".[103]

The issue of "apparent authority" often arises in arbitration, whether in relation to individuals, companies or government entities.[104] In common law countries, the principle is well accepted, in part in all likelihood because of the absence of the equivalent of a Commercial Registry. However, the trend may be to unification. The UNIDROIT Principles provide for apparent authority in art.2.2.5(2). According to that Article, "where the principal causes the third party reasonably to believe that the agent has authority to act on behalf of the principal and that the agent is acting within the scope of that authority, the principal may not invoke against the third party the lack of authority of the agent". This principle would appear to be applicable for all parties with respect to arbitration. **6–144**

Whether the subject matter is arbitrable[105]

National laws determine the matters that are subject to arbitration.[106] Article V(1) of the New York Convention reflects this basic principle, as it refers to arbitrability of the law governing the arbitration and the law of the place of arbitration. In enforcement of an Award, arbitrability under the law of the place of enforcement will also be relevant under art.V(2) of the New York Convention.[107] **6–145**

National laws vary as to matters that may be the subject to arbitration although there is a trend towards broadening the scope of arbitration. The general principle, **6–146**

arbitration); Grigera Naón, "Les contrats d'Etat: Quelques Réflexions" (2003) Rev Arb No.3, p.667; Silva Romero, "ICC Arbitration and State Contracts" (2002) ICC ICArb Bull Vol.13 No.1, p.35; Paulsson, "May a State Invoke its Internal Law to Repudiate Consent to International Commercial Arbitration?" (1986) Arb Int Vol.2 No.2, p.90. See also Paris, December 17, 1991, *Société Gatoil v National Iranian Oil Company* (1993) Rev Arb No.2, p.281, note Synvet.

103 See Pt III App.7; see also ICC case No.10947 (2002) (Interim Award), (2004) ASA Bull Vol.22 No.2 p.308. Briner, "Article 177" in *International Arbitration in Switzerland–An Introduction to and a Commentary on Articles 176-194 of the Swiss Private International Law Statute, op. cit.*, paras 21–18.

104 As it did in the *Himpurna* cases, see above, para.6–143 n.99.

105 Arbitrable is used in this instance with its meaning outside the US (where it encompasses the ability to arbitrate and whether the arbitration is within the scope of the arbitration agreement).

106 Baron and Liniger, "A Second Look at Arbitrability, Approaches in the United States, Switzerland and Germany" (2003) Arb Int Vol.19 No.1, p.27. For a comparative perspective, see for *France*, Delvolvé, Rouche & Pointon, *op. cit.*, para.62, p.38; for *England*, see Sutton, Gill & Gearing, *op. cit.*, para.1–033, p.14 and Maxwell, "England", in *Practitioner's Handbook on International Arbitration*, para.29, p.600.

107 Article V(2) of the New York Convention: "2. Recognition and enforcement of an arbitral award may also be refused if the competent authority in the country where recognition and enforcement is sought finds that: (a) The subject matter of the difference is not capable of settlement by arbitration under the law of that country; or (b) The recognition or enforcement of the award would be contrary to the public policy of that country". For an illustration, see the decisions of the Belgian Supreme Court in *Van Hopplynus Instruments v Coherent Inc*, November 16, 2006, case No.C020445F and *Colvi v Interdica*, October 15, 2004. According to the Belgian Supreme Court, the state court can apply its own law, i.e. lex fori, to decide whether the dispute is arbitrable and must be referred to arbitration. Distribution and agency agreements may give rise to issues of arbitrability. As regards Belgian distribution agreements, see Minjauw, "The Relationship Between the Belgian 1961 Act on the Termination of Exclusive Distributions Agreements and Arbitration" (2007) RDAI/IBLJ No.1, p.3; Verbist, "Arbitrability of Exclusive Distributorship Agreements in Belgium: Lex Fori (and Lex Contractus)?" (2005) J Int'l Arb Vol.22 No.5, p.427.

as reflected for example in the UNCITRAL Model Law, is that agreements for international commercial arbitration are valid.[108] But the Model Law also states that it "shall not affect any other law of this State by virtue of which certain disputes may not be submitted to arbitration or may be submitted to arbitration only according to provisions other than those of this Law".

6–147 In the United States of America, art.6(a) of the Uniform Arbitration Act of 2000 (which is not generally applicable to international arbitration but indicates the US approach) provides that "[a]n agreement contained in a record to submit to arbitration any existing or subsequent controversy arising between the parties to the agreement is valid, enforceable, and irrevocable except upon a ground that exists at law or in equity for the revocation of a contract".

6–148 In either situation, the basic principle is that agreements to arbitrate are valid subject to statutory exceptions. The issue is what those exceptions are and when they are applicable. Set out below are several common issues and a summary of the situation as to arbitrability with respect to each according to the nature of the agreement and the nature of the claim.

(i) Shareholder agreements

6–149 There appears to be no issue as to arbitrability as to shareholder agreements in most jurisdictions and there is no reason why they cannot be submitted to arbitration under the Rules.[109]

6–150 A closely related issue is that of shareholder rights in general and in particular shareholder rights by statute. These statutory rights provide for recourse to national courts to decide on remedies such as winding up and these appear to remain with the courts to the extent that they affect third parties. As regards other statutory rights the issue will usually depend on the interpretation of the relevant clause.[110] In a recent unreported ICC case, for example, the Tribunal held that it had jurisdiction to decide whether a party was entitled to certain statutory remedies based on oppression.

(ii) Employment agreements

6–151 In addition, there are frequently issues in Europe as to arbitrability of employment agreements. The French courts have upheld such agreements in the

[108] Article 1(1) of the UNCITRAL Model Law: "This Law applies to international commercial arbitration, subject to any agreement in force between this State and any other State or States". "Commercial" is defined broadly as is "international" but the essence is that the law is not intended to cover domestic arbitrations.

[109] The Bank for International Settlements Case provides an interesting illustration of an arbitration of a shareholder dispute where no national companies law was applicable (although not in the context of an ICC arbitration); see the Final Award of September 19, 2003 in the *Reineccius* case (2003) YBCA, Vol. XXVIII, p.100.

[110] For a discussion see In the matter of *James E McCabe Ltd* (2000) NICh 4 (April 14, 2000) where the court stated with respect to whether the statutory remedy of winding up was covered by the arbitration clause: "It would require very clear and specific words for the parties to be held to have agreed that a party should be debarred from pursuing a statutory remedy, assuming, without deciding, that a shareholder can contract out of the right to pursue such statutory remedies." See also *Fulham Football Club (1987) Ltd v Sir David Richards* [2011] EWCA Civ 855.
("96. . . .But the fact that a statutory power, which a court would not have at common law apart from the statutory provision, is given to the court does not mean that an arbitrator, to whom a dispute is properly agreed to be referred, does not have a similar power.")

international context, although the willingness to accept such agreements will presumably be affected by the position of the employee.[111] It may not be viewed as a matter of public policy that senior management be entitled to use the national courts. However, other employees of a lower income level may be deemed to require more protection.

In the United States, employment claims can be made subject to arbitration as a general rule, as was upheld in the *Circuit City Stores Inc v Adams* case.[112] However, as the Supreme Court noted in *Gilmer v Interstate/Johnson Lane Corp*, 500 US 20, 26 (1991), "[b]y agreeing to arbitrate a statutory claim, [an employee] does not forgo the substantive rights afforded by the statute; [he] only submits to their resolution in an arbitral, rather than a judicial forum". Therefore, the agreement to arbitrate an employment agreement in the United States may be struck down if it limits the remedies of the employee or is otherwise unconscionable.[113] **6–152**

(iii) Consumer agreements

As noted above, the Rules were not intended to cover agreements with consumers. Indeed, in the *Gateway* case, the court indicated that an ICC arbitration clause may be unenforceable as unconscionable due to cost under the Uniform Commercial Code. Analogous principles may be applicable in the EU.[114] However, the basic aim of the Rules is to cover business disputes and not consumer disputes. **6–153**

(iv) Agreements with public entities

Issues of arbitrability can also arise when disputes involve administrative, public or state contracts. This issue should be distinguished from the question whether one party to the agreement is a state or a public body and therefore has the capacity to enter into an arbitration agreement.[115] The issue is rather whether a contract or a decision, which is of public or administrative nature, is arbitrable. **6–154**

For example, in many Latin American countries, an administrative contract, e.g. a contract entered into by a public entity in a public capacity, can only be submitted to arbitration, if the law applicable to the contract is public, administrative or **6–155**

[111] For a comparative analysis between French and US systems, see Courtois-Champenois, "L'arbitrage des litiges en droit du travail: à la redécouverte d'une institution française en disgrâce. Etude comparative des droit français et américain" (2003) Rev Arb No.2, p.349; see also Webster, "Terms of Reference and French Annulment Proceedings" (2003) J Int'l Arb Vol.20 No.6, p.561; Grenoble, September 13, 1993, *SA CFTE v Jacques Dechavanne* (1995) YBCA Vol.XX p.656; (1994) Rev Arb No.2 p.337, note Moreau (the Court of Appeal held that an arbitration clause in an international employment agreement was valid); Aubert, "L'arbitrage en droit du travail" (2000) ASA Bull Vol.18 No.1, p.2; Paulsson, "Arbitration Unbound" (1981) Int'l Comp Law Quart, p.358 at p.369.

[112] See *Circuit City Stores Inc v Adams*, (99–1379) 532 US 105 (2001) 194 F.3d 1070, reversed and remanded; see also (2001) ASA Bull Vol.19 No.3 p.582.

[113] See *Circuit City Stores Inc v Saint Clair Adams*, 4-2-2002 F.App. (9th Cir.).

[114] In France, see Delvolvé, Rouche & Pointon, *op. cit.*, No.83, pp.49–50. The authors submit that "arbitration clauses are not prohibited as matter of principle in consumer contracts, but may be declared 'unfair' depending on the circumstances in each case. This opinion, however, is a matter of debate".

[115] See Slim, "Les contrats d'Etat et les spécificités des systèmes juridiques dualistes" (2003) Rev Arb No.3, p.691 at p.694, where the author explains that some countries which used to argue that public entities did not have the capacity to enter into arbitration agreements in order to deny the reference to arbitration, now argue that public contracts are not arbitrable.

constitutional law.[116] Colombian law for example does not restrict public entities from entering into arbitration agreements but prohibits the reference to arbitration of disputes arising from an administrative decision issued by a public law entity.[117]

6–156 In other countries, although contracts of administrative nature are considered as non-arbitrable, the frequent recourse of public entities to certain types of contracts, such as concession agreements or construction contracts, has led the legislator to enact laws explicitly authorising public entities to insert arbitration clauses in these contracts. This is the case for example in France for Public-Private Partnerships[118] or in Egypt and Lebanon for Build, Operate and Transfer (BOT) contracts.[119]

6–157 When issues involving public or administrative contracts are arbitrable, the law applicable to the arbitration usually is the public or administrative law of the State, whose entity or organ is a party to the agreement.[120] However, some authors consider that international law or international legal principles should also be applied to such contracts although the authors question the application of public international law to commercial transactions.[121]

(v) Antitrust/Competition claims

6–158 During the course of an arbitration, various claims may be made, including claims that there has been a breach of antitrust or competition law. Following the *Mitsubishi* case,[122] these claims may be subject to arbitration under US law. It is submitted that a similar situation would occur with respect to competition law claims in the EU.[123] The practical difficulty with respect to such claims may in

[116] Grigera Naón, "Les contrats d'Etat: Quelques Réflexions", *op. cit.*, para.6–143 n.102; Silva Romero, "ICC Arbitration and State Contracts", *op. cit.*, para.6–143 n.102, at p.40; the same applies under Algerian, Tunisian or Mauritanian law: Slim, "Les contrats d'Etat et les spécificités des systhèmes juridiques dualistes", *op. cit.*, at p.696. More generally on the situation in Latin America, see Kleinheisterkamp, *International Commercial Arbitration in Latin America* (Oceana Publication, Inc., 2005).

[117] Silva Romero, "ICC Arbitration and State Contracts", *op. cit.*, para.6–143 n.102, at p.39.

[118] Heitzmann, "The Contract de Partenariat: A new form of French Public Private Partnership" (2006) ICLR Vol.23 Pt 1, p.2; Audit, "Le contrat de partenariat ou l'essor de l'arbitrage en matière administrative" (2004) Rev Arb No.3, p.541; Delelis, "Partenariats public-private" in JurisClasseur Administratif (LexisNexis, 2005) Fasc. 670, para.81 p.11; CE October 29, 2004, *Monsieur Sueur et autres*, (2005) Rev Arb No.1 p.134, note Foussard.

[119] Slim, *op. cit.*, at p.698 and p.700 respectively.

[120] See for example ICC case No.8646, where the Tribunal considered that the contract was of administrative nature and therefore applied the State party's administrative law, *op. cit.* ICC ICArb Bull Vol.15 No.2, p.109.

[121] Leben, "L'évolution de la notion de contrat d'Etat" (2003) Rev Arb No.3, p.629 at p.637; Bernardini, "International Arbitration and A-National Rules of Law" (2004) ICC ICArb Bull Vol.15 No.2, p.58; Silva Romero, "The Dialectic of International Arbitration Involving State Parties, Observations on the Applicable Law in State Contract Arbitration", *op. cit.*, at p.134; Leboulanger, "Some Issues in ICC Awards relating to State Contracts" (2004), p.93.

[122] See para.6–80; see also Jarvin, "Arbitrability of Anti-Trust Disputes: The Mitsubishi v Soler Case" (1985) J Int'l Arb Vol.2 No.3, p.69; Smit, "Mitsubishi: It is Not What it Seems To Be" (1987) J Int'l Arb Vol 4 No.3, p.7; Liebscher, "Arbitration and EC Competition Law–The New Competition Regulation: Back to Square One?" (2003) IntlALR Vol.6 No.3, p.84; Fouchard, "Arbitrage et Faillite" (1998) Rev Arb No.3, p.471; Simont, "L'arbitrage et droit de la concurrence: quelques réflexions d'un arbitre" (1998) RDAI/IBLJ No.4/5, p.547.

[123] Dolmans and Grierson, "Arbitration and the Modernization of EC Antitrust Law: New Opportunities and New Responsibilities" (2003) ICC ICArb Bull Vol.14 No.2, p.37; Extracts from ICC Arbitral Awards relating to European Community Competition Law (2003) ICC ICArb Bull Vol.14 No.2, p.53; Ch.IV, "Arbitrage et droit de la concurrence" in *Les Cahiers de l'Arbitrage Volume II, op. cit.*,

fact relate not to arbitrability, but to the enforceability of an Award that does not take these matters into account. This subject is discussed in more detail under art.33 below.

(vi) Intellectual property claims

Many contracts submitted to ICC arbitration involve issues of intellectual property rights, be it the use of trademarks in distributorship agreements, the license to manufacture industrial equipment or pharmaceutical products based on patent and know-how rights, or the termination of a contract for the licensing of patents. It is widely accepted that the contractual issues concerning the exercise of intellectual property rights may be the subject of arbitration. The main advantage is that it allows the parties to maintain their trade secrets as confidential. However, since intellectual property rights, such as patents and trade marks are granted by the state, courts often consider that the validity or the existence of such rights cannot bind third parties and therefore, cannot be arbitrable. The US and Switzerland have a more liberal approach than most countries as they have accepted that any issues concerning intellectual property rights could be arbitrable, including patent infringement claims which require Tribunal's to decide on the validity of the patent (in the Tribunal's view) in the first place.[124] However, such arbitrations would generally not affect the rights of third parties. **6–159**

(vii) Issues of Illegality

Historically, one of the concerns about arbitration arose from the issue of enforcement of illegal contracts. Illegality is of course a concept that is found in each national legal system. The New York Convention includes the concept when it provides that one of the grounds for not enforcing an arbitral Award is that it offends international public policy. The issue of illegality has been dealt with extensively by various commentators, who provide reference to some of the basic case law on the subject.[125] **6–160**

The issue of corruption is raised from time to time in international arbitration either as a basis on which to colour the transaction or as grounds for refusing to enforce it. From a practical standpoint, if corruption is raised, then it should be raised with a legal argument as to its effect on the transaction and with evidence **6–161**

p.141; Jolivet, "Quelques exemples du traitement du droit communautaire dans l'arbitrage CCI", in *Les Cahiers de l'Arbitrage Volume II, op. cit.*, p.247.

124 See generally, Lew, "Final Report on Intellectual Property Disputes and Arbitration" (1998) ICC ICArb Bull Vol. 9 No.1, p.37; Hanotiau, "L'arbitrabilité des litiges de propriété intellectuelle: une analyse comparative" (2003) ASA Bull Vol.21 No.1, p.3; Park, "Irony in Intellectual Property Arbitration" (2003) Arb Int Vol.19 No.4, p.451; Caron, "The World of Intellectual Property and the Decision to Arbitrate" (2003) Arb Int Vol.19 No.4, p.441; Blessing, "Arbitrability of Intellectual Property Disputes" (1996) Arb Int Vol.12 No.2, p.191. See also Extracts from ICC Awards on Intellectual Property Rights–Part I, (1993) ICC ICArb Bull Vol.4 No.2, p.70 and Extracts from ICC Awards on Intellectual Property Rights–Pt II, (1994) ICC ICArb Bull Vol.5 No.1, p.65. For Germany, see Schäfer "Arbitration of Intellectual Property Law Disputes in Germany" in *Arbitration in Germany: The Model Law in Practice*, edited by K.-H. Bökstiegel, S. Kr\Ull and P. Nacimiento, (Kluwer, 2007), at p.953.

125 ICC, *Arbitration–Money Laundering, Corruption and Fraud* (ICC Dossier No.651, 2003); Kreindler, "Aspects of Illegality in the Formation and Performance of Contracts" (2003) *ICCA Congress Series No.11*, p.209.

to back up the claim. Raising the issue by innuendo without evidence is seldom effective and may reflect more on the party raising it than the other party. As noted by the Tribunal in the *Himpurna* Award, it is not sufficient to raise the issue, evidence must be provided to support the claim.[126]

6–162 The treatment of corruption in ICC Awards has varied and is beyond the scope of this book. However, there are very helpful indications in the literature both with respect to ICC Awards and generally.[127]

6–163 An arbitration agreement relating to what is fundamentally a prohibited activity will generally not be enforceable. In some instances, parties raise issues of illegality that do not go to the root of the transaction, but rather the failure to respect legal requirements as to activities or to obtain necessary authorisations. It is difficult to generalise in this area. However, in making these arguments parties should recall that the basic principle with most contracts is the objective intention of the parties. If neither party treated compliance with a legal requirement as essential, a Tribunal may be led to adopt the same approach. Therefore, the illegality may not affect the contract itself but may affect the measure of damages, as conducting a business without all necessary licenses involves a legal risk.[128] Where the essence of the relationship depended on these authorisations, a Tribunal may view the matter as going to the root of the transaction and therefore result in illegality of the contract.

6–164 Bribery does not invalidate contractual clauses for arbitration, and leaves the issue to the consideration of the Tribunal rather than the court. In the *Fiona Trust* case, the English Court of Appeal ruled in a decision upheld by the House of Lords that a dispute based on claims that a contract was procured by bribery and later rescinded on discovery of the bribery falls within the arbitration agreement contained in the contract.[129]

[126] See para.6–144 n.104.

[127] Scherer, "International Arbitration and Corruption–Synopsis of Selected Arbitral Awards" (2001) ASA Bull Vol.19 No.4, p.710; "Circumstantial Evidence in Corruption Cases Before International Arbitral Tribunals" (2002) Int'l ALR Vol.5 No.2, p.29; Sayed, "La question de la corruption dans l'arbitrage commercial international: Inventaire des solutions" (2001) ASA Bull Vol.19 No.4, p.653; Arfazadeh, "Considérations pragmatiques sur la compétence respective de l'arbitre et du juge en matière de corruption" (2001) ASA Bull Vol.19 No.4, p.672; Wetter, "Issues of Corruption before International Arbitral Tribunals: The Authentic Text and True Meaning of Judge Gunnar Lagergren's 1963 Award in ICC Case No.1110" (1994) Arb Int Vol.10 No.3, p.277.

[128] A claim for damages by a distributor without all of the proper local authorisations could be met with the argument that due to the absence of such authorisations it was less certain that the distribution agreement could have continued for its full term.

[129] See the *Fiona Trust* case as upheld before the House of Lords in the *Premium Nafta Products Ltd* case, cited at para.6–18 n.14. More generally, see Gee, "The Autonomy of Arbitrators, and Fraud Unravels All" (2006) Arb Int Vol.22 No.3, p.337. See for example ICSID case No.Arb/00/7, *World Duty Free Co Ltd v The Republic of Kenya*, October 4, 2006 (annulment of a contract for bribery by an ICSID Tribunal applying English law).

CHAPTER 3

MULTIPLE PARTIES, MULTIPLE CONTRACTS AND CONSOLIDATION

Articles 7–10

INTRODUCTION

Articles 7 – 10 of the 2012 Arbitration Rules form part of a new chapter called "Multiple Parties, Multiple Contracts and Consolidation". It deals with so-called complex arbitrations,[1] that is arbitrations with a plurality of parties (more than two), some of which may have been joined to the proceedings or voluntarily intervened in them, and/or with claims being brought under multiple contracts (*i.e.*, typically under more than one arbitration agreement), some of these claims being brought amongst multiple Claimants and/or multiple Respondents (so-called cross-claims).[2] The consolidation of arbitral proceedings falls also into the category of complex arbitrations. **7–1**

In 1998, the issue of a so-called multiple parties dispute was recognized for the first time by the Rules through the introduction of its Art. 10, which required multiple Claimants or Respondents to jointly agree upon an arbitrator, failing which, the ICC Court would step in for the constitution of the Tribunal. Article 10 of the 1998 Rules has now become Art. 12(8) of the 2012 Arbitration Rules. **7–2**

While in 1998 about one fifth of the cases involved multi-party disputes, that number has increased to one third some ten years later and since then.[3] Multi-party disputes reflect, simply put, the complexity of international business transactions, often involving more than two parties who may be bound by more than one contract for a given project.[4] Such disputes have become a reality for the ICC Court, and over the years forced it to adapt its practice to the needs and wishes of its users. In particular, the ICC Court developed a new practice allowing the joinder of a new party to an existing arbitration under certain circumstances. However, this practice remained in flux, and it would seem fair to say that even insiders of ICC arbitration had difficulties in describing it. More transparency and clarity regarding the ICC Court's practice was badly needed in the area of multiple party and multiple contract disputes. At the same time, the new chapter on **7–3**

[1] See Karrer, "Multi-party and complex Arbitration under the Zurich Rules: Art. 13 and 14 International Arbitration Rules of the Zurich Chamber of Commerce" in Aspekte des Wirtschaftsrechts – Festgabe zum Schweizerischen Juristentag (1994 Zürich, Ed. H.U. Walter et al.) at oo.261–271ff.; Briner, "Disputes that go beyond the two-party, one-contract scenario" in Special Supplement ICC International Court of Arbitration Bulletin (2003).

[2] See discussion under Art.6(4) at para. 6–84.

[3] (2013) ICC ICArb Bull Vol. 24 No. 1.

[4] See, *e.g.*, Bamford & Maidment, "" *All join in " or not? How well does international arbitration cater for disputes involving multiple parties or related claims?* (2009) ASA Bull. 27/1, p. 3.

multi-party disputes has set the yardstick for the conduct of such disputes under the Rules.

7–4 In the 2012 Arbitration Rules, at least seven articles now deal directly with multiple-party issues, four of which are entirely new, *i.e.* Arts 7 – 10. This explains in part the increase of articles from 35 to 41 in the 2012 Arbitration Rules. The seven relevant and new articles are:

(1) Article 7:	Joinder of Additional Parties;
(2) Article 8:	Claims between Multiple Parties;
(3) Article 9:	Multiple Contracts;
(4) Article 6(3)–(7):	Articles 7–9 are subject to Art. 6(3)–(7);
(5) Article 10:	Consolidation of Arbitrations;
(6) Article 12(6)–(8):	Constitution of Tribunal in multiple parties situations;
(7) Article 36(4):	Advances on costs in multiple parties situations.

7–5 The new ICC regime on multiple parties and multiple contracts is novel, although not revolutionary, and may be considered one of the most advanced set of rules in international institutional arbitration rules. The ICC has made substantial progress in setting out the requirements for, and limits of, multiple party arbitrations to be conducted under its 2012 Arbitration Rules.[5]

7–6 Today, the majority of national arbitration laws lacks provisions addressing the possibility for joinder, intervention or consolidation, and even the UNCITRAL Model Law in its revised 2006 version is silent in this respect. The Netherlands Arbitration Act of 1986 provides for joinder and intervention (Art.1045 of the DCCP) and consolidation: (Art.1046)) even absent parties' agreement. The English Arbitration Act contains no express provision on joinder or intervention of third parties, but regulates party-agreed consolidation at s. 35.[6] In Hong Kong, the Arbitration Ordinance Schedule 2.2 allows consolidation upon a party's application. However, Schedule 2 is an opt-in provision that automatically applies to domestic agreements entered into before the commencement of the ordinance (Section 100.a), arbitration agreements entered into at any time within a period of 6 years after the commencement of the ordinance which provides that arbitration under the agreement is a domestic arbitration (s. 100.b) and domestic construction sub-contracting cases (s. 101) but not to international arbitration. When it comes to international arbitration, parties must choose to have Schedule 2 apply. In New Zealand, Schedule 2.2 of the Arbitration Act provides for consolidation upon a party's application. However, when it comes to international arbitration, parties must choose to have Schedule 2 apply (Article 6.2) as it is an opt-in provision. Article 6.4.2 of the Australian Arbitration Act provides that arbitral tribunals can make orders to consolidate arbitral proceedings or hear related arbitral proceedings together or in sequence. Article 6.4.3 further states that where arbitral proceedings are consolidated, a new arbitral tribunal must be established in accordance with Articles 10 and 11 of the Model Law (2006). Where no agreement is made, the related arbitral proceedings will continue to be heard by separate arbitral tribunals.

[5] For a comparative analysis, see J. Gilbert, "Multi-Party and Multi-Contract Arbitration" in *Arbitration in England,*, *op.cit.*, pp. 455,465–467.

[6] J. Gilbert, *op.cit.*, p.455 et seq.

The Singapore International Arbitration Act does not contain provisions regarding consolidation. However, the Singapore Arbitration Act applicable to domestic arbitrations does. Article 26 addresses the questions of consolidation and concurrent hearings. It allows the parties to agree on consolidation (art. 26.1.a). However, Article 26.2 clearly states that arbitral tribunals do not have the power to order consolidation in the absence of a party's agreement. In *Stolt-Nielsen S.A. et al. v. AnimalFeeds International Corp.*, the US Supreme Court ruled that an arbitral tribunal that compelled class arbitration without concluding that the parties had contractually agreed to it (either expressly or as construed under the applicable law) exceeded its powers.[7] However, the US Supreme Court upheld arbitration where the issue of arbitrability was to be decided by the arbitrator and the arbitrator held that the relevant clause and rules permitted class action arbitration.[8]

Typically, given the consensual nature of arbitration, consent is required for joinder, intervention or consolidation. It can be direct (*e.g.* in a so-called umbrella arbitration agreement), indirect (by reference to arbitration rules, that contain appropriate provisions), or, in some cases, even implied (by reference to the parties' intention in light of the structure of their corporate transaction, and other considerations, such as efficiency).[9] 7–7

***

Article 7 Joinder of Additional Parties

1. **A party wishing to join an additional party to the arbitration shall submit its request for arbitration against the additional party (the "Request for Joinder") to the Secretariat. The date on which the Request for Joinder is received by the Secretariat shall, for all purposes, be deemed to be the date of the commencement of arbitration against the additional party. Any such joinder shall be subject to the provisions of Articles 6(3)–6(7) and 9. No additional party may be joined after the confirmation or appointment of any arbitrator, unless all parties, including the additional party, otherwise agree. The Secretariat may fix a time limit for the submission of a Request for Joinder.**
2. **The Request for Joinder shall contain the following information:**
   a) **the case reference of the existing arbitration;**
   b) **the name in full, description, address and other contact details of each of the parties, including the additional party; and**
   c) **the information specified in Article 4(3) subparagraphs c), d), e) and f).**

[7] *Stolt-Nielsen et al. v AnimalFeeds International Corp.*, 130 S.Ct. 1758, 1776 (2010).
[8] *Oxford Health Plans LLC v Sutter* 569 U. S. _ (2013). See discussion under Art. 6(4)(ii) at paras 6–51 and 6–52 and under Art. 6(9) at para. 6–135.
[9] In one unreported case, the arbitral tribunal in this case considered that, even though the parties did not expressly agree to consolidation in their arbitration agreement, the contracts formed part of one single economic transaction. Had the parties considered the question of consolidation, they would have agreed to arbitrate related claims arising from the contracts together. Thus, the arbitral tribunal ruled in favor of consolidation

The party filing the Request for Joinder may submit therewith such other documents or information as it considers appropriate or as may contribute to the efficient resolution of the dispute.

3. **The provisions of Articles 4(4) and 4(5) shall apply, *mutatis mutandis*, to the Request for Joinder.**

4. **The additional party shall submit an Answer in accordance, *mutatis mutandis*, with the provisions of Articles 5(1)–5(4). The additional party may make claims against any other party in accordance with the provisions of Article 8.**[10]

Introductory remarks

7–8 Article 7, an entirely new provision in the 2012 Arbitration Rules, allows to the joinder of a party, not originally named as such, as a party to an existing arbitration, at the request of one of the (existing) parties to that arbitration. Article 7 needs to be read in conjunction with Art. 6(4)(i) of the Rules. Articles 12(7) and (8), which deal with the constitution of the Tribunal in case of joinder of a new party, must also be considered in this context.

7–9 The traditional wisdom, which, for a long time, was the standing practice of the ICC Court, was that only the Claimant would determine the parties to the arbitration that it had initiated. If A had a contract with a joint-venture composed of B, C and D, it could decide whether to pursue a claim only against B, or against another party, or even both, of the contract parties. If it had started the arbitration only against B, then the latter could join C and D. Conversely, if B decided alone to bring claims against A, *i.e.* without its joint-venture partners C and D, A could not bring claims against C and D in the arbitration initiated by B. Under Art. 7, A (as the Respondent) can now bring a counterclaim against B (as the Claimant), and, at the same time, pursue claims against C and D by filing a Request for Joinder against the latter. Table [3] below illustrates this scenario:

[10] Article 7 is a new provision in the Rules.

Respondent's Request for Joinder

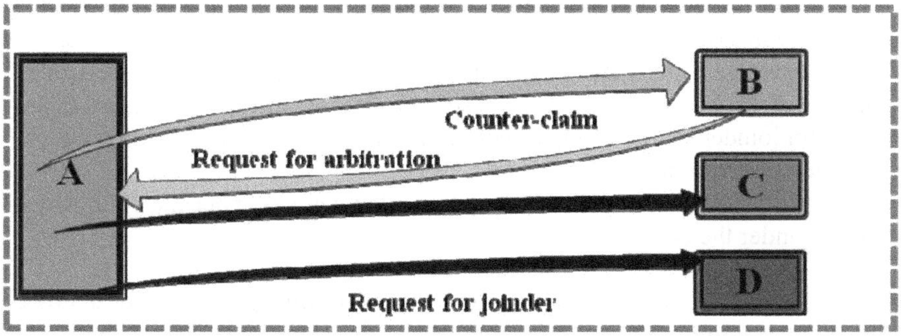

ICC Handbook, Table [3]

The consent of B to A's inclusion of C and D is not required under Art. 7. Nor 7–10
is the consent of B and C required. All four parties are bound by the same arbitration agreement and therefore could contemplate from the outset that one day they would all be parties to the same arbitration. As will be seen below, the scope of joinder under Art. 7 is rather limited, in particular as it only contemplates the situation where an arbitrator has not yet been confirmed or appointed.

Article 7 does not provide, however, for the intervention of a third party; the 7–11
latter's request to join pending proceedings is in fact not foreseen by the ICC Rules. In the scenario of Table 3, if A (as the respondent) does not decide to bring a Request for Joinder against C and D, C and D could not request to be joined to the proceedings pursuant to art. 7. This is not to say that if C and D wish to join the proceedings (assuming their joint venture partner A has made them aware of their existence), they could not do so if all participants to the arbitration would agree thereto. In other words, not only would the existing parties to the proceedings have to consent, but if the Tribunal were already constituted, it would also have to agree to such intervention.[11]

To conclude, while the possibility of intervention is nowhere provided for in 7–12
the ICC Rules, in the event of unanimous consent of all persons concerned, the

[11] Third party voluntary intervention was not provided for by the 1998 Rules. When a party requested to be joined to the arbitral proceedings, the Secretariat would usually reply that due to their confidential nature it could even acknowledge the existence of such proceedings. In 2009, a non-party which had signed one of the contracts upon which the proceedings were based, requested to take part in the arbitration. Its request was submitted to the parties for comments. One accepted the idea but the parties did not manage to reach an agreement preventing the non-party from joining. Greenberg & Feris, "Consolidation, Joinder, Cross-Claims, Multiparty and Multicontract Arbitrations, Recent ICC Experience", in "*Multiparty Arbitration, Dossier VII, ICC Institute of World Business Law*", (B. Hanotiau & E.A. Schwartz, eds 2010) ICC Publication No. 701 178 ; Unless all the parties to the arbitration agreement and the third-party that is to join the proceedings agreed to the addition of this third-party, there was no authority under the 1998 Rules to permit the intervention of a third party either at its request or that of one of the parties.

ICC Rules do not exclude *per se* the possibility of an intervention by a third party to pending proceedings.

7–13 As will be discussed under art. 10,[12] it is indirectly possible to also join an additional party in case of consolidation of two arbitral proceedings. If in the scenario of Table 3, where B starts an arbitration against A, A would start a separate arbitration against B, C and D, the same result as via a counterclaim against B and request for joinder against C and D, could be achieved by consolidating the second arbitration with the first.[13]

7–14 In 2012, the ICC received ten requests for joinder, six under the 1998 Rules, and four under the 2012 Rules.[14]

Article 7(1): "A party wishing to join an additional party to the arbitration shall submit its request for arbitration against the additional party (the "Request for Joinder") to the Secretariat. The date on which the Request for Joinder is received by the Secretariat shall, for all purposes, be deemed to be the date of the commencement of arbitration against the additional party. Any such joinder shall be subject to the provisions of Articles 6(3)–6(7) and 9. No additional party may be joined after the confirmation or appointment of any arbitrator, unless all parties, including the additional party, otherwise agree. The Secretariat may fix a time limit for the submission of a Request for Joinder."

Additional party

7–15 The term "additional party" has been newly introduced into the 2012 Rules, and refers to the new party that was not initially covered by the Request for Arbitration, and which is now to be added to the arbitration by way of a Request for Joinder. The term "additional party" was preferred over the more commonly used term "third party," since the latter may connote the idea that the third party need not be bound by the same arbitration agreement as the other parties to the arbitration.

7–16 It follows from Art. 2(ii) that the term "additional party" includes one or more additional parties.[15] A party becomes an "additional party" by the mere fact of having been included in, and notified with, a Request for Joinder. No prior authorization by the ICC Court is necessary for the filing of a Request for Joinder against an additional party. It is automatic in the same manner, in which a Respondent becomes a party to an ICC arbitration by the mere filing of a Request for Arbitration. However, an additional party may raise jurisdictional objections like any other Respondent, and in either case, it will be for the ICC Court, and eventually for the Tribunal to decide whether arbitral jurisdiction extends to that additional party (or a Respondent). In other words, if the ICC Court determines that

[12] See the discussion under Article 10 at paras. 10–7 et seq.

[13] See the discussion under Article 10 at paras. 10–6 to 10–9 as to the possible ways of achieving such consolidation.

[14] In 2011, the ICC received eighteen requests, of which eight were accepted. Information as per courtesy of Mr. Carlevaris, Secretary General.

[15] See the discussion under Article 2(ii) at paras. 2–13 to 2–14.

there exists no *prima facie* jurisdiction over the additional party, then the latter will be released from the arbitration, as would any Respondent for whom the ICC Court cannot establish *prima facie* jurisdiction. This follows form the application of Art. 6(3) – (6) of the Rules, to which the third sentence of Art. 7(1) expressly refers.[16]

Request for Joinder

Article 7(1) first sentence defines the Request for Arbitration against the additional party as the Request for Joinder. The content of the Request for Joinder is set out in detail in Art. 7(2) of the Rules.[17] The Request for Joinder against an additional party is the equivalent of a Request for Arbitration against a Respondent. The additional party enjoys the same rights and obligations as any Respondent that receives a Request for Arbitration from the Secretariat. **7–17**

The Request for Joinder is to be filed with the Secretariat, Art. 7(1), second sentence. **7–18**

No voluntary joinder

As mentioned above, Art. 7(1) does not contemplate the situation where a party wishes on its own to join a pending arbitration and requests, either the ICC Court's Secretariat or the Tribunal, to be joined to that arbitration (so-called intervention, *freiwillige Nebenintervention, intervention*). **7–19**

Prima facie jurisdiction over additional party

Article 7(1), third sentence refers to Art. 6(3) – (6) of the Rules and thus to the jurisdictional control exercised by the ICC Court's Secretary General, the ICC Court and/or the Tribunal. By making the Request for Joinder subject to these provisions, the additional party is granted the same protection of the *prima facie* test of jurisdiction as any Respondent that receives a Request for Arbitration. **7–20**

Article 6(3) of the Rules identifies four cases in which "any party against which a claim has been made" may be viewed as having raised, or may effectively have raised a jurisdictional objection. This applies to any additional party, as it is a "party against which a claim has been made." It follows from Art. 7(2)(c), and Art. 4(3)(c) and (d) of the Rules that the Request for Joinder must include a claim (or claims) against the additional party.[18] In the event of a jurisdictional objection from the additional party, it will be decided directly by the Tribunal, unless the Secretary General refers the matter to the ICC Court for a decision pursuant to Art. 6(4). **7–21**

In the case of Art. 7, the relevant text for the ICC Court's *prima facie* decision is to be found in Art. 6(4)(i), which is referred to here. In the example shown in Table **[3]** at paras 7 – 9 above, it would normally not be possible for A to seek to also join PB, the parent company of B, on the ground that it has obtained a parent company guarantee from PB, unless it could be shown *prima facie* that an **7–22**

[16] See discussion under Art. 6(3) at para. 6–34 and Art. 6(4) at paras. 6–39 – 6–44.
[17] See the discussion under Art. 7 at paras 7–31 et seq. below.
[18] See paras. 7–35 to 7–38.

arbitration agreement exists that binds all parties to the arbitration, including PB. Table **[4]** below illustrates the point where PB would not be a party to the contract entered into between A, on one side, and B, C, D, on the other side, and for that reason is called, for the purposes of this Table, a "third" party even though this term is not used by Art. 7. It would be for the ICC Court to decide whether PB is *prima facie* bound by the arbitration agreement between A, B, C and D. PB would most likely raise a jurisdictional objection, and the Court may, in all likelihood, find that absent specific factors, PB is not bound by the arbitration clause contained in the contract between A, B, C, and D. Therefore, A would be able to successfully pursue its Request for Joinder only against C and D.

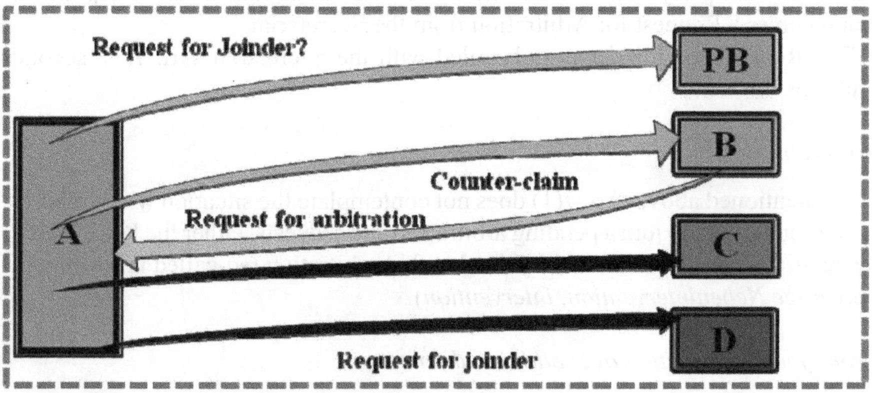

ICC Handbook, Table **[4]**

7–23 In this context, so-called umbrella arbitration agreements and complex arbitration clauses, which allow the joinder of parties although they are not parties to the same arbitration agreement as the Claimant and the Respondent, will require particular attention by the ICC Court.[19]

7–24 Article 7(1) third sentence makes the Request for Joinder also subject to Art. 9, which deals with claims made in the same arbitration under more than one contract. Thus, if a claim is brought against an additional party under a contract other than the contract on the basis of which the claim was made in the Request for Arbitration, the ICC Court's jurisdictional control will come into play pursuant to Art. 9 and Art. 6(4)(ii) of the Rules. The reference to Art. 9 significantly limits the possibility of bringing claims against an additional party on any basis other than the contract (or the contracts) underlying the Request for Arbitration.

[19] Regarding the possibility of umbrella arbitration agreements, see, *e.g.*, Bamford & Maindment, *op.cit.*, p. 20.

No joinder after appointment or confirmation of an arbitrator

Article 7(1) fourth sentence precludes the joinder of an additional party, once an arbitrator has been confirmed or appointed. In that way, the right of the additional party to participate in the constitution of the Tribunal is protected. This protection is essential, and so is the temporal limit set by Art. 7(1) for the joinder of an additional party.[20] There is an exception to this rule: If all parties to the arbitration, including the additional party that is to be joined to the arbitration, agree to the joinder, although one or more arbitrators have already been confirmed or appointed. It will be for the ICC Court's Secretariat to solicit such agreement, as long as the file has not been transmitted to the Tribunal. **7–25**

Article 7 does not contemplate the possibility of joining a party to the arbitration once the Tribunal has been constituted and seized with the file, not even in the event that all the parties, including the additional party to be joined, agree. **7–26**

Time limit to join additional party set by Secretariat

Article 7(1) fifth sentence expressly authorizes the ICC Court's Secretariat to set a time limit for the parties to file a Request for Joinder. The Secretariat will do so whenever it is in a position to proceed with the constitution of the Arbitral Tribunal, for instance by confirming the two party appointed arbitrators. Once it has done so, it will be too late to bring a Request for Joinder. Not in every case will it be necessary for the Secretariat to fix such time limit for the Parties. If the dispute relates to a contract signed between a seller and a buyer, and nothing indicates that any other party might be bound by that contract, there should be no reason to set a time limit to present a Request for Joinder, as there would appear no basis for such joinder. The Secretariat will therefore have to operate with some common sense in light of the information available to it when assessing the need whether or not to fix such time limit. **7–27**

By fixing a time limit for joining one or more additional parties, the Secretariat can prevent the risk of a series of joinder, which inevitably would bring significant delay to the constitution of the Tribunal.[21] **7–28**

Constitution of Tribunal in case of Joinder

Article 12(7) has been newly added to the Rules to respond to the fact that an additional party may be joined, and therefore has a right, and needs to be given the opportunity to participate in the constitution of the Arbitral Tribunal. **7–29**

In the example shown in Table **[3]** at para 7–9 above, the newly joined parties C and D, would have to choose their "camp" when appointing an arbitrator and trying to agree with the existing party upon an arbitrator. In that example, there could be hardly any doubt that C and D would side with B, which in the given example is in fact the Claimant. They would thus have to agree on the arbitrator on the Claimant's side. If B, C, and D would be unable to do so, Art. 12(8) of the **7–30**

[20] Bamford & Maidment, *op.cit.*, p. 6.

[21] A further deterrent for successive Requests of Joinder by the same party might be the fact that it would have to pay the filing fee each time, although this fee will be committed against its share of the advance on cost, see the discussion under Article 36(4) at paras. 36–34 to 36–35 below.

Rules would have to come into play.[22] The ICC Court could therefore appoint all three arbitrators, and often would do this on the basis of direct appointments rather than via soliciting proposals from different National Committees.[23]

Article 7(2): "The Request for Joinder shall contain the following information:

> **a) the case reference of the existing arbitration;**
> **b) the name in full, description, address and other contact details of each of the parties, including the additional party; and**
> **c) the information specified in Article 4(3) subparagraphs c), d), e) and f).**

The party filing the Request for Joinder may submit therewith such other documents or information as it considers appropriate or as may contribute to the efficient resolution of the dispute."

7–31 Article 7(2) lays down certain form requirements that must be met for a request for Joinder. They are fully aligned to those specified for a Request for arbitration in Art. 4(3) of the Rules.

Article 7(2)(a): "the case reference of the existing arbitration;"

7–32 Since the joinder concerns a matter already pending with the ICC Court, it is necessary to indicate the ICC file number of the pending case, followed by the initials of the counsel in charge of the file. The caption can be as follows: "Request for Joinder in ICC Case N° 18500/ABC."

Article 7(2)(b): "the name in full, description, address and other contact details of each of the parties, including the additional party;"

7–33 The name and contact details of each of the parties, including the additional party, *i.e.* the party to be joined, need to be indicated. It follows from Art. 7(3) that the ICC Secretariat will not only transmit a copy of the Request for Joinder to the additional party, but to all other parties in the arbitration.[24] It is for that reason that the name and contact details of the parties to the arbitration as well as that of the additional party must be stated in the Request for Joinder. The ICC Court's Secretariat is, of course, aware of the name and contact details of the parties to the existing arbitration. However, it remains the responsibility of the party seeking the joinder to provide these data, which in some cases may have changed since the filing of the Request for Arbitration without the Secretariat having been informed of that.

7–34 The comments made for Art. 4(3)(b) of the Rules apply to the same extent here.[25]

Article 7(2)(c): "the information specified in Article 4(3) subparagraphs c), d), e) and f)."

[22] See the discussion under Article 12(8) at paras. 12–60 to 12–68.
[23] See the discussion under Article 12(8) at para. 12-67.
[24] See para. 7–41.
[25] See the discussion under Article 4(3)(b) at paras. 4–37 to 4–38.

The additional party is treated like any Respondent that is to be notified with a Request for Arbitration.[26] It is normal that the Request for Joinder must set out the same information as is required for a Request of arbitration. This is why Art. 7(2)(c) simply refers to Art. 4(3)(c) – (f), and requires that the information specified in those subparagraphs also be included in the Request for Joinder. The comments made for Art. 4(3)(c) – (f) therefore apply to the same extent here.[27] **7–35**

Pursuant to Art. 4(3)(c) of the Rules, the nature and circumstances of the dispute giving rise to the claims and on the basis upon which the claims are made must be described. It is understood and implied in Art. 4(3)(c) that a Claimant will have claims against the Respondent. The same applies for a party seeking to join an additional party. It must assert claims against that party. At the minimum, such claim would entail a request for declaratory relief. **7–36**

We shall use again the example of the construction contract between A, as the general contractor, and the joint-venture consisting of B, C and D, as the sub-contractor, to explain the situation. Assuming, for instance, that Claimant A sues only the joint-venture partner B, but not C and D, B could bring a Request for Joinder against C and D with the request for a declaration that any findings made by the Tribunal in relation to the parties' rights and obligations under the construction contract binding all parties. If B were then to seek any redress from C and D under their joint-venture agreement, B could rely on the *res judicata* effect of the award rendered in the arbitration initiated by A. Since A is not a party to the joint venture agreement, B could not pursue claims arising out of that agreement against C and D in that same arbitration.[28] **7–37**

Concerning the arbitration agreement (Art. 4(3)(e)of the Rules), it will always be necessary to show that the party to be joined is bound by the same agreement as the one on which the Claimant has relied when starting the arbitration against Respondent unless the provisions of Art. 9 are applicable. **7–38**

"The party filing the Request for Joinder may submit therewith such other documents or information as it considers appropriate or as may contribute to the efficient resolution of the dispute."

The final subparagraph in Art. 7(2) is identical to the final subparagraph in both Art. 4(3) and Art. 5(1) of the Rules.[29] **7–39**

Article 7(3): "The provisions of Articles 4(4) and 4(5) shall apply, *mutatis mutandis*, to the Request for Joinder."

A Request for Joinder does not only have to follow the form requirements of a Request for Arbitration. It is also treated in the same way insofar as it requires that a sufficient number of copies are submitted (see Art. 4(4)(a) and (b) of the Rules) and the filing fee of USD 3,000 be paid to the Secretariat.[30] **7–40**

[26] See the discussion under Article 4(3)(c) to (f) at paras. 4–39 to 4–54.
[27] See the discussion under Article 4(3)(c) to (f) at paras. 4–39 to 4–54.
[28] See the discussion under Article 8(1) at para. 8–3.
[29] See the discussion under Article 4(3) at paras. 4–65 to 4–67.
[30] See the discussion under Article 4(4) at paras. 4–68 to 4–72 regarding these requirements.

7–41 Pursuant to Art. 4(5) of the Rules, the Request for arbitration is transmitted to the Respondent, once the Secretariat has received sufficient copies of the Request as well as the filing fee. The same applies for the Request for Joinder, which is transmitted to the Parties listed therein, that is, the additional party, as well as the existing party (or parties).

Article 7(4): "The additional party shall submit an Answer in accordance, *mutatis mutandis*, with the provisions of Articles 5(1)–5(4). The additional party may make claims against any other party in accordance with the provisions of Article 8."

7–42 Like any Respondent receiving a Request for Arbitration, the additional party must submit an Answer to the Request for Joinder. Its Answer to the latter will have to contain the same information as the Respondent's Answer to the Request for Arbitration. This is why Art. 7(4) refers in its first sentence to Art. 5(1) – (4) of the Rules.

7–43 Amongst others, the additional party will have to take position regarding the constitution of the Tribunal, as per Art. 5(1)(e).[31]

7–44 The second sentence of Art. 7(4) makes it clear that the additional party may bring claims against any other party to the arbitration, *i.e.* not only against the party that requested its joinder. The table **[5]** below gives an example of how an additional party might bring claims against the other parties. It would depend on the legal basis on which C and D rely for bringing their claims against B, and on which B relies for bringing its claim against C to determine whether such claims could at all be pursued in this arbitration. If the claims were based on the joint-venture agreement between B, C and D, this would not be possible, even if the arbitration clause in that agreement were fully compatible with the arbitration clause in the contract between A and B, C, D.[32]

Multiple claims

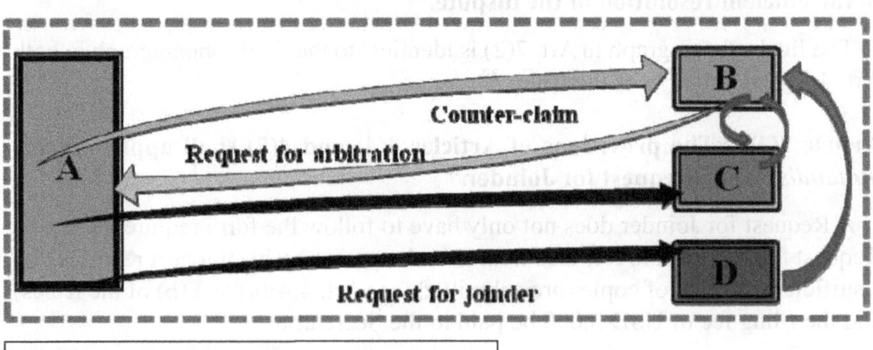

ICC Handbook, Table **[5]**

[31] See the discussion under Article 5(1)(e) at paras. 5–28 to 5–31.
[32] See para. 9–4 et seq.

Article 8 Claims between Multiple Parties

1. **In an arbitration with multiple parties, claims may be made by any party against any other party, subject to the provisions of Articles 6(3)–6(7) and 9 and provided that no new claims may be made after the Terms of Reference are signed or approved by the Court without the authorization of the arbitral tribunal pursuant to Article 23(4).**

2. **Any party making a claim pursuant to Article 8(1) shall provide the information specified in Article 4(3) subparagraphs c), d), e) and f).**

3. **Before the Secretariat transmits the file to the arbitral tribunal in accordance with Article 16, the following provisions shall apply, *mutatis mutandis*, to any claim made: Article 4(4) subparagraph a); Article 4(5); Article 5(1) except for subparagraphs a), b), e) and f); Article 5(2); Article 5(3) and Article 5(4). Thereafter, the arbitral tribunal shall determine the procedure for making a claim.**[1]

Introductory remarks

Article 8, like Art. 7, concerns arbitrations involving more than two parties, *i.e.*, multiple parties. More specifically, Art. 8 deals with claims multiple parties may have against each other in an arbitration, and sets a simple rule for such multi-party arbitrations: Any party can make claims against any other party. Article 8 is best understood by considering the definition of the terms "claim" or "claims" in the new Art. 2 (iv): These terms "include any claim by any party against any other party."[2] The 2012 Rules are no longer based on a bi-polar situation, in which a Claimant files a claim against a Respondent and the Respondent may file a counterclaim (or set-off claim) against the Claimant. Rather, the new Rules contemplate and recognize the possibility that any party which becomes a party to an ICC arbitration, including the additional party that is joined by way of a Request for Joinder pursuant to Art. 7, may have a claim against any other party to the arbitration. Article 8 embodies and reflects a simple principle. **8–1**

[1] This is a new provision of the Rules.
[2] See the discussion under Article 2(iv) at para. 2–**15**.

8–2 Article 8 therefore covers what in certain Anglo-Saxon jurisdictions are known as cross-claims, which are claims brought among parties on the same side of a dispute, *i.e.* claims by a Claimant against another Claimant, or claims by a Respondent against another Respondent.[3] If A as Claimant pursues claims against the joint-venture partners B, C and D as Respondents, B may have claims against C and/or D, and, if it should bring such a claim in the arbitration started by A, this claim would be considered a cross-claim.

8–3 Article 8 sets the requirements, and the limits, for such cross-claims, as well as any other claims that do not squarely fall into the initial Claimant-Respondent relation, as will be discussed at paras. 8-[7] and 8-[8] below.

8–4 Article 8 does not, however, deal with the constitution of the Tribunal in multiple parties settings. That is a matter dealt with in Art. 12(6)–(8) of the Rules.

Advances on costs

8–5 Claims between multiple parties that go beyond the traditional claim and counterclaim of a Claimant and a Respondent raise particular issues as regards the adequacy of a global advance on costs that would have to cover all claims made by the multiple parties. These issues are addressed by the new Art. 36(4) of the Rules.[4]

Article 8 (1): "In an arbitration with multiple parties, claims may be made by any party against any other party, subject to the provisions of Article 6(3)–6(7) and 9 and provided that no new claims may be made after the Terms of Reference are signed or approved by the Court without the authorization of the arbitral tribunal pursuant to Article 23(4)."

Claims by any party against any other party

8–6 As stated at para. 8–1 above, it follows from the definition of the term "claims" in Art. 2(iv) that this term covers indistinctly and invariably (i) claims by a Claimant against another Claimant (so-called cross-claims), against a Respondent and/or against an additional party, as well as (ii) claims by a Respondent against a Respondent, against a Claimant (so-called counter-claims) or against an additional party, and finally (iii) claims by an additional party against a Claimant, a Respondent or any other additional party.

Jurisdictional limits

8–7 Indeed, insofar as Art. 8(1) fixes the jurisdictional requirements and, at the same time, limits for claims between multiple parties, it does so more for the purpose of clarification than anything else. Claims between multiple parties remain subject to the jurisdictional limits of Art. 6(3) – (7) and of Art. 9. Claims between multiple parties, which arise out of the same arbitration agreement will be subject to the test of Art. 6(4)(i). If they arise under more than one arbitration

[3] See, *e.g.*, the definition in Fry, Greenberg & Mazza, op.cit., para. 3-326 ("Claims made by one or more respondents against another respondent, or by one or more claimants aganst another claimant").

[4] See the discussion under Article 36(4).

agreement, the test provided for under Art. 6(4)(ii) will also have to be made.[5] It can be concluded from the reference to both Art. 6(3)–(7) and Art. 9 that Art. 8 is not meant to extend in any way the scope of arbitral jurisdiction in the event of claims between multiple Parties. It remains, however, uncertain to what extent a Tribunal will be bound by the jurisdictional limits which the ICC Court is called upon to respect pursuant to Art. 6.[6]

Temporal limit

Article 8(1) also contains a temporal limit for claims between multiple parties by referring to Art. 23(4) of the Rules. Pursuant to this provision, after the Terms of Reference have been signed or approved by the ICC Court, new claims by any party are only allowed subject to the (prior) authorization by the Tribunal. **8–8**

Tribunal's jurisdiction over claims between multiple parties

Once the Tribunal has received the file, and before the Terms of Reference are signed or approved, and with the Tribunal's permission even thereafter, any party to the arbitration may introduce new claims against one or the other of the parties to that arbitration. Such claims will fall outside the (*prima facie*) control of the ICC Court, and it will therefore be for the Tribunal to decide whether it has jurisdiction over such new claims. The criteria set forth in Art. 6(4) for the ICC Court's *prima facie* jurisdictional control will apply *mutatis mutandis* to a Tribunal, which is required to make a positive jurisdictional finding in these circumstances.[7] **8–9**

Article 8(2): "Any party making a claim pursuant to Article 8(1) shall provide the information specified in Article 4(3) subparagraphs c), d), e) and f)."

A party making a claim against another party must provide the same type of information for that claim that is contemplated in Art. 4(3)(c)–(f) for a claim made in a Request of Arbitration. This subparagraph is consistent with the ICC's effort to have a Claimant provide as much information as possible when pursuing a claim in a Request for Arbitration, so as to give the Respondent an immediate understanding of what type of claim he has to respond to.[8] It adds clarity to the Rules, but is otherwise of limited relevance. In particular, it only applies until the Terms of Reference are signed or approved, by which time the Tribunal will be in charge and will be fixing the requirements for filing a claim. Likewise, if a party does not comply with the requirements of Art. 4(3)(c)–(f) in bringing a new claim, such failure will entail no sanctions whatsoever under the ICC Rules. It would not be a basis for declaring the new claim inadmissible, let alone for dismissing it. Such sanctions could only be imposed by the Tribunal, by setting them out in the Terms of Reference or Procedural Rules.[9] **8–10**

5 See Voser, "*Overview of the Most Important Changes in the Revised ICC Arbitration Rules*", (2011) ASA Bull. 29/4, p. 783(795).

6 See the discussion at para. 8–9 below.

7 In this sense see also Craig & Jaeger, "*The 2012 ICC Rules: Important changes and issues for future resolution*", (2012) *Les Cahiers de l'Arbitrage* (1), p. 15 (30) with respect to Art. 9.

8 See the discussion under Article 4(3)(c) at para. 4–40.

9 See the discussion under Article 24(1) at para. 24–**6**.

Article 8(3): "Before the Secretariat transmits the file to the arbitral tribunal in accordance with Article 16, the following provisions shall apply, *mutatis mutandis*, to any claim made: Article 4(4) subparagraph a); Article 4(5); Article 5(1) except for subparagraphs a), b), e) and f); Article 5(2); Article 5(3) and Article 5(4). Thereafter, the arbitral tribunal shall determine the procedure for making a claim."

8–11 As long as the ICC Court's Secretariat has not transmitted the file to the Tribunal, the Parties to the arbitration, including any additional party joined pursuant to Art. 7, may wish to bring new claims against each other, for which Art. 8(3) has set certain form requirements and procedures, which apply to the party bringing any such new claims, as well as to the party against which new claims are brought. In particular, they must submit all pleadings and other written communications in a number of copies sufficient to provide one copy for each party, plus one for each arbitrator and the Secretariat (Art.4(4)(a) and respond to the claims within 30 days from notification by the Secretariat, including comments as to the nature and circumstances of the dispute giving rise to the claims and the basis upon which the claims are made (Art.5(1)(c)), a response to the releif sought (Art.5(1)(d)), and such other documents or information as considered appropriate or as may contribute to the efficient resolution of the dispute (Art.5(1)).

8–12 Article 4(4)(a): A party filing a new claim must submit a sufficient number of copies thereof, *i.e.*, one for each of the other parties, one for each member of the Tribunal, and one for the ICC Court's Secretariat.[10] This reminder to the party seeking to file a new claim is important because the Secretariat will have to transmit the brief containing the new claim to all the other parties to the arbitration, as can be seen from the reference in Art. 8(3) to Art. 4(5) of the Rules.

8–13 Article 4(5): A brief containing a new claim – other than the counterclaim which normally is filed together with the Answer to the Request for Arbitration (Art. 5(5) of the Rules) and notified by the Secretariat together with the Answer (Art. 5(4) of the Rules) – will have to be notified by the Secretariat to all other parties to the arbitration.

8–14 While the party bringing any new claims must comply with the requirement foreseen for a Request for Arbitration, no separate filing fee will become due. The monetary amount of the new claims will be taken into account at the moment at which the ICC Court fixes the advance on cost or reconsiders the amount of such advance as per art. 36(4).[11]

8–15 Article 5(1) (c), (d): Article 8 makes art.5(1) applicable, except for its subparagraph (a), (b), (e) and (f), which leaves sub-paragraphs (c) and (d) and the last paragraph to apply *mutatis mutandis* to a brief containing a new claim. The answer to the new claim must therefore contain the opposing party's "comments as to the nature and circumstances of the dispute giving rise to the claims and the basis upon which the claims are made," as well as "its comments to the relief sought," Art. 5(1)(c) and (d).

[10] See the discussion under Article 4(4)(a) at paras. 4–**68 to 4–72.**

[11] See in that respect the discussion under Article 36(4) at paras. 36–34 to 36–35.

Article 5(2): The party against whom a new claim is directed and which has been invited by the Secretariat to answer that claim within a certain time-limit can seek an extension of that time-limit from the Secretariat. The requirement of having made "observations or proposals concerning the number of arbitrators and their choice", prior thereto, or at the same time, does not apply in this situation. **8–16**

Article 5(3): The opposing party's Answer to the new claim must be submitted in a sufficient number of copies. This is self-evident again, but it does not hurt to provide users guidance as to simple administrative matters, such as whether multiple copies of a brief are required or not by the ICC Court's Secretariat. **8–17**

Article 5(4): Once the Secretariat receives the opposing party's answer to a new claim, it will notify it to all other parties. It will, however, only have to do so as long as the file has not yet been transmitted to the Tribunal. Once the Tribunal is in possession of the file, it is incumbent upon the opposing party to send its answer directly to the Tribunal, as well as to all other parties, and to provide the Secretariat with a copy thereof. **8–18**

As soon as the Tribunal has received the file form the Secretariat, the Tribunal will have to fix the rules for introducing any new claim(s) and for the opposing party's answer thereto. It will either do so in the Terms of Reference (as per Art. 23(1)(g) of the Rules)[12] or in a Procedural Order setting forth the Procedural Rules that shall apply to a particular arbitration.[13] **8–19**

[12] See the discussion under Article 23(1)(g) at paras. 23–**54 to 23–64**.

[13] See the discussion under Article 22(1) at paras. 22–**3 to 22–5** and under Article 24(1) at para. 24–**6**.

Article 9 Multiple Contracts

Subject to the provisions of Articles 6(3)–6(7) and 23(4), claims arising out of or in connection with more than one contract may be made in a single arbitration, irrespective of whether such claims are made under one or more than one arbitration agreement under the Rules.

Introductory remarks

9–1 Article 9 deals with multiple contracts in a single arbitration. It represents a useful clarification inasmuch as it clearly states that parties may bring claims in the same ICC arbitration that are based on more than one contract. A classic example is where a seller and a buyer to a sales contract have, for instance, also entered into an after-sales service or maintenance contract. If the buyer has claims arising out of both contracts, he has two choices: He can start two separate arbitrations and pursue claims based on one of the two contracts in each. Or, he can start one single arbitration and pursue his claims based on the two contracts or, more precisely, on the basis of more than one arbitration agreement.

9–2 Article 9 applies irrespective of the number of parties to the arbitration, *i.e.* also when there are only two parties, as in the example of the preceding paragraph, which refers to a seller and a buyer having entered into two contracts. In addition, Article 9 does not distinguish as to whether or not the claims are pursued by the same or different parties. What matters for Art. 9 to apply is the fact that the claims are based on more than one contract.

9–3 Table **[6]** below illustrates the situation where A, as the owner, has entered into a construction contract with a consortium consisting of B and C as general contractor ("Contract 1"), and where the same parties have also entered into a maintenance contract ("Contract II"). Both contracts provide for ICC arbitration Paris.

9–4 During its works for the revision of the Rules, the Drafting Subcommittee discussed a few examples of typical situations with which the ICC Court has to deal with regularly, but for which the existing Rules gave.

9–5 Two party arbitrations, example No. 1: A Claimant may pursue two or more claims, each being based upon more than one contract.[1] In many cases, a Respondent will see no reason to object to Claimant's attempt to pursue claims arising out of different contracts in a single arbitration. In a few cases, however, Respondent may have good reasons to object, by stating that no agreement exists to arbitrate such combined claims in a single arbitration.

[1] See para. 9–**1** above the example of the seller and buyer having entered into a sales contract and a separate maintenance contract.

Multiple contracts

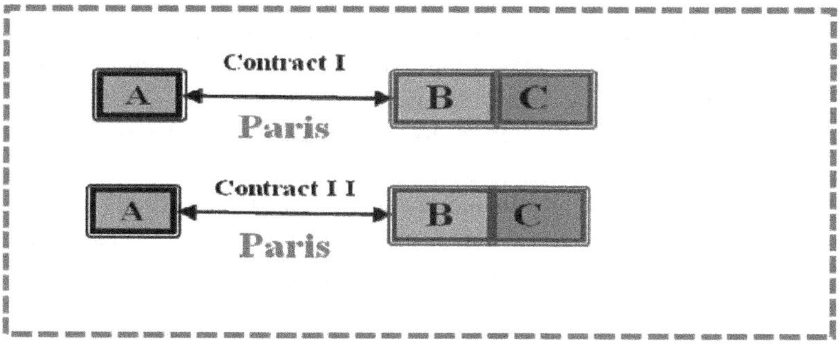

ICC Handbook, Table [6]

Two party arbitrations, example No. 2: The Claimant and the Respondent are bound by two contracts. Claimant starts the arbitration on the basis of Contract I, and respondent counterclaims on the basis of Contract II. In this scenario, Claimant may in few cases have good reasons to object in the same manner as Respondent in example No. 1. 9–6

Multiple party arbitration, example No. 3: A Claimant has a contract with three Respondents that are jointly and severally liable towards the Claimant under Contract I. The same Claimant has another contract with one of the three Respondents, Contract II. If the Claimant wishes to pursue in one arbitration, not only claims arising out of Contract I, but also claims against one Respondent on the basis of Contract II, any of the Respondents may object to arbitrating all of Claimant's claims in a single arbitration, on the ground that no agreement to arbitrate in such circumstances exists. 9–7

Multiple party arbitration, example No. 4: A Claimant has a Contract I with Respondent, against whom it files a claim. Respondent counterclaims on the basis of Contract I, and joins an additional party by pursuing against it a claim on the basis of Contract II, to which Claimant (i) is or (ii) is not a party. In this scenario, the objections to arbitrating the claims arising out of Contract I and Contract II in a single arbitration may come from Claimant, as well as from the additional party. 9–8

Many more examples, and variations of the above examples could be given, and are to be found in the ICC Court's practice. 9–9

Multiple contracts

The term "multiple contracts" is not defined in the 2012 Rules. What is meant is simply the fact that, in one single arbitration, claims are pursued that are based on more than one contract. This possibility is now also reflected in Art. 4(3)(c) and (f) for the Request for arbitration, and in Art. 5(5)(a) and (d) for the Counterclaim.[2] 9–10

[2] See respectively the discussion under Article 4(3)(c) and (f) at paras. 4–39 to 4–42, 4–53 to 4–54 and under Article 5(5)(a) and (d) at paras. 5–53 to 5–58.

More than one arbitration agreement

9–11 Claims arising out of two separate contracts may be based on the same arbitration agreement, for instance, a so-called umbrella arbitration agreement. These claims may also be based on the arbitration clause contained in each contract. Where the arbitration clauses are in all material respects identical, the Tribunal must decide whether it has jurisdiction to adjudicate these claims in one arbitration.

9–12 The ICC Court will, however, step in and, pursuant to the referral made to it by the Secretary General pursuant to Art. 6(3), exercise its *prima facie* control in accordance with Art. 6(4)(ii) of the Rules. That provision sets out two important conditions:

- **(i.) The ICC Court must be *prima facie* satisfied that the arbitration agreements in the two (or more) contracts are compatible. Examples of when this is or is not the case are discussed under art.6(4)(ii) above, and Table [7] in para 9–13 below illustrates the issue.**
- **(ii.) The ICC Court must also be *prima facie* satisfied that the Parties may have agreed that the claims based on contracts containing different arbitration agreements can be determined together in a single arbitration. Examples of such situation are discussed under art.6(4)(ii), and Table [8] below illustrates the issue.**

The compatibility issue

9–13 As stated in para. 9–12(i), the ICC Court must verify the compatibility of the arbitration agreements, on which parties to one arbitration rely in the pursuit of their claims. In the example given at para. 9–3, the two contracts contain identical arbitration clauses providing for Paris as place of arbitration. In the example at Table [7] below, the places of arbitration are different, making it impossible to pursue claims in the same arbitration arising both out of Contract I and Contract II.

Incompatible arbitration clauses

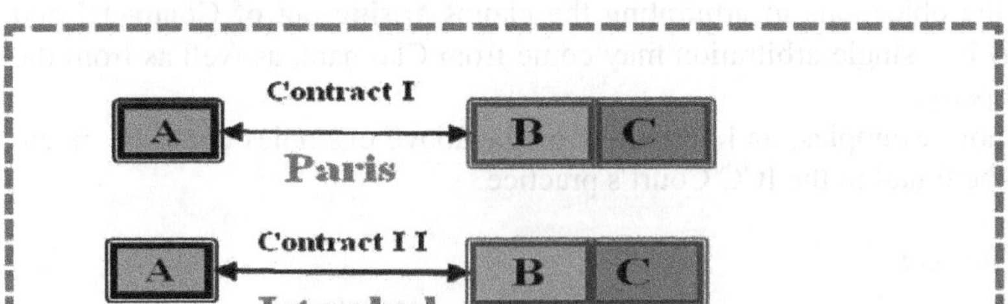

ICC Handbook, Table [7]

Lack of identity of parties

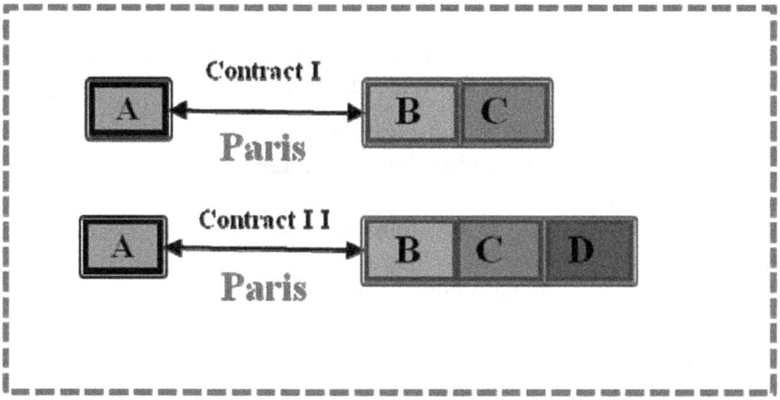

ICC Handbook, Table [8]

Lack of identity of parties

9–14 In the example given at para. 9–**3** above and illustrated in Table **[6]** above, the parties to Contract I and Contract II are identical. It is therefore possible to conclude, at least *prima facie*, that all parties would have agreed to a single arbitration as is discussed under Art.6(4). If, however, we add another party to Contract II, as in Table **[8]** below, the question of whether all parties may have agreed to a single arbitration becomes much more difficult to answer. We discuss the various criteria to be considered by the ICC Court in this context under Art. 6(4)(ii)(b) of the Rules.

Ultimate jurisdictional determination by Tribunal

9–15 Whenever claims are pursued under multiple contracts, a positive finding of jurisdiction will ultimately be required by the Tribunal. If the Court was asked, and thus had an opportunity, to take a *prima facie* decision on the basis of Art. 6(4), the Tribunal will nevertheless have the last (although not necessarily final) word in that respect, Art. 6(5). But even in cases where the ICC Court had no chance to take a decision on the basis of Art. 6(4), for instance, because the claims based on an additional contract were only made once the Tribunal was seized with the file, it will be for the Tribunal to determine its jurisdiction, and in doing so, it will have to consider the criteria set forth in Art. 6(4).

Article 10 Consolidation of Arbitration

The Court may, at the request of a party, consolidate two or more arbitrations pending under the Rules into a single arbitration, where:

a) the parties have agreed to consolidation; or
b) all of the claims in the arbitrations are made under the same arbitration agreement; or
c) where the claims in the arbitrations are made under more than one arbitration agreement, the arbitrations are between the same parties, the disputes in the arbitrations arise in connection with the same legal relationship, and the Court finds the arbitration agreements to be compatible.

In deciding whether to consolidate, the Court may take into account any circumstances it considers to be relevant, including whether one or more arbitrators have been confirmed or appointed in more than one of the arbitrations and, if so, whether the same or different persons have been confirmed or appointed.

When arbitrations are consolidated, they shall be consolidated into the arbitration that commenced first, unless otherwise agreed by all parties.[1]

Introductory remarks

10–1 Article 10 allows, within narrow conditions, the consolidation of an ICC arbitration case with an already pending ICC arbitration. Unless the parties otherwise agree, no consolidation of two or more ICC arbitration cases is permissible if the parties to all cases are not bound by the same arbitration agreement. Compared to Art. 4(6) of the 1998 Rules, Art. 10 broadens the scope of consolidation. Indeed, as long as the claims in the arbitration agreement are made under the same arbitration agreement, identity of the parties in these arbitrations is no longer required (see art. 10 b). Likewise, the signing of Terms of Reference in one of the arbitrations does, as such, no longer limit the ICC Court's possibility to consolidate the cases.

10–2 The decision to consolidate the arbitrations is to be taken exclusively by the ICC Court. It is an administrative decision, which is binding not only upon the Parties, but also upon the Tribunal.[2] The arbitrators have no power under the Rules to consolidate ICC arbitration proceedings, nor can they undo the ICC Court's decision to consolidate. This explains the relatively narrow scope of

[1] Article 10 replaces and expands the provision of Art.4(6) of the 1998 Rules.
[2] See the discussion under Article 1(2) at paras. 1–16 and 1–17 regarding the administrative nature of the ICC Court's decisions.

application of Art. 10, although it is slightly broader than the scope of Art. 4(6) of the 1998 Arbitration Rules.

When more than one arbitration is pending between the same parties or between related parties, concerning the same subject-matter or a related subject-matter, the question may arise whether for reasons of judicial economy and to avoid conflicting rules, the two (or more) arbitrations should not be consolidated so as to form one single arbitration. It is commonly accepted that, where disputes are based on a common or closely related set of facts, significant savings of time and money can be achieved in consolidating proceedings. Moreover, the risk of inconsistent awards disappears in such cases. The ICC Court's power to consolidate pending cases remains, however, restrictive, in particular with respect to cases commenced under more than one arbitration agreement. In those cases, the identity of the parties in both cases remains a strict requirement. **10–3**

This restriction is of particular importance in the construction and engineering industries, where a chain of contractors and sub-contractors is working to achieve a project for the account of its owner (also known as the employer). If a sub-contractor starts an arbitration against the general contractor, and the latter then decides to start an arbitration against the owner (employer) of the project, these two cases could not be joined by the ICC Court, absent unanimous consent of all parties concerned.[3] The lack of power of the ICC Court to consolidate cases in such circumstances absent full consent was considered an important protection in particular by users of ICC arbitration coming from the construction industry, including representatives of FIDIC. **10–4**

In 2012, the ICC Court considered ten applications for consolidation on the basis of Art. 10, seven of which were accepted. The year before, on the basis of Art. 4(6) of the 1998 Rules, eleven applications were considered, of which only two led to a consolidation.[4] **10–5**

Consolidation of Arbitral proceedings in three cases

Article 10 expressly lists three cases in which the ICC Court may consolidate two or more arbitrations. While the decision is in the ICC Court's discretion, the scope of discretion will vary depending on the circumstances before the Court. **10–6**

Article 10(a): "the parties have agreed to consolidation"

If the parties agree to have two or more cases consolidated, the ICC Court will normally want to respect that agreement, unless there existed circumstances making such consolidation inappropriate. This could be the case, for instance, if the arbitration clauses of the respective arbitration were not compatible, and the parties' agreement to consolidate would not cure the incompatibility. **10–7**

Article 10(b): "all of the claims in the arbitration are made under the same arbitration agreement"

[3] Such consent can take various forms in practice.

[4] Information provided by courtesy of the Secretary General of the ICC Court.

10–8 When all the claims are made under the same arbitration agreement, the Parties concerned by these claims will, by definition, be bound by the same arbitration agreement. It is therefore no longer required that there exists strict identity between the parties of the cases to be consolidated. The controlling factor is rather whether all parties are bound or not by the same arbitration agreement.

Article 10(c): "where the claims in the arbitrations are made under more than one arbitration agreement, the arbitrations are between the same parties, the disputes in the arbitrations arise in connection with the same legal relationship, and the Court finds the arbitration agreements to be compatible"

10–9 Where the claims are made under more than one arbitration agreement, identity of the parties to the arbitration is required. This safeguard is essential to avoid that in a chain of contracts more than the respective contract parties can be involved in one given arbitration. If a general contractor has a dispute with the owner, and another with one of his subcontractors, and starts an arbitration against each of them, a consolidation of these two arbitrations would not be possible.

"In deciding whether to consolidate, the Court may take into account any circumstances it considers to be relevant, including whether one or more arbitrators have been confirmed or appointed in more than one of the arbitrations and, if so, whether the same or different persons have been confirmed or appointed."

10–10 The decision to consolidate rests upon the ICC Court, and it has a reasonable amount of discretion in making this decision. The second full subparagraph of Art. 10 refers in general terms to "any circumstances [the ICC Court] considers to be relevant," and specifically mentions one of them (. . .).

"When arbitrations are consolidated, they shall be consolidated into the arbitration that commenced first, unless otherwise agreed by all parties."

10–11 The third subparagraph of Art. 10 contains a simple administrative rule: the case number and caption of the first case filed with the ICC will prevail in case of consolidation with one or more other cases, since the ICC Court will consolidate the cases into the arbitration that commenced first in time.

CHAPTER 4

THE ARBITRAL TRIBUNAL

Article 11 General Provisions

1 **Every arbitrator must be and remain impartial and independent of the parties involved in the arbitration.**

2 **Before appointment or confirmation, a prospective arbitrator shall sign a statement of acceptance, availability, impartiality and independence. The prospective arbitrator shall disclose in writing to the Secretariat any facts or circumstances which might be of such a nature as to call into question the arbitrator's independence in the eyes of the parties, as well as any circumstances that could give rise to reasonable doubts as to the arbitrator's impartiality. The Secretariat shall provide such information to the parties in writing and fix a time limit for any comments from them.**

3 **An arbitrator shall immediately disclose in writing to the Secretariat and to the parties any facts or circumstances of a similar nature to those referred to in Article 11(2) concerning the arbitrator's impartiality or independence which may arise during the arbitration.**

4 **The decisions of the Court as to the appointment, confirmation, challenge or replacement of an arbitrator shall be final, and the reasons for such decisions shall not be communicated.**

5 **By accepting to serve, arbitrators undertake to carry out their responsibilities in accordance with the Rules.**

6 **Insofar as the parties have not provided otherwise, the arbitral tribunal shall be constituted in accordance with the provisions of Articles 12 and 13**[1]

[1] Article 11 corresponds to art.7 of the 1998 ICC Rules. The main substantive change has been the introduction of reference to impartiality in art.11(1) and to the consequent changes in art.11(2) and art.11(3).

Introductory remarks

11–1 One of the basic features of ICC arbitration is the parties' freedom to choose the arbitrators. The ICC does not keep, let alone provide, a list of recommended or approved arbitrators. The Secretariat of the ICC Court will not generally offer any indication with respect to arbitrators or their qualities.[2] Another basic feature is that the ICC sets out its requirements for arbitrators under art.11(1), imposes disclosure requirements under art.11(2) and decides (under art.11(4)) whether to confirm arbitrators and therefore will consider whether arbitrators meet the requirements of the Rules prior to their appointment being effective. A third feature is that it is the ICC Court that decides on challenges to arbitrators under art.14 for failure to meet the requirements of art.11. Finally, pursuant to art.15 the ICC Court decides on the replacement of arbitrators due to their de facto or de jure inability to fulfill their obligations under the Rules. These matters are dealt with at Plenary and Committee Sessions as is outlined in Annex 1 Pt I. Therefore, the requirements discussed below are applied under other articles.

11–2 In addition to the ICC requirements, art.V(1) of the New York Convention provides that a national court may refuse enforcement of an Award if "[t]he composition of the arbitral authority or the arbitral procedure was not in accordance with the agreement of the parties, or, failing such agreement, was not in accordance with the law of the country where the arbitration took place".

11–3 Therefore, the framework provided by the Rules must be read not only in the light of the agreement of the parties, but also of the law of the place of arbitration. In respect of the latter, it is noteworthy that art.12(2) of the UNCITRAL Model Law provides that "[a]n arbitrator may be challenged only if circumstances exist that give rise to justifiable doubts as to his impartiality or independence, or if he does not possess qualifications agreed to by the parties". The standard of "impartiality and independence" has counterparts in the English Arbitration Act of 1996 (s.24(1)),[3] the US Federal Arbitration Act (s.10),[4] under French law based on art.341 of the NCPC[5] and art.180 of the Swiss PILA.[6] The main issue is how these provisions are applied in different situations, the main ones being discussed below, as well as under art.14 which deals with the challenge of arbitrators. The national law standards are applicable in any event. Therefore the addition of the reference to impartiality should not have a substantive effect on the standards applicable or the practice of the ICC Court (which always considered issues of impartiality as well in any event).

11–4 There are two aspects to the issue of the status of the arbitrator in an ICC arbitration that should be focused on from the outset and that are focused on in this chapter. The first aspect relates to what parties and arbitrators can do to avoid

[2] However, the ICC does feel that it has a role in introducing arbitrators, particularly younger arbitrators, into arbitration. This is done in part by educational programs and in part appointing, whenever possible, younger arbitrators as sole arbitrators or chairmen for smaller arbitrations. In such cases, the ICC, assumes particular appointment responsibilities, as it does have a duty to ensure that the arbitrators carry out their duties in accordance with the Rules as is discussed under art.12(2).

[3] See Pt III App.9.

[4] See Pt III App.8.

[5] See Pt III App.6.

[6] See Pt III App.7.

issues with respect to independence of arbitrators. The second aspect relates to what the parties and arbitrators can do once an issue as to the independence of an arbitrator has arisen. The first aspect is approached within the framework of "best practices" based on the rules of ethics discussed below. The second aspect is best approached by analysis of the case law in the major places of arbitration, which is the approach adopted under art.14 with respect to challenges to arbitrators.

With respect to best practices, the International Bar Association has published the IBA Guidelines on Conflict of Interest in International Arbitration in 2004 (the "IBA Guidelines"). These supersede in part the IBA's Rules of Ethics for International Arbitrators of 1987 and are themselves currently being revised.[7] In para.4 of the introduction, the IBA Committee states that: 11–5

> "[t]he Guidelines reflect the Working Group's understanding of the best current international practice firmly rooted in the principles expressed in the General Standards. The Working Group has based the General Standards and the Application Lists upon statutes and case law in jurisdictions and upon the judgment and experience of members of the Working Group and others involved in international commercial arbitration."

The IBA Rules of Ethics of 1987 do not appear to have been widely cited in the courts and their practical effect has been limited.[8] In the first edition of the Handbook the authors wrote that it was not clear that the IBA Guidelines will be relied upon extensively by the national courts or that they will in fact be used by arbitrators. With the benefit of several years of experience, it is now clear that the IBA Guidelines are discussed, in some ways critically, by international arbitration practitioners. The IBA Guidelines have been cited as a point of reference in some cases,[9] are referred to frequently by counsel in submissions to the ICC Court and are referred to by the Secretariat.

[7] The IBA Guidelines supersede the IBA's Rules of Ethics for International Arbitrators of 1987 with respect to the matters covered in the new guidelines but not with respect to other matters. Therefore, with respect to other matters it may be of interest to consult the 1987 IBA Rules of Ethics. More generally, see de Witt Witjnen, "The IBA Guidelines on Conflicts of Interest in International Arbitration—Three Years On" (2007) ICC Special Supplement, *Independence of Arbitrators*, p.107. Lawson, "Impartiality and Independence of International Arbitrators—Commentary on the 2004 IBA Guidelines on Conflicts of Interest in International Arbitration" (2005) ASA Bull Vol.23 No.1, p.22; Landoldt, "The IBA Guidelines on Conflicts of Interest in International Arbitration: An Overview" (2005) J Int'l Arb Vol.22 No.5, p.409; C′ardenas and Rivkin, "A Growing Challenge for Ethics in International Arbitration" in *Liber Amicorum in honour of Robert Briner, op. cit.*, p.191.

[8] According to the IBA Working Committee, "Almost every National Report noted that the IBA Rules of Ethics [of 1987] define the elements of bias more broadly and/or present more stringent disclosure requirements than do the relevant principles of the individual jurisdictions."; see also de Witt Wijnen, Voser and Rao, "Background Information on the IBA Guidelines on Conflicts of Interest in International Arbitration" (2004) Business Law International Vol.5 No.3, p.433.

[9] By the court of first instance in *Applied Industrial Materials Corp v Ovalar Makine Ticaret Ve Sanayi AS*, US Dist LEXIS 44789, (2007) Mealey's IAR Vol.21 No.#7 p.9 as upheld in *Applied Industrial Materials Corp v Ovalar Makine Ticaret Ve Sanayi AS*, 492 F.3d 132, C.A.2 (N.Y.), July 9, 2007. The principles were also cited in England but the court did not treat them as helpful. See *ASM Shipping Ltd of India v TTMI Ltd of England* [2005] EWHC 2238 (Comm) (October 19, 2005). See also *A v B, X v* [2011] EWHC 2345 (Comm) 2011 WL 2748602.

11–6 Several points should be noted with respect to the use of the IBA Guidelines. The first point is that the situations with respect to arbitrators are very individual and specific and it is difficult to fit them within the IBA Guidelines. For example, with respect to repeat appointments of an arbitrator, the IBA Guidelines do not consider the situation of "professional arbitrators" or the situation of arbitrators well-known in smaller countries or markets. The second point is that the principle in the IBA Guidelines that a failure to disclose is not in and of itself grounds for a challenge is inconsistent with the ICC approach requiring disclosure and rendering a failure to disclose a material factor in considering any challenge. The third point is that, although the IBA Guidelines state that they are based on case law, no references are provided (due to the international nature) and it is difficult to believe that some of the matters on the "orange list" could result in a successful challenge before national courts. Finally, the IBA Guidelines focus—understandably—on the position of the arbitrator and they do so independent of the stage of the proceedings. Challenges are decided at various points in the arbitral process and the timing of a challenge is bound to have a considerable influence on how it is treated.

11–7 Despite the various caveats, the IBA Guidelines are used in international arbitration, including in ICC arbitration as a reference point for both the parties and the arbitrators. The reason is that, however imperfect they may be, the IBA Guidelines provide general principles and concrete examples that can be invoked in the context of objection to confirmation to or challenge of arbitrators. Therefore, subject to the reservations that are noted below with respect to specific aspects of the IBA Guidelines, they do provide—as they suggest—an indication of problems and possible solutions in this area. Moreover, as the IBA Guidelines state, they are intended to provide the basis for further development[10] and have been accompanied by a helpful explanatory report on behalf of the Committee for their interpretation.[11] As a result, the IBA Guidelines are a useful reference point for "best practices" in this area where it is sometimes difficult to navigate from the general principles to the specific fact situations that arise in practice in ICC arbitration.

11–8 The IBA Guidelines are in no way binding upon the ICC Court. As mentioned in the Second Edition, an authoritative commentator has questioned how useful they are for the ICC as an institution due to the ICC's subjective standard for disclosure under art.11(1) and because many cases fall within the "orange list".[12] The comments are consistent with the limitations regarding the IBA Guidelines referred to above. However, the impression, which has been confirmed since the Second Edition, is that, as imperfect as they may be, the IBA Guidelines are considered by parties, ICC Court members and the Secretariat as an additional reference point.

11–9 In the United States, the American Bar Association and American Arbitration Association have adopted the non-binding Code of Ethics for Arbitrators in

[10] See para.7 of the Introduction to the IBA Guidelines, Pt III App.11.

[11] de Witt Wijnen, Voser and Rao, *op. cit.*, p.433.

[12] Whitesell, "Independence in ICC Arbitration: ICC Court Practice concerning the Appointment, Confirmation, Challenge and Replacement of Arbitrators" (2007) ICC Special Supplement, *op. cit.*, p.36/37. See also Fry & Greenberg, "The Arbitral Tribunal: Applications of Articles 7–12 of the ICC Rules in Recent Cases" (2009) Vol. 20 No. 2 ICC Int Court of Arb Bull 19.

Commercial Disputes of March 1, 2004 (the "Code of Ethics for Arbitrators") that replaced the Code of Ethics from 1977.[13] This Code of Ethics for Arbitrators covers both national and international arbitrations. Unlike the IBA Guidelines in some respects, and in particular with respect to disclosure, the Code of Ethics is based in part on a concurring Supreme Court opinion.[14]

Where the place of arbitration is in the United States, the Code of Ethics provides a good indication of "best practices" in this area. Breach of the Code would in and of itself probably provide no legal basis for challenge.[15] However, the Code is arguably based in part on authoritative case law. 11–10

Article 11(1): "Every arbitrator must be and remain impartial and independent of the parties involved in the arbitration."

Article 11(1) sets out the basic principle that an ICC arbitrator must be and remain impartial and independent of the parties. This essential principle is one of the keys to the wide acceptance of ICC arbitration internationally. Article 11(1) applies to all arbitrators, whether nominated by the parties or appointed by the ICC Court. There is no equivalent in ICC arbitration to the "non-neutral" arbitrator found in domestic US arbitration.[16] Likewise, the IBA Guidelines specifically exclude "non-neutral arbitrators" from their scope.[17] The legal requirements for a co-arbitrator are the same as those for a sole arbitrator or a chairman both at the time of appointment and throughout the arbitration, although there may be differences in interpretation for party-appointed arbitrators and chairmen under the national law of the place of arbitration.[18] 11–11

The formulation of art.11(1) is succinct, although it has been amended to expressly refer to impartiality. The IBA Guidelines express the principles in more detail in General Standard 1 by stating that: "Every arbitrator shall be impartial and independent of the parties at the time of accepting an appointment to serve and shall remain so during the entire arbitration proceeding until the final award has been rendered or the proceeding has otherwise finally terminated". The IBA 11–12

[13] For an explanation, see Sheppard, Jr, "A New Era of Arbitrator Ethics for the United States: The 2004 Revision to the AAA/ABA Code of Ethics for Arbitrators in Commercial Disputes" (2005) Arb Int Vol.21 No.1, p.91; Meyerson and Townsend, "Revised Code of Ethics for Commercial Arbitrators Explained" (2004) Dispute Resolution Journal Vol.59 No.1, p.10.

[14] *Canon II* was based on Justice White's opinion in *Commonwealth Coatings Corp v Continental Casualty Co*, 393 US 145 (1968). See also Meyerson and Townsend, *op. cit.*, p.10 at p.14.

[15] *York Hannover Holding AG v American Arbitration Ass'n*, 1993 US Dist. LEXIS 6192 (D.N.Y., 1993): "York alleges that these charges taken together demonstrate that Gant 'substantially departed' from the standards of conduct expected of arbitrators as specified in the Arbitration Act, the AAA Rules and the Canons of Ethics for Arbitrators . . . Petitioner cites no authority, however, and this court has found none, to support the proposition that a violation of those rules and canons constitutes bias or any other ground to review an arbitral award. Even assuming that York's allegations are true, they do not make a showing of bias or partiality under the case law as detailed above".

[16] Under the Code of Ethics, the presumption now is that arbitrators are neutral. However, the presumption can be rebutted. For a description of the rules applicable to a non-neutral arbitrator, see Canon X of the Code of Ethics. With respect to the treatment under national law, see the discussion under art.14.

[17] IBA Guidelines, General Standard 5.

[18] For a discussion of the role of a co-arbitrator, see Webster, "Selection of Arbitrators in a Nutshell", *op. cit.*, at p.262. For the treatment by different national courts of the situation of the co-arbitrator, see the discussion under art.14.

Guidelines provide further details with respect to this aspect in General Standard 2 (see Pt III).

11–13 Canon I of the Code of Ethics formulates the principle of fairness in general terms, but includes the basic requirement that the arbitrator be impartial and independent of "the parties, potential witnesses, and the other arbitrators". As discussed under art.14, Justice White in his authoritative opinion in the *Commonwealth Coatings* case expressed the standard somewhat differently giving the indication that, in American law, one should also consider the business practicalities of the arbitrator's situation.[19]

11–14 The Rules now refer to impartiality and independence of the arbitrator as a condition for his appointment or confirmation, and provide the obligation of "impartiality" in terms of fairness in the conduct of the proceedings. The terms "independence" and "impartiality" are not identical. The concept of independence can be analysed on the basis of objective criteria (e.g. existence of a relationship between the arbitrator and the parties) while the impartiality appears to be a state of mind, thus more subjective (bias of an arbitrator).

11–15 Article 11(2) also refers to the impartiality and independence "in the eyes of the parties". Before being confirmed or appointed as an arbitrator, every arbitrator has to fill out and send to the ICC the "Arbitrator Statement of Acceptance, Availability, Impartiality and Independence". This includes the statement that the declaration has been made "after [the arbitrator has] taken into account, *inter alia*, whether there exists any past or present relationship, direct or indirect, with any of the parties or their lawyers or other representatives, whether financial, professional or of another kind". The criteria referred to in the form are those of art.11(2). The form gives the following guideline to the prospective arbitrator "[a]ny doubt should be resolved in favour of disclosure".[20] In other words, any doubt as to whether certain facts or circumstances that could call into question the arbitrator's independence should be disclosed. The form also provides that "disclosure should be complete and specific, identifying *inter alia* relevant dates (both start and end dates), financial arrangements, details of companies and individuals, and all other relevant information".

11–16 The IBA Guidelines refer to the point of view of a "reasonable and informed third party". The distinction was deliberate. The IBA Working Group expressly sought to adopt an objective third party standard and rejected the standard of the parties. The practical effect of the distinction is not clear. It is not clear that art.11(1) was intended or would be interpreted to be a truly subjective standard. As with contracts in general, one would expect the standard would be that of reasonable parties in the situation of the parties to the arbitration. Moreover,

[19] Justice White stated in part: "The Court does not decide today that arbitrators are to be held to the standards of judicial decorum of Article III judges, or indeed of any judges. It is often because they are men of affairs, not apart from but of the marketplace, that they are effective in their adjudicatory function . . . This does not mean the judiciary must overlook outright chicanery in giving effect to their awards; that would be an abdication of our responsibility. But it does mean that arbitrators are not automatically disqualified by a business relationship with the parties before them if both parties are informed of the relationship in advance, or if they are unaware of the facts but the relationship is trivial. I see no reason automatically to disqualify the best informed and most capable potential arbitrators" in the *Commonwealth Coatings* case, see para.14–66.

[20] The form is reproduced in Pt II Document 7.1.

art.11(1) does not refer simply to the point of view of the challenging party but rather of both parties to the arbitration.

The IBA Guidelines give practical examples of the types of relationships that, under the Guidelines, do and do not raise issues as to whether an arbitrator is impartial and independent. The Red List is a checklist of examples where the relationship in general does give rise to issues as to the arbitrator's impartiality and independence. It is divided into two parts. The Non-Waivable Red List,[21] where the relationship should preclude the person from acting as an arbitrator, and the Waivable Red List,[22] where there is generally an issue as to the arbitrator's impartiality and independence, but where the parties may waive the objection. **11–17**

These lists have no binding effect as such unless adopted by the parties in their arbitration agreement. As mentioned before, the Secretariat will at best compare those lists with its own analysis, but not use the recommendations of the list as a basis for its own findings regarding a potential or actual challenge against an arbitrator since the ICC Court's decision is rendered on a case-by-case basis. However, the lists provide useful benchmarks for parties and arbitrators seeking to deal with practical problems and may end up being applied in national courts. **11–18**

The Non-Waivable Red List is as follows: **11–19**

> "1.1. There is an identity between a party and the arbitrator, or the arbitrator is a legal representative of an entity that is a party in the arbitration.
> 1.2. The arbitrator is a manager, director or member of the supervisory board, or has a similar controlling influence in one of the parties.
> 1.3. The arbitrator has a significant financial interest in one of the parties or the outcome of the case.
> 1.4. The arbitrator regularly advises the appointing party or an affiliate of the appointing party, and the arbitrator or his or her firm derives a significant financial income therefrom."

This is a list of relationships that cannot be waived in the view of the authors of the IBA Guidelines. In a sense, the relationship is such that it would undermine the arbitral process to have arbitrators act as such when they have an interest in the outcome, for example. It will depend upon the specific circumstances of each case submitted to the ICC Court whether the factors mentioned in the IBA Guidelines Red List would suffice to disqualify an arbitrator, but it should be the case.[23] At a minimum, the relationships described in the Non-Waivable Red List raise very serious issues relating to independence. **11–20**

The IBA Guidelines then set out a second list, "the Waivable Red List" which gives rise to doubts as to impartiality or independence but where the parties may, under the IBA Guidelines, waive a possible objection. That list is as follows: **11–21**

[21] For the complete list, see Pt III App.11.
[22] For the complete list, see Pt III App.11.
[23] Whether infringement of the rules in the Red List will result in a successful challenge to the arbitrator or the Award, is dealt with under arts 14 and 28.

"2.1. Relationship of the arbitrator to the dispute

2.1.1 The arbitrator has given legal advice or provided an expert opinion on the dispute to a party or an affiliate of one of the parties.

2.1.2 The arbitrator has previous involvement in the case.

2.2. Arbitrator's direct or indirect interest in the dispute

2.2.1 The arbitrator holds shares, either directly or indirectly, in one of the parties or an affiliate of one of the parties that is privately held.

2.2.2 A close family member of the arbitrator has a significant financial interest in the outcome of the dispute.

2.2.3 The arbitrator or a close family member of the arbitrator has a close relationship with a third party who may be liable to recourse on the part of the unsuccessful party in the dispute.

2.3. Arbitrator's relationship with the parties or counsel

2.3.1 The arbitrator currently represents or advises one of the parties or an affiliate of one of the parties.

2.3.2 The arbitrator currently represents the lawyer or law firm acting as counsel for one of the parties.

2.3.3 The arbitrator is a lawyer in the same law firm as the counsel to one of the parties.

2.3.4 The arbitrator is a manager, director or member of the supervisory board, or has a similar controlling influence, in an affiliate of one of the parties if the affiliate is directly involved in the matters in dispute in the arbitration.

2.3.5 The arbitrator's law firm had a previous but terminated involvement in the case without the arbitrator being involved himself or herself.

2.3.6 The arbitrator's law firm currently has a significant commercial relationship with one of the parties or an affiliate of one of the parties.

2.3.7 The arbitrator regularly advises the appointing party or an affiliate of the appointing party, but neither the arbitrator nor his or her firm derives a significant financial income therefrom.

2.3.8 The arbitrator has a close family relationship with one of the parties or with a manager, director or member of the supervisory board or any person having a similar controlling influence in one of the parties or an affiliate of one of the parties or with a counsel representing a party.

2.3.9 A close family member of the arbitrator has a significant financial interest in one of the parties or an affiliate of one of the parties."[24]

[24] For the purpose of the above a "close family member" is defined as "a spouse, sibling, child, parent or life partner." In reviewing the Red List and the other lists of the IBA Guidelines, one should note the comments of the Working Group with respect to law firms, groups and companies and barristers, discussed beginning of para.11–35.

Article 2 in general focuses on the arbitrator and not the arbitrator's law firm. With respect to legal advice (referred to in para.2.1.1), in a recent case, the ICC Court had to consider the situation where an arbitrator's former law firm provided an opinion on the agreement that gave rise to the dispute. In the authors' view this is a clear conflict of interest that is not dealt with as such in the IBA Guidelines. With respect to art.2.3.5 of the IBA Guidelines, the ICC Court had recently to consider the situation of a "beauty contest" in which the law firm of the future arbitrator had an initial meeting with one of the firm's lawyers and made some brief comments with a view to being hired as counsel in the arbitration. Ultimately, the firm was not retained for the arbitration. Another lawyer of that firm was then nominated by the other party (the Respondent) as its arbitrator. When the arbitrator then disclosed the initial contact of his firm with the Claimant, the latter objected to his appointment as arbitrator. In the particular circumstances of this case, the initial contact of the arbitrator's firm with one of the parties to the dispute was not held to give rise to a breach of art.11(1). **11–22**

The IBA Committee states that: **11–23**

> "[t]he waivable Red List encompasses situations that are serious but not as severe. Because of their seriousness, unlike circumstances described in the Orange List, these situations should be considered waivable only if and when the parties, being aware of the conflict of interest situation, nevertheless expressly state their willingness to have such a person act as arbitrator, as set forth in General Standard 4(c) [setting out the disclosure and express consent requirements]."

Whether the waiver approach set out in the IBA Guidelines provides an effective solution may ultimately be a matter for the national courts. It is not clear that, in all circumstances, the ICC Court would accept a waiver. For the ICC as an institution, there are interests with respect to ICC arbitration that may outweigh the principle of party autonomy. In some jurisdictions national courts may reject the waiver as being unenforceable if contrary to their interpretation of mandatory principles of law. Moreover, the waiver only applies to the disclosure of the relationship and not to the conduct of the arbitration. If a party perceives the arbitrator differently due to the relationship, it may colour the interpretation of conduct during the arbitration that may give rise to objection. In addition, an unsuccessful party may challenge the completeness of the disclosure and the nature of the waiver after the Award. Therefore, the waiver procedure has to be considered in the light of the relationship and the decisions of the national courts with respect to the relationship in question.[25] **11–24**

The IBA Guidelines indicate that the obligation of impartiality and independence should last until the final Award has been rendered but not during any annulment or enforcement proceedings. This approach appears to be reasonable as the Tribunal is, in principle, subject to remand discussed under art.35, functus officio with respect to the matter in dispute.[26] **11–25**

[25] See art.14 for a discussion of the national cases.

[26] For the possibility of a remand by a national court to the arbitrator, see the discussion under art.35.

Article 11(2): "Before appointment or confirmation, a prospective arbitrator shall sign a statement of acceptance, availability, impartiality and independence. The prospective arbitrator shall disclose in writing to the Secretariat any facts or circumstances which might be of such a nature as to call into question the arbitrator's independence in the eyes of the parties, as well as any circumstances that could give rise to reasonable doubts as to the arbitrator's impartiality. The Secretariat shall provide such information to the parties in writing and fix a time limit for any comments from them."

11–26 The arbitrator's duty of disclosure under art.11(2) can be subdivided into three issues: (i) what a prospective arbitrator is required to disclose; (ii) the effect of such disclosure; and (iii) whether a failure to disclose be in and of itself grounds for a refusal to confirm the arbitrator under art.11(4) or a challenge under art.14.

11–27 In ICC arbitration, disclosure is systematic; it is not left to the arbitrator. As mentioned above, the ICC requires prospective arbitrators to complete a disclosure form, the "Arbitrator Statement of Acceptance, Availability, Impartiality and Independence".[27] Also, every arbitrator in an ICC arbitration must be confirmed or appointed by the ICC Court. As a result, where there is an issue as to compliance with art.11(1), it will come before the ICC Court.

11–28 Article 11(2) refers to "facts and circumstances which may be of such a nature as to call into question the arbitrator's independence in the eyes of the parties". Therefore, the reference is once again to "independence" as in art.11(1) and the standard is that "in the eyes of the parties". In other words, the arbitrator should disclose any matters which may "reasonably" call into his independence vis-à-vis the parties. It is the arbitrator's responsibility to assess the need to make such a disclosure in consideration of the circumstances of the case as it is not the practice of the ICC Court and the Secretariat to second-guess, let alone verify the correctness of the arbitrator's statement.[28] The Secretariat does maintain that it conducts "spot checks" with the ICC database with respect to arbitrators and law firms. However, this review is not systematic and the ICC is not undertaking any obligation to the parties to carry out such checks.[29] Article 11(2) now requires disclosure of "any circumstances that could give rise to reasonable doubts as to the arbitrator's impartiality". These circumstances could relate, for example, to Awards rendered by Tribunals of which the arbitrator was a member or to the issue of parallel arbitration proceedings in which the arbitrator is participating.

[27] See also para.11–15 and Pt II Document 7.1.

[28] Failure to make a disclosure could give rise to a challenge of the arbitrator by one of the parties. See the discussion in art.14. As an illustration, see also Civ. Bruxelles, December 14, 2006, *s.a. CBC Banque v J.M.M., B.H., B.P. and J.C.*, (2007) Journal des Tribunaux p.208, note Keutgen (non-disclosure by a co-arbitrator who has been appointed in six similar arbitration cases admitting the liability in substance of the same Claimant, challenge admitted). Similarly, Henry, "Note—Cour d'appel de Paris (1re Ch. C), 29 janvier 2004. Cour d'appel de Paris (1re Ch. C), 10 février 2005; Cour d'appel (1re Ch. C), 17 février 2005; Tribunal de commerce de Paris (réf.), 6 juillet 2004" (2005) Rev Arb No.3, p.720. For a discussion, see r.3.3.7 of the IBA Guidelines, Orange List (obligation of disclosure by the arbitrator when he has been appointed within the last three years more than three times by the same counsel or the same law firm); Wislke and Stock, "Rule 3.3.7 of the IBA Guidelines on Conflicts of Interest in International Arbitration—The Enlargement of the Usual Shortlist?" (2005) ASA Bull Vol.23 No.1, p.45.

[29] The obligation to make disclosure is on the arbitrator. See, however, Fry, Greenberg & Mazza, *op. cit.* para. 3–391.

The Secretariat provides the statement of independence to the parties. If the arbitrator's statement is unqualified (and there is no disclosure), a party may comment based on information that it has in its possession. If the prospective arbitrator makes disclosure then the party may comment on other issues of which it has knowledge or on the matters disclosed. If a party has no objection based on the disclosure, usually the party either makes no comments or is neutral. If the party does object, it generally requests that the ICC Court decide not to confirm the arbitrator. Usually, the potential arbitrator will carefully consider any comments to determine whether they give rise to grounds for the ICC Court to refuse confirmation. A party should not intervene without justification in the confirmation procedure. However, where there is a substantive concern, it is preferable to have it dealt with early in the proceedings when the replacement of the arbitrator would be less problematic than later on. Since the perception of the parties (and the ICC Court) will depend on what the prospective arbitrator discloses (or fails to disclose), it is important to consider best practices for disclosure. 11–29

It is noteworthy that, while adopting the objective test with respect to the impartiality and independence requirement, the IBA Guidelines then adopt what they refer to as a subjective test ("in the eyes of the parties") with respect to disclosure. General Standard 3 of the IBA Guidelines provides as follows: 11–30

> "(a) If facts or circumstances exist that may, in the eyes of the parties, give rise to doubts as to the arbitrator's impartiality or independence, the arbitrator shall disclose such facts or circumstances to the parties, the arbitration institution or other appointing authority (if any, and if so required by the applicable institutional rules) and to the co-arbitrators, if any, prior to accepting his or her appointment or, if thereafter, as soon as he or she learns about them.
>
> (b) It follows from General Standards 1 and 2(a) that an arbitrator who has made a disclosure considers himself or herself to be impartial and independent of the parties despite the disclosed facts and therefore capable of performing his or her duties as arbitrator. Otherwise, he or she would have declined the nomination or appointment at the outset or resigned.
>
> (c) Any doubt as to whether an arbitrator should disclose certain facts or circumstances should be resolved in favour of disclosure."

Clearly, any matter in the Waivable Red List of the IBA Guidelines would, at the very least, have to be disclosed. The IBA Guidelines also set out an Orange List which it describes as a: 11–31

> "non-exhaustive enumeration of specific situations which (depending on the facts of a given case) in the eyes of the parties may give rise to justifiable doubts as to the arbitrator's impartiality or independence. The Orange List thus reflects situations that would fall under General Standard 3(a), so that the arbitrator has a duty to disclose such situations. In all these situations, the parties are deemed to have accepted the

arbitrator if, after disclosure, no timely objection is made. (General Standard 4(a))."

11–32 The Orange List is extensive and provides a useful checklist for parties and arbitrators to be engaged or actually involved in an ICC arbitration, although, as noted above, some of its provisions may be viewed as too strict. It should also be emphasised again that the ICC Court is not bound by the IBA Guidelines, and for arbitrators involved in an ICC arbitration they can only serve as what they are meant to be: guidelines. In light of their practical value in rendering parties and/or arbitrators sensitive to the issues that may arise, the Orange List is reproduced below in its entirety in Pt III.[30]

11–33 The striking difference between the IBA Guidelines and art.11(2) is to be found in s.3.3 of the Guidelines. Article 11(2) refers to independence from the parties; it does not mention counsel or the arbitrators. Nor does art.11(2) refer to the relationship between arbitrators, although the Statement of Acceptance, Availability, Impartiality and Independence does refer to the parties' lawyers or other representatives. There are cases in which the relationship between the arbitrator and the parties' lawyers or other representatives amounts to an indirect relationship with the party.[31] However, that depends in turn on the relationship between the counsel (or the other arbitrator) and the parties. In most cases, there is no identity between parties and their counsel: large groups consult various law firms and frequently have no systematic relationship with one law firm when it comes to international arbitration. The relationship with arbitrators is usually even more indirect as the arbitrators are usually selected by counsel and not by the parties themselves. Therefore, this distinction in drafting should be kept in mind at the stages of disclosure under art.11(2) and for a challenge under art.11.

11–34 The IBA Guidelines appear to try to set out "safe harbours" by defining the relevant time period (of three years) and in certain cases, the number of nominations. It is not clear that these "safe harbours" would be accepted by national courts, although the three-year time period and the number of nominations appear in themselves to be strict. As stated above in the context of the Red List, for the ICC Court, they are not relevant inasmuch as it will always look at the specific circumstances of each case.

11–35 The IBA Guidelines after some debate seek to adopt a flexible approach with respect to law firms, groups of companies and barristers' chambers. For the law firms, the principle in General Standard 6(a) is that the context should be "reasonably considered in each individual case".[32] The Working Group states in the explanatory note that "[i]n the opinion of the Working Group, the arbitrator

[30] See Pt III App.11.

[31] As noted above at para.11–15, the ICC form for the arbitrator's statement of independence refers to an arbitrator's relation with counsel of the parties as well. See also Whitesell, "Independence, in ICC Arbitration: ICC Court Practice concerning the Appointment, Confirmation Challenge and Replacement of Arbitrators" *op. cit.* at p.36.

[32] General Standard 6(a) provides: "When considering the relevance of facts or circumstances to determine whether a potential conflict of interest exists or whether disclosure should be made, the activities of an arbitrator's law firm, if any, should be reasonably considered in each individual case. Therefore, the fact that the activities of the arbitrator's firm involve one of the parties shall not automatically constitute a source of such conflict or a reason for disclosure".

must in principle be considered as identical to his or her law firm, but nevertheless the activities of the arbitrator's firm should not automatically constitute a conflict of interest. The relevance of such activities, such as the nature, timing and scope of the work by the law firm, should be reasonably considered in each individual case". There is a difference in interest between that of two partners in a 15-lawyer firm with one office and those in a firm with 500 partners with 30 offices. However, the partners in each case are in the same firm and the IBA Guidelines seek only to temper the traditional rule that an arbitrator is identical with his law firm.

With groups of companies, General Standard 6(b) provides for a similar reasonableness standard.[33] **11–36**

With respect to barristers, the background paper notes that the general rule is that barristers in chambers share expenses and not revenue. However, it also notes that chambers, perhaps increasingly, issue marketing material and then comments that: **11–37**

> "the Working Group considers that full disclosure to the parties of the involvement of more than one barrister in the same chambers in any particular case is highly desirable. Thus, barristers (including persons who are 'door tenants' or otherwise affiliated to the same chambers) should make full disclosure as soon as they become aware of the involvement of another member of the same chambers in the same arbitration, whether as arbitrator, counsel, or in any other capacity."

The treatment of barristers will of course depend on the place of arbitration as discussed in art.14. If the place of arbitration is England, then based on the *Laker* case,[34] there appears to be no issue with respect to barristers from the same chambers acting as counsel and arbitrator in the same arbitration. The problem remains for parties coming from jurisdictions where the chambers' system of barristers is unfamiliar to them, and where parties are therefore likely to have some difficulty, at least initially, to understand and accept this unique situation. The ICC Court has declined to confirm barristers who are from the same chambers as one of the arbitrators where the parties were not from the UK. It is not clear whether this would be the approach if all parties are represented by UK-based law firms who are familiar with the barrister system, although the better argument is that it should. If, despite their familiarity with the system, the UK-based law firm objects to confirmation due to such a relationship, then there is no reason why that should not be given the same weight as an objection by a non-UK-based law firm.

The IBA Guidelines go on to provide a "Green List" of matters that do not have to be disclosed. The Green List is perhaps not as helpful as it describes situations that, for many practitioners, have never raised issues of disclosure or challenge.[35] **11–38**

[33] General Standard 6(b) provides: "Similarly, if one of the parties is a legal entity which is a member of a group with which the arbitrator's firm has an involvement, such facts or circumstances should be reasonably considered in each individual case. Therefore, this fact alone shall not automatically constitute a source of a conflict of interest or a reason for disclosure".

[34] *Laker Airways v FLS Aerospace & Burnton* [1999] 2 Lloyd's Law Reports 45.

[35] See Pt III Document 11.

11–39 The IBA Guidelines refer to the problem of "over-disclosure" where a prospective arbitrator discloses minor or irrelevant information. However, General Standard 3(c) provides that "Any doubt as to whether an arbitrator should disclose certain facts or circumstances should be resolved in favour of disclosure". This approach is the one advocated by the ICC Court in its standard disclosure form for arbitrators[36] and has support elsewhere, including in the United States.[37]

Article 11(3): "An arbitrator shall immediately disclose in writing to the Secretariat and to the parties any facts or circumstances of a similar nature to those referred to in Article 11(2) concerning the arbitrator's impartiality or independence which may arise during the arbitration."

11–40 Article 11(1) requires that the arbitrators "be and remain" impartial and independent of the parties. Accordingly, art.11(3) requires ongoing disclosure during the arbitration and the arbitrator should not ignore new facts or seek to insulate him or herself from acquiring knowledge of new facts.[38]

11–41 The new facts are matters such as new intervening arbitrations. The new discovery of relevant facts is frequently a problem in larger law firms when, despite an initial conflicts check, some relationship is brought to the arbitrator's attention.

11–42 General Standard 3(d) of the IBA Guidelines states that "[w]hen considering whether or not facts or circumstances exist that should be disclosed, the arbitrator shall not take into account whether the arbitration proceeding is at the beginning or at a later stage". The standard is understandable as regards the arbitrator. However, the fact is that the ICC Court does appear to take into account the stage in the proceedings in deciding challenges as discussed under art.14.

11–43 The impact of new disclosure depends on the nature and stage of the arbitration and who makes the disclosure. If, prior to disclosure by the arbitrator, a party discovers the facts that arguably should have been disclosed, the effect is often

36 See Pt III App.11.

37 See *Commonwealth Coatings* case cited at para.11–9 n.14: "If arbitrators err on the side of disclosure, as they should, it will not be difficult for courts to identify those undisclosed relationships which are too insubstantial to warrant vacating an award".

38 See for example the *Applied Industrial Materials Corp* case cited at para.11–5 n.9 relying on the *Commonwealth Coatings* case cited at para.11–9 n.14, (2007) Mealey's IAR Vol.21 No.7 p.9 (annulment of an ad hoc Award for failure by the chairman of the Tribunal to disclose the commercial relationship between a company controlled by the arbitrator with one of the parties. The ongoing obligation of disclosure is even stronger when the parties had expressly stated in the submission agreement their expectations regarding disclosure of the arbitrators). *Positive Software Solutions Inc v New Century Mortgage et al*, No.01–11432, 436 F.3d 495, 504 (5th Cir. 2006) (Award vacated for failure of an arbitrator to disclose that seven years before the arbitration he worked with a firm that had an extensive litigation relationship with a firm that represented a party). In contrast, see *HSN Capital LLC et al v Productora Y Comercializador de Television, SA de CV*, July 5, 2006, 2006 WL 1876941 (M.D.Fla) (petition to vacate an ICC Award denied by the court under art.V of the New York Convention. Membership and professional relationship between the chairman of the Tribunal and one of the co-arbitrator during the arbitration proceedings are, alone, casual relationships that do not affect their independence. Failure by the challenging party to provide relevant evidence in this respect); see also *Merrill Lynch, Pierce, Fenner & Smith Inc v Lambros*, 1 F.Supp.2d 1337 (M.D.Fla. 1998) (petition to vacate the Award based on the fact that one of the arbitrators was a fraternity brother of one of Merrill Lynch's attorneys. The court found that the relationship between the arbitrator and the counsel was too remote to constitute a conflict of interest and create the appearance of partiality). See also the discussion under art.14.

negative. If the arbitrator discloses the facts spontaneously, the effect is frequently less negative. However, the stage in the proceedings is also crucial. If the Tribunal has issued important procedural orders or partial Awards, the disclosure can give rise to a challenge that may be suspected as being procedurally motivated.

Article 11(4): "The decisions of the Court as to the appointment, confirmation, challenge or replacement of an arbitrator shall be final, and the reasons for such decisions shall not be communicated."

Parties can and do object to the appointment of an arbitrator nominated by the other party or selected by the ICC Court, in the former case in particular when the arbitrator has submitted a so-called qualified statement of independence. Normally, such an objection is filed with as much support as possible: in the first instance, so as to persuade the potential arbitrator, particularly at the outset of the proceedings to withdraw his name from consideration. The objection may also take the form of questions seeking further disclosure, which the prospective arbitrator may prefer not to answer if it could lead to further grounds for objection. **11–44**

When such an objection is filed, the normal course is for the party who proposed the arbitrator to defend the proposal if it knew and had considered the relevant facts prior to making the appointment. As with the challenge, frequently case law and commentaries will be cited in support of this position. The object for both parties will be to provide the authority to convince the ICC Court of the position. **11–45**

Except in truly difficult cases, the ICC Court takes decisions as to confirmation of arbitrators at Committee Sessions. The ICC Court's decision with respect to the appointment, confirmation, challenge or replacement of the arbitrator is, like all other decisions it takes, an administrative decision, as further discussed under art.14.[39] Article 11(4) confirms that no reasons for the ICC Court's decision will be provided. **11–46**

Article 11(4) also states that the ICC Court's decision in this respect is "final". This means that the ICC Court will not reconsider its decision; that is, the ICC Court will not allow an "appeal" against its own decisions. There is in practice, however, one important exception to that rule: if a party can show new facts that were not before the ICC Court at the time it rendered its decision, the ICC Court may reconsider its decision. Moreover, the fact that a party has failed to block the confirmation of a co-arbitrator does not mean that the party cannot challenge the arbitrator later, on new grounds. The practical difference is that a challenge is dealt with at a Plenary Session and the confirmation of arbitrators is usually dealt with at a Committee Session. **11–47**

Decisions by the ICC Court regarding the subjects covered by art.11(4) are not "final" in the sense that they would be exempt of any judicial control. On the contrary, the ICC Court's decision regarding the constitution of the Tribunal is potentially subject to review by national courts, in particular the courts of the place of arbitration in the context of an annulment action against the Award or by **11–48**

[39] See Whitesell, "Independence in ICC Arbitration: ICC Court Practice concerning the Appointment, Confirmation, Challenge and Replacement of Arbitrators", *op. cit.* at p.38.

the courts of the place of enforcement.[40] The weight that will be given to the ICC decision is discussed under art.14. Since there are no reasons provided by the ICC Court, the state court may well consider the issue de novo.[41]

Article 11(5): "By accepting to serve, arbitrators undertake to carry out their responsibilities in accordance with the Rules."

11–49 By accepting to serve, an arbitrator is confirming that there is no obstacle, at least in the arbitrator's view, under art.11(1). Therefore, in the arbitrator's view, there is no issue as to his or her impartiality or independence from the parties.

11–50 In addition, the arbitrator is also confirming that disclosure has been made in accordance with the Rules. If disclosure has not been made in accordance with the Rules, arguably there is a breach of the Rules.

11–51 However, the obligations of an arbitrator extend beyond that of impartiality and independence of the parties and those additional obligations are implicitly referred to in art.11(5). As discussed under art.30, the Rules provide that the arbitration shall be completed, in principle, within six months after the signing of the Terms of Reference. Most ICC arbitrations are not completed within this period. In agreeing to be an arbitrator under the Rules, however, an arbitrator is undertaking to ensure that he or she has the time available to handle the arbitration. In notifying the potential arbitrator of the nomination, the Secretariat usually notes "the Rules contain strict time-limits for the conduct of the arbitral proceedings (see arts 24 and 30(1) of the Rules). Prior to accepting your nomination, you should therefore be satisfied, to the extent reasonably possible, that you will be in a position to devote the time and effort necessary to conduct the arbitration in accordance with the requirements of the Rules".

11–52 By accepting to serve, the arbitrator is also undertaking to assist in the conduct of the arbitration in accordance with the Rules and applicable law and for the fees set by the ICC Court. The arbitrator cannot simply resign during the proceedings unless he/she has some legitimate reasons in this respect.

11–53 In reviewing this obligation, one must keep in mind art.40 limiting the liability of the arbitrators (and the ICC) for claims by the parties under the Rules. The extent and effectiveness of that limitation of liability provision is discussed under art.40.

[40] See the discussion beginning at para.14–39. With respect to "indirect challenges", see the Swiss Supreme Court, December 14, 2004, *A. Ltd v B. Ltd* (2005) ASA Bull Vol.23 No.2 p.337 at p.344: "Decisions by bodies such as the Court of Arbitration of the International Chamber of Commerce cannot, as such, be contested under art.190 para.3 PIL Act in the form of proceedings to set aside. However, such decisions are indirectly subject to investigation within the scope of the proceedings to set aside the arbitrators' ruling. An objection on the grounds of irregular composition of the arbitral tribunal as defined by art.190 para.2 lit. a PIL Act is therefore admissible."

[41] The ICC Court decisions as based in large part on the material submitted by the parties and the experience of the ICC Court members. The prior decisions of the ICC Court are of course relevant. However, to the extent that they are relied upon as a database for rendering decisions and the parties are not informed of the contents of that database or asked to comment, then there may be a further due process issue as to the extent that state courts can rely upon the ICC Court decisions. See Fry, Greenberg & Mazza, *op. cit.* para. 3–374 stating "the Secretariat diligently briefs the Court on similar decisions it has taken in the past, particularly where the situation is difficult".

Article 11(6): "Insofar as the parties have not provided otherwise, the arbitral tribunal shall be constituted in accordance with the provisions of Articles 12 and 13"

Article 11(6) reiterates the principle of party autonomy. The parties' agreement as to the constitution of the Tribunal takes precedence over the provisions of arts 12 and 13. The basic limit on this provision is that the agreement of the parties must not undermine the nature of an ICC arbitration. **11–54**

Article 11(6) may play a role regarding the number of arbitrators. Article 12(1) provides that a dispute shall be decided by a sole arbitrator or three arbitrators. There is no reference to a contrary agreement in that article. The ICC standard arbitration clause puts no limit on the number of arbitrators, as it refers to "one or more arbitrators". Therefore, it is arguably possible in a joint venture agreement between three parties, to allow each party the right to appoint an arbitrator and to have a fourth arbitrator act as chairman (with a casting vote in case of a tie). This would be the kind of agreement contemplated under art.11(6), which would arguably take precedence over art.12(1). **11–55**

Article 12 Constitution of the Arbitral Tribunal

Number of Arbitrators

1 **The disputes shall be decided by a sole arbitrator or by three arbitrators.**

2 **Where the parties have not agreed upon the number of arbitrators, the Court shall appoint a sole arbitrator, save where it appears to the Court that the dispute is such as to warrant the appointment of three arbitrators. In such case, the claimant shall nominate an arbitrator within a period of 15 days from the receipt of the notification of the decision of the Court, and the respondent shall nominate an arbitrator within a period of 15 days from the receipt of the notification of the nomination made by the claimant. If a party fails to nominate an arbitrator, the appointment shall be made by the Court.**

Sole Arbitrator

3 **Where the parties have agreed that the dispute shall be resolved by a sole arbitrator, they may, by agreement, nominate the sole arbitrator for confirmation. If the parties fail to nominate a sole arbitrator within 30 days from the date when the claimant's Request for Arbitration has been received by the other party, or within such additional time as may be allowed by the Secretariat, the sole arbitrator shall be appointed by the Court.**

Three Arbitrators

4 **Where the parties have agreed that the dispute shall be resolved by three arbitrators, each party shall nominate in the Request and the Answer, respectively, one arbitrator for confirmation. If a party fails to nominate an arbitrator, the appointment shall be made by the Court.**

5 **Where the dispute is to be referred to three arbitrators, the third arbitrator, who will act as president of the arbitral tribunal, shall be appointed by the Court, unless the parties have agreed upon another procedure for such appointment, in which case the nomination will be subject to confirmation pursuant to Article 13. Should such procedure not result in a nomination within 30 days from the confirmation or appointment of the co-arbitrators or any other time limit agreed by the parties or fixed by the Court, the third arbitrator shall be appointed by the Court.**

6 **Where there are multiple claimants or multiple respondents, and where the dispute is to be referred to three arbitrators, the multiple claimants, jointly, and the multiple respondents, jointly, shall nominate an arbitrator for confirmation pursuant to Article 13.**

7 **Where an additional party has been joined, and where the dispute is to be referred to three arbitrators, the additional party may, jointly with the claimant(s) or with the respondent(s), nominate an arbitrator for confirmation pursuant to Article 13.**

8 **In the absence of a joint nomination pursuant to Articles 12(6) or 12(7) and where all parties are unable to agree to a method for the constitution of the arbitral tribunal, the Court may appoint each member of the arbitral tribunal and shall designate one of them to act as president. In such case, the Court shall be at liberty to choose any person it regards as suitable to act as arbitrator, applying Article 13 when it considers this appropriate.**[1]

Introductory remarks

Article 12 deals with the number, nomination and appointment of arbitrators. Article 12 deals in particular with whether there shall be one arbitrator or three, the failure by a party to appoint an arbitrator and the appointment of arbitrators in multiple party cases. The main substantive change in the Rules has been the addition of art.12(7) dealing with additional parties. The provisions of art.12(8) regarding multiple parties are very close to art.10 of the 1998 Rules. **12–01**

[1] Article 12 corresponds to arts 8 and 10 of the 1998 Rules. The main changes are discussed under the Introductory remarks.

Number of arbitrators

12–02 The Tribunal decides the dispute, not the ICC Court. This means that the Tribunal has the basic responsibility to establish the appropriate procedure to establish the facts of the case and to decide the case. The ICC Court's role is to ensure the application of the Rules.[2] Both the Rules and the standard ICC arbitration clause leave open the number of arbitrators. At first sight, this may seem odd; however, the overall objective is to permit the ICC Court and the parties to adapt the ICC arbitration procedure not just to the parties and the contract but also to the dispute itself.

12–03 A contract in a relatively small amount may give rise to a substantial and complex claim for damages. Large contracts may give rise to apparently intractable disputes as to smaller amounts that the parties to the contract may wish to have adjudicated, especially if they have an ongoing relationship. As a result, the amount in dispute may be relatively small although the contract itself is large. In other cases, the parties may wish to have an issue of principle decided without specifying the financial consequences of the resolution of the dispute.

12–04 This flexibility sometimes results in the first dispute between the parties being with respect to the arbitral procedure. One party may see an advantage in having a sole arbitrator and the other party may prefer to have three arbitrators. In case of dispute as to the number of arbitrators, the ICC Court will decide the issue in accordance with art.12.

12–05 Article 12 also provides for appointment by the ICC Court in certain circumstances of sole arbitrators and presidents. Those appointments are generally made at Committee Sessions of the ICC Court.

Multiparty arbitration

12–06 Article 12(6)–(8) deal with issues relating to multiparty arbitration, including joinder of additional parties under art.7. The 1998 Rules had dealt with multiparty arbitration briefly in art.10 of those Rules. The new Rules deal much more extensively with multiparty arbitration.

12–07 Arbitration under the ICC Rules is generally based upon the model of a single contract concluded by two parties who agree to arbitrate differences with respect to that contract. However, roughly 30 per cent of the arbitrations under the Rules involve multiple parties or multiple contracts or both. The situations are so diverse that it would be impossible to deal with them in detail and maintain the structural simplicity of the Rules. Moreover, one of the keystones of ICC arbitration is to adapt the procedure to the particularities of each case and this is particularly appropriate in multi-party and multi-contract arbitration.

12–08 Dealing with multiparty arbitration remains a problem in international commercial arbitration. The objective is a "one stop" resolution of disputes. However, to be able to resolve a dispute it may be necessary or desirable to have a number of parties appear in the same forum at the same time. This basic problem has given rise to both the "group of companies" doctrine (which appears to have been abandoned by the French courts) and, more recently, to the "chain of contracts"

[2] See para.1–18.

doctrine of the French Supreme Court.[3] Article 12 deals with one aspect of the problem where there is a basis for multipartite arbitration, the appointment of the members of the Tribunal if there is a three-person Tribunal.

Article 12 does not deal with all multiparty arbitrations. Article 12 is limited to cases where either the arbitration agreement provides that there shall be three arbitrators or where the ICC Court has decided in accordance with art.8(2) that there shall be three arbitrators. In situations where there is to be a sole arbitrator, the issue of equal treatment does not arise with respect to the nomination of the sole arbitrator. Either all the parties agree on the nominee or the arbitrator is appointed by the ICC Court. **12–09**

Article 12(8) is the direct result of the famous *Dutco* case of the French Supreme Court.[4] In that case, a Claimant brought proceedings against two Respondents. The Claimant nominated an arbitrator. The Respondents jointly agreed on a co-arbitrator but under protest and reserving their rights on the basis that the Claimant had been able to nominate a co-arbitrator on its own behalf. The Respondents sought to annul the Award based on breach of due process and succeeded at the level of the French Supreme Court, which held that "the principle of equal treatment of the parties in the designation of arbitrators is a matter of public policy that can only be waived after the dispute has arisen" and that by accepting the 1988 version of the Rules the Respondents had not waived the right to have the same treatment as the Claimant with respect to the nomination of a co-arbitrator. **12–10**

For some practitioners, the *Dutco* decision is a stark confirmation of the difference between the role of a co-arbitrator and that of a president. As discussed in art.11(1), all arbitrators are required to be independent of the parties. However, the *Dutco* decision is based on the realistic perception that, in the international context in particular, even if they are independent of the parties, the parties may have legitimate preferences for the approach of one co-arbitrator or another. This difference in approach is discussed below. It is the basic justification for the concern of equal treatment in multiparty arbitration. **12–11**

Article 12(1): "The disputes shall be decided by a sole arbitrator or by three arbitrators."

The reference to the "disputes" covers all matters submitted by the parties to the Tribunal for a decision. If there is a sole arbitrator, then that person decides the dispute. If there is a Tribunal of three arbitrators then, subject to art.31, the matter is decided usually by unanimity or by a majority. Under the Rules, whatever the number of Claimants or Respondents, there are never more than three arbitrators, but the parties can, to some extent, derogate from such rule, as reflected in art.11(6). **12–12**

Article 12(1) states that an uneven number of arbitrators is required under the Rules, at least in the absence of a contrary agreement under art.11(6) and subject to the provisions of the applicable law which can limit the choice of the parties. **12–13**

[3] Cass. 1re civile, March 27, 2007, 04–20.842, Arrêt No.513.

[4] Cass. 1re civ., January 7, 1992, Bull. civ. I, No.2.

This poses the problem of two-member Tribunals, which parties sometimes still foresee in their arbitration agreement with or without the subsequent intervention of an umpire.[5] It is doubtful whether the ICC Court would accept such arrangements as they are inconsistent with the spirit of the Rules which are based on the assumption that all members of the Tribunal establish and participate in the arbitral procedure.

12–14 In deciding whether there should be a sole arbitrator or three arbitrators, the main reason for preferring one arbitrator is the speed and cost. If there is a sole arbitrator, then it is possible to organise meetings more easily and there is no time devoted to coordination amongst arbitrators.

12–15 The main reason for preferring a Tribunal of three arbitrators is the concern about relying on the judgement of one person who the counsel or the parties may or may not be familiar with. The role of the co-arbitrator nominated by a party is in part to ensure that the personal reactions of the president are tempered by the ideas of his colleagues. This influence is important both for the procedure and for the substance of the dispute. Since in an international arbitration, there is generally no possibility of appeal against an Award and review of Awards is very often limited to procedural aspects, many parties feel more comfortable in having the responsibility of a binding and final decision of the merits of the dispute arrived at and shared by a panel of three arbitrators rather than a sole arbitrator.

Article 12(2): "Where the parties have not agreed upon the number of arbitrators, the Court shall appoint a sole arbitrator, save where it appears to the Court that the dispute is such as to warrant the appointment of three arbitrators. In such case, the claimant shall nominate an arbitrator within a period of 15 days from the receipt of the notification of the decision of the Court, and the respondent shall nominate an arbitrator within a period of 15 days from the receipt of the notification of the nomination made by the claimant. If a party fails to nominate an arbitrator, the appointment shall be made by the Court."

12–16 The parties can agree in their arbitration agreement or after the commencement of the proceedings that there will be one or three arbitrators and that will bind the Court. For cases submitted during the period from 2007–2011, parties agreed on the number of arbitrators in over 80 per cent of the cases.[6] Article 12(2) deals with the situation where there is no such agreement, which is contemplated by the ICC standard arbitration clause. It refers to "one or more arbitrators". The ICC Court generally decides the number of arbitrators at one of its weekly Committee Sessions.[7]

12–17 The presumption is that there will be one arbitrator "save where it appears to the Court that the dispute is such as to warrant the appointment of three arbitrators". For cases submitted during the period from 2007–2011, where the ICC was called upon to fix the number of arbitrators, it decided on a sole arbitrator in 80

[5] Section 15(3) of the English Arbitration Act provides for an uneven number of arbitrators. However, s.15(1) of the Act expressly provides for an umpire. Section 5 of the US Federal Arbitration Act does not expressly deal with the number of arbitrators and also expressly provides for umpires.

[6] Fry, Greenberg & Mazza, *op. cit.*, para.3–435.

[7] See Pt I para.Ann–36.

per cent of the cases.[8] In considering whether a Tribunal should consist of three members the factors that are usually considered are the amount in dispute, the complexity of the matter, the place of arbitration and whether there is a state entity involved.

In 2012, 24.9 per cent of the ICC's arbitrations involved claims for US$1million or less.[9] For those matters, unless the parties have agreed otherwise, one would expect the ICC Court to decide that there should be one arbitrator. Between US$1 million and US$10 million, the practice varies particularly based on the complexity of the dispute but the overwhelming tendency is for the ICC to decide on a sole arbitrator. For amounts above $10 million the practice is split.[10] **12–18**

The parties usually make submissions as to the number of arbitrators, seeking to highlight the various factors that, in accordance with ICC practice, would favour one or three arbitrators. This initial submission for each party should be in the Request and Answer. Sometimes, the parties supplement their submissions on those documents with letters addressed to the Secretariat. The Request and the Answer should, however, provide the basic information relating to the complexity of the dispute, the amount in dispute, and whether state entities are involved, all of which will be relevant in determining the number of arbitrators. **12–19**

In light of this background, and in particular the amount in dispute, the Secretariat usually draws the parties' attention to the financial consequences of having a three-member Tribunal as opposed to a sole arbitrator. Having three arbitrators instead of one arbitrator substantially increases the fees for the arbitration and increases the amount of the reimbursable expenses (e.g. for travel and accommodation). When notifying the Request, the Secretariat will indicate to the parties the average amount of the fees foreseen for the arbitrator(s) under the ICC fee schedule, and does so with reference to the ICC Cost Calculator, which can be accessed through the ICC's website (http://www.iccarbitration.com [accessed November 13, 2013]). **12–20**

The counsel at the Secretariat in charge of the file prepares the relevant documents for submission to the ICC Court and usually provides a recommendation as to whether appoint a sole arbitrator or a three-member Tribunal. A fairly typical recommendation is as follows[11]: **12–21**

> "The Secretariat makes its suggestion that the Court decide that this matter be submitted to one arbitrator in light of the:
>
> (i) presumption in Article 12(2) of the Rules in favour of one arbitrator:
> (ii) fact that the amount in dispute (US$ 7 232 718) is not so significant as to warrant a three-member Arbitral Tribunal: and

[8] Fry, Greenberg & Mazza, *op. cit.*, para.3–435.
[9] ICC ICArb Bull Vol.24 No.1, p.13.
[10] For 2011, see Fry, Greenberg & Mazza, *op. cit.*, para.3–440.
[11] ICC Case No.18565/ARP (Unpublished). The Secretariat also recommended as follows regarding the National Committee in that case: "[t]he Secretariat suggests inviting the Canadian National Committee to make a proposal in light of: (i) the nationalities of the parties (British Virgin Islands and France); (ii) the location of Claimant's counsel (London, United Kingdom); (iii) the place of arbitration (Geneva, Switzerland); and (iv) the applicable law ('Laws of Great Britain')".

(ii) fact that the subject matter (i.e., non-payment of commissions) does not appear to be overly complex."

12–22 The Secretariat will transmit the ICC Court's decision to the parties. The ICC Court does not provide any reasons for its decision. Moreover, it is difficult to imagine any recourse with respect to the decision. As stated in art.11(4), the ICC Court's decisions as to the appointment of an arbitrator are final, and that would seem to include the fixing of the number of arbitrators.

12–23 Where the ICC Court has decided that there should be three arbitrators, the Claimant has a period of 15 days to proceed with its nomination after it has received the Secretariat's notification of the decision of the Court. The Respondent then has 15 days after receipt of the Claimant's nomination to nominate a co-arbitrator. The Secretariat will generally extend these periods, upon request, and good cause, for a limited period of time, for example for 8–15 days. If a party fails to nominate a co-arbitrator then the ICC Court may appoint the co-arbitrator for that party. Prior to making such appointment, the ICC Court usually first consults with the National Committee or Group that it considers appropriate in accordance with art.12(4) (although it may appoint an arbitrator directly under art.13(4)). The ICC Court will review the issue of the appropriate National Committee or Group particularly with regard to the place of arbitration, nationality of the parties, the language of the arbitration and complexity of the dispute.[12] The ICC Court members will wish to be satisfied that the National Committee or Group will propose a person who is appropriate for this particular arbitration. Therefore, in choosing the National Committee or Group, the track record of that National Committee or Group and their approach to the proposal of arbitrators will be a factor that will be taken into account by the ICC Court. Many National Committees and Groups understand the importance of this factor and therefore seek to have a dialogue with the Secretariat as to who would be appropriate for a particular case. However, as discussed below, the decision as to whether to approve the proposal of the National Committee or Group is made solely by the ICC Court. Once the National Committee has been chosen, then the initial contact will be between the Secretariat and the National Committee, although the decision whether or not to confirm the proposed arbitrator will be made by the ICC Court at another Committee Session.

12–24 The ICC Court's right to appoint an arbitrator on behalf of the party that has failed to nominate an arbitrator within the required time limit, does not normally prevent the ICC Court from providing that party a further chance to nominate an arbitrator. In accepting the late nomination of an arbitrator by a party, the ICC Court tacitly extends the time limit it has previously set, and/or recognises that the

[12] In one example, the Secretariat stated as follows in its submission to the ICC Court: "[in] the light of the nationality of the parties (Czech and Bulgarian), the language of the arbitration (English), the applicable substantive law (Bulgarian law), the Secretariat suggests that the Court invite the Austrian National Committee to propose the Chairman in this matter". In another example, the Secretariat stated as follows: "[i]f the two co-arbitrators do not agree on a joint nomination for the Chairman of the Arbitral Tribunal, in light of the nationality of the parties (German and Algerian), of their legal advisors (Germany, France and Switzerland) and of the co-arbitrators (French and Swiss), of the place of arbitration (Geneva, Switzerland), of the language of the arbitration (French), the Secretariat suggests that the Court invite the Spanish National Committee to propose the Chairman of the Arbitral Tribunal". These examples are only indicative as to how the ICC Court is being put in a position to exercise its discretion.

time limits fixed by the ICC Court are purely administrative. In fact, if, even after the expiration of the time limits, a party nominates a co-arbitrator, the ICC Court would probably accept the nomination provided that it had not already appointed a co-arbitrator on behalf of the party.

Sole Arbitrator

Article 12(3): "Where the parties have agreed that the dispute shall be resolved by a sole arbitrator, they may, by agreement, nominate the sole arbitrator for confirmation. If the parties fail to nominate a sole arbitrator within 30 days from the date when the claimant's Request for Arbitration has been received by the other party, or within such additional time as may be allowed by the Secretariat, the sole arbitrator shall be appointed by the Court."

The parties may have agreed in the arbitration agreement that a sole arbitrator hear the matter. In addition, after the dispute has arisen, the parties may agree on a sole arbitrator. In the latter case, the parties will frequently seek to agree on the person to act as sole arbitrator. If the parties are unable to agree on the sole arbitrator within the time limit specified by the Rules or extended by the Secretariat, then the ICC Court will appoint the sole arbitrator in accordance with art.12. During the period from 2007–2011, 77 per cent of the Sole Arbitrators were appointed by the Court.[13] Upon the parties' joint request, the Secretariat will assist the parties in agreeing upon a sole arbitrator by providing a list of suitable arbitrators, from which the parties can choose one within a given time period. By proceeding in this way, the parties obtain proposals of suitable names from a neutral source, which often is found more attractive than to have to consider the name of a sole arbitrator proposed by one party to the other.[14] **12–25**

Three Arbitrators

Article 12(4): "Where the parties have agreed that the dispute shall be resolved by three arbitrators, each party shall nominate in the Request and the Answer, respectively, one arbitrator for confirmation. If a party fails to nominate an arbitrator, the appointment shall be made by the Court."

As revised, art.12 is only applicable where the parties have agreed that there are to be three arbitrators. Therefore, where there is no agreement, art.12(2) is applicable and there is no requirement that a party nominate an arbitrator in either the Request or the Answer. The parties are free to wait until the ICC has decided on the number of arbitrators. However, where a Respondent is granted an extension to file an Answer, then in applying for the extension the Respondent is required under art.5(2) to nominate a co-arbitrator. **12–26**

The nomination of an arbitrator is best viewed as an unilateral act of the party providing the nomination. The arbitrator only commits him or herself to the arbitration with the statement of acceptance and availability. The ICC Court only **12–27**

[13] See Fry, Greenberg & Mazza, *op. cit.*, para.3–445.

[14] See Seppala, "Obtaining The Right International Arbitral Tribunal: A Practitioner's View" (2007) Mealey's IAR Vol.22 No.10, p.26.

designates the arbitrator when it confirms the arbitrator at a Court Session. The ICC has permitted withdrawal of a nomination where a nominee has not yet been confirmed.[15] There may be timing issues with respect to withdrawal of a nomination but it may be preferable to challenging a nominee once confirmed.[16]

12–28 Article 12(4) raises two main issues. The first is the timing for the nomination of the co-arbitrators. The second is how to select the co-arbitrator.[17]

The procedure for nomination of the arbitrators

12–29 Article 12(4) covers situations where the arbitration agreement provides for three arbitrators. If the arbitration agreement expressly provides for three arbitrators, then the Claimant will usually nominate an arbitrator in its Request, unless it has a prior agreement with the Respondent that there should be a sole arbitrator. If there is no such express provision as to the number of arbitrators, but the Claimant is seeking to have a Tribunal composed of three arbitrators, frequently the Claimant will nominate an arbitrator in the Request as well. If there is no such express provision and the Claimant is seeking to have a sole arbitrator, usually the Claimant will not nominate an arbitrator in its Request as, in any event, the Claimant will have the possibility of nominating an arbitrator subsequently under art.12(2) once the ICC Court has decided on the number of arbitrators.

12–30 If a Respondent contests jurisdiction but makes submissions on jurisdiction, one would expect that it would nominate an arbitrator. However, if a Respondent has decided to ignore the proceedings then the Respondent is unlikely to nominate an arbitrator. In such a case, art.12 provides that the ICC Court will appoint the co-arbitrator for the Respondent. The Respondent's failure to nominate an arbitrator will therefore not prevent the Tribunal from being constituted.[18]

12–31 Article 12(4) provides for nominations of arbitrators in the Request or Answer. However, this provision is subject to other provisions of the agreement between the parties. The parties may agree on the timing of such nominations (as well as the qualifications of the arbitrators, for example) and in such circumstances the agreed timing is applicable.

[15] As to the ICC Court's practice, see Fry, Greenberg & Mazza, *op. cit.*, para.3–456.

[16] In one case, a party nominated as co-arbitrator a lawyer who the nominating party subsequently learned had worked with opposing counsel on a case, and was proposing to agree on a president who also had a prior relationship with opposing counsel. In such a case, the new information was the reason to withdraw the nomination, although the nominee withdrew on his own.

[17] Calvo, "The appointments, duties and rights of the ICC arbitrators (revisited under the new ICC rules)" (1999) RDAI/IBLJ No.3, p.361.

[18] For an example of the problems that can arise in ad hoc arbitration, see Cass civ 1re, *State of Israel v National Iranian Oil Company* (NIOC), February 1, 2005, case No.404. In that ad hoc case, the arbitration clause did not set the place of arbitration. Nor did it provide a default mechanism for appointment of a co-arbitrator, although it did provide that the president would be chosen by the president of the ICC Court. The State of Israel refused to appoint a co-arbitrator and, after an initial refusal, the French courts appointed an arbitrator in its stead on the basis that France was the least inappropriate jurisdiction to do so and that it would be a denial of justice not to do so. For a discussion of the case, see Tattevin, "NIOC v. Israel: 'The End' . . . Or Is It?" and Train, "Denial of Justice in International Arbitration: How the French 'Juge d'appui' Extends Its Jurisdiction', SIAR 2005:2, p.221 and p.230; Lazareff, "De l'amour du juge", Les Cahiers de l'arbitrage 2005/1 p.3 and Gazette du Palais, Special Arbitrage, October 21–22, 2005, p.3.

Selecting a co-arbitrator

One of the principles of ICC arbitration is that each party should have the right to nominate an arbitrator. In the international context, this possibility is seen as a safeguard to ensure that the arbitration will be conducted in a manner that takes best into consideration the positions of the parties. **12–32**

Parties nominate arbitrators usually because they are known to their lawyers or to the in-house counsel either on a professional level, because they have been involved in prior arbitrations, or because of publications, conferences, or other channels. Parties may seek the assistance of the ICC National Committee of their country to obtain a list of names of potential arbitrators. If they do so, the Secretariat of the ICC Court will not get involved in that type of discussion. The ICC does not maintain a list of approved arbitrators. **12–33**

In addition, lawyers (and sometimes parties) often wish to interview potential arbitrators either in person, by telephone or by videoconference. Most arbitrators accept interviews, although a diminishing group of arbitrators refuses them.[19] **12–34**

At the least, these interviews or at least some form of discussion are entitled in order to ensure that the potential co-arbitrator has no conflict of interest, is capable of acting, and wishes to act as arbitrator. Moreover, familiarity with the co-arbitrator is accepted and expected. The parties have opted for a system in which they nominate one arbitrator and are entitled to have some awareness of his or her approach to arbitration. **12–35**

In an effort to outline what a party can and cannot discuss with a co-arbitrator, the IBA has published the Guidelines on Party Representation in International Arbitration in 2013. These Guidelines are not binding unless adopted by the parties but they do provide a point of reference to judge contacts. As regards co-arbitrators, the Guidelines state: **12–36**

> "8. It is not improper for a Party Representative to have Ex Parte Communications in the following circumstances:
>
> (a) A Party Representative may communicate with a prospective Party-Nominated Arbitrator to determine his or her expertise, experience, ability, availability, willingness and the existence of potential conflicts of interest.
>
> (b) A Party Representative may communicate with a prospective or appointed Party-Nominated Arbitrator for the purpose of the selection of the Presiding Arbitrator.
>
> [. . .]
>
> (d) While communications with a prospective Party-Nominated Arbitrator or Presiding Arbitrator may include a general description of

[19] See Aksen, "The Tribunal's Appointment" in *The Leading Arbitrators' Guide to International Arbitration, op. cit.*, p.31; Lowenfeld, "The Party-Appointed Arbitrator: Further Reflections" in *The Leading Arbitrators' Guide to International Arbitration, op. cit.*, p.41; Bishop and Reed, "Practical Guidelines for Interviewing, Selecting and Challenging Party-Appointed Arbitrators in International Commercial Arbitration" (1998) Arb Int Vol.14 No.4, p.395 at p.423; Webster, "Selection of Arbitrators in a Nutshell", *op. cit.*, at p.262.

> the dispute, a Party Representative should not seek the views of the prospective Party-Nominated Arbitrator or Presiding Arbitrator on the substance of the dispute.
>
> Comments to Guidelines 7–8
>
> [. . .]
>
> The following discussion topics are appropriate in preappointment communications in order to assess the prospective Arbitrator's expertise, experience, ability, availability, willingness and the existence of potential conflicts of interest:
>
> (a) the prospective Arbitrator's publications, including books, articles and conference papers or engagements; (b) any activities of the prospective Arbitrator and his or her law firm or organisation within which he or she operates, that may raise justifiable doubts as to the prospective Arbitrator's independence or impartiality; (c) a description of the general nature of the dispute; (d) the terms of the arbitration agreement, and in particular any agreement as to the seat, language, applicable law and rules of the arbitration; (e) the identities of the Parties, Party Representatives, Witnesses, Experts and interested parties; and (f) the anticipated timetable and general conduct of the proceedings."[20]

12–37 The concern is that a party should not select an arbitrator in a manner that will result in a biased co-arbitrator. This can arise, for example, if an arbitrator has taken a position with regard to the dispute.[21] As a result, discussion of the merits in any interview should be limited to the nature of dispute.

12–38 As noted in the Guidelines there is no prohibition on a party interviewing a potential arbitrator to discuss the name of a potential president. Indeed, this is both necessary and expected because in choosing an arbitrator one is affecting the appointment of a president.

12–39 This occurs on several levels. Under ICC practice, if a party chooses an arbitrator with the nationality of the other party and the other party picks an arbitrator with the same nationality, the ICC will consider that there is no objection to having a president with the same nationality. For example, if a French company has an arbitration with a Swiss company and the French company and the Swiss company both nominate Swiss co-arbitrators, the ICC Court will assume that there is no objection to appointing a Swiss president.[22] This reflects in fact the view in many quarters that nationality is less important a factor than it may have once been.

12–40 With regard to the procedure, it is generally not appropriate to discuss specific issues of procedure that a party knows will arise in the arbitration. However, discussion of the general procedural approach would not appear to raise the same problems. One of the variants from arbitration to arbitration is the procedure to be

[20] See also the "green list" of the IBA Guidelines on Conflict of Interest in International Arbitration set out in Pt. III.

[21] See IBA Guidelines on Conflict of Interest in International Arbitration, s.4.5.1, Pt III App.11.

[22] This may be reinforced if both parties are, in the example, acting through Swiss counsel. Whenever doubts exist, the Court will normally make sure that there is no objection from the parties to having a president sharing the same nationality as one of the parties.

adopted. Indeed, under national law the Tribunal may be required to adapt the procedure to the circumstances of the case.[23] For example, it would not appear to raise any ethical issues to discuss the potential arbitrator's use of the IBA Rules of Evidence. Another aspect that one could reasonably discuss with a potential arbitrator is his general concept of the use of panels of witnesses or panels of experts or the appointment of Tribunal-appointed experts. It, however, would be wrong to assume that an arbitrator could or should not take a different approach, if he assumes that the circumstances of the case warrant so. Thus, while there is nothing wrong in asking these types of general questions, it is not certain that they will much help in the conduct of the actual case.

There is also a difference in approach among arbitrators as to the role of the Tribunal with respect to settlement. Lawyers with civil law backgrounds believe that it is the duty of the Tribunal to encourage settlement.[24] Other lawyers believe that this should be avoided at all costs. The IBA Guidelines now seek to address the issue. However, there would appear to be nothing wrong with discussing a potential arbitrator's views regarding the Tribunal's involvement in settlement discussions. **12–41**

It is expected that the parties will consider the technical competence and approach of the potential arbitrators in selecting them. Usually, a detailed résumé of the potential arbitrator is made available. That résumé should provide details as to the types of arbitrations that the arbitrator has dealt with. However, the summaries are usually without the names of the parties and usually brief. Therefore, it may be appropriate to discuss exactly the type of issues that the potential arbitrator has dealt with in past arbitrations (or litigations). Some relevant factors include the languages and legal systems that the arbitrator is familiar with. **12–42**

Another technical issue relates to how to manage the arbitration. There is a considerable difference in approach among arbitrators. Some are very computer literate; others are not. If a party wishes to make a computer-oriented presentation of its case, then it may be disappointed to realise that the Tribunal is reviewing only paper copies. If that is the case, it is unfortunate if it comes as a surprise at the hearings as it can be raised in the interview. **12–43**

Article 12(5): Where the dispute is to be referred to three arbitrators, the third arbitrator, who will act as president of the arbitral tribunal, shall be appointed by the Court, unless the parties have agreed upon another procedure for such appointment, in which case the nomination will be subject to

[23] Section 33(1)(b) of the English Arbitration Act 1996 states that the Tribunal shall "adopt procedures suitable to the circumstances of the particular case, avoiding unnecessary delay or expense, so as to provide a fair means for the resolution of the matters failing to be determined".

[24] See Schneider, "Combining Arbitration with Conciliation" (1996) *ICCA Congress Series No.8*, p.57 at p.77, summarising the results of a survey as follows: "with respect to the question whether it was appropriate for an arbitrator, at both parties' request, (a) to actively participate in settlement negotiations and (b) to propose a settlement formula, a predominantly negative answer came from American Respondents (71% and 58% respectively), an overwhelmingly positive answer from the German Respondents (92% and 100%) and a positive answer from the rest of continental Europe (65% and 58%)". In a situation where the practices vary widely, it is important to canvass the attitude of the potential arbitrator.

confirmation pursuant to Article 13. Should such procedure not result in a nomination within 30 days from the confirmation or appointment of the co-arbitrators or any other time limit agreed by the parties or fixed by the Court, the third arbitrator shall be appointed by the Court.

12–44 Article 12(5) is based on the second part of art.8(4) of the 1998 Rules with the addition of a default time limit of 30 days for the co-arbitrators to agree on the president.

12–45 Article 12(5) provides that the ICC Court shall appoint the president "unless the parties have agreed on another procedure for such appointment". Therefore, art.12(5) recognises expressly the autonomy of the parties,[25] subject to the time limit fixed by the parties or the ICC Court and the confirmation requirements in art.13. Depending on the circumstances, the president of the Tribunal can therefore be appointed by the ICC Court, the parties, the co-arbitrators or pursuant to any other procedure agreed by the parties.

12–46 For arbitrations between 2007–2011, in 39 per cent of the cases, the ICC appointed the president of the Tribunal. In 51 per cent of the cases, the co-arbitrators jointly proposed the president. In 8 per cent of the cases, the parties jointly proposed the president.[26] These figures demonstrate the importance of the procedures discussed below and those discussed under art.13 with respect to the selection and appointment of presidents.

12–47 As discussed below, usually the selection of the president is carried out through the co-arbitrators. However, in some instances, the parties deal directly with potential presidents. The IBA Guidelines on Party Representation in International Arbitration provide as follows with respect to party communications regarding a president:

> "8. It is not improper for a Party Representative to have Ex Parte Communications in the following circumstances:
>
> . . .
>
> (c) A Party Representative may, if the Parties are in agreement that such a communication is permissible, communicate with a prospective Presiding Arbitrator to determine his or her expertise, experience, ability, availability, willingness and the existence of potential conflicts of interest."

12–48 As regards the substance of the communications, the same rules would apply as with respect to co-arbitrators. Those rules are discussed above.

12–49 However, it is more frequent for the co-arbitrators to seek to agree on a president or a list of potential candidates for president and submit those lists to the parties. Some ICC arbitration clauses expressly authorise the co-arbitrators to select the president of the Tribunal, and thereby modify the ICC standard arbitration clause. But even where this is not the case, many parties will agree at the start of the arbitration to defer the selection process first to the co-arbitrators, and only

[25] Regarding party autonomy under the Rules, see above, para.0–46 (Re: Principle No.6).

[26] In 2 per cent of the cases, presidents were appointed by another method. Fry, Greenberg & Mazza, *op.cit.*, para.3–465.

if they cannot reach agreement on a president have the ICC Court make the choice. The reasoning is very simple: if the co-arbitrators select the president, he or she will have their full support and trust, and often, although certainly not always, the co-arbitrators would know the prospective president.

The appointment of the president by the ICC Court usually involves an element of surprise for both the parties and the arbitrators. The main incentive for the parties to agree on the president is a concern about the unknown. Many lawyers are satisfied with the presidents appointed by the ICC Court after the parties have failed to agree on the president. Others are much more reserved. Moreover, the position of the parties will vary based on the circumstances and the nature of the arbitration. If the parties are involved in a very technical or specialised field of arbitration, they may prefer to agree on a president. **12–50**

Frequently, the party-appointed arbitrators will, with the agreement of counsel, seek to agree on a list of possible candidates for president. Usually, the co-arbitrators will agree that they can discuss the persons on that list with the party appointing them. Therefore, in many cases, the discussion of who the president should be is done by the parties indirectly through the co-arbitrators. There is some discussion as to whether the co-arbitrators should be permitted to have these separate conversations with the lawyers who appointed them. Provided that the system is clear and applies to both parties, it is difficult to see the objection as art.12(4) gives the priority to agreement on the appointment procedure by the parties. However, there is generally no obligation of the co-arbitrators to review the names of the potential president with the party appointing them, unless this obligation has been specifically imposed on the co-arbitrators.[27] Nevertheless, the authors view it as far preferable for the co-arbitrators to obtain the approval of a nominee for president from the lawyers who nominated them. **12–51**

The importance of the agreement between the parties as to the method of appointment of the president is underlined in the case of *Encyclopaedia Universalis SA v Encyclopaedia Britannica*.[28] In that case, the co-arbitrators were to seek to agree on a president and if they were unable to agree the president was to be appointed by a court in Luxembourg.[29] The co-arbitrators were appointed and were in contact with regard to the arbitration and the procedure but failed to **12–52**

[27] TGI Paris, April 4, 2003, *SA Loris Azzaro v société Clarins et autre*, (2005) Rev Arb No.1 p.162, note Jaeger ("If it is common practice, in an arbitral proceeding, that the arbitrators have the parties' agreement on the choice of the third arbitrator, there is no such obligation on the contrary; indeed, the independence of the arbitrators towards the parties must lead them, where there is a difficulty, to find an agreement among themselves without having necessarily to take into account the opinion of the parties.") (Authors' translation).

[28] *Encyclopaedia Universalis SA v Encyclopaedia Britannica*, 2005 US App LEXIS 5157 (2d Cir., 2005). See also *Appellationsgericht Kanton Baselstadt*, September 6, 1968, (1976) YBCA p.200; Schweizerische Juristenzeitung Vol.64 (1967), p.378; Corte di Appello di Firenze, April 13, 1978, *Rederi Aktiebolaget Sally v S.r.l. Termarea* (1979) YBCA p.294. More generally, see Jarvin, "Irregularity in the composition of the Arbitral Tribunal and the Procedure" in *Enforcement of Arbitration Agreements and International Arbitral Awards—The New York Convention 1958 in Practice* edited by E. Gaillard and D. di Pietro (Cameron May, 2007). See also para.13–4 n.4.

[29] The contract provided "[u]pon the failure of the two arbitrators to reach agreement upon the choice of a third arbitrator, the third arbitrator, who must be fluent in French and English, shall be appointed by the President of the Tribunal of Commerce of the Seine from a list of arbitrators maintained by the British Chamber of Commerce in London at the request of the arbitrator who is first to make such a request".

discuss the selection of a president. One co-arbitrator then applied to the Luxembourg court to appoint a president. The other co-arbitrator learned of the application 15 days later and objected but the Luxembourg court had by then appointed a president. The Claimant's attempt to enforce the Award in New York was refused under the New York Convention due to the failure to follow the procedure to select the president. The US 2nd Circuit Court of Appeals rejected the argument that the appointment procedure was a matter of form stating:

> "Furthermore, contrary to [the Claimant]'s assertion, the District Court did not improperly elevate 'form over substance' in requiring that the two arbitrators disagree before [co-arbitrator appointed by the Claimant] petitioned the Tribunal. While we acknowledge that there is a strong public policy in favor of international arbitration, see *Compagnie Noga*, 361 F.3d at 683, we have never held that courts must overlook agreed-upon arbitral procedures in deference to that policy . . . Moreover, the issue of how the third arbitrator was to be appointed is more than a trivial matter of form. Article V(1)(d) of the New York Convention itself suggests the importance of arbitral composition, as failure to comport with an agreement's requirements for how arbitrators are selected is one of only seven grounds for refusing to enforce an arbitral award. As to the complaint that this result exalts form over substance, at the end of the day, we are left with the fact that the parties explicitly settled on a form and the New York Convention requires that their commitment be respected. We thus conclude that the District Court properly refused to confirm Plaintiff's arbitral award on the grounds that the appointment of a third arbitrator was premature, and, therefore, the composition of the arbitral authority was not in accordance with the parties' agreement."

12–53 Therefore, if there is an agreement between the parties as to the selection of a president, the parties and Tribunal should ensure that it has been complied with or that the parties have waived compliance. Otherwise, an Award may be subject to annulment or a refusal to enforce based on the argument that the Tribunal was improperly constituted.

Article 12(6): "Where there are multiple claimants or multiple respondents, and where the dispute is to be referred to three arbitrators, the multiple claimants, jointly, and the multiple respondents, jointly, shall nominate an arbitrator for confirmation pursuant to Article 13."

12–54 Article 12(6) sets out the basic principle that, where there are several Claimants or several Respondents, the parties "shall" nominate an arbitrator in accordance with art.13.

12–55 If the Claimants have jointly commenced arbitration proceedings, presumably it will be possible for them to agree on an arbitrator. For the Respondents, the issue is not as clear and it could be rendered more difficult by the timing. If the ICC Court has decided under art.12(2) that there shall be three arbitrators, then it generally provides 15 days for the Respondents to nominate an arbitrator. This may be too short a period for the Respondents to agree on a nominee and they may wish to request an extension. As noted in art.12(2), extensions are often granted to nominate co-arbitrators.

If there are multiple Claimants and Respondents, then each side will have to weigh the possibility of agreeing on a president. If there is one Claimant and several Respondents, or one Respondent and several Claimants (which have not agreed on a joint nominee), the issues may well be more unequal. The sole Claimant (or Respondent) will nominate the arbitrator of its choice. The Respondents (or Claimants) will then have to seek an agreement on the arbitrator to nominate. As a result, the parties who are seeking to agree on the person to be nominated will have to discuss and negotiate as to the appropriate profile. 12–56

For example, if the Respondents are from Italy and India, one may have a preference for a civil law lawyer and the other may have a preference for a common law lawyer. It may be difficult to bridge this gap, particularly if the Respondents have conflicting interests. In seeking to agree on an arbitrator, the Respondents will also have in mind the choice by the Claimant of its nominee. If the Respondents are unable to agree on a nominee, then the default mechanism of art.12(6) will be applicable and no party will be entitled to nominate an arbitrator and all three arbitrators will be appointed by the ICC Court. 12–57

The statement in art.12(6) that the multiple Respondents or Claimants "jointly, shall nominate an arbitrator" is best viewed as an admonition and not a requirement due to the *Dutco* case and the provisions of arts 7 and 12(7). 12–58

Article 12(7): "Where an additional party has been joined, and where the dispute is to be referred to three arbitrators, the additional party may, jointly with the claimant(s) or with the respondent(s), nominate an arbitrator for confirmation pursuant to Article 13."

As discussed under art.7, the provision for joinder of additional parties has been introduced in the Rules. As noted under art.7, an additional party may not be joined after the confirmation or appointment of an arbitrator unless all of the parties (including the additional party) agree. Therefore, the basic assumption is that the additional party is joined prior to even the partial constitution of the Tribunal (by confirmation of co-arbitrators, for example). In such cases, the additional party may seek to agree on a nominee as co-arbitrator with either the Claimants or Respondents. However, there is no obligation on the additional party to agree with any party as to such a nominee. 12–59

Article 12(8): "In the absence of a joint nomination pursuant to Articles 12(6) or 12(7) and where all parties are unable to agree to a method for the constitution of the arbitral tribunal, the Court may appoint each member of the arbitral tribunal and shall designate one of them to act as president. In such case, the Court shall be at liberty to choose any person it regards as suitable to act as arbitrator, applying Article 13 when it considers this appropriate."

Article 12(8) provides that if the parties fail to jointly nominate an arbitrator in accordance with art.12(6) or (7), the ICC Court may appoint all three arbitrators. For art.12(8) to be applicable, two conditions must be satisfied. First, there must be a failure by either multiple Claimants or multiple Respondents or the additional 12–60 parties to jointly nominate an arbitrator. Secondly, "all parties are unable to agree to a method for the constitution of the Arbitral Tribunal".

12–61 The first condition is drafted somewhat awkwardly. The intent of the article appears to be to cover the situation where there are multiple Claimants and multiple Respondents and either or both sets of parties is unable to agree on a joint nomination.

12–62 The second condition reaffirms the primacy of the agreement between the parties. However, it is not entirely satisfactory as it suggests that art.12(8) may no longer be applicable if the parties have agreed on a method but the method has broken down. Article 12(8) should also be read in the light of the purpose of the provision that is to provide a solution for the appointment of arbitrators in a multi-party setting. Therefore, if the parties have agreed on a method, but that method has failed, then art.12(8) should be applicable.

12–63 Article 12(8) provides that the ICC Court "may" appoint all three arbitrators. The Article was drafted and is applied by the ICC Court with respect to the specific facts of each case. These facts relate to whether the Claimants and Respondents are really independent and whether they have conflicting interests.

12–64 It is conceivable that the ICC Court will appoint two arbitrators and leave the two arbitrators to select a president; however, that would usually be in a situation where the parties had agreed with that procedure. The main justification for that approach would be to ensure that the two arbitrators agree with the choice of the president rather than having all three members imposed by the ICC Court.

12–65 It is also conceivable that the ICC Court will only nominate an arbitrator for the Claimants, or more often, the Respondents who cannot jointly agree upon an arbitrator. In doing so, the ICC Court would look very specifically at the circumstances of the case, and in particular why one side cannot jointly agree upon an arbitrator as well as the law of the place of arbitration.

12–66 It is also possible, that the ICC Court will confirm an arbitrator nominated but some but not by all of the parties on one side. In one case where the Claimants jointly nominated an arbitrator and all but one of the Respondents jointly nominated an arbitrator and the remaining Respondent, which was jointly owned by the parties, did not object, the ICC Court confirmed the appointments and did not apply the predecessor to art.12(8).[30]

12–67 Article 12(8) gives the ICC Court discretion to appoint any person who it deems appropriate as an arbitrator and to apply the procedure in art.13 when the ICC Court deems it appropriate. Therefore, the ICC Court is not required to consult one or more National Committees or Groups as provided for in art.13 unless the ICC Court chooses to do so.

12–68 Even if the parties are not able to agree on arbitrators or on a method for their appointment, the parties may seek to reach an agreement on the criteria for the arbitrators. Pursuant to art.11(6), such an agreement would take precedence over the provisions of art.12(8). For example, it may be useful for the parties to agree on the requirements of the three arbitrators, whether with respect to nationality, legal training or background, to reduce the uncertainty under art.12(8). The parties

[30] Fry, Greenberg & Mazza, *op. cit.*, para.3–485.

could also agree that the ICC Court should follow the procedure of art.13 and thus limit its discretion under art.12(8).

If the parties cannot agree on the criteria for selecting the arbitrators, they should consider making submissions as to whether or not the ICC Court should apply art.13 if they believe that the consultation with a National Committee or Group would be of assistance. **12–69**

Article 13 Appointment and Confirmation of the Arbitrators

1 In confirming or appointing arbitrators, the Court shall consider the prospective arbitrator's nationality, residence and other relationships with the countries of which the parties or the other arbitrators are nationals and the prospective arbitrator's availability and ability to conduct the arbitration in accordance with the Rules. The same shall apply where the Secretary General confirms arbitrators pursuant to Article 13(2).

2 The Secretary General may confirm as co-arbitrators, sole arbitrators and presidents of arbitral tribunals persons nominated by the parties or pursuant to their particular agreements, provided that the statement they have submitted contains no qualification regarding impartiality or independence or that a qualified statement regarding impartiality or independence has not given rise to objections. Such confirmation shall be reported to the Court at its next session. If the Secretary General considers that a co-arbitrator, sole arbitrator or president of an arbitral tribunal should not be confirmed, the matter shall be submitted to the Court.

3 Where the Court is to appoint an arbitrator, it shall make the appointment upon proposal of a National Committee or Group of the ICC that it considers to be appropriate. If the Court does not accept the proposal made, or if the National Committee or Group fails to make the proposal requested within the time limit fixed by the Court, the Court may repeat its request, request a proposal from another National Committee or Group that it considers to be appropriate, or appoint directly any person whom it regards as suitable.

4 The Court may also appoint directly to act as arbitrator any person whom it regards as suitable where:

a) one or more of the parties is a state or claims to be a state entity; or
b) the Court considers that it would be appropriate to appoint an arbitrator from a country or territory where there is no National Committee or Group; or
c) the President certifies to the Court that circumstances exist which, in the President's opinion, make a direct appointment necessary and appropriate.

5 The sole arbitrator or the president of the arbitral tribunal shall be of a nationality other than those of the parties. However, in suitable circumstances and provided that none of the parties objects within the time limit fixed by the Court, the sole arbitrator or the president

of the arbitral tribunal may be chosen from a country of which any of the parties is a national.[1]

Introductory remarks

Appointing or confirming arbitrators is a key part of the ICC Court's role in any ICC arbitration. The main changes in the Rules are the introduction of provisions to broaden the scope for direct appointment by the ICC Court without referring to National Committees or Groups in the last sentence of art.13(3) and in art.13(4). **13–1**

Under art.13, the ICC Court "confirms" arbitrators who are nominated by the parties or, in the case of a sole arbitrator or a president, jointly nominated by the parties. The ICC Court chooses and then "appoints" arbitrators where they have not been so nominated. As recognised for instance in the *Cubic* case,[2] the ICC's role is to organise a framework for an ICC arbitration. This framework includes the designation of the members of the Tribunal. However the ICC Court does not assume liability for the actions of the Tribunal. **13–2**

The context of the ICC Court's role under art.13 is as follows: where the parties have nominated their respective arbitrators (usually in the Request and Answer), the Secretariat will forward to the nominated person a blank Statement of Acceptance, Availability, Impartiality and Independence and curriculum vitae, requesting the person to complete each form and return it to the Secretariat.[3] If a proposal is to be made by a National Committee or Group, then the Secretariat will forward a copy of the blank Statement of Acceptance, Availability, Impartiality and Independence, the curriculum vitae and a document setting out the general characteristics of the dispute (including the names of the parties, the names of the counsel, the amount in dispute, the place of arbitration, the applicable law and any specific issues which the arbitration requires, e.g. the language of the arbitration to be other than that of the language of the country of the National Committee or Group). Once the above documents are returned to the Secretariat, the Secretariat verifies that they have been correctly filled in, signed and dated, and where the **13–3**

[1] Article 13 corresponds to art.9 of the 1998 ICC Rules. As discussed above, there have been substantive changes to this provision.
[2] See paras 1–16 and 1–80.
[3] See documents in Pt. II.

Statement is qualified, that reasons for the qualification have been provided. If the Statement is qualified, the other party will be provided the opportunity to comment. Those comments may include an objection to confirmation of the arbitrator. The completed documents, together with the comments of the parties, are then provided to the Court, which then determines whether to confirm the arbitrator(s). Thereafter, the Secretariat informs the parties and the arbitrators (whether confirmed or not) of the ICC Court's decision, without providing reasons for the decision.

13–4 The ICC Court's role under art.13 must be seen in the light of the overall legal framework applicable to international arbitration. Those requirements are set by the mandatory rules of the place of arbitration and the New York Convention. Article V(1)(d) of the New York Convention provides that a national court may refuse to enforce an arbitral Award if "[t]he composition of the arbitral authority or the arbitral procedure was not in accordance with the agreement of the parties, or, failing such agreement, was not in accordance with the law of the country where the arbitration took place".[4]

Article 13(1): "In confirming or appointing arbitrators, the Court shall consider the prospective arbitrator's nationality, residence and other relationships with the countries of which the parties or the other arbitrators are nationals and the prospective arbitrator's availability and ability to conduct the arbitration in accordance with the Rules. The same shall apply where the Secretary General confirms arbitrators pursuant to Article 13(2)."

13–5 The selection and appointment of sole arbitrators and presidents is of fundamental importance in international arbitration. During the period from 2007–2011, the ICC Court appointed 77 per cent of sole arbitrators and 39 per cent of the presidents, while the parties nominated 22 per cent of sole arbitrators and the parties or co-arbitrators proposed 59 per cent of the presidents.[5] However, at the same time, parties have a strong influence on the composition of Tribunals. In most cases, it is the parties who nominate co-arbitrators. As a result, in over half of the cases involving three arbitrators, all three arbitrators will have been chosen independently of the ICC. In most of the remaining cases, two of three of the arbitrators are nominated by the parties. It is only with multiparty arbitrations (discussed under art.12) and with respect to the appointment of sole arbitrators that the ICC Court's role in appointing arbitrators is preponderant.[6]

13–6 The parties have a key role in the composition of the Tribunal and how they exercise their right to nominate arbitrators subject often debated in international arbitration. This is in part due to the fact that each arbitration is different and therefore the best nominee for one arbitration is not necessarily the best nominee

[4] On the primacy of the parties' agreement as to the selection of the arbitrators, see the *Encyclopaedia Universalis* case discussed at para.12–52 for example.

[5] See (2007) ICC ICArb Bull. Vol.18 No.1, pp.8–9.

[6] And in the few cases where the ICC Court has to appoint an arbitrator on behalf of a defaulting party.

for another arbitration. The criteria used by the parties are discussed under art.12(4).

The ICC system for selection and appointment of co-arbitrators is unique. The ICC Court does not have a list of "ICC- approved" arbitrators.[7] The ICC system is based on the requirement that, generally but not always, the ICC Court consults with the National Committees or Groups with respect to prospective co-arbitrators (where a party has failed to nominate an arbitrator), sole arbitrators and presidents in accordance with the conditions set out in art.13(3). Two basic points should be noted. **13–7**

First, the parties have an opportunity to agree on a sole arbitrator or president and the ICC Court's role is limited to confirming the person. Thus, the ICC is unlike some other arbitration systems that basically impose the president from a list. Appointment by the ICC Court is a default mechanism. **13–8**

Secondly, the ICC Court generally selects the National Committee or Group. Article 13(1) provides the criteria for appointing co-arbitrators and one can assume that the ICC Court takes those criteria into account in selecting the National Committee. Moreover, the ICC Court also takes into account the responsiveness of the National Committee or Group in deciding which National Committees or Groups to approach. Therefore, the selection of the National Committee or Group is in most cases a matter of discretion for the ICC Court, but is not arbitrary. **13–9**

Confirmation of arbitrators nominated by the parties

The parties have the right to nominate the arbitrator of their choice; indeed, under the Rules they are required to nominate a co-arbitrator. The factors in the selection of a co-arbitrator are discussed under art.12(4). The arbitrator nominated by a party undertakes to meet the requirements of the Rules and in particular art.11(1) regarding impartiality and independence as regards the parties. The arbitrator nominated by a party must also meet the requirements of the arbitration agreement pursuant to which he was nominated. For example, if the arbitrators are required to be admitted to practice before certain courts or to be fluent in certain languages, this requirement must be respected or the nomination may be deficient. **13–10**

Article 13(1) refers to the "nationality, residence and other relationships with the countries of which the parties or the other arbitrators are nationals" as factors for the ICC Court to consider when appointing or confirming an arbitrator. However, these factors are generally relevant to the appointment of arbitrators by the ICC Court rather than to the confirmation of arbitrators nominated by the parties. For example, in the absence of other factors, a party is entitled to nominate an arbitrator with the party's nationality or residing in the same city as the party. Similarly, a party may nominate an arbitrator having the same nationality or residence as the other party. In each case, unless there are other factors that **13–11**

[7] Some National Committees of the ICC seem, however, to have internal lists, on which they put potential candidates for appointments by the ICC Court.

preclude a nominee from acting as arbitrator, the ICC Court or the Secretary General is likely to confirm the nomination.

13–12 As noted above, a prospective arbitrator is required to provide the ICC with a disclosure form, the so-called Statement of Acceptance, Availability, Impartiality and Independence, to be confirmed or appointed as arbitrator. The ICC Court will refuse to confirm or appoint an arbitrator if no statement of independence has been provided. As long as an arbitrator has not been confirmed, he cannot act as such under the ICC Rules.

13–13 Where the arbitrator who has been nominated provides a "qualified" statement of impartiality and independence or where it is not clear that the arbitrator meets the requirements of the arbitration agreement between the parties, the Secretariat will ask the other party (that is the party not nominating the arbitrator) to comment on the issues. The arbitrator who has been nominated as well as the party who has nominated him or her will usually have an opportunity to respond to any comments with respect to the arbitrator. If there is no objection, the Secretary General may confirm the arbitrator in accordance with art.13(2).

13–14 If the arbitrator has provided an "unqualified" statement of impartiality and independence or if the qualifications in the statement do not, in the opinion of the opposing party, deal with all relevant relationships, then the opposing party may raise the issue of confirmation with the Secretariat with a copy to the opposing counsel. This could lead to an objection to the confirmation. A party who objects to the nominee of the other party should raise the factual and legal issues that would justify a challenge to the nominee under art.14. As discussed in Annex 1 Pt. I, the ICC Court will usually decide whether or not to confirm the nominee at one of its weekly Committee Sessions.

13–15 If there is a qualified statement of impartiality and independence or if facts are brought to the attention of the Secretariat regarding the prospective arbitrator that call into question the arbitrator's independence, the issue is whether those facts are disqualifying under art.11. The Secretariat provides the nominee and the parties with an opportunity to comment on these aspects prior to submitting the issue of confirmation to the ICC Court. If the facts were disqualifying in the view of the ICC Court, then arguably the ICC would refuse to confirm the co-arbitrator under its duty referred to in the *Cubic* case, although the ICC Court exercises its discretion in evaluating the facts of the case.[8]

13–16 Article 13(1) requires the ICC Court to consider the prospective arbitrator's "availability and ability to conduct the arbitration in accordance with these Rules" and the ICC requires a statement of availability. Any arbitrator should have the time available to conduct expeditiously the arbitration, to meet either the requirements of the Rules (and in particular arts 23 and 30(1)) or the reasonably anticipated requirements of the arbitration.[9] As discussed under art.11(2), the arbitrator's statement deals with availability, and the Secretariat requires nominees to

[8] See paras 1–16 and 1–80.

[9] Article 30(1) sets out the basic principle that an arbitration should be completed within six months after the signing of the terms of references except in special circumstances. However, very few complex arbitrations are completed in that time frame. Therefore, unless the co-arbitrator is notified of special urgency in the matter, there would seem to be no reason for a potential arbitrator to assume that a complex arbitration will be completed within the six-month time period. The ICC

indicate when they are not available during the anticipated period of the arbitration. This does give rise to comments of the parties and could give rise to a refusal to confirm the nominee. However, as confirmed in a recent case, the ICC Court has not established practice in this regard.[10] As regards the capacity, in the absence of a contrary agreement between the parties, a party may nominate a person with little or no experience as an arbitrator to be a co-arbitrator. A proposed co-arbitrator does not need to have any specific legal or other training in the absence of any specific requirements in the arbitration agreement or the law applicable at the place of arbitration. A co-arbitrator does not have to be admitted to practice before the courts of the place of arbitration, unless there is a local requirement to that effect and such requirements appear to be very rare nowadays.[11] Therefore, despite the reservations that the other party may have with respect to a co-arbitrator, it is difficult to imagine an issue as to confirmation of a co-arbitrator based on lack of experience or specific knowledge or skills. The proposed arbitrator must also have the right to act as an arbitrator. In certain countries, national judges may not act as arbitrators, or may need from its administrative hierarchy a special authorisation to act as arbitrator.[12] If an arbitrator lacks such right, the ICC Court may in its decision and depending on the exact circumstances decide not to confirm the arbitrator nominated by a party. Here again, the ICC Court would be guided in its ultimate choice by the considerations of art.41, that is, to ensure the enforceability of the Award.

Another problem regarding an arbitrator's ability to conduct an arbitration relates to the linguistic skills he must have in order to act in the arbitration. Several situations are possible that should be analysed individually. If the parties have expressly agreed on the language of arbitration and that language is in widespread use in international arbitration, then the nomination of an arbitrator who does not speak that language may pose problems and indeed an issue as to confirmation of the co- arbitrator. Nominating an arbitrator without the reasonably expected linguistic capacity may be viewed as hindering the arbitral process, which a party is not entitled to do in particular in the light of art.41. If the parties have not agreed on a language of the arbitration and a party nominates a co-arbitrator who is fluent in the party's language but perhaps not in the language of the contract or the language of the correspondence between the parties, there may again be an issue as to confirmation, albeit a less acute one. If the case is conducted in two languages, the ICC Court does not normally require that the arbitrator be fluent in both languages. In each case, the ICC Court has in fact to balance the 13–17

may remove an arbitrator who does not devote adequate time to the arbitration. For example, see the cases discussed at para.15–7.

[10] ICC Case No. 18469/GZ (unpublished).

[11] Section 6125 of the California Business and Professions Code which provides that "[n]o person shall practice law in California unless the person is an active member of the State Bar". This gave rise to some uncertainty in California. Section 6125 is not however applicable to international commercial disputes. See Supreme Court of California, January 5, 1998, *Birbrower, Montalbano, Condon & Frank, P.C. v Esq Business Services Inc*, No.S.57125 (absence of a requirement that the arbitrator be a member of the California Bar). See 70 Cal.Rptr.2d at 310 and 312. ("The Legislature has recognized an exception to section 6125 in international disputes resolved in California under the state's rules for arbitration and conciliation of international disputes.")

[12] Aboukrat, "A propos du statut de l'arbitre et de celui de la magistrature: quelle place pour le droit français ?", in *Les Cahiers de l'Arbitrage* (Gazette du Palais, 2002), p.121.

fundamental interest of a party in nominating the co-arbitrator of its choice with the practicalities of conducting proceedings in international arbitration.

13–18 In reviewing whether to confirm nominees, the ICC Court will base its decision on the information provided by the nominee and the parties in any comments that the parties may provide. The Secretariat may be aware of prior issues with a nominee. However, it would be improper for the ICC Court to base its decision on any information held by the Secretariat without providing the nominee and the parties with an opportunity to comment on it. The solution appears to have been to request that the nominee disclose relevant information to the parties so that they may comment on it and to refuse to confirm a nominee if there is a refusal to disclose the information.[13] However, that in itself would only appear to be justified if there is an obligation of disclosure (which will often be the case under art.11) and a refusal to disclose.

13–19 In a recent case, the ICC Court had to consider an objection of confirmation of an arbitrator who had previously been a member of a Tribunal that had rendered a final Award between the same parties on the same contract. The Claimant sought to have the same Tribunal and nominated the same co-arbitrator in this new arbitration and in another new arbitration. The Respondent did not wish to have the same Tribunal and nominated different arbitrators. The Court declined to confirm the Claimant's arbitrator.[14]

13–20 In 2012, the ICC Court confirmed 939 arbitrators nominated by the parties. Thirty-three arbitrators nominated by the parties were not confirmed by the ICC Court.[15] Therefore, the ICC Court confirmed over 97 per cent of the arbitrators nominated by the parties. In most cases, these confirmations will have been unopposed. If the ICC Court refuses to confirm an arbitrator, it will provide the party a further chance to nominate another person as arbitrator.

Appointment of arbitrators by the ICC Court

13–21 In 2012, the ICC appointed 362 arbitrators, or slightly over 25 per cent of all arbitrators. The ICC Court appointed 40 per cent of all presidents and 7 per cent of the co-arbitrators.[16] As regards the arbitrators who are not nominated by the parties but who are appointed by the ICC, the ICC Court's review is more substantive because it is the ICC that is both selecting and appointing the arbitrator.

13–22 As discussed under art.13(3) one of the particularities of the ICC Rules is the use of National Committees or Groups to propose arbitrators. The decision whether to appoint an arbitrator nominated by a National Committee or Group is made by the ICC Court members in the Committee Session and not by the Secretariat. Usually, the ICC Court will only appoint sole arbitrators or presidents, although in some cases it will have to appoint co-arbitrators where a party fails to nominate a co-arbitrator or where there is a multipartite arbitration. If the ICC Court at the Committee Session does not approve the person proposed by a National Committee or Group, the ICC Court may decide that either: (i) the

[13] Fry, Greenberg & Mazza, *op. cit.*, para. 3–492.
[14] ICC Case No. 18469/GZ (unpublished).
[15] See ICC Statistical Report 2012, p.10.
[16] See ICC Statistical Report 2012, p.10.

Secretariat should consult the same National Committee or Group again; or (ii) whether it should consult another National Committee or Group; or (iii) the ICC Court should make a direct appointment. In any case, the new proposal will then have to be submitted to the ICC Court at another Committee Session.

In making an appointment, the ICC Court will be seeking to ensure that the ICC appointee meets all requirements of the Rules. It has been a common practice in this respect for the ICC Court to require that any appointees proposed by a National Committee provide an unqualified statement of impartiality and independence. The reasoning is that parties are not informed of the name and would not be informed of the qualifications in the arbitrator's statement prior to appointment. As a result, qualifications could give rise to challenges under art.14. Besides, there would rarely be a good reason for the ICC Court to appoint an arbitrator who cannot provide an unqualified statement, as there are normally equally qualified candidates available that would be free of any conflicts, whether actual or potential. Nevertheless, this procedure has been relaxed and the ICC Court now appoints arbitrators who have provided a qualified statement of impartiality and independence provided that the ICC Court does not consider the qualifications in the statement material. However, the ICC Court should not do so unless the Secretariat has followed up with respect to any qualifications to ensure that they are in fact minor.[17] **13–23**

Article 13(1) requires the ICC Court to consider "the prospective arbitrator's nationality, residence and other relationships with the countries of which the parties or the other arbitrators are nationals". As discussed under art.13(5), the sole arbitrator or president generally should not have the nationality of one of the parties. On the other hand, when appointing a co-arbitrator for a party (or in a multipartite setting) the ICC Court has usually sought to appoint a co-arbitrator with that nationality. **13–24**

The ICC Court will generally seek to have a balanced or neutral Tribunal taking into consideration the nationality and the status of the parties, the other arbitrators, and to a certain extent the parties' lawyers. Therefore, if, for example, there is an arbitration between a German Claimant and an American Respondent and the German Claimant appoints a German co-arbitrator and the American an American co-arbitrator, the ICC Court can be expected to appoint a non-German and non-American president. If, however, both the Claimant and Respondent appoint German arbitrators, the ICC Court may well assume that nationality is not an issue for the parties and appoint a German president. **13–25**

In addition, the ICC Court should not appoint an arbitrator unless it is satisfied with his/her "availability and ability to conduct the arbitration". Particularly if the appointee is to act as a sole arbitrator or president, the ICC Court will be concerned that he/she be in a position to meet the timing requirements of the Rules as set out in arts 23 and 30(1). With respect to the ability to conduct the arbitration, as discussed below, the ICC Court may well reject a proposal of a National Committee or Group if it is not satisfied that the person proposed as an arbitrator is able to **13–26**

[17] In some instances, the disclosure may be minimal but information on the internet or elsewhere provides the basis on which to object to the appointment of the arbitrator. If the Secretariat is proposing a nominee, it should have checked on this disclosure as the parties would have done. Otherwise, the appointment may place one of the parties in a situation where it feels that it should challenge the arbitrator under art.14.

conduct the arbitration in accordance with the Rules. For many members of the ICC Court, the proposed arbitrator should have the qualifications that the parties would have been expected to seek in a person that they would have proposed. In this respect, parties almost invariably prefer to have arbitrators with ICC experience together with international arbitration experience and one would expect the ICC Court to seek out persons with ICC arbitration experience whether as counsel or as arbitrator to ensure that they are familiar with the requirements of an ICC arbitration. This is often a material factor in deciding whether or not to appoint a person proposed by a National Committee or Group.

13–27 The ICC Court usually appoints lawyers and often seeks to appoint as a president or sole arbitrator a lawyer trained or with experience in the substantive law governing the agreement. Familiarity with the law of the place of arbitration, while relevant, is rarely a determining factor on its own. This is due to the fact that the law of the place of arbitration generally now imposes only minimum procedural requirements (although it may govern the arbitration agreement as well) and many international arbitrators are familiar with the basic principles applicable in the most common places of arbitration. The ICC Court sometimes prefers that the sole arbitrator or president be a resident at the place of arbitration so as to be familiar with the law and practice of the local courts and to avoid travel expenses.

13–28 The ICC Court will consider the technical expertise and the background of the arbitrators as well as the language abilities. With regard to language, in many if not most ICC arbitrations, the various arbitrators have different mother languages and one of the main issues is whether the president or sole arbitrator is capable of drafting an Award in the language of the arbitration. In some instances, where the language of the arbitration is not commonly used in international arbitration, this can result in a person being appointed with limited ICC arbitration experience, particularly with respect to smaller cases.

Article 13(2): "The Secretary General may confirm as co-arbitrators, sole arbitrators and presidents of arbitral tribunals persons nominated by the parties or pursuant to their particular agreements, provided that the statement they have submitted contains no qualification regarding impartiality or independence or that a qualified statement regarding impartiality or independence has not given rise to objections. Such confirmation shall be reported to the Court at its next session. If the Secretary General considers that a co-arbitrator, sole arbitrator or president of an arbitral tribunal should not be confirmed, the matter shall be submitted to the Court."

13–29 Article 13(2) reaffirms the autonomy of the parties by referring to persons nominated as arbitrators "by the parties or pursuant to their particular agreements". Parties have been very inventive about the types of arbitrators that they wish to have and the way that they should be nominated. The general rule is that the ICC will respect those agreements provided that the agreement does not undermine the nature of the arbitration as an ICC arbitration.

13–30 The Secretary General is permitted to confirm arbitrators if there has been an unqualified statement of impartiality and independence or no objection has been received after transmittal of a qualified statement of independence. This decision is not expressly stated to be final. However, since it is only to be "reported" to the ICC Court at its next session, it is intended to be legally effective when issued. Confirmation by the Secretary General is meant to accelerate the constitution of the Tribunal in particular also when the president of the Tribunal was selected by the parties or the co-arbitrators and has submitted an unqualified statement of independence.

The last sentence of art.13(2) suggests that it only covers situations where the Secretary General considers that the arbitrator should not be confirmed. It is conceivable for example that the Secretary General has doubts as to the issue of confirmation of an arbitrator when there are multiple Respondents and may prefer to leave the decision to the ICC Court on the issue. In each case, the counsel at the Secretariat handling the case prepares a report to the ICC Court outlining the reasons for the concern about confirming the arbitrator. 13–31

Article 13(3): "Where the Court is to appoint an arbitrator, it shall make the appointment upon proposal of a National Committee or Group of the ICC that it considers to be appropriate. If the Court does not accept the proposal made, or if the National Committee or Group fails to make the proposal requested within the time limit fixed by the Court, the Court may repeat its request, request a proposal from another National Committee or Group that it considers to be appropriate, or appoint directly any person whom it regards as suitable."

Article 13(3) provides the general mechanism for obtaining proposals for the sole arbitrator or president. This is subject to the exception in the last sentence in art.13(3) and in art.13(4) discussed below. 13–32

Article 13(3) is important and unique to ICC arbitration because the ICC Court has not maintained a list of "ICC approved" arbitrators and the members of the ICC Court are not always involved in proposing arbitrators. One of the goals of the Rules and the ICC Court is to ensure that the constituent members of the ICC, the National Committees and Groups, have a role in proposing arbitrators. This takes place in several steps. 13–33

The ICC Court has provided guidelines to the National Committees, from time to time. These guidelines are of course subject to change, but the basic points include the following: 13–34

(1) National Committees and Groups are not permitted to propose ICC Court Members as arbitrators.
(2) National Committees and Groups are not allowed to require that a person be a member of the National Committee as a condition for being proposed as an arbitrator (ICC Charter art.3). National Committees and Groups should not limit their proposals to persons on any list of arbitrators they might have. Nor are they permitted to request set fee or a percentage of the fees the person earns for work done as arbitrator on a particular case.
(3) National Committees and Groups are encouraged to propose persons experienced in ICC arbitration for relatively complex cases with larger

amounts in dispute, and newer and thus often younger arbitrators for relatively simple cases with lower amounts in dispute.

(4) In addition, when the amount in dispute is relatively small, the National Committee or Group should try to propose a person at or near the place of arbitration, in order to help keep the costs of the arbitration as low as possible.

13–35 The ICC Court therefore depends to a considerable extent on the National Committees and Groups for proposals as to nominees but has sought to provide guidelines to ensure that the proposals result in the appointment of an appropriate arbitrator for the case and it tends to seek proposals from National Committees and Groups that propose appropriate persons as arbitrators. National Committees and Groups can be of tremendous help in identifying appropriate profiles in their country, and by proposing them to the ICC Court introducing capable lawyers to whom the ICC Court would otherwise not have had access.

13–36 The first step is that the ICC Court will decide which National Committee or Group is appropriate to consult. In selecting the National Committee or Group, the ICC Court will have in mind the requirements of art.13(1) and in particular the requirement that it take into account "the prospective arbitrator's nationality, residence and other relationships with the countries of which the parties or the other arbitrators are nationals". In addition, the ICC Court will take into account the National Committee's or Group's available pool of arbitrators. The parties do not make any submission as to the National Committee Group that should be consulted, and the ICC Court will not consult the parties with respect to its choice of the National Committee or Group. The choice of the National Committee or Group is not communicated to the parties in order to avoid any possible pressure on the National Committee or Group by any of the parties. In practice, the ICC Court will decide on the choice of the National Committee or Group at Committee Sessions. The Secretariat will usually recommend at least one Committee in its agenda on the case. In one case, for example, the Secretariat recommended that the ICC Court invite the US National Committee (the USCIB)[18] to propose a president "in light of the nationalities of the parties (Hong Kong and Ghana), the nationalities of the co-arbitrators (United Kingdom and Italy) and the parties' counsel (United Kingdom), as well as the applicable law (laws of England, excluding the CISG)[. . .]". The Secretariat added that it was "aware of suitable candidates with substantial experience acting as Chairman in ICC arbitration and residing in the region of the place of arbitration". These proposals are usually discussed at the Committee Sessions because the factors that may point to different National Committees may be viewed somewhat differently by the Court members attending the Committee Session. On many occasions, the Secretariat's proposals are changed after such discussion.

13–37 An illustration of how the Secretariat chose the National Committee is provided in the following memorandum from the Secretariat to the ICC Court under the Rules[19]:

[18] (i.e. the United States Council for International Business also being the National Committee for North America). This is an ICC Case from May 2012.

[19] ICC Case from May 2012.

> "The parties have not agreed to any alternative method for appointing the President of the Arbitral Tribunal.
>
> Accordingly, in light of:
> the nationalities of the parties ([East European Country]);
> the location of the parties' counsel (France, [East European Country]);
> the nationalities of the co-arbitrators ([East European Country]);
> the applicable law ([East European Country law]);
> the place of arbitration (Paris, France);
> the language of arbitration (English);
> the Secretariat suggests that the Court invite the [East European Country National Committee] to propose the President of the Arbitral Tribunal, unless any of the parties objects within 5 days (Article 13(5)), in which case to invite the French National Committee to make a proposal (Article13(3))."

In this case, both parties had nominated co-arbitrators from the East European country. Therefore, the Secretariat proposed that the ICC Court designate the East European National Committee, although one of the parties was from that country, but provided for the opportunity for a party to object. If there is no such circumstance, the ICC Court will not provide the parties with notice of which National Committee it has selected or provide an opportunity to object. **13–38**

The second step is for the National Committee or Group to propose one or more persons as potential arbitrators within the time limit set by the ICC Court. The practice of the National Committees or Groups varies widely in this respect. Several National Committees and Groups seek a dialogue with the Secretariat to ensure that the names that they will propose will correspond to the profile of the arbitrator that is sought. Other National Committees and Groups tend to simply propose one person selected on whatever basis that National Committee or Group chooses. **13–39**

The Secretariat will include the name and the curriculum vitae of the proposed arbitrator in the agenda and attachments that it submits to the Committee Session. The ICC Court members generally discuss whether the profile of the proposed arbitrator is appropriate for the arbitration. One of the issues that often arises relates to the experience of the proposed arbitrator as an arbitrator in international arbitration in general and ICC arbitration in particular.[20] The National Committee or Group will request the prospective arbitrator to give specific information on his arbitral experience, including the number of times he has acted as counsel and/or arbitrator in ICC arbitrations and in other arbitrations. **13–40**

If the National Committee or Group fails to make a proposal of an arbitrator within the time limit set by the ICC Court or if the ICC Court finds that the persons proposed are not appropriate given the requirements of the Rules, it may repeat its request or go to another National Committee or make a direct appointment. When the ICC Court has doubts whether a given National Committee or Group will be in a position to come up with a suitable candidate, it may from the outset designate two National Committees or Groups to come up with a proposal. **13–41**

[20] See Pt I para.Ann–59 et seq.

13–42 In another case, the governing law was English law, and the European National Committee had proposed as sole arbitrator a person who initially did not indicate any experience in common law.[21] The Secretariat laid out the position with respect to that person (without making any recommendation) and then stated as follows:

> "In the event that the Court decides not to appoint X, in light of the following elements the Secretariat suggests that United Kingdom National Committee or, failing which, the Canadian National Committee could be invited to propose a suitable candidate to act as Sole Arbitrator:
>
> nationalities of the parties (Hong Kong, Germany);
>
> location of counsel (Singapore, Germany);
>
> place of arbitration (Zurich); and
>
> applicable law (English law, although Respondent claims that certain German statutes may be applicable),"

13–43 On this occasion, the Secretariat contacted or was willing to contact three National Committees to find the best match for the arbitration.

13–44 The National Committee or Group mechanism therefore should result in the national arbitration organisation of a country of which the parties are not nationals proposing names to the ICC Court through the Secretariat. The proposal should therefore be neutral as regards nationality and influenced by, but independent of, the ICC and the ICC Court. One of the Secretariat's goals is to work closely with National Committees and Groups to ensure that they propose the best persons as arbitrators and that they are open to newer and younger arbitrators.

Article 13(4): "The Court may also appoint directly to act as arbitrator any person whom it regards as suitable where:

> **a) one or more of the parties is a state or claims to be a state entity; or**
> **b) the Court considers that it would be appropriate to appoint an arbitrator from a country or territory where there is no National Committee or Group; or**
> **c) the President certifies to the Court that circumstances exist which, in the President's opinion, make a direct appointment necessary and appropriate."**

13–45 Article 13(4) is new, although art.13(4)(b) was also found in art.9(6) of the 1998 Rules. Under the 1998 Rules, the ICC Court was only permitted to appoint an arbitrator who had not been proposed by a National Committee (that is to make a direct appointment) if there was no National Committee in the country of the arbitrator and if no party objected or referral to a National Committee had not resulted in an appointment. The expansion of the ICC Court's authority to appoint directly was a significant change in the Rules.

[21] ICC Case from May 2012.

In 2012, the ICC Court made 53 direct appointments (as opposed to 309 appointments on proposals of National Committees or Groups). Therefore, 14 per cent of all appointments by the ICC Court in 2012 were direct appointments, although that represented less than 5 per cent of the all arbitrators confirmed or appointed. Direct appointments were made of sole arbitrators in 9 cases (and 169 appointments of sole arbitrators were made on proposal of the National Committees or Groups). Direct appointments were made of 29 co-arbitrators (and 21 such appointments were made on proposal of National Committees or Groups). Direct appointments were made of 15 presidents (and 119 appointments were made on proposal of National Committees or Groups). Therefore, while significant in each category, direct appointments are most frequent in the appointment of co-arbitrators. **13–46**

One of the justifications for the change was that the system under the 1998 Rules could be cumbersome. If a National Committee did not make an appropriate proposal, the ICC Court generally went back to that National Committee or to another National Committee for another proposal. This could result in delay and in some cases, significant delay. This issue is now dealt with under the last sentence of art.13(3) with the possibility of direct appointment by the ICC Court. **13–47**

A second justification for the change is that use of National Committees or Groups may have less attraction where state entities are involved. In 2012, approximately 9.9 per cent of the Requests for Arbitration involved state entities. In such instances, using a National Committee or Group, which is often related to the local chamber of commerce, has less relevance than in a commercial dispute. Thereforce, it is expected that, where state entities are involved direct appointments of co-arbitrators and presidents will be the norm. **13–48**

The justification for art.13(4)(c) is the need to deal with sensitive issues in certain cases. Since art.13(4)(a) already permits direct appointments in cases involving states or state entities, art.13(4)(c) is intended to cover other instances where sensitive issues may arise. This covers situations where a National Committee or Group may have ceased to exist or not be functional for some reason. It is also intended to cover situations where it is difficult to find an arbitrator for a matter due to language requirements or conflicts. If, for example, the pool of arbitrators speaking a language is limited, it may be appropriate to make a direct appointment of the arbitrator rather than going somewhat artificially through a National Committee or Group to have that person proposed. **13–49**

Article 13(5): "The sole arbitrator or the president of the arbitral tribunal shall be of a nationality other than those of the parties. However, in suitable circumstances and provided that none of the parties objects within the time limit fixed by the Court, the sole arbitrator or the president of the arbitral tribunal may be chosen from a country of which any of the parties is a national."

Article 13(5) applies to the appointment of the sole arbitrator or the president of the Tribunal by the ICC Court. The parties can derogate from this principle in accordance with art.11(6). Therefore, the parties may agree that the sole arbitrator or the president have the same nationality of the parties, subject to **13–50** the discretionary power of the ICC Court pursuant to art.13(1) with respect to confirmation of the sole arbitrator or president. The parties may also agree to waive this requirement indirectly where they have agreed that the co-arbitrators shall nominate the president and the co-arbitrators have chosen a president having the nationality of one of the parties.

13–51 Some commentators view nationality as a marginal criterion for an arbitrator. However, in selecting co-arbitrators—and seeking to agree on presidents—many practitioners have the impression that nationality remains an important factor. For most, nationality in and of itself is not the major factor. It is the legal background of the arbitrator that usually reflects his or her nationality that is relevant. Moreover, there are frequently issues as to dual nationals or persons with dual legal backgrounds. With regard to dual nationality, the oddity is that grammatically the dual national may be of a nationality "other than those of the parties" and yet have as a second nationality that of one of the parties. However, the general thrust of art.13(5) is that a party should not feel at a disadvantage due to the fact that a sole arbitrator or president has the nationality of the other party. Therefore, one would understand the basis for an objection based on nationality even for a dual national.

13–52 Article 13(5) reflects this approach in providing that the sole arbitrator or president will not have a nationality of the parties except in "suitable circumstances" and if neither party objects. There can be many suitable circumstances. However, in many cases in international arbitration the formal nationality of the party does not reflect the nationality of the ultimate owning or controlling shareholders. For example, a party to an arbitration may be a Brazilian subsidiary of a British-owned company. In such a case, the ICC denomination can be expected to list the nationality of the subsidiary as Brazilian. However, the parent company would be British. One would expect that the ICC Court would take the nationality of the parent into account under art.13(1). Indeed, the ICC Court may consider it appropriate to appoint a Brazilian sole arbitrator or president due to the nationality of the parent company. Many commercial transactions are carried out using corporate vehicles in so called offshore countries, for instance the British Virgin Islands and the Cayman Islands, to name but two. The shareholders of these corporate vehicles may be prominent business corporations, and be, for example, from the United States or Russia. In such cases, the ICC Court is likely to take into account the shareholders' nationality as well as one of the elements in making its choice.

Article 14 Challenge of Arbitrators

1 **A challenge of an arbitrator, whether for an alleged lack of impartiality or independence, or otherwise, shall be made by the submission to the Secretariat of a written statement specifying the facts and circumstances on which the challenge is based.**

2 **For a challenge to be admissible, it must be submitted by a party either within 30 days from receipt by that party of the notification of the appointment or confirmation of the arbitrator, or within 30 days from the date when the party making the challenge was informed of the facts and circumstances on which the challenge is based if such date is subsequent to the receipt of such notification.**

3 **The Court shall decide on the admissibility and, at the same time, if necessary, on the merits of a challenge after the Secretariat has afforded an opportunity for the arbitrator concerned, the other party or parties and any other members of the arbitral tribunal to comment in writing within a suitable period of time. Such comments shall be communicated to the parties and to the arbitrators.**[1]

Introductory remarks

ICC arbitration is built upon the principle that the arbitrators must be impartial and independent of the parties in accordance with art.11(1). ICC arbitrators must provide disclosure in accordance with art.11(2). In addition ICC arbitrators must meet the requirements of national law and must act in accordance with the Rules. As discussed under art.11, the express reference to impartiality has been added in the Rules. However, the substantive test for arbitrators has not changed. **14–1**

[1] Article 14 corresponds to art.11 of the 1998 ICC Rules. No substantive changes have been made other than the addition of reference to impartiality (as well as independence).

14–2 The challenge procedure in art.14 is a primary enforcement mechanism to ensure that these requirements are met during the arbitral proceedings.[2] During the 10-year period from January 1, 2001 to January 1, 2011, 397 challenges were filed of which 30 were successful. Therefore, 3.3 per cent of the arbitrators were challenged and only 7.6 per cent of the challenges were successful.[3] In 2012, 61 challenges were filed of which 13 were accepted by the ICC Court.[4] Both the number of challenges and the number of challenges that were accepted increased in 2012 in comparison with 2011. In addition, those figures do not reflect all of the difficulties with respect to constitution of Tribunals.

14–3 First, in an ICC arbitration there are also objections to confirmation, which in many instances amount to challenges, albeit prior to actual appointment of the arbitrator. In 2012, the ICC Court decided not to confirm arbitrators on 33 occasions and issues of impartiality or independence were at issue in 29 cases.[5]

14–4 Secondly, when challenged (or when there is an objection to confirmation) the arbitrators may prefer to withdraw. These statistics do not reflect withdrawal by arbitrators due to such objections.

14–5 Thirdly, as discussed below, a challenge, if unsuccessful may still be the subject of court proceedings in particular challenging the Award or its enforceability. As illustrated by the *Avax/Tecnimont* case discussed below, a challenge may be rejected by the ICC Court, but the grounds nevertheless successfully invoked to overturn or prevent enforcement of the Award.

14–6 Therefore, challenges or objections to confirmation are not infrequent. And the success rate with respect to them depends very much on the facts of the case. The role of the ICC Court is to ensure that it provides a mechanism to handle challenges that meets the requirements of applicable law, even if its decision is only administrative in nature.

14–7 Challenges were usually heard at the monthly Plenary Sessions of the ICC Court. However, in recent years, straightforward challenges have been dealt with at Committee Sessions. The ICC Court generally decides at least one challenge at each Plenary Session and in some instances will decide three or more challenges. As a result, the Court members have considerable experience in reviewing issues relating to challenges and the Secretariat has a considerable record with respect to challenges. The discussions of challenges at the Plenary Session reflect this extensive background with respect to these issues.

14–8 The challenge procedure under art.14 must be read with the other provisions of the Rules and in particular with the provision for removal of arbitrators by the ICC Court

2 For a general discussion on the challenge of arbitrators, see Cardenas and Rivkin, "A Growing Challenge for Ethics in International Arbitration" in *Liber Amicorum in honour of Robert Briner, op. cit.*, p.191; Koch, "Standards and Procedures for Disqualifying Arbitrators" (2003) J Int'l Arb Vol.20 No.4, p.325; Calvo, "The Challenge of the ICC Arbitrators: Theory and Practice" (1998) J Int'l Arb Vol.15 No.4, p.63; Rau, "On Integrity in Private Judging" (1998) Arb Int Vol.14 no.2, p.115; Hascher, "ICC Practice in Relation to the Appointment, Confirmation, Challenge and Replacement of Arbitrators" (1995) ICC ICArb Bull Vol.6 No.2, p.4. See also Whitesell, "Independence in ICC Arbitration: ICC Court Practice concerning the Appointment, Confirmation, Challenge and Replacement of Arbitrators", *op. cit.*, at pp.26–33.

3 Fry, Greenberg & Mazza, *op. cit.*, para.3–571.

4 (2013) ICArb Bull. Vol.24, p.10.

5 (2013) ICArb Bull. Vol.24, p.10.

under art.15(2). The requirements of the Rules must also be read against the background of the relevant national law. Some commentators have suggested that the ICC Court's decision on challenges is final. In a sense, in some jurisdictions that is correct. The national courts in some jurisdictions will not hear challenges of arbitrators or review the ICC Court's decision with respect to the challenge, although courts in other jurisdictions, such as in UNCITRAL Model Law countries and in England, will review challenges usually de novo. However, whether the challenge itself may be reviewed in some national courts, the grounds for challenge can and often are used in national courts to seek to annul Awards in the national courts of the major locations of ICC arbitration.[6] Therefore, the issue with respect to a challenge of an arbitrator has to be examined with respect to three phases in the proceedings: the conduct of the proceedings themselves, annulment proceedings under the law of the place of arbitration and enforcement proceedings in jurisdictions in which the successful party may seek to enforce the Award. Since the goal of any arbitral proceedings is an enforceable Award, the issue of whether there are grounds to challenge an arbitrator is an important one in each stage of the proceedings.

As discussed under art.11, national laws impose standards for the arbitrators as **14–9**
regards disclosure and their conduct of the arbitration. For example, art.12 of the UNCITRAL Model Law provides that:

> "(1) When a person is approached in connection with his possible appointment as an arbitrator, he shall disclose any circumstances likely to give rise to justifiable doubts as to his impartiality or independence. An arbitrator, from the time of his appointment and throughout the arbitral proceedings, shall without delay disclose any such circumstances to the parties unless they have already been informed of them by him.
>
> (2) An arbitrator may be challenged only if circumstances exist that give rise to justifiable doubts as to his impartiality or independence, or if he does not possess qualifications agreed to by the parties. A party may challenge an arbitrator appointed by him, or in whose appointment he has participated, only for reasons of which he becomes aware after the appointment has been made."

Under the UNCITRAL Model Law, disclosure is treated separately from other **14–10**
issues relating to challenge, although it can and often does provide a basis for challenge. Under art.11, "best practices" have been outlined with respect to disclosure and potential conflicts. Parties often refer to these "best practices" in challenges. However, as noted under art.11, they do not in and of themselves provide grounds for challenge, although they are referred to by the American courts in particular. A key standard for challenges is the national case law particularly in the place of arbitration and at the place of probable enforcement.

[6] In some jurisdictions, the ICC Court's decision on the challenge may be final, but the grounds for the challenge may be raised in annulment proceedings. Therefore, the grounds are no longer used to remove the arbitrator, but to annul the Award. In addition, as discussed below, the enforcement proceedings do not aim at removal of the arbitrator, but at a refusal to enforce an Award, the grounds for which may be the same as the grounds for the challenge. However, the practical effect in each case is that the Tribunal with the challenged arbitrator may not have rendered a valid or enforceable Award.

14–11 Under art.V(1) of the New York Convention, a national court may refuse to enforce an Award for reasons including:

> "(b) The party against whom the award is invoked was not given proper notice of the appointment of the arbitrator or of the arbitration proceedings or was otherwise unable to present his case; or (....)
>
> (d) The composition of the arbitral authority or the arbitral procedure was not in accordance with the agreement of the parties, or, failing such agreement, was not in accordance with the law of the country where the arbitration took place."

14–12 Under art.V(2) of the New York Convention, a national court may also refuse to enforce an Award where "the recognition or enforcement of the award would be contrary to the public policy of that country". In most countries, the independence and impartiality of the arbitrators is a matter of public policy. It would be difficult to draw up a complete list of possible grounds for challenging arbitrators or for challenging awards based on problems with the arbitrators. However, at the risk of some oversimplification, it should be noted that challenges often relate to a party's perception of: (i) inadequate disclosure either at the outset or during the course of the proceedings; or (ii) failure of the arbitrator to meet applicable requirements for appointment; or (iii) failure to conduct of the arbitral proceedings in accordance with legal requirements (usually of fairness).

14–13 Of these factors, the most important relate to failure to disclose a relationship with the parties and bias with regard to the conduct of proceedings. With regard to conduct of the proceedings, one or more parties may be dissatisfied with parts of the arbitral procedure. However, to give rise to an issue justifying a challenge the procedural issue must be a serious one.

14–14 To be valid and enforceable, an Award must not be subject to objection based on the status of the arbitrators or their conduct.[7] If one or both parties become dissatisfied with an arbitrator, the party must raise the issue promptly or run the risk that the issue will be waived under art.39, and the relevant national law.[8] Once the issue has been raised, the arbitrator either resigns or he or she maintains

[7] For a discussion, see for example Bagner, "Arbitrator Impartiality: Appearance Is Everything", Case T 6876/04 of May 5, 2006, (2006) Mealey's IAR Vol.21 No.6, p.26, regarding the challenge of the Award based on the failure of the president of the Tribunal to disclose that Respondent's group was a major client, if not of the largest client of a major Swedish law firm where the president, a former Supreme Court judge, was a consultant. The Court of Appeal held that the president should have disclosed such an information. However, the non-compliance with this obligation does not necessarily result in the arbitrator being unable to serve as arbitrator. The question of the arbitrator's impartiality must be decided on the basis of an objective test.

[8] Failure to raise an issue will result in waiver under many if not most national legal systems. See for example, for *France*: Paris, September 25, 2003, *BVD Laboratoires et al v BLC Talgo Cosmetic*, in *Les Cahiers de l'Arbitrage Volume II, op. cit.*, p.327; Paris, November 28, 2002, *Voith Turbo GmbH v Société Nationale des Chemins de Fer Tunisiens*, in *Les Cahiers de l'Arbitrage Volume II, op. cit.*, p.324 (failure to object to arbitrator participating in prior proceedings not raised in timely fashion). For *Switzerland*: Decision of June 10, 2003, 4P.263/2002 (failure to object to fee structure proposed by the arbitrators resulted in waiver). For *England: Locabail v Bayfield Properties*, [2000] 1 All ER 65. For the *United States: Andresen v State Farm Ins Co*, 1994 Minn. App. LEXIS 1335 (Minn. Ct. App., 1994); *Marino v Writers Guild of Am E Inc*, 992 F.2d 1480 (9th Cir., 1993) (waiver "extends even to questions such as arbitrator bias, that go to the very heart of arbitral fairness"); *Babcock & Wilcox Co v PMAC Ltd*, 863 S.W.2d 225 (Tex. App., 1993) (failure to object during

that there are no grounds for challenge. In an ICC arbitration, the party then has to decide whether to bring challenge proceedings under art.14 before the ICC Court.

Under art.41, the ICC Court is required to "make every effort to make sure that the Award is enforceable at law". Therefore, in deciding any challenge under art.14, it is submitted that the ICC Court should take into account national law of the place of arbitration and perhaps of the place of likely or probable enforcement.[9] However, the ICC Court will, to a certain extent, depend on the submissions of the parties with respect to the relevant law. In the absence of those detailed submissions, the practice of the ICC Court will usually prevail. 14–15

Dealing with a challenge under art.14 one should analyse not only the relevant national law, but also the relevant national procedure. Counsel to a party does not (and should not) challenge an arbitrator lightly. For some practitioners, if a challenge is made during the course of the proceedings, it should be made only if there is a strong probability of success and knowing whether or not a further national challenge is possible during the proceedings. For the challenged arbitrator, there is an initial issue of whether it would be better to resign or if the stage and developments in the arbitration tend to indicate that there should be no resignation. For the remaining arbitrators there is an issue as to how to conduct themselves in the face of a challenge and, in particular, whether to suspend the proceedings. Frequently, the party adverse to the challenging party will oppose the challenge. However, this natural support should again be tempered by a realistic view of the principles that will be applied at the place of arbitration and the place of probable enforcement, as the goal is to obtain a valid, enforceable Award within a reasonable time frame. 14–16

Therefore, set out beginning at para.14–41 is a discussion of the principles applicable in various major centres of arbitration with respect to the legal standards for challenges. This discussion deals with whether challenges before the 14–17

arbitration to the selection of arbitrator, or his alleged bias, held to waive party's rights); *Hunt v Mobil Oil Corp*, 654 F. Supp.1487 (SDNY, 1987).

[9] For a general discussion of the procedure, see Whitesell, "Independence in ICC Arbitration: ICC Court Practice concerning the Appointment, Confirmation, Challenge and Replacement of Arbitrators" *op. cit.* See also Clay, *L'arbitre* (Dalloz, 2001), p.231; Carter, "Rights and Obligations of the Arbitrator" (1997) J Chart Inst Arb Vol.63 No.3, p.170; Bellet, "Des arbitres neutres et non neutres" in *Etudes de droit international en l'honneur de Pierre Lalive* (Helbing & Lichtenhahn, 1993), p.399; Stevenson, "Regarding Selection of Arbitrators" in *Etudes de droit international en l'honneur de Pierre Lalive, op. cit.*, p.691; Art, "Challenge of Arbitrators: Is an Institutional Decision Final?" (1986) Arb Int Vol.2 No.3, p.261.

The ICC Court does not publish its challenge decisions. However, in a challenge under the UNCITRAL Arbitration Rules the following analysis was made: "This matter is governed by the UNCITRAL Arbitration Rules and its interpretation must be based on their text. However, assistance may be gleaned from jurisprudence in other jurisdictions. United States law, the law of the *lex fori*, is particularly relevant. This is because, *inter alia*, it is conceivable that judicial proceedings in relation to the arbitration process, including a challenge to the Award because of alleged bias, could be taken at the conclusion of the arbitration in the courts of the United States. The arbitration process, although apart from the judicial process, and notwithstanding that it may be international in character, is nevertheless subject to a modicum of judicial control on the part of those courts where it takes place in the US as it appears it will. Such control is provided for in the Federal Arbitration Act, 9 U.S.C. [Section] (1985). It applies in state as well as federal courts if the dispute arises, inter alia, out of an inter-state transaction or involves a non-American party, Challenge Decision of January 11, 1995, *Southland Corp. v Keating*, 465 US 1 (1984); Challenge Decision of January 11, 1995 Yearbook Commercial Arbitration, A.J. van den Berg (ed.), (1997) YBCA Vol.XXII, p.227 at p.231. See also Nicholas and Partasides, "LCIA Court Decisions on Challenge to Arbitrators: A Proposal to Publish" (2007) Arb Int Vol.23 No.1, p.1.

national courts are possible and required during the course of the proceedings and the effect on the validity and enforceability of Awards if grounds for challenge exist. The outline is not intended to be exhaustive. It is intended to provide the basic framework for handling the sensitive issue of challenges of arbitrators in an ICC arbitration before dealing with the actual procedure under art.14.

Article 14(1): "A challenge of an arbitrator, whether for an alleged lack of impartiality or independence, or otherwise, shall be made by the submission to the Secretariat of a written statement specifying the facts and circumstances on which the challenge is based."

14–18 Prior to filing a challenge, there is usually some correspondence with the arbitrator being challenged as to the circumstances relating to the challenge. In some cases, this will be the result of spontaneous disclosure by the arbitrator. In others, it will be because the challenging party has learned some information from another source that raises an issue as to past disclosure. In procedural challenges, it may have been that some procedural hearing has taken place that has raised issues as to the arbitrator's independence and lack of bias.

14–19 This pre-challenge correspondence has several functions. The first is to establish the facts so that all involved understand the issues. In some instances, there is a potential misunderstanding about the facts that can be clarified. The second is often to provide the arbitrator with an opportunity of considering whether or not to resign. Whether an arbitrator should—and is entitled to—resign is dealt with under art.15(1). The Secretariat's role with respect to establishing the facts is particularly important. The Secretariat must ensure that the parties and arbitrators are provided with an opportunity to comment on the facts and law relating to the challenge. In addition, the Secretariat has access to all of the procedural documents between the parties and the Tribunal in accordance with art.3(1) and will endeavor to provide key documents to the ICC Court for its review.[10]

14–20 Article 14(1) does not require that it be a party that files a challenge, although art.14(2) appears to anticipate that only parties will file challenges. If an arbitrator believes that there are grounds for a challenge, it is not clear that, under the Rules, that other arbitrator is entitled to file a challenge. In any event, one would expect that an arbitrator who has serious reservations about the conduct of his fellow arbitrators or the arbitration would choose to resign as provided for in art.15(1).

14–21 Article 14(1) does not prevent a party from challenging the arbitrator it nominated. However, since the basic principle is that a party can only challenge an arbitrator for grounds that have arisen since the appointment of the arbitrator, these challenges seem to be less frequent.

14–22 Article 14(1) refers to challenges "for an alleged lack of impartiality or independence or otherwise". The issue of lack of impartiality or independence is discussed under art.11(1) and in the introduction to the discussion of art.14. As noted above, for the parties, to determine the appropriate test for the lack of independence it is important to refer to national law at the place of arbitration in first

[10] There is a Rapporteur for the challenge. The Rapporteur can ask for any procedural documents that may be relevant to the challenge and the Secretariat will supply them.

place and to the law of the probable place of enforcement secondarily. The ICC Court will review the submissions of the parties on these issues. The ICC Court would not usually embark on a separate review of the potentially relevant laws with respect to a challenge unless the parties submit material with respect to those laws as part of the challenge procedure.

Article 14(1) refers to other grounds of challenges without defining them. It would appear that the other grounds would include a material breach of the Rules, although this must be read with art.15 as well. Sometimes, a challenge is based on breach of the requirements of the law of the place of arbitration. In this respect, as noted above, the standards do vary even among the principal places of arbitration. **14–23**

The party bringing a challenge must provide a written statement specifying the facts and circumstances on which the challenge is based. Very frequently, the facts are relatively uncontested and are submitted in documents or reflected in the pre-challenge exchange of letters. It is also not uncommon to file a witness statement if the facts are more complex. **14–24**

Although not mentioned by art.14(1), usually the challenging party files a legal argument to justify the challenge, although it is not required to do so. The legal argument would generally be based on the national law precedents of the law of the place of arbitration with references to non-binding material, such as the IBA Guidelines where appropriate. With respect to conflicts of interest, the ICC Court members have considerable experience and the authors' personal view is that the IBA Guidelines will be considered relevant by the ICC Court, when examining a challenge, but no more than that. One of the reasons is that the factual situations are almost invariably more complex than those set out in the IBA Guidelines. **14–25**

A party who has objected to the confirmation of an arbitrator cannot be prevented under the Rules from bringing a challenge against that arbitrator within the time limit provided in art.14(2) and include the arguments originally made against confirmation of the arbitrator. However, unless the challenging party provides new grounds or arguments, the challenge is virtually bound to fail before the ICC Court. **14–26**

Article 14(2): "For a challenge to be admissible, it must be submitted by a party either within 30 days from receipt by that party of the notification of the appointment or confirmation of the arbitrator, or within 30 days from the date when the party making the challenge was informed of the facts and circumstances on which the challenge is based if such date is subsequent to the receipt of such notification."

Article 14(2) sets out the basic rule that a party must file a challenge within 30 days after either the appointment or confirmation of the arbitrator or the date on which it was informed of the facts and circumstances on which the challenge was based. The 30-day period does not run from the date on which the other party nominated the arbitrator.[11] **14–27**

[11] Although not required under the Rules, it has been the practice of the ICC Court to examine a challenge on the merits even if the ICC Court considers that it was made out of time. As the reasons for rejecting a challenge are not provided to the parties, they will not know whether the challenge was rejected as being untimely, and thus inadmissible, and/or also on the merits.

14–28 A frequent issue in this respect is when the challenging party was informed of enough of the facts and circumstances to make a decision to bring the challenge. In such a situation, the ICC Court tends to rely or accept the statement of the challenging party unless it is clear that it could not have failed to know the facts earlier. Another issue is whether the notice can be constructive notice. For example, the French courts deemed that the fact that an arbitrator was a member of an association of lawyers was sufficient notice of that relationship,[12] as was information that was available on the internet.[13] Moreover, the IBA Guidelines provide that the parties have a duty to carry out the appropriate steps to check on conflicts.[14]

14–29 The timing of the challenge is important. Article 11 requires that an arbitrator be and remain impartial and independent of the parties. Article 11(1) provides for grounds for challenge that would include challenges based on the conduct of the arbitration. However, as a practical matter, a challenge that is brought at the outset of the arbitral proceedings is treated differently from a challenge brought after the Tribunal has become involved in the merits of the dispute or has rendered a partial Award.[15]

14–30 The main reasons for the difference are motivation and costs. If a challenge is brought after the Tribunal has issued procedural orders or partial Awards, it may appear that the challenge is motivated more by the challenging party's concerns as to the results of the arbitration than to the actual situation of the challenged arbitrator. Thus, if the challenge is brought in the middle of the arbitral proceedings, the challenged arbitrator, the other parties and the ICC Court may well place special emphasis on whether there has been a waiver.

14–31 As regards the costs, there are inherent additional costs, in replacing an arbitrator. The ICC Court will normally pay the outgoing arbitrator a proportional fraction of the fees in accordance with the fee schedule for his work in the

[12] See the *Voith Turbo* case, referred to above.

[13] See the *BVD Laboratoires* case, referred to above.

[14] General Standard 7 of the IBA Guidelines states: "(a) A party shall inform an arbitrator, the Arbitral Tribunal, the other parties and the arbitration institution or other appointing authority (if any) about any direct or indirect relationship between it (or another company of the same group of companies) and the arbitrator. The party shall do so on its own initiative before the beginning of the proceeding or as soon as it becomes aware of such relationship. (b) In order to comply with General Standard 7(a), a party shall provide any information already available to it and shall perform a reasonable search of publicly available information".

[15] As Lord Woolf noted in his judgment in the *AT&T Lucent* case (see above): "54. In any event, [the president] having been appointed an arbitrator and the arbitration having reached the stage it has, it would be inappropriate, in the absence of bias, to set aside the awards or to remove [the president]". See also the *Locabail* case cited above: "26. . . . What disclosure is appropriate depends in large measure on the stage that the matter has reached. If, before a hearing has begun, the judge is alerted to some matter which might, depending on the full facts, throw doubt on his fitness to sit, the judge should in our view inquire into the full facts, so far as they are ascertainable, in order to make disclosure in the light of them. But, if a judge has embarked on a hearing in ignorance of a matter which emerges during the hearing, it is in our view enough if the judge discloses what he then knows. He has no obligation to disclose what he does not know. Nor is he bound to fill any gaps in his knowledge which, if filled, might provide stronger grounds for objection to his hearing or continuing to hear the case. If, of course, he does make further inquiry and learn additional facts not known to him before, then he must make disclosure of those facts also. It is, however, generally undesirable that hearings should be aborted unless the reality or the appearance of justice requires that they should". See also Estreicher and Bennett, "Disqualification of Arbitrators: Before or After the Award?" New York Law Journal, Friday May 4, 2007 Vol.237 No.86.

arbitration. The incoming arbitrator will be entitled to a fee as for the period. This may lead to higher fees overall, in particular if the Tribunal has to hold additional hearings or to reconsider matters that it had considered previously.

Article 15(4) provides in this respect that "Once reconstituted, and after having invited the parties to comment, the Arbitral Tribunal shall determine if and to what extent prior proceedings shall be repeated before the reconstituted Arbitral Tribunal". Under national law, if a president is replaced, it may be necessary to repeat hearings. The costs of replacing an arbitrator do not provide a justification for requiring a party to accept an arbitrator that is not independent. However, it may be a factor in considering a challenge. 14–32

Article 14(3): "The Court shall decide on the admissibility and, at the same time, if necessary, on the merits of a challenge after the Secretariat has afforded an opportunity for the arbitrator concerned, the other party or parties and any other members of the arbitral tribunal to comment in writing within a suitable period of time. Such comments shall be communicated to the parties and to the arbitrators."

The issue of admissibility goes to whether the party bringing the challenge has filed it within the 30-day time period under art.14(2). The merits of the challenge are relevant only if the challenge is admissible. If the challenge is made within the 30-day period, there still may be an issue of whether there has been a waiver of the grounds for challenge. 14–33

The Secretariat is required to provide the challenged arbitrator, the other parties and the other arbitrators with an opportunity to comment in writing on the challenge. If the challenged arbitrator does not resign, the challenged arbitrator sometimes provides a reasonably detailed response as to the factual grounds for the challenge in particular. Some arbitrators will limit their response to simply presenting the facts on the assumption that the ICC Court will do what is appropriate in the circumstances. Other arbitrators like to cite key relevant authority to illustrate the challenged arbitrator's legal analysis of the issue. For many practitioners, aside from correcting factual errors, the challenged arbitrator should not become involved in the arguments relating to the challenge. In some instances it is the challenged arbitrators's submissions that have contributed to a successful challenge. 14–34

If the challenge is not well founded, or if there are issues as to waiver of the grounds for challenge, usually the party who has appointed the arbitrator being challenged responds to object to the challenge. This is a natural reflection of the adversarial process between the parties. In replying to the challenge, a party would usually respond both on the facts and on the law. 14–35

The other arbitrators are also provided with an opportunity to comment on the challenge. Many fellow arbitrators do not comment on challenges. The other arbitrators may be concerned that, by commenting on the challenge, they will be creating further issues in the mind of the challenging party as to the Tribunal as a whole. This concern is accentuated if the parties have adopted adversarial positions with respect to the challenge. Another concern for fellow arbitrators relate to divulging the contents of deliberations, particularly where the challenge is based on procedural grounds. With respect to procedural issues, the authors' personal view is 14–36 that the ICC Court will be reluctant to uphold a challenge based on an arbitrator's procedural decision, unless that procedural decision was so manifestly improper as to raise issues as to due process. Most arbitrators do not like to comment on a challenge brought against one of the members of the Tribunal, or if they do, will use considerable restraint. Indeed such comments require a delicate exercise between loyalty and respect towards the other arbitrator on the one hand, and the need to ensure the integrity of the arbitral process.

14–37 Once the documents relating to the challenge have been received, the Secretariat will prepare the file for the ICC Court. An ICC Court member is generally appointed to prepare a report on the challenge. The decision as to whether to accept or reject the challenge is taken by the ICC Court at a Plenary Session or, if the matter is straightforward, at a Committee Session. Neither the parties nor the challenged arbitrator have the occasion to address the ICC Court in person with respect to a challenge. Therefore, there will be no oral submissions by the parties regarding the challenge, although the members of the ICC Court attending the session will discuss the merits of the challenge.

14–38 The time it takes to decide a challenge varies as to whether the challenge is decided at a Plenary Session or a Committee Session. For example, in the *Avax/Tecnimont* case, which was heard at a Plenary Session, the challenge was filed on September 14, 2007 and decided on October 26, 2007. This corresponds to the normal practice for a Plenary Session challenge. The period should be much shorter for a challenge decided in a Committee Session.

14–39 As noted, the ICC Court does not provide reasons for accepting or rejecting the challenge. Nor does the ICC Court confirm whether the challenge was rejected as to admissibility or on the merits. Therefore, if national proceedings are brought to challenge the arbitrator, as is possible in England and UNCITRAL Model Law countries such as Germany and Singapore, the national court will not have the benefit of the ICC Court's reasoning. Similarly, if the grounds for challenge are raised as grounds for annulment, as is possible in many countries (including where direct challenges are possible before national courts as well, in countries such as France, Switzerland and the United States), the national court will generally consider the matter de novo.

14–40 The basic position of the national courts in France, England, Switzerland and the USA, as well as under the UNCITRAL Model Law is set out in a nutshell in the following paragraphs.

France

14–41 France distinguishes, for some purposes, between national and international arbitrations. Article 1506(1) of the French CPC provides that arts 1452–1458 and 1460 relating to the constitution of the Tribunal are applicable to international arbitration.

14–42 Article 1456 of the French CPC provides as follows:

> "The constitution of an arbitral tribunal shall be complete upon the arbitrators' acceptance of their mandate. As of that date, the tribunal is seized of the dispute.

Before accepting a mandate, an arbitrator shall disclose any circumstance that may affect his or her independence or impartiality. He or she also shall disclose promptly any such circumstance that may arise after accepting the mandate. If the parties cannot agree on the removal of an arbitrator, the issue shall be resolved by the person responsible for administering the arbitration or, where there is no such person, by the judge acting in support of the arbitration to whom application must be made within one month following the disclosure or the discovery of the fact at issue."[16]

The Paris Tribunal of First Instance has held based on the prior law that the court only had jurisdiction over challenges if there was no authority that had been designated to carry out this task.[17] The French Supreme Court has also held that it is not possible to bring an application for judicial review of the decision of the ICC Court, as it is a decision of a private body.[18] 14–43

Therefore, it is not possible to bring challenge proceedings for an ICC arbitration before the French courts directly, under art.1493 of the French CPC. However, issues as to the independence and conduct of arbitrators are to be raised before the Tribunal itself[19] and then may be the subject of annulment proceedings based on art.1520 of the CPC.[20] Therefore, the grounds for challenge are relevant in annulment proceedings. 14–44

Article 1520 of the French CPC provides that: 14–45

[16] The English translation is provided courtesy of Prof. Gaillard, Me. Leleu-Nobil and Ms. Pellarina of Shearman & Sterling.

[17] The Paris TGI in a decision dated April 1, 1993, *State of Dubai et al v Halcrow*, stated:

"Whereas the provisions of Article 1493(2) of the New Code of Civil Procedure do not limit the intervention of the national court in the exercise of its mission of 'technical assistance' and 'judicial cooperation' for arbitration solely to the aspects of the initial constitution of the arbitral tribunal; they also provide him with the power to decide, while respecting the intentions of the parties, any difficulty relating to a subsequent event affecting in one way or another the constitution of the arbitral tribunal and preventing it from continuing the exercise of the prerogative attached to its power to judge; that therefore the President of the Tribunal of First Instance has authority to decide on a challenge as is provided for in Article 1463 of the New Code Civil Procedure, applicable to international arbitration subject to French law. Whereas this provision is supplementary and the President of the Tribunal of First Instance only has authority to decide the merits of a challenge if no other institution has been designated by the arbitration agreement to decide the issue." (Authors' translation); (1993) Rev Arb No.3 p.455 at p.458, note Bellet.

[18] In Cass Civ 2e, October 7, 1987, *Opinter France v Dacomex*, the appeal against the judgment of the Paris Court of Appeal refusing to review the decision of the ICC Court with respect to a challenge was upheld in the following terms: "Whereas, the judgement holds correctly that the decision on the challenge rendered by the Court of Arbitration of the International Chamber of Commerce on October 20, 1982, which was simply entrusted with the organization of the arbitration and not with judicial functions cannot be considered as an arbitral award; And whereas the judgment notes that the Internal Rules of the Court of Arbitration, which the parties agreed to accept, provides in Article 16 that the reasons for the decision rendered on the requested challenge of an arbitrator will not be provided [to the parties]." (Authors' translation); (1987) Rev Arb No.4 p.479 at p.480, note Mezger.

[19] See the *BVD Laboratoires* case above.

[20] There appears to have been no issue as to the admissibility of the review of the independence of the arbitrators as grounds for annulment; see the *BVD Laboratoires* case above and the *Voith Turbo* case above: failure to object to arbitrator participating in prior proceedings not raised in timely fashion. If a party seeks to annul a partial Award, then presumably it would also raise the issue of the lack of independence or improper conduct of the arbitrators. Therefore, the situation in France could well be similar to that in Switzerland.

"An award may only be set aside where:

(1) the arbitral tribunal wrongly upheld or declined jurisdiction; or
(2) the arbitral tribunal was not properly constituted; or
(3) the arbitral tribunal ruled without complying with the mandate conferred upon it; or
(4) due process was violated; or
(5) recognition or enforcement of the award is contrary to international public policy."[21]

14–46 Article 1520(2) goes to the characteristics or the independence of the arbitrators. Article 1520(4) covers the failure to respect due process or procedural misconduct by the arbitrators. Article 1520(5) would cover various forms of misconduct by the arbitrators of such a type as to render the Award unenforceable under public international policy.

14–47 As regards the standards to be applied, as some authors have noted, French courts "closely investigate how the arbitral tribunal conducted the proceedings [. . .] and will decide [. . .] according to French standards of fairness and due process".[22] However, the standards should be analysed in a practical fashion and with due regard to waivers. The French courts have rejected annulment proceedings based on either actual or deemed notice of the grounds for objection.[23]

14–48 One example of what is covered is the issue of the independence of an arbitrator who had been nominated on a number of occasions by the same company in various arbitrations with respect to franchise arrangements. The French courts did not decide the issue but ordered an expert review of the facts to determine whether they provided grounds for annulment.[24]

14–49 In the *Avax/Tecnimont*, the issue was the disclosure by the president of a relationship between his law firm and an affiliate of one of the parties. Avax learned some details of this relationship in 2007 and filed a challenge with the ICC, which was rejected by the ICC Court on October 26, 2007. Avax reserved its rights and requested additional information. The Tribunal rendered a partial Award on December 10, 2007. Again, Avax sought additional information. Avax filed to annul the Award. The application was accepted by the Paris Court of Appeal in a judgment dated February 12, 2009. On November 4, 2010 the French Supreme Court overruled the Paris Court of Appeal and sent the case to the Reims Court of

[21] The English translation is provided courtesy of Prof. Gaillard, Me. Leleu-Nobil and Ms. Pellarina of Shearman & Sterling.

[22] Delvolvé, Rouche & Pointon, *op. cit.*, para.450, p.256.

[23] See the *Voith Turbo* case above: membership in network of lawyers publicly available and delay in objection resulted in waiver. See also above the *BVD Laboratoires* case above: deemed notice of information on the internet.

[24] Paris, April 2, 2003, *Fremac v ITM in Les Cahiers de l'Arbitrage Volume II, op. cit.*, p.325; See also Paris, May 16, 2002, *STPIF v SB Ballestero* in *Les Cahiers de l'Arbitrage Volume II, op. cit.*, p.322. Under French expert proceedings, an expert nominated by the Court investigates the relevant facts and reports to the Court. The court-appointed expert can and usually does request that the parties produce relevant documents and holds meetings with counsel to review the issues subject to the expertise.

Appeal for a new decision. The Reims Court of Appeal rendered its decision on November 2, 2011.

In the decision of the Reims Court of Appeal, the Court held that the decision of the ICC Court was administrative in nature and did not have res judicata effect. The Court held that it had the right to review the independence of the arbitrator under the predecessor to art.1520(2) of the French CPC. The Court then overturned the partial Award due to the client relationship that existed between the president's firm and Tecnimont referring in particular to the incomplete disclosure by the president.[25] **14–50**

Therefore, under French law, there is a possibility of raising the issue of lack of independence or other misconduct of the arbitrators in annulment proceedings. **14–51**

Switzerland

Article 180(2) of the Swiss PILA provides as follows: **14–52**

> "1 an arbitrator may be challenged:
>
> a. if he does not meet the requirements agreed upon by the parties;
> b. if a ground for challenge exists under the rules of arbitration agreed upon by the parties;
> c. if circumstances exist that give rise to justifiable doubts as to his independence.
>
> 2 No party may challenge an arbitrator nominated by it or whom it was instrumental in appointing, except on a ground which came to that party's attention after such appointment. The ground for challenge must be notified to the arbitral tribunal and to the other party without delay.
> 3 To the extent that the parties have not made provisions for this challenge procedure, the judge at the seat of the Arbitral tribunal shall make the final decision."

Article 190(2) of the Swiss PILA provides: **14–53**

> "2 The award may only be annulled:
>
> a. if the sole arbitrator was not properly appointed or if the arbitral tribunal was not properly constituted;
> b. if the Arbitral tribunal wrongly accepted or declined jurisdiction;
>
> [. . .]."

Under Swiss law, the Courts will not review a decision of the ICC Court with respect to a challenge directly. However, they will review the decision, based on Swiss law, when the court has to decide on the annulment of an arbitral Award **14–54**

[25] Reims Court of Appeal, November 2, 2011. The firm of one of the authors was involved in this case.

rendered in Switzerland.[26] Moreover, the decision to seek this ancillary review of the challenge is possible as soon as the Tribunal has rendered a partial Award and therefore has implicitly upheld its jurisdiction. In fact, it appears that the proceedings should be brought at that point in time.[27]

14–55 The national proceedings before the courts in Switzerland that are based on lack of independence of an arbitrator do not preclude the Tribunal from continuing the arbitration proceedings.[28]

14–56 Under Swiss law, arbitrators are held to the same standard as national judges and the issue is whether the concerns of the party making the challenge are

[26] As stated by the Swiss Federal Tribunal in a decision dated August 18, 1992, *K v X*, 118 BGE II 359: "It is correct that an appeal directly against a decision of refusal of a private body such as the ICC Court of Arbitration is not possible.[. . .] The possibility of an indirect review of the decision during the appeal procedure of the award itself is subject to different opinions in the commentaries. Bucher (Le nouvel arbitrage international en Suisse, Rz. 341) and Lalive/Poudret/Reymond (Le droit de l'arbitrage interne et inter- national en Suisse, S. 424 N 5 zu art.190 [Swiss PILA] permit during these appeal procedures only those grounds of refusal of which the parties have been notified after the award was rendered. Walter/Bosch/Bronnimann (a.a.O., S. 113), on the other hand, are of the opinion that the grounds for refusal can also include grounds that were known and raised before the award was rendered but which were refused by the private body deciding on the refusal. They maintain, in convincing fashion, that a legal system must reserve the right to review arbitral awards and procedures for their conformity with legal unobjectionability, the impartiality of the arbitrators being part of it. It is therefore for these authors to be assumed that such grounds for refusal can be raised in proceedings to set aside the award. [. . .] however, contrary to their opinion (p.113 and 217) it is not the one under article 190 para.2 lit. b [Swiss PILA] (incorrect decision on jurisdiction), but rather that of paragraph (a) (improper constitution of the tribunal). Therefore, the claim of lack of independence of the Claimant is to be reviewed insofar as it is relevant to the arbitrator who rendered the decision in question." (Authors' translation.) See also BGE 138 III 270 S of May 2, 2012 for a discussion which appears to confirm this approach.

[27] Proceedings in this respect are now governed by the Swiss Supreme Court Act of June 17, 2005 which entered into force on January 1, 2007 (RO 2006 1205) and in particular arts 77(1), 92 and 93. More generally on the Swiss Supreme Court Act, see Poudret, "Les recours au Tribunal fédéral suisse en matière d'arbitrage international (Commentaire de l'article 77 LTF)" (2007) ASA Bull. Vol.25 No.4, p.669; Besson, "Le recours contre la Sentence Arbitrale Internationale selon la Nouvelle LTF (Aspects procéduraux)" (2007) ASA Bull. vol.25 No.1, p.2. However, the principles of the prior case law appear to remain applicable. See Swiss Federal Tribunal, February 17, 2000, *Rhône Poulenc v Roche*: "The issue is whether this review may be raised against the final award or already against the partial awards. In this respect it should be noted that art.190 Abs. 3 [Swiss PILA] permits recourse against a preliminary award for improper constitution of the tribunal (art.190 Abs. 2 lit. a [Swiss PILA]) and lack of jurisdiction of the arbitral tribunal (art.190 Abs. 2 lit. b [Swiss PILA]). The legislator therefore, in the interests of procedural efficiency provided for direct recourse against preliminary and partial awards of an arbitral tribunal with regard to its constitution and jurisdiction to avoid that procedures that already are deficient at their commencement have to be continued.[. . .] This reflects the general procedural principle that organisational issues relating to the tribunal should be resolved before continuing the proceedings. (See: BGE 124 I 255 E. 1b/bb S. 259; 116 II 80 E. 3a S. 84). Based on the goal of art.190 Abs. 3 [Swiss PILA] it follows that the claim of improper constitution of the tribunal is to be made against the first decision of the arbitral tribunal which expressly or implicitly decides on its composition." (Authors' translation.)

[28] As the Swiss Federal Tribunal stated in its decision of June 10, 2003 cited above: "However, in the absence of a contrary provision in the arbitration rules, the removal procedure before the judge generally does not have a suspensive effect and does not prevent the arbitral procedure from being carried out. Poudret/Besson, Droit comparé de l'arbitrage international, n.428 p.381s.; Rüede/Hadenfeldt, Schweizerisches Schiedsgerichtsrecht, 2e ed., p.182 ch.3a and the authors cited at foot note 98). The arbitral tribunal retains therefore the jurisdiction to render an award at the risk of having it annulled if the grounds for removal are accepted. (Schwab/Walter, Schiedsgerichtsbarkeit, 6th ed., Munich 2000, p.141 n.26; Andreas Bücher, Le nouvel arbitrage international en Suisse, p.67 n.181; Pierre Jolidon, Commentaire du Concordat suisse sur l'arbitrage, n.43 ad art. 21 CA)." (Authors' translation.)

objectively justified. As the Swiss Federal Tribunal stated in the decision of June 10, 2003:

> "The principles developed by the Federal Tribunal on the basis of Article 58 para.(1) of the Constitution regarding removal of public judges and that it reviews freely are also applicable to members of arbitral tribunals. The guarantee of natural justice of Article 58 of the Constitution, included today in the procedural guarantees set out in Article 30(1) of the Constitution. (ATF 127 I 196 ground. 2b p. 198 and judgments cited therein) permits the request for removal of a judge whose situation or behaviour whose are of a nature to cause a legitimate doubt as to his impartiality. The key element is knowing whether the concerns of the party who requests removal are objectively justified (cf. Judgement 4P. 224/1997 of February 9, 1998, grounds 3a et 3b, reproduced in Bulletin ASA 1998 634 ff)" (Authors' translation).[29]

The Swiss Federal Tribunal has held that the review should not be as strict for party appointed arbitrators as for chairmen or sole arbitrators.[30] **14–57**

There are numerous cases in which challenges have been refused in Switzerland and only isolated cases in which they have been upheld.[31] **14–58**

As a result, in Switzerland, there is no direct recourse against the ICC Court's decision relating to a challenge. However, there is an indirect recourse that is possible once the Tribunal has rendered an Award. The standard of independence for arbitrators is generally the same as for that of national judges, but it does not appear to be applied as strictly to party nominated arbitrators. **14–59**

United States

The Federal Arbitration Act governs virtually all international arbitrations conducted within the United States. The state arbitration acts, which in many instances are based on the Uniform Arbitration Act or the Revised Uniform Arbitration Act of 2000, are pre-empted to the extent inconsistent with Federal law. **14–60**

The US courts have focused on the difference between domestic and non-domestic Awards under the New York Convention and an issue has arisen as to the applicable law with respect to setting aside international Awards rendered in the United States. In the *Yusuf* case, an Award was rendered in the United States with regard to a distribution agreement for Kuwait. The Court of Appeals for the Second District held that the Federal Arbitration Act was applicable stating: **14–61**

> "We read Article V(1)(e) of the Convention to allow a court in the country under whose law the arbitration was conducted to apply domestic arbitral law, in this case the FAA, to a motion to set aside or vacate that arbitral award. The district court in Spector v Torenberg,

[29] ibid.

[30] See above the *K v X* case above, at pp.361–362.

[31] For a discussion, see Patocchi & Geisinger, *IPRG Internationales Privatrecht* (Zurich 2000), pp.552–560.

852 F. Supp. 201 (S.D.N.Y. 1994), reached the same conclusion as we do now, reasoning that, because the Convention allows the district court to refuse to enforce an award that has been vacated by a competent authority in the country where the award was rendered, the court may apply FAA standards to a motion to vacate a nondomestic award rendered in the United States. See id. at 205–06 & n.4."[32]

14–62 As a result, when dealing with international Awards rendered in the United States, under the principles accepted by the Second Circuit Court of Appeals, the grounds are not limited to those set out in the New York Convention.

14–63 Article 10 of the US Federal Arbitration Act provides in relevant part as follows:

"(a) In any of the following cases the United States court in and for the district wherein the award was made may make an order vacating the award upon the application of any party to the arbitration

(1) Where the award was procured by corruption, fraud, or undue means.
(2) Where there was evident partiality or corruption in the arbitrators, or either of them.
(3) Where the arbitrators were guilty of misconduct in refusing to postpone the hearing, upon sufficient cause shown, or in refusing to hear evidence pertinent and material to the controversy; or of any other misbehavior by which the rights of any party have been prejudiced."

14–64 Article 10 of the US Federal Arbitration Act refers to vacating an Award. In *Certain Underwriters at Lloyd's, London v Argonaut Ins Co*,[33] the court stated:

"At the hearing, counsel for Certain Underwriters acknowledged there are, to his knowledge, no federal cases in which a court has issued an order disqualifying a neutral arbitrator once arbitration had commenced but prior to a final arbitration award. Although the Ninth Circuit appears not to have reached the issue, other courts have consistently held that courts do not have the power under the FAA to disqualify an arbitrator while proceedings are pending. See Gulf Guaranty Life Ins. Co. v Connecticut General Life Ins. Co., 304 F.3d 476, 490 (5th Cir.2002) ('Even where arbitrator bias is at issue, the FAA does not provide for removal of an arbitrator from service prior to an award, but only for potential vacatur of any award. The FAA appears not to endorse court

[32] *Yusuf Ahmed Alghanim & Sons WLL v Toys 'R' Us Inc and TRU Ltd*, 126 F.3d 15, 21 (2nd Cir. 1997); (1998) YBCA Vol.XXIII p.1058. See also *Karaha Bodas Company LLC v Perussahaan Pertambangan Minyak Dan Gas Bumi Negara*, 264 F. Supp. 2d 470: "The Court recognizes that, as an enforcing court, its review of the Arbitral Award was limited to the defenses listed in Article VI of the New York Convention, whereas a court of competent authority with jurisdiction to set aside the Arbitral Award is not so limited. See Yusuf 126 F.3d at 21 (a motion to set aside an international arbitral award is controlled by the domestic law of the rendering state)." *Frontera Res. Azer. Corp v. State Oil Co. of the Azer. Republic*, 582 F.3d 393 (2d Cir. 2009).

[33] *Certain Underwriters at Lloyd's, London v Argonaut Ins Co*, 264 F. Supp. 2d 926 (D. Cal., 2003); 2003 US Dist. Lexis 8796. See also *Island Territory of Curacao v Solitron Devices Inc*, 356 F. Supp. (SDNY, 1973).

power to remove an arbitrator for any reason prior to issuance of an arbitral award.'); Aviall, Inc., v Ryder Sys. Inc., 110 F.3d 892, 895 (2d Cir. 1997) ('Although the FAA provides that a court can vacate an award where there was evident partiality or corruption in the arbitrators, it does not provide for pre-award removal of an arbitrator.')."[34]

Therefore, the principle in the United States is that if grounds for challenge exist, they should be brought after the final Award has been issued. **14–65**

As regards the standard for arbitrators, the widely cited concurring opinion of Justice White in the *Commonwealth Coatings* case[35] confirms that arbitrators are not held to the same standards as judges.[36] **14–66**

This standard for arbitrators has been reaffirmed in many cases, including *Employers Ins v National Fire Ins*.[37] In that case, the court held "[to] hold arbitrators to the same rigorous standard of impartiality as judges would, in many cases, erase the salutary aspects of arbitration as opposed to litigation". As Justice White observed in the *Commonwealth Coatings* case, "[i]t is often because they [arbitrators] are men [and women] of affairs, not apart from but of the marketplace, that they are effective in their adjudicatory function". Consequently, "arbitrators are not automatically disqualified by a business relationship with the parties before them if both parties are informed of the relationship in advance".[38] **14–67**

As regards disclosure, the US standard appears to be reasonably strict. It should be noted that, in the *Commonwealth Coatings* case, the US Supreme Court held that the Award could be annulled due to the arbitrator's failure to disclose a sporadic financial relationship with a party. However, if the relationship is disclosed, then the fact that the arbitrator has some sort of connection with one of the parties might not suffice to justify a challenge. Not all arbitrators disqualified by failure to disclose they act as arbitrators in a similar arbitration. (*Scandinavian Reinsce v. St Paul Fire and Marine Insce Co* 668–F3d 60 (2nd Civ 2012)). Nevertheless, it is not sufficient that an arbitrator who made a partial disclosure insulated himself from obtaining further information by a "Chinese Wall". This created evident partiality as the arbitrator adopted this approach without disclosing it to the parties. (*Applied Indus. Materials Corp. v. Ovalar Makine Ticaret Ve Sanayi AS 492 F 3d 137* (2nd Civ 2007)) **14–68**

A practical illustration of the application of US principles is found in *Woods v Saturn*.[39] In that case, an automobile dealer had signed an arbitration clause providing that the arbitrators would include other automobile dealers handling the same vehicles. Two other dealers were appointed arbitrators. The dealer sought to challenge the Award due to this relationship. In the ruling on this bias claim, the court distinguished nondisclosure cases from bias cases. **14–69**

The Court held: **14–70**

[34] To the same effect, see *Certain Underwriters at Lloyd's, London v Continental Casualty Co* (1998) YBCA Vol.XXIII p.1046.

[35] See Epstein, "Arbitrator Independence and Bias: The view of Corporate In–House Counsel" (2007) ICC Special Supplement, *op. cit.*, p.55, at p.64.

[36] See para.11–9.

[37] *Employers Ins v National Fire Ins.*, 933 F.2d 1481 (9th Cir., 1991); *NHL Players' Ass'n v Bettman*, 1994 U.S. Dist. LEXIS 21715 (S.D.N.Y. November 9, 1994).

[38] *Commonwealth Coatings,* 393 US, 145, 150 (1968).

[39] *Woods v Saturn Distribution Corp,* 78 F.3d 424 (9th Cir., 1996).

> "In nondisclosure cases, vacatur is appropriate where the arbitrator's failure to disclose information gives the impression of bias in favor of one party. See Commonwealth Coatings Corp. v Continental Casualty Co., 393 US 145, 149, 89 S. Ct. 337, 21 L.Ed. 2d 301 (1969) (holding that impression of bias is sufficient to vacate arbitration award pursuant to 9 U.S.C. S 10(a)(2)); [. . .] In contrast, the integrity of the arbitrator's decision is directly at issue in actual bias cases. Id.[. . .] Therefore, 'the party alleging evident partiality [in actual bias cases] must establish specific facts which indicate improper motives.' Kinney, 756 F.2d at 746. In the instant case, the district court applied the legal standard used in actual bias cases and found that Woods failed to prove any facts to show that the arbitration award resulted from the arbitrators' alleged bias.[. . .] Woods relies solely on the financial relationship between the arbitrators and Saturn to support his allegation of evident partiality.[. . .] Woods offers no evidence to show that the arbitrators had a personal stake in the outcome of the arbitration.[. . .] Woods merely argues that they 'naturally tend to favor Saturn'.[. . .] In sum, Woods has presented no evidence to show that the arbitrators, two of whom were dealers and subject to the same arbitration procedure in the event they had a dispute with Saturn, were predisposed to favor Saturn."

14–71 It is important to note that, in domestic United States arbitration, there is a possibility of having a "non-neutral" co-arbitrator. These arbitrators are not required or expected to meet the same standard of independence as neutral co-arbitrators. However, the concept of the "non-neutral" arbitrator is inconsistent with art.11(1) and there is now arguably a presumption in the US that arbitrators are to be neutral.[40] Therefore, in an ICC arbitration, all arbitrators are expected to act as neutral arbitrators, whether or not they have been nominated by a party.[41]

14–72 In summary, there is no procedure for removal of an arbitrator during the course of an arbitration under the Federal Arbitration Act. The standard for arbitrators is different from that for judges due to the special role of arbitrators. The issue of disclosure is an important one. Failure to disclose creates a reasonable apprehension of bias. In other cases, however, to demonstrate bias the party must adduce evidence of actual bias and not mere apprehension of bias.

England

14–73 Section 24 of the English Arbitration Act 1996 provides as follows:

> "(1) A party to arbitral proceedings may (upon notice to the other parties, to the arbitrator concerned and to any other arbitrator) apply to the court to remove an arbitrator on any of the following grounds—

[40] See Canon IX A. of the ABA Rules of Ethics for Arbitrators which provides that "[i]n tripartite arbitrations to which this Code applies, all three arbitrators are presumed to be neutral and are expected to observe the same standards as the third arbitrator".

[41] Canon X of the ABA Rules of Ethics for arbitrators sets out the particular rules for non- neutral arbitrators. They include the limited and conditional right of arbitrators to have ex parte communications with the parties who appointed them.

(a) that circumstances exist that give rise to justifiable doubts as to his impartiality;
(b) that he does not possess the qualifications required by the arbitration agreement;
(c) that he is physically or mentally incapable of conducting the proceedings or there are justifiable doubts as to his capacity to do so;
(d) that he has refused or failed—
(i) properly to conduct the proceedings, or
(ii) to use all reasonable despatch in conducting the proceedings or making an award, and that substantial injustice has been or will be caused to the applicant.

(2) If there is an arbitral or other institution or person vested by the parties with power to remove an arbitrator, the court shall not exercise its power of removal unless satisfied that the applicant has first exhausted any available recourse to that institution or person.
(3) The arbitral tribunal may continue the arbitral proceedings and make an award while an application to the court under this section is pending.
(4) Where the court removes an arbitrator, it may make such order as it thinks fit with respect to his entitlement (if any) to fees or expenses, or the repayment of any fees or expenses already paid.
(5) The arbitrator concerned is entitled to appear and be heard by the court before it makes any order under this section.
(6) The leave of the court is required for any appeal from a decision of the court under this section."

Section 24 of the English Arbitration Act 1996 is noteworthy for various reasons. Under s.24 a party must first use the challenge procedure under art.14 before applying to the English court. The application can be made while the arbitral proceedings are pending but the Tribunal may continue with the arbitral procedure. The grounds for the application expressly include a failure to "properly conduct the proceedings" and failure "to use all reasonable despatch in conducting the proceedings and rendering an award, and that substantial injustice has been or will be caused to the applicant". Moreover, these provisions have to be read with s.33 of the English Arbitration Act 1996 that deals with the way in which arbitral proceedings are to be conducted.[42] **14–74**

[42] This provision could appear even stricter if read with s.68 of the Arbitration Act 1996. The High Court has held that this provision should be limited to areas of serious irregularity and not be used as a tool for intervention in arbitration in *Petroships Pte Ltd of Singapore v Petec Trading and Investment Corp of Vietnam* [2001] EWHC (Comm. 418 (May 22nd, 2001) citing the Departmental Advisory Committee on Arbitration Report stating in part: "7. Section 68 is designed as a longstop, only available in extreme cases, where the tribunal has gone so wrong in its conduct of the arbitration in one of the respects listed in s.68, that justice calls out for it to be corrected. 8. Section 68 must not be used as a means of circumventing the restrictions upon the court's power to intervene in arbitral proceedings". See also the reaffirmation by the House of Lords of the limited scope of court intervention in arbitration in the *Lesotho Highlands* case discussed under art.34. However, since those decisions, "serious irregularity" has been used to remove a president in the *ASM Shipping Ltd*

14–75 The grounds set out in s.24 overlap with art.12(2) to a certain extent and seem to go beyond situations that are normally viewed as challenges to give the English courts power to supervise arbitrations in England. However, there appear to have been relatively few cases where the English courts have intervened to basically supervise the procedure of an arbitration.

14–76 With regard to the standard of disclosure and independence, the leading case on arbitrators is *AT & T CorpLucent Technologies Inc v Saudi Cable Co.*[43] In that case, the president of the Tribunal had an assistant and a secretary who had two versions of his résumé. On the same day, the two résumés were faxed out. The one sent to the parties did not list the president's non-management directorship in a competitor to one of the parties. The other résumé did. It was sent to a third party in another matter. The Secretariat failed to forward its copy of the president's résumé that did mention the directorship. The president was challenged due to the lack of disclosure of this directorship. The ICC Court rejected the challenge and, with the arbitral proceedings pending, the challenging party brought court proceedings in London as the place of arbitration. The English Court of Appeal rejected the challenge. The Court held that arbitrators were held to be subject to the same standard as judges and Lord Woolf cited the following passage from *R. v Gough* with approval:

> "In conclusion, I wish to express my understanding of the law as follows. I think it possible, and desirable, that the same test should be applicable in all cases of apparent bias, whether concerned with justices or members of other inferior tribunals, or with jurors, or with arbitrators [. . .]. Finally, for the avoidance of doubt, I prefer to state the test in terms of real danger rather than real likelihood, to ensure that the court is thinking in terms of possibility rather than probability of bias. Accordingly, having ascertained the relevant circumstances, the court should ask itself whether, having regard to those circumstances, there was a real danger of bias on the part of the relevant member of the tribunal in question, in the sense that he might unfairly regard (or have unfairly regarded) with favour, or disfavour, the case of a party to the issue under consideration by him".[44]

14–77 Lord Woolf of the English Court of Appeal held that breach of the Rules could amount to misconduct and that the court was entitled to review it in the following terms:

> "49. Turning to the express provision of the ICC Rules which provides that a decision of the ICC Court should be final, I do not accept the view of Longmore J that the finality provision means that the English courts have no power to review the decision of the ICC Court. The finality

of India (cited under art.11 and a sole arbitrator in *Norbrook Laboratories Ltd v Tank* [2006] EWHC 1055 (Comm) (May 12, 2006).

[43] *AT & T CorpLucent Technologies Inc v Saudi Cable Co* [2000] 2 Lloyd's Rep. 127; [2000] EWCA Civ 154 CA, May 15, 2000.

[44] *R. v Gough* [1993] A.C. 646; for a discussion, see Lord Steyn, "England: The Independance and/or Impartiality of Arbitrators in International Commercial Arbitration" (2007) ICC Special Supplement, *op. cit.*, p.91; Eastwood, "A Real Danger of Confusion? The English Law Relating to Bias in Arbitrators" (2001) Arb Int Vol.17 No.3, p.287.

provision does not operate to exclude the English court's jurisdiction under s.23 of the 1950 Act. Accordingly, Longmore J was entitled to consider whether there had been 'misconduct' by breaching the terms of the arbitration agreement. When doing so the court, if required to interpret the ICC Rules, would naturally pay the closest attention to any interpretation of the ICC Rules adopted by the ICC Court, but the English courts retain their jurisdiction to determine whether the ICC Rules have been breached when entertaining an application to remove for alleged misconduct.

50. In this case, the decision of the ICC Court provides no assistance because the decision was not a reasoned one. We do not know the basis upon which the complaint of AT&T was dismissed."[45]

In the *Pinochet* case,[46] the issue was whether the prior decision of the House of Lords should be set aside because a law lord who had participated in the decision was a director of an Amnesty International affiliate. The House of Lords set out the standard in the following terms: **14–78**

"The fundamental principle is that a man may not be a judge in his own cause. This principle, as developed by the courts, has two very similar but not identical implications. First it may be applied literally: if a judge is in fact a party to the litigation or has a financial or proprietary interest in its outcome then he is indeed sitting as a judge in his own cause. In that case, the mere fact that he is a party to the action or has a financial or proprietary interest in its outcome is sufficient to cause his automatic disqualification. The second application of the principle is where a judge is not a party to the suit and does not have a financial interest in its outcome, but in some other way his conduct or behaviour may give rise to a suspicion that he is not impartial, for example because of his friendship with a party. This second type of case is not strictly speaking an application of the principle that a man must not be judge in his own cause, since the judge will not normally be himself benefiting, but providing a benefit for another by failing to be impartial.

In my judgment, this case falls within the first category of case, viz where the judge is disqualified because he is a judge in his own cause. In such a case, once it is shown that the judge is himself a party to the cause, or has a relevant interest in its subject matter, he is disqualified without any investigation into whether there was a likelihood or suspicion of bias. The mere fact of his interest is sufficient to disqualify him

[45] See above the *AT&T Lucent* case above. Lord Woolf's comment on the effect of the lack of reasons of the ICC Court is of interest. It is submitted that the growth of arbitration and reluctance of national courts to review the merits of arbitral decisions has resulted in focus on the arbitrators themselves which may, one way or another, be reviewed by national courts. The fact that the ICC Court does not provide reasons for challenges, means that the national courts are deprived of assistance of the ICC Court on this issue.

[46] *In re Pinochet* [1999] UKHL 1; [2000] 1 A.C. 119; [1999] 1 All E.R. 577; [1999] 2 W.L.R.272 (January 15, 1999).

unless he has made sufficient disclosure: see Shetreet, Judges on Trial, (1976), p.303; De Smith, Woolf & Jowel, Judicial Review of Administrative Action, 5th ed. (1995), p.525. I will call this 'automatic disqualification'."

14–79 The House of Lords went on to hold that the law lord's directorship in the Amnesty International affiliate was an automatic ground for disqualification notwithstanding the fact that it did not result in any financial advantage. In this respect, the House of Lords in effect extended the grounds for automatic disqualification. However, in doing so, the judgment notes that it is limited to the very special facts of the case where Amnesty International had participated in the proceedings.[47]

14–80 Therefore, in England, a decision of the ICC Court on a challenge is subject to court review. This review may take place while the arbitration proceedings are pending provided that the challenge procedure in art.14 is first used. In England, the standards for independence are the same for arbitrators as for national judges and it is whether there is a real danger of bias. This in turn is defined in terms of possibility rather than a probability of bias. The basis for arguing for removal appears to be broader than in many other countries as regards the procedure based on misconduct, although, as we noted in the first edition, it appeared to have been little used. Recently, the English courts have rendered three decisions relating to s.24 of the English Arbitration Act 1996.

14–81 In one case, a sole arbitrator in a specialised field was seeking to conduct what were in effect expedited and cost effective proceedings. In that context, the sole arbitrator had unilateral contact with the parties' counsel, with the parties and with the witnesses. The High Court disapproved of the unilateral contact with counsel even on administrative matters, but held that that did not justify removal of the sole arbitrator. However, the court annulled the Award under s.68 and ordered removal of the arbitrator for direct contact with the witnesses on the basis that he had improperly had access to information that could influence his decision.[48]

14–82 In another case, the issue was apparent bias of the president of a Tribunal who had been involved as a barrister in another case. In that other case, serious issues had been raised regarding the credibility of the challenging party's main witness and the issue was whether there was a risk of bias on the part of the president in the subsequent arbitration. The High Court found that there was a risk of bias and

[47] As Lord Browne-Wilkinson stated in the lead judgment "[i]t is important not to overstate what is being decided. It was suggested in argument that a decision setting aside the order of 25 November 1998 would lead to a position where judges would be unable to sit on cases involving charities in whose work they are involved. It is suggested that, because of such involvement, a judge would be disqualified. That is not correct. The facts of this present case are exceptional. The critical elements are (1) that AI [Amnesty International] was a party to the appeal; (2) that AI was joined in order to argue for a particular result; (3) the judge was a Director of a charity closely allied to AI and sharing, in this respect, AI's objects. Only in cases where a judge is taking an active role as trustee or Director of a charity which is closely allied to and acting with a party to the litigation should a judge normally be concerned either to recuse himself or disclose the position to the parties. However, there may well be other exceptional cases in which the judge would be well advised to disclose a possible interest".

[48] See the *Norbrook Laboratories Ltd* case cited at para.14–74 n.42.

held that the president should have recused himself.[49] The case is noteworthy in upholding of a challenge to an arbitrator based on his role as counsel.[50] The saga continued with the challenging party then challenging the two remaining arbitrators. In part this challenge was based on the view, expressed by the president, that the Tribunal as a whole had agreed that he should not recuse himself. Therefore, the challenging party maintained that the entire tribunal was tainted. The Court rejected this challenge holding that the claim of apparent bias was fanciful and on the basis that the matter was not raised in a timely fashion.[51]

[49] See the *Shipping Ltd v Harris* [2007] EWHC 1513 (Comm) (June 28, 2007). ("It is true that in specialist arbitrations prior contact between parties and their lawyers and arbitrators is to be expected. The mere fact, for example, that a person selected as arbitrator had previously had a trade dispute with one of the parties would not thereby have caused an objectionable situation. But even in such a case, much would depend on the facts: if the dispute had involved allegations of dishonesty of a similar nature to the allegations in the second arbitration, the position could well be different. Again, there would be no problem with a barrister sitting as an arbitrator in a case in which an expert witness whom he had previously cross-examined was to give evidence. But, again, if the contact had been a short time before, and allegations of dishonesty had been made, the position could be different. The Armageddon theory espoused by Mr Croall, were this application to succeed, is unreal. In this case there was a pattern of complaint amounting to dishonesty in relation to disclosure being made by the same solicitors in each case; and X QC had played a part in the B disclosure exercise 7 months before the arbitration. The nature of the allegations; the pattern of them; the involvement of the same solicitors; X QC's involvement in the disclosure process a short time before sitting as an arbitrator in judgment on the alleged dishonest party persuades me, for the reasons I have given that X QC should have recused himself after objection was taken.")

[50] See also District Court of The Hague, October 18, 2004, (Challenge No.13/2004; Petition No.HA/RK/2004.667) ASA Bulletin, Vol.23 No.1 (2005), pp.186–193 stating in part: "account should be taken of the fact that the arbitrator in the capacity of attorney will regard it as his duty to put forward all possibly conceivable objections against the RFCC/ Morocco award. This attitude is incompatible with the stance that [the arbitrator] has to take as an arbitrator in the present case, i.e. to be unbiased and open to all the merits of the RFCC/Morocco award and to be unbiased when examining these in the present case and consulting thereon in chambers with his fellow arbitrators.

Even if this arbitrator were able to sufficiently distance himself in chambers from his role as attorney in the annulment proceedings against the RFCC/Morocco award, account should in any event be taken of the appearance of his not being able to observe said distance. Since he has to play these two parts, it is in any case impossible for him to avoid giving the appearance of not being able to keep these two parts strictly separated. For this reason there will be justified doubts about his impartiality, if [the arbitrator] does not resign as attorney in the RFCC/Morocco case. Consequently the motion to challenge will in that case be upheld. To avoid any uncertainty [the arbitrator] should within ten days from this judgment have expressly and unreservedly notified the parties to this arbitration whether he will resign as attorney in the RFCC/Morocco case".

[51] See *ASM Shipping Ltd v Harris* [2007] EWHC 1513 (Comm) (June 28, 2007) ("59. Any objection to the two arbitrators continuing with the reference because Mr. Moustakas will be a witness would not be on the basis of any involvement that they themselves have had with Mr. Moustakas. It could only be made on the basis that there was a risk that they would be other than impartial because they have been influenced by discussions that they had with [the president]. It seems to me that this suggestion would be fanciful. The question is one of apparent bias, not actual bias, but it is to be considered against the background that [the president] stated during the hearing that he recalled nothing relating to the previous case that gave rise to any doubt in his mind as to the propriety of Mr. Moustakas' conduct, and there is no suggestion that that was not the case. This being so, I cannot accept that a fair minded and informed observer would conclude that there was any real possibility that there have been discussions between [the president] and the two arbitrators that might improperly influence their assessment of Mr. Moustakas' evidence or detract from their impartiality. 60. However that may be, the owners were aware of these matters well before 29 December 2005. They have lost the right to raise any objection of bias on this basis.")

UNCITRAL Model Law Countries (Germany, Singapore, Canada, Scotland)

14–83 The basic legal standard is set out in art.12 of the UNCITRAL Model Law that is set out at para.11–3.

14–84 The procedure is set out in art.13 of the UNCITRAL Model Law:

> "1. The parties are free to agree on a procedure for challenging an arbitrator, subject to the provisions of paragraph (3) of this article.
>
> 2. Failing such agreement, a party who intends to challenge an arbitrator shall, within fifteen days after becoming aware of the constitution of the arbitral tribunal or after becoming aware of any circumstance referred to in article 12(2), send a written statement of the reasons for the challenge to the arbitral tribunal. Unless the challenged arbitrator withdraws from his office or the other party agrees to the challenge, the arbitral tribunal shall decide on the challenge.
>
> 3. If a challenge under any procedure agreed upon by the parties or under the procedure of paragraph (2) of this article is not successful, the challenging party may request, within thirty days after having received notice of the decision rejecting the challenge, the court or other authority specified in article 6 to decide on the challenge, which decision shall be subject to no appeal; while such a request is pending, the arbitral tribunal, including the challenged arbitrator, may continue the arbitral proceedings and make an award."

14–85 Therefore, a party must first complete the challenge procedure pursuant to the Rules under art.14. However, the UNCITRAL Model Law then permits court proceedings on the challenge issue but those proceedings do not require the Tribunal to suspend the proceedings. The standard applied for challenges to arbitrators varies in general between jurisdictions. However, in the Commonwealth jurisdictions such as Australia and Canada, the principles set out in *R. v Gough* and applied in *AT&T Lucent* and *In re Pinochet* have not been followed.[52] Rather, as discussed in *Webb v The Queen* the test (in a jury case) is whether the circumstance "gives rise to a reasonable apprehension or suspicion on the part of a fair-minded and informed member of the public that the juror or jury has not discharged or will not discharge its task impartially".[53] It is not clear whether this test will also be followed with respect to international arbitration.

14–86 In such major centres of arbitration as Germany and Singapore, the UNCITRAL Model Law is applicable. However, in both cases, the Model Law has been adopted relatively recently and the case law appears to be limited. Other UNCITRAL Model Law countries include Canada (federally) and various provinces (including Ontario and British Columbia). The case law of those countries regarding bias is therefore of interest, although that case law has been developed

[52] See paras 14–76 n.43 and 14–78 n.46.

[53] *Webb and Hay v The Queen* [1994] HCA 30; (1994) 181 C.L.R. 41; (1994) 122 A.L.R. 41; (1994) 68 A.L.J.R. 582 F.C. 94/030 (June 30, 1994).

in the framework of national legal proceedings and not the UNCITRAL Model Law.

The Ontario Court of Appeal has re-affirmed the reasonable apprehension test after considering the decision in re Pinochet and declining to change the approach. As it stated in *Benedict v Ontario*: **14–87**

> "The test for reasonable apprehension of bias is that set out by de Grandpré J. in Committee for Justice and Liberty v Canada (National Energy Board), [1978] 1 S.C.R. 369, 68 D.L.R. (3d)
>
> 716.: [. . .] De Grandpré J. stated, at pp.394–95:
>
> '[. . .] the apprehension of bias must be a reasonable one, held by reasonable and right minded persons, applying themselves to the question and obtaining thereon the required information.[. . .] [T]hat test is "what would an informed person, viewing the matter realistically and practically—and having thought the matter through—conclude. Would he think that it is more likely than not that [the decision-maker], whether consciously or unconsciously, would not decide fairly'."[54]

[54] *Benedict v Ontario* (2000) 51 O.R. (3d) 147.

Article 15 Replacement of Arbitrators

1 An arbitrator shall be replaced upon death, upon acceptance by the Court of the arbitrator's resignation, upon acceptance by the Court of a challenge, or upon acceptance by the Court of a request of all the parties.

2 An arbitrator shall also be replaced on the Court's own initiative when it decides that the arbitrator is prevented *de jure* or *de facto* from fulfilling the arbitrator's functions, or that the arbitrator is not fulfilling those functions in accordance with the Rules or within the prescribed time limits.

3 When, on the basis of information that has come to its attention, the Court considers applying Article 15(2), it shall decide on the matter after the arbitrator concerned, the parties and any other members of the arbitral tribunal have had an opportunity to comment in writing within a suitable period of time. Such comments shall be communicated to the parties and to the arbitrators.

4 When an arbitrator is to be replaced, the Court has discretion to decide whether or not to follow the original nominating process. Once reconstituted, and after having invited the parties to comment, the arbitral tribunal shall determine if and to what extent prior proceedings shall be repeated before the reconstituted arbitral tribunal.

5 Subsequent to the closing of the proceedings, instead of replacing an arbitrator who has died or been removed by the Court pursuant to Articles 15(1) or 15(2), the Court may decide, when it considers it appropriate, that the remaining arbitrators shall continue the arbitration. In making such determination, the Court shall take into account the views of the remaining arbitrators and of the parties and such other matters that it considers appropriate in the circumstances.[1]

[1] Article 15 corresponds to art.12 of the 1998 ICC Rules. There have been no substantive changes.

Introductory remarks

Article 15 relates to several different issues arising in the context of an arbitrator's replacement. During 2012, the Court replaced 47 arbitrators pursuant to art.15 or its predecessor under the 1998 Rules.[2] Article 15(1) deals with replacement of the arbitrator due to the arbitrator's death or resignation or the acceptance of a challenge or the request of all parties. Article 15(2) deals with the removal and replacement of an arbitrator by the ICC Court on its own initiative. The remainder of Art.15 deals with the appointment of a new arbitrator and the effect on the proceedings. Where the replacement proceedings relate to the sole arbitrator, the issue is to ensure that the arbitral proceedings continue in an acceptable fashion. Where the replacement proceedings relate to a member of the Tribunal, then the basic underlying issue relates to the collegiality of the Tribunal.[3] Article 15 does not deal with the remuneration of replaced arbitrators. The general rule contained in art.37(1) will thus apply and the ICC Court will set the fees payable to the resigning arbitrator. Replacement of arbitrators is dealt with both in Committee Sessions and in Plenary Sessions of the ICC Court that are discussed in detail in Annex 1 Pt I. 15–1

The replacement of an arbitrator can therefore arise due to issues with the arbitrator him or herself that result in a successful challenge or his or her resignation or replacement of the arbitrator due to independent events. Article 15 does not address the issue of the effect of the replacement of the arbitrator on partial Awards that have been rendered prior to the replacement. Subject to annulment proceedings at the place of arbitration, such Awards remain valid and are res judicata. The reconstituted Tribunal therefore cannot reconsider those issues, although it can reconsider procedural issues. 15–2

Article 15(1): "An arbitrator shall be replaced upon death, upon acceptance by the Court of the arbitrator's resignation, upon acceptance by the Court of a challenge, or upon acceptance by the Court of a request of all the parties."

When an arbitrator accepts to act as such under the Rules, the arbitrator expressly undertakes to carry out his or her duties in accordance with the Rules. The most common view of this relationship is that of a contract between the arbitrator and the ICC. The contract is subject to various provisions, including the limitation of liability provision in art.40. 15–3

The arbitrator's undertakings are personal in nature and cease upon his death, or for that matter on his inability to act as discussed under art.15(2). In the case of the death of an arbitrator, some or all of the oral hearings may have to be carried out anew as is foreseen under art.15(4). There is sometimes discussion of 15–4

[2] ICC Int CtArb Bull Vol.24, No.1, p.10.

[3] See the discussion at para.31–2. See also Whitesell, "Independence in ICC Arbitration: ICC Court Practice Concerning the Appointment, Confirmation, Challenge and Replacement of Arbitrators", *op. cit.*, at pp.33–35.

insurance of the costs of arbitration. However, it is not clear that this insurance is available or that it has been used in practice, although it is apparently used in US litigation for example.

15–5 Arbitrators may choose to resign. If they do so, they must respect their obligations under the Rules as expressly provided in art.11(5). An arbitrator's resignation is subject to the acceptance of the ICC Court. It is possible that the ICC Court will refuse to accept an arbitrator's resignation if the ICC Court views the resignation as contrary to the Rules and as having an actual or potential detrimental effect on the arbitral proceedings. Therefore, the first issue is when an arbitrator can and should resign under the Rules. The second issue is the consequences of such resignation.

The necessary resignation

15–6 A resignation may be necessary due to an issue as to the independence of the arbitrator. If an arbitrator is unable to meet the requirements of the Rules, and in particular the requirement of art.11(1), then the arbitrator's resignation is necessary. However, if this lack of independence is the result of circumstances of which the arbitrator was or should have been aware at the time the appointment as arbitrator was accepted, there may be a breach of the Rules. If the lack of independence has arisen subsequently, then there is a further issue as to how the lack of independence has arisen. If the lack of independence has been caused by the arbitrator him or herself, then there is also arguably a breach of the Rules. However, even in the event of a breach of the Rules, the liability of arbitrators is limited by art.40.

15–7 Another supervening problem may be the arbitrator's availability. When the arbitrator accepts the appointment, he undertakes to participate in the arbitral proceedings in accordance with the Rules. The ICC Secretariat generally draws the arbitrator's attention in particular to the arts 23(2) and 30(1) relating to timing. Of course, after accepting the position as arbitrator, there may be other events that arise that affect the arbitrator's availability. For example, other arbitrations may take much more time than anticipated. Or the arbitral proceedings in question may demand far more time than was anticipated at the outset. Depending on the stage of the proceedings, and provided that the arbitrator has not caused the availability problems by accepting too much additional work, resignation for lack of availability may raise a legitimate issue as to whether the arbitrator should resign.

15–8 On occasion, the resignation is motivated by health or other personal reasons. These are generally justifiable grounds for resignation if they have arisen since the date of the arbitrator's appointment. When appointment as an arbitrator is accepted, the arbitrator does not warrant that his health will not change or that personal problems will not arise, such as a change of professional activity.

The quasi-voluntary resignation

15–9 The arbitrator may believe that he can meet the requirements of the Rules, but one party believes that the arbitrator should resign. A common situation is where the arbitrator has either made a subsequent disclosure or where a party has raised doubts about the arbitrator's disclosure with respect to conflicts of interest. For example, if an arbitrator has failed to make disclosure within the "best practices" referred to under art.11, a party may raise the issue of the possibility of a challenge. If under the Rules and the applicable law, there is, in the arbitrator's view, no basis for a challenge, the arbitrator will have to consider whether, nevertheless, he or she wishes to resign.[4] In some cases, the arbitrator will find it more important that the parties have full confidence in the members of the Tribunal and resign, rather than to continue as an arbitrator when at least one of the parties has doubts as to the arbitrator's lack of impartiality. The arbitrator also has to consider the effect of a resignation on the arbitral proceedings as a whole. For example, if a challenge is being made but it is manifestly unjustified and the effect of a resignation would be to disrupt the arbitral proceedings, the arbitrator may feel that he has the duty not to resign.

If the arbitral proceedings are at their commencement, then the disruption of a resignation may not be significant. However, if the arbitration is at an advanced stage, the resignation may have serious consequences. For example, a resignation after partial Awards have been rendered may result in an attempt to annul those Awards.[5] In addition, resignation after the oral hearings have been scheduled may result in delay due to the need to find a new date acceptable to the parties and the Tribunal. Moreover, as discussed under art.15(4), resignation after some oral hearings have taken place may result in having to conduct these hearings anew. **15–10**

The voluntary resignation

An arbitrator may consider resigning as an arbitrator although his resignation is not sought by either party or the ICC Court. In a sense, this type of resignation is "voluntary" in that the parties do not prompt it, although the facts giving rise to the resignation may be external to the arbitrator. **15–11**

An arbitrator should not resign so that the arbitrator or his law firm can undertake work for one of the parties. This would amount to the arbitrator rejecting the commitment to the current arbitration to benefit from the additional work and would generally be viewed as questionable. **15–12**

An arbitrator's resignation presupposes a change in circumstances from those that prevailed on the date on which the arbitrator accepted the nomination or appointment that cause the arbitrator to consider that his resignation is appropriate. The supervening events can be varied. Frequently, they relate to health, family or professional problems or for example a change in professional activity, such as appointment as a judge of a national or international court where judges are not permitted to act as arbitrators. In deciding whether to resign in the case of **15–13**

[4] See Glossner, "Sociological aspects of international commercial arbitration, The art of arbitration" in *Liber Amicorum Pieter Sanders* (Kluwer, 1982), p.143–145, who opined as follows: "In the case of a conflict of interest, whether existing before or during the arbitration proceedings, an arbitrator can be challenged. That arbitrator who decides before being officially challenged to give up his function deserves credit. Even after a challenge procedure has been started it is laudable for an arbitrator to withdraw voluntarily from his function, as there are certain ethical standards involved." (Footnote omitted.)

[5] By resigning, an arbitrator is not accepting that the grounds for challenge were valid. However, if a Court finds that the grounds were valid, then there is an argument that the Tribunal was improperly constituted from the outset and that any partial Awards are invalid. As regards annulment of Awards, see the discussion under art.34.

a conflict, the arbitrator has to consider the nature of the conflict and whether it is such as to require resignation based on the Rules and applicable national law. The ICC Court could refuse to accept an arbitrator's resignation if it would detrimentally affect the arbitration. This could arise, for example, if a co-arbitrator who was not in agreement with a draft Award, resigned immediately prior to the Award being signed. In other less extreme cases, an arbitrator's resignation may be a tactical manoeuvre designed to delay the proceedings. In such a case, the ICC Court may choose to decline to accept the resignation.

15–14 If the ICC Court does not accept an arbitrator's resignation, the arbitrator may cease to participate in the proceedings. In that case, the Tribunal could still continue to function, albeit in as a truncated Tribunal of two members, although the members of the Tribunal should ensure that reasonable steps are made to ensure that the third arbitrator has the possibility to participate.

The request of all parties

15–15 The parties have ultimate control over the procedure and it could be that they agree that an arbitrator should resign. In practice this joint request happens rarely, but it has happened, particularly where one party challenged an arbitrator and the other party accepted that challenge, for instance out of concern of the potential effect of the challenge on the challenged arbitrator.

15–16 The motives for a party accepting that an arbitrator should resign can be varied. However, if the arbitrator's presence could result in procedural complications, such as challenge proceedings or potential annulment proceedings, a party may wish to seek to avoid the problems by accepting that the arbitrator should resign. On some occasions, it is the arbitrator himself who suggests that the parties may agree on his resignation. Many arbitrators when faced with a potential challenge or challenge that they feel is entirely unjustified, object to the challenge but express the view that they are willing to resign if both parties so wish.

15–17 One of the modifications in the Rules is to provide that, even where there is agreement of the parties to replace an arbitrator, such agreement is nevertheless subject to the approval of the Court. It is not clear in what circumstances the Court would refuse a joint request of all parties to replace an arbitrator. However, it could presumably only arise where the Court as an institution considers that it is appropriate that the arbitrator remain despite the parties' views. In such a circumstance, the parties would have no alternative other than to terminate the proceedings if they did not wish to proceed with the arbitrator.

Article 15(2): "An arbitrator shall also be replaced on the Court's own initiative when it decides that the arbitrator is prevented *de jure* or *de facto* from fulfilling the arbitrator's functions, or that the arbitrator is not fulfilling those functions in accordance with the Rules or within the prescribed time limits."

15–18 Article 15(2) deals with a decision "on the Court's own initiative" to replace an arbitrator, and art.15(3) with the procedure that the ICC Court will follow for this replacement procedure. Replacement of an arbitrator on the ICC Court's initiative has been relatively infrequent, and occurred only on eight occasions during the period from 2007–2011. In 2011, the ICC Court took such initiative only twice due to inability or failure of the arbitrator to fulfill his functions.[6] ICC arbitration is not only an administered arbitration, but it is arguably one of the types of arbitration where the arbitral institution most closely monitors and supervises the arbitration proceedings. Therefore, it is possible that the Secretariat will become concerned about an arbitrator and whether he can de jure or de facto fulfill his functions and will inform the ICC Court.

As regards de jure problems, the Secretariat is familiar with the practices and rules in various countries. Therefore, the Secretariat may become aware of a legal issue that the arbitrator and the parties have overlooked.[7] **15–19**

For example, in some countries, such as Canada and France, judges are not permitted to act as arbitrators.[8] Since, the Secretariat is familiar with these requirements, the Secretariat rather than the parties may raise the issue with the arbitrator. As regards de facto problems, the Secretariat is very conscious of the timing requirements of the Rules. The Secretariat is also aware that these time limits are generally extended based on the facts of a particular case. The ICC Court will look at these problems on a case by case basis, and will have to ask itself whether the problem is likely to disappear in the near or a rather distant future. **15–20**

Factors that may influence the decision on whether to remove an arbitrator include the ease or difficulty that the Secretariat may have had in contacting the arbitrator, the extent to which the proceedings have been delayed without justification, the stage in the proceedings and the complexity and importance of the matter. In a drastic situation, such as where an arbitrator is detained by local authorities without any indication on the possible length of his incarceration, the ICC Court would likely decide to replace him due to the uncertainty when he may be able again to act as arbitrator.[9] Where the arbitral proceedings are being delayed for no good reason, the Secretariat may raise the issue with the ICC Court. **15–21**

The issue naturally arises as to the relationship between art.15 and art.14 relating to the challenge of arbitrators. It is not infrequent for the lawyers for the parties to contact the Secretariat, particularly if they are concerned about the procedure in an arbitration. These oral communications are ex parte as regards the Tribunal (and the other party).[10] The Secretariat will of course maintain a neutral position. If a party is basically complaining about matters that go to a challenge, the party should decide whether or not it should file a challenge. One would expect that the Secretariat would generally not invoke the replacement procedure if a party is basically making allegations as to a challenge, unless there is some overriding interest of the ICC Court in replacing the arbitrator. **15–22**

The ICC Court has an overriding interest in replacing an arbitrator where the arbitrator is undermining the arbitration as an ICC arbitration. This could be due **15–23**

[6] Fry, Greenberg & Mazza, *op. cit.*, para.3–611.

[7] Of course, it is incumbent upon the arbitrator and the lawyers to verify that there are no legal incompatibilities.

[8] See para.13–16.

[9] See Ming, "The Strange Case of Wang Shengchang" (2007) J Int'l Arb Vol.24 No.1, p.63 (detention of an arbitrator, former Vice chairman and Secretary General of CIETAC by the Chinese authorities on the basis of allegations that he was involved with "illegal distribution of state assets.")

[10] See para.3–20.

to very substantial and unjustified delays or a situation where the arbitrator is either legally prohibited from acting as an arbitrator or where the arbitrator is no longer of sound mind, or where he is engaging in improper conduct, such as seeking to enter into special fee arrangements directly with the parties.[11] The use of this provision may make most sense at the beginning of a case, before the Terms of Reference have been established. A more basic situation may be where the arbitrator is incapable of following the proceedings in the language of the arbitration despite having indicated otherwise on his curriculum vitae.[12] The impact of these facts may be such as to persuade the ICC Court to replace the arbitrator despite the fact that they could be grounds for a challenge as well.[13]

Article 15(3): "When, on the basis of information that has come to its attention, the Court considers applying Article 15(2), it shall decide on the matter after the arbitrator concerned, the parties and any other members of the arbitral tribunal have had an opportunity to comment in writing within a suitable period of time. Such comments shall be communicated to the parties and to the arbitrators."

15–24 Article 15(3) requires the ICC Court to provide the information relating to the grounds of replacement to the arbitrator concerned as well as to the other arbitrators and the parties. Article 15(3) also requires the ICC Court to provide an opportunity for the parties and the arbitrators to comment on the grounds for replacement. The ICC Court's communications are handled by the Secretariat.

15–25 In practice, the Secretariat contacts the arbitrator to express concerns about deadlines not being met and problems that appear to be reflected in the correspondence without raising the possibility of replacement. If the problems persist, the ICC Court, through its Secretariat, raises the reasons for removal of the arbitrator informally with the arbitrator to ensure that there was no misunderstanding relating to the grounds. The arbitrator may then wish to consider resigning under art.15(1) if he considers that a resignation is appropriate.

15–26 Assuming that there is no misunderstanding as to the potential reasons for the arbitrator's revocation, and that the arbitrator does not indicate an intention to resign, the Secretariat would generally set out the grounds for the arbitrator's replacement in a letter copied to the other arbitrators and the parties. As with challenges, the other arbitrators may prefer to adopt a neutral stance. However, if the

[11] Such arrangements are contrary to the Rules, see art.2(4) of App.III of the Rules. More generally, see Griffith and Pintos Lopez, "Renegociating arbitrators' Terms of Remunaration" (2002) J Int'l Arb Vol.19 No.6, p.581.

[12] See the discussion at para.13–17.

[13] The UNCITRAL Commentary on the Model Law states with respect to the grounds that:

"It is submitted that in judging whether an arbitrator failed to act the following consideration may be relevant: Which action was expected or required of him in the light of the arbitrator agreement and the specific procedural situation? If he has not done anything in this regard, has the delay been so inordinate as to be unacceptable in the light of the circumstances, including technical difficulties and the complexity of the case? If he has done something and acted in a certain way, did his conduct fall clearly below the standard of what may reasonably be expected from an arbitrator? Amongst the factors influencing the level of expectations are the ability to function efficiently and expeditiously and any special competence or other qualifications required of the arbitrator by agreement of the parties."

problem relates to how the Tribunal itself is functioning, then the best source of information may be the arbitrators themselves. In one case, the co-arbitrators provided spontaneously joint comments to the ICC Court with respect to the proposed removal of the president, thus confirming that the president was the problem. If the ICC Court commences a removal procedure but in the end does not remove and replace the arbitrator, the comments of the other members of the Tribunal may raise questions for the subsequent proceedings. This explains why the ICC Court will use its replacement power in only exceptional circumstances.

The parties may be neutral or may have different positions as to whether the arbitrator should be replaced. If both parties agree that the arbitrator should be replaced, then it would appear that art.15(1) becomes applicable, as it provides for resignation of an arbitrator upon the request of the parties. **15–27**

If the ICC Court decides that an arbitrator should not be replaced, then it is generally a matter for the law of the place of arbitration as to whether a party has further recourse against the decision. Article 14 of the UNCITRAL Model Law, for example, provides for recourse to the courts on this issue.[14] **15–28**

Article 15(4): "When an arbitrator is to be replaced, the Court has discretion to decide whether or not to follow the original nominating process. Once reconstituted, and after having invited the parties to comment, the arbitral tribunal shall determine if and to what extent prior proceedings shall be repeated before the reconstituted arbitral tribunal."

When an arbitrator is replaced, he or she is expected to return the file to the Secretariat for transmittal to the new arbitrator. **15–29**

If the Court decides to replace the arbitrator(s) then it is in the ICC Court's discretion as to whether to "follow the original nominating process". This decision is usually made at the same time as when the ICC Court decides to replace the arbitrator at its Committee Session. The process for nominating the arbitrator will depend on whether the arbitrator is a sole arbitrator, a co-arbitrator or a president. It is common for the ICC Court to seek to follow the original nominating process of the parties unless they request otherwise. In line with the principles in the *Dutco* case,[15] one would expect that a co-arbitrator nominated by a party should be replaced by a new co-arbitrator nominated by that party. This is in keeping with the overall purpose of the Rules to grant autonomy to the parties to determine certain aspects of the procedure that the Tribunal or the ICC Court is not obliged to decide. Similarly, one would expect the ICC to consult with the co-arbitrators and the parties with respect to the choice of a president. **15–30**

Under special circumstances, it may, however, be more appropriate for the ICC Court to appoint the new arbitrator. Since the nomination of an arbitrator is a basic right of a party, this would probably be limited to cases in which a party either cannot or will not nominate a replacement arbitrator or there are reasons to believe that the party will nominate an arbitrator who will seek to obstruct the proceedings. In the case of multiparty arbitration, where there was an agreement as to the **15–31**

[14] See art.14 of the UNCITRAL Model Law, Pt III App.5.

[15] Cass. 1re civ., January 7, 1992, Bull. civ. I, No.2. See paras 12–10 *et seq.*

co-arbitrator, then there may be an additional issue if the parties are unable to agree on the new nominee. Therefore, the discretion of the ICC Court with respect to the nominating process is subject to the overriding principles of the applicable law of the place of arbitration and perhaps the place of enforcement.

15–32 Once the Tribunal is reconstituted, art.15(4) provides that it is up to the Tribunal to decide the extent to which the prior proceedings shall be repeated and documents such as the Terms of Reference shall or shall not be reissued,[16] after having provided the parties with an opportunity to comment. The continuation of the arbitration and the extent to which proceedings must be repeated is also a matter for the law of the place of arbitration.[17] In many instances, the parties may agree that the proceedings continue with the use of the prior record. When the hearing has already taken place, the main factor in this respect is whether there is a transcript of the hearing. If so, then the parties may be satisfied that the new arbitrator will understand the hearing and the evidence based on that transcript. The crucial phase is the deliberation of the Tribunal and if this has not commenced or is in fact repeated, then the parties may prefer not to repeat hearings.[18] However, it is up to the Tribunal to decide subject to any mandatory limitations of applicable law.

15–33 In the *Pemex-Refinancion v Tblisi* case,[19] an arbitrator died in a case that had been pending for ten years. Substantial evidence had been filed and apparently the hearings had been completed, but the post-hearing brief of one of the parties had not been filed. A Federal District Court in New York summarised the US legal position as follows:

> "The 'general rule' established by the Second Circuit dictates that
>
> 'where one member of a three-person arbitration panel dies before the rendering of an award and the arbitration agreement does not anticipate that circumstance, the arbitration must commence anew with a fresh panel [. . .]
> In the instant case, the Charter [including the arbitration agreement] does not address the appointment of a new arbitrator following the death of a panel member. Furthermore, [the arbitrator] died not only 'prior to the rendering of an award', but before Tbilisi Shipping had the opportunity to submit its Main Post Hearing Brief, and before final panel deliberations commenced. Therefore, absent Pemex's demonstration of 'special circumstances', the general rule that the arbitration must commence anew is applicable here. [. . .] 'Special circumstances' meriting the appointment of a replacement arbitrator typically include instances where vacancies have occurred during the very early stages of arbitration or where a panel has rendered a final decision with respect to only some of the issues raised in the arbitration (i.e. a bifurcated arbitration)." (Citations deleted).

[16] Fry, Greenberg & Mazza, *op. cit.*, para.3–645.
[17] This is consistent with s.27(4) of the English Arbitration Act 1996 for example.
[18] During the hearing, the Tribunal will usually discuss the witness evidence. However, if the impact of the witness evidence is not reflected in the transcript and the documents submitted by the parties, then the Tribunal should perhaps repeat the witness evidence.
[19] *Pemex-Refinancion v Tblisi*, 2004 US Dist. LEXIS 17478 (SDNY 2004).

The "arbitration agreement" referred to by the court would appear to include the rules incorporated in the arbitration agreement. Therefore, in an ICC arbitration, there should be no requirement to commence new proceedings. However, there may be an issue as to due process if the Tribunal decides that certain proceedings will not be recommenced if a party objects. Article 15(4) leaves the matter of whether to repeat proceedings to the recomposed Tribunal. Therefore, in the case where a party has nominated a replacement arbitrator, that replacement arbitrator will have an opportunity to participate in the deliberations as to whether proceedings should be repeated. If the newly appointed arbitrator agrees that the proceedings need not be repeated, the procedural justification for not doing so is much stronger than if only the majority of the Tribunal decides to proceed without repeating the proceedings. 15–34

Article 15(4) does not deal with the fees to be paid to the replaced or to the replacement arbitrator, the amount of which is fixed in accordance with art.37. The ICC Court usually fixes the fees of the replaced arbitrator when deciding to replace the arbitrator. This is determined, upon recommendation of the Secretariat, pursuant to such things as the total number of hours undertaken by the arbitrator, if known. If it is not possible to gain an exact amount of time completed on the matter, then the Secretariat can gain an understanding from the other members of the Tribunal, or if a sole arbitrator, from the work undertaken by the sole arbitrator. This includes the arbitrator's involvement in the proceedings such as correspondence between the parties, the Tribunal and the Secretariat, as well as whether any Awards, procedural orders or other determinations have been rendered by the arbitrator. Regard will also be had to the procedural timetable to see whether, for example, a hearing was scheduled, and what, if any, preparations were made by the arbitrator(s) for the hearing, such as preparing the draft of an Award, setting out the procedural aspects of the case. 15–35

The amount of the fees to be paid to the replacement arbitrator is also set by the ICC Court, upon the Secretariat's recommendation. It is based on the stage at which the replacement arbitrator was appointed and the extent of his or her involvement in the proceedings. If the work done by the Tribunal is likely to be repeated, the ICC Court should take into account this possibility when fixing the fees of the replaced arbitrator in order to properly remunerate the newly appointed arbitrator without requesting an additional payment from the parties for the performance of the work twice. 15–36

Article 15(5): "Subsequent to the closing of the proceedings, instead of replacing an arbitrator who has died or been removed by the Court pursuant to Articles 15(1) or 15(2), the Court may decide, when it considers it appropriate, that the remaining arbitrators shall continue the arbitration. In making such determination, the Court shall take into account the views of the remaining arbitrators and of the parties and such other matters that it considers appropriate in the circumstances."

The Tribunal closes the proceedings in accordance with art.27, usually when the oral hearings have ended. It is after the proceedings have been closed, that the Tribunal deliberates with the view of rendering an Award. Article 15(5) thus 15–37 appears to deal mainly with two situations: first, when an arbitrator resigns or refuses to act late in an arbitration in order to disrupt the arbitration proceedings[20] and secondly, when there is a vacancy within the Tribunal, i.e. when an arbitrator dies or is rendered incapable of continuing after the deliberations have finished.

15–38 With respect to the death of an arbitrator, the situation may depend on how advanced the deliberations have been. One extreme is where the Tribunal has not yet met to deliberate. The other extreme is where the Tribunal has submitted a draft Award to the ICC Court for approval. In the latter case, there is, of course, a much stronger argument for simply continuing the arbitration without replacing the arbitrator who has died. However, if the deliberations have not yet begun or are far from having been completed, the situation is much more problematic, particularly if the deceased was an arbitrator nominated by one of the parties. Continuing the procedure with a president and a co-arbitrator nominated by the other party may create issues of fairness of treatment similar to the one of the *Dutco* case.

15–39 Article 15(5) refers to situations where an arbitrator has been "removed" by the ICC Court under arts 15(1) and (2). However, it appears that this provision is also intended to cover situations where the ICC Court has accepted an arbitrator's resignation under art.15(1). In fact, much of the discussion of whether to replace an arbitrator is conducted with respect to cases where it is perceived that a co-arbitrator nominated by a party either resigns or creates a legal impediment to continuing to act as an arbitrator after it has become apparent that he is in the minority with respect to the probable decision. In such a case, rather than accept the decision (or writing a dissent), the arbitrator resigns, thus creating a truncated Tribunal.[21] The ICC Court is conscious of this risk and therefore can be expected to carefully weigh in such circumstances whether to replace the arbitrator. It would be contrary to the basic objectives of an ICC arbitration if such a resignation could substantially delay the proceedings.

15–40 The ICC Court takes into consideration the views of the remaining arbitrators. One would generally expect this to be done by inviting written comments from the remaining arbitrators. Although not expressly provided for in art.15(5), the communications with the arbitrators would presumably be provided to the parties. The parties would similarly be provided with an opportunity to provide comments to the ICC Court through the Secretariat and such comments should be copied to the other parties and the remaining arbitrators. As with challenges and removal of arbitrators itself, parties (and the other arbitrators) have no opportunity to make oral presentations of their position with respect to the ICC Court's decision under art.15(5).

[20] Swiss Supreme Court, February 1, 2002, *X Ltd v Y BV*, 4P.226/2001 commented by Tchanz, "Uncooperative Arbitrators Need Not Delay Award", September 5, 2002 at http://www.internationallawoffice.com [accessed November 13, 2013] (the failure of an arbitrator to attend the deliberation of the Tribunal due to the pending challenge of a chairman (now president) before the Court is not a sufficient ground to set aside the Award). See also discussion at para.31–7.

[21] On this issue, see Schwebel, "The authority of truncated international arbitral tribunals" in *International Arbitration: three salient problems* (Grotius Publications Ltd, 1987); "The validity of an arbitral award rendered by a truncated tribunal" (1995) ICC ICArb Bull Vol.6 No.2, p.19; Philippe, "Difficultés procédurales causées par les clauses compromissoires paritaires et le tribunaux arbitraux tronqués" in *Les Cahiers de l'Arbitrage Vol.1, op cit*, p.24.

CHAPTER 5

THE ARBITRAL PROCEEDINGS

Article 16 Transmission of the File to the Arbitral Tribunal

The Secretariat shall transmit the file to the arbitral tribunal as soon as it has been constituted, provided the advance on costs requested by the Secretariat at this stage has been paid.[1]

Introductory remarks

Article 16 is intended to allow a rapid transmission of the file by the Secretariat to the Tribunal. Such transmission is made subject to two conditions: the Tribunal has been constituted and the advance on costs has been paid by either party. **16–1**

The Tribunal has been constituted when all arbitrators have been confirmed or appointed in accordance with art.13. The arbitrators are generally confirmed or appointed in Committee Sessions of the ICC Court. The Secretary General also has the power to confirm the arbitrator under art.13(2). Pursuant to art.36(1), a provisional advance on costs is fixed by the Secretary General after receipt of the Request. It is intended to cover the costs of arbitration for the period until finalisation of the Terms of Reference. Prompt payment can normally be expected from any Claimant eager to move its case forward without undue delay. As a result, the Secretariat is usually in a position to transfer the file to the Tribunal within a day or two after the appointment or confirmation of the president or the sole arbitrator. **16–2**

In accordance with art.36(2), a further amount may be (and often is) requested from both parties by way of an advance on cost, which is, however, fixed by the ICC Court itself. Article 16 provides that the Secretariat will not transmit the file until the advance on costs requested by the Secretariat has been paid. There is no reference to the "provisional" advance on costs set by the Secretary General under art.36(1), as art.16 is intended to provide the Secretariat some flexibility as to those advances.[2] **16–3**

When a provisional advance has been fixed pursuant to art.36(1), which is almost always the case, and received by the Secretariat, it will usually transmit the **16–4**

[1] Article 16 corresponds to art.13 of the 1998 ICC Rules. There have been no substantive changes.

[2] Fry, Greenberg, Mazza, *op cit.*, para.3–657 rightly point out that such flexibility is rarely needed.

file as of then to the Tribunal. It will not wait that at least half or even the full amount of the advance on cost fixed by the ICC Court pursuant to art.36(2) be paid in as well. Rather, quite often the Secretariat will only require payment of the advance on costs once it transmits the file to the Tribunal, by issuing to each party a so-called "Payment Request".

The arbitral file

16–5 The file transmitted to the Tribunal includes the Request, the Answer and counterclaim (if any), the Reply to the counterclaim (art.5), any Request for Joinder and any Answer to the Request for Joinder (art.7) and most, if not the entire correspondence between the Secretariat and the parties prior to the transmittal of the file.

16–6 In some cases, when the co-arbitrators are to choose the president of the arbitral Tribunal, the Secretariat may send them the file, or a portion of the file (i.e. at least the Request and Answer, where the latter is available) prior to the appointment of the president in order to give them information about the nature of the arbitration to assist in their selecting of a president. However, this is not a transmittal of the file within the meaning of art.16 with the consequences discussed below. In any event, the Secretariat has created a fact sheet called "Case Information", which it will send to the co-arbitrators to assist them in choosing an appropriate third arbitrator.[3]

16–7 A party may wish to have certain correspondence excluded from the file transmitted to the Tribunal. For example, if a party has expressed preferences as to the background of the president, it may prefer not to have such correspondence disclosed. If a party has such a concern, it should contact the Secretariat as otherwise it may well transmit the file with such correspondence to the Tribunal. Excluding correspondence relating to the preferences concerning the president, for example, would not appear to raise any procedural issues because the correspondence does not relate to the dispute itself.

16–8 The Secretariat establishes a list of the documents transmitted to the Tribunal, copied to the parties. This allows them to review this list to ensure that no important communications have been left out, and that they themselves are in possession of all these documents. The Secretariat will usually only send a copy of these documents to the parties on request (as they should already have received them).

16–9 In transmitting the file to the Tribunal, the Secretariat will point out to the parties that from then on, they should be writing directly to the Tribunal, with simultaneous copies to the other side and the Secretariat. As of this moment, the role of the Secretariat is more limited and the Tribunal will interact directly with the parties. Nevertheless, the Secretariat is copied on all correspondence with the parties and monitors compliance with the time limits under the Rules.

Note to the Arbitral Tribunal on the Conduct of the Arbitration

16–10 At the same time, the Secretariat will sent the arbitrators the "Note to the Arbitral Tribunal on the Conduct of the Arbitration", which provides practical details on matters such as:

[3] This fact sheet will quote the relevant arbitration clause, the language and place of the arbitration. It will also provide the amount in dispute with reference to a "Financial Table," which indicates, e.g. the range of the arbitrators' fees.

- the various time limits under the Rules to be respected by the Tribunal,
- the conduct of the arbitration, including the techniques for controlling time and costs,
- the advance on costs,
- the arbitrator's fees and entitlement to personal and Tribunal expenses,
- VAT applicable to arbitrator's fees,
- the replacement of arbitrators,
- the ICC Award Checklist,[4]
- the existence of the ICC's International Center for ADR, International Center for Expertise and Hearing Centre in Paris.

In addition, the Secretariat will point out that, in the absence of an extension, the Tribunal has two months to establish the Terms of Reference in accordance with art.23(2). As discussed under art.23(1) this deadline is important, and the Tribunal is expected to proceed swiftly upon receipt of the file in order to be able to meet the deadline. As a result, the obligation to deal with the case in a timely fashion starts from the moment of the transmission of the file pursuant to art.16. **16–11**

Under art.28(1), "[u]nless the parties have otherwise agreed, as soon as the file has been transmitted to it, the arbitral tribunal may, at the request of a party, order any interim or conservatory measure it deems appropriate". Therefore, once the file has been transmitted, the Tribunal may issue such interim or conservatory measures, whether or not the Terms of Reference have been signed. Prior to transmittal of the file under art.16, a party would have to seek interim measures from a national court, or apply for emergency arbitrator measures under art.29. **16–12**

Pursuant to art.24(1), the Case Management Conference must be convened when drawing up the Terms of Reference, or as soon as possible thereafter, i.e. within a relatively short period of the transmission of the file to the Secretariat. **16–13**

Under art.25(1), "[t]he arbitral tribunal shall proceed within as short a time as possible to establish the facts of the case by all appropriate means". Usually, the Tribunal deals with procedural issues after the Terms of Reference have been signed. However, nothing prevents the Tribunal from taking steps with respect to establishing the facts of the case as soon as it has received the file from the Secretariat and it may well be appropriate to do so to expedite the proceedings. **16–14**

As a practical matter, it may be that upon receipt of the file an arbitrator realises that there could exist an issue with respect to his impartiality and/or independence under art.11(1). This may arise in various ways. For example, the Request or Answer may provide further details of the parties or their action, or the probable witnesses that raise the issue of a conflict. The usual solution in such a case is for the arbitrator to disclose the fact and invite the comments of the parties. Such disclosure is required by art.11(3). Since the proceedings have just commenced, replacement of an arbitrator may be less problematic at this stage than later in the **16–15**

[4] For a discussion of that Checklist see the discussion under art.33.

proceedings. In addition, as the Tribunal will usually not have taken any substantive steps, a party may well waive a potential conflict as it may have little or no incentive to have an arbitrator replaced. Disclosure later in the proceedings may result in a more critical approach by the parties if they have become dissatisfied with the Tribunal's procedural or substantive decisions.

Article 17 Proof of Authority

At any time after the commencement of the arbitration, the arbitral tribunal or the Secretariat may require proof of the authority of any party representatives.[1]

Introductory remarks

This provision has been added to the Rules to deal with the issue of proof of authority. Article 17 expressly states that both the Secretariat and the Tribunal are permitted to request proof of authority. **17–1**

The inclusion of such a provision into the Rules, which is found in other institutional arbitration rules, was viewed by the ICC Task Force as necessary to fill a gap in the Rules, which was perceived to exist at least with respect to the Secretariat of the ICC Court.[2] In the past, there have been instances where a party challenged an attorney's power to represent more than one of the parties to the arbitration, or, where a power had been submitted, queried the scope of such power, in particular, whether it included the authority to appoint an arbitrator on behalf of the party(ies). Absent an express basis in the Rules to ask for a formal power of attorney, the Secretariat was generally reluctant to request such power, preferring to leave these matters to the Tribunal. **17–2**

In many national courts, when a lawyer makes an appearance on behalf of a party, the lawyer is representing that he or she has authority to represent the party. Often that lawyer will be admitted before the very court before which he or she is appearing. However, in international arbitration this is not the case, although the lawyer will be expected to actually have the authority to represent the party on behalf of whom he or she claims to appear. Therefore, it is common to require that parties provide a power of attorney or other proof of authority to the lawyers representing them. The ICC Rules refer at several places to a party's representative,[3] any person(s) representing a party in the arbitration,[4] and, with respect to hearings, to the parties' appearance "in person or through duly authorized representatives".[5] It is the power to represent a party, and the due authorisation to do so, which both the Secretariat and the Tribunal are permitted to verify on the basis of art.17. **17–3**

[1] No corresponding provision in the 1998 Rules.
[2] Regarding the guiding principles of the Drafting Sub-Committee and ICC Task Force, see above, Introduction, paras 0–12 to 0–17.
[3] See art.3(2) and (3).
[4] See art.4(3)(b) for the Claimant, art.5(1)(b) for the Respondent.
[5] See art.26(4).

17–4 In the past, ICC Tribunals have often requested counsel of the parties to submit a power of attorney, as the power to make such requests is inherent in the powers of the Tribunal to orderly conduct the proceedings and to ensure the respect of due process.[6]

Proof of authority requested by the Secretariat

17–5 The Secretariat may request proof of authority if it receives a Request (or any other pleading) and it is not clear for some reason whether the person transmitting it has authority to represent the party involved. The Secretariat may raise the issue spontaneously, but is more likely to do so only if the issue is raised by another party.[7] However, under art.17, the Secretariat can require proof of authority which would cover proof of corporate authorisation.

Proof of authority requested by the Tribunal

17–6 As soon as the Tribunal has received the file from the Secretariat pursuant to art.16, it may request proof of authority from the parties' representatives. Under art.17, it may do so at any time, but in practice, it is mostly when the Terms of Reference are being signed that Tribunals request a power of attorney. The Terms of Reference are a supplemental agreement among the parties and the Tribunal with respect to the arbitration and it is therefore important that the signatories be authorised.[8] As a matter of equal treatment of both parties and to avoid any suspicion of bias, it is advisable to ask for a power from all participants, even if the representation of one of the parties may only appear to be questionable.[9]

Emergency Arbitrator

17–7 Article 17 refers only to the Tribunal, which, pursuant to art.2, includes "one or more arbitrators", and as such does not cover the Emergency Arbitrator. There can be, however, no doubt that an Emergency Arbitrator has the power to ask counsel of the Applicant, for instance, for emergency measures to furnish proof of authority. Article 17 would be applicable by analogy, certainly via art.8(3) EAR, which allows the Emergency Arbitrator to act in all matters concerning emergency arbitrator proceedings not expressly provided for in the Appendix, "in the spirit of the Rules".[10]

17–8 The need to require a power of attorney may also arise in the course of the proceedings when there is a change of counsel on behalf of one of the Parties.

What constitutes proof of authority

17–9 In international arbitrations, there is no standard power of attorney or specific format for such power. Powers of attorney are normally signed and will refer to

6 See, e.g. Derains & Schwartz, *op. cit.*, p.241.
7 Fry, Greenberg, Mazza, *op.cit.*, para.3–665; Voser, Overview, p.802.
8 See below para.23–70.
9 Reiner & Aschauer, *op. cit.*, para.368.
10 See the discussion under art.29. See also the similar language in the more general provision of art.41.

the ICC arbitration, by giving the name of the parties involved therein and/or the ICC case number. Each lawyer will typically follow the practice prevailing in the lawyer's jurisdiction as regards the form and substance of the power of attorney. In many jurisdictions, local bar associations provide standard forms of powers of arbitration, and generally, they can be used as such for an ICC arbitration.

It is for each Tribunal to decide what it considers to be sufficient proof of authority for a party representative to represent one or more parties to the arbitration, in particular as regards the scope of the power and of the authority of the company's organ to issue such power. It may, for instance, require proof that the signatory of the power of attorney has the corporate authority to issue such power alone on behalf of the company. A current corporate certificate or extract from the Commercial Register may have to be submitted as well. The Tribunal may also wish to verify whether acts undertaken before the issuance of the power of attorney, such as the appointment of an arbitrator, require any form of confirmation or approval as a matter of the law applicable to the issuance of such power, and if so request that the party arrange for it, or, if no such measure is required, confirm this to the Tribunal. **17–10**

The original of the power of attorney and of supporting documents is normally sent to the president of the Tribunal alone, with copies to the opposing party and the other members of the Tribunal. If the opposing party has questions or comments to make about the validity of the power of attorney, it should raise them promptly. If the Tribunal considers them to be valid points, it will seek clarification. This provision has been added to the Rules to deal with issues of authority. Article 17 permits both the Secretariat and the Tribunal to require proof of authority. **17–11**

Article 18 Place of the Arbitration

1 **The place of the arbitration shall be fixed by the Court, unless agreed upon by the parties.**

2 **The arbitral tribunal may, after consultation with the parties, conduct hearings and meetings at any location it considers appropriate, unless otherwise agreed by the parties.**

3 **The arbitral tribunal may deliberate at any location it considers appropriate.**[1]

Introductory remarks

18–1 The basic principle implicit in art.18 and explicit in many laws on arbitration, including in art.20 of the UNCITRAL Model Law is that the parties may choose the place of arbitration. However, there must be a place of arbitration.[2]

International systems from a procedural point of view

18–2 ICC arbitration is a private form of justice, which is always linked to a national legal system, particularly as regards the conduct of the proceedings and the enforcement of the arbitral Award.[3] However, international arbitration is not

[1] Article 18 corresponds to art.14 of the 1998 ICC Rules. There have been no substantive changes.

[2] See Goode, "The Role of the Lex Loci Arbitri in International Commercial Arbitration" (2001) Arb Int Vol.17 No.1, p.19; Prof. Kaufmann-Kohler's comments on the fictional place of arbitration, "Le lieu de l'arbitrage à l'aune de la mondialisation—Réflexions à propos de deux formes récentes d'arbitrage" (1998) Rev Arb No.3, p.517; "Identifying and Applying the Law Governing the Arbitration Procedure—The Role of the Law of the Place of Arbitration" (1999) *ICCA Congress Series No.9*, p.336.

[3] This point has been well made by Goode as follows: "One can begin with the simple proposition relating to substantive rights that a contract is not law, and no award can be binding simply by virtue of the parties' agreement to be bound. A contract depends for its force on recognition by law. The point was made by Dr Francis Mann in characteristically trenchant style in a passage from his seminal piece 'Lex Facit Arbitrum', which has been cited on countless occasions but is worth repeating:

> No one has ever or anywhere been able to point to any provision or legal principle which would permit individuals to act outside the confines of a system of municipal law; even the idea of the

necessarily linked to a national legal system as regards the substantive law that the Tribunal applies to determine the merits of the case.[4]

The main link between arbitral proceedings and a national legal system is through the place of arbitration. The courts of the place of arbitration are the courts that deal with issues such as difficulties in the constitution of the Tribunal, challenges to arbitrators, requirements of due process, the annulment and sometimes also enforcement of arbitral Awards and remission of the Award to the Tribunal.[5] As the French courts state, they are the supporting court ("*juge d'appui*") for international arbitrations taking place in France. Article V(1)(a) of the New York Convention requires that an Award comply "the law of the country where the Award was made", thus rendering the law of the place of arbitration relevant to the enforcement proceedings in another country. **18–3**

Under the New York Convention, it is important to determine the place of arbitration as art.I(1) of that Convention sets out the basic rule that it applies to "arbitral awards made in the territory of a State other than the state where the recognition and enforcement of such awards are sought"[6] and art.I(3) of the New York Convention provides that "any State may on the basis of reciprocity declare that it will apply the Convention to the recognition and enforcement of awards made only in the territory of another Contracting State".[7] **18–4**

Although it is a main link between private ICC arbitration and a legal system, the role of the law of the place of arbitration has evolved over time. In major centres of arbitration, the relevant arbitration law does not seek to prescribe or unduly influence the method in which the proceedings are conducted. Instead, the law of the place of arbitration sets out minimum procedural standards for the arbitrators and the procedure and certain principles that are applicable to the jurisdiction of the Tribunal. **18–5**

In addition, recent English case law has raised the issue of whether the place of arbitration affects the law applicable to the arbitration clause itself. Building on a comment by Lord Mustill in *Black Clawson International*[8], in *C v D*,[9] the English court suggested that the law of the arbitration clause would generally be the law of the place of arbitration. In *Sulamerica*, the judge at first instance continued an injunction against court proceedings in Brazil where there was **18–6**

autonomy of the parties exists only by virtue of a given system of municipal law and in different systems may have different characteristics and effects. Similarly, every arbitration is necessarily subject to the law of a given State. No private person has the right or the power to act on any level other than that of municipal law. Every right or power a private person enjoys is inexorably conferred by or derived from a system of municipal law which may conveniently and in accordance with tradition be called the lex fori, though it would be more exact (but also less familiar) to speak of the lex arbitri or, in French, la loi d'arbitrage.", cited at para.18–1 n.2.

[4] See the discussion under art.17 on the *lex mercatoria* and the UNIDROIT Principles.

[5] See Webster, "Review of Substantive Reasoning of International Arbitral Awards by National Courts: Ensuring One-Step Adjudication" (2006) Arb Int Vol.22 No.3, p.431.

[6] The last sentence of art.I(1) of the New York Convention also provides that "[i]t shall also apply to arbitral awards not considered as domestic awards in the State where the recognition and enforcement are sought". Therefore, in some countries it may be applicable to international Awards rendered within the state.

[7] Approximately 135 States have adopted this "reciprocity" requirement.

[8] *Black Clawson International Ltd v Papierwerke Waldhof-Aschaffenburg AG* [1982] 2 Lloyd's Rep. 446.

[9] *C v D* [2007] EWCA Civ 1282.

an arbitration clause providing for arbitration in London but the underlying contract (an insurance policy) was governed by Brazilian law. The English Court of Appeal upheld the judgment despite the fact that the arbitration clause was apparently invalid as a matter of Brazilian law. This authority suggests that the place of arbitration has, at least in England, a particular importance with respect to the choice of law for the arbitration clause.[10]

18–7 The place of arbitration or "where the Award was made" is a legal concept. It provides the seat of the Tribunal and, under art.31(3) it is the place where the Award was "deemed to be made". The hearings, deliberations and the signing of the arbitral Award generally take place at the place of arbitration and it is generally recommended to have at least part of the arbitration actually take place at the place of arbitration.

18–8 The influence of the law of the place of arbitration is also felt indirectly as it may well affect the procedural approach chosen by the arbitrators under art.15 even if it does not amount to a choice of that law as the procedural law.[11] However, as noted in the discussion with respect to that article, the weight that the law of the place of arbitration should have is a matter of discussion.[12]

18–9 The approach of national courts to ICC arbitration varies considerably. There has also been an evolution of the case law in many national courts to further support arbitration. Therefore, in applying the ICC Rules, it is essential to keep in mind the principles applicable under the law of the place of arbitration and the legal principles applicable at the place of enforcement. The most striking aspect is the approach of national courts to Awards that have been annulled at the place of arbitration.[13] In France, for example, annulment at the place of arbitration as such has no effect on the Award and the French courts review whether, under French legal principles, the Award should be enforced or not notwithstanding the fact that it has been annulled. The US courts have tended in the same direction, although it now appears that they will do so only in exceptional cases.[14] In other countries, it is not possible to enforce an Award annulled at the place of arbitration.

The most frequent places of arbitration in ICC arbitration

18–10 For 2012, the places of arbitration for ICC arbitrations were as follows[15]:

[10] *Sulamerica CIA Nacional de Seguros SA v Enesa Engenharia SA* [2012] EWCA Civ 638.

[11] With reference to the seat under the "applicable procedural law" and connected problems, see ICC case No.1512 (1971) in *Collection of ICC Arbitral Awards 1974–1985*, Vol.1, *op. cit.*, p.3; see also ICC case No.5485 (1987), August 18, 1987, (1989) YBCA Vol.XIV p.156; ICC case No.4589 (1984) (Interim Award), (1986) YBCA Vol.XI p.148; ICC case No.5080 (1985), (1987) YBCA Vol.XII p.124; ICC case No.5073 (1986) (Partial Award), (1988) YBCA Vol.XIII p.53; ICC case No.5460 (1987), (1988) YBCA Vol.XIII p.104.

[12] Limitation periods in the common law are generally viewed as matters of procedure and not of substantive law. Therefore, there was the anomalous situation previously that an arbitration having England as its place of arbitration could result in English limitation periods to a dispute that had nothing to do with England. This has been eliminated by the English Foreign Limitation Periods Act 1984.

[13] For a general discussion see Webster, "Evolving Principles in Enforcing Awards Subject to Annulment Proceedings" (2005) J Int'l Arb Vol.23 No.3, pp.201–226.

[14] See the *Putrabali* case at para.0–59 n.39 and the discussion under art.34.

[15] 13 ICC ICArb Bull Vol.24 No.1, p.14.

Country-by-country breakdown: number of arbitrations seated in each country

Country	*Place chosen by the parties*	*Place fixed by the Court*	*Total*
Albania	1	0	1
Angola	1	0	1
Argentina	4	0	4
Austria	13	0	13
Bahrain	0	1	1
Belgium	5	1	6
Brazil	14	1	15
Canada	6	0	6
Chile	1	0	1
China*	10	2	12
Chinese Taipei	0	1	1
Costa Rica	1	0	1
Cyprus	1	0	1
Czech Republic	1	0	1
Denmark	2	1	3
Ecuador	1	0	1
Egypt	2	0	2
El Salvador	1	0	1
Estonia	1	0	1
Finland	3	0	3
France	80	21	101
Germany	18	1	19
Greece	6	0	6
Hungary	1	0	1
Iceland	1	0	1
India	11	0	11
Ireland	1	0	1
Italy	3	0	3
Japan	3	0	3
Kuwait	0	1	1
Lebanon	1	0	1
Malaysia	1	0	1
Mexico	11	1	12
Morocco	1	0	1
Netherlands	4	1	5
Norway	2	1	3

Country	*Place chosen by the parties*	*Place fixed by the Court*	*Total*
Panama	1	0	1
Peru	2	0	2
Philippines	1	0	1
Poland	2	0	2
Portugal	2	0	2
Qatar	4	0	4
Romania	8	1	9
Serbia	2	0	2
Singapore	31	5	36
Slovakia	1	0	1
South Africa	2	0	2
South Korea	2	0	2
Spain	7	0	7
Sri Lanka	3	0	3
Sweden	5	1	6
Switzerland	115	7	122
Thailand	0	1	1
Turkey	3	0	3
United Arab Emirates	8	0	8
United Kingdom	68	3	71
Uruguay	1	0	1
USA	33	8	41
Venezuela	1	0	1

18–11 The major countries of arbitration were France (101), Switzerland (122), the United Kingdom (71), the USA (41) and Singapore (36). Singapore is a UNCITRAL Model Law jurisdiction as are other countries that have also been widely used for ICC arbitration such as Germany (19).[16]

18–12 Parties usually agree upon the place of arbitration. In 2012, they did so in 90 per cent of cases, leaving the ICC Court to fix the place of arbitration for only 10 per cent of the cases under art.18(1). In fixing the place of arbitration, the ICC Court decided on France in 21 cases, the USA in eight cases and Switzerland in seven cases.

18–13 Therefore, with respect to issues such as challenges to arbitrators (see above, art.14), the due process requirements (see below, art.22) and annulment of Awards (see below, art.34), the authors have set out the basic principles with respect to each of these jurisdictions. With respect to other jurisdictions, the issue is how they deal with issues related to international arbitration.

[16] ICC Statistical Report 2012, p.16.

The list of places of arbitration is noteworthy with respect to various countries. The large number of arbitrations in France and Switzerland reflects not only historic tradition and their reputations as centres of arbitration, but also the fact that in many European countries the use of ICC arbitration clauses is widespread. In the case of France, where Paris is mostly chosen as place of arbitration, its choice can easily be explained by the presence of the ICC in Paris. In many contract negotiations, Paris appears to be an easy compromise for the parties for that reason. As to Switzerland, its reputation of neutrality and the large pool of experienced arbitration lawyers remain key factors in the choice of its cities as places of arbitration. The liberal arbitration laws in both France and Switzerland help in making these choices. **18–14**

Singapore is an UNCITRAL Model Law country where the arbitration activity has been, for a number of years, significant. There are a relatively large number of arbitrations in the Americas in comparison with the past. However the impact of the more favorable approach to international arbitration remains to be felt totally and varies from country to country. **18–15**

Article 18(1): "The place of the arbitration shall be fixed by the Court, unless agreed upon by the parties."

The basic rule is that the parties may freely choose, and agree on, the place of arbitration. If the parties agree on the place of arbitration, the ICC Court is generally viewed as having no power to change the place of arbitration. By choosing international arbitration, parties are opting out of national court systems. By choosing the place of arbitration, the parties are designating the national court system that will have supervisory jurisdiction over the arbitration. The fact that parties are free to choose whatever place of arbitration they wish is therefore an integral part of the respect for the autonomy of the parties in international arbitration.[17] **18–16**

Parties may choose the place of arbitration in their arbitration agreement or may agree on a place of arbitration after a dispute has arisen. In the latter case, the place of arbitration will presumably have been carefully considered. For places of arbitration that are set out in the arbitration agreement, there is a debate about the importance that should be attributed to the parties' agreement. The views range from treating the choice of the place of arbitration as a last-minute happenstance to attributing the matter to careful analysis of the merits of the proposed place of arbitration. Of course, the importance will depend on the facts of the case. **18–17**

If the parties have not agreed on a place of arbitration, it is set by the ICC Court. It is not for the Tribunal to fix the place of arbitration, unless the parties have given it the power to do so, which very rarely happens, and is not to be recommended.[18] **18–18**

[17] See para. 0–56 *et seq*.

[18] Indeed, the choice of the place of arbitration will not always suit both parties. Having the ICC Court rather than the Tribunal determine the place of arbitration, prevents the Tribunal from having to take a decision at the inception of the case which will be unpopular with one of the parties (although sometimes with both).

18–19 At the outset, there may be an issue of whether the parties have agreed on the place of arbitration. There are many variants on language that has been held to amount to or to not amount to an agreement as to the place of arbitration. A frequent issue concerns clauses such as the "ICC Paris arbitration" clause. The issue in these types of cases is whether the reference to Paris is intended to indicate a reference to the ICC (as it is mainly based in Paris) or whether it is intended to refer to the place of arbitration (as the ICC does not contain a reference to Paris in its name). In such situations, the Secretariat normally seeks the parties' comments so as to provide them to the ICC Court. Unless all the parties indicate that Paris was not intended to be the place of arbitration, the ICC Court may well find that Paris was the agreed place of arbitration rather than to find that there was no agreement as to the place of arbitration. If there is a reference such as "ICC Geneva", the ICC Court is likely to find that the reference to Geneva was intended to be a reference to the place of arbitration.

18–20 In construing these clauses to determine whether there has been an agreement as to the place of arbitration, the governing law is the law of the arbitration agreement. Therefore, the principles of interpretation will be based on that law as will the material that can be reviewed to determine whether there was an agreement between the parties.[19]

18–21 If it is not clear whether the parties have agreed on the place of arbitration, the ICC Court will decide whether there has been an agreement on the place of arbitration or whether the ICC Court is to fix the place of arbitration in accordance with art.18(1). The ICC Court usually decides these issues at one of its weekly Committee Sessions.

18–22 If the ICC Court decides whether the parties have agreed on the place of arbitration, the ICC Court is in fact interpreting the arbitration agreement. However, the ICC Court's decision is an administrative one and is rendered without providing reasons. Therefore, there is an issue as to whether the Tribunal should itself rule on whether or not the arbitration clause did amount to an agreement between the parties as to the place of arbitration. Given the consequences on the arbitration procedure, it would appear to be important that the Tribunal confirms its interpretation of the arbitration agreement and whether in the Tribunal's view it also determines the place of arbitration. Moreover, if the issue is the interpretation of the language of the arbitration agreement, then a final decision on the place of arbitration would appear to require an Award rather than a procedural order.[20]

18–23 However, whatever the place of arbitration may be, the Tribunal may hold hearings elsewhere in accordance with art.18(2) unless the parties agree otherwise.

[19] By way of example, art.4.3 of the UNIDROIT Principles with respect to interpretation of a contract provides:

"In applying Articles 4.1 and 4.2, regard shall be had to all the circumstances, including

(a) preliminary negotiations between the parties;
(b) practices which the parties have established between themselves;
(c) the conduct of the parties subsequent to the conclusion of the contract; (d) the nature and purpose of the contract;
(e) the meaning commonly given to terms and expressions in the trade concerned; (f) usages."

[20] As to the distinction between a procedural order and an Award, see the discussion under art.31.

In one ICC case,[21] the ICC Court was called to decide on the place of arbitration on the basis of the following arbitration agreement: 18–24

> "Arbitration shall be conducted in Madrid, Spain in accordance with Rules of Conciliation and Arbitration if X. is the respondent, and by the Japan Commercial Arbitration Association in Tokyo, Japan, in accordance with the Rules of Conciliation and Arbitration of the International Chamber of Commerce if Y. is the respondent".

The Claimant ("X") alleged that there was no agreement between the parties and requested that the ICC Court fix a neutral place of arbitration. The Respondent ("Y") opposed such request and submitted that Tokyo was the place of arbitration agreed between the parties. The ICC Court fixed Tokyo as place of arbitration, that is in the country of Respondent Y. In doing so, the ICC Court has considered that there was a valid agreement, and its decision to fix Tokyo as the place of arbitration was consistent with the agreement of the parties. If the ICC Court had felt that there was no agreement on the place of arbitration, it would have fixed the place of arbitration in a third neutral country to both parties.

In interpreting arbitrations clauses, the ICC Court's practice has been to fix Paris, France as the place of arbitration in circumstances where at least one party asserts that this was the intention. Therefore, if there is a reference to the "International Chamber of Commerce, Paris", the ICC will tend to designate Paris as the place of arbitration. In a recent case, the arbitration clause referred to the "International Chamber of Commerce, Paris". The Claimant proposed that Paris, France be the place of arbitration. The Respondent requested that it be in Switzerland as the reference to Paris was only meant as an indication of the arbitral institution. In addition, the parties could not decide at the time of signature of the Agreement on the place of arbitration in Paris. Prior to the submission of the case to the ICC Court, the Secretariat informed the parties that the usual practice of the ICC Court is to fix Paris, France, as the place of arbitration in circumstances where at least one of the parties asserts that this was the intention. Accordingly, the Secretariat suggested that the Court fix Paris, France as the place of arbitration. The ICC Court's practice does however vary, which makes it at times difficult to predict how the ICC Court will decide the issue of the place of arbitration in clauses referring to the "ICC, Paris", the "ICC in Paris", the "ICC of Paris" and the like, when no other place of arbitration is mentioned in the arbitration clause. 18–25

Prior to the decision of the ICC Court, the parties are generally required to comment on the place of arbitration in the Request pursuant to art.4(3)(h) and in the Answer pursuant to art.5(1)(f). Therefore, if a party wishes to argue that there was an agreement on the place of arbitration or that certain factors are relevant to the choice of the place of arbitration, it should set out its arguments in the Request or Answer, as the case may be. However, it is not infrequent that the parties file additional letters and materials with the Secretariat relating to the place of arbitration. 18–26

If the ICC Court decides that there is a real issue as to whether there is an agreement on the place of arbitration or where that place is, the ICC Court may provisionally decide on a place of arbitration and let the Tribunal decide the issue. 18–27

[21] ICC case No.14190 (2006), unreported; the parties settled their dispute without ever having had a meeting at the place of arbitration.

18–28 If the ICC Court decides that there has been no agreement on the place of arbitration, it will take various factors into account in fixing the place of arbitration, although, as with its other decisions, the ICC Court does not provide reasons in deciding on the place of arbitration. One point of reference for the factors relating to the selection of the place of arbitration is the UNCITRAL Notes. Those Notes deal with arbitration under the UNCITRAL Rules and not the ICC Rules and with the factors that a Tribunal should take into consideration in setting the place of arbitration. However, they nevertheless provide a useful list of comments and factors that have been referred to in international arbitral Awards, including by ICSID Tribunals.[22] Paragraph 22 of the Notes states:

> "22. Various factual and legal factors influence the choice of the place of arbitration, and their relative importance varies from case to case. Among the more prominent factors are: (a) suitability of the law on arbitral procedure of the place of arbitration; (b) whether there is a multilateral or bilateral treaty on enforcement of arbitral awards between the State where the arbitration takes place and the State or States where the award may have to be enforced; (c) convenience of the parties and the arbitrators, including the travel distances; (d) availability and cost of support services needed; and (e) location of the subject-matter in dispute and proximity of evidence."

18–29 Item (a) in this list is of course the arbitration law of the place of arbitration. It would be inappropriate to select as a place of arbitration a place with a law that does not support arbitration. Item (b) in many cases can be answered by ascertaining whether the country of the place of arbitration is a signatory of the New York Convention. Convenience referred to in (c) is always a factor. However, in many instances the parties neglect the importance of support services in the arbitration referred to in (d). The location of the subject matter of the dispute referred to in (e) may indicate that either the place of arbitration should or should not be in a specific country. The proximity of the evidence is also relevant. However, in most international arbitrations, there are alternatives such as site visits and holding hearings elsewhere than at the place of arbitration to deal with problems as to the evidence.

18–30 One of the major factors not referred to in the UNCITRAL Notes that is relevant for the ICC Court is neutrality. The ICC Court seeks to ensure in each case that the place of arbitration does not and will not be seen as favouring one party. Neutrality has many aspects. There is a geographic aspect but also a cultural or legal one. The reality is that parties do have recourse to national courts at the place of arbitration on some occasions.

18–31 Therefore, fixing as the place of arbitration a country with which one party is familiar and the other is not, may well be avoided.[23]

[22] See for example ICSID Case No. Arb (AF)/00/1, Procedural Order No.2 of July 11, 2001, *ADF Group Inc v United States of America* which can be found at http://icsid.worldbank.org [accessed November 14, 2013]. The ICSID site includes the submissions of the parties on the place of arbitration, which is also very helpful.

[23] For example, although Ireland and England have developed distinct arbitration statutes, they are still much closer than England and Belgium for example. Therefore, in an arbitration between a French and English company, a jurisdiction such as Switzerland or Germany may be viewed as

For the ICC Court, the above factors would also appear to be relevant. In addition, under art.41, the ICC Court "shall make every effort to make sure that the Award is enforceable at law". **18–32**

When fixing the place of arbitration, the ICC Court will decide on the city and not just the country. There does not appear to be any practical possibility of recourse against the ICC Court's decision of fixing the place of arbitration. Any such recourse would presumably be brought in Paris, where the ICC is based. However, as discussed under art.1, the ICC Court's decision is an administrative one and it would be very difficult to demonstrate that the ICC Court had somehow breached the Rules in selecting one place of arbitration over another. **18–33**

If the place of arbitration has been "agreed" by the parties, then the Tribunal would not generally be permitted to overturn that decision in the absence of factors that would otherwise enable a Tribunal to disregard an express agreement of the parties.[24] **18–34**

If the ICC Court decides that the arbitration agreement did not contain an agreement as to the place of arbitration and the Tribunal decided otherwise, then the decision of the Tribunal would prevail as that reflects the agreement of the parties. However, the authors are not aware of that having occurred. Presumably, this is because the ICC Court takes into account the possibility of an agreement on the place of arbitration in fixing the place of arbitration. **18–35**

If the place of arbitration has been "fixed" by the ICC Court, it remains unclear whether the decision of the ICC Court has vested the Tribunal with the power to fix another place of arbitration by giving its own interpretation of the arbitration agreement. In other words, is the Tribunal free to decide to modify or to confirm the place of arbitration previously fixed by ICC Court. Although nothing would prevent the Tribunal from considering this question as it has jurisdiction to construe this disputed aspect of the arbitration agreement, it seems that the Tribunal would have very limited possibilities to modify it, except that it could seek from the ICC Court a decision changing the originally fixed place to another. New factors not available to the ICC Court when it initially fixed the place of arbitration would normally be required to have the ICC Court change the place it had initially selected. Such change would also be very much subject to the comments made by the parties who would be consulted by the Secretariat before any decision is taken by the ICC Court.[25] Similarly to the right of the Tribunal to seek a modification of the place of arbitration which was initially fixed by the ICC Court, the parties are also entitled to request from the ICC Court a change of the place of arbitration because of modified circumstances. In both cases, the ICC Court has the authority to do so. In at least one case, the ICC Court did change the place of arbitration due to concern about enforceability of the Award, as it had **18–36**

more appropriate. For a general discussion by a then-counsel to the Secretariat, see Verbist, "The Practice of the ICC International Court of Arbitration With Regard to the Fixing of the Place of Arbitration, Arbitration International" (1996) ICC ICArb Bull Vol.12 No.3, p.347.

[24] These principles will depend on the legal system. Under art.7.2.2 of the UNIDROIT Principles, a party may not require performance where "(a) performance is impossible in law or in fact; (b) performance or, or where relevant, enforcement is unreasonably burdensome or expensive".

[25] Article 18 does not appear to prohibit reconsideration by the ICC Court of the place of arbitration, as art.18(1) is only applicable where the parties have not agreed on the place of arbitration. However, that would presumably only occur in very exceptional circumstances.

fixed the place of arbitration in a country that had not signed the New York Convention and there was apparently doubt about the enforceability of any resulting Award in relevant countries. In that case, the ICC Court's concern about ensuring that the Award was enforceable under art.26 of the 1988 ICC Rules (now art.41) led to reconsideration of the place of arbitration.[26]

18–37 A related issue is whether the ICC Court may change the place of arbitration upon request of one party because of changed circumstances, after the parties have "agreed" on the place of arbitration. Article 18(1) does not deal with the issue. In such a situation, the ICC Court tends to leave the question to the Tribunal to decide whether the arbitration agreement in which the place of arbitration is set out remains binding or not on the parties.

18–38 Whatever reasons may be invoked by the parties or the arbitrators to seek to change the place of arbitration due to concerns about security or interference of the courts at the place of arbitration fixed by the ICC Court or initially agreed by the parties themselves, these have to be balanced against the fact that the Tribunal is free to hold hearings elsewhere than at the place of arbitration. As a result, if there is an issue as to the place of arbitration, logically the issue should relate more to the functioning of the judicial system rather than to security.[27]

18–39 In some cases, the parties agree with a change of the place of arbitration upon a suggestion made by the Tribunal, in which case, it is often incorporated in the Terms of Reference.

Article 18(2): "The arbitral tribunal may, after consultation with the parties, conduct hearings and meetings at any location it considers appropriate, unless otherwise agreed by the parties."

18–40 The main initial meeting is the Case Management Conference discussed under art.24. In addition, there may be subsequent meetings and hearings to deal with procedural issues. The main hearing is the evidentiary hearing or hearings. In addition, there may be a hearing for legal argument.

18–41 The usual practical assumption is that the hearings and meetings will generally be held at the place of arbitration. Article 18(2) provides that the Tribunal may hold hearings and meetings at places other than the place of arbitration unless otherwise agreed by the parties. In some instances, parties may argue that the arbitration clause is phrased in a way that provides not only the place of arbitration, but also the place for the hearings. This is not the case under the standard ICC arbitration clause and is relatively rare.

[26] Jarvin, "The place of arbitration—A review of the ICC Court's guiding principles and practice when fixing the place of arbitration" (1996) ICC ICArb Bull Vol.7 No.2, p.58.

[27] Schwartz, "Do International Arbitrators Have a Duty to Obey the Orders of Courts at the Place of the Arbitration? Reflections on the Role of the Lex Loci Arbitri in the Light of a Recent ICC Award" in *Liber Amicorum in honour of Robert Briner, op. cit.*, p.795; Knoepfler, "Note—Sentence partielle du 11 octobre 2000 dans l'affaire CCI No.10439" (2004) Rev Arb No.2, p.421; Crivellaro "Note—Award of 7 December 2001 in Case No.10623—Summary of the Arbitral Proceedings—International Arbitrators and Courts of the Seat—Who Defers to Whom?" (2003) ASA Bull Vol.21 no.1, p.60; Scherer, "Note— Award of 7 December 2001 in Case No.10623—The Place or 'Seat' of Arbitration (Possibility, and/or Sometimes Necessity of its Transfer?)—Some Remarks on the Award in ICC Arbitration No.10623" (2003) ASA Bull Vol.21 No.1, p.112.

Article 18(2) is subject to the law of the place of arbitration. Therefore, it is conceivable that the law of the place of arbitration requires that some or all hearings be held at the place of arbitration or that the Award be signed at the place of arbitration. However, the laws of the major centres of arbitration do not appear to contain any such requirement and in some cases expressly permit the holding of hearings elsewhere than at the place of arbitration. Article 20 of the UNCITRAL Model Law provides a good example for that approach. **18–42**

There are various reasons for holding hearings and meetings at a place other than the place of arbitration. Where the place of arbitration was agreed upon by the parties, a Tribunal will have to consider that the so agreed place was probably the result of a bargain between the parties at the time the arbitration clause was negotiated. Arbitrators should therefore always have due regard to the parties' reasonable and legitimate expectations,[28] although that should of course be balanced against concern that the Tribunal may have as to interference by local courts. In the same way, the Tribunal should take into account sensitivities of the parties. **18–43**

The Tribunal may used to hold proceedings elsewhere "Especially when the place of arbitration is in the State of a party and that State or an emanation of it is itself a party in the arbitration."[29] When considering to meet at a place other than the place of arbitration, the Tribunal should explain to the parties why it considers its decision is appropriate. Costs saving and/or the convenience of the Tribunal, the parties and/or the witnesses are usually the most common reasons invoked although the list is not exhaustive. Another reason may be scheduling. Some arbitrators or lawyers may only be able to attend a hearing or meeting if it is held in a particular city due to other commitments. Usually, the parties are flexible about most hearings although, with respect to the evidentiary hearings, the prevailing practice seems to be to hold the hearings at the place of arbitration. **18–44**

Related to the issue of the place of hearings is the alternative means of communication, such as the use of video conferencing or telephone conferences. This is expressly anticipated in art.24(4) for the Case Management Conference. The use of this technology with respect to fact-finding is discussed under art.25. **18–45**

Article 18(3): "The arbitral tribunal may deliberate at any location it considers appropriate."

As is discussed under art.31, Tribunals are required to function in a collegial fashion. The Tribunal's deliberations are, of course, private. Usually, they are ongoing once the main evidentiary hearing has taken place. It is commonplace for arbitrators to discuss the credibility and weight to be given to each witness as the hearings are progressing. **18–46**

Many presidents seek to have the deliberations as to the final Award commence immediately after the last hearing, whether it is the evidentiary hearing or the **18–47**

[28] See Lalive, Poudret & Reymond, *op. cit.*, p.297; Poudret & Besson, *op. cit.*, p.111; Redfern & Hunter with Blackaby & Partasides, *op. cit.*, p.86.

[29] See Scherer, para.18–38 n.27. In ICC Case No. 17734, for example, at a hearing in Paris, the lawyer for a French government defence entity threatened criminal proceedings against witnesses. The Tribunal did not react. The opposing party ignored the threat but inserted the subsequent hearing be held outside France.

legal argument. Therefore, the initial deliberations may take place at the place of arbitration, if the hearing took place there.

18–48 Subsequent deliberations are often by email, fax or telephone with meetings held at places convenient to the members of the Tribunal. Frequently, deliberations are by email. The basic principle as outlined in art.31 is that each member of the Tribunal should have a full opportunity to participate in the deliberations.[30] One of the problems in some international arbitrations is organising these meetings due to travel requirements and time constraints. This should not, but in some cases does result in delay in rendering arbitral Awards. Depending on the issues to be decided, face-to-face meetings provide often the best results of deliberations, and art.18(3) gives the required flexibility to achieve this result.

[30] Paris, January 16, 2003, (2004) Rev Arb No.2 p.382, note Jaeger; Cass civ 2e, April 28, 1980, *Société Inex Film et autre v Société Universel Pictures* (1982) Rev Arb No.4 p.424, note Fouchard.

Article 19 Rules Governing the Proceedings

The proceedings before the arbitral tribunal shall be governed by the Rules and, where the Rules are silent, by any rules which the parties or, failing them, the arbitral tribunal may settle on, whether or not reference is thereby made to the rules of procedure of a national law to be applied to the arbitration.[1]

By choosing arbitration, parties are opting out of national courts in favour of private dispute resolution. The parties therefore are choosing another forum than the courts and another procedure than that applicable in the courts. When choosing ICC arbitration, the parties submit to the ICC Rules as the framework for dispute resolution. Article 19 is the same as art.15(1) of the 1998 Rules. Article 15(2) of the 1998 Rules has been moved to art.22(4). **19–1**

As discussed under art.18, an ICC arbitration is subject to the mandatory law of the place of arbitration. Therefore, the reference to the Rules and to the agreement of the parties as to the procedure is subject to the mandatory provisions of the place of arbitration. **19–2**

As discussed in the Introduction, one of the basic principles of international arbitration and ICC arbitration is that there is no code of civil procedure. Within the framework of the ICC Rules and mandatory law, the parties and the Tribunal are free to develop their own procedure. This accounts for the change that one observes with respect to international arbitration procedure from case to case and over time. **19–3**

Some of the agreed procedural rules will be set out in the Terms of Reference discussed under art.23. In addition, as discussed under art.23 and art.25, the Tribunal will decide procedural issues either in a procedural order or in a letter reflecting the decision itself. Examples of procedural orders are provided in Pt II. **19–4**

Article 19 deals with the procedure for an ICC arbitration and whether or not a national law should be applied to that procedure. Article 21 deals with the application of a national law to the merits of the dispute—normally including the governing law of the contract. As discussed under art.18, arbitration is linked to at least one national legal system through the place of arbitration, but that does not mean it adopts the procedure of that national legal system or of any national legal system. **19–5**

The fact that the parties have chosen one system of law to govern the merits of their dispute does not mean that they have chosen that system of law or any system of law in particular to govern the procedure. A Tribunal made this basic point, for example, in ICC case No.5029 in 1986. In that case, the Tribunal was faced with the interpretation of a clause providing that the contract was subject to Egyptian law. The Egyptian party argued that, as a result, Egyptian procedural law governed the arbitration. The Tribunal rejected this argument stating: **19–6**

[1] Article 19 corresponds to art.15(1) of the 1998 ICC Rules. No substantive changes have been made.

> "As it is recognized in virtually all legal systems around the world, a basic distinction must be made between the law governing the substance and the law governing the procedure. That distinction is also recognized in Egyptian conflict of laws: whereas Art. 19 of the Egyptian Civil Code provides for the law governing the substance of the dispute, Art. 22 is concerned with the law governing the procedure. Accordingly, if the parties had wished that the arbitration be governed by Egyptian procedural law, they should have made a specific agreement thereon. Art. 5(1)(b) of the Contract is not such a provision as it does not mention specifically that arbitration is governed by Egyptian law. Failing such agreement, the arbitration law of the place governs the arbitration."[2]

19–7 Article 19 confirms the distinction between the law on the merits and the law governing the procedure as well as the autonomy of the parties and of the Tribunal with respect to the arbitration procedure. Under the laws applicable in most major centres of arbitration, this autonomy as to the procedure is expressly confirmed. The basic principle is that, provided that the procedure of an ICC arbitration respects due process, the parties and the Tribunal may craft the procedure to suit the needs of the case.

19–8 Although not specifically mentioned in art.19, the arbitration agreement may set out details of the procedure. However, usually it does not. The standard ICC arbitration clause does not contain reference to the details of the procedure.

19–9 The arbitration agreement does also not incorporate by reference the procedural rules of any country. However, some clauses are drafted to suggest that the procedure will be that of a particular country or place. For example, the arbitration agreement may state that "the arbitration will be conducted in accordance with the civil procedure in Geneva, Switzerland".[3]

19–10 These types of references are somewhat problematic, as ICC arbitration is generally not carried out in accordance with the national procedure of the place of arbitration. Some parties seek to increase certainty with respect to the procedural conduct of the arbitration by inserting a reference to the procedural law at the place of arbitration. It remains, however, often unclear whether the reference is to the arbitration law only or the law of civil procedure in general. If reference is to the arbitration law only, the reference is of limited assistance as most modern arbitration laws contain very few guidelines as to how to conduct the arbitration, and leave it essentially to the discretion of the arbitrators. If the reference is to the local civil procedure, it may also be of little assistance as domestic civil procedure is applicable in the courts and may be difficult to adapt to an arbitration, let alone an international one.[4] Therefore, the better view is that these references to local procedure should be avoided and, if they are present, they should be clarified in the Terms of Reference.

[2] ICC case No.5029 (1986) (Interim Award), (1987) YBCA Vol.XII pp.113–123; more generally, see Fouchard, Gaillard & Goldman, *op. cit.*, para.1171 et seq., p.633.

[3] Hascher, "The Law Governing Procedure: Express or Implied Choice by the Parties— Contractual Practice" (1996) *ICCA Congress Series No.7*, p.322.

[4] See, for instance, art.19(2) of the UNCITRAL Model Law, Pt III App.5.

Article 19 confirms the precedence of an agreement between the parties as to the procedure as the procedural rules may be those "which the parties [. . .] may settle on". The parties may agree on procedural rules at any juncture. To the extent that the parties agree prior to the nomination of the arbitrators, they will be in the position of presenting to the Tribunal the procedure that should be followed. If the members of the Tribunal disagree with the proposed procedure, they should not accept the arbitration. If the parties agree on a procedure after the Tribunal has been constituted, the Tribunal may object to the procedure, although an agreement between the parties takes precedence under art.19. **19–11**

If the parties do not settle on the procedure, the Tribunal may do so itself, "whether or not reference is thereby made to the rules of procedure of a national law". In fact, Tribunals seldom make reference to national rules of procedure when they decide on the procedure. Usually the Tribunal will set out its own principles for the procedure in a procedural order. The nature of these orders does vary. Part II contains examples of the types of procedural orders that Tribunals may issue in an ICC arbitration. In setting out the procedure, the Tribunal may refer to the principles set out in the IBA Rules of Evidence,[5] which are discussed under art.25. More frequently, Tribunals either refer to the IBA Rules of Evidence as guidelines in the Terms of Reference or in a procedural order or acknowledge orally at the procedural hearing that the IBA Rules of Evidence are guidelines that will be referred to by the Tribunal in reaching its procedural decisions. **19–12**

[5] Pt III App.10.

Article 20 Language of the Arbitration

In the absence of an agreement by the parties, the arbitral tribunal shall determine the language or languages of the arbitration, due regard being given to all relevant circumstances, including the language of the contract.[1]

Introductory remarks

20–1 Unlike with national courts, in arbitral proceedings, the parties may agree on the language for the arbitral procedure. English has become increasingly important in international business and thus not surprisingly also in ICC arbitration. Three quarters of the ICC Awards rendered in 2012 were rendered in English.[2] However, the role of English should be seen within the overall context with respect to the parties, the arbitrators, the ICC Court and even the nature of the underlying contracts themselves.

20–2 In 2012, 7.12 per cent of the parties to ICC arbitrations were from the United States and 6.46 per cent were from the United Kingdom. Even allowing for parties from Australia and Canada, less than 25 per cent of the parties were from English-speaking countries.[3] In many if not most of even those cases, the other party or parties to the arbitration were from countries where English is not an official language. In 2012, the percentage of the parties from various countries was as follows: Germany (6.48 per cent), France (6.09 per cent), Switzerland (2.90 per cent), Italy (3.49 per cent), Latin American countries (38.47 per cent). These figures demonstrate the relevance of Spanish, Portuguese, German, French and Italian for ICC arbitration. In the recent past, several ICC arbitrations have also taken place in Turkish. Therefore, although English is not the language of most parties to ICC arbitration, it is the most important language used for international business and for ICC arbitration.[4]

20–3 Nor is English the mother language of most arbitrators in ICC arbitrations, as the origin of the arbitrators reveals. This being noted, many arbitrators from non-English speaking countries speak excellent English and are of course very used to handling arbitrations in English. However, for those arbitrators for whom English

[1] Corresponds to art.16 of the 1998 ICC Rules. There have been no substantive changes.
[2] (2013) ICC ICArb Bull Vol.24 No.1, p.16.
[3] (2013) ICC ICArb Bull Vol.24 No.1, p.10.
[4] On English as the arbitral *Weltsprache*, see Ulmer, "Language, Truth and Arbitral Accuracy" (2011) J. Int'l. Arb. Vol.28:4, p.295.

and legal English is a second language and no matter how frequently they deal with English, they will be open to influences from the other languages that they speak and from the civil law concepts with which they are familiar.

Finally, a review of the list of members of the ICC Court shows that the vast majority do not have English as their mother language, although most speak English fluently.[5] The official working languages of the ICC Court are English and French. **20–4**

Therefore, while English has become the leading language in ICC arbitration, it is English that is frequently spoken and understood by persons who are using it as a second or third language or who have been trained in a civil law vocabulary. Moreover, there are considerable variances in the English used in various parts of the world. Therefore, in preparing an ICC case, it is important to note this more complex linguistic background as compared to that in national court systems for example. **20–5**

Determining the language(s) for a specific ICC arbitration

Article 20 deals with the language(s) of the arbitration. The issue of the language to be used in the proceedings arises initially for the parties both in their relation with the Secretariat of the ICC Court, particularly when filing the Request and the Answer. However, art.20 leaves it to the Tribunal to decide on the language to the extent that there is no agreement between the parties. Therefore, until the Tribunal has been constituted and decided the issue, it may not be clear which language or languages will be applicable in the proceedings. Once the Tribunal has been constituted, the Tribunal will seek to establish the language of the arbitration as soon as possible and in any event at or shortly after the Case Management Conference. If the language of the arbitration has not been determined when the Terms of Reference are being prepared, the Tribunal may either expressly reserve the issue or draft the Terms of Reference in both languages. **20–6**

In respect of the parties' relations with the Tribunal, the language question becomes relevant when the parties: (i) engage their counsel; (ii) select an arbitrator; (iii) make their written submissions; (iv) submit documentary evidence; (v) have witnesses testify; and (vi) make oral arguments. As far as the members of the Tribunal are concerned, the language question arises not only in respect of the submissions of the parties, but also with regard to drafting the Terms of Reference, conducting the hearing, the internal deliberations and the rendering of the Award. **20–7**

Once an Award is made, the language question may also play a role when it comes to seeking the annulment of the Award at the place of arbitration, and/or its enforcement in the Respondent's country or elsewhere whenever the language of the arbitration is not identical to the language in the civil courts of the concerned country. In such a case, it is usually necessary to have a sworn translation prepared for submission to the national court. **20–8**

Article 20 provides that there may be one or more languages in the arbitration. The basic principle is again the autonomy of the parties as regards the language of the arbitration. The parties' agreement will prevail. The issue of whether there is an agreement between the parties as to the language is a question of interpretation of the arbitration agreement. Otherwise, the language of the arbitration is a **20–9**

[5] See http://www.iccwbo.org/court/ [accessed November 14, 2013].

question of procedure, not of substance so that the procedural rules governing the arbitration need to be examined. As noted under art.19,[6] in an ICC arbitration, the ICC Rules will govern the arbitration procedure, except where they may conflict with a mandatory rule of law of the place of arbitration.

20–10 As regards mandatory legal principles, none of the major centres of arbitration requires the parties to use a particular language with respect to an arbitration or a part of an arbitration. They place no restriction on the parties' agreement as to the language of an arbitration. This principle is also set out in art.22 of the UNCITRAL Model Law.[7] There is a diminishing list of countries in which there is either a requirement or a presumption that the local language will be used for international arbitrations.[8]

20–11 Many arbitration clauses contain an express agreement as to the language or languages to be used in arbitration.[9] In other instances, the parties may maintain that there was an agreement as to the language to be used in the arbitration. The question in each instance is to be determined under the law governing the arbitration agreement which relates to the interpretation of contracts (and the language provision in the contract where it would be separate from the arbitration agreement). Usually, the standard will be the objective intent of the parties as regards the language of the arbitration.

20–12 The Claimant will file the Request in a specific language and will often set out an initial argument as to the language of the arbitration if there is no express agreement in accordance with art.4(3)(h).

20–13 The Respondent then has the choice of either accepting the language proposed by the Claimant or of arguing that another language should be applicable in accordance with art.5(1)(f). If the Respondent maintains that another language should be applicable, it may well choose to file the Answer in that language. It may even decide to file no Answer on the ground that the Request was not submitted in the language agreed by the parties. If the arbitration clause contains a clear provision as to the language of arbitration, and the Claimant chooses to file the Request in a language other than the one of the arbitration clause, it runs the risk that the Respondent will refuse to submit an Answer, as long as no translation of the Request into the language of arbitration is provided, and/or as long as the Tribunal has not ordered the Respondent to file an Answer.

The Secretariat's correspondence with the parties

20–14 The Secretariat can usually understand (and respond) in most commonly spoken languages due to the language abilities of the members of the Secretariat.

[6] See the discussion under art.19 at paras 19–1 to 19–2.

[7] See Pt III App.5.

[8] See for example art.29 of Law No.27 for 1994 of Egypt (presumption of use of Arabic unless agreement between the parties or decision to the contrary by the Tribunal). See also art.212(6) of the Procedural Civil Law of the U.A.E. of March 8, 1992. For a general analysis, see Lamèthe "Les langues de l'arbitrage international: liberté raisonnée de choix ou contraintes réglementées? – D'autres intérêts économiques sont en jeu: ils sont culturels, moraux et sociaux et ils doivent être préservés. C'est au juriste de dire comment (Philippe Fouchard)" (2007) JDI No.4, p.1174.

[9] In some cases, a language provision concerning the contract as a whole is included in the contract, leading to the argument that it should also apply to the arbitration.

Therefore, the Secretariat may adopt one of several approaches. If there appears to be an agreement on the language in the arbitration agreement, the Secretariat may correspond in that language, if it has someone fluent in that language. However, the Secretariat has no obligation to correspond with the parties in languages other than English and French, which are the official working languages of the Court and its Secretariat.[10]

If there is no agreement on the language of arbitration, the Secretariat may decide to correspond in a language known by both counsel of the parties, even where this would be neither the language of the contract, nor one of the two official working languages. The Secretariat may in some exceptional cases send out communications in two languages. It is important to note that whatever language the Secretariat uses, the parties are always informed by the counsel in charge of the file that this is without prejudice to the Tribunal's right to decide upon the language (or languages) of the arbitration, in the absence of an agreement between the parties. The ICC Court has no right to decide the language(s) of the arbitration. That decision is reserved to the Tribunal. Likewise, once the Tribunal has decided the language of the arbitration, the Secretariat remains nevertheless free to correspond in the language it considers most appropriate in the given case. **20–15**

Since the two official languages of the ICC Court are English and French, the Secretariat will make its submissions to the ICC Court only in one of those languages. Therefore, when parties correspond in other languages, the Secretariat will generally provide a translation of the correspondence or relevant extracts translated into English or French if the material is to be used in ICC Court sessions. **20–16**

Tribunal's decision as to the language(s) of the arbitration

Once the Tribunal is constituted, it can decide: (i) whether there has been an agreement on the language(s) of the arbitration; and (ii) if not, which language(s) should be used for the arbitration. Therefore, if it is left to be decided by the Tribunal, it will only be decided after the Request, and Answer have been filed, perhaps in two different languages. **20–17**

If the issue is whether there has been an agreement as to the language of the arbitration, then the Tribunal will have to resolve it as one of the issues in the proceedings and reflect it generally in the Terms of Reference and subsequently in an Award. If the Tribunal decides that there is an agreement as to the language of the arbitration, one would expect that this would be reflected in the partial or final Award. The Award may itself become the subject of annulment proceedings. If the Tribunal is to decide the language of the arbitration pursuant to its power under art.20 (rather than its interpretation of whether there was an agreement as to the language of arbitration), the usual course would be to have the issue decided by a procedural order.[11] Where there is no agreement as to the language of the **20–18**

[10] Whenever the Secretariat corresponds in a language other than the official working languages, it needs to obtain translations of those documents it intends to submit to the Court. This is a time-consuming and costly exercise for the ICC, which it needs to cover from the revenues received through the administrative costs

[11] See in that sense, Paris Court of Appeal, February 26, 2013 (2013) Rev. Arb. No.2, p. 524; for a distinction between "Award" and "procedural order" see also discussion under art.33 at para.33–4.

arbitration, the most efficient way to proceed is to issue a procedural order at an early stage in the proceedings, that is, prior to the Terms of Reference, to enable the parties to know the language to be used in the arbitration. The procedural decision of the Tribunal would then usually be reflected in the Terms of Reference, as a matter that has already been decided by the Tribunal, and the Terms of Reference would then have to be drafted in that language. It may be seen as a sign of bias if the Tribunal provides the Parties with a draft on the Terms of Reference in a given language, without first having decided the language issue. However, if the Tribunal has reasons to believe that both Parties will understand the draft Terms of Reference in the language it has provisionally chosen for it, and describes the language issue as one of the issues to be decided, it would seem perfectly proper and sensible for a Tribunal to proceed in this manner.[12]

20–19 Article 20 requires the Tribunal to "determine the language or languages of the arbitration, due regard being given to all relevant circumstances, including the language of the contract". The wording of this provision indicates that the language of the contract will not necessarily be the sole factor, although it certainly is a strong and persuasive one, as will be further discussed below.

20–20 Usually, this analysis will result in the Tribunal deciding that one language shall be used in the arbitration. More infrequently, for the reasons referred to in para.20–31 below, Tribunals will decide to use more than one language for the arbitration. An illustration of the factors considered in deciding on the language of the arbitration is provided in ICC case No.9875,[13] where the Tribunal issued a procedural order including the following analysis:

> "This provision [corresponding to art.20 of the Rules] invites the Tribunal to give special, but not exclusive, attention to the language of the contract, which is English. In the practice of ICC arbitration, a certain proportion of procedures are actually conducted in a language other than that of the contract (cf. LAZAREFF, La langue de l'arbitrage institutionnel, Bull. Cour Arb. C.C.I. 1997, pp.18–27. 'The precedent version of the ICC Rules gave more weight to the language of the contract'). The modified formulation of the 1998 version ('in particular' replaced by 'including') reveals the admission that the language of the contract does not have such paramount importance. Other factors must also be considered ('all relevant circumstances').
>
> The Tribunal does not consider the neutral choice of [city], a bilingual if not polyglot place, as the seat of the arbitration a convincing factor in determining the language of the procedure. Nor does it consider there should be a necessary link between such language and the law applicable to the substance of the case, which will be discussed later.

Also see the ICC Court of Arbitration Bulletin 2010 for a discussion of procedural orders on languages.

[12] The situation may, however, be different again, if Respondent does not participate in the proceedings, and if therefore the Terms of Reference need to be approved by the ICC Court pursuant to art.23(3). In such case, the decision on the language might have to be taken before draft Terms of Reference are being circulated to the Parties. See Fry, Greenberg, Mazza, *op cit.,* para.3–860, who even consider that the Tribunal "must" do so in such case, which is, however, questionable.

[13] ICC case No.9875 (1999) (Partial Award), unreported.

The Tribunal has also taken the following factors into consideration. The parties are respectively [nationality] and [nationality]. Even though they have written their contract in English and used English to communicate, they (as well as the witnesses they may call to appear before the tribunal) may feel disadvantaged at certain stages of this legal procedure if they have to express themselves in a language other than their own. Both parties have chosen French-speaking counsel. The parties' choice of arbitrators, approved by the I.C.C. Court, includes a French arbitrator who has specified French as the only language in which he could conduct an arbitration without the assistance of an interpreter or translator and English arbitrator who has said the same about English, while adding he had a good knowledge of French.

The Tribunal is guided by the concern that this procedure should be concluded efficiently, in fairness to all parties involved. Under the above circumstances, it decides that English and French will be the languages of the arbitration, to be applied as follows:

- English will be the language used in the tribunal's correspondence to the parties, procedural orders, awards and other official documents.
- Oral debates may take place in French and English. Simultaneous translations will be organised.
- Written submission will be accepted in either of those languages.
- With prior notice, [language] will also be accepted in oral debates, with simultaneous translations into English and French.
- The costs of interpretation and translation will be included in the costs of the arbitration."

In the *Bombardier Transportation* case,[14] the challenging party attempted to have an ICC Award set aside, alleging violation by the Tribunal Terms of Reference, which provided for English as the language of the arbitration. It was argued that by allowing communications of exhibits in a language other than English, the Tribunal had exceeded its powers and mission (art.1502–3 of the French NCPC (now art.1520–3 of the French CPC)). The Paris Court of Appeal rejected the challenge stating: **20–21**

"Considering that, although the Terms of Reference signed by the parties on November 13, 2001, provide as regards procedural rules that 'the language used for the deliberations, files and other documents to be presented by the parties is English'; however a decision of the arbitral tribunal dated April 8, 2002 clarifies 'that documents which have been used in prior contractual dealings of the parties and have been used by both parties in a language other than English, can be communicated in that other language notwithstanding the possibility for the tribunal to ask for a translation, it appears unreasonable that a party who, during

[14] *La Société Bombardier Transportation Switzerland v La Société Siemens AG*, JurisData: 2005-287132.

the contract had accepted to work from French or German documents, would now object to the use of such documents, that the parties have been reminded of this decision in a letter from the tribunal dated April 30, 2002 as Bombardier which used documents written in languages other than English, objected nonetheless to the other side's German documents;

Moreover, taking into account that the tribunal has a jurisdictional prerogative which enabled it to regulate the proceedings, and that the tribunal rightly took care not to define the procedure too strictly in a way which would hinder its adaptibility to new circumstances during discovery, that the arbitrators have not exceeded their powers, the first argument for annulment is rejected." (Authors' translation)

20–22 As illustrated by this case, a Tribunal may consider keeping some flexibility in the Terms of Reference with respect to language issues, for instance, by providing that it may accept documents submitted in a language other than the language of the arbitration.

20–23 Nevertheless, the Paris Court of Appeal's recent ruling in *Blow Pack v Windmöller* underscores that a Tribunal's opting for such flexibility needs to be careful, as such practice may conflict with due process.[15] In *Blow Pack*, an ICC final award was partially set aside by the Paris Court on the ground that the Tribunal had breached due process when it allowed *Windmöller* to produce exhibits that it had translated in part only, on the ground that the translated extracts were the only relevant ones. Moreover, the president of the Tribunal took it upon himself to translate himself extracts of some additional documents filed by *Windmöller*. According to the Paris Court, this deprived the other party of the ability to address such evidence. Furthermore, the Court found that, although French was the language of the arbitration, the Tribunal based its Award exclusively on an expert report, to which the exhibits that had only been translated in part had been annexed.

20–24 In the UNCITRAL commentary on art.22 of the UNCITRAL Model Law, the point is made that the language of the arbitration must be determined by reference to art.19(3) of the UNCITRAL Model Law providing that "the parties shall be treated with equality and each party shall be given a full opportunity of presenting his case". This corresponds to the principle in art.22(4) that the parties be given a "reasonable opportunity" to present their case. Therefore, one of the legal circumstances will be the ability of the parties to present their cases in the arbitration.

20–25 If one party requires translation of the entire proceedings, this may have adverse consequences on its ability to defend itself. It may cause delay in counsel seeking and obtaining instructions from its client. This is therefore yet another factor the Tribunal will have to consider when deciding upon the language of the arbitration.

20–26 The sole factor expressly referred to in art.20 is the language of the contract. Generally, a Tribunal will anticipate that a party who signs a contract in one

[15] *Blow Pack v Windmöller et Hölscher KG*, Paris Court of Appeal, 1e Ch. April 2, 2013, No. 11/18244, (2013) Rev Arb. No.2, p.538.

language is at the very least able to understand that language for the purposes of an arbitration. This is frequently reinforced by the language of communications between the parties.

In the case of dual language contracts, the presumption may well be reversed. If parties sign a contract in English and Arabic, for example, it may well be taken as an indication that the parties are not comfortable in the other language, whether or not communications are in that language. **20–27**

The Tribunal will usually take into account the language abilities of the counsel to the arbitration and, to some lesser extent, of the arbitrators who have been appointed. If a party has signed a contract in one language and appoints an arbitrator fluent in that language, then the party is indirectly indicating that it is comfortable in the language. If a party appoints an arbitrator who is unable to conduct an arbitration in the language of the contract or in a commonly spoken international language in general, then there may be an issue as to whether that arbitrator is able to conduct arbitral proceedings in accordance with the requirements of art.11(5). **20–28**

As noted above, in many instances, the language of both the contract and the communications between the parties is English. Therefore, there is a tendency to have arbitrations in English even where neither of the parties has that language as its mother tongue. It is very frequent to have arbitrations conducted in English, for example in France or Switzerland, and the language of the place of arbitration in such cases is generally viewed as virtually irrelevant for the purpose of deciding the language of the arbitration. Likewise, if a project is located in a given country, the language spoken in that country is often also viewed as only marginally relevant in deciding the language of the arbitration. In addition, the applicable law on the merits would rarely, if ever, be a determining factor when fixing the language. This is true even though the need to translate the laws and judgments is often undesirable, in particular given the costs that such translations may entail. **20–29**

Dual language arbitrations

Article 20 contemplates the possibility of several languages being languages of the arbitration. The parties may agree on two languages for the arbitration or the Tribunal may decide that the arbitration (or parts of the arbitration) should be conducted in two languages. In some cases, the issue is what the parties have agreed on. In one recent case, the parties agreed that the arbitration be conducted in "Czech and English" and the issue was whether both languages should be used, and how. The common sense approach in such cases is that the parties should be able to make submissions and arguments in either language (and in this case in Czech or English), and not to require the simultaneous use of both languages. This is true in particular when the language is not an international language. **20–30**

Apart from specific circumstances such as those described above at para.20–20, the use of multiple languages as languages of the arbitration is not to be recommended for many reasons. First, it may be difficult to appoint an experienced arbitrator who has a full command of all the relevant languages. Secondly, his/her linguistic skills (or lack of) may give rise to an objection by a party to his/her confirmation as co-arbitrator by the ICC Court. In such a case, the ICC Court will **20–31** usually take into account the parties' intent as reflected in the arbitration agreement. If the parties have laid down very specific criteria on the arbitrator's linguistic abilities, there is a risk that the ICC Court may decide not to confirm the potential arbitrator if he/she does not meet those requirements. On the other hand, when the arbitration agreement contains no criteria relating to the arbitrator's linguistic skills, the ICC Court has more discretion and it may decide to confirm an arbitrator who does not speak one of the languages of the arbitration given that the services of an interpreter may be used.[16] It should however be noted that the decision of the ICC Court to confirm an arbitrator does not or should not affect the power of the Tribunal to determine the language or languages of the arbitration under art.20.[17] Thirdly, dual language arbitrations are more costly as is discussed in the following paragraph.

20–32 In deciding the issue of the languages of arbitration, Tribunals should have regard to the overall objective of the Rules to provide cost-effective dispute resolution. One of the advantages of international arbitration is to avoid costs of court proceedings where each document must generally be submitted in the language of the national court system. Therefore, Tribunals frequently adjust the procedure to reflect the linguistic abilities of the parties and their counsel. As a result, if all parties are fluent in certain languages (such as English or Spanish), then the Tribunal may permit the parties to make submissions in the language of their choice and submit documents in that language. Truly bilingual arbitration (where all documents and submissions are in two languages) is very cumbersome and expensive and for that reason alone should preferably be avoided.

20–33 In many national courts, a party submitting documents in a language other than that of the national court must submit a sworn translation of any foreign language document. That is often not the case in arbitration. Frequently, the approach in an ICC arbitration is to permit documents to be submitted with an unsworn or office translation with the opposing party having the possibility to question the translation, request a sworn translation, or simply submit its own translation.[18] If a Tribunal would request that a sworn translation be provided, it would normally leave it to the parties to select the sworn translator, who may not reside at the place of arbitration. In exceptional cases, the Tribunal may take it upon itself to appoint a sworn translator and have a specific document translated by him/her. The costs thereof would be paid by the Tribunal out of the parties' deposit made at the ICC Court.

20–34 With regard to legal authorities, usually parties will seek to limit the costs of translation of texts by translating brief extracts only (the original text being submitted as well). In ICC arbitrations in particular, many arbitrators allow the submission of legal authorities in the language in which they were originally

[16] Castineira & Petsche, "The Language of the Arbitration: Reflections on the Selection of Arbitrators and Procedural Efficiency" (2006) ICC ICArb Bull Vol.1 No.1, p.33 highlighting the difficulties for the parties when using more than one languages to find, for example, individuals who are able to satisfy the linguistic requirements without sacrificing the legal knowledge. In addition, the difficulties can be exacerbated in the absence of a fixed practice of the ICC Court, whose decisions are usually taken on a case-by-case basis.

[17] idem., at p.41.

[18] It is often not the translated document in its entirety, but only a few sentences or words with which the opposing party may have trouble and take issue.

published. Therefore, it is always advisable to provide a copy of the text in the original. In many cases, the parties agree that translations are not required where counsel and the parties are fluent in the language in which the legal authorities have been published.

With regard to the Award, the strong preference of most Tribunals will be to have an Award in one language. This would avoid the argument of inconsistencies between two versions of the Award. If the Award needs to be translated into a second language for enforcement purposes, the party seeking to enforce the Award may have to provide a sworn translation of the Award into the language used by that of the enforcing court.[19] **20–35**

Disclosure of documents

As discussed under art.25, parties generally submit the documents on which they wish to rely and there is much less Tribunal-ordered disclosure than in court proceedings or domestic arbitrations in the United States, for example. When documents are disclosed pursuant to orders of the Tribunal, they are disclosed in the original language. The disclosing party is not normally required to provide its opponent with a translation unless the disclosing party ends up submitting the documents as part of its case. If the recipient chooses to submit a document received through the discovery process, it will normally have the burden of translation into the language of the arbitration. **20–36**

Article 3(12)(d) of the IBA Rules on Evidence does not provide otherwise, but deals with the form of translations in the event that translations are produced: "[w]ith respect to the form of submission or production of Documents [. . .] translation of Documents shall be submitted together with the originals and marked as translations with the original language identified". Although the language of the article could be understood as requiring submission of translations of all original documents, art.3(12)(d) in fact only provides that, if translations of documents are submitted, they must be submitted with the originals, marked as translations, and identify their original language.[20] This interpretation is consistent with the French language version of art.3(12)(d) as well as the Commentary of the IBA Review Subcommittee. **20–37**

Effect of the language of the arbitration

As explained above, the language of the arbitration has a limited impact on the Secretariat's communications with the parties. It may have an impact on the selection of counsel by the parties, and of arbitrators, as discussed in the context of art.13(1).[21] **20–38**

Many ICC arbitrations are conducted by multilingual Tribunals. Therefore, as noted in the introductory remarks, while English may be the official language of the procedure, the impact of other languages, and particularly the language of the **20–39**

[19] See art.IV(2) of the New York Convention; see also Paris, 18 March 2004, *Sarl Synergie v Société SC Conect SA* (2004) Rev Arb No.4 p.917, note Garaud & Ziadé (absence of the translation of the Award by a sworn translator is not a ground for annulment of the *exequatur* decision granted by the French Court).

[20] Zuberbühler, Müller, & Habegger, *op. cit.*, at p.79.

[21] See the discussion under art.13(1) at paras 13–5 to 13–9.

members of the Tribunal, is important. There is no requirement that the Tribunal deliberate in the language of the arbitration and Tribunals generally deliberate in whatever language with which they are most comfortable.[22] However, if one of the members of the Tribunal is only familiar with the language of the arbitration, he or she will be able to insist that this language be used also for the deliberations, as well as for all internal communications between the members of the Tribunal.

20–40 Many contracts which are subject to civil law are written in English. The result in some instances is that the language of the contract does not correspond to the terms used in the civil law system.[23] The extent to which the Tribunal will consider the linguistic background of the parties in interpreting the contract will vary. It may well be a factor, especially if the issue is the interpretation of a clause that has a specific meaning under common law that may not be readily appreciated by some persons who do not speak English as their mother language.

[22] The Terms of Reference would not deal with the language of deliberations within the Tribunal and in most cases no reference is made in the Awards to the language used for deliberations by the Tribunal.

[23] See, e.g. Triebel, "Pitfalls of English as Contract Language", in: Olsen/Lorenz/Stein (eds), *Translation Issues in Language and Law* (2009, Palgrave Macmillan), p.158 ; Ulmer, *op. cit.*, p.304 ; see also von Breitenstein, "*La langue de l'arbitrage – une langue arbitraire*" (1995) ASA Bull. No.1, p.15.

Article 21 Applicable Rules of Law

1 **The parties shall be free to agree upon the rules of law to be applied by the arbitral tribunal to the merits of the dispute. In the absence of any such agreement, the arbitral tribunal shall apply the rules of law which it determines to be appropriate.**

2 **The arbitral tribunal shall take account of the provisions of the contract, if any, between the parties and of any relevant trade usages.**

3 **The arbitral tribunal shall assume the powers of an *amiable compositeur* or decide *ex aequo et bono* only if the parties have agreed to give it such powers.**[1]

[1] Article 21 corresponds to art.17 of the 1998 Rules. No substantive changes have been made.

Introductory remarks

21–1 Unlike art.19 regarding the law applicable to the arbitral procedure (*lex arbitri*), art.21 deals with the rules of law to be applied to the merits of the dispute. The difference between the two is discussed under art.19.[2] There is also a difference between the law applicable to the arbitration agreement or clause discussed under art.6 and the rules of law applicable to the dispute as a whole. It is important to understand that these may differ as is discussed in detail under art.6. The "rules of law" applicable to the merits of the dispute pursuant to art.21 include the law applicable to the relevant contract, as well as the various other rules of law that may be applicable in the circumstances of the case. The concept of "rules of law" is not limited to choosing between national legal systems. The Rules permit the parties to agree on and the Tribunal to apply *lex mercatoria* for example. The sole change from the prior version of the Rules is to delete reference to the phrase "In all cases . . ." at the introduction to art.21(2).

21–2 The general rule under ICC arbitration is that the Tribunal is required to decide the arbitration based on "rules of law". ICC Tribunals are not entitled to decide as *amiable compositeur* or *ex aequo et bono*, unless the parties expressly so agree in accordance with art.21(3). Therefore, as discussed under art.34,[3] although Awards with respect to interpretation of the rules of law are perhaps subject to less review by national courts than in the past, Tribunals are expected and required to apply the rules of law to resolve the dispute. Failure to do so can result in the annulment of an Award.

Article 21(1): "The parties shall be free to agree upon the rules of law to be applied by the arbitral tribunal to the merits of the dispute. In the absence of any such agreement, the arbitral tribunal shall apply the rules of law which it determines to be appropriate."

Rules of law

21–3 The reference in art.21(1) to the "rules of law" rather than to "the law" of a given country is a deliberate choice made in 1998 to signal that the parties or Tribunals were not restricted to the application of a country's national legal system. The parties might agree on free-standing legal rules, such as the principles of *lex mercatoria*, the UNIDROIT Principles of International Commercial Contracts, or a combination of national laws.[4]

Choice of law by the parties

21–4 Article 21(1) confirms the broad autonomy of the parties in the choice of the rules of law applicable to the dispute as well as the freedom of the Tribunal to determine the law applicable in the absence of an agreement. For Requests for Arbitration filed in 2012, the parties had agreed on a choice of law clause in

[2] See the discussion at paras 19–6 to 19–7.
[3] See the discussion at para.34–63.
[4] Derains & Schwartz, *op. cit.*, pp.217–220; Reiner & Aschauer, *op. cit.*, 419.

88 per cent of the cases. It is fair to say that nowadays a governing law clause is to be found in the vast majority of contracts dealing with international business transactions. The drafters of these contracts from all over the world consider it to be an essential element of such contracts, and parties will usually seek to agree in advance on the governing law. As a result, ICC tribunals are much less frequently called upon to decide upon the applicable law or rules of law to the dispute. The applicable law chosen by the parties was as follows in 2012[5]:

	Governing law	2012[6]:
1	English law	16.95%
2	Swiss law	13.43%
3	US law	9.78%
4	French law	7.17%
5	German law	5.35%
6	Brazilian law	3.52%
7	Chilean law	2.09%
8	Italian law	2.09%
9	Indian law	1.96%
10	Romanian law	1.96%

Although English law was chosen by the parties in 16.95 per cent of cases in 2012, English nationals made up only 2.4 per cent of parties this year. The gap, however, with regards to US and French parties is much smaller. And although Swiss law was chosen in 13.43 per cent of the cases, Swiss parties represented only 2.90 per cent of the total number of the parties in 2012.

The willingness of parties to agree on the applicable national law, before a dispute has arisen, is the result of several factors. The first is that parties sometimes agree as a compromise on a neutral applicable law. For example, in some instances the parties will agree that the substantive law will be English or Swiss law even where these laws have no relationship with the transaction or the parties. The second is the perception that, in many instances, there is no issue in accepting one or the other national legal system, as national legal systems are relatively neutral as between Claimants and Respondents of whatever nationality. The third is that, with respect to agreements drafted by lawyers, and in particular mergers and acquisition agreements, it is virtually automatic that the lawyers insert a governing law clause. **21–5**

Parties sometimes have a preference for one type of legal system over another. For example, many parties prefer either a civil law system or a common law system or vice versa. However, whatever system is preferred, it is submitted that one of the relevant factors for determining whether a party should accept the application of a particular system of law is the accessibility of legal materials in that legal system. In this respect, there has been a considerable **21–6**

[5] 2013 ICC ICArb Bull 24 No.1, p.13.
[6] (2013) ICC ICArb Bull Vol.24 No.1, p.13.

development of resources on the internet that render national systems readily accessible although advice from local practitioners remains, of course, essential.[7]

21–7 The statistics above relate to the choice of law with respect to the relevant contract. In addition to the law applicable to the contract, there may be various other rules of law applicable to the dispute between the parties. For example, other rules of law may be applicable with respect to torts or delicts, depending in part on the scope of the choice of law provision agreed to by the parties.

Choice of law by the Tribunal

21–8 Where the parties have not chosen the applicable law with respect to a legal issue in a case, the second sentence of art.21(1) gives the Tribunal wide discretion in determining the law: the Tribunal shall apply the rules of law that it determines to be appropriate. Thus, arbitrators are given the authority to engage the so-called *voie directe*, as opposed to applying a rule of conflict, in determining the applicable law. Tribunals are not bound to follow a specific set of national conflicts of law rules, and in that respect enjoy a freedom that the judges in a national court do not have.[8]

21–9 Although it is very liberal with respect to choice-of-law, art.21(1) nonetheless requires the determination of the applicable rules of law and its application by the Tribunal since it states that the Tribunal "shall apply the rules of law which it determines to be appropriate". The requirement in art.21(1) that the Tribunal apply rules of law is to be contrasted with the provision in art.21(3) that the parties may agree that the Tribunal decide *ex aequo et bono* or as *amiable compositeur*, and therefore without applying strict rules of law.

21–10 In some Awards, Tribunals appear to avoid relying on the applicable law and instead rely solely on the construction and interpretation of contract provisions. This approach does not appear to be compatible with art.21(1). Although Tribunals are to take into account the terms of the contract under art.21(2), a contract cannot be interpreted in a legal vacuum. The various legal systems and other rules of law, such as the UNIDROIT Principles discussed below, set out principles of interpretation. Moreover, terms used in a contract may have a special meaning depending on the relevant rules of law.[9] Therefore, with the exception of interpretation of arbitration clauses themselves and then only in

[7] Among the more complete systems, see, for example, the UK system (BAILLI) and the related Australian and Canadian sites, as well as the various sources of American Law (Findlaw, Cornell), the Swiss system (*http://www.bger.ch* [accessed November 19, 2013]) and the French system (*http://www.legifrance.gouv.fr*). The German site (*http://www.gesetze-im-internet.de* [accessed November 19, 2013]) is limited to laws and regulations.

[8] See below at paras 21–26 et seq.

[9] A Tribunal may of course decide that the appropriate rules of law in the absence of an agreement between the parties is some principle of *lex mercatoria*, such as by UNIDROIT and then apply the principles from that source to interpret the contract. However, if a Tribunal skips over that step and simply interprets the contract without reference to legal principles, it may well be caught between arts 21(1) and 21(3).

France, it appears that a Tribunal should determine which "rules of law" are applicable and apply those rules.[10]

The principle of party autonomy as regards the rules of law and the role of the Tribunal have to be read in the light of the law of the place of arbitration, the context of mandatory laws that are applicable to the transaction and the law applicable to torts or delicts. **21–11**

Choice of law and the law of the place of arbitration

In dealing with the issue of the applicable law, the Tribunal and the parties must consider the mandatory principles of the law of the place of arbitration. If there is a dispute as to the applicable law, the national authorities at the place of arbitration should be reviewed in detail with respect to those mandatory principles. However, as a general rule, the law applicable in the major centres of arbitration adopts a liberal approach, subject to several nuances referred to below. **21–12**

In France, art.1511 of the French CPC provides that "The arbitral tribunal shall decide the dispute in accordance with the rules of law chosen by the parties or, where no such choice has been made, in accordance with the rules of law it considers appropriate. In either case, the arbitral tribunal shall take trade usages into account".[11] **21–13**

The French courts have confirmed that "[t]o determine the law applicable to the merits, the arbitrator is not required to apply a conflicts rule of a specific national legislation".[12] Therefore French arbitration law grants wide discretionary powers to arbitrators as to the methods for determining the appropriate rule(s) of law. Arbitrators are permitted to refer to conflict of law principles, use the *voie directe* or even apply *lex mercatoria* if they think that it is the appropriate rule of law. The Tribunal must, however, give reasons for its decision and respect the mandatory rules that are applicable, failing which the Award may be subject to a challenge.[13] **21–14**

In Switzerland, art.187(1) of the Swiss PILA provides that "[t]he Tribunal shall decide the case according to the rules of law chosen by the parties or, in the absence thereof, according to the rules of law with which the case has the closest connection". **21–15**

Unlike French law, Swiss law refers to the use of the principle of the closest connection to determine the law applicable to the merits. Arguably, the second sentence of art.21(1) permits a Tribunal to use the *voie directe* in Switzerland. Article 187(1) of the Swiss PILA refers to the "rules of law chosen by the parties" and not to the method of choosing the applicable law. However, this distinction may be artificial as the Rules are intended to permit the *voie directe* and the parties have accepted this principle in accepting the Rules. **21–16**

[10] For a discussion of the French approach to the interpretation of arbitration clauses see para.6–104 et seq.

[11] Translation by Paris, The Home of International Arbitration, The 13 January 2011 Decree. The New French Arbitration Law, p.33.

[12] Paris, 13 July 1989, *Compania Valenciana de Cementos Portland SA v Primary Coal Inc* (1990) Rev Arb No.3 p.663, note Lagarde; (1990) JDI p.430, note Goldman; (1991) YBCA Vol.XVI p.142.

[13] Delvolvé, Rouche & Pointon, *op. cit.*, pp.144 et seq.

21–17 Many Tribunals will, in any event, apply the principle of the law with the closest connection to determine the applicable rules of law. In Switzerland, an arbitral Award should explain the basis on which the Tribunal found that the law was most closely connected with the dispute.[14]

21–18 In the United States, the Federal Arbitration Act contains no express provision regarding the choice of applicable law. Therefore, in most cases, one would expect that Tribunals would apply standard conflict of law principles to determine the applicable law. However, although not binding, art.187(2) of the Restatement (Second) of Conflict of Laws provides in pertinent part that:

> "[t]he law of the state chosen by the parties to govern their contractual rights and duties will be applied, even if the particular issue is one which the parties could not have resolved by an explicit provision in their agreement directed to that issue, unless either (a) the chosen state has no substantial relationship to the parties or the transaction and there is no other reasonable basis for the parties' choice, or (b) application of the law of the chosen state would be contrary to a fundamental policy of a state which has a materially greater interest than the chosen state in the determination of the particular issue [. . .]."

21–19 A detailed discussion of what constitutes a substantial relationship with the parties or the transaction within the meaning of the Restatement goes beyond the scope of this book. However, arguably the fact that an arbitration is being conducted in a specific country provides a substantial relationship. In addition, the issue with respect to US law is which state law is applicable and various states have enacted provisions expressly permitting parties to choose the applicable law in commercial transactions.[15]

21–20 In England, s.46(1) of the English Arbitration Act 1996 provides that in the absence of a choice of law by the parties, the Tribunal shall decide the dispute "(b) if the parties so agree, in accordance with such other considerations as are agreed by them or determined by the Tribunal". Section 46(2) goes on that for this purpose the choice of the laws of a country shall be understood to refer to the substantive laws of that country and not its conflict of laws rules. Section 46(3) gives the Tribunal the power to "apply the law determined by the conflict

[14] It is not clear under Swiss law whether it is possible to choose as an applicable law a non-national law, although it would appear to be permissible provided that the legal provisions are detailed; see the discussion in case 4C.1/2005, Tribunal Fédéral, 1e Cour civile, (2006) ASA Bull Vol.24 No.4 p.742. However, that case concerned a clause stating that "[t]his agreement is governed by FIFA rules and Swiss law", which was held to be a choice of Swiss law with an additional reference to the FIFA Rules.

[15] See for example para.5–1401 of the New York General Obligations Law provides in relevant part that: "Choice of law. 1. The parties to any contract, agreement or undertaking, contingent or otherwise, in consideration of, or relating to any obligation arising out of a transaction covering in the aggregate not less than two hundred fifty thousand dollars, including a transaction otherwise covered by subsection one of section 1–105 of the uniform commercial code, may agree that the law of this state shall govern their rights and duties in whole or in part, whether or not such contract, agreement or undertaking bears a reasonable relation to this state". There are exceptions for various specific types of contracts. However, this provision was aimed at permitting broad use of New York law in commercial transactions, although it would presumably be subject to any constitutional limitations.

of laws rules which it considers applicable" to the extent there is no choice or agreement of the parties.

Section 46 is not one of the mandatory provisions of the English Arbitration Act of 1996.[16] Therefore, parties can contract out of it, in particular, by accepting arbitration rules such as the ICC Rules. Under English law, the Tribunal is free to determine the conflict of laws rules applicable, but is expected to apply conflict of law principles in determining the law applicable to the dispute. However, the acceptance of the Rules should be viewed as a contrary agreement. If English conflicts rules are applied, one would generally expect the law to be applied to be that with which the contract is most closely connected by virtue of art.4(1) of the Rome I Regulation discussed below. **21–21**

The English High Court considered s.46 in the *Peterson Farms* case. In that case, the arbitrators relied in part of their Award on the "common intent of the parties" to apply the "group of companies doctrine" with respect to the parties to the arbitration.[17] The Court categorically rejected the approach stating: **21–22**

> "45. The predicate (paragraph 86) of the tribunal's approach was that the Agreement contained no choice of law with regard to the arbitration agreement in clause 17. Yet, as the tribunal also and rightly recognised, the issue raised a question of interpretation of the Agreement and such questions were expressly subject to Arkansas law by Clause 19. The identification of the parties to an agreement is a question of substantive not procedural law.
>
> 46. 'The autonomy' of the arbitration agreement is not in point. The question is whether it is governed by Arkansas law. In my judgment it plainly is.
>
> 47. There was, therefore, no basis for the tribunal to apply any other law whether supposedly derived from 'the common intent of the parties' or not. The common intent was indeed expressed in the Agreement: that is both English and Arkansas law (paragraph 17 of Mr Hollingsworth's statement). The 'law' the tribunal derived from its approach was not the proper law of the Agreement nor even the law of the chosen place of the arbitration but, in effect, the group of companies doctrine itself.
>
> 48. Mr Marriott submitted that the tribunal's approach was in accord with section 46 of the 1996 Act. It is not. Section 46(1)(a) sets out the basic rule that the tribunal 'shall' decide the dispute in accordance with the law chosen by the parties as applicable to the substance of the dispute. That was Arkansas law. Section 46(1)(b) provides only that 'if the parties agree' the tribunal shall decide in accordance with that agreement. There was no relevant agreement within this provision. It was (a) not (b) which should have been applied."[18]

[16] Sutton, Gill & Gearing, *op. cit.*, para.2–09, pp.79–80.

[17] See [2004] EWHC 121 (Comm); also see the discussion at para.6–99 in relation to the group of companies doctrine.

[18] (2004) Mealey's IAR Vol.19 No.2 A.5.

21–23 The English Court's approach is important because it basically limits Tribunals to the law chosen by the parties where they have expressed a choice. Moreover, if the parties have not expressed a choice, but the applicable law is determined in accordance with s.46, then once again the applicable law would appear to be the national law. Under the *Peterson Farms* case, the parties may well be able to apply non-national principles (such as the UNIDROIT Principles or perhaps even *lex mercatoria*), but it appears that they must do so expressly.[19]

21–24 In the countries which have followed the UNCITRAL Model Law, art.28 of the UNCITRAL Model Law will be the relevant provision when it comes to the applicable law:

> "(1) The arbitral tribunal shall decide the dispute in accordance with such rules of law as are chosen by the parties as applicable to the substance of the dispute. Any designation of the law or legal system of a given State shall be construed, unless otherwise expressed, as directly referring to the substantive law of that State and not to its conflict of laws rules.
> (2) Failing any designation by the parties, the arbitral tribunal shall apply the law determined by the conflict of laws rules which it considers applicable [. . .]"

21–25 The UNCITRAL Working Group Notes[20] make several basic points about art.28 of the UNCITRAL Model Law, which are of general interest for arbitration practitioners and therefore repeated here: First, "Article 28 deals with the question which law or rules the arbitral tribunal shall apply to the substance of the dispute". It does not deal with the arbitral procedure. Secondly, art.28 grants "the parties full autonomy to determine the issue (including the option of *amiable composition*) and, failing agreement, by entrusting the arbitral tribunal with that determination". Thirdly, art.28 refers to:

> "the freedom to choose 'rules of law' and not merely a 'law', which could be understood as referring to the legal system of one particular State only. This provides the parties with a wider range of options and allows them, for example, to designate as applicable to their case rules of more than one legal system, including rules of law which have been elaborated on the international level."

Principles used to determine the applicable law

21–26 The determination of the applicable law in the absence of an agreement between the parties is subject to some uncertainty, in part because any proposed solution is based on an assumed starting point and in part because art.21(1) provides for discretion but does not prescribe a solution.

21–27 A Tribunal has several possible approaches to determine the applicable law in the absence of a choice by the parties. One approach is for the Tribunal to consider which national legal system should be applicable and then to apply the conflict of

[19] Sutton, Gill & Gearing, *op. cit.*, para.2–091, p.80.
[20] A/CN.9/264 English, p.61.

law rules system or a particular rule of that national system. The second approach is to determine the potential national conflicts of law system that are applicable and to try to determine whether those systems provide any solution. The third approach is to use the closest connection test, which is in fact found in many legal systems. The fourth approach, which is provided for in art.21(1), is for the Tribunal to use the *voie directe* to determine the applicable national law based on criteria that the Tribunal would usually take from a traditional conflicts of law system.[21]

Traditionally, some arbitrators have looked to the law of the place of arbitration and used the conflicts of law principles of that country to determine the applicable law. This approach has fallen into disfavour due to the general acceptance that the place of arbitration may often have no relationship with the parties or the dispute.[22] In some instances, Tribunals have considered the law of the place of incorporation of the parties. However, this frequently gives rise to a conflict that can only be resolved by examining the common principles of conflicts of law in the various relevant national jurisdictions. **21–28**

The implicit reference in art.21(1) to the *voie directe* reflects the trend to seek to avoid the issues relating to national conflict of law systems. It appears that this tendency has been reinforced by a more generalised acceptance of the principle of the closest connection as reflected in Swiss and EU law. In European Union Countries, the Rome I Regulation sets out general rules that are applicable throughout the EU.[23] Article 4 of the Rome I Regulation deals with the applicable law in the absence of choice as follows: **21–29**

> "Applicable law in the absence of choice
>
> 1. To the extent that the law applicable to the contract has not been chosen in accordance with Article 3 and without prejudice to Articles 5 to 8, the law governing the contract shall be determined as follows:
>   (a) a contract for the sale of goods shall be governed by the law of the country where the seller has his habitual residence;
>   (b) a contract for the provision of services shall be governed by the law of the country where the service provider has his habitual residence;
>   (c) a contract relating to a right in rem in immovable property or to a tenancy of immovable property shall be governed by the law of the country where the property is situated;
>   (d) notwithstanding point (c), a tenancy of immovable property concluded for temporary private use for a period of no more than six consecutive months shall be governed by the law of the

[21] For a discussion, see for example, Blessing, "Choice of Substantive Law in International Arbitration" (1997) J Int'l Arb Vol.14 No.2, p.39; Wortmann, "Choice of Law by Arbitrators: The Applicable Conflict of Laws System in Arbitration International" (1998) Arb Int Vol.14 No.2, p.97.

[22] However, as discussed under art.18, the English courts have recently given weight to the place of arbitration to determine the law governing the arbitration agreement itself. See *C v D C v D* [2007] EWCA Civ 1282; and *Sulamerica CIA Nacional de Seguros SA v Enesa Engenharia SA* [2012] EWCA Civ 638, discussed under art.18.

[23] The provisions were enacted in national laws. However, the terms of the national legislation are intended to be identical throughout the EU. Under art.3(1) of that Convention, the parties are free to choose the applicable law.

country where the landlord has his habitual residence, provided that the tenant is a natural person and has his habitual residence in the same country;

(e) a franchise contract shall be governed by the law of the country where the franchisee has his habitual residence;

(f) a distribution contract shall be governed by the law of the country where the distributor has his habitual residence;

(g) a contract for the sale of goods by auction shall be governed by the law of the country where the auction takes place, if such a place can be determined;

(h) a contract concluded within a multilateral system which brings together or facilitates the bringing together of multiple third-party buying and selling interests in financial instruments, as defined by Article 4(1), point (17) of Directive 2004/39/EC, in accordance with non-discretionary rules and governed by a single law, shall be governed by that law.

2. Where the contract is not covered by paragraph 1 or where the elements of the contract would be covered by more than one of points (a) to (h) of paragraph 1, the contract shall be governed by the law of the country where the party required to effect the characteristic performance of the contract has his habitual residence.

3. Where it is clear from all the circumstances of the case that the contract is manifestly more closely connected with a country other than that indicated in paragraphs 1 or 2, the law of that other country shall apply.

4. Where the law applicable cannot be determined pursuant to paragraphs 1 or 2, the contract shall be governed by the law of the country with which it is most closely connected."

21–30 One of the most important features of art.4 of the Rome I Regulation is the list of factors in art.4(2). The Giuliano-Lagarde Report prepared in connection with the Rome Convention[24] includes helpful comments regarding those factors:

> "3. According to Article 4(2), it is presumed that the contract has the closest connection with the country in which the party who is to effect the performance which is characteristic of the contract has his habitual residence at the time when the contract is concluded, or, in the case of a body corporate or unincorporate, its central administration. [. . .]
>
> The submission of the contract, in the absence of a choice by the parties, to the law appropriate to the characteristic performance defines the connecting factor of the contract from the inside, and not from the outside by elements unrelated to the essence of the obligation such as

[24] Report on the Convention on the law applicable to contractual obligations (1) by Mario Giuliano Professor, University of Milan (who contributed the introduction and the comments on arts 1, 3–8, 10, 12, and 13) and Paul Lagarde, Professor, University of Paris I (who contributed the comments on arts 2, 9, 11, and 14–33). See [1980] J.O. C282/1.

> the nationality of the contracting parties or the place where the contract was concluded. [. . .]
>
> As for the geographical location of the characteristic performance, it is quite natural that the country in which the party liable for the performance is habitually resident or has his central administration (if a body corporate or unincorporate) or his place of business, according to whether the performance in question is in the course of his trade or profession or not, should prevail over the country of performance where, of course, the latter is a country other than that of habitual residence, central administration or the place of business. In the solution adopted by the Group the position is that only the place of habitual residence or of the central administration or of the place of business of the party providing the essential performance is decisive in locating the contract.
>
> Thus, for example, in a banking contract the law of the country of the banking establishment with which the transaction is made will normally govern the contract. It is usually the case in a commercial contract of sale that the law of the vendor's place of business will govern the contract. To take another example, in an agency contract concluded in France between a Belgian commercial agent and a French company, the characteristic performance being that of the agent, the contract will be governed by Belgian law if the agent has his place of business in Belgium. [. . .]
>
> For each category of contract it is the characteristic performance that is in principle the relevant factor in applying the presumption for determining the applicable law, even in situations peculiar to certain contracts, as for example in the contract of guarantee where the characteristic performance is always that of the guarantor, whether in relation to the principal debtor or the creditor."

These principles apply to contracts in general, but do not apply to arbitration agreements under art.1(2)(e) of the Rome I Regulation. However, the Giuliano-Lagarde Report noted that: **21–31**

> "[t]he exclusion of arbitration agreements does not relate solely to the procedural aspects, but also to the formation, validity and effects of such agreements. Where the arbitration clause forms an integral part of a contract, the exclusion relates only to the clause itself and not to the contract as a whole. This exclusion does not prevent such clauses being taken into consideration for the purposes of Article 3(1)."

Therefore, as regards the rules of law applicable to the merits, the existence of an arbitration clause does not prevent the Rome I Regulation from being applicable to the provisions other than the arbitration clause. Moreover, the reference to the principle of the closest connection in the Rome I Regulation is probably one of the main principles to be used by arbitrators in applying the *voie directe*. **21–32**

21–33 However, the difficulty in this area is summarised as follows in an article by a leading authority in reviewing the application of these principles in a series of ICC Awards[25]:

> "The summaries set out below confirm that as regards the determination of the law applicable to the merits of the dispute, there is a wide variance of approach in international arbitration. Certain tribunals adopt the traditional conflict of laws approach while others opt for the choice of law by the 'voie directe'. The factors that are considered to determine the closest relationship are varied: domicile, establishment or seat of the arbitration, etc. It is also apparent from these awards that the identification of the characteristic performance of the contract is in some cases difficult, permitting therefore the arbitrator to arrive at an original solution.
>
> These awards also illustrate the importance if not the primacy that the arbitrators of international commerce give to contractual agreements in comparison with national legislation or those resulting from international conventions. The determination of the national law applicable may be limited for example to the setting of an interest rate, with the dispute being decided by according to the contractual agreement.
>
> Finally, the method applied to decide on the applicable law, whether it is an international convention or one or more national laws (application of various systems being possible, although relatively rarely adopted by parties or arbitrators), is not always foreign to considerations of convenience, if not equity."

Claims in tort or delict

21–34 The standard ICC arbitration clause covers "all disputes arising out of or in connection with this contract". This language is often considered as covering tort or delict claims that are related to the contract.[26]

[25] Jolivet, "*La détermination du droit applicable au fond du litige*" (2008) Cahiers arb. Vol.2, p.15. (The extracts of ICC Awards quoted in the article are in French.) Prof. Jolivet is General Counsel of the ICC International Chamber of Commerce.

[26] As the Ontario Court of Appeal noted in *Dalimpex Ltd v Janicki*, 2003 CanLII 34234 (ON C.A.), the issue of whether the tort claims are covered by this type of wording is an issue for the Tribunal initially. The Court of Appeal overturned the lower court's holding that the clause did not extend to such claims. See also ICC case No.12167, (Final Award) (2007) JDI No.4 p.1270, note Jarvin and Truong-Nguyen (jurisdiction of the Tribunal to consider a counterclaim based on tort due to the broad scope of the arbitration agreement which provided that any disputes arising out or in connection with the contract shall be submitted to arbitration); ICC case No.12363 (Partial Award), (2006) ASA Bull Vol.24 No.3 p.462; Gonzales, "The Treatment of Tort in ICC Arbitral Awards" including extracts on ICC Arbitral Awards relating to Tort, (2002) ICC ICArb Bull Vol.13 No.2, p.39 and p.55; Reymond, "Conflits de lois en matière de responsabilité délictuelle devant l'arbitre international" in *Travaux du Comité français de droit international privé*, 1988–1989, Paris, CNRS 1991, p.97. Born, *op. cit.*, at p.319 citing *Consolidated Data Terminals v Applied Digital Data Systems Inc.*, 708 F 2nd 385 (9th Cir. 1983) (non application of the parties' chosen law to the contract to tort issues); *Knieriemen v Bache Halsey Stuart Shields*, 427 N.Y. S. 2d 10; 12–13 App. Div.) (New York law only permits a choice-of-law as to contract but not to tort claims), *Richie Enterprises v Honeywell Bull, Inc*, 730 F Supp. 1041 (D. Kan. 1990)

The law applicable to the tort or delict may well be different from that applicable to the contract itself. For example, it is possible that the parties have agreed that a distribution agreement between a French manufacturer and an English distributor will be governed by French law. However, if a tort occurs, the law governing the tort will generally be, although not necessarily exclusively, the law of the place where the tort occurs.[27] Therefore, if there is a tort in England, the Tribunal may be called upon to apply English law to the tort and French law to the contract if in fact the claims are distinct. **21–35**

The procedure for deciding the applicable rules of law

The Request should set out the Claimant's position regarding the applicable law in accordance with art.4(3)(h).[28] The Answer should contain a response with respect to the applicable law in accordance with art.5(1)(f).[29] Therefore, prior to the constitution of the Tribunal, it should be clear whether there is a dispute between the parties at least with respect to the rules of law applicable to the contract. Since it is up to the Tribunal to decide on the rules of law applicable to the contract, the matter will be one of the issues to be decided and possibly identified as such in the Terms of Reference pursuant to art.23(1)d). **21–36**

As regards the actual procedure for dealing with the parties, the International Law Association (ILA) adopted certain recommendations in 2008 that in many respects reflect best current practices in international arbitration. They provide in part as follows: **21–37**

> "*General considerations*
>
> 1. At any time in the proceedings that a question requiring the application of a rule of law (including a question of jurisdiction, procedure, merits or conflicts of laws) arises, arbitrators should identify the potentially applicable laws and rules and ascertain their contents insofar as it is necessary to do so to decide the dispute.
> 2. In ascertaining the contents of applicable law and rules, arbitrators should respect due process and public policy, proceed in a manner that is fair to the parties, deliver an award within the submission to arbitration and avoid bias or appearance of bias.
>
> [. . .]
>
> *Interaction with parties*
>
> 5. Arbitrators should primarily receive information about the contents of the applicable law from the parties.

(application of the parties' choice of law only to contract claims in absence of an "express and unambiguous" agreement to its application to tort claims as well). More generally, see also EC Regulation No.864/2007 of July 11, 2007 on the law applicable to non-contractual obligations (Rome II), O.J. L199/40).

[27] See for example s.11(1) of the English Private International Law (Miscellaneous Provisions) Act 1995: "The general rule is that the applicable law is the law of the country in which the events constituting the tort or delict in question occur".

[28] See the discussion at para.4–58 *et seq.*

[29] See the discussion at para.5–36.

> 6. In general, and subject to Recommendation 13, arbitrators should not introduce legal issues – propositions of law that may bear on the outcome of the dispute – that the parties have not raised.
>
> [. . .]
>
> 10. If arbitrators intend to rely on sources not invoked by the parties, they should bring those sources to the attention of the parties and invite their comments, at least if those sources go meaningfully beyond the sources the parties have already invoked and might significantly affect the outcome of the case. Arbitrators may rely on such additional sources without further notice to the parties if those sources merely corroborate or reinforce other sources already addressed by the parties.
>
> [. . .]
>
> 13. In disputes implicating rules of public policy or other rules from which the parties may not derogate, arbitrators may be justified in taking measures appropriate to determine the applicability and contents of such rules, including by making independent research, raising with the parties new issues (whether legal or factual), and giving appropriate instructions or ordering appropriate measures insofar as they consider this necessary to abide by those rules or to protect against challenges to the award."

21–38 As is clear from the ILA Recommendations, there may be a number of rules of law applicable to various aspects of the dispute. However, one of the central issues will be the law applicable to the contract if that is not clear in the contract itself. If the parties have not agreed on the rules of law applicable to the contract, the Tribunal may decide the matter at the outset normally by way of a partial Award. Unless one party requires a hearing, the partial Award will often be rendered based on written submissions of the parties. The decision as to the rules of law applicable would almost always be a final decision on a point in dispute. Therefore, as a matter of procedure, it would have to be set out in a partial Award that would be transmitted to the ICC Court for scrutiny (see art.33). It would be much less frequent for the Tribunal to rule on the law applicable to other issues that may arise in the dispute at the outset, other than perhaps the law applicable to extra-contractual claims.

21–39 The procedure required to obtain an Award on the rules of law applicable to a dispute will involve some delay. However, the delay should not be inordinately long. The issue can usually be briefed by the parties promptly and Tribunals are usually able and have a tendency to decide the issue quickly to enable the parties to deal with the merits of the case. The approval of the draft award by the ICC Court generally should not result in significant delay, as the Court deals with these types of Awards generally in Committee Sessions that are held every week.

21–40 In some cases, rather than having the arbitrators issue a partial Award, parties prefer to save the time required for such Award to be issued, and instead authorise the Tribunal to indicate to them in an informal manner the law the parties should refer to in their submissions. This indication can be in the form of a simple letter or procedural order, but should avoid taking the form of a decision. For instance, a Tribunal could say that having heard the parties, the Tribunal invites the parties to argue their case on the assumption that the laws of X apply to the merits of the dispute.[30] This way of proceeding is cost-effective but is not without risk. If the assumption is incorrect and the Tribunal applies another substantive law, then a party may argue that it was deprived of the opportunity of arguing the case based on that law. Moreover, if as the matter is argued, it is apparent that the "assumed" applicable law is unfavourable to a party, that party may argue that another law should be applied even at the risk of requiring further briefing of the applicable law. The preferred solution would therefore often be either for the parties to agree on an applicable law or for the Tribunal to decide the issue in an Award.

The Convention on Contracts for International Sale of Goods

One of the rules of law frequently invoked in ICC arbitration is the Vienna Convention also often referred to as the CISG.[31] In 2013, 79 countries have adopted the Vienna Convention, and it has become part of the national law of those countries. **21–41**

Article 1 of the Vienna Convention provides that: **21–42**

> "3(1) This Convention applies to contracts of sale of goods between parties whose places of business are in different States: (a) when the States are Contracting States; or (b) when the rules of private international law lead to the application of the law of a Contracting State."

Article 3[32] of the Vienna Convention specifies in particular that "[c]ontracts for the supply of goods to be manufactured or produced are to be considered sales unless the party who orders the goods undertakes to supply a substantial part of the materials necessary for such manufacture or production". However, art.3(2) provides that "[t]his Convention does not apply to contracts in which the preponderant part of the obligations of the party who furnishes the goods consists in the supply of labour or other services". **21–43**

When the Vienna Convention is applicable in an arbitration, its provisions displace some but not all of the provisions of the national law that would otherwise be applicable.[33] Many Tribunals view it as appropriate to raise the issue of **21–44**

[30] See also in that context two procedural orders, which dealt with the applicable law in the same way, an interim or partial award could have done so: Interim Order in ICC Case No. 11754 (2003), in: ICC ICArb. Bull., Spec. Suppl. (2010), p.20 and Procedural Order in ICC Case No. 12949 (2004), in: ICC ICArb. Bull., Spec. Suppl. (2010), p.86

[31] In 2012, in 3% of the contracts, the parties had chosen rules other than State law. In half of these cases, they had opted for the CISG, (2013) ICC ICArb Bull Vol.24 No.1, p.13. However, the authors have been faced with numerous situations where the Tribunal has applied the Vienna Convention or has considered applying it as part of the national law applicable to the dispute.

[32] In addition, art.2 of the Vienna Convention provides that "[t]his Convention does not apply to sales: (a) of goods bought for personal, family or household use, unless the seller, at any time before or at the conclusion of the contract, neither knew nor ought to have known that the goods were bought for any such use; (b) by auction; (c) on execution or otherwise by authority of law; (d) of stocks, shares, investment securities, negotiable instruments or money; (e) of ships, vessels, hovercraft or aircraft; (f) of electricity".

[33] If the parties have chosen a national law to be applicable, there is frequently a debate about whether the choice of the national law means the national law with or without the Vienna Convention; on this issue, see for example van Houtte, "The Vienna Sales Convention in ICC Arbitral Practice" including extracts of ICC Arbitral Awards referring to the Vienna Convention, (2000) ICC ICArb Bull Vol.11 No.2, p.22 and p.34.

the applicability of the Vienna Convention whether or not it is raised by the parties, on the basis that it is an integral part of the national law that may be applicable to the dispute.

Lex mercatoria as a rule of law

21–45 Some authors have discussed whether international Tribunals should not refer to *lex mercatoria* or the "common intent of the parties" with respect to certain contracts. The term *lex mercatoria* has different meanings to different authors.[34] However, to the extent that it refers to transnational legal rules, i.e. legal principles that are not those of a national legal system, the issue is how to identify them. In an article written in 2001, the current General Counsel of the ICC Court of Arbitration noted that: "Review of the recent arbitral jurisprudence of the International Chamber of Commerce (ICC) demonstrates that the contours of lex mercatoria are rather variable".[35]

21–46 Arguably, the Vienna Convention is part of *lex mercatoria*, although, as noted above, it has been incorporated in the national law of the various signatory states. Moreover, most of the case law interpreting the Vienna Convention is national case law and that is of course within the context of the national legal system.[36]

21–47 Perhaps the best example of *lex mercatoria* is the UNIDROIT Principles,[37] the most recent version of which has been published in 2004. The introduction of the UNIDROIT Principles explains their purpose as follows:

> "These Principles set forth general rules for international commercial contracts.
> They shall be applied when the parties have agreed that their contract be governed by them.
> They may be applied when the parties have agreed that their contract be governed by general principles of law, the *lex mercatoria* or the like.

[34] Gaillard, "La distinction des principes généraux du droit et des usages du commerce international" *in Etudes offertes à Pierre Bellet, op. cit.*, p.203; Mustill, "The New Lex Mercatoria: The First Twenty-Five Years" (1988) Arb Int Vol.4 No.2, p.86.

[35] Authors' translation. Jolivet, La Jurisprudence arbitrale de la CCI et la lex mercatoria, 2001 Cahiers arb p.36.

[36] See for example Audit, "The Vienna Sales Convention and the Lex Mercatoria" in Carbonneau, *Lex Mercatoria and Arbitration*, (Juris Publishing 1998), pp.173–194 and also available at *http://www.cisg.law.pace.edu/cisg/biblio/audit.htlm* ("The Vienna Convention represents a statutory framework of law created by states, whereas the *lex mercatoria* is a body of 'spontaneous' law—law created by standard commercial practices and arbitral decisions. Which of them stands for the law of transnational commerce? Despite their differences, the Vienna Convention and the *lex mercatoria* do not compete for the status of being the exclusive source of law for international trade. Although the rules of the Convention are approved by states, they operate in conjunction with international trade usages and the principle of contractual autonomy. Indeed, this chapter argues that the purpose of the Vienna Convention is not only to create new, state-sanctioned law, but also to give recognition to the rules born of commercial practice and to encourage municipal courts to apply them.")

[37] For a detailed discussion see Jolivet, The Unidroit Principles in ICC Arbitration, in: ICC Bulletin Spec. Sup. 2005, p.65. This article contains extracts from cases applying the Unidroit principles. See also, Fortier, "The New Lex Mercatoria, or, Back To The Future" (2001) Arb Int Vol.17 No.2, p.121, and more recently Bortolotti, "The Unidroit Principles and their Application in the Context of International Arbitration," in: *Liber Amicorum Lazareff*, (2011), p.81.

> They may be applied when the parties have not chosen any law to govern their contract.
> They may be used to interpret or supplement international uniform law instruments.
> They may be used to interpret or supplement domestic law. They may serve as a model for national and international legislators."

In ICC case No.10422,[38] the UNIDROIT Principles were applied by a Tribunal based on the following analysis: **21–48**

> "Article 12 of the Contracts makes reference to the ICC and to a 'neutral legislation specified by mutual agreement by the parties'. In view of the fact that no ICC legislation exists and that the parties have not specified by mutual agreement a neutral law, it must be concluded that the parties have not expressly chosen the applicable law.
> The Arbitral Tribunal will therefore have to determine the applicable law in conformity with the second sentence of Article 17(1) of the ICC Arbitration Rules according to which: 'In the absence of an agreement between the parties, the Arbitral Tribunal shall apply the rules of law it considers appropriate'.
> The Arbitral Tribunal holds that, in order to determine the most appropriate rules of law, the fact that the parties wanted a neutral solution had to be taken into account.
> Now, in the absence of an express indication as to the domestic law of a third country, the most appropriate solution in the case in which the parties express their desire for a neutral solution is to apply the general rules and principles of international contracts or *lex mercatoria*.
> In this context, for questions concerning general contract law, reference can be made to the 'UNIDROIT Principles of International Commercial Contracts' which represent—except for a few provisions (such as for example the provisions on hardship: see ICC award No.8873 of 1998, in Journal droit int., 1998, p.1017)—a 'restatement' of the rules that parties engaged in international trade consider to be consonant with their interests and expectations. This has been recognised in numerous arbitral awards in which the UNIDROIT Principles have been applied as an expression of the *lex mercatoria* or of international trade usages: see for example ICC partial award No.7110, in Bull. Arb. CCI, 2/1999, pp.40–50; ICC award No.7375, in Mealey's Inter- national Arbitration Report, vol.11 No.12 (December 1996), pp.A1–A69; ICC award n° 8502, in Bull. Arb. CCI, 2/1999, pp.74–77.
> The Tribunal will therefore apply the rules and principles generally recognised in international trade (*lex mercatoria*) and in particular the UNIDROIT Principles, to the extent that they represent rules

[38] ICC case No.10422 (2001), (2003) JDI p.1142, note Jolivet. More generally, see ICC ICArb Bull, Spec. Sup. (2005), *UNIDROIT Principles: New Developments and Applications*; Jolivet, "La jurisprudence arbitrale de la CCI et la *lex mercatoria*" (2001) Gazette du Palais—recueil mai-juin 2001 p.563; see also *http://www.unilex.info* [accessed November 19, 2013].

> recognised by international business people as being applicable to international contracts." (Authors' translation—original in French.)

21–49 In the *Andersen* arbitration held in Geneva,[39] the sole arbitrator, a Colombian lawyer, analysed the applicable law in the following terms:

> "The Tribunal found that the Member Firm Interfirm Agreements (MFIFAs) entered into between AWSC and the Andersen Worldwide Organization member firms, together with the AWSC Articles and Bylaws are the relevant rules of law chosen by the parties to govern the present arbitration; in interpreting the provisions of the MFIFAs the arbitrator is not bound to apply the substantive law of any jurisdiction but shall be guided by the policies and considerations set forth in the Preamble to the MFIFAs and the Articles and Bylaws of AWSC; if the MFIFAs and the AWSC Articles and Bylaws are silent or do not provide guidelines for a decision, the Tribunal shall, pursuant to Article 17.1 of the ICC Rules, apply the rules of law it deems appropriate; those rules of law shall be the general principles of law and the general principles of equity commonly accepted by the legal systems of most countries. The Unidroit Principles of International Commercial Contracts are a reliable source of international commercial law in international arbitration for they contain in essence a restatement of those 'principes directeurs' that have enjoyed universal acceptance and, moreover, are at the heart of those most fundamental notions which have consistently been applied in arbitral practice." (footnote deleted)

21–50 The approach of the sole arbitrator in the above case would appear to be consistent with the approaches of the French and Swiss courts that had to review ICC Awards applying the *lex mercatoria.* However, since the *Peterson Farms* case, it is less clear whether it would be in accordance with English law.

Mandatory law applicable to transactions

21–51 Whatever the rules of law applicable to the underlying contract, an arbitration may be subject to mandatory legal principles of other jurisdictions.

21–52 All major places of arbitration provide that Awards may be annulled for failure to respect some form of public policy.[40] Article 36 of the UNCITRAL Model Law provides that the Award may be annulled "if the court finds that. . . the recognition or enforcement of the Award would be contrary to the public policy of this State". Article V(2) of the New York Convention is of similar effect.

21–53 The autonomy of the parties with respect to the choice of the law on the merits does not permit the parties or the Tribunal to ignore mandatory law of the place of arbitration. Nor should the Tribunal ignore the mandatory law of the probable

[39] ICC case No.9797 (2000), *Andersen Consulting Business Unit Member Firms v Arthur Andersen Business Unit Member Firms* (2000) ASA Bull Vol.18 No.3 p.514; (2001) ICC ICArb Bull Vol.12 No.2 p.88.

[40] See art.1520 of the French CPC, art.190 of the Swiss PILA, s.10 of the US Federal Arbitration Act and s.68 of the English Arbitration Act 1996.

place of enforcement given its duties under art.41. ICC arbitrations frequently have to deal with several principles of mandatory law.

A particularly difficult issue arises with respect to the application of insolvency law and its consequences on a contract. In an article summarising a number of ICC Awards on this issue, a commentator stated[41]: **21–54**

> "Review of the ICC arbitral jurisprudence illustrates the diversity of the situations that are encountered and the variety of approaches that have been adopted by actors in arbitral proceedings. There does not appear to be uniformity in the solutions adopted either by legal systems or by the arbitrators applying the rules established by these systems, even if certain general principles of insolvency proceedings tend to be accepted. Thus the arbitrators apply the principle of equality amongst creditors and cessation of individual creditor proceedings either implicitly or by making express reference. If the rules of insolvency proceedings are considered by national courts as part of public international order, they may be overridden by principles of public policy that are really international that are superior to them. For example, this would be the case for the principle of good faith and pacta sunt servanda."

Capacity of the parties

As noted in the Rome I Regulation, the issue of the capacity of natural persons is not subject to that regulation, except for the provision of art.13.[42] The law of the place of incorporation governs the capacity of corporate entities.[43] **21–55**

Invalidity under the governing law or the law under which the Award was made

If the parties have subjected the arbitration to a law that does not permit arbitration of the relevant dispute, the Award may not be enforced under the New York Convention. Therefore, in exercising their freedom to choose the rules of law under art.21, the parties must have regard to the arbitrability of the dispute. **21–56**

[41] Authors' translation. E. Jolivet, "*Quelques exemples de traitement du droit des procédures collectives dans l'arbitrage*" (2006) Cahiers Arb. Vol.3, p.15.

[42] Article 13 of the Rome I Regulation provides: "In a contract concluded between persons who are in the same country, a natural person who would have capacity under the law of that country may invoke his incapacity resulting from the law of another country, only if the other party to the contract was aware of that incapacity at the time of the conclusion of the contract or was not aware thereof as a result of negligence".

[43] Article 1(2) of the Rome I Regulation provides that it does not apply to: "(f) questions governed by the law of companies and other bodies, corporate or unincorporated, such as the creation, by registration or otherwise, legal capacity, internal organisation or winding-up of companies and other bodies, corporate or unincorporated, and the personal liability of officers and members as such for the obligations of the company or body; (g) the question whether an agent is able to bind a principal, or an organ to bind a company or other body corporate or unincorporated, in relation to a third party . . .".

Public policy of the place of enforcement

21–57 In many arbitrations, it is reasonably clear where the major potential places for enforcement are located. There is debate about the scope of art.41 and the duty to which the Tribunal should make an effort to ensure that an Award is enforceable at law. A discussion of public policy is beyond the scope of this book. However, three issues frequently arise in this context: antitrust or competition law, protective national law relating to agencies and employment law issues.

21–58 With regard to competition law, whatever the rules of law applicable to the dispute, if an agreement has effect in a given country, then, in many countries, the competition law principles of that country are applicable. Therefore, an Award that is rendered under another rule of law, at a place of arbitration in another country may be refused enforcement if it is contrary to the law of the country in which the effects of the relevant contract are felt.[44]

21–59 Indeed, the principle may be expressed in two ways following the well-known *Mitsubishi* case decided by the US Supreme Court in 1985.[45] First, a Tribunal deciding an arbitration subject to Swiss law had the right to apply US antitrust law in addition to the law chosen by the parties. Secondly, US courts would exercise a control a posteriori over the arbitrator's application of the US antitrust law if the Award were presented for enforcement or recognition in the US. Thus, under US law principles, a Tribunal sitting outside the US applying foreign legal principles must also take into account US antitrust law if the effects of the underlying agreement were felt in the United States.

21–60 In the European Union, EU competition law is mandatory. Therefore, if a distribution contract or a joint venture agreement offends the provisions of EU competition law, an Award based on it may not be enforceable even if the distribution contract or joint venture agreement is governed by another system of law.[46]

21–61 With regard to agency and/or distribution agreements, there are still some countries, such as Belgium or Lebanon that prohibit arbitration with respect to the settlement of disputes relating to such agreements in favour of national courts.[47] The justification is that such agents and/or distributors are to be protected against

[44] Heymanns, *Public Policy and Arbitration—Cartel Law, Acts of State and Arbitration* (Verlag KG, 1997), p.61. For a general review, see Blank /Landolt, EU and US Antitrust Arbitration. A Practitioner's, Handbook (Kluwer 2011)

[45] See para.6–158 n.122.

[46] See also for example, Dolmans and Grierson, "Arbitration and the Modernization of EC Antitrust Law: New ICC Opportunities and New Responsibilities" including extracts on ICC Arbitral Awards relating to European Community Competition Law (2003) ICC ICArb Bull Vol.14 No.2, p.37 and p.53; Jolivet, "Chronique de jurisprudence arbitrale de la Chambre de Commerce Internationale (CCI): Quelques exemples du traitement du droit communautaire dans l'arbitrage CCI" (2003) Cahiers de l'Arbitrage 2e partie, p.3; von Mehren, "The Eco Swiss and International Arbitration" (2003) Arb Int Vol.19 No.4, p.465; Bensaude, "*Thalès Air Defence BV v GIE Euromissile*: Defining the Limits of Scrutiny of Awards Based on Alleged Violations of European Competition Law" (2005) J Int'l Arb Vol.22 No.3, p.239. Blanke, "Defining the Limits of Scrutiny of Awards Based on Alleged Violations of European Competition Law—A Réplique to Denis Bensaude's 'Thalès Air Defence BV v GIE Euromissile" (2006) J Int'l Arb Vol.23 No.3, p.249; see also Heitzmann and Grierson "SNF v Cytec Industrie: National Courts within the EC Apply Different Standards to Review International Awards Allegedly Contrary to Article 81 EC", SIAR 2007:2, p.39.

[47] See for example art.4 of the Belgian law of July 27, 1961 and art.5 of the Lebanese Decree- Law No.34 of August 5, 1967.

the principal or licensor when the contract is terminated.[48] Preferential treatment is thus granted to the agents and/or distributors under the national laws that are applied by Tribunals as *lois de police*. The concern that international Tribunals would not enforce agents' or distributors' rights appears to be misplaced in light of arbitral practice.[49]

With regard to employment agreements, the dramatic increase in employment arbitration in the US is not matched elsewhere. Indeed, the general principle in Europe is that even if arbitration is permitted, there will be either a mandatory choice of law or the mandatory application of certain principles of legal protection in accordance with art.6 of the Rome Convention. **21–62**

Proof of law; the Tribunal's right to raise legal issues on its own initiative

The application of rules of law to the merits under art.21 raises two additional issues. The first issue is whether the Tribunal should raise legal issues on its own initiative. The second issue is how the applicable rules of law should be proven. **21–63**

Given the general provision in art.41 that the Tribunal shall "make every effort to ensure that the Award is enforceable at law", it would appear incumbent upon a Tribunal to raise issues of mandatory law that would affect the enforceability of the Award. However, in doing so, the Tribunal must respect the requirements of due process discussed under art.22. In particular, if a Tribunal comes to the conclusion that a mandatory rule of law should be dealt with in the Award and the parties have not made submissions as to that law, it should provide the parties with an opportunity to comment on this aspect of law.[50] Generally speaking, this would appear true for any legal provision, including its application by way of analogy, which the parties did not have an opportunity to raise. Often, this will simply be the case, because they had not even thought about it. By the time the Tribunal comes to consider that a given legal provision should apply, it will have engaged in the deliberation process. At that point, the proceedings have normally been closed.[51] **21–64**

As regards the proof of law, there is no set practice in ICC arbitration. In many instances, issues of national law will be argued by the lawyers who represent the parties. In many other cases, however, the parties will submit legal opinions with **21–65**

[48] On the issue of arbitrability and jurisdiction of the Tribunal, see for example Truong, *op. cit.*, p.79 et seq.; for Belgium, see for example ICC case No.6379 (1990) in Truong, *op. cit.*, No.95, p.100; (1992) YBCA Vol.XVII p.212; Hanotiau commenting the decision No.C020216N dated October 15, 2004 of the Belgium Supreme Court on the issue of arbitrability in "Panorama de jurisprudence belge" (2005) Cahiers de l'Arbitrage No.1, p.46; Hollander, "State Courts May Apply *Lex Fori* in Assessing Arbitrability" *http://www.internationallawoffice.com* [accessed November 19, 2013]; for Lebanon, see ICC case No.8195 (1995) (Interim Award) and ICC case No.8606 (1997) in Truong, *op. cit.*, No.89 and No.91, p.92 and p.96; ICC case No.12193 (2004), (2007) JDI p.1276, note Silva Romero, for the United Arab Emirates, see ICC case No.8910 (1998) in Truong, *op. cit.*, No.93, p.97.

[49] Several ICC Tribunals have considered such a provision not to be a bar for a Lebanese distributor from arbitrating his claims against the foreign manufacturer.

[50] See also the discussion at para.33–31.

[51] Fry, Greenberg, Mazza, *op. cit.*, para.3–769 also caution arbitrators to rely on the principle of *iura novit curia*, which they consider to be an undesirable approach in international arbitration.

respect to matters of national law.[52] Most international arbitrators are experienced in various legal systems and therefore are quite flexible as to how the relevant rules of law are addressed in the proceedings.

Article 21(2): "The arbitral tribunal shall take account of the provisions of the contract, if any, between the parties and of any relevant trade usages."

Primacy of Contract, if any

21–66 In many if not most commercial arbitrations, the Tribunal begins its analysis with the terms of the contract and reverts to it as the central point in the deliberations. It is rare that a party succeeds in maintaining that the contract is null and void. In an analysis of a number of ICC Awards, Prof. Jolivet summarised the situation as follows[53]:

> "Reviews of arbitral awards since 1988 shows that the parties only rarely base their arguments on the nullity of the contract or of some of its provisions. When nullity is invoked, it is almost always in defence by the Respondent in the arbitral proceedings.
> Arbitral tribunals acting under the auspices of the ICC Rules appear to have accepted partial or total nullity only rarely.
> Applying Swiss law for example an arbitral tribunal, for example refused the annulment on the basis of Nemo auditor propriam turpitudinem allegans and good faith. Each party knew the provisions of the contract and to invoke nullity in violation of good faith would amount to an abuse of right.
> Only in several tens of cases since 1988 has the request to nullify the contract been accepted. For example, the nullity of the contract was accepted for the illegality of commissions paid to obtain a contract, or the negotiation or renegotiation of a contract. . . .
> The existence of parallel proceedings, whether before state courts or arbitral proceedings, may influence the decision of the arbitral tribunal. For example, a tribunal accepted the admissibility of a plea for annulment of a contract but deferred its decision pending a decision in a criminal case."

21–67 The principles of interpretation vary from jurisdiction to jurisdiction.[54] In particular, in most non-common law jurisdictions there is no equivalent to the "parole evidence rule". Therefore, the contract will frequently be read within the

[52] Kaufmann-Kohler, "The Arbitrator and the Law: Does He/She Know It? Apply It? How? And a Few More Questions" (2005) Arb Int Vol.21 No.4, p.631; "Iura Novit Arbiter"—Est- ce bien raisonnable? Réflexions sur le statut du droit de fond devant l'arbitre international" in *De Lege Ferenda—Réflexions sur le droit désirable en l'honneur du Professeur Alain Hirsch* (Editions Slatkine, 2004), p.71.

[53] Authors' translation. Jolivet, "L'annulation du contrat par les arbitres dans l'arbitrage CCI" (2005) Cahiers Arb., Vol.3, p.14. (The awards are in French.) The author of the article suggests that Tribunals are basically seeking to save the contract.

[54] Hence, the need to decide the applicable rules of law, where the parties have not done so; see above para. 21–11.

context of the drafts that were prepared of it and the actions that the parties took under it. In this respect, the UNIDROIT Principles are perhaps closer to the civil law approach. Article 4.3 of the UNIDROIT Principles states:

> "In applying Articles 4.1 and 4.2, regard shall be had to all the circumstances, including:
>
> (a) preliminary negotiations between the parties;
> (b) practices which the parties have established between themselves;
> (c) the conduct of the parties subsequent to the conclusion of the contract;
> (d) the nature and purpose of the contract;
> (e) the meaning commonly given to terms and expressions in the trade concerned;
> (f) usages."

As noted above, in revising the 1998 Rules, the role of States involved in ICC arbitrations, be it in commercial disputes, or treaty based investment disputes was given particular attention. As regards investment disputes, there exists "no privity," i.e. no contract between the investor and subsequent Claimant on the one side, and the investor's host state, and subsequent Respondent, on the other side.[55] In these cases, the invitation in art.21(2) to take into account the provisions of the Contract would be meaningless. By adding the words "if any", and deleting the reference to "in all cases", this provision better fits the situation prevailing in investment disputes.[56] **21–68**

Trade usages, if any

The reference in art.17(2) to "relevant trade usages" means that the parties to an ICC arbitration are accepting the application of such usages, if any,[57] by agreeing to ICC arbitration.[58] The term "trade usage" is itself given different meanings in different legal systems. However, in accepting the Rules, the parties are agreeing to an international interpretation of the term. The UNIDROIT Principles provide for example in art.1.9(1) that: **21–69**

> "(1) The Parties are bound by any usage to which they have agreed and by any practices which they have established between themselves."

Where the Vienna Convention applies to the parties' sales contract, they are bound "by any usage to which they have agreed and by any practices which they have established between themselves" pursuant to art.9(1) CISG. Article 9(2) CISG provides that the parties are "considered, unless otherwise agreed, to have impliedly made applicable to their contract . . . a usage of which the parties knew or ought to have known and which in international trade is widely known to, and **21–70**

[55] Paulsson, Arbitration without Privity, (1995) ICSID REV. Vol.10, p.232.
[56] Fry, Greenberg, Mazza, *op. cit.*, para. 3–779.
[57] The word "if any" was inserted to better fit the situation in investment disputes, where there would normally not be such usages, see para.21–13.
[58] Erdem, the Role of Trade Usages in ICC Arbitration, in: *Liber Amoricum Lazareff* (2011), p.247.

regularly observed by, parties to contracts of the type involved in the particular trade concerned".

21–71 The term "usage" is not defined in the CISG. It must be interpreted internationally and autonomously, without recourse to preconceived domestic notions.[59] A similar approach is required in relation to the interpretation of "trade usages" under the ICC Rules. There is no reason to believe that the term "trade usages" under the ICC Rules means anything different to the term "usages" under the CISG.

21–72 Definitions of "usages" or "trade usages" in legal commentary and international arbitral awards relating to the CISG and the ICC Rules show a number of significant similarities:

(a) "all those actions or modes of behaviour (including omissions) that are generally and regularly observed in the course of business transactions in a specific area of trade and/or a certain trade center,"[60]

(b) "rules of commerce which are regularly observed by those involved in a particular industry or market place,"[61]

(c) "a method of dealing or a way of conduct generally observed by in a particular line of business with such regularity that it is accepted as binding by those engaged in that line of business,"[62] and

(d) "Naturally, all of this applies only when there are true usages, *i.e.* usages widely known and regularly observed in the sector considered: consequently it is necessary to establish that these are rules that the parties engaged in international trade (and particularly in the sector in question) consider applicable with no need for an explicit reference, because they have become mandatory as a consequence of steady, widespread usage."[63]

21–73 This consensus is reflected in the UNIDROIT Principles which provide in art.19(2) that:

> "[t]he parties are bound by a usage that is widely known to and regularly observed in international trade by parties in the particular trade concerned except where the application of such a usage would be unreasonable."

21–74 The principal test is one of general acceptance by the relevant business community.[64] It is not necessary for all members of the relevant business community to be aware of the usage, but it must be known and observed by the majority and

[59] Kröll/Mistelis/Perales Viscasillas, UN Convention on Contracts for the International Sales of Goods (CISG), (2001), p.161, ¶ 20, see also Schlechtriem/Schwenzer, Commentary on the UN Convention on the International Sale of Goods (CISG), (2010), 3rd ed., C.H. Beck, art.187, ¶ 11.

[60] Ferrari/Flechtner/Brand, Draf Digest and Beyond (2003), p.194, quoted with approval in Kröll/Mistelis/Perales Viscasillas, *op. cit.*, p.162, ¶ 22.

[61] Schlechtriem/Schwenzer, *op. cit.*, p.187, ¶ 11.

[62] C. Schmitthoff, International Trade Usages (1987), ICC Publication No 440/4, p. 14, ¶ 12.

[63] ICC Case No. 8873(1997), published in: Collection of ICC Arbitral Awards 1996–2000, (2003), Kluwer/ICC Publishing, p.500 at 501/502 (original text in French).

[64] Schmitthoff, *op.cit.*, p.51, ¶ 6.

there must be no considerable group that is unaware of the usage.[65] In addition, the usage must be shown to have existed at the time the contract is concluded.[66]

The requirement of party knowledge (express or imputed) under art.9(2) of CISG is a corollary of the requirement that a usage be widely known and regularly observed in the relevant business community. As explained in the aforementioned ICC Award: **21–75**

> "Obviously, that judgement call [whether a trade usage exists] must be made with prudence, in order to prevent the parties from being subject to rules that they could not reasonably expect to apply."[67]

Unlike the Vienna Convention and the UNIDROIT Principles, art.21 does not refer to "practices". Such practices are based on a certain behavior and conduct of the parties which they have observed in their relations over time. They do not amount to trade usages. **21–76**

One of the arguments for arbitration is that its actors, in particular, the arbitrators, are in closer contact with the business community than national courts. In choosing arbitrators, frequently prior experience is sought in the particular area of business. Therefore, it is not surprising that relevant trade usages are expressly referred to in the Rules. **21–77**

Article 21(2) appears to place "trade usages" on the same level as the contract. In practice, the impact is more limited if one is to judge from the pleadings made by parties and/or the reasons given for Awards. Indeed, Tribunals tend to rely on provisions of a contract rather than trade usages. However, arguably a Tribunal may apply a relevant trade usage pursuant to art.21(2) even if the usage does not meet the requirements of custom under national law. The reason appears to be straightforward. Under national legal systems, custom must in some instances reach the level of justifying the use of the custom as an implied term of the contract. If the parties have agreed on ICC arbitration, they have automatically agreed to art.21(2). Therefore, relevant trade usages have become part of the parties' contract by incorporation of the Rules. **21–78**

Trade usages and Burden of proof

In practice, it appears to be difficult and rare for parties to successfully rely on trade usages in normal commercial transactions. Under the Vienna Convention,[68] as much as under art.21(2) of the Rules, the burden of proving the existence of a disputed (trade) usage, its content and fact that the other party knew or ought to have known of it, lies with the party seeking to rely on the (trade) usage. In a recent ICC arbitration, a Tribunal chaired by a Swiss President opined as follows in its final award: **21–79**

[65] Schlechtriem/Schwenzer, *op.cit.*, p.190, ¶ 16.
[66] Schlechtriem/Schwenzer, *op.cit.*, p.190, ¶ 15.
[67] ICC Case No. 8873 (1997).
[68] Schlechtriem/Schwenzer, *op.cit.*, p.192, ¶ 20.

> "[183] The question whether a usage and a trade usage respectively exists and what the content of such usage is [is] a question of fact. Accordingly, the burden of proof as regards all necessary elements for a trade usage lies with Claimant."[69]

21–80 The Tribunal went on:

> "[186] Irrespective whether under the provisions of CISG and the ICC Rules respectively, the term trade usage must be interpreted in an international and autonomous way. The minimum requirement for a trade usage is that it is a conduct that is generally and regularly observed by parties in a particular trade."[70]

Article 21(3): "The arbitral tribunal shall assume the powers of an *amiable compositeur* or decide *ex aequo et bono* only if the parties have agreed to give it such powers."

21–81 Article 21(3) is only applicable if the parties have agreed that the Tribunal shall have the power to act as *amiable compositeur* or to decide *ex aequo et bono*. Otherwise, the Tribunal is generally required to apply the applicable rule of law. If the parties have conferred upon the Tribunal the power to act as *amiable compositeur* or to decide *ex aequo et bono*, such power shall be mentioned in the Terms of Reference pursuant to art.23(1)g.

21–82 The fact that these terms have been left in French and Latin is an indication of the uncertainty of their meaning in English. The corresponding provision of the UNCITRAL Model Law is art.28(3). The UNCITRAL Commentary on that provision shows the uncertainty that is attached to the terms as also used in art.21(3).[71] The terms which are used in French law, are given roughly the same meaning in practice[72] and *amiable composition* is defined as "the arbitrators'

[69] ICC award No. 17648, (2013), unreported. One of the authors was Respondent's counsel.

[70] *Idem*; footnotes omitted.

[71] "7. Arbitration rules often provide that parties may authorize the arbitral tribunal to decide as *amiable compositeur* provided, however, that such arbitration is permitted by the law applicable to the arbitral procedure. Article 28(3) grants this permission and, thus, gives effect to an express authorization by the parties that the arbitral tribunal shall decide *ex aequo et bono*, as this arbitration is labelled in some legal systems, or, as labelled in others, as *amiable compositeur*. 8. Although this type of arbitration is not known in all legal systems, its inclusion in the Model Law seems appropriate for the following reasons. It is sound policy to accommodate features and practices of arbitration even if familiar only to certain legal systems. This is reasonable not merely because it would be contrary to the purpose of the Model Law to disregard or even prevent established practices but because it is in harmony with the principle of reducing the importance of the place of arbitration by recognizing types of arbitration not normally used or known at that place. Finally, such recognition does not entail a risk for any unwary party unfamiliar with this type of arbitration since an express authorization by the parties is required. 9. No attempt is made in the UNCITRAL Model Law to define this type of arbitration which comes in various and often vague forms. It is submitted, however, that the parties may in their authorization provide some certainty, to the extent desired by them, either by referring to the kind of *amiable composition* developed in a particular legal system or by laying down the rules or guidelines and, for example, request a fair and equitable solution within the limits of the international public policy of their two States. (A/CN.9/264 English page 63)."

[72] For a general discussion, see for example, Kiffer, "*Amiable Composition* and ICC Arbitration" including extracts of ICC Arbitral Awards relating to *Amiable Composition*, (2007) ICC Bull ICArb

power not to restrict themselves to applying rules of law, thereby allowing them not only to ignore rules of law altogether, but also to depart from them to the extent that their conception of equity requires".[73]

21–83 The terms have been used in French law and the French courts have set certain requirements on their use. For example, if a Tribunal is deciding a case as *amiable compositeur*, it is required to explain why the solution proposed is, in its eyes, just. As noted by the Paris Court of Appeal in the *Fotovista* case, an arbitrator-*amiable compositeur* deciding according to French law must explain to what extent his decision is rendered in conformity with equity, failing which the Award will be annulled.[74]

21–84 Therefore, if the parties agree that the Tribunal may act as *amiable compositeur* or decide *ex aequo et bono* they are giving the Tribunal the latitude to depart from the strict requirements of applicable law. Even when deciding as *amiable compositeur* or *ex aequo et bono* the Tribunal may be required to first determine the applicable law if the parties have not chosen a given law.[75] The Tribunal cannot act as *amiable compositeur* or *ex aequo et bono* unless the Tribunal is permitted to do so under the applicable law.

Vol.18 No.1, p.51; Derains & Schwartz, *op. cit.*, p.244; Craig, Park & Paulsson, *op. cit.*, p.112; Poudret & Besson, *op. cit.*, para.7.5, p.616; Lalive, Poudret & Reymond, *Le droit de l'arbitrage interne et international en Suisse* (Payot Lausanne, 1989), p.400. More generally, see ICC Task Force on *amiable composition* and *ex aequo et bono* which was created in September 2005 and was mandated to identify the essential features of *amiable composition* and *ex aequo et bono* and also to study the role of the arbitrators in this respect. A Guideline was published by the ICC Commission in 2008.

[73] Fouchard, Gaillard & Goldman, *op. cit.*, No.1502, p.837.

[74] Paris, 15 January 2004, *Société Centrale Fotovista v Vanoverbeke et autres*, (2004) Rev Arb No.4 p.907, see also Cass Civ 1e, 28 November 2007, *M. Yann X et al v M. Jacques y et al*, 06–16.835, case No.1363 at *http://www.courdecassation.fr* and Cass. Civ le Arret No. 98, 1 February 2012 (11–11, 084). [accessed November 19, 2013].

[75] Bühler & Jarvin, "L'amiable compositeur: Peut-il laisser la question du droit applicable au fond indéterminée?" in *Mélanges dédiés à François Knoepfler, Droit international privé, droit de l'arbitrage et droit comparé* (Helbing & Lichtenhahn, 2005), p.325.

Article 22 Conduct of the Arbitration

1. **The arbitral tribunal and the parties shall make every effort to conduct the arbitration in an expeditious and cost-effective manner, having regard to the complexity and value of the dispute.**
2. **In order to ensure effective case management, the arbitral tribunal, after consulting the parties, may adopt such procedural measures as it considers appropriate, provided that they are not contrary to any agreement of the parties.**
3. **Upon the request of any party, the arbitral tribunal may make orders concerning the confidentiality of the arbitration proceedings or of any other matters in connection with the arbitration and may take measures for protecting trade secrets and confidential information.**
4. **In all cases, the arbitral tribunal shall act fairly and impartially and ensure that each party has a reasonable opportunity to present its case.**
5. **The parties undertake to comply with any order made by the arbitral tribunal.[1]**

[1] Article 22(4) replaces art.15(2) and art.22 (3) replaces art.20(7) of the 1998 Rules.

Introductory remarks

Article 22(1) and (2) are new provisions introduced into the Rules. Despite the success of international arbitration, there has been increasing criticism of corporate users of international commercial arbitration in general, and of ICC arbitrations in particular, as regards the duration and costs of arbitration. This was a major concern for the ICC Task Force and the Drafting Committee when revising the Rules. The third guiding principle of the Task Force required the latter "to address concerns that have been raised about the time and cost efficiency of arbitration as a means of resolving disputes and seek to introduce provisions aimed at reducing the tie and cost of arbitration proceedings".[2] As explained in the Introduction, this concern was not new, neither to the ICC Court nor the ICC Commission. The 2007 report of the ICC Commission on "Techniques for Controlling Time and Costs in Arbitration" was a clear expression of that concern.[3] **22–1**

The concerns about the delays and costs in international arbitration are not new, as can be seen from the fact that even legislators have identified the problem and sought to address it. Thus, as discussed below, as early as 1996, the English Arbitration Act included at s.33(b) explicit provisions towards increasing efficiency and speedy resolution of arbitral disputes. More recently, s.1464(3) of the French Decree of January 13, 2011 included a provision expressly requiring that "[b]oth parties and arbitrators shall act diligently and in good faith in the conduct of the proceedings".[4] Efforts to reduce time and costs of international arbitration remain a major challenge for international arbitration, whose success will in the long run be very much dependent on the arbitral community's ability to meet that challenge. **22–2**

Article 22(1): "The arbitral tribunal and the parties shall make every effort to conduct the arbitration in an expeditious and cost-effective manner, having regard to the complexity and value of the dispute."

Article 22 (1) introduces into the 2012 Rules a new principle, which touches upon the essential advantages of international commercial arbitration over litigation in the local courts: speed and costs. For a long time, these advantages were taken for granted by the international arbitration community, but over the past they have come under considerable attack. It was therefore of paramount importance that the ICC expressly state in the Rules what its users are entitled to expect in the first place: An expeditious and cost-effective conduct of the arbitral **22–3**

[2] See also Principle 7 of ICC arbitration referred to in the Introduction, at para.0–52 et seq.
[3] See Introduction, at paras 0–52 to 0–55. For an updated version of the report see: Part III, Doc. 2
[4] Translation by Paris, The Home of International Arbitration, The 13 January 2011 Decree. The New French Arbitration Law, p.33.

proceedings. Parties and arbitrators alike must have that principle in mind when engaging in arbitral proceedings.

22–4 In 2007, the ICC Arbitration Commission published a *Report on Controlling Time and Costs in Arbitration* ("Report on Controlling Time and Costs") with the goal of introducing a series of techniques to increase the time and cost efficiency in conducting arbitral proceedings. The Report was updated in 2012, after the Drafting Sub-Committee, with the help of its two in-house counsel members, reached and consulted with arbitration users around the world on their needs to improve the regulatory framework of arbitral proceedings.[5] In its current form, the Report on Controlling Time and Costs includes provisions concerning the arbitration agreement, the initiation of proceedings, establishing the framework of the arbitral proceedings, subsequent procedure for arbitration, as well as special considerations for multiparty and multicontract arbitrations, consolidations of proceedings and emergency arbitrator proceedings.

22–5 Article 22(1) lays an important foundation for other ensuing ICC provisions, such as art.22(2) (procedural measures), art.23 (Terms of Reference) and art.24 (case management conferences and procedural timetable).[6] Its adoption was prompted at the demand of corporate users, always keen on pursuing time and cost efficiency.[7]

Expeditious and cost-effective conduct of arbitration

22–6 The duty to be expeditious and cost-effective is not novel, as far as the Tribunal is concerned. As mentioned above, s.33 of the English Arbitration Act 1996 provides that the arbitral Tribunal "shall [. . .] adopt procedures suitable to the circumstances of the particular case, avoiding unnecessary delay or expense, so as to provide a fair means for the resolution of the matters falling to be determined". Under art.22(1), the duty to be expeditious and cost effective rests, however, not only on the Tribunal, but also on the parties. This is in essence what the French Arbitration Decree of 2011 foresees in s.1464(3).[8] Thus, art.22(1) of the Rules spells out a concept that arbitration legislation has already embodied.

(1) The Tribunal

22–7 Throughout the proceedings, the Tribunal shall make every effort to conduct the proceedings in an efficient manner both from a timeline perspective, but also having regard to the financial resources involved in the conduct of the proceedings. Examples in this respect span a variety of tasks throughout the proceedings, such as reducing the costs associated with travelling, organisation and conduct of hearings (like minimising the costs for hearing venue hire), as well as interpretation and translation services.

[5] See Preface to Second Edition of the *ICC Arbitration Commission Report on Techniques for Controlling Time and Costs in Arbitration*.
[6] Fry, Greenberg, Mazza, *op. cit.*, para.3–791.
[7] As noted in the Introduction, para.0–4, two corporate users were members of the Drafting Sub-Committee. See also Fry, Greenberg, Mazza, *op. cit.*, para.3–793.
[8] See para.22–2.

Non-compliance with art.22(1) could lead, in extreme cases, to replacement under art.15(2)[9] and perhaps to a challenge under art.14. In any event, if the ICC Court determines that a Tribunal has failed to meet the requirements of art.22(1) it could well affect the amount that they are paid with respect to the arbitration.[10] However, the main purpose of art.22(1) is to focus the Tribunal and the parties on the need for expeditious and cost-effective conduct of the arbitration. Article 22(1), like s.33(b) of the English Arbitration Act sets out a principle that in many cases is difficult to enforce given the Tribunal's role with respect to conduct of the proceedings. **22–8**

While the duty to make every effort to act expeditiously and cost-efficiently should be reflected in the Tribunal's procedural conduct, the latter must also be in a position to adopt such conduct. If the members of the Tribunal have overloaded or conflicting agendas, their efforts to act expeditiously may be hampered for that reason alone. The relevance of the statement of availability, which each arbitrator needs to submit together with the statement of acceptance pursuant to art.11(2) becomes clear in this context.[11] **22–9**

(2) The Parties

Article 22(1) expressly requires the parties to make every effort to conduct the arbitration in an expeditious and cost-effective manner. Arbitrators are called to provide each party an adequate opportunity to present their case. Some parties seek to take advantage of this opportunity by adopting a procedural conduct, which in some cases amounts to so-called "guerilla tactics" in international arbitration proceedings.[12] **22–10**

In case the parties employ such dilatory techniques, the sanctions may be reflected in the allocation of costs depending on "the extent to which each party has conducted the arbitration in an expeditious and cost-effective manner" pursuant to art.37(5).[13] More importantly, art.22(1) constitutes a clear basis upon which a Tribunal may constantly remind the parties that they too need to act in an expeditious and cost-efficient manner. A Tribunal can refer to art.22(1) in justifying its procedural decisions regarding requests made by the parties. If such requests are not conducive to an expeditious and cost-efficient conduct of the proceedings, and absent any over-riding reasons, due, for example, to special circumstances, a Tribunal may refuse such requests on that basis. **22–11**

(3) The complexity and value of the dispute

Article 22(1) does not define what is to be understood as conducting the arbitration "in an expeditious and cost-effective manner", and what efforts precisely are expected from the Tribunal and the parties to meet that target. Each case being different, that would have been an impossible task. Article 22(1) sets, however, two criteria that the Tribunal and the parties must keep in mind when seeking to act expeditiously and cost-efficiently: the complexity of the dispute and the value in dispute. Simply put, it **22–12**

[9] See the discussion under art.15(2) at paras 15–18 to 15–23.
[10] See the discussion under art.37(2) at paras 37–45 to 37–46.
[11] See paras 11–26 to 11–39 concerning the statement of availability.
[12] Waincymer, *op. cit.*., p.412.
[13] See the discussion under art.37(5) at para.37–106.

should cost less to conduct small disputes and/or disputes which appear to involve straightforward issues as opposed to large and complex disputes.

(4) Two limitations

22–13 The duty to act expeditiously and cost-efficiently is subject to at least two limitations under the Rules. The first is contained in art.22(2). This provision, discussed below, requires the Tribunal to follow an agreement between the parties as to the procedure. The second limitation is also contained in art.22(4) which requires the Tribunal in all cases to "act fairly and impartially and ensure that each party has a reasonable opportunity to present its case". There may be a tension between the need to act expeditiously and cost-efficiently on the one hand, and on the other hand, the need to allow each party the possibility to properly present its case.

Article 22(2): "In order to ensure effective case management, the arbitral tribunal, after consulting the parties, may adopt such procedural measures as it considers appropriate, provided that they are not contrary to any agreement of the parties."

22–14 The obligation set forth in art.22(1) is to be implemented by the Tribunal pursuant to art.22(2), i.e. by adopting procedural measures that allow to ensure effective case management. It is for the Tribunal to decide the measures it considers to be appropriate for this particular dispute. ICC arbitral proceedings leave sufficient flexibility within a general framework to adopt each case to the needs of the parties. The proceedings should be adapted to the circumstances of each case.

In consultation with the parties

22–15 At least at the beginning of the proceedings, there is little risk that the Tribunal would seek to adopt procedural measures without first having consulted the parties. It follows from art.24(1) that when establishing the Terms of Reference or as soon as possible thereafter, the Tribunal must convene a case management conference "to consult the parties on procedural measures that may be adopted pursuant to art.22(2)". During that conference, or thereafter, the Tribunal must establish the procedural timetable as per art.24(2). But even once the procedural timetable has been adopted and the procedural rules applicable to the case established (as regards, for instance, the filing of exhibits, written witness statements, the production of documents, etc.), any procedural measure the Tribunal wishes to adopt pursuant to art.22(2) would require some kind of consultation of the parties.

The parties' agreement

22–16 Even after having consulted the parties, the Tribunal is not free to adopt the procedural measures it considers to be appropriate, if it turns out that such measures would be contrary to the parties' agreement. Such agreement can be found in the arbitration clause, or may have been reached by the parties after the start of the arbitral proceedings. From the Tribunal's perspective of an expeditious and cost-efficient arbitration, the parties' agreement may not be as cost-effective or expeditious as it could be. Article 22(2) requires the Tribunal to respect such an agreement. However, due to the Tribunal's duty to "make every effort to conduct the arbitration in an expeditious and cost-effective manner", the Tribunal may raise any concerns that it has with respect to the procedure with the parties.

In any event, the measures adopted by the Tribunal span upon a variety of procedural matters, depending on the complexity of the case and the amount in dispute. The case management conference introduced by art.24 is only one of the means facilitating an effective case administration. Article 22(2) is in this sense broader, and relates to all the measures that the arbitrators, after consulting with the parties, deem fit on a case-by-case basis. **22–17**

The range of measures that arbitrators may take under art.22(2) include deciding upon extension of deadlines, summary dispositions of claims or addressing issues not dealt with in the Terms of Reference because, for instance, they were not deemed necessary at that stage, like having a document production stage or ensuring translation services during the evidentiary hearings. Other more complicated examples include suspension due to other proceedings, like parallel arbitral proceedings, pending criminal proceedings, or anti-arbitration injunctions, which we will briefly address below. **22–18**

Suspension due to other proceedings

One issue with ICC proceedings is the pendency of other relevant proceedings. For example, in some cases, resolution of a dispute (or assessment of damages) may depend on the validity of a patent and there may be proceedings pending with respect to the validity of a patent. In other instances, there may be state proceedings pending as to the validity of a tax that may affect the calculation of damages, or even a criminal proceeding that may have an impact on the resolution of the dispute that it is to be adjudicated. Last, but not less important, another reason why arbitrators decide to stay a set of proceedings while others are pending is to avoid conflicting results, contradictory Awards, and ultimately a waste of financial resources and the threat of future connected litigation.[14] **22–19**

In each case, the Tribunal's approach must take into account any agreement between the parties. In the absence of such an agreement, the Tribunal has to weigh the various factors involved before it decides whether it is appropriate to suspend the procedure. It will normally do so by way of a Procedural Order, which it may revisit at any time, depending on any new developments. Since the situations are quite different, set out below is a discussion of parallel proceedings in general, then a discussion of pending criminal actions and finally a discussion of anti-arbitration injunctions. **22–20**

[14] In the ICC Case No.12510, the Arbitral Tribunal dismissed a request for consolidation and instead ordered a stay of the proceedings when the same commercial transaction between the same parties was being discussed by two ICC Tribunals, and many facts were very similar. The Tribunal's decision was prompted by the concern of avoiding potentially conflicting results, as follows: "This need to avoid possible inconsistencies and to try to prevent future problems is **paramount to this Tribunal**, which distinctively understands that its mission is, to the fullest extent possible, to render rulings that decide the disputes submitted by the Parties, without giving room for further litigation thereof" (emphasis in original). ICC ICArbBull., 2010 Suppl. "Decisions on ICC Arbitration Procedure", pp.59, 61.

Parallel proceedings generally

22–21 If the other proceedings concern arguably the same dispute, involving moreover the same parties, there may or may not be a serious issue of whether the arbitral proceedings should be stayed. There is no uniform practice either in ICC arbitration or before national courts as to how to deal with situations where two sets of legal proceedings are pending.

22–22 Article II(3) of the New York Convention sets out the basic principle:

> "The court of a Contracting State, when seized of an action in a matter in respect of which the parties have made an agreement within the meaning of this article, shall, at the request of one of the parties, refer the parties to arbitration, unless it finds that the said agreement is null and void, inoperative or incapable of being performed."

22–23 Therefore, if national court proceedings are brought in breach of an arbitration agreement there is no reason to stay the arbitral proceedings except as required under national law.

22–24 In many instances, however, the issue is not as clear-cut as the two proceedings will relate to somewhat different issues or involve different parties. As a result, the Tribunal may have to deal with a delimitation of the arbitration agreement in deciding whether and how to proceed. In such cases, the usual approach is for a Tribunal to weigh the various factors referred to below to decide whether or not the arbitral proceedings should be stayed.[15] In weighing the factors, the Tribunal will have to abide by mandatory principles applicable to arbitration at the place of arbitration.

22–25 The issue of pending proceedings was dealt with by the Swiss courts and by Swiss legislation as a result of the *Fomento* case. In that case, state proceedings were brought in Panama. The Claimant subsequently brought arbitration proceedings, but the Respondent maintained before the Panamanian courts that the Claimant had waived its right to arbitration. The Swiss Federal Tribunal held that the Tribunal, sitting in Geneva, should have stayed the proceedings pending a final decision by the Panamanian Supreme Court, as to whether the Claimant had waived its right to arbitration. As a result thereof, the Award on jurisdiction of the Tribunal was set aside by the Swiss Supreme Court.[16]

22–26 The *Fomento* case was heavily criticised since it opened the possibility for a party to circumvent the arbitral proceedings by bringing an action before a foreign court prior the initiation of an arbitration proceedings. The Swiss legislator saw

[15] Seraglini, "Brèves remarques sur les Recommandations de l'Association du droit international sur la litispendance et l'autorité de la chose jugée en arbitrage" (2006) Rev Arb No.4, p.909, at p.918; SIAR 2007:1 p.239; see also ILA website: *http://www.ila.hq.org* [accessed November 19, 2013].

[16] Swiss Federal Tribunal, May 14, 2001, *Fomento de Construcciones v Contratas SA v Colon Container Terminal SA*, ATF 127 III 279; (2004) YBCA Vol.XXIX p.809; Geisinger and Lévy, "*Lis Alibi Pendens* in International Commercial Arbitration" (2003) ICC ICArb Bull, Special Supplement, p.53; Oetiker, "The Principle of Lis Pendens in International Arbitration: The Swiss Decision in Fomento v Colon" (2002) Arb Int Vol.18 No.2, p.137; see also for a discussion of the *Fomento* case, Scherer, "Editors Note: When Should an Arbitral Tribunal Sitting in Switzerland Confronted with Parallel Litigation Abroad Stay the Arbitration?" (2001) ASA Bull Vol.19 No.3, p.451; Poudret, "Le tribunal fédéral suisse opte pour le régime de la *litispendence* entre le juge et l'arbitre: Note–Tribunal fédéral suisse, 14 mai 2001" (2001) Rev Arb No.4, p.835.

the risk that the Swiss Supreme Court's jurisprudence might endanger the attraction of Switzerland as a major place of arbitration, and decided promptly to amend the arbitration law. Section 1bis was added to art.186 of the Swiss PILA, which reads as follows: "1bis It [the arbitral Tribunal] shall decide on its jurisdiction notwithstanding an action on the same matter between the same parties already pending before a State Court or another arbitral tribunal, unless there are serious reasons to stay the proceedings".[17] The new amendment entered into effect on March 1, 2007.

In ICC case No.10947,[18] the issue was whether the Tribunal should stay the arbitral proceedings pending a court decision in Ecuador as to the nullity of the provision of the arbitration clause in the contract. The Tribunal accepted that the Ecuadorian proceedings were similar but not identical as they involved different parties in interest and decided that the Tribunal had been seized of the matter first. Therefore, the Tribunal held it was not required to stay the proceedings based on art.9 of the Swiss PILA.[19] The Tribunal also decided that it should not grant a stay as a matter of discretion and referred in particular to: **22–27**

- its finding that the Ecuadorian proceedings had not been filed as a delaying tactic;
- its finding that the issues were similar and that the validity of the arbitration clause arose in both of them;
- the effect of the Ecuadorian proceedings in resolving definitively the jurisdiction issue;
- the Tribunal's decision that the arbitration clause was valid under Ecuadorian law and that although "the Ecuadorian Courts are well placed to know and correctly apply Ecuadorian law [. . .]. However, to grant a stay now until the final resolution of the Nullity Proceeding simply for this reason [. . .] would be to reduce international arbitration to second rank status [. . .]. Moreover, it would be to disregard the

[17] More generally, see Temboury Redondo, "Preliminary Judgments, *Lis Pendens* and *Res Iudicata* in Arbitration Proceedings" *Liber Amicorum Bernardo Cremades* (2010), p.1131; "ILA Recommendations on *Lis Pendens* and *Res Judicata* and Arbitration" (2009) Arb. Int'l No. 1, 83; Arroyo, "*Lis Pendens* in International Arbitration–The Newly Adopted Swiss Approach", SIAR 2007:1 p.19; Poudret "Exception d'arbitrage et litispendance en droit suisse–Comment départager le juge et l'arbitre?" (2007) ASA Bull Vol.25 No.2, p.230; Tschanz, "Arbitrators May Decide Jurisdictional Issues Pending before Foreign Court", Arbitration–Switzerland, 17 May 2007, *http://www.internationallawoffice.com*; Ulmer, "Swiss Arbitration Update: First Amendments Of International Arbitration Law" (2006) Mealey's IAR Vol.21 No.12, p.35; Gaillard, "Switzerland Says Lis Pendens Not Applicable to Arbitration", New *York Law Journal*, 7 August 2006 and "La reconnaissance, en droit suisse, de la seconde moitié du principe d'effet négatif de la compétence-compétence" in *Liber Amicorum Robert Briner, op. cit.*, p.311. See also Söderlund, "Lis Pendens, Res Judicata and the Issues of Parallel Judicial Proceedings" (2005) J Int'l Arb Vol.22 No.4, p.301

[18] ICC case No.10947 (2002) (Interim Award), (2004) ASA Bull Vol.22 No.2 p.308.

[19] Article 9(1) of the Swiss PILA provides: "when an action having the same object is already pending between the same parties abroad, the Swiss Court shall stay the proceedings if it can be anticipated that the foreign Court will issue, within an appropriate time frame, a decision which may be recognised in Switzerland". This Award was issued prior to the amendment adding art.186(1)bis of the Swiss PILA.

intention of the parties as set out in article 17.2 of the Lease, namely that any dispute between them should be settled by arbitration and, as such, it would run contrary to the principle of pacta sunt servanda. We do not consider that this principle should be disregarded lightly."

- that "to grant a stay in these circumstances therefore entails acknowledging that we may well be causing an unnecessary and considerable delay to the final resolution of the substantive dispute between the parties. We consider that for us actively to cause such a delay would run contrary to the principle that 'justice delayed is justice denied' and also our (implicit) obligation to resolve the dispute before us with reasonable expedition."
- "by reason of Article 35 of the ICC Rules[20], we are under a duty to make every effort to ensure that our Award is enforceable at law [. . .], but that in the circumstances, the collateral challenge possibility should not be given great weight."

22–28 The Award in the above case illustrates the balancing of interests and provisions of law and the Rules to justify a stay in the proceedings. Of particular interest is the Tribunal's view that an international arbitration Tribunal should not have secondary status; that the Tribunal is in a position to interpret local law, even if the national court proceedings relate to that law; and the fact that the parties had agreed upon international arbitration to resolve disputes. The Tribunal also underlined that the Tribunal had been seized of the proceedings prior to the local court.[21]

22–29 The issue of a suspension of proceedings arises with respect to state court and parallel arbitration proceedings. In *Elektrim SA v Vivendi Universal SA*,[22] a dispute had arisen between the parties that had been the subject of LCIA arbitration proceedings. A partial Award upholding the validity of the relevant agreement was issued in the LCIA proceedings. The parties entered into settlement negotiations and the settlement agreement provided for ICC arbitration in Geneva. Vivendi Universal SA filed a Request for Arbitration under the settlement agreement for a declaration that the settlement agreement was binding. The LCIA Tribunal refused to stay the LCIA proceedings on four occasions and, as discussed below, the High Court refused to order a stay basically leaving the LCIA Tribunal to decide whether or not a stay was warranted stating in particular that:

> "[71] It is clear, therefore, that the Act contemplates that the tribunal will consider and decide such matters as whether there should be an adjournment or a stay of the arbitral proceedings. That is consistent with the general approach of the 1996 Act, which is to give as much power as possible to the parties and the arbitrators and to reduce the role

[20] Now replaced by art.41 of the 2012 Rules.

[21] To the same effect as regards *lis pendens*, see the decision of Swiss Supreme Court of August 7, 2001, *Nortrop Speditions–und Schifffahrtsgesellschaft mbH v TransRail AG* (2002) ASA Bull Vol.20 No.2 p.293.

[22] *Elektrim SA v Vivendi Universal* SA *(No.2)* [2007] EWHC 571 (Comm).

of the courts to that of a supporter of the arbitration process up to an Award being made."

On a more general level, the International Law Association adopted recommendations set out in Pt III with respect to lis pendens. Those recommendations set out a series of principles that highlight the issues that a Tribunal should consider in deciding whether or not to stay proceedings when there are other proceedings where the parties are the same and the issues are the same or substantially the same. In summary the Recommendations are: 22–30

(1) Where the court proceedings are pending before the courts of the place of arbitration, the Tribunal should take into account the law of that jurisdiction. (para.3)

(2) Where the court proceedings are pending before a court of a jurisdiction other than the place of arbitration, the Tribunal should proceed in the absence of a waiver. (para.4)

(3) Where the parallel proceedings are arbitration proceedings that have already been commenced, subject to various provisos, the Tribunal should decline jurisdiction at least temporarily. (para.5)

(4) A Tribunal may grant a request for a stay basically where it is not prohibited from doing so; where it is satisfied that the outcome of the parallel proceedings is material to the outcome of the proceedings; and where there would be no material prejudice to the party opposing a stay.

Pending criminal proceedings

In most jurisdictions,[23] it is generally admitted that the Tribunal has no obligation to stay the arbitration proceedings pending the outcome of the criminal proceedings which might be relevant for the arbitration.[24] The Tribunal has a 22–31

[23] For a general overview, see Poudret & Besson, *op. cit.*, para.583, p.502.

[24] See the Resolution No.22 of the International Law Association (ILA) adopted in 1996, *Report of 67th Conference* (1996) which considered that state court proceedings, either civil or criminal related to an arbitration proceedings, do not warrant a suspension of the arbitration proceedings, (1996) Rev Arb No.3 p.563, note Gaillard. In France, see for example Paris, June 20, 2002, *Odartech v W Management* in *Les Cahiers de l'Arbitrage–Volume II, op. cit.*, p.357; (2002) Rev Arb No.4 p.973, note Racine: "Although article 4 of the Criminal Procedure Code, which orders the civil judge to stay proceedings when the civil action and the public prosecution, arising from the same facts, are exercised separately or when the criminal decision is likely to influence the civil one, does not apply to the arbitrator when determining an international dispute because of the autonomy of arbitral procedure which has its own rules, nothing however forbids the arbitral tribunal from deciding that a criminal procedure is of such nature as to influence the outcome of the arbitration in question and from ordering for this reason a stay of the proceedings, the appreciation of which is part of his prerogatives."; Cass Civ 1e June 4, 2008, (2008) Rev Arb No.2 p.346, Cass Civ 1e, October 25, 2005, *Société Omenex v M Hugon* (2006) Rev Arb No.1 p.103, note Racine confirming Paris, January 17, 2002, (2002) Rev Arb No.2 p.401, note Racine and (2006) JDI No.3 p.996, note Train; Paris, February 23, 1996, December 14, 1999, (2000) Rev Arb No.3 p.471, note Racine; Cass Civ 1e, May 6, 2003, Paris, February 13, 2003 and Paris, September 10, 2003, (2004) Rev Arb No.2 p.311, note Racine; ICC case No.7986 (1999)(Award), (2002) JDI No.4 p.1071, note Derains. In Switzerland, see ATF 119 (1993) II 386; (1994) ASA Bull p.248 (the principle of "le criminel tient le civil en l'état" is not a mandatory provision, thus leaving a power appreciation to the arbitrators).

power of appreciation[25] which it exercises taking into consideration its duty to act expeditiously vis-à-vis the parties, i.e. to resolve the dispute which has been submitted to it pursuant to the parties' arbitration agreement.[26]

22–32 In deciding whether to suspend arbitral proceedings due to pending criminal proceedings, a Tribunal should consider various factors in addition to its obligation to act expeditiously and in a cost-effective manner as between the parties, and as required by art.22(1). One of those factors is the potential that the Award that it may render may turn out to be inconsistent with the findings in the criminal case and raise issues of international public policy. In such a case, there may be serious issues relating to the enforceability of an Award which is inconsistent with the criminal judgment. Another issue, is whether the Tribunal has access to the evidence that is relevant to the determination of factual issues that are also before the criminal court.[27] If the Tribunal's access to evidence is limited, it may militate for awaiting a decision in the criminal proceedings. However, despite these factors, except in cases where the issues in the criminal proceedings are central to the arbitration, there is a strong tendency for Tribunals to proceed with the arbitration.

Anti-arbitration injunctions

22–33 Another issue relates to anti-arbitration or anti-suit injunctions issued by national courts; despite the extensive commentary on this issue, there have been further developments since the second edition of this book.[28] Anti-arbitration

The same rule applies in the United States. See "Using equitable powers to coordinate parallel civil and criminal actions" (1985) 98 Harvard Law Review 1023, March 1985. See also Fouchard, Gaillard & Goldman, *op. cit.*, para.1660, at p.960; Sfeir-Slim, "L'application de la règle 'le criminel tient le civil en l'état' en matière d'arbitrage" in *Mélanges en hommage à Méliné Topakian, Le Droit en Mouvement* (Bruylant, Presse de l'Université Saint Joseph, 2005), p.255. See also para.6–129.

[25] See ICC case No.9800 (2000) (Award) (absence of obligation for the Tribunal to suspend the arbitration proceedings when there is a parallel state court proceedings), (2004) JDI No.4 p.1284, note Derains; see also ICC case No.6610 (1991) (Award), *Collection of ICC Arbitral Awards 1991–1995, Volume III, op. cit.*, p.280 (power of appreciation of the Tribunal to suspend the arbitration proceedings depending on the circumstances of the case).

[26] See ICC case No.9800 (2000), *op. cit.*, at p.1291; See also Mourre, "Arbitration and Criminal Law: Reflections on the Duties of the Arbitrator", *op. cit.*, at p.114; Levy and Schlaepfer, "La suspension d'instance dans l'arbitrage international" in *Les Cahiers de l'Arbitrage–Volume I, op. cit.*, p.132. See Ninth Circuit US Court of Appeals, *Dependable Highway Express Inc v Navigators Ins Co*, No.05–75033 (August 22, 2007), (2007) Mealey's IAR Vol.22 No.9 p.22 (a federal court's indefinite stay of an American company's action pending arbitration in England is an abuse of discretion).

[27] The Paris Court of Appeal suspended proceedings with respect to annulment of an Award stating "the facts referred to in the criminal complaint and in the annulment proceedings are the same and the [criminal] decision will therefore necessarily have an impact on the annulment proceedings; as a result it is appropriate to suspend the decision pending a decision on the [criminal] complaint". Paris, 1re Ch. April 20, 2004 *Société Ivoir Café v Banque Africaine de Développement.*

[28] See Noussia, "Anti-suit Injunctions and Arbitration Proceedings: What Does the Future Hold?" (2009) J. of Int'l Arb., p. 311; Phull, "U.S. Anti-suit Injunctions in Support of International Arbitration: Five Questions American Courts Ask" (2011) J. of Int'l Arb., p. 21; Gaillard, *Anti-Suit Injunctions in International Arbitration* (IAI series No.2, 2005), "Il est interdit d'interdire: réflexion sur l'utilisation des anti-suit injunctions dans l'arbitrage commercial international" (2004) Rev Arb No.1, p.47, "Anti-suit injunctions et reconnaissance des sentences annulées au siège: une évolution remarquable de la jurisprudence américaine" (2003) JDI, p.1105; Tan, "Enforcing Arbitration Agreements With Anti-suit Injunctions" (2006) Mealey's IAR Vol.21 No.7, p.39; Bachand, "Must An ICC Tribunal Comply with an Anti-Suit Injunction Issued by the Courts of the Seats of Arbitration–Comment on the Salini Costruttori Spa v Ethiopia" (2005) Mealey's IAR Vol.20 No.3,

injunctions issued against parties may raise issues as to due process as the parties may be concerned about breaching a court order by participating in the arbitral proceedings.

A complex issue arises with respect to state entities and the intervention of state courts. Again the causes of delay can be diverse. If the place of arbitration is in a neutral country, then the courts of the place of arbitration will be expected to be neutral. However, if the place of arbitration is in the Respondent's country, where there are doubts as to the independence or integrity of the judiciary, then the intervention of the national courts may become a serious threat to a pending arbitration. **22–34**

In a 2001 ICC case, one of the parties was a state entity from a country that is not a signatory to the New York Convention.[29] The place of arbitration was in that country and its courts issued an order that the proceedings should not proceed. The basis was that the arbitrators had been challenged for deciding to hold evidentiary hearings at a place other than the capital of the state. The Tribunal pointed out that the Terms of Reference had expressly provided that hearings could be held other than at the place of arbitration; that the challenge had been rejected by the ICC Court; that the arbitration involved a state entity and that there was a body of law precluding states from depriving arbitration clauses of their effect. The Tribunal decided to continue the proceedings stating: **22–35**

> "177. The Arbitral Tribunal accords great respect to the courts of State X, both in their own right and as the courts of the seat. Nevertheless, in this case, we are of the view that it would be improper, in light of our primary duty to the parties, to observe the injunctions issued by those courts, which have already significantly delayed these proceedings, given that they have the effect of frustrating the parties' agreement to submit disputes to international arbitration.
>
> 178. These arbitral proceedings will not be suspended, notwithstanding the injunctions issued by the Supreme Court and the First Instance Court of State X. Faced with the present situation, the Arbitral Tribunal will continue to prosecute these arbitral proceedings in accordance with its duty to the parties, in a manner consistent with their arbitration agreement."[30]

The Tribunal in this instance sought to avoid delay in the proceedings, while recognising the role of the courts of the place of arbitration. The Tribunal's approach was somewhat different from that in the *Karaha Bodas* case,[31] as in this **22–36**

p.47; Smith and Freeman, "Anti-Suit Injunctions in Europe: Another Advantage of Arbitration" (2005) Mealey's IAR Vol.20 No.3, p.45; Fellas, "Anti-Suit Injunctions in Aid of Arbitration" (2005) Mealey's IAR Vol.20 No.4, p.25. On the willingness of the US courts to issue injunctions, especially when there are some evidence suggesting that a foreign proceedings is being used by one of the parties to alter the parties' agreement to submit their dispute to arbitration, see for example *Storm LLC v Telenor Mobile Communication AS*, No.06 Civ 13157, 2006 WL 3735657 (SDNY December 15, 2006) and *Ibeto Petrochemical Industries Ltd v M/T Beffen*, No.05–6610 CV, 2007 WL 106165 (2nd Cir January 17, 2007).

[29] See ICC case No.10623 (2001), para.18–38 n.27.

[30] *Idem.* at p.99.

[31] *Karaha Bodas Co LLC v Pertamina and PT. PLN (Persero)*, 264 F Supp 2d 470 (2002), 2004 US App. Lexis 5445 (5th Cir 2004) Int'l Arb. Rep. March 2001, at C-2 et seq.

case the Tribunal did not attribute the court's actions to those of the State. It is not clear that the Tribunal would have taken that decision if the Terms of Reference had not expressly provided for hearings outside of State X.

22–37 In the *Elektrim* case discussed above, the English High Court refused to grant an anti-arbitration injunction with respect to the LCIA arbitration pending in London due to the parallel ICC arbitration in Geneva. Although, as noted above, it held that the courts should defer to the LCIA arbitral Tribunal as to the issue of the suspension of proceedings, the court also noted that the issues were different in the two arbitrations.[32]

22–38 In *Albon v Naza Motor Trading Sdn BHD*, the English Court of Appeal upheld an anti-arbitration injunction with respect to an arbitration in Malaysia governed by Malaysian law. The injunction was issued at the request of the party who maintained that the agreement in which the arbitration clause was found was a forgery and that the real agreement between the parties had been an oral agreement in England. In this case, the party bringing the English injunctive proceedings did so to rely on them as a valid reason for not attending the arbitration proceedings, although it is not clear whether the English court order would be enforceable in Malaysia, which was the place of arbitration.[33]

22–39 In the *West Tankers* case, the European Court of Justice clarified the intra-European Union position as regards anti-suit injunctions in favour of arbitration in light of Council Regulation 44/2001.[34] Despite the express exclusion of arbitration from the Regulation, the ECJ ruled that it is inconsistent with 44/2001 for an EU Member State Court to issue an anti-suit injunction forbidding a lawsuit to proceed in another Member State, even if the anti-suit injunction is issued in support of an arbitration agreement. The Court found that 44/2001 applied because the subject matter of the

[32] See the *Elektrim SA* case cited at para.22–29 n.22. However, since the Geneva arbitration in Elektrim dealt with the issue of whether the claims subject to the LCIA arbitration had been settled, the two proceedings were overlapping.

[33] *Albon (t/a NA Carriage Co) v Naza Motor Trading SDN BHD* [2007] EWCA Civ 1124 (November 6, 2007). In that case, the Court commented as follows on the relationship with the arbitration proceedings:

"16.That leaves for consideration the argument relating to the autonomy of the arbitration tribunal. It is said that the caution exercised by the court relating to anti-suit injunctions should be increased or even re-doubled in the case of an anti-arbitration injunction. It is further said that the judge is effectively case managing the arbitration and that it should be for the arbitrators, not the English Court, to decide whether the arbitration should proceed pending resolution of the genuineness of the JVA. 17. In the ordinary case there would be much to be said for this argument. But this is not an ordinary case because of the features set out in para.13 above. It is properly arguable that the agreement to arbitrate has been forged in order to defeat proceedings properly brought in England and, in addition to this, it is at present agreed that the English Court will determine that question. The autonomy of the arbitrators has thus already been undermined because they are, in any event, precluded for the present from determining that question. In these circumstances it is not right to say that the judge is attempting to case-manage the arbitration. It would be more accurate to say that he is case-managing the application before him which will determine in England the question whether the JVA is authentic or not."

[34] Case C-185/07 *Allianz SpA v West Tankers Inc (The Front Comor)*, February 10, 2009 (ECJ). See also Carducci, "Arbitration, Anti-suit Injunctions and Lis Pendens under the European Jurisdiction Regulation and the New York Convention", (2011) Arb. Int'l No. 2, p. 171; Pombo, "Arbitration and Anti Suit Injunctions in the Case Law of the European Court of Justice", *Liber Amicorum Bernardo Cremades* (2010), p. 975; Grierson, "Comment on *West Tankers Inc. v. RAS Riunione Adriatica di Sicurta S.p.A. (The Front Comor)*" (2009) J Int'l Arb, No. 6, p.891; Kessedjian, "Le Règlement 44/2001 et l'arbitrage" (2009) Rev. Arb. No. 4, p. 699.

dispute, i.e. the nature of the rights to be protected between the parties, fell within the scope of the Regulation (in the instant case, the applicability of an arbitration clause). The Court then concluded that using an anti-suit injunction to prevent a court of a Member State from ruling amounts to stripping that court of the power to rule on its own jurisdiction under the Regulation. This in turn is contrary to the mutual trust between legal systems and judicial institutions of the Union. Thus, anti-arbitration injunctions applicable to courts in the EU are incompatible with Regulation 44/2001.[35]

The *West Tankers* case has generated renewed interest in anti-suit injunctions issued by arbitrators.[36] Those that argue that Tribunals inherently have such power base their argument on the principle of *Kompetenz-Kompetenz*.[37] While certain Tribunals, such as ICSID[38] and the Iran-United States Claims Tribunal,[39] have had experience with anti-suit orders issued by arbitrators, the ICC also has had some history with this particular situation.[40] However, other commentators have opposed the idea anti-suit injunctions issued by arbitrators as a violation of the *Kompetenz-Kompetenz* of other Tribunals and Courts as well as of international comity.[41] **22–40**

In the case of *Sulamerica*,[42] the English Court of Appeal upheld a lower court decision continuing an injunction against Brazilian parties against bringing proceedings in Brazil with respect to an insurance policy governed by Brazilian law but providing for arbitration in London. The Brazilian parties maintained that, under Brazilian law, which was the express governing law for the policy, the arbitration clause was invalid. The Court of Appeal held that the arbitration clause was governed by English law as the law of the place of arbitration. **22–41**

The issue of injunctive relief was recently examined in *U&M Mining Zambia Ltd v Konkola Copper Mines Plc*[43] with respect to a dispute concerning the operation of a mine located in Zambia, between Zambian parties, with an LCIA arbitration agreement, with London as place of arbitration. In this case, Konkola Copper **22–42**

[35] See Lew *et al., Arbitration in England*, paras 1–43 et seq. regarding *Post West Tankers* anti-suit injunction preventing litigation outside the EU.

[36] See Moloo, "Arbitrators Granting Anti-suit Orders: When Should They and on What Authority?" (2009) J. of Int'l Arb., p. 675.

[37] Gaillard, "Introduction," Anti-Suit Injunctions in International Arbitration, (2005) IAI Series on Int'l Arb. No.2, p. .

[38] See *SGS Société Générale de Surveillance SA v Islamic Republic of Pakistan*, ICSID Case No. ARB/01/13, Procedural Order No.2, October 16, 2002, ICSID Rev. 305 (2002) (relying on ICSID's art.26 to grant an anti-suit order, confirming that, unless parties have otherwise stated, they have a right to have their disputes resolved by arbitration to the exclusion of any other remedy).

[39] See *E-Systems v.Islamic Republic of Iran*, Interim Award No. ITM 13–388–FT, February 4, 1983, (1984) YBCA, p.216.

[40] See ICC Case No.8307, Interim Award, (May 14, 2001) as cited in Moloo, above n.36 ("[T]he agreement to arbitrate implies that the parties have renounced to submit to judicial courts the disputes envisaged by the arbitral clause. If a party despite this commence[s] a judicial action when an arbitration is pending, it not only violates the rule according to which a dispute between the same parties over the same subject can be decided by one judge only, but also the binding arbitration clause."); ICC Award No. 3896 (December 23, 1982) JDI, 914 (1983) (issuing anti-suit injunction based on the fact that going before the courts risks aggravating the dispute and that it is against the spirit of good will that parties have demonstrated in signing the Terms of Reference).

[41] See Lévy, "Anti-Suit Injunctions Issued by Arbitrators", in Gaillard, *op. cit.*; Karrer, "Anti-Arbitration Injunctions: Theory and Practice," (2007) *International Arbitration 2006: Back to Basics*, p. 228.

[42] *Sulamerica CIA Nacional de Seguros SA v Enesa Engenharia SA* [2012] EWCA Civ 638.

[43] [2013] EWHC 260 (Comm).

Mines Pls (KCM) sought and obtained an injunction from the Zambian courts, pending arbitration proceedings. U&M obtained an anti-suit injunction before the English High Court against to restrain KCM from taking steps in the proceedings started in Zambia. The High Court lifted the Engish injunction stating that:

> "63. […] the power to grant interim relief is not confined to the court of the seat. […] a party may exceptionally be entitled to seek interim relief in some court other than that of the seat, if for practical reasons the application can only sensibly be made there, provided that the proceedings are not a disguised attempt to outflank the arbitration agreement. […]
>
> 71. […] This dispute arises between two Zambian companies. It concerns the operation of a copper mine in Zambia. Pending the appointment of the arbitrators, issues arise as to the possession of the mine, and the possession of the equipment within the guarantees. The matter is of national as well as local importance since, as I have been told, the mine contributes a substantial proportion of Zambia's total GDP. So far as judicial assistance by way of interim measures pending the appointment of the arbitrators is required, in my view the natural forum for such proceedings is in Zambia, not in England."

22–43 The issues of jurisdiction and of injunction not to bring or carry on proceedings in a forum outside the Brussels/Lugano regime,[44] whether or not the arbitration has started were recently addressed by the English Supreme Court. In *Ust -Kamenogorsk Hydropower Plant JSC v AES Ust-Kamenogorsk Hydropower Plant LLP*,[45] Ust – Kamenogorsk Hydropower Plant JSC ("JSC") brought proceedings against AES Ust-Kamenogorsk Hydropower Plant LLP ("AESUK") before the Kazakhstan courts which declared the ICC arbitration agreement as null and void and allowed matters to proceed. AESUK then brought proceedings in England (English law being the law of the arbitration) to ask for an anti-suit injunction although no arbitration was currently taking place, and itself having no intention to start proceedings. The UK Supreme Court decided that:

> "48. […]Where an injunction is sought to restrain foreign proceedings in breach of an arbitration agreement – whether on an interim or a final basis and whether at a time when arbitral proceedings are or are not on foot or proposed - the source of the power to grant such an injunction is to be found not in section 44 of the 1996 Act, but in section 37 of the 1981 Act. Such an injunction is not "for the purposes of and in relation to arbitral proceedings", but for the purposes of and in relation to the negative promise contained in the arbitration agreement not to bring foreign proceedings, which applies and is enforceable regardless of whether or not arbitral proceedings are on foot or proposed. […]

[44] See the discussion under Art.6 starting at para.6.126.

[45] Ust -Kamenogorsk Hydropower Plant JSC v AES Ust-Kamenogorsk Hydropower Plant LLP [2013] UKSC 35 (12 June 2013)

> 60. The power to stay domestic legal proceedings under section 9 and the power to determine that foreign proceedings are in breach of an arbitration agreement and to injunct their commencement or continuation are in truth opposite and complementary sides of a coin. Subject to the recent European inroad, that remains the position. The general power provided by section 37 of the 1981 Act must be exercised sensitively and, in particular, with due regard for the scheme and terms of the 1996 Act when any arbitration is on foot or proposed. It is also open to a court under section 37, if it thinks fit, to grant any injunction on an interim basis, pending the outcome of current or proposed arbitration proceedings, rather than a final basis. [...]
>
> 61. In some cases where foreign proceedings are brought in breach of an arbitration clause or exclusive choice of court agreement, the appropriate course will be to leave it to the foreign court to recognise and enforce the parties' agreement on forum. But in the present case the foreign court has refused to do so, and done this on a basis which the English courts are not bound to recognise and on grounds which are unsustainable under English law which is accepted to govern the arbitration agreement. In these circumstances, there was every reason for the English courts to intervene to protect the prima facie right of AESUK to enforce the negative aspect of its arbitration agreement with JSC."

Reconciling the various authorities (and the commentaries) on anti-arbitration injunctions is a difficult if not impossible task. For a Tribunal, the basic point is that there is a trend to permit the Tribunal to conduct its own case management of an arbitration and the Tribunal has an overriding obligation to ensure that an agreement to arbitrate is not nullified. For counsel when faced with a Tribunal that does not in its view take into account parallel court or arbitral proceedings, the avenues open to prevent the continuation of the proceedings will depend very much on the facts and state courts involved. **22–44**

Article 22(3): "Upon the request of any party, the arbitral tribunal may make orders concerning the confidentiality of the arbitration proceedings or of any other matters in connection with the arbitration and may take measures for protecting trade secrets and confidential information."

Confidentiality generally

The Rules do not contain a provision requiring an ICC arbitration, or the information shared during the course of the proceedings or the documents produced in connection with it, to be treated as confidential. Article 22(3) is based on art.20(7) of the 1998 ICC Rules but has been broadened to provide for confidentiality orders "in connection with the arbitration". Therefore, the Tribunal now has clear authority to issue orders relating to all matters not only relating to trade secrets and underlying confidential information but relating to the arbitration in and of itself. **22–45**

Article 22(3) deals with confidentiality orders issued by the Tribunal. Issues of confidentiality as regards the ICC Court and the Secretariat are dealt with and **22–46** discussed pursuant to Art. 1. In addition, art. 26(3) deals with the privacy of the hearings themselves. Article 22(3) does not deal with obligations of confidentiality of the arbitrators themselves. However, due to their quasi judicial role, arbitrators are widely viewed as subject to an obligation of confidentiality.

22–47 As regards the parties and the other participants in an arbitration (such as experts and counsel), the confidentiality will depend on the terms of the arbitration agreement (and underlying contract) itself, the rules of law governing the arbitration, the law of the place of arbitration as well as the measures taken by the Tribunal under Art.22(3). The lack of a confidentiality provision in the ICC Rules may appear surprising, as typically parties to an arbitration expect confidentiality, which is usually cited as one of the advantages of arbitration over litigation in the courts. However, in revising the ICC Rules both in 1998 and 2012, it was decided that it was not necessary or desirable to include a confidentiality provision due to the wide variance in national law and the practical difficulties with such a provision.

Confidentiality under applicable law

22–48 If the underlying contract contains a confidentiality provision, then a party can rely on that provision in the arbitration proceedings. In many instances, the party will seek confirmation from the other side that thenproceedings are to be treated as confidential. If there is agreement on the issue, then a confidentiality provision may be inserted in the Terms of Reference. There may be an argument that, under either the rules of law governing the arbitration agreement or under the laws of the place of arbitration, the arbitration should be treated as confidential.

Applicable laws

22–49 There may be an argument that, under either the rules of law governing the arbitration agreement and/or under the laws of the place of arbitration, the arbitration should be treated as confidential. However, relatively few national laws address the issue.

22–50 Under French law, the Decree of January 13, 2011 expressly provides that, subject to legal requirements and unless otherwise agreed by the parties, arbitral proceedings shall be confidential in domestic arbitrations.[46] This provision was not, however, declared applicable to international arbitrations,[47] unless the parties agree otherwise.[48] Article 1479 of the French CPC stipulates that the deliberations of arbitrators are confidential. This provision applies to both domestic and international arbitrations. For more than two decades, French courts had favoured

[46] The confidentiality principle under art.1464(4)French CPC is subject to certain exceptions deriving from other areas of law, such as fiscal and banking law obligations of disclosure. Moreover, such obligation is limited by a party's right to assert a legal right in annulment procedures before courts. See Derains, "Les nouveaux principles de procédure: confidentialité, célérité, loyauté" in T. Clay (ed.) *Le nouveau droit français de l'arbitrage* (Lextenso 2011), pp.91, 102.

[47] See art.1506 No.3 of French CPC. Derains,, "Les nouveaux principes de procédure: confidentialité, célérité, loyauté", *op cit.*, p.101, explaining that confidentiality is far from being a settled matter in international arbitration, and that in fact, other concerns like transparency and the public's right to be informed seem to gain more ground in the field.

[48] Derains, "Les nouveaux principes de procédure: confidentialité, célérité, loyauté", *op.cit.*, p.100.

a general principle of confidentiality in arbitration, finding in the *Aïta*[49] and *Bleustein* cases that arbitral proceedings are confidential. The Paris Commercial Court ("*Tribunal de Commerce*") held for example in *Bleustein* that "[w]hereas arbitration is a private proceeding of a confidential nature and that arbitration having been accepted by the parties, they must avoid any publicity relating to the dispute between them and the possible results".[50]

In a 2004 case, the Paris Court of Appeal, although admitting this principle, seemed to reduce the scope of the duty of confidentiality by requiring in the *Nafimco* case that the alleged breach of confidentiality be proved by the party requesting the payment of damages in this respect. The production of a party's financial books does not necessarily open the right to obtain the payment of damages for a party in absence of such a proof. **22–51**

Under Swiss law, there is an implied duty of confidentiality. In a recent case, the Swiss Federal Supreme Court admitted such a need for discretion in arbitration if the parties demonstrate that their interest outweighs the public interests to know how justice is administered and rendered. In other words, the Supreme Court is disposed to grant applications for the removal of the names of the parties, including the removal of certain portions of its judgments which relate to confidential information, such as the description of know-how.[51] **22–52**

Under US law, there appears to be no legal requirement of confidentiality in arbitration,[52] but at least one expert has opined, that there is no implied obligation of confidentiality although it would appear that it depends on an interpretation of the arbitration agreement.[53] **22–53**

There is a line of English authority in favour of confidentiality of arbitration hearings. As the Court of Appeals noted in the *City of Moscow* case, "[a]mong features long assumed to be implicit in parties" choice to arbitrate in England are privacy and confidentiality. The Act's silence does not detract from this. In its Report on the Arbitration Bill dated February 1996 (paras 10–17), the Departmental Advisory Committee ("DAC")(chaired by Lord Saville) recorded that there is [. . .] no doubt whatever that users of commercial arbitration in England place **22–54**

49 *G. Aïta v A. Ojjeh*, Cour d'Appel de Paris (1re Ch. suppl.), February 18, 1986, Rev. Arb. 1986, p.583.

50 *Bleustein et autres c/société True North Inc et société FCB* Tribunal de commerce de Paris (Ord. réf.) February 22, 1999 (2003) Rev. Arb. Vol.1, pp.189,190.

51 See Swiss Federal Supreme Court, June 19, 2006, 4P.74/2006, 24–4 ASA Bull., 724–725 (2006), available at: www.bger.ch/fr/index/juridiction/jurisdiction-inhe. . . . Search term 4P.74/2006. See also, for a comment on this decision, Tschanz, "Switzerland: Confidentiality of Swiss Supreme Court Review of Arbitral Awards", Mondaq Business Briefing, September 28, 2006, online publication available at: http://www.mondaq.com [accessed November 19, 2013]; Jolles, Stark-Traber and de Cediel, *op. cit.*, p.145.

52 See *US v Panhandle Eastern Corp*, 118 F.R.D. 346 (D. Del., 1988). For a more recent decision of the United States Court of Appeals for the Seventh Circuit confirming that arbitration materials may be disclosed in response to a subpoena, despite any previous confidentiality obligations undertaken by those in their possession, see *Gotham Holdings v Health Grades*, 580 F.3d 664 (7th Cir. 2009).

53 See Expert Report of Professor Hans Smit (in *Esso/BHP v Plowman*), (1995) Arb. Int'l Vol. 11 No.3, pp.297–298. See also, Pryles, "Confidentiality" in the *Leading Arbitrators' Guide in International Arbitration* (Juris Publishing/Staempfli Publishers, 2nd edn, 2008), p.415.

much importance" on privacy and confidentiality "as essential features".[54] In that case, the issue was confidentiality of annulment proceedings. However, the basic position is that the arbitration proceedings themselves are confidential.[55]

22–55 In countries that have adopted the UNCITRAL Model Law, the position appears to vary. There is no provision in the Model Law providing for confidentiality, unlike with the more recent UNCITRAL Model Law on Conciliation. Australian courts have held that there is no implied duty of confidentiality in arbitral proceedings.[56] Singapore has preferred the English approach.[57]

Confidentiality orders

22–56 As mentioned above, there is no need for a Tribunal generally to issue a confidentiality order with respect to attendance at the hearings, as this is covered by art.26(3). Tribunals may be called upon to issue confidentiality orders (i) with respect to the existence of the arbitration itself, (ii) with respect to submissions made in the arbitration, (iii) with respect to documents produced during the proceedings, or (iv) with respect to opinions expressed in the arbitration. A Tribunal may do so at its own initiative, but is more likely to do so at the request of a party.

22–57 In considering whether and to what extent to issue a confidentiality order with respect to any of these issues, the Tribunal must keep in mind the parties' agreements, the law applicable to the arbitration itself and the law applicable to the parties. For example, in the case of publicly-traded companies, those companies may be required to provide certain information with respect to the arbitration to meet their disclosure obligations. These are issues that are resolved on a case-by-case basis usually by seeking to work out a solution that meets such disclosure requirements but also protects to the extent possible the interests of other parties as to confidentiality.

22–58 In addition, in considering requests for confidentiality, to the extent that there is a government or state entity involved, the Tribunal should consider the issues of transparency to which those entities may be subject. This is particularly the case where the arbitration relates to an investment in a country as there is a growing trend to expect transparency in such situations.

22–59 As regards documentary disclosure, the IBA Rules of Evidence provide an indication of what most practitioners view as an acceptable general principle providing in Section 3(13) that:

[54] *Department of Economics, Policy and Development of the City of Moscow v Bankers Trust Co* [2004] EWCA Civ 314, [2]. For more details on the extent of the confidentiality obligation under English law, see Lew, "Confidentiality in Arbitrations in England, in Lew et al., *Arbitration in England, op.cit.*, pp.441–454.

[55] The English position on confidentiality was further reflected in art.30 of the LCIA Rules. For a commentary thereof, see Koepp, Farah and Webster, "Arbitration in London: Feature of the London Court of International Arbitration" in Giuditta Cordero-Moss (ed.) *International Commercial Arbitration. Different Forms and their Features* (Cambridge University Press, 2013), pp.217–270.

[56] *Esso Australia Resources Ltd v Sidney James Plowman*, 1–3 Arb. Int'l, 235 (1995).

[57] See, for example, *Myanma Yaung Chi Coo Ltd v Win Win Nu* [2003] 2 SLR (Singapore Law Reports), 547; *International Coal Pte Ltd v Kristle Trading Ltd* [2008] SGHC 182.

"13. Any Document submitted or produced by a Party or non-Party in the arbitration and not otherwise in the public domain shall be kept confidential by the Arbitral Tribunal and the other Parties, and shall be used only in connection with the arbitration. This requirement shall apply except and to the extent that disclosure may be required of a Party to fulfil a legal duty, protect or pursue a legal right, or enforce or challenge an award in bona fide legal proceedings before a state court or other judicial authority. The Arbitral Tribunal may issue orders to set forth the terms of this confidentiality. This requirement shall be without prejudice to all other obligations of confidentiality in the arbitration."

However, even this general principle may be subject to some modification – and need for clarification – where issues arise as to parallel proceedings with related parties. For example, this type of provision does not deal with the use of a related party to pursue a right in such parallel proceedings. Nevertheless, it is frequent that obligations along the lines of section 3(13) of the IBA Rules on Evidence are imposed with respect to documents disclosed during the arbitration in particular. **22–60**

Confidentiality orders under art.22(3) are directed at the parties but are generally applicable throught the parties to the various persons involved in the arbitration, such as the employees, lawyers and experts engaged by the parties. In some instances, the Tribunal will at the request of a party require that such persons sign a confidentiality obligation so that the persons assume obligations of confidentiality to the other parties in the arbitration directly. **22–61**

For Tribunal-appointed experts, one would normally expect that a confidentiality obligation be inserted in the terms of reference for the expert him or herself. A Tribunal may set out the fact that it will impose such an obligation or incorporate the terms of reference with that obligation in a procedural order relating to the appointment of the Tribunal-appointed expert as well. Nevertheless, a Tribunal-appointed expert is not a party and is retained pursuant to a contract. **22–62**

It is generally acknowledged that the enforcement of confidentiality agreements or orders is sometimes difficult due to the problems in assessing the damages for breach of those obligations. In the case of procedural orders issued by a Tribunal, this concern is somewhat reduced due to the concern that most parties have as to adverse inferences, whether official or inofficial, that a Tribunal may draw if a party chooses to breach a confidentiality order. **22–63**

Article 22(4): "In all cases, the arbitral tribunal shall act fairly and impartially and ensure that each party has a reasonable opportunity to present its case."

Article 22(4) is identical to the text of art.15(2) of the 1998 ICC Rules. The provision was integrated into art.22, which deals more generally with the conduct of the proceedings. **22–64**

This provision does not limit its reach solely to the provisions of art.22, but applies in all cases of the Tribunal's conduct of the arbitral proceedings, including when it proceeds "to establish the facts of the case by all appropriate means", art.25(1). **22–65**

22–66 When it settles on the procedural rules, the Tribunal must meet the requirements of the Rules, including art.22(4), and the requirements of the law of the place of arbitration. Article 22(4) requires that the Tribunal act fairly and impartially and provide each party with a "reasonable opportunity to present its case". This provision does not require the Tribunal to treat the parties in exactly the same fashion. Nor does it require the Tribunal to provide the parties with every opportunity to present their case. Under the Rules, the Tribunal is required simply to ensure that a party has a "reasonable opportunity" to present its case, leaving thus the requisite discretion to the Tribunal.

22–67 What constitutes a reasonable opportunity to present a case will depend on the nature of the case advanced by both parties and the nature of the procedure agreed upon by the parties or adopted by the Tribunal, and the stage of the proceedings. Therefore, although the Tribunal is to "make every effort to conduct the arbitration in an expeditious and cost-effective manner" pursuant to art.22(1), and although it is given broad powers under art.25 to establish the facts of the case by "all appropriate means", one of the duties of the Tribunal is to balance the procedural requirements of the parties to ensure that, as the proceedings advance, they are provided with a reasonable opportunity to present their case.[58] The requirements of the ICC Rules do not go as far as the UNCITRAL Model Law. Article 18 of that Law states that "[t]he parties shall be treated with equality and each party shall be given a full opportunity of presenting his case".[59] In practice, the safer course for a Tribunal is to seek to provide the parties with a full opportunity of presenting their case.

22–68 The *Bombardier Transportation* case which came before the French courts in 2005, provides a good illustration of the power granted to the Tribunal by art.22(4).[60] The Swiss Respondent in the ICC proceedings, attempted to challenge the Award on the basis of art.1502(4) of the French NCPC (now art.1520(4) of the French CPC) for violation of the principle of due process. It was argued that the German Claimant's failure to comply with the Rules and the procedural orders of the Tribunal including time limits for the submissions did not enable Respondent

[58] See below, para.23–92 to 23–95. See also Born, *International Arbitration: Law and Practice* (Kluwer Law International, 2012) p.151; Born, *International Commercial Arbitration* (Kluwer Law International, 2009) p.1763; Waincymer *op. cit.*, pp.80–81.

[59] Section 24(b) of the Singapore International Arbitration Act (Cap 143A) (b), which is based on UNCITRAL Model Law, provides one step further besides the grounds for annulment of Awards. Under that provision, the final Award can be set aside if "a breach of the rules of natural justice occurred in connection with the making of the Award by which the rights of any party have been prejudiced". See *Fairmount Development Pte Ltd v Soh Beng Tee & Co Pte Ltd* [2006] SGHC 189 of October 17, 2006. The Court of Appeals reversed and determined that arbitrator's decision to rule on the issue related to timing without having been raised by the parties and thus without giving them an opportunity to be heard was not a breach of natural justice. The issue of timing was not critical to the final Award—*Soh Beng Tee & Co Pte v Fairmont Development Pre Ltd* [2007] SGCA 28. For another example where a Singaporean court refused to set aside an Award based on the breach of natural justice, *see Government of the Republic of the Philippines v Philippine International Air Terminals Co, Inc* [2006] SGHC 206 of November 17, 2006; *Dongwoo Mann+Hummel Co Ltd v Mann+Hummel GmbH* [2008] SGHC 67 of May 8, 2008.

[60] Paris Court of Appeal, June 23, 2005, *La société Bombardier Transportation Switzerland v La société Siemens AG*, JurisData: 2005–287132. See also Paris Court of Appeal, September 9, 1997, *Heilmann v société Graziano Trasmissioni* (1998) Rev Arb No.4 p.712, note Derains. See also para.39–29.

to fully prepare its case before the hearing. The Paris Court of Appeal rejected the arguments in the following terms:

> "[. . .] time limits fixed by the arbitrators are not an end by itself [. . .] but are purported to ensure the equality between the parties, the loyalty of the debates and the efficient organization of the procedure, the procedural equality between the parties does not require, as alleged by the Respondent, that the decision taken for one party be extended to the other one, the proof that the time imbalance in favour of the Claimant has violated the Respondent's procedural rights remains to be given [. . .]" (Authors' translation).

The Hong Kong Court of Appeal reached a similar conclusion in *Pacific China Holdings v Grand Pacific Holdings*[61] and reversed a Court of First Instance decision to set aside an Award based on due process infringement. The alleged procedural violation involved a Tribunal's decision to order a sequential exchange of submissions in place of a previously ordered simultaneous exchange. By making this procedural change, Respondent obtained ten days to respond to Claimant's arguments, while Claimant received Respondent's submissions on the Friday night before the following Monday's hearing. While the Court of First Instance set aside the Award for not allowing the parties to present their case,[62] the Court of Appeal unanimously reversed and held that there had been no "serious" or even "egregious" procedural violations. Ultimately, it was emphasised that Hong Kong courts will not readily interfere with the decisions of Tribunals. **22–69**

The law of the place of arbitration also provides for basic rules as to the minimum requirements in arbitral proceedings and, in some instances, further requirements as to the conduct of the proceedings. To enforce any Award outside the place of arbitration, recourse will usually be made under the New York Convention, which also refers to the law of the place of arbitration as well as to the party's ability to present its case. **22–70**

Under art.V of the New York Convention: **22–71**

> "recognition and enforcement of the award may be refused, at the request of the party against whom it is invoked, only if that party furnishes to the competent authority where the recognition and enforcement is sought, proof that: [. . .] (b) The party against whom the award is invoked was [. . .] unable to present his case; or [. . .] (d) [. . .] the arbitral procedure was not in accordance with the agreement of the parties, or, failing such agreement, was not in accordance with the law of the country where the arbitration took place."

Therefore, under the New York Convention, a basic requirement is that the arbitration procedure meets the requirements of the "country where the arbitration took place". This is usually taken as a reference to the law of the place

[61] *Pacific China Holdings Ltd v Grand Pacific Holdings Ltd,* HCCT 15/2010, June 29, 2011.
[62] *Idem,* CACV 136/201, May 19, 2012.

of arbitration, although it could be interpreted to include the country where hearings have taken place.[63]

22–72 By requiring a Tribunal to meet the requirements of the law of the place of arbitration, art.V(1) of the New York Convention is not in contradiction with art.19 of the Rules, which gives arbitrators the freedom to make reference or not to "the rules of procedure of a national law". The national laws of the places of arbitration in all major centres of arbitration do not impose any requirement that a Tribunal follow the national procedure of that country. Rather, those laws require that Tribunals meet the requirements for due process or fairness set by national law for Tribunals in general.

22–73 Given that the Tribunal must ensure that the procedure meets the requirements of due process at the place of arbitration, the issue is what those basic requirements are and how they are interpreted in some of the major centres of arbitration. Set out in Pt III are the national laws (or excerpts of those laws) of the major centres of arbitration, France, Switzerland, the United States and England as well as the UNCITRAL Model Law. There are differences as to the approach, and differences in the standard of review for procedural due process. Section 68 of the English Arbitration Act 1996 in particular provides for the possibility of a broad scope for intervention due to "serious irregularity" with respect to procedure although, as discussed under art.34 this has been interrupt restrictively.

22–74 Above all, courts are not called to disagree with Tribunals on procedural matters when assessing, for example, a party's inability to present its case. Instead, courts should check whether "the party resisting enforcement somehow was deprived of its right to have its substantive case heard and determined by the arbitral tribunal".[64] Similarly, when dealing with a departure from the procedural rules agreed by the parties or, in absence thereof, from those of the law of the country where the arbitration took place, the Convention is not intended to afford the losing party with a right to appeal the Tribunal's procedural decisions or to refuse the recognition or enforcement if "the court called upon is of a different legal view than the arbitrators". According to the *ICCA Guide to the Interpretation of the 1958 New York Convention*, the Convention "is aimed at more fundamental deviations from the agreed procedure" such as instances where the parties' choice of institutional rules was disregarded by the Tribunal or where the Parties have agreed that no institutional rules would apply.[65]

Article 22(5): "The parties undertake to comply with any order made by the arbitral tribunal."

63 Taking into account the law of the place where hearings have taken place would not appear to have any policy basis. The arbitral procedure must be subject to one law of the place of arbitration to link it to a national legal system. There would seem to be no justification for linking it to two national legal systems, especially if the hearings were held in a certain country other than the place of arbitration for convenience, which is generally the case. On the application of art.V (1)(d) of the New York Convention, see Jarvin, "Irregularity in the composition of the Arbitral Tribunal and the Procedure", *op. cit.*, para.12–52 n.28.

64 Request for the Recognition and Enforcement of an Arbitral Award in *ICCA's Guide to the Interpretation of the 1958 New York Convention: A Handbook for Judges* (International Council for Commercial Arbitration 2011) pp.68, 89.

65 *Idem* at 98.

The Parties' duty to comply with the orders of the Tribunal was implied in the 1998 Rules,[66] but is now expressly stated. This is also the first time that the Rules make general reference to a Tribunal's order. Under the 1998 Rules, a Tribunal's order was only mentioned in the context of its decision to grant provisional relief, which can be in the form of an Award or of an Order.[67] **22–75**

In addition to art.22(5), the newly-introduced art.29(2) 2nd sentence also expressly states that the "parties undertake to comply with any order made by the emergency arbitrator". No similar provision was included in art.28(1) regarding a Tribunal's order granting provisional relief. In fact, it was only in the process of drafting the provisions of the Emergency Arbitrator, and in particular the 2nd sentence art.29(2), that the Drafting Sub-Committee realised that such general statement should now be made for any procedural order by a Tribunal. The Drafting Sub-Committee wanted to avoid the risk of an *a contrario* argument being made by the Parties. **22–76**

Consequence of non-compliance with the Tribunal's Order

Arbitrators lack *imperium*, and in so far as the parties refuse to voluntarily abide by their orders, the arbitrators cannot force compliance. Besides being able to draw adverse inferences from a party's non-compliance in certain circumstances,[68] arbitrators are only able to impose sanctions to the extent that they were given the power to do so. However, such practices are nonetheless rare. Under the Rules, if read together with art.22(3), art.22(5) generates a contractual obligation to comply with the orders of the Tribunal. Therefore, it can be argued that a breach thereof may lead, at least in theory, to a claim for damages. **22–77**

Local courts' assistance

Under certain national laws, local courts can assist arbitral Tribunals in the enforcement of their measures. For example, s.44 of the English Arbitration Act of 1996 provides that "[u]nless otherwise agreed by the parties, the court has for the purposes of and in relation to arbitral proceedings the same power of making orders [. . .] as it has for the purposes of and in relation to legal proceedings".[69] Local courts' assistance remains a matter to be decided on a case-by-case basis, depending on the issue at hand and ultimately by the provisions of the national law in respect thereof.[70] **22–78**

[66] Fry, Greenberg, Mazza, *op. cit.*, para.3–821. Derains & Schwartz explain that under the 1998 Rules non-compliance with the Tribunal's orders to produce documents was nonetheless rare, despite the arbitrators' inability to force compliance, and—we would add—an express provision to this effect. That was because the arbitrators retained at all times the power to draw adverse inferences whenever parties refused to produce the documents requested. See Derains & Schwartz, *op. cit.* at 283.

[67] See art.28(1), 2nd sentence of 1998 Rules, and art.28(1) 2nd sentence of current Rules.

[68] See Greenberg & Lautenschlager, "Adverse Inference in International Arbitral Practice" (2011) ICC ICArb Bull Vol. 22, No. 2, pp.43–56; see also "Extracts from ICC Arbitral Awards on the Subject of Adverse Inferences" (2011) ICC ICArb Bull Vol. 22, No. 2, pp.57–83.

[69] For a commentary of s.44, see, e.g. O'Callaghan & Finnis, "Support and Supervision by Courts" in Lew et al., *Arbitration in England, op.cit.*, pp.413,427 et seq.

[70] See, e.g. for more details, Poudret & Besson, *op.cit.*, 595–603; for court support for enforcement of interim relief, see, e.g. Waincymer, *op.cit.*, pp.640–642; for judicial assistance in taking evidence, see, e.g. Born, *op. cit*, pp.1922 et seq.

Article 23 Terms of Reference

1 **As soon as it has received the file from the Secretariat, the arbitral tribunal shall draw up, on the basis of documents or in the presence of the parties and in the light of their most recent submissions, a document defining its Terms of Reference. This document shall include the following particulars:**

a) the names in full, description, address and other contact details of each of the parties and of any person(s) representing a party in the arbitration;

b) the addresses to which notifications and communications arising in the course of the arbitration may be made;

c) a summary of the parties' respective claims and of the relief sought by each party, together with the amounts of any quantified claims and, to the extent possible, an estimate of the monetary value of any other claims;

d) unless the arbitral tribunal considers it inappropriate, a list of issues to be determined;

e) the names in full, address and other contact details of each of the arbitrators;

f) the place of the arbitration; and

g) particulars of the applicable procedural rules and, if such is the case, reference to the power conferred upon the arbitral tribunal to act as *amiable compositeur* or to decide *ex aequo et bono*.

2 **The Terms of Reference shall be signed by the parties and the arbitral tribunal. Within two months of the date on which the file has been transmitted to it, the arbitral tribunal shall transmit to the Court the Terms of Reference signed by it and by the parties. The Court may extend this time limit pursuant to a reasoned request from the arbitral tribunal or on its own initiative if it decides it is necessary to do so.**

3 **If any of the parties refuses to take part in the drawing up of the Terms of Reference or to sign the same, they shall be submitted to the Court for approval. When the Terms of Reference have been signed in accordance with Article 23(2) or approved by the Court, the arbitration shall proceed.**

4 **After the Terms of Reference have been signed or approved by the Court, no party shall make new claims which fall outside the limits of the Terms of Reference unless it has been authorized to do so by the arbitral tribunal, which shall consider the nature of such new claims, the stage of the arbitration and other relevant circumstances.**[1]

[1] Article 23 corresponds to art.18 and art.19 of the 1998 ICC Rules. There have been limited substantive changes discussed under the Introductory remarks.

Introductory remarks

As discussed in the Introduction and under art.19, one of the basic principles for an ICC arbitration is the autonomy of the parties. The parties are free to set the procedure that they wish within the overall framework of the ICC Rules and the law of the place of arbitration, taking into consideration, where appropriate and possible, the law of the probable place of enforcement. In an ICC arbitration, arbitrators will set out the details of the procedure in the Terms of Reference and even more so in procedural orders.[2] **23–1**

The Terms of Reference are to be signed by the parties and the Tribunal to indicate their agreement with the information set out therein. The Terms of Reference are intended to provide an "agreed framework" for the arbitration. If, and only if, signed by all parties, the Terms of Reference constitute a further agreement relating to the arbitration and will be enforceable as such.[3] The Terms of Reference can take the form of a "*compromis*" (or submission agreement), unless one party objects to the jurisdiction of the Tribunal, although it signed the Terms of Reference.[4] In order to comply with the requirements of arts II and IV(1) of the New York Convention, parties may consider including a special provision in the Terms of Reference providing that the Terms of Reference confirm the arbitration clause in the contract concluded by the parties, and that each original copy of the Terms of Reference shall form an original arbitration agreement for the purposes of arts II and IV(1) of the New York Convention. **23–2**

Since the Terms of Reference are intended to provide an agreed framework, a party is not required to accept provisions that go beyond the scope of the arbitration agreement. For example, a party may, but is not required to, agree to a provision on confidentiality in the Terms of Reference. At the same time, as discussed **23–3**

[2] Sanders, "The Terms of Reference in ICC Arbitration" in *Liber Amicorum Robert Briner, op. cit.*, p.693.

[3] In some non-ICC arbitrations, the Tribunal and the parties sign agreed procedural orders. Such an order was held to be an agreement between the parties *in Associated Electric & Gas Insurance Services Ltd v European Reinsurance Co of Zurich (Bermuda)* [2003] UKPC 11 (January 29, 2003), (2004) Mealey's IAR Vol.19 No.1 p.32.

[4] Cass Civ 1e, January 6, 1987, *Southern Pacific Properties Ltd and Southern Pacific Properties (Middle East) Ltd v The Arab Republic of Egypt* (1988) YBCA Vol.XIII p.152: "[. . .] the Court of Appeal, thus deciding on the assertions, decided correctly, on the one hand, that the arbitration agreement could only be constituted by the arbitration clause inserted in the contract of 12 December 1974 and not by the Terms of Reference, the object of which was only to define the issues and, on the other hand, that the Terms of Reference, in which the Republic of Egypt maintained that there was no arbitration agreement, could not replace such an agreement [. . .]"; see also Arnaldez, "L'acte déterminant la mission de l'arbitre" in *Etudes offertes à Pierre Bellet, op. cit.*, p.1 at p.20.

below, a party should not object to inclusion of statements regarding the other party's case provided that it is clear that those statements are not accepted as such.

23–4 The changes in the Rules from the 1998 Rules relate to the addresses for representatives and to quantification of claims in art.23(1)(a) and (c). These changes correspond to the changes in art.4(3) (for the Request), art.5(1) for the Answer, art.5(5) for the counterclaims. Another change from the prior rules is to insert as art.23(4), the provision of art.19 of the 1998 Rules regarding new claims.

23–5 Tribunals may and usually do set out the detailed procedure for an arbitration in procedural orders rather than in the Terms of Reference. Procedural orders are issued by the Tribunal and signed by the Tribunal or by the president of the Tribunal, if so provided in the Terms of Reference, but not by the parties.

23–6 Terms of Reference are a mandatory requirement in an ICC arbitration, and the parties are not allowed to conduct an ICC arbitration without such a document. Nor is the Tribunal. Article 23 requires the Tribunal to prepare Terms of Reference and sets out the points that the Terms of Reference must cover. The document is aimed in particular at setting out the undisputed facts relating to the arbitration, the claims of the parties and the issues to be decided at an early stage in the proceedings. More generally, the Terms of Reference are intended to define the scope of the Tribunal's mandate or mission so as to ensure that the Award will not be rendered either *ultra* or *infra petita*.[5] The Terms of Reference are also linked to the provisional timetable for the proceedings. Generally, that timetable is issued with or within a short time after the signing of the Terms of Reference.

23–7 ICC arbitration is an administered and supervised arbitration. Unlike most other arbitration institutions, the ICC not only monitors the progress of cases but also scrutinises Awards under art.33. This monitoring and scrutiny is carried out by reference to the Terms of Reference as well as to the correspondence between the Tribunal and the parties and to the procedural orders.[6] When an Award comes before the ICC Court for scrutiny, the Court is systematically provided with the Terms of Reference.

23–8 National courts refer to the Terms of Reference in deciding on annulment of Awards. Especially if all parties sign them, the Terms of Reference are seen as one of the best indications of the issues that the Tribunal was intended to deal with. The Terms of Reference are frequently signed at the case-management conference discussed under art.24. Usually, a copy of the Terms of Reference is signed for each party, for each member of the Tribunal and for the Secretariat.

23–9 The reluctance to use the Terms of Reference for details of the procedure is in part due to the fact that there is no provision for amending the Terms of Reference (except for adding new claims under art.23(4)). Therefore, where the Terms of Reference contain detailed procedural rules, there is an issue as to how they can be changed. The Tribunal has a general right to establish the rules of procedure pursuant to arts 19 and 22. However, that is subject to an agreement between the parties, and arguably signed Terms of Reference constitute such an agreement

[5] However, if the Terms of Reference do not list the issues to be decided but simply state that the Tribunal will decide the relevant issues raised in the parties' memorials, then the Terms of Reference will be of little assistance in this regard.

[6] As discussed under art.3(1) at para.3–21, all correspondence and filings exchanged by the Tribunal and the parties are normally transmitted at the same time to the Secretariat of the Court.

between the parties within the meaning of arts 19 and 22(2). If that is the case, the procedural rules set out in the Terms of Reference can presumably only be amended by a further agreement between the parties, which would give each party a veto over changes to the procedural rules set out in the Terms of Reference.[7] This situation is to be contrasted with procedural orders that are issued by the Tribunal and do not require the consent of the parties to be amended. Therefore, it will normally be much more practical to have aspects of the procedure decided by the Tribunal rather than agreed to by the parties.[8] Nonetheless, a Tribunal will most often seek to consult the parties and try to obtain their consent on as many aspects of the procedure as possible.[9]

Article 23(1): "As soon as it has received the file from the Secretariat, the arbitral tribunal shall draw up, on the basis of documents or in the presence of the parties and in the light of their most recent submissions, a document defining its Terms of Reference. This document shall include the following particulars:"

The Secretariat transmits the file to the Tribunal as soon as it has been constituted and the provisional advance on costs has been paid in accordance with art.16. **23–10**

Upon receipt of the file, the president will take the initiative to organise the work of the Tribunal and usually to prepare the initial draft of the Terms of Reference.[10] It is basically the president's responsibility to ensure that the Terms of Reference are signed within two months after transmittal of the file to the Tribunal. **23–11**

In the initial draft of the Terms of Reference, the Tribunal usually summarises the procedure to date. This is useful to provide the reader with an outline of the procedural aspects of the dispute and to ensure that no material communication or element has been omitted in the initial review of the file. **23–12**

The Terms of Reference are to be drawn up "on the basis of documents or in the presence of the parties and in the light of their most recent submissions". The Rules do not define what is meant by the "most recent submissions." The submissions include the Request and the Respondent's Answer thereto as well as any claims against the Claimant and the Reply to such claims or claims against an additional party and the latter's Reply thereto.[11] In addition, the general view is that parties' other submissions will be taken into consideration whether in the form of amendments to the Request or Answer or in the form of letters—including **23–13**

[7] In the *Bombardier Transportation* case referred to under art.20 at para.20–21, the party seeking annulment sought to argue that the Tribunal had failed to respect a provision of the Terms of Reference requiring that documents be submitted in English or French. The Paris Court of Appeal rejected the argument based in part on the flexibility that the Tribunal had retained for itself in the Terms of Reference.

[8] For a discussion of the issue of control of arbitration, see Webster, "Party Control in International Arbitration", *op. cit.*, at p.133.

[9] See the discussion under art.22(2) at paras 22–14 et seq.

[10] For the advantages of such meeting: Böckstiegel, "Case Management by Arbitrators: Experience and Suggestions" in *Liber Amicorum Robert Briner, op. cit.*, p.115. See also Bühler & Webster, *Handbook on ICC Arbitration* (2nd edn, 2008) at paras 18–16 to 18–22.

[11] See art.7(1) and (4).

letters sent as comments on drafts of the Terms of Reference. Such submissions may occur prior to transmission of the file or at any time prior to the signing of the Terms of Reference. It is not infrequent that the Respondent in such cases makes a submission relating to its defence or a counterclaim immediately prior to the signing of the Terms of Reference. The Tribunal then usually takes this submission into account in the Terms of Reference.

23–14 This relative flexibility in ICC arbitration may be surprising to lawyers used to complying with the pleading requirements of national court systems. However, arbitration, unlike court procedure, is intended to be flexible, so that each arbitration can resolve as many disputes between the parties as possible. With parties from different legal systems, the Tribunal will be conscious of the fact that some lawyers may not be familiar with general ICC practice and that such last-minute submissions may be a direct result of the relative novelty of the proceedings. There are seldom due process issues at this stage as claims or counterclaims added prior to signing of the Terms of Reference will be the subject of further memorials and evidence. What is more, a Tribunal always prefers to have a party participate in the proceedings, albeit with last-minute submissions.

23–15 As noted, the president usually prepares the first draft of the Terms of Reference that is submitted to the co-arbitrators for their comments. The president may well send the initial draft to the Secretariat to give it the possibility of an informal "compliance check", although the Secretariat will, in any event, receive a copy when the draft Terms of Reference are sent to the parties. After receiving the comments of the co-arbitrators, the president will then circulate a draft to the parties for their comments.[12] Based on those comments, the president will revise the Terms of Reference in consultation with the co-arbitrators. If there are no substantial difficulties, a final draft of the Terms of Reference will be prepared for signing either by way of correspondence, a telephone or videoconference or at a meeting. If there are substantial difficulties, the Tribunal may prefer to hold a meeting to clarify the issues. The discussion of any outstanding issues with the draft Terms of Reference is usually held at the case management conference discussed under art.24.

23–16 The key issues regarding drafting of the Terms of Reference relate to para.(c) the description of the claims of the parties and the relief sought, (d) the issues to be decided and (g) the applicable procedural rules to be followed. These points are discussed below.

23–17 Article 23 provides that the Terms of Reference may be drawn up "on the basis of the documents or in the presence of the parties". The initial drafting of the Terms of Reference occurs almost invariably prior to any such meeting. Whether a meeting will be held depends on a number of factors discussed under art.24.

Article 23(1)(a): "the names in full, description, address and other contact details of each of the parties and of any person(s) representing a party in the arbitration;"

[12] The Secretariat may provide comments too, and this is why it is always preferable to send the early draft to the Secretariat, particularly if the Respondent is not participating in the arbitration.

The Claimant identifies itself and provides its address and identifies the Respondent and provides its address in the Request. The Respondent confirms its name and address in the Answer. The Respondent may object to the inclusion of a Claimant (or of another Respondent) or may object to the address. Pursuant to art.23(1)(a) the Terms of Reference should include the exact name of each party, as reflected in its official documents as well as the physical address, telephone number and email address. The description of the parties usually includes the nature of the entity, if an incorporated entity and, if so, the nature and jurisdiction of incorporation. Usually a brief description of the area of activity of the party is inserted. 23–18

If there is an issue as to the proper parties, the ICC Court will have already decided whether there is a prima facie case that there may be jurisdiction under art.6(4). In such a case, the party to whom an objection has been made will usually be named in the Terms of Reference and asked to sign them subject to a decision of the Tribunal as to whether it is a proper party to the arbitration. 23–19

Article 23(1)(a) also provides for insertion of the contact details of the persons representing the parties. This change from the 1998 Rules reflects the change discussed in arts 4(3) and 5(1) regarding identification of the representatives of the parties. As discussed under those articles, this should include identification of all legal representatives of the parties who are involved as of the date of the Terms of Reference and who will be attending the hearings. 23–20

Article 23(1)(b): "the addresses to which notifications and communications arising in the course of the arbitration may be made;"

If the parties are represented by lawyers, the addresses for notification will almost invariably be the addresses of the lawyers and not those of the parties. Where there is co-counsel, in many instances the co-counsel also receives a copy of the notifications and filings. In some cases, in-house counsel of one or both parties is added for notification purposes. With the prevailing use of email communication of Tribunals with parties, adding more than one recipient on each side for notification purposes is not a problem. However, the Tribunal should be aware that when it is required to send hard copies by mail or courier to several recipients, having more than one recipient on each side may raise logistical problems. 23–21

When parties actually receive notifications (and how) is, surprisingly, often an issue in international arbitration, especially if the time frame for responses is rapid. In many instances, parties send letters and shorter memoranda by email, followed by a copy by fax, or post, or courier. 23–22

Article 23(1)(c): "a summary of the parties' respective claims and of the relief sought by each party, together with the amounts of any quantified claims and, to the extent possible, an estimate of the monetary value of any other claims;"

The Terms of Reference should be a self-standing document that is understandable for the ICC Court and any national court. To render it understandable, basic factual allegations must be set out. Therefore, although some Tribunals simply 23–23 refer to the claims made by the parties in their pleadings, this practice renders the Terms of Reference a much less useful document.[13]

23–24 To the extent possible, the Tribunal usually seeks to set out undisputed facts, although the extent to which that is possible will depend on the circumstances. In many instances, the parties will agree on little more than the fact that they signed a contract and that the contract contains specific provisions. This in itself may be very helpful as these provisions if quoted may give the third party an overview of the contractual situation.

23–25 The Terms of Reference also set out each of the parties' claims. These will usually include disputed facts and allegations. Therefore, in drafting the Terms of Reference it is important to ensure that a distinction is drawn between what is undisputed and what is disputed. In addition, the Terms of Reference should include an express statement that, by signing the Terms of Reference, a party is not accepting any claim whether of fact or law asserted by the other party.

23–26 The term "claim" is in some instances difficult to define.[14] However, this term is an essential feature of art.23(1) due to the impact of art.23(4). That article provides that no new claims may be added after the signature of the Terms of Reference that are "outside the limits of the Terms of Reference" unless authorised by the Tribunal. It follows from art.2(iv) that the term claims "include any claim by any party against any other party". The usual debate in this respect is whether a party is making a new "claim" or whether it is simply quantifying an existing claim or seeking additional relief with respect to it. In ICC case No.7453 (under the former 1988 ICC Rules), the sole arbitrator stated with respect to the 1988 ICC Rules:

> "To say that new claims may not be made (without the consent of the other party) after the Terms of Reference have entered into effect is not to say that new calculations of damages or new theories of quantification may not be subsequently introduced.
>
> The Terms of Reference, after all, enter into effect at an early stage of the proceedings, usually long before a detailed economic analysis has been made of the consequences of breach and before experts have been consulted. Claimants, to be sure, are well advised to ensure that their claims, as restated in the Terms of Reference, are in general terms and refer to general theories of recovery, with amounts claimed as damages carefully designated as 'estimates' or 'provisional estimates'. Failure to do so is not ordinarily fatal. New evidence, and new quantification, of damages does not constitute a new claim."[15]

[13] For a discussion, see Webster, "Terms of Reference and French Annulment Proceedings", *op. cit.*

[14] In the ICC Rules, the term "claim" is expressed in French as "prétention", in German as "Vorbringen", in Spanish as "pretensiones" and in Italian as "pretese", but only the French and English texts are official. This is not stated in the Rules itself, but on the first inner cover page of ICC Publication 850E, which contains the English version of the Rules.

[15] ICC case No.7453 (1994), (1997) YBCA Vol.XXII p.107; *Collection of ICC Arbitral Awards 1996–2000, Vol.IV, op. cit.*, p.94.

In ICC case No.7661 (also under the former 1988 ICC Rules), the Tribunal dealt with an alternative claim.[16] The Request had set out a warranty claim that the Claimant subsequently sought to modify to include a claim for damages. The Tribunal stated: **23–27**

> "[2] When it modified its claim, Claimant stated its principal claim as one for defendants to pay the amount of the Tax Debt (or a reasonable and proper lesser amount) on the basis of their contractual liability, and for defendants to pay damages '[a]s a further and/or alternative award'. The defendants protested against the introduction of the damages claim on the basis of this being excluded by the Terms of Reference.
> [3] It would go too far to fully exclude the modification of claimant's claim on the basis of perceived limitations imposed by the Terms of Reference and of the operation of art.16 of the [1988] ICC Rules. Claimant's initial formulation of its claim was ambiguous at best and this was reflected in the Terms of Reference, nothing in which can therefore be construed as prohibiting a correction such as applied by the Claimant through stating a principal warranty claim and an alternative damages claim.
> [4] However, the modification of the claim is not admissible to the extent that damages are claimed as a 'further award' as this is tantamount to introducing a new claim, outside the limits of the Terms of Reference, which are flexible enough to permit, in the circumstances, a choice of the basis of the claim, but not flexible enough to allow for amounts higher than the amount which Claimant clearly had stated as a maximum [. . .]. Thus, any claim for damages in addition to the warranty claim, instead of alternative to it, is outside the Terms of Reference and, in view of art.16 of the ICC Rules, inadmissible."

Most ICC arbitrations that concern commercial disputes (as opposed to investor-state disputes) revolve around allegations of breach of contract and one view is that each allegation of breach of contract is a separate claim. Therefore, if a party claims that the other has breached three provisions of a contract, but then wishes to amend that argument to allege a breach of a fourth provision of a contract or make a claim in tort, then the claim may amount to a new claim. Whether this claim would fall outside the limits of the Terms of Reference is discussed under art.23(4). **23–28**

In arbitration law, claims are sometimes referred to as *petita*. Hence claims that a Tribunal has acted beyond its authority are claims that the Tribunal has acted *ultra petita*. Claims that the Tribunal has failed to adjudicate an issue that it was required to adjudicate are claims that the Tribunal has acted *infra petita*. The consequences as regards annulment and enforcement of arbitral Awards are discussed under art.34. However, the Terms of Reference provide an important link in the review by the ICC Court and sometimes even state courts are appraised of the work of the Tribunal. **23–29**

[16] ICC case No.7661 (1995), (1997) YBCA Vol.XXII p.149; *Collection of ICC Arbitral Awards 1996–2000, Vol.IV, op. cit.*, p.135.

23–30 Usually, each party's claim will involve a mixture of fact and law. The factual allegations are necessary to understand the legal position. Many, but certainly not all Tribunals have each of the parties draft their own outline of their claims and insert this draft in the Terms of Reference.[17] This method has the advantage of showing each of the parties that their approach to the dispute is exactly reflected in the Terms of Reference. The approach has, however, been criticised in that it does not ensure that the Tribunal has actually understood the parties' positions, as the Tribunal is simply incorporating the parties' respective drafts in the Terms of Reference.

23–31 The summary of the claim can be quite brief, as there is no need for it, and it would not contain all the allegations of material fact that one would find even in a basic national pleading. Nor would it refer to or cite detailed documents. The overall approach is to permit the reader to understand on what basis the claim is being made. The details of the allegations and the documents relied upon will be filed with the subsequent submissions.[18]

23–32 The Terms of Reference should also state clearly whether the claims are in contract or tort (delict) as the nature of the claims may be important to determine the rules of law applicable to them. Details as to the law relied upon are generally not set out in the Terms of Reference.

23–33 The Terms of Reference should also set out exactly the relief sought by each of the parties. This relief is usually taken from the Parties' written submissions. Article 23(1)(c) requires that the parties insert the amount of quantified claims and to the extent possible an estimate of the monetary value of other claims. This provision was introduced in the Rules to seek an earlier quantification of claims as is discussed under art.4(3) and art.5(1) and (5).

23–34 Subsequent adjustments to the relief sought are also taken into account. Usually, the relief requested will consist of a request for damages, a request for a declaration or a request for an injunction.

23–35 Generally, in an ICC arbitration, parties are not expected at this stage to provide a detailed calculation of the damages that they are claiming. Many Tribunals expect that the exact quantification of a damage claim will be made after an expert has reviewed the matter. Usually, the parties provide a minimum amount claimed. This would enable the other party to ascertain roughly the amount at risk. It would also enable the ICC Court to set an amount for the provisional advance on the costs of arbitration. Some parties are reluctant to be precise about the amount claimed at the Terms of Reference stage due to the effect that it may have on the advance on costs ordered by the ICC. However, if the amount of a claim is increased at any point in the proceedings, then the ICC will usually take the amount of the increase into account and recalculate the amount of the advance on the costs of arbitration as is discussed under art.37.[19]

[17] The "ICC Arbitration Commission Report on Techniques for Controlling Time and Costs in Arbitration" rightly states that it is for the Tribunal to consider whether it is appropriate for it to draft the summary of claims and/or the relief sought, or whether it would assist if each party provided a draft summary for inclusion in the Terms of Reference. Bühler & Webster, *Handbook on ICC Arbitration* (2nd edn, 2008) at paras 18–32 to 18–39.

[18] See Pt II, Doc.15 for an example of Terms of Reference.

[19] See the discussion under art.37(2) at paras 37–59 to 37–64.

The request for relief should include alternative and ancillary requests. In particular, the currency of the damages should be set out (as well as the basis for the claim in that currency). If interest is sought, then the basis and amount claimed should be provided as well as the date from which the party is claiming interest. Moreover, it should be clear whether the interest is claimed by contract, under the rules of law applicable to the contract, or under the procedural rules of the place of arbitration. 23–36

Claims by way of set-off are generally viewed as claims under the ICC Rules.[20] To be entitled to set-off one claim against another, the claim must exist and be of a fixed amount. 23–37

Article 23(1)(d): "unless the arbitral tribunal considers it inappropriate, a list of issues to be determined;"

The issues are the questions of fact and law that the Tribunal has to decide upon the requests for relief of each party. 23–38

The summary of the parties' respective claims in the Terms of Reference sets out the factual and legal basis for the relief sought. Some of the factual and legal claims may not be in dispute. But others will provide the core of the dispute. 23–39

The issues to be determined vary with each arbitration. Frequently, there are issues of jurisdiction either generally or with respect to a particular party. Usually, there is a dispute as to whether a party has breached contractual or extra-contractual rights. Almost invariably, there is a request for interest on amounts awarded and for costs including legal costs. 23–40

In a typical arbitration regarding, for example, unlawful termination of a distribution agreement, the issues in dispute may well be issues such as: (1) the law applicable to the distribution agreement; (2) whether the distributor breached a provision of the agreement (such as an agreement not to compete or such as the agreement to pay in full and in a timely manner the invoices or to make minimum purchases); (3) whether such breach provided grounds for termination; (4) whether notice of termination was validly given; and (5) if the agreement was not validly terminated, the measure of damages for improper termination. In some rare instances, the issues will include issues of tort (such as fraud in the inducement of the contract) as well as the law applicable to the tort. 23–41

The Tribunal, in consultation with the parties, usually drafts the list of issues. The Tribunal will seek to include as an issue to be decided, any issue on which a party insists provided that it is within the scope of the arbitration agreement and the claims of the parties. The Tribunal will follow the claims of the parties, but may well raise issues of its own that are to be decided. For example, many Tribunals raise on their own initiative issues such as the application of the Vienna Convention to the transaction or part of it; the application of antitrust law; or issues as to the proper authorisation of the arbitration agreement or the underlying contract. 23–42

The drafting of the Terms of Reference takes place at an early stage in the proceedings where the complexities of the case may not have sufficiently 23–43

[20] See the discussion under art.36(7) at paras 36–55 to 36–56.

crystallised or the Tribunal may feel that based on the parties' submissions it is not yet sufficiently familiar with the case to set out an exhaustive list of all issues in the Terms of Reference. A lack of familiarity with the case will often be felt to exist when the parties have not provided a detailed description of their claims and defenses in the Request and Answer to the Request respectively. Moreover, there is frequently a concern that the issues may evolve during the course of the arbitration. As a result, some Tribunals prefer to use the option left open by art.23(1)(d) not to set out a list of issues to be decided.

23–44 When a party raises jurisdictional or procedural issues, it is good practice to list them in the Terms of Reference, since they will normally be addressed at the beginning of the arbitral proceedings.

23–45 A common approach is for the Tribunal to set out a list of issues but to include a statement that the list of issues will be subject to review and modification in accordance with the parties' submissions. Other Tribunals adopt language such as the following:

> "The issues to be determined by the Arbitral Tribunal shall be those resulting from the parties' submissions, including forthcoming submissions, and which in the Tribunal's view are relevant to adjudication of the parties' respective claims and defences, without prejudice to the provisions of Article 23(4) of the ICC Rules. Therefore, pursuant to Article 23(1)(d) of the Rules, the Tribunal considers it inappropriate to include at this stage a specific list of the issues to be determined."

23–46 This formulation is intended to leave the list of issues open while at the same time recognising that the Tribunal has considered the matter and decided, in accordance with art.23(1)(d), that it is inappropriate to draw up a list of issues for the Terms of Reference.

23–47 Yet another, and sometimes very helpful approach is to have both parties draft a list of issues to be decided, and to include them in the summary of each party's position in the Terms of Reference. This is not only a valuable exercise for each party, but can assist them in identifying and focusing on the truly dispositive issues in their subsequent written submissions. It will also help the Tribunal in gaining more quickly a better understanding of what the case is about, or of what the Parties believe it is about.

23–48 In deciding which approach to adopt, and which to argue for, the parties and the Tribunal have to be mindful of various consequences. For the parties, if there is no list of issues, there may well be less clarity as to what issues they are supposed to address. This lack of clarity can be compounded if the other party raises new or vague issues in subsequent submissions.

23–49 For the Tribunal, listing the issues to be decided does not only require a first serious study of the parties' submissions, but also an analysis of what decisions may be required by the Tribunal in order to decide on the parties' claims. The intellectual exercise which is required in identifying the key issues will often be stimulating for both the Tribunal and the parties, and its value in getting a better understanding of what are truly the key issues of the case should not be underestimated even at an early stage.

Parties have also been heard to complain that Tribunals did not address the issues in the Award that the parties thought should be addressed. The best way of ensuring that an issue is addressed in the Award is to have it listed as an issue in the Terms of Reference. That will not only draw the Tribunal's attention to the issue, but it will also ensure that the issue is scrutinised by the ICC Court under art.33 and, if necessary, reviewed by national courts.[21] **23–50**

This desire for certainty has to be balanced against the need to adapt the case to the submissions of the parties. Some issues will perhaps disappear during the course of the arbitration. Other issues may appear to gain importance as the further submissions are made. In addition, an unsuccessful party may seek to challenge the Award based on the failure to decide an issue. One approach to seek to reconcile these two concerns is to insert in the Terms of Reference a list of the issues to be determined while recognising that the list may evolve and then confirming with the parties shortly prior to the oral hearings that the Tribunal has in fact established an up-to-date list of the issues to be decided.[22] **23–51**

Article 24(3) expressly contemplates the possibility of having a further case management conference, once the initial conference has taken place. An additional case management conference, for instance prior to the evidentiary hearing, may be a good opportunity for both the Tribunal and the Parties to revisit and discuss the list of issues to be determined pursuant to the Terms of Reference.[23] **23–52**

Article 23(1)(e): "the names in full, address and other contact details of each of the arbitrators;"

The Terms of Reference set out the names and contact details of the arbitrators identifying whether they are members of a law firm, for example. If the arbitration agreement requires that the arbitrators meet certain requirements (such as being admitted to practice in a certain jurisdiction), the Terms of Reference should record the fact that the arbitrators either meet these requirements or that they have been waived if that is the case. **23–53**

It is also common to record the fact that the parties have no objection to the constitution of the Tribunal as at the date of the Terms of Reference, if in fact that is the case. This provision may prove useful if there is a requirement in the arbitration agreement that the parties have either settlement meetings or take other procedural steps prior to commencement of the arbitration. If the parties have decided to waive such steps and proceed directly with the arbitration, then it should be recorded, as it would constitute an express waiver of these procedural requirements. In essence, if there is an agreement that the Tribunal has been properly constituted, that agreement should be reflected in the Terms of Reference. **23–54**

[21] For a discussion of these issues, see Webster, "Party Control in International Arbitration", *op. cit.*, at p.133.

[22] For a discussion, see Webster, "Terms of Reference and French Annulment Proceedings", *op. cit.*, at p.564.

[23] See the discussion under art. 24(3) at paras 24–17 and 24–18.

Article 23(1)(f): "the place of the arbitration;"

23–55 The Terms of Reference are to set out the place of arbitration irrespective of whether it was agreed by the parties or not. If the parties have not agreed on the place of arbitration, the ICC Court of Arbitration fixes it pursuant to art.18(1).[24] In either case, it may assist the participants in the arbitration to verify in the Terms of Reference the place of arbitration. However, despite having been fixed by the ICC Court, there may be an issue as to whether there was an agreement between the parties as to the place of arbitration. If such is the case, whether there is an agreement on the place of arbitration may then be one of the issues to be decided by the Tribunal as it would involve the interpretation of the arbitration agreement as discussed under art.18.

23–56 The parties may decide to change the place of arbitration, subject to the Tribunal's agreement. If there is an issue as to the geographic aspects of the place of arbitration, the issue may be dealt with in the discussion of the place of the hearings, which is generally not dealt with in the Terms of Reference, but in a procedural order.

Article 23(1)(g): "particulars of the applicable procedural rules and, if such is the case, reference to the power conferred upon the arbitral tribunal to act as *amiable compositeur* or to decide *ex aequo et bono*."

23–57 As noted above, the Terms of Reference do not usually set out the detailed procedure for the arbitration.[25] Instead, Tribunals use their authority under art.19 and art.22 to establish such procedure by procedural orders, which they can and will establish in consultation with the parties, but for which they do not need the agreement of the parties, unlike in the case of the Terms of Reference. With respect to particulars of the applicable procedural rules in the Terms of Reference, the practice in ICC arbitration varies extensively.

23–58 Many Tribunals favour maximising discretion and hence flexibility for the Tribunal. Other Tribunals draft the Terms of Reference to set out a detailed outline for the procedure. The approach to adopt depends in many instances on the arbitrators and counsel involved in the arbitration. Therefore, it is perhaps more useful to examine certain procedural rules that generally are or are not found in Terms of Reference.

23–59 For example, it is rare for a Tribunal to provide that specific rules of national procedure will be followed in whole or in part.[26] Indeed, the Terms of Reference are sometimes used as an occasion to change from a national procedure if such a procedure has been provided for in the arbitration agreement. The reason is that international arbitration does not generally follow any national procedure.

23–60 Since their initial adoption in 1999 (and as revised in 2010), the IBA Rules on Evidence have been widely cited in legal materials.[27] Moreover, as discussed under art.25, various Tribunals have expressed the view either in the Terms of Reference or in procedural orders that they would be guided by those principles in

[24] See the discussion under art.18(1) at paras 18–16 to 18–39.
[25] See para.23–5.
[26] See the discussion under art.19 at para.19–12.
[27] See Pt III App.10.

deciding procedural issues that regard witness and/or documentary testimony.[28] It is preferable to have such a reference to the guidance of the IBA Rules of Evidence in the Terms of Reference if the parties agree, as it is then part of the parties argument as to the procedure.

The Terms of Reference may also set out certain evidentiary rules, such as that all documents are presumed to be authentic and complete even though furnished in photocopies, unless their authenticity is challenged by the other party.[29] **23–61**

The Terms of Reference may include a provision on the Tribunal's right, and that of any expert appointed by the Tribunal, to visit the site. Such a provision may also deal with the notice requirements and other procedural aspects of such site inspection. **23–62**

It is not unusual for the Terms of Reference to provide that the president of the Tribunal may take some decisions on his initiative. The Terms of Reference may state, for instance, that the president has the right to call meetings and to set and extend time limits on behalf of the Tribunal, or that the president may issue procedural orders with his signature alone, after such consultation with the co-arbitrators and counsel as he considers appropriate in light of the nature and urgency of the matters dealt with in such orders. In cases of urgency, the president may even be expressly authorised to act without a prior attempt to consult with his fellow arbitrators. **23–63**

Issues of confidentiality are specifically referred to in art.22(3). However, since many parties are interested in the confidentiality of the arbitral proceedings, they may find it opportune to include a clause on confidentiality in the Terms of Reference to protect their rights and the documents submitted by them during the course of the proceedings. The following language could be used if agreed to by all parties and the Tribunal: **23–64**

> "Confidentiality
>
> Unless the parties expressly agree in writing to the contrary, the parties undertake to keep confidential all awards and orders in the present arbitration, together with all materials in the proceedings created for the purpose of the arbitration and all other documents produced by any party in the proceedings, save to the sole extent that disclosure may be required of a party by a legal duty, to protect or pursue a legal right, or to enforce or challenge an award in bona fide legal proceedings before a State Court or other judicial authority. The parties also undertake to use their best efforts to ensure that the terms of the present paragraph are respected by witnesses, experts, counsel and any other individuals who may be granted access to the materials referred to above in the context of those proceedings."[30]

[28] See the discussion under art.25 at para.25–4 *et seq*.

[29] In order for such a challenge to be made in a timely fashion, it may be advisable to set a time limit in the Terms of Reference to challenge the authenticity of a document. If not challenged within that period the right to challenge the authenticity of the document would then shall be deemed to have been waived. In any event, the Tribunal should, at its discretion, be authorised to require the production of any originals.

[30] On the general issue on confidentiality in arbitration, see the discussion under art.22(3).

23–65 If one party does not accept the inclusion of a confidentiality undertaking in the Terms of Reference, the Tribunal may nevertheless consider ordering the confidential treatment of anything in relation to the arbitration by issuing a Procedural Order.

23–66 The power of the Tribunal to decide as *amiable compositeur* or *ex aequo et bono* has been discussed under art.21(3). In drafting the Terms of Reference, if it is proposed to insert such a provision, then the parties should seek to agree on its terms, as the terms do not have the same meaning in various jurisdictions.

23–67 A related issue is whether the Terms of Reference give the Tribunal the right to mediate the dispute. In arbitrations that are influenced by German, Austrian or Swiss law, the Tribunal may feel that it is appropriate and even prefer to have the Tribunal encourage a settlement of the dispute.[31]

23–68 However, this is not the tradition in the common law countries for example. One of the main issues in this respect is the extent to which the members of the Tribunal may have ex parte contact with one of the parties. The other aspect is that, in many instances, to be effective, a mediator expresses a preliminary view as to the merits. This can give rise to an objection by a party who feels that the member of the Tribunal or the Tribunal as a whole has pre-judged an issue.

Article 23(2): "The Terms of Reference shall be signed by the parties and the arbitral tribunal. Within two months of the date on which the file has been transmitted to it, the arbitral tribunal shall transmit to the Court the Terms of Reference signed by it and by the parties. The Court may extend this time limit pursuant to a reasoned request from the arbitral tribunal or on its own initiative if it decides it is necessary to do so."

23–69 Article 23(2) imposes an obligation on the parties and the members of the Tribunal to sign the Terms of Reference. Once signed, the Terms of Reference have a binding effect on the parties and the Tribunal.[32] However, a party should not and cannot be forced to waive any right it may have with respect to the arbitration by the signing of the Terms of Reference. Therefore, if a party believes that there is a danger that it will be waiving a right or that it will be accepting some additional obligation that it does not wish to accept, it may object to signing the Terms of Reference. In most instances, the Tribunal will then seek to clarify the Terms of Reference so that it is a neutral document and does not involve any commitment to which a party reasonably objects. If, despite the Tribunal's efforts, the party refuses to sign the Terms of Reference, the Tribunal may refer the matter to the ICC Court in accordance with art.23(3).

23–70 The parties sign either on their own behalf or through their authorised representatives. Normally, the Tribunal will ensure that the parties' representatives provide proof of due authorisation, such as a power of attorney, to sign the Terms of Reference; art.23(2) expressly permits the Tribunal to require the Parties to

[31] See Schneider, "Combining Arbitration with Conciliation" (1996) *ICCA Congress Series No.8*, p.57, who describes the differing positions in common law as well as civil law countries. In the author's experience, such differences are still existing nowadays.

[32] See above at para.23–2; Cass Civ 1e, March 8, 1988, *Société Sofidif et autres v O.I.A.E.T.I. et autre* (1989) Rev Arb No.3 p.481, note Jarrosson.

submit proof of authorisation.[33] It remains, however, for each Tribunal to decide whether it considers it appropriate to request a power of attorney or any other proof of authority to sign the Terms of Reference as provided for in art.17.

The Terms of Reference are to be signed within two months after the transmittal of the file to the Tribunal.[34] In many instances, this period can be met, unless there is a problem with travel schedules, with conflicting schedules of the Tribunal and counsel (for instance during the summer holiday break), or with corporate authorisations, for example. The Tribunal may request an extension with a brief letter setting out the reason for the delay. In fact, the ICC Court frequently will grant the initial extension automatically. Further extensions may also be granted by the ICC Court, although the delay may appear to the ICC Court to be unjustified. In this respect, one of the factors will be the attitude of the parties. 23–71

If the parties and the Tribunal sign the Terms of Reference, they are provided to the ICC Court after signature for information. However, the Secretariat is copied on drafts of the Terms of Reference prior to the signing and will review them to ensure that there are no missing elements. If there is a problem with the draft Terms of Reference, the Secretariat will inform the Tribunal (and in many cases the president of the Tribunal will specifically ask the Secretariat to review the draft Terms of Reference prior to signature). There is no reference in art.23 to the ICC Court rejecting Terms of Reference signed by the parties and the Tribunal. However, it is conceivable if the ICC Court sees a risk that the procedure set out would not be in compliance with the basic requirements of the Rules and/or raise issues as to the enforceability of any Award. In such a case, the ICC Court may well intervene and request the Tribunal to amend the Terms of Reference accordingly. Although the ICC Court is not a party to the Terms of Reference, it has a general duty of supervision of the Terms of Reference in each case. This duty is the direct result of the ICC Court's function to ensure the application of the Rules, art.1(2). 23–72

In some instances, one party may object to delays in signing or submitting the Terms of Reference. The delays can be caused by the other party or by the Tribunal or by a combination of the two. Usually, if delay is raised, the other persons involved raise various justifications for the delay. Since the ICC Court prefers to have Terms of Reference that are signed by all parties, reasonable delay tends to be tolerated provided that there is no overwhelming need to proceed urgently. At some point, delay in signing the Terms of Reference may amount to a breach of the Rules, and may give rise to a request for removal of the arbitrators. This is, however, conceivable only in most exceptional circumstances. 23–73

Article 23(3): "If any of the parties refuses to take part in the drawing up of the Terms of Reference or to sign the same, they shall be submitted to the Court for approval. When the Terms of Reference have been signed in accordance with Article 23(2) or approved by the Court, the arbitration shall proceed."

[33] Even prior to the 2012 Rules and its inclusion of art.17, Tribunals regularly asked for a power of attorney, where appropriate, see para.17–4.

[34] Similarly, see art.30 on the time limit for Awards to be rendered by the Tribunal.

23–74 Article 23(3) is intended to prevent one of the parties from blocking the Terms of Reference and the arbitration by refusing to sign them. Parties may refuse to sign the Terms of Reference because they intend to default on the entire procedure. Parties may also refuse to sign the Terms of Reference to avoid appearing to accept the jurisdiction of the Tribunal, although with properly drafted Terms of Reference this should not be an issue. Finally, parties, such as state entities, may argue that they are unable to obtain the required authorisations to sign the document.

23–75 With regard to jurisdictional objections, a party should ensure that the party not only records its objection as to jurisdiction, but also that it outlines in detail in its claims the reasons why it maintains that the Tribunal has no objection. Provided that the party does so, there is no reason for the party not to sign the Terms of Reference due to its jurisdictional objections.

23–76 As mentiond in para.23–72, the Secretariat will review the draft Terms of Reference to ensure that the draft complies with the requirements of the ICC Rules. This review is particularly important where a party is not participating in the procedure or is participating but has indicated that it has reservations about signing the Terms of Reference. After the Terms of Reference have been signed, the ICC Court will review the Terms of Reference submitted by the Tribunal to determine whether they meet the requirements of the Rules and, if a party has objected to particular provisions, whether the party's objection is justified. It may be, for example, that the drafting was inappropriate and that the party's refusal to sign was justified. In such a case the ICC Court would be expected to return the Terms of Reference to the Tribunal for modification. If the Tribunal has any questions as to the draft Terms of Reference where a party is refusing to sign them, the president may wish to go over the issues with the Secretariat to determine whether there is an issue based on prior ICC Court practice.

23–77 As discussed under art.1, the ICC Court will provide no reasons for its decision, as all the decisions of the ICC Court are administrative in nature and for that reason need not be reasoned. If the non-signing party objects to the approval of the Terms of Reference, it will usually have no recourse against the decision. However, if the ICC Court approves the Terms of Reference over the objection of a party, then the Terms of Reference would meet the requirements of the Rules.

23–78 Article 23(3) states that the arbitration shall proceed upon signature of the Terms of Reference or upon approval by the ICC Court of the Terms of Reference. However, in some instances, the Tribunal will take steps with respect to the procedure under art.19 prior to the signing of the Terms of Reference.[35]

23–79 As stated above, the signing or approval of the Terms of Reference is the starting point for the initial six-month period for the Tribunal to submit an Award in accordance with art.30(1).

[35] For example, if one or both parties are seeking to accelerate the arbitration, the Tribunal may indicate when it expects to receive submissions or even issue a procedural order to that effect. In effect, the time for the preparation of the submission will run prior to the signing of the Terms of Reference.

Sometimes, certain obligations are added to the Terms of Reference, such as an express agreement as to confidentiality. If one party signs the Terms of Reference, but not the other, two issues arise. The first issue is whether the ICC Court's approval of the Terms of Reference binds the non-signatory. The answer has two aspects: 23–80

(i) As far as obligations or undertakings are added to the Terms of Reference which go beyond the Rules and the arbitration agreement, the ICC Court's approval of the Terms of Reference will not extend new obligations upon the non-signatory.
(ii) Insofar as by approving the Terms of Reference a procedural requirement for rendering the Award will be deemed to have occurred and will allow the arbitration to move forward, then the Terms of Reference as approved by the ICC Court have a binding effect. Moreover, by accepting the ICC Rules the parties are agreeing that the Terms of Reference may be established in accordance with art.23(3).

A second issue is whether the party who signed the Terms of Reference is bound by a duty included in the Terms of Reference, when the opposing party will not be bound by the same duty by virtue of its refusal to sign the Terms of Reference. The issue does not arise if the Tribunal limits the Terms of Reference to the requirements of the Rules. If that is not the case, and there is no provision conditioning a party's obligations on acceptance by the other party, then the signatory may well have an argument that there is a lack of mutuality in the obligations if the other party has refused to sign the Terms of Reference. However, the effect on the signatory will depend on the law governing the arbitration agreement. 23–81

Article 23(4): "After the Terms of Reference have been signed or approved by the Court, no party shall make new claims which fall outside the limits of the Terms of Reference unless it has been authorized to do so by the arbitral tribunal, which shall consider the nature of such new claims, the stage of the arbitration and other relevant circumstances."

The Terms of Reference are intended to set out an agreed framework for an ICC arbitration. Although they are drafted at an early stage in the proceedings, they should give to the parties and the Tribunal an indication of the nature and subject matter of the dispute and the claims. 23–82

The purpose of art.23(4) is to avoid having the agreed framework of the arbitration unilaterally changed by one of the parties, and in particular any delay or disruption in the proceedings by that party. There must be a point in time when the parties can no longer present new claims, so that the arbitration can be brought to its end.[36] It is not, however, intended to limit the parties' right to make new factual allegations or legal arguments to support their claims, unless the new allegations or arguments would somehow amount to a new claim.[37] This sometimes causes 23–83

[36] See for example ICC case No.7184 (1994), (1997) ICC ICArb Bull Vol.8 No.2 p.64.

[37] See for example ICC case No.7047 (1994) ("A claim is new and not within the limits of art.16 of the ICC Rules only if it is raised issues of fact and of law which are completely new compared with the issue in dispute so far. If, however, a claim is subsequently based on different legal reasoning,

tension in the arbitration, as the late introduction of new allegations and/or arguments may be as disruptive for the arbitral proceedings as a new claim.[38]

23–84 The term "claim" is defined in art.2(iv), and its nature has been discussed under art.23(1). Article 23(4) is based on the assumption that certain claims that are not referred to in the Terms of Reference will by their nature fall within the overall scope of the Terms of Reference. The determination of what falls within or outside the limits of the Terms of Reference will depend on the manner in which the claims are framed in the Terms of Reference. The difficulty arises in part due to the absence of definition of what constitutes "new claims" in the Rules. However, the scope of the Terms of Reference can and should be examined with reference to the requests for relief. If the new claim leads to a modification of the relief sought, or to an additional request for relief then there may well be an issue as to whether it is within the scope of the Terms of Reference.[39]

23–85 In determining whether a claim is within the scope of the Terms of Reference, the Tribunal should verify whether the new relief is based on new facts and/or new legal arguments or whether it is a change in the nature of the relief sought. If a party claims declaratory relief (e.g. that the buyer owes the sales price as of a given date that has not yet occurred) and then changes the claim to seek performance, that is payment (in the example of payment of the purchase price, the due date having now occurred), the change of relief sought would not qualify as a new claim outside the limits of the Terms of Reference, unless there were indeed new facts and/or legal arguments that were not mentioned in the Terms of Reference.

23–86 The scope of the application of art.23(4) is, in practice, limited and based on the following rationale: the Terms of Reference describe the mission of the Tribunal. If new claims are being made by a party that are not covered by the Terms of Reference, then the mission of the Tribunal is being altered. Such alteration shall only be possible if the Tribunal has authorised it. The Tribunal has broad discretion in whether or not to authorise the new claim.

23–87 For example, if a new claim concerns the same contract and the factual basis for the claim is the same as that of existing claims, then a Tribunal may well conclude that the claim is within the Terms of Reference. Similarly, a new, although alternative claim for relief may well be treated in the same fashion. A totally new request for relief may be beyond the scope of the Terms of Reference.

23–88 In ICC case No.6197, the issue was whether a claim was a new claim and whether it was outside the Terms of Reference. The Tribunal held that:

> "[53] [. . .] Claimant requests the payment by the defendant of the equivalent value in the currency of country B of [an amount], as reimbursement of the sum which it had to pay to the subcontractor following

but still on the same facts, it is within the limits of art.16 [of the 1988] ICC Rules") and ICC case No.6223 (1991), (1997) ICC ICArb Bull Vol.8 No.2 at p.62 and p.70.

[38] This point was rightly made by Schwartz in his comprehensive analysis of art.19, see "New Claims in ICC Arbitration: Navigating Article 19 of the ICC Rules" (2006) ICC ICArb Bull Vol.17 No.2, p.55; see also Derains, "Amendments to the claims and new claims: where to draw the line?" in *Arbitral Procedure at the Dawn of the Millennium* (Bruylant, 2005), p.65.

[39] See Bühler & Jarvin, *op. cit.*, para.21–84. See also Derains & Schwartz, *op cit.*, at p.269; Webster, "Terms of Reference and French Annulment Proceedings", *op. cit*, at p.563 and p.583.

the substitution of the three-phase sedimentation tank by a two-phase system. The arbitral tribunal notes that this constitutes a new claim in the sense of art. 16 of the ICC Rules [predecessor to art.23(4)] because it is not explicitly mentioned in the Terms of Reference. However, the arbitral tribunal believes that this claim is within the limits of the Terms of Reference because there is a sufficient connection between the original claims by the Claimant and the new claim submitted by it (cf. Lazareff: 'L'Acte de mission selon le règlement d'arbitrage de la CCI de 1988, p.29).

[54] As a matter of fact, in the request for arbitration, the Claimant stated the poor functioning of the installation was caused by, among other things, the substitution by the defendant of the three-phase sedimentation tank by a two-phase system. The new claim of the Claimant does concern this substitution, since the Claimant is requesting that the defendant pay it an amount representing the difference between the cost of the two-phase sedimentation tank system and that of the three-phase system, plus the costs of the operation because according to the claimant, this operation should have been done without changing the price of the installation.

[55] In view of the above considerations, it must be allowed that this new request falls within the limits of the Terms of Reference (See also ICC case no.3267 in Yearbook Commercial Arbitration XII (1987) p.87 at pp.91–92)."[40]

In the above arbitration, which was decided under the 1988 ICC Rules, the Tribunal focused on the nature of the relief sought to determine whether there was a new claim. The Tribunal then focused on the factual allegations to determine whether the claim was within the Terms of Reference or not.[41] The nature of the sedimentation tank was a basic factual element that related to both the prior claim and the new claim. Therefore, for the Tribunal, there was a sufficient connection between the two claims to fall within the Terms of Reference. This reasoning is convincing because in an ICC arbitration, one of the key issues is ensuring that the parties have the possibility of presenting their factual and expert evidence relating to the dispute. If the evidentiary issues of the existing and the new claims are closely related, then not only is there no prejudice in accepting the new claim, but it is more cost-effective to have it dealt with in the same proceedings. **23–89**

Most Terms of Reference are specific about the contract(s) on which claims are brought. Therefore, if the Terms of Reference are based entirely on one contract between the parties and a party wishes to add a claim based on another contract (but containing an identical or at least compatible arbitration clause), which it can do in accordance with art.9, then it might well be outside the scope of the Terms of Reference. In that case, an authorisation by the Tribunal pursuant to art.23(4) would be required. An exception may arise where the subject matter of the two **23–90**

[40] ICC case No.6197 (1995), (1998) YBCA Vol.XXIII p.13 at p.27.

[41] The Tribunal's decision was important as ICC Tribunals did not have the right to permit new claims outside the limits of the Terms of Reference without the consent of all parties under the prior ICC 1988 Rules that were applicable to this arbitration.

contracts is closely connected and the underlying facts identical, or at least very similar, as may be the case in transactions with repeat purchase orders. In such a case under a broad view, it might still be held that the new claims fall within the Terms of Reference.[42]

23–91 An issue that is not often addressed is the effect of broad "saving" clauses on the scope of the Terms of Reference. It is commonplace for parties in the Request and the Answer to reserve their rights to add claims. If the Terms of Reference simply refer to the claims of the parties in these documents and in the submissions, there may be an issue of whether the parties have agreed that new claims may be added.[43]

23–92 In deciding whether to permit the addition of new claims that fall outside the limits of the Terms of Reference, the Tribunal "shall consider the nature of such new claims, the stage of the arbitration and other relevant circumstances".[44] As the words "other relevant circumstances" suggest, the Tribunal has broad discretion in deciding whether or not to authorise the new claim to be pursued in the pending arbitration. The closer a claim is to an existing claim, the more likely the claim is to be accepted. This will apply for all new requests for ancillary or incidental relief, such as a claim for interest, or for the costs of arbitration. If the new claim is raised shortly after the signing of the Terms of Reference, it is much more likely to be accepted than if it is made during or after the oral hearings. The Tribunal will also want to consider a party's ability to have introduced these claims at an earlier time. If new claims were withheld for purely tactical reasons, and are suddenly introduced into the proceedings, the Tribunal may take a restrictive attitude, provided there are other factors that might militate against the belated introduction of the new claims. Those factors would include the ability of the parties to submit evidence and arguments on the new claims. However, these examples reflect the basic principle that the addition of new claims outside the limits of the Terms of Reference should not be permitted if it would raise due process issues under the Rules,[45] the law of the place of arbitration or the law of the place of probable enforcement.

[42] See ICC case No.7184 (1997) ICC ICArb Bull Vol.8 No.2 p.64: "all seven orders appear, in fact to be commercially linked with each other to a substantial degree. They all contain the same identical arbitration clause [. . .]. Furthermore, all seven orders have the same object [. . .]. All contracts have been concluded within two meetings [. . .]. This is confirmed by the parties' subsequent conduct of not distinguishing in their further contractual behaviour between orders invoked by Claimant and those invoked by Respondent. The orders also highly resemble one another going by their outward appearance".

[43] When parties seek to insert such a general provision in the Terms of Reference, Tribunals will generally insist that there be a reference to art.23(4), which in effect limits the expansive nature of the clause.

[44] See, in turn, art.23(2) of the UNCITRAL Model Law which considers the delay in amending or supplementing a claim or defence during the course of the arbitral proceedings.

[45] In *Karaha Bodas Co LLC v Perusahaan Pertambangan Minyak Dan Gas Bumi Negara*, 190F Supp. 2d936 (D. Tex. 2001) the argument was made that that enforcement of an Award should be refused because: "[S]ix weeks before the hearing, in early May 2000, KBC filed a Rebuttal with the Tribunal. Pertamina contends that it was prejudiced by KBC's Rebuttal because KBC allegedly included an entirely new position on the financing of the Project, made new allegations of the conduct constituting Pertamina's breach, relied on newly-submitted awards in the arbitrations known as Himpurna and Patuha, identified additional witnesses, and presented new documentary evidence. Pertamina asserts that it was required to secure new experts and fact witnesses and to impose upon its existing experts and fact witnesses to review KBC's Rebuttal submissions in four

ICC arbitration is intended to be cost-effective, and art.22(1) explicitly requires the Tribunal and the Parties to conduct the arbitration "in an expeditious and cost-effective manner".[46] Therefore, to the extent possible, disputes between the parties that are covered by the relevant arbitration agreement should be resolved in one and the same proceeding. A party may therefore expressly agree that a new claim be added pursuant to art.23(4), or may decide not to object to the adding of the new claim, as the party may prefer to have the new claim dealt with in the pending arbitration rather than to be involved in a subsequent arbitration. In such a case, a Tribunal is likely to authorise the introduction of the new claim, irrespective of any other consideration. However, if a new claim is raised and a party objects that it would not have a "reasonable opportunity to present its case" within the meaning of art.22(4), and the Tribunal finds the objection justified, then there is a due process problem in including the new claim in the ongoing arbitration. In that case, the new claim needs to be pursued in a new arbitration. 23–93

If a Tribunal accepts that a new claim be added under art.23(4), the party against whom such a claim is asserted must register its objections or risk waiving them under art.39. The response from some Tribunals when faced with such an objection is to ask the party how it would propose to deal with the situation. If the party feels that it is not possible to deal with the issue, it must confirm its position and ensure that there is a record that any steps it takes to deal with the procedural problem are without prejudice to its basic position that the claim should not be added. Then, the issue of whether the new claim gives rise to due process issues will be dealt with if and when necessary by the national court dealing with the annulment or enforcement proceedings. 23–94

If the Tribunal refuses to accept a new claim, the party asserting it usually has the possibility of bringing new arbitration proceedings under the ICC Rules. However, pursuant to art.10, the factors to consider in a consolidation include whether arbitrators have been appointed or confirmed and whether different persons have been confirmed or appointed as arbitrators. 23–95

Another at least theoretical possibility for an unsuccessful party would be to bring proceedings in the place of arbitration based on an *infra petita* argument and argue that the court should remit the matter to the Tribunal to complete the arbitration. 23–96

The impact of art.23(4) should not be overestimated. The parties should make every effort to have all relevant claims within the Terms of Reference. In using the powers granted to it by art.23(4) to permit new claims, the Tribunal should in fact take into account the effect of admitting the new claims on the conduct of the 23–97

weeks. Pertamina further contends it had insufficient time post-Rebuttal to prepare for the hearing. The Court rejected this argument on the basis that: "In fact, KBC's Rebuttal did not assert any new claims or new legal theories for recovery. KBC's Rebuttal responded to specific defenses asserted in Respondents' Reply by specifying additional facts, argument, and authority supporting its claims, including the Himpurna and Patuha awards. The Court is aware of no rule or law that obligated KBC to specify in its Revised Statement of Claim all evidence it intended to submit, and every argument it intended to make, ultimately to support its claims at the hearing. Pertamina had notice of KBC's claims, and should have anticipated that KBC would contest its defenses". The court thus drew a distinction between "new claims or legal theories for recovery" (which arguably could raise a due process issue) and filing a defence (which raised no due process issue).

[46] See the discussion under art.22(1).

proceedings. If the new claim is filed at a time that allows the other side to respond to it without seriously delaying the timetable that was previously agreed, there would be no reason not to admit it, even if such claim could have been submitted before. On the contrary, if the admission of the new claim will delay the proceedings, consideration of fairness could lead a Tribunal to refuse to accept the claim if it is satisfied that the claim could reasonably have been submitted before.

23–98 Article 23(4) does not prescribe how the Tribunal should authorise the new claim or set limits as to the timing. Generally, one would expect the issue to be dealt with by way of a procedural order where a specific application has been made by one party and the other party has raised objections thereto. However, the Tribunal may deal with the issue by letter. It is conceivable that the Tribunal record the new claim in the Award but this could only be done if the Tribunal is satisfied that all parties are on notice of the new claim and have had a reasonable opportunity to be heard with respect to it in accordance with art.22(4) and applicable law.

Article 24 Case Management Conference and Procedural Timetable

1 When drawing up the Terms of Reference or as soon as possible thereafter, the arbitral tribunal shall convene a case management conference to consult the parties on procedural measures that may be adopted pursuant to Article 22(2). Such measures may include one or more of the case management techniques described in Appendix IV.

2 During or following such conference, the arbitral tribunal shall establish the procedural timetable that it intends to follow for the conduct of the arbitration. The procedural timetable and any modifications thereto shall be communicated to the Court and the parties.

3 To ensure continued effective case management, the arbitral tribunal, after consulting the parties by means of a further case management conference or otherwise, may adopt further procedural measures or modify the procedural timetable.

4 Case management conferences may be conducted through a meeting in person, by video conference, telephone or similar means of communication. In the absence of an agreement of the parties, the arbitral tribunal shall determine the means by which the conference will be conducted. The arbitral tribunal may request the parties to submit case management proposals in advance of a case management conference and may request the attendance at any case management conference of the parties in person or through an internal representative.[1]

Introductory remarks

Article 24 is intended to provide a framework for an efficient organisation of the arbitration. Article 24(2) is based on art.18(4) of the 1998 Rules. The remaining provisions of art.24 are new, although the idea behind them is not. **24–1**

[1] Article 24(2) corresponds to art.18(4) of the 1998 ICC Rules. The remaining provisions of art.24 are new.

24–2 The organisation of the written proceedings is discussed in detail in art.25 and the organisation of the hearings is discussed in art.26. The discussion at the case management conference should be based on the needs that have been identified for those stages of the proceedings. Therefore, in considering all of the procedural issues, it is important the parties review the details of what they wish or need under arts 25 and 26.

24–3 The case management conference takes place at the outset of the proceedings, usually at the same time as the signing of the Terms of Reference. It places a premium on an early review of the file by the Tribunal. In addition, it is important to separate out issues that can and cannot be decided at this stage. For example, the importance of some issues may not become apparent until the parties file their memorials. Therefore, issues of relevance and materiality may be difficult to ascertain at this stage. In addition, it may be that the parties prefer to deal with issues such as the detailed organisation of the evidentiary hearings, whether there should be a hearing for legal argument or whether there should be post-hearing submissions for later in the proceedings.

Article 24 (1): "When drawing up the Terms of Reference or as soon as possible thereafter, the arbitral tribunal shall convene a case management conference to consult the parties on procedural measures that may be adopted pursuant to Article 22(2). Such measures may include one or more of the case management techniques described in Appendix IV."

24–4 Pursuant to art.24(1), the case management conference is to be held when the Terms of Reference are drawn up or as soon as possible thereafter. As discussed under art.23, the Rules provide that the Terms of Reference are generally to be drawn up within two months after the file has been transmitted to the Tribunal. Therefore, as a general rule the case management conference should take place within approximately two months of the transmittal of the file to the Tribunal. Therefore, in accepting a position as arbitrator, an arbitrator is undertaking to have reasonable availability to meet this requirement either by attending an in-person case management conference or attending by way of video conference.

24–5 Article 24(1) is drafted in terms of a requirement that there be a case management conference. If the parties and the Tribunal agree, they can dispense with a case management conference. The ICC Court will not refuse to approve signed Terms of Reference or otherwise object if the parties and the Tribunal have agreed on the Terms of Reference and have agreed or made submissions on procedural issues without a case management conference.

24–6 If a party insists that there be a case management conference, however, the party is entitled to have that conference pursuant to art.24(1) and subject to the provisions of art.24(4) as to how that may be conducted.

24–7 Article 24(1) refers back to art.22(2), which provides as follows:

> "In order to ensure effective case management, the arbitral tribunal, after consulting the parties, may adopt such procedural measures as it considers appropriate, provided that they are not contrary to any agreement of the parties."

Therefore, art.24(1) is based on the principle that the parties may agree on the procedure and that, in any event, the parties should be consulted prior to adopting procedural measures. As mentioned above, the actual subject matter of those procedural measures is dealt with in various other provisions, and in art.25 and art.26 in particular. **24–8**

The case management conference is also intended to provide an occasion to discuss if need be any of the case management techniques described in App.IV of the 2012 "ICC Report Controlling Time and Costs in Arbitration".[2] Appendix IV states as follows: **24–9**

> "The following are examples of case management techniques that can be used by the arbitral tribunal and the parties for controlling time and cost. Appropriate control of time and cost is important in all cases. In cases of low complexity and low value, it is particularly important to ensure that time and costs are proportionate to what is at stake in the dispute.
>
> a) Bifurcating the proceedings or rendering one or more partial awards on key issues, when doing so may genuinely be expected to result in a more efficient resolution of the case.
> b) Identifying issues that can be resolved by agreement between the parties or their experts.
> c) Identifying issues to be decided solely on the basis of documents rather than through oral evidence or legal argument at a hearing.
> d) Production of documentary evidence:
>   (i) requiring the parties to produce with their submissions the documents on which they rely;
>   (ii) avoiding requests for document production when appropriate in order to control time and cost;
>   (iii) in those cases where requests for document production are considered appropriate, limiting such requests to documents or categories of documents that are relevant and material to the outcome of the case;
>   (iv) establishing reasonable time limits for the production of documents;
>   (v) using a schedule of document production to facilitate the resolution of issues in relation to the production of documents.
> e) Limiting the length and scope of written submissions and written and oral witness evidence (both fact witnesses and experts) so as to avoid repetition and maintain a focus on key issues.
> f) Using telephone or video conferencing for procedural and other hearings where attendance in person is not essential and use of IT that enables online communication among the parties, the arbitral tribunal and the Secretariat of the Court.

[2] Pt III, App. 2

g) Organising a pre-hearing conference with the arbitral tribunal at which arrangements for a hearing can be discussed and agreed and the arbitral tribunal can indicate to the parties issues on which it would like the parties to focus at the hearing.

h) Settlement of disputes:

(i) informing the parties that they are free to settle all or part of the dispute either by negotiation or through any form of amicable dispute resolution methods such as, for example, mediation under the ICC ADR Rules;

(ii) where agreed between the parties and the arbitral tribunal, the arbitral tribunal may take steps to facilitate settlement of the dispute, provided that every effort is made to ensure that any subsequent award is enforceable at law."

24–10 The list in App.IV is a checklist of elements that may, at some stage of the proceedings, be relevant. However, where experienced counsel are involved, they will be familiar with these techniques and will have considered them without the assistance of the Tribunal. Indeed, some of these techniques are appropriate for smaller cases only.

24–11 The usual approach is to raise various procedural issues with the parties prior to the case management conference so that the parties may express their preferences as to the procedure. In this context, it is useful to refer to the case management techniques but without seeking to discuss each of them at the case management conference. Some of the issues referred to in App.IV, such as bifurcation or the manner of producing documents, are frequently dealt with at this stage. Other issues, such as whether it is necessary to have hearings on certain issues should normally be limited to basic procedural issues, such as the language of the arbitration and perhaps the applicable law to the contract. In addition, at this stage, the Tribunal is not usually in an ideal position to decide on issues such as the length of submissions or witness evidence. Usually, at this stage, the parties may only be able to provide a rough indication as to the number of witnesses—subject to the evidence submitted by the other side. As regards settlement, the issue would also appear to be premature at this stage.

24–12 If one or more parties are not participating, there is an issue as to whether the Tribunal is required to hold a case management conference. Usually, if there is a party default, the Tribunal will propose a case management conference and invite the parties to confirm their availability. If the defaulting party confirms that it will not attend, then that defaulting party is waiving its right to participate in the case management conference and, if the other parties waive the case management conference, there is no need that it be held. If the defaulting party does not respond, then, usually the Tribunal will wish to hold the hearing, although it may be with just one party. To avoid unnecessary costs in such instances, if there is no indication that the defaulting party will attend and if the other parties do not wish to have an in-person case management conference, the most cost effective approach would be to hold the case management conference by telephone (with call-in numbers for each party) as is provided for in art.24(4).

If a hearing is held and the defaulting party does not attend, then the defaulting party has waived its right to object to the hearing itself under art.39. Nevertheless, as with any hearing, the Tribunal should notify the defaulting party of what transpired by preparing summary minutes. The better view is that a party failing to attend waives its right to challenge matters decided at that meeting, provided that there is a clear record of what was to be dealt with at the meeting. Therefore, although the defaulting party should be provided with minutes of the meeting, and a Tribunal should carefully consider any comments with respect thereto, it would be disruptive of the proceedings to permit the defaulting party to ignore the case management meeting and then challenge matters decided at it on the basis that it did not participate. **24–13**

Article 24(2): "During or following such conference, the arbitral tribunal shall establish the procedural timetable that it intends to follow for the conduct of the arbitration. The procedural timetable and any modifications thereto shall be communicated to the Court and the parties."

To establish the procedural timetable (which is also sometimes referred to as the provisional timetable), the Tribunal needs to have a clear idea as to the procedure to be followed and the time limits that are to be followed. Therefore, the procedural timetable is integrally linked to the procedure discussed under arts 22 and 25. **24–14**

Ideally, the timetable will cover the entire proceedings, up to the final hearing, and the ensuing Award. The scope of the timetable will very much depend on the structure of the proceedings. If they are bifurcated (with a liability phase and a damages phase, for example), the timetable will typically only cover the first phase of the proceedings. An example of a procedural timetable is to be found in Pt II, Document 16. In accordance with art.27, when it closes the proceedings, the Tribunal is required to provide the ICC Court and the parties with the date by which it expects to submit its draft Award. Since the procedural timetable relates not only to submissions of the parties and hearings but also to deliberations and rendering the Award, it is submitted that it is preferable to indicate at the outset the time period that the Tribunal will require after the last submission to prepare the draft Award. **24–15**

In order to assist the ICC Court in monitoring the arbitration, in particular pursuant to art.30(2), when extensions of time for rendering the Award are to be granted, the Tribunal is required to communicate any subsequent modifications of the procedural timetable to the Court. Naturally, the parties are to be informed of those modifications as well. The parties will often be the cause of the modifications, for example when they request an extension of time for making a certain submission. In any event, the Tribunal will generally consult the parties before the procedural timetable is modified. **24–16**

Article 24(3): "To ensure continued effective case management, the arbitral tribunal, after consulting the parties by means of a further case management conference or otherwise, may adopt further procedural measures or modify the procedural timetable."

Generally, there is a case management conference by telephone prior to the hearings. This type of case management conference is intended to ensure that **24–17** the hearings are organised smoothly and effectively and that any issues that can be dealt with prior to the hearings are so dealt with. In addition, there may be hearings, either by telephone, videoconference or in person to deal with specific procedural issues, such as disclosure of documents. However, these are generally oriented to the procedural issues and not case management.

24–18 The main aspect of art.24(3) is the recognition that the Tribunal may adopt further procedural measures and modify the procedural timetable. Usually, Tribunals will adopt a series of procedural orders to deal with issues as they arise (such as production of documents). In addition, there may be issues as to the timing of submissions and the need to modify the procedural timetable as a result. The Tribunal has the right to adopt such measures and change the procedural timetable after it has consulted with the parties and subject to the overriding duty to ensure that each party has a reasonable opportunity to present its case as discussed under art.22(4).

Article 24(4): "Case management conferences may be conducted through a meeting in person, by video conference, telephone or similar means of communication. In the absence of an agreement of the parties, the arbitral tribunal shall determine the means by which the conference will be conducted. The arbitral tribunal may request the parties to submit case management proposals in advance of a case management conference and may request the attendance at any case management conference of the parties in person or through an internal representative."

24–19 To be cost effective, it may be advisable to hold a case management conference by telephone or video conference. The second sentence of art.24(4) provides the Tribunal with the right to determine the method of holding the conference.

24–20 Tribunals can and usually do request that parties comment on the proposed organisation of the case management conference prior to it being held. The comments are usually intended to cover all matters to be dealt with at the case management conference including comments on the draft Terms of Reference, on the procedural issues to be adopted pursuant to art.22(2), the procedural timetable and, in some cases, whether the parties wish to consider the case management techniques in App.IV. The priority for many arbitrators is to encourage the parties not only to comment, but also to confer with or among each other with a view to arriving at joint proposals for the procedure.

Article 25 Establishing the Facts of the Case

1. **The arbitral tribunal shall proceed within as short a time as possible to establish the facts of the case by all appropriate means.**
2. **After studying the written submissions of the parties and all documents relied upon, the arbitral tribunal shall hear the parties together in person if any of them so requests or, failing such a request, it may of its own motion decide to hear them.**
3. **The arbitral tribunal may decide to hear witnesses, experts appointed by the parties or any other person, in the presence of the parties, or in their absence provided they have been duly summoned.**
4. **The arbitral tribunal, after having consulted the parties, may appoint one or more experts, define their terms of reference and receive their reports. At the request of a party, the parties shall be given the opportunity to question at a hearing any such expert.**
5. **At any time during the proceedings, the arbitral tribunal may summon any party to provide additional evidence.**
6. **The arbitral tribunal may decide the case solely on the documents submitted by the parties unless any of the parties requests a hearing.**[1]

Introductory remarks

To decide a dispute in an ICC arbitration, the Tribunal has to ascertain the facts and will receive submissions from the parties. Article 25 refers to "establishing the facts of the case", but the procedure will deal with both facts and law. Since the rules of law applicable to the merits of the dispute will frequently not be that of one or more of the arbitrators, legal submissions will usually be detailed. This is particularly the case if the dispute raises not just questions of **25–1**

[1] Article 25 corresponds to art.20 of the 1998 ICC Rules. No substantive changes have been made.

contractual interpretation and/or the principle of good faith but defences based on applicable law. In ICC arbitrations, there is no generally accepted concept that "foreign law is an issue of fact" or that specific rules of law must be proven by expert evidence.[2] However, in many cases the parties will submit expert reports on the rules of the governing law, particularly with respect to the law applicable to part of a dispute.[3]

25–2 The Terms of Reference provide the framework for the arbitral proceedings, but, as discussed under art.23, they generally do not set out the detailed procedure to be followed during the arbitral proceedings. That procedure is usually decided upon by the Tribunal and set out in procedural orders in accordance with art.22, after having solicited the view of the parties through written or oral submissions in accordance in particular with arts 22 and 24. The basic principle in international arbitration is that the parties, within certain limits, may agree on the procedure. Where the parties do not agree, the Tribunal generally sets the procedure. In practice, the Tribunal usually decides upon the procedure after consultation with the parties.

25–3 The fact that there is no procedural code for international arbitration makes this an area that varies the most from arbitration to arbitration. That is, perhaps, hardly surprising. International arbitration is flexible and evolving, as are the disputes that it aims to resolve.

25–4 However, within that broad framework, there are guidelines as to how the arbitral procedure may be arrived at. In the context of ad hoc arbitration, such a procedure is described in the UNCITRAL Notes on Organising Arbitral Proceedings.[4] Those principles can be adapted to ICC arbitration, which also provides comments on procedure. More importantly, a group of international practitioners developed the IBA Rules on Evidence, which are discussed further below (and which are set out in Pt III, App.10) and which are often referred to in ICC arbitration.[5] In addition, a Task Force created by the ICC Commission on Arbitration published a report updated in 2012 entitled "Techniques for Controlling Time and Costs in Arbitration".[6] That report provides comments on procedural aspects of arbitration, particularly with a view to reducing costs and time involved in the proceedings.

25–5 In previous editions of this Handbook, we have referred extensively in particular to the IBA Rules on Evidence. Since the first edition of the Handbook these rules or principles based on them have been increasingly accepted in international arbitration to the point, where in international arbitration

[2] On the subject of *iura novit euria*, see Kaufmann-Kohler, " 'Iura Novit arbiter'—est-ce bien raisonnable? Réflexions sur le statut du droit de fond devant l'arbitre international" in *De Lege Ferenda Réflexions sur le droit désirable en l'honneur du Professeur Alain Hirsch, op. cit.*

[3] For example, if Swiss law is the substantive governing law but one of the issues relates to corporate formalities under Cayman Islands law, parties may submit expert evidence on Cayman Islands law, while dealing with Swiss law as the law to be argued.

[4] *http://www.uncitral.org* [accessed November 20, 2013].

[5] Admittedly, many parties and their counsel who are not actively involved in international arbitration hear about the IBA Rules on Evidence for the first time when they are being referred to in an arbitration.

[6] http://www.iccwbo.org/Advocacy-Codes-and-Rules/Document-centre/2012/ICC-Arbitration-Commission-Report-on-Techniques-for-Controlling-Time-and-Costs-in-Arbitration [accessed November 2, 2013].

generally, and not just in ICC arbitration, these principles have become a standard point of reference.

Nevertheless, there is still an underlying theme with regard to procedure which is sometimes the relative influence of the common law and civil law approaches.[7] Article 25 provides that the Tribunal shall proceed to establish the facts of the case by all appropriate means. This provision reflects an obligation on the Tribunal to direct the proceedings, as one would expect in civil law proceedings given the inquisitorial approach of the judge in a civil law jurisdiction.[8] However, the reference to appropriate means gives the Tribunal the latitude—which most Tribunals use—to ensure that the parties take the proper steps to furnish the memorials and evidence required to establish the facts of the case. As discussed below, the appropriate means to establish the fact is frequently a hybrid of methods using elements from various civil and common law systems. **25–6**

As mentioned above, the Tribunal will consult with the parties prior to establishing the procedure and should do so at the case management conference discussed under art.24. When the Tribunal submits a draft of the Terms of Reference to the parties, it may well submit either a list of procedural points for consideration by the parties or a draft procedural order.[9] This permits the parties to comment on the proposed procedure in advance of the Terms of Reference or procedural hearing. To the extent that the parties agree on the procedure, the Tribunal will usually give this agreement considerable weight. Indeed, a failure to follow a procedure agreement by the parties may give rise to an objection under **25–7**

[7] The common law/civil law nomenclature is, in some respects, misleading. There are very significant differences in procedure between that in the United States and in England, for example, or between the procedure in France and Germany or Switzerland. However, to the extent that the terms are shorthand for differing national procedural approaches in certain jurisdictions, they are useful. Moreover, the view that international arbitration procedure is now independent of national procedure, while understandable, fails to reflect the ongoing interaction between national procedure and international arbitration. One of the advantages of international arbitration is that it can continue to adapt procedure to the requirements of each arbitration and it may be that national procedure provides very useful tools in this respect. For a general discussion, see for example Paulsson, "The Timely Arbitrator: Reflections on the Böckstiegel Method" (2006) Arb Int Vol.22 No.1, p.19 ("What the presiding arbitrator needs to do is to consult with counsel in order to understand their desiradata and expectations, and to explain those of the arbitral tribunal"; Lazareff, "L'arbitre singe ou comment assassiner l'arbitrage" in *Liber Amicorum in honour of Robert Briner, op. cit.*, p.477, at p.485, emphasising the necessity to make a distinction between the rules of procedure which must be respected by the Tribunal failing which the Award may be challenged and set aside (art.15) and the instruction of the case itself which is within the power and control of the Tribunal unless contractual restrictions have been imposed in the Terms of Reference (art.20); Pietrowski, "Evidence in International Arbitration" (2006) Arb Int Vol.22 No.3, p.373; Cordero Moss, "Is the Arbitral Tribunal Bound by the Parties' Factual and Legal Pleadings?" SIAR 2006:3, p.1; de Boisséson, "Comparative Introduction to the System of Producing Evidence in Common Law Countries and Countries of Roman Law Tradition" in ICC Publication no.440/8, *Taking of Evidence in International Proceedings* (1990); Reymond, "Civil and Common Law Procedures: Which is the More Inquisitorial? A Civil lawyer's Response" (1989) Arb Int Vol.5 No.4, p.357; see also Blessing, "The ICC Arbitral Procedure Under the 1998 ICC Rules—What Has Changed?" (1997) ICC ICArb Bull Vol. 8 No.2, p.16 at p.28 and "The ICC Arbitral Process (Part III): The Procedure before the Arbitral Tribunal" (1992) ICC ICArb Bull Vol. 3 No.2, p.18.

[8] Reymond, "Civil and Common Law Procedures: Which is the More Inquisitorial? A Civil lawyer's Response", *op. cit.*, p.357.

[9] An example of such a list is provided in Pt II, Document 14.

art.19 and art.22, the applicable law of arbitration[10] and/or the New York Convention.[11]

25–8 Tribunals will often ask the parties to comment on procedural aspects such as the following which are discussed under the provisions of arts 25 and 26 referred to in parenthesis:

(1) the number of memorials and the time required for their preparation (art.25(2));

(2) the timing and method of submission of documents (art.25(2));

(3) the use of witness statements and interviewing of factual witnesses (art.25(3));

(4) expert evidence through the Tribunal or the parties (art.25(4));

(5) whether and when there should be disclosure of documents, (art.25(5));

(6) confidentiality of documents submitted (art.22(3));

(7) whether there should be hearings and how the hearings are to be conducted and the use of cross examination (art.25(6) and art.26);

(8) whether there should be a transcript of the hearing (art.26);

(9) the submission of post-hearing briefs and/or the holding of a separate hearing for legal argument (art.26).

Article 25(1): "The arbitral tribunal shall proceed within as short a time as possible to establish the facts of the case by all appropriate means."

25–9 Under art.25(1), it is the obligation of the Tribunal to establish the facts of the case. Article 30(1) imposes a further obligation on the Tribunal as it states that the Tribunal is to render its final Award within six months from the Terms of Reference. This time frame is very difficult to follow and is not met in most cases submitted to ICC arbitration. Article 30(1) therefore provides for extensions. But the requirement that the Tribunal take the initiative to complete the proceedings within a certain time frame is unlike that in most national courts.

25–10 Management of the proceedings is important at all stages of the arbitration. Arbitral proceedings may have to be adapted to changing circumstances, and the parties may perceive ever more diverging interests as the procedure develops. Therefore, on each occasion on which the Tribunal changes the procedure, it should ensure that the result is not to derail subsequent proceedings.

25–11 The detailed means for establishing the facts of the case are discussed under the various other subsections of art.25. However, it should be noted that establishing the facts of the case depends basically on evidence provided by the parties and their counsel in ICC arbitration. It is seldom that a Tribunal will take the initiative

[10] Article 19(1) of the UNCITRAL Model Law gives priority to an agreement between the parties as to the procedure; s.34(1) of the English Arbitration Act 1996 is to the same effect: "It shall be for the tribunal to decide all procedural and evidential matters, subject to the right of the parties to agree any matter."

[11] Article V(1)(d) provides, inter alia, that recognition of an Award may be refused where "the arbitral procedure was not in accordance with the agreement of the parties [. . .]".

to collect and review evidence from sources other than the parties. Nevertheless, Tribunals may do so at the request of a party or to some extent even through a Tribunal-appointed expert.

In deciding on the appropriate means to establish the facts of the case, the Tribunal will have to take into account the basic procedural requirements discussed under arts 19 and 22 above. The Tribunal will also have to decide on several basic differences that may arise between the parties and between counsel and the Tribunal. **25–12**

The first difference is that Claimants (or counter-claimants) usually wish to pursue their claims actively. Claimants have the initiative as to bringing the proceedings and usually will do so after they have prepared for it. Claimants (or counter-claimants) stand to receive a payment if they win. Therefore, their financial incentive is to complete the proceedings rapidly. **25–13**

Respondents usually have not chosen the timing of the dispute, although they may well have advance warning of it and have had an adequate time to prepare. Respondents without a counterclaim are faced with a financial incentive to delay if there is a real risk of loss, although terminating legal proceedings may after all also be in a Respondent's interest from a cost and time point of view. However, in many cases, there is at least the perception that Respondents may seek to delay matters. Additional parties joined pursuant to art.7 may have particular procedual concerns as they may be peripheral or have conditional claims. **25–14**

The second difference is that ICC arbitration is applicable in a wide range of situations with parties having varying financial resources. The parties may be major groups or companies with substantial turnovers and revenue, governments or state enterprises. But the parties may also be relatively small distributors, contractors or buyers (for example, of industrial equipment), sometimes acting as individuals, or through small companies, of which these individuals are the sole or main shareholders. Funding the costs of an international arbitration, including the legal costs of foreign counsel and the travel of the party, its witnesses and experts to a foreign (and sometimes distant) place of arbitration will strain smaller parties and even more so when they come from developing countries. The appropriate means to establish the facts of the case for one company with large resources may be totally out of reach for smaller companies or individuals. As a result, an important issue in some arbitrations is providing dispute resolution that is accessible for smaller companies or individuals.[12] **25–15**

The third difference is that the Tribunal deals in general with counsel of the parties and not directly with the parties. Therefore, issues as to timing and expense are affected by the commitments—and preferences—of counsel. If both counsel agree on additional time periods, it will be difficult for the Tribunal not to respect that agreement. But if the additional time periods are requested by one counsel, **25–16**

[12] The issue has been reviewed in the consumer context in the *Gateway computer* cases in the United States. Gateway proposed AAA arbitration as a less costly alternative. See *Brower v Gateway* (and also *Klocek v Gateway*) case, cited at para.0–32, n.22 rejecting the enforceability of an ICC arbitration clause based on unconscionability. Section 33(1)(b) of the English Arbitration Act 1996 provides that the Tribunal shall "adopt procedures suitable to the circumstances of the particular case, avoiding unnecessary delay or expense, so as to provide a fair means for the resolution of the matters falling to be determined."

the Tribunal must keep in mind its obligation to establish the facts of the case "in as short a time as possible".

25–17 The fourth difference is that the parties may disagree strongly on whether to separate out legal issues to be decided: whether to bifurcate proceedings. The issue of whether the Tribunal holds separate, initial hearings on threshold matters that may make further evidence unnecessary is one of the early basic differences that may arise between the parties. But typical issues that are decided at the outset include decisions as to the applicable language, the applicable law and the jurisdiction of the Tribunal.[13]

25–18 The parties and their representatives are under a good faith obligation to cooperate in the arbitration procedure. The duty of party representatives has been the subject of a working group of the IBA that has resulted in the IBA Guidelines on Party Representation in International Arbitration. These Guidelines are not binding as such although they may be adopted by Tribunals. Moreover, the Guidelines deal with very sensitive issues such as the duty of the lawyers involved with respect to facts and provide for consequences for a failure to comply. Whether or not these will be widely-adopted, it is worth noting some of the principles that the Guidelines set out with respect to establishing the facts of the case. They include the following:

> 9. A Party Representative should not make any knowingly false submission of fact to the Arbitral Tribunal.
> 10. In the event that a Party Representative learns that he or she previously made a false submission of fact to the Arbitral Tribunal, the Party Representative should, subject to countervailing considerations of confidentiality and privilege, promptly correct such submission.
> 11. A Party Representative should not submit Witness or Expert evidence that he or she knows to be false. If a Witness or Expert intends to present or presents evidence that a Party Representative knows or later discovers to be false, such Party Representative should promptly advise the Party whom he or she represents of the necessity of taking remedial measures and of the consequences of failing to do so. Depending upon the circumstances, and subject to countervailing considerations of confidentiality and privilege, the Party Representative should promptly take remedial measures, which may include one or more of the following:
>
> (a) advise the Witness or Expert to testify truthfully;
> (b) take reasonable steps to deter the Witness or Expert from submitting false evidence;
> (c) urge the Witness or Expert to correct or withdraw the false evidence;
> (d) correct or withdraw the false evidence;
> (e) withdraw as Party Representative if the circumstances so warrant.

[13] Tallerico and Behrendt, "The Use of Bifurcation and Direct Testimony Witness Statements in International Commercial Arbitration Proceedings" (2003) J Int Arb Vol.20 No.3, p.295.

Many of these principles are in fact applicable amongst members of national bar associations. And there is no reason why a similar standard should not be applicable in international arbitration, although the issue of enforcement is a real one.[14] The main sanction for perceived misbehaviour in this respect is most likely to be in costs. 25–19

Article 25(2): "After studying the written submissions of the parties and all documents relied upon, the arbitral tribunal shall hear the parties together in person if any of them so requests or, failing such a request, it may of its own motion decide to hear them."

Article 25(2) requires that the Tribunal "hear the parties" after review of the submissions and documents. The Tribunal is therefore required to meet with the parties and receive their oral submissions. The wording of art.25(2) renders a hearing necessary, even if the parties have previously held an organisational hearing, unless the parties dispense with the hearing. As discussed under art.25(3), the Rules do not require the Tribunal to hear witnesses, although this may be necessary to meet due process requirements of the law of the place of arbitration for example. 25–20

The written submissions of the parties referred to in art.25(2) are usually the memorials of the parties. In a medium-size or large ICC arbitration, often each party will have the opportunity to submit two memorials prior to the hearing. The parties normally submit documents as exhibits with their memorials.[15] The details as to the organisation of the documents are set out in the procedural order. Witness statements are sometimes filed in connection with parties' memorials, although they are also frequently filed after the memorials themselves. The timing of filing witness statements is an important procedural step that the Tribunal will have to decide unless the parties have agreed on how to deal with it. 25–21

The Tribunal is required to hold the hearing after studying the parties' written submissions and all the documents that they rely on. However, this does not prevent the Tribunal from requesting additional documents pursuant to art.25(5) after the hearing and then deciding the case. The issue in each case will be whether the additional documents are of such a character and importance that the Tribunal should, under the Rules or applicable law, give the parties an opportunity to express their position orally with respect to them. 25–22

[14] The IBA Guidelines on Party Representation provide in part as follows regarding enforcement: "26. If the Arbitral Tribunal, after giving the Parties notice and a reasonable opportunity to be heard, finds that a Party Representative has committed Misconduct, the Arbitral Tribunal, as appropriate, may:
(a) admonish the Party Representative;
(b) draw appropriate inferences in assessing the evidence relied upon, or the legal arguments advanced by, the Party Representative;
(c) consider the Party Representative's Misconduct in apportioning the costs of the arbitration, indicating, if appropriate, how and in what amount the Party Representative's Misconduct leads the Tribunal to a different apportionment of costs;
(d) take any other appropriate measure in order to preserve the fairness and integrity of the proceedings."

[15] See App.IV suggesting that the Tribunal and the parties consider "requiring the parties to produce with their submissions the documents on which they rely".

25–23 The requirement of a hearing pursuant to art.25(2) appears to apply to the issue of any Awards, which includes a partial Award. Therefore, and although art.25(2) does not require that the Tribunal has to accept every request for a hearing by a party, there is an argument in such cases that the Tribunal must hold a hearing prior to rendering any Award under the Rules, including a partial Award on applicable law, for example.

25–24 Technically, the requirement of hearing the parties is probably best viewed as at least an opportunity to hear both parties at the same time and providing the parties with the opportunity to respond orally to the position of the other side and to comments and questions of the Tribunal. It is not clear that the requirements would be met with telephone conferences or video communication, let alone with online comments. If one party insists on a physical meeting for the hearing, that may be necessary to meet the requirements of art.25(2).[16]

25–25 Article 25(2) is silent as to whether and how the Tribunal should deliberate after having studied the parties' written submissions and prior to hearing the parties orally. In the authors' experience, the efficiency of the subsequent proceedings and sometimes even the quality of the ultimate Award is often improved if the Tribunal meets to discuss the issues raised by the parties' written submissions prior to attending the hearing. This holds true in particular if the Tribunal puts specific questions to the parties and/or sets out the areas or issues where it feels no further submissions are required or where the parties should put their focus. In setting out those areas or issues, Tribunals will usually seek to balance the enquiries so as to provide each party with an indication of the matters of concern to it with respect to their cases. The Tribunal's guidance and queries will always be preliminary and without prejudice to the Tribunal's ultimate determination of the case. However, the caveat is that such meetings require detailed preparation by the members of the Tribunal prior to the hearings and this may not be practical in some circumstances.

Article 25(3): "The arbitral tribunal may decide to hear witnesses, experts appointed by the parties or any other person, in the presence of the parties, or in their absence provided they have been duly summoned."

25–26 Article 25(3) is permissive. The Tribunal may decide whether or not to hear witnesses, experts or more generally any other person. However, a Tribunal must meet the requirements of the law of the place of arbitration discussed under art.19 and art.22(4) and should meet the due process requirements of the place of probable enforcement if that is ascertainable. Therefore, the permissive nature of art.25(3) is subject to limitations on due process, but also to the parties' agreement. If both parties request that the Tribunal hear witnesses, it will usually be obliged to do so and in light of the consensual nature of arbitration, it will normally be well advised to do so.[17] The key factor is that a Tribunal must balance its discretion under art.25(3) with the general requirement that it respect the parties' agreement as to the procedure.

[16] Videoconferencing has improved significantly, but it is not universally available. In addition, most practitioners prefer personal contact at hearings.

[17] But due to the lack of relevance, a Tribunal may refuse hearing a given witness.

The ICC Rules do not give a definition of the term "witness" and do not state whether any person can be a witness or not. The current practice, as reflected in art.4(2) of the IBA Rules on Evidence is that "any person may present evidence as a witness, including a Party or a Party's officer, employee or other representative".[18] Indeed, in an ICC arbitration, anyone capable of describing facts based on his own perception may be a witness, irrespective of his status as a party, employee, agent and the like. Any person can act as a witness under the ICC Rules. This only subject to the *lex arbitri*, and more precisely a mandatory rule of law applicable at the place of arbitration. 25–27

The ICC Rules do not give a definition either of the term "expert", and art.25(3) does not distinguish between experts appointed by the Tribunal and those by the parties, although the IBA Rules of Evidence do draw a distinction (in arts 5 and 6). The categories of expert evidence are very broad. 25–28

The Tribunal has a discretion to decide on its own initiative to hear a person if it believes that it is important for the outcome of the case. In such as case, the Tribunal will need however to seek the assistance of national courts having no coercive power or *imperium* vis-à-vis the third parties who refuse to appear before it. Although the situation is not clear in various circuit courts in the United States, it may be possible in some US states to use s.28 U.S.C. s.1782 to require a person to provide oral evidence (as well as documentary evidence as discussed below) in support of foreign arbitration.[19] 25–29

[18] See Oetiker Ch., "Witnesses before the International Arbitral Tribunal" (2007) ASA Bull Vol.25 No.2, p.253; Schlosser discussing the legal relationships between arbitrating parties and witnesses-whether witnesses of act or expert witnesses in "Generalizable Approaches to Agreements with Experts and Witness Acting in Arbitration and International Litigation" in *Liber Amicorum in honour of Robert Briner, op. cit.*, p.775; Derains, "Le témoin en matière d'arbitrage" in *Mélanges en l'honneur de François Knoepfler, op. cit.*, p.227; Gélinas, "Evidence through witnesses" in *Arbitration and Oral Evidence*, ICC Dossier No.689, *op. cit.*, p.29, at p.31; Bühler/Dorgan, "Witness Testimony Pursuant to the 1999 IBA Rules of Evidence in International Commercial Arbitration—Novel or Tested Standards?" (2000) J Int'l Arb Vol.17 No.1, p.3, at p.7.

[19] See the decision in *Re Oxus Gold PLC*, Misc:06–82, 2006 US Dist. LEXIS 74118 (D.N.J. Oct. 10, 2006) and in *Re Oxus Gold PLC*, 2007 WL 1037387, D.N.J., 2007. See also *Re Roz Trading Ltd.*, No.1:06–cv–02305–WSD, 2006 U.S. Dist. LEXIS 91461 (N.D. Ga. Dec. 19, 2006). However, it is not clear that this decision will be followed elsewhere. See Fellas, "Using Section 1782 In International Arbitration" (2007) Mealey's IAR Vol.22 No.2, p.39. Under s.1782 of Title 2 of the United States Court, a party to a proceeding in a foreign or international tribunal is allowed to apply directly to a United States court to take evidence in the United States for use in such proceedings ("The district court of the district in which a person resides or is found may order him to give his testimony or statement or to produce a document or other thing for use in a proceeding in a foreign or international tribunal, including criminal investigations conducted before formal accusation. The order may be made pursuant to a letter rogatory issued, or request made, by a foreign or international tribunal or upon the application of any interested person and may direct that the testimony or statement be given, or the document or other thing be produced, before a person appointed by the court"). Wessel and Eyre, "US Discovery in Aid of Foreign or International Proceedings: the Rise of 28 USC, s.1782", The Journal of the Dispute Resolution Section of the International Bar Association June 2007 Vol.1 No.1, p.23; Ostertag and Brosnik, "Stchottdorf: para.1782(a) in Discovery in Foreign Actions" in *New York Law Journal*, April 6, 2007. Lindsey, Hosking and Lahlou, "Application of US Discovery Law To Arbitration Upheld On Appeal" (2007) Mealey's IAR Vol.22 No.5, p.26. Sheppard, "US Discovery Can Be Obtained For Use in Foreign BIT Arbitration Proceedings" (2007) ASA Bull Vol.25 No.2, p.402. See also Dimolitsa, "Giving Evidence: Some reflections on oral evidence vs documentary evidence and on the obligations and rights of the witnesses" in *Arbitration and Oral Evidence*, ICC Dossier No.689, *op. cit.*, p.11, at p.16 and "Quid encore de la confidentialité?" *in Mélanges en l'honneur de François Knoepfler, op. cit., p.249*. See also the discussion in para.25–78 *et seq*.

25–30 If a Tribunal decides that certain evidence is not necessary to decide the arbitration, then the refusal to hear the witness or expert should be based on relevance.[20] If the Tribunal decides that a witness statement or expert report is relevant, and therefore intends to rely on it, the decision not to hear the witness or expert would raise serious procedural issues, as a witness should be made available for cross examination unless the opposing party waives the right to cross-examine the witness.

25–31 Cross-examination or questioning of witnesses is viewed as an important element in determining whether evidence is reliable or not. Cross-examination originated with the common law systems and is viewed as an essential element of due process in those systems. However, the importance of questioning of witnesses by counsel is now a widely accepted practice in international arbitration, although the method of questioning of witnesses and, above all, the time allowed for that questioning varies with the Tribunal.

25–32 In civil law countries, it is a basic principle that the due process ("*contradictoire*") must be respected. Therefore, the concept that one party could work with a witness or expert to prepare a statement or report and that the other party would not have the opportunity of questioning the witness or expert appears problematic, if much weight is to be given to such testimony.

25–33 The better view is that art.25(3) is permissive in the sense that it permits a Tribunal to rule that certain witness or expert testimony is not required for deciding the case.[21] However, art.25(3) does not permit the Tribunal to take written evidence of witnesses or experts into account and then refuse to hear the witness or expert, unless, of course, both parties would have waived such hearing.

25–34 Article 25(3) provides that the Tribunal can hear witnesses and experts in the absence of one of the parties if the party has been duly summoned. This provision is intended to preclude a defaulting party from blocking the procedure. If one party defaults, the Tribunal must, however, hear the relevant evidence, reach a decision and reflect that decision in a reasoned Award. In ICC arbitration, there is no possibility of "default Award", as there is in national court proceedings.

25–35 Article 25(3) does not set out any details as to how witness evidence should be presented. This is in part because the manner of presenting evidence will vary from case to case. However, the IBA Rules of Evidence provide an outline as to how witness evidence is often taken and the rules that Tribunals often apply in international arbitration. As noted above, the IBA Rules of Evidence do not appear to be adopted as such by most Tribunals, but provide useful guidelines, particularly so that parties receive equal treatment.[22]

25–36 Article 4(1) of the IBA Rules of Evidence provides that "within the time ordered by the Tribunal, each Party shall identify the witnesses on whose testimony it

[20] Article 19 of the UNCITRAL Model Law provides: "The power conferred upon the arbitral tribunal includes the power to determine the admissibility, relevance, materiality and weight of any evidence". See also Derains, "La pratique de l'administration de la preuve dans l'arbitrage commercial international" (2004) Rev Arb, No.4, p.781, at p.797; Pinsolle and Kreindler, "Les limites du rôle de la volonté des parties dans la conduite de l'instance arbitrale" (2003) Rev Arb No.1, p.41.

[21] Derains, "La pratique de l'administration de la preuve dans l'arbitrage commercial international", *op. cit.*, at p.796.

[22] See Lévy, "Witness Statements" in *De Lege Ferenda—Réflexions sur le droit désirable en l'honneur du Professeur Alain Hirsch, op. cit.*, p.95.

intends to rely and the subject matter of that testimony". Parties exchange either witness summaries or witness statements discussed below. Usually this will take place with or after the exchange of memorials and well prior to the evidentiary hearings.

Unlike in some civil law jurisdictions, parties or their representatives may be witnesses under art.4(2) of the IBA Rules of Evidence and it is not improper for the parties to interview witnesses and to discuss their testimony with them under art.4(3) of the IBA Rules of Evidence.[23] **25–37**

Article 4(4) of the IBA Rules of Evidence provides for witness statements and art.4(5) of those Rules states that each witness statement shall contain: **25–38**

> "(a) the full name and address of the witness, a statement regarding his or her present and past relationship (if any) with any of the Parties, and a description of his or her background, qualifications, training and experience, if such a description may be relevant to the dispute or to the contents of the statement;
> (b) a full and detailed description of the facts, and the source of the witness's information as to those facts, sufficient to serve as that witness's evidence in the matter in dispute. Documents on which the witness relies that have not already been submitted shall be provided;
> (c) a statement as to the language in which the Witness Statement was originally prepared and the language in which the witness anticipates giving testimony at the Evidentiary Hearing;
> (d) an affirmation of the truth of the Witness Statement; and
> (e) the signature of the witness and its date and place."[24]

The ICC Rules contain no requirement of that sort and in practice, the format, content and quality of witness statements varies greatly. Counsel of the parties may seek to follow the prescription of art.4(4) of the IBA Rules of Evidence when submitting witness statements. **25–39**

Article 4(6) of the IBA Rules of Evidence provides for supplemental witness statements. In many ICC arbitrations, parties sometimes submit two sets of witness statements. As discussed under art.20, witness statements must be provided in the language of the arbitration, although this is not expressly stated in the IBA Rules of Evidence. If the witness is not sufficiently competent in that language, a translation of his statement into the language of arbitration by the party providing the statement has to be submitted. **25–40**

In the Working Group's Commentary on Witness Statements for the 2010 version of the IBA Rules, it was noted in particular that: **25–41**

> "If witness statements are used, the evidence that a witness plans to give orally at the hearing is known in advance. The other party can thereby

[23] Bühler and Dorgan, "Witness Testimony Pursuant to the 1999 IBA Rules of Evidence in International Commercial Arbitration—Novel or Tested Standards?", *op. cit.*, at p.7; Thorens, "L'arbitre international au point de rencontre des traditions du droit civil et de la common law" *in Etudes de droit international en l'honneur de Pierre Lalive, op. cit.*, p.693.

[24] The IBA Rules of Evidence do not require that the witness statement be sworn.

better prepare its own examination of the witness and select the issues and witnesses it will present. The tribunal is also in a better position to appreciate the testimony and put its own questions to these witnesses. Witness statements may in this way contribute to a shortening of the length of oral hearings. For instance, they may be considered as the 'evidence in chief' ('direct evidence'), so that extensive explanation by the witness becomes superfluous and examination by the other party can start almost immediately.

In order to save on hearing time and expense, witnesses need not appear unless their presence is requested by a party or the arbitral tribunal (Article 8.1). Often the arbitral tribunal and the parties may agree that a witness whose statement is either not contested or not considered material by the opposing party need not be present at the oral hearing. [. . .]

Article 4.4 of the IBA Rules of Evidence leaves it to the arbitral tribunal to specify when the written statements have to be submitted. There is a basic choice to be made in this respect: the parties may exchange their statements simultaneously or consecutively. The second round of witness statements should address only information contained in witness statements, expert reports or submissions submitted by another party in the first round or otherwise not previously presented in the arbitration (see Article 4.6)."

25–42 Simultaneous witness statements provide for a more rapid procedure, but in some cases, a Respondent may feel that this is unfair, as he should see the Claimant's testimony first. It will ultimately be for the Tribunal to decide the sequence of witness statements, and in doing so, it will seek to strike a balance between efficiency and fairness. To the extent that the parties have, or are supposed to have set out all relevant factual allegations in their written pleadings, a Respondent should in the normal case suffer no prejudice if a simultaneous exchange of written statements is ordered. Having two rounds of witness statements permits the Tribunal to have the comments of the witnesses on the evidence submitted by the other side, but adds to the duration and costs of the proceedings.[25] A further variant, is to permit counsel who has filed one or more witness statements to question that witness to a limited extent in his introduction on evidence that has been submitted since the last witness statement has been filed. In that manner, the outstanding factual or expert issues may be narrowed for the Tribunal and the witness can present in person his or her evidence on these limited points in person.

25–43 Article 4(7) of the IBA Rules of Evidence makes provision for excusing witnesses, usually where their evidence is not contentious. Where there are numerous witnesses, it is not infrequent that witnesses of secondary importance are not heard, as the failure to hear the witness does not mean that the evidence as such is accepted (and it may well be contradicted by documentary evidence).

[25] See Bühler, "Costs in arbitration. Some further considerations" in *Liber amicorum in honour of Robert Briner, op. cit.*, p.179.

Article 4(9) of the IBA Rules of Evidence provides for seeking to obtain evidence of a witness who will not voluntarily testify. The possibility of this will depend in most instances on the national law of the place where the person is located or perhaps the law of the place of arbitration. It is relatively seldom that a Tribunal seeks to compel testimony due to the complications involved and in particular the delay that can result in the proceedings.[26] **25–44**

Article 4(10) of the IBA Rules of Evidence provides the Tribunal with the possibility of requiring a party to assist in obtaining evidence. However, most Tribunals are more reluctant to seek to require testimony than to order production of documents. **25–45**

A related issue is how to treat a third party or former party who is in effect providing evidence against the interests of his or her former employer. The often-repeated expression is that "there is no property in a witness". However, witnesses may be subject to confidentiality undertakings that effectively limit their ability to testify. Frequently, if these issues are raised, the parties seek to work out some form of arrangement so that the witness can testify subject to limitations to protect issues such as trade secrets. However, the issue of testimony of these witnesses can rapidly become complex and a Tribunal may be faced with witness statements from the same witness being filed by both parties.[27] **25–46**

Article 25(4): "The arbitral tribunal, after having consulted the parties, may appoint one or more experts, define their terms of reference and receive their reports. At the request of a party, the parties shall be given the opportunity to question at a hearing any such expert."

In many ICC arbitrations involving technical matters, the parties designate experts and submit expert reports. As discussed below, the Tribunal may designate an expert as well, but in ICC arbitration Tribunals seldom do so. This is the case whether the parties originate in common law or civil law jurisdictions. The usual procedure is to have party-appointed experts.[28] **25–47**

[26] Bühler and Dorgan, "Witness Testimony Pursuant to the 1999 IBA Rules of Evidence in International Commercial Arbitration—Novel or Tested Standards?", *op. cit.*, at p.18.

[27] In examining the competing witness statements from the same witness, the role of the lawyers in the preparation of the witness statement may become an important issue.

[28] With respect to party-appointed experts, art.5(2) of the IBA Rules of Evidence states that the report of the expert shall contain:

"(a) the full name and address of the Party- Appointed Expert, a statement regarding his or her present and past relationship (if any) with any of the Parties, their legal advisors and the Arbitral Tribunal, and a description of his or her background, qualifications, training and experience;
(b) a description of the instructions pursuant to which he or she is providing his or her opinions and conclusions;
(c) a statement of his or her independence from the Parties, their legal advisors and the Arbitral Tribunal;
(d) a statement of the facts on which he or she is basing his or her expert opinions and conclusions;
(e) his or her expert opinions and conclusions, including a description of the methods, evidence and information used in arriving at the conclusions. Documents on which the Party-Appointed Expert relies that have not already been submitted shall be provided;
(f) if the Expert Report has been translated, a statement as to the language in which it was originally prepared, and the language in which the Party Appointed Expert anticipates giving testimony at the Evidentiary Hearing;

25–48 Article 25(4) therefore deals with a situation, which in practice has probably become the exception. Usually, the appointment of an expert by the Tribunal will be at the request of one or both parties and if one or both parties agree to bear the cost.[29] If the Tribunal refuses a request to appoint an expert, it should justify that decision in a Procedural Order or in the Award to avoid due process issues.[30]

(g) an affirmation of his or her genuine belief in the opinions expressed in the Expert Report;
(h) the signature of the Party-Appointed Expert and its date and place; and
(i) if the Expert Report has been signed by more than one person, an attribution of the entirety or specific parts of the Expert Report to each author."

[29] Bühler, "Technical Expertise: An additional Means for Preventing or Settling Commercial Disputes" (1989) J Int'l Arb Vol.6 No.1, p.135. See also Voser and Mueller, "Appointment of Experts by the Arbitral Tribunal: the Civil Law Perspective" (2006) Business Law International Vol.7 No.1, p.73; For examples of a Tribunal appointed expert, see ICC case No.6057 (1990), (1993) J Int'l Arb No.4 p.1067, and ICC case No.6673 (1992), (1992) J Int'l Arb No.4 p.992, note Hascher. Regarding the consequences of failure of one party to cooperate with the Tribunal appointed expert, see ICC case No.6497 (1994), (1999) YBCA Vol.XXIV p.71. For an example of a Tribunal appointed expert and a discussion of his procedure and report in the context of the Iran-US Claims Tribunal, see *Ebrahimi v Iran* Award in cases Nos 44 46 47 (560–44/46/47–3) of October 12, 1994, 30 Iran-US C.T.R. 170.

[30] See ICC case No.13772 (2006) (Procedural Order), unreported (refusal of the Tribunal to appoint an expert upon request of a party) ("[32].There is very little in the ICC Rules and the Terms of Reference upon which to ground the proposition that the tribunal-appointed experts are subsidiary to an obligation upon the parties themselves to put forth the evidence they wish to rely on and make their case[. . .] [35]. The leading commentaries on the ICC Rules provide support for the proposition that in ICC arbitrations the appointment of an expert by the arbitral tribunal is subsidiary to an obligation upon the parties themselves to put forth the evidence they wish to rely on and make their case. [36]. Bühler and Webster state that: The usual procedure is to have party-appointed experts. Article 25(4) therefore deals with a situation, which in practice has probably become the exception. [37]. Derains and Schwartz affirm in relation to Article 25(4) of the ICC Rules that: The [tribunal-appointed] expert also should not be used to discharge either party of any obligation that it may have to prove its case, although the extent of a party's related burden may be perceived differently in various legal systems [. . .] [39]. In this case Respondents have not provided a statement from an accountant or auditor at arm's length from Respondents. That is the nature of the expert whom Respondents would have the Arbitral Tribunal appoint in the Request. [40]. Respondents have contended that the Confidentiality Agreement entails a material restriction on an expert of this nature appointed by Respondents from having access to Claimant's documents and that a tribunal-appointed expert would be better positioned to do so. [41]. This is, however, not the case [. . .] [44]. Again, Respondent could commission an expert from outside of their organizations . . . The Arbitral Tribunal is of the view that Respondents are at no material disadvantaged in obtaining their own expert's report on the matters indicated in the Request. In view of the subsidiarity of the tribunal-appointed experts, this is a sufficient ground upon, which to reject the Request [. . .]"); ICC case No.4629 (1989), (1993) YBCA Vol.XVIII p.11. In this case, the Tribunal denied a request for a second expert in the following terms: "[t]he arbitrators are at liberty to decide whether such an appointment is necessary for the solution of the case. Such an expert may be useful or even necessary for technical questions. In the present situation, such utility is in no way established. On the contrary, the questions which are typically in the field of activity of an expert have already been covered by the [first expert's] report. This report describes the work done by the defendant party and is necessary for the determination of the payment claimed by the Claimants. Other questions such as the ones quoted by Respondent are to be resolved by the arbitrators. Moreover, it is their duty to interpret the contractual documents and evidences filed by the parties. Appointing a second expert would lead to a replacement of the arbitrators by an expert. Therefore, independently from the question of the cost of an expertise, the request of Respondent is to be dismissed". See also Fouchard, Gaillard & Goldman, *op. cit.*, para.1290, at p.704 (". . . the arbitral tribunal is never required to grant a party's request for the appointment of an expert. In its 1980 decision in the *Air Intergulf v. S.E.C.A.* case, the Paris Court of Appeal held that where the tribunal considers that it has sufficient information to make its decision, 'its refusal to order . . . the expert investigation requested by a party does not contravene the rights of defense").

One of the basic issues with a Tribunal-appointed expert is the selection of the appropriate person.[31] The Tribunal has recourse to an expert because of a lack of expertise in an area. The parties frequently have this expertise. Therefore, a Tribunal may find it useful to request from the parties either a list of potential experts or an agreement on the name of an expert to be appointed by the Tribunal. **25–49**

The Tribunal may consult the ICC International Centre for Expertise to locate an expert. The Centre is part of the ICC headquarters in Paris and has a list of potential experts in various areas, and enjoys contacts with experts and technical institutions all over the world that may assist it in identifying the proper expert.[32] A flat fee of US$2,500 is charged by the Centre to appoint or propose an expert. However, Tribunals that act under the ICC Rules are exempt from such charge for the proposal of an expert. **25–50**

The costs of the expert are dealt with in art.1(12) of App.III of the Rules which provides: **25–51**

> "Before any expertise ordered by the arbitral tribunal can be commenced, the parties, or one of them, shall pay an advance on costs fixed by the arbitral tribunal sufficient to cover the expected fees and expenses of the expert as determined by the arbitral tribunal. The arbitral tribunal shall be responsible for ensuring the payment by the parties of such fees and expenses."

The costs of the expert are not part of the general costs of the arbitration and the advance on costs of the expert must be paid prior to commencement of the expert's work.[33] **25–52**

The Tribunal drafts the terms of reference for the expert.[34] Whether the obligation to consult the parties applies grammatically to the terms of reference (as well as the appointment) of the expert is not clear.[35] However, Tribunals would usually consult the parties to ensure that the expert will deal with all technical issues that the parties reasonably deem appropriate. **25–53**

Article 25(4) does not deal with how the expert conducts his or her activities. Article 6 of the IBA Rules of Evidence provides as follows with respect to Tribunal-appointed experts[36]: **25–54**

> "1. The Arbitral Tribunal, after consulting with the Parties, may appoint one or more independent Tribunal-Appointed Experts to report to it on

[31] In national court proceedings, this seems to be a lesser issue, as there are lists of approved experts and there is generally no concern about neutrality of the nationality of the expert.

[32] Wolrich, "ICC Expertise—The New, Revised ICC Rules for Expertise: A presentation and Commentary" (2002) ICC ICArb Bull Vol.13 No.2, p.11; see also *http://www.iccexpertise.org* [accessed November 20, 2013].

[33] Otherwise the arbitrator engages his personal liability. The arbitrator can open a separate trust account, into which the advance to cover the expert's costs can be paid.

[34] Bühler, "Technical Expertise: An Additional Means for Preventing or Settling Commercial Disputes", *op. cit.*, p.138.

[35] It would not make sense to require consultation with the parties prior to receiving the expert report. Therefore, grammatically the consultation requirement appears to solely apply to the appointment of the expert.

[36] As noted above, the IBA Rules of Evidence are not applicable unless adopted by the parties. However, they provide useful guidelines as to current practice.

specific issues designated by the Arbitral Tribunal. The Arbitral Tribunal shall establish the terms of reference for any Tribunal-Appointed Expert Report after consulting with the Parties. A copy of the final terms of reference shall be sent by the Arbitral Tribunal to the Parties.

[. . .]

4. The Tribunal-Appointed Expert shall report in writing to the Arbitral Tribunal in an Expert Report.

The Expert Report shall contain:

(a) the full name and address of the Tribunal Appointed Expert, and a description of his or her background, qualifications, training and experience;
(b) a statement of the facts on which he or she is basing his or her expert opinions and conclusions;
(c) his or her expert opinions and conclusions, including a description of the methods, evidence and information used in arriving at the conclusions. Documents on which the Tribunal-Appointed Expert relies that have not already been submitted shall be provided;
(d) if the Expert Report has been translated, a statement as to the language in which it was originally prepared, and the language in which the Tribunal-Appointed Expert anticipates giving testimony at the Evidentiary Hearing;
(e) an affirmation of his or her genuine belief in the opinions expressed in the Expert Report;
(f) the signature of the Tribunal-Appointed Expert and its date and place; and
(g) if the Expert Report has been signed by more than one person, an attribution of the entirety or specific parts of the Expert Report to each author.

5. The Arbitral Tribunal shall send a copy of such Expert Report to the Parties. The Parties may examine any information, Documents, goods, samples, property, machinery, systems, processes or site for inspection that the Tribunal-Appointed Expert has examined and any correspondence between the Arbitral Tribunal and the Tribunal-Appointed Expert. Within the time ordered by the Arbitral Tribunal, any Party shall have the opportunity to respond to the Expert Report in a submission by the Party or through a Witness Statement or an Expert Report by a Party-Appointed Expert. The Arbitral Tribunal shall send the submission, Witness Statement or Expert Report to the Tribunal-Appointed Expert and to the other Parties.

6. At the request of a Party or of the Arbitral Tribunal, the Tribunal-Appointed Expert shall be present at an Evidentiary Hearing. The Arbitral Tribunal may question the Tribunal-Appointed Expert, and he or she may be questioned by the Parties or by any Party-Appointed

> Expert on issues raised in his or her Expert Report, the Parties' submissions or Witness Statement or the Expert Reports made by the Party-Appointed Experts pursuant to Article 6.5."

As art.6(7) of the IBA Rules of Evidence states, it is up to the Tribunal to decide the issues and not up to the expert to decide the issues. The expert, whether party-appointed or Tribunal-appointed, is intended to provide a technical opinion. The drafters of the Rules may have seen no need to state the obvious, but it cannot hurt to sometimes reiterate a basic point of procedure, as does art.6(7) of the IBA Rules of Evidence. **25–55**

In ICC case No.12131, a Tribunal sitting in Switzerland set out its position as to the respective roles of the Tribunal and the Tribunal-appointed expert in the following terms: **25–56**

> "207. Given the Arbitral Tribunal did not have the specialized knowledge with respect to the technical issues raised by the determination of each item of the claimed X know- how set forth in Claimant's Annex A, it appointed upon Claimant's request and notwithstanding Respondent's objection thereto a tribunal-appointed expert [. . .].
>
> 209. In terms of weighing the evidence, one should bear in mind that the Tribunal is not bound by the Expert's finding. However, should the arbitrators decide to have differing opinions from those of the Expert, they ought to provide grounds for their solution in order to preclude any oversight or violation of the right to be heard (see Poudret/Besson, *Droit comparé de l'arbitrage international*, ed.2002, p.595). In other words, there are no reasons for the Arbitral Tribunal to divert from the Expert's findings, unless there is an objectively justified material and different solution [. . .]."[37]

Article 25(5): "At any time during the proceedings, the arbitral tribunal may summon any party to provide additional evidence."

Article 25(5) refers to requests by the Tribunal to provide evidence. In most instances, the request to provide documents is initiated by the opposing party in the proceedings. **25–57**

The issue of whether, when and under what conditions a Tribunal should require production of documents from a party in international arbitration has been a matter of much debate, and is a matter of great concern to many parties.[38] The **25–58**

[37] ICC case No.12131 (2006) (Partial Award), unreported.

[38] Lionnet, "Once Again: Is Discovery of Documents Appropriate in International Arbitration?" in *Liber Amicorum Robert Briner, op. cit.*, p.492; Kaufman-Kohler, "Discovery in International Arbitration: How Much is Too Much?" (Jan./Feb. 2004) SchiedvsVZ, p.13; Bernini, "The civil law approach to discovery: a comparative overview of the taking of evidence in the anglo-american and continental arbitration systems" in *The Leading Arbitrators' Guide in International Arbitration, op. cit.*, p.269; Brower and Sharpe, "Determining the extent of discovery and dealing with request for discovery: perspectives from the common law" in *The Leading Arbitrators' Guide in International Arbitration, op. cit.*, p.307; King and Bosman "Rethinking Discovery in International Arbitration: Beyond the Common Law, Civil Law Divide" (2001) ICC ICArb Bull Vol.12 No.1, p.24; Cremades, "Powers of the arbitrators to decide on the admissibility of evidence and to organise the production

origin of the debate is the difference in practice between common law countries and civil law countries with respect to providing evidence. For American litigators, documentary discovery, interrogatories and deposition discovery are an integral part of the judicial fact-finding process.[39] In addition, in American procedure, third parties can be required to provide evidence with respect to court proceedings. English court procedure provides for documentary disclosure of documents by one party to the other party if the documents relate to the matters in issue in the case and, in exceptional cases, for disclosure by third parties. These common law approaches have been contrasted with the civil law approach, where it is basically up to each party to obtain and submit the evidence on which it relies.[40] However, in considering these approaches, it should be noted that American courts and English law both favour limited discovery in arbitration,[41] although the difficulty lies in the practical application of this rule to concrete requests for document production.

25–59 The IBA Rules of Evidence set out what is meant to be a compromise between the common and civil law approaches as regards documentary disclosure. Tribunals (and parties) often decide not to adopt the Rules as such, but to agree that the principles in the IBA Rules of Evidence will be a point of reference for the Tribunal in considering issues such as requirements that the parties disclose documents. In this respect, the approach of the Tribunal in the *Reineccius* case appears to reflect practice of some international arbitrators to refer to the IBA Rules of Evidence as guidelines.[42] In addition, even if the IBA Rules of Evidence have not been accepted as such by the Tribunal, parties dealing with international Tribunals use them.[43]

Requests to Produce by Parties

25–60 Article 3(2) of the IBA Rules of Evidence provides that any party may submit a "Request to Produce". The timing of such "Request to Produce" is not specified although art.3(11) of those Rules provides for subsequent requests which may

of evidence" (1999) ICC ICArb Bull Vol.10 No.1, p.49; Goldman, "Instance judiciaire et instance arbitrale internationale" in *Etudes offertes à Pierre Bellet, op. cit.*, p.219; Briner, "The Evaluation of Evidence: Some Observations Based on the Practice of the Iran-United States Claims Tribunal" in *Liber Amicorum Thomas Bär and Robert Karrer* (1997), p.41.

[39] Deposition discovery involves questioning of a witness by the opposing lawyer, under oath and almost invariably not in the presence of the judge or arbitrator.

[40] This is not to say that judges in civil law countries cannot provide a party significant assistance in obtaining documents, although not as a matter of routine and in specific circumstances only.

[41] See for example, *COMSAT Corp v NSF*, 190 F.3d 269 (4th Cir., 1999): "Parties to a private arbitration agreement forego certain procedural rights attendant to formal litigation in return for a more efficient and cost-effective resolution of their disputes" cited by Webster, "Party Control in International Arbitration", *op. cit.*, p.125, n.15; see also s.33 of the English Arbitration Act 1996.

[42] See *Reineccius* case, para.25–72; Procedural Order No.3 of that arbitration appears to be based on the IBA Principles and the Tribunal ordered that any objection to production be filed with reference to the grounds set out in art.9.2 of the IBA Rules of Evidence.

[43] The IBA Rules of Evidence may be of less weight when the parties and the Tribunal all originate from common law countries (in which case they may be viewed as permitting too narrow disclosure) or if all arbitrators have a similar civil law tradition (in which case they may be viewed as permitting too broad disclosure). However, this is not always or even usually the case.

imply that the initial request will be made shortly after the Terms of Reference.[44] However, frequently in international arbitration, unlike in American litigation, the Request to Produce will be made after certain memorials have been filed.

Pursuant to art.3(3) of the IBA Rules of Evidence, a Request to Produce shall contain: **25–61**

> "(a) *(i)* a description of each requested Document sufficient to identify it, or *(ii)* a description in sufficient detail (including subject matter) of a narrow and specific requested category of Documents that are reasonably believed to exist; in the case of Documents maintained in electronic form, the requesting Party may, or the Arbitral tribunal may order that it shall be required to, identify specific files, search terms, individuals or other means of searching for such Documents in an efficient and economical manner;
> (b) a statement as to how the Documents requested are relevant to the case and material to its outcome; and
> (c) *(i)* a statement that the Documents requested are not in the possession, custody or control of the requesting Party or a statement of the reasons why it would be unreasonably burdensome for the requesting Party to produce such Documents, and *(ii)* a statement of the reasons why the requesting Party assumes the Documents requested are in the possession, custody or control of another Party."

The last point is sometimes overlooked in practice, as it means that any correspondence exchanged between the parties falls outside the boundaries of admissible discovery requests, and therefore does not have to be disclosed.[45] The most important and at the same time most difficult point in practice relates to the second item, the need to show relevance and materiality to the outcome of the case. These are discussed below. **25–62**

Article 3(4) of the IBA Rules of Evidence sets out the basic requirement that a party produce the requested documents, unless the party makes an objection under art.3(5), which provides that: **25–63**

> "If the Party to whom the Request to Produce is addressed has an objection to some or all of the Documents requested, it shall state the objection in writing to the Arbitral Tribunal and the other Parties within the time ordered by the Arbitral Tribunal. The reasons for such objection

[44] Article 3(11) of the IBA Rules of Evidenced provides: "11. Within the time ordered by the Arbitral Tribunal, the Parties may submit to the Arbitral Tribunal and to the other Parties any additional Documents on which they intend to rely or which they believe have become relevant to the case and material to its outcome as a consequence of the issues raised in Documents, Witness Statements or Expert Reports submitted or produced, or in other submissions of the Parties". See also Hafter, "The Provisions on the Discovery of Internal Documents in the IBA Rules of 1999" in *Liber Amicorum Robert Briner, op. cit.*, p.347.

[45] Unless the requesting party is no longer in possession of the correspondence it sent to and received from the other party.

shall be any of those set forth in Article 9.2 or a failure to satisfy any of the requirements of Article 3.3."[46]

25–64 Article 3(6) of the IBA Rules of Evidence provides that:

> "6. Upon receipt of any such objection, the Arbitral Tribunal may invite the relevant Parties to consult with each other with a view to resolving the objection."

25–65 Article 3(8) of the IBA Rules of Evidence provides for review of a disputed document by either the Tribunal or an expert.

25–66 Article 3(9) of the IBA Rules of Evidence makes provision for requests for documents from persons or organisations that are not parties.[47] This provision fits in with various provisions of national law that allow arbitrators or parties in arbitrations to have recourse to national courts for production of evidence from third parties.[48]

25–67 As regards the procedure, the Request to Produce provides an opportunity for the lawyer requesting the documents to educate the Tribunal as to a specific issue

[46] Article 9.2 of the IBA Rules of Evidence states: "2. The Arbitral Tribunal shall, at the request of a Party or on its own motion, exclude from evidence or production any Document, statement, oral testimony or inspection for any of the following reasons: (a) lack of sufficient relevance to the case or materiality to its outcome; (b) legal impediment or privilege under the legal or ethical rules determined by the Arbitral Tribunal to be applicable; (c) unreasonable burden to produce the requested evidence; (d) loss or destruction of the document that has been shown with reasonable likelihood to have occurred; (e) grounds of commercial or technical confidentiality that the Arbitral Tribunal determines to be compelling; (f) grounds of special political or institutional sensitivity (including evidence that has been classified as secret by a government or a public international institution) that the Arbitral Tribunal determines to be compelling; or (g) considerations of procedural economy, proportionality, fairness or equality of the Parties that the Arbitral Tribunal determines to be compelling".

Article 3.3 of the IBA Rules of Evidence states: "3. A Request to Produce shall contain: (a) *(i)* a description of each requested Document sufficient to identify it, or *(ii)* a description in sufficient detail (including subject matter) of a narrow and specific requested category of Documents that are reasonably believed to exist; in the case of Documents maintained in electronic form, the requesting Party may, or the Arbitral Tribunal may order that it shall be required to, identify specific files, search terms, individuals or other means of searching for such Documents in an efficient and economical manner; (b) a statement as to how the Documents requested are relevant to the case and material to its outcome; and (c) *(i)* a statement that the Documents requested are not in the possession, custody or control of the requesting Party or a statement of the reasons why it would be unreasonably burdensome for the requesting Party to produce such Documents, and *(ii)* a statement of the reasons why the requesting Party assumes the Documents requested are in the possession, custody or control of another Party".

[47] Article 3(9) of the IBA Rules of Evidence provides: "9. If a Party wishes to obtain the production of Documents from a person or organisation who is not a Party to the arbitration and from whom the Party cannot obtain the Documents on its own, the Party may, within the time ordered by the Arbitral Tribunal, ask it to take whatever steps are legally available to obtain the requested Documents, or seek leave from the Arbitral Tribunal to take such steps itself. The Party shall submit such request to the Arbitral Tribunal and to the other Parties in writing, and the request shall contain the particulars set forth in Article 3.3, as applicable. The Arbitral Tribunal shall decide on this request and shall take, authorize the requesting Party to take, or order any other Party to take, such steps as the Arbitral Tribunal considers appropriate if, in its discretion, it determines that *(i)* the Documents would be relevant to the case and material to its outcome, *(ii)* the requirements of Article 3.3, as applicable, have been satisfied and *(iii)* none of the reasons for objection set forth in Article 9.2 applies".

[48] For a discussion, see Webster, "Obtaining Evidence from Third Parties in International Arbitration" (2001) Arb Int Vol.17 No.2, p.143 at p.147.

in the case and the documents that the other side should have in its control with respect to that issue. Therefore, aside from obtaining the documents or an adverse inference if the documents are not produced, the highlighting of a material issue is of importance given the quantity of submissions that the parties frequently make in arbitrations.

The first issue with respect to a Request to Produce is the relevance of the documents. Unlike courts in common law countries, Tribunals generally wish to see a demonstrated relevance of the document request to the issues in the case. For many international arbitrators, the fact that documents may be relevant is not sufficient and documents that are relevant only to qualify the credibility of a witness may be considered irrelevant to the issues in the case. In addition, art.3(7) of the IBA Rules of Evidence refers to issues that one party "wishes to prove" to support its case and not simply to contest the case of the other side.[49] Therefore, it raises the issue of whether a Request to Produce should be granted if it is aimed solely at the production of documents that are required to contest the case of the other side.[50] **25–68**

Another issue is what is meant by a "narrow and specific requested category of documents". Here practices vary widely and, in many instances, the difference in approach between common law and civil law jurisdictions becomes evident. For example, for common law lawyers, requests for "minutes of directors' meetings" or "account statements for account no.1234" or "import authorisations relating to computer hard drives" are narrow and specific categories of documents. For other lawyers, the issue may be which directors' meetings and why, which account statements and which import authorisations. Dealing with these issues will depend on various factors, including the composition of the Tribunal, the origin of the parties and/or their counsel, and perhaps the place of arbitration.[51] Another issue is the production of electronic documents, which has been the subject of a report by the ICC Arbitration Commission entitled "Managing E-Document Production". **25–69**

Article 6(3) of the IBA Rules of Evidence provides that a Tribunal-appointed expert has the same right to request documents as the Tribunal itself.[52] This is **25–70**

[49] A party has the burden of proving the case it advances. If a party fails to provide evidence to support its case, it generally will fail. The other party is not required to disprove the case and therefore some arbitrators deem it inappropriate to request documents that are solely designed for that purpose.

[50] The justification for the limitation is that documentary production should be restricted to areas in which the requesting party has the burden of proof.

[51] The Working Group gave the following example in its commentary of the IBA Rules of Evidence (at p.7): "For example, if an arbitration involved the termination by one party of a joint venture agreement, the other party may know that the notice of the termination was given on a certain date, that the Board of the other party must have made the decision to terminate at a meeting shortly before that notice and that certain documents must have been prepared for the Board's consideration of that decision and minutes must have been taken concerning the decision. The requesting party cannot identify the dates or the authors of such documents, but nevertheless the requesting party can identify with some particularity the nature of the documents sought and the general time frame in which they would have been prepared. Such a Request may qualify as a 'narrow and specific category of documents as permitted under Article 3.3(a)(ii)' ".

[52] The provision states: "3. Subject to the provisions of Article 9.2, the Tribunal-Appointed Expert may request a Party to provide any information or to provide access to any Documents, goods, samples, property, machinery, systems, processes or site for inspection, to the extent relevant to the case and material to its outcome. The authority of a Tribunal-Appointed Expert to request such

typical of civil law expertise proceedings where a court-appointed expert regularly demands explanations and documents from the parties. In fact, such proceedings can be as intrusive as common law discovery.[53]

25–71 The issue of privilege also arises in document production. The issue of which law governs the issue of privilege is a thorny one that is unresolved. Several factors are usually relevant in dealing with issues of privilege. The parties have to be treated equally. Therefore, ordering production from one party of documents that would be privileged if in the position of the other party may raise due process issues. Privilege is related to national law and the place where a lawyer (or other professional) practices. Therefore, at least initially the law of that place should be used to determine the scope of the privilege.[54]

25–72 In the *Reineccius* case,[55] the Tribunal analysed a claim for privilege in an ad hoc arbitration applying, in part, international law, in the following terms:

> "The attorney-client privilege, which is widely applied in domestic legal systems, has been recognized in public international and international commercial arbitration rules and arbitral awards. The privilege applies to corporate entities as well as to individuals; when claimed for corporate entities, it obtains with respect to those who are authorised to participate in the decisions. The attorney-client privilege has, in addition, been recognized and applied with respect to international organisations. At the core of the attorney-client privilege in both domestic and international law is the appreciation that those who must make decisions on their own or others' behalf are entitled to seek and receive legal advice and that the provision of a full canvass of legal options and the exploration and evaluation of their legal implications would be chilled, were counsel and their clients not assured in advance that the advice

information or access shall be the same as the authority of the Arbitral Tribunal. The Parties and their representatives shall have the right to receive any such information and to attend any such inspection. Any disagreement between a Tribunal-Appointed Expert and a Party as to the relevance, materiality or appropriateness of such a request shall be decided by the Arbitral Tribunal, in the manner provided in Articles 3.5 through 3.8. The Tribunal-Appointed Expert shall record in the Expert Report any non-compliance by a Party with an appropriate request or decision by the Arbitral Tribunal and shall describe its effects on the determination of the specific issue".

53 Common law discovery is based on correspondence and requests. In court-appointed expert hearings, they are frequently made immediately. The requests for explanations or documents are subsequently confirmed in writing by the expert. See also, Jarrosson, "L'expertise Juridique" in *Liber amicorum Claude Reymond, op. cit.*, p.127; Poudret, "Expertise et droit d'être entendu dans l'arbitrage international" in *Etudes de droit international en l'honneur de Pierre Lalive, op. cit.*, p.607.

54 See for example European Court of First Instance, September 17, 2007, *Akzo Nobel Chemicals Ltd and Akcros Chemicals Ltd v Commission of the European Communities*, joined case 62003A0253 (T–122/03 and T–253/03) (Commission's powers of investigation— documents seized in the course of an investigation—legal professional privilege protecting communications between lawyers and their clients—admissibility). See also Rosher, "Legal privilege et confidentialité des communications avocat-client en matière d'arbitrage international—Vers une possible harmonisation?", Les Cahiers de l'Arbitrage No.2007/3, p.21 and "The Application and Scope of Attorney-Client Privilege in International Arbitration" SIAR 2007:2, p.1.

55 See *Dr Horst Reineccius v Bank for International Settlements, Respondent (Claim No. 1); First Eagle SoGen Funds, Inc., Claimant v Bank for International Settlements, Respondent (Claim No.2); Pierre Mathieu and la Société Hippique de la Châtre, Claimants v Bank for International Settlements, Respondent (Claim no. 3)*, June 11, 2002, Procedural Order No.6.

> proffered, along with communications related to it, would remain confidential and immune to discovery.
>
> Ratione materiae, the legal communications which are entitled to an attorney-client privilege must be related to making a decision that is in or is in contemplation of legal contention; ratione personae, the legal communications must be between an attorney (whether in-house or outside) and those who are afforded his or her professional advice for purposes of making or in contemplation of that decision. Legal communications which would qualify for privilege on the basis of these criteria may lose their privileged status if the party entitled to it waives the privilege by word or deed or voluntarily publicizes the substance of the legal communications beyond the circle of those who are authorised to make or participate in the making of the decision. In addition, in circumstances in which the privilege is abused by using it in ways that would unfairly benefit the party entitled to it and unfairly prejudice the other party—the so-called 'sword and shield rule' as it is called in United States' federal jurisprudence—the privilege will not be given effect. As the Court said in *US v Bilzerian*, the attorney-client privilege cannot be used as a shield and a sword . . . A defendant may not use the privilege to prejudice his opponent's case or to disclose some selected communications for self-serving purposes." (footnote deleted)

The *Reineccius* case is a useful discussion of the principles; the fundamental one is that a Tribunal must address the issue of the *rationae materiae* (the material to be covered), *rationae personae* (the persons to be covered) and the issue of waiver. Depending on the national origins of the parties, each of these issues may be treated somewhat differently. However, there are a number of cross-border examples of principles[56] and a more generalised acceptance that privilege applies to persons such as in-house counsel. **25–73**

Requests to Produce from the Tribunal

Article 3(10) of the IBA Rules of Evidence permits the Tribunal to request production of documents in the following terms: **25–74**

> "10. At any time before the arbitration is concluded, the Arbitral Tribunal may *(i)* request any Party to produce Documents, *(ii)* request any Party to use its best efforts to take or *(iii)* itself take, any step that it considers appropriate to obtain Documents from any person or organisation. A Party to whom such a request for Documents is addressed may object to the request for any of the reasons set forth in

[56] See for example the Code for Conduct for Lawyers in the European Union which provides: "5.3.1. If a lawyer sending a communication to a lawyer in another Member State, which the sender wishes it to remain confidential or without prejudice he or she should clearly express this intention prior to communicating the documents 5.3.2. If the prospective recipient of the communication is unable to ensure their status as confidential or without prejudice he or she should inform the sender accordingly without delay" (www.ccbe.org/doc).

Article 9.2. In such cases, Article 3.4 to Article 3.8 shall apply correspondingly."

25–75 It would appear that art.25(5) provides a Tribunal with at least a similarly broad power, whether or not there exists any reference to the IBA Rules of Evidence.

25–76 Tribunals are generally reluctant to take the initiative in ordering production of documents. However, this reluctance is sometimes overcome if there are repeated references by one or both parties to existing documents that are relevant to deciding the dispute. A Tribunal is judging a case. It is important, both for the Tribunal and for any national courts that review the Award, that the Tribunal take any necessary steps to ensure that the proceedings are just in a broad sense of that term.

25–77 Pursuant to art.9(5) of the IBA Rules of Evidence, the sanction for a failure to produce a document pursuant to an order of the Tribunal is an adverse inference.[57] In addition, parties may have alternatives to force production through local courts.

Obtaining of documents through local court proceedings

25–78 Parties may, with or without the consent of the Tribunal, seek to obtain the production of documents through court proceedings.[58] The scope of production and manners in which this may be obtained go beyond the scope of this book. However, the recent developments with respect to US law should be kept in mind, although the US law in this respect is in a state of flux.

25–79 Article 1782 of the US Code provides as follows:

"Assistance to foreign and international tribunals and to litigants before such tribunals

(a) The district court of the district in which a person resides or is found may order him to give his testimony or statement or to produce a document or other thing for use in a proceeding in a foreign or international tribunal, including criminal investigations conducted before formal accusation. The order may be made pursuant to a letter rogatory issued, or request made, by a foreign or international tribunal or upon the application of any interested person and may direct that the testimony or statement be given, or the document or other thing be produced, before a person appointed by the court. By virtue of his appointment, the person appointed has power to administer any necessary oath and take the testimony or statement. The order may prescribe the practice and procedure, which may be in whole or part the practice and procedure of the foreign country or the international tribunal, for taking the testimony or statement or

[57] Article 9(5) of the IBA Rules of Evidence provides: "5. If a Party fails without satisfactory explanation to produce any Document requested in a Request to Produce to which it has not objected in due time or fails to produce any Document ordered to be produced by the Arbitral Tribunal, the Arbitral Tribunal may infer that such document would be adverse to the interests of that Party".

[58] In practice, it would normally seem wise to first seek a Tribunal's permission to do so, or at least to inform the Tribunal. For a discussion, see Webster, "Obtaining Documents from Adverse Parties in International Arbitration" (2001) Arb Int Vol.17 No.1, p.41 at p.42.

> producing the document or other thing. To the extent that the order does not prescribe otherwise, the testimony or statement shall be taken, and the document or other thing produced, in accordance with the Federal Rules of Civil Procedure.

A person may not be compelled to give his testimony or statement or to produce a document or other thing in violation of any legally applicable privilege."

For a number of years, after some hesitation, various US courts of appeal decided that s.1782 did not apply to arbitral tribunals.[59] However, in *Intel Corp v Advanced Micro Devices, Inc*, the US Supreme Court considered the application of s.1782 and took a broad view of its scope holding that the EU competition directorate fell within the scope of s.1782. In its discussion of the legislative history of the section it stated in part: **25–80**

> "Moreover, when Congress established the Commission on International Rules of Judicial Procedure in 1958, see *supra*, at 3–4, it instructed the Rules Commission to recommend procedural revisions 'for the rendering of assistance to foreign courts *and quasi- judicial agencies*.' para.2, 72 Stat. 1743 (emphasis added). Section 1782 had previously referred to 'any judicial proceeding.' The Rules Commission's draft, which Congress adopted, replaced that term with 'a proceeding in a foreign or international tribunal.' See *supra*, at 4. Congress understood that change to 'provid[e] the possibility of U.S. judicial assistance in connection with [administrative and quasi-judicial proceedings abroad].' S. Rep. No. 1580, at 7–8; see Smit, International Litigation 1026–1027, and nn. 71, 73 ('[t]he term 'tribunal' . . . includes investigating magistrates, administrative and arbitral tribunals, and quasi-judicial agencies, as well as conventional civil, commercial, criminal, and administrative courts'; in addition to affording assistance in cases before the European Court of Justice, para.1782, as revised in 1964, "permits the rendition of proper aid in proceedings before the [European] Commission in which the Commission exercises quasi-judicial powers").[60]

In the *Intel Corp* case, the US Supreme Court did not hold that international arbitral tribunals fell within s.1782 but with its broad interpretation of the provision and reference to the quotation from Professor Smit's article, it appeared to give that indication. **25–81**

In the *Oxus Gold* case, the District Court of New Jersey referred to the prior cases holding that s.1782 did not apply to Tribunals but distinguished them on the basis that the Tribunal in that instance had been set up pursuant to a bilateral investment treaty and therefore had a different status.[61] In effect, the **25–82**

[59] See the decisions in *NBC v Bear Stearns & Co*, 165 F.3d 184 (2d Cir. 1999); and *Republic of Kazakhstan v Biedermann Int'l*, 168 F.3d 880 (5th Cir. 1999).

[60] *Intel Corp v Advanced Micro Devices, Inc*, 542 US 241 (2004), citing Hans Smit, "International Litigation Under the United States Code" 65 Colum. L. Rev. 1015, 1026–27 n.71, 73 (1965).

[61] See the *Re Oxus Gold PLC*, Misc:06–82, 2006 US Dist. LEXIS 74118 (D.N.J. Oct. 10, 2006) ("In the case at bar, however, Article 8 of the BIT Agreement between the United Kingdom and Kazakhstan specifically mandates that disputes between nationals of the two countries would be

court gave a broader reading to s.1782 but without dealing with the pre-Intel Corp cases.

25–83 In the *Roz Trading* case, the district court of the Northern District of Georgia held that the "international commercial arbitral body located in Austria was a 'tribunal' within the meaning of federal statute permitting domestic discovery for use in foreign proceedings".[62] In that decision, the Court followed the broad interpretation in Intel Corp and expressly rejected the narrower interpretation of s.1782 that had been previously adopted by the Second and Fifth Circuit Courts of Appeal.

25–84 If the *Roz Trading* case is followed, parties will have the opportunity to pursue US discovery in the aid of international arbitration. The potential scope is very broad as it could cover documents and witness evidence from parties and third parties to the arbitral proceedings, subject to the US courts having personal jurisdiction over the defendants and to discretion of the US court before which the application is brought. However, any party considering this course of action should carefully consider the law in the relevant circuit court in the US in which the application would be brought. Moreover, it would be important also to consider the impact on the arbitral proceedings themselves, as such an application will necessarily result in more time being taken for the proceedings.[63] In *In re Application of Mesa Power Group, LLC* the US District Court for the Southern District of Florida allowed the application of art.1782 enabling a party to obtain evidence from a third party for claims brought in a North American Free Trade Agreement arbitration.[64]

Article 25(6): "The arbitral tribunal may decide the case solely on the documents submitted by the parties unless any of the parties requests a hearing."

resolved by arbitration governed by international law. The Arbitration at issue in this case, between two admittedly private litigants, is thus being conducted within a framework defined by two nations and is governed by the Arbitration Rules of the United Nations Commission on International Trade Law (the 'UNCITRAL rules'). In light of these facts, this Court concludes that the Magistrate Judge's holding that the arbitration panel in the case at bar constituted a 'foreign tribunal' for purposes of a 28 U.S.C. s.1782 analysis was not clearly erroneous or contrary to law.").

[62] See the decision in the *Roz Trading Ltd* case cited at para.25–29 n.19. See also the decision in *Re Oxus Gold PLC*, Misc: 06–82, cited at para.25–29, n.19.

[63] An illustration of the impact is provided in a Canadian case relating to the use of depositions in international arbitration. In that case, the parties had agreed that the procedural rules would be those of the Province of Alberta in Canada. Alberta procedural rules are similar to US rules on discovery. The Tribunal ordered depositions of non-parties and the other party sought to have the decision annulled. The Alberta Court of Appeals refused to annul the Tribunal's decision and the Canadian Supreme Court refused to hear an appeal from that decision. As a result, the parties to the arbitration were in fact permitted to conduct deposition discovery with respect to the arbitration. In addition, the proceedings were stayed pending the various appeals. In addition, the proceedings were almost certainly longer than those in other arbitrations without discovery. However, it is noteworthy that it was the Tribunal itself that permitted the deposition discovery in a matter where the amount in dispute was very substantial; see *Jardine Lloyd Thompson Canada Inc Jardine Lloyd Thompson Group Plc and JLT Risk Solutions Ltd v Western Oil Sands Inc, Western Oil Sands L.P., In the Matter of the International Commercial Arbitration Act*, 2005, 2005 A.B.Q.B. 509 (CanLII).

[64] *In re Mesa Power Group, LLC*, 878 F. Supp. 2d 1296 (S.D. Fla. 2012).

Unlike some other types of arbitration, ICC arbitration is a "documents only" arbitration only if the parties so agree. Any party to an ICC arbitration may request a hearing. Most parties—and most arbitrators—assume that there will be a hearing. **25–85**

It is unusual that the Tribunal will not hold a hearing before rendering a final Award. However, it is much more frequent that a Tribunal will render an interim or partial Award without a hearing. In many instances, the parties may feel that it is not strictly necessary to have an issue such as jurisdiction or the applicable law or applicable language decided by the Tribunal with a hearing and that it is more cost effective to skip the oral hearing step. **25–86**

Article 26 Hearings

1 When a hearing is to be held, the arbitral tribunal, giving reasonable notice, shall summon the parties to appear before it on the day and at the place fixed by it.

2 If any of the parties, although duly summoned, fails to appear without valid excuse, the arbitral tribunal shall have the power to proceed with the hearing.

3 The arbitral tribunal shall be in full charge of the hearings, at which all the parties shall be entitled to be present. Save with the approval of the arbitral tribunal and the parties, persons not involved in the proceedings shall not be admitted.

4 The parties may appear in person or through duly authorized representatives. In addition, they may be assisted by advisers.[1]

Introductory remarks

26–1 The oral hearings are the focal point of any ICC arbitration. The hearings may be split into a hearing of the evidence and a separate hearing for legal argument. If so, the hearings are usually linked, so that the hearing for the legal argument takes place reasonably promptly after the evidentiary hearings or the submission of post hearing briefs. Some arbitrators seek to limit this period to two to three weeks after the closing of the hearings or receipt of the post-hearing briefs if they are filed.

26–2 When the Tribunal establishes the provisional timetable pursuant to art.24(2), the various steps in the procedure are often planned with regard to a specific date for the oral hearings. The parties usually make substantial written submissions during the period from the establishment of the Terms of Reference to the oral hearings and Tribunals will give particular attention to those submissions immediately prior to the hearings.

[1] Article 26 corresponds to art.21 of the 1998 ICC Rules. No substantive changes have been made.

In the preparation of their cases, the parties have the advantage of discussing the events relating to the dispute with the factual and expert witnesses. The oral hearings are important because they provide the Tribunal with the opportunity to have this personal contact with the witnesses to, in essence, bring the evidence to life. Therefore, although the Tribunal will have studied the submissions, and have noted the differences in the positions of the parties, the oral hearings provide an opportunity to focus on these differences to weigh the related evidence. 26–3

In preparing for the oral hearings, several basic principles should be kept in mind. The Tribunal will have read the submissions in detail. The Tribunal will also have read the witness statements and the key documents in detail, although one of the basic points of hearings is often to deal with contradictions amongst witnesses and between witnesses and documents. Frequently, although not always, one of the key issues is a question of interpretation of the contemporaneous documentary record, as many arbitrators view this record as inherently more reliable than the undocumented recollections of witnesses. 26–4

Article 26(1): "When a hearing is to be held, the arbitral tribunal, giving reasonable notice, shall summon the parties to appear before it on the day and at the place fixed by it."

The date (or a series of alternative dates) for the oral hearings is frequently established in the provisional timetable under art.24(2). Given the commitments of the parties, their lawyers and the arbitrators, establishing dates for the hearings is often complicated. Therefore, once the dates are set, it is often very difficult to change them. 26–5

As noted under art.25(2), as a general matter, there must be a hearing prior to rendering an Award, unless the parties agree otherwise. Usually, if there is only one hearing, it will be an evidentiary hearing with or without legal argument at the end of the hearing. If there is more than one hearing, then one may be for evidentiary purposes and the other for legal argument. 26–6

As to whether there should be more than one hearing, the UNCITRAL Notes on Organising Arbitral Proceedings reflect the differing positions, which apply also to the considerations arbitrators will make in an ICC arbitration: 26–7

> "76. Attitudes vary as to whether hearings should be held in a single period of hearings or in separate periods, especially when more than a few days are needed to complete the hearings. According to some arbitrators, the entire hearings should normally be held in a single period, even if the hearings are to last for more than a week. Other arbitrators in such cases tend to schedule separate periods of hearings. In some cases issues to be decided are separated, and separate hearings set for those issues, with the aim that oral presentation on those issues will be completed within the allotted time. Among the advantages of one period of hearings are that it involves less travel costs, memory will not fade, and it is unlikely that people representing a party will change. On the other hand, the longer the hearings, the more difficult it may be to find early dates acceptable to all participants. Furthermore, separate periods

of hearings may be easier to schedule, the subsequent hearings may be tailored to the development of the case, and the period between the hearings leaves time for analysing the records and negotiations between the parties aimed at narrowing the points at issue by agreement."[2]

26–8 Given the overriding concern about costs and timing,[3] for smaller more straightforward arbitrations it may be possible and advisable to have one set of hearings dealing with both the presentation of the oral evidence and the legal argument. If the amount in dispute is substantial and the legal issues are complex, then providing for a separate hearing for legal argument is often the preferred approach.

26–9 Article 26(1) envisages a hearing in person and not by telecommunications. Therefore, if there is to be a hearing, the Tribunal should seek to ensure that all parties can be physically present. It would be unorthodox, for example, to have one party attend in person and the other party attend by video link.

26–10 As discussed above, the Tribunal sets the date of the hearings in consultation with the parties, often at the initial procedural hearing. The Tribunal summons the parties to appear on a specific date. This can be done by letter or a procedural order. In either case, there should be a clear record of transmission and receipt of the summons concerning the date. The date will usually have been known well in advance of the hearing, in particular when it was set at the time of establishing the procedural timetable established under art.24(2). If the parties have accepted the dates, it is for the parties and their witnesses to make themselves available for the hearing date, and to ensure that they will have no conflicting commitments. If the parties have not accepted the dates, then it is arguably an obligation of the Tribunal to propose a reasonable number of alternative dates to ensure that the parties can be represented by the counsel of their choice and that the parties' witnesses can attend.

26–11 Generally, the hearing is held at the place of arbitration. In practice, there are a number of exceptions to this general rule. The Tribunal may hold the hearings elsewhere than at the place of arbitration in accordance with art.18(2) provided that the Tribunal first consults with the parties, and that the parties do not agree to the contrary. If there is more than one set of evidentiary hearings, the Tribunal may hold the hearings at a more convenient place for the witnesses. Other reasons for changing the venue of the hearings may relate to the need for, or at least the Tribunal's wish to have, a site visit,[4] the convenience of the members of the Tribunal and the parties or the availability of support for the hearings.

[2] See *http://www.uncitral.org* [accessed November 20, 2013]; see also for the ICC Part III, App. 2 to be found also at http://www.iccwbo.org/Advocacy-Codes-and-Rules/Document-centre/2012/ICC-Arbitration-Commission-Report-on-Techniques-for-Controlling-Time-and-Costs-in-Arbitration/ [accessed November 3, 2013].

[3] *Ibid.* para.72.

[4] The construction site may be in the country of one of the parties, so that holding the hearing in that country may be giving an advantage to that party. The Tribunal will have to consider such situation with due care. In some cases, it may be preferable to separate the site visit from the evidentiary hearing, at the risk of increasing the costs and possible the duration of the arbitration.

On a practical level, it is important to reserve adequate space for the hearings (and accommodation for the participants) well in advance. Usually, Tribunals prefer neutral venues such as arbitration centres (including the ICC) or hotels.[5] The parties are left to organise their facilities, such as separate conference rooms to prepare for the hearings, or can seek in this respect the assistance of the Secretariat, through the counsel in charge of the file.[6] **26–12**

The issue of whether a party has been "duly summoned" is important in case one party fails to attend the hearing as discussed under art.26(2). The Tribunal (and if need be the other party) should ensure that there is a clear documentary record of the notice of the date of the hearing and that such notice was given in accordance with the Terms of Reference. In addition, if there is a chance that a party will fail to attend, some arbitrators ensure that the notice is given to the official address of the party as provided in the Registry of Commerce, for example. The issue of insolvent companies is discussed at para.26–18 below. As regards notice, the most prudent course is to give notice to the legal representative of the company and any person appointed by the court either to approve or direct the affairs of the insolvent company. **26–13**

Article 26(1) deals with notice to the parties only. Therefore the Tribunal is to give notice to the parties' representatives in the arbitration, in accordance with the Terms of Reference. A Tribunal is not obliged under art.26(1) or any other article of the Rules, to summon any of the parties' witnesses, and will normally not do so. It is the responsibility of each party who submits a witness statement to ensure that the witness appears at the hearing. **26–14**

Article 26(2): "If any of the parties, although duly summoned, fails to appear without valid excuse, the arbitral tribunal shall have the power to proceed with the hearing."

Article 26(2) permits the Tribunal to hold the hearing in case of default by one party. A party is in default, when it does not attend the hearing, although duly summoned by the Tribunal to do so. A "valid excuse" within the meaning of the article would generally be expected to be an event beyond the control of the party involved. **26–15**

If a party is prevented from attending by a legal impediment, then there may be an issue of whether that is truly independent of the party or not. For example, if a party has created or contributed to the impediment, the Tribunal may decide that the excuse is not valid. **26–16**

It is difficult to see a financial issue as giving rise to a "valid excuse", unless the issue is such as to virtually render the arbitration agreement unconscionable. **26–17**

In the case of insolvency proceedings, it may be that, under the law of the place of incorporation of the insolvent party, the proceedings are stayed or stayed **26–18**

[5] If the hearings are to be held in Paris, the ICC facilities are advantageous due to the presence of the Secretariat, which can provide assistance at any time, but also to the neutrality and the availability of recording and interpreting facilities.

[6] Bühler & Jarvin, *op. cit.*, p.245.

pending completion of certain formalities as a result of the insolvency.[7] However, the general trend is to seek to continue arbitration proceedings even in such a case. The trustee in bankruptcy or receiver of the insolvent company should have some funding to deal with outstanding issues, although the trustee may seek a delay to decide on whether to appear and what resources to commit to the hearing. Basically, however, the bankruptcy of a party should not deprive the other party of being able to proceed with the arbitration within a reasonable time period taking into account the circumstances, provided that the arbitration may continue under applicable law. In such cases, Tribunals can sometimes use various methods to ensure that the parties are able to present their case in a cost-effective manner.[8]

26–19 In an analysis of the ICC Awards regarding insolvency, a commentator has noted in an article summarising a number of Awards that:

> "Another practical consequence if the Arbitral Tribunal decides to continue the proceedings is the need to keep informed and to consider as a participant in the arbitral proceedings the trustee in bankruptcy or any other person designated as legal representative in the insolvency proceedings. Particular attention should be paid to respect of due process as commencement of insolvency proceedings frequently results in the temporary disorganization of the insolvent party due to the change in its representatives."[9]

26–20 ICC arbitration does not permit default Awards but allows the Tribunal to proceed if one of the parties fails to appear or participate in the proceedings.[10] Therefore, if a party fails to attend, the Tribunal should exercise maximum care to avoid any possible due process concern. It is the duty of the Tribunal to review the evidence and question the witness to satisfy itself that the case has been proven and, to specify the circumstances in the text of the Award.

[7] For a discussion under American and French law see for example Rosell and Prager, "International Arbitration and Bankruptcy: United States, France and the ICC" (2001) J Int'l Arb Vol.18 No.4, p.417; see also Fouchard, "Arbitrage et faillite" (1998) Rev Arb No.3, p.471; For Swizerland, see Lévy, "Insolvency in Arbitration (Swiss Law)" (2005) IntALR Issue No.1, p.23; Brown-Berset and Lévy, "Faillite et arbitrage" (1998) ASA Bull Vol.16 No.4, p.664; Kaufmann-Kohler and Lévy "Insolvency and International Arbitration" in "The Challenge of Insolvency Law Reform in 21st Century" Schulthess 2006, p.257; Mantilla-Serrano, "International Arbitration and Insolvency Proceedings" (1995) Arb Int Vol. 11 No.1, p.51; Croze and Reinhard, "Procédures collectives et arbitrage: Conseils pratiques aux parties et aux arbitres" (2005) JCP Entreprises et Affaires No.14, p.614; see also Cass Com, January 14, 2004, *Prodim v Logidis* (2004) Rev Arb No.3, p.591, note Ancel; Cass Com, June 2, 2004, *Gaussin v Société Alstom Power Turbomachines and Industry v Société Alstom Power Turbomachines* (2004) Rev Arb No.3 p.596, note Ancel.

[8] This may be the type of situation where video conferencing permits a reduction in costs, for example.

[9] Authors' translation. E. Jolivet, "*Quelques exemples de traitement du droit des procédures collectives dans l'arbitrage*", Cahiers Arb 2006 vol. 3, p. 15.

[10] More generally, see for example Lew, Mistelis & Kroll, *Comparative International Commercial Arbitration, op. cit.*, p.544.

Article 26(3): "The arbitral tribunal shall be in full charge of the hearings, at which all the parties shall be entitled to be present. Save with the approval of the arbitral tribunal and the parties, persons not involved in the proceedings shall not be admitted."

The basic principle is that the Tribunal is responsible for the conduct of proceedings. Usually, after consulting the parties, the Tribunal will set out the way in which it intends to conduct the hearings in advance of the hearing, either in writing or through a telephone conference with the parties, followed by a procedural order.[11] The hearings usually have two main objectives, to hear the arguments of the parties and the evidence of the witnesses. **26–21**

One of the issues that arises in organising the hearing relates to the allocation of time between the parties. The comment in the UNCITRAL Notes on Organising Arbitral Proceedings highlights the issues: **26–22**

> "78. Some arbitrators consider it useful to limit the aggregate amount of time each party has for any of the following: (a) making oral statements; (b) questioning its witnesses; and (c) questioning the witnesses of the other party or parties. In general, the same aggregate amount of time is considered appropriate for each party, unless the arbitral tribunal considers that a different allocation is justified. Before deciding, the arbitral tribunal may wish to consult the parties as to how much time they think they will need.
>
> 79. Such planning of time, provided it is realistic, fair and subject to judiciously firm control by the arbitral tribunal, will make it easier for the parties to plan the presentation of the various items of evidence and arguments, reduce the likelihood of running out of time towards the end of the hearings and avoid that one party would unfairly use up a disproportionate amount of time."[12]

If there is to be only one set of hearings, the parties may each present a brief introduction on the first day and will present closing statements on the last day of the hearings, but neither are required in an ICC arbitration. If separate hearings or post-hearing briefs are scheduled for legal argument, there is generally no oral argument at the end of the evidentiary hearings. Arbitral hearings are less formal than court hearings. In small and medium-sized arbitrations, the hearings may be held in a conference room with the parties and the counsel seated at a conference table. Where more persons are present, there is usually a separate conference table **26–23**

[11] On the power of the Tribunal to organise the proceedings and the binding nature of its procedural orders, see for example Karrer, "Freedom of an arbitral tribunal to conduct proceedings" (1999) ICC ICArb Bull Vol.10 No.1, p.14; Orrego Vicuna, "The binding nature of procedural orders in international arbitration" (1999) ICC ICArb Bull Vol.10 No.1, p.38; Donovan, "Powers of the arbitrators to issue procedural orders, including interim measures of protection, and the obligations of parties to abide by such orders" (1999) ICC ICArb Bull Vol.10 No.1, p.57; Böckstiegel, "Major Criteria for International Arbitrators in Shaping an Efficient Procedure" (1999) ICC ICArb Bull, Special Supplement, p.49.

[12] See *http://www.uncitral.org* [accessed November 20, 2013]; see also ICC publication, *Techniques for Controlling Time and Costs in Arbitration, op. cit.*, para.75 (Agenda and timetable), para.76 (Avoiding repetition).

for the Tribunal and for the parties.[13] In either case, there is direct personal interaction between the Tribunal, the parties and witnesses, which personalises the impact of allegations in witness statements, for example.

26–24 With regard to time allocation, frequently one member or the secretary (if any) of the Tribunal (as well as the lawyers for the parties) keeps a record of the time used by each party and provides that summary to the parties on a daily basis. This enables the Tribunal to pay overall attention to equitable use of time although it should be made clear in the procedural order that there is no commitment to more than rough equality as to the allocation of time. In this respect, one issue that sometimes arises is unequal numbers of witnesses on each side. If the Claimant calls one witness for example and the Respondent calls eight, then the Claimant will usually argue that it needs more time for cross examination. Usually, the issue is resolved with a compromise solution that reflects the number of witnesses to be cross examined on each side but also the scope of the cross examination for each witness (which will naturally be broader for the Claimant's sole witness in this example).

26–25 During the hearings, procedural issues may arise that the Tribunal will have to decide rapidly, and often on the spot. Therefore, it is not infrequent for the Tribunal to issue procedural orders during the hearings, first orally, and sometimes subsequently in written form. No formal requirement exists under the Rules, and the best way to proceed will be left to the Tribunal. It would normally be sufficient if the minutes of the hearing, or a verbatim hearing transcript records the Tribunal's order.

26–26 If factual witnesses and experts testify, then there is an initial issue as to how such questioning will be carried out and by whom. The civil law approach in national court proceedings is to have questioning mainly by the judge. The common law approach is generally to have questioning mainly by the lawyers.

26–27 These differences in approach have been attenuated in international arbitration.[14] However, they are subject to certain recent developments such as "witness conferencing", that are briefly discussed below.

26–28 The evidence submitted to a Tribunal is generally not subject to any specific rules of evidence. As noted for example in the IBA Rules of Evidence, it is up to the Tribunal to decide the weight to be given to particular items of evidence.[15]

The Witness Procedure in the IBA of Rules of Evidence

26–29 The IBA Rules of Evidence set out a procedure for taking evidence at hearings. Although not usually adopted by Tribunals as such, art.8 of the IBA Rules of Evidence helps in identifying the issues and potential solutions. It provides as follows:

[13] Where there is a court reporter, he or she may sit next to the Tribunal or between the Tribunal and the witnesses. He or she will often seek to be close to the place from where witness testimony will be given.

[14] See, for example, Elsing and Townsend, "Bridging the Common-Law Civil Divide in Arbitration" (2002) Arb Int Vol.1 No.1, p.59.

[15] The text of the IBA Rules of Evidence is set out in Pt III, App.10.

"1. Within the time ordered by the Arbitral Tribunal, each Party shall inform the Arbitral Tribunal and the other Parties of the witnesses whose appearance it requests. Each witness (which term includes, for the purposes of this Article, witnesses of fact and any experts) shall, subject to Article 8.2, appear for testimony at the Evidentiary Hearing if such person's appearance has been requested by any Party or by the Arbitral Tribunal. Each witness shall appear in person unless the Arbitral Tribunal allows the use of videoconference or similar technology with respect to a particular witness.
2. The Arbitral Tribunal shall at all times have complete control over the Evidentiary Hearing. The Arbitral Tribunal may limit or exclude any question to, answer by or appearance of a witness, if it considers such question, answer or appearance to be irrelevant, immaterial, unreasonably burdensome, duplicative or otherwise covered by a reason for objection set forth in Article 9.2. Questions to a witness during direct and re-direct testimony may not be unreasonably leading.
3. With respect to oral testimony at an Evidentiary Hearing:

    (a) the Claimant shall ordinarily first present the testimony of its witnesses, followed by the Respondent presenting the testimony of its witnesses;
    (b) following direct testimony, any other Party may question such witness, in an order to be determined by the Arbitral Tribunal. The Party who initially presented the witness shall subsequently have the opportunity to ask additional questions on the matters raised in the other Parties' questioning;
    (c) thereafter, the Claimant shall ordinarily first present the testimony of its Party-Appointed Experts, followed by the Respondent presenting the testimony of its Party-Appointed Experts. The Party who initially presented the Party- Appointed Expert shall subsequently have the opportunity to ask additional questions on the matters raised in the other Parties' questioning;
    (d) the Arbitral Tribunal may question a Tribunal-Appointed Expert, and he or she may be questioned by the Parties or by any Party-Appointed Expert, on issues raised in the Tribunal-Appointed Expert Report, in the Parties' submissions or in the Expert Reports made by the Party-Appointed Experts;
    (e) if the arbitration is organised into separate issues or phases (such as jurisdiction, preliminary determinations, liability and damages), the Parties may agree or the Arbitral Tribunal may order the scheduling of testimony separately for each issue or phase;
    (f) the Arbitral Tribunal, upon request of a Party or on its own motion, may vary this order of proceeding, including the

arrangement of testimony by particular issues or in such a manner that witnesses be questioned at the same time and in confrontation with each other (witness conferencing);

(g) the Arbitral Tribunal may ask questions to a witness at any time.

4. A witness of fact providing testimony shall first affirm, in a manner determined appropriate by the Arbitral Tribunal, that he or she commits to tell the truth or, in the case of an expert witness, his or her genuine belief in the opinions to be expressed at the Evidentiary Hearing. If the witness has submitted a Witness Statement or an Expert Report, the witness shall confirm it. The Parties may agree or the Arbitral Tribunal may order that the Witness Statement or Expert Report shall serve as that witness's direct testimony.

5. Subject to the provisions of Article 9.2, the Arbitral Tribunal may request any person to give oral or written evidence on any issue that the Arbitral Tribunal considers to be relevant to the case and material to its outcome. Any witness called and questioned by the Arbitral Tribunal may also be questioned by the Parties."

26–30 The above procedure is adopted in many international arbitrations, as it provides the lawyers of the parties with the flexibility of testing the evidence while allowing for questioning by the Tribunal.[16] It has become less common to have the Tribunal begin the questioning, although this can arise particularly in the case of witness conferencing discussed below. However, early questioning by the Tribunal may in many instances well be in the interest of an efficient and focused evidentiary hearing. This is not only a matter of culture and preferences, but also of the circumstances in each case.

26–31 At evidentiary hearings, one of the first issues to be clarified is whether witnesses, whether of fact or expert witnesses, are allowed to be in the hearing room, and if so as of what moment. The difference of treatment between fact and expert witnesses is due to the consideration that an expert should be opining on the basis of all relevant facts, and should therefore not be deprived of a fact witness' oral testimony. Although not mentioned in the IBA Rules of Evidence, usually a witness of fact, unlike an expert witness, will not attend the evidentiary hearings prior to providing his or her testimony. Therefore after a brief welcome by the Tribunal of the parties' and the persons attending on their behalf, witnesses are excluded from the hearing room, until their turn has come to testify.[17] Thus, if

[16] See Bühler and Dorgan, "Witness Testimony Pursuant to the 1999 IBA Rules of Evidence in International Commercial—Novel or Tested Standards?", *op. cit.*, at p.17; see also ICC Institute of World Business Law Dossiers, *Arbitration and Oral Evidence* (ICC Publishing SA, 2005), ICC Publication No.689.

[17] See Bühler and Dorgan, "Witness Testimony Pursuant to the 1999 IBA Rules of Evidence in International Commercial—Novel or Tested Standards?", *op. cit.*, at p.27; Fouchard, Gaillard & Goldman, *op. cit.*, para.1287, at p.698. Dissenting: Oetiker, "Witness before the International Arbitral Tribunal", *op. cit.*, at p.270 ("Many arbitration rules provide that the decision in this regard lies with the arbitral tribunal. In practice, arbitral tribunals often permit the presence of witnesses

the parties are to make opening statements at the beginning of the hearing, none of the fact witnesses will normally be present in the hearing room. In some instances, an exception to that rule can be made if one of the witnesses is at the same time a party representative (discussed under art.26(4) below).

In medium and larger arbitrations, it is frequent that there is a daily transcript of the witness evidence. In some cases, the transcript may be prepared on a real time basis subject to rectification of errors in the evening. In smaller arbitrations, the Tribunal may simply make a tape recording of the proceedings, which the Tribunal and the parties can consult, if need be, after the hearings. Although court reporters will add to the costs of arbitration (albeit often only marginally), whenever a party expects significant witness testimony, the most convenient, most efficient and safest approach over tape recording is a verbatim transcript.[18] **26–32**

Certain basic principles applicable to cross examination in American litigation, for example, are not found in normal ICC arbitrations. For example, although a factual foundation should be present for questioning of a witness to make the cross-examination more effective, it is infrequent for a Tribunal to permit a party to object to questions on that basis. Similarly, although there is reference in the IBA Rules of Evidence to certain questions not being "unreasonably leading", it is generally not possible to object to a question on that basis, although it is possible to comment in argument on the nature of the questioning. In addition, cross-examination of witnesses in ICC arbitrations is usually based on the documents that have been filed in the proceedings and it is rare that the Tribunal permits cross-examination on documents that have not previously been submitted. Likewise, it is uncommon in an ICC arbitration to object to the testimony of a witness on the basis of hearsay. The strict evidentiary rules of court proceedings are normally not applicable in an ICC arbitration, and will often only distract, and sometimes annoy the Tribunal.[19] **26–33**

Witnesses frequently testify in a language that is not their mother language. Therefore, there is in some (but certainly not all) cases somewhat less precision as to what exactly is meant under questioning. If the witness is unable to speak the language of the arbitration fluently, then an interpreter will be required. With a professional interpreter the questioning of the witness can usually be conducted with no great difficulty. Generally, parties are not permitted to use their own employees as interpreters for their witnesses. **26–34**

There is a continuing difference in approach as to the time allowed for questioning of witnesses. Common law lawyers tend to expect to be able to question witnesses for much longer than civil law lawyers. As a result, witness hearings that one side may expect to take two weeks, may well be held in half that time. **26–35**

who will be called later, even if they must subsequently testify on the facts that are the subject matter of the hearing.").

[18] Unless the hearing would be limited strictly to legal argument, a tape recording should be the very minimum parties should be insisting on at any hearing, in order to avoid a subsequent dispute over what was said and agreed.

[19] More generally, see Newman & Klieman, *Take the Witness: The Experts Speak on Cross-Examination* (Jurispublishing Inc, 2006), in particular, Newman, "Cross-examination in International Arbitration" at p.55.

26–36 This difference in approach may give rise to due process issues. In *Generica Ltd v Pharmaceutical Basics Inc*,[20] the arbitrator refused to permit further cross examination of a third party when it became apparent that the questioning involved his liability and when the arbitrator held that the issue was not determinative. The US Seventh Circuit Court of Appeals permitted enforcement of the Award on the basis that "The arbitrator's curtailment of cross-examination of [the witness] was not such a fundamental procedural defect that it violated our due process jurisprudence and therefore the New York Convention".

26–37 In *Tempo Shain Corp v Bertek Inc*,[21] the Tribunal was faced with a witness who had become unavailable for an undetermined period due to serious illness in the family. The Tribunal proceeded without the testimony on the basis that the evidence was reflected in letters. The court vacated the arbitral Award stating:

> "Because [the potential witness] as sole negotiator for Bertek was the only person who could have testified in rebuttal of appellees' fraudulent inducement claim, and in support of Bertek's fraudulent inducement claim, and the documentary evidence did not adequately address such testimony, there was no reasonable basis for the arbitrators to conclude that [the witness's] testimony would have been cumulative with respect to those issues. The record showed that the witness would have testified to facts that only he could have known, making his testimony essential."

26–38 These cases highlight the potential impact of exclusion of witness evidence as a due process issue in the place of arbitration and the place of enforcement. Therefore, prior to taking a decision as to the exclusion of witnesses, the Tribunal and the parties would be well advised to consider the case law in these countries on the issue.

26–39 Lawyers also have different approaches with regard to electronic presentations. In larger, complex cases, the use of electronic presentations can be very helpful for the Tribunal, particularly where it focuses on the documents being presented to the witness. However, it should not have the effect of taking the other party by surprise and therefore there should be some coordination as regards electronic presentation prior to the hearings. Usually, this can be dealt with in the pre-hearing (telephone) conference in which the parties confirm whether or not they will be using presentation media. In addition, the electronic means should not be a way of presenting new evidence, but rather of presenting evidence that has already been submitted to the Tribunal (and the other party).

26–40 Other aspects of due process are discussed under art.22. One of the basic points made by the courts is that it is up to the Tribunal to weigh the evidence, but that the lawyers should have an opportunity to present their case subject to the overall management of the proceedings by the Tribunal.

[20] *Generica Ltd v Pharmaceutical Basics Inc*, 125 F.3d 1123 (7th Cir., 1997).
[21] *Tempo Shain Corp v Bertek Inc*, 120 F.3d 16 (2d Cir., 1997).

Testimony by video conferencing or telephone

The general rule is that witnesses are expected to be present in person at the evidentiary hearing. Therefore, any alternative arrangement is subject either to consent of the parties or an order of the Tribunal. In issuing any order permitting video conferencing, the Tribunal will have to keep in mind the importance of the witness, his relationship with the parties and the requirements of due process.[22] **26–41**

If a party insists on questioning a key factual witness for the other side who is in fact employed by the other side and does not have a convincing reason for not physically attending the hearing, the Tribunal will generally give that insistence considerable weight. If the evidence to be provided is that of a third party with no current relationship with the parties to the arbitration, the Tribunal will most likely take reasonable steps to accommodate the witness to obtain his or her testimony. With respect to experts, testimony by video conferencing can be quite satisfactory, although the party proposing the expert should consider whether the expert's impact would be reduced if he were not physically present. **26–42**

Witness conferencing

In some civil law countries, such as France, there is a tradition in the criminal law of having the witnesses "confront" each other. Some arbitrators have introduced a new method of hearing witnesses in which the factual witnesses are heard together.[23] This method is viewed as one of the best ways of cutting through rhetoric and establishing what really happened. For example, at a construction site, representatives of the contractor and a subcontractor may have worked together on a project for months and in some instances if they testify together they will establish where the real problems were. Witness conferencing is also a way of hearing more witnesses rapidly, which can be particularly appropriate where there is a large number of witnesses to be heard. **26–43**

By its nature, witness conferencing calls more upon the Tribunal, and particular the president, to organise the testimony and to ensure that each factual witness has a chance to express him or herself. Otherwise, there is a danger that, instead of assisting in establishing the facts of the case, the witness conference does the contrary. For the lawyers, witness conferencing leaves less control over the proceedings and may therefore be less predictable than traditional questioning. **26–44**

Expert witnesses and conferencing

Experts are questioned much like factual witnesses with focus on their credentials, the material reviewed and the basis for their opinions. The IBA Rules of Evidence provide for early meetings of experts (as in fact is carried out in some national courts, such as in England), and this practice is developing more broadly in international arbitration. Many Tribunals now prefer a joint report from experts on both sides identifying their areas of agreement and disagreement. **26–45**

[22] Schäfer, "Videoconferencing in Arbitration" (2003) ICC ICArb Bull Vol.14 No.1, p.35 describes in much detail the many aspects a Tribunal needs to consider prior to authorising and proceeding with videoconferencing.

[23] Peter, "Witness 'Conferencing" (2002) Arb Int Vol.18 No.1, p.47.

26–46 It is also possible to have the experts testify as a panel or to have the experts testify initially individually and then as a panel. The objective is to see whether the experts can reach common ground on the issues and in many instances, there would appear to be no reason why this would not work. The main concern is that by having the experts testify as a panel, the Tribunal is encouraging the most assertive expert rather than necessarily the best.

Factual witness and expert witness conferencing

26–47 In some instances, the factual and expert issues are so intertwined that the Tribunal may wish to hear a panel of factual witnesses and experts. This type of procedure basically relegates the lawyers to the role of observers and can be very difficult to manage. In fact, the joint panel approach may be most appropriate where the factual witnesses are engineers who have worked on the litigious project and have technical expertise that is on the level of that of an expert.

Persons in attendance

26–48 Article 26(3) expressly provides for the privacy of the arbitration hearings. In many jurisdictions, this provision reflects the implied requirement of confidentiality of arbitral proceedings. In other proceedings, by accepting the Rules, the parties are accepting the privacy of the hearings.

26–49 The president typically prepares an attendance list for each day of the hearings recording the persons who are in attendance and their capacity. The various attendees sign that list, which the president keeps in his file to provide the parties with a copy of the attendance list, during or after the hearing.[24]

26–50 The issue of privacy becomes more complicated if the parties are using live transmission of the transcript to parties outside the hearing room. This is usually dealt with by adding such persons to the attendance list of the arbitration. However, if that is the case, steps have to be taken to ensure that the persons who have not yet testified are not thereby permitted to hear the testimony. A similar issue arises with respect to daily transcripts. If witnesses are excluded until they testify, then they should not be permitted to review the transcripts prior to their testimony. The usual course in this situation would be to rely on an undertaking of counsel to restrict access to transcripts.

Article 26(4): "The parties may appear in person or through duly authorized representatives. In addition, they may be assisted by advisers."

26–51 In an ICC arbitration, parties have the right to be represented by the persons of their choice. A distinction should however be made between "authorized representatives" and "advisors". Usually, the parties have attorneys represent them in the arbitration. Thus, an attorney may have both capacities, but this may not always be the case. As an adviser, he or she would not need a power of attorney. On the other hand, as a representative of a party, he or she might need a power of attorney. In addition, lawyers are often not admitted to practice in the place of

[24] See for an example, Pt II, Document 21.

arbitration. The major centres of arbitration do not appear to have restrictions on the right of lawyers from other countries to argue cases in those countries, although there appears to still be an issue in this respect in California.[25]

Lawyers who attend hearings are generally not required to present powers of attorney, although powers of attorney may have been filed at the time of the Terms of Reference or pursuant to art.17. **26–52**

It is relatively frequent in ICC arbitration to have co-counsel. One law firm may represent the party on a regular basis and be familiar with its activities and personnel and be located in the same country as the party. The other law firm may be more familiar with the rules of law governing the arbitration or ICC arbitration in general. One of the law firms will need to have a power of attorney from the party it acts for, and may have the right to delegate the power to another lawyer. **26–53**

Usually, in addition to the attorney, a party will be represented by an executive at the hearings. The presence of an executive is viewed as being important to ensure that the attorney is in a position to obtain instructions from his client as to any procedural issue that may arise during the hearings. It may be that with respect to major issues it is necessary to refer to persons who are not at the hearing. However, the presence of an executive at the hearing is helpful and virtually expected. **26–54**

If the client representative is also a witness in the proceedings, then a party may wish to have the executive attend throughout the hearings. In such cases, frequently the Tribunal will have the executive testify either first, or if the person is an executive of the Respondent, prior to any other witnesses of the Respondent. Tribunals vary in their approach but most seek to find a solution that allows a party to effectively instruct their lawyers during the proceedings while at the same time ensuring that witness evidence is not coloured by prior witness testimony. **26–55**

[25] See Caron and Harhay "By Prohibiting Foreign Lawyers from Participating, California is missing out" http://www.law.berkeley.edu/9181.htm [accessed November 3, 2013].

Article 27 Closing of the Proceedings and Date for Submission of Draft Awards

As soon as possible after the last hearing concerning matters to be decided in an award or the filing of the last authorized submissions concerning such matters, whichever is later, the arbitral tribunal shall:

- **a) declare the proceedings closed with respect to the matters to be decided in the award; and**
- **b) inform the Secretariat and the parties of the date by which it expects to submit its draft award to the Court for approval pursuant to Article 33.**

After the proceedings are closed, no further submission or argument may be made, or evidence produced, with respect to the matters to be decided in the award, unless requested or authorized by the arbitral tribunal.[1]

27–1 ICC arbitration is intended to be cost-effective. Accordingly, art.25 requires the Tribunal to establish the facts of the case "within as short a time as possible". Article 30(1) provides that ICC arbitrations are to be completed in six months, unless an extension is granted. To finalise the Award, the Tribunal must be able to impose a cut-off on submission of evidence and argument by the parties. That is what art.27 is designed to provide. By agreeing to ICC arbitration, the parties are accepting this basic rule that is typical of civil law systems. The purpose of art.27 is to streamline the proceedings, and also to protect the arbitral process from being interrupted by late (and unexpected) submissions of a party. Both parties will be advised that they will, as of the time of the closing of the proceedings, have to expect a decision from the Tribunal.

27–2 Article 27 provides, unlike its predecessor under the 1998 Rules, that the proceedings shall be closed as soon as possible after the last hearing or last set of authorised submissions. This change was made to expedite proceedings and to avoid having the Tribunal wait until it finalised an Award to close the proceedings. The determination of when it is possible to close the proceedings will vary. Nevertheless, there is a tendency to only close the proceedings once the Tribunal has had initial deliberations. Prior to closing the proceedings, the Tribunal may wish to ensure that it has all of the evidence and legal authorities that the Tribunal considers it needs to finalise an Award. This approach is not required by or in conformity with the spirit of the Rules. A Tribunal may always re-open the proceedings under art.27 if, during deliberations, the Tribunal considers that it does not have sufficient evidence or legal authority on a point.

27–3 Article 27 also provides that the Tribunal may close the proceedings with respect to the matters to be decided in the Award. Therefore, if the Award is to

[1] Article 27 is based on art.22 of the 1998 Rules. The new provision provides for partial closing of proceedings and for closing of proceedings as soon as possible after the hearings or last submissions.

decide solely jurisdictional issues, the Tribunal may close the proceedings with respect to the jurisdictional issues.

In addition, art.27 provides that the Tribunal shall inform the parties as well as the Secretariat of the date by which it anticipates submitting a draft Award for scrutiny pursuant to art.33. **27–4**

Article 27 relates directly to art.22(4). The Tribunal shall declare the proceedings closed when it is satisfied that each party has had "a reasonable opportunity to present its case". Prior to closing the proceedings, the Tribunal should ensure that the due process requirements of the Rules and the place of arbitration are respected. As discussed under arts 18 and 22,[2] the perception of what will constitute a reasonable opportunity to present a case will depend to a certain extent on the approach of the national courts. **27–5**

In many instances, especially with smaller or mid-size arbitrations, oral submissions are made and the hearings are closed at the end of the hearing. In other instances, the parties submit post-hearing briefs either reflecting their final positions or responding to specific points that have been raised by the Tribunal. In such cases, the Tribunal frequently announces that the proceedings are closed subject to the submission of the post-hearing briefs and the submissions on costs. Post-hearings are normally not allowed to contain new factual evidence, but Tribunals may allow and sometimes even solicit legal material in support of the parties' legal submissions. Many Tribunals find it helpful to have the post-hearing briefs submitted promptly after the oral hearings so that the members of the Tribunal can recall it in more detail. Frequently, the Tribunal will close the procedure at the end of the evidentiary hearings and oral argument. At that time, the Tribunal will usually invite the parties to submit at a later date their costs in the arbitration, as is discussed under art.37. **27–6**

Article 27 requires no specific form for closing the proceedings. The Tribunal will normally record its decision in writing, in a Procedural Order or simply in a letter to the parties. The same result would be achieved if at the end of the hearing the Tribunal declares the proceedings closed and such declaration is recorded, for instance, by a court reporter's verbatim transcript. In practice, it often happens that the Secretariat invites the Tribunal to close the proceedings, once it has received the draft Award from the Tribunal. Such practice defeats somewhat the purpose of art.27. Ideally, however, the Secretariat would be asking Tribunals at a much earlier point in time, whether they consider that the proceedings should be closed, and in the affirmative to require the Tribunal to inform the parties accordingly. **27–7**

Prior to closing the proceedings, many Tribunals ask the parties if they have any objection to the way the proceedings have been conducted and whether they accept that the proceedings be now closed. This question is intended to cover whether the parties feel that they have had a reasonable opportunity to present their cases. If the parties do not object, then they will usually be deemed to have waived their right to object under art.39. This confirmation may in fact even cover **27–8**

[2] See paras 18–2, 22–64 *et seq.*

objections that were made prior to the oral hearings. As the US Court of Appeals for the Fifth Circuit said in the *Karaha Bodas* case[3]:

> "In the Final Award, issued in December 2000, the Tribunal stated that all parties had 'waived their respective requests for discovery' at the conclusion of the hearing. Pertamina asserts that it did not waive its requests for discovery because the Tribunal denied the request before the hearing, when the discovery could have been of use. Pertamina ignores the fact that in international commercial arbitration, it is not uncommon to ask for additional discovery or information after a hearing, to request additional sessions of a hearing to submit more evidence, or to file posthearing submissions. Rather than renew its requests for discovery into FPL's willingness to finance the project or to assert a request for discovery into FPL's political risk insurance, Pertamina's counsel expressly stated that the record had been 'fully made' and that he was 'prepared to rest on the record.' The record supports the Tribunal's conclusion that the discovery requests made before the hearing had been waived. Pertamina did not ask for discovery into political risk insurance until it filed its Rule 60(b) motion in the district court. The Tribunal's denial of a continuance and additional discovery did not prevent Pertamina from presenting its case, so as to deprive it of a fair hearing. Pertamina presented ample evidence in support of its position that KBC would be unable to find financing. The Tribunal considered Pertamina's evidence and gave it considerable weight, awarding KBC damages substantially lower than the amount it sought."

27–9 In the *Karaha Bodas* case, the party's confirmation therefore covered not only the conduct of the hearings, but arguably the discovery request prior to the hearings. This type of confirmation of the parties is particularly relevant if a party later argues that it could have submitted additional evidence or additional argument. The confirmation is less useful if the party subsequently alleges bias in the conduct of the proceedings, as a party may only waive what the party knows of and some forms of bias that are not subject to waiver.[4] In addition, such a confirmation places counsel in an awkward position with respect to the Tribunal. It is submitted that one way to deal with this situation is for counsel to respond confirming that there is no objection to the conduct of the oral hearings if that is its case, but that counsel maintain its position with respect to procedural matters that were raised prior to the hearing.[5]

[3] *Karaha Bodas Co LLC v Perusahaan Pertambangan Minyak Dan Gas Bumi Negara*, 364 F.3d 274 (5th Cir. 2004); (2004) YBCA Vol.XXIX, p.1262.

[4] Parties may hesitate to raise procedural issues immediately prior to deliberation of the Tribunal on the merits. In some instances, the circumstances may act to vitiate any waiver argument. If the Tribunal has adopted a procedure with the consent of the parties, the situation is quite different from one where the Tribunal has adopted a procedure over the objection of the party and then seeks at the end of the proceedings a confirmation that the party has no objection to the procedure.

[5] In the *Karaha Bodas* case, the discovery issue was apparently raised during the enforcement proceedings. If a party has made a disclosure request and the Tribunal has ruled and rejected it, then it is difficult to see a justification for the Tribunal to ask for a waiver of rights at the end of the

Article 27 provides that parties may make submissions when requested or authorised by the Tribunal. The need for further submissions may sometimes appear to the Tribunal on very specific points that it is able to fully consider only during the deliberation stage. It may concern clarification of a factual or legal point. Any such submissions must be made in a manner that ensures that the other party has the right to comment on them in accordance with due process. The Tribunal is not required as a general matter to hold further hearings after such submission. If, as it may happen in very exceptional circumstances, the additional submission contains a factual witness statement, then the other party should have the right to test that witness statement and, depending on the circumstances and the importance of the evidence, a further hearing may be appropriate. However, in organising a further hearing, the practicalities and costs should be taken into account. Therefore, it may be that a hearing by video conference or by telephone is adequate and that a hearing in person is not required. 27–10

The circumstances in which the Tribunal may decide to reopen the proceedings and authorise further submissions are varied.[6] With regards to requests by the parties to consider further submissions, the Tribunal will wish to consider the nature and type of documents, the time that has elapsed since the closing of the proceedings, the reasons for the late submission, and the impact the admission of the new documents may have on the proceedings, when deciding to reopen the proceedings with respect to such documents. The classic circumstance where late-filed documents may be admitted is when new evidence arises that was not available to the parties previously and which is material to the resolution of the dispute. For example, in a case evolving around the validity of patented and unpatented technology, a Tribunal in an unreported Award permitted further submissions after the patent had been held presumptively invalid. These further submissions should not permit a party to re-argue the entire case. In another unreported Award, an arbitrator declined to permit expert evidence of damages when both parties had argued the damages point extensively in their memorials. 27–11

As mentioned, the Tribunal may during its deliberations conclude that certain matters have not been covered adequately for whatever reason. In such a case, the desire to do justice has to be reconciled with the need to complete the arbitration. Frequently, Tribunals resolve such issues based on the burden of proof: it is up to the party who has the burden of proof to satisfy that burden or its claim fails. 27–12

Moreover, when the Tribunal reopens the hearing on a given point at its own initiative, this may provide the parties a clear hint in what direction the Tribunal seems to be going. This route is therefore not always appropriate, but may nevertheless in some cases be the better course of action. 27–13

hearing. The rejection was the Tribunal's decision and the Tribunal is required to meet the requirements of due process.

[6] For instance, art.38(2) of the ICSID Rules is rather specific on this point, when it states: "(2) Exceptionally, the Tribunal may, before the award has been rendered, reopen the proceeding on the ground that new evidence is forthcoming of such a nature as to constitute a decisive factor, or that there is a vital need for clarification on certain specific points". More generally, see Taylor and Baruti, "Reopening The Case After The Hearing–To What Extent And Under What Circumstances Should It Be Allowed?" in *ASA Special Series* No.29, September 2007, *The Resolution of the Dispute–from the Hearing to the Award*, Conference of January 26, 2007 in Geneva, p.8 with references to cases of the Iran-United States Claims Tribunal.

27–14 Article 27 requires the Tribunal to provide the Secretariat and the parties with an approximate date for the submission of the draft Award for scrutiny when the proceedings are closed. Article 27 was inserted to permit the parties, Secretariat, and thus the ICC Court, to better monitor the progress in rendering the Award. As noted above, the provision has now been expanded to provide that the Tribunal is to inform the parties as well.

27–15 There is no sanction for failing to submit an Award by the date indicated by the Tribunal.[7] At the same time, deliberations in a three-member Tribunal may prove to be difficult and may oblige the president to take a cautious approach as regards informing the Secretariat by which date the draft Award will be submitted, as long as he has the support of the co-arbitrators in that respect.[8] The deliberations of the Tribunal are discussed in detail under art.31.[9] The deliberations may begin in an informal fashion during the evidentiary hearings when the Tribunal will discuss the evidence. Further deliberations may follow immediately after the hearings. Part of the deliberations must be with respect to the question whether to declare the proceedings closed, and if so as of when, as this is a basic decision of the Tribunal.

[7] See Bühler & Jarvin, *op. cit.*, para.17, at p.251; see also Bühler, "Cost of arbitration: some further considerations" in *Liber Amicorum in honour of Robert Briner, op. cit.*, at p.182.

[8] See Reiner, "Le Règlement d'Arbitrage de la CCI, Version 1998" (1998) Rev Arb No.1, p.25 at p.60.

[9] See paras 31–4 et seq.

Article 28: Conservatory and Interim Measures

1 **Unless the parties have otherwise agreed, as soon as the file has been transmitted to it, the arbitral tribunal may, at the request of a party, order any interim or conservatory measure it deems appropriate. The arbitral tribunal may make the granting of any such measure subject to appropriate security being furnished by the requesting party. Any such measure shall take the form of an order, giving reasons, or of an award, as the arbitral tribunal considers appropriate.**

2 **Before the file is transmitted to the arbitral tribunal, and in appropriate circumstances even thereafter, the parties may apply to any competent judicial authority for interim or conservatory measures. The application of a party to a judicial authority for such measures or for the implementation of any such measures ordered by an arbitral tribunal shall not be deemed to be an infringement or a waiver of the arbitration agreement and shall not affect the relevant powers reserved to the arbitral tribunal. Any such application and any measures taken by the judicial authority must be notified without delay to the Secretariat. The Secretariat shall inform the arbitral tribunal thereof.**[1]

Introductory remarks

Effective dispute resolution depends on ensuring that the parties have access to evidence and obtain the benefit of the proceedings by being able to realise on any Award. It is important that production of evidence and enforcement of the Award is not frustrated by actions of the other party. National courts have developed various methods to ensure that this will be the case, using the enforcement mechanisms that are available to them. Private arbitral tribunals are by their nature different in that they lack the "*imperium*" to enforce certain measures. Therefore, **28–1**

[1] Article 28 replaces art. 23 of the 1998 Rules. There have been no substantive changes.

the issue of conservatory and interim relief depends on the interaction between national courts and Tribunals.[2]

28–2 Article 28 is unchanged from the corresponding article of the 1998 Rules. However, there has been a major change in ICC procedure with the introduction of the Emergency Arbitrator provisions in art.29. Those provisions are intended to deal with "urgent interim or conservatory measures that cannot await the constitution of the Tribunal". Therefore, although the provisions of art.28 govern conservatory and interim measures decided upon by Tribunals, there is an alternative under art.29 that the parties should consider at the outset. As discussed under art.29, the decisions of the Emergency Arbitrator may be revisited by the Tribunal.

28–3 The need to ensure that international arbitration is effective was the main impetus for the first revision to the UNCITRAL Model Law since it was enacted over twenty years ago. The UNCITRAL Model Law as so modified in 2006 has, of course, not been widely adopted as yet.[3] However, the concepts and issues that it deals with in art.17 of the Model Law are helpful with respect to the issues that arise in this context. Many of those provisions will be familiar to practitioners, as they are commonly found in state law proceedings relating to interim measures. As such, and although not directly applicable to an ICC arbitration, the new provisions of art.17 of the UNCITRAL Model Law contain a useful checklist of what parties and Tribunals may always wish to consider with respect to such measures.

28–4 Article 17 of the UNCITRAL Model Law begins by drawing a distinction between "interim measures" that are issued upon notice to the other party and "preliminary orders" that are made ex parte (art.17 B). It was the preliminary orders discussed beginning at para.28–23 below that gave rise to the greatest divergences of opinion amongst practitioners. The material on "interim measures" in large part is an uncontroversial reflection of current practice and will be referred to as such below.

28–5 As discussed under art.18, in general the link between the Tribunal and the national courts is through the courts of the place of arbitration. However, with respect to enforcement of conservatory or interim measures, this is not necessarily the case. The relevant national court for conservatory and interim measures will usually be the court where the conservatory or interim measure is to be carried out. This is frequently not the country of the place of arbitration, although it may well be the country of enforcement. Therefore, one of the key aspects of the revi-

[2] Poudret, "Les mesures provisionnelles et l'arbitrage. Aperçu comparatif des pouvoirs respectifs de l'arbitre et du juge" in *Mélanges en l'honneur de François Knoepfler, op. cit.*, at p.289. The importance of the interaction was also noted by the Federal Court of the Southern District of New York in *Discount Trophy & Co v Plastic Dress-Up Co*, No.Civ. 3:03cv2167, 2004 US Dist LEXIS 2659, at 29 (D. Conn., 2004) in the following terms: "Even though this case will be stayed pending the parties' arbitration, the Second Circuit has made it clear in a series of decisions that the Court has both the power and duty to entertain a motion for a preliminary injunction pending the results in the arbitration. And this is true even though, as is the case here, the parties are entitled under the rules of the arbitral tribunal they have chosen to seek pendente lite relief directly from the arbitrator". However, see the discussion of the *McCreary Tire* case at para.28–47; more generally on the role of the courts and problems related to the execution of conservatory and provisional measures, see (1993) ICC ICArb Bull, Special Supplement, *Conservatory and Provisional Measures in International Arbitration*.

[3] See art.17 of the UNCITRAL Model Law with amendments as adopted in 2006, *http://www.uncitral.org* [accessed November 23, 2013] and Pt III App.5.

sion to the UNCITRAL Model Law was to seek to provide a legal mechanism for the enforcement of interim measures.[4]

For example, to order production of documents, the parties will frequently seek the approval of the courts of the Respondent's place of business. Therefore, where the Respondent in one case was based in the United States, the party seeking an order for inspection addressed itself to the US courts.[5] In the case of inspection of a ship located in the United States, the court proceedings were brought in the United States, although the place of arbitration was London.[6] To order the attendance of a witness, usually the competent court will be the court of the place of residence of the witness. In some instances, the place of arbitration and the place of inspection or of residence of a witness will coincide. However, that is not always or even usually the case. Indeed, to obtain the assistance of the local courts, Tribunals may well hold hearings in places other than the place of arbitration.[7] 28–6

Article 28 refers to "conservatory or interim measures". Article 28 provides that those measures may be taken by reasoned procedural order or by Award at the Tribunal's option. The distinction between Awards and procedural orders is important. Final measures include Awards for damages, declarations and injunctions. In an ICC arbitration, final measures are set out in an Award (whether interim, partial or final) and that Award is subject to the scrutiny of the ICC Court under art.33.[8] Conservatory or interim measures are measures that are intended to be put in place prior to the rendering of a final Award. These measures are intended to cover, for example, preservation of evidence, financial issues, prevention of damage and maintenance of status quo and confidentiality.[9] 28–7

A fundamental characteristic common to provisional and conservatory measures relates to the fact that they are intended to protect the rights of a party solely pending the final resolution of the dispute, and are therefore temporary in 28–8

[4] Article 17H provides for enforcement and art.17 I provides grounds for refusal of enforcement. As regards enforcement, art.17H provides:
"(1) An interim measure issued by an arbitral tribunal shall be recognized as binding and, unless otherwise provided by the arbitral tribunal, enforced upon application to the competent court, irrespective of the country in which it was issued, subject to the provisions of article 17 I.
(2) The party who is seeking or has obtained recognition or enforcement of an interim measure shall promptly inform the court of any termination, suspension or modification of that interim measure.
(3) The court of the State where recognition or enforcement is sought may, if it considers it proper, order the requesting party to provide appropriate security if the arbitral tribunal has not already made a determination with respect to security or where such a decision is necessary to protect the rights of third parties."

[5] See *Publicis Communication v True North Communications Inc*, 206 F.3d 725 (7th Cir., 2000); (2000) YBCA Vol.XXV p.641; (2000) Mealey's IAR, Sect. B-1; (2000) ASA Bull Vol.18 No.2 p.830, note Goldstein; (2000) Rev Arb No.4 p.657, note Pinsolle; discussed in Webster, "Obtaining Documents from Adverse Parties in International Arbitration", *op. cit.*, p.41 at p.42, N.3 and p.54. See also para.33–7.

[6] *In the Matter of the Application of Deiulemar Compagnia di Navigazione SpA v M/V Allegra*, 198 F.3d 473, 480 (4th Cir., 1999), the court granted an inspection order stating: "In the present case, Pacific Eternity was repairing the ship's main engine and hull and the condition of these items was crucial to Deiulemar's arbitration claim. Deiulemar's effort to preserve the evidence on the Allegra was disrupted by Pacific Eternity, which denied Deiulemar access to the ship."

[7] See Webster, "Obtaining Evidence from Adverse Parties in International Arbitration", *op. cit.*, at p.54.

[8] See para.33–1.

[9] See for example Voser, "Interim Relief in International Arbitration: The Tendency Towards More Business-Oriented Approach" (2007) Dispute Resolution International Vol.1 No.2, p.171 at p.179

nature.[10] Although such measures will normally imply an assessment of the prima facie chances of the requesting party to win the case on the merits, the measure should not lead to a prejudgment of the case.

28–9 At the risk of some oversimplification, there are three basic categories of conservatory and interim measures: (1) evidentiary measures; (2) financial measures; and (3) standstill measures.[11] These categories, which are referred to below, are similar to those adopted in art.17 of the amended UNCITRAL Model Law.[12]

28–10 This being said, there is no fixed list of provisional and conservatory measures as stated by Tribunal in ICC case No.9691, "[t]he categories of provisional or conservatory measures which may be granted in international arbitration are not closed. These are broad and flexible remedies which may be tailored to meet the needs of parties in a wide range of circumstances, particularly in the context of ICC arbitration".[13] There are variations in the way that these matters are treated under national law.

28–11 There are various procedural issues with respect to provisional or conservatory measures that are highlighted in the provisions of the UNCITRAL Model Law. As regards the conditions to be fulfilled to issue interim measures for standstill and financial matters (as defined in arts 17(2)(a), (b) and (c) quoted at para.28–9, art.17A(1) provides that the applying party shall satisfy the Tribunal that:

> "(a) Harm not adequately reparable by an award of damages is likely to result if the measure is not ordered, and such harm substantially outweighs the harm that is likely to result to the party against whom the measure is directed if the measure is granted; and
>
> (b) There is a reasonable possibility that the requesting party will succeed on the merits of the claim. The determination on this possibility shall not affect the discretion of the arbitral tribunal in making any subsequent determination."

[10] See, for example, Bernardini, "The Powers of the Arbitrator" (1993) ICC Court of International Arbitration, Special Supplement, p.21, at p.28.

[11] More generally, see Poudret & Besson, *op. cit.*, para.6.3, p.518; Lew, "Commentary on Interim and Conservatory Measures in ICC Arbitration Cases" (2000) ICC ICArb Bull Vol.11 No.1, p.28; Yesilirmak, "Interim and Conservatory Measures in ICC Arbitration Cases" (2000) ICC ICArb Bull Vol.11 No.1, p.31 including Extracts from ICC Awards referring to Interim and Conservatory Measures; Reiner, "Les mesures provisoires et conservatoires et l'arbitrage international notamment l'arbitrage CCI" (1998) JDI, p.853; Besson, *Arbitrage international et mesures provisoires–Etude de droit comparé* (Schulthess, 1998); Goldman, "Provisional Measures in International Arbitration" (1993) RDAI/IBLJ No.1, p.3; Giardina, "Provisional Measures in Europe–Some Comparative Observations" in *Etudes de droit international en l'honneur de Pierre Lalive, op. cit.*, p.499; Schwartz, "The practices and experience of the ICC Court" (1993) ICC ICArb Bull, Special Supplement, p.45.

[12] Article 17(2) of the UNCITRAL Model Law provides the following definition:
"(2) An interim measure is any temporary measure, whether in the form of an award or in another form, by which, at any time prior to the issuance of the award by which the dispute is finally decided, the arbitral tribunal orders a party to:
(a) Maintain or restore the status quo pending determination of the dispute;
(b) Take action that would prevent, or refrain from taking action that is likely to cause, current or imminent harm or prejudice to the arbitral process itself;
(c) Provide a means of preserving assets out of which a subsequent award may be satisfied; or
(d) Preserve evidence that may be relevant and material to the resolution of the dispute."

[13] Procedural Order No.7 of 2000 at para.43, which contained the following footnote: "S. Besson, Arbitrage international et mesures provisoires, Zürich (1998) at pp.264-265; P. Lalive, J.-F. Poudret, C. Reymond, *Le droit de l'arbitrage–interne et international en Suisse*, Lausanne (1989) at pp.362–365."

For evidentiary applications, art.17A(2) (d) of the UNCITRAL Model Law states that with regard to a request for an interim measure under art.17(2)d, the requirements under art.17(1) (a) and (b) "shall apply only to the extent the arbitral tribunal considers appropriate". Therefore there is a lesser burden in those instances. This is understandable as the purpose of those measures is to ensure that evidence is available for the arbitral proceedings. **28–12**

More generally, in the practice of international arbitration, a Tribunal will normally wish to ensure that the following conditions have been satisfied before it decides that the applicant deserves provisional protection: **28–13**

— request by a party setting out the reasons and providing adequate evidence;

— prima facie jurisdiction of the Tribunal over both parties, based on the existence of a valid agreement to arbitrate;

— prima facie establishment of a valid claim on the merits, that is likelyhood of success on the merits;

— risk of imminent irreparable or substantial harm, which cannot be compensated by a subsequent award damages;

— no pre-judgement of the case.

Usually, a party making an application for a conservatory or interim measure will provide the evidentiary support for that application by way of documents. The party may, in addition, file a witness statement. If the Tribunal is proposing to issue an Award with respect to the measure, then pursuant to art.25(2) it is necessary to hold a hearing unless the parties waive that requirement. In many instances, these measures are viewed as very important by the parties and therefore it is desirable to have a hearing in person, although such matters may also be dealt with in telephone or video conferences, where appropriate. If the measure is an Award, it will be subject to scrutiny of the ICC Court under art.33. Given the urgency of getting approval, a decision by the President of the ICC Court pursuant to art.1(3) may be sought by the Tribunal. **28–14**

Article 17E of the UNCITRAL Model Law provides that: "(1) The arbitral tribunal may require the party requesting an interim measure to provide appropriate security in connection with the measure". The issue of security is linked to the liability of the applying part for the damage resulting from the granting of an interim measure.[14] In addition to security, art.17F of the UNCITRAL Model Law also leaves open the possibility of requiring that it be updated by the party as regarding the circumstances giving rise to the interim measure.[15] **28–15**

[14] Article 17G of the UNCITRAL Model Law provides: "The party requesting an interim measure or applying for a preliminary order shall be liable for any costs and damages caused by the measure or the order to any party if the arbitral tribunal later determines that, in the circumstances, the measure or the order should not have been granted. The arbitral tribunal may award such costs and damages at any point during the proceedings".

[15] Article 17F of the UNCITRAL Model Law provides:
"(1) The arbitral tribunal may require any party promptly to disclose any material change in the circumstances on the basis of which the measure was requested or granted.

Evidentiary measures

28–16 These conservatory and interim measures relate to evidence and include orders and Awards relating to preservation of evidence, site visits, inspection of evidence, disclosure of documents, access to witnesses and appointments of experts in relation to these matters. In general, national law in major centres of arbitration supports the granting of evidentiary measures by a Tribunal to ensure that it can carry out a fact-finding role.

Financial measures

28–17 These conservatory or interim measures relate to issues such as security for either the costs of arbitration or for the damages that may result therefrom. These measures may well be treated differently in various jurisdictions depending on whether such relief is generally available in state courts and its perceived effect on due process. In very exceptional circumstances, they may even lead to an order for a provisional payment, although in practice this is extremely rare. In a recent case, a Claimant requested provisional payment of what it considered to be undisputed sums. The Tribunal rejected this claim as follows:

> "The mere *possibility*, which of course cannot be excluded, that Claimant's claims will, in the end, be held justified, in all or in part, does not provide a sufficient basis for an order for provisional payment, unless Claimant convinces the Tribunal that money is of existential importance for it, or that Respondent organizes its own insolvency during the course of the proceedings to escape the consequences of a potentially unfavourable award.It is not generally the case, in commercial matters, that money is of existential importance for a party (see Berti, *International Arbitration in Switzerland*, ed. Berti/Vogt/Schnyder, Kluwer Law International, 2000, n 10 to art. 183 SPILA), and Claimant has not brought forward arguments of such kind in the present arbitration."[16]

Standstill orders

28–18 These conservatory or interim measures are intended to preserve the *status quo* pending the resolution of the dispute. These measures would include, for example, continuation of performance of a contract, an injunction preventing the call and/or cashing of first demand bank guarantees by the employer, or an injunction

(2) The party applying for a preliminary order shall disclose to the arbitral tribunal all circumstances that are likely to be relevant to the arbitral tribunal's determination whether to grant or maintain the order, and such obligation shall continue until the party against whom the order has been requested has had an opportunity to present its case. Thereafter, paragraph (1) of this article shall apply."

16 ICC case No.13646, Procedural Order No.6 (2006), unreported. The Tribunal then went on to explain why the Claimant's arguments had no merit and could not be accepted in the instant case.

ordering a party to suspend legal proceedings before a state court pending the Tribunal's decision on jurisdiction.[17]

One of the basic issues with conservatory and interim measures is enforcement. With regard to evidentiary issues, Tribunals have the power to draw an adverse inference.[18] In such cases, the remedy corresponds to and can be gauged based on the breach of the measure. With regard to financial issues, there is generally no such remedy and the effect is usually dependent on enforcement by national courts.[19] With regard to standstill orders, the effect will depend on national law. However, there is often an innate enforcement mechanism as the effect of a breach of such an order may well be to increase the claim for damages. 28–19

Article 28 approaches this area first from the point of view of the Tribunal and then from the point of view of the parties and their application to national courts. 28–20

Although the ICC Rules for a Pre-Arbitral Referee Procedure have been in effect since January 1990, they were almost never used in the past. These Rules are designed to reduce the need for recourse to the national courts with respect to interim or conservatory measures before the Tribunal is put in place. Pursuant to art.2.1 of those Rules, the referee has the right: 28–21

> "(a) to order any conservatory measures or any measures of restoration that are urgently necessary to prevent either immediate damage or irreparable loss and so to safeguard any of the rights or property of one of the parties; (b) to order a party to make to any other party or to another person any payment which ought to be made; (c) to order a party to take any step which ought to be taken according to the contract between the parties, including the signing or delivery of any document or the procuring by a party of the signature or delivery of a document; (d) to order any measures necessary to preserve or establish evidence."[20]

The ICC Rules of Pre-Arbitral Referee Procedure must have been specifically agreed to be applicable between the parties to a dispute. In the past, very few parties thought of including a reference to the ICC Rules of Pre-Arbitral Referee 28–22

[17] A Tribunal may be reluctant to make such an order, if it felt that it would interfere with the power of the state court to rule on its own jurisdiction. The Tribunal is often more likely to defer to the state court to rule on its own jurisdiction rather than to seek to decide itself that the state court is incompetent.

[18] See arts 9(4) and (5) of the IBA Rules of Evidence:
"4. If a Party fails without satisfactory explanation to produce any document requested in a Request to Produce to which it has not objected in due time or fails to produce any document ordered to be produced by the Arbitral Tribunal, the Arbitral Tribunal may infer that such document would be adverse to the interests of that Party.
5. If a Party fails without satisfactory explanation to make available any other relevant evidence, including testimony, sought by one Party to which the Party to whom the request was addressed has not objected in due time or fails to make available any evidence, including testimony, ordered by the Arbitral Tribunal to be produced, the Arbitral Tribunal may infer that such evidence would be adverse to the interests of that Party."

[19] It is difficult to see any basis for a Tribunal to draw any inference from a failure to provide security, if ordered by the Tribunal for example.

[20] More generally, see Garaud and de Taffin, "The ICC Rules for a Pre-Arbitral Referee Procedure", (2005) ICC ICArb Bull, Vol. 16 No.1, p.33; Berger, "Pre-Arbitral Referees: Arbitrators, Quasi-Arbitrators, Hybrids or Creatures of Contract Law?" in *Liber Amicorum in honour of Robert Briner, op. cit.*, p.73.

Procedure into their contract. To remedy that situation, the ICC has revised its standard arbitration clause by incorporating by reference these rules in addition to the ICC Rules of Arbitration. However, although not withdrawn, the ICC Rules of Pre-Arbitral Referee Procedure have been largely supplanted by the provision in art.29 for an Emergency Arbitrator.

Ex parte orders

28–23 The most controversial part of the modification to the UNCITRAL Model Law relates to ex parte orders. Article 17B provides as follows:

> "(1) Unless otherwise agreed by the parties, a party may, without notice to any other party, make a request for an interim measure together with an application for a preliminary order directing a party not to frustrate the purpose of the interim measure requested.
> (2) The arbitral tribunal may grant a preliminary order provided it considers that prior disclosure of the request for the interim measure to the party against whom it is directed risks frustrating the purpose of the measure.
> (3) The conditions defined under article 17A apply to any preliminary order, provided that the harm to be assessed under article 17A(1)(a), is the harm likely to result from the order being granted or not."[21]

28–24 The initial question is whether the Rules constitute an "agreement to the contrary" so as to preclude ex parte orders. Despite various procedural safeguards, the better view appears to be that it is not the case. However, with respect to ex parte or preliminary orders, the UNCITRAL Model Law does not appear to reflect accepted practice in the major centres of arbitration. Therefore, a Tribunal would have to carefully consider whether it has the power to issue an ex parte preliminary order, in particular under the law of the place of arbitration.

28–25 A second question is whether the structure of the Rules is such as to provide an indication that a Tribunal should not act ex parte. In this respect, the general, albeit perhaps conservative reaction is that it is always better to hear both parties. One of the reasons for this is that, despite the obligation under art.17 for example of disclosure by the applying party of the relevant circumstances, there is not as yet a well-settled concept in international arbitration such as the requirement of "full and fair disclosure" as understood in England for example. In addition, hearing both sides permits the Tribunal to apprehend or fully appreciate arguments to which it may not otherwise give adequate weight.

28–26 Another question is whether a preliminary order would be effective in the circumstances of the case and how the Tribunal should act after the preliminary order has been issued. The effectiveness of a preliminary order will in many

[21] See Malinvaud, "Modification de la loi modèle CNUDCI sur les mesures intérimaires: un texte de compromis sur les mesures ex parte", Les Cahiers de l'Arbitrage 2007/1 p.12 ; Van Houtte," Ten Reasons Against a Proposal for Ex Parte Interim Measures of Protection in Arbitration; Derains, "L'arbitre et l'octroi de mesures provisoires *ex parte*", Les Cahiers de l'Arbitrage 2003/2 1re partie, p.45; Gaffney, "*Ex Parte* Measures in International Arbitration" (2002) Mealey's IAR Vol.17 No.11 p.39.

instances depend on enforceability in state courts, a subject that is dealt with in the UNCITRAL Model Law. As regards the procedure to be followed after the preliminary order has been issued, art.17C of the UNCITRAL Model Law provides overall guidance.[22] However, a corresponding provision is not generally available in most arbitration laws and therefore there is an issue as to enforceability.

Article 28(1): "Unless the parties have otherwise agreed, as soon as the file has been transmitted to it, the arbitral tribunal may, at the request of a party, order any interim or conservatory measure it deems appropriate. The arbitral tribunal may make the granting of any such measure subject to appropriate security being furnished by the requesting party. Any such measure shall take the form of an order, giving reasons, or of an award, as the arbitral tribunal considers appropriate."

The Tribunal has the power to order "interim or conservatory measures" unless the parties have otherwise agreed.[23] The parties may otherwise agree in the arbitration agreement itself, in an agreement immediately prior to the arbitration or by their choice of procedural law, if any. In arbitration agreements, one tends to see language to broaden rather than limit the right to issue interim or conservatory measures. In some instances, there is express reference to the right of a party to seek interim relief from a national court and/or from the Tribunal. Immediately prior to the arbitration, the parties frequently have difficulty on agreeing on any aspects of the procedure. However, it may be in their interest to avoid disruption through an interim agreement as to how to conduct their relationship pending resolution of their dispute. It is less frequent that the parties agree on a specific system of law that would govern the granting of conservatory relief, although there are important differences between national legal systems with respect to certain forms of relief. Therefore, in most instances, the Tribunal will have to determine whether, under the rules and the law that would be applicable with respect to the conservatory or interim measure, it is permitted to grant the relief.[24] **28–27**

[22] "Article 17 C. Specific regime for preliminary orders

(1) Immediately after the arbitral tribunal has made a determination in respect of an application for a preliminary order, the arbitral tribunal shall give notice to all parties of the request for the interim measure, the application for the preliminary order, the preliminary order, if any, and all other communications, including by indicating the content of any oral communication, between any party and the arbitral tribunal in relation thereto.

(2) At the same time, the arbitral tribunal shall give an opportunity to any party against whom a preliminary order is directed to present its case at the earliest practicable time.

(3) The arbitral tribunal shall decide promptly on any objection to the preliminary order.

(4) A preliminary order shall expire after twenty days from the date on which it was issued by the arbitral tribunal. However, the arbitral tribunal may issue an interim measure adopting or modifying the preliminary order, after the party against whom the preliminary order is directed has been given notice and an opportunity to present its case.

(5) A preliminary order shall be binding on the parties but shall not be subject to enforcement by a court. Such a preliminary order does not constitute an award."

[23] On the possibility for the parties to restrict or exclude on a contractual basis the recourse to courts to seek interim measures, see Fouchard, Gaillard & Goldman, *op. cit.*, para.139 p.718.

[24] See for example art.183 of the Swiss PILA, art.1468 of the French CPC, s.44 of the English Arbitration Act 1996; s.7502(c) of the US Civil Practice Laws and Rules authorizing New York courts to grant provisional measures in international arbitration, *New York Law Journal*, October 12,

28–28 As discussed under art.16, the file is transmitted to the Tribunal once it has been formed and the initial provisional advance on costs has been paid. The Tribunal would thus be able to order provisional measures as soon as it has received the file from the Secretariat, subject, however, to possible mandatory provisions of the law of the place of arbitration or exclusive jurisdiction of the courts.[25] In particular, there is no reason why the Tribunal would first have to establish Terms of Reference, even when it wishes to render its decision in the form of an Award rather than procedural order.[26]

Evidentiary matters

28–29 In all major centres of arbitration, a Tribunal can issue orders or Awards regarding what has been referred to above as "evidentiary matters". In France, art.1468 of the French CPC provides that:

> "[t]he arbitral tribunal may order upon the parties any conservatory or provisional measures that it deems appropriate, set conditions for such measures and, if necessary, attach penalties to such order. However, only courts may order conservatory attachments and judicial security. The arbitral tribunal has the power to amend or add to any provisional or conservatory measure that it has granted".[27]

28–30 In Switzerland, art.183(1) of the Swiss PILA provides that "[u]nless the parties have agreed otherwise, the Arbitral tribunal may, on motion of one party, order provisional or conservatory measures".

28–31 In England, s.38(4) of the English Arbitration Act 1996 provides:

> "(4) The tribunal may give directions in relation to any property which is the subject of the proceedings or as to which any question arises in the proceedings, and which is owned by or is in the possession of a party to the proceedings–
>
> (a) for the inspection, photographing, preservation, custody or detention of the property by the tribunal, an expert or a party, or
> (b) ordering that samples be taken from, or any observation be made of or experiment conducted upon, the property."

28–32 In the United States, s.7 of the Federal Arbitration Act provides that:

2005, by Caher. More generally, see Rau, "Provisional Relief in Arbitration: How Things Stand in the United States" (2005) J Int'l Arb Vol.22 No.1, p.1. See also "La nécessaire collaboration des juges et arbitres pour assurer l'efficacité de l'arbitrage international: les mesures conservatoires et provisoires et la question des tiers en France et aux Etats-Unis" Par Pauline Pietrois-Chabassier http://m2bde.u-paris10.fr/node/2433 [accessed November 23, 2013].

[25] See Lew, "Commentary on Interim and Conservatory Measures in ICC Arbitration Cases", *op. cit.*, p.28; Besson, *Arbitrage international et mesures provisoires–Etude de droit comparé, op. cit.*, para.21, p.31.

[26] See Bühler & Jarvin, *op. cit.*, art.28(1) N.13, p.254.

[27] Translated by Emmanuel Gaillard, Nanou Leleu-Knobil and Daniela Pellarini of Shearman & Sterling LLP.

"[t]he arbitrators selected either as prescribed in this title or otherwise, or a majority of them, may summon in writing any person to attend before them or any of them as a witness and in a proper case to bring with him or them any book, record, document, or paper which may be deemed material as evidence in the case."

As discussed in detail at paras 25–78 et seq., it now appears that s.1782 of the USC may be used to obtain evidence for arbitration proceedings held outside of the United States. It is not clear the extent to which this article has been used to date. In addition, this provision creates potential problems with respect to coordinating the US discovery measures and arbitration proceedings. However, this may be an area in which there is considerable development in the future.

As noted above, art.17(2)A(d) of the UNCITRAL Model Law specifically provides for interim measures relating to evidence. **28–33**

Financial measures

There are three main types of financial measures: **28–34**

(1)security for costs of the arbitration;

(2)security for an Award;

(3)a freezing order on property subject of the proceedings.

Security for costs of the arbitration

In most jurisdictions, a Tribunal would appear to be entitled to order that a party provide security for costs of the arbitration. The English Arbitration Act 1996 expressly provides for such orders and in most other jurisdictions, there would appear to be no impediment to such an order.[28] However, the prevalence of such orders varies significantly. In English court proceedings, security for costs is relatively commonplace. In American and French court proceedings, they are virtually unknown.[29] In German court proceedings, a Claimant indirectly provides such security by depositing an amount based on the amount of the dispute to secure the court's costs, not, however, the legal costs of the other side.[30] The difficulty is **28–35**

[28] Section 38(3) of the English Arbitration Act 1996 provides: "[t]he tribunal may order a Claimant to provide security for the costs of the arbitration. This power shall not be exercised on the ground that the Claimant is–(a) an individual ordinarily resident outside the United Kingdom, or (b) a corporation or association incorporated or formed under the law of a country outside the United Kingdom, or whose central management and control is exercised outside the United Kingdom". The well-known *Ken Ren* case of the House of Lords, where the English Courts were requested to, and did, order the Kenyan Claimant, an insolvent project company, to post security for cost in an ICC arbitration, was based on the law prior to the English Arbitration Act: [1994] 2 All E.R. 449 and (1995) YBCA Vol.XX p.228. See also Paulsson, "The Unwelcome Atavism of Ken Ren: The House of Lords Shows is Meddle" (1994) ASA Bull Vol. 12, No.3/4, p.439.

[29] Moreover, art.1468 of the CPC states in part that "only courts may order conservatory attachments and judicial security".

[30] Only when the party is a resident in a foreign country with which Germany is not bound through a multilateral or bilateral treaty regarding civil or commercial matters, would the Claimant have to

compounded in international arbitration, because the parties have to pay advances on the costs of arbitration. An Award under the Rules of the Zurich Chamber of Commerce decided that an insolvent company should be ordered to provide security for the costs of arbitration, and analysed the position as follows:

> "The traditional view in Switzerland was that, lacking the parties' explicit agreement to the contrary, a Swiss Arbitral Tribunal had no authority to order security for a party's legal costs. The authorizing agreement between the parties may be indirect, that is by way of reference to institutional rules that contain an explicit authorizing provision.
>
> In casu, neither the PILA [Swiss Private International Law] nor the ZCC [Zurich Chamber of Commerce] Arbitration Rules nor the arbitration agreement between the parties contain an authorisation according to which the Sole Arbitrator would have authority to order security for a party's legal costs.
>
> [. . .]
>
> However, the modern view expressed in Swiss legal doctrine and arbitral practice is that the authority granted to the arbitrators by art. 183 PILA also extends to orders requesting a party to provide security for the opposing party's legal costs.
>
> Recent arbitral decisions appear to signal differing views regarding the circumstances under which security for costs may be ordered. In an unpublished arbitral decision of December 1995, it was held that security should only be ordered in exceptional circumstances, that is if there is a clear and present danger that a future cost award would not be enforceable, e.g. because of a party's insolvency as proven by the applicant.
>
> A party's insolvency is a common ground for granting security for costs. p 73, para.2 to 5 of the Zurich Civil Procedure Code lists various grounds on which a court is allowed to request a Claimant to provide security for costs all of which are based on the risk of Claimant's insolvency.
>
> A recent arbitral decision, by contrast, appears to consider a mere potential risk of non-enforceability of a future cost award as insufficient grounds; it rather emphasizes the requirement that an order for security shall not unduly restrict the party's access to arbitral justice and that the principle of equal treatment of the parties should be observed." (citations omitted)[31]

28–36 In a relatively recent ICC case, a Swiss Respondent requested that a Tribunal sitting in Geneva order security for costs, covering inter alia the Claimant's share of the ICC arbitration and its own legal costs, against a Nigerian Claimant. The

post security for costs for the legal costs of the other party. This is true for the United States, the Philippines and Uganda, to give but three examples.

31 ZCC Arbitration Proceedings No.415 of November 2001, (2002) ASA Bull Vol.20 No.3 p.467 at p.469.

Respondent based its request on the alleged fact that the Claimant would encounter difficulties to effect a payment abroad in favour of the Respondent, and that enforcing an Award in Nigeria would require lengthy and costly procedures. The Tribunal rejected the Respondent's request given the absence of any special circumstances justifying such a decision. In so doing, the Tribunal emphasised in its Procedural Order the necessity for it to use such a power in a restrictive manner:

> "It is generally admitted, however, that such power must be used in a restrictive manner. In Switzerland, this is, in particular, the opinion of Jean-François Poudret and Sebastien Besson: 'Un security for costs n'est à notre avis justifié que dans des cas très particuliers' (*Droit comparé de l'arbitrage international*, Bruylant L.G.D.J. Schulthess, 2002, §610). The abovementioned procedural order issued by a tribunal sitting in Zurich expresses the same view: 'Arbitral precedents [. . .] show that security for costs should only be granted in exceptional circumstances and with the greatest reluctance' (*ASA Bulletin* 2005, at p. 112). As far as ICC Arbitration is concerned, Y. Derains and E. Schwartz confirm that 'those drafting the 1998 Rules were reluctant to mention security for costs expressly because they did not wish to encourage the proliferation of such applications, which, apart from being rare, are generally disfavoured in ICC arbitration' (op. cit., p. 297).
>
> This Arbitral Tribunal shares the view that the mere existence of doubt as to the possibility of enforcing a future award against the other party is not a sufficient ground for granting a request for security for costs. To impose such burden on a party requires more than the ordinary risk that the party ordered to pay may not be willing and may not be easily forced to do so; it requires the existence of special circumstances. Such necessity might be lightened if a very serious likelihood, if not near certainty that the alleged debt exists or will exist could be established [. . .]"[32]

In ICC case No.13070,[33] a Tribunal sitting in Paris, rejected the Respondent's request for security for costs against the Claimant based on the lack of any exceptional circumstances. The Tribunal, however, appeared to consider deterioration of the financial situation of a Claimant as constituting exceptional circumstances, the case considered that the Respondent had failed to provide specific proof thereof in the case: **28–37**

> "Security for costs should only be granted in exceptional circumstances and with the greatest reticence (Karrer/Desax, Security for Costs in International Arbitration, in: Briner/Fortier/Berger/Bredow (eds.), Liber

[32] ICC case No.13646, Procedural Order No.3 (2005), unreported. See also *Puerto Rico Hospital Supply Inc v Boston Scientific Corp*, October 21, 2005 First Circuit US Court of Appeals, Mealey's IAR Vol.20 No.10 p.16 (denial of injunctive relief pending ICC arbitration by US court in absence of any irreparable harm for the requesting party); *Plama Consortium Ltd v Republic of Bulgaria*, ICSID case No.ARB/03/24 of September 6, 2005, Mealey's IAR Vol. 20 No.10 p.8 (denial of a request for urgent provisional measures to protect a party's right to non aggravation of a pending arbitration claim in absence of a change of circumstances that threatens the ability of the Tribunal to grant the relief sought by a party and the capability of giving effect to the relief).

[33] ICC case No.13070 (2006) (Interim Award), unreported.

Amicorum Karl-Heinz Böckstiegel, Köln et al. 2001, Weigand (Ed.), Practitioner's Handbook on International Arbitration, Copenhague 2002, p.253). Insolvency must be considered as one of these exceptional circumstances (ASA Bull 1997, p.377), as well as the situation, where a claimant did no longer conduct its commercial activity (ASA Bull 1999, p.59).

As a general rule, security for costs may only be ordered if, *inter alia*, the following conditions are fulfilled: there must be a situation of urgency and a risk of substantial damage for the requesting party. It is usually required to be in presence of a 'fundamental change of the situation since the basic agreement between the parties was entered into' (Karrer/Desax, op. cit., p.345). In other words, the financial situation of the counterparty must have deteriorated since the time when the parties concluded their agreement.
Respondent does nowhere provide for specific proof for any such deterioration of Claimant's financial situation. Neither has it established that Claimant's financial situation has changed, either since the validity of the agreement or since the beginning of the arbitral proceedings. On the other hand, Claimant rightly observes that 1/ so far, it has assumed the entirety of the arbitration costs, 2/ it is a public institution under the Government monitoring. This last element, indeed, precludes by principle any serious risk of insolvency or bankruptcy."

28–38 The analysis of the Tribunals in the above cases reflects current practice in ordering security for costs particularly for arbitrations held in Switzerland, France or Germany, if not elsewhere as well.[34] More generally, a fundamental change of the parties' situation since the arbitration agreement was signed, may result in a serious risk of non-enforcement of an Award on costs. The mere existence of a doubt as to the possibility of enforcing a future Award against the other party is not a sufficient ground for the granting of such request. This is rather part of the commercial risk parties take when entering into commercial agreements (provided a party does not attempt to organise its own insolvency, hide assets or to otherwise act fraudulently). In this respect, although the UNCITRAL Model Law now provides for preliminary measures as security for an Award that is to be issued (which would include the claim for legal expenses), it is not clear to what extent Tribunals will adopt that approach in the future.

Security for the Award

28–39 It is not as clear that a Tribunal has the jurisdiction to order security for an Award due to the concern about due process. In this respect, in national court

[34] Veit, "Note–Procedural Order No.14 of November 27, 2002-Security for Costs in International Arbitration–Some Comments to Procedural Order No.14 of November 27, 2002" (2005) ASA Bull Vol.28 No.1, p.116; Besson, Arbitrage international et mesures provisoires–Etude de droit comparé, *op. cit.*, para.37, p.38 and para.358 p.220; Sandrock, "The Cautio Judicatum Solvi in Arbitration Proceedings or The Duty of an Alien Claimant to Provide Security for the Costs of the Defendant" (1997) J Int'l Arb Vol. 4 No.2, p.17 at p.28; Karrer and Desax, "Security for Costs in International Arbitration; Why, When and What if [. . .]" in *Liber Amicorum Karl-Heinz Böckstiegel, op. cit.*, p.339.

procedures there is a significant difference in approach in court proceedings between English and American practice, for example.[35] This influence may well affect a court's interpretation of the validity of such an order. However, even in England, it may be difficult to justify such an order in arbitral proceedings. In the *Kastner v Jason* case,[36] the issue was the validity of an order of the arbitrator that a party not dispose of his home. This had the effect of ensuring that the property would be available to satisfy a judgment. The Court of Appeal held that the arbitrator did not have the power to grant the freezing order under the applicable procedural law or for that matter under the English Arbitration Act 1996, as the power to issue a freezing order was limited to final Awards.

Many ICC arbitrations involve distribution agreements and in some cases the issue is the validity of the termination of the agreement. In such cases, it may be appropriate for the Tribunal to consider ordering the parties to continue to honour the agreement pending a decision on validity. The main problem with this type of order would perhaps be supervision of the performance of the agreement. Once there is a dispute, parties tend to be much less cooperative in a commercial context. However, in many instances this remedy would be appropriate and could serve to reduce the amount of any claim for damages.[37] **28–40**

Awards and procedural orders

Article 28(1) leaves open the possibility of use by the Tribunal of a reasoned procedural order or an Award for a conservatory or interim relief.[38] **28–41**

The distinction between final and conservatory or interim measures is not always easy to define. For example, an order for the production of documents may constitute a final or provisional matter. If a party has a contractual right to inspect documents, then the Tribunal's decision with respect to that contractual right involves the interpretation and enforcement of that right.[39] If, on the other hand, a party is seeking a procedural order of disclosure that is not based on the contract, it is arguably seeking an interim measure. Nevertheless, the decision to use a procedural order or an Award on provisional measures is left to the appreciation **28–42**

[35] The use of freezing orders (formerly referred to as "Mareva orders") in England is well known. Those orders are often issued prior to any judgment being awarded. In the United States, it is very difficult to obtain an order for security without having a judgment. The basic approach is reflected in *Contichem LPG v Parsons Shipping Co Ltd*, 229 F.3d 426, 430 (2d Cir., 2000), and (2001) YBCA Vol.XXVI p.1013 at p.1015: "As a preliminary matter, we agree with the district court's determination that because ContiChem did not have a judgment against Parsons, the court had no equitable power to issue a preliminary injunction preventing any entity from disposing of Parsons' assets pending arbitration of the dispute".

[36] *Kastner v Jason* [2004] EWCA Civ 1599.

[37] For an example where a Court considered continuation of performance of an agreement pending arbitration, see above *Discount Trophy & Co v Plastic Dress-Up Co*, para.28–1 n.2.

[38] Similarly, see art.17(2) of the UNCITRAL Model Law: "An interim measure is any temporary measure, whether in the form of an award or in another form, by which, at any time prior to the issuance of the award by which the dispute is finally decided, the arbitral tribunal orders a party to [. . .]".

[39] See Webster, "Obtaining Documents from Adverse Parties in International Arbitration", *op. cit.*, p.41.

of the Tribunal subject to the final control on the nature of such decision by the national court.[40]

28–43 The distinction is important for two reasons: first, if the decision takes the form of an Award, it will have to undergo the scrutiny and notification process of Awards pursuant to arts 33 and 34. Secondly, an Award, unlike a procedural order, can be enforced with the help of the courts, in particular under the New York Convention.

28–44 Another and related issue that quite often arises concerns the interim nature of the proposed order. In ICC case No.11761,[41] an American Claimant requested that a Tribunal sitting in Paris and applying Texas law issue an injunction compelling a Guatemalan Respondent, which declined to take part in the ICC proceedings, to proceed before the ICC rather than before Guatemalan courts. The question that was to be addressed by the Tribunal was in fact to decide whether the Tribunal should make an order against the Respondent in the form of a permanent injunction or restraining order. The Tribunal declined to grant the Claimant's request in the following terms:

> "Although the injunction sought might be described as a conservatory measure, Article 23 [now art.28] is aimed at protecting parties' rights pending the final resolution of the dispute by a final Award (see commentary on Interim and Conservatory Measures in ICC Arbitration Case by Dr Julian D M Lew [. . .] (2000) ICC Court Bulletin vol 11 no 1 pages 28, 25). Nevertheless, at least one Tribunal appointed under the ICC Rules of Arbitration and sitting in Paris has decided that it had power derived from the those rules to make a permanent injunction (see ICC Award 7895 extracted in the ICC Court Bulletin referred to above).
>
> Leaving aside any issue of whether in view of the Texas Uniform Declaratory Judgement Act this Tribunal has the power to issue what in effect is an anti-suit injunction, the grant of such relief is an extraordinary remedy. Although an injunction is directed against a party in default and not the court, an arbitral tribunal (assuming it has the power) should be satisfied that such a measure is essential to do justice between the parties. Where, as here, parties have bound themselves to enforce the contractual bargain, it is essential, however, that the party seeking to enforce its rights to arbitrate should not only assert that right (as was done here), but also apply without delay to the Tribunal for interim measures.

40 See art.12(2) of the French CPC: "He [The judge] must give or restore their proper legal definitions to the disputed facts and deeds notwithstanding the denominations given by the parties". See also Bensaude, "*SA Otor Participations v S.A.R.L. Carlyle (Luxembourg) Holdings 1: Interim Awards on Provisional Measures in International Arbitration*" (2005) J Int'l Arb Vol.22 No.4, p.357; Jacquet, "Qualification et conséquences des mesures provisoires prises par un tribunal arbitral" (2005) JCP G No.22, June 1, 2005, p.1027. See also Paris, April 4, 2002 (*Nafimco* case) and April 11, 2002 (*ABC International* case), (2003) Rev Arb No.1 p.130, note Bensaude; Paris, July 1, 1999, *Braspetro Oil Services Company (Brasoil) v The Management and Implementation Authority of the Great Man-Made River Project (GMRA)*, (2000) ASA Bull Vol.18 No.2 p.376.

41 ICC case No.11761 (2003) (Final Award), unreported.

> In this case, the Claimant did not seek an interim injunction of this Tribunal when [Respondent] commenced proceedings in Guatemala. Instead, the Claimant instructed its counsel to file objections in Guatemala to Respondent's proceedings [. . .] The Guatemalan courts have been informed of this arbitration and will no doubt be informed of this Award [. . .] In our opinion, such action by the Claimant's attorney is more appropriate than our ordering [Respondent] to discontinue the proceedings to discontinue the proceedings at this late stage. Having carefully considered the Claimant's request for an injunction, and because at this stage of the proceedings in Guatemala, we have decided not to grant this relief [. . .]."

It is difficult to obtain a permanent injunction from an ICC Tribunal other than through a final Award. This case also underlines the interplay between a Tribunal and the national courts. The Claimant had sought relief before the Guatemalan courts with respect to the Respondent's proceedings in Guatemala. Having done so, the Tribunal was apparently reluctant to intervene in the matter and in effect to direct that a party should not proceed before the state court. **28–45**

Article 28(2): "Before the file is transmitted to the arbitral tribunal, and in appropriate circumstances even thereafter, the parties may apply to any competent judicial authority for interim or conservatory measures. The application of a party to a judicial authority for such measures or for the implementation of any such measures ordered by an arbitral tribunal shall not be deemed to be an infringement or a waiver of the arbitration agreement and shall not affect the relevant powers reserved to the arbitral tribunal. Any such application and any measures taken by the judicial authority must be notified without delay to the Secretariat. The Secretariat shall inform the arbitral tribunal thereof."

Prior to constitution of the Tribunal, it is generally accepted that parties may apply to national courts for conservatory or interim relief.[42] Article 9 of the UNCITRAL Model Law states that "[i]t is not incompatible with an arbitration agreement for a party to request, before or during arbitral proceedings, from a court an interim measure of protection and for a court to grant such measure".[43] **28–46**

[42] For example, in France, see Versailles, October 8, 1998, *Société Akzo Nobel v SA Elf Atochem* (1999) Rev Arb No.1 p.57, note Houry: "[w]hereas it is a principle of positive French law that the parties to an agreement with an arbitration clause giving jurisdiction to an arbitral tribunal of the ICC may have recourse to the state courts to obtain conservatory measures having in particular as their objective to preserve the situation, the rights or the evidence and in particular the existence of an arbitration clause does not preclude action by the judge for urgent matters" (Authors' translation); see also art.185 of the Swiss PILA, s.38 of the English Arbitration Act 1996. See also Cass. civ 1re, November 18, 1986, *Atlantic Triton Co v (1) Republic of Guinea and (2) Soguipêche* (1987) YBCA Vol.XII p.183, note Gaillard (art.26 of the ICSID Convention does bar one of the parties from resorting to national courts to attach assets until an Award is rendered by the Tribunal).

[43] Discussed for example in Federal Court of Canada, *Frontier International Shipping Corp v Tavros* [2000] 2 F.C. 427; 1999 CanLII 9389 (F.C.). See also *Brunswick Corp, Mercury Marine Division v Yamaha Motor Co Ltd*, US District Court Eastern District of Wisconsin, case No.04-C-0584 (October 1, 2004) (preliminary injunction ordering the Respondent to continue the performance of the contract pending the final resolution of the dispute based on the wording of the contract, the

This has now been confirmed and broadened in art.17J of the UNCITRAL Model Law that provides that:

> "[a] court shall have the same power of issuing an interim measure in relation to arbitration proceedings, irrespective of whether their place is in the territory of this State, as it has in relation to proceedings in courts. The court shall exercise such power in accordance with its own procedures in consideration of the specific features of international arbitration."

28–47 In the *McCreary Tire* case,[44] the US Court of Appeals for the Fifth District held that under art.II(3) of the New York Convention a domestic court did not have the jurisdiction to issue a pre-award attachment. However, this decision has not been followed in other US Districts such as the Second District[45] and the Fourth District[46] and is seen as an anomaly as regards the obtaining of support for evidentiary matters at any rate.

28–48 After constitution of the Tribunal, a request for interim or conservatory measures should be made to the Tribunal except in "appropriate circumstances". Therefore, art.28(2) appears to anticipate the decision of a Tribunal and then either voluntary compliance or enforcement under the New York Convention or pursuant to national court proceedings. This is consistent with the approach that it is the Tribunal that is most familiar with the proceedings and is in the better position to judge whether such measures are required.

28–49 In various national jurisdictions, there is support for the principle that a party should first make a request to the Tribunal before going to court.[47] Two examples

court declining to rule on the substance which is left to the arbitrators); *Peabody Coalsales Co v Tampa Elec Co*, 36 F.3d46 (8thCir 1994) (preliminary injunction ordered by the court based on the contractual provision stating "Unless otherwise agreed in writing by the parties during the dispute resolution process". According to the court, an order compelling arbitration "in accordance with the terms of the agreement" must necessarily include an order requiring continued performance); *RGI Inc v Tucker & Assocs Inc*, 858F.2d 227 (5th Cir.1988) (a preliminary injunction is appropriate in light of the contract language providing "[i]n the event that a dispute is submitted for arbitration pursuant to this paragraph, this Subcontract shall continue in full force and effect until such decision is rendered [. . .] in such a circumstance, the court needs not involve itself in balancing the various factors to determine whether a preliminary injunction should be issued").

44 *McCreary & Tire & Rubber Co v CEAT SpA*, 501 F. 2d 1032 (1974).

45 See for example *James Associates Ltd v Anhui Machinery & Equipment Import and Export Corp*, 171 F. Suppl. 2d 1146 (D.Colo.2001), 2001 US Dist. LEXIS 18682 and *Signature Marketing Pty Ltd v Slim Print International LLC*, 2001 US Dist. LEXIS 21222: "There is presently a circuit split on the issue of whether courts are stripped of subject matter jurisdiction once arbitration is ordered pursuant to the Convention and thus, whether they may order provisional remedies in aid of such arbitration. The Second Circuit has held, however, that the Convention does not divest a court of jurisdiction and does not preclude a court from issuing Provisional remedies in aid of arbitration" (citation deleted). For a discussion see Martin, "Court ordered Interim Measures in Support of International Arbitration" 17 American Review of Int'l Arb.299.

46 See *In the Matter of the Application of Deiulemar* case, para.28–6 n.6.

47 See for example s.44 of the English Arbitration Act 1996 which provides for the primacy of the Tribunal when it states with respect to applications to court that "(3) If the case is one of urgency, the court may, on the application of a party or proposed party to the arbitral proceedings, make such orders as it thinks necessary for the purpose of preserving evidence or assets. (4) If the case is not one of urgency, the court shall act only on the application of a party to the arbitral proceedings (upon notice to the other parties and to the tribunal) made with the permission of the tribunal or the agreement in writing of the other parties. (5) In any case the court shall act only if or to the extent that the arbitral tribunal, and any arbitral or other institution or person vested by the parties with power in

where there may be "appropriate circumstances" for making an application first to the national court involve ex parte measures and requests for emergency relief.

As discussed above, under the ICC Rules, a Tribunal generally does not have **28–50**
the right to act ex parte (although a Tribunal may have such power under the law of the place of arbitration if a provision such as art.17B of the UNCITRAL Model Law is applicable).[48] Therefore, to freeze a bank account a party may feel that it is necessary to go directly to a national court. Similarly, if a ship is about to depart, then there may not be time to make an application to the Tribunal.[49] However, the availability of this remedy will depend on the national courts and in some jurisdictions it may not be able to obtain freezing orders for example ex parte.

Although under art.28(2), an application to the national courts does not divest **28–51**
the Tribunal of jurisdiction to grant interim or conservatory measures, the party taking such an initiative should nevertheless take care that its action will not be considered as a waiver or violation of the arbitration agreement. It should also be aware that such an action may affect the willingness of the Tribunal to grant the relief.[50]

Several years ago, a Tribunal sitting in Paris and applying Swiss law on the **28–52**
merits of the dispute was requested by the Claimant to issue an interim measure of protection against the Respondent in a dispute relating to the validity of the termination of a distribution agreement for luxury branded goods. Subject to the final decision of the Tribunal, the Claimant (and distributor) contended that the agreement was to remain in force, and the Respondent (and manufacturer) was not entitled to open a store within the Claimant's territory. Prior to the start of the ICC arbitration, the Claimant applied before the US District court for the Southern District of New York which issued an Order (i) temporarily restraining termination of the agreement; and (ii) enjoining the Respondent from refusing to perform its obligation under said agreement. The opening of the store was not restrained by the New York Court's Temporary Restraining Order ("TRO"). Shortly after, the Claimant filed the Request for Arbitration, it submitted a request for interim measures to the Tribunal, seeking namely that Respondent (i) be directed to perform the agreement; and (ii) not to supply the store which Respondent had opened in the meantime pending the final Award. The request was rejected by the Tribunal as the Claimant failed to demonstrate on a prima facie basis, any urgency or irreparable damages it would suffer if its application was denied. The Tribunal

that regard, has no power or is unable for the time being to act effectively". See also *Cetelem SA v Roust Holdings Ltd*, where an order freezing Respondent's assets was granted on the basis of s.44(3) of the Act. Lord Justice Clarke, writing for the English Court of Appeal's ruling dated May 24, 2005, wrote:

"I do not think that this decision in any way usurps the functions or powers of the arbitral tribunal. The whole purpose of giving the court power to make such orders is to assist the arbitral process in cases of urgency before there is arbitration on foot. Otherwise it is all too easy for a party who is bent on a policy of non-co-operation to frustrate the arbitral process. Of course, in any case where the court is called upon to exercise the power, it must take great care not to usurp the arbitral process and to ensure, by exacting appropriate undertakings from the Claimant, that the substantive questions are reserved for the arbitrator or arbitrators" [2005] EWCA Civ 618.

[48] See the discussion under paras 28–23 et seq.

[49] For an illustration, see the *In the Matter of the Application of Deiulemar* case cited at, para.28–6 n.6.

[50] More generally, on the waiver of the arbitration agreement, see Jarvin, "La renonciation à la convention d'arbitrage" in *Liber Amicorum Dobrosav Mitrovic*, Belgrade, (2007).

felt the necessity to affirm its power to take such a decision based on the parties' agreement despite the saisine of the New York court in the following terms:

> "The Parties are in agreement that the Arbitral Tribunal has jurisdiction to hear the Claimant's Application and to order interim and conservatory measures. Although the arbitration agreement contained in Section [. . .] of the Distribution Agreement does not expressly confer such power, it follows from Article [28 (1)] of the ICC Rules of Arbitration, which are incorporated in the Parties' arbitration agreement. The Parties are also in agreement that there exist no mandatory law at the place of arbitration, that is to say Paris, that would prevent or limit the Arbitral Tribunal from exercising its power to grant interim relief.
>
> The only question which may presently arise regarding the power of the Arbitral Tribunal to grant interim relief, or rather whether it should make use of such power, relates to the TRO of the New York Court. The TRO was issued before this Arbitral Tribunal was even constituted, and was heard before Judge [NN.] before this Arbitral Tribunal had received the file. However, the TRO [Order] of the New York Court does not preclude the Arbitral Tribunal from granting interim relief, given, in particular, the Parties' agreement that it should do so."[51]

28–53 In another recent case, the Tribunal adopted the following reasoning regarding interim relief sought from a national court in the presence of an arbitration agreement:

> "If the state court orders or declines to order a measure, the parties cannot subsequently resort to the arbitral tribunal to obtain a more favourable ruling, and *vice-versa*. Even if the state court was first approached solely for the reason that the arbitral tribunal was not yet properly constituted, the tribunal cannot later on, after its constitution, reverse or modify the measure ordered by the state judge. What if a subsequent request for reversal or modification of an order is based on changed circumstances? Arguably, such a request should be dealt with by the arbitral tribunal once it is constituted."[52]

28–54 This reasoning is convincing to the extent that it seeks to avoid a multiplicity of applications and it is with such applications that international arbitration becomes more complicated and expensive. However, it does not address the issue of whether the application may have been rejected based on a different procedural standard from that to be applied by the Tribunal.

28–55 Article 28(2) provides that application to a state court "shall not be deemed to be an infringement or a waiver of the arbitration agreement". A party is entitled to seek interim or conservatory measures from a national court and yet insist that the

[51] ICC case No.11770, Procedural Order No.1 (2001), unreported.

[52] ICC Order No.5 of April 2, 2002, regarding Claimant's Request for Interim Relief (2003) ASA Bull Vol.21 No.4 p.810 at p.816.

overall dispute be submitted to arbitration rather than the national courts.[53] This provision may be important as the court before which the interim measures are sought is often the court where the other party is based and therefore may be a court before which the party seeking the measures does not wish to litigate. The actual standard and procedural requirements to avoid a waiver of a right to arbitrate are a matter for national law. However, it should be remembered that art.II(3) of the New York Convention requires a party to apply to dismiss the national court proceedings and to thus compel arbitration if national proceedings are brought.

A party seeking interim or conservatory measures from a national court must notify the Secretariat of both the application and the measures taken without delay. Therefore, even in the case of ex parte measures, the Secretariat should be informed promptly after they have been granted or refused. Article 28(2) provides that the Secretariat will then inform the Tribunal. However, one would imagine that most parties would inform the Tribunal of such measures as well as the Secretariat, as it is the Tribunal that is responsible for the arbitral proceedings. **28–56**

[53] Supreme Court of Philippines, May 19, 2006, *Transfield Philippines Inc v Luzon Hydro Corp, Australia and New Zealand Banking Group Ltd and Security Bank Corp* (ICC case No.11264 with Singapore as place of arbitration): "As a fundamental point, the pendency of arbitral proceedings does not foreclose resort to the courts for provisional relief. The Rules of the ICC, which govern the parties' arbitral dispute, allow the application of a party to a judicial authority for interim or conservatory measures. Likewise, s.14 of the Republic Act No.876 recognizes the rights of any party to petition the court to take measures to safeguard and/or conserve any matter which is the subject of the dispute in arbitration," *http://elibrary.supremecourt.gov.ph.*

Article 29 Emergency Arbitrator

1 **A party that needs urgent interim or conservatory measures that cannot await the constitution of an arbitral tribunal ("Emergency Measures") may make an application for such measures pursuant to the Emergency Arbitrator Rules in Appendix V. Any such application shall be accepted only if it is received by the Secretariat prior to the transmission of the file to the arbitral tribunal pursuant to Article 16 and irrespective of whether the party making the application has already submitted its Request for Arbitration.**

2 **The emergency arbitrator's decision shall take the form of an order. The parties undertake to comply with any order made by the emergency arbitrator.**

3 **The emergency arbitrator's order shall not bind the arbitral tribunal with respect to any question, issue or dispute determined in the order. The arbitral tribunal may modify, terminate or annul the order or any modification thereto made by the emergency arbitrator.**

4 **The arbitral tribunal shall decide upon any party's requests or claims related to the emergency arbitrator proceedings, including the reallocation of the costs of such proceedings and any claims arising out of or in connection with the compliance or noncompliance with the order.**

5 **Articles 29(1)–29(4) and the Emergency Arbitrator Rules set forth in Appendix V (collectively the "Emergency Arbitrator Provisions") shall apply only to parties that are either signatories of the arbitration agreement under the Rules that is relied upon for the application or successors to such signatories.**

6 **The Emergency Arbitrator Provisions shall not apply if:**

a) the arbitration agreement under the Rules was concluded before the date on which the Rules came into force;
b) the parties have agreed to opt out of the Emergency Arbitrator Provisions; or
c) the parties have agreed to another pre-arbitral procedure that provides for the granting of conservatory, interim or similar measures.

7 **The Emergency Arbitrator Provisions are not intended to prevent any party from seeking urgent interim or conservatory measures from a competent judicial authority at any time prior to making an application for such measures, and in appropriate circumstances even thereafter, pursuant to the Rules. Any application for such**

measures from a competent judicial authority shall not be deemed to be an infringement or a waiver of the arbitration agreement. Any such application and any measures taken by the judicial authority must be notified without delay to the Secretariat.[1]

[1] Article 29 is a new provision.

Introductory remarks

29–1 Article 29 is one of the truly novel provisions of the 2012 Arbitration Rules and corresponds to similar provisions adopted with respect to a number of international arbitration rules.[2] It allows parties bound by an ICC arbitration agreement to obtain provisional relief[3] from a so-called Emergency Arbitrator prior to the transmission of the file to the Tribunal. Article 29 is not applicable to arbitration agreements entered into prior to January 1, 2012. For arbitration agreements providing for ICC arbitration that entered into after January 1, 2012, art.29 is applicable unless it has been excluded. It remains to be seen, therefore, whether, in practice, much use will be made of art.29, as its scope of application is rather narrow. Up to October 31, 2013, six applications for Emergency Arbitrator Measures had been filed with the ICC, one of which was successful.[4]

29–2 Article 29 allows interim and conservatory relief that cannot await the constitution of the Tribunal. Article 29 does not contemplate or allow any kind of fast-track or summary proceedings on the merits. The Emergency Arbitration proceedings will normally precede an arbitral procedure, but will not substitute

[2] For a comparison of emergency arbitration procedures, see: *http://www.klgates.com/files/Publication/33e561cb-b459-47f5-bab1-856c51d8459b/Presentation/PublicationAttachment/f5e1a648-049e-4f63-afcf-f8d4dc91bae2/Emergency-Arbitration-Procedures_A-Comparative-Analysis.pdf* [accessed on November 10, 2013].

[3] See the definition of the term at para.28–7.

[4] Two in 2012, one of which was considered inadmissible by the ICC, and two in 2013. Courtesy information of the Secretary General of the ICC Court.

such a procedure.[5] Article 29 does not preclude recourse to national courts under art.28(2) in particular. In many circumstances, parties may prefer to apply to national courts for relief and not to use art.29. This is particularly the case where the national court in the relevant jurisdiction is open to applications for interim relief and where the court order for relief can be directly enforced.

Article 29 allows a party to obtain Emergency Arbitrator Measures, but at a cost of US$40,000 payable up-front by the applicant. This covers the ICC administrative costs and the fees and expenses of the Emergency Arbitrator. The lump sum fee can, in some circumstances, be increased, but will never be decreased; it applies irrespective of the amount in dispute.[6] 29–3

Article 29(1)–(7) is the cornerstone provision in the Rules for the new Emergency Arbitrator mechanism. It needs to be read in conjunction with App.V of the Rules, which is entitled "Emergency Arbitrator Rules", the "**EAR**". For ease of references the EAR together with Article 29(1)–(4) of the Rules are referred to as the "Emergency Arbitrator Provisions" ("**EAP**"). These new provisions are quite elaborate and mirror the comparable provisions in the 2012 Arbitration Rules to a large extent, without, however, referring to them. In that sense, the EAP set up a standalone regime for Emergency Measures. 29–4

It is not clear how often the EAP will be invoked. To date, there have been six applications, only one of which has been successful. The experience of other arbitration institutions suggests, however, that there is a significant role for provisions such as the EAP.[7] However some commentators are reserved.[8] 29–5

Overview of Article 29 and Appendix V

Article 29 has seven paragraphs, which deal with the following matters: 29–6

(1) the definition of "Emergency Measures";

(2) the decision of the Emergency Arbitrator as an order, not an award;

(3) the lack of binding nature for the Tribunal of the emergency arbitrator's order;

(4) the power of the Tribunal to deal with a party's request or claim related to the emergency arbitrator proceedings;

(5) the applicability of the EAP only to signatories of the arbitration agreement and their successors;

(6) the exclusion of the EAP in three specific circumstances;

(7) the possibility to have at any time recourse to the state courts to obtain provisional relief.

[5] Parties that have received a decision from an Emergency Arbitrator may, of course, use it as a basis for settling their dispute rather than pursuing arbitral proceedings on the merits.

[6] See para.29–94 below as to the costs of the Emergency Arbitrator Proceedings.

[7] As of September 2012, the ICDR EA rules have been invoked 20 times. Reports on the four first cases filed are available, more details at *http://www.adr.org/aaa* p. 25 [accessed November 24, 2013]. According to the SCC, six applications based on the EA provisions were filed since their entry into force, more details at *http://www.sccinstitute.se* [accessed November 24, 2013].

[8] See, for example Johansen, "The Ermergency Arbitrator in Construction. Disputes" (2013) Int'l Constr Law R, vol. 3 p.266.

29–7 Appendix V of the Rules contains eight articles, which deal with the actual proceedings to obtain emergency arbitration measures as follows:

Article 1:	The application for Emergency Measures
Article 2:	The appointment of the Emergency Arbitrator, and transmission of the file
Article 3:	The challenge of an Emergency Arbitrator
Article 4:	The Place of the Emergency Arbitrator Proceedings
Article 5:	The Conduct of the Emergency Arbitrator Procedure
Article 6:	The Order of the Emergency Arbitrator
Article 7:	The Costs of the Emergency Arbitrator Proceedings
Article 8:	A general rule

EAP in a Nutshell

29–8 Table **[1]** below describes in a nutshell how the system of Emergency Arbitrator Proceedings works as per App.V. There are six different steps that can be distinguished:

29–9 *Step 1*: A party, called "the applicant", submits its Application for Emergency Measures (the "Application" as per art.1(1) EAR) with the Secretariat of the ICC Court of Arbitration ("ICC Secretariat").

29–10 *Step 2*: The Secretariat will check whether in the dispute between the parties to the arbitration the file has already been transmitted to the Tribunal. Only if this is not the case will the Secretariat transmit the Application to the President of the ICC Court. The President checks whether, on the face of the Application, the EAP are applicable, art.1(5) EAR.

29–11 *Step 3*: In the affirmative, the Secretariat will notify the Request to the opposing party. This party is referred to in art.1(5), first sentence EAR as the "responding party".

29–12 *Step 4*: Within two days, the President of the ICC Court will have to appoint the Emergency Arbitrator, and possibly have to fix the place of the emergency arbitration proceedings.

29–13 *Step 5*: Provided the proposed candidate has submitted an unqualified statement of independence, the Secretariat will hand over the file to the Emergency Arbitrator, once appointed.

29–14 As of *Step 6*, the matter will be fully in the hands of the Emergency Arbitrator: He or she will first have to get in touch with both parties and establish a procedural timetable. He or she will then have to hear the parties, and thereafter render an Order, which normally will include a decision on costs. Finally, the Emergency Arbitrator will send the Order directly to the parties, without any further involvement of the Secretariat.

Timeline for Emergency Arbitrator Proceedings

29–15 The EAP provide a timeline of 18 days from the day of filing the Application with the Secretariat until the notification of the Order by the Emergency Arbitrator. This timeline can be shorter if things move quickly, but may need to be extended, if the circumstances require more time.

EAR in a Nutshell

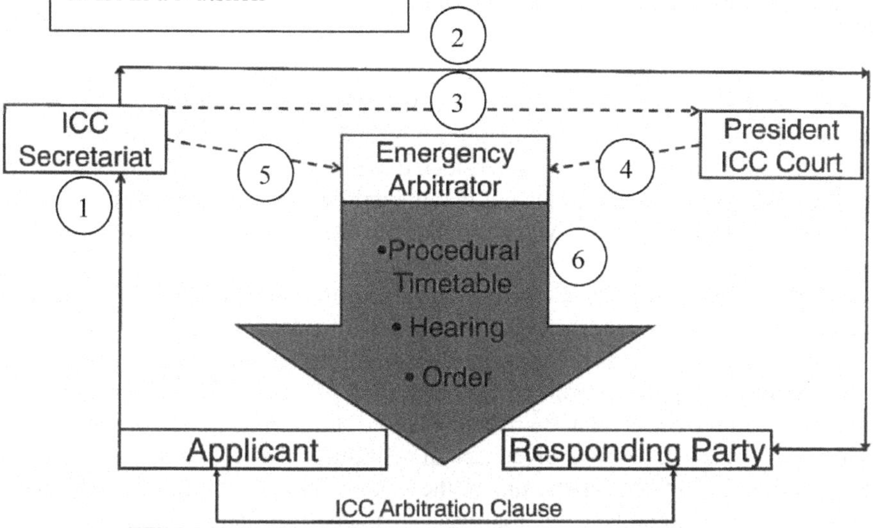

ICC Handbook, Table 1

They are as follows: **29–16**

- on Day 1, the Application for Emergency Measures is filed;
- on Day 3, the Emergency Arbitrator is appointed and receives the file from the Secretariat;
- on Day 5, the Emergency Arbitrator has established the procedural timetable;
- on Day 11, ten days after filing of the Request, the applicant must file its Request for Arbitration;
- on Day 18, 15 days after receipt of the file from the Secretariat, the Emergency Arbitrator has issued the Order.

These 18 days need to be compared with the time it takes to constitute a Tribunal under the 2012 Arbitration Rules. Upon receipt of a Request for Arbitration, a Respondent has 30 days alone to nominate an arbitrator, and to submit an Answer. Under the Emergency Arbitrator regime, the Respondent will have received a decision from the Emergency Arbitrator before even having submitted the Answer to a Request for Arbitration. **29–17**

Article 29 is a novelty in the ICC Arbitration Rules. However, ICC dispute resolution was familiar with the possibility of providing parties with provisional relief prior to the constitution of a Tribunal. Since 1990, by agreeing to the ICC Pre-Arbitral Referee Rules, parties were able to obtain a decision from a pre-arbitral referee.[9] **29–18**

[9] For a comparison of the ICC Pre-Arbitral Referee Rules with the emergency arbitrator provisions of the 2012 Arbitration Rules, see Bühler, "ICC Pre-Arbitral Referee and Emergency Arbitrator Proceedings Compared" (2011) ICC ICArb Bull vol. 22 Special Supplement, p. 93.

The major defect of the ICC Pre-Arbitral Referee Rules was the need to have the parties separately agree on them and parties rarely did so. During the last 20 years there have been only 10 cases administered by the ICC under its ICC Pre-Arbitral Referee Rules.

29–19 One of the key guiding factors of the Task Force was to fill any gaps in the Rules. The impossibility of obtaining provisional relief under the Rules prior to the constitution of a Tribunal was considered by the Task Force to be a serious gap of the 1998 version of the Rules but that the only way to remedy that gap was to provide that generally the EAP are applicable if the parties have agreed to ICC arbitration after 1 January 2012.

29–20 As discussed under art.28, provisional measures help preserve the subject matter of the dispute, and can be a vital need for one of the parties. This need occurs in many cases prior to the contribution of the Tribunal. While state courts are generally equipped to grant provisional relief, parties to international business transactions may be reluctant to refer matters to state courts to obtain such relief. There may exist a real or perceived lack of neutrality of state courts in some countries, and/or the judicial functioning of these courts may not be guaranteed. There may also be an apprehension for reasons of confidentiality, and many other reasons that may deter a party in a given case from seeking interim relief before the state courts.[10] Thus, where parties have agreed to arbitration, it was considered appropriate to provide them also with the possibility of provisional relief under the Rules prior to the constitution of the Tribunal.

The Term "Emergency Arbitrator"

29–21 The EAP use the term "arbitrator" to designate the Emergency Arbitrator. The Emergency Arbitrator is called upon to adjudicate a request for interim measures.

29–22 The Emergency Arbitrator has all the attributes of an arbitrator and for all purposes should be treated as such.[11] The Emergency Arbitrator is not a mediator or settlement facilitator, and although his mandate is similar, albeit narrower than that of a dispute board adjudicator or of a pre-arbitral referee, he is neither an adjudicator nor a referee, but an arbitrator with a very specific and limited mandate.[12] Unlike a normal arbitrator, the Emergency Arbitrator can only provide temporary relief, but not decide the merits of the dispute.

"Opting out" of the Emergency Arbitrator

29–23 As noted above, art.29 is not applicable to arbitration agreements entered into prior to January 1, 2012. Parties to an ICC arbitration clause, who do not want the emergency arbitrator provisions to apply must exclude them from the arbitration agreement, see art.29(6)(b).

[10] Castineira, *idem*, para 3, pp.65–66.
[11] This is discussed further at paras 29–107 *et seq*. in the context of the issue regarding the legal effect of the Emergency Arbitrator's Order.
[12] Article 2(1) of the Singapore International Arbitration Act includes the "emergency arbitrator" in its definition of the term "arbitral tribunal".

To that effect, an alternative ICC model arbitration clause is being proposed by the ICC to those users who wish to choose the "opt-out" solution. They must insert an additional sentence to the model arbitration clause as follows: 29–24

> "Arbitration without emergency arbitrator
>
> All disputes arising out of or in connection with the present contract shall be finally settled under the Rules of Arbitration of the International Chamber of Commerce by one or more arbitrators appointed in accordance with the said Rules. The Emergency Arbitrator Provisions shall not apply." [emphasis added]

Interaction between Article 29 and Appendix V

Article 29 has seven paragraphs and as such is one of the longest articles in the 2012 Arbitration Rules. Appendix V, which contains the "Emergency Arbitrator Rules," consists of eight articles. These provisions, defined above on the EAP, provide an autonomous set of procedural rules for an emergency arbitrator. However, with regard to the substantive issue of whether interim measures should be granted the provisions of art.28 and the discussion thereunder is highly relevant. 29–25

The procedural autonomy of the EAP is confirmed by the General Rule implemented in art.8 of App.V. Pursuant to art.8(1). The President has the power to discretionarily decide all administrative questions that were not dealt with in art.29 and App.V. Article 8(3), which echoes art.41 of the ICC Rules, provides that in all matters not addressed in the Appendix, the President and the Emergency Arbitrator should act "in the spirit of the Rules and this Appendix". This general provision aims at allowing the President and the Emergency Arbitrator to fill any lacunae in art.29 and App.V, to carry out the purposes of art.29. 29–26

Article 29(1): "A party that needs urgent interim or conservatory measures that cannot await the constitution of an arbitral tribunal ("Emergency Measures") may make an application for such measures pursuant to the Emergency Arbitrator Rules in Appendix V. Any such application shall be accepted only if it is received by the Secretariat prior to the transmission of the file to the arbitral tribunal pursuant to Article 16 and irrespective of whether the party making the application has already submitted its Request for Arbitration."

Application for Emergency Measures

The Application for Emergency Measures dealt with in detail in art.1 EAR. That provision mirrors art.4 of the Rules regarding the filing of a Request for Arbitration. Like the latter, the Application is to be filed with the Secretariat of the ICC Court. Article 1(1) EAR clarifies that the Application can be submitted to any of the offices of the ICC Court's Secretariat specified in the Internal Rules of the Court in App.II to the Rules.[13] Although sending an electronic copy to the Secretariat will be sufficient to start the process, the Secretariat will require at 29–27

[13] See para.1–84 above.

least three hard copies of the Application, one for the opposing party, one for the Emergency Arbitrator and one for itself. Once the ICC Court will make it possible to have online filing of Requests for arbitration and other pleadings,[14] this procedure will also impact the filing of Applications under art.29.

Content of the Application

29–28 Article 1(3) EAR describes the content of the Application for Emergency Measures, in its sub-paragraphs a) through i):

(a) "*the name in full, description, address and other contact details of each of the parties*". – This is the same type of information as required for a Request for Arbitration pursuant to art.4(3) a) of the Rules.

(b) "*the name in full, address and other contact details of any person(s) representing the applicant*". – This is the same type of information as required for a Request for Arbitration pursuant to art.4(3) b) of the Rules.

(c) "*a description of the circumstances giving rise to the Application and of the underlying dispute referred or to be referred to arbitration.*" – The description must cover two different points: First, it should provide an explanation of the reasons why the applicant is seeking Emergency Measures. Secondly, it should provide a description the underlying dispute between the parties. If at the time of the Application a Request for Arbitration has already been filed, it will be sufficient to refer to the description of the dispute made therein.[15] In that case, but also when the Request for Arbitration has not yet been filed, the dispute between the parties must be described in at least a summary fashion with reference in particular to the reasons for the application.

(d) "*A statement of the Emergency Measures sought*:" This refers to the provisional relief the applicant is seeking to obtain from the Emergency Arbitrator. (. . .)

(e) "*The reasons why the applicant needs urgent interim or conservatory measures that cannot await the constitution of an arbitral Tribunal.*" This requirement reflects the very definition of Emergency Measures in art.29(1).

(f) "*any relevant agreements and, in particular, the arbitration agreement*". – Submitting the arbitration agreement is important to establish and prove the signatory requirement under art.29(5), and to show that none of the exclusionary grounds of art.29(6) exists. Other relevant agreements may be those evidencing, for instance, the fact that a party has become a successor to a signatory of the arbitration agreement.

(g) "*any agreement as to the place of the arbitration, the applicable rules of law or the language of the arbitration*". – This information will normally be contained in the arbitration agreement. It may facilitate the President's choice of

[14] See para.3–5 above.

[15] It follows from art.29(1) 2nd sentence that the filing of a Request for Arbitration is not necessary at the time of filing an Application.

an Emergency Arbitrator if the place of arbitration, the law applicable to the contract and the language of the arbitration is highlighted in the Application. Where the arbitration agreement is silent in respect to the place of arbitration, the President will have to fix the place of the emergency arbitrator proceedings, art.(1) EAR.[16] Nothing prevents the applicant from making proposals and explaining the reasons behind such proposals.[17]

(h) "*proof of payment of the amount referred to in Article 7(1) of this Appendix*". – The applicant must furnish proof of payment of the sum of US$40,000, which is meant to cover the costs of the Emergency Arbitrator Proceedings, art.7(1) EAR. Proof of payment can be in the form of payment itself, e.g. a check made out to the order of the ICC. The ICC will not take payments in cash for such amount. A copy of a bank wire transfer to the ICC's account will normally constitute sufficient proof of payment.

The EAR do not say expressly what will happen if the applicant fails to provide (sufficient) proof of payment. If the filing fee required for a Request for Arbitration is not paid, the Secretariat may fix a time limit for Claimant to do so, art.4(4), 2nd para. of the Rules. Unless it has received the filing fee, it will not notify the Request for Arbitration. Undoubtedly, in case of an Application, the Secretariat is not required to take action prior to having received (sufficient) proof of payment.

(i) "*any Request for Arbitration and any other submissions in connection with the underlying dispute, which have been filed with the Secretariat by any of the parties to the emergency arbitrator proceedings prior to the making of the Application.*" – If a Request for Arbitration has been filed, this information must be mentioned in the Application, and a copy of the Request supplied. It is not necessarily the applicant that will have filed a Request for Arbitration with the ICC; it may be any other party covered by the Application.

Article 1(3)(i) EAR mentions also "any other submission in connection with the underlying dispute". Since such other submission will have to be filed with the Secretariat, an applicant will rarely be in a situation where such other submissions could be filed.[18] It could be, for instance, the Answer to the Request for Arbitration, or simply a letter sent by the Respondent to the Secretariat upon receipt of the Request for Arbitration.

The final paragraph of art.1(3) EAR contains a catch-all clause inviting the applicant to provide "*such other documents or information as the applicant considers appropriate or as may contribute to the efficient examination of the Application*". Similar language can be found in the last paragraph of art. 4(3) and 5(1) of the Rules for the Request for Arbitration and Answer respectively. The applicant might already have filed a request for interim relief before a state court, **29–29**

[16] See paras 29–59 et seq. below.

[17] See para.29–64 below regarding the criteria to be taken into account by the ICC Court's President when fixing the place of Emergency Arbitrator proceedings.

[18] Fry, Greenberg, Mazza, Guide, *op. cit.*, para.3–1077.

and might have filed for interim relief. This could further justify the need to obtain urgent interim relief under the ICC Rules.

Language of the Application

29–30 Pursuant to art.1(4) EAR, the language of the Emergency Arbitration proceedings will be the language of the arbitration. This requirement presupposes that the parties have agreed upon the language of the arbitration in their arbitration clause.[19] If no such agreement exists, the language of the Emergency Arbitration proceedings shall be the language of the arbitration agreement, i.e. typically the language of the contract, which contains the arbitration clause. It follows that the Application is to be drafted in the language foreseen for the arbitration and, where the parties have not provided for any such language, in the language of the contract. If the contract has been written in two languages (e.g. English and Russian), the applicant can choose either language for drafting the Application.

Three Admissibility Conditions for the Application

29–31 An Application is subject to three conditions of admissibility. First, pursuant to Article 29(1), the application must be received by the Secretariat of the ICC Court "prior to the transmission of the file to the Tribunal pursuant to art.16". Thus, in a dispute that is covered by the Application the Tribunal must not have been constituted or the Tribunal must not have received the file from the Secretariat.

29–32 Secondly, pursuant to art.29(5) of the Rules, the EAP "shall apply to parties that are signatories to an ICC arbitration agreement or to the successors of such parties". In other words, emergency relief cannot be obtained against non-signatories to the arbitration agreement.

29–33 Thirdly, art.29(6), lists three situations in which the application of the EAP is excluded:

(1) where the arbitration agreement was signed prior to the coming into force of the 2012 Rules, i.e. prior to January 1, 2012; or

(2) where the parties have opted out of the EAP; or

(3) if the parties have agreed to another pre-arbitral procedure, which takes priority.

29–34 Article 29(6) is a negative condition, i.e. satisfied if under none of the three aforementioned cases the EAP are or have been excluded.

29–35 The second and third admissibility conditions are discussed below when dealing with art.29(5) and (6) of the Rules respectively. They are for the President of the ICC Court to assess; it is enough for the President "to consider" that these conditions are met, art.1(5) EAR. The EAP do not state what level of evidence is required for the President to consider the signature or successor requirements to be satisfied. In practice, the ICC Court's President should proceed with the matter

[19] Article 20 of the Rules refers to an agreement by the parties, which typically is to be found in the arbitration clause, but can also be reached once the arbitration has started, see paras 20–17 *et seq.* above.

if on the balance of probabilities the condition was met. The Emergency Arbitrator him or herself can render a final decision on admissibility. If the President considers one or both of these two conditions not to be satisfied, the Emergency Arbitrator proceedings will come to an immediate halt, unless the President requests further information and clarification from the applicant.

Under the EAP, nothing prevents the President of the ICC Court from requesting the applicant provide further clarification and/or evidence on one or both of these two conditions. The power to ask additional information is inherent to the administrative function of the President. It can also be based on art.8(1) EAR, which gives the President the right to fill any gaps under the Rules. It is implied in art.1(5) EAR, which states that "if and to the extent" the President considers the conditions with respect to art.29(5) and (6) of the Rules to be satisfied. **29–36**

Under art.2(1) EAR, the President is expected to appoint the Emergency Arbitrator within "as short a time as possible, normally within two days from the Secretariat's receipt of the Application". **29–37**

In the President's absence, the aforementioned admissibility check can also be carried out by one of the Vice-Presidents pursuant to art.8(2) EAR.[20] To allow prompt attention to the matter, the Secretariat will have to alert the President, and possibly one of the Vice-Presidents, of the need to carry out the admissibility check.[21] **29–38**

Consequences of Admissibility Check by ICC Court President

In case of admissibility, i.e. if the President has assessed that the second and third conditions are met, the Secretariat will send the Application to the "responding party", that is the opposing party (or parties)[22] named in the Application, and which the President has considered to be signatories (or successors) of an ICC arbitration agreement, see art.1(5) EAR. Ideally, the notification of the Application to the responding party would take place within 24 hours upon receipt by the Secretariat. **29–39**

In case of the non-admissibility of the Application, the Secretariat informs the parties that the Emergency Arbitrator proceedings "shall not take place with respect to some or all of the parties and shall transmit a copy of the Application to them for information", art. 1(5) EAR. In other words, the responding party (or parties) will be informed of the relief requested from it (or them) by the applicant, even if the Application is considered not admissible by the ICC Court's President. This notification will be made for information, so as to allow full transparency. This solution differs from the comparable situation of the filing of a Request for Arbitration. Pursuant to art.4(4) of the Rules, where the Claimant fails to comply with certain requirements for the Request for Arbitration, in particular fails to pay the filing fee, the Secretariat may close the file, without the Respondent ever finding out that such Request had been filed with the ICC. **29–40**

[20] Article 1(3) of the Rules, which gives the President, and in his absence or otherwise, at the President's request, also the Vice-Presidents the power to take urgent decisions on behalf of the ICC Court, is not applicable to the present situation.

[21] The Secretariat will make a submission to that effect to the President.

[22] It can be concluded by way of analogy, and thus indirectly from art.2(ii) that the singular word "responding party" includes one or more responding parties. The next revision of the Rules will have to amend them, so as to cure a minor drafting oversight.

29–41 The decision of the ICC Court's President to accept or not to accept an Application is a purely administrative decision. There is no requirement that the President give reasons. Likewise, no recourse can be brought against such decision within the ICC arbitration system. The President's decision is to be treated in a way analogous to any decision taken by the ICC Court under the Rules.[23]

29–42 If the Application is considered not to be admissible by the ICC Court's President, the Emergency Arbitration proceedings come to an end. Out of the US$40,000 advance on costs paid by the applicant, the ICC retains at least US$5,000 to cover its administrative costs, art.7(5) EAR.

Appointment of Emergency Arbitrator

29–43 The Emergency Arbitrator is appointed by the President of the ICC Court, normally within two days upon the Secretariat's receipt of the Application, art.2(1) EAR.

29–44 The ICC Court is not involved in the appointment process, except as discussed below, in the event of a challenge against an Emergency Arbitrator.[24] The President of the ICC Court does not need to solicit the proposal of an ICC National Committee or Group. He has unfettered discretion in the selection of an Emergency Arbitrator.

29–45 Article 3(1) EAR does not provide for the appointment of an Emergency Arbitrator by agreement of the Parties, as in practice this situation is unlikely to occur.[25] If it did, it would then be incumbent upon the President of the ICC Court to confirm the Emergency Arbitrator jointly chosen by the parties.[26]

29–46 In light of the urgency involved with Emergency Measures, having the President of the ICC Court make the appointment was the most sensible solution. The President will no doubt rely on recommendations of the Secretariat, which may wish to establish an internal list of potential candidates upon which the President may seek to call when asked to appoint an Emergency Arbitrator.[27] It can be assumed that when faced with requests for appointment, the President will reach out to the most experienced arbitrators, with a proven track record in ICC arbitrations.[28]

29–47 An applicant may wish to inform the ICC Court's Secretariat of the imminent filing of an Application, so as to give the Secretariat more lead time for organising the appointment process.

Statement of Acceptance, Availability, etc.

29–48 The candidate selected by the ICC Court's President to act as Emergency Arbitrator must fill out and sign a Statement of Acceptance, Availability, Impartiality and Independence, pursuant to art.2(5) EAR. Its content is identical

[23] As to the administrative nature of the ICC Court's decisions, see para.6–40 above.

[24] See para.29–58 below.

[25] However, it is conceivable that the parties have agreed already in their arbitration agreement who will be the Emergency Arbitrator.

[26] In the same way, the ICC Court will confirm a sole arbitrator chosen by the parties, art.12(3) of the Rules.

[27] It is the authors' understanding that the ICC has so far no intention to establish such list. The AAA/ICDR Rules provide for a list of emergency arbitrators, art.37(3). See also r.14.5 of the CPR Arbitration Rules.

[28] Castineira, *op.cit.*, at 95, p. 89.

to the one foreseen in art.11(2) of the Rules for any arbitrator that is to be appointed or confirmed under the Rules. The prospective Emergency Arbitrator is therefore required to disclose in writing to the Secretariat any facts or circumstances which might be of such a nature as to call into question the Emergency Arbitrator's independence in the eyes of the parties. If the prospective Emergency Arbitrator submits a qualified statement of independence, it is unlikely that the ICC Court's President will proceed with the appointment, as any risk of challenge and objections by a party must be avoided in these circumstances.

The requirement of availability will need particular attention by the prospective Emergency Arbitrator and by the President of the ICC Court. In essence, the Emergency Arbitrator must be in a position to confirm substantial availability for a period of at least the subsequent 15 days, since that is the time the Emergency Arbitrator has to issue an Order. **29–49**

The Secretariat shall provide a copy of the Emergency Arbitrator's statement to the parties, pursuant to art.2(5) 2nd sentence EAR. In practice, this will be done at the same time the appointment of the Emergency Arbitrator is notified to the parties as per art.2(3) 1st sentence EAR. **29–50**

No Appointment of Emergency Arbitrator in case Tribunal has received the File

The President will refrain from appointing an Emergency Arbitrator in the event that the Secretariat has transmitted the file to the Tribunal at the same time the Application was submitted to the President, art.2(2) EAR. In practice, this scenario is unlikely to happen, since any applicant will be able to know, in consultation with the Secretariat. **29–51**

Article 2(2) EAR underscores the fact that the first condition of admissibility of the Application must still be satisfied when the President is about to appoint the Emergency Arbitrator, which normally will occur 24 or 48 hours after the Secretariat concluded that this first condition is met, and therefore transferred the Application to the ICC Court's President. Article 2(2) EAR is important inasmuch as it clearly tells any applicant that under the Rules it will not be entitled to the appointment of an Emergency Arbitrator once the Tribunal has been seized with the file. **29–52**

Transmission of File to Emergency Arbitrator

Immediately upon appointment of the Emergency Arbitrator by the ICC Court's President, the Secretariat will send the file to the Emergency Arbitrator, art.2(3) EAR. It is noteworthy that up to this stage the "responding party" will not have been requested by the ICC to state its position in respect of the Application, as will be discussed further below. **29–53**

Challenge of Emergency Arbitrator

The EAR provide in art.3 for a separate regime for challenging an Emergency Arbitrator. Article 14 of the Rules does not apply in that respect. **29–54**

The Emergency Arbitrator may be challenged by either party within three days from the notification of the appointment by the Secretariat pursuant to art.3(1) EAR. **29–55**

29–56 The ICC Court, not its President, will decide upon any such challenge. It will do so after having received submissions from the Emergency Arbitrator and the parties. This is the normal procedure regarding challenges of arbitrators under art.14 of the Rules. Normally, the ICC Court examines challenges against arbitrators at its monthly plenary sessions, but in recent years also at its weekly Committee Sessions.[29] In all likelihood, the challenge against an Emergency Arbitrator will be brought before a Court's Committee, since it would not be consistent with the urgency of a request for Emergency Measures to await a Plenary Session. But even to wait for a weekly Committee Session of the Court, which normally takes place every Thursday of any given week, might defeat the purpose of such a request. It may well therefore become necessary to have the President (or one of the Vice-Presidents) decide upon a challenge on behalf of the ICC Court in accordance with art.1(3) of the ICC Rules, or to convene a special ad hoc session of a Court's Committee to have the latter examine the challenge.[30] Unless the challenge is manifestly unfounded, the latter solution would seem preferable, as at least three members of the ICC Court would be examining the challenge. To increase the impartiality of the process, it would also seem advisable that the person who made the appointment of the Emergency Arbitrator, i.e. the President or a Vice-President of the ICC Court, abstain from deciding the challenge.

29–57 As will be further discussed below, the challenge brought against an Emergency Arbitrator has no suspensive effect. It does not bring the proceedings to a standstill and the Emergency Arbitrator continues enjoying the power to issue the Order, as long as the ICC Court has not decided upon the challenge.[31]

Replacement of Emergency Arbitrator

29–58 The EAP do not provide for the possibility of a replacement of the Emergency Arbitrator. In practice, in view of the short time span of the Emergency Arbitrator's expectation, there should hardly ever be a need for such replacement. Although art.15(1) of the Rules does not apply directly, on the basis of art.8(1) EAR, the President of the ICC Court undoubtedly has the power to replace an Emergency Arbitrator under the same conditions as those applicable for arbitrators.

Place of Emergency Arbitrator Proceedings

29–59 The place of Emergency Arbitrator proceedings shall be identical to the place of arbitration agreed upon by the parties in the arbitration agreement or otherwise, see art.4(1) EAR. If no agreement exists, it is incumbent upon the President of the ICC Court to fix such a place. The EAP do not say when the President shall fix the place. Presumably, the President will do so at the time of appointing the Emergency Arbitrator.[32]

[29] Fry, Greenberg, Mazza, *op. cit.*, para.3–590.

[30] In the past, it appears that no decisions on challenges were taken on the basis of art.1(3), see Fry, Greenberg, Mazza, *op. cit.*, para.3–36 for the period 2007–2010.

[31] See para.29–108 below.

[32] Fry, Greenberg, Mazza, *op. cit.*, para.3–1056, who expect the President to do so already when determining, pursuant to art.1(5) of App.V whether the Application may be notified.

Pursuant to the annual case statistics of the ICC Court, for many years now, in well over 80 per cent of the cases parties to ICC arbitrations have agreed upon the place of arbitration.[33] Accordingly, the need for the President of the ICC Court to fix the place of Emergency Arbitrator proceedings should not arise often. **29–60**

Under art.18(1) of the Rules, the ICC Court fixes the place of arbitration (unless agreed upon by the parties). The criteria taken into consideration by the ICC Court in doing so will apply mutatis mutandi to the ICC Court's President when fixing the place of Emergency Arbitrator proceedings. **29–61**

There is, however, a significant difference between the place of arbitration and the place of Emergency Arbitrator proceedings. Unlike the latter, the former has a legal significance when it comes to seeking the annulment and/or the enforcement of an arbitral award.[34] National arbitration laws and the New York Convention expressly refer to the place of arbitration and attach legal consequences to its existence in any given dispute. The concept and term of a place (or seat)[35] of Emergency Arbitrator proceedings is, however, unknown in statutory rules or international conventions on arbitration. **29–62**

This raises the question of the legal relevance of the place of Emergency Arbitrator proceedings, which will be discussed when addressing the possibility of seeking the enforcement of the Emergency Arbitrator's Order with judicial help. **29–63**

Among the criteria the President of the ICC Court may use when fixing the place for Emergency Arbitrator proceedings may be the place of residence of the prospective Emergency Arbitrator. Considerations of enforcement of the Emergency Arbitrator's Order may also play a role. This is something that the applicant would have to raise in the Application. **29–64**

Venue for Meetings/Hearings

Pursuant to art.4(2) EAR, the venue for meetings and hearings with the parties may be any location that the Emergency Arbitrator considers appropriate. The place of Emergency Arbitrator proceedings will certainly be the starting point for the Emergency Arbitrator's decisions, but may not always be the most appropriate under the circumstances. If the parties should agree on a hearing venue at a place other than the place of Emergency Arbitrator proceedings, the Emergency Arbitrator will normally be expected to respect such agreement. **29–65**

Rather than convening a physical meeting with the parties, the Emergency Arbitrator may decide to hold a video and/or telephone conference instead. Article 4(2) EAR mentions expressly that possibility, in line with art.24(4) of the 2012 Arbitration Rules. **29–66**

[33] See para.18–12 above. In 2012, the parties agreed upon the place of arbitration in 90 per cent of the cases.

[34] See the discussion at paras 18–2 et seq. above.

[35] The SCC Rules App.II art.5, refer to the seat of the emergency proceedings. Since the ICC Rules use the term "place" for the seat of arbitration, the same term "place" was also used for the seat of emergency arbitrator proceedings.

No Involvement of "Responding Party" up to File Transmission to Emergency Arbitrator

29–67 When the Secretariat sends the Application to the responding party, it does so purely for information, with no request to comment on the Application. At this stage, the responding party is not invited to state its position regarding the fulfillment of the second and third admissibility conditions, which the President of the ICC Court is to assess on the basis of the Application alone. Likewise, the responding party will not be asked to give its view regarding the profile of the Emergency Arbitrator and the choice, if any, of the place of Emergency Arbitration proceedings, although the applicant can, address such issues in the Application. The tension that exists between the right of due process and the need to promptly put an Emergency Arbitrator in place will require particular care by the ICC Court's President in the appointment process.

29–68 A responding party should, however, keep in mind that nothing under the EAP prevents it from submitting, on its own initiative, any (relevant) comments it may have to the ICC Court's Secretariat and/or President before the latter appoints the Emergency Arbitrator. For such comments to be taken into consideration and to have any effect, the responding party will have to react extremely quickly. Not every responding party will be in a position to do so.

29–69 In practice, a responding party will often reply to the Application only once the Emergency Arbitrator has been appointed, and once the latter has invited that party to do so within a specified and, by definition, short time limit.

Need to File Request for Arbitration

29–70 It follows from art.1(6) EAR that an applicant must generally file a Request for Arbitration within ten days upon having submitted its Application to the ICC Court's Secretariat unless the Emergency Arbitrator determines that a longer period is necessary. This requirement was added to test from the outset the seriousness of the Application, and thus to protect the responding party. The applicant must follow suit with its claim on the merits, if it wishes to obtain pre-arbitral provisional relief from an Emergency Arbitrator. The drafters of the 2012 Arbitration Rules wanted to avoid the risk that a party initiates Emergency Arbitrator proceedings for purely tactical and possibly abusive reasons.[36]

Emergency Arbitrator Procedure

29–71 Upon receipt of the file from the Secretariat, the Emergency Arbitrator is given two days to establish the procedural timetable, art.5(1) EAR. The Emergency Arbitrator will therefore have to get in contact with the parties immediately by any available means, including by telephone.

29–72 In establishing the procedural timetable, it would appear that the Emergency Arbitrator has to make at least three different considerations: first, the Order of the Emergency Arbitrator must be made within 15 days after the Emergency Arbitrator's receipt of the file under art.6(4) first sentence EAR. Secondly, the

[36] Castineira, *op. cit.*, para.10, pp.67–68.

Emergency Arbitrator will have to assess the nature and urgency of the Application under art.5(2) 1st sentence EAR. Thirdly, the Emergency Arbitrator will have to consider the need to provide the responding party with an opportunity to submit an answer to the Application, as no ex parte Order can be rendered under the EAP. Normally, the responding party will only at this stage provide the response to the provisional relief sought, and comment on the description of the nature and circumstances of the dispute giving rise to the Application and the measures sought.

Procedural Directions

It is the duty of the Emergency Arbitrator to always act fairly and impartially, and to afford both parties a reasonable opportunity to present their case under art.5(2) 2nd sentence EAR. Within these limits, it is entirely left to the discretion of the Emergency Arbitrator to issue appropriate procedural directions to the parties. This may include the filing of written submissions, of certain documents, the hearing of witnesses or even experts. The EAP do not provide for any minimum time limit for the responding party to submit an answer to the Application. It is for the Emergency Arbitrator to fix it. In fixing the time limit, the Emergency Arbitrator may also have to consider the time possibly taken by the applicant to prepare its Application then urgency and the nature of the matter and the relief sought. If a physical hearing with the parties is to take place, the Emergency Arbitrator will have to take the appropriate steps, which may include, for instance, the hiring of a court reporter. One way or the other, the Emergency Arbitrator will need to be rather proactive in his or her approach towards the parties, so that an Order can be issued as quickly as possible, and in any event, within the 15 days time limit. **29–73**

Prior to issuing the procedural directions, the Emergency Arbitrator should consider inviting the parties to comment on the procedure to be followed for the determination of the Application. The Emergency Arbitrator will have to set very short time limits for the parties to make such comments; in some cases, the parties may only be given a few hours to do so. **29–74**

No ex parte Order

It follows clearly from art.1(5) and art.5(2) EAR that ex parte Orders are not allowed in ICC Emergency Arbitrator Proceedings. The responding party will always be informed by the Secretariat of the Application, and the Emergency Arbitrator will have to hear the responding party, or at least give it an opportunity to present its case, before issuing the Order. **29–75**

Article 29(2): "The emergency arbitrator's decision shall take the form of an order. The parties undertake to comply with any order made by the emergency arbitrator."

Order

Although the word order is nowhere defined in the 2012 Arbitration Rules, it is clear that the decision of the Emergency Arbitrator is not to be an Award, but an **29–76**

Order, not different from any other procedural order a Tribunal will take when conducting an arbitration. By not giving the Emergency Arbitrator the possibility to grant provisional relief in the form of an (interim) Award,[37] a marked difference exists with the provisional relief a Tribunal can grant pursuant to art.28(2) of the Rules: it can either be in the form of an Award or of an Order.[38] Unlike the ICC, other arbitral institutions have given the Emergency Arbitrator the power to issue either an award or an order.[39]

29–77 Since the decision is rendered only in the form of an Order, it follows logically that it is not open, or subject, to the scrutiny process under art.33 of the Rules, which is exclusively reserved to Awards. In that respect, the Order of the Emergency Arbitrator is not treated any differently from the procedural order of a Tribunal. Neither the ICC Court, nor its Secretariat formally review procedural orders of a Tribunal. Accordingly, the EAP do not provide for any kind of scrutiny or review of the Order issued by the Emergency Arbitrator.

29–78 In order to facilitate the task of the Emergency Arbitrator, the Secretariat has prepared a checklist to assist in drafting the order, and will volunteer, upon the request of the Emergency Arbitrator, to review the draft Order.[40]

29–79 Article 6(1) EAR reiterates the statement of art.29(2) 1st sentence of the Rules that the decision of the Emergency Arbitrator is to be in the form of an Order.

29–80 It is implied by the 1st sentence of art.29(2) of the Rules that the Order must be in writing. Article 6(3) EAR expressly states this, and further states that the Order must contain reasons. It shall also be dated and signed by the Emergency Arbitrator.

Content of the Order

29–81 The Order of the Emergency Arbitrator will have to contain at least five different points:

29–82 First, it will have to address the admissibility requirement for the Application under art.29(1) of the Rules, which concerns the need for urgent interim or conservatory measures that cannot await the constitution of a Tribunal pursuant to art.6(2) EAR. Urgency is one of the conditions of admissibility, which art.29(1) qualifies by referring to measures that "cannot await the constitution of a Tribunal". Thus, art.29(1) sets a special degree of urgency, which the Emergency Arbitrator needs to assess. If the Emergency Arbitrator will come to the conclusion that no such degree of urgency exists and that it is possible to "await the constitution of a Tribunal", he or she is likely to dismiss the Application on this basis alone.

29–83 In making such an assessment, the Emergency Arbitrator will first have to consider how long it may take the ICC to have the Tribunal put in place. This may depend on a variety of factors, such as whether a Sole Arbitrator or a three member panel is to be constituted, whether the president of the Tribunal is to be appointed

[37] For a discussion of the pros and cons of the ICC's policy decision, see Castineira, *op. cit.*, at 92, pp.87–88.

[38] See para.28–7 above.

[39] See SCC Rules art.32(3) and SIAC Rules Sch.1(6).

[40] Fry, Greenberg, Mazza, *Guide*, *op. cit.*, p.303 ("Note to Parties and Emergency Arbitrator").

by the ICC Court or by the co-arbitrators. In addition, the Emergency Arbitrator will have to estimate how long it may take for the Tribunal, once constituted, to do exactly what he or she is supposed to do, that is, to examine and decide upon a request for provisional relief. It is clear, from the purpose of this provision that the possibility of the newly constituted Tribunal to effectively act and order provisional relief is what matters. This point will have to be addressed by the applicant in its Application pursuant to art.1(3)(e) EAR, and possibly in subsequent submissions to the Emergency Arbitrator.[41]

Secondly, pursuant to art.6(2) EAR, the Emergency Arbitrator must also confirm that he or she has jurisdiction to order Emergency Measures. The ICC Court's President will have already made a preliminary determination when confirming that the signatory requirement under art.29(5) of the Rules is fulfilled.[42] However, the Emergency Arbitrator is not, and cannot be, bound by this determination, which is only administrative in nature.[43] He or she will have to make such a determination after having heard the responding party as well, unlike the President of the ICC Court. The determination by the Emergency Arbitrator will be made on a first impression or prima facie basis, bearing in mind that it is ultimately for the Tribunal to decide upon the existence of arbitral jurisdiction over the parties.[44] **29–84**

Thirdly, the Emergency Arbitrator will have to examine the merits of the request for Emergency Measures, and, in doing so, will either uphold or dismiss the applicant's request for urgent relief in full or in part. In principle, the substantive conditions required to be entitled to provisional relief from a Tribunal,[45] will have to be satisfied, to obtain Emergency Measures as well. Thus, an Emergency Arbitrator will have to apply the same diligence in assessing the clauses of success on the merits as would a Tribunal seized with a request for interim relief.[46] As a result, the factors discussed in art.28 for rendering interim or conservatory relief are equally applicable under art.29. **29–85**

The analysis as to the substantive conditions that will normally have to be satisfied to obtain Emergency Measures will have to be made by arbitrators when granting provisional relief. These conditions may include the existence of imminent serious harm that neither outweighs the likely harm to the other party ("balance of interests test") nor prejudgment of the case, and the likelihood or reasonable chance of success on the merits.[47] **29–86**

Fourthly, the Order needs to contain the holding or ruling of the Emergency Arbitrator. In this context, art.6(7) EAR expressly states that such ruling can be made with conditions, such as that the applicant furnish appropriate security. Considering the potential damage that may be caused to one party if the provisional relief granted does not prove to have been justified, for the applicant's **29–87**

[41] See para.29–51 above, Castineira, *op. cit.*, para.54.
[42] See paras 29–31 et seq. above and paras 29–132 et seq. below.
[43] See para.29–41 regarding the administrative nature of the decisions of the ICC Court's President.
[44] Castineira, *idem*, para 94, p.88, and paras 29–127 et seq. below, discussing the right of the Tribunal to revisit the Emergency Arbitrator's Order.
[45] See paras 28–13 et seq.
[46] Reiner & Aschauer, *op. cit.*, para.598 and at n.362.
[47] See paras 28–13 et seq. above regarding the substantive conditions to obtain interim relief.

lack of a substantive right (or otherwise), it is important that the Emergency Arbitrator can require appropriate security as a pre-condition for granting the requested relief.

29–88 Fifthly, the Order must contain a decision on costs pursuant to art.7(3) EAR.

Time limit for Issuing the Order

29–89 Pursuant to art.6(4) EAR, the Order is to be issued at the latest within 15 days after receipt of the file by the Emergency Arbitrator.

29–90 This time limit can be extended by the President of the ICC Court pursuant to art.6(4) EAR. In doing so, the President will consider the Procedural Timetable established by the Emergency Arbitrator in the first place.

29–91 As long as the time limit for issuing the Order runs, with or without extension, the Emergency Arbitrator remains empowered to render the Order even if the Tribunal has in the meantime received the file from the Secretariat, art.2(2) EAR.

Notification of the Order

29–92 The Order is notified to the parties directly by the Emergency Arbitrator, thus without the intervention of the ICC Court's Secretariat, art.6(5) EAR. The situation here is not any different from the one where a Tribunal issues and sends a procedural order to the parties. It does so without involving the Secretariat. Allowing direct notification of the Order to the parties by the Emergency Arbitrator, rather than by the Secretariat, and by any of the means of communication permitted by art.3(2) of the Rules, is in the interest of speed; it was therefore sensible to choose a different solution from the one prevailing under the ICC Pre-Arbitral Referee Rules .[48]

Costs of Emergency Arbitrator Proceedings

29–93 The issue of the costs of the Emergency Arbitrator Proceedings is dealt with by art.7 EAR. These costs will normally consist of (i) the ICC administrative expenses; (ii) the fees and expenses of the Emergency Arbitrator; and (iii) the parties' reasonable legal and related costs. In the normal case, the first two cost items will be covered by the US$40,000 lump sum payment that the applicant had to pay when filing the Application (the "ICC Costs"). This is the amount of the ICC costs to be stipulated in the Order. US$10,000 will cover the ICC administrative expenses, and the balance of US$30,000 will cover both the expenses and fees of the Emergency Arbitrator. In the normal case, the expenses of the Emergency Arbitrator should be minimal, so that the bulk of the US$30,000 balance should go to his or her fees.

29–94 Neither the ICC Court's President or the ICC Court, nor its Secretariat need to intervene to fix the ICC costs, as they represent a fixed lump sum. The Emergency

[48] See art.6(1) and (5) of the ICC Pre-Arbitral Referee Rules pursuant to which *"[t]he decisions taken by the Referee shall be sent by him to the Secretariat in the form of an Order giving reasons"* and "*[t]he Secretariat shall notify the parties of the Order of the Referee provided it has received the full amount of the advance on costs fixed by the Secretariat. Only Orders so notified are binding upon the parties*".

Arbitrator will therefore not have to await a decision by one of the ICC's organs for the fixing of the ICC costs. They are, in fact, pre-fixed.

In exceptional cases, the ICC Court's President can increase the ICC costs, either at the level of the ICC administrative expenses or of the Emergency Arbitrator's fees under art.7(2) 1st sentence EAR. In that case, the Secretariat will provide the applicant with a (short) time frame in which to pay the increased amount. If no payment is received, the Application shall be considered withdrawn pursuant to art.7(2) 2nd sentence EAR. Although the EAR do not say so expressly, the Secretariat has the power to extend this time limit. **29–95**

The lump sum increased by the ICC Court's President will represent the ICC costs, which the Emergency Arbitrator simply has to allocate in the Order, but will, as such, not fix. **29–96**

As a Tribunal must do so in its Award, the Emergency Arbitrator must decide in the Order "which of the parties shall bear [the costs] or in what proportion they shall be borne by the parties", art.7(3) EAR. Like an arbitrator, the Emergency Arbitrator enjoys discretion in allocating costs, be it the ICC costs or the parties' costs. In practice, it would appear, however, that the options in allocating the costs are rather limited: **29–97**

(i) if the applicant is unsuccessful in its request for provisional relief, it will have to bear the ICC costs, and possibly also pay some compensation for the responding party's legal costs,[49] unless the Emergency Arbitrator decides that each party should bear its own legal costs;
(ii) if the applicant is successful in its request for provisional relief, the Emergency Arbitrator may allocate all or part of the costs to the Respondent party, or have each party bear the costs it has incurred (which would include the ICC costs advanced by Claimant).

Finally, in both situations, the Emergency Arbitrator might defer the allocation of the costs to the Tribunal. Since the ICC costs are known in advance, it is the parties' costs which would then also have to be fixed by the Tribunal. This possibility would seem to follow from art.29(4) of the Rules, which allows the Tribunal to reallocate the costs of the Emergency Arbitrator proceedings. If it can reallocate the costs, there should be no reason why it could not allocate the costs of these proceedings ultimately in the final award.[50] **29–98**

Because the applicant will normally have to file a Request for Arbitration prior to obtaining an Order, the US$3,000 filing fee for the former is closely associated with the cost necessary for the applicant to obtain Emergency Measures. **29–99**

Termination of the Emergency Arbitration Proceedings without an Order

The Order of the Emergency Arbitrator, and its notification to the parties is the last step in any Emergency Arbitration Proceeding. The EAP expressly foresee one situation where the Emergency Arbitration Proceedings are brought to an end **29–100**

[49] Given the short time frame, there may be practical difficulties for the parties to submit their actual costs, but the Emergency Arbitrator may also ask at least for an estimate, which would then serve as a basis for fixing an amount designed to compensate the legal costs incurred by the prevailing party.

[50] See also below as to the power of the Tribunal to reallocate the costs of the Emergency Arbitrator proceedings; see also Fry, Greenberg, Mazza, *Guide*, *op. cit.*, para.3–1092.

without an Order having been issued by the Emergency Arbitrator. Article 1(6) EAR authorises the ICC Court's President to terminate the Emergency Arbitrator Proceedings, if the applicant has failed to file a Request for Arbitration within 10 days upon having filed the Application. The requirement to do so follows from art.1(6) EAR.

29–101 Thus, the ICC Court's President will first have to consult the Emergency Arbitrator before taking such a radical measure. Article 1(6) EAR expressly authorises the Emergency Arbitrator to determine that a longer period of time is necessary for filing the Request for Arbitration. This may be the case in multitier arbitration clauses that provide for a "cooling off" period before a party can file its Request for Arbitration. The dispute resolution mechanism in the FIDIC Conditions of Contract provide, a good example of cooling-off periods that are not compatible with the 10 days under art.1(6) EAR. Such provisions should not per se prevent a party from seeking Emergency Measures pending the cooling-off period.[51] In the case of the FIDIC Conditions, the question arises, however, whether they do not take precedence over and, in fact, exclude the EAP, as per art.29(6)(c).[52]

29–102 The possibility to extend the time limit for filing the Request for Arbitration, based on the Emergency Arbitrator's assessment, attenuates the stringent and very short ten day time limit, and effectively allows the Emergency Arbitrator to determine the deadline by which the applicant must file the Request for Arbitration.

29–103 The Emergency Arbitrator will have to inform not only the ICC Court's President, but also the parties of his or her decision to allow a longer period for the filing of the Request for Arbitration, and may have to invite the latter for comments prior to making such decision. The extension will have to be notified by the Secretariat to both parties. The EAR do not indicate the criteria that are to be considered in determining that a longer period is necessary. If the arbitration clause conditions the filing of the Request for Arbitration on a lapse of time, be it for a simple "cooling off" period prior mediation proceedings,[53] an extension of the time limit is likely to be justified. The ten day time limit in art.1(6) EAR is particularly short, compared, for instance, to the 30 days that the SCC Rules provide in the similar situation.[54] In practice, any plausible explanation of why the drafting of the Request for Arbitration could not yet have been completed, coupled with a request for a reasonable extension of time, should normally be sufficient for the Emergency Arbitrator's determination. An extension of 20 days (or less) would normally seem to be reasonable.

[51] One of the ICC's standard clauses expressly states that if the dispute has not been settled pursuant to the ADR Rules within 45 days following the filing of a Request for ADR, the dispute shall then be settled under the ICC Rules of Arbitration, see ICC model clause "Obligation to submit to ADR, followed by arbitration if required." – In such case, it would also be possible for the applicant to file the Request for Arbitration, and at the same time ask the ICC Court's Secretariat to suspend the arbitration until the end of the "cooling off" period.

[52] This issue is discussed at paras 29–146 *et seq.* below.

[53] See para.29–142 below.

[54] SCC Rules App.II art.9(4)(iii).

Legal Effect of the Order

The second sentence of art.29(2) of the Rules expressly states that the parties' undertake "to comply with any order made" by the Emergency Arbitrator. The Order is therefore binding upon the parties as soon as it has been issued and notified to them. **29–104**

It would seem incorrect, however, to qualify the Order of the Emergency Arbitrator as a decision purely contractual in nature rather than a judicial decision. However, this is the position the Paris Court of Appeal took in 2003 in the well-known *Congo* case, where the legal qualification of an order issued by an ICC Pre-Arbitral Referee was at stake. The Paris Court of Appeal considered the order to have no more binding effect than that of a contractual provision and that it was deprived of the binding effect of a decision as being res judicata.[55] **29–105**

The Emergency Arbitrator has each and every attribute of an arbitrator, the only limit being that he or she can only render an interim decision, not, however, a final Award. To take, as an example the French judicial system, in which provisional measures ("*mesures provisoires*") are rendered by the so-called "*juge des référés*," no one seriously suggests that the *juge des référés* is not as much a judge as any other judge deciding upon the merits of the dispute.[56] **29–106**

The Emergency Arbitrator acts as an independent and impartial person, in proceedings in which both parties are given the opportunity to be heard, and where a decision is to be rendered concerning the rights of one party over the other, albeit on an interim basis.[57] Admittedly, on the merits, the order of the Emergency Arbitrator is only provisional, but the order as such is to be immediately binding and enforceable. This should, in the authors' view, be sufficient to qualify it as a judicial decision, and to assimilate it with an order for interim relief issued by an arbitral tribunal. **29–107**

Duration of Binding Effect of Order

In its sub-paras (a)–(d), art.6(6) EAR lists four situations when the Order shall cease to be binding upon the parties: **29–108**

(a) "*the President's termination of the emergency arbitrator proceedings pursuant to Article 1(6) of this Appendix*": – An applicant advances US$ 40,000 and bound to lose at least US$ 5,000 in the event the proceedings are terminated by the ICC Court's President. Therefore, the applicant will presumably seek to file the Request for Arbitration with 10 days or any longer period set by the Emergency Arbitrator.

[55] CA Paris, 1ère ch. C, April 29, 2003, *Sté Nationale des Pétroles du Congo et République du Congo c/ Sté Total Fina Elf TEP Congo*; Gaillard & Pinsolle, *op. cit.*, p.13; Berger, "Pre-Arbitral Referees. Arbitrators, Quasi-Arbitrators, Hybrids or Creates of Contract Law?" in *Liber Amicorum in honour of R. Briner* (2005), p.73; Castineira, para.93, p.85.

[56] Clay, "*La première application du référé pré-arbitral de la CCI*" (2003) Recueil Dalloz, p. 2478; Mourre, "*Référé pré-arbitral de la CCI, to be or not to be a judge*," (29/05/2003) Gazette Du Palais No.149 p.5 ; and Loquin, "*De la nature juridique du référé pré-arbitral de la CCI*," (2003) RTD Com., p. 482.

[57] Clay, *idem*; Mourre, *idem*.

(b) "*the acceptance by the Court of a challenge against the emergency arbitrator pursuant to Article 3 of this Appendix*": – As stated above, as long as the ICC Court has not decided upon the challenge, the Emergency Arbitrator Proceedings will continue their course. Thus, the Emergency Arbitrator may even render an Order before the ICC Court has made its decision. If the ICC Court accepts a challenge against an Emergency Arbitrator, the Order would automatically lose its effect. It would appear appropriate for the Secretariat to mention this effect in the notification letter to the parties with reference to art.6(6)(b) EAR.

(c) "*the arbitral Tribunal's final award, unless the arbitral Tribunal expressly decides otherwise*": – The Order being interim in nature, it is the Tribunal's award which will ultimately decide, one way or the other, but in any event in a final manner, on the relief covered by the Order. Thus, normally, the Order of the Emergency Arbitrator ceases to have binding effect upon the parties at the latest once an Award is rendered by the Tribunal provided either that it is a Final Award or that it deals with the interim relief that was the subject of the Emergency Arbitrator's Order.

(d) "*the withdrawal of all claims or the termination of the arbitration before the rendering of a final award*": – If a party withdraws its claims that were the subject of, or underlied the Order, or if the arbitration is terminated for whatever reason, the Order will automatically lose its effect. The termination may be due to non-payment of the advance on cost, and may thus have been triggered by the Secretariat. It may also have been the result of a settlement agreement by the parties.

29–109 There are at least two other situations when the Order ceases to have binding effect: First, the Emergency Arbitrator him or herself may terminate or annul the Order pursuant to art.6(8) EAR.[58] Secondly, the Tribunal has the same right to do so pursuant to art.29(3) of the Rules.[59]

Right of Emergency Arbitrator to Revisit the Order

29–110 As long as the Tribunal has not been seized with the file by the Secretariat,[60] the Emergency Arbitrator may, upon a reasoned request by either party, "modify, terminate or annul the order" pursuant to art. 6(8) EAR. Strictly speaking, it was not necessary to expressly provide for such right, which is analogous to a Tribunal's right to change procedural decisions taken in the course of arbitral proceedings. It was, however, necessary to expressly stipulate until what moment the Emergency Arbitrator holds the power to revisit or even vacate his or her Order. Once the Tribunal has received the file, the Emergency Arbitrator loses that power, which, in fact, is transferred from that moment on to the Tribunal, in accordance with art.29(3).

[58] See para.29–110 below.
[59] See paras 29–123 et seq. below.
[60] As per art.16 of the Rules.

Article 6(8) EAR does not expressly refer to the right to correct material errors, or to provide an interpretation, as is provided in art.35(1) and (2) of the Rules for a Tribunal's award. There can be no doubt that the Emergency Arbitrator has such a right,[61] but there was no need to state so in the Rules. First, the right to modify necessarily includes the right to correct any material error or to clarify the decision by providing an interpretation. Secondly, in light of the interim nature of the Order, which is not different from a procedural order of a Tribunal in any material way,[62] there should be no doubt that the Emergency Arbitrator can make corrections or give an interpretation of the Order, if requested to do so. **29–111**

Consequences of (non-) compliance with Order

The enforceability of the Emergency Arbitrator's Order is one of the most critical issues facing Emergency Measures under the Rules. The 2012 Arbitration Rules are silent in that respect, and in no way exclude such enforceability. Rather, this is a matter of the law applicable in the country where a party would wish to seek judicial assistance for enforcing such an order. **29–112**

Pursuant to art.17 H(1) of the UNCITRAL Model Law, as amended in 2006, "an interim measure by an arbitral Tribunal shall be recognized as binding and, unless otherwise provided by the arbitral Tribunal, enforced upon application to the competent court [. . .]". While this provision refers to a Tribunal, not an emergency arbitrator, courts in countries following art.17H of the Model Law[63] will have to consider whether to treat the Emergency Arbitrator's Order like an interim measure of a Tribunal.[64] **29–113**

However, whether or not judicial aid is available to enforce the Order, the parties will most probabaly comply. Then question is based on, when the high degree of compliance with provisional measures in ICC arbitration,[65] and with orders issued by ICC Pre-Arbitral referees.[66] **29–114**

Exclusion of Emergency Arbitrator's Liability

Article 40 of the 2012 Arbitration Rules also expressly covers the Emergency Arbitrator, and thus exclude him or her from any liability "to any person for any act or omission in connection with the arbitration". **29–115**

Although no specific confidentiality obligation is imposed on the Emergency Arbitrator by the EAP, the latter is expected to keep the information relating to the Emergency Arbitrator Proceedings confidential, in the same way an arbitrator is expected to keep the information relating to the arbitration confidential. **29–116**

[61] Castineira, *idem*, pp. 90–91.

[62] See Poudret/Besson, para.640 p.548; Redfern & Hunter para.5-28, p.321 as to the right of a Tribunal to modify its procedural orders.

[63] For example, the 1998 German Arbitration Act foresees the possibility of enforcement of interim measures of a Tribunal, see s.1041(2) of the German Code of Civil Procedure. See also s.593(3)–(5) of the Austrian Code of Civil Procedure, and s.183(2) of the Swiss PILA.

[64] See also Castineira, *op. cit.*, at 94; Webster, Handbook of UNCITRAL Arbitration, 26–28.

[65] See Fry, Greenberg, Mazza, *op. cit.*, para.3–1086.

[66] Castineira, *op. cit.*, at 95 states that all orders of ICC Pre-Arbitral referees had always been complied with, including the one challenged before the French courts.

Right of Emergency Arbitrator to Act as Arbitrator

29–117 Article 2(6) EAR excludes the right of the Emergency Arbitrator from acting subsequently as arbitrator in the same matter.

29–118 It would seem, however, that, with the agreement of both parties, an Emergency Arbitrator should be permitted to become sole arbitrator or president of the Tribunal. In certain cases, the parties might find it advantageous to have someone who has already gained familiarity with the dispute, and shown his or her qualities in understanding the intricacies of the case, become the sole or third arbitrator. At the same time, the parties must then accept that the chances of having the Tribunal later revisit the Order in the same way a totally different Tribunal would do so.

Article 29(3): "The emergency arbitrator's order shall not bind the arbitral tribunal with respect to any question, issue or dispute determined in the order. The arbitral tribunal may modify, terminate or annul the order or any modification thereto made by the emergency arbitrator."

Interplay between Emergency Arbitrator and Tribunal

29–119 Article 29(3) is one of the provisions that deals with the interplay between the Emergency Arbitrator and the Tribunal, by declaring that the Order of the former shall not be binding upon the latter. The fact that the Emergency Arbitrator's Order does not bind the Tribunal is discussed below.

29–120 Article 29(4) of the Rules is another provision that reflects the interplay between the Emergency Arbitrator and the Tribunal. The latter is expressly given the power to deal with parties' requests or claims related to the Emergency Arbitrator proceedings.

29–121 Finally, it should be noted that the submission of the file to the Tribunal by the ICC Court's Secretariat has two immediate consequences upon the Emergency Arbitration proceedings: first, the appointment of an Emergency Arbitrator by the ICC Court's President is no longer possible, art.2(2) EAR. Secondly, the Emergency Arbitrator can no longer revisit his or her Order, art.6(8) EAR.

No Binding Effect of the Emergency Arbitrator's Order on the Tribunal

29–122 The Order issued by an Emergency Arbitrator does not bind a Tribunal constituted under the ICC Rules. However, the Emergency Arbitrator's Order remains in place until terminated or modified by the Tribunal. The Tribunal does not need to confirm the Order to maintain its binding effect upon the parties.

Right of Tribunal to Revisit Emergency Arbitrator's Order

29–123 The 2nd sentence of art.29(3) of the Rules expressly grants the Tribunal the power to revisit the Order issued by the Emergency Arbitrator, in particular to "modify, terminate or annul the order or any modification thereto made by the emergency arbitrator". This is the logical consequence of the rule that the Emergency Arbitrator's Order not be binding upon the Tribunal. Normally, the Tribunal will have been seized by a request of the parties prior to revisiting an Order as a result of an application by a party, but the Tribual may do so of its initiative.

Should the Tribunal modify the Order, it will incidentally confirm it, however by adopting the Order in a way it considers appropriate. It might restrain or increase the scope of the injunctive relief; it might ask for new or additional security, and the like. **29–124**

Should the Tribunal terminate or annul the Order, it will bring the latter to an end. In the event of termination, the Order will cease to have its effects *ex nunc*, that is for the future. In the event of annulment, the Order would cease to have its effect *ex tunc*, that is, from the time it was issued. Thus, the annulment of the Order will have retroactive effect, which may have far-reaching consequences that need to be carefully considered by the Tribunal. **29–125**

The right to revisit the Emergency Arbitrator's Order explains in part why art.2(6) EAR disqualifies an Emergency Arbitrator from acting subsequently as an arbitrator. The Parties may, however, agree otherwise, and allow the Emergency Arbitrator also to act as either Sole Arbitrator or chairman of the Tribunal.[67] **29–126**

Article 29(4): "The arbitral tribunal shall decide upon any party's requests or claims related to the emergency arbitrator proceedings, including the reallocation of the costs of such proceedings and any claims arising out of or in connection with the compliance or noncompliance with the order."

This provision expressly recognises the power of the Tribunal to deal with requests or claims of a party related to the Emergency Arbitrator proceedings. Article 29(4) expressly provides for claims "arising out of or in connection with the compliance or non-compliance with order". If, for example, an order has been granted based on a misrepresentation and the party against who the order was made has suffered damage, that the party would have recourse under art.29(4) with respect to that damage, in the related arbitration proceedings. Similarly, if a party has failed to comply with an order and the other party suffers damage, that could give rise to a claim under art.29(4). **29–127**

Article 29(4) makes it also clear that the decision on cost in the Order may be changed by the Tribunal which may foresee a different cost allocation than the one provided for by the Emergency Arbitrator. **29–128**

Article 29(5): "Articles 29(1)–29(4) and the Emergency Arbitrator Rules set forth in Appendix V (collectively the "Emergency Arbitrator Provisions") shall apply only to parties that are either signatories of the arbitration agreement under the Rules that is relied upon for the application or successors to such signatories."

Signatory requirement

Article 29(5) of the 2012 Arbitration Rules sets a clear and narrow requirement for the EAP to be applicable: the parties' covered by the Application must have **29–129**

[67] Fry, Greenberg, Mazza, *Guide*, *op. cit.*, para.3–1056 lit. e).

signed the (ICC) arbitration agreement, upon which the applicant relies in order to justify its Application for Emergency Measures. A successor to a party having originally signed the ICC arbitration agreement will be bound likewise, provided it can show that it is indeed a successor to the original signatory.[68]

29–130 Article 29(5) has a much narrower scope and uses a more stringent test than art.6(3) and (4) of the Rules, which simply requires "that the Court is *prima facie* satisfied that an arbitration agreement under the Rules may exist", for an ICC arbitration to proceed pursuant to art.6(4) 1st sentence.[69] However, although the President of the ICC Court makes a preliminary determination with respect to the scope of jurisdiction, it will be for the Emergency Arbitrator to address the issue substantively in his or her order.

29–131 In light of the immediate and far-reaching character of the interim or provisional relief, and the harm it could cause to a party, such relief is only to be made available against a party that has signed an ICC arbitration agreement. This signature requirement is incumbent upon the ICC Court's President to determine in the first place,[70] and then for the Emergency Arbitrator to confirm in the Order as part of his or her jurisdictional analysis.[71] Non-signatories of ICC arbitration agreements are therefore protected against the risk of becoming subject to an Order from an ICC Emergency Arbitrator Proceedings in the first place.

29–132 As noted above, the test in art.29(5) is quite different from the test in art.6(4) of the Rules. If it would have been enough for the ICC Court's President to carry out a prima facie test prior to appointing an Emergency Arbitrator, this might have put the ICC Court in a delicate position when having to make the same test once the Request for Arbitration is filed. The Task Force wanted to avoid such a situation, and thereby the risk of conflicting decisions. Such a risk would have been real, since, under the EAP, the President does not hear the responding party, whereas the ICC Court will normally be confronted with "one or more pleas concerning the existence, validity or scope of the arbitration agreement", art.6(3) of the Rules.[72]

The Successor Requirement

29–133 The party or parties having originally signed the arbitration agreement may not be or become parties to emergency arbitration proceedings, since their rights might have been transferred to a third party, which will have become its successor. In such cases, the applicant will have to show how the succession operated and why the signatory requirement extends to the successor. In order for the ICC Court's President to promptly assess whether a party is a successor to a signatory

[68] See the discussion starting at para.29–136 below.
[69] See paras 6–39 et seq. regarding the ICC Court's prima facie test.
[70] See paras 29–31 et seq. above.
[71] See para.29–84 above.
[72] The situation would be comparable where the Respondent does not submit an Answer, and yet the Secretary General sees the need to refer the matter to the ICC Court for a decision pursuant to art.6(4).

of the arbitration agreement, a clear documentary record will have to be filed with the Application.[73]

Exclusion in case of investment treaties

The signatory requirement excludes treaty-based investment disputes from the scope of application of the EAP.[74] **29–134**

Article 29(6): "The Emergency Arbitrator Provisions shall not apply if:

- **a) the arbitration agreement under the Rules was concluded before the date on which the Rules came into force;**
- **b) the parties have agreed to opt out of the Emergency Arbitrator Provisions; or**
- **c) the parties have agreed to another pre-arbitral procedure that provides for the granting of conservatory, interim or similar measures."**

Article 29(6) excludes the application of the EAP in three specific cases: **29–135**

a) Post January 2012 Agreements Required

The ICC Rules have a global reach and are of universal application. Allowing the EAP to have immediate effect, in accordance with art.6(1) of the Rules,[75] on any ICC arbitration agreement was not felt to be appropriate by the Task Force, as the possibility of pre-arbitral Emergency Measures is far-reaching and might not necessarily have been expected by parties having adopted ICC arbitration clauses in their contracts prior to the 2012 Arbitration Rules coming into force.[76] Article 29(6)(a) therefore expressly requires that the ICC arbitration agreement post-dates the coming into force of the 2012 Arbitration Rules for the EAP to apply. From then on, parties are considered as being aware of the Emergency Arbitration provisions in the current Rules. **29–136**

The additional standard ICC arbitration clause, entitled "Arbitration without emergency arbitrator", which is published on the ICC Secretariat's website and in the ICC booklet containing the ICC arbitration and ADR Rules,[77] is designed to increase users' awareness of the new Emergency Arbitrator regime, and of the possibility to opt out from it. **29–137**

[73] Castineira, *op. cit.*, para.30, p.73, recommends that the applicant should produce unambiguous documentary evidence of a successor-signatory relationship.

[74] Castineira, *op. cit.*, paras 34–37 ; Reiner & Aschauer, *op. cit.*, para.612.

[75] Although other well-known international arbitration institutions had, in the meantime, adopted emergency arbitrator provisions in their arbitration rules, this, in and of itself, would hardly have been enough to make ICC arbitration users understand that a similar provision was to be expected in the Rules in the forthcoming edition. Besides, one would have argued against such an expectation given the fact that the ICC has its ICC Pre-Arbitral Referee Rules, which parties are free to adopt or not.

[76] See para.6–123 above concerning the ipso facto application of the 2012 Arbitration Rules at the date of the start of an arbitration, irrespective of when the arbitration agreement was entered into.

[77] ICC Publication No.850 at p.78, and para.29–19 above.

29–138 Needless to say, the parties are free at any point in time to agree on the application of the EAP, even if their original agreement predates January 1, 2012, or if they had originally chosen to exclude them. The ICC Court's President will have no choice but to respect such agreement when checking the admissibility of the Application.[78]

b) "Opting-out" of the Emergency Arbitrator Provisions

29–139 Parties that are wary of the possibility of being subject to pre-arbitral Emergency Measures must exclude the application of the EAP from their ICC arbitration agreement. To that effect, the ICC has provided for a standard arbitration clause providing for ICC arbitration "without emergency arbitrator".[79] This reflects the opting-out method, which, in all likelihood, few users of ICC arbitration clauses will adopt.

29–140 The agreement to opt-out of the EAP can be reached when making the original ICC arbitration agreement, and at any time thereafter. In the latter case, it may be more difficult for the ICC Court's President to become aware of it when deciding whether or not to appoint an Emergency Arbitrator.[80]

29–141 It is worth pointing out here that art.29 is the only provision in the 2012 Arbitration Rules, which expressly provides that the parties can exclude its application by way of agreement. Therefore, they do not form "mandatory" provisions of the Rules, since the parties are authorised to exclude them.[81]

c) "Overriding" pre-arbitral procedure mechanism

29–142 Article 29(6)(c) of the Rules contains a third case, which renders the EAP inapplicable. Unlike in the first and second case, this article contains no clear-cut rule, and may be difficult to apply in practice.[82] The ICC Court's President (and possibly the Emergency Arbitrator) will have to assess whether the parties have agreed (i) "to another pre-arbitral procedure"; and (ii) whether it "provides for the granting of conservatory, interim or similar measures". The underlying rationale of this exclusionary rule is that, where the parties have agreed to some other kind of pre-arbitral provisional relief mechanism, they do not want the EAP to apply in addition thereto. It is therefore thought that implicitly the parties have opted-out the EAP.[83]

29–143 Since in these circumstances, the opting-out of the EAP can at best be implied, the President of the ICC Court will have to be very careful in the analysis of this negative condition.

29–144 In particular, where the parties to an ICC arbitration agreement have agreed to the ICC Pre-Arbitral Referee Rules, the latter should apply instead of the EAP,

[78] See paras 29–33 et seq. above.

[79] See para.29–34 above.

[80] See para.29–35 above regarding the third admissibility condition to be verified by the ICC Court's President.

[81] See a discussion of such "mandatory" provisions of the Rules, above paras 6–23 et seq.

[82] Voser, "Overview of the Most Important Clauses in the Revised ICC Arbitration Rules", 29 ASA Bulletin 4/2011 (December), 783(814).

[83] Fry, Greenberg, Mazza, *Guide*, *op. cit.*, para.3–1102 refer to an "implied opt-out".

since under art.2 of the ICC Pre-Arbitral Referee Rules, the Pre-Arbitral Referee has the power to order conservatory measures.[84] The ICC Pre-Arbitral Referee Rules have not been abolished by the ICC, and, although they are no longer actively marketed, they remain in force.[85]

The ICC Pre-Arbitral Referee Rules were designed to reduce the need for recourse to the national courts with respect to interim or conservatory measures before the Tribunal is put in place. Pursuant to art.2.1 of the ICC Pre-Arbitral Referee Rules, the referee has the right "(a) to order any conservatory measures or any measures of restoration that are urgently necessary to prevent either immediate damage or irreparable loss and so to safeguard any of the rights or property of one of the parties; (b) [. . .]; (d) to order any measures necessary to preserve or establish evidence".[86] **29–145**

FIDIC's Dispute Adjudication Boards

In construction contracts exceeding a certain volume, one finds provisions for Dispute Adjudication Boards ("DAB") quite often, whether standing or ad hoc. Various organisations offer rules for DAB proceedings. In 2004, the ICC issued the ICC Dispute Board Rules governing the creation and operation of dispute boards.[87] In the FIDIC Conditions of Contract for Construction, DABs are foreseen in the so-called Red, Yellow, Silver and Gold Books in their respective art.20.4.[88] Under the Red Book, the most widely used set of the FIDIC Conditions, once a dispute is referred to a DAB, a "binding" decision must be made by the DAB within 84 days of its seizure. If a notice of dissatisfaction is filed, amicable settlement shall take place within a maximum of 56 days. If no settlement can be reached within that time limit, the dissatisfied party may then, but only then have recourse to ICC arbitration. **29–146**

Pursuant to art.20.4 of the Red Book, a DAB can order interim and conservatory measures in the context of its adjudicatory powers. The scope of measures that a DAB can order is, however, large; and goes well beyond what an Emergency Arbitrator can do. A DAB may, for instance, order the employer to pay out advances or milestone payments, thereby alleviating the cash-flow needs of the contractor. In such cases, while the Emergency Arbitrator may in principle not order such measures, as they would go beyond the scope of provisional injunctive relief. **29–147**

[84] For a comparison of the powers of the decision-maker under these two sets of Rules, see Bühler, "ICC Pre-Arbitral Referee and Emergency Arbitrator Proceedings Compared" (2011) ICC Arb. Bull., vol. 22 Special Supplement, pp.93 et seq.

[85] As mentioned at para.29–18 above, ICC Publication Nos 838 and 846 contained both the 1998 Arbitration Rules and the 1990 ICC Pre-Arbitral Referee Rules. ICC Publication No.850 reproduces the 2012 Arbitration Rules, now together with the ICC's ADR Rules of 2004, but without the ICC Pre-Arbitral Referee Rules. The latter can still be downloaded from the ICC's website, *http://www.iccwbo.org* [accessed November 24, 2013].

[86] Reiner & Aschauer, *op. cit.*, para.616.

[87] ICC publication No.829.

[88] Red Book (1999), Yellow Book (1999), Silver Book, (1999), and Gold Book (2008). In 2011, FIDIC published its "Conditions of Subcontract for Construction", which is "back-to-back" with the Red Book.

29–148 As mentioned, DABs can be ad hoc or standing.[89] For the President to exclude the application of the EAP, it would seem necessary that a DAB is already in place when an Application is filed under art.29. It is not infrequent, that parties agree in their construction contracts upon standing DABs, but then fail to appoint them. In such cases, it would not seem appropriate to imply that the mere reference in the contract to a DAB is meant to be an exclusion of the EAP under the 2012.

Article 29(7): "The Emergency Arbitrator Provisions are not intended to prevent any party from seeking urgent interim or conservatory measures from a competent judicial authority at any time prior to making an application for such measures, and in appropriate circumstances even thereafter, pursuant to the Rules. Any application for such measures from a competent judicial authority shall not be deemed to be an infringement or a waiver of the arbitration agreement. Any such application and any measures taken by the judicial authority must be notified without delay to the Secretariat."

29–149 This provision is identical to art.28(2) as regards access to state courts to obtain interim relief, whether prior or after having seized the Emergency Arbitrator.

29–150 This provision was necessary to avoid the risk that a state court faced with a request for provisional relief denies such a request on jurisdictional grounds, by arguing that, by agreeing to ICC arbitration and its Emergency Arbitrator regime, the parties have effectively ruled out the state court's jurisdiction to entertain requests for interim or conservatory measures.[90]

29–151 The EAP are not intended to exclude the jurisdiction of state courts to grant any kind of interim or conservatory measures. The new EAP were designed to provide parties to an ICC arbitration agreement with an additional option to obtain swift provisional relief, and are thus premised on concurrent jurisdiction with the state courts.[91] By providing an alternative to recourse to state courts to obtain provisional relief, the "one-stop shop" approach under the Rules is meant to increase the overall attraction and effectiveness of the 2012 Arbitration Rules. However, whenever the chances of obtaining effective and prompt provisional relief exist only in the State courts, which for instance would be true whenever it is necessary to have an order issued by surprise and thus ex parte, parties should have the possibility of seeking relief from state courts.

[89] Castineira, *idem*, para.25, p.71.

[90] Voser, *idem*, at 814 ; Castineira, *idem*, at para.15; see Berger, *op. cit.*, with respect to the pre-arbitral referee procedure, at p.86.

[91] It is an altogether different option whether, as a matter of public policy, parties can exclude in advance the jurisdiction of state courts to grant provisional relief.

CHAPTER 6

AWARDS

Article 30 Time Limit for the Final Award

1. **The time limit within which the arbitral tribunal must render its final award is six months. Such time limit shall start to run from the date of the last signature by the arbitral tribunal or by the parties of the Terms of Reference or, in the case of application of Article 23(3), the date of the notification to the arbitral tribunal by the Secretariat of the approval of the Terms of Reference by the Court. The Court may fix a different time limit based upon the procedural timetable established pursuant to Article 24(2).**
2. **The Court may extend the time limit pursuant to a reasoned request from the arbitral tribunal or on its own initiative if it decides it is necessary to do so.**[1]

Introductory remarks

The ICC seeks to expedite arbitration proceedings to ensure that ICC arbitration is cost effective.[2] Therefore, the ICC sets a two-month limit from the transmission of the file to the arbitral Tribunal to the signing of the Terms of Reference and a six-month limit after signing the Terms of Reference for the rendering of the Award. Both limits are subject to extension and in almost every case the six-month limit for rendering the Award is extended at least once, and often several times. **30–1**

Pursuant to art.24(2), the Tribunal is required to provide a procedural timetable as soon as possible after the signing of the Terms of Reference. This procedural timetable is usually arrived at after consultation with the parties. Frequently, it will provide for a schedule for submitting memorials and evidence that exceeds that six-month period provided for in art.30(1). This will be an indication to the **30–2**

[1] Article 30 corresponds to art.24 of the 1998 Rules. The only substantive change is the addition of the last sentence in art.30(1).

[2] See Introduction, para.0–52 regarding Principle 7 of ICC arbitrations.

ICC Court that the extensions to the six-month period should be granted to accommodate the period set out in the procedural timetable. However, despite the existence of a procedural timetable, it was the practice of the ICC Court to extend the time limit only on a three-month basis in order to be able to monitor the proper progress of the proceedings.[3] In recent years, not the least due to the increase of cases pending at the ICC that need to be monitored all alike, the ICC Court has changed its practice and fully integrates the requirements of the procedural timetable when fixing, and, if necessary, extending the time limit for rendering the award. A new third sentence was added to art.30(1) to reflect that new practice and to provide a clear basis for it.

30–3 The procedural timetable may have to be adjusted based on external factors, such as the delays encountered by the parties in preparing and submitting their evidence. In many instances, the parties will be agreeable to grant the other party additional time for filing memorials and evidence, provided that they are granted a similar extension. The effect may, however, be to render the original dates for the hearings impractical, which in itself often raises problems due to the commitments of the members of the Tribunal, as well as the parties that may result in further delay.[4]

30–4 In addition, there may be related or parallel disputes between or involving the parties. This gives rise to issues of lis pendens, staying of proceedings and state court injunctions. These issues are discussed under art. 22(2).

Article 30(1): "The time limit within which the arbitral tribunal must render its final award is six months. Such time limit shall start to run from the date of the last signature by the arbitral tribunal or by the parties of the Terms of Reference or, in the case of application of Article 23(3), the date of the notification to the arbitral tribunal by the Secretariat of the approval of the Terms of Reference by the Court. The Court may fix a different time limit based upon the procedural timetable established pursuant to Article 24(2)."

Six month time limit

30–5 The time limit for rendering a final award remains six months. Despite some renewed debate during the revision of the 1998 Rules, the ICC Task Force decided not to change this time limit in the first sentence of art.30(1). While in most cases, this time limit is not met, it is intended to provide a target date.

30–6 The last signature on the Terms of Reference, i.e. typically that of the sole arbitrator, or of the president of the Tribunal, is the starting point of the six month time limit. The Secretariat always advises the Parties and the Tribunal of the starting date, once it has received a signed original copy of the Terms of Reference. In case of non-signature of the Terms of Reference by one of the parties, the

[3] The practice has been criticised as unrealistic as the procedural timetable sets out the realistic—and often agreed—timeline for the arbitration. However, the ICC Court maintained this practice for decades due to its concern that the ICC Court with the help of the Secretariat follow developments in the arbitral proceedings, i.e. to allow the ICC Court to fulfil its supervisory function at regular intervals.

[4] See para.23–73.

six-month time limit only starts to run upon the Secretariat's notification of the approval of the Terms of Reference by the ICC Court in the second sentence of art.30(1). In practice, the starting date of the six-month time limit is not an issue in either case.

Article 30(1) refers to a final Award, which means an Award resolving the dispute and bringing the arbitration to its end.[5] It is of course conceivable that the Tribunal with or without the consent of the parties will issue interim or partial Awards. The fact that the Tribunal has issued interim or partial Awards may well reflect the complexity of the proceedings and therefore provide a basis for an extension of the period in art.30(1) to render the final Award. However, it is the final Award that is referred to in the Rules. **30–7**

For a Tribunal to meet the six-month time limit, it is not enough to send the draft award to the Secretariat. Rather, the latter will have to be scrutinised and approved, and signed by the Tribunal prior to the expiry of the time limit. For instance, if delays occur in obtaining the signature from one of the members of the Tribunal, the Court will have to extend the time limit pursuant to art.30(2).[6] **30–8**

The actual length of ICC arbitrations varies widely. For mid-size arbitrations, the period is generally longer than 12 months from the date on which the Tribunal is constituted. Therefore, in accepting ICC arbitration and in conducting proceedings parties and the Tribunal must keep in mind both the requirements of the Rules and the practicalities of conducting the arbitration when drafting the procedural timetable. **30–9**

There is a broad range of reasons for the fact that most ICC arbitrations are not completed within six months after the signing of the Terms of Reference and that many take two years or more to complete. The most acceptable reason for additional time for the proceedings is an agreement between the parties. The principle of party autonomy is found throughout the Rules and if the parties agree on a more extended time frame for the proceedings, then, within reasonable limits, there appears to be no justification for that not to be accepted.[7] **30–10**

In many cases, extending the period is not a matter of agreement, but is the result of external factors. If the factor is the availability of the members of the Tribunal, then the criticism has to take into account the legal obligations of the member of the Tribunal to conduct the proceedings in accordance with the Rules, reasonable commitments of arbitrators and the possibility that all parties have under art.15(1) to request that an arbitrator be replaced. Moreover, it is submitted that, if a co-arbitrator occasions the delay, it is the responsibility of the president to take whatever steps are available to ensure that the co-arbitrator does not cause undue delay in the proceedings. **30–11**

If the delay is caused by the parties (e.g. request for extension of time to submit their statements, long hearing period), then the Tribunal will have to weigh the justification for such a request, the delay and the concerns with due process **30–12**

[5] See art.2(iii) for a description of the term Award, which includes inter alia, an interim, partial or final Award; see also Hunter, "Final Report on Interim and Partial Award" (1990) ICC ICArb Bull. Vol.1 No.2, p.26. As to the meaning of the term award, as opposed to procedural order, see the discussion under art.33 at paras 33–4 et seq.

[6] Reiner & Aschauer, *op. cit.*, para.624.

[7] See para.0– 46.

against the Tribunal's obligations under the Rules to "conduct the arbitration in an expeditious and cost-effective manner", art.30(1).

30–13 Some Tribunals seek to address the issue of the incentive for delay by discussing a detailed procedural order at the same time as the Terms of Reference. To the extent that the Tribunal is able to obtain the parties' agreement on the procedure at an early stage, it will provide a baseline for future reference if there are attempts to delay the proceedings. Moreover, the lawyers involved in the proceedings will generally work to the deadlines that they have agreed to.

Time limit commensurate with needs under procedural time table

30–14 Pursuant to the 2012 Rules, the ICC Court is now expressly empowered to fix a different time limit pursuant to the procedural timetable established in accordance with art.24(2). This provision is consistent with a practice that it started in recent years. Essentially, when receiving the Procedural Timetable, the ICC Court will fix a time limit, which will go by one month or more beyond the last event mentioned in the Timetable.

30–15 The time limit for rendering the final award will be a result of the duration foreseen in the procedural timetable to allow a Tribunal to reach such award. Often the procedural timetable is silent about the dates of post-hearing activities, i.e. the post-hearing briefs or the oral argument that will follow the (evidentiary) hearing, as well as the submission of costs and the target date for rendering the Award.

30–16 Article 38(1) provides the parties may shorten the various time limits set out in the Rules. Where this happens, it is likely to be reflected in the procedural timetable. In these cases, which are very rare, the ICC Court might fix an even shorter time limit than the standard six months to render the award.[8] It follows, however, from art.38(2) that even where the parties have agreed on a time limit shorter than six months for rendering the award, the ICC Court maintains the power to extend it if necessary.

Article 30(2): "The Court may extend the time limit pursuant to a reasoned request from the arbitral tribunal or on its own initiative if it decides it is necessary to do so."

30–17 Article 30(2) deals with extensions for the time to render Awards under the Rules. If there is no extension of the time limit to render an Award in accordance with art.30(1), then the Tribunal is arguably functus officio. However, generally extensions are virtually automatic, and are never refused, as it is difficult to conceive that the ICC Court would oblige the Tribunal to either proceed or to accept that it becomes functus officio.[9] What the ICC Court may do in some instances is to extend the period for a limited period of one or two months to put pressure on the Tribunal to submit a draft Award.

30–18 Article 30 does not as such deal with the requirements of national law. However, by accepting the Rules, parties are agreeing that the ICC Court may extend these

[8] Reiner & Aschauer, *op. cit.*, paras 625 and 626.

[9] Fry, Greenberg, Mazza, *Guide, op. cit.*, para.3–1130.

time limits in accordance with art.30. Therefore, it is difficult to see how national time limits on the time to render arbitral Awards can be applicable. Indeed, the better view is that this provision permits the ICC Court to extend deadlines even where national law at the place of arbitration would otherwise limit the period in which the Tribunal would have to render an Award.

The ICC Court's right to extend the time limits at its own initiative as provided by art.30(2) is characteristic for an administered and supervised arbitration, such as the ICC's.[10] This is a great advantage compared to ad hoc arbitration where arbitrators have to take care of prolongations of the time limit to render the award, where applicable, by appropriate means.[11] In the *Consorts Juliet* case, the Award was set aside by the French Supreme Court because it was rendered after the time limit set by French law and the Tribunal failed to obtain an extension from the French courts in accordance with art.1456 (current art.1463) of the French CPC.[12] **30–19**

The ICC Court generally deals with issues relating to extensions at Committee Sessions described in Annex 1 Pt I. At those sessions, the Secretariat provides background as to the reason for an extension if the extension is out of the ordinary. An extension that is in accordance with the procedural timetable transmitted with the Terms of Reference or subsequently amended would be approved generally as a matter of course. However, where there is an unexplained delay in rendering the Award, the ICC Court will grant an extension, but at the same time instruct the Secretariat to contact the Tribunal to discuss the situation. **30–20**

Once the draft award has become due, as per the Tribunal's notification of its date of submission pursuant to art.27(b), the ICC Court will generally grant short extensions only, i.e. a month, and will request appropriate updates from the sole arbitrator or president of the Tribunal. Phone calls from the counsel in charge of the case, the Secretary General or even the President of the ICC Court to enquire about the status may follow. The purpose of this hands-on control of the arbitrators' work is to reduce the still far too long delays in draft awards reaching the ICC Court. **30–21**

In extreme cases, where the Tribunal is not proceeding with the arbitration, the result may be for the ICC Court to apply the replacement procedure under art.15(2). Nevertheless, this would have to be a case in which the ICC Court saw no reasonable prospect for an Award as it would result in substantial duplication of costs.[13] As a result, it is much more likely that an extension will be granted but that the issue of the time taken by the Tribunal to prepare the Award will be taken into account in setting the fees for the Tribunal under art.31. **30–22**

As mentioned above, the ICC Court extends the time limit on a case-by-case basis, generally distinguishing cases in which one or several procedural steps remain to be completed and those in which only the final award remains to be **30–23**

[10] See Introduction, para.0–18 regarding Principle 1 of ICC arbitrations.

[11] In ad hoc arbitration agreements, it is not rare to see a time limit for rendering the award.

[12] Cass civ 1re, December 6, 2005, *Consorts Juliet v Castagnet et al*, SIAR 2006:1 p.149, note Degos; (2006) Rev Arb No.1 p.126, note Jarrosson; (2006) JCP G II 10066 p.852, note Clay; Paillusseau, "L'arbitre responsable du délai d'arbitrage" (2006) JCP I 129, p.666; Fouchard, Gaillard & Goldman, *op. cit.*, para.868, p.500 and para.1149, p.621. See also para.40–30 regarding contractual liability of the arbitrator.

[13] Removal proceedings under art.15 are very rare and they are much more likely to occur with respect to issues arising much earlier in the proceedings, such as with respect to drafting of the Terms of Reference under art.18.

drafted, in which case the ICC Court will be more cautious in granting an extension, looking at whether the Tribunal is the cause of any delay in issuing the Award.[14]

30–24 Under art.30(2), the ICC Court is not required to consult with or notify the extension of the period to render the Award to the parties. In the *Skanska* case, the Paris Court of Appeal held that this did not cause the period for the arbitration to expire and noted that the party challenging the Award participated in the proceedings after the expiration of the period in question.[15] If a party is dissatisfied with the extensions, it may raise the issue with the Secretariat informally or in writing. Since it is the ICC Court's[16] (and therefore the Secretariat's) responsibility to monitor the proceedings, this informal contact seems appropriate. Once the arbitral proceedings have been closed by the Tribunal, the parties are put into a "waiting position", and will not have to take any further steps as part of their participation in the arbitration. In practice, the Secretariat informs the Tribunal of the extension and normally always sends a copy to the parties as well.[17] There is nothing wrong with the Tribunal writing to the parties as well to report on the status, in particular once the proceedings have been closed.[18]

30–25 According to a recent Paris Court of Appeal decision, the ICC may be liable for its failure to extend the time limit for the final award.[19] Finding that a contractual relationship existed between the ICC and a litigant, the Court found that the exclusion of liability in art.34 of the 1998 Rules was invalid and that, pursuant to its contractual obligations, the ICC must organise and administer an efficient arbitration. However, the Court rejected Claimant's assertion that the ICC had failed to properly control time limits, finding that parties also have obligations to cooperate with procedure regarding time limits. Previously, the French Supreme Court had ruled that arbitrators are contractually liable for the setting aside of an award they render when they could have requested an extension from the *juge d'appui*, but did not.[20]

14 See para.30–10 above; Fry, Greenberg, Mazza, *Guide, op. cit.*, pp.313–314.

15 Cass civ 1re, July 6, 2005, *Société AIC v Société Skanska*: "[. . .] by virtue of the provisions of the Arbitration Rules of the International Chamber of Commerce, extensions of time need not to be notified to the parties themselves; AIC, by its active behaviour and payment of the advance on costs made during the deliberation, has undoubtedly accepted to participate in the arbitration until the rendering of the award and the extensions of time limit, and has waived to claim any irregularity on this ground. [. . .]" (Authors' translation); (2006) Rev Arb No.2 p.429, note Pic; (2005) Dalloz p.3061, note Clay; Paris, March 6, 2003, Société *AIC v Société Skanska* (2004) Rev Arb no.3 p.886, note Bensaude; see also Paris, June 12, 2003, *SA Citel v Mungovan* (2004) Rev Arb No.1 p.135: "by virtue of Article 24 of the Rules of Arbitration of the ICC, the period set for the Tribunal to decide is extended either pursu=ant to a reasoned decision of the Tribunal or spontaneously by the Court; that it therefore is to the Court of Arbitration within the framework of its institutional functions organising and monitoring the procedure to extend it for the parties without being required to notify the parties" (Authors' translation).

16 Bruna "Control of time limits by the International Court of Arbitration" (1996) ICC ICArb Bull Vol.7 No.2, p.72.

17 Thereby learning the lessons from the French *Skanska* case, where the claimant complained about the lack of notification of the ICC Court's time extension, see n.15 above with further references.

18 See art.27 regarding the closing of the proceedings and the date for submission of draft awards.

19 CA Paris, *SNF v International Chamber of Commerce,* January 22, 2009, (2010) Rev. Arb. No. 2, 314. See Jarrosson, "Note – 22 janvier 2009, Cour d'appel de Paris (1re Ch. C.)" (2010) Rev. Arb., No. 2, 320; Kiffer, "Comment on the Paris Court of Appeal Decision in *SNF v. International Chamber of Commerce*" (2009) J Int'l Law No. 4, 579.

20 Jarrosson, "Note – Cour de Cassation (1re Ch. Civ.) 6 décembre 2005" (2006) Rev. Arb. No.1, 127.

Article 31 Making of the Award

1. **When the arbitral tribunal is composed of more than one arbitrator, an award is made by a majority decision. If there is no majority, the award shall be made by the president of the arbitral tribunal alone.**
2. **The award shall state the reasons upon which it is based.**
3. **The award shall be deemed to be made at the place of the arbitration and on the date stated therein.**[1]

Introductory remarks

Article 31 is a central provision of the ICC Rules, as it deals with the making of the Award, and thus the decision of the Tribunal that will ultimately end the parties' dispute, at least before the Tribunal.[2] Article 31 deals with three different matters. The first paragraph refers to the requirement of a majority within the Tribunal, and the possibility for the President to decide alone. The second paragraph imposes the obligation to provide reasons for the Award. Finally, the third paragraph refers to the place and the date where the Award is made. **31–1**

Article 31(1): "When the arbitral tribunal is composed of more than one arbitrator, an award is made by a majority decision. If there is no majority, the award shall be made by the president of the arbitral tribunal alone."

[1] Article 31 corresponds to art.25 of the 1998 Rules. There have been no changes to the text from the 1998 Rules.

[2] See Lloyd, Darmon, Ancel, Dervaird, Liebscher & Verbist, "Drafting Awards in ICC Arbitration" (2005) ICC ICArb Bull Vol.16 No.2, p.12.

31–2 Tribunals are intended to be collegial in nature. The objective of most presidents is to reach a unanimous agreement on an Award or agreement on an Award that all members of the Tribunal are willing to sign even if they have reservations about specific findings. This preference for unanimity is a reflection of various factors, including the perception that unanimously-rendered Awards are more likely to be accepted by the parties and enforceable before the courts. Most Awards rendered in ICC arbitrations are rendered by unanimity.[3] In 2002 and 2012, 359 and 460 Awards respectively were approved by the ICC Court. Of those Awards 16 (4.5 per cent) in 2002 and 52 (19 per cent) in 2012 were not based on unanimity.[4] There is no easy explanation as to why the number of dissents has increased over the 10-year period in question. However, as the number of arbitrations and arbitrators has increased, there is perhaps less collegiality or pressure to conform amongst arbitrators.

31–3 If no unanimity can be reached, art.31(1) comes into play, as it allows a Tribunal's decision to become effective by majority decision or by a decision of the president if there is no majority. Almost invariably, the arbitrator who is unwilling to support the vote of the majority is the one nominated by the party against whom the decision is rendered. But there may be cases, where the president is not even able to reach a majority. In such case, the second sentence of art.31(1) permits the president to render the decision alone. The aim of art.31(1) is to allow the arbitral process to be completed by an Award, even if there exists no unanimity or majority within a three-member Tribunal.[5]

Tribunal's deliberations

31–4 Article 31 applies to Awards whether final, interim or partial.[6] To arrive at an Award, the Tribunal will have to deliberate. The deliberations of the Tribunal are confidential[7] and require a lot of trust among the members of the Tribunal.[8] While the arbitrators' deliberations often constitute an ongoing pro-

[3] See the ICC Statistical reports for 2002 and 2012, respectively (2003) ICC Bull ICArb Vol. 14 No.1, p.16 and (2013) ICC Bull ICArb Vol. 24 No. 1, p.15. See also Bühler & Jarvin, *op. cit.*, art.25(1) para.2, p.261.

[4] Note, however, that the number of 359 and 460 Awards does not include 36 and 31 Awards by consent, where by definition, there is no room for dissent.

[5] In 2012, no case was reported where a president had to render an Award alone. See (2013) ICC ICArb Bull Vol. 24 No.1, at p.15. The same situation applied in 2002, see (2003) ICC Bull ICArb Vol. 14 No.1, p.16.

[6] See para. 2–16.

[7] *Certain Underwriters at Lloyd's, London v Argonaut Insurance Co* (United States District Court, Northern District of California, para.14–64 n.33. (Footnote 11: "Certain Underwriters cite other procedural irregularities. It contends Interim Order No.2 was issued before Certain Underwriters' arbitrator ever learned of [. . .] it. But this claim gets into the internal deliberation of the panel, which the Court concludes is not warranted in this case." In the Matter of the *Petition of Fertilizantes Fosfatados Mexicanos, S.A.*, 751 F.Supp. 467, 468 n.1 (S.D.N.Y. 1990), 2003 US Dist. LEXIS 8796. ('This case should not be viewed as a precedent in any way for inquiry into the deliberations of an arbitration panel. Such matters should remain confidential and inviolate.')." (2003) YBCA Vol.XXVIII p.1248; 2003 US Dist. LEXIS 8796. More generally as to arbitrators' obligation of confidentiality, see para.22–45 above.

[8] Madsen & Eriksson, "Deliberations of the Arbitral Tribunal–Analysis of Reasoned Awards from a Swedish Perspective" (2006) SIAR 2006:2, p.1; Derains, "La pratique du délibéré arbitral" in *Liber Amicorum in honour of Robert Briner, op. cit.*, p.221 and *ASA Special Series No.29* (September 2007), *op. cit.*, p.16; Leboulanger, "Principe de collégialité et délibéré arbitral" in *Mélanges en*

cess, they usually begin at the latest during the evidentiary hearings with respect to the credibility of various witnesses. Oral testimony frequently has a significant impact on Tribunals, as it brings the evidence to life and may highlight discrepancies. The natural tendency of the arbitrators—like counsel—is to review the impact of each day's testimony as the hearings progress. This immediate impact of oral testimony may be affected if there is a transcript of the proceedings, particularly if that transcript is available on a same day basis. The Tribunal's deliberations may continue immediately after the evidentiary hearings or after the legal argument and, in many cases, the Tribunal will wish to set aside dates to review the material in detail.

The role of each arbitrator in deliberations is important. As noted by the French Supreme Court in the *Dutco* case,[9] one of the basic requirements in ICC arbitration is that the parties be treated equally as regards the selection of the members of the Tribunal. It is a natural consequence of this principle that this equality of treatment continues as regards the participation of the members of the Tribunal in the decision-making process. **31–5**

As the Paris Court of Appeal stated: **31–6**

> "the requirement of deliberations is a basic principle of the procedure which guarantees the judicial nature of the decision arrived at by the arbitral tribunal; [. . .] the principle of collegiality supposes, as indicated above, that each arbitrator will have the possibility of discussing each decision with his colleagues."[10] (Authors' translation.)

Therefore, usually, there will be meetings among the three members of the Tribunal to discuss certain issues. If one member is not available, then the president will have to ensure that the arbitrator is apprised of the deliberations and given an opportunity to express his opinion prior to any decision being taken. The absence of an arbitrator, however, should not prevent or unduly delay the completion of the Award. As with hearings, the usual principle should be reasonable notice to the arbitrator so that he can participate in the deliberations. If a an arbitrator fails to participate in deliberations, the other arbitrators may proceed as long as he has been granted the opportunity to participate in the deliberations.[11] **31–7**

l'honneur de François Knoepfler, op. cit., p.259; Fortier, "The Tribunal's deliberation" in *The Leading Arbitrators' Guide to International Arbitration, op. cit.*, p.391; Bredin, "Le secret du délibéré arbitral" in *Etudes offertes à Pierre Bellet, op. cit.*, p.71 and "Retour au délibéré arbitral" in *Liber Amicorum Claude Reymond, op. cit.*, p.43; Alonso, "Deliberation and Drafting Awards in International Arbitration", in M.A. Fernández-Ballesteros & David Arias (eds.), Liber *Amicorum Bernardo Cremades* (2010), 131.

[9] See para.12–10 n.4.

[10] Paris, January 16, 2003, *Société des télécommunications internationales du Cameroun (Intelcam) v SA France Télécom* (2004) Rev Arb No.2 p.369.

[11] The replacement of arbitrators is discussed under art.15. For an illustration of how an arbitrator was apparently rendered unavailable see the *Himpurna* case, para.6–143. See also Swiss Supreme Court, *X Ltd v Y BV*, February 1, 2002, *http://www.bger.ch* [accessed November 24, 2013] (refusal of the court to set aside an Award on the ground that an arbitrator failed to attend the deliberation. The challenge against an arbitrator does not impose an ipso facto a stay of the arbitration proceedings).

31–8 Deliberations are now frequently carried out in part by exchanges in writing; email permits attaching of relevant documents in electronic format and tripartite discussion of the issues. At various times the arbitrators may meet to deliberate, and according to the Rules, they may so do "at any location [the Tribunal] considers appropriate" (art.18(3)). Very often, the arbitrators' deliberations will take place over the phone, sometimes even by videoconference. Depending on the complexity of the issues, and each arbitrator's participation, these deliberations can last several hours, and depending on the complexity, variety or number of issues, may be going on over an extended period of time.

31–9 The participants in deliberations should be the arbitrators. If the Tribunal has an administrative secretary,[12] then the secretary may in some instances attend the deliberations. However, the secretary's role should be that of assisting in locating the evidence (e.g. a specific document or reference in the hearing transcript) and thus be of logistical help (in particular in cases with numerous and voluminous exhibit files) and observing, rather than acting as an active participant in the deliberations. The secretary may also assist in the drafting of certain parts of the Award, provided it leaves him or her with no discretion in the assessment of facts or analysis of legal argument.[13] As stated by a learned author "the judgment making really takes place only at the time and through the drafting of the decision – form and substance being not separable".[14] When the secretary appointed by the Tribunal is a paralegal rather than a trained lawyer, then it is very unlikely that the secretary will assume any drafting role.

31–10 Deliberations take time, and are only productive if and once the arbitrators are fully familiar with the files. It is therefore most sensible to have the Tribunal deliberate shortly after the final hearing. An efficient president of the Tribunal will therefore ensure in advance of the final hearing that in each of the arbitrator's diaries time is reserved for joint deliberation either immediately after the final hearing or shortly after receipt of the post-hearing submissions, if any.[15]

31–11 The deliberation process will be facilitated if the truly dispositive issues have been identified, and if all three arbitrators know the arguments advanced

[12] See also Donovan, "Introduction to the Sixteenth Annual Workshop of the Institute for Transnational Arbitration" (2007) Arb Int Vol.23 No.2, p.163, at pp.250-251; Clay, "Le Secrétaire arbitral" (2005) Rev Arb No.4, p.931; Partasides, "The Fourth Arbitrator? The Role of Secretaries to Tribunals in International Arbitration" (2002) Arb Int Vol.18 No.2, p.147; Schwartz, "On the Subject of Administrative Secretaries" (1996) ASA Bull Vol.14 No.1, p.32. In 2012, the ICC Court revised its note on the appointment, duties and remuneration of administrative secretaries which sets out the policy and practice of the ICC International Court of Arbitration ("Court") and its Secretariat regarding the engagement of Administrative Secretaries by Arbitral Tribunals. It applies with respect to any Administrative Secretary appointed on or after August 1, 2012. See also, Joint Report of the International Commercial Disputes Committee and the Committee on Arbitration of the NYC Bar Association, Secretaries to International Arbitral Tribunals, 2006, 17 Am. Rev. Int'l Arb. 575.

[13] Reiner & Aschauer, para.641 n.382 refer to the formal elements of the Award, such as the names of the parties and the procedural history.

[14] Lalive, "*Dérives Arbitrales I*" (2005) ASA Bull. Vol. 23 No 1, p. 587 (590). Author's translation ("l'acte de juger ne se réalise vraiment qu'au moment et dans la rédaction de la décision – forme et fond étant inséparables").

[15] Tschanz, "The Award–How To Structure it, How Detailed? Orders And Reasons, Adding Insult To Injury" *ASA Special Series No.29* (September 2007), *op. cit.*, p.25.

by the parties in that respect. Through deliberations, it may suddenly become clear that the parties have wrongly focused on certain points, or that even if one legal requirement would be met, others would still not be satisfied.

Reasons for disagreements amongst members of the Tribunal

To the extent that a Tribunal is not unanimous on an issue, one would expect the majority or the president, if there is no majority, to set out the reasons for the decision. The minority arbitrator may insert his or her comments and reasons for disagreement in the Award, but sign the Award. Or the minority arbitrator may file a dissent, in particular if he or she is unwilling to sign the overall Award. The reasons that can lead to one or the other solution depend on the personalities involved and the nature of the disagreement. Although the dissent is sometimes attributed to pressure from the party who appointed an arbitrator, it may well have a more fundamental basis. The minority arbitrator may feel that the decision of the majority or the president is fundamentally contrary to justice and therefore be unwilling to cooperate with respect to it. **31–12**

If there is a disagreement in the Tribunal, then there is an issue as to what can and should be discussed in the Award given the principle of confidentiality of deliberations. If one of the issues in the proceeding is, for example, whether the Tribunal acted on a collegial basis, the extent of the minority arbitrator's participation in the deliberations is relevant. If the issue is not procedural but a question of weighing the evidence, then it is arguably the evidence and not the deliberations that are relevant. However, in the end, the weight that will be attributed to a dissent (or to a discussion of the different positions of the members of the Tribunal in the Award itself) will depend on the court of the annulment or enforcement proceedings. **31–13**

As discussed under arts 2 and 31(2), an Award is made up of various elements of procedure, fact and law together with a dispositive section. With respect to issues as to which the parties are in disagreement and that are relevant to the decision, the Tribunal will have to reach a decision. An Award will usually consist of a series of decisions as to which the members of the Tribunal may agree on some and disagree on others. **31–14**

A majority decision with respect to each matter decided by the Tribunal is sufficient under the Rules. As noted above, if there is no majority, the president may decide the issue under art.31(1). **31–15**

As a result, an Award may consist of a series of decisions as to which there are varying majorities (or lack of a majority) on various issues. If all arbitrators sign the Award, the Tribunal does not usually identify the arbitrators who agreed or disagreed with respect to decisions arrived at by majority given the confidentiality of the deliberation of the Tribunal. An arbitrator who signs an Award without reservation is approving its contents, although those contents may include reservations by one arbitrator. If the arbitrator signs the Award indicating that he or she is making reservations (set out in a dissent, for example), then his or her signature basically confirms he or she has participated in the process of making the collegial decision resulting in the Award.[16] **31–16**

[16] See paras 31–2 et seq.

31–17 If one arbitrator does not agree with the Award or part of it, he or she may write a dissent based on the fact that he or she has a "diverging decision" or a "diverging argumentation".[17] Dissenting arbitrators will normally sign the award, despite their disagreement, as part of their duties as an arbitrator. If they are reluctant to do so, the Secretariat can play a useful role by explaining the situation to them. If the minority arbitrator nevertheless refuses to sign the award, the president of the Tribunal will mention so in the award and reason why a signature could not be obtained from that arbitrator.[18] The ICC Court generally communicates dissents to the parties although they are not scrutinised by the ICC Court and are not part of the Award.[19] In France, for example, they are considered as "elements of fact" by the courts in annulment proceedings and have no legal value as such.[20]

31–18 An interesting question arises when the ICC Court has approved the draft majority Award subject to either suggested or proposed modifications. In such a case, the dissenting arbitrator remains involved by the majority in the deliberation and final drafting of the final version of the Award. The dissenting arbitrator must be provided with an opportunity to participate in the deliberation given the collegial nature of the Tribunal's work. However, if the dissenting arbitrator is provided with the opportunity to participate in the deliberations and fails to do so, then it is difficult to see any breach of the obligation of collegiality. As noted by the Lebanese Supreme Court in ICC case *Henco v Moawad*,[21] the participation to the deliberation is not the sole responsibility of the president of the Tribunal, but of all arbitrators. It is therefore incumbent to the dissenting arbitrator, like any members of the Tribunal, when appropriate, to express his or her additional opinion to the majority, as soon as the decision of the ICC Court has been communicated to the Tribunal.

Article 31(2): "The award shall state the reasons upon which it is based."

Requirement of reasoned Awards

31–19 It is a basic requirement of an ICC Award that it be reasoned. Therefore, whether the law of the place of arbitration or the rules of law applicable to the arbitration require a reasoned Award or not, a Tribunal must furnish one under the Rules, unless both the parties and the ICC Court agree otherwise. This has happened in the practice of ICC arbitrations in a few cases, but the ICC Court will accept such derogation from its Rules only on a case-by-case basis and

[17] Hunter, "Final Report on Dissenting and Separate Opinions", *op. cit.*; Smit, "Dissenting Opinions in Arbitration" (2004) ICC ICArb Bull Vol.15 No.1, p.37. See also Tercier, "Dissenting Opinions and Majority Decision", ASA Conference of January 26, 2007; Geneva, *The Resolution of the Dispute (from the Hearing to the Award)*; Rees, "Dissenting Opinions: Can they Fulfil a Beneficial Role?", (2009) Arb. Int'l No. 3, 329; Arroyo, "Dealing with Dissenting Opinions in the Award: Some Options for the Tribunal," (2008) ASA Bulletin No. 3, 437.

[18] See art.31(1) of the UNCITRAL Model Law.

[19] *Fry, Greenberg & Mazza, Guide, op. cit.*, para.3–1147.

[20] See the *Société des Télécommunications Internationales du Cameroun* case cited above, para.31–6 n.9 where the Paris Court of Appeal held that the dissenting opinion reflected the fact that there had been collegial deliberations.

[21] Lebanese Supreme Court, 5th Chamber, April 27, 2006, *Henco v Moawad, MBV and Triple M*, unreported.

provided the parties have agreed in writing.[22] The ICC Court would seem well advised to allow such derogation in only the most exceptional cases.

The requirement of reasoned awards is a fundamental guarantee of the arbitral process. It forces arbitrators to carefully review and weigh the evidence submitted by the Parties, and to properly consider and apply the law to the dispute.[23] It allows parties to understand why and based on which argument they have won or lost the case. **31–20**

In practice, it will very much depend on the experience, legal and writing skills and diligence of the Tribunal whether the parties will obtain an award that sets out the factual and legal basis, with reference to, and citations from the relevant documents and material on record. **31–21**

In ICC arbitrations, Awards are subject to scrutiny by the ICC Court pursuant to art.33. This scrutiny should ensure that the minimum requirements of a reasoned award are met satisfactorily. The issue of the scope and nature of the review by national courts of the reasons of an Award varies considerably and forms an integral part of their approach with regard to annulment or enforcement, as briefly discussed under art.34.[24] However, several basic points can be noted at the outset regarding the preparation of Awards. **31–22**

Preparation of the draft Award

Some presidents prepare initial drafts of the Award prior to the oral hearings as a checklist for procedural and substantive issues of fact and law to be decided in the final Award. The purpose is not to prejudge the issues: an experienced arbitrator will wish to hear all the evidence and arguments before reaching a decision. The purpose is to ensure that there will be no gaps when the Tribunal is deliberating after the proceedings have been closed. The president is not required to share his preliminary draft with the co-arbitrators. Whatever draft the president prepares, it should normally not contain a view or recommendation as to how a certain issue is to be decided, as long as the arbitrators have not had a chance to deliberate.[25] Prior to any such deliberations, and in particular where such way of proceeding was not agreed, it may well be viewed as being unfair for a president to send his or her fellow arbitrators a fully reasoned draft. Except when such draft deals with truly straightforward issues, such a way of proceeding cannot in the authors' view be considered as good practice. A president should always find the time to solicit from both arbitrators their views and to allow a debate of these views. Anything else puts the other arbitrators before a fait accompli and is an affront. **31–23**

To the extent that disputes among the arbitrators as to the proper handling of the deliberations become an issue, it does not appear to be the role of the ICC Court, let alone that of the President of the ICC Court to step in, even when this matter is brought to their attention. The President of the ICC Court may, however, try to use the moral authority, which the President normally enjoys, to encourage the arbitrators to come to an agreement as to their dispute. **31–24**

22 Fry, Greenberg, Mazza, *Guide, op. cit.*, para.3–1152.
23 Webster, Review of Substantive Reasoning, *op.cit.*, (2006) Arb Int Vol. 22 No.3 p.431.
24 See paras 34–63 et seq.
25 Reiner & Aschauer, para.640.

Relationship with the Terms of Reference

31–25 As discussed under art.23, the Terms of Reference are intended to provide the agreed framework for the arbitration. They set out the claims and requests for relief of the parties, and possibly also the issues to be decided. The reasons of the Award should deal with those issues or explain why they have not been dealt with. The ICC Court will review the Award with reference to the Terms of Reference. Some arbitrators update the issues as identified initially in the Terms of Reference prior to the evidentiary hearings to ensure that all issues are dealt with at the hearings and in the Award.

Procedural issues

31–26 Usually the Award will deal with all important procedural steps in the arbitration. In particular, it will provide the names and addresses of the parties and their counsel, and refer to the constitution of the Tribunal, the establishing of the Terms of Reference, the exchange of briefs and witness statements, the date and object of a hearing or of the hearings. If summary minutes or a verbatim transcript of the hearing have been made, the Award will usually refer also to such documents, as it will mention all procedural orders issued by the Tribunal.

31–27 The reasons for the Award should set out the basis for the material procedural decisions. For example, if evidence has been excluded, it is important to explain the basis.[26] If the cross-examination of a witness has been curtailed, it is helpful to provide the reasons for curtailing that evidence.[27] If the Tribunal proceeded in the absence of one of the parties or a witness, the reasons for the Award should explain on which basis.[28]

Factual issues

31–28 Many arbitrators set out the respective positions of the parties and then have a discussion by the Tribunal with the reasons for the Tribunal's decision with respect to the issues. To the extent that the Tribunal's discussion refers to the evidence on which it provides this decision it will provide an "audit trail" for the documentation relied upon.[29] In most jurisdictions, the national courts will not review the substance of this "audit trail". However, the requirement that an Award

[26] *Phoenix Aktiengesellschaft v Ecoplas, Inc*, (2nd Cir.) December 10, 2004, 391 F. 3d 433. As regards a claim an Award should not be enforced as a party was unable to present its case the Court noted: "Given the arbitrator's careful consideration of the issue, Ecoplas's claim that it was 'unable to present [its] case' is groundless". See also January 10, 2012, *Sharikat Al Ikarat Wal Abnieh SAL v Butec SAL,* note Jaeger, (2003) Cahiers de l'arbitrage, No. 1 p. 71. As regards evidence, each party must be granted the same opportunity to present the witnesses whose testimony it intends to rely upon. In this case, "the procedural rules clearly established the requirements and timetable for testimonial evidence, so there could be no breach of party equality". The Court, in this case, reinforced its position not to interfere with the arbitral tribunal's procedural decisions, as long as they derive from "unambiguous procedural rules, which were accepted by the parties".

[27] See the *Himpurna* case, para. 6–143.

[28] For a discussion of circumstances leading to proceeding without one of the parties (and one of the arbitrators), see the *Himpurna* case, para.6–143.

[29] An "audit trail" is much more convincing than a general statement that the Tribunal has reviewed the evidence carefully.

is reasoned means that there should be some evidentiary explanation for the decision in the Award.

Weighing the evidence is a crucial part of the Tribunal's fact-finding mission. Each arbitrator has an approach to weighing the evidence. However, it is submitted that, in international arbitration, there are tendencies that one finds with arbitrators from different backgrounds. One of those tendencies is to place weight on the documentation contemporaneous to factual issues if it was prepared for normal business purposes and not with a view to defend a legal position. Oral testimony may in some instances be very persuasive as well. However, if there is a conflict between oral testimony and the contemporaneous record, arbitrators tend to prefer the contemporaneous record. Likewise, when there exists only oral evidence, even though contemporaneous evidence would have been plausible, a Tribunal will be very cautious in relying primarily on such evidence. **31–29**

Another tendency is to try to analyse the evidence of all types in the light of the commercial transaction to which the parties agreed. ICC arbitration is business arbitration and many arbitrators will seek to understand, for example, whether there was an express or implied allocation of risks as part of the basic contract. For some arbitrators, this is one of the prisms through which the factual evidence should be analysed. A further tendency is to focus more on whether a witness was credible on a certain issue relevant to the case rather than the credibility of a witness overall. Therefore, the time and weight that Tribunals devote to peripheral credibility issues is less than what may be expected by some lawyers. **31–30**

Legal issues

Each Award has to provide the reasons for the Tribunal's decisions also with respect to legal issues that are in dispute between the parties. In deciding these legal issues, Tribunals will be weighing their views as to the applicable law as it will have been presented and argued by the parties. Parties may present some of their legal case through expert evidence. However, in the end it is the Tribunal that will have to decide which legal interpretation it prefers. **31–31**

There are several challenges in this respect. Unlike national judges, Tribunals are frequently providing reasons with respect to a legal system in which they have not received their initial legal training. In some cases, the Tribunal will be reviewing the legal material in translated form. In other cases, even the approach of the legal system, whether it be of common law or civil law, may be different from that of the individual members of the Tribunal. **31–32**

These aspects are of course a natural result of the preference of the parties to have a neutral Tribunal or president. In practice, these issues are felt by most practitioners to be less problematic for various reasons. Many international arbitrators are used to dealing with arbitrations under various legal systems and, in any event, many national legal systems have either similar origins or have been subject to similar influences that render adapting oneself to the legal system much less difficult. Finally, most arbitrations involve an allegation of breach of contract and many principles relating to contracts are similar. **31–33**

Providing legal reasons is often the most difficult part of drafting the Award, which in many cases turns out to be the weakest part of the Award. Parties expect **31–34** a detailed legal analysis of their case with a reasoned explanation of why their position was rejected, if in fact that is what has occurred. Detailed legal reasoning can be a very powerful argument for accepting the Tribunal's decision. For example, if the Tribunal has rejected an argument based on several cases under the applicable law, it is helpful to have in the Award a detailed analysis of those cases with an explanation as to why the cases did not assist the relevant parties in the circumstances.

31–35 Some view the weakness in legal reasoning as in part a result of the fact that most ICC Awards are not published and that if published, this is often without the names of the arbitrators who participated in their drafting. This contrasts with the situation under the ICSID Rules for example, where Awards are systematically published with the names of the members of the Tribunal (and even the names of the parties).[30] This is due to the difference between commercial disputes, which form the bulk of ICC arbitration, and state-investor disputes, in ICSID arbitrations, and the need for transparency in the latter cases.

Amiable compositeur, ex aequo et bono

31–36 If the Tribunal is not required to decide the case based on legal principles but on fairness, then the reasons in the Award should set out the basis on which the Tribunal decided that the Award is fair. It has been held as inadequate for a Tribunal in such circumstances to simply base itself on the application of the legal principles.[31]

Damages

31–37 The rules of law governing the causation and quantification of damages are generally those applicable under the rules of law applicable pursuant to art.21. The Award should set out the reasons based on which it holds that these requirements are met particularly as to the causation of the damages and the probability that the damages will occur. Damages frequently cover claims for future lost profits, which by their nature require the Tribunal to estimate what could happen in the future.

Cost issues

31–38 As discussed under art.37, the issue of the allocation of costs is one of the areas of international arbitration for which the general guidelines are not clear. A Tribunal has discretion in the allocation of costs; however, the Tribunal must

[30] Rule 48(4) of the ICSID Arbitration Rules provides: "The Centre shall not publish the award without the consent of the parties. The Centre may, however, promptly include in its publication excerpts of the legal rules applied by the Tribunal", SIAR 2006:1 at p.205.

[31] See July 10, 2003, *Pion v Dumas*, (2003) Rev Arb No.4 p.1362, note Betto; Cass Civ 1re, October 18, 2001, *SARL grenobloise d'investissement v Société Eurovia* (2002) Rev Arb p.361, confirmed by Paris, March 14, 2006, *C v S*, Paris, May 10, 2007, *Caisse Centrale de Réassurance SA v Société Arianespace SA*, and Paris, July 3, 2007, *L v B*, (2007) Rev Arb No.1 p.821 note Chantebout; see also Bühler and Jarvin, "L'amiable compositeur: peut-il laisser la question du droit applicable indéterminé?" in *Mélanges François Knoepfler, op. cit.*, para.21–84 n.75.

provide reasons for the exercise of this discretion and those reasons should be relevant to the level of the costs and the Tribunal's overall decision on the merits.

Interest issues

The Award must provide reasons for the period of the interest and the rate. In particular, the Tribunal cannot award interest for a period prior to that requested by a party. Therefore, the reasons for the Award must set out the basis on which the rate of interest has been arrived at. **31–39**

The Award should also provide reasons for granting of or declining to grant compound interest, i.e. "interest on interest" or the capitalisation of interest. Although the ICC Rules are silent on the interest question, the power of a Tribunal to grant compound interest is generally admitted as part of its authority to award compensation to the aggrieved party.[32] Indeed, the French Court of Appeal ruled that a Tribunal that awards compound interest 14 years after issuing its initial award does not overstep its jurisdiction so long as the arbitration clause gives the Tribunal the authority to decide all disputes arising out of contract performance or the contract, more generally.[33] **31–40**

Article 31(3): "The award shall be deemed to be made at the place of the arbitration and on the date stated therein."

Article 31(3) refers to where the Award is "deemed to be made", and not where it was signed. As discussed under art.18, the place of arbitration is a legal concept. The place of arbitration provides the link with the place of the proceedings relating to the conduct of the arbitration and any annulment proceedings, as has been recognised by courts of many countries.[34] **31–41**

The ICC Court requires that at the end of every Award the following words be inserted prior to the date and signature block of the arbitrators: "Place of Arbitration:–".[35] By doing so, the impression shall be avoided that the arbitrators actually signed the Award on the given date at the place of arbitration. When none **31–42**

[32] See for example, Brower, "Awarding Interest–Ex Officio or Only If Requested, At What Rate, As of When, Compound or Not?", *ASA Special Series No.29, op. cit.*, at p.70; Brower & Sharpe, "Award of Compound Interest in International Arbitration: The *Aminoil* Non-Precedent" in *Liber Amicorum in honour of Robert Briner, op. cit.*, p.155; Baude-Texidor, "Les intérêts moratoires postérieurs à la sentence devant l'arbitre et devant le juge" (2005) Gazette du Palais, May 27 and 28, 2005, p.2; Gotanda, "Compound Interest in International Disputes" (2004); Hammoud & Secomb, "Interest in ICC Arbitral Awards: Introduction and Commentary" (2004) ICC ICArb Bull Vol.15 No.1, p.53; Affolder, "Awarding Compound Interest in International Arbitration" (2001) Am Rev Int'l Arb Vol.12, p.45.

[33] Dupeyré, "Note – Département de commercialization du pétrole – Petroleum Marketing Department (Syrtol) v. SARL Babanapht, Cour d'appel de Paris (Pôle 1 – Ch. 1), 3 February 2011" (2011) Rev. Arb. No. 2, 472.

[34] See for example the decision rendered in 2004 in the *Karaha Bodas* case discussed above at paras 27–9 and below at para.34–39: "In selecting Switzerland as the site of the arbitration, the parties were not choosing a physical place for the arbitration to occur, but rather the place where the award would be 'made'. Under Art.16(1) of the UNCITRAL Rules, the 'place' designated for an arbitration is the legal rather than physical location of the forum. The arbitration proceeding in this case physically occurred in Paris, but the Award was 'made in' Geneva, the place of the arbitration in the legal sense and the presumptive source of the applicable procedural law" (citations deleted). See also the *Titan* case of the Swedish Court of Appeal February 2, 2005 case no.T103 8–05, (2007) Mealey's IAR Vol 20 No. 7 p.42, note Jarvin and Dorgan.

[35] See Pt II, Document 25.

of the arbitrators reside at the place of arbitration, it is most unlikely for the Award to be signed there. It is rather standard practice that the president will circulate the original copies of the Award for signature by the co-arbitrators by way of courier or mail, and that once he signs the Award himself, he will date it and then transmit it to the Secretariat for notification to the parties. The authors are not aware of an arbitration law requiring physical signature of the Award at the place of arbitration.

31–43 The award is also to be dated, the relevant date being the one "stated in" the Award. There is no need for all three arbitrators to put a date next to their signature. If they do so, it is advisable to state which date shall prevail and they are free to chose the date of the award, as long as it does not predate the ICC Court's approval of the Award. It would normally be the most recent one, and that should be the one of the president of the Tribunal as he will be typically the one to sign last.

Article 32 Award by Consent

If the parties reach a settlement after the file has been transmitted to the arbitral tribunal in accordance with Article 16, the settlement shall be recorded in the form of an award made by consent of the parties if so requested by the parties and if the arbitral tribunal agrees to do so.[1]

***

Article 32 permits Awards by consent of the parties. In 2012, 31 Awards by consent were rendered under the ICC Rules, i.e. about 6 per cent of the total number of awards.[2] This figure is to be compared with the overall number of cases that are withdrawn each year from the ICC Court's docket before a final award is issued, i.e. about one out of two cases.[3] Consent Awards are either expressly provided for or permitted under the law of most major centres of arbitration.[4] 32–1

Article 32 requires that the Tribunal must have been constituted prior to the consent Award being issued. In other words, there must have been a dispute between the parties, the dispute must have been submitted to arbitration, and the arbitral process must have been put into motion in such way that allowed the constitution of the Tribunal and its receipt of the file in accordance with art.16. Article 32 does not appear to contemplate the parties agreeing that a dispute in their contract be resolved by a consent Award prior to these steps being taken.[5] 32–2

Under art.32, it is not necessary for Terms of Reference to have been signed before an Award by consent can be issued. It would be a futile formality for the ICC Court to require Terms of Reference, as a condition for approving Awards by consent.[6] In a recent case, the parties settled the matter prior to the signing of the 32–3

[1] Article 32 corresponds to art.26 of the 1998 Rules. There have been no changes to the text of the rule.

[2] (2013) ICC ICArb Bull Vol.24 No.1, p.15.

[3] Fry, Greenberg, Mazza, Guide, *op. cit.*, para.3–1163 refer to a figure of approximately 47 per cent.

[4] See for example s.51 of the English Arbitration Act 1996, art.30 of the UNCITRAL Model Law. In Switzerland, art.34 of the Concordat on Arbitration expressly refers to the Award by consent in domestic arbitration. It is however accepted for international arbitration proceedings under the Swiss PILA, although it does not contain any specific rules as to how the proceedings can be terminated upon settlement of the dispute by the parties. See Lalive, Poudret & Reymond, *op. cit.*, p. 418 n.20 re art.189; Wirth, "Article 189" in *International Arbitration in Switzerland, An Introduction to and a Commentary on Article 176-194 of the Swiss Private International Law Statute, op. cit.*, para. 41, p.558. The same observation applies in France where there is no express provision on this subject in the CPC. See Delvolvé, Rouche & Pointon, *op. cit.*, para. 305, p.169.

[5] For the parties to have a Tribunal constituted, then these requirements would have to be met. For the parties to agree to waive these provisions in order to obtain a consent Award would not appear to have been contemplated in art.32 as there is no reference to a contrary agreement between the parties; see Newmark and Hill, "Can a Mediated Settlement Become an Enforceable Arbitration Award?" (2000) Arb Int Vol.16 No.1, p.81; Lazareff, "Aux frontières de l'arbitrage et de l'ADR: la sentence d'accord parties" in *Les Cahiers de l'Arbitrage, Vol.I, op. cit.*, p.8; Tchakoua, "The Status of the Arbitral Award by Consent: The limits of the Useful" (2002) RDAI/IBLJ No.2, p.775; Kreindler, "Settlement Agreements and Arbitration in the Context of the ICC Rules" (1998) ICC ICArb Vol. 9 No.2, p.22.

[6] Fry, Greenberg, Mazza, *Guide, op. cit.* para.3–1171 assert that the waiver to have Terms of Reference signed before an Award by consent is issued should be in writing and communicated to the

Terms of Reference but requested an Award by consent. The Tribunal agreed provided that the parties waived the signing of the Terms of Reference. The parties did so and the ICC Court approved the Award by consent.

32–4 Article 32 does not deal with how this settlement has come about. As discussed under art.23(1), there are different views as to the involvement[7] of the Tribunal in settlement discussions.[8]

32–5 One commentary described the process as follows with respect to the English Arbitration Act of 1996:

> "If the parties compromise or settle their differences, it is the frequent practice for parties to agree that their settlement is to be set out in an Award made by consent. It provides a written record of the settlement; and if the settlement were not complied with, it allows the aggrieved party to enforce the Award rather than begin fresh arbitration proceedings on the original cause of action. The Tribunal (although not bound to do so) will usually make such an Award in agreed terms unless there is something objectionable in the settlement, e.g. an attempt to mislead third parties; and almost invariably it will be evident from the face of the Award that it is an agreed Award. Indeed, it is usual for the parties also to sign the consent Award."[9]

32–6 This commentary reflects practice outside of England as well, although generally it appears that the parties do not sign consent awards, and it is not contemplated by the Rules.

32–7 In international arbitration, a consent Award may be of great effect due to the New York Convention. A consent Award issued in one country can currently be enforced under the New York Convention in 150 countries. In this respect, a consent Award is treated in the same fashion as any other Award under the Rules.[10] Like any Awards, it is also confidential and does not come into the public domain.

Secretariat as well as the tribunal. The Parties' settlement agreement, requesting the tribunal to issue an award by consent should be viewed as an implied waiver, and sufficient for all purposes.

[7] More generally, see Nater-Bass, "Consent Awards–How to Draft Them", *ASA Special Series No. 29*, *op. cit.*, at p.36; Bertrand, "Sur le bon usage des sentences d'accord parties" (2006) ASA Bull Vol.24 No.1, p.13; Lörcher, "Enforceability of Agreed Awards in Foreign Jurisdictions" (2001) Arb Int Vol. 17 No.3, p.275.

[8] See above para.23; see also ICC publication No.843, *Techniques for Controlling Time and Costs in Arbitration, op. cit.*, para.43, at p.28 (the Tribunal's role in promoting settlement); Schneider, "Combining Arbitration with Conciliation" (1996) *ICCA Congress Series No. 8*, p.57: "The admissibility and appropriateness for an arbitrator to act as conciliator is among the most controversial issues among international arbitration practitioners. The views and practices in this respect differ widely". See also U. Draetta, "Leveraging the Arbitral Process to Encourage Settlement: Some Practical and Legal Issues", in Evelio Verdera y Tuells and José Carlos Fernández Rozas (eds), Arbitraje: Revista de Arbitraje Comercial y de Inversiones (2009), 761.

[9] Veeder, "Report on England", *ICCA Handbook*, J. Paulsson (ed) Supp. 23 (March 1997), p.24.

[10] On the enforceability of an Award by consent under the New York Convention, see Lörcher, *op. cit.*, at p.277; see also *United States v Sperry Corp*, 493 US 52 (1989) (the US Supreme Court admitted that an Award on Agreed Terms or Award by consent, is, like all Awards "final and binding" and "enforceable [. . .] in the court of any nation in accordance with its laws". In France, see Cass Civ 2e, October 2, 1981, *Société Guilliet et al v Consorts Gillet* (1984) Rev Arb No.3 p.361 (the French Supreme Court denied the qualification of an Award to a settlement agreement or transaction reached by the parties and endorsed by the Tribunal in absence of a decision of the arbitrator condemning one or another party).

Despite these advantages, parties may prefer not to obtain a consent Award but to keep the terms of their settlement confidential, with perhaps a suspension of the proceedings until the settlement agreement has been complied with. In this way, the parties avoid divulging the terms of the settlement or involving the Tribunal or the ICC Court in the terms of the settlement. In such a case, the Secretariat will take note of the parties' indication that they have settled their dispute and wish to withdraw the proceedings accordingly. The Secretariat will thereafter invite the ICC Court to take note of the withdrawal and to fix the costs of arbitration costs. **32–8**

A consent Award is also subject to the same provisions of the Rules as any form of Award, in particular, as regards the need for approval by the ICC Court, the possibility of correction and interpretation, as well as annulment and enforcement.[11] **32–9**

The Award by consent will, like any final Award, bring the arbitral proceedings to an end. It will therefore also have to contain a ruling on the costs of arbitration, as fixed by the ICC Court in accordance with art.37, and decided by the Tribunal based on the parties' agreement. Frequently, each party will bear half of the ICC costs of arbitration, and its own costs itself. **32–10**

A consent Award is normally final, as it ends the dispute submitted to arbitration in its entirety and brings the proceedings to an end. Where the parties have reached only a partial settlement, a partial Award by consent is possible. In either case, as regards the issues decided, the issues will usually be res judicata as between the parties and the Tribunal will be functus officio with respect to those aspects of the dispute. The effect is an aspect that should be carefully considered by the parties, as it is one of the fundamental distinctions between a settlement and a consent Award. A settlement is a contract and has the effect as such. A consent Award is an adjudication of issues and has the ancillary effects of an adjudication. Therefore, if there is a subsequent dispute between the parties, for example, the effect of a consent Award may be different from that of a settlement. **32–11**

By contrast, if a settlement is reached before the arbitration hearing, courts are divided as to whether to enjoin a hearing over the existence of such a settlement. Recently, the Singapore High Court refused to declare a Tribunal functus officio for this reason and enjoin arbitration proceedings.[12] Similarly, the English High Court has previously ruled that the question of whether an arbitrator is functus officio falls under the jurisdiction of the arbitrator, and is thus a matter for an arbitrator to decide.[13] However, the Supreme Court of Appeal of South Africa has held that, under South African common law, a settlement agreement reached prior to an arbitration automatically terminated the arbitrators' powers and necessarily formed an arbitration award, despite the fact that the South African Arbitration Act does not make a provision for an award by consent.[14] **32–12**

The basic principle for ICC arbitration is the autonomy of the parties subject to overall limitations based on public policy and the rights of the Tribunal under the **32–13**

[11] For an illustration of enforcement of an Award by consent, see Indian Supreme Court, May 13, 1999, *Harendra H. Mehta v Mukesh H. Mehta* (2000) YBCA Vol.XXV p. 641.

[12] *Doshion Ltd v Sembawang Engineers and Constructors Pte Ltd* [2011] SGHC 46.

[13] *Martin Dawes v Treasure & Son Ltd* [2010] EWHC 3218.

[14] *Guido Bruno Bidoli v Bidoli AS*, Supreme Court of Appeal, Case No. 436/10, May 27, 2011.

Rules. The parties may first enter into a binding settlement agreement and then submit the text of a draft of the proposed consent Award to the Tribunal. In this case, the parties have undertaken to settle their disputes and the agreement should indicate clearly whether or not that settlement is conditional upon the issuance of a consent Award. If the agreement is unconditional, then presumably the dispute will be resolved in any event and there will be little or no concern about further proceedings. If the agreement is conditional upon the issuance of a consent Award, then there will be the possibility of further proceedings. In that situation, the parties and the Tribunal should provide that, if the consent Award is not issued, the Tribunal should continue the proceedings and issue an Award.

32–14 The members of the Tribunal are not required to agree to a consent Award under the terms of art.32 based on the exercise of their discretion. Therefore, the terms of the consent Award must be acceptable to all the parties to the arbitration and the Tribunal. If presented in draft form, the Tribunal may have comments, in particular, it may identify potential problems that may arise to future disagreements, such as, an allocation of costs.[15] The Tribunal will also wish to ensure that the consent Award is in accordance with the law of the place of arbitration and that it cannot be used to mislead third parties. In this respect, the Tribunal may have issues as to statements of fact accepted by the parties or with respect to whether mandatory principles of applicable law have been applied. In addition, the Tribunal may be concerned about questions of illegality, and may wish to make sure that it does not become the instrument of money laundering or related illegal activities.

32–15 Typically, a Tribunal will ask the Parties whether they want to be assisted in having their settlement incorporated into an Award by consent, once the Parties have advised the Tribunal that they are in the process of settling their dispute. Parties are sometimes reluctant to have a Tribunal make an award by consent, since this will increase the overall costs of the arbitration. The ICC Court will often be inclined to award full fees to the Tribunal, once it has rendered an Award, be it an Award by consent. This practice is as such not objectionable, but depends on a case by case analysis and on the work carried out by the Tribunal.

[15] Fry, Greenberg, Mazza, *Guide, op. cit.,* para.3–1171 "Note to Arbitrators" and para.3–1174.

Article 33 Scrutiny of the Award by the Court

Before signing any award, the arbitral tribunal shall submit it in draft form to the Court. The Court may lay down modifications as to the form of the award and, without affecting the arbitral tribunal's liberty of decision, may also draw its attention to points of substance. No award shall be rendered by the arbitral tribunal until it has been approved by the Court as to its form.[1]

Introductory remarks

As discussed in the Introduction and under art.1, ICC arbitration is an administered and supervised arbitration. One of the key elements in the involvement of the administering institution in the arbitral process concerns the scrutiny and approval of draft Awards by the ICC Court. It is part of the organisational framework that the ICC Rules provide. In 2012, 491 Awards were scrutinised by the ICC Court. This number included 31 Awards by consent. Eight Awards were approved by the ICC Court without any comment, 483 Awards were approved subject to modifications. In 59 cases, the ICC Court requested, however, that the draft Award be resubmitted by the Tribunal for scrutiny (and possibly subsequent approval) by the ICC Court.[2] **33–1**

The ICC Court's scrutiny is consistent with the ICC's role and distinguishes it from other forms of international arbitration.[3] As the French Supreme Court stated in the *Cubic* case: **33–2**

> "the [Court of Appeal] noted that the arbitration rules of the ICC maintain a distinction between the function of the organisation of the arbitration through the 'International Court of Arbitration' and the decision-making function which is left exclusively to the arbitrators, the Court having no decisional power; that, in this respect, the Court of Appeal properly held that the transmission of a draft of the award to the International Court of Arbitration did not result in any interference in the decisional role of the arbitrator but had as its purpose solely to

[1] Article 33 corresponds to art.27 of the 1998 Rules. There have been no changes to the text of the Article.

[2] (2013) ICC ICArb Bull Vol.24 No.1, p.15.

[3] Abedian, "Judicial Review of Arbitral Awards in International Arbitration – *A Case for an Efficient System of Judicial Review*" (2011) J. of Int'l Arb, No.6, 553; Greenberg., "Arbitral awards under scrutiny: An assessment", *op. cit.*, p.89(90), explains that scrutiny of awards was first introduced in the 1927 version of the ICC Rules.

ensure the effectiveness of the arbitration; and that the Court correctly upheld in its reasons the validity of the contract organizing the arbitration as regards the requirements of public international law."[4] (Authors' translation)

33–3 The ICC's scrutiny of Awards raises various issues, some of which are frequently misunderstood. The first of these issues is what is scrutinised and in particular the distinction between Awards and procedural orders. The second issue is the submission of the draft Award and the comments as to form and substance. The third issue is the treatment of dissenting opinions and the fourth issue is the timing of the scrutiny of Awards. Each of these issues is discussed below.

Awards and Procedural Orders

33–4 A Tribunal is required to submit a draft Award to the ICC Court and a failure to do so may result in the annulment of the Award. Article 2 of the Rules describes the term Award as to include "*inter alia*, an interim, partial or final Award". In fact, it also includes an Award by consent within the meaning of art.32 of the Rules, and thus, any type of Award falls under the scrutiny and approval requirement of art.33 of the Rules.[5]

33–5 The ICC Rules do not define what decision of an arbitral tribunal constitutes an arbitral Award, and the laws of arbitration do not either. More than once, the state courts in various jurisdictions had to come in and define what qualifies as an Award. It is the substance of the Tribunal's decision that determines whether the decision is an Award or procedural order, not the description that the Tribunal gives to it. An Award is a decision that finally decides an issue in the case, or records an agreement of the parties settling the dispute.[6]

33–6 The distinction between an Award and a procedural order has become the subject of decisions by American courts and by French courts. It is clear from both of the following decisions that state courts look at the substance of the decision by

[4] See para.1–8 n.10.

[5] Greenberg, *op. cit.*, p.91.

[6] In that sense, see the constant case law of the French courts, in particular CA Paris, March 25, 1994, *Société Sardisud et autre v société Technip* (1994) Rev Arb No.2 p.391 note Jarrosson (an Award is "the decision of an arbitral tribunal which finally settles, in whole or in part, the underlying dispute either on the merits, on jurisdiction or on any procedural issue which terminates the arbitral proceedings"); see also Paris, July 1, 1999, *Société Braspetro Oil Services (Brasoil) v The Management and Implementation Authority of the Great Man-Made River Project (GMRA)* (2000) ASA Bull Vol.18 No.2 p.376; (1999) YBCA Vol.XXIVa p.296; (1999) Rev Arb No.4 p.834; CA Paris, April 11, 2002, *Société ABC International v Société Diverseylever Ltd* (2003) Rev Arb No.1 p.778 and p.160, note Bensaude, (2003) YBCA Vol.XXVIII p.209; SAR 2002:1 p.185, note Kaplan and Cuniberti; Cass. 1re civ., June 17, 2009, Sté française de rentes et de financement Crédirente c/Sté Compagnie générale de garantie : Rev. Arb 2009, p. 741 (1re esp., 2e déc), note C. Chainais; Cass. 1re civ., October 12, 2011, Sté Groupe Antoine Tabet c/République du Congo: D. 2011, p.2483; Procédures 2011, comm. 369, note L. Weiller, JCP G 2011, p. 2545, obs. J. Ortscheidt; Centre français d'arbitrage et reassurance et d'assurance; Rév. Arb. 2012, p. 86, note F.-X. Train; see also Jarvin, "To What Extent Are Procedural Decisions of Arbitrators Subject to Court Review?" (1999) *ICCA Congress Series No.9*, p.366; Carlevaris, "*La qualification des décisions des tribunaux arbitraux dans le Règlement d'arbitrage CCI et dans la jurisprudence française*" in *Les Cahiers de l'Arbitrage Volume I*, *op. cit.*, p.153.

the Tribunal, not just the form, to determine whether it is an Award or a procedural order.

In the *Publicis* case,[7] the US Court of Appeals for the Seventh Circuit decided that an order for production of documents rendered by a Tribunal in England could be enforced in the United States. In doing so, the Court dealt with the difference between procedural orders and Awards in the following terms: **33–7**

> "[4] Publicis says the tribunal's decision was an interim order and, under the convention, only arbitral 'awards' are final and subject to confirmation [. . .]
> [5] Publicis' position is that an arbitral ruling can be final in every respect, but unless the document bears the word 'award' it is not final and is unenforceable. This is extreme and untenable formalism. The New York Convention, the United Nations arbitration rules, and the commentators' consistent use of the label 'award' when discussing final arbitral decisions does not bestow transcendental significance on the term. Their treatment of 'award' as interchangeable with final does not necessarily mean that synonyms such as decision, opinion, order, or ruling could not also be final. The content of a decision–not its nomenclature–determines finality. [. . .]
> [6] [. . .] Discovery involves compiling information needed to reach a resolution; it is an early step in moving toward the end result. In the situation at hand, whether or not Publicis had to turn over the tax records is the whole ball of wax. The tribunal's order resolved the dispute, or was supposed to, at any rate. Producing the documents wasn't just some procedural matter–it was the very issue True North wanted arbitrated. The finality of the tribunal's ruling is demonstrated by the deadline. [. . .] A ruling on a discrete, time-sensitive issue may be final and ripe for confirmation even though other claims remain to be addressed by arbitrators. (citations omitted)
> [8, 9] [. . .] Despite some possible superficial technical flaws, and despite its designation as an 'order' instead of an 'award', the arbitral tribunal's decision–as to this chunk of the case–was final."[8]

In the *Braspetro* case, a Tribunal in an ICC arbitration had issued a document that it entitled an order. The Tribunal did not submit the order to the ICC Court for scrutiny and an application was made to annul it for failure to meet the procedural requirements of the Rules regarding scrutiny. The Paris Court of Appeal annulled the order, which it viewed as an Award.[9] The Paris Court of Appeal stated as follows: **33–8**

[7] See also Smith & Turner, "Enforcement by US Court of International Arbitration Interim Orders and Awards under the New York Convention, *Publicis Communication v True North Communications Inc*" SAR 2001:1, p.47.

[8] 206 F.3d 725 US Court of Appeals, 7th Circ., March 14, 2000, (2000) YBCA Vol.XXV at pp.1153–1155.

[9] See the *Braspetro* case, 2000 ASA Bull Vol.18, No.2, p.376.

> "[1] The qualification of [a decision as an] award does not depend on the terms used by the arbitrators or by the parties. On 15 October 1997, Brasoil requested the arbitrators to review the partial award of 5 March 1995, alleging that GMRA had fraudulently withheld essential documents which it already had in its possession at the beginning of the arbitration and which could have affected the decision on who was responsible for the malfunctioning [of the wells], and that in any case these documents revealed an essential fact of which Brasoil was unaware through no fault of its own. GMRA maintained that the request was inadmissible and unfounded. The parties exchanged statements on this issue and were heard at the hearing of 19 December 1997 together with their 'respective experts'.
>
> [2] In the light of all these elements and after a five-month deliberation, the arbitral tribunal rendered the 'order' of 14 May 1998, by which, after a lengthy examination of the parties' positions, it declared that the request could not be granted because Brasoil had not proven that there had been fraud as alleged. This reasoned decision–by which the arbitrators considered the contradictory theories of the parties and examined in detail whether they were founded, and solved, in a final manner, the dispute between the parties concerning the admissibility of Brasoil's request for a review, by denying it and thereby ending the dispute submitted to them–appears to be an exercise of its jurisdictional power by the arbitral tribunal.
>
> [3] GMRA's objection that the 'order' at issue refuses to open an appellate instance and thus amounts to 'decisions on the administration of the proceedings' made by arbitral institutions to refuse commencement of an arbitration or joinder of a third party, is unfounded. Even if the similarity were perfect, the main reason for which the decisions of the ICC, whatever the nature of the problems they solve and the procedure followed, are not awards, is that they are not rendered by an arbitral tribunal, which clearly is not the case here.
>
> [4] Contrary to GMRA's opinion and notwithstanding its qualification as an 'order', the decision of 14 May 1998, which did not concern the evidence-taking in the arbitration, is thus indeed an award. Hence, Brasoil's request [to the Court of Appeal] is admissible."[10]

33–9 Therefore, in this case, because it "solved, in a final manner, the dispute between the parties concerning the admissibility of Brasoil's request for a review" and "did not concern evidence taking", the Tribunal's decision was an Award subject to arts 33–35 and not an order and was annulled because the procedure in art.33 had not been followed.

33–10 Another way of approaching the same issue is to examine whether the Tribunal is functus officio with respect to the relief it has granted. The essence of an Award is to finally decide an issue. If the Tribunal issues an order and reserves the right to modify it, then it is not finally deciding the issue.

[10] (1999) YBCA Vol.XXIVa at pp.297–298.

In reviewing a decision of a Tribunal, the key aspect is the substantive nature of that decision, not how it is entitled or presented. If the decision finally deals with an issue in the case, it will be viewed as an Award even if other issues remain to be decided. If the decision is a procedural step in the organisation of the proceedings, however, such as the appointment of an expert for the inspection of goods, it will be viewed as a non-final procedural order. The difficulty arises when the final decision relates to an issue, such as in the *Publicis* case, of the production of documents. **33–11**

In ICC arbitration, Tribunals will render procedural orders without submitting the draft first to the Secretariat to have the latter indicate whether or not the order should rather be in the form of an Award and thus made subject to the ICC Court's approval pursuant to art.33. Although the Secretariat normally receives copies of all procedural orders issued by a Tribunal in a given case, one can assume that it will not, as a matter of routine, verify whether the content of the procedural order would qualify it as an Award. These decisions will therefore often go unnoticed by the ICC Court, as in the *Braspetro* case referred to above. **33–12**

Conversely, where a Tribunal submits to the ICC Court a draft Award for approval, which in the Court's view is solely of procedural substance, the ICC Court will in most instances approve the Award, rather than invite the Tribunal to issue a procedural order. In some cases, the Secretariat may express doubts to the Tribunal as to the need to issue an Award rather than a procedural order. If a Tribunal maintains the view that its decision should take the form of an Award, and requests its approval by the ICC Court, the latter would exceed its administrative functions if it were to refuse the approval.[11] **33–13**

ICC Award Checklist

Since 2010, the Secretariat provides a checklist to all arbitrators,[12] which it sends with its letter transmitting the case file to the arbitral Tribual. The Secretariat considered that, too often, it had needed to remind arbitrators of the same points, and that rather than using its resources for this somewhat daunting task, it was now up to arbitrators to check these points themselves.[13] This checklist includes formalities that arbitrators must mention in their Award.[14] The Checklist also provides drafting guidelines, which an arbitrator may, and often will consider, without being required to do so.[15] The Checklist is helpful, both for arbitrators, newcomers in particular, but also for the Secretariat. The aim of the Checklist is to improve the overall quality of ICC Awards, render them more uniform, and, in particular, ensure their enforceability. It is the latter point which the ICC Court has in mind when scrutinising draft Awards. **33–14**

The document lists general points (such as numbering of paragraphs and pages and mention of the ICC case reference number in full on the front page), **33–15**

[11] See also Greenberg, *op. cit.*, p.92 for the opposite situation.

[12] (2010) ICC ICArb Bull. Vol.21 No.1, p.20.

[13] Fry, Greenberg, Mazza, *Guide*, *op. cit.*, para.3–1197.

[14] The "ICC Award Checklist 2012 Rules" can be found in Pt II Document 25. The Checklist was updated with the coming into force of the 2012 Rules, so that its references are in conformity with the numbering of the new Rules but, but has otherwise remained unchanged.

[15] The Checklist expressly mentions that "it does not constitute an exhaustive, mandatory or otherwise binding document".

identification of the parties, their representatives, and arbitrators, mention of any arbitration and choice of law agreements, the history of proceedings, jurisdiction, cost of the Arbitration (for Final Awards), a dispositive section, place of arbitration, date and signature.

33–16 The ICC Court may lay down modifications as to form that are required for such approval. Modifications as to form can cover matters such as:

- whether the Award clearly identifies whether it is a partial Award or a final Award;
- whether it mentions which version of the Rules are applicable;
- whether the Award deals with all issues in the Terms of Reference;
- whether reasons have been provided with respect to all issues to be decided, including quantum and interest;
- a reference to the parties and their addresses (by their corporate name or if there has been a merger or insolvency), their representatives and the arbitrators;
- a quotation of the entire arbitration agreement;
- the date of various procedural steps such as the commencement of the arbitration;
- the date of constitution of the Tribunal, in particular by whom each arbitrator was appointed and when;
- a recital of the extensions of time granted by the ICC Court for rendering the Award;
- details of the hearings (place, date);
- the date the proceedings were closed;
- aspects relating to the drafting of the dispositive provisions;
- aspects relating to the decision on costs, in particular as regards the distinction between the ICC costs of arbitration (fixed by the ICC Court) and party cost, fixed by the Tribunal, which in both cases will also have to decide upon the allocation of these costs;
- details of the place of arbitration;
- issues of jurisdiction, e.g. reference to an art.6(4) decision;
- issues relating to the applicable rule of law; and
- any formal requirements of the place of arbitration to the extent known by the Secretariat.

33–17 To the extent that the ICC Award Checklist contains simple guidelines, it should therefore not lead the Secretariat to become overly zealous in seeking to impose upon the Tribunal formalistic additions or unnecessary translations.

Submission of the draft Award and the ICC Court's scrutiny

The procedure by which the Tribunal arrives at a draft Award and the contents of that Award are discussed under art.30. The draft Award is not submitted to the ICC Court until there is agreement on its terms by the Tribunal or if the members of the Tribunal have agreed that there can be no agreement. Therefore, the draft Award submitted to the ICC Court is not a rough or preliminary draft, but rather a complete draft that is in a proposed final form. **33–18**

The president of the Tribunal usually submits the draft Award to the Secretariat. He or she should also copy the co-arbitrators. The Secretariat then reviews the draft particularly with reference to the Terms of Reference and prepares the file for submission to the ICC Court.[16] However, prior to submitting the matter to the ICC Court, the counsel at the Secretariat may wish to discuss with the president potential problems of form that the ICC Court might raise. This preliminary review is usually very helpful as draft Awards are established over time with the participation of each arbitrator, which can lead to simple errors in drafting. After that initial review by the Secretariat, the president may wish to proceed, in consultation with his co-arbitrators, with certain corrections in the draft Award and confirm to the Secretariat that the corrected draft Award should be submitted to the ICC Court. The interaction with regard to submission of the draft Award is between the Tribunal (usually the president) and the Secretariat. The other members of the Tribunal have no direct contact with the members of the ICC Court with respect to the scrutiny of the Award. **33–19**

As discussed in Annex 1 Pt I, depending on the complexity of the case, the draft Award will be submitted either to a Plenary Session of the ICC Court or to a Committee of the ICC Court.[17] In very rare cases of true urgency, draft Awards can also be approved by the President of the ICC Court pursuant to art.1(3).[18] If there is a dissenting opinion or if a government or state entity is a party to the arbitration, it is a longstanding practice of the ICC Court to submit the draft Award to a Plenary Session of the ICC Court. A member of the ICC Court will then be asked by the Secretariat to review the detail of the draft Award and report back on it at the Plenary Session. When an Award was submitted, but not approved at a Plenary Session, the revised version does not necessarily need to go back before the Plenary Session of the ICC Court, but may be scrutinised and approved by a Committee of the ICC Court. **33–20**

Article 33 draws a distinction between issues of form with respect to an Award and issues of substance. Article 33 makes Awards subject to approval of the ICC **33–21**

[16] See Pt 1 para. Ann.24 et seq. At the level of the Secretariat, primary responsibility for reviewing the award falls upon the counsel in charge of the file; in principle, the Managing Counsel, the Secretary General or his deputy and/or the ICC's General Counsel will also review the draft award before it goes before the ICC Court. See also Greenberg, *op. cit.*, p.97.

[17] Since 2009, the ICC Court holds special foreign language sessions, in particular in Spanish, but also German and Portuguese, so as to allow the review and approval of awards rendered in these languages without the need to have them translated into English or French, i.e. the ICC Court's official working languages. This allows the ICC Court to save considerable time and cost, as it dispenses it of having the draft awards, sometimes several hundred pages long, translated before they come before the ICC Court. Fry, Greenberg, Mazza, *Guide*, *op. cit.*, paras 3–32 and 3–1200; also Greenberg, *op. cit.*, p.107.

[18] See paras 1–62 et seq. above; Fry, Greenberg, Mazza, *Guide*, *op. cit.*, para.3–1202.

Court as to form. Article 33 permits the ICC Court to make comments on the substance of the Award "without affecting the Arbitral Tribunal's liberty of decision".[19]

33–22 In many instances, the points of form raised by the ICC Court will be minor, and will require little time by the Tribunal to comply with. In some instances, the comments as to form overlap with comments as to the substance. For example, lack of reasoning is a question of form and can be dealt with by providing the Tribunal's reasoning on the point. However, in some instances the reasoning is inadequate but exists, in which case the comment may become one of substance which the Tribunal is free to consider, but also to disregard.

33–23 In the majority of cases, the ICC Court approves the draft Award with reservations ("subject to . . ."),[20] an approval without any comments being the exception. In case of non-approval, the Tribunal is expected to resubmit the draft for the approval of the ICC Court after having addressed the issues raised by the Court. In either case, the Secretariat will verify whether the Tribunal has complied with the modifications requested by the ICC Court. If a Tribunal decides not to make a given change of form, the Secretariat will resubmit the draft Award to the ICC Court for a decision. Depending upon the explanation that is given by the Tribunal for not making a certain change, the ICC Court will or will not approve the draft Award as it is, or decide to return the draft Award with comments to the Tribunal. The situations in this respect are as varied as are formal issues raised by draft Awards. If an issue as to form is such as to call into question the enforceability of the Award, then there is a very real question as to whether an Award should be approved if it does not meet the formal requirements of the ICC Rules. However, in practice, it is not issues of form that cause the main tension between the ICC Court and Tribunals but rather comments on substance.

33–24 The issues of substance that the ICC Court may raise under art.33 are varied.[21] There may be an apparent issue with respect either to contradiction in certain elements of the draft Award or a finding as to the applicable law. This is the aspect of the scrutiny of draft Awards that perhaps gives rise to most difficulties in practice. The ICC Court is not a court of appeal and does not scrutinise the draft Award to see whether the decisions are correct or not. The ICC Court is, however, the first outside body to see the reasoning contained in a draft Award and therefore is in a position to provide comments—but not recommendations—as to issues that are either not addressed or addressed inadequately or in a contradictory fashion.

33–25 The quality and detail of Awards varies. However, members of the ICC Court are sometimes frustrated by the lack of detailed reasoning on the truly dispositive issues and the lack of legal reasoning on the applicable law. Awards that simply

[19] On the "mandatory" or "advisory" power of the ICC Court as to the modifications of form and substance, see for example High Court, Queen's Bench Division (Commercial Court), January 12, 1988, *Bank Mellat v GAA Development Construction Co* (1990) YBCA Vol.XV p.521; see also the French Cubic case, CA Paris, September 15, 1998 (1999) Rev. Arb. No.1, p.103 (111), which refers to the drafting advice ("*conseil rédactionnel*") being given by the ICC Court.

[20] See para. 33–1, and the outcome of scrutiny process by type of award for the period 2007–2011, Fry, Greenberg, Mazza, *Guide*, *op. cit.*, para.3–1205.

[21] For examples, see Greenberg, *op. cit.*, pp.99 et seq.

indulge in minimal reasoning, with the statement that the Tribunal has carefully reviewed the arguments of the parties, do not normally meet the parties' expectations. In a recent construction dispute, the Tribunal dismissed many claims based on the report of a Tribunal appointed expert by repeating for each claim the following language: "With regard to Respondent's claim for [. . .], the Arbitral Tribunal believes that the Expert's analysis and findings are reasonable and have not been convincingly refuted by the Parties".[22] This type of reasoning is not sufficient as it does not explain why the Expert's analysis was preferred to that of the parties and therefore lacks an element of reasoning.

The ICC Court "draws [the Tribunal's] attention to points of substance" but does so by suggesting that it may be useful to have the Award deal with certain issues. It is not the role of the ICC Court to criticise the results in an Award, even if a member of the ICC Court such as the *Rapporteur* believes the decision to be wrong, the Tribunal is to reach the decision on the merits and even the comments on the points of substance will be oriented towards ensuring that issues are dealt with and not the results of the analysis. Moreover, the Tribunal is free to disregard the comments of the ICC Court and the Award will still be approved, as the ICC Court approves Awards solely as to form. The reactions of Tribunals to these comments are varied. However, most experienced arbitrators either seek to reflect the modifications suggested by the Court or provide an explanation to the Secretariat of the reasons why they do not feel it appropriate to do so. **33–26**

In a case from 1978, the ICC Court's scrutiny of a draft Award was illustrated as follows: **33–27**

> "On January 23, 1978, the Secretary General of the ICC wrote to the three arbitrators inter alia: 'I would inform you that the Court of Arbitration examined the award in this case at its session on the 18th January, 1978, but decided that it could not approve it.
> The Court considered that paragraph 1 of the decision contained an apparent contradiction. If the defendant was entitled to reject the ship, how can they now be obliged to accept it with a price reduction for the faults?
> The precise meaning and legal effect of rejection and any new facts since the rejection which lead to the result of the award should be explained in the reasons.
> Secondly as a matter of form the award must be expressed either as unanimous or as a majority award as a whole. If an arbitrator wishes to dissent, this may be treated in the appropriate manner. Bearing in mind that the place of arbitration is Paris, the dissenting arbitrator can refuse to sign the award but this refusal has to be confirmed by the two other arbitrators."[23]

[22] ICC Award, case No.16978 rendered in 2013.

[23] See extracts from the ICC Award of 1978, *Götaverken v GMTC* (1981) YBCA Vol.VI p.133 to p.140; see also Delvolvé, Rouche & Pointon, *op. cit.*, para.410, p.233.

33–28 The draft Award was then resubmitted and after further comments, it was approved. The comments therefore focused on apparent contradiction and on the formal requirement for signatures where one arbitrator refused to sign the Award.

33–29 After approval by the Court, the draft Award should not be modified beyond the corrections required by the ICC Court, except to deal with minor issues such as typographical errors, which may have remained undetected.

The treatment of dissenting opinions

33–30 When an arbitrator has drafted a dissenting opinion, the dissenting arbitrator is expected to submit the dissent to the ICC Court within a reasonable time after the submission of the draft Award for scrutiny. The ICC Court will take note of the dissent while scrutinising the draft Award of the majority. The ICC Court will not comment upon the dissenting opinion, which is neither scrutinised nor approved since it is not part of the Award. To the extent that the ICC Court feels that a valid point has been raised by the dissenting arbitrator which the majority does not seem to have considered, but with which it should have dealt with in the draft Award, it will draw the majority's attention to such point. The most important points in this respect often relate to the procedure. In some instances, the dissent raises issues as to the collegiality with respect to the deliberations. For example, if a dissenting arbitrator maintains that he or she was not consulted with respect to the draft Award or that the dissenting arbitrator was excluded from some deliberations, the ICC Court may well draw the chairman's attention to the issue and may well invite the president to consider re-opening the deliberations. However, in most cases, the ICC Court will be reluctant to become involved in the deliberation process as, by submitting the draft Award for approval, the majority has indicated its view on the merits.

33–31 Since the ICC Court's quality control of Awards should ultimately ensure their enforceability, the ICC Court will also consider, as far as possible, whether the Award is compatible with the public policy at the place of arbitration. This is precisely what the Internal Rules of the ICC Court prescribe: "When the Court scrutinizes draft Awards in accordance with Art.33 of the Rules, it considers, to the extent practicable, the requirements of mandatory law at the place of arbitration".[24] This raises the question whether it falls upon the ICC Court to require an arbitral Tribunal to verify the compatibility of the Award, for example, with anti-trust laws, where the parties have not even raised possible anti-trust violations. In the 2009 *Linde* case, the Paris Court of Appeal noted that the ICC Court had not made any comments regarding the possible violation of EU competition law while verifying the validity of the draft Award. The Paris Court of Appeal used this lack of comment as a further argument for its conclusion that such violation could not have been "manifest" as now alleged by the applicant.[25]

[24] App. II Art.6.
[25] CA Paris, October 22, 2009, (2010) Rev Arb. No 1, p.124.

The ICC Court's approval and the State Courts

The ICC Court's decision leading to the approval of a draft Award is communicated by its Secretariat only to the Tribunal, never to the parties. Its decision, as well as the underlying reasons are treated in a confidential manner. Even upon a party's subsequent request, the ICC Court's Secretariat will normally not communicate the Court's approval to the Parties. **33–32**

However, as the *Linde* decision shows, the ICC Court provided the Paris Court of Appeal with its decision regarding the approval of the draft Award. This allowed the Paris Court of Appeal to state that the ICC Court had not made any comments regarding the possible violation of EU competition law rules. It is undoubtedly important that the ICC Court be at all times in a position to show to the annulment judge the basis for its approval decision. This is what the ICC Court has done in a few instances before the Paris Court of Appeal, in particular in those cases, where it was also made a party to the proceedings, like in the well-known *SNF* case.[26] **33–33**

However, when seized with an annulment action or request for enforcement of an ICC Award, the state courts have to make their independent judgment based on the legal standard applicable for their decisions. In the normal case, there should be no reason for them to be concerned with the reasoning of the ICC Court during the Court's approval of a draft Award. **33–34**

Timing

Once a draft Award is submitted to the ICC Court it will be reviewed first by the Secretariat with a view to preparation of the outline referred to in Annex 1 Pt I. In the case of draft Awards that are dealt with at Committee Sessions, once the Secretariat has completed its review, the matter can be dealt with at the next weekly Committee Session. For matters dealt with at Plenary Sessions, the draft Award (and dissent) will be transmitted for review by a member of the ICC Court, the *Rapporteur* of the case. **33–35**

The timing required for the Secretariat to consider a draft Award will vary with the workload. However, generally a draft Award (and any relevant dissent) to be considered at a Plenary Session should be provided two to three weeks prior to the Plenary Session. For draft Awards dealt with at Committee Sessions, the duration is somewhat shorter. In urgent cases, it may be scrutinised by the Chairman of the ICC Court or a Vice Chairman designated by him pursuant to art.1(3). **33–36**

As discussed under Annex 1 Pt I, the Secretariat transmits the Court's comments to the arbitrators generally within a few days after the Court's session. Thereafter, the time taken to incorporate or respond to the comments depends on the arbitrators themselves. In some instances, a revised version of the Award is available in a short period of time. In other cases, particularly where the ICC Court has not approved the Award, the preparation of a revised draft may take considerable **33–37**

[26] CA Paris, January 22, 2009, *SNF SAS v Chambre de commerce internationale (CCI)* (2010) Rev Arb No.2, p.314.

time. The duration of the scrutiny process is a matter of irritation in some ICC arbitrations. Pursuant to art.27(2), when the Tribunal closes the proceedings, the Tribunal is required to provide the Secretariat and the parties with "an approximate date by which the draft award will be submitted to the Court for approval pursuant to Article 33".

Article 34 Notification, Deposit and Enforceability of the Award

1. **Once an award has been made, the Secretariat shall notify to the parties the text signed by the arbitral tribunal, provided always that the costs of the arbitration have been fully paid to the ICC by the parties or by one of them.**
2. **Additional copies certified true by the Secretary General shall be made available on request and at any time to the parties, but to no one else.**
3. **By virtue of the notification made in accordance with Article 34(1), the parties waive any other form of notification or deposit on the part of the arbitral tribunal.**
4. **An original of each award made in accordance with the Rules shall be deposited with the Secretariat.**
5. **The arbitral tribunal and the Secretariat shall assist the parties in complying with whatever further formalities may be necessary.**
6. **Every award shall be binding on the parties. By submitting the dispute to arbitration under the Rules, the parties undertake to carry out any award without delay and shall be deemed to have waived their right to any form of recourse insofar as such waiver can validly be made.**

Introductory remarks

Article 34 covers both administrative and substantive aspects of Awards. Article 34(1)–(5) deal with the mechanics of transmitting Awards to the parties and seek **34–1** to exclude national formalities with respect to them. Article 34(6) then deals with the substantive effect of Awards and the Rules.

Article 34(1): "Once an award has been made, the Secretariat shall notify to the parties the text signed by the arbitral tribunal, provided always that the costs of the arbitration have been fully paid to the ICC by the parties or by one of them."

34–2 Once the draft Award has been approved by the ICC Court pursuant to art.33 the Award is signed and dated by the arbitrators.[1] The president of the Tribunal usually circulates copies of the Award for signature and submits the signed copies to the Secretariat. The number of original copies required will depend on the number of recipients. The president should circulate an original for each party, for the ICC and for each arbitrator. The Secretariat then "notifies" an original copy to each of the parties and confirms to the members of the Tribunal that the Award has been notified to the parties. The notification is normally made by using international courier services, or registered letters against return receipt. Thus, unlike procedural orders, under the Rules, Awards must be sent to the parties by the Secretariat, not by the Tribunal.

34–3 At this time, the parties are also invited to submit their overall appreciation on how the ICC arbitration was conducted by the arbitrators and also the assistance provided by the Secretariat in the ICC Evaluation Form. The evaluation, which is confidential, is meant to assist the ICC Court and its Secretariat in measuring the parties' expectations or satisfaction and also to anticipate the needs to improve its own practice and possibly the Rules themselves.

34–4 In accordance with art.31(1), if one arbitrator refuses to sign the Award, then the Award may be signed by the remaining arbitrators. Although seldom, it is possible that the two co-arbitrators agree on the Award and that the president is the minority member. If that is the case, and the president refuses to sign the Award, the Award would be rendered by the two arbitrators. If both co-arbitrators do not concur with the Award, then the Award may be made and signed by the president alone.

34–5 The Secretariat generally sends a copy of any dissenting opinion with the Award, although, as discussed in art.31, the dissenting opinion has no legal standing as such under the Rules.[2]

34–6 Prior to sending the Award to the parties, the Secretariat will review the level of the advance on costs to determine whether the costs as fixed by the ICC Court and set out in the Award have been fully covered. If payment of the full amount of the advance on costs has not been made to the ICC, then the ICC Court will require the parties to make that payment. If one party refuses to make the payment, the other party may substitute itself for the defaulting party. As long as such payment

[1] The president of the Tribunal may ask the co-arbitrators to sign the last page of the Award prior to approval by the Court. However, any signature is subject to approval and to a final determination by the ICC Court of the costs of arbitration under art.37(1). The president of the Tribunal will generally be the last one to sign and date the Award. It is not necessary, and not even recommended, that the co-arbitrators add the date of signature. One date, which will be the date of the Award as per art.31(3), is sufficient for all purposes.

[2] See para.31–13.

has not been made, the Secretariat will not notify the Award. The Secretariat does not require that the parties pay amounts due to the members of the Tribunal for value added tax, even if the account for collection of value added tax is being maintained by the ICC, as the collection of value added tax is a matter between the arbitrators and the parties.

The Secretariat will send the Award to the addresses for notifications indicated in the Terms of Reference in accordance with art.23(1)(b), or any other address it may have subsequently been advised of by the parties. The Secretariat sends one original of the Award for each party. If the party is represented by outside counsel, the latter will receive the original copy or copies for the party(ies) he or she represents. Generally the Secretariat uses international courier services for notifying of Awards rather than registered mail with return receipt. If a party's counsel is based in Paris, hand delivery by messenger will normally be chosen by the Secretariat.[3] If all parties or their representatives are in Paris, they may agree that the Award be simultaneously remitted to all of them at the ICC headquarters. Depending on the location and time zones of the parties' counsel, the parties will invariably receive the Award at different times. In some cases, one party may receive an Award a day or several days before the other party.[4] There is no practice of simultaneous transmittal by email or by access to a website for example, although that would deal with the problem. 34–7

As was noted in the second edition of this Handbook, it was not possible for parties to obtain from the Secretariat a meaningful indication as to whether a draft Award was received from the Tribunal and when the draft Award should be approved by the ICC Court. This was not in the interest of transparency of the approval process and the preference of many parties is to have a reasonable expectation of when the Award will be rendered. Whether justified or not, there is a perception that the drafting of some Awards tends to be delayed as the members of the Tribunal are taken up with other matters. An expected date for rendering the Award can help defuse this concern and provide an impetus for having the Award issued. In the 2012 Rules, this issue has now been addressed, and to some extent solved by art.27(b). Once the Tribunal has closed the proceedings, it is to inform the parties and the Tribunal of the date on which the Tribunal expects to submit its draft Award to the ICC. The ICC does not automatically inform the parties (or the Tribunal) generally of the time that scrutiny will involve. However, if requested by the Tribunal, the Secretariat may provide an indication. On some occasions, if there is a delay in scrutiny of the Award, the president of the Tribunal will so inform the parties. 34–8

The situation may be particularly difficult if a shares of a publicly-traded entity are involved or if a government entity is concerned. In several recent cases involving such entities, the president of the Tribunal has sought to inform the parties on the status of and the scrutiny process. In one case, at the request of the 34–9

[3] To avoid Paris-based counsel to receive the Award earlier than counsel which resides elsewhere, the Secretariat normally delays by one day the messenger delivery to Paris-based counsel.

[4] The Secretariat will confirm to the lawyers whether an Award has been sent out and can be prevailed upon to provide a copy by fax. Therefore, if contacted by the other side, there are ways of verifying the status of the Award.

parties, the parties were informed of the date on which the Award would be made available at the ICC and a copy was sent by email to the parties at the same time.

34–10 Article 34(1) is applicable to all Awards, including partial or interim Awards or Awards by consent. Prior to sending a partial or interim Award, the ICC may be less concerned about verifying the status of the payment of advances on costs, although the financial status of the file will generally be reviewed by the Secretariat before it notifies any Award.

Article 34(2): "Additional copies certified true by the Secretary General shall be made available on request and at any time to the parties, but to no one else."

34–11 For annulment or enforcement proceedings parties generally require an original of the Award or a certified copy of the Award. The Secretariat of the ICC Court will provide a party at its request one or more certified copies, normally within 48 hours or less. This service is rendered by the ICC free of charge, although the ICC generally asks the requesting party to complete a form as to why the original or certified copy is needed. The provision under art.34(2) for certified copies of the Award is very useful for the parties as it is always possible to obtain from the ICC a copy of the Award that can be used for enforcement purposes.[5] This is particularly useful if a party is, for example, a joint venture and each member of the joint venture wishes to have a certified copy through the Secretariat.

34–12 National courts usually accept certified copies of Awards. There have, however, been instances where the original was requested. If parties see a risk of being requested to provide the state courts with the original copy of the Award, they would be well advised to request more than one original copy from the Tribunal at the outset.

34–13 ICC Awards are confidential as far as the ICC and the arbitrators are concerned. Therefore, art.34(2) specifies that additional copies of an Award are not available for other persons. This is a contractual restriction and therefore would appear to be subject to limitations if disclosure is sought by a public authority with a right to require disclosure. However, there appear to have been no recorded instances of public authorities seeking to require disclosure of Awards from the ICC.[6]

Article 34(3): "By virtue of the notification made in accordance with Article 34(1), the parties waive any other form of notification or deposit on the part of the arbitral tribunal."

34–14 Under some national laws, such as in Saudi Arabia or in Germany, prior to the adoption of the UNCITRAL Model Law in 1997, an Award had to be deposited with the local court to be effective. These requirements are not found in the UNCITRAL Model Law or in the laws of most major centres of arbitration, e.g. Paris, France.

[5] In ad hoc arbitration, if one of the members of the Tribunal dies or is incapacitated, it may not be possible to obtain additional copies of an Award.

[6] There have, however, been instances where the terms of an Award have been sought from the parties or from the arbitrators.

Under each national legal system, there is a limited period for parties to seek the annulment of an Award. The date on which this period begins to run will depend on the terms of the national law and, in particular, whether the Award must be notified in a particular form or not. The details of national procedure—and the time limits for filings—must be analysed in detail in each instance. However, set out below are basic provisions relating to the time periods applicable in major centres in arbitration that should be reviewed at the appropriate time. 34–15

In France, the party seeking to enforce an Award files an original or certified copy with the court and obtains an order permitting its enforcement (known as "*exequatur*"). Under art.1522 of the French CPC, the other party then has one month from the date of notification of this order to seek to annul the Award. Therefore, the time within which to begin annulment proceedings will only begin to run once there has been a filing to declare the Award enforceable and the initial decision has been notified to the parties in accordance with French court procedure and subject to the time limits of that procedure.[7] 34–16

In Switzerland, art.191 of the Swiss PILA provides that "[t]he sole judicial authority to set aside is the Swiss Federal Supreme Court. The procedure follows Art. 77 of the Swiss Federal Statute on the Swiss Federal Supreme Court of June 17, 2005".[8] The time limit is "30 days from the notification of the decision in accordance with cantonal law" and the time period begins to run with the notification of the Award.[9] 34–17

In the United States, under s.12 of the Federal Arbitration Act, "[n]otice of a motion to vacate, modify, or correct an award must be served upon the adverse party or his attorney within three months after the award is filed or delivered". 34–18

In England, under s.70(3) of the English Arbitration Act 1996, "[a]ny application or appeal must be brought within 28 days of the date of the award or, if there has been any arbitral process of appeal or review, of the date when the applicant or appellant was notified of the result of that process". 34–19

Article 34(4): "An original of each award made in accordance with the Rules shall be deposited with the Secretariat."

The Sole Arbitrator or president will provide the ICC Secretariat with original copies of the Award for each party, as the case may be, each arbitrator, and for the ICC itself.[10] The ICC maintains an original in its records to permit it to issue certified copies of the Award. 34–20

The Secretariat also requests that the Sole Arbitrator or president provide an electronic version of the Award for use in the ICC's database and for easy access to extracts that the ICC publishes from time to time in its Bulletin. 34–21

[7] The limitation period of one month is however extended by one month where the party to be served is resident or has its registered office in a French overseas department or territory, and by two months if such residence or registered office is situated abroad (art.643 of the French CPC). See Delvolvé, Rouche & Pointon, *op. cit.*, para.468, p.267.

[8] Unofficial translation by the Swiss Arbitration Association.

[9] Article 100 al.1 of the Swiss Supreme Court Act.

[10] For further details, see para.34–2.

Article 34(5): "The arbitral tribunal and the Secretariat shall assist the parties in complying with whatever further formalities may be necessary."

34–22 The formalities referred to in art.34(5) are usually formalities that are required to enforce an Award. Often the formality that may be required is the signing of an additional original of an Award for enforcement proceedings. In lieu of that, a certified copy of the Award is sometimes sufficient. In some instances, it may be necessary to obtain an *apostille* under the Hague Convention of October 5, 1961 Abolishing the Requirement of Legalisation for Foreign Public Documents.

Article 34(6): "Every award shall be binding on the parties. By submitting the dispute to arbitration under the Rules, the parties undertake to carry out any award without delay and shall be deemed to have waived their right to any form of recourse insofar as such waiver can validly be made."

34–23 By agreeing to ICC arbitration, parties are agreeing to be bound by Awards. Moreover, they are waiving "any form of recourse insofar as such waiver can validly be made".

Effect of waiver in general

34–24 The predecessors to art.34(6) were intended, in particular, to effect a waiver of any national rights to appeal an Award. These rights existed under various legal systems but have been virtually eliminated in major centres of arbitration. Waiver of a right to appeal is also not required under the UNCITRAL Model Law as the grounds for court review of Awards are limited under art.40 of that Law.

34–25 Article 34(6) was not intended to and does not amount to a waiver of basic rights of parties, including the right to have the Award set aside under applicable law or to object to its enforcement under the grounds set out in the New York Convention discussed below. Nor does it permit a party to execute on the Award without judicial formality on the Award. As the French courts have held:

> "Whatever its obligatory effect the undertaking [in art.34(6)] does not have the effect of conferring on the arbitral award the status of an automatically executory judgment as claimed by the defendants; that it cannot deprive the parties not only of the possibility of seeking to have the award annulled, which is a matter of public policy, but also of that to invoke the generally applicable provisions of the [Code of Civil Procedure] to seek to block the temporary execution if, as in the present case, it has been ordered; Article 34(6) of the above rules and the obligation of good faith in the carrying out of the award which follows from it imply solely a strict interpretation of the cases in which one can derogate even temporarily from the enforcement of the award and therefore

the objection as to admissibility of the defendants must be rejected."[11] (Authors' translation)

The position of the Paris Court of Appeal was confirmed in the *République du Congo* case where the French Supreme Court took the view that the reference to the equivalent of art.34 under the prior Rules is not to be construed as a waiver of the suspensive nature of the annulment action ("*recours en annulation*").[12] Under the text of art.1506 of the French CPC prior to the 2011 reform, the *recours en annulation* of the Award was suspensive unless the parties had expressly agreed to waive its suspensive effect or when the Tribunal had granted a provisional enforcement of the Award in accordance with art.514 of the French CPC.[13] In other words, in the context of international arbitration, if provisional enforcement had been ordered in the Award, it could only be stopped by the judge on appeal on specific grounds, i.e. if it was prohibited by law or would have patently excessive consequences. However, following its 2011 reform, the French CPC no longer provides for a suspensive nature to the annulment action, instead stating explicitly that "the annulment action formed against an award and the appeal of the enforcement order are not suspensive". (Author's translation)[14] **34–26**

No exclusion of setting aside actions

Article 34(6) does not amount, and should not be considered as a (valid) agreement of excluding a setting aside (annulment) action against an ICC Award.[15] Some jurisdictions, such as Switzerland, expressly allow the parties to enter into exclusion agreements regarding setting aside actions prior to the issuance of an Award, even at the time of entering into the arbitration agreement.[16] **34–27**

The Swiss Federal Court has taken the position on several occasions that the waiver in the ICC Rules does not qualify as an exclusion agreement within the meaning of art.192 PILA.[17] **34–28**

Since the 2011 reform of French arbitration law, art.1522 of the French CCP expressly allows parties to agree to an exclusion of setting aside actions. The **34–29**

[11] CA Paris, February 5, 2003, *Société Thalès Air Defence v GIE Euromissile et Eads* (2004) Rev Arb No.1 p.94.

[12] CA Paris, March 10, 2005, *République du Congo v SA Total E&P Congo* (2005) Rev Arb No.3 p.788. See also Cass Civ 1re, July 4, 2007, *Groupe Antoine Tabet v République du Congo et Société Totale E&P Congo*, No.05-16.586; see also (2007) Rev Arb No.3 p.648; see, however, the contrary decision of the Paris TGI, December 2002, *Banque Centrale de Syrie et République arabe de Syrie v Société Papillon Group Corp (PGC)* (2003) Rev Arb No.1 p.245; Farhad, "Provisional Enforcement of International Arbitral Awards Made in France–The Dilatory Effect of the French Set Aside Application" (2006) J Int'l Arb Vol.23 No.2, p.115; Fouchard, Gaillard & Goldman, *op. cit.*, p.1011.

[13] CA Paris, June 2, 2005, *Bacque v Société Carlyle Luxembourg Holding* (2005) Rev Arb No.4 p.1015, note Callé.

[14] See art.1526 of the French CPC. See Seraglini & Ortscheidt, "La nouvelle articulation des recours en arbitrage international" in Clay, *Le nouveau droit français de l'arbitrage* (2011), p.195.

[15] Mandatory law at the place of arbitration and the law applicable to the ICC arbitration agreement is likely to make an advance waiver against an annulment action, see Reiner & Aschauer, para.689.

[16] Article 1925 PILA is reproduced in Pt III. Regarding the formal requirements of exclusion agreements under Swiss law see Levy and Besheda "Recent Swiss Developments on Exclusion Agreements" SIAR 2008:3, p.67.

[17] ATF 133 III 235 ; 134 III 260 ; *Tribunal Fédéral*, Decision of August 21, 2008 (4A-194/208).

parties can do so at any time, as long as their agreement is express and takes the form of a special agreement ("*convention spéciale*"). It is understood, however, that the parties' agreement under art.34(6) of the ICC Rules does not suffice to qualify waiver pursuant to art.1522.[18]

Effect of waiver on state entities

34–30 In the *Creighton Ltd v Qatar* case, the issue was whether, by accepting the ICC arbitration, the Qatari state entity was waiving its claim to immunity from execution as well as the immunity from jurisdiction. The Paris Court of Appeal held that that was not the case, and Creighton brought the matter before the French Supreme Court. The French Supreme Court ruled in favour of Creighton, holding that the state entity had waived its claim to immunity in the following terms:

> "[1] A waiver of immunity from execution may be deduced in particular from the acceptance by the State by the signing of an arbitration clause or a submission to arbitration; the rules of arbitration of the International Chamber of Commerce at the time of the signing of the contract between the State of Qatar and Creighton Limited provided expressly that in submitting their dispute to arbitration of the International Chamber of Commerce the parties undertook to carry out without delay the award and that the award was 'enforceable' (Art.24); in deciding that the State of Qatar did not waive its immunity from execution when it is apparent from the documents in the file that state agreed to arbitration under the rules of the International Chamber of Commerce, the [Court of Appeal] erred in law with regard to Articles 1142, 1147 and 1098 of the New Code of Civil Procedure [and] the principles of private international law governing the immunity of states."[19]

34–31 More recently, the French Supreme Court, in *NML v Argentina*, has significantly tightened the rule with respect to waiver of sovereign immunity in the context of attempts by a hedge fund to enforce obligations against Argentina. In one of three cases rendered in March 2013, the French Supreme Court held that:

> "Whereas pursuant to customary international law, as reflected in the United Nations Convention of 2 December 2004 on jurisdictional immunity of states and of their property, although states can waive their immunity of execution by written agreement with respect to their property or a category of property destined for public use, such waiver must

[18] Seraglini, *L'efficacité et l'autorité renforcées des sentences arbitrales en France après le décret n° 2011–48 du 13 janvier 2011* (2011) Les Cahiers de l'Arbitrage, No.2011/2, p.375; Jarosson & Pellerin, *Le droit français de l'arbitrage après le décret du 13 janvier 2011* 1 (2011) Rev. Arb. 5, at 70–71.

[19] (2000) YBCA Vol.XXV at pp.459–460, see also (2000) ASA Bull Vol.18 No.3, p.605; Gaillard, "Convention d'arbitrage et imunités de juridiction et d'exécution des Etats et des organisations internationales" (2000) ASA Bull Vol.18 No.3, p.471; Annacker & Greig, "State Immunity and Arbitration" (2004) ICC ICArb Bull Vol.15 No.2, p.70.

be express and identify the property or the category of property for which the waiver is granted." (Authors' translation)[20]

Creighton Ltd sought to enforce the Award in the United States. The Court of Appeals for the District of Columbia Circuit found that the acceptance of international arbitration was not a waiver of sovereign immunity.[21] The court did find that acceptance of international arbitration amounted to a waiver of objections to subject matter jurisdiction under the 1988 amendment to the US Foreign Sovereign Immunities Act.[22] However, the court held that Qatar did not have the minimum contacts required to justify personal jurisdiction and therefore held that it did not have jurisdiction in the case.[23] **34–32**

[20] Cass Civ 1re, March 28, 2013, No.395. See also Cass Civ 1re, March 28, 2013, Nos 394 and 396. For a discussion in English see Kleiman and Spinelli "*NML v Argentina*: Supreme Court tightens waiver of sovereign immunity test" http://www.internationallawoffice.com/newsletters/detail.aspx?g=52a47656-8854-4c26-9892-5d7205148277 [accessed November 19, 2013]. As correctly noted by those authors, the UN Convention relied upon by the French Supreme Court is not yet in force, although it has been signed and ratified by France.

[21] *Creighton Ltd v Govt of Qatar*, 181 F.3d 118 (DC Cir. 1999); (2000) YBCA Vol.XXV p.458 at p.459. In that case, the Court noted: "The closest Creighton comes to arguing that Qatar intended to waive its sovereign immunity is in pointing to this statement in the House Report accompanying the FSIA: 'the courts have found [implicit] waivers in cases where a foreign state has agreed to arbitration in another country.' H.R. Rep. No.94-1487, at 18 (1976), reprinted in 1976 U.S.C.C.A.N. 6604, 6617. Creighton claims Qatar's agreement to arbitrate in France should be deemed an implicit waiver of its sovereign immunity in US courts. Cf. id. (explaining courts have also found such waivers 'where a foreign state has agreed that the law of a particular country should govern a contract'). We follow the Second Circuit in rejecting such a broad reading of the 'implicit waiver' exception".

[22] The Court stated: "The Congress added the following exception to the FSIA in 1988: 'A foreign state shall not be immune from the jurisdiction of courts of the United States or of the States in any case [. . .] in which the action is brought. [. . .] to confirm an award made pursuant to [. . .]an agreement to arbitrate, if [. . .] the agreement or award is or may be governed by a treaty or other international agreement in force for the United States calling for the recognition and enforcement of arbitral awards.' 28 U.S.C. p 1605 (a)(6). Qatar does not contest Creighton's assertion that because the New York Convention calls for enforcement of any arbitral award rendered within the jurisdiction of a signatory country, the quoted exception applies by its terms to this action. Indeed, it has been said with authority that the New York Convention 'is exactly the sort of treaty Congress intended to include in the arbitration exception".

[23] Under the Fifth Amendment to the US Constitution, for a court to assert jurisdiction over a defendant, the defendant must have certain minimum contacts with the jurisdiction. The US Court of Appeals for the DC Circuit held that Qatar did not have these minimum contacts given the fact that the project was to take place in Qatar and payments were made in Qatar. In *S. Davis International, Inc v Yemen* 218 F. 3d 1292 (11th Cir. 2000), the 11th Circuit held that the there were the minimum contacts with the Yemeni state agency in the following terms: "In Creighton, the district court for the District of Columbia, held that Qatar was not subject to personal jurisdiction under a minimum contacts and purposeful availment analysis, because the contract 'was offered, accepted, and performed in Qatar pursuant to a sponsorship arrangement between Creighton and a Qatari contractor.' Id. at 127–28. In addition, the contract specified that it was subject to the laws of Qatar, payment was made in Qatari riyals to Creighton's bank account in Qatar, and the alleged breach occurred in Qatar. Id. at 128 .[. . .] Having determined that the Ministry was involved in more than 'one regulatory act,' the contract itself anticipates further contacts between the two nations. One of the parties to this contract was a United States corporation who was required to provide 'U.S. wheat No.2 or better' (none of which is grown in Yemen) to be imported to Yemen. Performance logically required contact and interaction with the United States, as discussed in the contract (such as designating a U.S. bank for payment and a point of departure for shipping). Unlike the facts of Creighton, the contract did not state it was subject to the laws of Yemen, there were direct dealings between parties of both countries, [. . .]and the direct effect occurred with the defendants' failure to open the letter of credit at the New York bank.' When minimum contacts have been established, often the interests of the plaintiff and the forum in the exercise of jurisdiction will justify even the serious

34–33 However, some jurisdictions have found that, while acceptance of the ICC Rules (in an arbitration clause, for example) presumes a waiver of any right to claim immunity for jurisdiction, it does not do so for enforcement. In *FG Hemisphere Associates LLC v Democratic Republic of Congo*, the High Court of Hong Kong ruled this way, finding that submission to arbitration rules is not sufficient on its own and that clear conduct which is at variance with claiming immunity from execution was required as art.34(6) does nothing more than waive the right of challenging the Award.[24] The Court specifically addressed the *Creighton* decision stating, "With respect I do not think that [Creighton] can be right insofar as it was there suggested that submission to an ICC arbitration is without more tantamount to a waiver of immunity from execution. I do not think such conclusion logically follows from the premise". Indeed, in *Orascom Telecom Holding SAE v Republic of Chad*, a UK court applying French law, and, in particular, the *Creighton* decision, found that the decision had done no more than reaffirm that waiver of immunity would be presumed in respect of assets held for "commercial purposes".[25] The Court therefore found that the finding in regards to the ICC Rules was secondary to the nature of the property being seized or attached.

34–34 In the United States, enforcement of a foreign state's assets must proceed under the Foreign Sovereign Immunity Act (FSIA) rather than the Federal Arbitration Act because the FSIA is the sole basis for obtaining jurisdiction over a foreign state in the courts of the United States. Some courts have found that a foreign state's agreement to adjudicate all disputes under the contract at issue by arbitration under the rules of an arbitral institution such as the ICC constitutes a waiver of sovereign immunity under the Act.[26] Most courts, however, have construed the relevant sections of the FSIA narrowly and refused to find an implicit waiver of immunity to suit in US courts from an arbitration clause stipulating in favour of arbitration in a country outside of the United States.

34–35 In the case of *Svenska Petroleum Exploration AB v (1) Government of the Republic of Lithuania (2) Ab Geonafta*,[27] the English Court of Appeal decided that, when a foreign state has agreed in writing to submit a dispute to arbitration within s.9(1) of the State Immunity Act 1978, that state cannot claim immunity in respect of proceedings in United Kingdom courts under s.101(2) of the English Arbitration Act of 1996 to enforce a foreign arbitration award and stated as follows:

burdens placed on the alien defendant.' Asahi Metal Industry Co. Superior Court of California, 480 US 102, 114 (1987)".

[24] *FG Hemisphere Associates LLC v Democratic Republic of Congo* Hong Kong, SAR No.24. High Court of the Hong Kong Special Administrative Region, Court of Appeal, May 5, 2010; Civil Appeal No.43 of 2009.

[25] *Orascom Telecom Holding SAE v Republic of Chad*, July 28, 2008 QBD (Comm).

[26] See *Ipitrade Int'l, SA v Fed Rep of Nigeria*, 465 F.Supp 824 (D.C.D.C. 1978); *Libyan American Oil Co v Socialist People's Libyan Arab Jamahirya*, 482 F.Supp. 1175 (D.C.D.C. 1980).

[27] *Svenska Petroleum Exploration AB v (1) Government of the Republic of Lithuania (2) Ab Geonafta, op. cit.*

> "[. . .] in our view the judge was right to hold that the Government agreed to submit disputes with Svenska to arbitration under the ICC Rules in accordance with the provisions of article 9 of the agreement. [. . .]
> Under Lithuanian law an arbitration clause is regarded as an autonomous agreement, that is, an agreement which gives rise to rights and obligations which existing independently of the contract within which it is found, and an agreement to arbitrate under the ICC rules confers on the arbitrators jurisdiction to decide whether they have jurisdiction in any given case. In the present case by agreeing to ICC arbitration the parties conferred on the arbitrators jurisdiction to determine that question and are therefore bound by their award. [. . .]
> The judge held that there was no basis for construing section 9 of the State Immunity Act (particularly when viewed in the context of the provisions of section 13 dealing with execution) as excluding proceedings relating to the enforcement of a foreign arbitral award. We think that is right. Arbitration is a consensual procedure and the principle underlying section 9 is that, if a state has agreed to submit to arbitration, it has rendered itself amenable to such process as may be necessary to render the arbitration effective. [. . .]
> We therefore agree with the judge that Svenska's application for leave to enforce the second award falls within section 9(1) of the State Immunity Act and that the Government is unable to claim immunity in respect of it."

The impact of art.34(6) on state entities will therefore depend on the jurisdiction of enforcement. If the French and now English approach is adopted it will be very significant as it will be a major distinction between arbitration under the ICC Rules and other international arbitration rules. **34–36**

The primary jurisdiction

Article V(1)(e) of the New York Convention provides that the courts of the place of enforcement "may" refuse enforcement if "[t]he award [. . .] has been set aside or suspended by a competent authority of the country in which, or under the law of which, that award was made". The country in which the Award is made is the country of the place of arbitration. This is generally viewed as the country with primary jurisdiction over annulment proceedings. **34–37**

The reference to the "country [. . .] under the law of which" an Award has been made is a matter of considerable debate. As discussed under art.21, the parties are free to select the "rules of law" that are to be applied to the merits of the dispute and, in the absence of such an agreement, the Tribunal "shall apply the rules of law which it determines appropriate". The law applicable to the merits is to be distinguished from the law applicable to the procedure. As discussed under arts 18 and 19, most ICC arbitrations do not follow any national procedure. However, all arbitrations are required to meet the mandatory requirements of the law of the place of arbitration. Therefore, although a matter of considerable debate, many view the "country [. . .] under the law of which" an Award is rendered as the **34–38** mandatory law of the place of arbitration, at least in the absence of extraordinary factors.

34–39 An illustration of this approach is found in *Karaha Bodas Co LLC v Perusahaan Pertambangan Minyak Dan Gas Bumi Negara*, referred to above.[28] In that case, the place of arbitration was Geneva; the law governing the contract was Indonesian law and there were certain references to Indonesian procedure in the contract, although there was no specific reference to Indonesian procedural law.[29] When the Indonesian party sought to argue that the Award had been properly annulled by Indonesian courts, the Fifth Circuit Court of Appeals held:

> "[11] Under the New York Convention, an agreement specifying the place of the arbitration creates a presumption that the procedural law of that place applies to the arbitration. Authorities on international arbitration describe an agreement providing that one country will be the site of the arbitration but the proceedings will be held under the arbitration law of another country by terms such as 'exceptional'; 'almost unknown'; a 'purely academic invention'; 'almost never used in practice'; a possibility 'more theoretical than real'; and a 'once-in-a-blue-moon set of circumstances'. Commentators note that such an agreement would be complex, inconvenient, and inconsistent with the selection of a neutral forum as the arbitral forum [. . .]
>
> [12] [. . .] Under Art.16(1) of the UNCITRAL Rules, the 'place' designated for an arbitration is the legal rather than physical location of the forum. The arbitration proceeding in this case physically occurred in Paris, but the Award was 'made in' Geneva, the place of the arbitration in the legal sense and the presumptive source of the applicable procedural law [. . .]
>
> [13] The references in the contracts to certain Indonesian civil procedure rules do not rebut the strong presumption that Swiss procedural law applied to the arbitration. These references fall far short of an express designation of Indonesian procedural law necessary to rebut the strong presumption that designating the place of the arbitration also designates the law under which the award is made." (citations deleted)[30]

[28] See above paras 27–8 and 27–9.

[29] The reference was as follows (as set out in footnote No.7 of the case): "The award rendered in any arbitration commenced hereunder shall be final and binding upon the Parties and judgment thereon may be entered in any court having jurisdiction for its enforcement. The Parties hereby renounce their right to appeal from the decision of the arbitral panel and agree that in accordance with Section 641 of the Indonesian Code of Civil Procedure [neither] Party shall appeal to any court from the decision of the arbitral panel and accordingly the Parties hereby waive the applicability of [certain Indonesian laws]. In addition, the Parties agree that [neither] Party shall have any right to commence or maintain any suit or legal proceeding concerning a [dispute hereunder until the] dispute has been determined in accordance with the arbitration procedure provided for herein and then only to enforce or facilitate the execution of the award rendered in such arbitration" (at p. 6).

[30] *op. cit.*, para.27–8 n.4. The same approach was adopted in *Belize Soc Dev, Ltd v Gov't of Belize*, 668 F.3d 724, where the Court of Appeals for the District of Columbia rejected the argument that an LCIA Award rendered in London should not be enforced in the US because it was contrary to Belize law as the governing law.

The Court held that the Swiss courts had jurisdiction over the annulment proceedings and the Swiss court had rejected annulment of the Award.[31] **34–40**

Although the *Karaha Bodas* decision conforms to the prevailing view in Europe, there are decisions to a contrary effect, such as in India. In the *Nirma* case,[32] the Indian court dealt with an ICC arbitration held in London where the law applicable to the merits was Indian law. The High Court of Gujarat held that the Indian Courts had jurisdiction to annul the Award under art.40 of the International Arbitration Act (which adopted the UNCITRAL Model Law). The Court stated: **34–41**

> "[20] According to the principle stated by Lord Denning M.R. in International Tank and Pipe Sak v Kuwait Aviation Fuelling Co. KSC, [1975] 1 All ER 242, if the parties had agreed that the proper law of the contract should be the law in force in India, but had also provided for arbitration in a foreign country, the laws of India would undoubtedly govern the validity, interpretation and effect of all clauses, including the arbitration clause in the contract as well as the scope of the arbitrators' jurisdiction. It is Indian law which governs the contract, including the arbitration clause, although in certain respects regarding the conduct of the arbitration proceedings, the foreign procedural law and the competent Courts of that country may have a certain measure of control.
> [21] The Supreme Court has also observed in NTPC case (supra) that the arbitration clause must be considered together with the rest of the contract and the relevant surrounding circumstances. In that case, the choice of the place of arbitration was, as far as the parties were concerned, merely accidental. On the other hand, apart from the expressly stated intention of the parties, the contract itself, including the arbitration agreement contained in one of its clauses, was redolent of India and matters Indian. The disputes between the parties under the contract had no connection with anything English, and they had the closest connection with Indian Laws, Rules and Regulations. In those circumstances, the mere fact that the venue chosen by the ICC Court for the conduct of arbitration was London did not support the case of [the party] on the point. Any attempt to exclude the jurisdiction of the competent Courts and the laws enforceable in India was held to be totally inconsistent with the agreement between the parties.
> [22] In view of the above, we have no hesitation in holding that the Indian Court was the Court of competent jurisdiction to entertain an application under Sect. 34 for setting aside the award, subject to the other provisions of Part I of the Act."[33]

[31] See *Yusuf Ahmed Alghanim & Sons, WLL v Toys 'R' Us, Inc, op. cit.*, para.14–[61] n.32 ("only the state under whose procedural law the arbitration was conducted has jurisdiction under Art.V(1)(e) to vacate the award").

[32] High Court, Gujarat, December 19, 2002, No.1787 of 2002 with Civil Application Nos 6301, 6556 and 8562 of 2002, *Nirma Ltd v Lurgi Energie und Entsorgung GmbH* (2003) YBCA Vol.XXVIII p.790.

[33] (2003) YBCA Vol.XXVIII at p.803.

34–42 The *Nirma* case is particular in that it is a case under the UNCITRAL Model Law. However, it appears to be an anomaly. The better view is that annulment will almost invariably be solely the prerogative of the courts of the place of arbitration.

Law of the place of arbitration: enforcement of annulled Awards

34–43 The place of arbitration is the primary jurisdiction and for many years it was assumed that an Award[34] annulled by the courts of the place of arbitration had no further legal existence. Therefore, under that view, the annulled Award could no longer be enforced under the New York Convention.[35]

34–44 That situation changed with a series of cases in Belgium, France and the United States.[36] The basic principle following those cases is that an Award that has been annulled at the place of arbitration may nevertheless be enforced in some circumstances in another New York Convention state. In some quarters, this was viewed as very surprising, especially when the French Supreme Court stated that "the award rendered in Switzerland is an international award which is not integrated in the legal system of that State, so that it remains in existence even if set aside and its recognition in France is not contrary to international public policy".[37]

34–45 However, the enforcement of annulled Awards continues to evolve. Therefore, set out below is a discussion of the situation under French and US law, which now show very divergent approaches to this issue.

34–46 In the first *Hilmarton* Award,[38] the Tribunal held that a contract providing for the payment of a commission was contrary to Algerian law and contrary to Swiss public policy and therefore not enforceable, although the contract was subject to Swiss law and the place of arbitration was Geneva. The Swiss court annulled the Award under art.36(f) of the Intercantonal Convention as being arbitrary.[39]

34–47 The French Supreme Court permitted enforcement of the first *Hilmarton* Award holding the contract unenforceable in stating:

[34] For a general discussion, see Webster, "Evolving Principles in Enforcing Awards Subject to Annulment Proceedings", Vol. 23 Jul of Int. Arb 261 (2006).

[35] The former para.44 of the UNCITRAL Official Commentary on the Model Law stated for example: "[t]he setting aside of an award at the place of origin prevents enforcement of that award in all other countries by virtue of article V(1)(e) of the 1958 New York Convention and article 36(1)(a)(v) of the Model Law". This sentence has been deleted from para.48, which replaces the old para.44 in the version of the UNICTRAL Official Commentary on the Model Law (as amended in 2006).

[36] For a discussion of the evolution, see Gaillard, "L'exécution des sentences annulées dans leur pays d'origine" (1997) JDI p.645; Fouchard, "La portée internationale de l'annulation de la sentence arbitrale dans son pays d'origine" (1998) Rev Arb No.3, p.329 ; and in *Philippe Fouchard–ECRITS–Droit de l'arbitrage–Droit du commerce international* (Comité français de l'arbitrage, 2007) p.441.; Moreau, "Les effets de la nullité de la sentence arbitrale" in *Etudes offertes à Pierre Bellet, op. cit.*, p.403.

[37] (1995) YBCA Vol.XX p.663.

[38] Cass Civ 1re, March 23, 1994, *Hilmarton Ltd v Omnium de traitement et de valorisation–OTV* (1995) YBCA Vol.XX p. 663.

[39] The Swiss Intercantonal Convention is no longer applicable to international arbitration and the Swiss PILA does not provide for annulment of Awards based on them being held arbitrary.

> "[4] Further, the lower decision correctly held that, applying Art.VII of the [1958 New York Convention], OTV could rely upon the French law on international arbitration concerning the recognition and enforcement of international arbitration awards rendered abroad, and especially upon Art.1502[40] CPC, which does not list the ground provided for in Art.V of the 1958 Convention among the grounds for refusal of recognition and enforcement. [5] Lastly, the award rendered in Switzerland is an international award which is not integrated in the legal system of that State, so that it remains in existence even if set aside and its recognition in France is not contrary to international public policy."[41]

After the first Award was annulled in Switzerland, a new sole arbitrator was appointed who held that the payment of the commission was valid under Swiss law, which was the governing law of the contract. This was the second *Hilmarton* Award.[42] In that Award, the fact that the payment of the commission was invalid under Algerian law was held by the sole arbitrator not to prevent enforceability under Swiss law, as there was no finding that the commission amounted to bribery. The Claimant sought to enforce the second Hilmarton Award in France and the Respondent invoked the French Supreme Court's decision upholding the first *Hilmarton* Award. The French Supreme Court held that the matter was res judicata in France and annulled the lower court decision permitting enforcement of the second *Hilmarton* Award. Therefore, in France, the final result was that the first *Hilmarton* Award was enforceable and the underlying contract was unenforceable. 34–48

However, an application by the Claimant to enforce the second *Hilmarton* Award was accepted in England. As a result, in Switzerland and England, the second *Hilmarton* Award was enforced and the contract was held enforceable although in France the contract was held unenforceable. The result is an anomaly due to the fact that there are two Awards on the same matter with inconsistent decisions in two EU jurisdictions as to enforceability of the underlying contract.[43] 34–49

The French Supreme Court adopted the same approach in the *Putrabali* case.[44] In that case, an arbitral Award was rendered on April 10, 2001 (the 2001 Award) in favour of the Respondent. The Respondent sought and obtained enforcement of the 2001 Award in France pursuant to a judgment dated March 31, 2005. However, the 2001 Award was partially annulled in review on a point of law before the English High Court. The matter was remitted to arbitration and this resulted in a second Award on August 21, 2003 (the 2003 Award) in favour of the Claimant, Putrabali. Claimant sought to enforce the 2003 Award in France. The French 34–50

[40] Current art.1520 of the CPC.

[41] (1995) YBCA Vol.XX at p.665. More recently, see the *Putrabali* case see 29 June 2007, 2007 Rev Art No.3 p.507.

[42] English High Court of Justice, Queen's Bench Division, May 24, 1999, *Omnium de Traitement et de Valorisation SA v Hilmarton* (1999) YBCA Vol.XXIVa p.777.

[43] The fact that state courts in two countries decide the issue of whether a contract is contrary to public policy is, of course, not infrequent. Under the New York Convention, it is quite possible that a state court will refuse to enforce an Award based on grounds of public policy although the courts of the place of arbitration or other state courts dealing with enforcement have upheld the underlying contract.

[44] See the *Putrabali* case. 29 June 2007, 2007 Rev Art No.3 p.507.

Supreme Court held that the 2003 Award could not be enforced in France due to the res judicata effect of the French enforcement proceedings relating to the 2001 Award, although the enforcement proceedings relating to the 2001 Award were only commenced in France after the 2001 Award has been partially annulled in England.

34–51 In the *Chromalloy* case,[45] the Award was rendered in favour of an American corporation against an Egyptian government entity. The place of arbitration was Cairo. The applicable law was Egyptian law. The Egyptian courts annulled the Award for failure to apply Egyptian administrative law.[46] The US court, however, permitted enforcement of the annulled Award, stating:

> "[10] Like the arbitrator in Al-Harbi, the arbitrators in the present case made a procedural decision that allegedly led to a misapplication of substantive law. After considering Egypt's arguments that Egyptian administrative law should govern the contract, the majority of the arbitral panel held that it did not matter which substantive law they applied–civil or administrative. Id. At worst, this decision constitutes a mistake of law, and thus is not subject to review by this Court. See Al-Harbi, 85 F.3d at 684.
> [11] In the United States, '[W]e are well past the time when judicial suspicion of the desirability of arbitration and of the competence of arbitral tribunals inhibited the development of arbitration as an alternative means of dispute resolution.' Mitsubishi Motors Corp v Soler Chrysler-Plymouth, Inc, 473 U.S. 614, 626-627, 105 S.Ct. 3346, 3354, 87 L.Ed.2d 444 (1985). In Egypt, however, '[I]t is established that arbitration is an exceptional means for resolving disputes, requiring departure from the normal means of litigation before the courts, and the guarantees they afford.' Egypt's complaint that, '[T]he Arbitral Award is null under Arbitration Law, [. . .] because it is not properly "grounded" under Egyptian law', reflects this suspicious view of arbitration, and is precisely the type of technical argument that US courts are not to entertain when reviewing an arbitral award [. . .]."

34–52 Similarly, the Court in the *Chromalloy* case upheld the enforcement of the annulled Award and this position has been adopted by the US Court of Appeals for the Fifth Circuit.

34–53 In the *Termorio* case, the United States Court of Appeals for the District of Columbia decided not to enforce an ICC Award which has been annulled by the competent authority, the Colombian Council of State ("*Consejo de Estado*") as contrary to the law of Colombia. According to the Council of State, in absence of an express agreement of the parties to submit their dispute to international arbitration, the submission of a domestic arbitration to ICC arbitration is a violation of

[45] United States District Court, District of Columbia, July 31, 1996, Civil No.94-2339, *Chromalloy Aeroservices Inc v The Arab Republic of Egypt* (1997) YBCA Vol.XXII p.1001; see also Schwartz, "A Comment on Chromalloy Hilmarton, à l'américaine" (1997) J Int'l Arb Vol. 14 No. 2, p.125.

[46] In many civil law countries, contracts with state agencies are subject to a code of administrative law rather than the civil code, see para.6–154.

public policy. In so deciding, the US Court of Appeals did not take into account the *Chromalloy* case which was heavily relied on by the appellant because:

> "as appellees point out 'the present case is plainly distinguishable from *Chromalloy* where an express contract provision was violated by pursuing an appeal to vacate the Award. Here, Electranta preserved its objection that the panel was not proper or authorized by law, promptly raised it in the Colombian courts, and received a definitive ruling by the highest court on this question of law."[47]

In COMMISA,[48] the US Federal Court in New York enforced an ICC Award that had been annulled in Mexico, which was the place of arbitration. The Court so decided on the grounds that the annulment was based on what appeared to be a retroactive law creating issues regarding the rescission of non-arbitrable administrative contracts and the lack of an alternative forum. **34–54**

The enforcement of annulled awards also arose in the Netherlands and the UK with the *Yukos* cases. Basically, the Claimant in that case had obtained an arbitration award in Russia against a company which was private at the time but later came under state ownership. The Award was annulled in Russia. The Claimant sought to enforce the Award in the Netherlands and the Amsterdam Court of Appeal permitted the enforcement on the basis that the Russian courts were partial and dependent of the state.[49] In the UK, the High Court judge held that the defendant was estopped by the decision of the Amsterdam Court of Appeal from maintaining that the Russian annulment decision was not partial and dependent and held that the doctrines of act of state and non-justiciability were not applicable. The English Court of Appeal overturned the High Court on issue estoppel but upheld the decision on act of state. Therefore, it was open to the Claimant to seek to enforce the annulled award in England but the Claimant would have to demonstrate that the annulment decision was partial and dependent and therefore should be ignored.[50] **34–55**

The basic point with respect to the above is the discretion as to the enforcement of an annulled Award under the New York Convention. This discretion, as the public policy exception under the New York Convention, permits different results in different jurisdictions, although it rarely results in a situation such as that in the *Hilmarton* cases. The basic position that appears to be emerging is that if a party is seeking to enforce on Award that has been annulled that party has the burden of demonstrating that the enforcing court should not give effect to the annulment decision due to issues relating ro basic procedural fairness in the annulment proceedings. **34–56**

[47] United States Court of Appeals for the District of Columbia Circuit, May 25, 2007, *Termorio SA ESP and LeaseCo Group LLC v Electranta SP*, No.06-7058, *http://www.ll.georgetown.edu/federal/judicial* [accessed November 25, 2013], and (2007) ASA Bull Vol.25 No.3, p.643, note Goldstein; SIAR 2007:2 p.133, note Schimmel and Ryan; (2007) Rev Arb No.3 p.553, note Paulsson.

[48] *Corporación Mexicana de Mantenimiento Integral, S De RL de CV v Pemex-Exploración y Producción*, No.10 Civ. 206 (AKH), 2013 WL 4517225, (S.D.N.Y. August 27, 2013).

[49] For a discussion see: http://www.eversheds.nl/uploads/publications/Amsterdam_court_of_appeals_rules_on_enforcement_of_award_set_aside_by_russian_courts.pdf [accessed November 16, 2013].

[50] *Yukos Capital SARL v OJSC Rosneft Oil Co* [2012] EWCA 855, paras 154 et seq.

Whether enforcement should be stayed pending a final decision of the courts of the place of arbitration.

34–57 A related issue is whether the courts of the place of enforcement should suspend the enforcement of an Award pending a final decision of the courts of the place of arbitration as to the annulment of the Award. Article VI of the New York Convention provides:

> "If an application for the setting aside or suspension of the award has been made to a competent authority referred to in article V(1)(e), the authority before which the award is sought to be relied upon may, if it considers it proper, adjourn the decision on the enforcement of the award and may also, on the application of the party claiming enforcement of the award, order the other party to give suitable security."

34–58 Under US law (at least in the Second Circuit, covering New York), the decision as to whether to grant a stay is a matter of discretion for the enforcing court. In *Sarhank Group v Oracle Corp*, the court set out various factors relating to whether a stay should be granted.[51] In Germany, the Bavarian Court of Appeal refused to suspend enforcement of an Award that was subject to annulment proceedings on the basis that it did not believe that there were reasonable grounds for the proceedings to annul the Award in California.[52] In most New York Convention countries, one would expect that the local courts would be reluctant to suspend enforcement proceedings based on annulment proceedings at the place of arbitration unless the annulment proceedings had a reasonable prospect of success. In some instances, the court of enforcement may suspend enforcement upon conditions as to security.

34–59 In *Powerex Corp v Alcan Inc ("Powerex")*,[53] the place of arbitration was Portland, Oregon. Powerex was awarded US$100 million under the Award. Alcan sought to set aside the Award before the lower court in Oregon and, when that application failed, sought to appeal the decision to the Court of Appeals. While that appeal was pending, Powerex sought to enforce the Award in British Columbia (which has adopted the UNCITRAL Model Law). The trial court found that it was required to weigh the balance of convenience and irreparable harm and stated:

[51] United States District Court, Southern District of New York, October 9, 2002, No. 01 Cov. 1285 (DAB), (2003) YBCA Vol.XXVIII p.1043; 2002 US Dist. LEXIS 19229: "[13] [. . .] Therefore, the Second Circuit has concluded that, when considering a stay, a proper balancing should lead a district court to consider several factors, including (1) the general objectives of arbitration–the expeditious resolution of disputes and the avoidance of protracted and expensive litigation; (2) the status of the foreign proceedings to be resolved; (3) whether the award sought to be enforced will receive greater scrutiny in the foreign proceedings under a less deferential standard of review; (4) the characteristics of the foreign proceedings including (i) whether they were brought to enforce an award (which would tend to weigh in favor of a stay); (ii) whether they were initiated before the underlying enforcement proceeding so as to raise concerns of international comity; (iii) whether they were initiated by the party now seeking to enforce the award in federal court; and (iv) whether they were initiated under circumstances indicating an intent to hinder or delay resolution of the dispute; (5) a balance of the possible hardships to each of the parties [. . .] and (6) any other circumstances that could tend to shift the balance in favor of or against adjournment". The decision was reversed by the Second Circuit Court of Appeals on the grounds that the Respondent non-signatory was not a proper party to the arbitration. See *Sarhank Group v Oracle Corp*, 404 F.3d 657 (2005).

[52] Bavarian Higher Court of Appeal November 22, 2002 No.4 Z Sch 13/02.

[53] *Powerex Corp v Alcan Inc*, June 30, 2004; [2004] B.C.S.C. 876.

"In weighing the balance of convenience and irreparable harm, the court will give heed to judicial comity and the possibility of inconsistent judgments. The court will recognize that a party seeking to enforce the arbitration award will necessarily be prejudiced by delay. Also, there is a potential prejudice to the party seeking the adjournment should the court refuse the adjournment and enforce the award, only to have the original jurisdiction set aside the award.

In assessing the balance of convenience, the court will consider a number of factors, including the estimated time to complete the case in the originating jurisdiction; whether the party opposing enforcement is merely delaying the inevitable; whether a court in the originating jurisdiction has already refused to set aside the award; the availability of security and the possibility of asset removal prior to enforcement; and the willingness of the party resisting enforcement to undertake diligent prosecution of the action in the originating jurisdiction [. . .]

Here, both parties have filed affidavits to establish the likelihood of Alcan succeeding on the appeal. Alcan has filed affidavit material from an eminent jurist in the United States indicating that the appeal has some prospect of success. Powerex has filed affidavits of two experienced jurists indicating that Alcan's appeal has very little prospect of success. As a result, I cannot conclude that Alcan's action has no prospect of success. I conclude that there is an issue to be tried. I am mindful, however, that Alcan's argument has already been rejected by a magistrate and a judge of the United States District Court. Therefore, it cannot be said that Alcan's appeal has more than a chance of success.

Powerex has been and will continue to be prejudiced by delay in payment of the award. Although the award accrues interest, Powerex is unable to use the proceeds which have been awarded to it and confirmed by the U.S. District Court.

Alcan appears to have proceeded expeditiously; it has advised the court that it will continue to do so and that it is not pursuing the appeal as a delaying tactic. No decision on the appeal is likely until mid-to-late 2005.

Alcan is a very substantial entity and is well able to pay the outstanding award.

In my view, it is appropriate that this matter be adjourned, on Alcan posting security in a manner that will allow Powerex use of the funds pending conclusion of these matters in the United States. The security will be similar to that ordered in Voth Brothers Construction (1974) Ltd v. National Bank of Canada (1987), 12 B.C.L.R. (2d) 43 (C.A.): Alcan will pay the amount of the award, together with accrued interest to Powerex's solicitors, in trust. Powerex will then have access to these funds on the following conditions: (1) should Alcan succeed in its appeal in the United States, Powerex will immediately repay all the monies which it has received, together with interest at the rate currently accruing on the award; and (2) Powerex will provide security satisfactory to Alcan to secure repayment of all monies, including interest, to Alcan.(76)"

34–60 The security provision in Powerex was such that it made the victory pyrrhic in nature and Alcan appealed. Although Alcan was granted leave to appeal on the security ordered, the matter was apparently settled prior to hearing of the appeal.

34–61 The *IPCO (Nigeria)* case[54] concerned an application to enforce an arbitration Award rendered in Nigeria under Nigerian law. IPCO (Nigeria) had been granted an ex parte order requiring payment of the amount of the Award. The Respondent, the Nigerian National Petroleum Corp, sought to have the order set aside and to have the enforcement adjourned pending completion of annulment proceedings before the Nigerian courts. The Claimant sought to maintain enforcement and, in the alternative, sought security of US$50 million if the enforcement was adjourned. Judge Gross set out the principles in the following terms:

"[10] By the provisions of section 103 as set out above, the Act carries into English Law the substance of Arts. V.1(e), V.2(b) and VI of the New York Convention.

[11] For present purposes, the relevant principles can be shortly stated. First, there can be no realistic doubt that section 103 of the Act embodies a predisposition to favour enforcement of New York Convention Awards, reflecting the underlying purpose of the New York Convention itself; indeed, even when a ground for refusing enforcement is established, the court retains a discretion to enforce the award: MUSTILL & BOYD, COMMERCIAL ARBITRATION, 2nd edition, 2001 Companion, at p. 87.

[12] Secondly, section 103(2)(f) is only applicable when there has been an order or decision suspending the award by the court in the country of origin of the award ('the country of origin'). Section 103(2)(f) is not triggered automatically by a challenge brought before the court in the country of origin.

[13] Thirdly, considerations of public policy, if relied upon to resist enforcement of an award, should be approached with extreme caution: *DST v. Rakoil* [1987] 2 Lloyd's Rep. 246, at p. 254. The reference to public policy in section 103(3) was not intended to furnish an open-ended escape route for refusing enforcement of New York Convention awards. Instead, the public policy exception in section 103(3) is confined to the public policy of England (as the country in which enforcement is sought) in maintaining the fair and orderly administration of justice: MUSTILL & BOYD, at pp. 91–92.

[14] Fourthly, section 103(5) 'achieves a compromise between two equally legitimate concerns': FOUCHARD, at p.981. On the one hand, enforcement should not be frustrated merely by the making of

[54] *IPCO (Nigeria) Ltd v Nigerian National Petroleum Corp* [2005] EWHC 726 (QB Com) (April 27, 2005).

an application in the country of origin; on the other hand, pending proceedings in the country of origin should not necessarily be pre-empted by rapid enforcement of the award in another jurisdiction. Pro-enforcement assumptions are sometimes outweighed by the respect due to the courts exercising jurisdiction in the country of origin–the venue chosen by the parties for their arbitration: MUSTILL & BOYD, at p. 90.

[15] Fifthly, the Act does not furnish a threshold test in respect of the grant of an adjournment and the power to order the provision of security in the exercise of the court's discretion under section 103(5). In my judgment, it would be wrong to read a fetter into this understandably wide discretion (echoing, as it does, Art.VI of the New York Convention). Ordinarily, a number of considerations are likely to be relevant: (i) whether the application before the court in the country of origin is brought *bona fide* and not simply by way of delaying tactics; (ii) whether the application before the court in the country of origin has at least a real (i.e., realistic) prospect of success (the test in this jurisdiction for resisting summary judgment); (iii) the extent of the delay occasioned by an adjournment and any resulting prejudice. Beyond such matters, it is probably unwise to generalise; all must depend on the circumstances of the individual case [. . .]."

The court went on to review in detail the grounds for the appeal, concluding that the defendant had reasonable grounds on some bases and therefore decided that the order should stand but that its enforcement would be adjourned subject to the Respondent paying US$13 million that was due under the contract and providing security in England of US$50 million. Subsequently, the Claimant obtained enforcement of part of the Award due to delay in the proceedings in Nigeria.[55] **34–62**

Annulment in the major centres of arbitration

The case law on the annulment of Awards in the major centres of arbitration is extensive and for research on this issue, the best recourse is to refer to one of the leading works on arbitration referred to with respect to each country. However, set out below are the basic provisions together with comments on particular issues relating to annulment of Awards in these countries.[56] **34–63**

In France, pursuant to art.1522 of the French CPC, the grounds for annulment of international arbitral Awards rendered in France are the same as those for a refusal to enforce Awards rendered abroad. Those grounds are set out in art.1520 of the French CPC.[57] **34–64**

[55] *IPCO (Nigeria) Ltd v Nigerian National Petroleum Corp* [2008] EWHC 797 (Comm).

[56] See generally Webster, "Review of Substantive Reasoning of International Arbitral Awards by National Courts: Ensuring One-Stop Adjudication," *op. cit.*, p.436 (France), p.440 (England), p.446 (USA) and p.451 (Switzerland).

[57] Art.1520 of the French CPC:

"The annulment action is only open if:

1 the arbitral tribunal has wrongly declared itself competent or incompetent;

34–65 One of the themes in French annulment proceedings was the argument that the Tribunal had failed to carry out its mission if the reasoning in the Award is contradictory based on the argument that contradictory reasoning is the same as no reasoning whatsoever. However, this argument required the Court to review in detail the reasoning of the Awards. The French legal requirements changed with the *Rivers* case[58] of the French Supreme Court, where the court stated that "the argument of the contradiction of reasoning in the arbitral award dealt with by the Paris Court of Appeal tends in reality to criticize the merits of the reasoning of the award and is therefore inadmissible". (Authors' translation) Since that date, the trend of the French courts has been to eschew review of the merits of Awards and to focus on procedural issues. Most commentators have approved this evolution of the case law. The prior theory of "contradiction of reasoning" had resulted in detailed review of the merits of Awards in an attempt to find some basis for attack. ICC Awards in particularly were not often annulled but it undermined the effectiveness of arbitration in France due to the detail on the annulment proceedings.

34–66 One of those procedural issues relates to Awards rendered as *amiable compositeur*. The French Supreme Court has held that an Award rendered on that basis must provide reasons based on fairness for the Award; a reasoning based solely on the legal position is inadequate.

34–67 In Switzerland, art.190(2) of the Swiss PILA Law provides the basis for annulment proceedings.[59]

34–68 The Swiss PILA "has considerably limited the possibilities of setting aside an award compared to the Concordat [the prior law]".[60] In particular, it is no longer possible to have an Award set aside for arbitrariness including determinations of fact contrary to the record or errors in law. It is thus not possible to obtain from the Supreme Court any review of the merits of the Tribunal's evaluation of the

2 the arbitration tribunal has been unlawfully constituted;
3 the arbitral tribunal has ruled upon the matter contrary to the assignment given to it;
4 due process has not been respected;
5 recognition or enforcement would be contrary to public international order."

[58] Cass. Civ 1re, May 11, 1999, *Société Rivers v Fabre–Paris*, October 26, 1999, *J. Patou Parfumeur Société Edipar* (1999) Rev Arb No.4 p.811, note Gaillard. For a further illustration, see also Paris, March 2, 2006, *Société Fashion Box Group SpA v Société A.J. Heelstone LLC*, case No.01/15038 reported by Clay *in arbitrage-adr$EMyahoogroupes.fr* on May 6, 2006.

[59] Art.190(2) of the Swiss PILA:

"The award may only be annulled:

a) if the sole arbitrator was not properly appointed or if the Arbitral tribunal was not properly constituted;
b) if the Arbitral tribunal wrongly accepted or declined jurisdiction;
c) if the Arbitral tribunal's decision went beyond the claims submitted to it, or failed to decide one of the items of the claim;
d) if the principle of equal treatment of the parties or the right of the parties to be heard was violated;
e) if the award was incompatible with public policy."

More generally, see Dasser, "International Arbitration and Setting Aside Proceedings in Switzerland: A Statistical Analysis" (2007) ASA Bull Vol.25 No.3, p.444.

[60] See Müller, *International Arbitration: A Guide to the Complete Swiss Case Law, (Unreported and Reported), op. cit.*, p.142.

evidence submitted by the parties or of its interpretation of the substance.[61] Therefore, it is not clear that the first *Hilmarton* Award would have been subject to annulment under the new law.[62]

Under art.192 of the Swiss PILA, it is possible for parties that are not domiciled and do not reside or have their place of business in Switzerland to exclude by an express agreement all or some of the grounds for review under art.190(2) of the Swiss PILA. However, the effect of such an exclusion is limited. If the successful party seeks to enforce the Award in Switzerland, it is subject to review based on the principles of the New York Convention under art.192(2) of the Swiss PILA. Moreover, art.28 does not amount to a waiver within the meaning of art.192(2) of the Swiss PILA.[63] **34–69**

In the United States, the Federal Arbitration Act provides the basis for vacating an Award.[64] **34–70**

Practitioners based outside the United States are often concerned with the procedural requirements of due process as interpreted by American courts. For litigators accustomed to depositions and extensive cross examination, some of the procedures typical in an ICC arbitration may be surprising. However, the US case **34–71**

[61] Swiss Supreme Court, March 7, 2003, 4P.250/2002, *X SA v Y & Co* (2006) ASA Bull Vol.24 No.1 at p.53 and p.76. See also Dasser and Gabus, "Waiver of Appeal against State Court Decision", May 8, 2007, Litigation–Switzerland, *http://www.internationallaw office.com.* Hirsch, "Contractual Exclusion of Annulment Actions Against International Arbitral Awards Made in Switzerland", SIAR 2006:2, p.43.

[62] See the discussion at para.34–46.

[63] See the discussion at para.34–28 n.20. See also ATF 4P198/2005, *X AS (Turkey) v Motorola Corp (USA)* (2006) ASA Bull Vol.24 No.2 at p.265 and p.339.

[64] US Federal Arbitration Act s.10:

"(a) In any of the following cases the United States court in and for the district wherein the award was made may make an order vacating the award upon the application of any party to the arbitration

(1) Where the award was procured by corruption, fraud, or undue means.

(2) Where there was evident partiality or corruption in the arbitrators, or either of them.

(3) Where the arbitrators were guilty of misconduct in refusing to postpone the hearing, upon sufficient cause shown, or in refusing to hear evidence pertinent and material to the controversy; or of any other misbehavior by which the rights of any party have been prejudiced.

(4) Where the arbitrators exceeded their powers, or so imperfectly executed them that a mutual, final, and definite award upon the subject matter submitted was not made.

(5) Where an award is vacated and the time within which the agreement required the award to be made has not expired the court may, in its discretion, direct a rehearing by the arbitrators.

(b) The United States district court for the district wherein an award was made that was issued pursuant to section 590 of title 5 may make an order vacating the award upon the application of a person, other than a party to the arbitration, who is adversely affected or aggrieved by the award, if the use of arbitration or the award is clearly inconsistent with the factors set forth in section 582 of Title 5." As an example, see *Stephen B Sawtelle, Hackett Associates Inc v Waddell & Reed Inc Torchmark Corp*, NY Sup, App Div, 1st Dept, cited in Mealey's IAR Vol.20 No.10 October 2005 pp.24–25 (punitive award grossly disproportionate: "Where an award has been vacated on the ground that it is in manifest disregard of law [. . .]here, because it is grossly disproportionate to any actual harm sustained by petitioner–arbitral prerogative does not permit a panel to ignore the ruling of obdurately issue an identical determination [. . .]An award of punitive damages that is some 23 times actual damages is irreconcilable with prevailing authority and can only be construed as arbitrary".) More generally, see Wilske and Mackay, "The Myth of the 'Manifest Disregard of the Law' Doctrine: Is this Challenge to the Finality of Arbitral Awards Confined to U.S. Domestic Arbitrations or Should International Arbitration Practitioners be Concerned?" (2006) ASA Bull Vol.24 No.2, p.216.

law endorses the principle that arbitration is intended to be different from court proceedings and therefore the procedures will be different.[65]

34–72 A more troubling issue is the dicta in the *Wilko v Swan* case[66] that "the interpretations of the law by the arbitrators in contrast to manifest disregard are not subject, in the federal courts, to judicial review for error". Many parties have sought to use this argument to have the substance of arbitral Awards reviewed, usually with little success. The test has been set out by the Second Circuit Court of Appeals in the following terms:

> "The two-prong test for ascertaining whether an arbitrator has manifestly disregarded the law has both an objective and a subjective component. We first consider whether the 'governing law alleged to have been ignored by the arbitrators [was] well defined, explicit, and clearly applicable'. We then look to the knowledge actually possessed by the arbitrator. The arbitrator must 'appreciate[] the existence of a clearly governing legal principle but decide[] to ignore or pay no attention to it'. Both of these prongs must be met before a court may find that there has been a manifest disregard of law." (citations deleted)[67]

34–73 The two-pronged test rendering annulment of Awards on this basis is exceptional rather than common. A Tribunal may make a mistake as to the interpretation of the law. To be annulled on this ground, the mistake must have been virtually deliberate. Nevertheless, the possibility of review for "manifest disregard" holds out hope to losing parties, and may provoke and prolong annulment proceedings, although there is currently a split in the US Circuits as to whether the doctrine is applicable.[68]

34–74 On March 25, 2008, in *Hall Street Associates, LLC v Mattel, Inc*[69] the US Supreme Court held that parties to an arbitration agreement did not have the right to expand the grounds for judicial review of arbitration Awards beyond the categories set out in ss.9 and 10 of the Federal Arbitration Act. In *Hall Street*, the arbitration clause purported to extend the scope for judicial review to cover situations: "(i) where the arbitrator's finding of facts are not supported by substantial evidence; or (ii) where the arbitrator's conclusions of law are erroneous". Justice Souter for the majority summarised the position as follows:

> "Federal Arbitration Act (FAA or Act), 9 U. S. C. §1 *et seq.*, provides for expedited judicial review to confirm, vacate, or modify arbitration

[65] See for example, *Comsat Corp v National Science Foundation*, 190 F.3d 269, US App. LEXIS 20017 (4th Cir. Va. 1999).

[66] 346 US 427 (1953).

[67] *Westerbeke Corp v Daihatsu Motor Co Ltd*, 304F. 3d 200, 209 (2d Cir. 2002).

[68] As summarised by Quinn Emmanuel "It is now debatable whether the 'manifest disregard of the law' ground is available to vacate an award, as conflicting opinions have emerged since Hall Street. See Ramos-Santiago v. United Parcel Service, 524 F.3d 120, 124 n.3 (1st Cir. 2008)(noting, in dicta, that manifest disregard of law is not a valid ground for vacating or modifying an award under the FAA); *Comedy Club, Inc. v. Improv West Associates*, 553 F.3d 1277, 1281, 1283 (9th Cir. 2009) (noting that an arbitrator's manifest disregard of the law remains a valid ground for vacatur in the form of a judicial gloss on the statutorily enumerated grounds in the FAA); Affymax, Inc. v. Ortho-McNeil- Janssen Pharmaceuticals, Inc., 660 F3d 281, 285 (7th Cir 2011) (noting that 'manifest disregard of the law is not a ground on which a court may reject an arbitrator's award under the Federal Arbitration Act')." (http://quinnemanuel.com/ [accessed November 25, 2013])

[69] No.06-989 (Justices Stevens, Kennedy and Breyer dissenting).

> awards. §§9–11 (2000 edn and Supp. V). The question here is whether statutory grounds for prompt vacatur and modification may be supplemented by contract. We hold that the statutory grounds are exclusive."

As the Supreme Court noted: "The Courts of Appeals have split over the exclusiveness of these statutory grounds when parties take the FAA shortcut to confirm, vacate, or modify an Award, with some saying the recitations are exclusive, and others regarding them as mere threshold provisions open to expansion by agreement". The Court opted for the restrictive interpretation based on the mandatory wording of s.9 of the act. However, the Supreme Court did leave open the possibility of judicial review on grounds other than the act in certain circumstances.[70] **34–75**

As regards the review of jurisdiction itself, the US Supreme Court has recently confirmed that judicial review should be limited. In *Oxford Health Plans LLC v Sutter*, the US Supreme Court was called upon to deal with whether an arbitration clause permitted class action arbitration. The arbitrator had held that it did. The US Supreme Court held that it was not for the courts to reconsider the arbitrator's interpretation of the arbitration clause. Provided that the arbitrator was construing the arbitration clause he was not exceeding his jurisdiction. Therefore, the potential for US court review of even the interpretation of the jurisdictional clause is limited.[71] This situation is to be contrasted with the scope of jurisdictional review elsewhere, which is basically de novo. **34–76**

In England, the Arbitration Act 1996 was intended to restrict the supervisory role of the English courts with respect to international arbitration. The key provisions are ss.67 and 68 of the Act (which in turn refers back to s.33 of the Act).[72] **34–77**

[70] The Court stated in particular: "In holding that §§10 and 11 provide exclusive regimes for the review provided by the statute, we do not purport to say that they exclude more searching review based on authority outside the statute as well. The FAA is not the only way into court for parties wanting review of arbitration awards: they may contemplate enforcement understate statutory or common law, for example, where judicial review of different scope is arguable. But here we speak only to the scope of the expeditious judicial review under §§9, 10, and 11, deciding nothing about other possible avenues for judicial enforcement of arbitration awards".

[71] 569 U. S. _ (2013). The Court stated (footnotes deleted): "In sum, Oxford chose arbitration, and it must now live with that choice. Oxford agreed with Sutter that an arbitrator should determine what their contract meant, including whether its terms approved class arbitration. The arbitrator did what the parties requested: He provided an interpretation of the contract resolving that disputed issue. His interpretation went against Oxford, maybe mistakenly. But still, Oxford does not get to rerun the matter in a court. Under §10(a)(4), the question for a judge is not whether the arbitrator construed the parties' contract correctly, but whether he construed it at all. Because he did, and therefore did not 'exceed his powers,' we cannot give Oxford the relief it wants. We accordingly affirm the judgment of the Court of Appeals".

[72] English Arbitration Act 1996:

"67.–(1) A party to arbitral proceedings may (upon notice to the other parties and to the tribunal) apply to the court–

(a) challenging any award of the arbitral tribunal as to its substantive jurisdiction; or
(b) for an order declaring an award made by the tribunal on the merits to be of no effect, in whole or in part, because the tribunal did not have substantive jurisdiction. [. . .]

68–(1) A party to arbitral proceedings may (upon notice to the other parties and to the tribunal) apply to the court challenging an award in the proceedings on the ground of serious irregularity affecting the tribunal, the proceedings or the award.

A party may lose the right to object (see section 73) and the right to apply is subject to the restrictions in section 70(2) and (3).

(2) Serious irregularity means an irregularity of one or more of the following kinds which the court considers has caused or will cause substantial injustice to the applicant–

At the outset, jurisdictional issues are reviewed de novo in England and such review can take place despite the fact that the party challenging the Award did not appear in the proceedings.[73] Therefore, the main issue is the scope for review on other matters.

34–78 In the *Lesotho Highlands* case, the Court of Appeal upheld the annulment of an Award based on an error in appreciation of ss.48 and 49 of the English Arbitration Act 1996 with respect to the arbitrators' determination of the conversion and interest rates. In essence, the Court of Appeal held that the tribunal was required to apply the law of Lesotho and was not entitled to exercise its discretion under those provisions. The House of Lords overturned the decision of the Court of Appeal and re-emphasised the limited scope of review of arbitral Awards in England noting that "[s]ection 68(2)(b) does not permit a challenge on the ground that the tribunal arrived at a wrong conclusion as a matter of law or fact. It is not apt to cover a mere error of law".[74]

34–79 Therefore, despite the list of grounds for annulment, it appears that the House of Lords has given a clear signal that the review of arbitral Awards rendered in England should not extend to review of the merits of the decision. As Lord Steyn stated in the *Lesotho Highlands* case:

(a) failure by the tribunal to comply with section 33 (general duty of tribunal);
(b) the tribunal exceeding its powers (otherwise than by exceeding its substantive jurisdiction: see section 67);
(c) failure by the tribunal to conduct the proceedings in accordance with the procedure agreed by the parties;
(d) failure by the tribunal to deal with all the issues that were put to it;
(e) any arbitral or other institution or person vested by the parties with powers in relation to the proceedings or the award exceeding its powers;
(f) uncertainty or ambiguity as to the effect of the award;
(g) the award being obtained by fraud or the award or the way in which it was procured being contrary to public policy;
(h) failure to comply with the requirements as to the form of the award; or
(i) any irregularity in the conduct of the proceedings or in the award which is admitted by the tribunal or by any arbitral or other institution or person vested by the parties with powers in relation to the proceedings or the award

(3) If there is shown to be serious irregularity affecting the tribunal, the proceedings or the award, the court may–
(a) remit the award to the tribunal, in whole or in part, for reconsideration,
(b) set the award aside in whole or in part, or
(c) declare the award to be no effect, in whole or in part.

The court shall not exercise its power to set aside or to declare an award to be of no effect, in whole or in part, unless it is satisfied that it would be inappropriate to remit the matters in question to the tribunal for reconsideration".

[73] *Dallah Real Estate and Tourism Holding Co v The Ministry of Religious Affairs, Government of Pakistan [2010] UKSC 46*, paras 23, 26 and 96.

[74] *Lesotho Highlands Development Authority (Respondents) v Impregilo SpA (Appellants)* [2005] UKHL 43 (June 30, 2005). See Park, "The Nature of Arbitral Authority: A Comment on Lesotho Highlands" (2005) Arb Int Vol.21 No.4, p.483. For a confirmation of the House of Lords principles in the *Lesotho* case, see *Mohammed Abdulmohsin Al-Kharafi & Sons for General Trading, General Contracting and Industrial Structures WLL v Big Dig Construction (Proprietary) Ltd (in liquidation, formerly known as Protech Projects Construction (PTY) Ltd)* [2005] EWHC 2165 (Comm) (challenge of an ICC Award rejected in absence of any serious irregularity which has caused or will cause substantial injustice to the applicant). See also *Bermuth Lines Ltd v High Seas Shipping Ltd* [2005] EWHC 3020 (Comm) (December 21, 2005); and *ABB AG v Hochtief Airport GmbH & Athens International Airport SA* [2006] EWHC 388 (Comm) (March 8, 2006) cited in (2006) ASA Bull Vol. 24 No.3 at p.460.

"I am glad to have arrived at this conclusion [upholding the award]. It is consistent with the legislative purpose of the 1996 Act, which is intended to promote one-stop adjudication. If the contrary view of the Court of Appeal had prevailed, it would have opened up many opportunities for challenging awards on the basis that the tribunal exceeded its powers in ruling on the currency of the award. Such decisions are an everyday occurrence in the arbitral world. If the view of the Court of Appeal had been upheld, a very serious defect in the machinery of the 1996 Act would have been revealed. The fact that this case has been before courts at three levels and that enforcement of the award has been delayed for more than three years reinforces the importance of the point."[75]

Secondary jurisdiction

As discussed above with respect to enforcement of annulled Awards, the primary jurisdiction is the country of the place where the Award was rendered. A secondary jurisdiction is another country where a party seeks to enforce the Award. **34–80**

The issue for any successful party is ensuring that it has the benefit of an Award, which is usually the payment of monetary damages. To obtain that payment, the successful party may seek to enforce the Award in the unsuccessful party's country or in any other country in which the unsuccessful party has assets. **34–81**

Enforcement of international Awards depends on the national law including the applicable international conventions. By far the most important convention is the New York Convention. However, it is noteworthy that, in some jurisdictions, and in particular in France and the United States, there are instances in which the national law will permit enforcement of an international Award even if not required by the New York Convention. Therefore, the New York Convention is becoming a minimum standard rather than an absolute standard enforcement. **34–82**

The New York Convention is now in force in some 150 countries,[76] each of which has its own case law with respect to it. Moreover, in some jurisdictions, such as the United States, the case law varies somewhat as between the different areas. Therefore, in seeking to enforce an Award due regard has to be had to the case law of the court of the area or state of enforcement.[77] This topic is too vast for this book and there are excellent materials on the subject. However, in planning an arbitration and the procedures to be adopted, the parties to the arbitration **34–83**

[75] [2005] UKHL 43 at p.21. See also *Primera Maritime (Hellas) Ltd v Jiangsu Eastern Heavy Industry Co Ltd* [2013] EWHC 3066 (Comm) (6. In order to succeed under section 68 an applicant needs to show three things. First of all, a serious irregularity. Secondly, a serious irregularity which falls within the closed list of categories in section 68(2). Thirdly, that one or more of the irregularities identified caused or will cause the party substantial injustice. As Hamblen J. said in *Abuja International Hotels v Meridian SAS* [2012] EWHC 87 (Comm) at [48]–[49], "the focus of the enquiry under section 68 is due process, not the correctness of the tribunal's decision".)

[76] See Introduction para.0–13.

[77] The most complete digest of the case law is provided in the *Yearbook Commercial Arbitration*, A.J. van den Berg (ed.). That digest includes excerpts from cases around the world broken down by topic and is a very helpful point of reference in the matter.

are well advised to consider any particularities that might arise under the law of the place of probable enforcement. This is illustrated in particular by the *Hilmarton* cases discussed above and the *Dallah* cases discussed under art.6. In addition, it is important to note that, in most jurisdictions, it is not necessary for a party to participate in arbitral proceedings or to seek to annul an Award in order to object to enforcement.[78]

[78] See for example *Dallah Estate and Tourism Holding Co v The Ministry of Religious Affairs, Government of Pakistan* [2010] UKSC 46; and *The London Steam Ship Owners Mutual Insurance Association Ltd v The Kingdom of Spain* [2013] EWHC 2840 (Comm).

Article 35 Correction and Interpretation of Award; Remission of Awards

1 On its own initiative, the arbitral tribunal may correct a clerical, computational or typographical error, or any errors of similar nature contained in an award, provided such correction is submitted for approval to the Court within 30 days of the date of such award.

2 Any application of a party for the correction of an error of the kind referred to in Article 35(1), or for the interpretation of an award, must be made to the Secretariat within 30 days of the receipt of the award by such party, in a number of copies as stated in Article 3(1). After transmittal of the application to the arbitral tribunal, the latter shall grant the other party a short time limit, normally not exceeding 30 days, from the receipt of the application by that party, to submit any comments thereon. The arbitral tribunal shall submit its decision on the application in draft form to the Court not later than 30 days following the expiration of the time limit for the receipt of any comments from the other party or within such other period as the Court may decide.

3 A decision to correct or to interpret the award shall take the form of an addendum and shall constitute part of the award. The provisions of Articles 31, 33 and 34 shall apply *mutatis mutandis*.

4 Where a court remits an award to the arbitral tribunal, the provisions of Articles 31, 33, 34 and this Article 35 shall apply *mutatis mutandis* to any addendum or award made pursuant to the terms of such remission. The Court may take any steps as may be necessary to enable the arbitral tribunal to comply with the terms of such remission and may fix an advance to cover any additional fees and expenses of the arbitral tribunal and any additional ICC administrative expenses.[1]

[1] Article 35 corresponds to art.29 of the 1998 Rules. The main substantive change is the addition of art.35(4) regarding remanding to the Tribunal.

Introductory remarks

35–1 An Award, whether final, partial or interim, finally decides an issue in dispute in the arbitration. From the moment that a Tribunal renders an Award, it is functus officio with respect to that issue, subject to the provisions of art.35 and the provisions of the law of the place of arbitration. Article 35 gives the arbitrators the right to correct and/or interpret their Award under certain conditions; art.35 does not cover the right to supplement the Award in case a claim was omitted.[2]

35–2 The figures concerning corrections were as follows in the four year period from 2008–2011.[3]

Year	Number of Awards	Requests for correction/interpretation	%
2008	407	42 (32 granted, 10 rejected)	9.7
2009	415	59 (28 granted, 31 rejected)	7.0
2010	479	53 (34 granted, 23 rejected)	9.0
2011	508	78 (45 granted, 33 rejected)	6.5

35–3 Under some national laws, it is possible that the courts will refer a matter back to the Tribunal, in a sense instructing the Tribunal to complete the task. The effect is to reopen issues for which the Tribunal was functus officio prior to the remand. Prior to the 2012 Rules, no express rules existed in the Rules providing for the possibility of remanding a matter back to the Tribunal, once an Award had been set aside in full or in part. This was viewed as a gap in the 1998 Rules, which has now been filled with the introduction of art.35(4).

Article 35(1): "On its own initiative, the arbitral tribunal may correct a clerical, computational or typographical error, or any errors of similar nature contained in an award, provided such correction is submitted for approval to the Court within 30 days of the date of such award."

35–4 Article 35(1) permits the Tribunal to act on its own initiative with respect to corrections. Despite the care that the Tribunal and the ICC Court take with respect to Awards, it remains possible that an error slips through and that one of the members of the Tribunal notices it after the Award has been signed and notified to the parties.

35–5 Article 35(1) is limited to "a clerical, computational or typographical error, or any errors of similar nature". The provision is not aimed at substantive matters or at dealing with an interpretation of the Award. The classic type of problem is when there has been a failure to insert a "not" before a verb. Other examples are where from the context it is evident that it should read Claimant instead of Respondent or where the figures awarded by the Tribunal either do not add up or do not correspond to those in the discussion part of the Award. The reference to errors of a "similar nature" appears to be intended to cover mechanical errors as well. In interpreting an analogous provision, the English court noted that "[t]he authorities

[2] See generally Hauser-Morel & Nedden, "Correction and Interpretation of Arbitral Awards and Additional Awards" in *Post Award Issues* (ed. Tercier) (2011 JurisNet), p.19.

[3] See (2009) ICC Bull ICArb Vol.20 No.1, pp.15–16; (2010) ICC Bull ICArb Vol.24 No.1, p.14; (2011) ICC Bull ICArb Vol.22 No.1, p.15; (2012) ICC Bull ICArb Vol.23 No.1, p.15.

draw distinctions between errors affecting the expression of the tribunal's thought (which can be corrected) and errors in the tribunal's thought process (which cannot) and to not permitting corrections to reflect 'second thoughts' ".[4]

The correction must be submitted by the Tribunal, either unanimously, at the majority or even by the president alone, to the ICC Court. However the submission is made to Secretariat. **35–6**

The 30-day time limit starts to run from the date of the Award,[5] which will normally be a few days before the Parties receive the Award from the ICC Court's Secretariat. With respect to a correction relating to a particular partial or interim Award, the time also starts to run with the date of that Award. If the Tribunal detects a clerical error on its own initiative, there is normally no need to seek the Parties' comments. However, the Tribunal may, and often should inform the Parties that it has detected such error and that it has or will send a corrected version of the Award, as per art.35(3) in the form of an Addendum, to the ICC for approval by the ICC Court. **35–7**

Once the Secretariat has received the draft Addendum, no time limit exists for the ICC Court to approve it. Once the ICC Court has approved the Addendum, the Tribunal will have to sign and date it. It continues to have the power to do so, as long as it respected the original 30-day time limit to submit its corrections to the ICC Court for approval.[6] **35–8**

Article 35(2): "Any application of a party for the correction of an error of the kind referred to in Article 35(1), or for the interpretation of an award, must be made to the Secretariat within 30 days of the receipt of the award by such party, in a number of copies as stated in Article 3(1). After transmittal of the application to the arbitral tribunal, the latter shall grant the other party a short time limit, normally not exceeding 30 days, from the receipt of the application by that party, to submit any comments thereon. The arbitral tribunal shall submit its decision on the application in draft form to the Court not later than 30 days following the expiration of the time limit for the receipt of any comments from the other party or within such other period as the Court may decide."

A party may apply for a correction or for an interpretation of an Award by submitting a corresponding request to the Secretariat within 30 days after the party's receipt of the Award. The applicant must provide the same number of copies of this application as provided for a Request. Therefore, if there are two parties and a Tribunal of three members, an applicant must forward to the Secretariat five copies of the application. The Secretariat then forwards copies to the members of the Tribunal and to the other party. **35–9**

Article 35(2) refers expressly to art.3(1) as to the manner of notification. However, many applications for interpretation are simply sent by email with a **35–10**

[4] *Gannet Shipping Ltd v Eastrade Commodities Inc* [2001] EWHC Commercial 483 (December 6, 2001).

[5] As to the date of the Award, see the discussion under art.31(3) at para.31–43.

[6] Reiner/Aschauer, *op. cit.*, para.699, consider that the Parties should be given the opportunity to comment on the intended correction, provided this can be done within the 30-day time limit.

confirming hard copy. Parties use email to ensure that the 30-day requirement is met[7] because the application usually consists of a letter or brief setting out the nature of the request without any supporting documents. In practice, the Secretariat will normally be satisfied with the receipt of an electronic copy, which it will pass on to the Tribunal and the other side.[8]

35–11 The scope for corrections is the same as that under art.35(1). The scope for interpretation is less clear and would depend in part on the nature of the relief granted. With respect to monetary relief, one can imagine that a party might seek to clarify an issue such as the basis for commissions (as was the issue in the *Behr* case).[9] With respect to injunctive or declaratory relief, the issue may be the interpretation of the terms of the Tribunal's order.

35–12 There is a natural tendency for a party who has lost on an issue, to seek to highlight what it views as inconsistencies in the Tribunal's reasoning in a request for interpretation. In many instances, this is not helpful to that party's case, in particular if it were to consider an annulment action or to resist enforcement of the Award. As noted above, except to the extent provided for in art.35 or by remand under applicable law, the Tribunal is functus officio with respect to the issues decided. Generally, a Tribunal will not have the opportunity to modify or explain its Award. Therefore, in annulment or enforcement proceedings, the Award will generally have to stand on its own. By seeking an interpretation in such a case, the party may in fact be worsening its situation in annulment or enforcement proceedings, by giving the Tribunal an opportunity to deal with issues of concern to the party.

35–13 Article 35(2) does not indicate the material to be supplied with an application for correction or interpretation. Usually, reference will be made to the Award and possibly also to submissions made by the parties. With respect to interpretation of the Award, reference will often be made to specific documents in the file and particularly the underlying contract, but there exists no requirement to submit these documents or extracts thereof.

35–14 The Tribunal is seized of the matter when it receives a copy of the application from the Secretariat. It follows from art.2(10) of Annex II of the Rules that the transmission of the application to the Tribunal may be made "subject to the prior cash payment in full to the ICC" of a special advance fixed by the ICC Court "to cover additional fees and expenses of the arbitral Tribunal and additional ICC administrative expenses".[10] The Tribunal then sets a time limit for comments from the other party that normally should not exceed 30 days. This is the time limit, which in practice is most often set by Tribunals to the other party, although shorter time limits will often be more appropriate. This may be the case where the request is for correction, particularly if straight forward.

35–15 Article 35(2) provides that the Tribunal has a period of 30 days after the expiration of the time-limit for receipt of any comments from the other party to submit any draft of the correction or interpretation that it proposes to make. If no such comments are made within the time-limit, the Tribunal must proceed with

[7] It would then seem prudent to immediately double-check with the Counsel in charge of the file at the Secretariat that the application has been well received.

[8] Fry, Greenberg, Mazza, *op. cit.*, para.3–1267.

[9] See below at paras 35–37 et seq.

[10] See Reiner & Aschauer, para.841 as to the Secretariat's practice.

submitting its draft decision to the ICC Court. Tribunals virtually systematically provide a written notification of their acceptance or rejection of a request for correction or interpretation and the Tribunal's decision in this respect is presented to the ICC Court as a "Decision". In many instances, a request for correction of clerical errors and the like will have merit, and as a consequence the Tribunal will make the requested correction. The same is not true for requests for interpretation, which in fact rather rarely succeed.

As noted by the Tribunal in a 2006 ICC case,[11] the purpose of art.35(2) is to permit the clarification of an Award so as to allow its correct execution by the parties: 35–16

> "It is not to be used to require the tribunal to explain, or to reformulate, its reasons. It does not provide an occasion for the reconsideration of the tribunal's decisions. Should this be the basis of the party's application, the tribunal will be quite justified in finding it unnecessary or inappropriate to render the requested interpretation [. . .]
> Interpretation thus consists of eliminating any ambiguities or uncertainties, if any, and clarifying the genuine meaning of the decision without modifying it. In other words, interpretation consists of restoring the true meaning of the decision where it has been improperly expressed in the operative part, where the latter is at odds with the findings or contains uncertainties or ambiguities. Interpretation does not entail a modification or an addition to the initial decision and thus cannot jeopardize *res judicata*."

Another Tribunal had stated in an earlier ICC case that "there is virtual unanimity that an application [for interpretation] cannot be used to seek revision, reformulation or additional explanations of a given decision".[12] 35–17

A related issue, but one which does not arise often in practice, is whether a Tribunal, when seized of an application by a party to correct and interpret an Award under art.35(2) may correct another aspect of the Award after the 30-day period in art.35(1) has expired. Of course, the Tribunal could not do so without giving notice to the parties but even with such notice, arguably the Tribunal is not entitled to do so unless the further correction relates to the issue that has been raised by the party in its application under art.35(2).[13] 35–18

The issue of the scope of the Tribunal's authority to the deal with corrections and interpretations may also be affected by the provisions of the applicable law, and in particular the law of the place of arbitration to the extent that those provisions provide additional possibilities with respect to correction or interpretation of the Award. 35–19

Article 35(3): "A decision to correct or to interpret the award shall take the form of an addendum and shall constitute part of the award. The provisions of Articles 31, 33 and 34 shall apply *mutatis mutandis*."

[11] ICC case No.12131 (Decision of the Tribunal dismissing a request for interpretation) (2006), unreported.

[12] ICC case No.16451, (2010) ICC ICArb Bull, Spec. Supplement, p.18.

[13] For a discussion, see Fróes, "Correction and Interpretation of Arbitral Awards" in *Liber Amoricum Robert Briner, op. cit.*, at p.289.

35–20 Article. 35(3) covers the situation where the Tribunal decides that it should correct or interpret the Award. Its decision becomes part of the Award through an Addendum. The Addendum is not an additional, let alone separate Award, but forms an integral part of the original Award, which it corrects and/or interprets.[14]

35–21 If the Tribunal decides that it should not correct or interpret the Award, it will issue a document entitled "Decision". The Decision briefly sets out the parties' requests and positions, as well as the Tribunal's reason for rejecting the party's request for correction or interpretation. Although the "Decision" is not referred to in art.35(3), in the practice of the ICC Court, a "Decision" is treated in the same way as the Addendum to the Award, to which art.35(3) refers expressly.

35–22 Article 35(3) refers to arts 31, 33 and 34, which it declares applicable mutatis mutandis. As noted above, the Addendum and the Decision, by which a request for correction and/or interpretation, are respectively accepted and denied, are treated by the ICC Court like any Award. As discussed in Annex 1 Pt I, Addenda and Decisions are usually dealt with at Committee Sessions of the ICC Court.

35–23 The reference to art.31 means that reasons must be provided for the Addendum and Decision, which must be dated and signed. Both the Addendum and the Decision are subject to the scrutiny of the ICC Court in accordance with art.33; the provisions regarding notification of the Award under art.34 are equally applicable to the Addendum and Decision. As part of the Award, the Addendum is subject to review on the same basis by the national courts involved in any annulment or enforcement proceedings.

Costs

35–24 Article 34(1) provides that "[o]nce an award has been made, the Secretariat shall notify to the parties the text signed by the arbitral tribunal, provided always that the costs of the arbitration have been fully paid to the ICC by the parties or by one of them". Prior to issuing the initial Award, the ICC shall have ensured that the amount of all costs of arbitration as set out in the Award has been paid. To the extent that the interpretation of the Award may require significant time, the ICC may ask for an additional advance on costs and refuse to issue the Addendum until that advance has been paid. For corrections, one would anticipate that this would not be the case, since the need for corrections is always the result of a deficiency, be it minor, of the Tribunal, and possibly also of the Secretariat and the ICC Court, who each should normally have detected the error.[15] Thus, in practice, normally no additional advances on cost for corrections are fixed by the ICC Court.[16]

35–25 For interpretations, especially if the parties are seeking guidance for their further relationship, the ICC may decide that it is appropriate to provide a supplemental payment to the members of the Tribunal, and thus to call for a special advance on cost. It is, however, rare for a Tribunal to ask on its own for an advance

[14] Bühler & Jarvin, *op. cit.*, art.29 at p.1344. The Swiss Supreme Court took the same view in its decision of January 12, 2005, case No.4 P. 219/2004, (2005) ASA Bull Vol. 13 No. 2, p.352.

[15] See para.Ann–29.

[16] Fry, Greenberg, Mazza, *op. cit.*, para.3–1285.

on costs, except when the request appears to be manifestly ill-considered. In both situations (correction or interpretation), the Tribunal has the same powers, as in the Award, to award costs according to art.37 in the Addendum or the Decision.

The Secretariat will invite the Court to fix an additional advance only where the costs of arbitration have already been fixed by the Court pursuant to art.37, i.e. where the application is for the correction or interpretation of a final Award.[17] The Court's power to fix a special advance under art.2(10) of App.III is discretionary. It will almost certainly fix an additional advance in cases where applications are attempts to appeal an Award, i.e. applications are lengthy and complicated, requiring the arbitral Tribunal to undertake significant work before rejecting the application as falling outside the scope of art.35(2). The amount of the advance has recently been between US$5,000 and US$10,000. **35–26**

As long as the time limit for requesting a correction of an Award has not lapsed, it does not seem prudent for the Secretariat to pay out the arbitrators' fees in their totality. Once a request is made under art.35, retaining a small percentage of the fees payable is the best way for the Secretariat to ensure that the Tribunal will render the Addendum or Decision as promptly as possible. **35–27**

Correction/Interpretation of an Addendum

Article 35(3) does not state whether the provisions of art.35 apply to the Addendum. In other words, the issue is whether a request of a party for correction and interpretation of the Addendum is itself admissible. Article 35, by its terms, provide only for corrections and interpretation of an Award, and not of an Addendum to the Award. However the better position is that an Addendum is subject to correction or interpretation since it is part of the Award. Otherwise the part of the Award represented by the Addendum could not be corrected or interpreted. A Decision, on the other hand, does not modify the Award, and there would appear to be no basis under art.35 to seek to correct or interpret a Decision, as the essence of the application would be to reconsider it. **35–28**

Article 35(4): "Where a court remits an award to the arbitral tribunal, the provisions of Articles 31, 33, 34 and this Article 35 shall apply *mutatis mutandis* to any addendum or award made pursuant to the terms of such remission. The Court may take any steps as may be necessary to enable the arbitral tribunal to comply with the terms of such remission and may fix an advance to cover any additional fees and expenses of the arbitral tribunal and any additional ICC administrative expenses."

Remanding a matter to the Tribunal

The 2012 Rules do now expressly provide for the possibility of remanding or remitting an award to the Tribunal once it was annulled. The lack of such provision in the Rules was a gap in the 1998 rules. **35–29**

[17] Fry, Greenberg, Mazza, *op. cit.*, paras 3–1281 to 3–1284.

35–30 Article 35(4) deals with the consequences of a court's order to remit an award to the Tribunal. The ICC Rules do not state when and under what circumstances such remission is possible. They also do not fix any time limit by which a request following a Court's order for remission must reach the ICC Court.

35–31 The state court annulling an ICC award will normally determine if and under what conditions an award is to be remitted to the arbitral tribunal. If the annulment court does not do so, the laws applicable at the place of arbitration may provide the answer as to the conditions of such remand.[18]

35–32 Under art. 35(4), the ICC Court "may take any steps as may be necessary to enable the arbitral tribunal to comply with the terms of such remission". The ICC Rules are silent as to the Tribunal's power to render a new award and if so within what limits it may do so. It will be for the Tribunal, whether consisting of the original arbitrators—provided they are still available—or of newly appointed ones, to decide in accordance with the *lex arbitri*.[19]

35–33 In France, s.1485(1) of the French CPC provides that "[o]nce an award is made, the arbitral tribunal shall no longer be vested with the power to rule on the claims adjudicated in that award". Section 1485(2) makes the following exception to this rule:

> "However, on application of a party, the arbitral tribunal may interpret the award, rectify clerical errors and omissions, or make an additional award where it failed to rule on a claim. The arbitral tribunal shall rule after having heard the parties or having given them the opportunity to be heard."

35–34 In other words, if the Tribunal cannot be reconvened, such power shall be vested in the court which would have had jurisdiction if there had been no arbitration.[20]

35–35 In Switzerland, a remand to the Tribunal is possible, although art.190 of the Swiss PILA refers only to annulment of the Awards. The Federal Supreme Court has also admitted the possibility of a revision of the Award in an international arbitration proceeding.[21]

[18] This affirmation is based on the conflict of laws rule according to which a French judge would have had jurisdiction to interpret, rectify or complete international Awards (B. Golfman, J. Cl. International, fasc. No.586–5–1, No.91; Ph. Grandjean, "La durée de la mission des arbitres", Rev Arb 1995, p.39). Some scholars take the view that this solution does not truly correspond to the simplification targeted by the parties resorting to arbitration (Garnier, "Interpréter, rectifier et compléter les sentences arbitrales internationales" (1995) Rev Arb No.4, p.565, para.12; See Devolvé, Rouche, & Pointon, *op. cit.*, para. 341, p.190). For a general review, see Webster, Functus Officio and Remand in International Arbitration, Vol. 27 ASA Bulletin No.3, p. 441.

[19] See also Reiner & Aschauer, *op. cit.*, para.708.

[20] See Delvové, Rouche & Pointon, *op. cit.*, para.341, p.190. See also Garnier, "Interpéter, rectifier et compléter les sentences arbitrales internationales" (1995) Rev Arb No. 4, p. 565.

[21] Kaufmann-Kohler & Rigozzi, *Arbitrage international–Droit et pratique à la lumière de la LDIP*, Schulthess 2006, at p.348; Müller, *International Arbitration–A Guide to the Complete Swiss Case Law (Unreported and Reported), op. cit.*, p.199. Similarly, there is no express provision for remand to the Tribunal under the UNCITRAL Model Law. See, however, e.g. art.1059(4) of the German Code of Civil Procedure.

In the United States, the federal law specifically provides for remand to the Tribunal.[22] In *M&C Corp v Erwin Behr GmbH & Co and Heinz Etzel*,[23] the issue of referring or remanding a matter back to the arbitrator arose in the context of an ICC arbitration and a series of litigations referred to as "Behr I", "Behr II" and "Behr III". 35–36

The arbitrator in that case awarded damages on several heads including based on "orders" that were received within a given period after the Award. An issue arose as to which orders were covered. The lower court remanded the matter to the arbitrator and the matter was appealed to the Court of Appeals. In discussing the issue of remanding the matter to the arbitrator, the Court of Appeals stated: 35–37

> "[12] A remand is proper, both at common law and under the federal law of arbitration contracts, to clarify an ambiguous award or to require the arbitrator to address an issue submitted to him but not resolved by the award. [. . .] The authority to order a remand derives from a recognised exception to the *functus officio* doctrine, which holds that an arbitrator's duties are generally discharged upon the rendering of a final award, when the arbitral authority is terminated. [. . .] However, "where the award, although seemingly complete, leaves doubt whether the submission has been fully executed, an ambiguity arises which the arbitrator is entitled to clarify."

The Court of Appeals thus upheld the principle of referring a matter back to the arbitrator and went on to deal with two issues relating to the remand. The first was whether the remand should be to the same arbitrator. The second was whether such a remand was permitted under the 1988 version of the ICC Rules. The Court of Appeals held that the referral should be back to the same arbitrator[24] and that it was permitted under the 1988 version of the Rules,[25] even though the latter, unlike the 2012 Rules, did not expressly provide for such remission. 35–38

However, the Court of Appeals went on to reverse the lower court and to direct that the lower court specify the matters that were ambiguous in the award and 35–39

[22] US Federal Arbitration Act s.10.

[23] United States Court of Appeals, Sixth Circuit, April 21, 2003, No.01–1949, *M&C Corp v Erwin Behr GmbH & Co, KG and Heinz Etzel* (2003) YBCA Vol.XXVII p.1120; 2003 US App. LEXIS 7426.

[24] In this respect, the Court stated: "[16] Behr argues that, assuming remand was appropriate, it was error for the district court to remand the award to the original arbitrator rather than directing the parties to start the whole process over again before a brand new arbitrator. In making this argument, Behr fails to account for our observation in Green that 'courts usually remand to the original arbitrator for clarification of an ambiguous award when the award fails to address a contingency that later arises or when the award is susceptible to more than one interpretation'. Green, 200 F.3d at 977".

[25] The Court relied on both the ICC Rules and the law of the place of arbitration (England) in stating:

> "[17] Hoping to avoid remand, Behr makes a two-pronged argument that remand is improper even if the award is ambiguous. First, Behr contends that the International Chamber of Commerce (ICC) Rules that govern this dispute pursuant to the parties' arbitration agreement do not expressly permit remand.
>
> [18] However, as M&C points out, Art. 34 [now Art.41] of the same rules demonstrates that a guiding principle behind the rules is to ensure that the award is ultimately susceptible of enforcement [. . .] We read this provision to permit remand in this case, given that clarification by the original arbitrator is critical in order to make the Eighth Award enforceable at law."

require a remand. After the lower court specified those matters, its decision was once again appealed (in *Behr III*) and the Court of Appeals refused to permit a further remand to the arbitrator stating:

> "Although federal courts have jurisdiction to enforce arbitrations awards, courts may not go beyond the arbitration award to decide questions that the arbitrator did not decide. Behr II, 143 F.3d at 1037–38 (citing United Steelworkers of America v. Enter. Wheel & Car Corp., 363 U.S. 593, 599 (1960)). 'An ambiguous award may not be enforced but should be remanded to the arbitrator.'. [. . .] As discussed below, the relevant portions of the arbitration award, as well as the parties' contract, are unambiguous and, therefore, the district court erred in remanding to the arbitrator for further clarification on the scope of products for which Behr must pay commissions."[26]

35–40 The *Behr* trilogy illustrates both the possibilities and the possible detriments of remands in arbitration. The Court of Appeals in *Behr III* noted in June 2005:

> "According to the United States Supreme Court, '[a]rbitration agreements allow parties to avoid the costs of litigation.' Circuit City Stores, Inc. v Adams, 532 U.S. 105, 123 (2001). This litigation proves the exception to that rule. This is now the fourth appeal to this Court regarding an arbitration award that was finalized in 1994, three years after Defendant Edwin Behr GmbH & Co. ('Behr') terminated its contract with Plaintiff M & C Corporation, who had been acting as the exclusive sales agent for Behr's automotive parts."

35–41 In England, the Arbitration Act of 1996 specifically provides for remand to the arbitrators under s.68 of that Act which, amongst other things, allows the parties to ask the courts that the Award be remitted to the Tribunal in cases where there has been a serious irregularity which falls within the list of s.68(2)[27] and which has caused the party substantial injustice.[28]

[26] *M&C Corp v Erwin Behr GmbH & Co, KG and Heinz* Etzel, 411 F.3d 749 (6th Cir 2005).

[27] Section 68(2) provides as follows:

"Serious irregularity means an irregularity of one or more of the following kinds which the court considers has caused or will cause substantial injustice to the applicant—

(a) failure by the tribunal to comply with section 33 (general duty of tribunal);
(b) the tribunal exceeding its powers (otherwise than by exceeding its substantive jurisdiction: see section 67);
(c) failure by the tribunal to conduct the proceedings in accordance with the procedure agreed by the parties;
(d) failure by the tribunal to deal with all the issues that were put to it;
(e) any arbitral or other institution or person vested by the parties with powers in relation to the proceedings or the award exceeding its powers;
(f) uncertainty or ambiguity as to the effect of the award;
(g) the award being obtained by fraud or the award or the way in which it was procured being contrary to public policy;
(h) failure to comply with the requirements as to the form of the award; or
(i) any irregularity in the conduct of the proceedings or in the award which is admitted by the tribunal or by any arbitral or other institution or person vested by the parties with powers in relation to the proceedings or the award".

[28] On the application of s.68(2)(d), see *Petrochemical Industries Co (KSC) v The Dow Chemical Co* [2012] EWHC 2739 (Comm); and *Primera Maritime (Hellas) Ltd, Astra Finance Inc, Comet*

However, s.67 of the 1996 Act (relating to jurisdictional issues) contains no such provision. Nevertheless, in *Hussman (Europe) Ltd v Ahmed Pharaon* [2003] EWCA Civ 266, the Court of Appeal held that it did have the power to remit the matter to the arbitrator where a prior Award had been annulled as having been in favour of the wrong party.[29] The Court did so in stating: **35–42**

> "It is true that there is no express power to remit [to the tribunal] under section 67(3)(compare section 68(3)(a)). However, on the basis of the principle which we have preferred, there would appear to be no need of such a power: the arbitration merely carries on or revives as necessary.
>
> If, in the present case, the arbitrators had merely made an award as to their jurisdiction (to make an award against or in favour of the Company), but had not entered on the merits, we do not see how it could possibly be argued that the setting aside of that award, or its being declared to be of no effect, could deprive the arbitrators of jurisdiction to make a final award on the merits, if they were in a position to do so. We do not consider that the present situation, where they have gone on to make an award on the merits in favour of the Company alters the principle. A valid final award on the merits will of course exhaust the arbitrators' jurisdiction, subject to any remission from the courts: but we can see no good reason in principle why an invalid final award, in excess of jurisdiction, should lead to the same result, when once that award has been declared to be of no effect by the courts."

The *Behr* and *Hussman* cases reflect the fact that, even where a Tribunal has rendered an Award and therefore rendered itself functus officio, the jurisdiction of a Tribunal may be revived by order of the courts of the place of arbitration. Otherwise, the sole right of a Tribunal is to interpret or correct within a limited period of time an Award as provided for in art.35.[30] **35–43**

Finance Inc v Jiangsu Eastern Heavy Industry Co Ltd, Ningbo Ningshing International Inc [2013] EWHC 3066 (Comm).

29 The facts were as follows: Mr Pharaon had previously conducted business as a Saudi establishment, which is an entity without legal personality. The establishment entered into a contract with Hussman (Europe) Ltd (Hussman). Subsequently, Mr Pharaon assigned the business to a Saudi company, but that assignment did not assign the contract with Hussman. The Tribunal initially issued a final award in favour of the Saudi company and not the establishment or Mr Pharaon personally. The Award was declared "of no effect" by the English courts under s.67 of the English Arbitration Act of 1996, Mr Pharaon then sought to have the Tribunal issue an Award in his name.

30 More generally, see Fróes, "Correction and Interpretation of Arbitral Awards," *op. cit.*, at p.289 and p.291; Daly, "Correction and Interpretation of Arbitral Awards under the ICC Rules of Arbitration" including Extracts from ICC Addenda and Decisions on the Correction and Interpretation of Arbitral Awards, (2002) ICC ICArb Bull Vol.13 No.1, p.61 and p.72; Note of the Secretariat of the International Court of Arbitration of the International Chamber of Commerce Regarding the Correction and Interpretation or Arbitral Awards (1999) ICC ICArb Bull Vol.10 No.2 p.4; Bühler, "Correction and Interpretation of Awards and Advance on Costs" (1997) ICC ICArb Bull, Special Supplement, p.53; Kühn, "Rectification and Interpretation of Arbitral Awards" (1996) ICC ICArb Bull Vol.7 No.2, p.78.

Costs

35–44 Pursuant to art.35(4), the ICC Court may "fix an advance to cover any additional fees and expenses of the arbitral tribunal and any additional ICC administrative expenses". It follows from art.2(10) of App.III to the Rules, that the ICC Court is no longer bound by the ICC Cost Schedule to fix an advance on costs, and subsequently the arbitrators' fees and the ICC's administrative expenses. The ICC can fix these amounts at its discretion.

CHAPTER 7

COSTS

Article 36 Advance to Cover the Costs of the Arbitration

1 **After receipt of the Request, the Secretary General may request the claimant to pay a provisional advance in an amount intended to cover the costs of the arbitration until the Terms of Reference have been drawn up. Any provisional advance paid will be considered as a partial payment by the claimant of any advance on costs fixed by the Court pursuant to this Article 36.**

2 **As soon as practicable, the Court shall fix the advance on costs in an amount likely to cover the fees and expenses of the arbitrators and the ICC administrative expenses for the claims which have been referred to it by the parties, unless any claims are made under Article 7 or 8 in which case Article 36(4) shall apply. The advance on costs fixed by the Court pursuant to this Article 36(2) shall be payable in equal shares by the claimant and the respondent.**

3 **Where counterclaims are submitted by the respondent under Article 5 or otherwise, the Court may fix separate advances on costs for the claims and the counterclaims. When the Court has fixed separate advances on costs, each of the parties shall pay the advance on costs corresponding to its claims.**

4 **Where claims are made under Article 7 or 8, the Court shall fix one or more advances on costs that shall be payable by the parties as decided by the Court. Where the Court has previously fixed any advance on costs pursuant to this Article 36, any such advance shall be replaced by the advance(s) fixed pursuant to this Article 36(4), and the amount of any advance previously paid by any party will be considered as a partial payment by such party of its share of the advance(s) on costs as fixed by the Court pursuant to this Article 36(4).**

5 **The amount of any advance on costs fixed by the Court pursuant to this Article 36 may be subject to readjustment at any time during the arbitration. In all cases, any party shall be free to pay any other party's share of any advance on costs should such other party fail to pay its share.**

6 **When a request for an advance on costs has not been complied with, and after consultation with the arbitral tribunal, the Secretary General may direct the arbitral tribunal to suspend its work**

and set a time limit, which must be not less than 15 days, on the expiry of which the relevant claims shall be considered as withdrawn. Should the party in question wish to object to this measure, it must make a request within the aforementioned period for the matter to be decided by the Court. Such party shall not be prevented, on the ground of such withdrawal, from reintroducing the same claims at a later date in another proceeding.

7 **If one of the parties claims a right to a set-off with regard to any claim, such set-off shall be taken into account in determining the advance to cover the costs of the arbitration in the same way as a separate claim insofar as it may require the arbitral tribunal to consider additional matters.**[1]

Introductory remarks

36–1 As discussed under art.1, the ICC is a non-profit association that provides various services, including the arbitration services under the Rules. The ICC's funding comes from various sources, including the administrative fees it charges for arbitrations conducted under the ICC Rules.

36–2 The ICC keeps a bank account with UBS in Geneva (Switzerland), to which Parties pay the advances on cost fixed by the ICC Court. It has been the consistent practice of the ICC not to credit parties any interest on their deposit of the advances on cost, let alone to reimburse any such interest to them at the end of the proceedings. In the past, the ICC Court's practice has been criticised, although it is by far not the only institution to follow such a practice. Another concern regarded the fact that the Court's practice to keep any interest earned through the deposit of the Parties' advances was not mentioned in the Rules or its Appendices. Article 1(13) of App.III, which was issued together with the 2012 Rules, has remedied the situation. It states: "The amounts paid as advances on costs do not yield interest for the parties or the arbitrator". In any event, given the extremely low interest available on US Dollar deposits in recent years, the issue of interest has been less of a concern.

36–3 Article 36 deals with the advances on costs to cover ICC arbitration. It has been amended from the corresponding provision of the 1998 Rules to expressly

[1] Article 36 corresponds to art.30 of the 1998 Rules. The text has been modified in particular to provide that the filing fee is to be taken into account in calculating the advances paid by the parties and to provide in art.36(4) for multi-party cases subject to arts 7 and 8. In addition, there have been drafting and organizational modifications to the text.

provide that the filing fee is to be taken into account in calculating the advances paid by the parties (in art.36(1)) and to take into account multiparty arbitration (in art.36(4)). In addition, various drafting and organisational changes were made.

The costs of arbitration are divided into the administrative costs of the ICC and the fees for the arbitrators. Appendix III sets out tables showing the range of those costs and fees which in both cases are calculated on the basis of the amount in dispute. It is possible to check the range of the ICC administrative costs and the range of the arbitrators' fees online through the ICC website[2] and by reference to the tables reproduced in Pt III App.1. The ICC Court sets the actual amount of the costs for each case based on a number of factors, including the amount in dispute, the complexity of the dispute, the actions of the parties and the time spent by the Tribunal. The expenses incurred by the members of the Tribunal in the course of the arbitration need to be added to these costs. **36–4**

As of January 1, 2012, a new Costs Schedule applies to ICC arbitration. The new Cost Schedule applies to all ICC arbitrations started as of January 1, 2012. The minimum administrative charge (expenses) is US$3,000 for disputes worth US$50,000 or less, and is capped at the maximum of US$113,215 for disputes worth US$500 million or more. As regards the arbitrators' fees, the rates in the fees table have been increased from those under the previous table. As discussed under art.37, the fees payable to the arbitrators will range between the minimum and the maximum amount of the fee schedule depending on the complexity of the case, the time spent by the arbitrators, as well as other factors.[3] **36–5**

The ICC Court Costs Schedule has historically been denominated in US Dollars. Whenever a party submits a claim in a currency other than US Dollars, the Secretariat will convert the amount into US Dollars, irrespective of the geographic origin of the parties, the place of arbitration or the domicile of the arbitrators. Therefore, any fluctuation in the value of the Dollar against other currencies may have an impact on the cost of the arbitration including the fees of the arbitrators. The result is not very satisfactory, but it is not easy to imagine or implement an alternative. The four major centres of arbitration primarily considered in this Handbook use varying currencies, from the US Dollar to the Swiss Franc, the British Pound Sterling to the Euro. As a result, there are almost bound to be fluctuations between the US Dollar and foreign currencies and it is viewed as impractical to offer parties an alternative scale of fees in various currencies. **36–6**

As the ICC table on costs reflects, the costs of an ICC arbitration other than the legal costs depend largely on the amount in dispute. Therefore, there is a strong incentive for a party asserting a claim to set the amount at a reasonable level and an incentive for the parties in some instances to bring non-monetary claims. **36–7**

Article 36 deals with the advances on costs covering the administrative costs of the ICC, the fees of the arbitrators and the expenses they are likely to incur. The advance to cover such costs is fixed by the ICC Court, and, within certain limits, also by the Secretary General. The parties do not have to and should not discuss **36–8**

[2] http://www.iccwbo.org [accessed November 28, 2013].
[3] See the discussion at paras 37–43 to 37–57 below.

their fees with the arbitrators. Article 2(4) of App.III to the Rules expressly states: "The arbitrator's fees and expenses shall be fixed exclusively by the Court as required by the Rules. Separate fee arrangements between the parties and the arbitrator are contrary to the Rules". The same applies for the advance on costs. If a party wishes to raise any issue with respect to the costs of the arbitration in general or the advance on costs fixed by the ICC Court it should do so with the Secretariat. If the arbitrators wish to discuss the level of fees and/or the advance on costs, they too should do so with the Secretariat. The fact that the parties do not have to interact with the arbitrators on the issue of fees is considered by many as a very distinct advantage of ICC arbitration.

Article 36(1): "After receipt of the Request, the Secretary General may request the claimant to pay a provisional advance in an amount intended to cover the costs of the arbitration until the Terms of Reference have been drawn up. Any provisional advance paid will be considered as a partial payment by the claimant of any advance on costs fixed by the Court pursuant to this Article 36."

36–9 Article 36(1) is intended to permit the Secretary General to provide for the initial coverage of the ICC's costs pending a decision by the ICC Court as to the amount of the advance to be paid by both parties under art.36(2). Article 36(1) does not depend on a decision of the ICC Court. As a result, the Secretary General's request is made independently of any Committee or Plenary Session of the ICC Court.

36–10 The Claimant pays an initial (and non-refundable) amount of US$3,000 when the Request is filed which is credited to the Claimant's portion of the advance on costs.[4] After receipt of the Request, the Secretary General, through the Secretariat, may and, in practice, virtually always does request that the Claimant pay a provisional amount or advance to cover the costs of arbitration for the first stage of the proceedings, until the Terms of Reference have been drawn up. This provisional advance on costs is to be paid by the Claimant before the file will be transmitted to the Tribunal.[5] This mechanism is intended to ensure that the administrative fees and the fees for the arbitrators will be covered for this initial period of the arbitration. It should be noted that the initial period is intended to be relatively brief, as under art.23(1), the Terms of Reference are to be signed within two months of the date of transmittal of the file to the Tribunal.

36–11 Usually, the Secretariat provides 30 days for the Claimant to pay the provisional advance under art.36(1). If the Claimant fails to make the payment, the file will not be transmitted to the Tribunal.

36–12 The provisional advance is calculated on the basis of the amount in dispute quantified in the Request. Article 1(2) of App.III to the Rules sets out a cap for the amount of the provisional advance under art.36(1). That cap is calculated based on the administrative expenses, the minimum fees for the arbitrators as set out in the table to App.III of the Rules, and a sum calculated to cover the expenses the

[4] Article 1(1) of App.III to the Rules, see at para.4–69 above.
[5] See Pt II Document 12, the Secretariat's Transmittal of the File to the Tribunal.

Tribunal may incur up to the Terms of Reference. The amount of the provisional advance may be less than this amount, particularly if the intention is to have the ICC Court set the amount of the advance on costs for both parties within a reasonably short period of time after transmittal of the file to the Tribunal. If the sum in dispute is not quantified, the Secretary General can fix the amount of the provisional advance at its discretion.[6]

The Secretary General's practice has recently been to establish the amount of the provisional advance by adding (i) one half of the administrative costs according to ICC's Cost Schedule; (ii) half of the minimum arbitrator's fees resulting from the Cost Schedule times the number of arbitrators; and (iii) an estimated amount for the reimbursable expenses for the Tribunal up to the signing of the Terms of Reference.[7] 36–13

Article 36(2): "As soon as practicable, the Court shall fix the advance on costs in an amount likely to cover the fees and expenses of the arbitrators and the ICC administrative expenses for the claims which have been referred to it by the parties, unless any claims are made under Article 7 or 8 in which case Article 36(4) shall apply. The advance on costs fixed by the Court pursuant to this Article 36(2) shall be payable in equal shares by the claimant and the respondent."

Article 36(2) deals with fixing the advance on costs in cases other than those in which additional parties have been joined (art.7) or where claims are between multiple parties (art.8). Advances are fixed in those cases under art.36(4). To obtain an overall amount for these fees, the ICC has made available the ICC Arbitration Cost Calculator on its website.[8] 36–14

The ICC Court sets the amount of the advance on costs for an arbitration "as soon as practicable". This language is intended to deal with the fact that the ICC Court will need certain basic elements to determine the amount of this advance on costs. As discussed in Annex 1 Pt I, the ICC Court generally sets the amount of the advance at a Committee Session at the same time as it deals with various other issues such as the number of arbitrators. The ICC Court renders this decision at an early stage in the proceedings, generally when the Tribunal is constituted and well in advance of the signing of the Terms of Reference. Therefore, the information that will be available to the ICC Court at this stage will generally be limited to the Request and the Answer, and any counterclaim as well as any answer to the counterclaim. In addition, in many cases, the ICC Court will not seek to set an advance on costs intended to cover the total costs associated with the arbitration. Although there is no uniform practice in this regard, in the authors' view, in many if not most instances, the ICC Court will anticipate that it may be necessary to have a further adjustment of the costs later on in the proceedings.[9] 36–15

[6] Fry, Greenberg, Mazza, *op. cit.*, para.3–350.

[7] Fry, Greenberg, Mazza, *op. cit.*, para. 3–333.

[8] Available online at: *http://www.iccwbo.org/products-and-services/arbitration-and-adr/arbitration/cost-and-payment/cost-calculator/* [accessed November 28, 2013].

[9] There are two schools of thought as to the initial advance. The first school of thought is that the amount of the advance should be set at an amount intended to cover the anticipated costs of the arbitration. The second school of thought is that the initial advance should be set at an amount to

36–16 Article 1(4) of App.III to the Rules provides that: "The advance on costs fixed by the Court according to Articles 36(2) or 36(4) of the Rules comprises the fees of the arbitrator or arbitrators (hereinafter referred to as 'arbitrator'), any arbitration-related expenses of the arbitrator and the ICC administrative expenses".

36–17 The level of the ICC administrative costs is set based on the aggregate amount in dispute of the claims and the counterclaims. Determining the amount in dispute sometimes represents a major difficulty for the parties. This is a problem for the ICC Court, as well, and sometimes also for Tribunals. The ICC Court is entitled to fix the arbitrators' fees and the ICC administrative expenses "at its discretion" (see App.III arts 2(1) and 2(5)).[10] A party's claim for arbitration costs and/or for accrued interest is generally not taken into account by the ICC Court when assessing the amount in dispute, unless the costs or interest claim forms the very subject matter of the dispute. Where declaratory relief is sought in addition or as an alternative to monetary relief, the question arises how the ICC Court should value this relief. In some instances, there is a figure associated with the declaratory relief.[11] However, the request for a declaration may be made according to conditions that may or may not arise. In other words, unlike a request for an order of payment, the conditions may not be met and the party may thus never end up with a right to payment. In such a case, where declaratory relief is sought for contingent payment, the amount of the underlying claim for which declaratory relief is sought, may in effect be discounted in calculating the amount of the advance on costs.

36–18 As discussed under art.37, the amount of the fees payable to the arbitrators will depend also on the amount in dispute between the parties.[12] With damage claims, the parties may set out in the Request and Answer the exact amounts in dispute, if the amounts are quantified, as well as estimates for unquantified claims. These provisions have been reinforced for the Request, Answer, Request for Joinder and the Terms of Reference in an effort to obtain a better view of the amounts in dispute. However, as discussed under arts 4 and 5, it may be difficult for a party to provide even an estimate of the amount in dispute at that point.

36–19 The ICC Court will also take into account the estimated arbitration-related expenses of the Tribunal in setting the amount of the advance. Therefore, if it is anticipated that the arbitrators will incur travel and accommodation expenses, then the advance will take into account these expenses.

36–20 This general rule is subject to several exceptions relating to the expenses that are to be incurred in connection with an arbitration, and in particular expenses that may be incurred with respect to experts and hearings.

cover the first stage in the proceedings based on the assumption that there will be an adjustment later in the proceedings when the ICC Court has more information as to the procedure and claims. The authors' view is that the circumstances may call for a different treatment of different cases. In a straightforward arbitration regarding termination of a distribution agreement, it may be appropriate to seek to estimate the full amount of the costs to give the parties adequate warning of the costs of the arbitration. With complex lengthy proceedings, an interim advance, which is thus subject to adjustments, may well be more appropriate as the parties and their counsel understand that there will have to be adjustments but at the same time prefer to pay the advance in stages.

[10] Schwartz, "The ICC Arbitral Process – Part IV: The Costs of ICC Arbitration" (1993) ICC ICArb Bull Vol.4 No.1, p.13.

[11] For example, a Claimant may seek a declaration that US$10 million are due, when certain conditions are met pursuant to the contract.

[12] See para. 37–10.

With regard to experts appointed by the Tribunal, art.1(12) of App.III to the Rules provides that: **36–21**

> "[b]efore any expertise ordered by the arbitral tribunal can be commenced, the parties, or one of them, shall pay an advance on costs fixed by the arbitral tribunal sufficient to cover the expected fees and expenses of the expert as determined by the arbitral tribunal. The arbitral tribunal shall be responsible for ensuring the payment by the parties of such fees and expenses . . .".

Tribunals often ask the parties to organise the advance and the payment for significant additional costs, such as those for meeting rooms and court reporters. Indeed, the ICC Court will normally not have taken such expenses into account when fixing the advance on costs. Nevertheless, such expenses can also be paid out of the advance on costs fixed by the ICC Court, which, from a purely practical perspective, may be more convenient for the Parties. In such a case, an increase of the advance on costs by the ICC Court is likely to occur so as to avoid reducing the amount of expenses reduces the sums available to pay the arbitrators' fees. Whenever the Secretariat reserves conference rooms, be it at the ICC headquarters, or the ICC Hearing Centre in Paris or elsewhere, the Secretariat will normally also take charge of the financial side of these room reservations. **36–22**

The basic rule set out in the first sentence of art.36(2) is that the parties are expected to pay the advance on costs in equal shares. In calculating the amount of the payment, the filing paid by the Claimant upon filing the Request, as well as the provisional advance is taken into account. Article 1(5) of App.III states that each party shall pay its share of the total advance on costs "in cash". In fact, the ICC accepts payments only by cheque or wire transfer at its account at UBS Geneva,[13] but no payment in cash as such.[14] **36–23**

Once the advance on costs has been fixed by the ICC Court, the parties are generally granted 30 days to make the requested payment. To that effect, the Parties receive a letter from the Secretariat enclosing a Payment Request for both the Claimant and the Respondent. If the Secretariat receives no payment within the initial 30-day time limit, it will almost automatically grant the Parties additional time to pay the required amounts. **36–24**

Under art.1(5) of App.III, in cases where the share of the advance on costs is greater than US$500,000, parties may provide a guarantee instead of making payment under art.36(2). The ICC Court's current practice has been to cap the advance on costs to US$650,000 even if the amount of the dispute would result in a substantially higher amount in order that the parties not be faced with too onerous payment obligations at the start of proceedings.[15] **36–25**

The last sentence of art.36(2) imposes an obligation on the parties as it states that "[t]he advance on costs [. . .] shall be payable in equal shares by the claimant and the respondent". If a party fails to make payment, the other party may substitute for that party by paying that sum pursuant to art.36(5) 2nd sentence. In prac- **36–26**

[13] See para.36–2.

[14] This is also one way for the ICC to protect against money laundering, see Bühler, *op. cit.*, p.__.

[15] Fry, Greenberg, Mazza, *op. cit.*, para.3–355.

tice, the Secretariat will not leave that party much choice. If, following several reminders, the Respondent fails to pay its share, the Secretariat will invite the Claimant to pay in lieu of the Respondent. To that effect, it will set the Claimant a time limit, which it will automatically extend if no payment is received within that period. If no payment is received even within the extended time limit, the Secretariat will warn the Claimant that the Tribunal will be advised to suspend its work and that a final time limit will be set. If the Claimant still fails to make payment, the Secretariat will generally invite the Tribunal to suspend its work in relation to the claims concerned by the advance on costs and set a final limit, usually of 15 days. If the advance on costs remains unpaid after this, the claims will be considered withdrawn. The party substituting for the other party can recover the amount of the advance (depending on the results of the arbitration) pursuant to the final Award. However, there is an issue as to whether the party has a right to obtain payment from the defaulting party prior to the final Award. Article 36(5) provides that "any party shall be free to pay any other party's share of any advance on costs should such other party fail to pay its share".

36–27 Several ICC Awards have held that there is a contractual obligation to the other party and not just an obligation to the ICC.[16] However, certain commentators disagree,[17] and in an Award dated March 26, 2002, the sole arbitrator held that there was no such legal obligation to the other party.[18] However, in that interim Award, the sole arbitrator ordered the defaulting party to make payment of US$75,000, which was the amount of the advance on costs pursuant to art.23(1). Therefore, the basic difference between the positions appears to be whether the

[16] See for example ICC Case No.17502 Interim Award of November 12, 2010 (2010) ASA Bull Vol.29 No.3 p.634; ICC case No.13853 (Partial Award on costs—reimbursement of the Respondents' share of the advance on costs to Claimants; award on costs), unreported ("13.The Tribunal considers that payment should be made direct to the Claimants rather than to the ICC. The Claimants' submission that this is a contract debt is accepted. That debt is owed to the Claimants and it is they, not the ICC, who should receive payment"); see also ICC Partial Award of March 27, 2001, *X Co, Panama, v Y SA, Suisse* (2001) ASA Bull Vol.19 No.2, p.285.

[17] See on the subject generally, Bühler, "Note – Sentence Partielle du 1er juin 2004 dans l'affaire CCI No.12491/KGA/EC—Non-payment of the advance on costs by the Respondent party—is there really a remedy?" (2006) ASA Bull Vol.24 No.2, p.290; Secomb, "Awards and Orders Dealing with the Advance on Costs in ICC Arbitration: Theoretical Questions and Practical Problems" (2003) ICC ICArb Bull Vol.14 No.1, p.59; Fadlallah, "Payment of the Advance on Costs in ICC Arbitration: The Parties' Reciprocal Obligations" (2003) ICC ICArb Bull Vol.14 No.1, p.53; Scherer, "Jurisprudence—Introduction to Case Law Section—Advance on the costs of the arbitration" (2003) ASA Bull Vol.21 No.4, p.749; Rouche, "Le paiement par le défendeur de sa part de provision sur les frais d'arbitrage: simple faculté ou obligation contractuelle?" (2002) Rev Arb No.4, p.841; Favre-Bulle, "Les conséquences du non-paiement de la provisions pour frais de l'arbitrage par une partie—Un tribunal arbitral peut-il condamner un défendeur au paiement de sa part de l'avance de frais?" (2001) ASA Bul Vol.19 No.2, p.227; Reymond: "Note sur l'avance des frais de l'arbitrage et sa répartition", in *Etudes de procédure et d'arbitrage en l'honneur de Jean-François Poudret* (Lausanne, 1999) p.495; Rohner & Lazopoulos, "Respondent's Refusal to Pay its Share of the Advance on Costs" (2011) ASA Bull. No.3, p.549.

[18] See ICC Interim Award of March 26, 2002 (2003) ASA Bull Vol.21 No.4, p.802 ("[17] The Arbitrator considers that this power of the ICC Court of Arbitration to discharge the parties from the obligation to pay each half of the global advance on costs, by fixing separate advances, implies that the parties are not contractually bound (each towards the other) to pay half of the advance on costs when a counterclaim is raised. This aspect seems not having been considered by the legal literature and the arbitral awards mentioned hereabove (No 14 and 15), but it had been raised by the Arbitrator (letter of July 26, 2001) and has been discussed with the parties at the October 29–30, 2001 hearing").

party which has made payment by substitution for the other party has a contractual right to reimbursement which may be the subject of a partial Award or whether that party has the possibility of seeking payment of a similar amount as interim relief. One would anticipate that any claims in this respect would be made in the alternative to cover both possibilities.

If a party fails to make payment in accordance with art.36(2), one should keep in mind that art.37(3) provides that "[a]t any time in the arbitral proceedings, the arbitral tribunal may make decisions on costs other than those fixed by the Court, [i.e. the parties' legal and other costs], and order payment". Therefore, a Tribunal may issue a partial Award dealing with costs—and in essence deal with the failure to pay an advance on costs. **36–28**

In a 2006 case, the Claimant submitted to the Tribunal a request for injunction asking that the Respondent—who had challenged the Tribunal's jurisdiction—be ordered to pay half of the advance on costs fixed by the ICC Court pursuant to art.36.[19] According to Respondent, the Tribunal could not issue such an injunction before it has decided whether or not it had jurisdiction over Respondent. In other words, a challenge of the jurisdiction of the Tribunal is a challenge of its power to entertain interim measures as well. Although such a situation is not provided by the ICC costs system, it is however a case in which a Tribunal, irrespective of the view that it takes of the nature of the obligation set forth in art.36(2), may be reluctant to render a decision ordering a non-paying party to pay before it has decided on its jurisdiction.[20] **36–29**

In one instance, a Tribunal ruled in a procedural order that it did not have jurisdiction to order a defaulting party to pay its share of the advance on costs based on the wording of the predecessor to art.36(2) and the provision that a party may substitute for the non-paying party (as is now provided for in art.36(5)). The authors disagree with that approach (and with dealing with a jurisdictional issue in a procedural order), although it does highlight a procedural issue: until a party has substituted for the defaulting party, a request to order the defaulting to make payment of its share of the advance on fees may be viewed as premature.[21] **36–30**

[19] ICC case No.13645 (2006), unreported.

[20] See Bühler, "Costs in ICC Arbitration: A Practitioner's View" (1992) Am Rev Int'l Arb Vol.3 at pp.148–149; See also ICC case No.10439 (2002) (Partial Award) dismissing the non-defaulting party's request "[s]ince the issue of jurisdiction over [the Respondent] is still pending, the relief sought by the [Claimant] cannot be granted" cited by Secomb, "Awards and Orders Dealing with the Advance on Costs in ICC Arbitration: Theoretical Questions and Practical Problems", *op. cit.*, at p.63.

[21] In ICC case No.12895, Procedural Order No.10 (2005), unreported, a three-member Tribunal refused to order a Respondent to pay its share of the advance on costs in the following terms:

> "10. (. . .) Article 30(3) of the ICC Rules [corresponding to Art.36(2) of the current Rules deals with the case where one party refuses to pay its share of the advance on costs. It provides that in that event, the other party is free to substitute for the non-paying party and to pay the full advance on costs. That is the mechanism foreseen in the Rules for dealing with this situation. It is not clear to the Arbitral Tribunal that it has authority to modify that rule.
>
> 11. This is so for yet another reason. Under the ICC Rules, it is the Court or the Secretary General, and not the Arbitral Tribunal, who has authority to deal with circumstances where a party fails to pay its share of the advance on costs. The underlying rationale for the Court or Secretary General being the competent authority is that the arbitrators have a personal interest in being paid their fees. If an arbitral tribunal were to order a party to pay its share of the advance on costs, its decision might be viewed as self- serving and lacking in independent and

36–31 Assuming that a Tribunal decides that it has jurisdiction to grant interim relief over a party challenging the basis of its jurisdiction, and assuming that the Claimant would have paid the full advance on costs, the Tribunal would have to consider whether the conditions for interim relief are met. One of these conditions is the existence of irreparable, or at least substantial harm to the requesting party.[22] In addition, the Tribunal should consider the temporary nature of the payment of the advance on costs itself since under art.37(3), it has the power to decide, in its final Award, which party has to bear the costs of the arbitration. Decisions on a party's request for injunction should thus be carefully weighed by the Tribunal.[23]

36–32 As discussed above, where the advances on costs for claims and counterclaims have been separated out pursuant to art.36(3) sets out the principle that each party is required to pay for its claim or counterclaim as the case may be.[24] The same principle applies in multi-party situations, where the ICC Court fixes advances for one party's claims pursuant to art.36(4).

Article 36(3): "Where counterclaims are submitted by the respondent under Article 5 or otherwise, the Court may fix separate advances on costs for the claims and the counterclaims. When the Court has fixed separate advances on costs, each of the parties shall pay the advance on costs corresponding to its claims."

36–33 Article 36(3) provides for the possibility of setting of separate advances on costs for the parties to the arbitration. The ICC Court fixes separate advances on costs generally on the application of one of the parties to the arbitration. Any party may make a request that the ICC fix separate advances on costs, whether it is a Claimant, Respondent or additional party. A party usually makes such an application when (i) the party is concerned that the other party will not pay its share of

unbiased judgment. Such is not the case when one party has already paid the full advance on costs and requests the tribunal to order the non-paying party to reimburse it.

12. For these reasons, the Arbitral Tribunal considers that in the circumstances of the present case, it does not have the power under the ICC Rules to order Respondents to pay its share of the advance on costs."

[22] See ICC case No.7289 (1996)(Partial Award): "Although the Arbitral Tribunal found that it had authority to make the order requested by the Claimant and that the Respondent was, in fact, obligated under the ICC Rules to pay its share of the advance, it nevertheless decided not to order the Respondent to do so because the Claimant had not established that it would be irreparably harmed" cited in Derains & Schwartz, *op. cit.*, at p.346; See also Rouche, "Le paiement par le défendeur de sa part de provisions sur les frais d'arbitrage: simple faculté ou obligation contractuelle?", *op. cit.*, at p.841 and (2002) Rev Arb No.4, p.1001; See also ICC case No.11392 (2002) (Partial Award), cited in Secomb, "Awards and Orders Dealing with the Advance on Costs in ICC Arbitration: Theoretical Questions and Practical Problems", *op. cit.*, at p.65. In that case, the Tribunal held that "it is only when it is convinced that the failure by the [Respondent] to pay its share of the advance on costs would cause injustice that an arbitral tribunal must, if so requested, do what it can to prevent such injustice". The Tribunal decided that irreparable harm had been shown because the party lacked the financial resources to pay the totality of the claim. More generally on conservatory and interim measures, see above, paras 28–27 et seq.

[23] See ICC case No.7289 (1996) (Partial Award), *op. cit.*: "In light of the fact that the definitive responsibility for the costs will be decided by the Arbitrator in his final award, and that the Court's application of the ICC Rules has allowed the provisional financing of the arbitral procedure, the Arbitrator must examine with the greatest prudence whether his 'interference' at this stage of the procedure is justified by the facts" (Authors' translation).

[24] See para.36–23.

the advance on costs; or (ii) the claims of the two parties are disproportionate; or (iii) both of these conditions are met.

An example of this situation (i) is when the Claimant has a claim for US$5 million and the Respondent has a claim for US$4.8 million. In such a case, the advances on costs would be similar if not the same with respect to the claim and the counterclaim. However, the Claimant may be concerned that the Respondent will not pay for 50 per cent of the advance on costs for the claim. If the advances on costs are not separated, then the Claimant may end up paying 100 per cent of the costs for its claim and of the costs for the Respondent's counterclaim. If the Claimant has this type of concern, the Claimant may request separate advances for the claim and the counterclaim under art.36(3) in order to oblige the Respondent to pay for the counterclaim. The Claimant will then pay the full amount of the advance on costs for the claim. If the Respondent wishes to proceed with the counterclaim, the Respondent must pay the full amount of the advance on costs for the counterclaim pursuant to art.36(3). Therefore, the Respondent will have to pay its share of the overall advance on costs if both the claim and the counterclaim are proceeded with. **36–34**

Situation (ii) arises, for example, where the Claimant is making a claim for US$1 million and the Respondent is making a claim for US$20 million. The amount of the advance on costs for the US$1 million claim will be a fraction of the amount of the advance on costs for the US$20 million counterclaim. Therefore, the Claimant may prefer to separate out the advance on costs and pay 100 per cent of the advance on costs for the claim while leaving the Respondent to pay 100 per cent of the advance on costs for the counterclaim in accordance with art.36(3). **36–35**

When requesting such a decision from the ICC Court, the parties should be aware that the fixing of separate advances on costs is more expensive for them due to the graduated nature of the fee calculation. The Secretariat will usually draw the attention of the parties to the financial consequences of the fixing of separate advances on costs before the request is submitted to the ICC Court. To that effect, it will provide the parties an estimate of the advance on costs to be fixed for the principal claims and the counterclaims, which varies between a minimum and a maximum of fees of the Tribunal, excluding the sum set aside to cover the Tribunal's expenses.[25] **36–36**

As regards the payment of the separate advance on cost, art.1(8) of App.III to the Rules expressly provides: "When the Court has fixed separate advances on costs pursuant to Article 36(3) of the Rules, the Secretariat shall invite each party to pay the amount of the advance corresponding to its respective claim(s)". **36–37**

Article 36(4): "Where claims are made under Article 7 or 8, the Court shall fix one or more advances on costs that shall be payable by the parties as decided by the Court. Where the Court has previously fixed any advance on costs pursuant to this Article 36, any such advance shall be replaced by the advance(s) fixed pursuant to this Article 36(4), and the amount of any advance previously paid by any party will be considered as a partial payment by such party of its share of the advance(s) on costs as fixed by the Court pursuant to this Article 36(4)."

[25] The increase is due to the progressive nature of the ICC costs schedule.

36–38 Article 36(4) is a new provision of the Rules. Article 36(4) deals with advances on costs where there are additional parties (art.7) and multiparty claims (art.8). In such circumstances, the bipolar approach as to the advances on costs may have to be adjusted to reflect the number of parties and number of claims, and to avoid putting an unjust and unjustified burden on some of the parties. Article 36(2) specifically excludes matters that fall under art.36(4). If an advance has already been set under art.36(2) and the arbitration has evolved in such way that the matter now falls under art.36(4), the amount of the advance on costs and the number of advances on costs may be re-adjusted.

36–39 The Court has discretion to fix one advance on costs or several and to allocate payment as it sees fit.[26] The ICC's general practice remains to set one amount for the advance on costs and require equal treatment by all parties. However, the ICC Court is not required to request equal payment from each party and may allocate the amounts differently depending on the circumstances. Nevertheless, prior to doing so, and given that the ICC Court is very reluctant to reconsider a decision, the ICC Court will normally request the comments from the parties, to avoid imposing a burden based on its view of the matter that may end up being inaccurate. The parties are free to agree to a different allocation of the advance(s) on costs, which shall be taken into consideration by the Court when fixing the advance(s) on costs. In addition, where there are three or more parties to a dispute, the ICC Court may decide on separate advances on costs. It is noteworthy that in multiparty arbitration, while the total amount of a single advance on costs does not increase even though its payment may be allocated in various proportion to the parties, the fixing of several advances on costs will certainly significantly increase the amount of the total of the advances on costs that will be paid by the parties to the Secretariat.[27]

36–40 However, as explained above, it may be necessary to request separate advances on costs, even in multiparty arbitration, especially when one or more of the parties refuse to pay their share of the advance on costs. Failure to pay the advance(s) on costs fixed under art.36(4) have the same consequence as those fixed under art.36(2): they fall under art.36(5) and art.36(6).

Article 36(5): "The amount of any advance on costs fixed by the Court pursuant to this Article 36 may be subject to readjustment at any time during the arbitration. In all cases, any party shall be free to pay any other party's share of any advance on costs should such other party fail to pay its share."

36–41 Article 36(5) provides that the ICC Court may adjust the amount of the advance on costs "at any time during the arbitration". This sentence is intended in particular to cover adjustments to the advances on costs that are made after the Terms of Reference have been signed and after the parties provided much more detail as to the nature and amount of their claims, as well as the procedure that they propose for the arbitration. These adjustments to the advance are made at various times prior to rendering of the Award. The most appropriate times are when there are

[26] Fry, Greenberg, Mazza, *op. cit.*, para.3–1383.

[27] For a detail explanation of how the advance on costs is calculated in multiparty arbitration, see Fry, Greenberg, Mazza, *op. cit.*, paras 3–1394 et seq.

specific developments in the procedure, such as (i) completion of briefing of the case or an issue; (ii) completion of hearing on the case or a part of the case; and (iii) prior to or after rendering of a partial Award. It is axiomatic that if the adjustment is made later in the proceedings and one party is dissatisfied with the procedural or substantive aspects at that stage, that party may be less willing to meet a request for a further advance on costs.

The Secretariat follows the procedure in the arbitration and will therefore be aware of any increase in the amount of the claims and counterclaims or any quantification of any unquantified claim. In addition, the Secretariat will be aware of the procedural complications that may be involved in the case and of any additional expenses incurred by the members of the Tribunal. As a result, in many instances, it is the Secretariat that contacts the Tribunal (and in particular the president) to determine whether an adjustment in the level of the advance on costs is appropriate. **36–42**

In some instances, the president of the Tribunal will take the initiative of indicating to the Secretariat when the work involved in the arbitration has reached the point where a reconsideration of the amount of the advance on costs should be considered. The president will usually do this in a letter sent to the Secretariat (and not copied to the parties) in which the president outlines the work done to date, the work that remains to be done and the level of complexity of the matter. **36–43**

All of these can result in a readjustment of the amount of the advance on costs in accordance with art.36(2) or art.36(4). Any such readjustment is notified to the parties, and a time limit is set for the payment of the balance of the advance. Where a party disagrees with the decision of the ICC Court, it may ask its reconsideration. New elements will, however, be required to make the ICC Court change its decision.[28] **36–44**

Article 36(5) provides that a party may substitute for another party who fails to pay an advance on costs. This is intended to ensure that the arbitration can proceed despite the failure of a party to pay its share of the advance on costs as is discussed under art.36(6). As discussed above, art.36(2) imposes an obligation on the parties to pay the advance on costs. Absent payment by one party of its advance on costs, the Secretariat will invite the other to pay in the non-paying party's place and will set a time limit to do so. This amount may be recovered in the final Award, and perhaps earlier. **36–45**

Article 36(6): "When a request for an advance on costs has not been complied with, and after consultation with the arbitral tribunal, the Secretary General may direct the arbitral tribunal to suspend its work and set a time limit, which must be not less than 15 days, on the expiry of which the relevant claims shall be considered as withdrawn. Should the party in question wish to object to this measure, it must make a request within the aforementioned period for the matter to be decided by the Court. Such party shall not be prevented, on the ground of such withdrawal, from reintroducing the same claims at a later date in another proceeding."

[28] See the discussion under art.11(4) as to the "finality" of the ICC Court's administrative decisions taken under the Rules above at paras 11–45 to 11–49.

36–46 Article 36(6) deals with the situation where either of the parties fail to make a payment of the advance on costs or if one party fails to make a payment and the other party fails to substitute for the defaulting party. The usual procedure followed in this respect is outlined in Annex 1 Pt I. Article 36(6) is noteworthy in that the decision is that of the Secretary General and not the ICC Court in the first instance. The Secretary General cannot delegate this authority. However, if a party is dissatisfied with the Secretary General's decision, the party may apply to the ICC Court for a decision provided that it does so within the time limit set by the Secretary General.

36–47 If there is only a claim (and no counterclaim) or if there is a claim and a counterclaim, but no separate advances on cost have been fixed, the failure to pay the advance in accordance with art.36(2) will usually result in a stay and ultimately deemed withdrawal of all claims in the arbitration.

36–48 More frequently, the failure to pay an advance on costs is a failure with respect to the counterclaim as, in bringing the proceedings, a Claimant has usually made the decision to pay the entire advance on costs if the Respondent defaults in payment of its share of the costs. Therefore, the Claimant will often make the payment of its share and the Respondent's share of the advance on costs for the principal claim, but nothing will prevent Claimant from seeking the fixing of a separate advance on costs for the counterclaim to force the Respondent to finance the counterclaim.

36–49 If the Respondent fails to pay the separate advance on costs for the counterclaim, then the ICC's practice has been to invite the Tribunal not to proceed with the counterclaim. A recent case, however, has caused some concern with regard to this practice. In this case, the Paris Court of Appeal set aside an ICC Award, in which a Tribunal was ordered by the Secretariat not to hear a counterclaim due to the bankrupt party's failure to pay the advance on costs.[29] The Court of Cassation confirmed the Court of Appeal's ruling, which found that the Award violated the counterclaiming party's right to access justice and due process by upsetting the equality of the parties (art.1520–4 and 1520–5 of the French CCP[30]), and added only that the counterclaims must be inseparable from the claims in order not to violate art.1520.[31] This case was unique because an Award was set aside precisely due to the fact that the Tribunal abided by the ICC Rules and the directions of the ICC Court.[32] However, it illustrate, the basic principle that the ICC Court and the Tribunal must ensure comphance with mandatory provisiond of applicable law.

36–50 Prior to directing the Tribunal to suspend the work on the relevant claims or counterclaims, the Secretariat consults with the Tribunal. It is possible that the Tribunal will consider it appropriate to continue its work on the claims or coun-

[29] Recently, the Paris Court of Appeal ruled that the refusal to hear counterclaims due to failure to pay the advance on costs violated the party's right to access justice and party equality and justified the setting aside of the Award. *Société Licensing Projects v Société Pirelli & C.SPA*, Paris Court of Appeal, November 17, 2011, (2012) Rev. Arb., pp.387–392. In a decision dated 28 March 2013 (Pirellli & Co. v. Licensing Products) the French Supreme Court limited the application of the principle to where the claims and counter claims were intrinsically linked

[30] The text of these provisions is reproduced in Pt III App.6.

[31] Cass. Civ. 1e, March 28, 2013, No.11–27.770.

[32] C. Dupeyron & F. Poloni, "Procédure de liquidation d'une partie, arbitrage et droit d'accès à la justice: l'impossible équation" (2012) ASA Bul. Vol.30 No.2, p.468.

terclaims given issues of timing or other special circumstances. In such case, the Tribunal's view does not bind the Secretary General. Moreover, the Tribunal will continue to work at its financial risk. However, it remains to be seen whether recent French case law will have any effect on the ICC's practices.

Article 36(6) gives the Tribunal no power to suspend the arbitral proceedings for lack of payment of the advance on cost, unless it was authorised by the Secretariat to do so. A Tribunal may, however, indicate to the Secretariat that it considers further activities to be inappropriate, as long as uncertainty exists as to the payment of, e.g. separate advances on costs. It will be for the Secretary General to consider the situation and to instruct the Tribunal. As ICC arbitration is primarily concerned with commercial disputes,[33] most Tribunals expect that the rules on payment of the advance on costs should be complied with. 36–51

When directing the Tribunal to suspend its works, the Secretary General usually gives a time limit of 15 days to the defaulting party(ies) to fulfill its/their financial obligations. Should the party in question wish to make an objection in this respect, it may submit its request for decision to the ICC Court. However such request must be made within the 15 day time limit. If not made within that time limit, the ICC Court will not consider the matter. In the event a timely objection is raised, the time limit for payment is suspended until the ICC Court renders its decision. The ICC Court is free to confirm or to extend the time limit granted by the Secretary General. If the ICC Court extends the time limit for payment, the party in question must ensure that the requested payment be effectively received by the ICC before the end of the time limit. If not paid within that time limit, its claims or counterclaims will be automatically considered as withdrawn. 36–52

Failure to pay the advance on costs may result in a deemed withdrawal of the claim or counterclaim. A party may object to the deemed withdrawal and one would imagine that this would either be on the basis that the amount of the advance is too high or that the party requires additional time to obtain the funds. 36–53

The deemed withdrawal of the claims or counterclaims does not prevent the party from reintroducing the claims or counterclaims in another proceeding. However, the date of the reintroduction will generally be considered the date on which the claim or counterclaim has been filed. Therefore, the deemed withdrawal and reintroduction may raise issues under applicable law based on limitation periods. In addition, art.36(6) refers to reintroduction in another proceeding, that is in a newly filed ICC arbitration. 36–54

Article 36(7): "If one of the parties claims a right to a set-off with regard to any claim, such set-off shall be taken into account in determining the advance to cover the costs of the arbitration in the same way as a separate claim insofar as it may require the arbitral tribunal to consider additional matters."

In most legal systems, to assert a set-off, a party must assert a claim that is in a defined amount that has some connection with the claim of the other party.[34] 36–55

[33] See Introduction, paras 0–25 to 0–35.

[34] See for example art.8.1 of the UNIDROIT Principles:

"(1) Where two parties owe each other money or other performances of the same kind, either of them ('the first party') may set off its obligation against that of its obligee ('the other party') if

Article 36(7) provides that the amount of the set-off is taken into account in determining the advance on costs. However, the amount should not be double counted. Therefore, if a party asserts that its counterclaim gives right to a right of set-off, it is the amount of the counterclaim that should be taken into account in determining the level of the advance on costs. For example, a party may counterclaim for breach of contract for US$1 million and maintain that this amount should be set-off against any amount awarded to the other party.

36–56 A set-off can be particularly important in case of insolvency. A party making a claim or counterclaim against a potentially insolvent opponent will wish to ensure that it pays the net amount due to the other party rather than pay the full amount and be a creditor for the amount of its claim against the other (insolvent) party. As a creditor (and usually an unsecured one), the party may only receive a fraction of its claim from the insolvent company.

at the time of set-off, (a) the first party is entitled to perform its obligation; (b) the other party's obligation is ascertained as to its existence and amount and performance is due.
(2) If the obligations of both parties arise from the same contract, the first party may also set off its obligation against an obligation of the other party which is not ascertained as to its existence or to its amount."

Article 37 Decision as to the Costs of the Arbitration

1 The costs of the arbitration shall include the fees and expenses of the arbitrators and the ICC administrative expenses fixed by the Court, in accordance with the scale in force at the time of the commencement of the arbitration, as well as the fees and expenses of any experts appointed by the arbitral tribunal and the reasonable legal and other costs incurred by the parties for the arbitration.

2 The Court may fix the fees of the arbitrators at a figure higher or lower than that which would result from the application of the relevant scale should this be deemed necessary due to the exceptional circumstances of the case.

3 At any time during the arbitral proceedings, the arbitral tribunal may make decisions on costs, other than those to be fixed by the Court, and order payment.

4 The final award shall fix the costs of the arbitration and decide which of the parties shall bear them or in what proportion they shall be borne by the parties.

5 In making decisions as to costs, the arbitral tribunal may take into account such circumstances as it considers relevant, including the extent to which each party has conducted the arbitration in an expeditious and cost-effective manner.

6 In the event of the withdrawal of all claims or the termination of the arbitration before the rendering of a final award, the Court shall fix the fees and expenses of the arbitrators and the ICC administrative expenses. If the parties have not agreed upon the allocation of the costs of the arbitration or other relevant issues with respect to costs, such matters shall be decided by the arbitral tribunal. If the arbitral tribunal has not been constituted at the time of such withdrawal or termination, any party may request the Court to proceed with the constitution of the arbitral tribunal in accordance with the Rules so that the arbitral tribunal may make decisions as to costs.[1]

[1] Article 37 corresponds to art.31 of the 1998 Rules. The substantive changes are the addition of arts 37(3), (5) and (6) to the text of the Article.

Introductory remarks

37–1 In opting out of national courts with international arbitration, the parties are agreeing to pay the costs associated with international arbitration. The costs of international arbitration include the costs of the ICC and the arbitrators; these costs are in many instances much higher than those that a party is required to pay to bring national proceedings. Article 37 has been modified from the corresponding provision of the 1998 Rules to expressly provide that the Tribunal may consider additional factors including the extent to which a party has conducted the proceedings in an expeditious and cost-effective manner (art.37(5)) and to provide for the possibility of constitution of a Tribunal to deal with costs on termination of proceedings (art.37(6)).

37–2 Article 37 provides the tool for deciding upon the amount of the costs of arbitration and for allocating such amount as between the parties. Given the substantial costs incurred in many ICC arbitrations, art.37 is a provision with which every user or prospective user of ICC arbitration needs to be familiar. The first subsection defines the costs of arbitration, and expressly refers to the parties' reasonable legal costs. The second subsection deals with the setting of the arbitrators' fees and ICC administrative fees by the ICC Court. The third subsection deals with the Tribunal's role in setting the costs of arbitration and allocating all costs between the parties.

Article 37(1): "The costs of the arbitration shall include the fees and expenses of the arbitrators and the ICC administrative expenses fixed by the Court, in accordance with the scale in force at the time of the commencement of the arbitration, as well as the fees and expenses of any experts appointed by the arbitral tribunal and the reasonable legal and other costs incurred by the parties for the arbitration."

ICC Arbitration Costs and Party Costs

In an ICC arbitration, there are two basic types of costs of the arbitration, which are covered by art.37(1). The first type of costs (the "**ICC Arbitration Costs**") are those relating to the ICC administrative costs and the fees and expenses of the arbitrators and Tribunal-appointed experts.[2] The overall amount of these costs is set by the ICC Court in accordance with art.37(2) and the Tribunal decides on their allocation between the parties in accordance with art.37(3). 37–3

The second type of costs (the "**Party Costs**") are the "legal and other costs incurred by the parties". The Tribunal decides on the amount of such costs and their allocation between the parties. These costs and the procedure for arriving at them are discussed under art.37(3). 37–4

The term "**costs of arbitration**" in art.37(1) therefore covers both ICC Arbitration Costs (fixed by the Court) and Party Costs. The Tribunal allocates the costs of arbitration as between the parties in its final Award. To do so it allocates the ICC Arbitration Costs determined by the Court and determines and allocates the Party Costs. 37–5

The ICC strives for arbitrations conducted under its Rules to be cost-effective.[3] As a result, the ICC's Commission on Arbitration prepared a study entitled "Techniques for Controlling Time and Costs in Arbitration" first published in 2007.[4] As its title indicates, the study was aimed at reducing costs and time associated with ICC arbitration. For the study, an analysis was made of the proportion of the ICC Arbitration Costs and the Party Costs in ICC arbitrations for which a final Award was rendered in 2003 and 2004. The proportions of the relative costs were as follows: 37–6

Costs borne by the parties to present their case:	
(including, as the case may be, lawyers' fees and expenses, expenses related to witness and expert evidence, and other costs incurred by the parties for the arbitration other than those set forth below)	82%

[2] See Schwartz, "The ICC Arbitral Process, Part IV: The Cost of ICC Arbitration" including Extracts from ICC Awards on Arbitration Costs, (1993) ICC ICArb Bull Vol.4 No.2, p.8 and p.31; Bühler, "Costs in ICC Arbitration: A Practitioner's View" *op. cit.*, p.110; Wetter and Priem, "Cost and their Allocation" (1991) Am Rev Int'l Arb Vol.2, p.249.

[3] See the discussion under art.23(1).

[4] A revised version is set out in Pt III.

Arbitrators' fees and expenses:	16%
Administrative expenses of ICC:	2%

37–7 The survey covered a period of only two years, and therefore the exact proportions may differ over a longer period. However, the basic relative importance of the Party Costs and the ICC Arbitration Costs corresponds roughly to what many practitioners would have expected. It is quite normal that the lawyers' fees and thus the Party Costs are much higher than the ICC Arbitration Costs. The lawyers spend more time in investigating the facts, putting the case together, interviewing potential witnesses and experts, and presenting their case to the Tribunal. The submission of a brief to the Tribunal constitutes solely the tip of the iceberg of the lawyers' work.[5]

37–8 The level of Party Costs depends in particular on the procedure that the parties agree on or that the Tribunal sets for the arbitration. In this respect, the Commission's Report provides valuable ideas as to how Tribunals can assist in limiting the Party Costs in particular. However, the parties basically control the amount of the Party Costs and the issue under art.37 is limited to how the Tribunal allocates those costs. The ICC Arbitration Costs and in particular the arbitrators' fees are set by the ICC Court and not by the parties. Therefore, the issue with respect to the ICC Arbitration Costs is to establish the amount (which is done by the ICC Court) and to allocate them (which is done by the Tribunal).

Fees of the arbitrators

37–9 The ICC Court sets the amount of the fees of the arbitrators. It is not permissible for the parties to have private fee arrangements with the arbitrators. Article 2(4) 2nd sentence of App.III of the Rules expressly stipulates: "Separate fee arrangements between the parties and the arbitrator are contrary to the Rules". This rule suffers only a limited exception with regard to value added tax (VAT) on arbitrator's fees and expenses, as discussed below.[6]

37–10 In an ICC arbitration, the fees of the arbitrators are fixed upon an *ad valorem* basis, by applying the fee scale in App.III of the Rules. The scale of Arbitrators' Fees effective as of January 1, 2012 applies to all arbitrations commenced on or after such date, and irrespective of the version of the Rules applying to such arbitrations.[7] The ICC applies, however, no pure *ad valorem* approach, as it takes other factors than the amount in dispute into account in fixing the fees. Indeed, art.2(2) of App.III to the Rules provides:

> "In setting the arbitrator's fees, the Court shall take into consideration the diligence and efficiency of the arbitrator, the time spent, the rapidity

[5] Mistelis, "International Arbitration—Corporate Attitudes and Practices—12 Perceptions Tested: Myths, Data and Analysis—Research Report", *op. cit.*, para.0–6; see also Bühler, The Arbitrator's Remuneration – too much, too little?, in *Liber Amoricum Lazareff* (2011), p.103; and Lalive, *Dérives Arbitrales (I)*, (2005) ASA Bull. Vol.4, p.587 at 591.

[6] See paras 37–62 to 37–66 below.

[7] Art.4(1) of App.III to the Rules.

of the proceedings, the complexity of the dispute and the timeliness of the submission of the draft award, so as to arrive at a figure within the limits specified or, in exceptional circumstances (Article 37(2) of the Rules), at a figure higher or lower than those limits."[8]

The Secretariat is copied on the various communications between the parties and the Tribunal and therefore can form an idea as to the diligence of the arbitrator. However, the speed with which the proceedings are conducted will depend on the parties as well and frequently either the parties agree on a period of one year or so to file the various memorials. In addition, the arbitration may be complex and as such require substantial time even from the Tribunal. The Secretariat will also ask the arbitrators to inform it of the time that the members have spent on the file. The ICC prefers to have proceedings carried out promptly. Therefore, if the proceedings have been conducted rapidly and effectively within the context of the procedure adopted by the parties, then the fees of the arbitrators should reflect the results (as well as the time spent). In most cases, the fees will be within the limits specified in art.37(2). **37–11**

Article 2(3) of App.III to the Rules provides: **37–12**

"When a case is submitted to more than one arbitrator, the Court, at its discretion, shall have the right to increase the total fees up to a maximum which shall normally not exceed three times the fees of one arbitrator."

If there is a Tribunal rather than a sole arbitrator, the fees for the arbitrators will be higher than for a sole arbitrator. As a general rule, the allocation of the fees among the members of the Tribunal is 30 per cent for each co-arbitrator and 40 per cent for the president. However, this may be modified either by the ICC Court or by agreement amongst the arbitrators. In recent years, the ICC Court has disregarded the traditional 40/30/30 breakdown on occasion, but has not departed from it as the starting point for allocating fees amongst arbitrators.[9] **37–13**

The president usually does the bulk of the drafting, which is the most difficult and most time-consuming task in an arbitration. The president provides the other arbitrators with draft letters to the parties, draft Terms of Reference, draft Procedural Orders and the draft Award. Producing the first draft of such documents takes far more time than providing the president with comments thereon. In addition, the president has to manage the case on a permanent basis, by sending reminders either to his co-arbitrators or to the parties in order to have the case move forward. **37–14**

In some instances, although the arbitrators acknowledge that the president does carry out more than 40 per cent of the work for the Tribunal, the traditional allocation is followed on the basis that it tends to be the same persons over time who act as both co-arbitrators and president. Therefore, any disadvantage to a president in one case may well be offset by an advantage to the same person when sitting as a **37–15**

[8] Some of these factors were considered by the ICC Cout at least since 1980, when it first published its Internal Rules, see Bühler, *op.cit.*, p.105.

[9] See Bühler/Webster, *Handbook of ICC arbitration* (2nd edn, 2008), para.31–40; see also Bühler, *op. cit*, p.108.

co-arbitrator in another case. It is often difficult for a president to request the two other members of the panel to agree on a different fee allocation than the 40/30/30.

37–16 If the Tribunal (or a sole arbitrator) wishes to appoint an administrative secretary to the Tribunal, it should do so as soon as possible and provide the Secretariat and the parties with an estimate of the fees, so that they could be taken into account when the Court fixes the advance on costs. The fees of the administrative secretary to the Tribunal are thus paid out of the fees awarded to the arbitrators and are not normally treated as expenses of the Tribunal.[10] Under the ICC's current practice, the administrative secretary of the Tribunal needs to keep time-records, which the ICC Secretariat will communicate to the parties. An alternative would be to indicate to the parties the amount of time spent over a given period of time, and if this raises a question, the parties might then contact the Secretariat to obtain further explanations.

37–17 An arbitrator's duties are personal and cannot be delegated. Therefore, the basic view is that, with the exception of the cases of administrative secretaries, the time of other legal personnel assisting an arbitrator or president is not taken into account in setting the fees for the arbitrators. In this respect, there is a natural tension between the personal nature of an arbitrator's duties and the reality that, particularly with large complex arbitrations, some professional assistance is often required to find documents and check references for example.

37–18 If an arbitration is settled or if a matter is withdrawn, then the ICC Court will adjust the fees of the arbitrators. Article 2(8) of App.III to the Rules provides in this respect:

> "If an arbitration terminates before the rendering of a final Award, the Court shall fix the costs of the arbitration at its discretion, taking into account the stage attained by the arbitral proceedings and any other relevant circumstances."

37–19 In case of settlement or withdrawal of the claim, the ICC Court will refund the amount by which the advance on costs exceeds the costs as set by the ICC Court.

37–20 The ICC Court calculates the arbitrators' fees (and the administrative costs) in US Dollars. However, for most arbitrators, the currency of the arbitrator's expenses is not the US Dollar but a different currency.[21] The issue can be taken into account automatically (because the amount of the claims is also in Dollars). However, there is a perception that arbitrators are at risk due to the fluctuations of the value of the US Dollar. With respect to expenses incurred there should be no real currency risk and it is reasonable to use the exchange rate at the time the expense was incurred or at the time the request for reimbursement is made.

37–21 The ICC Court's decision as to the fees of the arbitrators is an administrative decision that is not subject to appeal or review. By accepting the Rules, the parties are agreeing that the ICC has the discretion to set the arbitrators' fees and by accepting appointment, the arbitrators are also accepting the ICC Court's discretion as to the fees. Like for any other of its decisions, the ICC Court does

[10] See Pt II Document 12.2, ICC Note on the Appointment, Duties and Remuneration of Administrative Secretaries.

not have, and will not give reasons for its decisions, by which it sets the arbitrators' fees.

Fees of the Emergency Arbitrator

As regards the Emergency Arbitrator, his or her fees are based on a lump sum, which is not covered by art.37 and not fixed by the ICC Court. It is also not dependent on the amount in dispute, but the time spent by the Emergency Arbitrator may in exceptional cases be taken into account by the President of the ICC Court when increasing the costs payable by the Applicant.[11] **37–22**

Expenses of the arbitrators

Arbitrators are entitled to reimbursement of their personal expenses in accordance with the principles set out in the ICC Note on Personal and Arbitral Tribunal Expenses (September 1, 2013), a copy of which is provided to each arbitrator upon his appointment or confirmation.[12] **37–23**

From time to time during the arbitration, the arbitrators will submit the expenses that they incur either personally or with respect to the proceedings. The Secretariat reviews the request for reimbursement and the supporting documentation to ensure that it falls within the approved categories of reimbursable expenses as described in the Notice on Arbitrators' Expenses. The parties are generally not involved in such matters and are only informed of the total amount of the expenses of the Tribunal, and not those of each arbitrator. **37–24**

Under the ICC Note on Personal and Arbitral Tribunal Expenses of September 1, 2013,[13] arbitrators are entitled to a flat per diem allowance of US$1,200 for each night spent on an ICC arbitration away from a place of residence. If no hotel accommodation is required, the per diem is US$400. Reimbursable expenses include costs for hotels, meals, transportation, communication, etc. Airline travel is generally in business class. Entertainment expenses (such as theatre tickets and expensive restaurants) are not reimbursed. **37–25**

The Tribunal may also incur expenses in relation to the conduct of the hearings. These expenses may include the cost of renting hearing rooms, and the cost of interpreters or court reporters (if these are not paid directly by the parties). To be reimbursable, the expenses incurred should relate directly to the conduct of the arbitration. General overhead costs, such as charges for secretarial time or overtime are considered not reimbursable. **37–26**

The Tribunal sets the amount of the deposit and the amount to be paid for Tribunal-appointed experts who are appointed in accordance with art.25(4). The ICC Court does not set the amount of the deposit for these experts. Usually, the Tribunal will request that the parties each pay one half of the amount of the deposit for the fees for the Tribunal-appointed expert. In many instances, the Tribunal will open a separate bank account for payment of the advance for these fees. The Tribunal should ensure that the fee arrangements with the Tribunal-appointed **37–27**

[11] See the discussion under art.29 as to the fees of the Emergency Arbitrator.
[12] See Pt II Document 12.4.
[13] See Pt II Document 12.4.

experts are clear so that the deposit covers the expert's fees. The Tribunal then sets the amount payable to the expert in the final Award that should not exceed the amount of the deposit and should of course be in accordance with the fee arrangements with the expert.

VAT on arbitrators' fees and expenses

37–28 Article 2(13) of App.III to the Rules provides as follows with respect to VAT:

> "Amounts paid to the arbitrator do not include any possible value added tax (VAT) or other taxes or charges and imposts applicable to the arbitrator's fees. Parties have a duty to pay any such taxes or charges; however, the recovery of any such charges or taxes is a matter solely between the arbitrator and the parties."

37–29 This provision was inserted due to uncertainty about the imposition of value added tax on services rendered by arbitrators domiciled within the European Union. In the *von Hoffman* case,[14] the European Court of Justice held that an arbitrator's fees were subject to VAT even if the services were rendered for export to another EU country. As a result most arbitrators based in the EU seek to charge VAT and art.2(9) of App.III leaves them free to do so. The ICC now provides a service for the administration of VAT from the parties, although collecting VAT is a matter for the individual arbitrator.

37–30 The VAT situation with respect to arbitration has still not been solved in a satisfactory manner for arbitrators domiciled in the European Union. Where both parties are within the EU and are subject to VAT, then there should be no financial issue as the parties obtain a credit for the VAT. However, where one of the parties is not an EU party, there may well be a real cost to imposing the VAT. Many arbitrators deal with the issue by providing in the Terms of Reference that the parties agree to pay VAT on the amount of the fees and expenses if the arbitrators are required to change and pay VAT on such amount.

37–31 Since the European Union now has 27 members, a large number of arbitrators residing in Europe are concerned by the VAT issue. Swiss arbitrators remain a notable exception within Europe.[15]

37–32 Where arbitrators, who are subject to VAT, wish to secure the payment of the VAT due on their fees, since November 2006, they may request assistance from the ICC, one sentence as indicated in the ICC Note to the Arbitral Tribunal on the Conduct of The Arbitration.[16] Basically, the ICC acts as the depositary:

[14] ECJ, 6th Chamber, September 16, 1997, Bernd von Hoffman and Finanzamt Trier, (1997) Mealey's IAR Vol.12 No.10, H–1; (1998) YBCA Vol. XXIII p.175; see also Lazareff and Le Gall, "L'assujetissement des arbitres à la TVA sous l'empire de l'article 259 du code général des impôts" (2006) Rev Arb No.2, p.543; Le Gall, "The fiscal status of the arbitrator" (1995) ICC ICArb Bull, Special Supplement, p.100; ICC case No.12711 (2004) (Procedural Order), JDI 2006 No.4 p.1454, note Jolivet.

[15] See Patocchi, "Deciding on the costs of the arbitration. Selected Topics" in *ASA Special Series No.29, op. cit.*, p.49 at p.60.

[16] See Pt II Document 12.4, ICC Note to the Arbitral Tribunal on the Conduct of the Arbitration.

> "of the fund for the payment of VAT. The ICC receives funds from the parties who have been instructed to this effect by an arbitrator (president of arbitral tribunal on behalf of the other members of the arbitral tribunal, member of an arbitral tribunal subject to VAT or sole arbitrator subject to VAT), and makes the payments corresponding to the VAT at the request of the arbitrators when the latter bill the parties for their fees".

> Calls of advances for the payment of VAT on fees and payments on the basis of the amounts deposited by the parties lie however solely with the arbitrators and not the ICC. Some arbitrators prefer that the foreseeable amount of VAT be paid into a fiduciary account opened by the president. Some other arbitrators will forego any request for security and invoice the parties their share of the required VAT once they have been paid their fees and/or expenses by the ICC.

ICC administrative costs

The ICC Court fixes the amount for the ICC administrative costs. The ICC administrative costs are calculated based on the schedule in App.III to the Rules that was in force when the arbitration was commenced. Article 2(5) of that Appendix provides that "[i]n exceptional circumstances, the Court may fix the administrative expenses at a lower or higher figure than that which would result from the application of such scale, provided that such expenses shall normally not exceed the maximum amount of the scale". **37–33**

One would expect that the "exceptional circumstances" would relate to the level of service required for the arbitration from the ICC Court and the Secretariat. For example, if the parties agree that matters should be expedited then additional time spent by the Secretariat in that connection may be taken into account. **37–34**

Appendix III was amended to provide as follows: **37–35**

> "6) At any time during the arbitration, the Court may fix as payable a portion of the ICC administrative expenses corresponding to services that have already been performed by the Court and the Secretariat.
>
> 7) The Court may require the payment of administrative expenses in addition to those provided in the scale of administrative expenses as a condition for holding an arbitration in abeyance at the request of the parties or of one of them with the acquiescence of the other."

The introduction of a "pay as you go" possibility for payment of the ICC fees is particularly appropriate where cases are long and complicated. The ICC Court has for some years imposed an abeyance on fees where arbitrations have been suspended at the request of the parties. If the arbitration is settled or withdrawn, then the ICC Court will normally set a lower amount for the ICC administrative fees based on the reduction of the amount of work to be carried out by the ICC in connection with the arbitration. This reduction will depend on the stage of the proceedings at the time of settlement or withdrawal. **37–36**

Which costs are recoverable and what is reasonable

37–37 The basic requirement of the Rules is that the Party Costs (that is, the "legal and other costs") must be "reasonable" to be recoverable. It is the Tribunal that decides whether Party Costs are reasonable, and the Tribunal does so in the overall context of art.37(4).

37–38 The ICC sets the costs of arbitration based generally on the amount in dispute and it is submitted that this is an indication that, in establishing whether Party Costs are reasonable, the amount in dispute should be a central factor. One of the major factors tempering the application of this principle relates to complexity. Some ICC arbitrations are straightforward, but many deal with technical or legal issues that are complex and novel. Those factors will increase the level of cost for all participants in an ICC arbitration.

37–39 ICC arbitration is also international in the vast majority of cases. It is based on the participation of lawyers and professionals from different countries with very different staffing and billing practices. Therefore, it is also important that a Tribunal takes into account the backgrounds of the parties and their counsel in establishing what is reasonable.[17]

37–40 The general preference is to permit the parties to present their cases as they see fit. However, where the place of arbitration is in England or Wales, two provisions of the English Arbitration Act of 1996 should be kept in mind. Section 33(2) of the Act requires Tribunals to "adopt procedures suitable to the circumstances of the particular case, avoiding unnecessary delay or expense, so as to provide a fair means for the resolution of the matters falling to be determined". Section 65 of the 1996 Act permits Tribunals to limit the costs of the arbitration.[18] Section 65 of the 1996 Act should be considered early in the proceedings and not at the end. However, the fact that this right exists and that the Tribunal has an obligation to avoid unnecessary expense may be relevant to the issue of whether the costs incurred (and recoverable) are reasonable in the circumstances.

[17] See for example, ICC case No.8528 (1996) (Final Award). The Award dealt with a dispute between a Turkish and American company. The Tribunal noted that: "[65] If the amount claimed by Claimant is compared with legal costs presented by defendant, Claimant's legal costs are more than double the comparable costs incurred by defendant. [66] In respect of the costs incurred by Claimant we considered that these costs are mainly attributable to the fact that the Leader's decision had already been implemented and that this decision was also made in respect of the future accounting of the JV. Therefore it was essential for Claimant to take the greatest efforts in this Arbitration in order to obtain a revision of the Leader's decision. We furthermore took into consideration that Claimant incurred much higher costs for experts and for travel expenses to the place of arbitration. But even if these factors as well as the outcome of this matter are considered, it nevertheless appears to us that there is a certain imbalance in the legal costs incurred by both. In view thereof we find that defendant has only to contribute (approximately 60% of) the legal costs of Claimant." (2000) YBCA Vol. XXV p.11; *Collection of ICC Arbitral Awards, Volume IV*, 1996–2000, *op. cit.*, p.402.

[18] Section 65 provides:

"(1) Unless otherwise agreed by the parties, the tribunal may direct that the recoverable costs of the arbitration, or of any part of the arbitral proceedings, shall be limited to a specified amount.

(2) Any direction may be made or varied at any stage, but this must be done sufficiently in advance of the incurring of costs to which it relates, or the taking of any steps in the proceedings which may be affected by it, for the limit to be taken into account."

Lawyers' fees

In many ICC arbitrations, more than one law firm is involved. This is usually justified based on the different legal systems applicable or on the law of the place of arbitration. In addition, some firms have recourse to lawyers specialised in ICC arbitration. The presence of more than one firm is seldom an issue in the allocation of costs. **37–41**

The awarding of costs to the Claimant is occasionally challenged by the Respondent, when the legal costs claimed by the Claimant have in fact been borne by a third party, such as an insurer or an affiliate company of the Claimant. The Respondent will then argue that the Claimant has not effectively incurred such costs. The authors are aware of two cases where such a defense failed. **37–42**

In a final Award rendered in 1992, the Tribunal held that the Respondent could recover the legal costs which had been billed and paid by an indemnifier, stressing in particular: **37–43**

> "[. . .] Defendant rather than the [indemnifier] mandated counsel to represent them in the arbitration. By doing so, they incurred the primary obligation to pay such counsel's fees and expenses— one not negated by the fact that someone else, through prior arrangement, paid them on their behalf."[19]

In a final Award rendered in 2006, it was the Claimant that objected to the ability of the Respondent, a holding company of a large group of companies, to recover its legal costs paid on its behalf by one of its subsidiaries. The Tribunal rejected the Claimant's attempt to benefit from the financial arrangements between the Respondent and its subsidiary.[20] The Tribunal did not take into account these arrangements which had been made as "a matter of convenience within the Respondent's group for invoicing of such fees and expenses", but rather considered that the fees and expenses submitted by the Respondent constituted reasonable costs incurred by or on behalf of the Respondent within the meaning of what was the predecessor of art.37(1).

Tribunals generally request a simultaneous submission of the amounts claimed with respect to legal fees. Often these submissions are made together with a break-down of the time spent by the lawyers and other professionals on the matter. Usually, Tribunals are reluctant to review in detail the time spent by the lawyers in preparing the case. Certainly, it would be very unusual for a Tribunal to "tax" the amounts claimed as a taxing officer might in some common law countries. The general view is that the break-down is submitted to establish who spent the time, that the time spent was reasonable and that it related to the arbitration. **37–44**

Tribunals will generally compare the amounts claimed by the two parties for their legal fees, taking into account the legal backgrounds of the parties and there will probably be a tendency to find one party's claim for legal fees reasonable if it is significantly less than that of the other party.[21] However, this weighing of the claims is a very rough measure of reasonableness. **37–45**

[19] ICC case No.7006 (1992) (Final Award), (1993) ICC ICArb Bull Vol.4 No.1, p.49. See also Derains & Schwartz, *op. cit.*, at pp.366–367.

[20] ICC case No.13645 (2006), unreported, cited at para.4–31 n.27.

[21] In some cases, the lawyers for one party will submit a claim which is significantly less than the amount that they have actually billed the client. This reduces the risk of the effect of a comparison

37–46 It has also become the practice to allow each side to briefly comment on the cost submission of the other side. Parties are free to take this invitation up, and a party will not always challenge the other side's costs, even if they are higher than its own costs. In a recent ICC Award, where the Respondent had challenged the Claimant's fees and costs as being excessively high, the Tribunal took the following position[22]:

> "559. As to Claimant's attorneys fees and costs, the Arbitral Tribunal is not surprised that Claimant had somewhat higher amounts than Respondent, since Claimant had to bring a complex case forward and had to carefully select the available options. Respondent's position is normally somewhat easier as, generally speaking, the Claimant carries the bulk of the burden of proof whilst Respondent may confine itself to contest the claims. In spite of this, the gap between Claimant and Respondent's invoices is enormous in this case. When comparing just attorneys' fees, Claimant's cost compensation claim is more than twice that of Respondent. When looking at the costs for the Parties' experts, these are approximately equal, at around EUR 2 million on each side.
>
> 560. In order to take account of the big difference in attorney fees and to bring the relation to a reasonable level, the Arbitral Tribunal deducts EUR 1 million from Claimant's attorneys' fees, thereby reducing Claimant's total costs to be considered for compensation purposes to EUR 7'415'555."

Fees for in-house lawyers

37–47 The current trend, although modestly implemented, is to treat in-house lawyers in a similar fashion to outside lawyers provided that their costs are provable and that they are incurred in connection with the arbitration.[23]

37–48 Many companies have internal costing and accounting for in-house lawyers. Those costs are then attributed to profit centres in calculation of overall results. However, the rates established for these allocations may be arbitrary, as they are in effect cost allocations within a group. This aspect renders the costs less convincing than the costs of outside lawyers. In some instances, this is offset by a relatively lower hourly rate for the charge.[24] If the costing per hour for the in-house lawyer is, for example, significantly lower than that for an outside lawyer, the

and may reflect the fact that the expenditure in legal fees was viewed as necessary to defend a principle going beyond the amounts at issue in the relevant case. See also Swiss Supreme Court, January 9, 2006, 4P.280/2005, *X v Y* (2006) ASA Bull Vol.24 No.2, p.347, note Scherer, at p.266.

22 ICC case No.17648 (2013) (Final Award), unreported. One of the authors was Respondent's counsel.

23 The Tribunal accepted a significant amount for in-house legal costs in ICC case No.8786 (1997), (2002) ASA Bull Vol.20 No.1 p.67; (2000) ICC ICArb Bull Vol.11 No.2 p.71.

24 Of course the in-house lawyers' contribution may be as, or more, valuable than that of the outside lawyer. However, one of the incentives for having in-house lawyers carry out work is that there is believed to be a lower cost for their time. It would seem curious to build into a claim for reimbursement of costs a profit element on the in-house lawyers by charging more per hour than they actually cost the party.

overall amount charged may appear reasonable even if the time the in-house lawyer spent on the matter is more difficult to verify. Another approach is to apply the similar hourly rate as outside lawyers but to then apply the same principles for time spent on the matter.[25]

The allocation of an in-house lawyer's time as between arbitration activities and non-arbitration activities may also raise issues. Therefore, particularly with regard to in-house lawyers, the time sheet or other documentation of the activity of the lawyer may be particularly useful and even essential to establishing the claim. 37–49

In another case, French Claimants requested the payment of the equivalent of over US$2 million in internal costs incurred by their employees in relation to a very large arbitration. The all-American New York based Tribunal was unmoved by the fact that the Claimants' cost claim included internal costs and simply reduced them with a broad brush approach for lack of detailed description and justification: 37–50

> "[837]. The Claimants' bill of costs also includes internal costs in the amount of €[ ] in respect of the time and expense incurred by their employees in relation to this arbitration. The Tribunal sees no reason in principle not to award internal costs since, if not organized and performed internally, the matters usually encompassed within these types of costs would likely be incurred at a higher cost from outside providers. As the Claimants have not provided a detailed description and justification of these internal costs, the Tribunal believes it appropriate to reduce the internal costs claimed in respect of this arbitration by 50 percent."[26]

Fees for paralegals and expert assistance

Some larger companies provide their own paralegals or other experts to assist in arbitration. For example, it is frequent in construction arbitration to have engineers made available to the outside lawyers to assist in the conduct of the arbitration, or where significant data are to be projected during the hearing, to be assisted by outside IT specialists. Some Tribunals will accept claims for these costs on the basis that they correspond directly to (and may be less costly than) similar services offered by outside lawyers, or simply because they consider them justified for the purpose of presenting a party's case. 37–51

Costs of expert witnesses

Reasonable time and expenses for expert witnesses is generally recoverable provided that the Tribunal determines that the expert evidence was material for the case even if, in the end, the expert testimony was not essential for the decision. 37–52

[25] This is the suggestion in the Chartered Institute of Arbitrators "Guidelines for Arbitrators on Making Orders Relating to the Costs of Arbitration", *op. cit.*, at para.37–93 fn.35 below, p.139.

[26] ICC case No.12124 (2006) (Final Award), unreported.

Costs of fact witnesses

37–53 Parties almost invariably claim for travel expenses for fact witnesses, whether they are employees of the party or not. For fact witnesses that are not employees of a party, the parties may enter into arrangements to reimburse them for lost income and for the time spent in rendering their services. Such arrangements would be subject to disclosure on questioning at the witness hearing. However, there appears to be no reason in principle why these costs, if reasonable, cannot be recovered.

37–54 There is said to be a tendency to permit claims for time spent by internal witnesses. However, it is not clear to what extent these have actually been recovered in ICC arbitrations. With many construction cases, the witnesses have hourly or daily rates and therefore can be charged to the arbitration with reasonable accuracy. However, in many other cases there are simply no time records to permit that allocation and the issue becomes much more complicated. Moreover, these types of claims are generally not recoverable, even in jurisdictions such as England.

Management time

37–55 The conduct of an arbitration may involve extensive management time. Some commentators believe that this should be recoverable. The Chartered Institute of Arbitrators approach is that this is generally not recoverable, but that it may be in some contexts (basically if it reduced other costs).[27] Most arbitrators would not be sympathetic to this type of claim. Management time and cost spent on an arbitration is difficult to quantify, and difficult to allocate. In most cases, the review of this type of claim for costs will therefore be difficult to make. As with time of witnesses who are in the employment of a party, these types of costs are generally not recoverable, even in England.

Proof of payment

37–56 Generally costs must have been paid or be outstanding to be recoverable. This is usually dealt with by having a confirmation from the party that it has paid the outstanding fees or a portion thereof (although the last invoice has frequently not been paid when the submission on costs is transmitted to the Tribunal). Such confirmation is sometimes given by a letter from the company's chief financial officer.

37–57 Further issues may arise with respect to contingency or conditional payments. If, under the law applicable to the arbitration, contingent or conditional fees are possible, there would be no issue of principle as to including them. With respect to the amount, usually contingent fees reflect the inherent risk either with a percentage fee arrangement or with a premium over the normal rates. In most instances the law firm involved will also have the usual backup to show work carried out on an hourly basis. Therefore, the Tribunal will have the option of

[27] Chartered Institute of Arbitrators, "Guidelines for Arbitrators on Making Orders Relating to the Costs of Arbitration", 5.7.3.2.

relying on the amount of time spent or on the fee arrangement in deciding the allocation of costs.

Third party funding

A more recent trend in international arbitration, third party funding, presents further questions with regard to the allocation of costs. The fact that many third party funding schemes often include contingency or conditional payment elements presents the same difficulties as when counsel enters into such an agreement independent of third party funding.[28] In addition, if the case is lost by the funded party, arbitration costs cannot be collected directly against the third party funder because this party was not a party to the arbitration.[29] Tribunals are often faced with the question of whether to take into account the fact that an arbitration is funded by a third party when awarding costs. In a recent ICSID case, a Tribunal stated that it "knows of no principle why any such third party financing arrangement should be taken into consideration in determining the amount of recovery by the Claimants of their costs".[30] Accordingly, the Tribunal allowed Claimants' fees of about US$6.2 million which it found to be reasonable. **37–58**

Article 37(2): "The Court may fix the fees of the arbitrators at a figure higher or lower than that which would result from the application of the relevant scale should this be deemed necessary due to the exceptional circumstances of the case."

As discussed under art.36, the starting point for determining the ICC Arbitration Costs is the amount in dispute. That amount results in minimum and maximum figures for those costs in accordance with App.III to the Rules. **37–59**

Although ICC arbitrators are not paid on an hourly basis, it is the constant practice of the ICC Court to request an indication from the arbitrators of the time they have devoted to the case. The Secretariat will therefore always ask arbitrators to provide it with the amount of hours, (not, however, with their time-sheets). Prior to or at the time of submitting the draft Award to the Secretariat, the president of the Tribunal will submit information as to the hours spent and expenses incurred by himself. The president may include the hours which were communicated to him or her by the other members of the Tribunal or invite them to submit their time directly to the Secretariat. The president may also provide comments as to any specific procedural aspects relating to the time spent by the Tribunal. Co-arbitrators may also provide comments, although these comments are often coordinated through the president. Each member of the Tribunal will at that point in time have to provide the Secretariat with a final accounting of the expenses it has incurred, and not yet submitted for reimbursement by the Secretariat. **37–60**

At the outset as discussed under art.36, the ICC Court will normally fix the advance on cost by taking the average of the arbitrators' fees based on the ICC **37–61**

[28] Pinsolle, "Le financement de l'arbitrage" (2011) Rev Arb Vol.2, p.408.

[29] Bertrand, "The Brave New World of Arbitration: Third-Party Funding" (2011) ASA Bul., p.612.

[30] *Kardassopoulos & Ron Fuchs v The Republic of Georgia, Award*, ICSID Case No. ARB/07/15, March 3, 2010, p.168.

cost calculator's figures. Depending on the development of the case, the advances may be increased, so as to allow the ICC Court to fix higher fees than the average. Article 36(2) gives the Court a lot of flexibility, since it can set the fees even below the minimum, but also above the maximum of the fee schedule. The former situation is unlikely to happen when a case is brought to an end by way of a final Award. It may happen where, early in the proceedings, an award by consent is issued by the Tribunal.

Advances on fees

37–62 Although the Rules do not contemplate the possibility for arbitrators to receive an advance on fees during the proceedings, it is the ICC Court's constant and longstanding practice to grant advances on fees, provided a certain phase in the arbitration has been reached (e.g. Terms of Reference signed, a partial Award rendered) and a request for payment of such advance is made by the Tribunal. The request is submitted to the Secretariat by the president on behalf of the Tribunal and need not be copied to the parties.

37–63 In the Court's practice, a Tribunal is permitted to request a first advance on fees once the Terms of Reference have been established, and transmitted to the Court.[31] The Tribunal will then be asked to indicate to the Secretariat the time each of its members has so far spent on the matter, and how much time the arbitrators estimate spending through the end of the case. At this stage of the proceedings, i.e. Terms of Reference signed, it has been the practice of the Court to grant an advance on fees equivalent to half of the minimum fees provided for under the ICC Fee Schedule. The Court is not bound by this guideline, and will for instance depart from it when the amount in dispute is on the high side. In such a case, the Court may only grant 25 per cent of the minimum fees, or any other figure it considers appropriate, in particular in light of the time spent up to that stage by the arbitrators. Since the Court has no control as to when the Parties wish to end their case, the Court seeks to avoid an over-payment of the arbitrators at the time of the Terms of Reference. The risk of over-payment can also arise when an arbitrator needs to be replaced before the end of the proceedings. The ICC Court wishes to preserve the parties against these risks, and therefore avoids paying high advances on fees to arbitrators. Any amounts paid to the arbitrators by way of an advance granted by the Court, are considered to be due to the arbitrators, and not subject to subsequent requests for reimbursement by the Court.

37–64 The advances on fees will generally be paid to the arbitrators on the same 40/30/30 basis on which their fees are currently fixed, in the absense of special circumstances, such as a separate agreement among the arbitrators. This split is without prejudice to the ICC Court's faculty to foresee a different allocation of the arbitrators' fees at the end of the case, as discussed above.[32]

[31] The request is normally transmitted by the president to the Secretariat on behalf of the Tribunal. Before making such request, the president should, of course, ensure that the two other members of the panel agree with making such request.

[32] See para.37–13.

Article 37(3): "At any time during the arbitral proceedings, the arbitral tribunal may make decisions on costs, other than those to be fixed by the Court, and order payment."

Article 37(3) deals with the Tribunal's rights to make a costs order at any time in the proceedings.[33] This provision existed already in the 1998 Rules, where it was introduced for the first time. In practice, Tribunals have, however, rarely made use of the possibility of issuing early cost orders in the proceedings. **37–65**

Success or failure in an ICC arbitration can occur at various steps in a proceeding, including with jurisdictional and procedural applications as well as with regard to liability and damages. As a result, the Tribunal may decide on the costs of an application when the application is dealt with rather than leave the matter for the final Award. **37–66**

The basic principles on which Tribunals allocate costs are discussed under art.37(4) and those principles are generally equally applicable to decisions on costs during the proceedings. However, there are some particularities with respect to decisions as to costs prior to the final Award. **37–67**

With jurisdictional applications, it is commonplace that the party who is unsuccessful in a jurisdictional argument is required to pay the other party's costs with respect to that application. The basic justification for that approach is that the unsuccessful application should not have been made. However, there are exceptions to this principle.[34] **37–68**

With other applications, such as applications for security for costs and for disclosure of documents, costs would normally follow the event provided that the procedural application is not viewed as excessive in the circumstances. For example, if there are multiple requests for disclosure of documents, there is an issue of who was successful in the application. In addition there may be an issue as to the relative importance of the documents in the hearings. Therefore, even if a party is successful in applications, the Tribunal may have reservations about the effort that is committed to the applications. **37–69**

[33] Article 37(3) is the same as the 2nd sentence in art.37(2) of the 1998 Rules.

[34] In ICC case No.9302 (1998), the Tribunal held that it did not have jurisdiction in the final Award where one of the issues was whether the Respondent was the successor to a signatory to the arbitration agreement. However, it ordered that each party bear its costs in the following terms: "[41] For the reasons set out below, the arbitral tribunal holds that the ICC costs of arbitration shall be shared equally by the parties and that each party shall bear its own legal fees and costs. Although S has prevailed in its defense on lack of jurisdiction and, hence, in this arbitration overall, equal sharing of costs is the most appropriate solution under the circumstances. [42] The issue of jurisdiction was a complex one, the outcome of which was difficult to predict. When engaging in this arbitration, both parties, but especially D, which, for reasons of the tribunal's lack of jurisdiction, has not prevailed, can be said to have had legitimate expectations of success. This balanced situation is also reflected if one looks at the positions during contract performance. Apparently, both parties operated in good faith in the genuine belief that different rules governed their relationship. Further- more, S, which was in control of the facts and the documents surrounding the changes which occurred within its group in 1971, failed to provide conclusive evidence of the lack of jurisdiction early in the proceedings. This being said, the arbitral tribunal wishes to acknowledge that both parties have fully co-operated in the arbitration, and acted, through their counsel, in a highly professional manner, which the tribunal appreciated." (2003) YBCA Vol. XXVIII p.54; (2003) Gazette du Palais, Special Issue on Arbitration, November 8, 2003, No.311 and 312 p.38.

37–70 If the jurisdictional or procedural costs are not allocated on a "pay as you go" basis, then the Tribunal will tend to consider the overall procedural aspect at the end of the hearing. This remains the prevailing practice in ICC arbitration.

Article 37(4): "The final award shall fix the costs of the arbitration and decide which of the parties shall bear them or in what proportion they shall be borne by the parties."

37–71 The ICC Court decides the amount of the ICC Arbitration Costs and the Tribunal decides which of the parties shall bear those Party Costs. In addition, the Tribunal decides which of the parties shall bear the Party Costs, and in doing so, the Tribunal will have to decide whether the Party Costs are reasonable. The issue of reasonableness is discussed above under art.37(1).

37–72 Article 37(3) permits the Tribunal to take decisions on costs at any time in the proceedings. However, whether or not the Tribunal has made decisions under art.37(3), as a general rule, the overwhelming bulk of the Party Costs and the allocation of all costs are decided in the final Award.

37–73 When the Tribunal submits a draft Award to the Secretariat for the ICC Court's scrutiny and approval, the amount of the ICC Costs of Arbitration are left blank as they must be determined by the ICC Court. The draft Award will however deal with the allocation of these costs as well as the amount and allocation of the party costs, i.e. "legal and other costs" as between the parties.

37–74 Usually, a party makes a claim for reimbursement of its legal costs in its Request or Answer. This claim should be reflected in the Terms of Reference. To obtain an order from the Tribunal with respect to reimbursement of its costs, as a general rule, each party must ensure that it has made a claim for those costs in the arbitration.

37–75 At the close of the oral hearings, the Tribunal will generally give the parties a short period in which to make a submission as to their Party Costs. As noted before, some Tribunals also provide that each party has the option of submitting brief comments on the claims of the other party as to their Party Costs, although often the parties do not necessarily avail themselves of this opportunity.

37–76 Article 37(4) covers all final Awards. Therefore, it would appear to cover an Award in which the Tribunal decided that it did not have jurisdiction over a case. A Tribunal has the right to decide on its own jurisdiction (*Kompetenz-Kompetenz*). However, there is an issue as to whether it has the right to award costs where the Tribunal decides that it does not have jurisdiction.

37–77 If a Claimant brings proceedings under the Rules asserting that the Tribunal has jurisdiction, then it would appear to be logical and defensible that, by doing so, the Claimant is accepting that the Tribunal has jurisdiction to decide on jurisdiction and to award costs based on the Rules. Moreover, by signing the Terms of Reference, the Claimant may either be expressly or implicitly accepting the Tribunal's authority, depending on the wording of the Terms of Reference. Similarly, if a Respondent brings a counterclaim, which is rejected on jurisdictional grounds, then the same principles would appear to be applicable. In a sense, if there is a decision that there is no jurisdiction, it will involve a ruling against a party who has specifically relied upon the ICC Rules and who should be estopped from denying the right of the Tribunal to act under them.[35]

Article 37(5): "In making decisions as to costs, the arbitral tribunal may take into account such circumstances as it considers relevant, including the extent to which each party has conducted the arbitration in an expeditious and cost-effective manner."

Article 37(5) has been added in the Rules to provide some direction as to how the Tribunal should exercise its right to allocate costs under art.37(4). However, there is an initial issue as to whether a Tribunal in an ICC arbitration is required to or should refer to any rules of law in deciding the issue of costs and, if so, which legal system. A secondary issue is how to interpret the reference in art.37(5) to the method in which the arbitration has been conducted. **37–78**

Law of the place of arbitration or place of enforcement

The first step in the analysis is to determine whether there are mandatory principles under the law of the place of arbitration as to costs. **37–79**

No arbitration law in a major centre of arbitration requires Tribunals to follow cost principles applicable before national courts. This would in fact be contrary to the basic principle that it is up to the Tribunal to establish the rules governing the proceedings under art.19. As discussed under art.18, the laws of the place of arbitration as a general matter establish only minimum procedural requirements for arbitration. **37–80**

In France, Switzerland and countries in which the UNCITRAL Model Law is applicable, there are no mandatory principles that would override the discretion vested in the Tribunal pursuant to art.37(5). In the United States and England, the application of that provision appears to be somewhat more complex. **37–81**

The United States

In American courts, except where a statute or contract expressly so provides, the losing party in legal proceedings does not pay the successful party's legal costs. For American courts therefore, for the Tribunal to have the power to award costs against the losing party, it must be empowered to do so by the arbitration agreement or under applicable law. In *August Aasma v American Steamship Owners Mutual Protection and Indemnity*,[36] the US Federal Court in Ohio dealt with whether a foreign arbitration Award should be refused enforcement as it awarded costs against the unsuccessful party. The Court upheld the Award of costs stating: **37–82**

> "[i]n the instant action, Plaintiffs assert that the award of costs is beyond the scope of the parties' arbitration agreement because 'nowhere are costs or attorneys' fees specifically mentioned, much less agreed upon' [. . .] However, the parties' agreement established that the arbitration

[35] See Bühler, "Costs in ICC Arbitration: A Practitioner's View", *op. cit.*, at p.139.

[36] 238 F. Supp.2d (N.D. Ohio 2003) 918–923. Extracts published in (2003) YBCA Vol.XXVIII, p.1140.

was to be conducted in accordance with the Arbitration Act 1996. Sections 59–64 of the [English Arbitration] Act specifically provide for the awarding of costs and set forth default provisions in the absence of an agreement between the parties as to costs."

The Court went on to reject the argument that enforcement of the Award of costs was contrary to public policy.[37]

37–83 In an ICC arbitration, art.37(1) expressly permits a Tribunal to award "reasonable legal and other costs". The New York courts accept that legal costs can be awarded in an ICC arbitration, art.37 constituting an agreement of the parties to have such costs reimbursed.[38] Therefore, within the context of American decisions there would appear to be an agreement permitting the Tribunal—in the context of an ICC arbitration under the Rules—to award costs provided that the arbitration agreement does not limit the application of the provision.[39] However, in drafting the Award, where the place of arbitration or probable place of enforcement is in the United States, it is desirable to reflect the basis in the agreement or Rules on which the Tribunal decided that the parties have agreed that it has the authority to award costs.

37–84 In a 2007 ICC arbitration, where the merits of the dispute were governed by New York law, a Tribunal sitting in New York ordered the Respondent to bear 50 per cent of the Claimant's legal costs which were found to be reasonable in accordance with the wording of a specific clause of the contract which provided that where a "legal action or other proceedings is brought for the enforcement" of the contract, "the successful or prevailing party or parties shall be entitled to recover reasonable attorneys' fees and other costs incurred in that action". The Tribunal also relied on the provisions of art.37 to order Respondents to bear the entire ICC Arbitration Costs.[40]

[37] "Plaintiffs protest largely on the grounds that the award is contrary to the American Rule regarding attorney's fees. Plaintiffs characterize the award of costs and fees as 'exorbitant and immoderate', punitive in nature, and issued by 'an unsympathetic arbitrator in a foreign land'. Plaintiffs argue that fees should not be awarded absent a showing of bad faith litigation tactics. Plaintiffs further assert that confirmation of the instant arbitral award would 'reward West for hiring phalanxes of attorneys who ran up legal fees with unfettered abandon' ... Though under the American Rule parties normally bear their own costs of litigation, parties are free to contract regarding the apportionment of fees. In the instant action, the parties' arbitration agreement was silent as to the award of fees, thus implicating the default provisions of the Arbitration Act 1996. Costs of arbitration are routinely awarded under the Act, and Plaintiffs were presumably aware of this fact but nonetheless chose to pursue the arbitration. Plaintiffs even concede that the award of costs under the Act 'is left to the discretion of the arbitrator' [. . .]" (footnotes deleted), 238 F. Supp.2d (N.D. Ohio 2003) 918–923. Extracts published in the (2003) YBCA Vol.XXVIII, p.1140.

[38] Bühler & Conybeare Williams, "New York Law: Awards of Attorney's Fees in International Arbitration" (2005) Mealey's IAR Vol.20 No.5, p.36. See also Minnerop and Johns, "Attorneys' Fees in Arbitration" (2006) *The Business Lawyer* Vol.61 February 2006, p.589, at p.604. See also *Stone & Webster Inc v Triplefine International Corp* 118 Fed Appx 546 (2d Cir 2004) (The parties' agreement to submit their dispute before the ICC Court had the effect of making the ICC Rules part of their agreement which expressly allow ICC arbitrators to award attorneys' fees. The arbitrators did not thus disregard the law of New York in granting attorney fees to Taiwanese corporation and the Award was confirmed by the court).

[39] In exceptional cases, the parties may agree on the allocation of costs. In many contracts involving US companies, there is a specific reference to the awarding of attorneys' fees in the arbitration agreement itself.

[40] ICC case No.12125 (2007) (Final Award), unreported.

England

The allocation of costs is an essential part of the English court system and that emphasis continues to influence arbitration in England. The cost system is also found in other common law systems, such as in Australia and Canada. However, those countries have frequently adopted the UNCITRAL Model Law whereas England declined to do so and instead adopted the Arbitration Act 1996. That Act has a number of particular provisions relating to costs. Moreover, case law and arbitration practice in England show that the treatment of costs in arbitration in England is expected to be similar in some respects to the treatment by the courts. **37–85**

The English Arbitration Act 1996 deals with the awarding of costs in the following terms: **37–86**

> "60. An agreement which has the effect that a party is to pay the whole or part of the costs of the arbitration in any event is only valid if made after the dispute in question has arisen.
>
> 61. (1) The tribunal may make an award allocating the costs of the arbitration as between the parties, subject to any agreement of the parties.
> (2) Unless the parties otherwise agree, the tribunal shall award costs on the general principle that costs should follow the event except where it appears to the tribunal that in the circumstances this is not appropriate in relation to the whole or part of the costs."

Section 60 of the Arbitration Act 1996 appears to apply to an agreement as to payment of fees in any event. It is less clear whether it applies to an agreement that a party will not be able to recover its costs even if successful.[41] Section 60 is a mandatory provision for arbitrations having their seat in England and Wales under the Arbitration Act 1996. Therefore, that provision would prevail even if the rules of law governing the English arbitration provided otherwise. **37–87**

Section 61 of the Arbitration Act 1996 sets out the principle that the costs should follow the event. In other words, the successful party should be entitled to recover all or a substantial part of its costs from the unsuccessful party. Section 61 is not one of the mandatory provisions of the Arbitration Act 1996. Therefore, parties can derogate from it either by specific agreement or by reference to arbitration rules. But it is not clear that art.37(4) would constitute an agreement to exclude application of s.61. As a result, given s.61, a Tribunal having a place of arbitration in England should generally directly address the issue of the award of costs taking into account this provision. **37–88**

In directing itself to those issues, a Tribunal should also keep in mind the particularity of English procedure relating to costs. Although the Arbitration Act 1996 no longer requires an arbitrator to act "judicially" with respect to costs, a serious irregularity with respect to costs may result in annulment of an Award or remittal of the Award to the Tribunal for a further decision on costs. **37–89**

[41] Section 60 is based on s.18(3) of the Arbitration Act 1950 and was retained on the basis of public policy in the current Act.

37–90 In the *Newfield* case,[42] the arbitrator defined the "event" in terms of the issue in the arbitration pursuant to letters rather than the pleadings that had been filed in the arbitration. As a result, in applying the principle of costs follow the event, he ordered that the Claimant pay the Respondents costs. The English High Court decided the case on other grounds. However, it also stated as follows with respect to the decision on costs:

> "[43] I have found that the Arbitrator construed 'the event' not by reference to all the pleadings, but by reference to two other, irrelevant documents which, to put it at the very lowest, all the pleadings expressly contradicted. That was not what the parties wanted him to do: the whole point of the pleadings was to define and, as actually happened here, to narrow the disputes between the parties; the parties wanted the Arbitrator to construe the 'event' by reference to their pleadings and were entitled to have it so construed; his complete failure to do so therefore amounted to a serious irregularity [. . .]. In my judgment the Arbitrator's letter of 28.5.04 makes clear that what I have found to be the serious irregularity has caused substantial injustice because, but for the irregularity, the Arbitrator himself explains that his Award on costs would have been completely reversed."[43]

37–91 In an ICC arbitration, if the issues to be decided are described in some detail in the Terms of Reference, then those issues constitute elements of the "event" and can be used for this analysis.

37–92 Moreover, various other English authorities, such as the Chartered Institute of Arbitrators Guidelines for Arbitrators on Making Orders Relating to the Costs of Arbitration[44] show that, for domestic arbitration in any event, the approach in England is still inspired by court practice. Therefore, in this respect special caution should be exercised to meet the English requirements in drafting an Award if the place of arbitration is in England or Wales to reflect the consideration of issues relating to allocation of costs as discussed below with respect to s.63 of the Arbitration Act 1996.

37–93 A further particularity of English procedure is the relevance of settlement offers and reverse settlement offers. In English court proceedings a party may make an offer to settle the case by payment of a certain sum. If the Claimant does not recover more than that sum in the case, then the Respondent's liability for costs will be reduced or eliminated. With a "reverse settlement offer" it is the Claimant who is offering to settle a counterclaim and the same principles are applicable. In *Linpave v Gillingham*,[45] the Claimant made a reverse settlement offer. The Award made no mention of that offer in its reasoning regarding the allocation of costs. The court remitted the Award to the arbitrator due to this failure to deal with the reverse settlement offer. This suggests that, for arbitrations in England, settlement

[42] *Newfield Construction Ltd v John Lawton Tomlinson and Kathleen Christine Tomlinson* [2004] EWHC 3051 (TCC).

[43] [2004] EWHC 3051 (TCC) at p.16.

[44] (2003) Arbitration, Vol.69, No.2 pp.130 et seq.

[45] (TCC July 29, 2002) (2003) Arbitration Vol.69 No.2 pp.144 et seq.

offers must be taken into account in deciding on the costs or a reason must be provided for failing to do so.[46]

The application of English procedural law does not seem, however, to be viewed as a condition for the application of the effects of a settlement offer by the Tribunal. Indeed, in a recent case, a Tribunal, sitting in Paris and applying English law as the governing law on the merits, took into account the Respondent's (apparent) absence of any settlement offer for the allocation of costs of the arbitration as follows: **37–94**

> "The Respondent never made any proposal to compromise these proceedings by payment of a sum of money greater than that which has been awarded by the Tribunal. Accordingly the Respondents took no effective steps to protect itself from the sort of result which has occurred in this case."[47]

However, the use of settlement offers in ICC arbitration is fraught with practical problems. The English system is based on an understanding of the rules and the risks associated with failing to accept an offer. A key element is that the offer is only to be brought to the attention of the Tribunal after the Tribunal has decided the issues as to liability and the measure of damages. However, to implement the system, the parties have to understand and accept that it is applicable.[48] **37–95**

Generally applicable principles in allocating costs

Tribunals also have an issue as to which law, if any, should govern the awarding of costs. In most cases, the underlying agreement will be governed by one system of law and some authority interprets the recovery of costs as an additional element of damage. However, in state court settings, recovery of costs is not usually viewed as a head of damages, but rather as a procedural right.[49] In many legal systems, bringing or defending a claim is not an actionable wrong, unless there is either an element of bad faith or abuse of rights. **37–96**

If the arbitration agreement contains provisions regarding the allocation of costs, then, subject to the mandatory principles of applicable law, those provisions should be analysed in accordance with the rules of law applicable to the arbitration agreement. The standard ICC arbitration clause does not deal with costs. However, many contracts have very specific rules as to costs and this type of rule **37–97**

[46] For a discussion of the use of settlement offers or sealed offers, see Sutton, Gill & Gearing, *op. cit.*, p.332. See also Tweeddale, *Arbitration of Commercial Disputes— International and English Law and Practice* (Oxford University Press, 2007), para.29.40, p.843.

[47] ICC case No.13078 (2006) (Final Award), unreported.

[48] A party who wishes to consider this type of procedure would ideally prefer to have it reflected in the Terms of Reference. However, that party may be quite unwilling to raise it due to the concern that it is an implicit admission that the party has a significant risk of some liability. Therefore, unless the Tribunal raises the issue, it may not be included in the Terms of Reference. The issue is whether Tribunals sitting in England should propose it.

[49] See discussion in Kreindler, "Final Rulings on Costs: Loser Pays All?" *in Best Practices in International Arbitration, op. cit.*, p.4; Bühler, "Awarding Costs in International Commercial Arbitration: an Overview" (2004) ASA Bull Vol.2 No.2, p.249. See also ICC Study of the final Awards of 1991 cited in Derains & Schwartz, *op. cit.*, at p.371.

would generally amount to an agreement between the parties on that issue which is enforceable under art.19 or under art.21.

37–98 If the arbitration agreement is silent on one or more issues of costs, then, under art.19, the Tribunal is to settle, on the procedure, "whether or not reference is thereby made to rules of procedure of a national law to be applied in the arbitration". It is submitted that national principles of costs are ill-suited to be applied as such in ICC arbitrations.[50] International arbitration represents a decision to opt out of the national court system. The national procedure of the law governing the contract is seldom applied as such. As discussed under art.18 the law of the place of arbitration is not usually used for a detailed procedure but rather sets out the minimum procedural standards for international arbitration. Subject to the particularities in the United States and England, these standards do not impose specific requirements as to costs.

37–99 Traditionally, there are three approaches to the allocation of the arbitration costs: (i) the parties bear the costs equally; (ii) the arbitration costs are divided between the parties based on the outcome of the case; and (iii) the losing party that is unsuccessful on the merits bears the entire costs of the arbitration.[51] There appears to be a consensus in ICC arbitration that Tribunals do generally apply the principle that the costs of an ICC arbitration should follow the event, taking into account various particularities of international arbitration. As one Tribunal stated:

> "The Rules do not contain any rules or criteria for the decision that the Tribunal must take [regarding costs]. The decision is left to the discretion of the arbitrator. Nevertheless, the results of the arbitration play a predominant role in the exercise of this discretion by the arbitrator. A party who loses his case is, in principle ordered to pay the costs of arbitration. However, other criteria can be taken into account, and notably the manner in which the case was conducted and the costs caused by reckless or abusive request or by delaying tactics."[52]

37–100 Therefore, instead of setting out rules as to costs, it is more useful to discuss factors that have been used by ICC Tribunals in exercising their discretion with respect to costs.

[50] ICC case No.8786 (1997) (Final Award): "The Arbitrator has to decide within his own discretion to what extent attorney's fees may be determined to be 'normal'. Thereby, the Arbitrator is not bound by 'any local procedural law or practice' (cf. W. Laurence Craig/ William W. Park/Jan Paulsson, *International Chamber of Commerce Arbitration*, 2nd ed., New York/London/Rome/Paris 1990, p.338). Therefore, it is not relevant what attorney's fees would be customary or provided for, e.g., by Turkish law. It is within the free discretion of the Arbitrator to decide to what extent attorney's fees are 'normal' and how the attorney's fees are allocated between the parties." (2002) ASA Bull Vol.20 No.1, p.67; (2000) ICC ICArb Bull Vol.11 No.2, p.83.

[51] See Derains & Schwartz, *op. cit.*, p.371; Webster, "Efficiency in Investment Arbitration: Recent Decisions on Preliminary and Costs Issues" (2009) Arbitration Int. Vol.25, No.4, pp.469–514.

[52] ICC case No.11670 (2003) (Final Award), (2004) ASA Bull Vol.22 No.2, p.333; see also ICC case No.8547 (1999)(Final Award)("This arbitral tribunal applies the general rule, that costs should follow the event. The party losing an arbitration is therefore burdened with its costs. Since it is the defendant who is winning this arbitration because the claim of Claimant was either withdrawn during the oral hearing or is dismissed by this final award, it is the Claimant who is to carry its costs.") (2003) YBCA Vol. XXVIII p.27, (2001) ICC ICArb Bull Vol.12 No.2 p.57.

Relative success in claims

With many types of relief, determination of which party is successful is relatively easy. For monetary claims for damages, however, the results may not be clear-cut. A party may succeed on liability and fail on damages. Or a party may succeed on liability and be awarded a fraction of the damages that it has sought. The general approach in ICC arbitrations is to take into account the success of a party relative to the relief that the party sought.[53] In countries such as Germany, Austria and Switzerland, the civil procedural rules require a proportional allocation reflecting each party's relative success of the claims and defences. Under English arbitration law prior to the Arbitration Act 1996, this approach was criticised and may have amounted to an abuse of discretion.[54] Under English legal principles the winner is entitled to its costs unless the Award of costs is nominal. However, it is not clear that that would be the case under the 1996 Act although the Guidelines of the Chartered Institute of Arbitrators adopt the traditional English approach.[55] **37–101**

Cause of the dispute

Some arbitrators examine which of the parties caused the dispute and use this as a mitigating factor. In ICC case No.7661, the Tribunal stated for example that "[t]he Arbitrator is of the opinion that the fact that the Claimant prevails should **37–102**

[53] See ICC case No.10188 (1999) (Final Award): "Each party has sought recovery of its legal costs and the costs of the arbitration. The tribunal considers these claims under Art. 31 [now 37] of the ICC Rules. Having regard to the amounts claimed by software distributor M and counterclaimed by software developer E, the extent to which the tribunal has accepted software distributor M's claim and software developer E's counterclaim, the amount of time devoted in the course of the action to the parties' respective claims and counterclaims, and other relevant factors, the tribunal awards software distributor M 25 per cent of its legal costs [. . .]. The tribunal also concludes that software developer E shall bear 75% of the costs of the arbitration and software distributor M shall bear 25% of the costs of the arbitration, based upon the same factors." (2003) YBCA Vol. XXVIII p.68.
See also the somewhat laconic formulation in the final Award in ICC case No.9466 (1999): "Taking into account that damages have been granted to the Claimant in a smaller amount than requested, and that defendant's counterclaim for the payment of arrears of charter fees was justified, the tribunal unanimously decides that the costs of the arbitration be borne by the parties in equal proportions (50/50) and that each party shall bear its own legal costs." (2002) YBCA Vol. XXVII p.170.
See also ICC case No.8445 (1996) (Final Award): "[53] "Given the finding by the arbitrators that the defendant breached the Agreement, and the granting of an Award in Claimant's favor, the Tribunal determines that a large part of such costs and fees should be assessed against defendant. However, not all of Claimant's claims were allowed, and the final amount awarded by the Tribunal is considerably less than the total amounts claimed. Therefore, it is not appropriate to assess all such costs against the defendant. [54] "Taking the above into consideration, the Tribunal determines that 75% of the costs of arbitration be assessed against the defendant . . . [55] "The Tribunal similarly determines that the defendant shall reimburse to the Claimant 75% of Claimant's legal costs." (2001) YBCA Vol. XXVI p.167.

[54] See *Channel Islands Ferries v Cenargo Navigation Ltd, The Times*, April 5, 1994; [1994] 2 Lloyd's Rep. 161.

[55] Chartered Institute of Arbitrators, "Guidelines for Arbitrators on Making Orders Relating to the Costs of Arbitration", http://www.ciarb.org/information-and-resources/PracticeGuideline9.pdf [accessed on November 30, 2013]. ("If a Claimant recovers a monetary award, he is normally regarded as successful since he had to bring the arbitration in order to recover the sum in question. The "event" is the recovery of money. It is normally no ground for depriving the Claimant of his costs that the amount recovered is less than that claimed unless the recovery is so small that it can be regarded as nominal or derisory.")

not result in an award on costs in its favour. As was noted already before, only the strength of the contract has caused this success, which is no reflection of either party's behaviour, which has been reproachable both towards each other with regard to their contractual relationship and procedurally during this arbitration".[56] Although somewhat unorthodox, as the parties should have analysed the contract in detail before commencing the arbitration, the reference to the parties' behaviour both under the contract and in the procedure is perhaps a realistic view of the relevance of these factors for some arbitrators.

37–103 In a 2007 case, a Tribunal sitting in France ordered the Respondent to bear its own legal costs in addition to 50 per cent of the Claimant's costs. The ICC Arbitration Costs were to be born equally by the parties. The Tribunal took into account the cause of action of the parties together with the outcome of the arbitration:

> "Most of the efforts made by the parties concentrated on the question whether the early termination of the [. . .] Agreement was justified. Indeed, both the disputed part of the principal claims and the decisions on the counterclaims largely hinged on the resolution of this central question. It was finally resolved against Respondent and, as mentioned above, Claimant was then successful at the rate of 25% on the disputed part of the principle claims and fully victorious in respect of the counterclaims."[57]

37–104 In two recent cases, ICC Tribunals made use of their discretionary power in similar ways. In the first case, the Tribunal applied the rule that "costs follow the event" for the ICC costs of arbitration, and thus burdened the loosing Claimant with those costs, and thus dismissed prevailing Respondent's claim for such costs amounting to more than US$17.7 million. The Tribunal based this decision on the view that Claimant had acted reasonably in pursuing its claim in arbitration against the Respondent, which in fact was a governmental entity[58]:

> "140. (. . .) [T]he Claimant may have had reasonable expectations from a business and investment point of view, consistent with past practice [in Respondent's country] that it would be able to take an assignment from its departing partner, [X], who was also acting as Operator, based on Claimant's recognized financial competence and its ability, not seriously contested, to bring in another party, with technical competence to act as operator. [. . .]."[59]
>
> "141. Nevertheless, the Claimant had a legitimate entitlement to clarify the legal situation and an important economic incentive to do so since the position supported by the [Respondent] entailed the loss of its entire investment."[60]

[56] ICC case No.7661 (1995) (Final Award), (1997) YBCA Vol. XXII p.149; *Collection of ICC Arbitral Awards, Volume IV*, 1996–2000, *op. cit.*, p.135.

[57] ICC case No.13686 (2007) (Final Award), unreported.

[58] The dispute arose out of a Production Sharing Agreement and whether Respondent was obliged to approve an assignment thereunder, as requested by Claimant.

[59] The Tribunal then explains that Respondent had no firm legal obligation to approve the assignment.

[60] ICC Case No.16845 (2013), unreported. One of the authors was counsel to one of the Parties.

In the second case, in which Claimant's claims were also dismissed as being unfounded, the Tribunal took the following view: **37–105**

> "424. In the experience of this Tribunal in international commercial arbitrations taking place in Continental Europe, and ICC arbitrations in particular, nowadays' prevailing practice is that costs follow the event, *i.e.* the losing party has to bear the procedural costs, totally or in part, and compensate its opponent for the legal fees and other costs incurred by the latter, again totally or in part (but only insofar as the Tribunal determines such costs to be reasonable). While it has also been observed that there exists no uniform approach in allocating costs in international commercial arbitration, this Tribunal believes that the 'cost follow the event' rule is in any event a good starting point for both the procedural costs and the parties' costs for an ICC arbitration seated in Vienna (Austria).
>
> 427. In the present case, Claimants fail in their claims because they have not been able to show that [Respondent's] conduct [. . .].
>
> 431. Under the circumstances, the Tribunal feels that the costs of the arbitration, *i.e.* those fixed by the ICC Court, as well as Parties' own cost, best lie where they were incurred, and decides that both Parties shall bear half of the ICC Costs of arbitration, and bear their own legal and other costs."[61]

Procedural behaviour

As stated in the previous edition of this Handbook, ICC arbitration is intended to be cost-effective and a party who presents a case in a particularly time-consuming fashion may well be penalised when the Tribunal allocates the costs. This has been expressly reinforced in art.37(5). Procedural behavior relates not only to the procedural motions but also the length of the submissions and the hearings proposed by the parties and presentation of the evidence at an appropriate time.[62] In extreme cases, this can even result in the party being ordered to pay the other party's costs although the other party has failed on much if not most of its **37–106**

[61] ICC Case No.17043, (2013), unreported. One of the authors was the president of the Tribunal whose decision was unanimous.

[62] See the final Award in ICC case No.9302 (1998) which cited as a factor for not awarding costs against the Claimant: "Furthermore, [the Respondent], which was in control of the facts and the documents surrounding the changes which occurred within its group in 1971, failed to provide conclusive evidence of the lack of jurisdiction early in the proceedings" (2003) YBCA Vol. XXVIII p.54; Gazette du Palais, Special Issue on Arbitration, November 8, 2003, Nos 311 and 312 p.38. See also ICC case No.8786 (1997), (1995) ASA Bull p.57, the prevailing Respondent was awarded only 80% of its legal costs because it had applied for an interim Award on security which the Tribunal dismissed; ICC case No.13078 (2006) cited at para.37–95 fn.38. The Tribunal took into account the amount of evidence and exhibits submitted by the parties as a criteria for the allocation of the costs of the arbitration: "The parties have not been sufficiently selective in the number and type of documents put before the Tribunal. As a result this arbitration has been unnecessarily overloaded with paper which has prolonged these proceedings and the preparation of this Award".

claim.[63] This admonition has now been reflected in art.37(5) with its reference to the procedural behaviour of the parties.

Reasoning for decision on costs[64]

37–107 ICC Awards generally refer to the discretion of the Tribunal in awarding costs. The Award itself must set out the reasons for the exercise of that discretion,[65] but in many instances that reasoning tends to be very summary in nature, and sometimes totally unconvincing given the outcome of the case, and thus truly disappointing for at least one of the parties. Without the reasoning being present in the Award the ICC Court will not approve it as the Award may be subject to annulment (at least in respect of the cost decision).

37–108 The English Arbitration Act 1996 is more explicit than other arbitration laws with respect to the allocation of costs as it provides in s.63:

> "(3) The tribunal may determine by award the recoverable costs of the arbitration on such basis as it thinks fit. If it does so, it shall specify—
> (a) the basis on which it has acted, and
> (b) the items of recoverable costs and the amount referable to each.
>
> (4) If the tribunal does not determine the recoverable costs of the arbitration, any party to the arbitral proceedings may apply to the court (upon notice to the other parties) which may—
> (a) determine the recoverable costs of the arbitration on such basis as it thinks fit, or

63 See ICC case No.8486 (1996) (Final Award): "In the present case the defendant loses its counterclaim, but the Claimant's claim is granted only in part. Further, the Claimant must pay the costs related to its partial claim renunciation to the defendant [. . .]. [26] "Nonetheless, the costs of the arbitration shall be borne totally by the defendant. According to the general principles of international arbitration law, the arbitral tribunal must take into account for its decision on costs not only the result of the proceedings but also the behaviour of the parties during the proceedings [. . .]. According to good faith, the parties to an international arbitration must in particular facilitate the proceedings and abstain from all delaying tactics [. . .]. The behaviour of the defendant during the entire proceedings did not comply with these requirements in any way. The defendant made none of the advance payments on costs which are required for the proceedings. Further, not only did it file its counterclaim belatedly, that is, only after the first draft of the terms of reference; it also refused to sign the terms of reference, which had been modified according to its wishes, notwithstanding a detailed explanation by the arbitral tribunal of the terms' meaning and legal consequences, and it did not participate in the oral hearings although it had been given sufficient notice to appear. Further, it also contributed to unnecessary delay and confusion in the proceedings by appointing counsel at the last moment, that is, after the closing of the oral hearings and shortly before the expiry of the latest time limit for a statement concerning the minutes of the hearings; compounded by counsel's renunciation to the mandate only a few days afterward. The proceedings were further complicated by the same counsel again accepting his mandate on the same day, a fact which had not been communicated to the arbitrator. For the above reasons, the defendant shall also reimburse to the Claimant the advance payment on costs, which the latter paid for these proceedings" (1999) YBCA Vol. XXIVa p.162; see also ICC case No.6955 (1993) (Final Award), (1999) YBCA Vol. XXIVa p.107; *Collection of ICC Arbitral Awards, Volume IV*, 1996–2000, *op. cit.*, p.267.

64 For a discussion on cost allocation problems see James H. Carter, "A KISS for arbitration costs allocation", The American Review of International Arbitration. See also Webster, "Efficiency in Investment Arbitration: Recent Decisions on Preliminary and Costs Issues" (2009) Arbitration Int. Vol.25 No.4, pp.469–514.

65 See above the discussion under art.31 at paras 31–20 to 31–23.

(b) order that they shall be determined by such means and upon such terms as it may specify.

(5) Unless the tribunal or the court determines otherwise—

(a) the recoverable costs of the arbitration shall be determined on the basis that there shall be allowed a reasonable amount in respect of all costs reasonably incurred, and

(b) any doubt as to whether costs were reasonably incurred or were reasonable in amount shall be resolved in favour of the paying party."

Section 63 is not a mandatory provision of the English Arbitration Act 1996. There is an open issue as to whether it is excluded by art.31(3) of the Rules or whether the two provisions should be read together. If so, then the failure to meet the requirements of s.63(3) of the Act could result in a "serious irregularity" and annulment of the Award pursuant to s.68 of the Act.[66] **37–109**

In addition, the English approach, which is influenced by the taxing of costs in national court procedure, creates an expectation of a more detailed analysis of the heads of costs than is found in many ICC cases. The ICC Awards quoted above appear to reflect a tendency to allocate by percentage or on a more global level than would be frequent in English proceedings influenced by High Court procedure. **37–110**

Finally, as noted above, if a settlement offer has been made between the parties, under the principle set out in the *Linpave* case,[67] the Tribunal should address the issue of whether it took that settlement offer into account in arriving at its decision on costs and, if not, the reasons why it did not do so. **37–111**

Article 37(6): "In the event of the withdrawal of all claims or the termination of the arbitration before the rendering of a final award, the Court shall fix the fees and expenses of the arbitrators and the ICC administrative expenses. If the parties have not agreed upon the allocation of the costs of the arbitration or other relevant issues with respect to costs, such matters shall be decided by the arbitral tribunal. If the arbitral tribunal has not been constituted at the time of such withdrawal or termination, any party may request the Court to proceed with the constitution of the arbitral tribunal in accordance with the Rules so that the arbitral tribunal may make decisions as to costs."

Article 37(6) was introduced into the 2012 Rules to fill what was perceived as a gap. It deals with termination prior to the rendering of a final Award. It permits the Tribunal to decide on the costs, although it does not state whether this is to be in an Award or in a termination order. The better view is that this should be contained in an Award, because it is a final decision on an issue, albeit a limited one. There is no provision in the Rules that expressly provides for a termination order, for example.[68] If the Tribunal has not been constituted and the settlement fails to deal with costs or the parties do not agree on costs, the ICC Court may constitute the Tribunal to deal with the costs issue. **37–112**

[66] See, for example, the *Newfield Construction* case cited at para.37–94 fn.45.

[67] See discussion at Arbitration Vol.69 No.2 (May 2003) pp.144 et seq. As mentioned above, the use of sealed offers or Calderbank offers presents practical problems for an international Tribunal.

[68] For a discussion of termination orders under the UNCITRAL Arbitration Rules, see Webster, *Handbook of UNCITRAL Arbitration* (Thomson/Sweet & Maxwell, 2010), paras 36–11 et seq.

CHAPTER 8

MISCELLANDUS

Article 38 Modified Time Limits

1. **The parties may agree to shorten the various time limits set out in the Rules. Any such agreement entered into subsequent to the constitution of an arbitral tribunal shall become effective only upon the approval of the arbitral tribunal.**
2. **The Court, on its own initiative, may extend any time limit which has been modified pursuant to Article 38(1) if it decides that it is necessary to do so in order that the arbitral tribunal and the Court may fulfil their responsibilities in accordance with the Rules.**[1]

Introductory remarks

38–1 The ICC Arbitration Rules, prior to their 1998 version, did not contain a provision for fast track or accelerated arbitration. The predecessor to the current art.38(1) was introduced in 1998 to bring into the Rules the flexibility required for organising fast track arbitrations with the agreement of the parties. When reviewing the 1998 Rules, the ICC Task Force did not consider it appropriate to adopt and integrate parallel fast track arbitration rules into the 2012 Rules. No genuine need to change the Rules in this respect had been identified. Unlike most other articles, art.38 is only applicable if there is an agreement by the parties to use it.

38–2 Article 38 is intended to provide for a flexible approach where both parties have an interest in having the arbitration carried out on an expedited basis. This common interest of adverse parties in speed may arise in at least three scenarios: (i) Where the parties have an ongoing relationship and the dispute relates to a specific aspect of that relationship, the parties may wish to have a rapid decision on an issue so that they can adapt their practice to the situation. (ii) One or both parties may have a right to assert against a third party. Such a situation may arise where there is an issue of liability as between the two parties to the arbitration and

[1] Article 38 corresponds to art.32 of the 1998 Rules. There have been no changes to the text of the article.

one or both of the parties wish to be indemnified by a third party who, for one reason or another, is not a party to the arbitration. (iii) Both parties may believe that expedited proceedings will be less costly and therefore agree to shorten the time limits for the arbitral proceedings. In the authors' view, expeditious conduct of the arbitration within the time limits provided by the rules can be very cost-effective, provided that the Tribunal and the parties are available.

Article 38 deals with shortening time limits, in particular those set out in art.23 (providing that the Terms of Reference shall be signed within two months after transmittal of the file to the Tribunal) and art.30 (providing that the Award shall be rendered within six months after the signing of the Terms of Reference). These basic time limits are of course seldom met, but if the parties and the Tribunal are able to meet them, the proceedings can be expeditious. As discussed under art.22(1), both the Tribunal and the Parties shall make every effort to be expeditious. It will depend on the facts of the case whether a further shortening of the time periods pursuant to art.38(1) will reduce or increase costs. In straightforward cases with no need for an oral hearing, that may well be the result. In more complex cases, the situation is not as clear. The main cost in any arbitration is legal fees and, generally, for a complex but expedited arbitral proceeding, one would expect to see a larger team of lawyers. **38–3**

Article 38 does not deal with procedural methods of cutting short arbitral procedure, such as motions for summary judgment or dispositive motions. Those measures are in essence procedural issues to be dealt with under arts 19, 22(2) and 25. Indeed, with the aim of speeding up the arbitral process and reducing costs, such measures have since some time become the subject of discussion in international arbitral circles.[2] Suffice to note here that the ICC Rules do not contemplate any such measures, which may be suitable in court proceedings allowing for appeal, and thus re-trial, but which for that very reason would seem extraneous to the arbitral process, unless expressly agreed to by the parties. **38–4**

In ICC cases No.7385 and No.7402, which were conducted under the 1988 ICC Rules, the Tribunal dealt with an arbitration clause that provided for fast track arbitration of "specific" issues under the agreement.[3] The Tribunal managed to deal with the proceedings in some 80 days (with oral hearings) and brought into focus the issue of expediting arbitrations in certain cases. **38–5**

[2] See, for example, most recently Raviv, "No More Excuses: Towards a Workable System of Dispositive Motions in International Arbitration" (2012) Arb. Int'l Vol.28 No.3, p.487; IAI Seminar on the "Dispositive Motions in International Arbitration" November 9, 2006, Paris, reported in (2007) ASA Bull Vol.25 No.1, p.197, note Knoll and (2006) Rev Arb No.4, p.1129, note Train.

[3] ICC cases No.7385 (1992) and No.7402 (1992), (1993) YBCA Vol.XVIII, p.68. The fast track provision was as follows: "If either party elects that any Proposed Redetermination is to be arbitrated, the provisions of clause 13.2 of the . . . [Basic Contract] shall apply, provided, however, that: (a) the arbitrator(s) shall establish procedures such that a final decision will be rendered no later than sixty (60) days after the Redetermination Date; (b) no additional issues shall be arbitrated in the proceeding unless buyer and seller otherwise shall agree; (c) no [local] purchaser other than the [Ultimate Buyer] may participate in the proceedings; (d) the costs related to the arbitration shall be divided equally between seller and buyer; (e) in deciding the matter the arbitrator(s) shall keep in mind the criteria set forth in clause 9D.6.4; and (f) at any time prior to the issuance of the decision of the arbitrator(s), buyer and seller may agree to commodity charges and/or minimum volume obligations to be effective as of such date as buyer and seller shall agree, and upon submission of such agreement to the arbitrator(s), the arbitration proceeding as to that issue shall be terminated and of no force or effect".

38–6 One of the main concerns about fast track arbitrations is the effect on due process, i.e. on the parties' reasonable opportunity to present their case, as required by art.22(4).[4] If the periods are so short that a party does not have a proper opportunity to present its case, then there may, at least in some cases, be problems with enforcement or annulment of the Award. Where the parties have agreed on a fast track procedure those concerns are reduced but not eliminated. Prior to the existence of any dispute, the parties may agree to shorten time limits, for example by agreeing that the final Award be rendered within 90 days after the date of the Request. However, these agreements may be unrealistic in light of the dispute when it arises either due to the factual complexity, the legal complexity or the intervention of state courts.

38–7 Given the limitations on art.38, it is seldom used in practice. The premise for use of the Article is an agreement between the parties and the parties have various alternatives to deal with specific issues that would otherwise warrant expedited arbitration. If the agreement to reduce the time limits is in the arbitration agreement itself (and therefore agreed to well in advance of the dispute), then it may not reflect the complexities or the situation of the parties at the time of the dispute. In addition, although one party may have agreed to the arbitration agreement with the shortened time periods at the time it was entered into, it may object, particularly on due process grounds, during the arbitration itself.

38–8 Where the parties both agree after the dispute has arisen that there is an urgent issue to be resolved, the most common manner is probably with a standstill agreement in which the parties reach agreement as to how to deal with the issue pending the results of the arbitration. Another manner is for the parties to agree on bifurcation of the proceedings so that specific issues can be dealt with in partial Awards on a more rapid basis. ICC arbitration provides a flexible framework, especially where the parties have a common goal to deal with an issue reasonably promptly and shortening the time limits in the Rules is a subsidiary method in this respect. A subsequent agreement to reduce the time limits in the Rules is perhaps less likely, although possible particularly with respect to the time limit for the Tribunal to render an Award.[5]

Article 38(1): "The parties may agree to shorten the various time limits set out in the Rules. Any such agreement entered into subsequent to the constitution of an arbitral tribunal shall become effective only upon the approval of the arbitral tribunal."

38–9 The Rules set out specific time periods for various steps in the procedure, from filing an Answer (art.5) and appointing an arbitrator (art.12) to signing of the Terms of Reference (art.23) and rendering the Final Award (art.30). However, in

[4] Kreindler, "Speedier arbitration as a response to changes in world trade: a necessary goal or a threat to the expectations of the parties?" in *Liber Amicorum Michel Gaudet, op. cit.*, p.180.

[5] One complaint with regard to expedited arbitration proceedings is the time taken by the Tribunal to render an Award. An ICC Award should meet a high standard and therefore does take time to draft. However, on more than some occasions the delay is due to the Tribunal's conflicting time commitments.

some cases, particularly where there is an ongoing relationship between the parties, these time limits are viewed as too long.

Article 38(1) sets out a basic principle that any agreement to shorten the various time limits set out in the Rules is subject to the agreement of the parties. It is not possible under the Rules for one party to impose shortened time limits on the other party. This basic limitation on the scope of the provision has rendered it less significant than it would have been if the Tribunal could order a reduction in such time limits. The ICC Rules do not require the shortened time limits to be already inserted in the arbitration agreement, although parties tend to sometimes include shortened periods, in particular for the appointment of the president of the Tribunal, or for rendering the Award, in the arbitration agreement itself. It is not rare that the ICC Court's Secretariat will encourage parties to extend the time limit or otherwise apply art.38(2) if the ICC Court or the Secretariat regards the time limit set by the parties as potentially problematic.[6] **38–10**

If the agreement to shorten the time limits is entered into after the dispute has arisen, it will usually be tailored to the circumstances of the dispute. There may be a difference of opinion between the parties, who wish to resolve the dispute rapidly, and the Tribunal that wishes to ensure that it has the time to render an Award that reflects the facts and law and is enforceable. **38–11**

Under the second sentence of art.38(1), the consent of the Tribunal is also required to shorten the time limits, if the Tribunal has already been constituted. Therefore, if the parties agree on shortening the time limits prior to the constitution of the Tribunal, the members of the Tribunal will be deemed to have accepted the shortened time limits. Where it is possible that the parties may agree on fast-track arbitration, one would expect the parties to ensure that their nominees have the necessary availability to carry it out not only as regards hearings but also as regards the rendering of an Award. **38–12**

With regard to arbitration agreements calling for some form of fast-track arbitration, it is the Secretariat's practice to inform the nominees of the timing in the arbitration agreement to ensure that they are available for an expedited arbitration. As regards subsequent agreement between the parties, one of the most likely venues for discussing a fast track proceeding is at the initial organisational or Terms of Reference hearing. **38–13**

Article 38(2): "The Court, on its own initiative, may extend any time limit which has been modified pursuant to Article 38(1) if it decides that it is necessary to do so in order that the arbitral tribunal and the Court may fulfil their responsibilities in accordance with the Rules."

Article 38(2) provides a safeguard in case the Tribunal cannot meet the time limit initially agreed by the parties where the parties have modified those limits. The ICC Court retains the power to modify, and in fact to prolong, any agreed time limits if necessary for either the Tribunal or the ICC Court to fulfil their responsibilities.[7] If the parties have agreed on shortened time limits in their arbi- **38–14**

[6] Fry, Greenberg, Mazza, *Guide*, para.3–1511 ("Note to Parties").

[7] See for example ICC case No.11183 (2001), unreported. The arbitration agreement provided that the Award shall be rendered within four months from the appointment of the arbitrator. The

tration agreement, the Secretariat will note these shortened limits when it receives the Request. The first step would usually be to contact the parties to determine whether the time limits are reasonable given the complexity of the matter and the other factors involved. If there is no agreement with the parties, then the matter will be decided by the ICC Court.

38–15 In theory, the parties' agreement could exclude the power of the ICC Court to extend any shortened time limits. It is unlikely that the ICC Court will accept such opting out of art.38(2); it may instead refuse the administration of the arbitration under its Rules.[8]

38–16 If the parties have agreed on shortened time limits after the arbitration has commenced and the Tribunal has given its consent, the ICC Court may intervene at its own initiative to extend the time limits, so the conduct of the proceedings can be completed. In most cases, the extension will have been requested by the Tribunal, and/or by one party, sometimes even both parties. But if no such request is made, or is not presented in a timely manner, the ICC Court will step in at its own initiative to avoid the lapse of the time limit before the Award is rendered. Pursuant to art.41, the ICC Court and the Tribunal "shall make every effort to make sure that the Award is enforceable at law". Therefore, the Rules provide a solution to the potential problem that is created when parties agree on unrealistically short periods for example. By accepting the Rules, the parties are accepting the right of the ICC Court to modify the agreed time limits.[9] This is an advantage of ICC arbitration over ad hoc arbitration where the parties (and the Tribunal) may have more difficulty in dealing with sometimes unrealistic time limits.

38–17 It should be noted that, by its terms, art.38(2) deals with situations where the time limits have been modified pursuant to art.38(1). The provision refers to situations where the parties have shortened the time limits in the Rules. Therefore, if the parties have agreed on a time limit that is equal to or greater than the time limit set out in the Rules, art.38 is not applicable. This could occur where the parties have committed to rendering an Award within six months after the Terms of Reference has been signed. That time limit would in most cases be difficult to meet. However, art.38 is not applicable to extending the time limits set by the parties generally but only to extending time limits that have been shortened by the parties. In such other instances, the Court may rely on art.40 and the requirements of due process to justify an extension of a time limit which is equal to or greater than the time limit in the Rules but that could cause due process issues if not modified.

four-month time limit has been extended by the ICC Court in accordance with (the predecessor version of) art.38(2) in order to enable the Tribunal to fulfil its task. The Award was finally rendered within six months.

[8] Derains & Schwartz, *op. cit.*, p.378; see also Reiner & Aschauer, para.775, who consider the possibility of partial nullity of the agreed time limits.

[9] For a discussion of the problem, see Cass civ 1re, June 15, 1994, *Communauté urbaine de Casablanca v Société Degrémont* (1995) Rev Arb No.1, p.88, note Gaillard.

Article 39 Waiver

A party which proceeds with the arbitration without raising its objection to a failure to comply with any provision of the Rules, or of any other rules applicable to the proceedings, any direction given by the arbitral tribunal, or any requirement under the arbitration agreement relating to the constitution of the arbitral tribunal, or to the conduct of the proceedings, shall be deemed to have waived its right to object.[1]

Introductory remarks

Article 39 sets out the waiver principle that is found in various legal systems, albeit subject to different legal requirements.[2] For example, art.4 of the UNCITRAL Model Law provides: **39–1**

> "A party who knows that any provision of this Law from which the parties may derogate or any requirement under the arbitration agreement has not been complied with and yet proceeds with the arbitration without stating his objection to such non-compliance without undue delay or, if a time-limit is provided therefor, within such period of time, shall be deemed to have waived his right to object."

[1] Article 39 corresponds to art.33 of the 1998 Rules. There have been no changes to the text of the article.

[2] The concept is related to that of estoppel and to the principle of *venire contra factum proprium*, while in civil law jurisdiction it finds its basis in the principle of good faith. More generally, see Poudret & Besson, *op. cit.*, para.555, p.480; Pinsolle, "Les applications du principe de l'interdiction de se contredire au détriment d'autrui en droit du commerce international" in *L'interdiction de se contredire au détriment d'autrui*, colloque du CEDAG, Economica 2001, at p.37; Gaillard, "L'interdiction de se contredire au détriment d'autrui comme principe général du droit du commerce international" (1985) Rev Arb p.241; Cadiet, "La renonciation à se prévaloir des irrégularités de la procédure arbitrale" (1996) Rev Arb No.1, p.3; Rosher, "L'estoppel à la française,"(2011) Les Cahiers de l'Arbitrage 2011/1, p.119.

39–2 In international arbitration, waiver is particularly relevant due to the fact that the procedure varies from arbitration to arbitration and therefore the potential grounds for objection to the procedure are numerous. A rather striking example of the internationalisation of the concept of waiver is found in the *Golshani* case,[3] where the French Supreme Court used the concept of estoppel to reject a party's attempts to revisit procedural issues. In that case, the Claimant had brought arbitral proceedings before the American Iranian Claims Tribunal and pursued the arbitration for nine years. The claim was rejected and the Respondent sought to obtain *exequatur* of the Award in France. Mr Golshani objected that the Tribunal had no jurisdiction. The Court stated:

> "The decision [of the Court of Appeal], without any distortion, validly decided that Mr. Golshani who himself presented the request for arbitration before the American Iranian Claims Tribunal and who had participated for nine years without reservation in the arbitral proceedings is not permitted by reason of estoppel to maintain that the tribunal had decided without having an agreement to arbitrate or an invalid one not applicable to him."[4]

39–3 More recently, in *Merial v Société Klocke Verpackungs-Service GMBH*, the French Supreme Court ruled that the Court of Appeal was wrong in qualifying as estoppel the fact that Claimant did not protest the Tribunal's decision on Respondent's counterclaims and signed the minutes of the hearing, but then attempted to have the award set aside based on the Tribunal's decision on counterclaims.[5] However, some commentators have sought to distinguish *Merial* from *Golshani*, noting that the mere act of signing the minutes of a hearing does not rise to the procedural inconsistency present in *Golshani* that can be identical to estoppel.[6]

39–4 Article 39 and the corresponding provisions under applicable law raise the issue of the type of provisions that can be waived, the requirements to constitute a waiver and what must be undertaken to make and maintain a waiver. Finally, it raises the issue of the request by many Tribunals at the end of the oral hearings that the parties confirm whether they have any complaints to make about the conduct of the proceedings.[7]

[3] Cass Civ 1e, July 6, 2005, *Golshani v Gouvernement de la République d'Iran* (2005) Rev Arb No.4 p.993, note Pinsolle.

[4] Authors' translation from the French.

[5] *Société Merial v Société Klocke Verpackungs-Service GMBH*, February 3, 2010, Cass Civ. 1e (2010) Rev Arb No.1, p.94. See, however, *SA Jean Lion*, Cass Civ. 1e, May 6, 2009, (2009) RTD com. P. 546, Obs. Loquin; *BotasPetroleum*, Cass. Civ. 1e, December 19, 2012, No.11–13269, Obs. Maire du Poset, (2013) Petites Affiches, No.86, p.7.

[6] S. Adeline, "L'édification de la notion d'estoppel par la Cour de cassation (France) – Société Merial c. Société Klocke Verpackungs-Service GMBH" (2010) ASA Bull., p.406.

[7] One of the main waiver issues in international arbitration relates to whether a party has waived its right to arbitration. This issue is one for the national courts in proceedings under art.II(3) of the New York Convention. ("3. The court of a Contracting State, when seized of an action in a matter in respect of which the parties have made an agreement within the meaning of this article, at the request of one of the parties, refer the parties to arbitration, unless it finds that the said agreement is null and void, inoperative or incapable of being performed.")

Limits on waiver under applicable law

The laws of the place of arbitration and of the place of enforcement will generally be relevant as to the limits of a party's waiver of a right (and the requirements for a waiver to be effective). 39–5

The basic limit under most legal systems is based on public policy concerns. Arbitration is a private form of justice and, if the result of the waiver would be to deprive a party of a basic right, that waiver may not be enforceable.[8] 39–6

With respect to the independence of arbitrators, it is possible to waive the right to challenge an arbitrator under art.14 after disclosure of certain facts by that arbitrator. However, the IBA Guidelines provide a list of matters in the non-waivable Red List for which the authors believe that no waiver is possible based on the principle that a party cannot be a judge and party in the same case.[9] 39–7

With respect to the conduct of the procedure, within certain limits it is possible for a party to waive unequal treatment. However, other forms of conduct may so offend the relevant public policy as to be unenforceable. If treatment is so unequal as to amount to a breach of basic due process, then national courts may hold that the unequal treatment may not be waived. 39–8

With respect to applicable law, certain substantive rules of law cannot be waived. For example, proceeding with an arbitration without raising a competition law issue may also not result in a waiver due to the public policy aspects of competition law of the European Union. In the *Eco Swiss* case, neither party to the arbitration had raised the issue of invalidity of the relevant agreement under EU competition law. The European Court of Justice held that the Dutch courts were required to apply competition law in the following terms: 39–9

> "[37] It follows that where its domestic rules of procedure require a national court to grant an application for annulment of an arbitration award where such an application is founded on failure to observe national rules of public policy, it must also grant such an application where it is founded on failure to comply with the prohibition laid down in Art. 85(1) of the Treaty."[10]

As a matter of EU law, the fact that a party does not raise EU competition law does not mean that the Tribunal should not deal with the issue.[11] In other words, claims arising out of competition law "must" be arbitrated, failing which, the 39–10

[8] For a discussion, see Sheppard, "Interim ILA Report on Public Policy as a Bar to Enforcement of International Arbitral Awards" (2003) Arb Int Vol.19 No.2, p.217.

[9] See the discussion at para.14–78 above.

[10] See para.6–57 n.43; see also von Mehren, "The Eco Swiss and the International Arbitration", *op. cit.*, p.465; Dhúner, "EC Competition Law and National Implications on Arbitration" and von Quitzow, "The Benetton Judgment and its Practical Implications on Arbitration" SAR 2000:1, pp.23 et seq.; Mourre, "Les rapports de l'arbitrage et du droit communautaire après l'arrêt Eco Swiss de la Cour de Justice des Communautés Européennes" in *Les Cahiers de l'Arbitrage–Vol. I, op. cit.*, p.77; Poillot and Perruzzetto, "L'ordre public international en droit communautaire. A propos de l'arrêt de la Cour de justice des Communautés du 1er juin 1999–Affaire Eco Swiss China Time Ltd" (2000) JDI, p.299.

[11] See the discussion of the arbitrability of antitrust issues under para.6–125.

issue may well be raised in annulment proceedings under domestic law and/or in an action to enforce under the New York Convention.

39–11 The position under US law is similar. In the *Mitsubishi* case,[12] the issue was whether antitrust claims were subject to arbitration where the governing substantive law was that of Switzerland. The US Supreme Court held not only that the claims were arbitrable but also that they must be dealt with by the Tribunal in the following terms:

> "[21] Having permitted the arbitration to go forward, the national courts of the United States will have the opportunity at the award enforcement stage to ensure that the legitimate interest in the enforcement of the antitrust laws has been addressed. The Convention reserves to each signatory country the right to refuse enforcement of an award where the 'recognition or enforcement of the award would be contrary to the public policy of that country'. Art. V(2)(b) 21 U.S.T., at 2520; see Scherk, 417 U.S., at 519, n.14, 94 S.Ct., at 2457, n.14. While the efficacy of the arbitral process requires that substantive review at the award-enforcement stage remain minimal, it would not require intrusive inquiry to ascertain that the tribunal took cognizance of the antitrust claims and actually decided them."[13]

39–12 Therefore, the US Supreme Court has confirmed that the issue of whether antitrust laws have been applied will be considered not only in annulment proceedings but also in enforcement proceedings under the New York Convention. This would be so even if a party failed to raise the claims, as US antitrust claims are not subject to waiver because the result could be to enforce an agreement in restraint of trade.

39–13 Recently, French courts have adopted a more flexible position, as reflected by the *Thalès* case and subsequent cases.[14] In the *Thalès* case, a party sought to have the Award annulled based on a violation of EU competition law. None of the parties had, however, raised this issue during the arbitral proceedings, nor did the Tribunal. The Paris Court of Appeal rejected the annulment action in the following terms:

[12] See paras 6–57 n.41 and 6–125 n.115.

[13] (1986) YBCA Vol. XI at p.564.

[14] See *Société Thalès v S La Marine de la République de Chine*, CA Paris, May 11, 2010, No.2009/14280; Cass Civ 1e, February 11, 2009 (2009) Rev Arb 2009/3, p.517; *Société SNF v Société Cytec Industries BV*, Cass Civ 1e, June 4, 2008 (2008) Rev Arb 2008/3, p.473. See also Webster, "Review of Substantive Reasoning of International Arbitral Awards by National Courts: Ensuring One-Stop Adjudication", *op. cit.*, para.14–3 n.4; Mourre & Radicati di Brozolo, "Towards Finality of Arbitral Awards: Two Steps Forward and One Step Back" (2006) J Int'l Arb Vol.23 No.2, p.171; Senkovic and Lastenouse, "International Arbitration And Antitrust Law; Eco Swiss Judgment Revisited By the Paris Court of Appeal" (2005) Mealey's IAR Vol.20 No.2, p.1; (2005) RTD Com p.263, note Loquin; Radicati di Brozolo, "L'illicéité qui crève les yeux: critère de contrôle des sentences au regard de l'ordre public international (à propos de l'arrêt Thalès de la Cour d'appel de Paris)" (2005) Rev Arb. No.3, p.529; Racine, "Réflexions sur l'autonomie de l'arbitrage commercial international (II.–L'arbitrage, Deuxième Séance)" (2005) Rev Arb No.2 p.305, at p.324. See also Kurkela, Levin, Liebscher and Sommer, "Certain Procedural Issues in Arbitrating Competition Cases" (2007) J Int'l Arb Vol.24 No.2, p.189.

"The violation of public international order within the meaning of article 1502(5) of the New Code of Civil Procedure must be flagrant, effective and concrete. Although the judge in annulment proceedings may review elements of law and fact that are in the award subjected to his review, the judge cannot review the merits of a complex litigation which has not yet been pleaded nor argued before an arbitrator concerning the simple possibility of illegality of certain contractual provisions;

There is no reason to permit Thalès to benefit from the gaps, intentional or not, in the defence of its own interests before the arbitrators. [This is the case whether Thalès] considered, at the relevant time, that the clauses in question were compatible with EC competition law or, on the contrary, sought to avoid a sanction of the Commission, and in any case in order to reserve its arguments for proceedings to annul the award against it;

It is clear that the judge in the annulment proceedings should not, in the absence of fraud or, as it has been said, manifest violation, review the application of the competition rules to the contracts in dispute, as there is no automatic annulment simply because the arbitrators, as maintained by Thalès, did not raise of their own initiative the EC competition law questions. Otherwise it would cast doubt on the definitive character of the decision of the arbitrators [...]. The Court of Justice of the European Communities acknowledges itself in the *Eco Swiss* decision the limited nature of the review of awards. The to imperative rules of national law, solely require that the necessity of [the application of EC law] application be weighed against the principles of legal security and the respect of the basic rules of arbitration." (Authors' translation)[15]

In the *Thalès* case, the French Supreme Court acknowledged the applicability of EC competition law, but also noted that the review of Awards is limited under French law. Therefore, review of the merits, including the treatment of competition law issues, is limited to situations where there is a "manifest violation" of competition law,[16] i.e. in the words of the court: "[t]he violation of public international order within the meaning of article 1502(5) of the New Code of Civil Procedure must be flagrant, effective and concrete [. . .]".[17] In the *Linde* case, the Paris Court of Appeal dismissed a motion to set aside a final Award for violation of public policy, ruling that, absent a manifest violation of EC competition law, **39–14**

[15] See *Société Thalès v S La Marine de la République de Chine*, CA Paris, May 11, 2010 (No.2009/14280).

[16] See Paris, March 23, 2006, *Société SNF SAS v Société Cytec Industries BV* (2006) Rev Arb No.2, p.483; for a comparison, see Tribunal de Première Instance de Bruxelles, March 8, 2007, *Société SNF SAS v Société Cytec Industries* (2007) Rev Arb No.2, p.303, note Mourre and Radicati di Brozolo; (2007) ASA Bull Vol.25 No.3, p.630, note de Meulemeester and Piers. See also *Note 22 octobre 2009, CA de Paris*, (2010) Rev Arb No. 1, p.128; *Note 22 juin 2009*, CA de Bruxelles, (2009) Rev Arb No.3, p.594.

[17] *Société Thalès v S La Marine de la République de Chine*, CA Paris, May 11, 2010 (No.2009/14280) Authors' translation.

French judges should not review contractual provisions and their conformity to competition law.[18] In the *SNF* case, the Paris Court of Appeal dismissed a party's action for damages against the ICC alleging failure to comply with its Rules in its failure to verify the draft Award's compliance with EC competition law.[19] The Court held that the Rules ensure the distinction between the administrative function of the arbitration and its legal function, reserved solely to the arbitrators, and that the documents produced by the ICC showed that it had effectively conducted a formal review of the Award. In the same *SNF* matter, the Belgian Courts followed the French position in this respect.[20]

39–15 In the *Tensacciai* case, Swiss courts have gone one step further than the French courts.[21] In that case, a party sought to annul an Award based on the fact that the Award did not take into account EU and Italian competition law and an exclusivity clause in the contract violated those laws and was therefore invalid. The Swiss Federal Tribunal rejected the argument stating that:

> "the provisions of competition law, whatever they may be, do not belong to the essential and widely recognized values which, according to the prevailing concepts in Switzerland, should constitute the foundation of any legal system. Consequently, the violation of such a provision does not fall within the scope of art. 190(2)(e) PILA . . .".

39–16 Swiss courts leave the issue of whether or not to apply competition law to the Tribunal, which is not a position that is adopted (or that could be adopted) in the EU or the United States.

Waiver of "any provision of these Rules"

39–17 The Rules provide for a particular form of administered arbitration. In a properly directed ICC arbitration, there should be no issue as to a waiver of a basic right defining an ICC arbitration. For example, it is essential that the Tribunal establish Terms of Reference and it is difficult to imagine that this provision could be waived unless the proceedings are terminated by a consent Award. However, it is possible that the issue will arise in other contexts. For example, a Respondent may file its Answer late and the Claimant may well decide not to object. Generally, these types of timing provisions can be waived. If a party receives a procedural order that is in essence an Award and the party does not object, there is an issue as to whether that can result in a waiver. One of the basic provisions of the Rules is

[18] *Société Linde Aktiengesellschaft v Société Halyvourgiki AE*, Paris Court of Appeal, October 22, 2009, (2010) Rev Arb, pp.124–128.

[19] *SNF SAS v Chambre de commerce international*, Paris Court of Appeal, January 22, 2009 (2010) 2 Rev Arb 2010, pp.314–320.

[20] Brussels CA, June 22, 2009 (2009) Rev Arb 574, note Mourre.

[21] Swiss Federal Tribunal, March 8, 2006, *Tensacciai v Terra Armata*, 4P.278/2005 (ICC arbitration–Italian law–place of arbitration: Lausanne), *http://www.bger.ch*; Radicati di Brozolo, "Note–Tribunal Fédéral Suisse, 8 mars 2006" Rev Arb No.3, p.769. More generally, see Arfazadeh, "*Ordre public et arbitrage international à l'épreuve de la mondialisation*" (Bruylant, LGDJ, Schulthess, 2006), 2nd edn.

that the ICC Court scrutinises all Awards.[22] This is a right that cannot be waived under the ICC Rules.[23]

Waiver of "any other rules applicable to the proceedings"

As discussed under art.19, usually Tribunals do not agree that any specific procedural rules are applicable, although a reference may, for example, be made to the IBA Rules of Evidence in the Terms of Reference. If the IBA Rules are adopted, then art.39 applies equally with respect to those Rules. Similarly, art.39 would apply to a failure to follow procedural rules set out in the Terms of Reference. **39–18**

The effect of art.39 would also be to result in a waiver, to the extent permissible under applicable law, for the failure by a party to object to the fact that some local rules were not applied. For example, although most Tribunals do not apply national procedural rules in any event, if a party wishes to object to the failure to apply those rules, it must do so promptly under art.39. **39–19**

Waiver of rights with respect to "any direction given by the Arbitral Tribunal"

On some occasions, a Tribunal will issue a direction, for the production of a document, for example, and a party will fail to comply. The general remedy in the case of the failure to produce documents is an adverse inference on the party who fails to produce the document. If a party is unsuccessful in the arbitration, it may feel that the failure to follow the direction had serious consequences and therefore seek to rely on that failure (and perhaps the failure of the Tribunal to follow up on the direction). If a party wishes to raise such an issue, it must do so under art.39. **39–20**

Waiver of "any requirement under the arbitration agreement relating to the constitution of the Arbitral Tribunal"

Arbitration agreements sometimes impose requirements as to the procedure to be followed prior to commencement of the arbitration, as to the qualifications of the arbitrators or as to the nationality of the president, for example. Usually, in the Terms of Reference, the parties expressly waive any objection to the constitution of the Tribunal. If they fail to do so in the Terms of Reference, then art.39 would in any event generally result in a waiver unless an objection was made. **39–21**

Waiver with respect to the "conduct of the proceedings"

One of the most basic goals of art.39 is to ensure that any objection as to the conduct of the proceedings is made promptly. Some objections cannot be waived or remedied. A procedural issue can often be dealt with in an equitable fashion. A common situation is where a party submits a new document late in the proceedings together with a reasonable explanation of why the document was not produced previously. If the other party objects, the Tribunal may be able to take measures to **39–22**

[22] See above the discussion under art.33.

[23] See the *Braspetro* case, para.33–8. See also Smit, "Mandatory ICC Arbitration Rules" in *Liber Amicorum Robert Briner, op. cit.*, p.845.

permit the objecting party to rebut or comment on the new document. If the other party does not object, then it may well be deemed to have waived its right to object pursuant to art.39. There is no need to waive in writing, although as a matter of proof an objection to waiver should be in writing or in the transcript or be clear from the conduct.[24]

39–23 Another issue is if the Tribunal asks the parties to inform them whether they have any objection to the manner in which the proceedings have been carried out. The purpose of this invitation is to remedy any issues that can be remedied and to strengthen the enforcement of the Award to the extent possible in the spirit of art.34(6). However, it cannot remedy the conduct of the proceedings to which a party has previously objected. The weight that will be given to these types of formal waivers is not clear. If the Tribunal asks for such a statement at a time when the issue of conduct could be remedied, then there is no reason why it should not be effective.

What constitutes an objection

39–24 To be effective, a waiver will have to be accepted as such by the national courts of the place of arbitration and of any place of enforcement. The basic concept of waiver is frequently seen as requiring awareness of a specific right and a failure to use that right. The assumption in art.39 appears to be that the waiver can be implied, but this may not always suffice. In the context of the IBA Guidelines, the working group stated:

> "The waivable Red List encompasses situations that are serious but not as severe. Because of their seriousness, unlike circumstances described in the Orange List, these situations should be considered waivable only if and when the parties, being aware of the conflict of interest situation, nevertheless expressly state their willingness to have such a person act as arbitrator, as set forth in General Standard 4(c)."

39–25 This comment suggests that the specific requirements for waiver may vary with the element that is allegedly waived and that, in some instances at any rate, the waiver must be express. The specific requirements for what constitutes a waiver are an issue of national law under the law of the place of arbitration and the law of the place of enforcement.

39–26 A practical issue that arises with respect to procedural matters relates to what steps are required to avoid a waiver of a right. Parties frequently make submissions with respect to procedural matters and the Tribunal decides the issue in a procedural order or a direction. Those submissions are sometimes couched in terms of fairness of the proceedings or the requirements of due process. If, despite those submissions, the Tribunal rules against the party, there is an issue of whether the objection "survives" the exchange. To maintain the objection, a party will sometimes confirm that it is carrying out the procedural order without waiving its prior objections. It is not clear that such confirmation is necessary.

[24] For a Hong Kong example of waiver by continuing the proceedings, see *Gao Haiyan v Keeneye Holdings Ltd* [2011] HKCA 459; [2012] 1 HKLRD 627; [2012] 1 HKC 335; CACV79/2011 (December 2, 2011).

In the *Karaha Bodas* case,[25] the Fifth Circuit Court of Appeals held that there had been a waiver of procedural rights in the following circumstances: 39–27

> "[44] Pertamina asserts that it did not waive its requests for discovery because the Tribunal denied the request before the hearing, when the discovery could have been of use. Pertamina ignores the fact that in international commercial arbitration, it is not uncommon to ask for additional discovery or information after a hearing, to request additional sessions of a hearing to submit more evidence, or to file post-hearing submissions. Rather than renew its requests for discovery into FPL's willingness to finance the project or to assert a request for discovery into FPL's political risk insurance, Pertamina's counsel expressly stated that the record had been 'fully made' and that he was 'prepared to rest on the record.' The record supports the Tribunal's conclusion that the discovery requests made before the hearing had been waived. Pertamina did not ask for discovery into political risk insurance until it filed its Rule 60(b) motion in the district court."[26]

The court's ruling suggests that, in some cases, requests for discovery (and perhaps other procedural rights) must be renewed or they will be deemed waived and that the general acceptance of the procedure will be given weight in determining whether a party has waived a procedural right. 39–28

If there are objections to the procedure, they must be identified and in general substantiated. In the *Bombardier* case,[27] the Respondent raised general procedural objections and the Tribunal on several occasions requested that the Respondent specify the procedural objections so that they could be dealt with. The Respondent failed to do so and eventually brought proceedings to annul the Award. The Paris Court of Appeal rejected the request for annulment and noted in particular that: 39–29

> "Considering that in order to be heard in annulment proceedings, the grievance needs to have been invoked in front of the arbitral tribunal each time it was possible to do so; that this rule, which protects procedural loyalty and arbitral awards, would be rendered useless if it was enough to utter menaces and critics in front of the arbitrator, as shown by Bombardier, in order to keep its options open when the time has come, to isolate an element of the procedure and present it as a violation of the adversarial principle."

In the *Butec* case of January 10, 2012, the Paris Court of Appeal followed accepted case law, which has since become part of the French CPC,[28] when it held: 39–30

[25] See paras 27–9 to 27–10.

[26] (2004) YBCA Vol.XXIX at pp.1288–1289.

[27] See the *Bombardier Transportation* case cited at paras 15–11 and 20–21 (author's translation).

[28] CA Paris, January 10, 2012, No.10/21671 (author's translation); Cass. Civ. 1e, May 28, 2008 (2008) in Rev Arb Vol.4, p.693. See also art.1466 of the French CCP as in force since January 13, 2011. For a discussion and further French case law references see Jaeger, "The administration and assessment of testimonial evidence," (2013) *Les Cahiers de l'Arbitrage*, Vol.1, p.71.

> "To be admissible before the annulment judge, the complaint made against an arbitral award must be raised before the arbitral tribunal itself where it is possible to do so."

39–31 The Swiss Federal Supreme Court has consistently held that a party that considers itself to be the victim of a due process violation, must protest immediately during the arbitral proceedings. Otherwise, it can no longer invoke such violation in the course of an annulment action. For the Swiss Supreme Court, it constitutes a violation of the principle of good faith for a party to await the outcome of the arbitrations and to raise procedural objections only once it learns that the outcome of the case is unfavourable to it.[29]

39–32 In a recent decision, the Swiss Federal Supreme Court ruled that, not only must a procedural violation be raised without delay in arbitral proceedings under penalty of forfeiting the right to raise such a violation, but it must be done so with the utmost clarity.[30] Counsel for Appellants, the Respondent in the ICC arbitration, had "politely" inquired as to the arbitrators view on a procedural issue, also noting on another issue that equal treatment was at stake and his clients were at a disadvantage due to an imbalance in time for questioning witnesses. The Swiss Federal Supreme Court ruled that neither constituted a valid complaint within the meaning of art.190(2)(d) PIL and thus the right to raise these procedural violations had been waived. The Court noted that, as Appellants had not made an attempt to give the Tribunal an opportunity to remedy these alleged violations and simply waited to see if the Award would be in their favour, they forfeited their right to argue these violations before the Swiss Federal Supreme Court.

The timeliness of art.39 objections

39–33 Article 39 does not provide for any time limit during which to raise an objection and imposes no requirement of "promptness" or the like. Nor does it state that objections must be made in a "prompt" manner, in contrast with the LCIA, WIPO and UNCITRAL Rules.[31] However, it is usually limited in those circumstances to challenges to the arbitrators. Article 39 does nevertheless provide an indication as to when the objection should be made when it states that the waiver occurs "when the party proceeds with the arbitration without raising its objection". The basic principle is that the party should object prior to further steps being taken in the arbitration. If the party fails to do so, then the waiver may arise. In the normal course of arbitral proceedings, the parties will be called upon to proceed with the arbitration promptly, and therefore objections will have to be made generally in rather prompt fashion to effectively prevent a waiver of rights under art.39.

[29] ATF 119 II 386; See also the Swiss Supreme Court decision of July 25, 1997 [4P. 221/1996] ASA Bull., pp.96, 103; *X, SE & Y, GmbH v Z, BV*, February 20, 2013, 4A_407/2012, (http://www.swissarbitrationdecisions.com/sites/default/files/20%20fevrier%202013%204A%20407%202012.pdf [accessed December 3, 2013]).

[30] *X, SE & Y, GmbH v Z, BV*, February 20 2013, *op. cit.*

[31] More generally, see Poudret & Besson, *op. cit.*, para.838, p.779.

However, waiver is not intended to be a trap for the unwary and the illustrations of where the principle has been applied show that the courts have used it in cases where the party was clearly aware of the right and decided not to pursue the objection.[32] **39–34**

[32] See the *Bombardier Transportation* case, cited above at paras 15–11 and 20–21 and 39–29.

Article 40 Limitation of liability

The arbitrators, any person appointed by the arbitral tribunal, the emergency arbitrator, the Court and its members, the ICC and its employees, and the ICC National Committees and Groups and their employees and representatives shall not be liable to any person for any act or omission in connection with the arbitration, except to the extent such limitation of liability is prohibited by applicable law.[1]

Introductory remarks

40–1 Article 40 is the provision in the Rules dealing with limitations on liability for the ICC, its constituent elements, its employees, as well as the persons, such as arbitrators appointed or confirmed by the ICC Court, or the emergency arbitrator appointed by the ICC Court's President. Article 40 has been modified from the corresponding provision of the 1998 Rules. The title has been changed from exclusion of liability to limitation of liability. The text of the article has been broadened as to the scope. And the last phrase has been added stating that the exclusion on liability is not applicable to the extent such limitation of liability is prohibited by applicable law. This is a recognition in the Rules that, there can be no absolute exclusion of liability; that whatever limitation in liability the Rules seek to introduce, there are limitations on liability under the law applicable to the various actors in an ICC arbitration. As pointed out in the prior editions of this Handbook, these limitations were applicable in any event.[2] The Rules have been amended to reflect that fact.

[1] Article 40 corresponds to art.34 of the 1998 Rules. The scope of the persons covered by the provision has been broadened and an exception has been inserted to cover situations where limitation of liability is prohibited by applicable law.

[2] See Bühler/Webster, *Handbook of ICC Arbitration* (2nd edn), paras 34–5 et seq.

Arbitrators are individuals, who are entrusted by parties with a private mission under the Rules. As discussed under art.1, the ICC is a private entity, which performs its services at the request of parties seeking such services under and in accordance with the ICC Rules of arbitration.[3] In an ICC arbitration, the arbitrators as well as the ICC, through the ICC Court and its Secretariat,[4] act in a private capacity, as a result of an agreement between parties to submit their disputes to the ICC Rules of arbitration. The ICC's realtionship with the parties is a contractual one. **40–2**

As the French Supreme Court confirmed in the *Cubic* case,[5] the role of the ICC is to provide through the ICC Court administrative services and to render administrative decisions in connection with arbitration.[6] The arbitrators are also providing services, but of a judicial nature. The basic purpose of art.40 is to set out the principle that, to the extent possible, the arbitrators, the ICC and the various other actors involved in arbitration under the Rules should not be liable for acts or omissions in connection with the arbitration. **40–3**

The policy justification for art.40 is the need to avoid obstruction of the ICC arbitration system by claims of liability against arbitrators, the ICC or other persons involved.[7] With national courts, this need is reflected in the immunity of judges in many jurisdictions from claims by parties to national court proceedings. As far as arbitrators act in a judicial function, there seems to exist no reason why they should be less protected than the judge of a state court. The judicial immunity should apply to arbitrators as well in order to protect as much as possible the integrity of the arbitral process. **40–4**

The exclusion of liability has to be analysed as to its validity, scope and limitations under national law, as will be discussed below. However, it is important to note from the outset what art.40 does not cover despite its broad wording. **40–5**

Article 40 does not operate to exclude or limit any recourse to challenge or remove arbitrators. The effect of such a challenge or removal, if successful, may be to deprive the arbitrator of substantial fees, which he or she would have earned, if the challenge had been rejected by the ICC Court.[8] Article 40 seeks to exclude claims against the arbitrator or the ICC for further amounts, for example relating to costs that were incurred due to the successful challenge. **40–6**

Article 40 does not limit any right to annul any resulting Award or to challenge its enforcement. The grounds for annulment or a refusal to enforce an Award may be directly related to failures by the arbitrators or the ICC. The party objecting to such actions has the basic remedy (against the Award), but does not have the follow-up remedy (against the arbitrators or the ICC). **40–7**

3 See above at para.1–55.

4 See para.1–8 regarding the structure of the ICC and the absence of legal autonomy of the ICC Court.

5 See the *Cubic* case, para.1–8 n.10 and confirmed recently in the *SNF* case, *op. cit.*, para.1–8 n.10.

6 See also above, para.1–16.

7 Fouchard, "Final Report on the Status of the Arbitrator—A Report of the ICC's Commission on International Arbitration", *op. cit.*, p.27; see also ICC Special Bulletin (1995), *The Status of the Arbitrator*. For an analysis of the comparable provision under the UNCITRAL Arbitration Rules, see Webster, *Handbook of UNCITRAL Arbitration* (Thomson/Sweet & Maxwell, 2010), paras 16–1 et seq.

8 As noted under art.11, most challenges submitted to the ICC Court are in fact rejected. If successful, the arbitrator will normally receive a fee for the services rendered until the challenge.

40–8 Article 40 does not limit claims by one party against another party. Therefore, to the extent that the other party has contributed to an action by the Tribunal or the ICC that a party feels is wrongful, the party may have recourse against the other party depending on the terms of their contract and the underlying legal principles.

Liability with respect to "any act or omission in connection with the arbitration"

40–9 Article 40 is phrased in broad terms provided that the act or omission is "in connection" with the arbitration. The act or omission can therefore be a procedural act or a failure to act, including the rendering of an Award or matters relating to the organisation of the hearings for example.[9] The phrase would not cover acts or omissions that have no relationship with the arbitration, such as where they relate to another, non-ICC arbitration. The reference to "act or omission" should cover claims of whatever nature, whether contractual or in delict (tort).

40–10 Article 40 covers in one provision the liability limitation of arbitrators, as well as of emergency arbitrators on the one hand, and of the arbitral institution and its constituents on the other hand. While arbitrators act in a judicial (or at least quasi-judicial) function, the arbitral institution does not. Its acts are administrative in nature, and yet, it is well accepted that both arbitrators and the arbitral institution act on a contractual basis.[10]

Limitation of liability of (emergency) arbitrators and any person appointed by the arbitral tribunal

40–11 Article 40 covers arbitrators, irrespective of who has appointed them. Before being appointed by the ICC Court, or confirmed by the latter or by the Secretary General,[11] a prospective arbitrator needs to sign a statement of acceptance, and provide certain information, which the ICC Court will consider when making the appointment or confirmation. The ICC Court/Secretary General will rely on the veracity of that information as much as the parties.

40–12 With the introduction of the emergency arbitrator in art.29, the liability protection of art.40 was extended to cover the emergency arbitrator as well.

40–13 The liability protection now also extends to persons appointed by the Tribunal, such as experts, but also, albeit less relevant, court reporters, interpreters or other auxiliaries. In some instances, the Tribunal will designate its own expert. The Tribunal's expert would therefore benefit from this limitation in liability, although party-appointed experts would not.

40–14 Professional experts will often make their appointment subject to an express liability limitation, for example linking monetary damages to the amount of their

[9] Van Houtte/McAsey, "The Liability of Arbitrators and Arbitral Institutions," in: Habegger *et al.*, (eds), *Arbitral Institutions under Scrutiny* (Juris 2013) p.133 (146 et seq.), distinguishes types of duties in the context of the contractual basis for an arbitrator's liability: (i) the duty to render an award, (ii) the duty to render a "good" decision, and (iii) the duty to behave diligently.

[10] See van Houtte/McAsey, *op.cit.*, pp.137 et seq., and pp.161 et seq.

[11] See art.13(1) and (2).

fees. Before making the appointment, the Tribunal will normally seek the Parties' agreement with the terms of their engagement.

The law applicable to liability of the arbitrators is not entirely clear but the most appropriate appears to be the law of the place of arbitration.[12] The law of the place of arbitration is the law of the place where the Award is deemed to have been made and where often, although not always, the hearings are conducted. The law of the place of arbitration governs many other aspects of arbitrations, including imposing the minimum procedural standards. The law of the place of arbitration applies to all three arbitrators, who may be based in three different countries and their liability could thus be subject to three different laws, if the law of the place of arbitration were not to apply to their status as arbitrator under the ICC Rules. **40–15**

Liability of arbitrators under the various national legal systems differs significantly. As the UNCITRAL Working Group on International Arbitration has stated: **40–16**

> "93. National arbitration laws, including a number of laws enacting the Model Law, have added provisions dealing with liability of the arbitrator. These provisions differ on whether arbitrators should be immune from professional liability and on the parameters of the immunity. There is a tendency amongst common law jurisdictions to equate arbitrators with judges and extend an equivalent immunity, and amongst civil law jurisdictions to focus on arbitrators' contractual function as experts. Nevertheless, there is considerable diversity even within the same legal families, and no clear line of distinction can be drawn between the approaches taken by each."[13]

Liability of "the Court and its members, . . . the ICC and its employees, . . . the ICC National Committees and Groups and their employees and representatives"

As discussed under art.1, the ICC is a private legal entity established under French law. The ICC Court is the part of the legal entity that deals with arbitration under the Rules.[14] Therefore, art.40 covers the ICC as a legal entity and specifically refers to the ICC Court as part of that entity. The ICC as such is responsible for the administrative acts of the ICC Court and of the Secretariat of the ICC Court.[15] Article 40 also expressly covers the members of the ICC Court, including its President (and the Vice-Presidents), who actually review the matters and decide the various issues, such as the validity of challenges and whether to approve the terms of an Award. Under the 2012 Rules, the powers of the ICC Court's President have been increased, in particular as regards the appointment of the emergency arbitrator.[16] **40–17**

Article 40 also covers the employees of the ICC, and in particular the Secretary General, the General Counsel and the counsel and staff employed by the Secretariat **40–18**

[12] This view is also shared by Reiner & Aschauer, *op. cit.*, para.787 n.488.

[13] United Nations Commission On International Trade Law Thirty-second session, Vienna, May, 17—June, 4 1999 Document A/CN.9/460 April 6, 1999.

[14] See para.1–8 n.10.

[15] For a recent confirmation, see the Paris Court of Appeal decision of January 22, 2009 in the *SNF* case cited at para.1–8 n.11 and discussed below.

[16] See discussion under art.29 and see also paras 13–46 to 13–50.

of the ICC Court.[17] This is in keeping with most limitation of liability provisions that seek to cover employees as well as entities themselves.[18]

40–19 Article 40 goes one step further in covering the ICC National Committees and Groups and their employees and representatives. The ICC National Committees and Groups are involved in ICC arbitration as they propose arbitrators for appointment by the ICC Court as sole arbitrators, presidents, and, sometimes co-arbitrators. They assist the ICC Court in fulfilling its obligations under the Rules, and act as mere auxiliaries of the ICC.[19]

Relationship between the parties and the ICC

40–20 The existence of art.34 in the 1998 Rules, now replaced by and amended by art.40 of the 2012 Rules, has not discouraged parties from suing the ICC, in particular before the French courts, by seeking damages and/or a refund of the administrative charges. The limitation of liability under the Rules is one way for the ICC to protect itself from lawsuits of disgruntled parties. The predecessor provision of art.40 has been tested in court, in particular before the Paris Court of Appeal in the 2009 *SNF* case, which will be discussed below.

40–21 The French Supreme Court has confirmed in the *Cubic* and *SNF* cases that the relationship between the ICC and the parties is a contractual one.[20] Moreover, the court held that the decisions of the ICC Court were administrative in nature.

40–22 To determine the effect of an exclusion of liability clause in the contractual context, one must first determine the applicable rule of law and the limits of exclusion of liability clauses under that national law.[21] However, as mentioned above,[22] art.40 extends beyond purely contractual claims and would extend to claims in delict (tort). Therefore, another issue that may arise under the relevant national system is the extent to which a party can limit its liability in tort.

40–23 As regards the ICC, the Paris Court of Appeal took the view in the 2009 *SNF* case that the arbitration contract that is formed between the ICC and the parties to an ICC arbitration, is governed by French law, since the ICC furnishes its services in Paris via the intermediary of the ICC Court.[23] *SNF* had sued the ICC in 2005. In October 2007, the Paris Court of First Instance issued a judgment in a case brought by the Respondent (SNF) in an ICC arbitration against the ICC. An award had been rendered against SNF. Both parties sought an interpretation of the award under art.29 (now art.35) of the Rules. The Tribunal issued an Addendum. Following receipt of the Addendum, SNF sought clarification on procedural points with respect to the Addendum from the ICC relating to a missing signature and as to the date on which the Award should be considered final. The ICC did not

[17] Technically speaking, the President of the ICC Court is not an employee of the ICC, but has a consultancy agreement with the ICC.

[18] See for example s.74 of the English Arbitration Act 1996.

[19] Reiner & Aschauer, para.794 n.498.

[20] See the discussion on the *Cubic* and the *SNF* cases cited above at para.1–8 n.11.

[21] See for a discussion of the applicable law and competent country in relation to the civil liability of arbitral institutions, van Houtte/McAsey, *op. cit.*, pp.163 et seq.

[22] See para.40–10.

[23] Paris Court of Appeal, January 22, 2009, (2010) Rev Arb No.2, p.314 at 317; (2009) Yearbook Com Arb, p.262.

respond. SNF then brought proceedings in France against the ICC for allegedly breaching the Rules, particularly with respect to scrutiny of the Award and Addendum.[24] The Paris Court of First Instance rejected SNF's claims, essentially considering that art.34, the predecessor of art.40, was a valid exclusion of liability in an international contract, and that SNF had not proven a fault on the part of the ICC, whether in contract or in tort, and any damages resulting therefrom. SNF's appeal was unsuccessful, although the Paris Court of Appeal declared art.40 to be at least partially void. It held:

> "The clause exclusive of liability, which authorizes the ICC not to perform its essential obligation as provider of non–judicial services has to be considered as non-written [void] as regards the relations between the ICC and SNF inasmuch as the clause contradicts the scope of the arbitration contract." (Authors' translation)[25]

The French Arbitration Act, unlike the arbitration laws in some other countries, such as England or Singapore,[26] contains no provision dealing with liability of arbitral institutions. This may be surprising since the ICC Court is based in Paris. It is, however, to be noted that to date, the French courts have not held the ICC liable for breach of contract for an alleged violation of the Rules. Although the ICC Commission was of course familiar with the view taken by the Paris Court of Appeal when revising the 1998 Rules, it essentially maintained the limitation of liability clause, albeit by adding a reference to the prohibition by applicable law of such limitation of liability. **40–24**

In the authors' view, it would be from a legal perspective more sensible, and in the better interest of the ICC, as the service provider, to expressly submit its relations, with the parties that accept the ICC Arbitration Rules, to French law as the governing law, and to provide for the exclusive jurisdiction of the Paris Courts in case of any claims brought against the ICC in relation to the arbitration services performed by the ICC Court and its Secretariat.[27] This would allow the ICC to more clearly and better limit its liability. This could be done in an article in the Rules separate from the article dealing with the arbitrator's immunity. **40–25**

The situation in the United States is different, as arbitration institutions are generally entitled to the same type of immunity as arbitrators (as discussed below). As summarised in the commentary to the Revised Uniform Arbitration Act: **40–26**

> "Section 14(a) [of the Revised Uniform Arbitration Act] also provides the same immunity as is provided to an arbitrator to an arbitration organisation. Extension of judicial immunity to those arbitration

[24] See the *SNF* case cited at para.1–8 n.11. Paris TGI, October 10, 2007, *Société SNF v Chambre de Commerce Internationale*, and the Paris Court of Appeal decision of January 22, 2009.

[25] Paris Court of Appeal, January 22, 2009 (2010) Rev Arb No.2, p.314 at 317/318; (2009) Yearbook Com Arb, p.262.

[26] See s.74 of the English Arbitration Act 1996, and s.25A of the Singapore International Arbitration Act as amended and revised on December 31, 2002. For further examples see van Houtte/McAsey, *op.cit.*, pp.158 et seq. Interestingly, the UNCITRAL Model Law does not limit the liability of arbitral institutions.

[27] From a policy perspective, and possibly for other reasons, the ICC may wish to avoid of being suddenly seen as a French institution, even though the French Courts have qualified it as a NGO recognised by the United Nations.

> organisations is appropriate to the extent that they are acting 'in certain roles and with certain responsibilities' that are comparable to those of a judge. *Corey v New York Stock Exch.*, 691 F.2d 1205, 1209 (6th Cir. 1982). This immunity to neutral arbitration organisations is appropriate because the duties that they perform in administering the arbitration process are the functional equivalent of the roles and responsibilities of judges administering the adjudication process in a court of law. There is substantial precedent for this conclusion."[28]

40–27 This principle was illustrated in 2008 in the *Global Gold Mining* case,[29] a decision of the United States District Court of the Southern District of New York. In that case, the ICC Court rendered a decision under art.6(2). That decision permitted the arbitration to proceed against certain signatories of an agreement containing an arbitration clause but refused to permit the arbitration to proceed against an individual who was a non-signatory of the agreement. The Claimant brought proceedings in New York to compel the ICC to permit the arbitration to proceed so that the issue of jurisdiction could be decided by the Tribunal. The District Court rejected the application stating in part as follows (footnote deleted):

> "[P]arties seeking 'review' of an arbitrator's ultimate decision do not normally sue the arbitrator; instead, they bring an action against the counterparties to the arbitration seeking to confirm or vacate the arbitrators' decision. See 9 U.S.C. §§ 9–12. As the Second Circuit mentioned in passing in Shaw, where the ICC Court had determined, pursuant to Rule 6(2), that a petitioner had an arbitrable dispute against one party but not others, an action in federal court involving both that petitioner and those other parties—but not the ICC Court or the ICC—would satisfy Rule 6(2) by allowing the petitioning party 'to seek review of the arbitrator's [i.e. the ICC Court's] decision' that the petitioner's dispute against the other parties was not prima facie arbitrable. Shaw, 322 F.3d at 122 n. 3. Here, therefore, in order to put the question whether a binding arbitration agreement with Ayvazian exists before a court, GGM must bring a motion to compel arbitration against Ayvazian himself, not in injunctive action against the ICC respondents.
>
> [...]
>
> The rationale of arbitral immunity is that such immunity 'is essential to protect the decision-maker from undue influence and protect the decision-making process from reprisals by dissatisfied litigants.' Austern v. Chicago Bd. of Options Exch., Inc., 898 F.2d 882, 886 (2d Cir. 1990), quoting Corey v. New York Stock Exch., 691 F.2d 1205, 1211 (6th Cir.1982); see also Pfannenstiel v. Merrill Lynch, Pierce, Fenner & Smith, 477 F.3d 1155, 1158 (10th Cir.2007), quoting New England Cleaning Servs., Inc. v. American Arbitration Ass'n, 199 F.3d 542, 545

[28] The Revised Uniform Arbitration Act (2000) is not generally applicable to international arbitrations which are governed by the Federal Arbitration Act. However, the commentary provides a useful and authoritative summary of the case law, see also below fn.44.

[29] *Global Gold Mining, LLC v Peter Robinson & the ICC*, 533 F. Supp. 2d 442 S.D.N.Y., 2008.

(1st Cir.1999). In order to protect the decision-making process, courts should be wary of 'claim[s] [which], regardless of [their] nominal title, effectively seek to challenge [a] decisional act' made during the arbitration process. Pfannenstiel, 477 F.3d at 1159. That rationale extends equally to claims against arbitral administrative institutions, when they perform 'functions that are integrally related to the arbitral process.' Austern, 898 F.2d at 886. Nor does that rationale apply only to suits for damages. If administrative institutions such as the ICC or the ICC Court can be required to defend their decisions in the national courts of any country in the world, the expenses of defending such potentially far-flung suits could constrain their judgment, and increase the costs of arbitration procedures, every bit as much as potential liability for damages. The real parties in interest to litigate the question of arbitrability are the parties seeking and resisting arbitration, not the arbitrators or arbitral administrators, whose role is solely to render neutral judgment. Any action to ask this or another court 'whether or not there is a binding arbitration agreement' must be brought as a motion to compel arbitration against the party resisting arbitration."

Liability to "any person"

Article 40 is not limited to the parties to the arbitration. It is expressed to cover "any person". This would cover any successor in interest to a party to the arbitration. In addition, it would presumably cover any person claiming through a party to an ICC arbitration. Whether the limitation on liability provision binds parties who have never agreed to arbitrate under the Rules will depend on national law. If a third party makes a claim based on an ICC arbitration, there appears to be no reason not to apply art.40, as well as the other Rules that may be relevant to that claim. **40–28**

France

Under French law, an arbitrator may be liable to the parties for his conduct in the arbitration.[30] In one case involving an international arbitration, an arbitrator accepted employment from one of the parties immediately after rendering his Award. The Award was annulled and a claim was filed against the arbitrator for the costs. The court held the arbitrator liable for a portion of the costs.[31] **40–29**

Besides, under French law, if a party disagrees with the Award, it should attack the Award and not the arbitrators. In the *Bompard* case,[32] the Paris Court of Appeal described the status of the arbitrator and potential liability in the framework of a domestic arbitration as follows: **40–30**

[30] For a detailed discussion, see Fouchard, "*Le statut de l'arbitre dans la jurisprudence française*" (1996) Rev Arb No.3, p.325.

[31] Paris, October 12, 1995, *V v société Raoul Duval* (1999) Rev Arb No.2 p.327, note Fouchard; TGI Paris, May 12, 1993, *Société Raoul Duval v V* (1996) Rev Arb No.3 p.411.

[32] Paris, May 22, 1991, *Bompard v Consortis C* (1996) Rev Arb No.3 p.476.

"Whereas the regime of liability of the arbitrator cannot therefore be strictly of a contractual nature due to the double nature of the arbitral institution, contractual in its basis and judicial in its function;
In the current situation the criticism of the arbitrators of having made a grave error in calculations in attributing a debit to Mr Bompard without any reason or logical ground could as such only provide grounds for annulment under Article 1482 of the New Code of Civil Procedure.
Thus, the alleged fault is related directly to the content of the judicial act and constitutes a criticism of the reasons in the award and does not constitute personal fault which is the sole type [of fault] permitting an action for liability against the arbitrators." (Authors' translation)

40–31 Failure to disclose a relationship with the parties may result in personal liability of the arbitrator. In the *L'Oréal* case,[33] which concerned an international arbitration, an arbitrator was held personally liable based on art.1382 of the French Civil Code where he failed to disclose his relationship with the parties as a result of which the Award was annulled. Moreover, the arbitrator was ordered to reimburse the amount of his fees.

40–32 In one case, the French court appeared to suggest that an arbitrator could be held liable for a sudden resignation that apparently had the effect of delaying the proceedings. However, the case did not directly concern the liability of the arbitrator.[34]

40–33 In the *Consorts Juliet* case, concerning a domestic ad hoc arbitration, the French Supreme Court held the arbitrators liable on a contractual basis for having failed to seek an extension of time to render the Award.[35] However, in a more recent case, *Conselho National de Carregadores*,[36] the French Supreme Court held that arbitrators were only subject to an obligation of means (*de moyens*) and not of results and that the arbitrators were not liable for the procedural delays or for suspension of their work as that had been demanded by the parties.

Switzerland

40–34 There appears to be little authority on the liability of arbitrators in Switzerland. One would generally expect that their liability would be decided on the same basis as for judges given the similarity of the mandate.[37] There are limits to the immunity applicable to the arbitrators for non-judicial acts. As an example, an arbitrator could in some circumstances be held liable for breach of the obligation to disclose information that might affect his or her independence in the eyes of the parties.[38]

[33] TGI Paris, December 9, 1992, *Société Annahold BV et D Frydman v société L'Oréal et B* (1996) Rev Arb No.3 p.483.
[34] TGI Paris, February 15, 1995, *Société chérifienne des pétroles v Société Mannesmann Industria Iberica* (1996) Rev Arb No.3 p.503.
[35] See the *Consorts Juliet* case: Civ 1e, December 6, 2005, No.03–13.166. The question of the arbitrator's liability has been referred back to the Court of Appeal of Orléans.
[36] Cass. Civ 1e, November 17, 2010, No.12352.
[37] See Lalive, Poudret & Reymond, *op. cit.*, p.93; Poudret & Besson, *op. cit.*, para.446, p.373.
[38] Zuberbühler, Müller & Habbeger, *Swiss Rules of International Arbitration—Commentary* (Kluwer, Schulthess, 2005), para.N 2–5, p.370.

United States

Under American law, the Federal Arbitration Act does not specifically address the issue of liability of arbitrators,[39] but case law establishes the principle of immunity comparable to that of judges (sometimes referred to as "quasi-judicial" immunity). The limitation on liability is based on and limited to the exercise by the arbitrators of judicial authority. As a result art.40 appears to be consistent with the strong policy of immunity for arbitrators in the exercise of their functions in the United States. The *Global Gold Mining* case referred to above dealt with the liability of the ICC Court and not the liability of arbitrators. However, the premise to that decision is that the arbitrators are generally immune from liability.[40] **40–35**

England

The issue of the nature of an arbitrator's role was extensively canvassed in the case leading to the judgment of the UK Supreme Court in *Jivraj v Hashwani* [2011] UKSC 40. In that case, Lord Clarke described the role as follows (at para.45): **40–36**

> "Further, in so far as dominant purpose is relevant, I would hold that the dominant purpose of appointing an arbitrator or arbitrators is the impartial resolution of the dispute between the parties in accordance with the terms of the agreement and, although the contract between the parties and the arbitrators would be a contract for the provision of personal services, they were not personal services under the direction of the parties."

As a result, under English law, the issue of liability of the arbitrators would begin with a contractual analysis, subject to the provisions of applicable law, the arbitration agreement and the relevant arbitration rules. **40–37**

Section 29 of the English Arbitration Act 1996 provides: **40–38**

[39] Article 14(a) of the Revised Uniform Arbitration Act (2000), which is generally not applicable to international arbitrations, provides: "An arbitrator or an arbitration organisation acting in that capacity is immune from civil liability to the same extent as a judge of a court of this State acting in a judicial capacity". The commentary summarises the position as follows: "Arbitral immunity has its origins in common law judicial immunity; most jurisdictions track the common law directly. The key to this identity is the 'functional comparability' of the role of arbitrators and judges. See *Butz v Economou*, 438 U.S. 478, 511–12 (1978) (establishing the principle that the extension of judicial-like immunity to non- judicial officials is properly based on the 'functional comparability' of the individual's acts and judgments to the acts and judgments of judges); see also *Corey v New York Stock Exch.*, 691 F.2d 1205, 1209 (6th Cir. 1982) (applying the 'functional comparability' standard for immunity); *Antoine v Byers & Anderson, Inc.*, 508 U.S. 429, 435–36 (1993) (holding that the key to the extension of judicial immunity to non-judicial officials is the 'performance of the function of resolving disputes between parties or of authoritatively adjudicating private rights')".

[40] There has been discussion in arbitration circles of the case of *Gulf Petro Trading Company, Inc v Nigerian Nat Petroleum Corp*, 2008 WL 62546 (CA 5 (Tex.)). In that case, Gulf Petro made various claims, including the claim that the arbitrators had been bribed. The US Court of Appeals for the 5th Circuit did not have to consider the issue of the arbitrators' liability (which is generally not applicable for bribery) as it upheld the lower court decision rejecting the claim as a collateral attack on an arbitration Award rendered in Switzerland.

"29.—(1) An arbitrator is not liable for anything done or omitted in the discharge or purported discharge of his functions as arbitrator unless the act or omission is shown to have been in bad faith.
(2) Subsection (1) applies to an employee or agent of an arbitrator as it applies to the arbitrator himself.
(3) This section does not affect any liability incurred by an arbitrator by reason of his resigning (but see section 25)."[41]

40–39 Section 29 is a mandatory provision of the Arbitration Act 1996. Therefore, it appears that a limitation on liability of an arbitrator would not be effective if it were shown that the arbitrator acted in bad faith.

40–40 To the extent that art.40 does not provide an effective protection against liability, the issue of insurance coverage for arbitrators is sometimes raised, in particular by individual arbitrators who may not have general professional liability insurance.

[41] Section 25 of the English Arbitration Act 1996 is reproduced in full in Pt III App.9.

Article 41 General Rule

In all matters not expressly provided for in the Rules, the Court and the arbitral tribunal shall act in the spirit of the Rules and shall make every effort to make sure that the award is enforceable at law.[1]

Introductory remarks

Article 41 addresses two distinct issues. The first issue is dealing with matters "not expressly provided for in these Rules". The second issue is the requirement to "make every effort to make sure that the Award is enforceable at law". The provisions of Art.41 apply to the ICC Court as well as to the Tribunal with respect to filling in gaps in the Rules, i.e. in all matters not expressly provided for in the Rules.[2] **41–1**

The Rules are not a comprehensive code of civil procedure, and are not intended to be one. Nor are the Rules a detailed list of principles applicable to arbitration in general. The Rules provide a flexible framework for arbitration that is intended to be adapted to the requirements of each case. Article 41 addresses matters that are "not expressly provided for" in the Rules, and how to address situations when there is a gap in the Rules.[3] The gap is to be filled by acting in the spirit of the Rules, and by ensuring the award's enforceability. Applying certain provisions of the Rules by analogy may be one way of filling a gap. In such cases, Art.41 requires the ICC Court and Tribunals to act "in the spirit of" the Rules in dealing with issues arising in the arbitration. **41–2**

In rendering the various decisions at the Plenary Sessions and Committee Sessions discussed in Annex 1 Pt I, the ICC Court will frequently refer to the spirit of the Rules and its duty to seek to ensure that there is an enforceable Award. This is one of the particular concerns in scrutiny of Awards under Art.33, as well as in constituting the arbitral tribunal. Following the coming into force of the 2012 Rules, the need for the ICC Court to fill gaps in the Rules should be limited, as one of the very objectives of the Rules revision was precisely to fill such gaps.[4] **41–3**

The *Behr* case, which is discussed at paras 35–37 to 35–41, represents a prominent example of a case where the ICC Court expressly relied on the predecessor provision of Art.41 to allow a remission of the award, even though the 1998 Rules did not contain an express provision to this effect.[5] **41–4**

[1] Article 41 corresponds to Art.35 of the 1998 Rules. There have been no changes to the text of the article.

[2] Fry, Greenberg, Mazza, *op. cit.*, para.3–1537; see also Reiner & Aschauer, *op. cit.*, para.797 n.500, which refers to a comprehensive gap-filling competence.

[3] Derains & Schwartz, *op. cit.*, p.385.

[4] See also Fry, Greenberg, Mazza, *op. cit.*, para.3–1539.

[5] See para.35–39 fn.37, where the US Court of Appeals, Sixth Circuit, stated that it read the predecessor of Art.41 "to permit remand in this case, given that clarification by the original arbitrator is critical in order to make the Eight Award enforceable at law".

The Spirit of the Rules

41–5 The spirit of the Rules is based on several concepts. The Rules are based on party autonomy to adapt the procedure to the requirements of each case; on neutrality towards the parties and their equal treatment, the independence and impartiality of the members of the Tribunal and generally the requirement that the procedure be fair to both parties, and that they are both given a reasonable opportunity to present their case. The Rules are also based on the application of the rules of law agreed upon by the parties, or applicable pursuant to the Tribunal's decision, unless the parties have agreed that the Tribunal is to act *ex aequo et bono* or as *amiable compositeur*.[6]

Ensuring enforceability of the Award

41–6 Article 41 also requires the ICC Court and the Tribunal to "make every effort to make sure that the award is enforceable at law". Article 41 recognises the importance of the law applicable to the arbitration. That law may be the law of the place of arbitration, the law of the arbitration agreement (if different from that of the law of the place of arbitration) and the law of the place of enforcement. Therefore, it is important, and indeed essential to consider the Rules, the administrative practice of the ICC Court and the actions of the Tribunal in the light of those legal requirements.

41–7 The wording of Art.41 is strong in referring to "every effort", but, as noted above, it addresses primarily matters not expressly covered by the Rules. In all other matters, if the arbitrator acts in accordance with the Rules, there is normally no reason to believe that the Award would not be enforceable. This does not mean that, although the arbitrator acted fully in accordance with the Rules, the award might not be declared enforceable in a specific country.[7]

41–8 Article 41 refers only to the Tribunal, not the Emergency Arbitrator.[8] Appendix V of the Rules, i.e. the EAR, contains, however, a similar provision which in Art.8(3) expressly refers to the Emergency Arbitrator, and the acting in the spirit of the Rules and of App.V, for all matters concerning the emergency arbitrator proceedings "not expressly provided for in [that] Appendix".

41–9 Article 41 refers to enforceability and not validity, which seems to suggest that the ICC Court and the Tribunal should take into account not only the law of the place of arbitration, but, to the extent practicable, also the law of the probable place of enforcement. In that context, one of the basic elements that any Tribunal should take into consideration is the New York Convention. However, the extent to which the Tribunal or the ICC Court can take such matters into account depends on the facts of the case and the briefing by the parties. The parties have the most accurate view of where enforcement may take place and, if they are concerned about a particular aspect, they can then seek to have it covered in the Award in particular by raising it as an issue to be decided under the Terms of Reference.

6 As to the power to act as *amiable compositeur*, see the discussion under Art.21(3) at para.21–__.
7 See van Houtte/McAsey, *op. cit.*, p.147.
8 This is true for Art.17 as well as regards the proof of authority, see para.17–7.

A Tribunal should meet the legitimate expectation of the parties at the time they agreed to submit their disputes to arbitration. Presumably, the expectation was that the Award would be enforceable and would not be set aside at the place of arbitration. For this reason a Tribunal should, in principle, always take into account the law prevailing at the seat of arbitration. This being said, if local courts at the place of arbitration make a travesty of justice by denying an international Tribunal from enforcing the parties' legitimate expectations, a Tribunal may decide to ignore the decision of those courts. In such cases, it will be for the Tribunal to decide whether, as a matter of fairness and of providing access to (arbitral) justice, it is appropriate to follow a local court's decision if doing so would frustrate the arbitration agreement. **41–10**

Some parties who challenged the jurisdiction of a Tribunal have argued that a Tribunal would breach its obligation to render an enforceable Award if it concluded that it had jurisdiction over the parties, as the courts would hold to the contrary. On that basis, the parties have suggested that the Tribunal deny jurisdiction. In an interim Award of 1984, an ICC Tribunal in case No.4695 dealt with this rather circular argument in the context of Art.26 of the 1988 Rules (predecessor of Art.41): **41–11**

> "Art. 26 of the ICC Rules must be understood as requiring every arbitral tribunal to avoid any grounds of nullity, since if the award is unenforceable the whole arbitration proceeding will have been a waste of time and energy.
> But this requirement of Art. 26 is not relevant to the question of jurisdiction. It is obvious that if a tribunal would decline to exercise jurisdiction on the basis of the possible difficulties of a future enforcement in a given country, then there would be no award at all, susceptible of being enforced in other jurisdictions.
> In this case there may be difficulties, perhaps not insuperable, in the enforcement of this tribunal [sic] awards, in some national jurisdictions.
> But if the tribunal finds, as it does, that it has jurisdiction, it cannot fail to exercise it. Otherwise, it would be concurring in a failure to exercise jurisdiction and could even be accused of a denial of justice."[9]

Some 15 years later, another ICC Tribunal in ICC case No.10623 followed that view, in its interim Award of 2001. The case dealt with an arbitration between state "X" and a private party. The place of arbitration was in state "X". The Tribunal commented as follows on the requirements of Art.35 (which is the predecessor under the 1998 Rules to Art.41): **41–12**

> "[140.] A generally accepted principle of international arbitration, reflected in Article 35 of the ICC Rules, compels the Arbitral Tribunal to make every effort to ensure that any award it renders is enforceable at law. In this contact, complying with the law and the judicial decisions of the seat is clearly an important objective, in light of the fact that the

9 ICC case No.4695 (1986) in *Collection of ICC Arbitral Awards, Vol. II, op. cit.*, p.33.

courts have the power to set aside an award rendered in their country [. . .].

[142.] This does not mean, however, that the arbitral tribunal should simply abdicate to the courts of the seat the tribunal's own judgment about what is fair and right in the arbitral proceedings. In the event that the arbitral tribunal considers that to follow a decision of a court would conflict fundamentally with the tribunal's understanding of its duty to the parties, derived from the parties' arbitration agreement, the tribunal must follow its own judgment, even if that requires non-compliance with a court order.

[143.] To conclude otherwise would entail a denial of justice and fairness to the parties and conflict with the legitimate expectations they created by entering into an arbitration agreement. It would allow the courts of the seat to convert an international arbitration agreement into a dead letter, with intolerable consequences for the practice of international arbitration more generally.

[144.] This conclusion is consistent with principles that are already well established in international arbitration. In particular, it is clear from arbitral case law that the obligation to make every effort to render an enforceable award does not oblige an arbitral tribunal to render awards that are fundamentally unfair or other- wise improper. An arbitral tribunal should not go so far as to frustrate the arbitration agreement itself in the interests of ensuring enforceability. Such an outcome would be, to say the least, a paradox."[10]

41–13 A key factor for the Tribunal in the above case was that the arbitration involved the state and the courts of a state are an emanation of that state. Therefore, in this exceptional case, the Tribunal decided to ignore the anti-arbitration injunction of the courts of the place of arbitration. The reference in the Award to cases where annulled Awards have been enforced is the litmus test. If a Tribunal does not believe that any Award it renders will be enforced either at the place of arbitration or elsewhere, then it will hardly ignore the courts of the place of arbitration.

41–14 The Tribunal's duty under Art.41 is to ensure that it abides by the procedural requirements of the law of the place of arbitration, but also take into consideration the parties' legitimate procedural expectations with respect to the jurisdictions of enforcement.

41–15 For example, if a Tribunal is sitting in Switzerland, but the probable place of enforcement is in the United States, then it may be appropriate to deal expressly with certain issues relating to the power of the Tribunal to award costs in the Award. As discussed under Art.37, the basic rule in the United States is that the power to award costs must have been conferred on the arbitrators by the arbitration agreement, the relevant rules of arbitration or the law of the place of arbitration.

[10] ICC case No.10623, *op. cit.*, paras 0–57 n.42, 18–37 n.25.

A more complex issue relates to the duty of a Tribunal to consider mandatory principles of law that may affect enforcement.[11] In the *Eco Swiss* case for example,[12] neither party raised issues of EU competition law during the course of the arbitration. Nor did the Tribunal. The result was that the Award was annulled on public policy grounds based on EU competition law. This suggests that the Tribunal may, and possibly should raise issues of public policy if they appear to be relevant to the validity or the enforceability of the Award. **41–16**

With regard to the law of the probable place of enforcement, the degree to which a Tribunal may take into account the local requirements may be subject to limitations and is the subject of discussion in arbitration circles. The practical limitation is that the Tribunal may not be aware of local requirements to the extent that they are not those common under the New York Convention. Another limitation may be the concern of the Tribunal to resolve a dispute in accordance with the applicable rules of law in an appropriate period of time notwithstanding legal issues in a potential or probable place of enforcement. **41–17**

In ICC case No.6474,[13] the Tribunal dealt with the argument that the Award rendered in Switzerland would not be enforceable in the "territory" against a state entity in a country because the country was not recognised, the documents were not validly signed by a representative of the state entity and the transaction was illegal due to bribery. The Tribunal stated with respect to Art.26 of the 1988 Rules corresponding to Art.41: **41–18**

> "[134] "As to the 'dilemma' which, in defendant's submission, is created by the co-existence of Art. 26 of the ICC Rules and Art. 177(1) PILA,[[14]] it must be considered as non-existent or purely theoretical, in the following sense: it is not the purpose of Art. 26 of the ICC Rules[[15]] to be in any way a substitute for the law governing the international arbitration under the common will of the Parties or to bypass the law of the seat of the arbitration. It is at most, as recognised by the defendant's language, a 'general directive' and not a rule of law in the sense of Art. 177(1), which, in any case, would have to prevail over the ICC Rules if a real contradiction arose, which is not the case.
> [135] "Moreover, it is not enough to state that an application of Art. 177(1), 'could result in an arbitral award not being enforceable elsewhere'—which is undeniable and has been intentionally accepted as a risk, although a limited one, by the Swiss legislator. It would fall upon the defendant to establish that an application of Art. 177(1), did result or would result in the arbitral award not being enforceable, not

[11] See for a discussion of the latter above at para.41–6.

[12] European Court of Justice, *Eco Swiss China Time Ltd v Benetton International NV*, Case C–126/97.

[13] ICC case No.6474 (1992) (Partial Award), ICC ICArb Bull Vol.15 No.2, p.102; *Collection of ICC Arbitral Awards, Volume IV, 1996–2000, op. cit.*, p.341; (2000) YBCA Vol. XXV p.11.

[14] Article 177(1) of the Swiss PILA provides: "Any dispute of a financial nature may be the subject of an arbitration". Article 177(2) of the law limits the right of a state entity to invoke its own law to maintain it does not have capacity to be a party in international arbitration. Footnote added by the authors.

[15] Article 26 of the 1988 Rules is the predecessor to Art.41 of the Rules. Footnote added by the authors.

'elsewhere'—which is undeniable and has been intentionally accepted as a risk, although a limited one, by the Swiss legislator. It would fall upon the defendant to establish that an application of Art. 177(1), did result or would result in the arbitral award not being enforceable, not 'elsewhere' in general, but in the country or countries having the closest connection with questions of enforcement. In the Arbitral Tribunal's opinion, the territory's law, just as the law of the European country, may prima facie have to be taken into consideration, especially or exclusively if and when the Tribunal comes to decide on the merits of the case.

[136] "Be that as it may, the defendant has not satisfied the Tribunal that a decision affirming the Arbitral Tribunal's jurisdiction in the present case could not be recognised or would not be recognised in the territory. Even if that had been established, however, the question would remain open whether the Claimant does not have a legitimate interest in obtaining an award which would be enforceable in some other countries, though not in the territory." [Footnotes added by the authors.]

41–19 ICC case No.6474 reflects the secondary role of the law of the country of the place of enforcement, even where the parties have directly raised that issue. The primary goal is usually to meet the requirements of the law of the place of arbitration. However, Tribunals may even, in some instances, be led to disregard issues under the law of the place of arbitration.

ANNEX 1

THE ICC COURT'S SESSIONS IN A NUTSHELL

Article 1(2) of the Rules provides that: "[t]he Court does not itself resolve disputes. It administers the resolution of disputes by arbitral tribunals, in accordance with the Rules of Arbitration of the ICC (the 'Rules')". The ICC Court ensures the application of the Rules in particular by taking decisions provided for in the Rules. The decisions of the ICC Court relate to many different aspects of an ICC arbitration.[1] However, the ICC Court's power is that of an administrative body. It is the Tribunal that decides the merits of each case. **Ann–01**

To understand how the ICC Court functions in practice set out below is a description of the ICC Court's sessions, first of the monthly "Plenary Session" (A.), followed by its weekly "Committee Sessions" (B.) at which most material decisions are taken.[2] In addition to these sessions, there is an annual working session of the ICC Court, usually in September, which reviews developments with respect to international arbitration in general and ICC arbitration in particular. **Ann–02**

All sessions of the ICC Court are confidential. Except with the consent of the President of the ICC Court only Court Members are permitted to attend. Members of the Secretariat also attend. Moreover, the ICC Court does not provide the parties with reasons of its decisions. Some users have therefore complained about what they consider to be an opaque decision-making process. The following comments are intended to render this process more transparent. **Ann–03**

The comments set out below are based on the authors' experience with respect to the sessions of the ICC Court. These comments should be read together with the commentary regarding the relevant articles of the Rules dealing with the functions and prerogatives of the ICC Court. The comments are for the purpose of illustrating how the administrative body of ICC arbitration functions in practice. Each case which comes before the ICC Court is different from another, and decisions taken by the ICC Court in one case can for that reason alone not be binding in another. Each decision taken by the ICC Court involves the exercise of some discretion, and that discretion is exercised by the members attending a specific session of the ICC Court. **Ann–04**

[1] The decisions to be taken by the ICC Court under the Rules are referred to in Arts 6(4), 10, 12(2), 12(3), 12(4), 12(5), 12(8), 13(1), 13(3), 13(4), 14(3), 15(1)–(5), 18(1), 23(2), 23(3), 30(1), 33, 35(1), 35(2), 37 and 38.

[2] As discussed below, the President of the ICC Court is entitled to take certain decisions which are then communicated to the ICC Court. In addition, the Rules provide that the Secretariat may take certain administrative decisions.

Ann–05 The material submitted by the Secretariat to the ICC Court, either at a Plenary Session or at Committee Sessions, includes invariably some basic information about the matter to be dealt with at the ICC Court session:

(i) the name of the parties and of their counsel, if they are represented in the proceedings;

(ii) the name of the arbitrator(s);

(iii) a summary of the main characteristics of the dispute submitted to arbitration;

(iv) the place of arbitration;

(v) the arbitration agreement;

(vi) the language(s) of the file;

(vii) the financial aspects of the file;

(viii) the Secretariat's comments regarding the general background and past practice relevant to the decisions to be taken by the ICC Court, and the Secretariat's recommendation for consideration by the ICC Court.

Where the circumstances of the matter so require only, additional information will be provided by the Secretariat, including comments as to past practice (which does not bind the ICC Court but is used as an indicator) and certain documents, as will be explained, by way of examples, below.

A. The Monthly Plenary Session of the ICC Court

Introductory Notes

Ann–06 Plenary Sessions occur once a month, normally the last Thursday of the month, based on a calendar set prior to the start of each calendar year. All members and alternate members of the ICC Court are invited to attend the ICC Court's Plenary Session. Between 20 and 30 members of the ICC Court usually attend at a minimum; for a quorum, at least six members of the ICC Court must be in attendance.[3]

Ann–07 The members of the ICC Court, who have indicated to the Secretariat that they intend to attend a Plenary Session, are provided with the binder of information in advance of the session. Set out below is a list of the information that is generally provided in such binder with respect to each specific matter with an illustration from a recent case.

Approval of Minutes of Prior Plenary Session

Ann–08 The minutes of the prior Plenary Session are available for review by the ICC Court members and are approved at the session.

[3] See Pt III Appendix 1, Statutes of the International Court of Arbitration at Art.4.

Appointment of Committee Members for the Following Month

The Plenary Session appoints the Committee members for the following month upon proposal of the President of the ICC Court.[4] **Ann–09**

New Matters

There is a list of Requests for Arbitration filed during the prior month setting out the names and nationalities of parties to the arbitration. This list is circulated to allow Court members attending the Plenary Session of the following month to see whether they may have a conflict of interest. In such a case, they will receive no papers concerning that case and are not allowed to participate at the session of the ICC Court dealing with such matters, as they are "interested", and thus "excused". **Ann–10**

Committee Matters

The allocation of matters between the Plenary Session and the Committee Sessions is a matter for the ICC Court. Matters dealt with at Committee Sessions are dealt with at para.Ann–36, below. **Ann–11**

Matters that are generally dealt with at Committee Sessions of the ICC Court may be deferred to the Plenary Session. This can occur where the Committee is unable to reach a unanimous decision or where the matter raises a question of principle that the Committee would prefer to have considered at the Plenary Session. If a matter from a Committee Session is referred to a Plenary Session, the material for the Plenary Session will generally include the material submitted to the Committee Session as well as a report by a reporter (the "*Rapporteur*"). **Ann–12**

A.1. Challenge of Arbitrators

Challenges per Art.14 are usually submitted to the Plenary Session of the ICC Court unless they are repetitive or in some cases very straightforward.[5] **Ann–13**

Report of the Secretariat

The Secretariat's reports outlines the circumstances relating to the case and provides background as to prior ICC Court practice that may be relevant. Attached to this report is a copy of the key correspondence relating to the challenge. **Ann–14**

Report by a member of the ICC Court selected by the Secretariat

This report which the other members of the ICC Court will receive in writing at the beginning of the ICC Court Sessions usually summarises the grounds for the challenge as regards admissibility and merits. The report is expected to be brief and to deal with the main issues. The report frequently, but does not always provide a recommendation as to a decision to be adopted by the ICC Court. **Ann–15**

[4] See Pt III Appendix 1, Statutes of the International Court of Arbitration at Art.5.

[5] See the discussion under Art.14. See also (2007) ICC Bull ICArb Vol.8 No.1, p.9.

Deliberations at the Plenary Session

Ann–16 After the *Rapporteur* has presented his or her report, the counsel at the Secretariat provides any update that may be appropriate with respect to the positions of the parties and the arbitrators. There is then generally a discussion of the admissibility and the merits of the challenge based on the experience of the members of the ICC Court and the practice of the Secretariat and ICC Court in the past.

Ann–17 If there is a consensus as to how to deal with the challenge, then it is dealt with without a vote. Otherwise, the President of the ICC Court will proceed with a vote of Court members in attendance at the Plenary Session. The vote relates to whether the challenge should be accepted or rejected overall. The vote does not relate to whether specific grounds of a challenge should be accepted or rejected. Therefore, there may be a consensus among Court members as to how to deal with a challenge without there being necessarily any agreement as to the specific grounds of the challenge.

Notification of the Decision

Ann–18 The Secretariat records the decision which is then notified by the Secretariat to the parties and arbitrators involved in the arbitration. No reasons are provided for the decision either in the letter of notification or at any other time.

Ann–19 If the challenge is rejected, the Secretariat will inform in writing the parties and the Tribunal accordingly, without providing any reasons for it.

Ann–20 If a challenge is accepted with respect to a co-arbitrator nominated by a party, the ICC Court has discretion as to the appointment of a replacement pursuant to Art.15(4) of the Rules.[6] However, in many instances the party who nominated the arbitrator who has been successfully challenged will be provided with a limited period of time (15 days) in which to nominate another co-arbitrator. If the challenge is accepted with respect to a President or a sole arbitrator, then the procedure for selection of the President will be followed, usually providing the parties with a limited period in which to nominate a replacement.

A.2. Removal of Arbitrators

Ann–21 Article 15 deals with replacement and removal of arbitrators. The ICC Court generally decides upon the removal of arbitrators at Plenary Sessions, except for arbitrators who have died or who have tendered their resignation, which are dealt with at Committee Sessions. Where replacement proceedings are brought upon the request of all the parties under Art.15(1) or on the ICC Court's own initiative under Art.15(2), the matter is generally first brought before the ICC Court at its Committee Session, at which the ICC Court considers whether to initiate a removal procedure against the arbitrator(s).

[6] A relevant factor in deciding whether to follow the original procedure for nomination of the arbitrator will be the urgency of the replacement. If hearings are scheduled for the near future, a more expeditious replacement procedure may be considered appropriate.

In the event that the Committee Session of the ICC Court decides that removal proceedings should be initiated against the arbitrator(s) or that the matter should be decided by the Plenary Session, then the matter is referred to the Plenary Session of the ICC Court to decide whether to remove the arbitrator(s) in accordance with Art.15(3). **Ann–22**

The same procedure as for challenges applies mutatis mutandis with removal. **Ann–23**

A.3. Scrutiny of Awards

Draft Awards are generally scrutinised by the ICC Court pursuant to Art.33, generally at a Committee Session of the ICC Court except in four cases: (i) where the draft Award involves a state or state entity; (ii) where there is a dissenting opinion; (iii) where the draft Award is of particular concern (due to the amount in issue or some issue of principle); or (iv) where the Committee has been unable to reach a decision as to the Award. **Ann–24**

The ICC Court does not scrutinise, let alone approve the dissent or make any comments on it. However, the dissent is a relevant document in considering the draft Award itself. **Ann–25**

The ICC Court's scrutiny is intended to focus on "modifications as to the form of the Award" and the ICC Court "without affecting the arbitral tribunal's liberty of decision, may also draw its attention to points of substance" in accordance with Art.33 of the Rules. In addition, as provided in Art.6 of App.II (Internal Rules of the ICC Court): **Ann–26**

> "When the Court scrutinizes draft Awards in accordance with Article 33 of the Rules, it considers, to the extent practicable, the requirements of mandatory law at the place of arbitration."

The members of the ICC Court scrutinise anywhere from four to eight draft Awards at every Plenary Session. This provides a unique perspective in which to compare the method and quality of draft Awards. **Ann–27**

The Secretariat's Report

This provides the basic background regarding the case and the main characteristics of the dispute. It also covers the financial aspects of the file as the ICC Court will also have to deal with the level of fees. It sets out the Secretariat's comments on the background of the parties' dispute, provides the structure and main findings of the draft Award, as well as the content of the dissenting opinion (if any), highlights issues that may arise under the law of the place of arbitration and any prior practice that may be considered relevant. **Ann–28**

The Report of the Rapporteur

The report by the ICC Court member dealing with an Award is expected to focus on the following issues: **Ann–29**

(i) clerical and similar errors in the Award;

(ii) whether adequate reasoning is found in the Award;

(iii) whether the reasoning given in the draft Award is consistent with the dispositive section of the Award;

(iv) whether the issues that were to be decided pursuant to the Terms of Reference have indeed been decided, and if no decision was required, that it be stated so in the Award;

(v) where a dissenting opinion raises what appears to be a plausible point, the majority will have dealt with it in the draft Award;

(vi) violation of any public policy rule applicable at the place of arbitration.

The report usually provides a recommendation as to a decision to be adopted by the ICC Court.

A.4. National Court Decisions on Arbitration

Ann–30 The Secretariat receives documentation on national case law and court cases relating to ICC arbitration and international arbitration in general from all over the world. Copies of relevant cases are provided to the ICC Court members for their information.

B. The Weekly Committee Session of the ICC Court

Introductory Notes

Ann–31 Committee Sessions occur once a week. Normally they are held based on a calendar set prior to the start of each calendar year. Committees generally consist of three members of the ICC Court. The President or a Vice-President of the ICC Court presides over each Committee Session. All members and alternate members of the ICC Court may attend Committee Sessions. However, in most cases, only the Committee members attend.

Ann–32 The members of the ICC Court who are participating as Committee members are provided with the binder containing the documents referred to below for review prior to the Committee Session generally a week prior to the session. This material is usually updated the day before the session with additional material relating to the cases that have been listed for the Committee Session.

Ann–33 The deliberations at the Committee Sessions are under the direction of the President or Vice President presiding over the session. The Committee members are provided with an opportunity to comment on each matter. The Secretariat is invited to provide background and to provide details as to the practice of the ICC Court. Decisions at Committee Sessions must be unanimous or the matter will be deferred to the next Plenary Session of the ICC Court.

Ann–34 Parties are generally not informed whether a decision is to be taken or has been taken at a Plenary Session or a Committee Session. This practice is adopted by the Secretariat with the view to preserve the serenity of the work of the Tribunal and the ICC Court, thus avoiding unnecessary pressure from the parties. The decisions are notified to the parties by the Secretariat.

Ann–35 Article 5 of App.I and Art.4 of App.II of the Rules set out the provisions relating to Committees of the ICC Court.

Overview of Issues Covered in the Committee Sessions

The following issues are covered in the Committee Sessions of the ICC Court: **Ann–36**

(i) First Submissions of cases to the ICC Court. It is common for First Submissions to include the following issues for determination by the ICC Court:

(a) jurisdictional objections pursuant to Art.6(4);
(b) deciding upon the number of arbitrators pursuant to Art.12, and as the case may be, choice of the appropriate National Committee(s);
(c) confirming or appointing arbitrators pursuant to Art.13;
(d) fixing the place of arbitration pursuant to Art.18;
(e) fixing the advance on costs, or re-examination of the advance on costs pursuant to Art.36.

(ii) Joinder of parties (Arts 6 and 7).

(iii) Withdrawal of cases (Art.36(6)).

(iv) Scrutiny of draft Awards, pursuant to Art.33 (concerns any type of Awards, including Awards by consent).

(v) Scrutiny of a correction and/or interpretation of the Award pursuant to Arts 33 and 35.

(vi) Determining the costs of arbitration pursuant to Art.37, in the case of withdrawals, Awards by consent or final Awards.

(vii) Transmission of the Terms of Reference and Provisional Timetable to the ICC Court pursuant to Art.23(2).

(viii) Extension to the time limit for rendering the Terms of Reference pursuant to Art.23(2).

(ix) Approval of the Terms of Reference pursuant to Art.23(3).

(x) Extensions to the time limit for rendering the Award pursuant to Art.30(2).

(xi) Granting the Tribunal an advance on fees.

Decisions of the ICC Court on the matters listed above involve a fair amount of discretion. The members of the ICC Court attending a specific session will exercise this discretion within the limits of the Rules and with due regard to the practice of the ICC Court. The members of the Secretariat, and in particular its Secretary General and General Counsel, will point out the practice of the ICC Court to the members of the Court at each session. **Ann–37**

Prior to the commencement of any discussion of those matters set out below, any member of the ICC Court who is involved in the arbitration or may have some interest in the matter will be invited to leave the room in which the Committee Session takes place. That member will not have received any information of that case in the binder provided to the members attending the ICC Court sessions. **Ann–38**

Ann–39 With respect to various matters referred to below, the Secretariat will always provide a report. In addition to the specific information relating to the type of decision to be taken, the Secretariat's reports will generally include the information mentioned at para.Ann–5 above.

Ann–40 The Secretariat records the decision at the Committee Session and notifies it promptly, generally no later than within one or two working days to the parties involved in the arbitration. No reasons are provided for the decision either in the letter of notification or at any other time.

B.1 Article 6(4): Effect of the Arbitration Agreement (Jurisdictional Objections)

Ann–41 Jurisdictional objections per Art.6(4) are almost invariably submitted to a Committee Session of the ICC Court if the Secretary General refers the matter to the ICC Court under Art.6(3).

Ann–42 Jurisdictional objections arise generally in three ways. The Respondent(s) may raise the objection prior to the constitution of the Tribunal (usually in their Answer). The Secretariat or the ICC Court may raise the issue if there is a non-participating Respondent(s) where there is concern that the ICC Court should decide whether it is satisfied that an arbitration agreement "may exist" so that the arbitration may proceed. The Secretariat may also raise the issue if the Respondent(s) does not file its Answer in time under Art.5(1), in which case the ICC Court will once again be invited to consider whether an arbitration agreement "may exist" so that the arbitration may proceed.

Ann–43 The Secretariat will submit to the ICC Court the key relevant documents. The parties are generally not informed of the documents that are submitted to the Committee Sessions. The documents submitted with the objection will vary from case to case. In one recent case, the documents with respect to an Art.6(4) decision were as follows:

(1) extracts of the agreement between the parties containing the arbitration clause and the signature page thereto;

(2) correspondence between counsel for the Claimant and the Secretariat setting out the Claimant's submissions on jurisdiction;

(3) correspondence between counsel for some but not all Respondents and the Secretariat regarding their submissions on the jurisdictional objection, together with supporting evidence;

(4) a further submission of the Claimant to the ICC Court;

(5) copies of specific articles of a separate agreement between some of but not all the parties to the arbitration.

Ann–44 At the Committee Session, the counsel at the Secretariat provides any update that may be appropriate with respect to the positions of the parties. Then there is generally a discussion of the jurisdictional objection amongst the Committee members as to the merits of the objection.

The parties are notified of the decision as described above. In addition, the Secretariat notifies the Tribunal of the ICC Court's decision when the Tribunal is constituted, and will confirm that such decision by the ICC Court is administrative in nature only, and that the Tribunal is required to make a substantive finding of the jurisdictional objection in an Award. **Ann–45**

If the ICC Court accepts the jurisdictional objection, the decision is still notified to the party against whom the arbitration will no longer proceed. It is at that party's discretion to elect whether to remain a non-participating party to the arbitration or not. **Ann–46**

B.2 Articles 6(4): Joinder of parties

The addition of parties may arise pursuant to Art.4 (at the request of the Claimant) or Art.5 (at the request of the Respondent) or under Art.7. In each case, there may be an issue as to the scope of the agreement to arbitrate under Art.6. **Ann–47**

As discussed under Art.7, there is now a provision in the Rules expressly permitting, under certain conditions, the joinder of additional parties. However, the conditions set forth in that article must be met. **Ann–48**

The Secretariat will submit to the ICC Court the key relevant documents. The documents submitted with the objection will vary from case to case. In one recent case, the documents with respect to an Art.6(4) decision were as follows: **Ann–49**

(1) copy of the section of the Respondents' counterclaim seeking the joinder of the third party;

(2) copy of the section of the agreement showing the parties to the agreement and the signature page thereto;

(3) copy of the section of the agreement setting out the guarantee provisions of the agreement between the parties to the arbitration and the third party, being the party which the Respondent seeks to join to the arbitration.

The Secretariat notifies the Tribunal of the ICC Court's decision when the Tribunal is constituted. With respect to the ICC Court's determination of the jurisdictional objection, the Secretariat will confirm that such decision is administrative in nature only, and that the Tribunal is required to make a substantive finding of the jurisdictional objection in an Award. **Ann–50**

B.3 Article 12: Number of Arbitrators

The issue of the number of arbitrators is usually raised by the parties in the Request and Answer. Where the parties differ as to whether there should be one or three arbitrators, the ICC Court will decide the issue in accordance with Art.12. **Ann–51**

The Secretariat will provide the ICC Court with comments on the background and apparent complexity of the dispute as well as the comments of the parties. **Ann–52**

If the Secretariat recommends a three-member Tribunal, it will generally recommend setting a time limit for the two co-arbitrators or the parties to agree on a President. If the Secretariat recommends that the matter be submitted to a sole **Ann–53** arbitrator, it will recommend also that a National Committee or Group be consulted should the parties fail to agree on the sole arbitrator.

Ann–54 When the ICC Court confirms the co-arbitrators, the Secretariat will also recommend, as a "fall-back position", a National Committee or Group to be consulted with respect to the appointment of a President in accordance with Art.13(3) if the co- arbitrators or the parties do not agree on a nomination.

Ann–55 The ICC Court will review the issue of the appropriate National Committee or Group particularly with regard to the place of arbitration, nationality of the parties, the language of the arbitration and complexity of the dispute.

Ann–56 The ICC Court members will wish to be satisfied that the National Committee or Group will propose a person who is appropriate for this particular arbitration. Therefore, in choosing the National Committee the track record of that National Committee and their approach to the proposal of arbitrators will be a material factor that will be taken into account.

Ann–57 Once the National Committee or Group has been chosen, then the initial contact will be between the Secretariat and the National Committee, although the decision whether or not to confirm the proposed sole arbitrator or President will be made by the ICC Court at another Committee Session.

Ann–58 The ICC Court usually decides at the same time as the number of arbitrators the advance on costs for the arbitration pursuant to Art.36.

B.4 Article 13: Appointment and Confirmation of the Arbitrators

Ann–59 Arbitrators are "appointed" by the ICC Court generally upon "proposal" of a National Committee or Group pursuant to Art.13 (and in 2012 in 15 per cent of the cases on direct proposal of the ICC Court). Arbitrators are "confirmed" by the ICC Court if they are "nominated" by the parties.

Ann–60 With respect to persons proposed by a National Committee or Group, the ICC Court will consider whether the person is appropriate for the arbitration. In addition, as discussed under Art.13(4), the ICC Court has the right in certain circumstances to make direct appointments without going through National Committees or Groups. There is no formal list of potential direct appointees by the Court.

Ann–61 The curriculum vitae of the arbitrator(s) considered for appointment/confirmation and any statement of qualification given by the arbitrator(s) are provided to the ICC Court.

Appointment Upon the Proposal of a National Committee

Ann–62 Pursuant to Art.13, an arbitrator may be proposed by a National Committee or Group where either the ICC Court is to appoint the President or sole arbitrator, or to appoint an arbitrator on behalf of a party which has failed to nominate one.

Ann–63 Generally, the ICC Court did not appoint arbitrators who are proposed by National Committees or Groups who file a qualified statement of independence. However, the practice has evolved and limited qualifications are now accepted.

Ann–64 With regard to other proposals, the Committee will review whether the person proposed is suitable for the arbitration. The decision whether to appoint an arbitrator nominated by a National Committee or Group is made by the ICC Court members composing the Committee and not by the Secretariat.

Where the parties have nominated their respective arbitrators (usually in the Request and Answer), the Secretariat will forward to the nominated person a blank Statement of Independence and curriculum vitae, requesting the person to complete each form and return it to the Secretariat. (For an example see Pt II Documents 7.1 and 7.2). **Ann–65**

If a proposal is to be made by a National Committee or Group, then the Secretariat will forward to the National Committee a copy of the blank Statement of Independence, the curriculum vitae and a document setting out the general characteristics of the dispute (including the names of the parties, the names of the counsel, the amount in dispute, the characteristics of the dispute, the place of arbitration and any specific issues which the arbitration requires, e.g. the language of the arbitration to be other than that of the language of the country of the National Committee or Group). **Ann–66**

Once the above documents are returned to the Secretariat, the completed documents are then provided to the ICC Court, which then determines whether to confirm or, as the case may be, appoint the arbitrator(s). **Ann–67**

Thereafter, the Secretariat informs the parties and the arbitrators (whether confirmed/appointed or not) of the ICC Court's decision, without providing reasons for the decision. **Ann–68**

Appointment made by the President of the ICC Court

Some arbitration clauses provide for the President of the ICC Court to propose and appoint the Chairman, or sole arbitrator to an arbitration. **Ann–69**

Although not specifically provided for in the Rules, the practice of the ICC Court is to receive the appointment from the President of the ICC Court, and then to confirm such appointment. **Ann–70**

B.5 Article 15: Replacement of Arbitrators

If replacement proceedings are brought before the ICC Court due to (i) the death of the arbitrator; (ii) the acceptance by the ICC Court of the arbitrator's resignation; (iii) the acceptance by the ICC Court of a challenge; or (iv) upon the request of all the parties under Art.15(1), then the replacement proceedings are brought before and decided at the Committee Session of the ICC Court. **Ann–71**

Where replacement proceedings are brought on the ICC Court's own initiative under Art.15(2), the proceedings are first brought before the ICC Court at its Committee Session, where the ICC Court considers whether or not to initiate a removal procedure against the arbitrator(s). **Ann–72**

If the Committee Session of the ICC Court decides that removal proceedings should be initiated against the arbitrator(s), then the matter is referred to the Plenary Session of the ICC Court to decide whether to remove the arbitrator(s) in accordance with Art.15(3). **Ann–73**

Pursuant to Art.15(4), if the ICC Court decides to replace the arbitrator(s) then it is in its discretion as to whether to "follow the original nominating process". This decision is usually made at the same time as when the ICC Court is deciding to replace the arbitrator at its Committee Session. **Ann–74**

Ann–75 It is common for the ICC Court to seek to follow the original nominating process of the parties unless the parties request otherwise. This is in line with the overall purpose of the Rules to grant autonomy to the parties to determine certain aspects of the procedure that the Tribunal or the ICC Court is not obliged to decide. The ICC Court also usually fixes the fees of the arbitrator when deciding to replace the arbitrator.

B.6 Article 18: Place of the Arbitration

Ann–76 Where the ICC Court is to determine the place of Arbitration under Art.18, it takes into consideration various factors, including the nationality of the parties; the law of the arbitration, if agreed, or where not agreed, the law governing the agreement between the parties and the location of counsel; and the amount in dispute. The Secretariat's report sets out the relevant factors and frequently provides a recommendation based on ICC Court practice discussed under Art.18.

Ann–77 Once the Tribunal is constituted, the Secretariat informs the Tribunal of the ICC Court's decision to fix the place of arbitration. It usually includes the comments of the parties, if any, with respect to their selection of the place of arbitration.

B.7 Article 23: Terms of Reference; Procedural Timetable

Ann–78 There are two situations with respect to Terms of Reference. If the Terms of Reference are signed by the parties and the members of the Tribunal, they are "transmitted" to the ICC Court pursuant to Art.23(2).

Ann–79 If the Terms of Reference are not signed by all the parties, they are "submitted" to the ICC Court for approval in accordance with Art.23(3). In either case, the Tribunal will be expected to transmit the Procedural Timetable to be established in accordance with Art.24(2).

Ann–80 With respect to approval of the Terms of Reference, the issue for the Secretariat and the ICC Court is whether there is a legitimate reason for the party to refuse to sign the Terms of Reference. This could be the case where, for example, the Terms of Reference seek to record an agreement on a procedural or substantive point, with which a party disagrees.

Ann–81 Once the Terms of Reference are approved by the ICC Court in accordance with Art.23(3), the arbitration may proceed.

B.8 Article 33: Scrutiny of the Draft Award by the Court

Ann–82 As discussed with respect to Plenary Sessions, in certain circumstances, draft Awards are scrutinised at Committee Sessions. The issues with respect to scrutiny are the same and reference is made to the documents that are submitted to the Plenary Sessions with respect to scrutiny of draft Awards.

Ann–83 The major difference is that, instead of having a report from a member of the ICC Court, all Committee members will have reviewed and made notes on the draft Award to discuss it at the Committee Session. As with Awards scrutinised in Plenary Sessions, the members of the Secretariat will usually submit comments on the draft Award.

B.9 Article 35: Correction and Interpretation of the Award

The correction and interpretation of an Award goes through the standard scrutiny process for Awards. It must "state the reasons upon which it is based" (Art.31(2)). The notification procedures which apply to Awards also apply to the "Addendum", as well as to the "Decision". **Ann–84**

The draft Addendum or Decision is submitted to the ICC Court. The Secretariat provides a report on it and may provide a recommendation as to whether the draft Addendum should be approved or not. The Secretariat will also comment on issues such as whether (i) the contents of the draft Addendum; and (ii) whether the application was filed timely, and whether this is set out in the draft Addendum. **Ann–85**

The Tribunal is required to submit the draft Addendum "not later than 30 days following the expiration of the time limit for the receipt of any comments from the other party or within such other period as the Court may decide". **Ann–86**

The ICC Court may therefore extend this time limit. This is generally done upon application by the Secretariat to the ICC Court, by submission of a report. The report usually contains a suggested date for the extension to expire. **Ann–87**

The ICC Court's decision regarding draft Addendums is notified to the Tribunal by the Secretariat in the same manner that it notifies the ICC Court's decisions on draft Awards. The ICC Court's comments are set out in a letter to the Tribunal, which is usually sent no later than one to two days following the ICC Court session. **Ann–88**

Once the Secretariat receives the signed and dated Addendum, it verifies that any amendments which were to be made in accordance with Art.33 have been made. If that is the case, the Secretariat then notifies the Addendum to the parties. **Ann–89**

B.10 Article 36(3): Separate Advances on Costs

Separate advances on costs usually arise in two ways. Either one of or more than one of the parties to the arbitration requests separate advances on costs, or the parties have failed to pay the advance on costs as fixed by the ICC Court, so the ICC Court may fix separate advances on its own motion. **Ann–90**

Prior to seeking the ICC Court's determination on this matter, the Secretariat informs the parties of the consequences of fixing separate advances on costs and in particular that this can result in a higher total amount of the two deposits taken together. This higher amount results from the fact that the scales for advances on costs are graduated. **Ann–91**

If the parties request separate advances on costs, then the ICC Court is requested to decide whether there should be separate advances on costs. **Ann–92**

The Secretariat reports to the ICC Court on the financial aspect of the arbitration under the advance of costs set by the ICC Court, and the new financial aspect should the ICC Court decide that separate advances on costs are appropriate. **Ann–93**

B.11 Article 36(6): Claims Considered Withdrawn due to Non-Payment of Advance on Costs

Article 36(6) concerns the procedure for dealing with parties who do not pay the advance on costs. In practice, the procedure is as follows: **Ann–94**

(1) Once the ICC Court has fixed the advance on costs in accordance with Art.36(2) or 36(4), the Secretariat notifies the ICC Court's decision to the parties and requests payment within a specified time limit, usually 30 days.

(2) The parties are free to request an extension of this time limit, within reason, and the Secretariat is able to grant such extension in its discretion.

(3) However, if that payment is not made, either after the initial time limit or subsequent extension(s) have expired, then the Secretariat is required to "consult" with respect to the non-payment with the Tribunal. This usually involves the counsel at the Secretariat contacting the sole arbitrator or President and discussing the non-payment, as well as informing the Tribunal that it is considering invoking Art.36(6). The discussion is also aimed at obtaining the Tribunal's views on the issue.

(4) Thereafter, if the Secretariat considers it appropriate, the Secretary General "directs" the Tribunal to "suspend its work and set a time limit, which must be not less than 15 days, on the expiry of which the relevant claims, or counterclaims, shall be considered as withdrawn". This is usually done by letter from the Secretary General to the parties informing them of the time limit within which payment must be made. The time limit to pay the advance on costs is therefore set by the Secretary General. A separate letter is also sent to the Tribunal directing it to suspend its work.

(5) Alternatively, pursuant to Art.36(5), either party is able to "pay any other party's share of any advance on costs should such other party fail to pay its share." If this occurs, then the suspension is lifted and the arbitration may proceed.

(6) Article 36(6) does provide for recourse against the procedure of claims being considered withdrawn. The party whose claims are to be considered withdrawn may, within the time limit set to make payment, instead request that the matter of withdrawal of its claims be decided by the ICC Court. If such a request is made, then the ICC Court decides whether the initial time limit as set by the Secretary General still applies, and accordingly whether the claims or counterclaims are considered withdrawn.

(7) If the ICC Court does not accept the withdrawal of the claims or counterclaims, then it also decides a final time limit within which the parties are to make payment. Failure to pay within this time limit results in the claims being considered withdrawn.

(8) The effect of making a request to the ICC Court is that it usually extends the time limit within which payment must be made.

(9) If the claims or counterclaims are considered withdrawn from the proceedings, then this does not prevent the same claims from being brought again, although they must be done "at a later date in another proceeding".

If the ICC Court decides that the claims or counterclaims are not considered withdrawn pursuant to the Secretary General's letter, then the Secretariat will also notify the parties of the ICC Court's decision to grant the party/parties a further time limit within which to make payment. It will also usually state that failure to pay within this new time limit will render the claims and or counterclaims as being considered withdrawn. **Ann–95**

B.12 Reconsideration of a Decision

The ICC Court is able to reconsider any of its decisions. This is done either (i) when a direct request is made by either the parties or the Tribunal to the Secretariat to have the ICC Court reconsider its decision; or (ii) when a request is made by the Secretariat to the ICC Court. **Ann–96**

When a request is made by the Secretariat to the ICC Court, this is usually done as the initial decision taken by the ICC Court is no longer appropriate in the circumstances following the decision. In this case, a request will be made to the ICC Court only when necessary; that is, the Secretariat is unable to amend the decision at its own discretion as the Rules specifically require such issue be decided by the ICC Court: **Ann–97**

(1) the amount of the advance on costs, and increases or decreases thereto;

(2) the amount of each separate amount for the separate advances on costs, and increases or decreases thereto;

(3) the amount of the fees of the Tribunal as fixed by the ICC Court.

The ICC Court usually only reconsiders its decision if material new elements are presented by the parties or the Tribunal. **Ann–98**

B.13 Extensions of Time Limits

The ICC Court grants extensions with respect to the time to sign the Terms of Reference (under Art.23) and the time to render an Award (under Art.30). The ICC Court's practice is generally now to review the extensions in the light of the procedural timetable to determine whether the extension is justified and for how long. The extensions are therefore tied to the circumstances of the case. However, in some instances, the Secretariat still issues extensions for a time period that is far shorter than the period that the parties and the Tribunal have set themselves in the procedural timetable. In such a case, a further extension can be requested and will almost invariably be granted. **Ann–99**

PART II

II. Models, Precedents and Examples

A. List of Models, Precedents and Examples

Document 1	Standard ICC Arbitration Clauses
Document 2	List of addresses for notification of the Request
Document 3	Secretariat's Letter Notifying the Request for Arbitration to the Respondent
Document 4	Request for additional time and details of arbitrator (art.5 of the Rules)
Document 5	Secretariat's Notification of the Answer
Document 6	Notification from Secretariat of ICC Court Decision setting in Motion Arbitration
Document 7	Notification from Secretariat to the Claimant's nominee as Arbitrator
Document 7.1	ICC Arbitrator's Statement of Acceptance, Availability, Impartiality and Independence (art.11 of the Rules)
Document 7.2	ICC Model Curriculum vitae for Arbitrators
Document 7.3	Secretariat's Case Information Summary
Document 7.4	Financial Table
Document 8.1	Transmittal of Statement of Acceptance, Availability, Impartiality and Independence and curriculum vitae of Claimant's nominee to Respondent when the nominee provided an unqualified statement of independence
Document 8.2	Transmittal of Statement of Acceptance, Availability, Impartiality and Independence and curriculum vitae of Claimant's nominee to Respondent when the nominee provided a qualified statement of independence
Document 9.1	Notification from Secretariat to Respondent to Propose an Arbitrator
Document 9.2	Respondent's nomination of an Arbitrator and comments on the qualified statement of independence of Claimant's nominee
Document 10.1	Secretariat's Notification of Confirmation of the Two Co-arbitrators
Document 10.2	Secretariat's Notification of Confirmation of the Two Co-arbitrators by the Secretary General
Document 11	Secretariat's Notification of Appointment of the President of the Arbitral Tribunal by the Court
Document 12	Secretariat's Transmittal of the File to the Tribunal (art.18 of the Rules)
Document 12.1	ICC Notice to Arbitrators on Personal and Arbitral Tribunal Expenses (September 2013)
Document 12.2	Explanatory Note By The President Of The Court On *Per Diem* Allowances To All Serving Arbitrators And To All Newly Constituted Tribunals
Document 12.3	ICC Note Concerning the Appointment of Administrative Secretaries by Arbitral Tribunals

B. Introduction regarding Models, Precedents and Examples

1. There is no procedural code for ICC arbitration. The basic principle is that the parties are free to structure their case within the overall framework of the Rules and applicable law. However, in part because of this freedom, it is sometimes of assistance to review the types of documents that are usually produced in connection with an ICC arbitration. Set out below is an overall view of the types of documents produced in an ICC arbitration.

2. The Secretariat, the parties and the members of the Tribunal prepare the documents referred to below. The ICC Court does not itself send documents to the parties or the Tribunal. The ICC Court communicates with the parties and the Tribunal through the Secretariat.

3. Set out below is a procedural outline for an arbitration in which particular issues arise, such as the challenge on jurisdiction. However, the variety of issues that can arise in an ICC arbitration is almost unlimited. With regard to the precedents themselves, in some instances the documents are reproduced in their entirety and in some instances only extracts are reproduced due to limitations of space. In each instance, the language is that taken from the precedents and is to be adapted to the situation and the preferences of each practitioner.

4. The authors have included examples of letters issued by the Secretariat based on a review of their own files with respect to ICC arbitration to prepare counsel for the types of letters that have in the past been used in the context of ICC arbitration. However, the Secretarial adapts its letters to the circumstances of each case and the practice of the Secretarial evolves over time. Therefore, these letters serve as illustrations of the types of letters that may be issued and counsel should be prepared for variations in the approach by the Secretariat.

Pre-dispute documents

(1) *Arbitration Agreement.* (Document 1) The basic element in any ICC arbitration is the agreement to arbitrate. Set out examples of clauses.

(2) *Pre-arbitration dispute resolution documents.* (Not reproduced) The arbitration agreement requires the parties to seek to settle the dispute prior to going to

arbitration. The attempts to settle the dispute may take various forms. However, one of the key issues is whether the documents created in that connection are privileged or not. As discussed under art.25, the issue of privilege is a thorny one and the party who intends to rely on privilege with respect to a document should clearly indicate that it is privileged on its face.

Commencement of the dispute

(3) *Request for Arbitration.* (Not reproduced) The Request for Arbitration not only initiates the proceedings. The Request also contains the nomination of the co-arbitrator for the Claimant. If the Claimant wishes to proceed quickly, and the arbitration agreement does not set out the number of arbitrators, the Claimant may seek to have the dispute settled by a sole arbitrator. Document 2 sets out the addresses at which a Request may be filed.

(4) *Letter of Notification of the Request to the Respondent.* (Document 3) This is a standard letter from the ICC Secretariat notifying the Respondent of the Request and stating the time to submit the Answer.

(5) *Respondent's Letter Requesting Extension.* (Document 4) As discussed in Pt I para.5–1, the Respondent frequently requests an extension to file the Answer. In many instances, the Claimant will consent to the extension provided that it is of limited duration.

(6) *Secretariat's letter granting or not the extension.* (Not reproduced) As discussed in Pt I para.5–42, the Secretariat grants these requests for extension but requires comments from the Respondent on the number of arbitrators.

(7) *Answer to the Request for Arbitration.* (Not reproduced) The Answer contains may be a full answer or a jurisdictional objection. There may be a counterclaim.

(8) *Secretariat's Notification of the Answer.* (Document 5) The Secretariat notifies the Claimant of the Answer and the jurisdictional objection and provides a limit time (frequently 10 days) for comments on the jurisdictional issue. These comments are submitted to the ICC Court to permit it to take a decision under art.6(4) as to whether there is a prima facie case that jurisdiction may exist.

(9) *Request for Joinder.* (Not Reproduced). Where a party wishes to file a claim against an additional party, it must file a Request for Joinder (art.7)

(10) *Secretariat's Notification of the Decisions of the ICC Court.* (Document 6) These decisions frequently deal with (i) whether there is a prima facie case that there may be jurisdiction; (ii) the number of arbitrators; and (iii) the amount of the advance on costs. No reasons are provided for the decision.

Constitution of the Tribunal

(If there is no agreement as to three arbitrators, then there will usually be further correspondence regarding the issue. In addition, there is often jurisdictional correspondence where a party is seeking an art.6(4) decision.)

(11) *Claimant's Nomination of an Arbitrator.* (Not reproduced) In the Request, the Claimant usually nominates an arbitrator as is discussed at para.4–56. If the Claimant has sought to have the matter heard by a sole arbitrator, then the Claimant would not nominate an arbitrator. If the ICC Court then decides that there should be three arbitrators, the Claimant will be invited to nominate an arbitrator within a limited period of time (usually ten days). Respondent will be invited afterwards to nominate an arbitrator within the same time limit once Claimant's appointment of an arbitrator has been made.

(12) *Notification from Secretariat to the Claimant's Nominee as Arbitrator*. (Document 7) This invitation is accompanied by a request that the nominee complete (i) the Statement of Acceptance, Availability, Impartiality and Independence (Document 7.1); (ii) *Curriculum Vitae* (Document 7.2).

(13) *Transmittal of Statement of Acceptance, Availability, Impartiality and Independence*. (Document 8) The Respondent is provided with a limited time period to make any comments (usually seven days) if Claimant's proposed arbitrator has submitted a "qualified" Declaration of Independence.

(14) *Notification from Secretariat to Respondent to Propose an Arbitrator*. (Document 9) The Secretariat invites the Respondent to provide comments if any within a short period (usually seven days).

(15) *Respondent's Nomination of an Arbitrator*. (Not reproduced) This would be similar to the Claimant's nomination, with a reservation as to jurisdiction, if that is the case.

(16) *Notification from Secretariat to the Respondent's Nominee as Arbitrator*. (Not reproduced) This invitation is accompanied by a request that the nominee complete (i) the Declaration of Acceptance and Statement of Independence; (ii) *Curriculum Vitae*. This would be the same as the notification to the Claimant's nominee.

(17) *Transmittal of Declaration of Independence and Curriculum Vitae of Respondent's Nominee to Claimant*. (Not reproduced) The Secretariat invites the Claimant to provide comments if any within a short period (usually seven days). This would be the same as the notification relating to the Claimant's nominee.

(18) *Secretariat's Notification of Confirmation of the Two Co-arbitrators*. (Document 10) This notification sets a time limit for agreement on the chairman. As indicated in the text of the letter, the Secretariat usually writes to the co-arbitrators separately setting out the requirements and information to be provided to the potential President and transmits a copy of the Request and Answer to provide background information regarding the dispute and potential conflicts.

(19) *Secretariat's Notification of Designation of President*. (Document 11) If the parties or the co-arbitrators (depending on the nomination process) have agreed on the chairman, then the President is confirmed by the ICC Court or the Secretary General. (Document 11.1) If the parties have not agreed on the chairman, then the President is appointed by the ICC Court. (Document 11) If appointed by the ICC Court, the Secretariat's letter will indicate the National Committee or Group that proposed the president if not a direct appointment.

(20) *Secretariat's Reminder of the Parties to Pay the Balance of the Advance on Costs*. (Not reproduced) The Secretariat will not transmit the file to the Tribunal until the advance on costs has been paid and may use the procedure provided for under art.35(4) of the Rules.

(21) *Secretariat's Transmittal of the File to the Tribunal*. (Document 12) This notification includes (i) ICC Note on Expenses (Document 12.1); (ii) the Rules,; (iii) the *Curriculum Vitae* of the arbitrators; (iv) ICC Note concerning the Appointment of Administrative Secretaries (Document 12.2); (v) ICC Note on VAT, Taxes and Charges applicable to the Arbitrators' fees (Document 12.3).

Tribunal's Establishment of the Terms of Reference and the Procedure

(22) *Notification by the Tribunal to the Parties regarding the Case Management Conference and Invitation to Comment on the Claims.* (Document 13) Many Tribunals invite the parties to provide a summary description of their claims. Attached to this letter is an extract of the ICC Commission Report on Saving Time and Costs (2nd edition) regarding the Case Management Conference.

(23) *Transmittal of Points for Consideration for the Procedure.* (Document 14) As discussed in Pt I art.24, the Tribunal is required to establish a Procedural Timetable when or immediately after it establishes the Terms of Reference. To establish the Procedural Timetable, the Tribunal should have a precise idea of the procedure to be followed. Many Tribunals therefore invite the parties to comment on the procedure by transmitting a list of points for consideration.

(24) *Terms of Reference.* (Document 15) The draft provided includes a confidentiality provision. This provision goes beyond the Rules, although under applicable law, similar principles may be applicable.

(25) *Procedural Timetable.* (Document 16)

(26) *Procedural Order No 1.* (Hearing on Jurisdiction) (Document 17) In many instances, the jurisdictional issue will be heard prior to other issues.

(27) *Summary Minutes of Hearing.* (Document 18)

(28) *Partial Award on Jurisdiction.* (Not reproduced) Some practitioners refer to an Award on jurisdiction as an interim Award as the final decision belongs to the national courts. Note that to finally decide jurisdiction there should be an Award that is scrutinised by the ICC Court.

(29) *Secretariat's Reminder of the Parties to Pay the Balance of the Advance on Costs.* (Not reproduced) The Secretariat is attentive to the development of the proceedings and seeks to ensure that there are enough funds available to cover the costs of the arbitration. When it becomes apparent that this is not the case, the ICC Court will reconsider the advance on costs and the Secretariat will notify the parties of the ICC Court's decision. Should the parties not pay, they will get a letter from the Secretariat reminding them to pay the advance on costs.

Hearings on the Merits and Award

(30) *Procedural Order No.2 (regarding the hearing on the merits).* (Document 19)

(31) *List of Attendance.* (Document 20) The hearing is confidential. Therefore, on a daily basis, the President should ensure that a list of attendees is prepared.

(32) *Power of Attorney.* (Document 21) This is usually provided prior to the hearings in accordance with art.17.

(32) *Letter closing the proceedings and indicating an expected date for submitting the Award to the ICC Court for scrutiny* (art.27). (Document 22)

(33) *Letter extending the date to render the Award.* This document does not necessarily indicate when the Award will be rendered, as it is intended to extend the time limit under art.30 and to encourage the Tribunal to issue the Award promptly (Document 23)

(33) *Checklist for the Award.* (Document 24)

(34) *Final Award.* (Not reproduced) The example provided is a very brief Award. In many instances, Tribunals will set out in much greater detail the positions of the parties.

(35) *Secretariat's Notification of the Award to the Parties.* (Not reproduced) When the Award has been scrutinised by the Court in accordance with art.33 of the Rules and signed by the Arbitral Tribunal, it will then be notified to the parties in accordance with art.34 of the Rules.

(36) *ICC Note on Correction of Awards.* (Not reproduced) As discussed under art.35 Tribunal may prepare an Addendum (where a correction to the Award is made) or a Decision (where it declines to make a correction to the Award.

DOCUMENT 1

STANDARD ICC ARBITRATION CLAUSES

Below are standard and suggested clauses for use by parties who wish to have recourse to ICC arbitration and/or ICC ADR under the foregoing Rules.

Arbitration

All disputes arising out of or in connection with the present contract shall be finally settled under the Rules of Arbitration of the International Chamber of Commerce by one or more arbitrators appointed in accordance with the said Rules.

Arbitration without emergency arbitrator

All disputes arising out of or in connection with the present contract shall be finally settled under the Rules of Arbitration of the International Chamber of Commerce by one or more arbitrators appointed in accordance with the said Rules. The Emergency Arbitrator Provisions shall not apply.

Optional ADR

The parties may at any time, without prejudice to any other proceedings, seek to settle any dispute arising out of or in connection with the present contract in accordance with the ICC ADR Rules.

Obligation to consider ADR

In the event of any dispute arising out of or in connection with the present contract, the parties agree in the first instance to discuss and consider submitting the matter to settlement proceedings under the ICC ADR Rules.

Obligation to submit dispute to ADR with an automatic expiration mechanism

In the event of any dispute arising out of or in connection with the present contract, the parties agree to submit the matter to settlement proceedings under the ICC ADR Rules. If the dispute has not been settled pursuant to the said Rules within 45 days following the filing of a Request for ADR or within such other period as the parties may agree in writing, the parties shall have no further obligations under this paragraph.

Obligation to submit dispute to ADR, followed by arbitration if required

In the event of any dispute arising out of or in connection with the present contract, the parties agree to submit the matter to settlement proceedings under the ICC ADR Rules. If the dispute has not been settled pursuant to the said Rules within 45 days following the filing of a Request for ADR or within such other period as the parties may agree in writing, such dispute shall be finally settled under the Rules of Arbitration of the International Chamber of Commerce by one or more arbitrators appointed in accordance with the said Rules of Arbitration.

How to use these clauses

Parties wishing to use ICC arbitration and/or ICC ADR should choose one of the above clauses, which cover different situations and needs.

If the parties do not want the Emergency Arbitrator Provisions to apply, they must expressly opt out by using the second of the two arbitration clauses.

Parties are free to adapt the chosen clause to their particular circumstances. For instance, when providing for arbitration, they may wish to stipulate the number of arbitrators, given that the Rules of Arbitration contain a presumption in favour of a sole arbitrator. They may also wish to stipulate the language and place of the arbitration and the law applicable to the merits. When providing for ADR, they may wish to specify the settlement technique to be applied, failing which mediation, the default mechanism, will be used.

The last clause above is a two-tiered clause providing for ADR followed by arbitration. Other combinations of services are also possible. Combined and multi-tiered dispute resolution clauses may help to facilitate dispute management. However, it is also possible for parties to file requests under the ICC ADR Rules or the ICC Rules for Expertise at any time, even after a dispute has arisen or in the course of other dispute resolution proceedings.

At all times, care must be taken to avoid any risk of ambiguity in the drafting of the clause. Unclear wording causes uncertainty and delay and can hinder or even compromise the dispute resolution process.

When incorporating any of the above clauses in their contracts, parties are advised to take account of any factors that may affect their enforceability under applicable law. For instance, they should have regard to any mandatory requirements at the place of arbitration and the place of enforcement.

Translations of the above clauses and clauses providing for other procedures and combinations of procedures can be found at <www.iccarbitration.org>.

DOCUMENT 2

LIST OF ADDRESSES FOR NOTIFICATION OF THE REQUEST

The Secretariat of the International Court of Arbitration
International Chamber of Commerce
Headquarters
33–43 avenue du Président Wilson
75116 Paris
France

Tel.: +33 1 49 53 28 78

Fax: +33 1 49 53 29 33

Email: arb@iccwbo.org

or

Secretariat of the ICC International Court of Arbitration – Asia Office
Suite 2, 12/F, Fairmont House
8 Cotton Tree Drive
Central
Hong Kong

Tel.: +852 3607 5601

Fax: +852 2523 1619

Email: ica8@iccwbo.org

International Chamber of Commence (ICC) ICC International Court of Arbitration
Sicana Inc.
1212, Avenue of the Americas
New York
NY 10036
United States

Tel.: 1 646 699 5704

Fax: 1 212 221 1295

Email: ica9@iccwbo.org

DOCUMENT 3

SECRETARIAT'S LETTER NOTIFYING THE REQUEST FOR ARBITRATION TO THE RESPONDENT

Dear Mesdames, Dear Sirs,

The Secretariat of the International Court of Arbitration of the International Chamber of Commerce ("Secretariat") notifies you that, on [•] 2012, it received a Request for Arbitration ("Request") from [•] represented by [•],[•] and [•] that names you as Respondent.

Pursuant to Article 4(2) of the ICC Rules of Arbitration ("Rules"), this arbitration commenced on that date.

The caption and reference of this arbitration are indicated above. Please include the reference [•] in all future correspondence.

In all future correspondence, any capitalised term not otherwise defined will have the meaning ascribed to it in the Rules and references to Articles of the Rules generally will appear as: "(Article ***)".

We enclose a copy of the Request and the documents annexed thereto (Article 4(5)).

Answer to the Request

Your Answer to the Request ("Answer") is due within 30 days from the day following your receipt of this correspondence (Article 5(1)).

Please send us [•] copies of your Answer.

You may apply for an extension of time for submitting your Answer by providing your comments on the number of arbitrators and, where appropriate, nominating an arbitrator (Article 5(2)). Such information will enable the International Court of Arbitration of the International Chamber of Commerce ("Court") to take steps towards the constitution of the Arbitral Tribunal.

If any of the parties refuses or fails to take part in the arbitration or any stage thereof, the arbitration will proceed notwithstanding such refusal or failure (Article 6(8)).

Joinder of Additional Parties

No additional party may be joined to this arbitration after the confirmation or appointment of any arbitrator, unless all parties including the additional party otherwise agree (Article 7(1)). Therefore, if you intend to join an additional party and seek an extension of time for submitting your Answer, please inform us in your application for such extension.

Constitution of the Arbitral Tribunal

The arbitration agreement provides for three arbitrators. Claimant has nominated [•] as co-arbitrator

You are required to nominate a co-arbitrator in your Answer or in any request for an extension of time for submitting your Answer (Article 12(4)). If you fail to nominate an arbitrator within **30 days** from the day following your receipt of this correspondence, the Court will appoint an arbitrator on your behalf (Article 12(4)).

We will invite the prospective arbitrator to complete a Statement of Acceptance, Availability, Impartiality and Independence, which we will send to all parties.

Claimant has proposed that the President be nominated by the co-arbitrators, within a time limit of 30 days following their confirmation.

Respondent is invited to give its comments on Claimant's proposal within **30 days** from the day following your receipt of this correspondence. Failing the parties' agreement on the procedure for the appointment of the President, the latter will be appointed by the Court (Article 12(5)).

Place of Arbitration

The arbitration agreement provides for London, England as the place of arbitration.

Language of Arbitration

The arbitration agreement provides for English as the language of arbitration.

Claimant proposes that the parties be authorised to submit documents drafted in the French language without a translation into English. This issue will be decided by the Arbitral Tribunal once constituted.

Representation

If you are represented by counsel, please provide the relevant contact details.

Communication with the Secretariat

Please provide your fax number/s and email address/es, as we may transmit correspondence by fax or email.

Efficient Conduct of the Arbitration

The Rules require the parties and the Arbitral Tribunal to make every effort to conduct the arbitration in an expeditious and cost-effective manner having regard to the complexity and value of the dispute (Article 22(1)).

In making decisions as to costs, the Arbitral Tribunal may take into account such circumstances as it considers relevant, including the extent to which each party has conducted the arbitration in an expeditious and cost effective manner (Article 37(5)).

Amicable Settlement

Parties are free to settle their dispute amicably at any time during an arbitration. The parties may wish to consider conducting an amicable dispute resolution procedure pursuant to the ICC ADR Rules. These Rules provide for a wide range of amicable settlement procedures including mediation. ICC can also assist the parties in finding a suitable mediator. Further information is available from the ICC International Centre for ADR at +33 1 49 53 30 53 or adr@iccwbo.org or www .iccadr.org.

Your Case Management Team

[•]

Finally, please find enclosed a note from the Court's Secretary General that highlights certain key features of ICC arbitration, as well as a Note on Administrative Issues.

Yours faithfully,

[•]

Counsel

Secretariat of the ICC International Court of Arbitration

encl. (for Respondent only)

- All correspondence exchanged to date
- Request for Arbitration with documents annexed thereto
- ICC Rules of Arbitration *(see also www.iccarbitration.org)*
- ICC Dispute Resolution Brochure *(see also www.iccarbitration.org)*
- Note to the Parties from the Secretary General
- Note on Administrative Issues

DOCUMENT 4

REQUEST FOR ADDITIONAL TIME AND DETAILS OF ARBITRATOR (ART.5 OF THE RULES)

Dear Sirs

[•] v [•]

Arbitration Reference: [•]

We confirm that [•] acts as counsel on behalf of the Respondents in the above arbitration.
Answer – Extension of Time

The Respondents received your letter dated [•] 2012 plus enclosures, including the Request for Arbitration, on [•] September.

Accordingly, pursuant to Article 5(1) of the Rules, the Respondent's Answer is due within 30 days from [•].

The Request for Arbitration places reliance on a number of documents which appear material to the claims which have been advanced. However, certain of such documents have not previously been provided by the Claimants to the Respondents and such documents are not exhibited to the Request for Arbitration.

Such documents include:

1 an email from [•] to [•] dated [•] 2010 (paragraph 35, page 5 of the Request);

2 an external report issued on [•] 2008 (paragraph 64, page 9 of the Request);

3 claims from [•] (paragraph 65, page 9 of the Request);

4 two credit note requests issued in [•] and [•] 2008 in favour of [•] (paragraph 67, page 9 of the Request); and

5 three analysis reports dated 2000, 2002 and 2004 (paragraph 77, page 10 of the Request)

Under article 5(2) of the Rules we, therefore, request an extension of time for the Respondents to serve the Answer to 30 days from receipt of such documents and any necessary translations so that the Answer can refer to and, if necessary, respond to the claims reliant upon such documents.

We have sought the extension of time for service of the Answer at an early stage and we have copied this letter direct to the Claimants' counsel (as set out in paragraph 128 of the Request for Arbitration) in the hope that the provision of such documents and translations can be expedited as much as possible to minimise any delay.

Arbitrators

In accordance with the provisions of Article 5(2) of the Rules, we confirm that the Claimants and the Respondents have agreed under the terms of Clause 13.23.3 of the SPA (as defined in the Request) that:

"The arbitral tribunal shall be composed of three (3) arbitrators."

Accordingly, under Article 12(4) of the Rules, where the parties have agreed that the dispute shall be resolved by three arbitrators, each party shall nominate in the Request and the Answer, respectively, one arbitrator for confirmation.

Arbitrator – Claimants

The Respondents note the Claimants' nomination of [•] and their statement that [•] is independent and has no relationship with any of the Parties involved.

At this stage, unless and until we have received [•]'s Statement of Acceptance, Availability, Impartiality and Independence, we have no comments to make on the Claimants' nomination.

Arbitrator – Respondents

The Respondents nominate [•].

To the knowledge of the Respondents, [•] is independent and has no relationship with any of the Parties involved.

The contact details for [•] are:

[•]

Applicable law

We confirm that the Claimants and the Respondents have agreed under the terms of Clause 13.23.1 of the SPA that the applicable law of the substantive dispute is English law:

> *"This Agreement and the documents to be entered into pursuant to it, save as expressly referred to therein, and any non-contractual obligations arising out of or in connection with the Agreement and such documents shall be governed by and construed in accordance with English Law."*

Further, we confirm that the procedural law applicable to the arbitration shall be Swiss law.

Communications

We confirm that all future communications in this arbitration should be referred to ourselves as set out below:

[•]

FAO: [•] and [•]

We look forward to hearing from you.

Yours faithfully

[•]

DOCUMENT 5

SECRETARIAT'S NOTIFICATION OF THE ANSWER

1. [•] 2. [•] 3. [•] vs/ 1. [•] 2. [•] 3. [•]

Dear Madame and Sirs,

The Secretariat acknowledges receipt of 7 copies of Respondents' Answer dated [•] 2012. Respondents have sent a copy of the Answer to Claimants by email. A hard copy is enclosed to this letter for Claimants' files.

Constitution of the Arbitral Tribunal

The Secretariat of the ICC International Court of Arbitration ("Secretariat") informs you that, pursuant to Article 13(2) of the Rules, on [•] 2012 the Secretary General confirmed:

- [•], as co-arbitrator upon Claimants' joint nomination;
- [•], as co-arbitrator upon Respondents' joint nomination;

Their confirmation will be reported to the International Court of Arbitration of the International Chamber of Commerce ("Court") (Article 13(2)).

Further to our letter dated [•] 2012, we are looking forward to hearing from the parties regarding the President's nomination. Failing the parties agreement within the time limit granted (*i.e.* [•] 2012), unless the parties jointly agree to extend it, the President will be appointed by the Court.

Provisional Advance and Advance on Costs

As the provisional advance has been fully paid, we will transmit the file to the Arbitral Tribunal, once constituted (Article 16).

The Court will be invited to fix the advance on costs (Article 36(2)) at one of its next sessions.

Yours faithfully,

[•]

Counsel

Secretariat of the ICC International Court of Arbitration

encl. – Respondents' Answer *(for Claimants only)*

DOCUMENT 6

SECRETARIAT'S NOTIFICATION OF ICC COURT DECISION(S) SETTING IN MOTION THE ARBITRATION*

The parties normally receive a letter from the Secretariat of the ICC Court, addressed jointly to the parties' respective counsel, along the following lines:

Dear Sirs,

The Secretariat is pleased to inform you that, at its session of [•], the Court took the following decisions for the setting in motion of the procedure. The Court decided:

— that this matter shall proceed in accordance with Article 6(4) of the Rules,

— that the dispute shall be submitted to a three-member Arbitral Tribunal, and

— to fix the advance on costs at US$ [•], subject to later readjustments.

Pursuant to Article 12(2) of the Rules, Claimant is invited to nominate an arbitrator within 15 days from the date of receipt of this letter, and Respondent will be invited to nominate an arbitrator in a time limit of 15 days as from receipt of the notification of appointment made by Claimant.

Pursuant to Article 36(2) of the Rules and Article 1(4) of Appendix III, the advance on costs is fixed to cover the fees of the Arbitral Tribunal, the out-of-pocket expenses, if any, and the ICC administrative expenses. In the present matter, said advance has been fixed by reference to (i) the information available to the Court to date (ii) an amount in dispute of US$ [•], and (iii) taking into account that there shall be a three-member Arbitral Tribunal.

Depending on the evolution of the matter, the Court may readjust the advance on costs at a later date.

In conformity with Article 30(3) of the Rules, the parties shall be invited to pay within 30 days from the day following the date of transmission of the file to the Arbitral Tribunal, the advance on costs in the following manner:

Claimant: US$ [•] (US$ [•] less US$ [•] already paid), and

Respondent: US$ [•]

The provisional advance having been fully paid by Claimant pursuant to Article 16 of the Rules, the file will be transmitted to the Arbitral Tribunal once fully constituted.

Yours faithfully,

Counsel
Secretariat of the ICC International Court of Arbitration

Document 7

SECRETARIAT'S NOTIFICATION TO THE CLAIMANT'S NOMINEE AS ARBITRATOR

[•] vs/ [•]

Dear Sir,

The Secretariat of the ICC International Court of Arbitration ("Secretariat") informs you that you have been nominated by Claimant for confirmation as co-arbitrator.

Please complete and email a signed PDF and Word version of the enclosed Statement of Acceptance, Availability, Impartiality and Independence ("Statement"), as well as your *curriculum vitae*, to ica5@iccwbo.org by [•] 2012. In completing the Statement, please take the time to respond to the question concerning your availability at the top of page 2.

If you have questions, please do not hesitate to contact us.

Yours faithfully,

encl. – Case Information
– ICC Rules of Arbitration *(see also www.iccarbitration.org)*
– Statement of Acceptance, Availability, Impartiality and Independence Form
– *Curriculum vitae Form*
– Note to the Arbitral Tribunal on the Conduct of the Arbitration

DOCUMENT 7.1

ICC ARBITRATOR'S STATEMENT OF ACCEPTANCE, AVAILABILITY, IMPARTIALITY AND INDEPENDENCE (ART.11 OF THE RULES)

CASE No.[•]

Family Name(s): ____________________ **Given Name(s):**____________________

Please tick all relevant boxes.

1 – ACCEPTANCE

❑ **I agree** to serve as arbitrator under and in accordance with the 2012 ICC Rules of Arbitration ("**Rules**"). I confirm that I am familiar with the Rules. I accept that my fees and expenses will be fixed exclusively by the ICC Court (Article 2(4) of Appendix III to the Rules).

NON-ACCEPTANCE

❑ I decline to serve as arbitrator in this case. (*If you tick here, simply date and sign the form without completing any other sections.*)

2 – AVAILABILITY

❑ **I confirm**, on the basis of the information presently available to me, that I can devote the time necessary to conduct this arbitration diligently, efficiently and in accordance with the time limits in the Rules, subject to any extensions granted by the Court pursuant to Articles 23(2) and 30 of the Rules. I understand that it is important to complete the arbitration as promptly as reasonably practicable and that the ICC Court will consider the duration and conduct of the proceedings when fixing my fees (Article 2(2) of Appendix III to the Rules). My current professional engagements are as below for the information of the ICC Court and the parties.

Principal professional activity
(e.g. lawyer, arbitrator, academic): ________________________________

Number of currently pending cases in which I am involved *(i.e. arbitrations and activities pending now, not previous experience; additional details you wish to make known to the ICC Court and to the parties in relation to these matters can be provided on a separate sheet)*:

	As tribunal chair / sole arbitrator	As co-arbitrator	As counsel
Arbitrations			
Court litigation	*Not applicable*	*Not applicable*	

Furthermore, I am aware of commitments which might preclude me from devoting time to this arbitration during the following periods (*please provide details regarding such periods below or on a separate sheet*):

3 – INDEPENDENCE AND IMPARTIALITY *(Tick one box and provide details below and/or, if necessary, on a separate sheet.)*

In deciding which box to tick, you should take into account, having regard to Article 11(2) of the Rules, whether there exists any past or present relationship, direct or indirect, between you and any of the parties, their related entities or their lawyers or other representatives, whether financial, professional or of any other kind. Any doubt must be resolved in favour of disclosure. Any disclosure should be complete and specific, identifying *inter alia* relevant dates (both start and end dates), financial arrangements, details of companies and individuals, and all other relevant information.

- ❑ **Nothing to disclose:** I am impartial and independent and intend to remain so. To the best of my knowledge, and having made due enquiry, there are no facts or circumstances, past or present, that I should disclose because they might be of such a nature as to call into question my independence in the eyes of any of the parties and no circumstances that could give rise to reasonable doubts as to my impartiality.
- ❑ **Acceptance with disclosure:** I am impartial and independent and intend to remain so. However, mindful of my obligation to disclose any facts or circumstances which might be of such a nature as to call into question my independence in the eyes of any of the parties or that could give rise to reasonable doubts as to my impartiality, I draw attention to the matters below and/or on the attached sheet.

Date:____________________________ Signature:______________________________

The information requested in this form will be considered by the ICC Court and its Secretariat solely for the purpose of your appointment or confirmation as arbitrator in ICC proceedings. The information will remain confidential and will be stored in a case management database system. However, it may be disclosed solely to the parties and their counsel in the case referenced above for the purposes of that proceeding. According to Article 32 and, in particular, Article 40 of the French law "Informatique et Libertés" of 6 January 1978, you may access this information and ask for rectification by writing to the Secretariat of the Court.

ICC MODEL CURRICULUM VITAE FOR ARBITRATORS

CASE No. [•]

CURRICULUM VITAE

For the confidential use of the ICC International Court of Arbitration and communication to the parties. To be completed in English.

❑ Mr. ❑ Mrs. ❑ Miss ❑ Ms.

Family Name(s): Given Name(s):

Date of birth: Nationality(ies):

Personal Address:

Telephone: Telefax:

E-Mail:

Business Address *(Including company or firm name where applicable)*:

Telephone: Telefax: Mobile:

E-Mail: Website:

Please indicate which address you wish to be used for any correspondence:

❑ Personal ❑ Business

Please indicate which email you wish to be used for all notifications and communications:

❑ Personal ❑ Business

For the confidential use of the ICC International Court of Arbitration and communication to the parties. To be completed in English.

Academic degrees / Qualifications:

Current professional activity(ies) and position(s):

Professional Experience:

Additional information *(Use separate sheet if necessary)*:

Languages *(Mark all languages, including your native language, in which you consider yourself able to conduct an arbitration and to draft an award without the assistance of an interpreter or translator)*

❑ English	❑ French	❑ German	❑ Italian
❑ Spanish	❑ Portuguese	❑ Russian	❑ Polish
❑ Arabic	❑ Chinese	❑ Japanese	❑ Other ________

Please indicate other languages of which you have good knowledge:

Date: ______________________________ Signature: ____________________________

For the confidential use of the ICC International Court of Arbitration only. To be completed in English.

Family Name(s): ____________________ Given Name(s): ____________________

Fields of legal expertise:

- ❑ Civil law — ❑ specify jurisdiction(s):
- ❑ Common law — ❑ specify jurisdiction(s):
- ❑ European law
- ❑ International law
- ❑ Islamic law — ❑ specify jurisdiction(s):
- ❑ Other laws — ❑ please specify:

Specialization *(Mark the appropriate box or boxes)*:

- ❑ Administrative Law
- ❑ Agency (Representation)
- ❑ Competition
- ❑ Construction, Engineering
- ❑ Corporate Law
- ❑ Criminal Law
- ❑ Distribution, Franchising
- ❑ Employment
- ❑ Energy and Natural Resources
- ❑ Environment
- ❑ Finance and Banking
- ❑ Information and Communication Technologies
- ❑ Insurance
- ❑ Intellectual Property
- ❑ Joint Ventures, Consortia, Cooperation
- ❑ Pharmaceutical
- ❑ Real Estate
- ❑ Sales, Purchases
- ❑ Taxation
- ❑ Transport
- ❑ Other ________________________

For the confidential use of the ICC International Court of Arbitration only. To be completed in English.

Arbitration Experience:

Number of arbitration cases in which you have acted as:

		Chair of Tribunal	Sole Arbitrator	Co-arbitrator	Party's Counsel	Secretary or Other
International Institutional Arbitration	ICC					
	Other					
International *Ad Hoc* Arbitration						
Domestic Arbitration						

Other alternative dispute resolution experience:

Date:____________________________ Signature:____________________________

The information requested in this curriculum vitae is necessary for your appointment or confirmation as arbitrator. It will be stored in a case management system and used for the ICC's sole purposes. According to Article 32 and, in particular, Article 40 of the French law "Informatique et Libertés" of 6 January 1978, you may access this information and ask for rectification by writing to the Secretariat of the Court.

DOCUMENT 7.3

SECRETARIAT'S CASE INFORMATION SUMMARY

CASE INFORMATION Date: [•] 2012

[•] vs/ [•]

The information below comes from the documents submitted by the parties. Such information is intended to give the Arbitral Tribunal an overview of this arbitration and is not intended to affect any assessment or decision of the Arbitral Tribunal.

Team in Charge of this Arbitration [•]

Parties [•]

- Claimant
- Respondent

Counsel [•]

- Claimant's counsel
- Respondent's counsel

Other Relevant Entities

- Name of entity
- [•]
- [•]

Arbitral Tribunal

- Co-arbitrator nominated by Claimant
- [•]

Agreement upon which the Request is Based

- License and Distribution Agreement ("Agreement") dated [•] 2007, signed by the Parties

Arbitration Agreement

- Article 25.5 of the Agreement:
Any dispute arising out of or in relation to this Agreement or the interpretation, making, performance, breach or termination thereof, shall be settled by binding arbitration in London, England, in accordance with the Rules of Arbitration of the International Chamber of Commerce by a panel of three arbitrators appointed in accordance with the said Rules. Prior to the initiation of any arbitration proceeding under this section, each party agrees that they will notify the other party in writing of the nature of any such dispute, and the parties will meet and confer in good faith in an effort to resolve any such dispute. No party will initiate an arbitration proceeding until the parties have engaged in the meet and confer process. Should the meet and confer efforts prove unsuccessful and an arbitration proceeding is initiated by one or more of the parties, the award of the arbitrator shall be final and binding upon the parties, and the prevailing party may apply to any court of competent jurisdiction for enforcement of such award. The arbitration panel shall be guided by the following principles with respect to the license rights: The rights and licenses granted pursuant to this Agreement are revocable only upon termination of this Agreement. Termination of this Agreement or such rights and licenses should not be ordered unless all three of the following conditions are met: (i) a breach by [•] that entitles [•]to terminate the Agreement as set forth in Section 23 has been established by clear and convincing evidence; and (ii) [•] is not in the process of making good faith efforts to cure such breach or cannot cure such breach within 180 days of such breach and (iii) such breach has had material adverse effect on [•]'s business. In addition, if the foregoing three conditions have been met, the limitations and exclusions set forth in Section 19 shall not limit [•]'s liability. With respect to breaches of the Agreement by [•], the arbitration panel should take into account the fact that termination of the agreement by [•] is not an adequate remedy. Therefore, notwithstanding anything in this Agreement to the contrary, if the arbitration panel finds by clear and convincing evidence that [•] has intentionally, recklessly or repetitively breached material obligations of this Agreement and that such breaches cannot be cured and that such breaches have had a material adverse impact on [•]'s business, the limitations and exclusions set forth in Section 19 shall not limit [•]'s liability. Except as may be necessary to enter judgment upon the award or to the extent required by applicable law, and except as required by any governmental or judicial authority with competent jurisdiction, all claims, defenses and proceedings (including, without limiting the generality of the foregoing, the existence of the dispute and the fact that there is an arbitration proceeding) shall be treated in a confidential manner by the arbitrator, the parties and their counsel, and each of their agents, employees and all others acting on behalf of or in concert with them. Nothing contained in this Section 25 shall prevent either party from resorting to judicial process to seek injunctive or other equitable relief, including injunctive

relief to compel a party to comply with its obligation hereunder. In the event of any action by the parties under this Agreement, the prevailing party shall be entitled to costs and reasonable attorney's fees and expert's fees.

Applicable Law	
- Article 25.4 of the Agreement	the laws of the Commonwealth of Massachusetts (U.S.A.)
Language of Arbitration	
- Not determined	Claimant requests English
Place of Arbitration	
- Article 25.5 of the Agreement	London (United Kingdom)

Number of Arbitrators
- Article 25.5 of the Agreement: 3

Amount in Dispute
See the attached Financial Table.

DOCUMENT 7.4

FINANCIAL TABLE

FINANCIAL TABLE Date: [•] 2012

[•] vs/ [•]

The following table reflects the financial situation of the arbitration.

PROVISIONAL ADVANCE

AMOUNT IN DISPUTE

Amount in dispute	**US$ 4 800 000**	(partially quantified principal claims)

PROVISIONAL ADVANCE FIXED BY THE SECRETARY GENERAL

Amount	US$ 85 000

RANGE OF ARBITRATOR'S FEES

Arbitrators' fees may vary		
between a minimum of	US$ 32 017 × 3 = US$ 96 051	
and a maximum of	US$ 139 118 × 3 = US$ 417 354	

PAYMENT RECEIVED

Claimant	US$ 3 000

PAYMENT REQUESTED

Claimant	US$ 82 000

DOCUMENT 8.1

TRANSMITTAL OF STATEMENT OF ACCEPTANCE, AVAILABILITY, IMPARTIALITY AND INDEPENDENCE AND CURRICULUM VITAE OF CLAIMANT'S NOMINEE TO RESPONDENT WHEN THE NOMINEE PROVIDED AN UNQUALIFIED STATEMENT OF INDEPENDENCE

[•] vs / 1. [•] 2. [•]

Dear Mesdames and Sirs,

The Secretariat encloses a copy of the Statement of Acceptance, Availability, Impartiality and Independence, as well as the *curriculum vitae* of [•] whom Claimant has nominated as co-arbitrator.

We are now in a position to invite the Secretary General to examine whether to confirm the co-arbitrators. We remind you that no party may be joined after the confirmation or appointment of any arbitrator, unless all parties including the additional party otherwise agree (Article 7(1)). Unless we are informed otherwise by [•], we will proceed with the constitution of the Arbitral Tribunal.

Yours faithfully,

[•]
Counsel
Secretariat of the ICC International Court of Arbitration

encl. – Statement of Acceptance, Availability, Impartiality and Independence of [•]
– *Curriculum vitae* of [•]

DOCUMENT 8.2

TRANSMITTAL OF STATEMENT OF ACCEPTANCE, AVAILABILITY, IMPARTIALITY AND INDEPENDENCE AND CURRICULUM VITAE OF CLAIMANT'S NOMINEE TO RESPONDENT WHEN THE NOMINEE PROVIDED A QUALIFIED STATEMENT OF INDEPENDENCE

1. [•] 2. [•] 3. [•] vs/ 1. [•] 2 [•] 3 [•]

Dear Mesdames and Sirs,

The Secretariat encloses a copy of the Statement of Acceptance, Availability, Impartiality and Independence, as well as the *curriculum vitae* of [•] whom Claimants have nominated jointly as co-arbitrator.

As the prospective arbitrator has made a disclosure, we invite you to provide your comments, if any, by [•] (Article 11(2)).

If a party does not provide comments within the time limit granted, we will consider that said party does not object to [•]'s confirmation.

Upon receipt of the parties' comments or expiry of the time limit granted, the Court or the Secretary General will decide whether to confirm the prospective arbitrator.

Yours faithfully,

Counsel,
Secretariat of the ICC International Court of Arbitration

encl. – Statement of Acceptance, Availability, Impartiality and Independence of [•]
– *Curriculum vitae* of [•]

DOCUMENT 9.1

SECRETARIAT'S NOTIFICATION TO THE RESPONDENT TO PROPOSE AN ARBITRATOR

In the Request and Answer set out above, both parties have nominated co-arbitrators. If that has not been the case and there has been a difference between them as to the number of arbitrators, the ICC Court will resolve the matter. After the ICC Court's decision has been communicated to the parties, the Claimant will then have a limited period to nominate an arbitrator and the Respondent will have a limited period as well to nominate an arbitrator.

The parties normally receive a letter from the Secretariat of the ICC Court, addressed jointly to the parties' respective counsel, along the following lines:

Dear Sirs,

The Secretariat acknowledges receipt of Claimant's fax dated [•], by which it designated Mr. [•] as co-arbitrator in this case, copied directly to Respondent.

Pursuant to the Court's decision during its session of [•], a time limit of [•] days is now granted to Respondent as of receipt of this notification of nomination made by Claimant, to propose a co-arbitrator, failing which an arbitrator will be appointed on its behalf.

Yours faithfully,

Counsel
Secretariat of the ICC International Court of Arbitration

DOCUMENT 9.2

RESPONDENTS' NOMINATION OF AN ARBITRATOR AND COMMENTS ON THE QUALIFIED STATEMENT OF INDEPENDENCE OF CLAIMANTS' NOMINEE

Dear Sirs
1 [•] 2 [•] [•] 3 [•] v1 [•] 2 [•] 3 [•]

Arbitration Reference: [•]

Thank you for your letter dated [•] 2012.

Answer – Extension of Time

Thank you for the extension of time to **[•] 2012** for the Respondents to submit their Answer.

Arbitrator – Claimants

We confirm receipt of the information completed by [•] in the ICC Arbitrator Statement of Acceptance, Availability, Impartiality and Independence.

We note the declarations made by [•] in relation to Rule 11(2) of the ICC Rules in connection with [•]'s past and present relationships, direct or indirect with any of the parties, related entities or their lawyers or representatives.

We further note that you required a response regarding any objections to this appointment by [•] 2012. For the avoidance of doubt, the Respondent confirms that it has no objection to [•]'s appointment.

Arbitrator – Respondents

We also note that on the morning of [•], the arbitrator nominated by the Respondent, [•], declined to serve as arbitrator in this case.

In light of [•] unavailability, the Respondents nominate [•].

To the knowledge of the Respondents, [•] is independent and has no relationship with any of the Parties involved.

The contact details for [•] are:

[•]

We look forward to hearing from you.

Yours faithfully

[•]

DOCUMENT 10.1

SECRETARIAT'S NOTIFICATION OF CONFIRMATION OF THE TWO CO-ARBITRATORS BY THE COURT

[•] v [•]
Dear Mesdames and Sirs,

At its session of [•], the International Court of Arbitration of the International Chamber of Commerce ("Court"):

- confirmed [•] as co-arbitrator upon Claimant's nomination (Article 13(1)).
- confirmed [•] as co-arbitrator upon Respondent's nomination (Article 13(1)).
- took the necessary steps for the appointment of the President of the Arbitral Tribunal (Article 13(3)).

Advance on Costs

The Court will fix the advance on costs to cover the Arbitral Tribunal's fees and expenses, as well as the ICC administrative expenses (Article 36(2) and Article 1(4) of Appendix III) upon receipt of Respondent's Answer to the Request for Arbitration. We will inform you of the Court's decision and invite you to pay the advance on costs upon the transmission of the file to the Arbitral Tribunal (Article 36(2)).

Yours faithfully,
[•]
Counsel
Secretariat of the ICC International Court of Arbitration

Document 10.2

SECRETARIAT'S NOTIFICATION OF CONFIRMATION OF THE TWO CO-ARBITRATORS BY THE SECRETARY GENERAL

1 [•] 2 [•] 3 [•] vs./ 1 [•] 2 [•] 3 [•]

Dear Madame and Sirs,

The Secretariat acknowledges receipt of 7 copies of Respondents' Answer dated [•] 2012.

Respondents have sent a copy of the Answer to Claimants by email. A hard copy is enclosed to this letter for Claimants' files.

Constitution of the Arbitral Tribunal

The Secretariat of the ICC International Court of Arbitration ("Secretariat") informs you that, pursuant to Article 13(2) of the Rules, on [•] 2012 the Secretary General confirmed:

- [•], as co-arbitrator upon Claimants' joint nomination;
- [•], as co-arbitrator upon Respondents' joint nomination;

Their confirmation will be reported to the International Court of Arbitration of the International Chamber of Commerce ("Court") (Article 13(2)).

Further to our letter dated [•] 2012, we are looking forward to hearing from the parties regarding the President's nomination. Failing the parties agreement within the time limit granted (*i.e.* [•] 2012), unless the parties jointly agree to extend it, the President will be appointed by the Court.

Provisional Advance and Advance on Costs

As the provisional advance has been fully paid, we will transmit the file to the Arbitral Tribunal, once constituted (Article 16).

The Court will be invited to fix the advance on costs (Article 36(2)) at one of its next sessions.

Yours faithfully,

[•] Counsel
Secretariat of the ICC International Court of Arbitration

encl. – Respondents' Answer *(for Claimants only)*

DOCUMENT 11

SECRETARIAT'S NOTIFICATION OF APPOINTMENT OF THE PRESIDENT OF THE ARBITRAL TRIBUNAL BY THE COURT

[•] (Country) **vs/** [•] (Country)

Dear Mesdames,

Dear Sirs,

At its session of [•] 2013, the International Court of Arbitration of the International Chamber of Commerce ("Court"):

- appointed [•] as President of the Arbitral Tribunal upon the Canadian National Committee's proposal (Article 13(3)); and
- fixed the advance on costs at US$ [•], subject to later readjustments (Article 36(2)).

A copy of the Statement of Acceptance, Availability, Impartiality and Independence, as well as the *curriculum vitae*, of [•] are enclosed for your information.

Advance on Costs

The Secretariat acknowledges receipt of Claimant's letter dated [•] 2013, a copy of which was sent directly to Respondent and the co-arbitrators, and a copy of which is enclosed for the Chairman.

The Court fixed an advance at its discretion based on an amount in dispute quantified at US$ [•], and three Arbitrators. Depending on the evolution of the arbitration, the Court may readjust the advance on costs.

Normally, the advance on costs is intended to cover the Arbitral Tribunal's fees and expenses, and the ICC administrative expenses (Article 36(2) and Article 1(4) of Appendix III). However, the Court has fixed a lower advance than would normally be the case. Based on the current amount in dispute, the Cost Calculator (available on www.iccarbitration.org) suggests an advance in excess of US$ [•]. We will closely monitor this arbitration and foresee a readjustment and increase of the advance on costs. Accordingly, the parties must not assume that the current advance will cover the costs of arbitration through the end of the arbitration.

We enclose the Financial Table. We also enclose Payment Requests that indicate the amounts to be paid and when such payments are due.

As the provisional advance has been fully paid, we are transmitting the file to the Arbitral Tribunal today (Article 16). The parties should correspond directly with the Arbitral Tribunal and send copies of their correspondence to the other party and to the Secretariat.

Yours faithfully,
[•]
Counsel
Secretariat of the ICC International Court of Arbitration

encl.
- Statement of Acceptance, Availability, Impartiality and Independence of [•]
- *Curriculum vitae* of [•]
- Claimant's letter dated [•] 2013 (*for the Chairman only*)
- Financial Table
- Payment Requests
- Note on Article 36(4)

DOCUMENT 12

SECRETARIAT'S TRANSMITTAL OF THE FILE TO THE TRIBUNAL (ART.16 OF THE RULES)

[•] vs/ [•]

Dear Sirs,

The Secretariat transmits the file to you (Article 16).

Efficient Conduct of the Arbitration

The Arbitral Tribunal and the parties must make every effort to conduct the arbitration in an expeditious and cost effective manner, having regard to the complexity and value of the dispute (Article 22(1)). We draw your attention to Appendix IV of the Rules, which contains suggested case management techniques.

We enclose a Note on the Conduct of the Arbitration which sets forth the time limits under the Rules that you must observe and relevant information concerning the conduct of the proceedings.

Financial Information

We enclose a Financial Table.

Communications

As from now, the parties should correspond directly with you and send copies of their correspondence to the other party and to us. Please provide us with copies of all your correspondence with the parties.

Amicable Settlement

Parties are free to settle their dispute amicably at any time during an arbitration. The parties may wish to consider conducting an amicable dispute resolution procedure pursuant to the ICC ADR Rules. These Rules provide for a wide range of amicable settlement procedures including mediation. ICC can also assist the parties in finding a suitable mediator. Further information is available from the ICC International Centre for ADR at +33 1 49 53 30 53 or adr@iccwbo.org or www.iccadr.org.

ICC International Centre for Expertise

If the assistance of an expert is required, the ICC International Centre for Expertise ("Centre") can, upon request, make proposals of experts from a wide range of specializations. This service is provided free of charge to arbitrators. Further information is available from the Centre on +33 1 49 53 30 53 or expertise@iccwbo.org or www.iccexpertise.org.

Yours faithfully,

[•]
Counsel
Secretariat of the ICC International Court of Arbitration

encl. – List of Documents as well as documents mentioned therein (*By FedEx only*)
– Case Information
– Financial Table
– Note to the Arbitral Tribunal on the Conduct of Arbitration
– Note on Administrative Issues
– Note on the Appointment, Duties and Remuneration of Administrative Secretaries
– ICC Award Checklist
– *Curriculum vitae* of fellow arbitrators

DOCUMENT 12.1

NOTE ON PERSONAL AND ARBITRAL TRIBUNAL EXPENSES

(This Note replaces the previous Note dated 1 September 2009.)

Expenses of arbitrators and arbitral tribunals which are incurred on or after 1 September 2013 will be reimbursed by the Secretariat of the ICC International Court of Arbitration in accordance with this Note.

How to submit a request for expenses

1. The Secretariat will reimburse expenses and pay *per diem* allowances only upon receipt of a request in a readily comprehensible form including a cover page listing each payment claimed and the reason for it. Expense reimbursement claims must be supported by an original receipt. This is necessary so that the Secretariat can carry out its accounting responsibilities and, from time to time, provide the parties with comprehensive statements of expenses incurred by arbitrators.

When to submit a request for expenses

2. Arbitrators should submit their requests for the reimbursement of expenses and/or the payment of *per diem* allowances, together with any required supporting documentation as specified below, as soon as possible after expenses are incurred. This will help ensure that the advance on costs paid by the parties is adequate to cover the costs of the arbitration.

3. All requests for the reimbursement of expenses and/or the payment of *per diem* allowances relating to any period prior to the submission of the draft final award must be provided at the latest when the draft final award is submitted to the Secretariat. When there is a three-member arbitral tribunal, the co-arbitrators and the chairman should co-ordinate their submission of requests for the reimbursement of expenses and/or the payment of *per diem* allowances in order to ensure that they reach the Secretariat no later than the draft final award. Requests for the reimbursement of expenses and/or the payment of *per diem* allowances submitted after the Court has approved the final award will not be taken into account by the Court when fixing the costs of the arbitration and will not be paid save in exceptional circumstances as decided by the Secretary General.

4. If an arbitration terminates before the rendering of a final award, all requests for the reimbursement of expenses and/or the payment of *per diem* allowances must be submitted within the time limit granted by the Secretariat. Requests for the reimbursement of expenses and/or the payment of *per diem* allowances submitted after the date the Court fixes the costs of arbitration will not be taken into account by the Court and will not be paid.

Travel expenses

5. If required to travel for the purpose of an ICC arbitration, an arbitrator will be reimbursed for the actual travel expenses he or she incurs travelling from and returning to

his or her usual place of business as indicated on the *curriculum vitae* filed for the relevant ICC arbitration. Travel expenses will be reimbursed in accordance with paragraphs 6 to 8.

6. A request for reimbursement of travel expenses must be accompanied by the originals of all receipts claimed or other proper substantiation if receipts are unavailable. Travel expenses that are not fully and comprehensively justified will not be reimbursed.

7. The reimbursement of travel expenses is subject to the following strict limits:

(a) Air travel: an airfare equivalent to the applicable standard business class airfare.
(b) Rail travel: the applicable first class train fare.
(c) Transport to and from airport(s) and/or train station(s): the applicable standard taxi fare.
(d) Travel by private car: a flat rate for every kilometre driven, plus all necessary actual parking and toll charges incurred. The flat rate is US$ 0.80 per kilometre.

8. Except for expenses claimed pursuant to paragraph 7(d) above, travel expenses will, where possible, be reimbursed in the same currency in which they were incurred. An arbitrator may alternatively request reimbursement in US dollars provided that the request is accompanied by a statement of the US dollar amount and evidence of the exchange rate (for example, a print out from <www.oanda.com>). The date for the currency conversion should be the date the expense was incurred.

Per diem allowance

9. In addition to travel expenses, an arbitrator will be paid a flat-rate *per diem* allowance in accordance with paragraphs 10 to 14 for every day of an ICC arbitration that he or she is required to spend outside his or her usual place of business as indicated on the *curriculum vitae* filed for the relevant ICC arbitration. The arbitrator is not required to submit receipts in order to claim the *per diem* allowance, but simply evidence of the travel for purposes of the arbitration.

10. If the arbitrator is not required to use overnight hotel accommodation, the flat-rate *per diem* allowance is US$ 400.

11. If the arbitrator is required to use overnight hotel accommodation, the flat-rate *per diem* allowance is US$ 1.200.

12. The applicable *per diem* allowance is deemed to cover fully <u>all</u> personal living expenses of whatever nature and of whatever actual value (other than travel expenses) incurred by an arbitrator. In particular, the applicable *per diem* allowance is deemed to cover, among other expenses, the total cost of:

- Accommodation (except where paragraph 10 above applies)
- Meals
- Laundry/ironing/dry cleaning and other housekeeping or similar services
- Inner-city transport
- Telephone calls, faxes, emails and other means of communication
- Gratuities

13. For the avoidance of doubt, no *per diem* allowance will be paid in respect of time spent by an arbitrator travelling to or from the relevant destination.

14. Since the *per diem* allowance is deemed to cover <u>all</u> personal living expenses incurred by an arbitrator while outside his or her usual place of business on ICC arbitration business, the Secretariat will <u>not</u> reimburse expenses over and above the applicable *per diem* allowance under any circumstances.

General office expenses and courier charges

15. General office expenses and overheads incurred in the ordinary course of business by an arbitrator or an arbitral tribunal in connection with an ICC arbitration will not be reimbursed. However, an arbitrator or an arbitral tribunal may request to be reimbursed at cost for any courier, photocopying, facsimile or telephone charges incurred for the purposes of an ICC arbitration, provided such request is accompanied by detailed receipts.

Advance payments on expenses

16. An arbitrator may request an advance payment of travel expenses and/or the applicable *per diem* allowance in accordance with paragraphs 5 to 14 above. If an advance is granted, the arbitrator must subsequently submit the relevant supporting documentation to the Secretariat, including all receipts and a statement of working days and nights spent outside of his or her usual place of business on ICC arbitration business.

Document 12.2

EXPLANATORY NOTE BY THE PRESIDENT OF THE COURT ON *PER DIEM* ALLOWANCES TO ALL SERVING ARBITRATORS AND TO ALL NEWLY CONSTITUTED TRIBUNALS

The Bureau of the Court has recently concluded a review of the '*per diem*' allowances, which are in place at present.

It has concluded that an increase in the '*per diem*' is now appropriate; that any adjustment should continue to be based upon a fixed '*per diem*' allowance of universal application, *i.e.* without adjustment to reflect case-specific factors, such as the amount in dispute or the venue of hearings; and that, in future, the level of the '*per diem*' allowances should be reviewed regularly and at least every two years.

The Bureau of the Court has taken account of the fact that inflation in US$ terms has been running at just under 2.5% p.a., in the period (2005–2013), such that US$ 800 at the time that rate was first introduced has the buying power of US$ 1.000 today. It has in mind, too, that the US Dollar has fallen against most major currencies (in the case of the Euro, a little more than 10%).

There is a further factor: inflation has been higher in some sectors than in others. In particular, hotel and restaurant prices have risen – in many cities dramatically, Paris being a case in point. Anecdotal evidence is indicative of recent increases of 20%, if not more.

The Bureau of the Court considered whether a scale of '*per diem*' rates should be introduced to reflect variations in the cost of living in cities around the World, bearing in mind that government foreign services and many firms, which operate in multiple centres, apply "country factors" to take into account local cost differences.

The Bureau of the Court has decided against such a 'city by city' approach. While it may be appropriate in circumstances in which provision for employees embarking upon long-term permanent international postings of three years or more has to be made, that is a very different proposition from the '*per diem*' arrangements made for arbitrators serving away from home for short periods from time to time on an '*ad hoc*' basis.

Further, the plain fact is that the cities, which host the majority of ICC arbitrations are high cost centres.

A final factor, which weighed with the Bureau of the Court, was that the reintroduction of a system, which might be susceptible to elements of 'special pleading' or case by case review would inevitably involve the Secretariat in additional administrative work, as it had done in the past. The introduction of the universal flat rate '*per diem*' allowance in 2009 was intended precisely to alleviate that administrative burden.

The Bureau of the Court is well aware of the need to keep the costs of arbitration within sensible bounds. It has approached this review with that overriding principle very much in mind.

The Bureau of the Court has sought to strike a balance. Its concern to ensure that arbitrators serving on ICC tribunals should be in a position to find accommodation appropriate to their needs and commensurate with that selected by the parties or their representatives is to be seen in the context of the Bureau of the Court's decisions to set business class travel as the norm for long haul journeys of more than six hours' duration, rather than first class; and to determine that administrative secretaries may no longer be the subject of 'off balance sheet' separate fee arrangements with the parties. (For the avoidance of doubt, no '*per diem*' allowance is payable to administrative secretaries in any event).

The '*per diem*' allowances have remained unchanged for eight years. As a result of its deliberations, the Bureau of the Court has concluded that, with effect from 1 September 2013, they should be increased in line with inflation and with other factors which have impacted the US$ exchange rate.

Accordingly, the '*per diem*' allowance applicable to an overnight stay will be increased to US$ 1.200. The rate for an attendance, which does not involve an overnight stay will be increased to US$ 400.

In accordance with its new policy, the '*per diem*' allowances will be reviewed again prior to 1 September 2015.

The President

DOCUMENT 12.3

NOTE ON THE APPOINTMENT, DUTIES AND REMUNERATION OF ADMINISTRATIVE SECRETARIES

The ICC Rules of Arbitration ("**Rules**") are silent as to the appointment, duties and remuneration of Arbitral Tribunal administrative secretaries or other assistants ("**Administrative Secretaries**"). This Note replaces the Secretariat's previous note on the same subject. It sets out the policy and practice of the ICC International Court of Arbitration ("**Court**") and its Secretariat regarding the engagement of Administrative Secretaries by Arbitral Tribunals. It applies with respect to any Administrative Secretary appointed on or after 1 August 2012. Any Arbitral Tribunal proposing to appoint an Administrative Secretary shall provide the parties with a copy of this Note.

1. Appointment

Administrative Secretaries can provide a useful service to the parties and Arbitral Tribunals in ICC arbitration. While principally engaged to assist three-member Arbitral Tribunals, an Administrative Secretary may also assist a Sole Arbitrator. Administrative Secretaries can be appointed at any time during an arbitration.

If an Arbitral Tribunal envisages the appointment of an Administrative Secretary, it shall consider carefully whether in the circumstances of that particular case such an appointment would be appropriate.

Administrative Secretaries must satisfy the same independence and impartiality requirements as those which apply to arbitrators under the Rules. ICC staff members are not permitted to serve as Administrative Secretaries.

There is no formal process for the appointment of an Administrative Secretary. However, before any steps are made to appoint an Administrative Secretary, the Arbitral Tribunal shall inform the parties of its proposal to do so. For this purpose, the Arbitral Tribunal shall submit to the parties the proposed Administrative Secretary's *curriculum vitae*, together with a declaration of independence and impartiality, an undertaking on the part of the Administrative Secretary to act in accordance with the present Note and an undertaking on the part of the Arbitral Tribunal to ensure that this obligation on the part of the Administrative Secretary shall be met.

The Arbitral Tribunal shall make clear to the parties that they may object to such proposal and an Administrative Secretary shall not be appointed if a party has raised an objection.

2. Duties

Administrative Secretaries act upon the Arbitral Tribunal's instructions and under its strict supervision. The Arbitral Tribunal shall, at all times, be responsible for the Administrative Secretary's conduct in relation to the arbitration.

An Administrative Secretary may perform organizational and administrative tasks such as:

- transmitting documents and communications on behalf of the Arbitral Tribunal;
- organizing and maintaining the Arbitral Tribunal's file and locating documents;
- organizing hearings and meetings;
- attending hearings, meetings and deliberations; taking notes or minutes or keeping time;
- conducting legal or similar research; and
- proofreading and checking citations, dates and cross-references in procedural orders and awards as well as correcting typographical, grammatical or calculation errors.

Under no circumstances may the Arbitral Tribunal delegate decision-making functions to an Administrative Secretary. Nor should the Arbitral Tribunal rely on the Administrative Secretary to perform any essential duties of an arbitrator.

The Administrative Secretary may not act, or be required to act, in such a manner as to prevent or discourage direct communications among the arbitrators, between the Arbitral Tribunal and the parties, or between the Arbitral Tribunal and the Secretariat.

A request by an Arbitral Tribunal to an Administrative Secretary to prepare written notes or memoranda shall in no circumstances release the Arbitral Tribunal from its duty personally to review the file and/or to draft any decision of the Arbitral Tribunal.

When in doubt about which tasks may be performed by an Administrative Secretary, the Arbitral Tribunal or the Administrative Secretary should contact the Secretariat.

3. Remuneration

With the exception of the Administrative Secretary's reasonable personal disbursements as detailed in this Note, the engagement of an Administrative Secretary should not pose any additional financial burden on the parties. Accordingly, the Arbitral Tribunal may not look to the parties for the reimbursement of any costs associated with an Administrative Secretary beyond the scope prescribed in this Note.

Any remuneration payable to the Administrative Secretary shall be paid by the Arbitral Tribunal out of the total funds available for the fees of all arbitrators, such that the fees of the Administrative Secretary will not increase the total costs of the arbitration.

In no circumstances should the Arbitral Tribunal seek from the parties any form of compensation for the Administrative Secretary's activity. Direct arrangements between the Arbitral Tribunal and the parties on the Administrative Secretary's fees are prohibited. Since the fees of the Arbitral Tribunal are established on an *ad valorem* basis, any compensation to be paid to the Administrative Secretary is deemed to be included in the Arbitral Tribunal's fees.

4. Disbursements

The Arbitral Tribunal may seek reimbursement from the parties of the Administrative Secretary's justified reasonable expenses for hearings and meetings.

Document 12.4

NOTE ON ADMINISTRATIVE ISSUES

Communications

1 Parties and arbitrators must send copies of all written correspondence directly to all other parties, arbitrators and the Secretariat of the International Court of Arbitration of the International Chamber of Commerce ("Secretariat").

2 The Secretariat prefers to receive and generally will send correspondence by email or fax. As such, parties, their counsel and prospective arbitrators must provide the Secretariat with their email addresses and fax numbers.

Dispatch of Materials to the ICC and Customs Fees

3. Materials sent to the ICC (correspondence, submissions, binders, tapes, CDs, etc.) must be sent exclusively as "Documentation". No other description should be indicated on the transportation slip or waybill. Generally, documentation is not subject to customs tax. Other material may be subject to tax, which varies according to the origin, content and weight of such material. Customs fees, if any, will increase the costs of arbitration.

Representation

4. If the parties foresee being represented by counsel, they must inform the Secretariat of the name and address of such counsel.

ICC International Centre for Expertise

5. If a party requires the assistance of an expert, the ICC International Centre for Expertise ("Centre") can, upon request, propose experts from a wide range of specializations. The fee for this service is US$2,500. Further information is available from the Centre at +33 1 49 53 30 53 or expertise@iccwbo.org or www.iccexpertise.org.

ICC Hearing Centre

6. The ICC Hearing Centre in Paris, France offers flexible packages and a range of specialized facilities and services for hearings and meetings. Further information is available on our website at www.icchearingcentre.org.

Post-Arbitration Services

7. Disbursements in connection with services requested after this arbitration is closed may be charged to the requesting party.

DOCUMENT 12.5

NOTE TO THE ARBITRAL TRIBUNAL ON THE CONDUCT OF THE ARBITRATION

This Note is intended to provide the arbitral tribunal with information concerning the conduct of arbitration under the ICC Rules off Arbitration ("**Rules**").

Time limits under the Rules

1. Rapid resolution of arbitrations is a priority of the International Court of Arbitration of the International Chamber of Commerce ("Court"). Arbitrators should devote the time and effort necessary to conduct the arbitration within the requirements of the Rules. The Rules contain strict time limits, in particular:

    - **Terms of Reference:** must be established within **two months** from the transmission of the file to the arbitral tribunal (Article 23(2))).
    - **Case Management Conference:** must be convened with the parties when drawing up the Terms of Reference or as soon as possible thereafter (Article 24(1)).
    - **Procedural Timetable:** must be established during or immediately following the case management conference and transmitted to the Court and the parties (Article 24(2)).
    - **Closing off the proceedings:** must be done as soon as possible after the last hearing concerning matters to be decided in an award, or the filing of the last authorised submissions concerning such matters (Article 27).
    - **Date for submission of draft awards:** must be indicated to the Secretariat and the parties when the arbitral tribunal closes the proceedings in relation to the award (Article 27).
    - **Final award:** must be rendered within the time limit fixed by the Court based upon the procedural timetable or, if the Court does not fix such time limit, within **six months** from the date of the last signature or notification of the approval of the Terms of Reference. ((Article 30((1)). The Court expects sole arbitrators to submit draft awards within **two months** and three-member arbitral tribunals to submit draft awards within **three months** of the last hearing concerning matters to be decided in such award or the filing of the last authorised submission concerning such matters, whichever is later (Article 27).

Conduct of the Arbitration and Techniques for Controlling Time and Costs

2 The Rules require the arbitral tribunal and the parties to make every effort to conduct the arbitration in an expeditious and cost-effective manner, having regard to the complexity and value of the dispute (Article 22(1)).

3 In order to ensure effective case management, the arbitral tribunal, after consulting the parties, may adopt such procedural measures at it considers appropriate, provided that they are not contrary to any agreement of the parties (Article 22(2)). The arbitral tribunal should consider the case management techniques in Appendix V to the Rules

and the Techniques for Controlling Time and Costs in Arbitration (available under Tools on the Court's website www.iccwbo.org/court/arbitration).

4 Although extensions of the time limits indicated above may be granted by the Court, in setting an arbitrator's fees, the Court considers the diligence and efficiency of the arbitrator, the time spent, the rapidity of the proceedings, the complexity of the dispute and the timeliness of the submission of the draft award when fixing arbitrators' fees(Article 2(2) of Appendix III).

5 The Court can replace an arbitrator when it decides that such arbitrator is not fulfilling his or her functions within the prescribed time limits (Article 15(2)).

ICC International Centre for ADR

6. Parties are free to settle their dispute amicably prior to or at any time during an arbitration. Where appropriate, arbitrators may wish to remind the parties about the ADR Rules of the International Chamber of Commerce. The ADR Rules provide for a wide range of amicable settlement procedures including mediation. ICC can also assist the parties in finding a suitable mediator. Further information is available from the ICC International Centre for ADR at +33 1 49 53 30 53 or adr@iccwbo.org or www.iccadr.org.

ICC International Centre for Expertise

7. If the assistance of an expert is required, the ICC International Centre for Expertise can, upon request, propose experts from a wide range of specializations. This service is provided free of charge to arbitrators. Further information is available from the Centre at +33 1 49 53 30 53 or expertise@iccwbo.org or www.iccexpertise.org.

Replacement of Arbitrators

8. When an arbitrator is replaced, the reconstituted arbitral tribunal shall invite the parties to comment and then determine if and to what extent prior proceedings shall be repeated (Article 15(4)).

9. When fixing the arbitral tribunal's fees, the Court generally deducts the fees of the previous arbitrator from the fees of the replacement arbitrator.

10. Subsequent to the closing of the proceeding, taking into account the views of the remaining arbitrators and the parties, instead of replacing an arbitrator who has died or been removed by the Court pursuant to Article 15(1) or 15(2), the Court may decide, when it considers it appropriate, that the remaining arbitrator shall continue the arbitration (Article 15(5)).

ICC Award Checklist ("Checklist")

11. The Checklist is intended to provide arbitrators with some guidance when drafting awards and is not an exhaustive, mandatory or otherwise binding document. It does not reflect the opinion of the Court, its Secretariat or its members, and is intended to facilitate the arbitrators' mission. It may not be published or used for any purpose other than the conduct of ICC arbitrations. The Checklist is not exhaustive of issues that may be raised by the Court under Article 33 of the Rules.

ICC Hearing Centre

12. The ICC Hearing Centre in Paris, France offers flexible packages and a range of specialized facilities and services for hearings and meetings. Further information is available on our website at www.icchearingcentre.org.

Advance on Costs

13. The advance on costs is intended to cover the arbitral tribunal's fees and arbitration related expenses, as well as the ICC administrative expenses (Article 36 and Article 1(4) of Appendix III).

14. Depending on the evolution of the arbitration, the Court may readjust the advance on costs (Article 36).

15. The arbitral tribunal should clarify with the parties whether they will be directly responsible for the costs of any hearing or whether such costs should be included in the arbitration-related expenses. If hearing costs will be included in the arbitration-related expenses, the arbitral tribunal should provide the Secretariat with an estimate of such costs. Thereafter, we will examine whether it is appropriate to invite the Court to reconsider the advance on costs.

16. The arbitral tribunal should inform the Secretariat of any development concerning the value and complexity of the arbitration, and any other issues that it considers relevant.

The Arbitral Tribunal's Fees

17. The arbitral tribunal is encouraged to consult the Cost Calculator on our website (www.iccarbitration.org). Fees are fixed exclusively by the Court. Separate fee arrangements between the parties and arbitrators are not permitted.

18. The Court fixes arbitrators' fees at the end of the arbitration, although advances on fees may be granted upon completion of concrete steps in the arbitration.

19. In setting an arbitrator's fees, the Court considers the diligence and efficiency of the arbitrator, the time spent, the rapidity of the proceedings, the complexity of the dispute and the timeliness of the submission of draft award, so as to arrive at a figure within the time limits specified or, in exceptional circumstances (Article 37(2)), at a figure higher or lower than those limits (Article 2(2) of Appendix III to the Rules). The Court does not consider the arbitrator's usual hourly rates or remuneration.

20. When there is a three-member arbitral tribunal, arbitrators should consider the time spent and the work done by each arbitrator and inform the Secretariat of their opinion of a fair and appropriate allocation of the fees for each arbitrator. Unless we are advised in writing that the arbitral tribunal has agreed to a different allocation, the Court normally fixes the arbitrators' fees so that the president receives 40% of the total fees and each co-arbitrator receives 30%. The Court may decide upon a different allocation based on the circumstances. Unless otherwise agreed, the same allocation will apply to any advances on fees granted by the Court.

21. Under French tax laws, the ICC is required to declare the amount of fees, including advances on fees, paid to any arbitrator during each calendar year, as well as any expenses reimbursed during the same period.

Personal and Arbitral Tribunal Expenses

[See Document 12.1]

VAT, Taxes, Charges and Imposts applicable to Arbitrators' Fees *(as of 13 October 2010)*

38. Amounts paid to an arbitrator do not include any possible value added taxes (VAT) or other taxes or charges and imposts applicable to the arbitrator's fees (Article 2(13) of Appendix III). Parties have a duty to pay any such taxes or charges; however, the recovery of any such charges or taxes is a matter solely between the arbitrator and the parties.

39. ICC nonetheless offers arbitrators subject to VAT and other taxes, charges and imposts (hereinafter 'VAT'), who expressly request in writing, a service allowing them to have the funds corresponding to their estimate of the VAT due on their fees and expenses (hereinafter 'fees') administered by ICC.

40. This service is totally separate from, and has no effect on, the procedure for paying advances as set out in the Rules. Should the parties fail to pay the VAT on the arbitrators' fees, this cannot be invoked by the arbitrators before the Court, for instance as a ground for suspending the arbitral proceedings.

41. Any arbitrator subject to VAT may take advantage of this service. ICC acts as the 'depositary' of the funds, receives funds from parties who have been instructed to this effect by an arbitrator, and makes the payments corresponding to the VAT at the arbitrator's request.

42. The initiative of requesting that a VAT account be opened, of calling advances for the payment of VAT on fees ('VAT advance') and paying arbitrators on the basis of the amounts deposited lies solely with the arbitrators.

43. This service is available to arbitrators from any country.

44. The VAT advance is only administered in US dollars and does not yield interest for the parties or the arbitrators.

45. It is the arbitrators' sole responsibility to ensure that the procedure described below complies with the tax law provisions applicable to the exercise of their profession as arbitrators, including the payment of their fees. Arbitrators are encouraged to check the basis on which they should calculate the amount of VAT due.

46. The ICC acts exclusively as depositary and is not in a position to advise the arbitrators on any tax law.

47. **Procedure**

Step 1: Request for VAT account

Any arbitrator wishing to use this service shall inform the Secretariat in writing and request ICC to act as depositary for the sums paid by the parties as an advance on the VAT due on the arbitrators' fees.

Step 2: Estimation of amounts

The arbitrator determines the amount of VAT on his or her fees in light of the rules that apply at the place where he or she is taxable.

Arbitrators may use the cost calculator on the website of the International Court of Arbitration (www.iccarbitration.org) to estimate the amount of the fees that may be payable. They are however reminded that the proportions in which the total amount of the fees is divided between the members of the arbitral tribunal (40% for the President, 30% for each coarbitrator) are given merely as a guide and may be changed by the Court.

If, in the course of an arbitration, the amount of the advance is increased pursuant to a decision of the Court, this step may be repeated.

Step 3: Disclosure of the estimated amounts of VAT

The arbitrator fixes a time limit in this respect and requests the parties:

- to pay the VAT advance in US dollars
- bear any banking charges associated with the payment
- use the following banking instructions:

Beneficiary (*Account holder*):	International Chamber of Commerce 38, cours Albert 1er 75008 Paris, France
Bank of Beneficiary:	UBS SA 35, rue des Noirettes P.O. Box 2600 1211 Geneva 2, Switzerland
IBAN:	CH44 0024 0240 2245 3463 G
Code SWIFT/BIC:	UBSWCHZH80A
Reference of the case:	*****/***/VAT Arbitrators

The arbitrator must also inform the Secretariat of the substance of this request. If the president calls for a VAT advance on behalf of the members of the arbitral tribunal subject to VAT, he or she shall inform the Secretariat of the breakdown of this advance arbitrator-by-arbitrator.

Step 4: Acknowledgement of payments and administration

The Secretariat confirms to the arbitrator and the parties the receipt of the amounts paid by the parties.

In the absence of communication to the arbitrator by the Secretariat of any receipt of payments on the advance on VAT made by the parties, it is up to the arbitrator to renew his or her request to the parties and to fix a time limit in this respect.

ICC administers the VAT advance on behalf of the arbitrator.

Step 5: Payments to the arbitrator

When drawing up his or her invoice, the arbitrator requests ICC to pay the amount corresponding to the VAT on the fees due by the parties. This applies at the time of the final award, but also in the event that the Court decides to pay an advance on fees to arbitrators who reside in countries where, under local tax law, VAT becomes payable to the tax authorities when fees are paid in advance.

Payments are made to the arbitrators by ICC on behalf of the parties and within the limits of the VAT advances already provided.

Step 6: Balance of account

At the end of the arbitration proceedings the Secretariat seeks instructions from the arbitrator for closing the VAT advance. On the basis of the information provided by the arbitrator and in accordance with his or her instructions, the Secretariat closes the VAT account and returns to the parties any amounts remaining from the VAT advance deposited with ICC.

After advising the arbitrator, ICC may close the account if no balance remains. The account will be closed even if the parties have not paid any additional VAT advance requested by the arbitrator.

DOCUMENT 13

NOTIFICATION BY THE TRIBUNAL TO THE PARTIES OF THE CASE MANAGEMENT CONFERENCE AND INVITATION TO COMMENT ON THE CLAIMS (WITH EXTRACT FROM THE COMMISSION REPORT ON SAVING TIME AND COSTS (2ND EDITION) REGARDING THE CASE MANAGEMENT CONFERENCE)

[Letterhead of President]

[Counsel]

Re: ______________________) (ICC Case No. _____/MHM)

[•] 2012

Dear Colleagues:

Attached is an initial draft of the Terms of Reference as well as a list of points for consideration in the procedural order. The Tribunal has the following comments:

1. We would ask the parties to provide the draft insert of their claims and requests for relief within seven days after the date of this letter.
2. We would encourage the parties to discuss the extent to which they may be able to agree on the procedural issues. We would like to hear back from the parties three days prior to the case management conference as to areas of agreement or disagreement with respect to the procedure.
3. The Tribunal tends to think that a case management conference would be useful and proposes January 4, 2013 either in Paris (beginning at 13:00) or in London (whenever most convenient for those coming from Paris).
4. The purpose of the case management conference is to finalize the Terms of Reference, discuss the procedure, seek to agree on a preliminary timetable and to deal with any other issue that the parties may have. In the present case, the Request for Arbitration and Answer set out the parties' positions in some detail. However, if both parties agree on making a brief presentation of 5–10 minutes, the Tribunal would not object.
5. The parties' attention is drawn to Appendix IV of the ICC Rules as to some basic case management techniques. Discussion of these is often part of an overall discussion of the procedure.
6. The Tribunal looks forward to hearing from the parties as soon as possible and in any event within one week as to their views on the usefulness, place and date of the case management conference. Once again, if the parties reach a joint position, that will be given considerable weight by the Tribunal.

Thank you for your cooperation.

Yours truly

cc. Co-arbitrators

ICC

Extract
Case management conferences

25 Timing

Article 24(1) requires the arbitral tribunal to convene a case management conference when drawing up theTerms of Reference or as soon as possible thereafter. Consider whether it is most convenient and efficient to hold the case management conference immediately after the signing of the Terms of Reference and at the same meeting.

26 Preparation

For the case management conference to be most effective, the tribunal should consider asking the parties well in advance of the conference to submit joint or separate case management proposals. This will encourage them actively to consider and exchange views on the procedures and case management techniques that may be appropriate for the case. Any joint or separate proposals from the parties, any agreements between the parties, and any suggestions from the tribunal should be discussed at the case management conference. It should be noted that, in accordance with Article 22(2) of the Rules, the arbitral tribunal may not adopt procedural measures that are contrary to an agreement of the parties.

27 Use of the Techniques

Appendix IV of the Rules sets out examples of available case management techniques. These and additional examples are also contained in this Report. They can be used by the arbitral tribunal and the parties at the case management conference to assist in arriving at the most appropriate procedures for the case (see the section entitled "Subsequent procedure for the arbitration" below).

28 Providing information in advance of the conference

The more information the arbitral tribunal has about the issues in the case prior to the conference, the better placed it will be to assist the parties in devising a procedure that will deal with the dispute as efficiently as possible. For example, a tribunal that has made itself familiar with the details of the case from the outset can be proactive and give appropriate, tailor made suggestions on the issues to be addressed in documentary and witness evidence, the areas in which it will be assisted by expert evidence, and the extent to which disclosure of documents by the parties is needed to address the issues in dispute.

29 Scope

Whenever possible, the procedure for the entire arbitration should be determined at the first case management conference and reflected in the procedural timetable to be established pursuant to Article 24(2) of the Rules. However, it may not always be possible to do so, for example in very complex cases or in cases where insufficient detail has been provided prior to the first case management conference. In such situations, the procedural timetable would lay out the procedure as far as can be done (e.g. through a first round of briefs) and a second case management conference would be held promptly to determine the remainder of the procedure for the arbitration.

30 Client attendance

Article 24(4) of the Rules expressly allows the arbitral tribunal to request the attendance at the case management conference of the parties in person or through an internal representative. The tribunal should consider requiring such attendance. When clients are present at the case management conference, they can play an active role in the decision-making process. They should be empowered to make case management decisions. Such decisions call for a cost benefit analysis. For example, is an additional round of briefs worth the time and expense? Is a degree of discovery-style document production likely to produce benefits justifying the time and cost?

31 Need for a physical meeting

As with the drawing up of the Terms of Reference (see paragraph 22 above) and as permitted by Article 24(4), consider whether it is appropriate to hold the case management conference by way of telephone, video conference or similar means of communication that do not involve a physical meeting. If the case management conference is to be held at the same time as the Terms of Reference are signed, consider whether that would justify a physical meeting for both purposes.

32 Use of discretion in apportionment of costs

Pursuant to Article 37(5) of the Rules, the extent to which each party has conducted the arbitration in an expeditious and cost-effective manner may be taken into account by the arbitral tribunal in determining who shall bear what portion of the costs of the arbitration. The arbitral tribunal should consider informing the parties at the case management conference that in exercising its discretion to allocate costs pursuant to the Rules, it will take into consideration any unreasonable failure to comply with procedures agreed upon or ordered in the arbitration or any other unreasonable conduct (see paragraph 82 below).

33 Further case management conferences

Consider holding further case management conferences during the course of the arbitration, as appropriate. Such conferences may be held prior to significant phases in the procedure (e.g. the exchange of witness statements) so as to ensure that the procedure provided for that phase remains appropriate. Short telephone conferences may also be held at regular intervals (e.g. once a month) to enable the arbitral tribunal to check on progress and discuss with the parties any unforeseen procedural issues that have arisen or may shortly arise.

DOCUMENT 14

POINTS FOR CONSIDERATION FOR THE PROCEDURE

[Note: The chairman would usually transmit to the parties an invitation to submit their comments on their claims together with a list of points on the procedure that he or she would like them to consider. Set out below is a list of points for consideration in the procedure.]

Preliminary Draft

POINTS FOR CONSIDERATION IN THE PROCEDURAL ORDER

1. Submissions of the Parties

1.1 Timing: after exchange of relevant documents

1.2 Requests for documents

1.3 Simultaneous or consecutive submissions

1.4 Post-hearing briefs

1.5 Documents relied on to be submitted with submissions

1.6 Translations submitted with the documents

2. Documentary evidence

2.1 Time limits for submission; effect of late submission; documents for cross examination

2.2 Should assertions about the origins and receipt of documents and about the correctness of photocopies be assumed as accurate

2.3 Are the parties willing to submit jointly a set of documentary evidence

2.4 Numbering of documents

3. Witnesses

3.1 Advance notice of witnesses whom a party intends to present (contents if no witness statements)

3.2 Use of witness statements

3.2.1 Timing: simultaneous or consecutive
3.2.2 Scope and effect of omissions
3.2.3 Effect on examination in chief
3.2.4 Availability for cross-examination
3.2.5 Formalities: signed, affirmation or oath

3.3 Manner in which oral testimony will be taken

3.3.1 Questioning by the parties and the Tribunal
3.3.2 Formalities
3.3.3 Whether witnesses can attend the hearings when not testifying
3.3.4 Order in which witnesses to be called
3.3.5 Hearing party representatives

4. Experts and expert testimony

4.1 Expert testimony presented by the parties

4.2 Whether the Tribunal will appoint an expert

5. Hearings

5.1 Whether one set or several hearings

5.2 Time required for each side to present its case

5.2.1 Opening statements
5.2.2 Presenting their evidence
5.2.3 Cross-examination

5.3 Length of the hearings

5.4 Bifurcation of jurisdiction issue

5.5 Arrangements for a record of the hearings

5.6 Submissions of notes at the time of the hearing

6. Preliminary Schedule

7. Compliance with ICC timing requirements

DOCUMENT 15

TERMS OF REFERENCE

ICC ARBITRATION NO. /MHM

---

1. **X SA (FRANCE)**
2. **X Gestein GMBH (GERMANY)**
3. **X Stone SAS (FRANCE)**

v.

1. **Y INTERNATIONAL SARL (LUXEMBOURG)** 2. **Y INTERNATIONAL HOLDINGS B.V. (NETHERLANDS)** 3. **Y GROUP LIMITED (UNITED KINGDOM)**

Arbitral Tribunal:

A, Co-arbitrator
B, QC Co-arbitrator
C, President

Pursuant to Article 23 of the Rules of Arbitration effective January 1, 2012 (the "Rules") of the International Court of Arbitration of the International Chamber of Commerce, the Tribunal and the Parties hereby establish the following terms of reference (the "Terms of Reference") for the above-mentioned arbitration:

I. THE PARTIES AND THEIR COUNSEL

1. The Claimants in these proceedings are:

   X SA, a French company with its registered office at:
   [address]

   X Gestein GmbH, a German company with its registered office at:
   [address]

   X Stone SAS, a French company with its registered office at:
   [address]

2. The Claimants are part of a group that specializes in__________________.
3. Counsel representing the Claimants in these proceedings and to whom all communications should be sent is:

   [name and address]
4. The Respondents in these proceedings are:

   Y International SARL, a Luxembourg company with its registered office at:
   [address]

   Y International Holdings BV, a Dutch company with its registered office at:
   [address]

Y Group Limited, an English Company with its registered office located at: [address]

5. The Respondents are part of the Y Group. The Y companies are also active in road construction, transportation infrastructure and quarry exploitation.

6. The Respondents are represented in these proceedings by counsel and all communications should be sent to:

   [name and address]

II. PROCEDURE TO DATE; CONSTITUTION OF THE TRIBUNAL

9. On [•] 2012, the Claimants filed a Request for Arbitration (the "Request"). The Request included Exhibits numbered 1 to 5.

10. The Claimants submitted as Attachment No. 1 a copy of the agreement between the Claimants and the Respondents, as well as Y France SAS, dated [•] 2010 (the "Agreement") pursuant to which this arbitration was brought.

11. The Agreement provides in particular as follows:

> *"13.23.1 This Agreement and the documents to be entered into pursuant to it, save as expressly referred to therein, and any non-contractual obligations arising out of or in connection with the Agreement and such documents shall be governed by and construed in accordance with English law.*
>
> *13.23.2 Any dispute arising out of, or in connection with, this Agreement shall be finally settled by arbitration in accordance with the Rules of Arbitration of the International Chamber of Commerce.*
>
> *13.23.3 The place of arbitration shall be Geneva. The language to be used in the arbitral proceedings shall be English."*

12. On [•] 2012, the Respondents requested an extension to file their answer to the Request (the "Answer") and requested that the Claimants produce certain documents referred to in the Request.

13. On [•] 2012, the Claimants provided the Respondents with certain of the documents requested on [•] 2012.

14. On [•] 2012, the ICC Secretariat granted the Respondents until [•] 2012 to file their Answer.

15. On [•] 2012, the Claimants provided the Respondents with additional documents requested by the Respondents on [•] 2012.

16. On [•] 2012, the Respondents filed the Answer together with Annexes 1–5. In their Answer, the Respondents agreed that the relationship between the parties is governed by the Agreement; that the provisions of Articles 13.23.1, 13.23.2 and 13.23.3 of the Agreement are applicable, and agreed with the statements in paragraph 123 of the Request:

    (a) *that all of the claims advanced in this Request for Arbitration shall be finally resolved by arbitration under the ICC Rules of Arbitration;*

    (b) *that the arbitration shall be legally seated in Geneva, Switzerland and that Swiss law shall be the applicable law for the proceedings;*

    (c) *that the language of the arbitration shall be English;*

    (d) *that the governing law of the SPA shall be the substantive law of England and Wales subject to the mandatory provisions of the law of the forum and the laws in which the Companies are registered and operating; and*

    (e) *that there shall be three arbitrators.*

17. The Claimants jointly nominated as co-arbitrator in the Request:

A
[address]

18. The Respondents jointly nominated as co-arbitrator on [•] 2012:

B, QC
[address]

19. On [•] 2012, the ICC International Court of Arbitration ("ICC Court") confirmed the co-arbitrators.

20. On [•] 2012, upon proposal of the Canadian National Committee of the ICC, the ICC Court appointed as President:

C
[address]

21. This matter is being handled by the following members of the Secretariat:

[•] Counsel
[•] Deputy Counsel
[•] Deputy Counsel
Secretariat of the ICC International Court of Arbitration

33–43 avenue du Président Wilson
75116 Paris
France
Tel: +33 1 49 53 28 34
Fax: +33 1 49 53 57 76
E-mail: ica6@iccwbo.org

22. The Tribunal received the file on [•] 2012. On [•] 2012, the President wrote to the Parties to inform them that they would be receiving a draft of the Terms of Reference and an outline of points for the procedural order as soon as possible and asking them to prepare a brief outline of their claims and requests for relief.

23. On [•] 2012, the Tribunal transmitted to the parties a draft of the Terms of Reference together with a list of points for consideration in the procedural order and proposing that the case management conference be held on [•] 2013.

24. The parties exchanged further correspondence relating to the procedure and to the draft Terms of Reference during the period up to (and including) [•] 2013.

25. On [•] 2012, the Tribunal confirmed that the case management conference would be held in London on [•] 2013.

26. In accordance with Article 24 of the Rules, a case management conference was scheduled on [•] 2013 to permit:

(i) the parties to provide an original of their powers of attorney authorizing the persons signing the Terms of Reference to sign that document to the extent not previously provided;

(ii) the Terms of Reference to be signed;

(iii) the Parties to discuss with the Tribunal the procedure to be adopted with respect to the arbitration in the light of Article 22 of the Rules and the case management techniques in Appendix IV to the Rules;

(iv) the Tribunal to establish a procedural timetable.

<u>Summary of the Procedural Aspects of the Arbitration</u>

27. The Parties confirm the principles set out in paragraph 16 above. Therefore, on the basis of the Request and Answer, there is no jurisdictional issue at present in these proceedings.

28. The Parties confirm that they have no grounds to object to any of the arbitrators.

III. CLAIMS AND ISSUES

29. The following summary of the Parties' respective claims and pleadings submitted to date constitutes a framework designed to enable the Tribunal and the Parties to focus on the issues in the present arbitration. It does not foreclose the making of arguments or the introduction of evidence not expressly referred to herein. The making of new claims or counterclaims is, however, governed by Article 23(4) of the Rules.

30. The claims of the Parties have been established based on the Parties' filings to date. The Claimants' Claims identify their claims. All figures therein are provisional. The signing of these Terms of Reference shall in no way be interpreted as the acceptance of either Party of any claims or requests for relief of the other Party.

31. The Claimants' Claims. The Claimants make the following five claims (with certain capitalized terms referred to below being defined in the Request for Arbitration):

    All amounts stated below as claimed are subject to adjustment and amendment. Certain are estimates only. There are five claims.

    Claim no. 1: [details of claim].

    Claim no. 2: [details of claim]

    Claim no. 3: [details of claim]

    Claim no. 4: [details of claim].

    Claim no. 5: [details of claim]

32. The Claimants' Request for Relief.

    The Claimants seek an award granting them the following relief:

    (i) damages in the foregoing amounts, alternatively in such amount(s) as may be determined by the Tribunal;

    (ii) interest;

    (iii) costs of arbitration as per Article 31 of the ICC Rules.

33. The Respondents' Claims. The Respondents confirm that they have made no counterclaims against the Claimants and do not intend to do so. Relief sought by the Respondents.

    (i) The Respondents have denied, and continue to deny, that:

        (1) any of the losses alleged by the Claimants are recoverable from the Respondents under the SPA or otherwise; and

        (2) the Claimants are entitled to any of the relief they seek.

    (ii) Consequently, the only relief sought by the Respondents is:

        (1) for the Claimants' claims to be dismissed in their entirety; and

        (2) for the Respondents to be awarded their costs of this Arbitration.

The Issues to be Determined

34. The Tribunal shall decide the issues that it determines necessary with respect to the requests for relief filed by each party, including, without limitation, whether the Tribunal has jurisdiction with respect to such request for relief. Based on the claims of the Parties as of the date hereof and the requests for relief, the Tribunal has identified the Claimants' five claims and the Respondents response thereto as the specific issues that should be addressed.

35. The issues set out above may evolve during the course of the proceedings subject to the provisions of the Rules and in particular Article 23(4) of the Rules.

IV. PROCEDURAL ISSUES

36. The Rules shall apply to the arbitration procedure. All issues not covered by those Rules shall be decided by agreement between the Parties and, in case of disagreement, by the Tribunal.

37. As noted above, the place of arbitration is Geneva, Switzerland. These proceedings shall be subject to the Private International Law of Switzerland applicable to international arbitration proceedings, being Chapter 12 of the Swiss Federal Private International Law Act of 18 December 1987.

38. The Parties have agreed that the language of this arbitration shall be English. The parties agree that Article 13.23.1 of the Agreement sets out the applicable law with respect to disputes under the Agreement.

39. Documents submitted to the Arbitral Tribunal in any language other than English shall be accompanied by a translation into English of the relevant parts on which a Party relies. When a Party submits a partial translation into English, the opposing Party may request that a more extensive translation or a full translation be provided. The Parties will make good faith efforts to agree on the extent of the needed translation, and any unresolved question will be submitted to the Tribunal for resolution.

40. Written statements of witnesses shall be ranked as testimony and considered as evidence in chief at the evidentiary hearing before the Arbitral Tribunal. A Party may call a witness or witnesses who have submitted written statements to give oral evidence. The Arbitral Tribunal, or either Party, shall have the right to examine any witness, but a reasonable time, as determined by the Arbitral Tribunal, shall in such event be allocated to each of the Parties for examination/cross-examination. The Parties' legal representatives may also make oral arguments to the Arbitral Tribunal for such reasonable time as the Arbitral Tribunal may allow within the overall time allocated in the procedural timetable for the substantive hearing.

41. The Arbitral Tribunal shall remind each witness before giving their oral evidence of the requirement for witnesses to provide truthful evidence and of the risk of criminal sanctions under the Swiss Penal Code (Article 309) in the event that the witness provides false evidence.

42. Witnesses may give oral evidence in the language of their choice, provided that arrangements for consecutive or simultaneous interpretation to the satisfaction of the Arbitral Tribunal are made by the Party calling the witnesses in question, initially at its own cost, such costs to form part of the costs of the arbitration.

43. A full written record of a verbatim transcript shall be made of all proceedings, including oral evidence, presented to the Arbitral Tribunal, unless the Arbitral Tribunal directs otherwise. The cost of such written records shall be shared equally between the Parties prior to an Award on the costs of the arbitration.

44. The Tribunal shall have the right to determine any conclusion(s), claim(s) or counterclaim(s) raised by the parties in a partial Award if it deems it appropriate in the circumstances of the case.

45. All communications in the course of the arbitration shall be sent to the parties by any means of communication *via* their respective counsel at their above stated addresses and to the Tribunal at the above stated addresses.

46. Any change in address shall be notified to the representatives of the other parties, the members of the Tribunal and the ICC promptly and in the same fashion.

47. The Parties will address all communications to the Tribunal, to the opposing party and to the Secretariat of the ICC Court (the "Secretariat") simultaneously. Documents may be validly communicated from one party to another, provided that a copy is simultaneously sent to the Secretariat and to the Tribunal.

48. Notifications and communications shall be sent by email. Any email submission should be limited to the text of the submission and must be followed by a full hard copy, including any documentary memorials, evidence and exhibits, sent by express courier service or by hand delivery no later than the next business day. The email addresses are set out above for the Parties, the Tribunal and the Secretariat.

49. Each page of each document submitted in these proceedings should be given a unique number by the party submitting it, and this should be marked on the document itself: the Claimants' numbering is to start with "C" and the Respondents' numbering is to start with "R".

50. The paginated bundle of documents for the substantive hearing will be prepared in accordance with the index which is to be agreed, with a single copy only of each document.

51. Time limits for submissions set by the Tribunal are considered respected if the submissions are sent up to and including the last day of the time limit until midnight Geneva time. Where submissions are due from both sides simultaneously, the local time in Geneva applies.

52. If either Party fails, within the prescribed time, to present its case or comply with the directions of the Arbitral Tribunal at any stage of the proceedings, the Tribunal may, of its own volition, or at the request of the other Party, after giving reasonable notice to the Parties, proceed with the arbitration and make an Award.

53. The Parties agree to keep confidential all orders and awards in this arbitration, together with all materials in the proceedings, either created for the purposes of the arbitration, such as correspondence, memorials, submissions, etc. and all other documents produced by another party in the proceedings not otherwise in the public domain, save and to the extent that disclosure may be required of a party by law or by order of a court or to enforce an award issued pursuant hereto. This undertaking of all parties will not prevent the Tribunal from taking additional measures for protecting trade secrets and other confidential information (Article 22(3) of the Rules).

54. The Arbitral Tribunal may be guided by the *IBA Rules on the Taking of Evidence in International Arbitration (2010)* but shall not be bound to apply these rules. The Parties hereby confirm their agreement, for the duration of this arbitration, to take all reasonable steps to retain and preserve any documents (whether hard copy and/or electronic documents in any format, whether currently in existence or which come into existence in the future) which are or may be reasonably anticipated to be of relevance to any issues in the arbitration.

55. All interlocutory applications shall be made in writing. In addition:

- Requests for the fixing of time limits or for extensions of time shall be determined by the President of the Arbitral Tribunal alone, after such consultation with the other members of the Arbitral Tribunal and, if, the President considers it appropriate, after consultation with the Parties. Any requests for extensions of time must state until which date the extension is requested, why the extension is necessary and why the request could not have been made earlier.

- Interlocutory applications other than requests for the fixing of time limits or for extensions of time will be determined by the Arbitral Tribunal. It shall be within the discretion of the Arbitral Tribunal to hold a hearing prior to the determination of such interlocutory applications.

- All procedural orders to be issued by the Arbitral Tribunal may be signed by the President alone, on behalf of the Arbitral Tribunal.

<u>Value Added Tax</u>

56. The Parties shall pay any amount that may be due with respect to Value Added Tax on the amounts due to the Tribunal; however, the recovery of those taxes is a matter between the Tribunal and the Parties.

57. To the extent that Value Added Tax might be due on the Tribunal's fees under the applicable tax rules, the undersigning Party/Parties undertake to pay the applicable Value Added Tax upon request and submission of an invoice addressed to them by the Tribunal.

58. The place of arbitration is Geneva (Switzerland).

59. These Terms of Reference are signed in 12 copies and may be signed in counterparts.

Date: [•] 2013

X SA	**Y INTERNATIONAL SARL**
X GESTEIN GMBH	**Y INTERNATIONAL HOLDINGS B.V.**
X STONE SAS	**Y GROUP LIMITED**
A, Co-arbitrator	**B, QC, Co-arbitrator**

C
President

PROCEDURAL TIMETABLE

EXHIBIT A TO PROCEDURAL ORDER NO. 1

ICC ARBITRATION NO. _______/MHM/EMT

---

1. **X SA (FRANCE)**
2. **X Gestein GMBH (GERMANY)**
3. **X Stone SAS (FRANCE)**

v.

1. **Y INTERNATIONAL SARL (LUXEMBOURG)** 2. **Y INTERNATIONAL HOLDINGS B.V. (NETHERLANDS)** 3. **Y GROUP LIMITED (UNITED KINGDOM)**

PROCEDURAL TIMETABLE

No.	Action	Party	Time Period	Date
1.	Request for Arbitration	Claimants	N/A	August 20, 2012
2.	Answer to the Request for Arbitration	Respondents	N/A	November 9, 2012
3.	File received by members of the Tribunal	N/A	N/A	December 7, 2012
4.	Case Management Conference (Finalization of the Terms of Reference, Procedural Timetable and Procedural Rules)	Tribunal and Parties	N/A	February 6, 2013
5.	Procedural Order No. 1 (with Procedural Timetable)	Tribunal	N/A	February 7, 2013
6.	Statement of Claim (with exhibits, witness statement(s) and expert report(s))	Claimants	14 weeks after Case Management Conference	April 29, 2013
7.	Statement of Defence (with exhibits and witness statement(s) and expert report(s))	Respondents	25 weeks after receipt of Statement of Claim	October 21, 2013

8.	Request(s) for Production of Documents	Both Parties *(inter partes)*	2 weeks after receipt of Statement of Defence	November 4, 2013
9.	Response(s) to Request(s) for Production of Documents and Voluntary Production of Requested Documents	Both Parties *(inter partes)*	2 weeks after relevant Requests for Production	November 18, 2013
10.	Application(s) to Arbitral Tribunal for Production of Documents (with submission of completed Redfern schedules)	Both Parties	2 weeks after Responses to Requests for Production	December 2, 2013
11.	Procedural Order on Contested Request(s) for Production	Tribunal	2 weeks after receipt of Parties' Applications	Target date: December 9, 2013
12.	Production of Documents pursuant to Procedural Order	Both Parties	2 weeks after receipt of Procedural Order	December 23, 2013
13.	Claimants' Reply (with exhibits and supplemental witness statement(s)/expert report(s))	Claimants	12 weeks after receipt of Respondents' Statement of Defence	January 13, 2014
14.	Respondents' Rejoinder (with exhibits and supplemental witness statement(s)/expert report(s))	Respondents	11 weeks after receipt of Claimants' Statement of Reply	April 3, 2014
15.	Experts to prepare list of agreed and not agreed issues	Experts		April 30, 2014
16.	Agreement of contents of trial bundle	Both Parties		May 9, 2014
17.	Procedural Hearing by Telephone (Organisation of Witness Hearing)	Tribunal and Parties	2 weeks before Main Hearing	May 16, 2014
18.	Trial bundle to be produced and filed with the Tribunal	Both Parties	2 weeks before Main Hearing	May 16, 2014
19.	Main Hearing (including Witness Hearing and Closing Argument)	Tribunal and Parties	Either in Geneva or in London as agreed by the parties by February 28, 2013.	June 2–20, 2014
20.	Post-Hearing Procedure [to be discussed at the Procedural Hearing or the Hearing itself]	Tribunal and Parties		

21.	Deliberations of Tribunal	Tribunal	To begin as soon as all submissions have been completed	
22.	Award	Tribunal	Target date for submission to the ICC: Within three months after all submissions have been completed	

DOCUMENT 17

PROCEDURAL ORDER NO. 1

ICC ARBITRATION NO.:

BETWEEN :

D Limited

vs.

M Limited

R
W

T (President)

Background

1. D Limited ("Claimant") filed a Request for Arbitration under the ICC Rules dated [•] 2013 against M Limited ("Respondent").
2. Respondent responded on [•] 2013 to appoint an arbitrator and contest jurisdiction and confirmed on [•] 2013 that Respondent would not file a substantive response but disputed liablity to Claimant.
3. On [•] 2013, Claimant noted the provisions of Section 31 of the Arbitration Act and invited Respondent to set out any jurisdictional objection promptly.
4. On [•] 2013, Respondent responded stating that the most reasonable course in its point of view would be to file the substantive jurisdiction application once the Tribunal had been appointed.
5. The Tribunal was constituted on [•] 2013.
6. On [•] 2013, Respondent applied to have the arbitration dismissed on jurisdictional grounds.
7. On [•] 2013, Claimant objected to having the jurisdictional issue dealt with at the outset.
8. On [•] 2013, Respondent clarified its application for dismissal by email.
9. The Tribunal deliberated on [•] 2013 and agreed on the following procedural order.

The Tribunal therefore decides as follows:

1. Claimant filed a Request for Arbitration based on an agreement dated [•] 2012 (the "Agreement") (signed in two somewhat different versions by the two parties) seeking the following relief: [not reproduced]

2. Respondent maintains that the claim should be dismissed and that this matter should be decided at the outset. Respondent relied in particular on the following factors with respect to dismissal of the application:

    (1) With regard to the defamation claim, Respondent maintains that it is not a "*dispute arising out of or in connection with*" the Sale Contract and therefore it is not subject to the arbitration provision;

    (2) With regard to the other claims, Respondent maintains that the claims were the subject of a settlement agreement dated [•] 2012 among the parties; and

    (3) In addition, the guarantee letter dated [•] 2012 is also subject to LMAA arbitration.

3. Claimant noted that it was unclear that Respondent was seeking to have the jurisdictional issue decided at the outset [brief summary of position]

4. In an email dated [•] 2013 Respondent confirmed that it wished the jurisdictional issue decided at the outset stating: [brief summary of position]

5. The preliminary issue for the Tribunal is whether it would be appropriate at this stage to have the jurisdictional issue further briefed prior to taking a decision as to whether to accept or reject the jurisdictional objection or to defer any decision on the jurisdictional objection until the Tribunal decides issues on the merits.

6. The Tribunal has decided that it would be appropriate to have further briefing on the jurisdictional issue prior to deciding the issue for the following reasons:

    (1) Respondent has set out detailed objections to jurisdiction based in part on a settlement agreement among the parties and a third party and the Tribunal would like to receive further information from Claimant regarding this settlement agreement.

    (2) In conjunction with that further information, it may be of assistance to provide witness evidence. However, it is not clear that this evidence will be necessary or that it will overlap with evidence on the merits.

    (3) The timetable for these submissions need not be lengthy and therefore it will not result in substantial delay. In addition, the Tribunal may proceed in parallel to establish the procedure for the merits in case the Tribunal either finds that it has jurisdiction or decides not to decide the jurisdictional issue as a preliminary matter.

7. Therefore, the Tribunal orders as follows:

    (1) Respondent shall make any further filing that it wishes to make by the close of business on [•] 2013.

    (2) Claimant shall make any further filing that it wishes to make by the close of business on [•] 2013.

    (3) Respondent may file a reply by the close of business on [•] 2013

    (4) Claimant may file a rejoinder by the close of business on [•] 2013.

    (5) In their filings, the parties are invited in particular to address any issues of lis pendens that may exist with respect to any LMAA arbitration proceedings pending at the present time. The parties may file witness statements and exhibits with their filings.

    (6) The Tribunal shall hold a hearing to deal either with the jurisdictional issue or the procedure on the merits or both at the request of either party in the second half of [•] 2013 and the parties are invited to confirm the dates

on which they are available for such hearing as well as the proposed venue for the hearing.

8. This Procedural Order is issued on behalf of the Tribunal. The Tribunal reserves the right to modify this Procedural Order.

[•] 2013

__________, President

Document 18

SUMMARY MINUTES OF THE HEARING ON JURISDICTION

In the ICC Arbitration Case No. [•] between:

B, LLC (United States) as Claimant and A, SA (France) as Respondent

SUMMARY MINUTES OF THE HEARING
ON [•]

Place: [•]

Attendance: The Tribunal composed of Messrs [•] (Chairman), [•] and [•]

Parties: As per the attached attendance lists

1. The Hearing on jurisdiction was opened on [•] 2013 at [•] AM and ended on [•] 2013 at [•] PM.

2. It was agreed that the Parties would first present their arguments in respect of the issue on jurisdiction. After the conclusion of the Parties' opening statement in respect of the issue on jurisdiction, clarifying questions were addressed by the Tribunal to the Parties as well as further interventions on behalf of the Parties. The following witnesses called by the Parties were heard in the following order: For Claimant, [•]; for Respondent, [•]. The examination of the witnesses was completed on [•] at [•] AM. Claimant's total time of examination was two hours thirty minutes and Respondent's one hour seventeen minutes. This does not include the time used by the Tribunal in questioning the witnesses.

3. The cross-examination of [•] was waived by Respondent, and they were therefore not heard. The cross-examination of [•] by Claimant was waived in view of the illness of that witness.

4. A verbatim transcript was taken of the entire hearing by Mr. [•] and Mr. [•] of Irish Stenographers.

5. Before declaring the hearing closed, the President noted that the Parties had no further requests, and thanked counsel for both Parties for their professional and courteous attitude throughout the proceedings.

6. The Tribunal indicated to the Parties that Post Hearing briefs shall be submitted by both Parties on [•]. Thereafter the proceedings will be closed as regards jurisdiction, and the Tribunal shall endeavour to issue a partial award on jurisdiction as soon as feasible thereafter. Once said award is rendered and subject to its findings, the hearings shall be held to determine liability and to evaluate quantum of either the Claimant or the Respondent. The Tribunal endeavours to have the arbitration concluded before the end of the year by sending a final Award.

[•] 2013

On behalf of the Tribunal

President

Document 19

SECRETARIAT'S NOTIFICATION OF PARTIAL AWARD

[•] vs/ 1. [•] 2. [•] 3. [•]

Dear Mesdames and Sirs,

Pursuant to Article 34 of the ICC Rules of Arbitration, the Secretariat of the ICC International Court of Arbitration notifies you the Partial Award dated [•] 2013 and rendered by the Arbitral Tribunal, which was approved by the Court at its session of [•] 2013.

We draw your attention to Article 34(6) of the Rules which states: *"Every Award shall be binding on the parties. By submitting the dispute to arbitration under these Rules, the parties undertake to carry out any Award without delay and shall be deemed to have waived their right to any form of recourse insofar as such waiver can validly be made"*.

Yours faithfully,

[•]
Deputy Counsel
Secretariat of the ICC International Court of Arbitration

Encl: Original of the Partial Award dated [•] 2013

DOCUMENT 20

PROCEDURAL ORDER NO. 2

ICC ARBITRTION NO._____

BETWEEN :

A

vs.

(1) B
(2) C, AND
(3) D

____________ (Sole Arbitrator)

Background

1. The Sole Arbitrator invited the parties to confer with respect to the procedure for the arbitration.
2. The Claimant and the Second and Third Respondents conferred and transmitted separate comments on [•] 2013.
3. The Claimant provided follow up comments on [•] 2013 and the Second and Third Respondents provided follow up comments on [•] 2013.
4. On [•] 2013, the Sole Arbitrator circulated a letter and a draft procedural timetable for the arbitration inviting the parties to comment on the procedural timetable within three days.
5. The Claimant provided comments on the draft procedural timetable on [•] 2013 (with follow up comments on [•] 2013) and the Respondents provided those comments on [•] 2013 (with a follow up subsequently on [•] 2013).

The Sole Arbitrator decides as follows:

1. In accordance with Article 22 Rules, the Sole Arbitrator is to decide on the procedure to the extent there is no agreement among the parties.
2. Attached as Exhibit A is the Procedural Timetable for the arbitration.
3. As regards the details of the procedure, as I noted in my letter of [•] 2013, the IBA Rules on the Taking of Evidence in International Arbitration (2010) (the "IBA Rules") have become a standard reference in international arbitration. The parties have not adopted the IBA Rules in these proceedings, and the Claimant disagrees with some aspects of

them. However, they are regularly invoked as providing guiding principles for international arbitration[1] and I intend to use them as guidelines for the procedure subject to certain clarifications noted below.

4. As regards documentary production, the criteria are set out in the IBA Rules and in particular in Article 3 and Article 9 of the IBA Rules and will be addressed, if need be, during the documentary production phase. In particular I note the following in Article 3(3)(a) of the IBA Rules:

   3. A Request to Produce shall contain:

   (a) (i) a description of each requested Document sufficient to identify it, or

   (ii) a description in sufficient detail (including subject matter) of a narrow and specific requested category of Documents that are reasonably believed to exist; in the case of Documents maintained in electronic form, the requesting Party may, or the Arbitral Tribunal may order that it shall be required to, identify specific files, search terms, individuals or other means of searching for such Documents in an efficient and economical manner;

   (b) a statement as to how the Documents requested are relevant to the case and material to its outcome; and

   (c) (i) a statement that the Documents requested are not in the possession, custody or control of the requesting Party or a statement of the reasons why it would be unreasonably burdensome for the requesting Party to produce such Documents, and

   (ii) a statement of the reasons why the requesting Party assumes the Documents requested are in the possession, custody or control of another Party.

5. In response to the query of the Claimant, the IBA Rules do not permit a party to refuse to disclose documents on the basis that they are adverse to the party, for example. The grounds for refusing to disclose are set out in Article 9 of the IBA Rules.

6. In response to a query of the Second and Third Respondents, Article 3(4) of the IBA Rules requires disclosure of "all the Documents requested in its possession, custody or control" (subject to objections and decision of the Sole Arbitrator). Therefore, the obligation is limited to documents requested by the opposing party in respect of which no objection to production is made or production of which is ordered by the Sole Arbitrator and it is generally expected that party will not request (and therefore the Sole Arbitrator will not order production of documents in the possession custody or control of the requesting Party (Article 3(3)(c)(i) of the IBA Rules).

7. A Request to Produce (as defined in the IBA Rules) should meet the requirements of Article 3 of the IBA Rules quoted above. A Request to Produce may be submitted in the form of a schedule (referred to as a Redfern Schedule in some cases) or otherwise. However, I expect that the contents will address the issues in Article 3 of the IBA Rules or provide an explanation as to why those issues are not addressed.

8. The Sole Arbitrator orders that any factual witnesses on which a party relies is required to provide witness statements within the time frame provided for in the Procedural Order. In accordance with Article 4(5)(b) of the IBA Rules, the witness statement shall be sufficient to serve as the witness's evidence in the arbitration. Therefore, it should represent the evidence in chief of the witness and direct examination should be (i) of a limited duration agreed by the parties (usually 15–20 minutes) and (ii) provide for an introduction of the witness and deal with issues that have arisen after the witness's last witness statement that a witness could not reasonably have been expected to address previously.

[1] See for example Redfern & Hunter, International Arbitration (5th edn), para.1.245

9. In accordance with Article 7 of the IBA Rules, all witnesses must attend the hearings unless excused. The main purpose of the witnesses attending the hearing is for questioning by the adverse party and the Tribunal.

10. The Sole Arbitrator orders that any expert witness on which a party relies is required to provide an expert report within the time frame provided for in the Procedural Order. In accordance with Article 8(5) of the IBA Rules, Expert Witnesses are expected to attend the hearing. If Expert Evidence is submitted it has become frequent to order the experts to meet and confer as is provided for in Article 8(4) of the IBA Rules. The Procedural Timetable provides for this possibility. The issue of whether a direction will be issued will be addressed if the parties do not agree and an application is made by any party after the initial expert reports have been filed.

11. All parties to the arbitration are to participate in the proceedings. This includes Respondent No.1 who has not participated to date in the proceedings.

12. The Procedural Timetable provides for the preparation of bundles. It is expected that these bundles will be paper bundles with the pleadings, submissions, witness statements and documentary record of a type and in a format that the parties find appropriate for the hearings. The Claimant is to prepare the initial bundles, as the hearings are in London and usually the Claimant does prepare the initial draft. The costs of preparation of the bundles will be costs of arbitration.

13. The bundles should include in particular: (i) all documents relied upon by each party and (ii) all documents that have been submitted by the cut off date including the documents that have been produced by one party to the other parties. For good order, the parties should note that documents that have been produced pursuant to a Notice to Produce but that have not been submitted with the submissions or prior to the cut off date are not considered part of the record for the arbitration and should not be included in the bundles. Therefore, any submission of such documents whether for cross examination or any other purpose would require my consent as Sole Arbitrator.

14. Submissions and witness statements shall be sent out electronically and by courier on the due date. Voluminous documents should also be sent out electronically by the due date but, if this raises a technical issue for a party and it cannot be agreed as among the parties, I will give directions in that respect.

15. For good order, supplying documents in pdf format in chronological order is requested but not required.

16. As Sole Arbitrator, I reserve the right to modify this Procedural Order.

Seat of Arbitration: [•]

[•] 2013

___________, Sole Arbitrator

DOCUMENT 21

LIST OF ATTENDANCE

ICC Arbitration Case No. [•]

between

B, LLC (Claimant) and A (Respondent) List of Attendance

(place of the meeting)

[•] 2008 (Date and time)

NAME	FUNCTION	SIGNATURE

Document 22

POWER OF ATTORNEY

[Letterhead of [•]]
POWER OF ATTORNEY

We, the undersigned, acting as duly authorised representatives for and on behalf of

[•] (name of the Company), whose registered office is at [•], hereby appoint: [•] (name of the Law firm) acting through [•] (name of the Counsel), or any other person designated by him/her

[•] (address) (Tel.: [•]; Fax: [•])

to represent [•] (name of the Company) as its Attorney in respect of the following:

(a) in general in respect to the arbitration commenced by B, LLC, the Claimant, before the International Chamber of Commerce (ICC) against A, the Respondent, ICC case No. [•]

(b) in particular all acts as the Attorney shall deem necessary and appropriate under this representation in the interests of [•] in connection with the conduct of the whole ensuing arbitration proceedings including, without limitation, the constitution and the appointment of the Arbitral Tribunal, the execution and submission of all documents, the making of all pleadings, oral and written, the receipt and acknowledgement of any funds pertaining to the arbitration on behalf of [•], and

(c) the execution of any settlement agreement in connection with the arbitration.

[•], date/month/year

For [•] [•] (Name)

Attached: Documents reflecting the authority of signatories (Board resolution appointing representative of a US company or Commercial Registry Extract for European company, for example.)

DOCUMENT 23

LETTER CLOSING THE PROCEEDINGS

[Letterhead of President of the Tribunal]

[Counsel to Claimant]

[Counsel to Respondent]

[Date]

Re: ICC Case No. [•]

X (France) v Y (United Kingdom)

Dear Madam, dear Sirs:

On behalf of the Tribunal, and pursuant to Article 27 of the ICC Rules, I write formally to declare the proceedings closed with respect to the matters to be decided by final award in this case and to notify the Parties that the Tribunal expects to submit its draft award to the ICC Court for approval pursuant to Article 33 of the ICC Rules within the next 30 days.

Sincerely,
C.
President
cc:
ica5@iccwbo.org

DOCUMENT 24

SECRETARIAT'S LETTER EXTENDING THE DATE FOR RENDERING THE AWARD

[•] vs [•]
Counsel: [•]
Deputy Counsel: [•]

(Email: ica5@iccwbo.org)

Dear Sirs,

On [•] 2013, the International Court of Arbitration of the International Chamber of Commerce extended the time limit for rendering the final award until **[•] 2013** (Article 30(2)).

Yours faithfully,

[•]
Deputy Counsel
Secretariat of the ICC International Court of Arbitration

Document 25

ICC AWARD CHECKLIST (2012 RULES)

Disclaimer: This list is intended to provide arbitrators acting under the ICC Rules of Arbitration with guidance when drafting Awards and in no way constitutes an exhaustive, mandatory or otherwise binding document. It should not be thought to reflect the opinion of the ICC Court, its Secretariat or its members, but is intended simply to facilitate the arbitrators' mission. It may not be published or used for any purpose other than the conduct of ICC arbitration. Moreover, this checklist is not exhaustive of issues that may be raised by the ICC Court under Article 33 of the Rules.

1. General
   - □ A. ICC case reference number mentioned in full on front page.
   - □ B. Award clearly identified in its title as Interim, Partial, Final or Award by Consent.
   - □ C. Paragraphs numbered.
   - □ D. Pages numbered.
   - □ E. Table of contents included (unless Award is short and does not need one).
   - □ F. Abbreviations defined and used consistently.
   - □ G. Translations of quotations in languages other than the language(s) of the arbitration.
   - □ H. Indication of the applicable version of the ICC Rules of Arbitration (*e.g.* 2012).
2. Identification of the parties, their representatives and the arbitrator(s)
   - □ A. Parties' complete addresses and correct names. Clarify the identity of any parties to the arbitration that are different from the parties to the contract(s).
   - □ B. Addresses of parties' representatives.
   - □ C. Arbitrators' addresses.
3. Arbitration and choice-of-law agreements
   - □ A. Quotation of entire arbitration agreement(s).
   - □ B. Record of any agreed amendments to the arbitration agreement(s).
   - □ C. Precise indication of the parties to and/or signatories of the arbitration agreement(s).
   - □ D. Quotation of relevant choice-of-law clause.
4. History of the arbitral proceedings
   - □ A. Summary of all procedural steps to date (*e.g.* Request for Arbitration, Answer, Terms of Reference, date of the case management conference, procedural timetable, parties' submissions, hearing).
   - □ B. Indication of the ICC Court's decisions regarding (if applicable):

- □ i. Article 6(4);
- □ ii. Place of arbitration;
- □ iii. Number of arbitrators.

□ C. Description of the constitution of the Arbitral Tribunal (including confirmation or appointment decisions).

□ D. If applicable, reference to the parties' agreement on an alternative method of nominating or appointing the president of the Arbitral Tribunal.

□ E. Date of closing of the proceedings under Article 27 (for every award).

□ F. Indication of the time limit for rendering the final award, including any extensions granted by the Court under Article 30(2) and the date on which it was granted. It is recommended that all extensions granted by the Court and the date(s) on which they were granted be specified, especially when Paris is the place of arbitration.

□ G. If there has been a prior Award, no need to repeat the procedural history set out in the prior Award, but simply:

- □ i. restate the information mentioned in sections 1, 2 and 3 above;
- □ ii. refer to the previous Award, the date on which it was notified to the parties by the Secretariat, the issues it decided, and the fact that its procedural background is incorporated by reference into the present Award;
- □ iii. describe the procedure subsequent to that set out in the previous Award.

5. Jurisdiction

□ Wherever jurisdiction has been contested, or there is a non-participating party, or the ICC Court has made an Article 6(4) decision, the award should ordinarily include the Arbitral Tribunal's decision on jurisdiction or state why it is not necessary.

6. Costs of the Arbitration (Final Awards only)

□ A. Costs of arbitration fixed by the ICC Court and each party's legal costs dealt with separately in both the body of the Award and in the dispositive section.

□ B. Reference to Article 37 and to the discretion in Article 37(5) to allocate costs (i.e. costs of arbitration fixed by the Court and parties' legal costs) and fix the amount to be borne by each party.

7. Dispositive section, place of arbitration, date, signature

□ A. Award contains a dispositive section mentioning all orders (including the decision on jurisdiction, if applicable) and nothing more.

□ B. Award deals with all of the issues and parties' claims (which should be stated clearly and precisely somewhere in the Award and compared to the Terms of Reference), including the parties' most recent requests for relief, and decides nothing more than those issues and claims (state clearly if certain claims are reserved for one or more future Awards).

□ C. State in the dispositive section of Final Awards that all other requests and claims are rejected (unless the nature of the Award makes this unnecessary).

□ D. After the dispositive section, add the date on which the Award is made and the signatures in the following manner:

Place of arbitration: City (Country)

Date: _/_/____ *[date must be later than the Court session at which the Award was approved and not earlier than when the last arbitrator signs]*

Signature(s):____________

DOCUMENT 26

ICC NOTE ON CORRECTION AND INTERPRETATION OF ARBITRAL AWARDS

27 May 2013

Procedure

Article 35 of the 2012 Rules provides:

> *"1. On its own initiative, the arbitral tribunal may correct a clerical, computational or typographical error, or any errors of similar nature contained in an award, provided such correction is submitted for approval to the Court within 30 days of the date of such award.*
>
> *2. Any application of a party for the correction of an error of the kind referred to in Article 35(1), or for the interpretation of an award, must be made to the Secretariat within 30 days of the receipt of the award by such party, in a number of copies as stated in Article 3(1). After transmittal of the application to the arbitral tribunal, the latter shall grant the other party a short time limit, normally not exceeding 30 days, from the receipt of the application by that party, to submit any comments thereon. The arbitral tribunal shall submit its decision on the application in draft form to the Court not later than 30 days following the expiration of the time limit for the receipt of any comments from the other party or within such other period as the Court may decide.*
>
> *3. A decision to correct or to interpret the award shall take the form of an addendum and shall constitute part of the award. The provisions of Articles 31, 33 and 34 shall apply mutatis mutandis."*

Furthermore Appendix III Article 2(10) provides:

> *"In the case of an application under Article 35(2) of the Rules [.|.|.], the Court may fix an advance to cover additional fees and expenses of the arbitral tribunal and additional ICC administrative expenses and may make the transmission of such application to the arbitral tribunal subject to the prior cash payment in full to the ICC of such advance. The Court shall fix at its discretion the costs of the procedure following an application [.|.|.], which shall include any possible fees of the arbitrator and ICC administrative expenses, when approving the decision of the arbitral tribunal."*

Article 35(1)

If the Arbitral Tribunal decides to correct the award on its own initiative, it should inform the parties and the Secretariat of its intention to do so and grant the parties a short time limit to comment. The Arbitral Tribunal should submit the draft *Addendum* to the Court for scrutiny within 30 days of the date of the Award.

Article 35(2)

Upon receipt of an Article 35(2) application, the Secretariat may submit the matter to the Court for it to consider whether, in view of the circumstances of the case, an advance to cover additional fees and expenses of the Arbitral Tribunal and additional ICC administrative expenses is warranted. Should the Court fix an additional advance, such advance must be paid before the Secretariat will transmit the application to the Arbitral Tribunal. Otherwise, the Secretariat will transmit the application directly to the Arbitral Tribunal. As such, the Arbitral Tribunal should not address an application until the Secretariat transmits it to them.

If the Court did not ask for an advance on costs at the time when the application was submitted to the Secretariat, it can, in exceptional circumstances, take a decision on costs at the time of the scrutiny and make the notification of the *Addendum* or the Decisioncontingent upon the payment by one or both parties of the costs fixed by the Court.

Upon receipt of the application from the Secretariat the Arbitral Tribunal should grant theother parties a short time limit, normally not exceeding 30 days, for comments.

The Arbitral Tribunal should then submit its draft decision to the Court for scrutiny not laterthan 30 days following the expiration of the time limit granted for comments. Should the Arbitral Tribunal require an extension of such time limit, it should inform the Secretariat.

Depending upon the Arbitral Tribunal's decision, such decision can take one of four forms:

1. ***Addendum***: if the Arbitral Tribunal decides to correct or interpret the award, as this shall constitute part of the award.
2. **Decision**: if the Arbitral Tribunal decides that the award does not need to be corrected or interpreted and does not take a decision on costs.
3. ***Addendum* and Decision**: if there are two or more applications and the Arbitral Tribunal decides to correct or interpret the award on the basis of one or more, but not all applications.
4. **Decision and *Addendum* on Costs**: if the Arbitral Tribunal decides that the award does not need to be corrected or interpreted but takes a decision on costs related to the application.

General Considerations

All decisions should contain the reasons upon which they are based (Article 31(2)). They should also include operative conclusions ("*dispositif*") or a finding that the application is rejected. For further guidance about what should be included in the draft decision, see the ICC Checklist on Correction and Interpretation of Arbitral Awards. The Court will scrutinise the draft decision (Article 33), and upon approval thereof it should be signed by the Arbitral Tribunal (Article 31(1) and (3)) and sent to the Secretariat for notification to the parties (Article 34).

In all cases the Arbitral Tribunal must first ensure that mandatory rules of law at the place of arbitration do not exclude the correction or interpretation of an award by the Tribunal.

Where the relevant national law or court practice provide specific circumstances in which an Arbitral Tribunal may render certain decisions other than corrections or interpretation regarding an award which had been approved and notified, such situations shall be treated in the spirit of this Note.

PART III

TABLE OF CONTENTS

APPENDICES AND FURTHER MATERIALS

Appendices

APPENDIX 1

ICC RULES OF ARBITRATION WITH APPENDICES TO THE RULES

In force as from 1 January 2012.

ICC dispute resolution service. Also available in the ICC Dispute Resolution Library at <www.iccdrl.com>.

ICC ARBITRATION RULES

INTRODUCTORY PROVISIONS

Article 1: International Court of Arbitration

1. The International Court of Arbitration (the "Court") of the International Chamber of Commerce (the "ICC") is the independent arbitration body of the ICC. The statutes of the Court are set forth in Appendix I.

2. The Court does not itself resolve disputes. It administers the resolution of disputes by arbitral tribunals, in accordance with the Rules of Arbitration of the ICC (the "Rules"). The Court is the only body authorized to administer arbitrations under the Rules, including the scrutiny and approval of awards rendered in accordance with the Rules. It draws up its own internal rules, which are set forth in Appendix II (the "Internal Rules").

3. The President of the Court (the "President") or, in the President's absence or otherwise at the President's request, one of its Vice-Presidents shall have the power to take urgent decisions on behalf of the Court, provided that any such decision is reported to the Court at its next session.

4. As provided for in the Internal Rules, the Court may delegate to one or more committees composed of its members the power to take certain decisions, provided that any such decision is reported to the Court at its next session.

5. The Court is assisted in its work by the Secretariat of the Court (the "Secretariat") under the direction of its Secretary General (the "Secretary General").

Article 2: Definitions

In the Rules:

(i) "arbitral tribunal" includes one or more arbitrators;

(ii) "claimant" includes one or more claimants, "respondent" includes one or more respondents, and "additional party" includes one or more additional parties;

(iii) "party" or "parties" include claimants, respondents or additional parties;

(iv) "claim" or "claims" include any claim by any party against any other party;

(v) "award" includes, *inter alia*, an interim, partial or final award.

Article 3: Written Notifications or Communications; Time Limits

1. All pleadings and other written communications submitted by any party, as well as all documents annexed thereto, shall be supplied in a number of copies sufficient to provide one copy for each party, plus one for each arbitrator, and one for the Secretariat. A copy of any notification or communication from the arbitral tribunal to the parties shall be sent to the Secretariat.

2. All notifications or communications from the Secretariat and the arbitral tribunal shall be made to the last address of the party or its representative for whom the same are intended, as notified either by the party in question or by the other party. Such notification or communication may be made by delivery against receipt, registered post, courier, email, or any other means of telecommunication that provides a record of the sending thereof.

3. A notification or communication shall be deemed to have been made on the day it was received by the party itself or by its representative, or would have been received if made in accordance with Article 3(2).

4. Periods of time specified in or fixed under the Rules shall start to run on the day following the date a notification or communication is deemed to have been made in accordance with Article 3(3). When the day next following such date is an official holiday, or a non-business day in the country where the notification or communication is deemed to have been made, the period of time shall commence on the first following business day. Official holidays and non-business days are included in the calculation of the period of time. If the last day of the relevant period of time granted is an official holiday or a non-business day in the country where the notification or communication is deemed to have been made, the period of time shall expire at the end of the first following business day.

Commencing The Arbitration

Article 4: Request for Arbitration

1. A party wishing to have recourse to arbitration under the Rules shall submit its Request for Arbitration (the "Request") to the Secretariat at any of the offices specified in the Internal Rules. The Secretariat shall notify the claimant and respondent of the receipt of the Request and the date of such receipt.

2. The date on which the Request is received by the Secretariat shall, for all purposes, be deemed to be the date of the commencement of the arbitration.

3. The Request shall contain the following information:

   a) the name in full, description, address and other contact details of each of the parties;

   b) the name in full, address and other contact details of any person(s) representing the claimant in the arbitration;

   c) a description of the nature and circumstances of the dispute giving rise to the claims and of the basis upon which the claims are made;

   d) a statement of the relief sought, together with the amounts of any quantified claims and, to the extent possible, an estimate of the monetary value of any other claims;

   e) any relevant agreements and, in particular, the arbitration agreement(s);

   f) where claims are made under more than one arbitration agreement, an indication of the arbitration agreement under which each claim is made;

g) all relevant particulars and any observations or proposals concerning the number of arbitrators and their choice in accordance with the provisions of Articles 12 and 13, and any nomination of an arbitrator required thereby; and

h) all relevant particulars and any observations or proposals as to the place of the arbitration, the applicable rules of law and the language of the arbitration.

The claimant may submit such other documents or information with the Request as it considers appropriate or as may contribute to the efficient resolution of the dispute.

4. Together with the Request, the claimant shall:

a) submit the number of copies thereof required by Article 3(1); and

b) make payment of the filing fee required by Appendix III ("Arbitration Costs and Fees") in force on the date the Request is submitted.

In the event that the claimant fails to comply with either of these requirements, the Secretariat may fix a time limit within which the claimant must comply, failing which the file shall be closed without prejudice to the claimant's right to submit the same claims at a later date in another Request.

5. The Secretariat shall transmit a copy of the Request and the documents annexed thereto to the respondent for its Answer to the Request once the Secretariat has sufficient copies of the Request and the required filing fee.

Article 5: Answer to the Request; Counterclaims

1. Within 30 days from the receipt of the Request from the Secretariat, the respondent shall submit an Answer (the "Answer") which shall contain the following information:

a) its name in full, description, address and other contact details;

b) the name in full, address and other contact details of any person(s) representing the respondent in the arbitration;

c) its comments as to the nature and circumstances of the dispute giving rise to the claims and the basis upon which the claims are made;

d) its response to the relief sought;

e) any observations or proposals concerning the number of arbitrators and their choice in light of the claimant's proposals and in accordance with the provisions of Articles 12 and 13, and any nomination of an arbitrator required thereby; and

f) any observations or proposals as to the place of the arbitration, the applicable rules of law and the language of the arbitration.

The respondent may submit such other documents or information with the Answer as it considers appropriate or as may contribute to the efficient resolution of the dispute.

2. The Secretariat may grant the respondent an extension of the time for submitting the Answer, provided the application for such an extension contains the respondent's observations or proposals concerning the number

of arbitrators and their choice and, where required by Articles 12 and 13, the nomination of an arbitrator. If the respondent fails to do so, the Court shall proceed in accordance with the Rules.

3. The Answer shall be submitted to the Secretariat in the number of copies specified by Article 3(1).

4. The Secretariat shall communicate the Answer and the documents annexed thereto to all other parties.

5. Any counterclaims made by the respondent shall be submitted with the Answer and shall provide:

a) a description of the nature and circumstances of the dispute giving rise to the counterclaims and of the basis upon which the counterclaims are made;

b) a statement of the relief sought together with the amounts of any quantified counterclaims and, to the extent possible, an estimate of the monetary value of any other counterclaims;

c) any relevant agreements and, in particular, the arbitration agreement(s); and

d) where counterclaims are made under more than one arbitration agreement, an indication of the arbitration agreement under which each counterclaim is made.

The respondent may submit such other documents or information with the counterclaims as it considers appropriate or as may contribute to the efficient resolution of the dispute.

6. The claimant shall submit a reply to any counterclaim within 30 days from the date of receipt of the counterclaims communicated by the Secretariat. Prior to the transmission of the file to the arbitral tribunal, the Secretariat may grant the claimant an extension of time for submitting the reply.

Article 6: Effect of the Arbitration Agreement

1. Where the parties have agreed to submit to arbitration under the Rules, they shall be deemed to have submitted *ipso facto* to the Rules in effect on the date of commencement of the arbitration, unless they have agreed to submit to the Rules in effect on the date of their arbitration agreement.

2. By agreeing to arbitration under the Rules, the parties have accepted that the arbitration shall be administered by the Court.

3. If any party against which a claim has been made does not submit an Answer, or raises one or more pleas concerning the existence, validity or scope of the arbitration agreement or concerning whether all of the claims made in the arbitration may be determined together in a single arbitration, the arbitration shall proceed and any question of jurisdiction or of whether the claims may be determined together in that arbitration shall be decided directly by the arbitral tribunal, unless the Secretary General refers the matter to the Court for its decision pursuant to Article 6(4).

4. In all cases referred to the Court under Article 6(3), the Court shall decide whether and to what extent the arbitration shall proceed. The arbitration

shall proceed if and to the extent that the Court is *prima facie* satisfied that an arbitration agreement under the Rules may exist. In particular:

(i) where there are more than two parties to the arbitration, the arbitration shall proceed between those of the parties, including any additional parties joined pursuant to Article 7, with respect to which the Court is *prima facie* satisfied that an arbitration agreement under the Rules that binds them all may exist; and

(ii) where claims pursuant to Article 9 are made under more than one arbitration agreement, the arbitration shall proceed as to those claims with respect to which the Court is *prima facie* satisfied

(a) that the arbitration agreements under which those claims are made may be compatible, and

(b) that all parties to the arbitration may have agreed that those claims can be determined together in a single arbitration.

The Court's decision pursuant to Article 6(4) is without prejudice to the admissibility or merits of any party's plea or pleas.

5. In all matters decided by the Court under Article 6(4), any decision as to the jurisdiction of the arbitral tribunal, except as to parties or claims with respect to which the Court decides that the arbitration cannot proceed, shall then be taken by the arbitral tribunal itself.

6. Where the parties are notified of the Court's decision pursuant to Article 6(4) that the arbitration cannot proceed in respect of some or all of them, any party retains the right to ask any court having jurisdiction whether or not, and in respect of which of them, there is a binding arbitration agreement.

7. Where the Court has decided pursuant to Article 6(4) that the arbitration cannot proceed in respect of any of the claims, such decision shall not prevent a party from reintroducing the same claim at a later date in other proceedings.

8. If any of the parties refuses or fails to take part in the arbitration or any stage thereof, the arbitration shall proceed notwithstanding such refusal or failure.

9. Unless otherwise agreed, the arbitral tribunal shall not cease to have jurisdiction by reason of any allegation that the contract is non-existent or null and void, provided that the arbitral tribunal upholds the validity of the arbitration agreement. The arbitral tribunal shall continue to have jurisdiction to determine the parties' respective rights and to decide their claims and pleas even though the contract itself may be non-existent or null and void.

Multiple Parties, Multiple Contracts And Consolidation

Article 7: Joinder of Additional Parties

1. A party wishing to join an additional party to the arbitration shall submit its request for arbitration against the additional party (the "Request for Joinder") to the Secretariat. The date on which the Request for Joinder is received by the Secretariat shall, for all purposes, be deemed to be the date of the commencement of arbitration against the additional party. Any such joinder shall be subject to the provisions of Articles 6(3)–6(7) and 9. No additional

party may be joined after the confirmation or appointment of any arbitrator, unless all parties, including the additional party, otherwise agree. The Secretariat may fix a time limit for the submission of a Request for Joinder.

2. The Request for Joinder shall contain the following information:

   a) the case reference of the existing arbitration;

   b) the name in full, description, address and other contact details of each of the parties, including the additional party; and

   c) the information specified in Article 4(3) subparagraphs c), d), e) and f).

The party filing the Request for Joinder may submit therewith such other documents or information as it considers appropriate or as may contribute to the efficient resolution of the dispute.

3. The provisions of Articles 4(4) and 4(5) shall apply, *mutatis mutandis*, to the Request for Joinder.

4. The additional party shall submit an Answer in accordance, *mutatis mutandis*, with the provisions of Articles 5(1)–5(4). The additional party may make claims against any other party in accordance with the provisions of Article 8.

Article 8: Claims Between Multiple Parties

1. In an arbitration with multiple parties, claims may be made by any party against any other party, subject to the provisions of Articles 6(3)–6(7) and 9 and provided that no new claims may be made after the Terms of Reference are signed or approved by the Court without the authorization of the arbitral tribunal pursuant to Article 23(4).

2. Any party making a claim pursuant to Article 8(1) shall provide the information specified in Article 4(3) subparagraphs c), d), e) and f).

3. Before the Secretariat transmits the file to the arbitral tribunal in accordance with Article 16, the following provisions shall apply, *mutatis mutandis*, to any claim made: Article 4(4) subparagraph a); Article 4(5); Article 5(1) except for subparagraphs a), b), e) and f); Article 5(2); Article 5(3) and Article 5(4). Thereafter, the arbitral tribunal shall determine the procedure for making a claim.

Article 9: Multiple Contracts

Subject to the provisions of Articles 6(3)–6(7) and 23(4), claims arising out of or in connection with more than one contract may be made in a single arbitration, irrespective of whether such claims are made under one or more than one arbitration agreement under the Rules.

Article 10: Consolidation of Arbitrations

The Court may, at the request of a party, consolidate two or more arbitrations pending under the Rules into a single arbitration, where:

a) the parties have agreed to consolidation; or

b) all of the claims in the arbitrations are made under the same arbitration agreement; or

c) where the claims in the arbitrations are made under more than one arbitration agreement, the arbitrations are between the same parties, the disputes in the arbitrations arise in connection with the same legal relationship, and the Court finds the arbitration agreements to be compatible.

In deciding whether to consolidate, the Court may take into account any circumstances it considers to be relevant, including whether one or more arbitrators have been confirmed or appointed in more than one of the arbitrations and, if so, whether the same or different persons have been confirmed or appointed.

When arbitrations are consolidated, they shall be consolidated into the arbitration that commenced first, unless otherwise agreed by all parties.

THE ARBITRAL TRIBUNAL

Article 11: General Provisions

1. Every arbitrator must be and remain impartial and independent of the parties involved in the arbitration.

2. Before appointment or confirmation, a prospective arbitrator shall sign a statement of acceptance, availability, impartiality and independence. The prospective arbitrator shall disclose in writing to the Secretariat any facts or circumstances which might be of such a nature as to call into question the arbitrator's independence in the eyes of the parties, as well as any circumstances that could give rise to reasonable doubts as to the arbitrator's impartiality. The Secretariat shall provide such information to the parties in writing and fix a time limit for any comments from them.

3. An arbitrator shall immediately disclose in writing to the Secretariat and to the parties any facts or circumstances of a similar nature to those referred to in Article 11(2) concerning the arbitrator's impartiality or independence which may arise during the arbitration.

4. The decisions of the Court as to the appointment, confirmation, challenge or replacement of an arbitrator shall be final, and the reasons for such decisions shall not be communicated.

5. By accepting to serve, arbitrators undertake to carry out their responsibilities in accordance with the Rules.

6. Insofar as the parties have not provided otherwise, the arbitral tribunal shall be constituted in accordance with the provisions of Articles 12 and 13.

Article 12: Constitution of the Arbitral Tribunal

Number of Arbitrators

1. The disputes shall be decided by a sole arbitrator or by three arbitrators.

2. Where the parties have not agreed upon the number of arbitrators, the Court shall appoint a sole arbitrator, save where it appears to the Court that the

dispute is such as to warrant the appointment of three arbitrators. In such case, the claimant shall nominate an arbitrator within a period of 15 days from the receipt of the notification of the decision of the Court, and the respondent shall nominate an arbitrator within a period of 15 days from the receipt of the notification of the nomination made by the claimant. If a party fails to nominate an arbitrator, the appointment shall be made by the Court.

Sole Arbitrator

3. Where the parties have agreed that the dispute shall be resolved by a sole arbitrator, they may, by agreement, nominate the sole arbitrator for confirmation. If the parties fail to nominate a sole arbitrator within 30 days from the date when the claimant's Request for Arbitration has been received by the other party, or within such additional time as may be allowed by the Secretariat, the sole arbitrator shall be appointed by the Court.

Three Arbitrators

4. Where the parties have agreed that the dispute shall be resolved by three arbitrators, each party shall nominate in the Request and the Answer, respectively, one arbitrator for confirmation. If a party fails to nominate an arbitrator, the appointment shall be made by the Court.

5. Where the dispute is to be referred to three arbitrators, the third arbitrator, who will act as president of the arbitral tribunal, shall be appointed by the Court, unless the parties have agreed upon another procedure for such appointment, in which case the nomination will be subject to confirmation pursuant to Article 13. Should such procedure not result in a nomination within 30 days from the confirmation or appointment of the co-arbitrators or any other time limit agreed by the parties or fixed by the Court, the third arbitrator shall be appointed by the Court.

6. Where there are multiple claimants or multiple respondents, and where the dispute is to be referred to three arbitrators, the multiple claimants, jointly, and the multiple respondents, jointly, shall nominate an arbitrator for confirmation pursuant to Article 13.

7. Where an additional party has been joined, and where the dispute is to be referred to three arbitrators, the additional party may, jointly with the claimant(s) or with the respondent(s), nominate an arbitrator for confirmation pursuant to Article 13.

8. In the absence of a joint nomination pursuant to Articles 12(6) or 12(7) and where all parties are unable to agree to a method for the constitution of the arbitral tribunal, the Court may appoint each member of the arbitral tribunal and shall designate one of them to act as president. In such case, the Court shall be at liberty to choose any person it regards as suitable to act as arbitrator, applying Article 13 when it considers this appropriate.

Article 13: Appointment and Confirmation of the Arbitrators

1. In confirming or appointing arbitrators, the Court shall consider the prospective arbitrator's nationality, residence and other relationships with the

countries of which the parties or the other arbitrators are nationals and the prospective arbitrator's availability and ability to conduct the arbitration in accordance with the Rules. The same shall apply where the Secretary General confirms arbitrators pursuant to Article 13(2).

2. The Secretary General may confirm as co-arbitrators, sole arbitrators and presidents of arbitral tribunals persons nominated by the parties or pursuant to their particular agreements, provided that the statement they have submitted contains no qualification regarding impartiality or independence or that a qualified statement regarding impartiality or independence has not given rise to objections. Such confirmation shall be reported to the Court at its next session. If the Secretary General considers that a co-arbitrator, sole arbitrator or president of an arbitral tribunal should not be confirmed, the matter shall be submitted to the Court.

3. Where the Court is to appoint an arbitrator, it shall make the appointment upon proposal of a National Committee or Group of the ICC that it considers to be appropriate. If the Court does not accept the proposal made, or if the National Committee or Group fails to make the proposal requested within the time limit fixed by the Court, the Court may repeat its request, request a proposal from another National Committee or Group that it considers to be appropriate, or appoint directly any person whom it regards as suitable.

4. The Court may also appoint directly to act as arbitrator any person whom it regards as suitable where:

a) one or more of the parties is a state or claims to be a state entity; or

b) the Court considers that it would be appropriate to appoint an arbitrator from a country or territory where there is no National Committee or Group; or

c) the President certifies to the Court that circumstances exist which, in the President's opinion, make a direct appointment necessary and appropriate.

5. The sole arbitrator or the president of the arbitral tribunal shall be of a nationality other than those of the parties. However, in suitable circumstances and provided that none of the parties objects within the time limit fixed by the Court, the sole arbitrator or the president of the arbitral tribunal may be chosen from a country of which any of the parties is a national.

Article 14: Challenge of Arbitrators

1. A challenge of an arbitrator, whether for an alleged lack of impartiality or independence, or otherwise, shall be made by the submission to the Secretariat of a written statement specifying the facts and circumstances on which the challenge is based.

2. For a challenge to be admissible, it must be submitted by a party either within 30 days from receipt by that party of the notification of the appointment or confirmation of the arbitrator, or within 30 days from the date when the party making the challenge was informed of the facts and circumstances

on which the challenge is based if such date is subsequent to the receipt of such notification.

3. The Court shall decide on the admissibility and, at the same time, if necessary, on the merits of a challenge after the Secretariat has afforded an opportunity for the arbitrator concerned, the other party or parties and any other members of the arbitral tribunal to comment in writing within a suitable period of time. Such comments shall be communicated to the parties and to the arbitrators.

Article 15: Replacement of Arbitrators

1. An arbitrator shall be replaced upon death, upon acceptance by the Court of the arbitrator's resignation, upon acceptance by the Court of a challenge, or upon acceptance by the Court of a request of all the parties.

2. An arbitrator shall also be replaced on the Court's own initiative when it decides that the arbitrator is prevented *de jure* or *de facto* from fulfilling the arbitrator's functions, or that the arbitrator is not fulfilling those functions in accordance with the Rules or within the prescribed time limits.

3. When, on the basis of information that has come to its attention, the Court considers applying Article 15(2), it shall decide on the matter after the arbitrator concerned, the parties and any other members of the arbitral tribunal have had an opportunity to comment in writing within a suitable period of time. Such comments shall be communicated to the parties and to the arbitrators.

4. When an arbitrator is to be replaced, the Court has discretion to decide whether or not to follow the original nominating process. Once reconstituted, and after having invited the parties to comment, the arbitral tribunal shall determine if and to what extent prior proceedings shall be repeated before the reconstituted arbitral tribunal.

5. Subsequent to the closing of the proceedings, instead of replacing an arbitrator who has died or been removed by the Court pursuant to Articles 15(1) or 15(2), the Court may decide, when it considers it appropriate, that the remaining arbitrators shall continue the arbitration. In making such determination, the Court shall take into account the views of the remaining arbitrators and of the parties and such other matters that it considers appropriate in the circumstances.

THE ARBITRAL PROCEEDINGS

Article 16: Transmission of the File to the Arbitral Tribunal

The Secretariat shall transmit the file to the arbitral tribunal as soon as it has been constituted, provided the advance on costs requested by the Secretariat at this stage has been paid.

Article 17: Proof of Authority

At any time after the commencement of the arbitration, the arbitral tribunal or the Secretariat may require proof of the authority of any party representatives.

Article 18: Place of the Arbitration

1. The place of the arbitration shall be fixed by the Court, unless agreed upon by the parties.
2. The arbitral tribunal may, after consultation with the parties, conduct hearings and meetings at any location it considers appropriate, unless otherwise agreed by the parties.
3. The arbitral tribunal may deliberate at any location it considers appropriate.

Article 19: Rules Governing the Proceedings

The proceedings before the arbitral tribunal shall be governed by the Rules and, where the Rules are silent, by any rules which the parties or, failing them, the arbitral tribunal may settle on, whether or not reference is thereby made to the rules of procedure of a national law to be applied to the arbitration.

Article 20: Language of the Arbitration

In the absence of an agreement by the parties, the arbitral tribunal shall determine the language or languages of the arbitration, due regard being given to all relevant circumstances, including the language of the contract.

Article 21: Applicable Rules of Law

1. The parties shall be free to agree upon the rules of law to be applied by the arbitral tribunal to the merits of the dispute. In the absence of any such agreement, the arbitral tribunal shall apply the rules of law which it determines to be appropriate.
2. The arbitral tribunal shall take account of the provisions of the contract, if any, between the parties and of any relevant trade usages.
3. The arbitral tribunal shall assume the powers of an *amiable compositeur* or decide *ex aequo et bono* only if the parties have agreed to give it such powers.

Article 22: Conduct of the Arbitration

1. The arbitral tribunal and the parties shall make every effort to conduct the arbitration in an expeditious and cost-effective manner, having regard to the complexity and value of the dispute.
2. In order to ensure effective case management, the arbitral tribunal, after consulting the parties, may adopt such procedural measures as it considers appropriate, provided that they are not contrary to any agreement of the parties.
3. Upon the request of any party, the arbitral tribunal may make orders concerning the confidentiality of the arbitration proceedings or of any other matters in connection with the arbitration and may take measures for protecting trade secrets and confidential information.
4. In all cases, the arbitral tribunal shall act fairly and impartially and ensure that each party has a reasonable opportunity to present its case.
5. The parties undertake to comply with any order made by the arbitral tribunal.

Article 23: Terms of Reference

1. As soon as it has received the file from the Secretariat, the arbitral tribunal shall draw up, on the basis of documents or in the presence of the parties and in the light of their most recent submissions, a document defining its Terms of Reference. This document shall include the following particulars:

   a) the names in full, description, address and other contact details of each of the parties and of any person(s) representing a party in the arbitration;

   b) the addresses to which notifications and communications arising in the course of the arbitration may be made;

   c) a summary of the parties' respective claims and of the relief sought by each party, together with the amounts of any quantified claims and, to the extent possible, an estimate of the monetary value of any other claims;

   d) unless the arbitral tribunal considers it inappropriate, a list of issues to be determined;

   e) the names in full, address and other contact details of each of the arbitrators;

   f) the place of the arbitration; and

   g) particulars of the applicable procedural rules and, if such is the case, reference to the power conferred upon the arbitral tribunal to act as *amiable compositeur* or to decide *ex aequo et bono*.

2. The Terms of Reference shall be signed by the parties and the arbitral tribunal. Within two months of the date on which the file has been transmitted to it, the arbitral tribunal shall transmit to the Court the Terms of Reference signed by it and by the parties. The Court may extend this time limit pursuant to a reasoned request from the arbitral tribunal or on its own initiative if it decides it is necessary to do so.

3. If any of the parties refuses to take part in the drawing up of the Terms of Reference or to sign the same, they shall be submitted to the Court for approval. When the Terms of Reference have been signed in accordance with Article 23(2) or approved by the Court, the arbitration shall proceed.

4. After the Terms of Reference have been signed or approved by the Court, no party shall make new claims which fall outside the limits of the Terms of Reference unless it has been authorized to do so by the arbitral tribunal, which shall consider the nature of such new claims, the stage of the arbitration and other relevant circumstances.

Article 24: Case Management Conference and Procedural Timetable

1. When drawing up the Terms of Reference or as soon as possible thereafter, the arbitral tribunal shall convene a case management conference to consult the parties on procedural measures that may be adopted pursuant to Article 22(2). Such measures may include one or more of the case management techniques described in Appendix IV.

2. During or following such conference, the arbitral tribunal shall establish the procedural timetable that it intends to follow for the conduct of the arbitration. The procedural timetable and any modifications thereto shall be communicated to the Court and the parties.

3. To ensure continued effective case management, the arbitral tribunal, after consulting the parties by means of a further case management conference or otherwise, may adopt further procedural measures or modify the procedural timetable.

4. Case management conferences may be conducted through a meeting in person, by video conference, telephone or similar means of communication. In the absence of an agreement of the parties, the arbitral tribunal shall determine the means by which the conference will be conducted. The arbitral tribunal may request the parties to submit case management proposals in advance of a case management conference and may request the attendance at any case management conference of the parties in person or through an internal representative.

Article 25: Establishing the Facts of the Case

1. The arbitral tribunal shall proceed within as short a time as possible to establish the facts of the case by all appropriate means.

2. After studying the written submissions of the parties and all documents relied upon, the arbitral tribunal shall hear the parties together in person if any of them so requests or, failing such a request, it may of its own motion decide to hear them.

3. The arbitral tribunal may decide to hear witnesses, experts appointed by the parties or any other person, in the presence of the parties, or in their absence provided they have been duly summoned.

4. The arbitral tribunal, after having consulted the parties, may appoint one or more experts, define their terms of reference and receive their reports. At the request of a party, the parties shall be given the opportunity to question at a hearing any such expert.

5. At any time during the proceedings, the arbitral tribunal may summon any party to provide additional evidence.

6. The arbitral tribunal may decide the case solely on the documents submitted by the parties unless any of the parties requests a hearing.

Article 26: Hearings

1. When a hearing is to be held, the arbitral tribunal, giving reasonable notice, shall summon the parties to appear before it on the day and at the place fixed by it.

2. If any of the parties, although duly summoned, fails to appear without valid excuse, the arbitral tribunal shall have the power to proceed with the hearing.

3. The arbitral tribunal shall be in full charge of the hearings, at which all the parties shall be entitled to be present. Save with the approval of the arbitral tribunal and the parties, persons not involved in the proceedings shall not be admitted.

4. The parties may appear in person or through duly authorized representatives. In addition, they may be assisted by advisers.

Article 27: Closing of the Proceedings and Date for Submission of Draft Awards

As soon as possible after the last hearing concerning matters to be decided in an award or the filing of the last authorized submissions concerning such matters, whichever is later, the arbitral tribunal shall:

a) declare the proceedings closed with respect to the matters to be decided in the award; and

b) inform the Secretariat and the parties of the date by which it expects to submit its draft award to the Court for approval pursuant to Article 33.

After the proceedings are closed, no further submission or argument may be made, or evidence produced, with respect to the matters to be decided in the award, unless requested or authorized by the arbitral tribunal.

Article 28: Conservatory and Interim Measures

1. Unless the parties have otherwise agreed, as soon as the file has been transmitted to it, the arbitral tribunal may, at the request of a party, order any interim or conservatory measure it deems appropriate. The arbitral tribunal may make the granting of any such measure subject to appropriate security being furnished by the requesting party. Any such measure shall take the form of an order, giving reasons, or of an award, as the arbitral tribunal considers appropriate.

2. Before the file is transmitted to the arbitral tribunal, and in appropriate circumstances even thereafter, the parties may apply to any competent judicial authority for interim or conservatory measures. The application of a party to a judicial authority for such measures or for the implementation of any such measures ordered by an arbitral tribunal shall not be deemed to be an infringement or a waiver of the arbitration agreement and shall not affect the relevant powers reserved to the arbitral tribunal. Any such application and any measures taken by the judicial authority must be notified without delay to the Secretariat. The Secretariat shall inform the arbitral tribunal thereof.

Article 29: Emergency Arbitrator

1. A party that needs urgent interim or conservatory measures that cannot await the constitution of an arbitral tribunal ("Emergency Measures") may make an application for such measures pursuant to the Emergency Arbitrator Rules in Appendix V. Any such application shall be accepted only if it is received by the Secretariat prior to the transmission of the file to the arbitral tribunal pursuant to Article 16 and irrespective of whether the party making the application has already submitted its Request for Arbitration.

2. The emergency arbitrator's decision shall take the form of an order. The parties undertake to comply with any order made by the emergency arbitrator.

3. The emergency arbitrator's order shall not bind the arbitral tribunal with respect to any question, issue or dispute determined in the order. The arbitral

tribunal may modify, terminate or annul the order or any modification thereto made by the emergency arbitrator.

4. The arbitral tribunal shall decide upon any party's requests or claims related to the emergency arbitrator proceedings, including the reallocation of the costs of such proceedings and any claims arising out of or in connection with the compliance or non-compliance with the order.

5. Articles 29(1)–29(4) and the Emergency Arbitrator Rules set forth in Appendix V (collectively the "Emergency Arbitrator Provisions") shall apply only to parties that are either signatories of the arbitration agreement under the Rules that is relied upon for the application or successors to such signatories.

6. The Emergency Arbitrator Provisions shall not apply if:

a) the arbitration agreement under the Rules was concluded before the date on which the Rules came into force;

b) the parties have agreed to opt out of the Emergency Arbitrator Provisions; or

c) the parties have agreed to another pre-arbitral procedure that provides for the granting of conservatory, interim or similar measures.

7. The Emergency Arbitrator Provisions are not intended to prevent any party from seeking urgent interim or conservatory measures from a competent judicial authority at any time prior to making an application for such measures, and in appropriate circumstances even thereafter, pursuant to the Rules. Any application for such measures from a competent judicial authority shall not be deemed to be an infringement or a waiver of the arbitration agreement. Any such application and any measures taken by the judicial authority must be notified without delay to the Secretariat.

AWARDS

Article 30: Time Limit for the Final Award

1. The time limit within which the arbitral tribunal must render its final award is six months. Such time limit shall start to run from the date of the last signature by the arbitral tribunal or by the parties of the Terms of Reference or, in the case of application of Article 23(3), the date of the notification to the arbitral tribunal by the Secretariat of the approval of the Terms of Reference by the Court. The Court may fix a different time limit based upon the procedural timetable established pursuant to Article 24(2).

2. The Court may extend the time limit pursuant to a reasoned request from the arbitral tribunal or on its own initiative if it decides it is necessary to do so.

Article 31: Making of the Award

1. When the arbitral tribunal is composed of more than one arbitrator, an award is made by a majority decision. If there is no majority, the award shall be made by the president of the arbitral tribunal alone.

2. The award shall state the reasons upon which it is based.

3. The award shall be deemed to be made at the place of the arbitration and on the date stated therein.

Article 32: Award by Consent

If the parties reach a settlement after the file has been transmitted to the arbitral tribunal in accordance with Article 16, the settlement shall be recorded in the form of an award made by consent of the parties, if so requested by the parties and if the arbitral tribunal agrees to do so.

Article 33: Scrutiny of the Award by the Court

Before signing any award, the arbitral tribunal shall submit it in draft form to the Court. The Court may lay down modifications as to the form of the award and, without affecting the arbitral tribunal's liberty of decision, may also draw its attention to points of substance. No award shall be rendered by the arbitral tribunal until it has been approved by the Court as to its form.

Article 34: Notification, Deposit and Enforceability of the Award

1. Once an award has been made, the Secretariat shall notify to the parties the text signed by the arbitral tribunal, provided always that the costs of the arbitration have been fully paid to the ICC by the parties or by one of them.

2. Additional copies certified true by the Secretary General shall be made available on request and at any time to the parties, but to no one else.

3. By virtue of the notification made in accordance with Article 34(1), the parties waive any other form of notification or deposit on the part of the arbitral tribunal.

4. An original of each award made in accordance with the Rules shall be deposited with the Secretariat.

5. The arbitral tribunal and the Secretariat shall assist the parties in complying with whatever further formalities may be necessary.

6. Every award shall be binding on the parties. By submitting the dispute to arbitration under the Rules, the parties undertake to carry out any award without delay and shall be deemed to have waived their right to any form of recourse insofar as such waiver can validly be made.

Article 35: Correction and Interpretation of the Award; Remission of Awards

1. On its own initiative, the arbitral tribunal may correct a clerical, computational or typographical error, or any errors of similar nature contained in an award, provided such correction is submitted for approval to the Court within 30 days of the date of such award.

2. Any application of a party for the correction of an error of the kind referred to in Article 35(1), or for the interpretation of an award, must be made to the

Secretariat within 30 days of the receipt of the award by such party, in a number of copies as stated in Article 3(1). After transmittal of the application to the arbitral tribunal, the latter shall grant the other party a short time limit, normally not exceeding 30 days, from the receipt of the application by that party, to submit any comments thereon. The arbitral tribunal shall submit its decision on the application in draft form to the Court not later than 30 days following the expiration of the time limit for the receipt of any comments from the other party or within such other period as the Court may decide.

3. A decision to correct or to interpret the award shall take the form of an addendum and shall constitute part of the award. The provisions of Articles 31, 33 and 34 shall apply *mutatis mutandis*.

4. Where a court remits an award to the arbitral tribunal, the provisions of Articles 31, 33, 34 and this Article 35 shall apply *mutatis mutandis* to any addendum or award made pursuant to the terms of such remission. The Court may take any steps as may be necessary to enable the arbitral tribunal to comply with the terms of such remission and may fix an advance to cover any additional fees and expenses of the arbitral tribunal and any additional ICC administrative expenses.

Costs

Article 36: Advance to Cover the Costs of the Arbitration

1. After receipt of the Request, the Secretary General may request the claimant to pay a provisional advance in an amount intended to cover the costs of the arbitration until the Terms of Reference have been drawn up. Any provisional advance paid will be considered as a partial payment by the claimant of any advance on costs fixed by the Court pursuant to this Article 36.

2. As soon as practicable, the Court shall fix the advance on costs in an amount likely to cover the fees and expenses of the arbitrators and the ICC administrative expenses for the claims which have been referred to it by the parties, unless any claims are made under Article 7 or 8 in which case Article 36(4) shall apply. The advance on costs fixed by the Court pursuant to this Article 36(2) shall be payable in equal shares by the claimant and the respondent.

3. Where counterclaims are submitted by the respondent under Article 5 or otherwise, the Court may fix separate advances on costs for the claims and the counterclaims. When the Court has fixed separate advances on costs, each of the parties shall pay the advance on costs corresponding to its claims.

4. Where claims are made under Article 7 or 8, the Court shall fix one or more advances on costs that shall be payable by the parties as decided by the Court. Where the Court has previously fixed any advance on costs pursuant to this Article 36, any such advance shall be replaced by the advance(s) fixed pursuant to this Article 36(4), and the amount of any advance previously paid by any party will be considered as a partial payment by such party of its share of the advance(s) on costs as fixed by the Court pursuant to this Article 36(4).

5. The amount of any advance on costs fixed by the Court pursuant to this Article 36 may be subject to readjustment at any time during the arbitration.

In all cases, any party shall be free to pay any other party's share of any advance on costs should such other party fail to pay its share.

6. When a request for an advance on costs has not been complied with, and after consultation with the arbitral tribunal, the Secretary General may direct the arbitral tribunal to suspend its work and set a time limit, which must be not less than 15 days, on the expiry of which the relevant claims shall be considered as withdrawn. Should the party in question wish to object to this measure, it must make a request within the aforementioned period for the matter to be decided by the Court. Such party shall not be prevented, on the ground of such withdrawal, from reintroducing the same claims at a later date in another proceeding.

7. If one of the parties claims a right to a set-off with regard to any claim, such set-off shall be taken into account in determining the advance to cover the costs of the arbitration in the same way as a separate claim insofar as it may require the arbitral tribunal to consider additional matters.

Article 37: Decision as to the Costs of the Arbitration

1. The costs of the arbitration shall include the fees and expenses of the arbitrators and the ICC administrative expenses fixed by the Court, in accordance with the scale in force at the time of the commencement of the arbitration, as well as the fees and expenses of any experts appointed by the arbitral tribunal and the reasonable legal and other costs incurred by the parties for the arbitration.

2. The Court may fix the fees of the arbitrators at a figure higher or lower than that which would result from the application of the relevant scale should this be deemed necessary due to the exceptional circumstances of the case.

3. At any time during the arbitral proceedings, the arbitral tribunal may make decisions on costs, other than those to be fixed by the Court, and order payment.

4. The final award shall fix the costs of the arbitration and decide which of the parties shall bear them or in what proportion they shall be borne by the parties.

5. In making decisions as to costs, the arbitral tribunal may take into account such circumstances as it considers relevant, including the extent to which each party has conducted the arbitration in an expeditious and cost-effective manner.

6. In the event of the withdrawal of all claims or the termination of the arbitration before the rendering of a final award, the Court shall fix the fees and expenses of the arbitrators and the ICC administrative expenses. If the parties have not agreed upon the allocation of the costs of the arbitration or other relevant issues with respect to costs, such matters shall be decided by the arbitral tribunal. If the arbitral tribunal has not been constituted at the time of such withdrawal or termination, any party may request the Court to proceed with the constitution of the arbitral tribunal in accordance with the Rules so that the arbitral tribunal may make decisions as to costs.

MISCELLANEOUS

Article 38: Modified Time Limits

1. The parties may agree to shorten the various time limits set out in the Rules. Any such agreement entered into subsequent to the constitution of an arbitral tribunal shall become effective only upon the approval of the arbitral tribunal.

2. The Court, on its own initiative, may extend any time limit which has been modified pursuant to Article 38(1) if it decides that it is necessary to do so in order that the arbitral tribunal and the Court may fulfil their responsibilities in accordance with the Rules.

Article 39: Waiver

A party which proceeds with the arbitration without raising its objection to a failure to comply with any provision of the Rules, or of any other rules applicable to the proceedings, any direction given by the arbitral tribunal, or any requirement under the arbitration agreement relating to the constitution of the arbitral tribunal or the conduct of the proceedings, shall be deemed to have waived its right to object.

Article 40: Limitation of Liability

The arbitrators, any person appointed by the arbitral tribunal, the emergency arbitrator, the Court and its members, the ICC and its employees, and the ICC National Committees and Groups and their employees and representatives shall not be liable to any person for any act or omission in connection with the arbitration, except to the extent such limitation of liability is prohibited by applicable law.

Article 41: General Rule

In all matters not expressly provided for in the Rules, the Court and the arbitral tribunal shall act in the spirit of the Rules and shall make every effort to make sure that the award is enforceable at law.

APPENDIX I

STATUTES OF THE INTERNATIONAL COURT OF ARBITRATION

Article 1: Function

1. The function of the International Court of Arbitration of the International Chamber of Commerce (the "Court") is to ensure the application of the Rules of Arbitration of the International Chamber of Commerce, and it has all the necessary powers for that purpose.

2. As an autonomous body, it carries out these functions in complete independence from the ICC and its organs.

3. Its members are independent from the ICC National Committees and Groups.

Article 2: Composition of the Court

The Court shall consist of a President[1], Vice-Presidents[2], and members and alternate members (collectively designated as members). In its work it is assisted by its Secretariat (Secretariat of the Court).

Article 3: Appointment

1. The President is elected by the ICC World Council upon the recommendation of the Executive Board of the ICC.
2. The ICC World Council appoints the Vice-Presidents of the Court from among the members of the Court or otherwise.
3. Its members are appointed by the ICC World Council on the proposal of National Committees or Groups, one member for each National Committee or Group.
4. On the proposal of the President of the Court, the World Council may appoint alternate members.
5. The term of office of all members, including, for the purposes of this paragraph, the President and Vice-Presidents, is three years. If a member is no longer in a position to exercise the member's functions, a successor is appointed by the World Council for the remainder of the term. Upon the recommendation of the Executive Board, the duration of the term of office of any member may be extended beyond three years if the World Council so decides.

Article 4: Plenary Session of the Court

The Plenary Sessions of the Court are presided over by the President or, in the President's absence, by one of the Vice-Presidents designated by the President. The deliberations shall be valid when at least six members are present. Decisions are taken by a majority vote, the President or Vice-President, as the case may be, having a casting vote in the event of a tie.

Article 5: Committees

The Court may set up one or more Committees and establish the functions and organization of such Committees.

Article 6: Confidentiality

The work of the Court is of a confidential nature which must be respected by everyone who participates in that work in whatever capacity. The Court lays down the rules regarding the persons who can attend the meetings of the Court and its Committees and who are entitled to have access to materials related to the work of the Court and its Secretariat.

[1] Referred to as "Chairman of the International Court of Arbitration" in the Constitution of the International Chamber of Commerce.

[2] Referred to as "Vice-Chairman of the International Court of Arbitration" in the Constitution of the International Chamber of Commerce.

Article 7: Modification of the Rules of Arbitration

Any proposal of the Court for a modification of the Rules is laid before the Commission on Arbitration before submission to the Executive Board of the ICC for approval, provided, however, that the Court, in order to take account of developments in information technology, may propose to modify or supplement the provisions of Article 3 of the Rules or any related provisions in the Rules without laying any such proposal before the Commission.

APPENDIX II

INTERNAL RULES OF THE INTERNATIONAL COURT OF ARBITRATION

Article 1: Confidential Character of the Work of the International Court of Arbitration

1. For the purposes of this Appendix, members of the Court include the President and Vice-Presidents of the Court.

2. The sessions of the Court, whether plenary or those of a Committee of the Court, are open only to its members and to the Secretariat.

3. However, in exceptional circumstances, the President of the Court may invite other persons to attend. Such persons must respect the confidential nature of the work of the Court.

4. The documents submitted to the Court, or drawn up by it or the Secretariat in the course of the Court's proceedings, are communicated only to the members of the Court and to the Secretariat and to persons authorized by the President to attend Court sessions.

5. The President or the Secretary General of the Court may authorize researchers undertaking work of an academic nature to acquaint themselves with awards and other documents of general interest, with the exception of memoranda, notes, statements and documents remitted by the parties within the framework of arbitration proceedings.

6. Such authorization shall not be given unless the beneficiary has undertaken to respect the confidential character of the documents made available and to refrain from publishing anything based upon information contained therein without having previously submitted the text for approval to the Secretary General of the Court.

7. The Secretariat will in each case submitted to arbitration under the Rules retain in the archives of the Court all awards, Terms of Reference and decisions of the Court, as well as copies of the pertinent correspondence of the Secretariat.

8. Any documents, communications or correspondence submitted by the parties or the arbitrators may be destroyed unless a party or an arbitrator requests in writing within a period fixed by the Secretariat the return of such documents, communications or correspondence. All related costs and expenses for the return of those documents shall be paid by such party or arbitrator.

Article 2: Participation of Members of the International Court of Arbitration in ICC Arbitration

1. The President and the members of the Secretariat of the Court may not act as arbitrators or as counsel in cases submitted to ICC arbitration.

2. The Court shall not appoint Vice-Presidents or members of the Court as arbitrators. They may, however, be proposed for such duties by one or more of the parties, or pursuant to any other procedure agreed upon by the parties, subject to confirmation.

3. When the President, a Vice-President or a member of the Court or of the Secretariat is involved in any capacity whatsoever in proceedings pending before the Court, such person must inform the Secretary General of the Court upon becoming aware of such involvement.

4. Such person must be absent from the Court session whenever the matter is considered by the Court and shall not participate in the discussions or in the decisions of the Court.

5. Such person will not receive any material documentation or information pertaining to such proceedings.

Article 3: Relations between the Members of the Court and the ICC National Committees and Groups

1. By virtue of their capacity, the members of the Court are independent of the ICC National Committees and Groups which proposed them for appointment by the ICC World Council.

2. Furthermore, they must regard as confidential, vis-à-vis the said National Committees and Groups, any information concerning individual cases with which they have become acquainted in their capacity as members of the Court, except when they have been requested by the President of the Court, by a Vice-President of the Court authorized by the President of the Court, or by the Court's Secretary General to communicate specific information to their respective National Committees or Groups.

Article 4: Committee of the Court

1. In accordance with the provisions of Article 1(4) of the Rules and Article 5 of its statutes (Appendix I), the Court hereby establishes a Committee of the Court.

2. The members of the Committee consist of a president and at least two other members. The President of the Court acts as the president of the Committee. In the President's absence or otherwise at the President's request, a Vice-President of the Court or, in exceptional circumstances, another member of the Court may act as president of the Committee.

3. The other two members of the Committee are appointed by the Court from among the Vice-Presidents or the other members of the Court. At each Plenary Session the Court appoints the members who are to attend the meetings of the Committee to be held before the next Plenary Session.

4. The Committee meets when convened by its president. Two members constitute a quorum.

5. (a) The Court shall determine the decisions that may be taken by the Committee.

(b) The decisions of the Committee are taken unanimously.

(c) When the Committee cannot reach a decision or deems it preferable to abstain, it transfers the case to the next Plenary Session, making any suggestions it deems appropriate.

(d) The Committee's decisions are brought to the notice of the Court at its next Plenary Session.

Article 5: Court Secretariat

1. In the Secretary General's absence or otherwise at the Secretary General's request, the Deputy Secretary General and/or the General Counsel shall have the authority to refer matters to the Court, confirm arbitrators, certify true copies of awards and request the payment of a provisional advance, respectively provided for in Articles 6(3), 13(2), 34 (2) and 36(1) of the Rules.

2. The Secretariat may, with the approval of the Court, issue notes and other documents for the information of the parties and the arbitrators, or as necessary for the proper conduct of the arbitral proceedings.

3. Offices of the Secretariat may be established outside the headquarters of the ICC. The Secretariat shall keep a list of offices designated by the Secretary General. Requests for Arbitration may be submitted to the Secretariat at any of its offices, and the Secretariat's functions under the Rules may be carried out from any of its offices, as instructed by the Secretary General, Deputy Secretary General or General Counsel.

Article 6: Scrutiny of Arbitral Awards

When the Court scrutinizes draft awards in accordance with Article 33 of the Rules, it considers, to the extent practicable, the requirements of mandatory law at the place of the arbitration.

APPENDIX III
ARBITRATION COSTS AND FEES

Article 1: Advance on Costs

1. Each request to commence an arbitration pursuant to the Rules must be accompanied by a filing fee of US$ 3,000. Such payment is non-refundable and shall be credited to the claimant's portion of the advance on costs.

2. The provisional advance fixed by the Secretary General according to Article 36(1) of the Rules shall normally not exceed the amount obtained by adding together the ICC administrative expenses, the minimum of the fees (as set out in the scale hereinafter) based upon the amount of the claim and the expected reimbursable expenses of the arbitral tribunal incurred with respect to the drafting of the Terms of Reference. If such amount is not quantified, the provisional

advance shall be fixed at the discretion of the Secretary General. Payment by the claimant shall be credited to its share of the advance on costs fixed by the Court.

3. In general, after the Terms of Reference have been signed or approved by the Court and the procedural timetable has been established, the arbitral tribunal shall, in accordance with Article 36(6) of the Rules, proceed only with respect to those claims or counterclaims in regard to which the whole of the advance on costs has been paid.

4. The advance on costs fixed by the Court according to Articles 36(2) or 36(4) of the Rules comprises the fees of the arbitrator or arbitrators (hereinafter referred to as "arbitrator"), any arbitration-related expenses of the arbitrator and the ICC administrative expenses.

5. Each party shall pay its share of the total advance on costs in cash. However, if a party's share of the advance on costs is greater than US$ 500,000 (the "Threshold Amount"), such party may post a bank guarantee for any amount above the Threshold Amount. The Court may modify the Threshold Amount at any time at its discretion.

6. The Court may authorize the payment of advances on costs, or any party's share thereof, in instalments, subject to such conditions as the Court thinks fit, including the payment of additional ICC administrative expenses.

7. A party that has already paid in full its share of the advance on costs fixed by the Court may, in accordance with Article 36(5) of the Rules, pay the unpaid portion of the advance owed by the defaulting party by posting a bank guarantee.

8. When the Court has fixed separate advances on costs pursuant to Article 36(3) of the Rules, the Secretariat shall invite each party to pay the amount of the advance corresponding to its respective claim(s).

9. When, as a result of the fixing of separate advances on costs, the separate advance fixed for the claim of either party exceeds one half of such global advance as was previously fixed (in respect of the same claims and counter-claims that are the subject of separate advances), a bank guarantee may be posted to cover any such excess amount. In the event that the amount of the separate advance is subsequently increased, at least one half of the increase shall be paid in cash.

10. The Secretariat shall establish the terms governing all bank guarantees which the parties may post pursuant to the above provisions.

11. As provided in Article 36(5) of the Rules, the advance on costs may be subject to readjustment at any time during the arbitration, in particular to take into account fluctuations in the amount in dispute, changes in the amount of the estimated expenses of the arbitrator, or the evolving difficulty or complexity of arbitration proceedings.

12. Before any expertise ordered by the arbitral tribunal can be commenced, the parties, or one of them, shall pay an advance on costs fixed by the arbitral tribunal sufficient to cover the expected fees and expenses of the expert as determined by the arbitral tribunal. The arbitral tribunal shall be responsible for ensuring the payment by the parties of such fees and expenses.

13. The amounts paid as advances on costs do not yield interest for the parties or the arbitrator.

Article 2: Costs and Fees

1. Subject to Article 37(2) of the Rules, the Court shall fix the fees of the arbitrator in accordance with the scale hereinafter set out or, where the amount in dispute is not stated, at its discretion.

2. In setting the arbitrator's fees, the Court shall take into consideration the diligence and efficiency of the arbitrator, the time spent, the rapidity of the proceedings, the complexity of the dispute and the timeliness of the submission of the draft award, so as to arrive at a figure within the limits specified or, in exceptional circumstances (Article 37(2) of the Rules), at a figure higher or lower than those limits.

3. When a case is submitted to more than one arbitrator, the Court, at its discretion, shall have the right to increase the total fees up to a maximum which shall normally not exceed three times the fees of one arbitrator.

4. The arbitrator's fees and expenses shall be fixed exclusively by the Court as required by the Rules. Separate fee arrangements between the parties and the arbitrator are contrary to the Rules.

5. The Court shall fix the ICC administrative expenses of each arbitration in accordance with the scale hereinafter set out or, where the amount in dispute is not stated, at its discretion. In exceptional circumstances, the Court may fix the ICC administrative expenses at a lower or higher figure than that which would result from the application of such scale, provided that such expenses shall normally not exceed the maximum amount of the scale.

6. At any time during the arbitration, the Court may fix as payable a portion of the ICC administrative expenses corresponding to services that have already been performed by the Court and the Secretariat.

7. The Court may require the payment of administrative expenses in addition to those provided in the scale of administrative expenses as a condition for holding an arbitration in abeyance at the request of the parties or of one of them with the acquiescence of the other.

8. If an arbitration terminates before the rendering of a final award, the Court shall fix the fees and expenses of the arbitrators and the ICC administrative expenses at its discretion, taking into account the stage attained by the arbitral proceedings and any other relevant circumstances.

9. Any amount paid by the parties as an advance on costs exceeding the costs of the arbitration fixed by the Court shall be reimbursed to the parties having regard to the amounts paid.

10. In the case of an application under Article 35(2) of the Rules or of a remission pursuant to Article 35(4) of the Rules, the Court may fix an advance to cover additional fees and expenses of the arbitral tribunal and additional ICC administrative expenses and may make the transmission of such

application to the arbitral tribunal subject to the prior cash payment in full to the ICC of such advance. The Court shall fix at its discretion the costs of the procedure following an application or a remission, which shall include any possible fees of the arbitrator and ICC administrative expenses, when approving the decision of the arbitral tribunal.

11. The Secretariat may require the payment of administrative expenses in addition to those provided in the scale of administrative expenses for any expenses arising in relation to a request pursuant to Article 34(5) of the Rules.

12. When an arbitration is preceded by an attempt at amicable resolution pursuant to the ICC ADR Rules, one half of the ICC administrative expenses paid for such ADR proceedings shall be credited to the ICC administrative expenses of the arbitration.

13. Amounts paid to the arbitrator do not include any possible value added tax (VAT) or other taxes or charges and imposts applicable to the arbitrator's fees. Parties have a duty to pay any such taxes or charges; however, the recovery of any such charges or taxes is a matter solely between the arbitrator and the parties.

14. Any ICC administrative expenses may be subject to value added tax (VAT) or charges of a similar nature at the prevailing rate.

Article 3: ICC as Appointing Authority

Any request received for an authority of the ICC to act as appointing authority will be treated in accordance with the Rules of ICC as Appointing Authority in UNCITRAL or Other Ad Hoc Arbitration Proceedings and shall be accompanied by a non-refundable filing fee of US$ 3,000. No request shall be processed unless accompanied by the said filing fee. For additional services, ICC may at its discretion fix ICC administrative expenses, which shall be commensurate with the services provided and shall normally not exceed the maximum amount of US$ 10,000.

Article 4: Scales of Administrative Expenses and Arbitrator's Fees

1. The Scales of Administrative Expenses and Arbitrator's Fees set forth below shall be effective as of 1 January 2012 in respect of all arbitrations commenced on or after such date, irrespective of the version of the Rules applying to such arbitrations.

2. To calculate the ICC administrative expenses and the arbitrator's fees, the amounts calculated for each successive tranche of the amount in dispute must be added together, except that where the amount in dispute is over US$ 500 million, a flat amount of US$ 113,215 shall constitute the entirety of the ICC administrative expenses.

3. All amounts fixed by the Court or pursuant to any of the appendices to the Rules are payable in US$ except where prohibited by law, in which case the ICC may apply a different scale and fee arrangement in another currency.

A. ADMINISTRATIVE EXPENSES

Amount in dispute (in US Dollars)				Administrative expenses*
up to			50,000	$3,000
from	50,001	to	100,000	4.73%
from	100,001	to	200,000	2.53%
from	200,001	to	500,000	2.09%
from	500,001	to	1,000,000	1.51%
from	1,000,001	to	2,000,000	0.95%
from	2,000,001	to	5,000,000	0.46%
from	5,000,001	to	10,000,000	0.25%
from	10,000,001	to	30,000,000	0.10%
from	30,000,001	to	50,000,000	0.09%
from	50,000,001	to	80,000,000	0.01%
from	80,000,001	to	500,000,000	0.0035%
over	500,000,000			$113,215

* For illustrative purposes only, [the third table] indicates the resulting administrative expenses in US$ when the proper calculations have been made.

B. ARBITRATOR'S FEES

Amount in dispute (in US Dollars)				Fees**	
				minimum	maximum
up to	50,000			$3,000	18,0200%
from	50,001	to	100,000	2.6500%	13.5680%
from	100,001	to	200,000	1.4310%	7.6850%
from	200,001	to	500,000	1.3670%	6.8370%
from	500,001	to	1,000,000	0.9540%	4.0280%
from	1,000,001	to	2,000,000	0.6890%	3.6040%
from	2,000,001	to	5,000,000	0.3750%	1.3910%
from	5,000,001	to	10,000,000	0.1280%	0.9100%
from	10,000,001	to	30,000,000	0.0640%	0.2410%
from	30,000,001	to	50,000,000	0.0590%	0.2280%
from	50,000,001	to	80,000,000	0.0330%	0.1570%
from	80,000,001	to	100,000,000	0.0210%	0.1150%
from	100,000,001	to	500,000,000	0.0110%	0.0580%
over	500,000,000			0.0100%	0.0400%

** For illustrative purposes only, [the fourth table] indicates the resulting range of fees in US$ when the proper calculations have been made.

AMOUNT IN DISPUTE (in US Dollars)	A. ADMINISTRATIVE EXPENSES (in US Dollars)	B. ARBITRATOR'S FEES (in US Dollars)	
		Minimum	Maximum
up to 50,000	3,000	3,000	18.0200% of amount in dispute
from 50,001 to 100,000	3,000 + 4.73% of amt. over 50,000	3,000 + 2.6500% of amt. over 50,000	9,010 + 13.5680% of amt. over 50,000
from 100,001 to 200,000	5,365 + 2.53% of amt. over 100,000	4,325 + 1.4310% of amt. over 100,000	15,794 + 7.6850% of amt. over 100,000
from 200,001 to 500,000	7,895 + 2.09% of amt. over 200,000	5,756 + 1.3670% of amt. over 200,000	23,479 + 6.8370% of amt. over 200,000
from 500,001 to 1,000,000	14,165 + 1.51% of amt. over 500,000	9,857 + 0.9540% of amt. over 500,000	43,990 + 4.0280% of amt. over 500,000
from 1,000,001 to 2,000,000	21,715 + 0.95% of amt. over 1,000,000	14,627 + 0.6890% of amt. over 1,000,000	64,130 + 3.6040% of amt. over 1,000,000
from 2,000,001 to 5,000,000	31,215 + 0.46% of amt. over 2,000,000	21,517 + 0.3750% of amt. over 2,000,000	100,170 + 1.3910% of amt. over 2,000,000
from 5,000,001 to 10,000,000	45,015 + 0.25% of amt. over 5,000,000	32,767 + 0.1280% of amt. over 5,000,000	141,900 + 0.9100% of amt. over 5,000,000
from 10,000,001 to 30,000,000	57,515 + 0.10% of amt. over 10,000,000	39,167 + 0.0640% of amt. over 10,000,000	187,400 + 0.2410% of amt. over 10,000,000
from 30,000,001 to 50,000,000	77,515 + 0.09% of amt. over 30,000,000	51,967 + 0.0590% of amt. over 30,000,000	235,600 + 0.2280% of amt. over 30,000,000
from 50,000,001 to 80,000,000	95,515 + 0.01% of amt. over 50,000,000	63,767 + 0.0330% of amt. over 50,000,000	281,200 + 0.1570% of amt. over 50,000,000
from 80,000,001 to 100,000,000	98,515 + 0.0035% of amt. over 80,000,000	73,667 + 0.0210% of amt. over 80,000,000	328,300 + 0.1150% of amt. over 80,000,000
from 100,000,001 to 500,000,000	99,215 + 0.0035% of amt. over 100,000,000	77,867 + 0.0110% of amt. over 100,000,000	351,300 + 0.0580% of amt. over 100,000,000
over 500,000,000	113,215	121,867 + 0.0100% of amt. over 500,000,000	583,300 + 0.0400% of amt. over 500,000,000

Appendix IV

Case Management Techniques

The following are examples of case management techniques that can be used by the arbitral tribunal and the parties for controlling time and cost. Appropriate control of time and cost is important in all cases. In cases of low complexity and low value, it is particularly important to ensure that time and costs are proportionate to what is at stake in the dispute.

a) Bifurcating the proceedings or rendering one or more partial awards on key issues, when doing so may genuinely be expected to result in a more efficient resolution of the case.

b) Identifying issues that can be resolved by agreement between the parties or their experts.

c) Identifying issues to be decided solely on the basis of documents rather than through oral evidence or legal argument at a hearing.

d) Production of documentary evidence:

   (i) requiring the parties to produce with their submissions the documents on which they rely;

   (ii) avoiding requests for document production when appropriate in order to control time and cost;

   (iii) in those cases where requests for document production are considered appropriate, limiting such requests to documents or categories of documents that are relevant and material to the outcome of the case;

   (iv) establishing reasonable time limits for the production of documents;

   (v) using a schedule of document production to facilitate the resolution of issues in relation to the production of documents.

e) Limiting the length and scope of written submissions and written and oral witness evidence (both fact witnesses and experts) so as to avoid repetition and maintain a focus on key issues.

f) Using telephone or video conferencing for procedural and other hearings where attendance in person is not essential and use of IT that enables online communication among the parties, the arbitral tribunal and the Secretariat of the Court.

g) Organizing a pre-hearing conference with the arbitral tribunal at which arrangements for a hearing can be discussed and agreed and the arbitral tribunal can indicate to the parties issues on which it would like the parties to focus at the hearing.

h) Settlement of disputes:

   (i) informing the parties that they are free to settle all or part of the dispute either by negotiation or through any form of amicable dispute resolution methods such as, for example, mediation under the ICC ADR Rules;

   (ii) where agreed between the parties and the arbitral tribunal, the arbitral tribunal may take steps to facilitate settlement of the dispute, provided that every effort is made to ensure that any subsequent award is enforceable at law.

Additional techniques are described in the ICC publication entitled "Techniques for Controlling Time and Costs in Arbitration".

Appendix V

Emergency Arbitrator Rules

Article 1: Application for Emergency Measures

1. A party wishing to have recourse to an emergency arbitrator pursuant to Article 29 of the Rules of Arbitration of the ICC (the "Rules") shall submit its Application for Emergency Measures (the "Application") to the Secretariat at any of the offices specified in the Internal Rules of the Court in Appendix II to the Rules.

2. The Application shall be supplied in a number of copies sufficient to provide one copy for each party, plus one for the emergency arbitrator, and one for the Secretariat.

3. The Application shall contain the following information:

   a) the name in full, description, address and other contact details of each of the parties;

   b) the name in full, address and other contact details of any person(s) representing the applicant;

   c) a description of the circumstances giving rise to the Application and of the underlying dispute referred or to be referred to arbitration;

   d) a statement of the Emergency Measures sought;

   e) the reasons why the applicant needs urgent interim or conservatory measures that cannot await the constitution of an arbitral tribunal;

   f) any relevant agreements and, in particular, the arbitration agreement;

   g) any agreement as to the place of the arbitration, the applicable rules of law or the language of the arbitration;

   h) proof of payment of the amount referred to in Article 7(1) of this Appendix; and

   i) any Request for Arbitration and any other submissions in connection with the underlying dispute, which have been filed with the Secretariat by any of the parties to the emergency arbitrator proceedings prior to the making of the Application.

The Application may contain such other documents or information as the applicant considers appropriate or as may contribute to the efficient examination of the Application.

4. The Application shall be drawn up in the language of the arbitration if agreed upon by the parties or, in the absence of any such agreement, in the language of the arbitration agreement.

5. If and to the extent that the President of the Court (the "President") considers, on the basis of the information contained in the Application, that the Emergency Arbitrator Provisions apply with reference to Article 29(5) and Article 29(6) of the Rules, the Secretariat shall transmit a copy of the Application and the documents annexed thereto to the responding party. If and to the extent that the President considers otherwise, the Secretariat shall inform the parties that the emergency arbitrator proceedings shall not take place with respect to some or all of the parties and shall transmit a copy of the Application to them for information.

6. The President shall terminate the emergency arbitrator proceedings if a Request for Arbitration has not been received by the Secretariat from the applicant within 10 days of the Secretariat's receipt of the Application, unless the emergency arbitrator determines that a longer period of time is necessary.

Article 2: Appointment of the Emergency Arbitrator; Transmission of the File

1. The President shall appoint an emergency arbitrator within as short a time as possible, normally within two days from the Secretariat's receipt of the Application.

2. No emergency arbitrator shall be appointed after the file has been transmitted to the arbitral tribunal pursuant to Article 16 of the Rules. An emergency arbitrator appointed prior thereto shall retain the power to make an order within the time limit permitted by Article 6(4) of this Appendix.

3. Once the emergency arbitrator has been appointed, the Secretariat shall so notify the parties and shall transmit the file to the emergency arbitrator. Thereafter, all written communications from the parties shall be submitted directly to the emergency arbitrator with a copy to the other party and the Secretariat. A copy of any written communications from the emergency arbitrator to the parties shall be submitted to the Secretariat.

4. Every emergency arbitrator shall be and remain impartial and independent of the parties involved in the dispute.

5. Before being appointed, a prospective emergency arbitrator shall sign a statement of acceptance, availability, impartiality and independence. The Secretariat shall provide a copy of such statement to the parties.

6. An emergency arbitrator shall not act as an arbitrator in any arbitration relating to the dispute that gave rise to the Application.

Article 3: Challenge of an Emergency Arbitrator

1. A challenge against the emergency arbitrator must be made within three days from receipt by the party making the challenge of the notification of the appointment or from the date when that party was informed of the facts and circumstances on which the challenge is based if such date is subsequent to the receipt of such notification.

2. The challenge shall be decided by the Court after the Secretariat has afforded an opportunity for the emergency arbitrator and the other party or parties to provide comments in writing within a suitable period of time.

Article 4: Place of the Emergency Arbitrator Proceedings

1. If the parties have agreed upon the place of the arbitration, such place shall be the place of the emergency arbitrator proceedings. In the absence of such agreement, the President shall fix the place of the emergency arbitrator proceedings, without prejudice to the determination of the place of the arbitration pursuant to Article 18(1) of the Rules.

2. Any meetings with the emergency arbitrator may be conducted through a meeting in person at any location the emergency arbitrator considers appropriate or by video conference, telephone or similar means of communication.

Article 5: Proceedings

1. The emergency arbitrator shall establish a procedural timetable for the emergency arbitrator proceedings within as short a time as possible, normally within two days from the transmission of the file to the emergency arbitrator pursuant to Article 2(3) of this Appendix.

2. The emergency arbitrator shall conduct the proceedings in the manner which the emergency arbitrator considers to be appropriate, taking into account the nature and the urgency of the Application. In all cases, the emergency arbitrator shall act fairly and impartially and ensure that each party has a reasonable opportunity to present its case.

Article 6: Order

1. Pursuant to Article 29(2) of the Rules, the emergency arbitrator's decision shall take the form of an order (the "Order").

2. In the Order, the emergency arbitrator shall determine whether the Application is admissible pursuant to Article 29(1) of the Rules and whether the emergency arbitrator has jurisdiction to order Emergency Measures.

3. The Order shall be made in writing and shall state the reasons upon which it is based. It shall be dated and signed by the emergency arbitrator.

4. The Order shall be made no later than 15 days from the date on which the file was transmitted to the emergency arbitrator pursuant to Article 2(3) of this Appendix. The President may extend the time limit pursuant to a reasoned request from the emergency arbitrator or on the President's own initiative if the President decides it is necessary to do so.

5. Within the time limit established pursuant to Article 6(4) of this Appendix, the emergency arbitrator shall send the Order to the parties, with a copy to the Secretariat, by any of the means of communication permitted by Article 3(2) of the Rules that the emergency arbitrator considers will ensure prompt receipt.

6. The Order shall cease to be binding on the parties upon:

   a) the President's termination of the emergency arbitrator proceedings pursuant to Article 1(6) of this Appendix;

   b) the acceptance by the Court of a challenge against the emergency arbitrator pursuant to Article 3 of this Appendix;

   c) the arbitral tribunal's final award, unless the arbitral tribunal expressly decides otherwise; or

   d) the withdrawal of all claims or the termination of the arbitration before the rendering of a final award.

7. The emergency arbitrator may make the Order subject to such conditions as the emergency arbitrator thinks fit, including requiring the provision of appropriate security.

8. Upon a reasoned request by a party made prior to the transmission of the file to the arbitral tribunal pursuant to Article 16 of the Rules, the emergency arbitrator may modify, terminate or annul the Order.

Article 7: Costs of the Emergency Arbitrator Proceedings

1. The applicant must pay an amount of US$ 40,000, consisting of US$ 10,000 for ICC administrative expenses and US$ 30,000 for the emergency arbitrator's fees and expenses. Notwithstanding Article 1(5) of this Appendix, the Application shall not be notified until the payment of US$ 40,000 is received by the Secretariat.

2. The President may, at any time during the emergency arbitrator proceedings, decide to increase the emergency arbitrator's fees or the ICC administrative expenses taking into account, *inter alia*, the nature of the case and the nature and amount of work performed by the emergency arbitrator, the Court, the President and the Secretariat. If the party which submitted the Application fails to pay the increased costs within the time limit fixed by the Secretariat, the Application shall be considered as withdrawn.

3. The emergency arbitrator's Order shall fix the costs of the emergency arbitrator proceedings and decide which of the parties shall bear them or in what proportion they shall be borne by the parties.

4. The costs of the emergency arbitrator proceedings include the ICC administrative expenses, the emergency arbitrator's fees and expenses and the reasonable legal and other costs incurred by the parties for the emergency arbitrator proceedings.

5. In the event that the emergency arbitrator proceedings do not take place pursuant to Article 1(5) of this Appendix or are otherwise terminated prior to the making of an Order, the President shall determine the amount to be reimbursed to the applicant, if any. An amount of US$ 5,000 for ICC administrative expenses is non-refundable in all cases.

Article 8: General Rule

1. The President shall have the power to decide, at the President's discretion, all matters relating to the administration of the emergency arbitrator proceedings not expressly provided for in this Appendix.

2. In the President's absence or otherwise at the President's request, any of the Vice-Presidents of the Court shall have the power to take decisions on behalf of the President.

3. In all matters concerning emergency arbitrator proceedings not expressly provided for in this Appendix, the Court, the President and the emergency arbitrator shall act in the spirit of the Rules and this Appendix.

Appendix 2

TECHNIQUES FOR CONTROLLING TIME AND COSTS IN ARBITRATION

Second Edition

Report of the ICC Commission on Arbitration and ADR Task Force on Reducing Time and Costs in Arbitration

Preface To The Second Edition

Arbitration is a valuable tool for the resolution of disputes. However, if it is to serve the needs of its users, it must be time and cost effective. The first edition of this Report, published in August 2007, provided a range of techniques that could be used to increase the time and cost efficiency of arbitration. The final paragraph of the preface to that edition expressed the hope that the Report would be of use in the crafting of efficient arbitration procedures. That hope has become a reality. Since its publication, the Report has been positively received by the users of arbitration, as well as by arbitrators and counsel, and the techniques set out in the Report have been widely applied in institutional and ad hoc arbitrations all over the world. The need to focus on the time and cost efficiency of arbitration has become generally recognized, and the ideas in the Report have inspired much discussion as well as a large number of other publications.

In 2009, the ICC Commission on Arbitration (as it was then known) began its revision of the 1998 ICC Rules of Arbitration. A drafting subcommittee (the "DSC") was established to propose modifications to the Rules, taking into account suggestions received from national committees, the ICC International Court of Arbitration and its Secretariat, and the arbitration community at large. The DSC included two in-house counsel who consulted with the user community worldwide. The users proposed that the approach to time and cost efficiency taken in the Report should be incorporated into the Rules. This was accomplished in Articles 22–24 and Appendix IV of the 2012 ICC Rules of Arbitration. Article 22(1) places an explicit obligation on both the arbitral tribunal and the parties to make every effort to conduct the arbitration in an expeditious and cost-effective manner, having regard to the complexity and value of the dispute. Article 22(2) empowers the arbitral tribunal, in the absence of an agreement of the parties, to adopt appropriate procedural measures to ensure effective case management. Article 24(1) requires the arbitral tribunal to convene a case management conference to consult the parties on appropriate procedural measures to be adopted pursuant to Article 22(2). It is expressly stated that those measures may include one or more of the techniques described in Appendix IV. Those techniques are taken directly from the Report.

In sum, the tailor-making of the arbitral procedure referred to in the preface to the first edition of the Report has become a formal requirement in the 2012 Rules, accomplished through the case management conference. Ideally, party representatives will be present so that they can participate in the choice of appropriate procedures for the case. To make an arbitration faster and cheaper, it may be necessary to forego certain steps, such as additional rounds of briefs, excessive document production, longer hearings, more experts, and the like. The goal at the case management conference is to arrive at procedures that are genuinely useful and necessary for the effective presentation of the case. Any additional procedures are likely to result in time and cost inefficiencies.

What, then, is the nature and function of this second edition of the Report? First, the Report has been updated to reflect the various modifications made in the 2012 Rules. Second, and more importantly, this edition of the Report should be seen as an adjunct to the 2012 Rules. It can be used to enhance the tailor-making process required by the Rules. In this edition the techniques set out in Appendix IV to the Rules are further discussed and explained. Additional techniques beyond those in Appendix IV are also presented. The hope that may be expressed for this edition of the Report is that it will help ensure the success of the tailor-making process under the 2012 Rules and thereby contribute to the increased effectiveness and attractiveness of international arbitration.

Peter M. Wolrich

Chairman, ICC Commission on Arbitration and ADR

Preface To The First Edition

One of the salient characteristics of arbitration as a dispute resolution mechanism is that the rules of arbitration themselves present a framework for arbitral proceedings but rarely set out detailed procedures for the conduct of the arbitration. For example, rules of arbitration do not generally specify whether there should be one, two or more exchanges of briefs. They do not contain any detailed provisions concerning document production. They do not specify how hearings should be conducted and how witnesses, if any, should be heard.

This important characteristic entails that the specific procedures can be tailor-made as appropriate for each dispute and adapted to the legal cultures of the parties and the arbitrators. In order to establish the appropriate procedures for a given arbitration, it is useful and efficient for the parties and the tribunal to make conscious decisions as early as possible on the procedures best suited to the dispute at hand. In making those decisions, it is possible to shape the arbitral proceedings so that the duration and cost of the arbitration are commensurate with what is at stake in the case and appropriate in light of the claims and issues presented.

With the above in mind, the Task Force on Reducing Time and Costs in Arbitration, set up by the ICC Commission on Arbitration and excellently co-chaired by Yves Derains and Christopher Newmark, has prepared the following document setting out a large number of techniques which can be used for organizing the arbitral proceedings and controlling their duration and cost. This document can provide valuable assistance to the parties and the tribunal in developing appropriate procedures for their arbitration. It is intended to encourage them to create a new dynamic at the outset of an arbitration, whereby the parties can review the suggested techniques and agree upon appropriate procedures and, if they fail to agree, the tribunal can decide upon such procedures. For example, an arbitral tribunal can send this document to the parties at the start of the proceedings, indicating that early in the proceedings they might seek to agree upon appropriate procedures in consultation with the tribunal. In that process, all may agree upon the use of certain techniques. If one party wishes to use a particular technique and the other party does not, the tribunal, after obtaining the views of each party on the matter, can decide whether or not to adopt that procedure. The use of this approach, coupled with the proactive involvement of the tribunal in the management of the proceedings, can result in meaningful savings of time and cost in the arbitration.

The techniques suggested in the document are not intended to be exhaustive. On the contrary, they are open-ended, and the parties and the tribunal are encouraged to think of this document as a basis from which to develop the procedures to be used. Indeed, it is the intention of the ICC Commission on Arbitration to revise and republish this document in the future, taking into account further suggestions which will emerge from the use of the document. As a corollary, it should be clear that parties and arbitrators are in no way obligated to follow any of the techniques. Moreover, the document is a product of the ICC Commission on Arbitration and not of the ICC International Court of Arbitration and thus it is not part of or interpretative of the ICC Rules of Arbitration or in any way binding upon the Court. Rather, it is a practical tool designed to stimulate the conscious choice of arbitral procedures with a view to organizing an arbitration which is efficient and appropriately tailor-made. Finally, while this document was conceived with the ICC Rules of Arbitration in mind, the vast majority of the techniques as well as the dynamics generated by the document can be used in all arbitrations.

It is the sincere hope of the Task Force that this document will be used and be of use in the crafting of efficient arbitration procedures in which time and cost will be proportionate to the needs of the dispute.

Peter M. Wolrich

Chairman, ICC Commission on Arbitration

Introduction

Costs incurred by the parties constitute the largest part of the total cost of international arbitration proceedings. It follows that if the overall cost of the arbitral proceedings is to be reduced, special emphasis needs to be placed on steps aimed at lowering the costs connected with the parties' presentation of their cases. Such costs are often caused by unnecessarily long and complicated proceedings with unfocused requests for disclosure of documents and unnecessary witness and expert evidence. Costs can also be unnecessarily increased when counsel from different legal backgrounds use procedures familiar to them in a manner that leads to needless duplication.

The increasing and, on occasion, unnecessary complication of the proceedings seems to be the main explanation for the long duration and high cost of many international arbitrations. The longer the proceedings, the more expensive they will be. The 2012 ICC Rules of Arbitration (the "Rules") have expressly addressed these concerns.

These Techniques for Controlling Time and Costs in Arbitration (the "Techniques") are designed to assist arbitral tribunals, parties and their counsel in devising tailor-made procedures for individual arbitrations pursuant to Articles 22–24 of the Rules.

In particular, the Techniques may be of benefit to the parties and the tribunal when preparing the case management conference and seeking agreement on procedures suitable for their case. If the parties cannot reach agreement, the Techniques may also assist the arbitral tribunal in adopting procedures that it considers appropriate, taking into account its obligation to conduct the arbitration in an expeditious and cost-effective manner. The Techniques are freely accessible online on the ICC's website (www.iccwbo.org) and in the ICC Dispute Resolution Library (www.iccdrl.com). They are in no way prescriptive. Rather, they provide suggestions that may assist in arriving at procedures that are efficient and will reduce both cost and time. Certain procedures will be appropriate for one arbitration, but inappropriate for another. There may be other procedures not mentioned here that are well suited to a particular case. In all instances, it is for the parties and the arbitral tribunal to select the procedures that are best suited for the case. The table of contents to this document can serve as a checklist of points to consider.

While the main focus of the Techniques is to provide guidance on the procedure during the arbitration, the first two sections give suggestions on the drafting of arbitration agreements and the initiation of arbitral proceedings.

Arbitration Agreement

1 Keeping clauses simple

Simple, clearly drafted arbitration clauses will avoid uncertainty and disputes over their meaning and effect. They will minimize the risk of time and costs being spent on disputes regarding, for example, the jurisdiction of the arbitral tribunal or the process of appointing arbitrators. In all cases, ensure that the arbitration clause conforms with any relevant applicable laws.

2 Use of the ICC model clause

Use of the standard ICC arbitration clause is recommended. It provides as follows:

> All disputes arising out of or in connection with the present contract shall be finally settled under the Rules of Arbitration of the International Chamber of Commerce by one or more arbitrators appointed in accordance with the said Rules.

Modifications to the standard clause can result in unintended and undesirable consequences and therefore should be made only with great care and for specific purposes. In addition to the standard clause, the parties may wish to specify in separate sentences the place of the arbitration, the language of the arbitration and the rules of law governing the contract. Be cautious about adding to this clause further provisions relating to the procedure for the arbitration.

The Rules permit any party in need of urgent or conservatory measures that cannot await the constitution of an arbitral tribunal to make an application to the ICC International Court of Arbitration (the "Court") for the appointment of an emergency arbitrator to decide upon the request for such measures. The parties should consider whether the Emergency Arbitrator Provisions as set out in Article 29 and Appendix V of the Rules are desirable in their particular situation. If the parties do not want the Emergency Arbitrator Provisions to apply, they must agree to opt out of those provisions and may do so by using the following model clause:

> All disputes arising out of or in connection with the present contract shall be finally settled under the Rules of Arbitration of the International Chamber of Commerce by one or more arbitrators appointed in accordance with the said Rules. The Emergency Arbitrator Provisions shall not apply.

3 Selection and appointment of arbitrators

High-value and complex contracts can give rise to small disputes for which a three-member tribunal may be too expensive. Although parties may desire the certainty of appointing either a one- or a three-member tribunal in their arbitration agreement, consideration should be given to staying with the standard ICC arbitration clause and providing for one or more arbitrators. This will enable the ICC to appoint, or the parties to agree on, a sole arbitrator where the specific nature of any subsequent dispute does not warrant a three-member tribunal (Rules, Article 12(2)).

If the parties wish the ICC to select and appoint all members of the arbitral tribunal (see paragraph 11 below), then the following wording can be used: "All arbitrators shall be selected and appointed by the ICC International Court of Arbitration."

Adding special requirements regarding the expertise and qualifications of arbitrators to be appointed will reduce the pool of available arbitrators and may increase the time taken to select a tribunal.

4 Fast-track procedures

Consideration may be given to setting out fast-track procedures in the arbitration clause. Indeed, Article 38(1) of the Rules enables the parties to shorten time limits provided for in the Rules, while Article 38(2) enables the Court to extend those shortened time limits when necessary. Fast-track procedures are designed to enable an arbitration to proceed quickly, given the specific nature of the contract and the disputes that are likely to arise. However, experience shows that in practice it is difficult at the time of drafting the clause to predict with a reasonable degree of certainty the nature of disputes and the procedures that will be suitable for those disputes. Also, disagreements can arise later over the interpretation or application of fast-track clauses. Careful thought should therefore be given before such provisions are included in an arbitration agreement. Once a dispute has arisen, the parties could at that time agree upon a fast-track procedure, if appropriate.

5 Time limits for rendering the final award

One commonly used provision that can give rise to significant difficulties is the requirement that a final award be produced within a certain number of weeks or months from the commencement of the arbitration. Such specific time limits can create jurisdictional and enforcement problems if it turns out that the time limit specified is unrealistic or not clearly defined.

6 More detailed arbitration agreement after the dispute has arisen

If the parties agree to submit a dispute to ICC arbitration after the dispute has arisen, they can consider specifying in some detail the procedure for the arbitration, taking into account the nature of the dispute in question. This procedure may include some of the suggestions set out below to control time and costs.

INITIATION OF PROCEEDINGS

Selection of counsel

7 Counsel with experience

Consider appointing counsel with the skills necessary for handling the arbitration at hand and who are sensitive to the need for appropriate time and cost efficiency. Such counsel are more likely to be able to work with the arbitral tribunal and the other party's counsel to devise an efficient procedure for the case.

8 Counsel with time

Ensure that the counsel you have selected has sufficient time to devote to the case.

Selection of arbitrators

9 Use of a sole arbitrator

After a dispute has arisen, consider agreeing upon having a sole arbitrator, when appropriate. Generally speaking, a one-member tribunal will be able to act more quickly than a three-member tribunal, since discussions between tribunal members are not needed and diary clashes for hearings will be minimized. A one-member tribunal will obviously also be cheaper.

10 Arbitrators with time

Whether selecting a sole arbitrator or a three-member tribunal, it is advisable to make sufficient enquiries to ensure that the individuals selected have sufficient time to devote to the case in question. If there is a particular need for speed, this must be made clear to the ICC so that it can be taken into consideration when making any appointments.

11 Selection and appointment by the ICC

Consider allowing the ICC to select and appoint the arbitral tribunal, whether it be a sole arbitrator or a three-person tribunal. This will generally be the quickest way to constitute the arbitral tribunal if there is no agreement between the parties on the identity of all arbitrators. It will also reduce the risk of challenges, facilitate the constitution of a tribunal having a variety of specialist skills and create a different dynamic within the arbitral tribunal. If the parties wish to have input into the selection of the tribunal by the ICC, they can request that the ICC provide a list of possible arbitrators to be selected in accordance with a procedure to be agreed upon by the parties in consultation with the ICC.

12 Avoiding objections

Any objection to the appointment of an arbitrator will delay the constitution of the arbitral tribunal. When selecting an arbitrator, give careful thought to whether or not the appointment of that arbitrator might give rise to an objection.

If the parties wish the ICC to select and appoint all members of the arbitral tribunal (see paragraph 11 below), then the following wording can be used: "All arbitrators shall be selected and appointed by the ICC International Court of Arbitration."

Adding special requirements regarding the expertise and qualifications of arbitrators to be appointed will reduce the pool of available arbitrators and may increase the time taken to select a tribunal.

13 Selecting arbitrators with strong case management skills

A tribunal that is proactive and skilled in case management will be able to play its role in managing the arbitration so as to make it as cost and time effective as possible, given the issues in dispute and the number and nature of the parties. Careful consideration should therefore be given to selecting tribunal members, especially the sole arbitrator or chair.

Request for Arbitration and Answer

14 Complying with the Rules

The claimant should ensure that the Request for Arbitration includes all of the elements required by Article 4(3), subparagraphs (a)—(h), of the Rules. Failure to do so may make it necessary for the Secretariat to revert to the Claimant before the Request can be forwarded to the Respondent in accordance with Article 4(5). This causes delay. Similarly, when filing its Answer, the Respondent should include all elements required by Article 5(1), subparagraphs (a)—(f), of the Rules.

15 Setting out a detailed statement of case

The Rules do not require a Request for Arbitration or an Answer to set out a full statement of case for either the claim or the defence (or, where applicable, a counterclaim). Whether or not a full statement is made in the Request can have an impact on the efficient management of the arbitration. Where the Request does contain detailed particulars of the claim, and a similar approach is taken by the respondent in the Answer, the parties and the arbitral tribunal will be in a position to make informed decisions at a very early stage in the proceedings regarding the procedural measures and case management techniques that are appropriate for the case. This will help to optimize the first case management conference held pursuant to Article 24(1).

16 Submitting additional information

The Rules expressly allow the parties to submit with a Request or an Answer any further documents or information that may contribute to the efficient resolution of the dispute (see Articles 4(3) and 5(1)). Those provisions allow for the submission of a full statement of case but also allow the parties simply to submit additional useful information. Consideration should be given to exercising this option, whether or not a full statement of case is provided.

Language of the arbitration

17 Determination of the language by the arbitral tribunal

If the parties have not agreed on the language of the arbitration, the arbitral tribunal, when determining the language, should consider doing so by means of a procedural order pursuant to Article 20 of the ICC Rules, prior to drawing up the Terms of Reference and after ascertaining the positions of the parties.

18 Proceedings involving two or more languages

Having two or more languages of the arbitration will normally increase time and cost. Consideration should be given to whether the use of two or more languages truly justifies the additional time and cost. On the other hand, where there is a single language of the arbitration, the use of an additional language should be considered if it would reduce time and cost. For example, where appropriate, the parties can agree that documents, legal materials and witness testimony in a particular language need not be translated into the language of the arbitration.

If the parties have agreed, or the arbitral tribunal has decided, that the arbitration will be conducted in two or more languages, the parties and the arbitral tribunal should consider agreeing upon practical means to avoid duplication. In cases where the members of the arbitral tribunal are fluent in all applicable languages, it may not be necessary for documents to be translated. Consideration should also be given to avoiding having the Terms of Reference, procedural orders and awards in more than one language. If this cannot be avoided, the parties would be well advised to agree upon the language that will prevail.

Establishing The Framework Of The Arbitral Proceedings

The Rules call for the framework of the arbitral proceedings to be established in three steps: the Terms of Reference; the case management conference; and the procedural timetable. The paragraphs that follow provide suggestions on how to use each of these steps to optimize time and cost efficiency.

Terms of Reference

19 Summaries of claims and relief sought

The arbitral tribunal should consider whether it is appropriate for it to draft the summary of claims and/or the relief sought itself, or whether it would assist if each party were to provide a draft summary for inclusion in the Terms of Reference in accordance with Article 23(1), subparagraph (c), of the Rules. In the latter case, the arbitral tribunal should consider requesting the parties to limit their summaries to an appropriate fixed number of pages. Further guidance on preparing Terms of Reference can be found in the article of Serge Lazareff, "Terms of Reference", ICC International Court of Arbitration Bulletin, Vol. 17/No. 1 (2006).[1]

20 Empowering the president of the arbitral tribunal on procedural issues

Where there is a three-member tribunal, it may not be necessary for all procedural issues to be decided upon by all three arbitrators. The parties should consider empowering the president of the arbitral tribunal to decide on certain procedural issues alone. In all events, consider authorizing the president to sign procedural orders alone.

21 Administrative secretary to the arbitral tribunal

Consider whether or not an administrative secretary to the arbitral tribunal would assist in reducing time and cost. If it is decided to use such a secretary, the parties and the arbitral tribunal should take into account the Note of the Secretariat of the Court on the Appointment, Duties and Remuneration of Administrative Secretaries. It is distributed to arbitrators in all cases and is reproduced in the ICC International Court of Arbitration Bulletin, Vol. 23/No. 1 (2012).

22 Need for a physical meeting

Consider whether it is appropriate to agree upon and sign the Terms of Reference without a physical meeting (e.g. by way of a telephone or video conference). In making that

[1] The ICC International Court of Arbitration Bulletin is available from the ICC Bookstore (www.iccbooks.com) and online in the ICC Dispute Resolution Library (www.iccdrl.com).

decision, the advantages of having a physical meeting at the start of the proceedings should be weighed against the time and cost involved. The holding of the case management conference should also be taken into account when deciding whether or not to hold a physical meeting (see paragraph 31 below).

23 Counterparts

If there is no physical meeting for signing the Terms of Reference, the arbitral tribunal should consider having the Terms of Reference signed in counterparts.

24 Compliance with Article 23(3)

If a party refuses to take part in drawing up the Terms of Reference or refuses to sign them, the arbitral tribunal should make certain that the Terms of Reference to be submitted to the Court for approval pursuant to Article 23(3) of the Rules do not contain any provisions that require the parties' agreement or a decision by the arbitral tribunal.

Case management conferences

25 Timing

Article 24(1) requires the arbitral tribunal to convene a case management conference when drawing up the Terms of Reference or as soon as possible thereafter. Consider whether it is most convenient and efficient to hold the case management conference immediately after the signing of the Terms of Reference and at the same meeting.

26 Preparation

For the case management conference to be most effective, the tribunal should consider asking the parties well in advance of the conference to submit joint or separate case management proposals. This will encourage them actively to consider and exchange views on the procedures and case management techniques that may be appropriate for the case. Any joint or separate proposals from the parties, any agreements between the parties, and any suggestions from the tribunal should be discussed at the case management conference. It should be noted that, in accordance with Article 22(2) of the Rules, the arbitral tribunal may not adopt procedural measures that are contrary to an agreement of the parties.

27 Use of the Techniques

Appendix IV of the Rules sets out examples of available case management techniques. These and additional examples are also contained in this Report. They can be used by the arbitral tribunal and the parties at the case management conference to assist in arriving at the most appropriate procedures for the case (see the section entitled "Subsequent procedure for the arbitration" below).

28 Providing information in advance of the conference

The more information the arbitral tribunal has about the issues in the case prior to the conference, the better placed it will be to assist the parties in devising a procedure that will deal with the dispute as efficiently as possible. For example, a tribunal that has made itself familiar with the details of the case from the outset can be proactive and give appropriate, tailor-made suggestions on the issues to be addressed in documentary and witness evidence, the areas in which it will be assisted by expert evidence, and the extent to which disclosure of documents by the parties is needed to address the issues in dispute.

29 Scope

Whenever possible, the procedure for the entire arbitration should be determined at the first case management conference and reflected in the procedural timetable to be established pursuant to Article 24(2) of the Rules. However, it may not always be possible to do so, for example in very complex cases or in cases where insufficient detail has been provided prior to the first case management conference. In such situations, the procedural timetable would lay out the procedure as far as can be done (e.g. through a first round of briefs) and a second case management conference would be held promptly to determine the remainder of the procedure for the arbitration.

30 Client attendance

Article 24(4) of the Rules expressly allows the arbitral tribunal to request the attendance at the case management conference of the parties in person or through an internal representative. The tribunal should consider requiring such attendance. When clients are present at the case management conference, they can play an active role in the decision-making process. They should be empowered to make case management decisions. Such decisions call for a cost-benefit analysis. For example, is an additional round of briefs worth the time and expense? Is a degree of discovery-style document production likely to produce benefits justifying the time and cost?

31 Need for a physical meeting

As with the drawing up of the Terms of Reference (see paragraph 22 above) and as permitted by Article 24(4), consider whether it is appropriate to hold the case management conference by way of telephone, video conference or similar means of communication that do not involve a physical meeting. If the case management conference is to be held at the same time as the Terms of Reference are signed, consider whether that would justify a physical meeting for both purposes.

32 Use of discretion in apportionment of costs

Pursuant to Article 37(5) of the Rules, the extent to which each party has conducted the arbitration in an expeditious and cost-effective manner may be taken into account by the arbitral tribunal in determining who shall bear what portion of the costs of the arbitration.

The arbitral tribunal should consider informing the parties at the case management conference that in exercising its discretion to allocate costs pursuant to the Rules, it will take into consideration any unreasonable failure to comply with procedures agreed upon or ordered in the arbitration or any other unreasonable conduct (see paragraph 82 below).

33 Further case management conferences

Consider holding further case management conferences during the course of the arbitration, as appropriate. Such conferences may be held prior to significant phases in the procedure (e.g. the exchange of witness statements) so as to ensure that the procedure provided for that phase remains appropriate. Short telephone conferences may also be held at regular intervals (e.g. once a month) to enable the arbitral tribunal to check on progress and discuss with the parties any unforeseen procedural issues that have arisen or may shortly arise.

Procedural timetable

34 Compliance with the procedural timetable

Consistent with their obligation under Article 22(1) of the Rules to make every effort to conduct the arbitration in an expeditious and cost-effective manner, the arbitrators and the parties should make all reasonable efforts to comply with the procedural timetable. Extensions and revisions of the timetable should be made only when justified. Any revisions should be promptly communicated to the Court and the parties in accordance with Article 24(2) of the Rules.

35 Need for a hearing

Consider whether or not it is necessary for there to be a hearing in order for the arbitral tribunal to decide the case. If it is possible for the arbitral tribunal to decide the case on documents alone, this will significantly reduce costs and time.

36 Fixing the hearing date

If a hearing is necessary, then early in the proceedings (ideally at the first case management conference) consider fixing the date for this hearing. This will reduce the likelihood that the arbitral proceedings become drawn out and will enable the procedure leading up to the hearing to be adapted to the time available.

37 Pre-hearing conference

Consider organizing a conference with the arbitral tribunal, which may be by telephone, to discuss the arrangements for any hearing. At such a prehearing conference, held a suitable time before the hearing itself, the parties and the arbitral tribunal can discuss matters such as time allocation, use of transcripts, translation issues, order of witnesses and other practical arrangements that will facilitate the smooth conduct of the hearing. The arbitral tribunal may consider using the occasion of the pre-hearing conference to indicate to the parties the issues on which it would like them to focus at the forthcoming hearing.

38 Short and realistic time periods

When deciding upon the length of the final hearing and the amount of time required for all procedural steps leading up to that hearing, choose the shortest times that are realistic. Unrealistically short periods of time are likely to result in longer rather than shorter proceedings, should they need to be rescheduled.

39 Bifurcation and partial awards

The arbitral tribunal should consider, or the parties could agree on, bifurcating the proceedings or rendering a partial award when doing so may genuinely be expected to result in a more efficient resolution of the case.

40 Briefing everyone involved in the case

As soon as the proceedings start, parties should give thought to the input that will be needed for each step in the anticipated timetable. Once the timetable is set, the parties should consider precisely what is required of them to comply with the timetable. It will be useful for all relevant personnel to be briefed accordingly (e.g. management within the client organization, witnesses, internal and external lawyers, experts). This will greatly assist in enabling everyone to reserve the time needed to provide input at the relevant point in the procedure and will assist in enabling each party to adhere to deadlines set in the timetable.

Settlement

41 Arbitral tribunal's role in promoting settlement

The arbitral tribunal should consider informing the parties that they are free to settle all or part of the dispute at any time during the ongoing arbitration, either through direct negotiations or through any form of ADR proceedings. For example, ADR proceedings can be conducted under the ICC ADR Rules, further information on which can be found in the article of Peter Wolrich entitled "ICC ADR Rules: The Latest Addition to ICC's Dispute Resolution Services" in *ADR—International Applications*, 2001 Special Supplement of the ICC International Court of Arbitration Bulletin.

42 Settlement initiatives taken with the parties' agreement

The parties may request the arbitral tribunal to suspend the arbitration proceedings for a specific period of time while settlement discussions take place. The parties may also agree that the arbitral tribunal should take other steps to facilitate settlement of their dispute, provided that such steps are not inconsistent with the tribunal's duty under Article 41 of the Rules to make every effort to make sure that its award is enforceable at law.

SUBSEQUENT PROCEDURE FOR THE ARBITRATION

The paragraphs that follow give guidance on the points to be discussed by the parties and the arbitral tribunal at the case management conference. They provide suggestions that may assist in reducing the cost and duration of the proceedings.

Written submissions

Written submissions come in different forms and are given different names. They include the Request for Arbitration and the Answer, statements of case and defence, memorials and other written arguments, and opening and closing written submissions. These comments apply to written submissions generally.

43 Setting out the case in full early in the proceedings

If the parties set out their cases in full early in the proceedings, the parties and the arbitral tribunal will be better able to understand the key issues at an early stage. Doing so will help ensure that the procedure defined at the case management conference is efficient and that time and money are not wasted on matters that turn out to be of no direct relevance to the issues to be determined.

44 Avoiding repetition

Avoid unnecessary repetition of arguments. Once a party has set out its position in full, it should not be necessary to repeat the arguments at later stages (e.g. in pre-hearing memorials, oral submissions or post-hearing memorials), and the arbitral tribunal may direct that there be no such repetition.

45 Sequential or simultaneous delivery

Consider whether it is more effective for written submissions to be sequential or simultaneous. Whilst simultaneous submissions enable both parties to inform each other of their cases at the same time (and this may make things quicker), it can also result in inefficiency if the parties raise different issues in their submissions and extensive submissions are required in response.

46 Specifying form and content

Consider specifying the form and content of written submissions. For example, clarify whether the first round of written submissions should or should not be accompanied by witness statements and/or expert reports.

47 Limiting the length of submissions

Consider agreeing on limiting the length of specific submissions. This can help focus attention on the key issues to be addressed and is likely to save time and cost.

48 Limiting the number of submissions

Consider limiting the number of rounds of submissions. This may help to avoid repetition and encourage the parties to present all key issues in their first submissions.

Documentary evidence

49 Organization of documents

From the outset of the case the parties should consider using a coherent system for numbering or otherwise identifying documents produced in the case. This process can start with the Request for Arbitration and the Answer, and a system for the remainder of the arbitration can be established with the arbitral tribunal at the time of the first case management conference.

50 Producing documents on which the parties rely

The parties will normally each produce the documents upon which they intend to rely. Each party should consider avoiding requests for production of documents from another party unless such production is relevant and material to the outcome of the case. When the parties have agreed upon non-controversial facts, no documentary evidence should be needed to prove those facts.

51 Establishing procedure for requests for production

Consider whether requests for production of documents are genuinely necessary. If they are, the parties and the arbitral tribunal should consider establishing a clear and efficient procedure for the submission and exchange of documents. In that regard, they could consider referring to Article 3 of the IBA Rules on the Taking of Evidence in International Arbitration for guidance. In addition, the parties and the arbitral tribunal should consider establishing an appropriate time frame for the production of documents. In most situations, this is likely to be after the parties have set out their cases in full for the first time. If issues concerning the production of electronic documents arise, consider referring to the ICC Commission Report *Managing E-Document Production*[2] for information and guidance on how to manage such production in an efficient and cost-effective manner.

52 Managing requests for production efficiently

Time and costs associated with requests for production of documents, if any, can further be reduced by agreeing upon one or more of the following:

- Limiting the number of requests;
- Limiting requests to the production of documents (whether in paper or electronic form) that are relevant and material to the outcome of the case;
- Establishing reasonable time limits for the production of documents;
- Using the Schedule of Document Production devised by Alan Redfern (often referred to as the Redfern Schedule) in the form of a chart containing the following four columns:
    - First Column: identification of the document(s) or categories of documents that have been requested;
    - Second Column: short description of the reasons for each request;
    - Third Column: summary of the objections by the other party to the production of the document(s) or categories of documents requested; and
    - Fourth Column: left blank for the decision of the arbitral tribunal on each request.

53 Avoiding duplication

It is common for each of the parties to produce copies of the same documents, appended to their statements of case, witness statements or other written submissions. Avoiding duplication where possible will reduce costs.

[2] Available in print as ICC Publication 860 and online at www.iccdrl.com.

54 Selection of documents to be provided to the arbitral tribunal

It is wasteful to provide the arbitrators with documents that are not material to their determination of the case. In particular, it will usually not be appropriate to send to the arbitral tribunal all documents produced pursuant to production requests. This not only generates unnecessary costs, but also makes it harder for the arbitral tribunal to prepare efficiently.

55 Keeping hard copies to a minimum

Consider minimizing the volume of paper documents that need to be produced. Exchanging documents in electronic form can reduce costs (see the ICC Commission Report *Managing E-Document Production* and the 2004 Special Supplement of the ICC International Court of Arbitration Bulletin, *Using Technology to Resolve Business Disputes*).

56 Translations

Try to agree how translations of any documents are to be dealt with. Reducing the need for certified translations will help to lower costs. Certified translations may be required only where translation issues emerge from unofficial translations.

57 Authenticity of documents

Consider providing that documents produced by the parties are deemed to be authentic unless and until such authenticity is challenged by another party.

Correspondence

58 Correspondence between counsel

Avoid unnecessary correspondence between counsel. The arbitral tribunal may consider informing the parties that the persistent use of such correspondence may be viewed as unreasonable conduct and be taken into consideration by the arbitral tribunal when exercising its discretion in allocating costs pursuant to the Rules (see paragraph 82 below).

59 Sending correspondence to the arbitral tribunal

Avoid sending correspondence between counsel to the arbitral tribunal unless a decision of the arbitral tribunal is required. Any such correspondence that is addressed to the arbitral tribunal should be copied to the Secretariat in accordance with Article 3(1) of the Rules.

Witness statements

60 Limiting the number of witnesses

Every witness adds to the costs, both when a witness statement is prepared and considered and when the witness attends to give oral evidence. Costs can be saved by limiting the number of witnesses to those whose evidence is required on key issues. The arbitral tribunal may assist in identifying those issues on which witness evidence is required and focusing the evidence from witnesses on those issues. This whole process will be facilitated if the parties can reach agreement on non-controversial facts that do not need to be addressed by witness evidence.

61 Minimizing the number of rounds of witness statements

If there are to be witness statements, consider the timing for the exchange of such statements so as to minimize the number of rounds of statements that are required. For example, consider whether it is preferable for witness statements to be exchanged after all documents on which the parties wish to rely have been produced, so that the witnesses can comment on those documents in a single statement.

Expert evidence

62 Presumption that expert evidence not required

It is helpful to start with a presumption that expert evidence will not be required. Depart from this presumption only if expert evidence is needed in order to inform the arbitral tribunal on key issues in dispute.

63 ICC International Centre for Expertise

If either the parties or the arbitral tribunal require assistance in identifying an expert witness, recourse can be had to the ICC International Centre for Expertise pursuant to the ICC Rules for Expertise. Where an ICC arbitral tribunal seeks a proposal from the Centre for a tribunal-appointed expert, the services of the Centre are available at no cost. Further information regarding the operation of the ICC Rules for Expertise and the services of the Centre can be found in Jason Fry, Simon Greenberg, Francesca Mazza, *The Secretariat's Guide to ICC Arbitration* (ICC Publication 729).[3]

64 Clarity regarding the subject matter and scope of reports

It is essential for there to be clarity at an early stage (by agreement, if possible) over the subject matter and scope of any expert evidence to be produced. This will help to ensure that the experts appointed by the parties have similar expertise and address the same issues.

65 Number of experts

Other than in exceptional circumstances, it should not be necessary for there to be more than one expert per party for any particular area of expertise.

66 Number of reports

Consider agreeing on a limit to the number of rounds of expert reports and consider whether simultaneous or sequential exchange will be more efficient.

[3] Available from www.iccbooks.com and online at www.iccdrl.com.

67 Meetings of experts

Experts will often be able to narrow the issues in dispute if they can meet and discuss their views after they have exchanged reports. Consideration should therefore be given to providing that experts shall take steps to agree on issues in advance of any hearing at which their evidence is to be presented. Time and cost can be saved if the experts draw up a list recording the issues on which they have agreed and those on which they disagree.

68 Use of single expert

Consider whether a single expert appointed either by the arbitral tribunal or jointly by the parties might be more efficient than experts appointed by each party. A single, tribunal-appointed expert may be more efficient in some circumstances. An expert appointed by the arbitral tribunal or jointly by the parties should be given a clear brief and the expert's report should be required by a specified date consistent with the timetable for the arbitration.

Hearings

69 Minimizing the length and number of hearings

Hearings are expensive and time-consuming. If the length and number of hearings requiring the physical attendance of the arbitral tribunal and the parties are minimized, this will significantly reduce the time and cost of the proceedings.

70 Choosing the best location for hearings

Pursuant to Article 18(2) of the Rules, hearings do not need to be held at the place of the arbitration. The arbitral tribunal and the parties can select the most efficient place to hold hearings. In some cases, it may be more cost-effective to hold hearings at a location that, for example, is convenient to the majority of the witnesses due to give evidence at that hearing.

71 Telephone and video conferencing

For procedural hearings in particular, consider the use of telephone and video conferencing, where appropriate. Also, consider whether certain witnesses can give evidence by video link, so as to avoid the need to travel to an evidentiary hearing.

72 Providing submissions in good time

The arbitral tribunal should be provided with all necessary submissions (e.g. pre-hearing briefs, if any) sufficiently in advance of any hearing to be able to read them, prepare and become fully informed of the issues to be addressed.

73 Cut-off date for evidence

In advance of any evidentiary hearing, consider setting a cut-off date after which no new documentary evidence will be admitted unless a compelling reason is shown.

74 Identifying core documents

Consider providing the arbitral tribunal, in advance of any hearing, with a list of the documents it needs to read in preparation for the hearing. Where appropriate, this can be done by preparing and delivering to the arbitral tribunal a bundle of core documents on which the parties rely.

75 Agenda and timetable

Consider agreeing on an agenda and timetable for all hearings, with an equitable division of time between each of the parties. Consider the use of a chess clock to monitor the fair allocation of time.

76 Avoiding repetition

Consideration should be given to whether it is necessary to repeat pre-hearing written submissions in opening oral statements. This is sometimes done because of concern that the arbitral tribunal will not have read or digested the written submissions. If the arbitral tribunal has been provided with the documents it needs to read in advance of the hearing and has prepared properly, no such repetition will be necessary.

77 Need for witnesses to appear

Prior to any hearing, consider whether all witnesses need to give oral evidence. This is a matter on which the parties' counsel can confer and seek to reach agreement.

78 Use of written statements as direct evidence

Cost and time can be saved by limiting or avoiding direct examination of witnesses. When appropriate, witness statements can substitute for direct examination at a hearing.

79 Witness conferencing

Witness conferencing is a technique in which two or more fact or expert witnesses presented by one or more of the parties are questioned together on particular topics by the arbitral tribunal and possibly by counsel. Consider whether this technique is appropriate for the arbitration at hand.

80 Limiting cross-examination

If there is to be cross-examination of witnesses, the arbitral tribunal, after hearing the parties, should consider limiting the time available to each party for such cross-examination.

81 Closing submissions

Consider whether post-hearing submissions can be avoided in order to save time and cost. However, if post-hearing submissions are required, consider providing for either oral or written closing submissions. The use of both will result in additional time and cost. In order to give focus, the arbitral tribunal should consider providing counsel with a list of questions or issues to be addressed by the parties in the closing submissions. Any written closing submissions should be provided by an agreed date as soon as reasonable following the hearing.

Costs

82 Using allocation of costs to encourage efficient conduct of the proceedings

The allocation of costs can be a useful tool to encourage efficient behaviour and discourage unreasonable behaviour. Pursuant to Article 37(5) of the Rules, the arbitral tribunal has discretion to award costs in such a manner as it considers appropriate. It is expressly stated that, in making its decisions on costs, the tribunal may take into consideration the extent to which each party has conducted the arbitration in an expeditious and cost-effective manner. The tribunal should consider informing the parties at the outset of the arbitration (e.g. at the case management conference) that it intends to take into account the manner in which each party has conducted the proceedings and to sanction any unreasonable behaviour by a party when deciding on costs. Unreasonable behaviour could include: excessive document requests, excessive legal argument, excessive cross-examination, dilatory tactics, exaggerated claims, failure to comply with procedural orders, unjustified applications for interim relief, and unjustified failure to comply with the procedural timetable.

Deliberations and awards

83 Anticipating the time required

Before closing the proceedings, the arbitral tribunal should ensure that time has been reserved in each of the arbitrators' diaries for deliberation promptly thereafter. The arbitral tribunal should promptly comply with Article 27 of the Rules and indicate to the Secretariat and the parties the date by which it expects to submit its draft award to the Court.

84 Prompt completion of the award

The arbitral tribunal must use its best efforts to submit the draft award as quickly as possible and should follow the guidance on drafting awards in the ICC Award Checklist sent to all arbitrators when the case file is transmitted to them. Further guidance can be found in the article "Drafting Awards in ICC Arbitrations" by Humphrey LLoyd, Marco Darmon, Jean-Pierre Ancel, Lord Dervaird, Christoph Liebscher and Herman Verbist, published in the ICC International Court of Arbitration Bulletin, Vol. 16/No. 2 (2005).

SPECIAL CONSIDERATIONS

Multiparty and multicontract arbitrations

85 Conditions imposed by Articles 7–9 of the Rules

Subject to certain conditions set forth in the Rules, Article 7 expressly permits the joinder of additional parties; Article 8 expressly permits claims between multiple parties; and Article 9 expressly permits claims arising out of more than one contract to be brought in a single arbitration, even if the claims are made under more than one arbitration agreement. Clearly, time and cost will be wasted if a party seeks to apply those provisions when the conditions set forth in the Rules are not met. For example, a Request for Joinder pursuant to Article 7 will be successful only if the joined party is bound by the arbitration agreement under which the claims in the arbitration are made; in addition, no additional party may be joined after the confirmation or appointment of any arbitrator, unless otherwise agreed. While Article 9 allows claims to be made in a single arbitration under more than one arbitration agreement, those claims will be sustained only if the different arbitration agreements are compatible. The conditions imposed by Articles 7, 8 and 9 should be carefully studied so as to avoid wasting time and money by making claims that will be rejected or by claiming against parties over whom the tribunal will have no jurisdiction.

86 Adapting procedures to multiparty and multicontract cases

The presence of one or more additional parties, the existence of one or more claims between claimants or between respondents, and the existence of claims under more than one contract are likely to complicate the proceedings. Care should be taken at the case management conference to devise tailor-made procedures, appropriate to the specifics of the case at hand, for dealing with the presence of additional parties, cross-claims and multicontract claims.

Consolidation

87 Consider consolidating related cases

Article 10 of the Rules provides for the consolidation of two or more separate arbitrations brought under the Rules when all of the parties to those arbitrations consent to the consolidation. Consider whether giving such consent would result in a more efficient resolution of the disputes.

Emergency arbitrator proceedings

88 Issues to consider before initiating emergency arbitrator proceedings

Subject to the conditions set forth in the Rules, the Emergency Arbitrator Provisions allow a party to seek urgent interim or conservatory measures from an emergency arbitrator acting under the Rules. The emergency arbitrator offers an alternative forum to state courts for seeking such relief. In deciding whether to file an Application for Emergency Measures, a party should consider a number of issues: first, whether it is genuinely useful and necessary to spend time and money on seeking to obtain interim or conservatory measures; second, whether an application for Emergency Measures under the Rules is preferable to seeking interim measures in a state court. Furthermore, the party should make sure that the conditions for bringing emergency arbitrator proceedings under the Rules are met. For example, the party making the application must be able to demonstrate that it needs urgent interim or conservatory measures that cannot await the constitution of the arbitral tribunal. Also, emergency arbitrator proceedings may only be brought against a signatory of the arbitration agreement or the signatory's successor. An attempt to bring emergency arbitrator proceedings that do not meet all of the conditions will result in needless expenditure and loss of time.

APPENDIX 3

LIST OF OTHER ICC DISPUTE RESOLUTION SERVICES

Note: The text of the other Rules of the ICC's Dispute Resolution Services and corresponding model clauses recommended by the ICC are available on the ICC websites cited below.

ADR Rules and Guide to ICC ADR (as from 1 July 2001)	*http://www.iccwbo.org/court*
Dispute Board Rules (as from 1 September 2004)	*http://www.iccwbo.org/court/dispute_boards*
DOCDEX Rules (as from 15 March 2002)	*http://www.iccwbo.org/court/docdex*
Pre-arbitral Referee Procedure (as from 1 January 2003)	*http://www.iccwbo.org/court/arbitration*
Rules for Expertise (as from 1 January 2003)	*http://www.iccwbo.org/court/expertise*
Rules of ICC as Appointing Authority in UNCITRAL or Other Ad Hoc Arbitration Proceedings (as from 1 January 2004)	*http://www.iccwbo.org/court/arbitration*
Mediation Rules (as from 1 January 2014)	*http://www.iccwbo.org/products-and-services/arbitration-and-adr/mediation/rules*

APPENDIX 4

NEW YORK CONVENTION

United Nations Conference on International Commercial Arbitration
Convention On The Recognition and Enforcement of Foreign Arbitral Awards

Article I

1. This Convention shall apply to the recognition and enforcement of arbitral awards made in the territory of a State other than the State where the recognition and enforcement of such awards are sought, and arising out of differences between persons, whether physical or legal. It shall also apply to arbitral awards not considered as domestic awards in the State where their recognition and enforcement are sought.

2. The term "arbitral awards" shall include not only awards made by arbitrators appointed for each case but also those made by permanent arbitral bodies to which the parties have submitted.

3. When signing, ratifying or acceding to this Convention, or notifying extension under article X hereof, any State may on the basis of reciprocity declare that it will apply the Convention to the recognition and enforcement of awards made only in the territory of another Contracting State. It may also declare that it will apply the Convention only to differences arising out of legal relationships, whether contractual or not, which are considered as commercial under the national law of the State making such declaration.

Article II

1. Each Contracting State shall recognize an agreement in writing under which the parties undertake to submit to arbitration all or any differences which have arisen or which may arise between them in respect of a defined legal relationship, whether contractual or not, concerning a subject matter capable of settlement by arbitration.

2. The term "agreement in writing" shall include an arbitral clause in a contract or an arbitration agreement, signed by the parties or contained in an exchange of letters or telegrams.

3. The court of a Contracting State, when seized of an action in a matter in respect of which the parties have made an agreement within the meaning of this article, shall, at the request of one of the parties, refer the parties to arbitration, unless it finds that the said agreement is null and void, inoperative or incapable of being performed.

Article III

Each Contracting State shall recognize arbitral awards as binding and, enforce them in accordance with the rules of procedure of the territory where the award is relied upon, under the conditions laid down in the following articles. There shall not be imposed

NOTE:
FOR AN UPDATED LIST OF THE SIGNATORIES SEE: *http://www.uncitral.org/uncitral/en/uncitral-texts/arbitration/NYConvention-status.html*

substantially more onerous conditions or higher fees or charges on the recognition or enforcement of arbitral awards to which this Convention applies than are imposed on the recognition or enforcement of domestic arbitral awards.

Article IV

1. To obtain the recognition and enforcement mentioned in the preceding article, the party applying for recognition and enforcement shall, at the time of the application, supply:

(a) The duly authenticated original award or a duly certified copy thereof;

(b) The original agreement referred to in article II or a duly certified copy thereof.

2. If the said award or agreement is not made in an official language of the country in which the award is relied upon, the party applying for recognition and enforcement of the award shall produce a translation of these documents into such language. The translation shall be certified by an official or sworn translator or by a diplomatic or consular agent.

Article V

1. Recognition and enforcement of the award may be refused, at the request of the party against whom it is invoked, only if that party furnishes to the competent authority where the recognition and enforcement is sought, proof that:

(a) The parties to the agreement referred to in article II were, under the law applicable to them, under some incapacity, or the said agreement is not valid under the law to which the parties have subjected it or, failing any indication thereon, under the law of the country where the award was made; or

(b) The party against whom the award is invoked was not given proper notice of the appointment of the arbitrator or of the arbitration proceedings or was otherwise unable to present his case; or

(c) The award deals with a difference not contemplated by or not falling within the terms of the submission to arbitration, or it contains decisions on matters beyond the scope of the submission to arbitration, provided that, if the decisions on matters submitted to arbitration can be separated from those not so submitted, that part of the award which contains decisions on matters submitted to arbitration may be recognized and enforced; or

(d) The composition of the arbitral authority or the arbitral procedure was not in accordance with the agreement of the parties, or, failing such agreement, was not in accordance with the law of the country where the arbitration took place; or

(e) The award has not yet become binding on the parties, or has been set aside or suspended by a competent authority of the country in which, or under the law of which, that award was made.

2. Recognition and enforcement of an arbitral award may also be refused if the competent authority in the country where recognition and enforcement is sought finds that:

(a) The subject matter of the difference is not capable of settlement by arbitration under the law of that country; or

(b) The recognition or enforcement of the award would he contrary to the public policy of that country.

Article VI

If an application for the setting aside or suspension of the award has been made to a competent authority referred to in article V(1)(e), the authority before which the award is sought to be relied upon may, if it considers it proper, adjourn the decision on the enforcement of the award and may also, on the application of the party claiming enforcement of the award, order the other party to give suitable security.

Article VII

1. The provisions of the present Convention shall not affect the validity of multilateral or bilateral agreements concerning the recognition and enforcement of arbitral awards entered into by the Contracting States nor deprive any interested party of any right he may have to avail himself of an arbitral award in the manner and to the extent allowed by the law or the treaties of the country where such award is sought to be relied upon.

2. The Geneva Protocol on Arbitration Clauses of 1923 and the Geneva Convention on the Execution of Foreign Arbitral Awards of 1927 shall cease to have effect between Contracting States on their becoming bound and to the extent that they become bound, by this Convention.

Article VIII

1. This Convention shall be open until 31 December 1958 for signature on behalf of any Member of the United Nations and also on behalf of any other State which is or hereafter becomes a member of any specialized agency of the United Nations, or which is or hereafter becomes a party to the Statute of the International Court of Justice, or any other State to which an invitation has been addressed by the General Assembly of the United Nations.

2. This Convention shall be ratified and the instrument of ratification shall be deposited with the Secretary-General of the United Nations.

Article IX

1. This Convention shall be open for accession to all States referred to in article VIII.

2. Accession shall be effected by the deposit of an instrument of accession with the Secretary-General of the United Nations.

Article X

1. Any State may, at the time of signature, ratification or accession, declare that this Convention shall extend to all or any of the territories for the international relations of which it is responsible. Such a declaration shall take effect when the Convention enters into force for the State concerned.

2. At any time thereafter any such extension shall be made by notification addressed to the Secretary-General of the United Nations and shall take effect as from the ninetieth day after the day of receipt by the Secretary-General of the United Nations of this notification, or as from the date of entry into force of the Convention for the State concerned, whichever is the later.

3. With respect to those territories to which this Convention is not extended at the time of signature, ratification or accession, each State concerned shall consider the possibility of

taking the necessary steps in order to extend the application of this Convention to such territories, subject, where necessary for constitutional reasons, to the consent of the Governments of such territories.

Article XI

In the case of a federal or non-unitary State, the following provisions shall apply:

(a) With respect to those articles of this Convention that come within the legislative jurisdiction of the federal authority, the obligations of the federal Government shall to this extent be the same as those of Contracting States which are not federal States;

(b) With respect to those articles of this Convention that come within the legislative jurisdiction of constituent states or provinces which are not, under the constitutional system of the federation, bound to take legislative action, the federal Government shall bring such articles with a favourable recommendation to the notice of the appropriate authorities of constituent states or provinces at the earliest possible moment;

(c) A federal State Party to this Convention shall, at the request of any other Contracting State transmitted through the Secretary-General of the United Nations, supply a statement of the law and practice of the federation and its constituent units in regard to any particular provision of this Convention, showing the extent to which effect has been given to that provision by legislative or other action.

Article XII

1. This Convention shall come into force on the ninetieth day following the date of deposit of the third instrument of ratification or accession.

2. For each State ratifying or acceding to this Convention after the deposit of the third instrument of ratification or accession, this Convention shall enter into force on the ninetieth day after deposit by such State of its instrument of ratification or accession.

Article XIII

1. Any Contracting State may denounce this Convention by a written notification to the Secretary-General of the United Nations. Denunciation shall take effect one year after the date of receipt of the notification by the Secretary-General.

2. Any State which has made a declaration or notification under article X may, at any time thereafter, by notification to the Secretary-General of the United Nations, declare that this Convention shall cease to extend to the territory concerned one year after the date of the receipt of the notification by the Secretary General.

3. This Convention shall continue to be applicable to arbitral awards in respect of which recognition or enforcement proceedings have been instituted before the denunciation takes effect.

Article XIV

A Contracting State shall not be entitled to avail itself of the present Convention against other Contracting States except to the extent that it is itself bound to apply the Convention.

Article XV

The Secretary-General of the United Nations shall notify the States contemplated in article VIII of the following:

(a) Signatures and ratifications in accordance with article VIII;

(b) Accessions in accordance with article IX;

(c) Declarations and notifications under articles I, X and XI;

(d) The date upon which this Convention enters into force in accordance with article XII;

(e) Denunciations and notifications in accordance with article XIII.

Article XVI

1. This Convention, of which the Chinese, English, French, Russian and Spanish texts shall be equally authentic, shall be deposited in the archives of the United Nations.

2. The Secretary-General of the United Nations shall transmit a certified copy of this Convention to the States contemplated in article VIII.

Appendix 5

UNCITRAL MODEL LAW ON INTERNATIONAL COMMERCIAL ARBITRATION AS AMENDED IN 2006 WITH COMMENTARY AND RECOMMENDATION REGARDING THE NEW YORK CONVENTION.

The UNCITRAL Model Law was amended in 2006 to add Article 2A and Articles 17A-C. Most countries that have adopted the Uncitral Model Law adopted the original version of the law. In December 2013, UNCITRAL stated on its website that:

> "Legislation based on the UNCITRAL Model Law on International Commercial Arbitration as adopted in 1985 has been enacted in:
>
> **Armenia, Australia, Austria, Azerbaijan, Bahrain, Bangladesh, Belarus, Belgium, Brunei Darussalam, Bulgaria, Cambodia, Canada, Chile, China (Hong Kong, Macau), Costa Rica, Croatia, Cyprus, Denmark, Dominican Republic, Egypt, Estonia, Georgia, Germany, Greece, Guatemala, Honduras, Hungary, India, Iran (Islamic Republic of), Ireland, Japan, Jordan, Kenya, Lithuania, Madagascar, Malaysia, Malta, Mauritius, Mexico, New Zealand, Nicaragua, Nigeria, Norway, Oman, Paraguay, Peru, Philippines, Poland, Republic of Korea, Russian Federation, Rwanda, Serbia, Singapore, Slovenia, Spain, Sri Lanka, Thailand, the former Yugoslav Republic of Macedonia, Tunisia, Turkey, Uganda, Ukraine, within the United Kingdom of Great Britain and Northern Ireland: (Scotland, Bermuda), the United States of America (California, Connecticut, Florida, Georgia, Illinois, Louisiana, Oregon and Texas), Venezuela (Bolivarian Republic of), Zambia, Zimbabwe."**

Part One

UNCITRAL Model LAW ON INTERNATIONAL COMMERCIAL ARBITRATION
(United Nations documents A/40/17, annex I and A/61/17, annex I)

(As adopted by the United Nations Commission on International Trade Law on 21 June 1985, and as amended by the United Nations Commission on International Trade Law on 7 July 2006)

Chapter I. General Provisions

Article 1. Scope of application[1]

(1) This Law applies to international commercial[2] arbitration, subject to any agreement in force between this State and any other State or States.

[1] Article headings are for reference purposes only and are not to be used for purposes of interpretation.

[2] The term "commercial" should be given a wide interpretation so as to cover matters arising from all relationships of a commercial nature, whether contractual or not. Relationships of a commercial nature include, but are not limited to, the following transactions: any trade transaction for the supply

(2) The provisions of this Law, except articles 8, 9, 17 H, 17 I, 17 J, 35 and 36, apply only if the place of arbitration is in the territory of this State.

(Article 1(2) has been amended by the Commission at its thirty-ninth session, in 2006)

(3) An arbitration is international if:

(a) the parties to an arbitration agreement have, at the time of the conclusion of that agreement, their places of business in different States; or

(b) one of the following places is situated outside the State in which the parties have their places of business:

(i) the place of arbitration if determined in, or pursuant to, the arbitration agreement;

(ii) any place where a substantial part of the obligations of the commercial relationship is to be performed or the place with which the subject-matter of the dispute is most closely connected; or

(c) the parties have expressly agreed that the subject matter of the arbitration agreement relates to more than one country.

(4) For the purposes of paragraph (3) of this article:

(a) if a party has more than one place of business, the place of business is that which has the closest relationship to the arbitration agreement;

(b) if a party does not have a place of business, reference is to be made to his habitual residence.

(5) This Law shall not affect any other law of this State by virtue of which certain disputes may not be submitted to arbitration or may be submitted to arbitration only according to provisions other than those of this Law.

Article 2. Definitions and rules of interpretation

For the purposes of this Law:

(a) "arbitration" means any arbitration whether or not administered by a permanent arbitral institution;

(b) "arbitral tribunal" means a sole arbitrator or a panel of arbitrators;

(c) "court" means a body or organ of the judicial system of a State;

(d) where a provision of this Law, except article 28, leaves the parties free to determine a certain issue, such freedom includes the right of the parties to authorize a third party, including an institution, to make that determination;

or exchange of goods or services; distribution agreement; commercial representation or agency; factoring; leasing; construction of works; consulting; engineering; licensing; investment; financing; banking; insurance; exploitation agreement or concession; joint venture and other forms of industrial or business cooperation; carriage of goods or passengers by air, sea, rail or road.

(e) where a provision of this Law refers to the fact that the parties have agreed or that they may agree or in any other way refers to an agreement of the parties, such agreement includes any arbitration rules referred to in that agreement;

(f) where a provision of this Law, other than in articles 25*(a)* and 32(2) *(a)*, refers to a claim, it also applies to a counter-claim, and where it refers to a defence, it also applies to a defence to such counter-claim.

Article 2 A. International origin and general principles
(As adopted by the Commission at its thirty-ninth session, in 2006)

(1) In the interpretation of this Law, regard is to be had to its international origin and to the need to promote uniformity in its application and the observance of good faith.

(2) Questions concerning matters governed by this Law which are not expressly settled in it are to be settled in conformity with the general principles on which this Law is based.

Article 3. Receipt of written communications

(1) Unless otherwise agreed by the parties:

(a) any written communication is deemed to have been received if it is delivered to the addressee personally or if it is delivered at his place of business, habitual residence or mailing address; if none of these can be found after making a reasonable inquiry, a written communication is deemed to have been received if it is sent to the addressee's last-known place of business, habitual residence or mailing address by registered letter or any other means which provides a record of the attempt to deliver it;

(b) the communication is deemed to have been received on the day it is so delivered.

(2) The provisions of this article do not apply to communications in court proceedings.

Article 4. Waiver of right to object

A party who knows that any provision of this Law from which the parties may derogate or any requirement under the arbitration agreement has not been complied with and yet proceeds with the arbitration without stating his objection to such non-compliance without undue delay or, if a time-limit is provided therefor, within such period of time, shall be deemed to have waived his right to object.

Article 5. Extent of court intervention

In matters governed by this Law, no court shall intervene except where so provided in this Law.

Article 6. Court or other authority for certain functions of arbitration assistance and supervision

The functions referred to in articles 11(3), 11(4), 13(3), 14, 16(3) and 34(2) shall be performed by . . . [Each State enacting this model law specifies the court, courts or, where referred to therein, other authority competent to perform these functions.]

Chapter II. Arbitration Agreement

Option I

Article 7. Definition and form of arbitration agreement (As adopted by the Commission at its thirty-ninth session, in 2006)

(1) "Arbitration agreement" is an agreement by the parties to submit to arbitration all or certain disputes which have arisen or which may arise between them in respect of a defined legal relationship, whether contractual or not. An arbitration agreement may be in the form of an arbitration clause in a contract or in the form of a separate agreement.

(2) The arbitration agreement shall be in writing.

(3) An arbitration agreement is in writing if its content is recorded in any form, whether or not the arbitration agreement or contract has been concluded orally, by conduct, or by other means.

(4) The requirement that an arbitration agreement be in writing is met by an electronic communication if the information contained therein is accessible so as to be useable for subsequent reference; "electronic communication" means any communication that the parties make by means of data messages; "data message" means information generated, sent, received or stored by electronic, magnetic, optical or similar means, including, but not limited to, electronic data interchange (EDI), electronic mail, telegram, telex or telecopy.

(5) Furthermore, an arbitration agreement is in writing if it is contained in an exchange of statements of claim and defence in which the existence of an agreement is alleged by one party and not denied by the other.

(6) The reference in a contract to any document containing an arbitration clause constitutes an arbitration agreement in writing, provided that the reference is such as to make that clause part of the contract.

Option II

Article 7. Definition of arbitration agreement (As adopted by the Commission at its thirty-ninth session, in 2006)

"Arbitration agreement" is an agreement by the parties to submit to arbitration all or certain disputes which have arisen or which may arise between them in respect of a defined legal relationship, whether contractual or not.

Article 8. Arbitration agreement and substantive claim before court

(1) A court before which an action is brought in a matter which is the subject of an arbitration agreement shall, if a party so requests not later than when submitting his first statement on the substance of the dispute, refer the parties to arbitration unless it finds that the agreement is null and void, inoperative or incapable of being performed.

(2) Where an action referred to in paragraph (1) of this article has been brought, arbitral proceedings may nevertheless be commenced or continued, and an award may be made, while the issue is pending before the court.

Article 9. Arbitration agreement and interim measures by court

It is not incompatible with an arbitration agreement for a party to request, before or during arbitral proceedings, from a court an interim measure of protection and for a court to grant such measure.

CHAPTER III. COMPOSITION OF ARBITRAL TRIBUNAL

Article 10. Number of arbitrators

(1) The parties are free to determine the number of arbitrators.

(2) Failing such determination, the number of arbitrators shall be three.

Article 11. Appointment of arbitrators

(1) No person shall be precluded by reason of his nationality from acting as an arbitrator, unless otherwise agreed by the parties.

(2) The parties are free to agree on a procedure of appointing the arbitrator or arbitrators, subject to the provisions of paragraphs (4) and (5) of this article.

(3) Failing such agreement,

(a) in an arbitration with three arbitrators, each party shall appoint one arbitrator, and the two arbitrators thus appointed shall appoint the third arbitrator; if a party fails to appoint the arbitrator within thirty days of receipt of a request to do so from the other party, or if the two arbitrators fail to agree on the third arbitrator within thirty days of their appointment, the appointment shall be made, upon request of a party, by the court or other authority specified in article 6;

(b) in an arbitration with a sole arbitrator, if the parties are unable to agree on the arbitrator, he shall be appointed, upon request of a party, by the court or other authority specified in article 6.

(4) Where, under an appointment procedure agreed upon by the parties,

(a) a party fails to act as required under such procedure, or

(b) the parties, or two arbitrators, are unable to reach an agreement expected of them under such procedure, or

(c) a third party, including an institution, fails to perform any function entrusted to it under such procedure,

any party may request the court or other authority specified in article 6 to take the necessary measure, unless the agreement on the appointment procedure provides other means for securing the appointment.

(5) A decision on a matter entrusted by paragraph (3) or (4) of this article to the court or other authority specified in article 6 shall be subject to no appeal. The court or other authority, in appointing an arbitrator, shall have due regard to any qualifications required of the arbitrator by the agreement of the parties and to such considerations as are likely to secure the appointment of an independent and impartial arbitrator and, in the case of a sole or third arbitrator, shall take into account as well the advisability of appointing an arbitrator of a nationality other than those of the parties.

Article 12. Grounds for challenge

(1) When a person is approached in connection with his possible appointment as an arbitrator, he shall disclose any circumstances likely to give rise to justifiable doubts as to his impartiality or independence. An arbitrator, from the time of his appointment and throughout the arbitral proceedings, shall without delay disclose any such circumstances to the parties unless they have already been informed of them by him.

(2) An arbitrator may be challenged only if circumstances exist that give rise to justifiable doubts as to his impartiality or independence, or if he does not possess qualifications agreed to by the parties. A party may challenge an arbitrator appointed by him, or in whose appointment he has participated, only for reasons of which he becomes aware after the appointment has been made.

Article 13. Challenge procedure

(1) The parties are free to agree on a procedure for challenging an arbitrator, subject to the provisions of paragraph (3) of this article.

(2) Failing such agreement, a party who intends to challenge an arbitrator shall, within fifteen days after becoming aware of the constitution of the arbitral tribunal or after becoming aware of any circumstance referred to in article 12(2), send a written statement of the reasons for the challenge to the arbitral tribunal. Unless the challenged arbitrator withdraws from his office or the other party agrees to the challenge, the arbitral tribunal shall decide on the challenge.

(3) If a challenge under any procedure agreed upon by the parties or under the procedure of paragraph (2) of this article is not successful, the challenging party may request, within thirty days after having received notice of the decision rejecting the challenge, the court or other authority specified in article 6 to decide on the challenge, which decision shall be subject to no appeal; while such a request is pending, the arbitral tribunal, including the challenged arbitrator, may continue the arbitral proceedings and make an award.

Article 14. Failure or impossibility to act

(1) If an arbitrator becomes *de jure* or *de facto* unable to perform his functions or for other reasons fails to act without undue delay, his mandate terminates if he withdraws from his office or if the parties agree on the termination. Otherwise, if a controversy remains concerning any of these grounds, any party may request the court or other authority specified in article 6 to decide on the termination of the mandate, which decision shall be subject to no appeal.

(2) If, under this article or article 13(2), an arbitrator withdraws from his office or a party agrees to the termination of the mandate of an arbitrator, this does not imply acceptance of the validity of any ground referred to in this article or article 12(2).

Article 15. Appointment of substitute arbitrator

Where the mandate of an arbitrator terminates under article 13 or 14 or because of his withdrawal from office for any other reason or because of the revocation of his mandate by agreement of the parties or in any other case of termination of his mandate, a substitute arbitrator shall be appointed according to the rules that were applicable to the appointment of the arbitrator being replaced.

CHAPTER IV. JURISDICTION OF ARBITRAL TRIBUNAL

Article 16. Competence of arbitral tribunal to rule on its jurisdiction

(1) The arbitral tribunal may rule on its own jurisdiction, including any objections with respect to the existence or validity of the arbitration agreement. For that purpose, an arbitration clause which forms part of a contract shall be treated as an agreement independent of the other terms of the contract. A decision by the arbitral tribunal that the contract is null and void shall not entail *ipso jure* the invalidity of the arbitration clause.

(2) A plea that the arbitral tribunal does not have jurisdiction shall be raised not later than the submission of the statement of defence. A party is not precluded from raising such a plea by the fact that he has appointed, or participated in the appointment of, an arbitrator. A plea that the arbitral tribunal is exceeding the scope of its authority shall be raised as soon as the matter alleged to be beyond the scope of its authority is raised during the arbitral proceedings. The arbitral tribunal may, in either case, admit a later plea if it considers the delay justified.

(3) The arbitral tribunal may rule on a plea referred to in paragraph (2) of this article either as a preliminary question or in an award on the merits. If the arbitral tribunal rules as a preliminary question that it has jurisdiction, any party may request, within thirty days after having received notice of that ruling, the court specified in article 6 to decide the matter, which decision shall be subject to no appeal; while such a request is pending, the arbitral tribunal may continue the arbitral proceedings and make an award.

CHAPTER IV A. INTERIM MEASURES AND PRELIMINARY ORDERS

(As adopted by the Commission at its thirty-ninth session, in 2006)

SECTION 1. INTERIM MEASURES

Article 17. Power of arbitral tribunal to order interim measures

(1) Unless otherwise agreed by the parties, the arbitral tribunal may, at the request of a party, grant interim measures.

(2) An interim measure is any temporary measure, whether in the form of an award or in another form, by which, at any time prior to the issuance of the award by which the dispute is finally decided, the arbitral tribunal orders a party to:

(a) Maintain or restore the status quo pending determination of the dispute;

(b) Take action that would prevent, or refrain from taking action that is likely to cause, current or imminent harm or prejudice to the arbitral process itself;

(c) Provide a means of preserving assets out of which a subsequent award may be satisfied; or

(d) Preserve evidence that may be relevant and material to the resolution of the dispute.

Article 17 A. Conditions for granting interim measures

(1) The party requesting an interim measure under article 17(2)*(a)*, *(b)* and *(c)* shall satisfy the arbitral tribunal that:

(a) Harm not adequately reparable by an award of damages is likely to result if the measure is not ordered, and such harm substantially outweighs the harm that is likely to result to the party against whom the measure is directed if the measure is granted; and

(b) There is a reasonable possibility that the requesting party will succeed on the merits of the claim. The determination on this possibility shall not affect the discretion of the arbitral tribunal in making any subsequent determination.

(2) With regard to a request for an interim measure under article 17(2)*(d)*, the requirements in paragraphs (1)*(a)* and *(b)* of this article shall apply only to the extent the arbitral tribunal considers appropriate.

SECTION 2. PRELIMINARY ORDERS

Article 17 B. Applications for preliminary orders and conditions for granting preliminary orders

(1) Unless otherwise agreed by the parties, a party may, without notice to any other party, make a request for an interim measure together with an application for a preliminary order directing a party not to frustrate the purpose of the interim measure requested.

(2) The arbitral tribunal may grant a preliminary order provided it considers that prior disclosure of the request for the interim measure to the party against whom it is directed risks frustrating the purpose of the measure.

(3) The conditions defined under article 17A apply to any preliminary order, provided that the harm to be assessed under article 17A(1)*(a)*, is the harm likely to result from the order being granted or not.

Article 17 C. Specific regime for preliminary orders

(1) Immediately after the arbitral tribunal has made a determination in respect of an application for a preliminary order, the arbitral tribunal shall give notice to all parties of the request for the interim measure, the application for the preliminary order, the preliminary order, if any, and all other communications, including by indicating the content of any oral communication, between any party and the arbitral tribunal in relation thereto.

(2) At the same time, the arbitral tribunal shall give an opportunity to any party against whom a preliminary order is directed to present its case at the earliest practicable time.

(3) The arbitral tribunal shall decide promptly on any objection to the preliminary order.

(4) A preliminary order shall expire after twenty days from the date on which it was issued by the arbitral tribunal. However, the arbitral tribunal may issue an interim measure adopting or modifying the preliminary order, after the party against whom the preliminary order is directed has been given notice and an opportunity to present its case.

(5) A preliminary order shall be binding on the parties but shall not be subject to enforcement by a court. Such a preliminary order does not constitute an award.

SECTION 3. PROVISIONS APPLICABLE TO INTERIM MEASURES AND PRELIMINARY ORDERS

Article 17 D. Modification, suspension, termination

The arbitral tribunal may modify, suspend or terminate an interim measure or a preliminary order it has granted, upon application of any party or, in exceptional circumstances and upon prior notice to the parties, on the arbitral tribunal's own initiative.

Article 17 E. Provision of security

(1) The arbitral tribunal may require the party requesting an interim measure to provide appropriate security in connection with the measure.

(2) The arbitral tribunal shall require the party applying for a preliminary order to provide security in connection with the order unless the arbitral tribunal considers it inappropriate or unnecessary to do so.

Article 17 F. Disclosure

(1) The arbitral tribunal may require any party promptly to disclose any material change in the circumstances on the basis of which the measure was requested or granted.

(2) The party applying for a preliminary order shall disclose to the arbitral tribunal all circumstances that are likely to be relevant to the arbitral tribunal's determination whether to grant or maintain the order, and such obligation shall continue until the party against whom the order has been requested has had an opportunity to present its case. Thereafter, paragraph (1) of this article shall apply.

Article 17 G. Costs and damages

The party requesting an interim measure or applying for a preliminary order shall be liable for any costs and damages caused by the measure or the order to any party if the arbitral tribunal later determines that, in the circumstances, the measure or the order should not have been granted. The arbitral tribunal may award such costs and damages at any point during the proceedings.

SECTION 4. RECOGNITION AND ENFORCEMENT OF INTERIM MEASURES

Article 17 H. Recognition and enforcement

(1) An interim measure issued by an arbitral tribunal shall be recognized as binding and, unless otherwise provided by the arbitral tribunal, enforced upon application to the competent court, irrespective of the country in which it was issued, subject to the provisions of article 17 I.

(2) The party who is seeking or has obtained recognition or enforcement of an interim measure shall promptly inform the court of any termination, suspension or modification of that interim measure.

(3) The court of the State where recognition or enforcement is sought may, if it considers it proper, order the requesting party to provide appropriate security if the arbitral tribunal has not already made a determination with respect to security or where such a decision is necessary to protect the rights of third parties.

Article 17 I. Grounds for refusing recognition or enforcement[3]

(1) Recognition or enforcement of an interim measure may be refused only:

(a) At the request of the party against whom it is invoked if the court is satisfied that:

(i) Such refusal is warranted on the grounds set forth in article 36(1)*(a)*(i), (ii), (iii) or (iv); or

(ii) The arbitral tribunal's decision with respect to the provision of security in connection with the interim measure issued by the arbitral tribunal has not been complied with; or

(iii) The interim measure has been terminated or suspended by the arbitral tribunal or, where so empowered, by the court of the State in which the arbitration takes place or under the law of which that interim measure was granted; or

(b) If the court finds that:

(i) The interim measure is incompatible with the powers conferred upon the court unless the court decides to reformulate the interim measure to the extent necessary to adapt it to its own powers and procedures for the purposes of enforcing that interim measure and without modifying its substance; or

(ii) Any of the grounds set forth in article 36(1)*(b)*(i) or (ii), apply to the recognition and enforcement of the interim measure.

(2) Any determination made by the court on any ground in paragraph (1) of this article shall be effective only for the purposes of the application to recognize and enforce the interim measure. The court where recognition or enforcement is sought shall not, in making that determination, undertake a review of the substance of the interim measure.

SECTION 5. COURT-ORDERED INTERIM MEASURES

Article 17 J. Court-ordered interim measures

A court shall have the same power of issuing an interim measure in relation to arbitration proceedings, irrespective of whether their place is in the territory of this State, as it has in relation to proceedings in courts. The court shall exercise such power in accordance with its own procedures in consideration of the specific features of international arbitration.

[3] The conditions set forth in article 17 I are intended to limit the number of circumstances in which the court may refuse to enforce an interim measure. It would not be contrary to the level of harmonization sought to be achieved by these model provisions if a State were to adopt fewer circumstances in which enforcement may be refused.

CHAPTER V. CONDUCT OF ARBITRAL PROCEEDINGS

Article 18. Equal treatment of parties

The parties shall be treated with equality and each party shall be given a full opportunity of presenting his case.

Article 19. Determination of rules of procedure

(1) Subject to the provisions of this Law, the parties are free to agree on the procedure to be followed by the arbitral tribunal in conducting the proceedings.

(2) Failing such agreement, the arbitral tribunal may, subject to the provisions of this Law, conduct the arbitration in such manner as it considers appropriate. The power conferred upon the arbitral tribunal includes the power to determine the admissibility, relevance, materiality and weight of any evidence.

Article 20. Place of arbitration

(1) The parties are free to agree on the place of arbitration. Failing such agreement, the place of arbitration shall be determined by the arbitral tribunal having regard to the circumstances of the case, including the convenience of the parties.

(2) Notwithstanding the provisions of paragraph (1) of this article, the arbitral tribunal may, unless otherwise agreed by the parties, meet at any place it considers appropriate for consultation among its members, for hearing witnesses, experts or the parties, or for inspection of goods, other property or documents.

Article 21. Commencement of arbitral proceedings

Unless otherwise agreed by the parties, the arbitral proceedings in respect of a particular dispute commence on the date on which a request for that dispute to be referred to arbitration is received by the respondent.

Article 22. Language

(1) The parties are free to agree on the language or languages to be used in the arbitral proceedings. Failing such agreement, the arbitral tribunal shall determine the language or languages to be used in the proceedings. This agreement or determination, unless otherwise specified therein, shall apply to any written statement by a party, any hearing and any award, decision or other communication by the arbitral tribunal.

(2) The arbitral tribunal may order that any documentary evidence shall be accompanied by a translation into the language or languages agreed upon by the parties or determined by the arbitral tribunal.

Article 23. Statements of claim and defence

(1) Within the period of time agreed by the parties or determined by the arbitral tribunal, the claimant shall state the facts supporting his claim, the points at issue and the relief or remedy sought, and the respondent shall state his defence in respect of these particulars, unless the parties have otherwise agreed as to the required elements of such statements. The parties may submit with their statements all documents they consider to be relevant or may add a reference to the documents or other evidence they will submit.

(2) Unless otherwise agreed by the parties, either party may amend or supplement his claim or defence during the course of the arbitral proceedings, unless the arbitral tribunal considers it inappropriate to allow such amendment having regard to the delay in making it.

Article 24. Hearings and written proceedings

(1) Subject to any contrary agreement by the parties, the arbitral tribunal shall decide whether to hold oral hearings for the presentation of evidence or for oral argument, or whether the proceedings shall be conducted on the basis of documents and other materials. However, unless the parties have agreed that no hearings shall be held, the arbitral tribunal shall hold such hearings at an appropriate stage of the proceedings, if so requested by a party.

(2) The parties shall be given sufficient advance notice of any hearing and of any meeting of the arbitral tribunal for the purposes of inspection of goods, other property or documents.

(3) All statements, documents or other information supplied to the arbitral tribunal by one party shall be communicated to the other party. Also any expert report or evidentiary document on which the arbitral tribunal may rely in making its decision shall be communicated to the parties.

Article 25. Default of a party

Unless otherwise agreed by the parties, if, without showing sufficient cause,

(a) the claimant fails to communicate his statement of claim in accordance with article 23(1), the arbitral tribunal shall terminate the proceedings;

(b) the respondent fails to communicate his statement of defence in accordance with article 23(1), the arbitral tribunal shall continue the proceedings without treating such failure in itself as an admission of the claimant's allegations;

(c) any party fails to appear at a hearing or to produce documentary evidence, the arbitral tribunal may continue the proceedings and make the award on the evidence before it.

Article 26. Expert appointed by arbitral tribunal

(1) Unless otherwise agreed by the parties, the arbitral tribunal

(a) may appoint one or more experts to report to it on specific issues to be determined by the arbitral tribunal;

(b) may require a party to give the expert any relevant information or to produce, or to provide access to, any relevant documents, goods or other property for his inspection.

(2) Unless otherwise agreed by the parties, if a party so requests or if the arbitral tribunal considers it necessary, the expert shall, after delivery of his written or oral report, participate in a hearing where the parties have the opportunity to put questions to him and to present expert witnesses in order to testify on the points at issue.

Article 27. Court assistance in taking evidence

The arbitral tribunal or a party with the approval of the arbitral tribunal may request from a competent court of this State assistance in taking evidence. The court may execute the request within its competence and according to its rules on taking evidence.

Chapter VI. Making of Award and Termination of Proceedings

Article 28. Rules applicable to substance of dispute

(1) The arbitral tribunal shall decide the dispute in accordance with such rules of law as are chosen by the parties as applicable to the substance of the dispute. Any designation of the law or legal system of a given State shall be construed, unless otherwise expressed, as directly referring to the substantive law of that State and not to its conflict of laws rules.

(2) Failing any designation by the parties, the arbitral tribunal shall apply the law determined by the conflict of laws rules which it considers applicable.

(3) The arbitral tribunal shall decide *ex aequo et bono* or as *amiable compositeur* only if the parties have expressly authorized it to do so.

(4) In all cases, the arbitral tribunal shall decide in accordance with the terms of the contract and shall take into account the usages of the trade applicable to the transaction.

Article 29. Decision-making by panel of arbitrators

In arbitral proceedings with more than one arbitrator, any decision of the arbitral tribunal shall be made, unless otherwise agreed by the parties, by a majority of all its members. However, questions of procedure may be decided by a presiding arbitrator, if so authorized by the parties or all members of the arbitral tribunal.

Article 30. Settlement

(1) If, during arbitral proceedings, the parties settle the dispute, the arbitral tribunal shall terminate the proceedings and, if requested by the parties and not objected to by the arbitral tribunal, record the settlement in the form of an arbitral award on agreed terms.

(2) An award on agreed terms shall be made in accordance with the provisions of article 31 and shall state that it is an award. Such an award has the same status and effect as any other award on the merits of the case.

Article 31. Form and contents of award

(1) The award shall be made in writing and shall be signed by the arbitrator or arbitrators. In arbitral proceedings with more than one arbitrator, the signatures of the majority of all members of the arbitral tribunal shall suffice, provided that the reason for any omitted signature is stated.

(2) The award shall state the reasons upon which it is based, unless the parties have agreed that no reasons are to be given or the award is an award on agreed terms under article 30.

(3) The award shall state its date and the place of arbitration as determined in accordance with article 20(1). The award shall be deemed to have been made at that place.

(4) After the award is made, a copy signed by the arbitrators in accordance with paragraph (1) of this article shall be delivered to each party.

Article 32. Termination of proceedings

(1) The arbitral proceedings are terminated by the final award or by an order of the arbitral tribunal in accordance with paragraph (2) of this article.

(2) The arbitral tribunal shall issue an order for the termination of the arbitral proceedings when:

(a) the claimant withdraws his claim, unless the respondent objects thereto and the arbitral tribunal recognizes a legitimate interest on his part in obtaining a final settlement of the dispute;

(b) the parties agree on the termination of the proceedings;

(c) the arbitral tribunal finds that the continuation of the proceedings has for any other reason become unnecessary or impossible.

(3) The mandate of the arbitral tribunal terminates with the termination of the arbitral proceedings, subject to the provisions of articles 33 and 34(4).

Article 33. Correction and interpretation of award; additional award

(1) Within thirty days of receipt of the award, unless another period of time has been agreed upon by the parties:

(a) a party, with notice to the other party, may request the arbitral tribunal to correct in the award any errors in computation, any clerical or typographical errors or any errors of similar nature;

(b) if so agreed by the parties, a party, with notice to the other party, may request the arbitral tribunal to give an interpretation of a specific point or part of the award.

If the arbitral tribunal considers the request to be justified, it shall make the correction or give the interpretation within thirty days of receipt of the request. The interpretation shall form part of the award.

(2) The arbitral tribunal may correct any error of the type referred to in paragraph (1)*(a)* of this article on its own initiative within thirty days of the date of the award.

(3) Unless otherwise agreed by the parties, a party, with notice to the other party, may request, within thirty days of receipt of the award, the arbitral tribunal to make an additional award as to claims presented in the arbitral proceedings but omitted from the award. If the arbitral tribunal considers the request to be justified, it shall make the additional award within sixty days.

(4) The arbitral tribunal may extend, if necessary, the period of time within which it shall make a correction, interpretation or an additional award under paragraph (1) or (3) of this article.

(5) The provisions of article 31 shall apply to a correction or interpretation of the award or to an additional award.

Chapter VII. Recourse Against Award

Article 34. Application for setting aside as exclusive recourse against arbitral award

(1) Recourse to a court against an arbitral award may be made only by an application for setting aside in accordance with paragraphs (2) and (3) of this article.

(2) An arbitral award may be set aside by the court specified in article 6 only if:

(a) the party making the application furnishes proof that:

(i) a party to the arbitration agreement referred to in article 7 was under some incapacity; or the said agreement is not valid under the law to which the parties have subjected it or, failing any indication thereon, under the law of this State; or

(ii) the party making the application was not given proper notice of the appointment of an arbitrator or of the arbitral proceedings or was otherwise unable to present his case; or

(iii) the award deals with a dispute not contemplated by or not falling within the terms of the submission to arbitration, or contains decisions on matters beyond the scope of the submission to arbitration, provided that, if the decisions on matters submitted to arbitration can be separated from those not so submitted, only that part of the award which contains decisions on matters not submitted to arbitration may be set aside; or

(iv) the composition of the arbitral tribunal or the arbitral procedure was not in accordance with the agreement of the parties, unless such agreement was in conflict with a provision of this Law from which the parties cannot derogate, or, failing such agreement, was not in accordance with this Law; or

(b) the court finds that:

(i) the subject-matter of the dispute is not capable of settlement by arbitration under the law of this State; or

(ii) the award is in conflict with the public policy of this State.

(3) An application for setting aside may not be made after three months have elapsed from the date on which the party making that application had received the award or, if a request had been made under article 33, from the date on which that request had been disposed of by the arbitral tribunal.

(4) The court, when asked to set aside an award, may, where appropriate and so requested by a party, suspend the setting aside proceedings for a period of time determined by it in order to give the arbitral tribunal an opportunity to resume the arbitral proceedings or to take such other action as in the arbitral tribunal's opinion will eliminate the grounds for setting aside.

CHAPTER VIII. RECOGNITION AND ENFORCEMENT OF AWARDS

Article 35. Recognition and enforcement

(1) An arbitral award, irrespective of the country in which it was made, shall be recognized as binding and, upon application in writing to the competent court, shall be enforced subject to the provisions of this article and of article 36.

(2) The party relying on an award or applying for its enforcement shall supply the original award or a copy thereof. If the award is not made in an official language of this State, the court may request the party to supply a translation thereof into such language.[4]

(Article 35(2) has been amended by the Commission at its thirty-ninth session, in 2006)

Article 36. Grounds for refusing recognition or enforcement

(1) Recognition or enforcement of an arbitral award, irrespective of the country in which it was made, may be refused only:

(a) at the request of the party against whom it is invoked, if that party furnishes to the competent court where recognition or enforcement is sought proof that:

(i) a party to the arbitration agreement referred to in article 7 was under some incapacity; or the said agreement is not valid under the law to which the parties have subjected it or, failing any indication thereon, under the law of the country where the award was made; or

(ii) the party against whom the award is invoked was not given proper notice of the appointment of an arbitrator or of the arbitral proceedings or was otherwise unable to present his case; or

(iii) the award deals with a dispute not contemplated by or not falling within the terms of the submission to arbitration, or it contains decisions on matters beyond the scope of the submission to arbitration, provided that, if the decisions on matters submitted to arbitration can be separated from those not so submitted, that part of the award which contains decisions on matters submitted to arbitration may be recognized and enforced; or

(iv) the composition of the arbitral tribunal or the arbitral procedure was not in accordance with the agreement of the parties or, failing such agreement, was not in accordance with the law of the country where the arbitration took place; or

(v) the award has not yet become binding on the parties or has been set aside or suspended by a court of the country in which, or under the law of which, that award was made; or

(b) if the court finds that:

[4] The conditions set forth in this paragraph are intended to set maximum standards. It would, thus, not be contrary to the harmonization to be achieved by the model law if a State retained even less onerous conditions.

(i) the subject-matter of the dispute is not capable of settlement by arbitration under the law of this State; or

(ii) the recognition or enforcement of the award would be contrary to the public policy of this State.

(2) If an application for setting aside or suspension of an award has been made to a court referred to in paragraph (1)*(a)*(v) of this article, the court where recognition or enforcement is sought may, if it considers it proper, adjourn its decision and may also, on the application of the party claiming recognition or enforcement of the award, order the other party to provide appropriate security.

[NOTE: For the interpretation of the UNCITRAL MODEL LAW see the "Explanatory Note by the UNCITRAL Secretariat on the 1985 model law on International Commercial Arbitration as amended in 2006". This Note has not been reproduced due to limitations on space but can be found on the UNCITRAL website (*www.uncitral.org*).]

PART THREE

Recommendation regarding the interpretation of article II, paragraph 2, and article VII, paragraph 1, of the Convention on the Recognition and Enforcement of Foreign Arbitral Awards, done in New York, 10 June 1958, adopted by the United Nations Commission on International Trade Law on 7 July 2006 at its thirty-ninth session

The United Nations Commission on International Trade Law,

Recalling General Assembly resolution 2205 (XXI) of 17 December 1966, which established the United Nations Commission on International Trade Law with the object of promoting the progressive harmonization and unification of the law of international trade by, inter alia, promoting ways and means of ensuring a uniform interpretation and application of international conventions and uniform laws in the field of the law of international trade,

Conscious of the fact that the different legal, social and economic systems of the world, together with different levels of development, are represented in the Commission,

Recalling successive resolutions of the General Assembly reaffirming the mandate of the Commission as the core legal body within the United Nations system in the field of international trade law to coordinate legal activities in this field,

Convinced that the wide adoption of the Convention on the Recognition and Enforcement of Foreign Arbitral Awards, done in New York on 10 June 1958,[1] has been a significant achievement in the promotion of the rule of law, particularly in the field of international trade,

Recalling that the Conference of Plenipotentiaries which prepared and opened the Convention for signature adopted a resolution, which states, inter alia, that the Conference "considers that greater uniformity of national laws on arbitration would further the effectiveness of arbitration in the settlement of private law disputes",

[1] United Nations, *Treaty Series*, vol. 330, No. 4739.

Bearing in mind differing interpretations of the form requirements under the Convention that result in part from differences of expression as between the five equally authentic texts of the Convention,

Taking into account article VII, paragraph 1, of the Convention, a purpose of which is to enable the enforcement of foreign arbitral awards to the greatest extent, in particular by recognizing the right of any interested party to avail itself of law or treaties of the country where the award is sought to be relied upon, including where such law or treaties offer a regime more favourable than the Convention,

Considering the wide use of electronic commerce,

Taking into account international legal instruments, such as the 1985 UNCITRAL Model Law on International Commercial Arbitration,[2] as subsequently revised, particularly with respect to article 7,[3] the UNCITRAL Model Law on Electronic Commerce,[4] the UNCITRAL Model Law on Electronic Signatures[5] and the United Nations Convention on the Use of Electronic Communications in International Contracts,[6]

Taking into account also enactments of domestic legislation, as well as case law, more favourable than the Convention in respect of form requirement governing arbitration agreements, arbitration proceedings and the enforcement of arbitral awards,

Considering that, in interpreting the Convention, regard is to be had to the need to promote recognition and enforcement of arbitral awards,

1. *Recommends* that article II, paragraph 2, of the Convention on the Recognition and Enforcement of Foreign Arbitral Awards, done in New York, 10 June 1958, be applied recognizing that the circumstances described therein are not exhaustive;

2. *Recommends also* that article VII, paragraph 1, of the Convention on the Recognition and Enforcement of Foreign Arbitral Awards, done in New York, 10 June 1958, should be applied to allow any interested party to avail itself of rights it may have, under the law or treaties of the country where an arbitration agreement is sought to be relied upon, to seek recognition of the validity of such an arbitration agreement.

[2] *Official Records of the General Assembly, Fortieth Session, Supplement No. 17* (A/40/17), annex I, and United Nations publication, Sales No. E.95.V.18.

[3] Ibid., *Sixty-first Session, Supplement No. 17* (A/61/17), annex I.

[4] Ibid., *Fifty-first Session, Supplement No. 17* (A/51/17), annex I, and United Nations publication, Sales No. E.99.V.4, which contains also an additional article 5 bis, adopted in 1998, and the accompanying Guide to Enactment.

[5] Ibid., *Fifty-sixth Session, Supplement No. 17* and corrigendum (A/56/17 and Corr.3), annex II, and United Nations publication, Sales No. E.02.V.8, which contains also the accompanying Guide to Enactment.

[6] General Assembly resolution 60/21, annex.

APPENDIX 6

EXCERPT FROM THE FRENCH CODE OF CIVIL PROCEDURE

REPUBLIC OF FRANCE

Ministry of Justice and Civil Liberties

NOR: JUSC1025421D

Decree No. 2011-48 of 13 January 2011,*
reforming the law governing arbitration.

The Prime Minister,
Upon the report of the Keeper of the Seals, Minister of Justice and Civil Liberties;
Considering the Civil Code, in particular Articles 2059 through 2061;
Considering the Code of Civil Procedure, in particular Book IV;
Having heard the *Conseil d'Etat (Section de l'intérieur)*,

Decrees that:
Article 1 – Articles 1508 through 1519 of the Code of Civil Procedure shall become Articles 1570 through 1582 respectively.
Article 2 – Book IV of the Code of Civil Procedure shall be drafted as follows:

BOOK IV – ARBITRATION

TITLE I – DOMESTIC ARBITRATION[1]

CHAPTER I – THE ARBITRATION AGREEMENT

Article 1442

An arbitration agreement may be in the form of an arbitration clause or a submission agreement.

An arbitration clause is an agreement by which the parties to one or more contracts undertake to submit to arbitration disputes which may arise in relation to such contract(s).

A submission agreement is an agreement by which the parties to a dispute submit such dispute to arbitration.

Article 1443

In order to be valid, an arbitration agreement shall be in writing. It can result from an exchange of written communications or be contained in a document to which reference is made in the main agreement.

* Translated by Emmanuel Gaillard, Nanou Leleu-Knobil and Daniela Pellarini of Shearman & Sterling LLP. Thanks go to Charles Kaplan of Herbert Smith LLP for his valuable comments.

[1] Articles or paragraphs preceded by three asterisks (***) also apply to international arbitration.

Article 1444

An arbitration agreement shall designate, including by reference to arbitration rules, the arbitrator or arbitrators, or provide for a procedure for their appointment. Alternatively, Articles 1451 through 1454 shall apply.

Article 1445

In order to be valid, a submission agreement shall define the subject matter of the dispute.

***** Article 1446**

Parties may submit their dispute to arbitration even where proceedings are already pending before a court.

***** Article 1447**

An arbitration agreement is independent of the contract to which it relates. It shall not be affected if such contract is void. If an arbitration clause is void, it shall be deemed not written.

Article 1448

*** When a dispute subject to an arbitration agreement is brought before a court, such court shall decline jurisdiction, except if an arbitral tribunal has not yet been seized of the dispute and if the arbitration agreement is manifestly void or manifestly not applicable.

*** A court may not decline jurisdiction on its own motion.

Any stipulation contrary to the present article shall be deemed not written.

***** Article 1449**

The existence of an arbitration agreement, insofar as the arbitral tribunal has not yet been constituted, shall not preclude a party from applying to a court for measures relating to the taking of evidence or provisional or conservatory measures.

Subject to the provisions governing conservatory attachments and judicial security, application shall be made to the President of the *Tribunal de grande instance* or of the *Tribunal de commerce* who shall rule on the measures relating to the taking of evidence in accordance with the provisions of Article 145[2] and, where the matter is urgent, on the provisional or conservatory measures requested by the parties to the arbitration agreement.

2 Article 145 provides as follows: If, before legal proceedings commence, there is a legitimate reason to preserve or establish evidence upon which the resolution of a dispute may depend, measures relating to the taking of evidence may be ordered, upon the request of any concerned party, by way of a petition to a court or expedited proceedings.

Chapter II – The Arbitral Tribunal

Article 1450

Only a natural person having full capacity to exercise his or her rights may act as an arbitrator.

Where an arbitration agreement designates a legal person, such person shall only have the power to administer the arbitration.

Article 1451

An arbitral tribunal shall be composed of a sole arbitrator or an uneven number of arbitrators.

If an arbitration agreement provides for an even number of arbitrators, an additional arbitrator shall be appointed.

If the parties cannot agree on the appointment of the additional arbitrator, he or she shall be appointed by the other arbitrators within one month of having accepted their mandate or, if they fail to do so by the judge acting in support of the arbitration (*juge d'appui*) referred to in Article 1459.

*** Article 1452

If the parties have not agreed on the procedure for appointing the arbitrator(s):

(1) Where there is to be a sole arbitrator and if the parties fail to agree on the arbitrator, he or she shall be appointed by the person responsible for administering the arbitration or, where there is no such person, by the judge acting in support of the arbitration;

(2) Where there are to be three arbitrators, each party shall appoint an arbitrator and the two arbitrators so appointed shall appoint a third arbitrator. If a party fails to appoint an arbitrator within one month following receipt of a request to that effect by the other party, or if the two arbitrators fail to agree on the third arbitrator within one month of having accepted their mandate, the person responsible for administering the arbitration or, where there is no such person, the judge acting in support of the arbitration, shall appoint the third arbitrator.

*** Article 1453

If there are more than two parties to the dispute and they fail to agree on the procedure for constituting the arbitral tribunal, the person responsible for administering the arbitration or, where there is no such person, the judge acting in support of the arbitration, shall appoint the arbitrator(s).

*** Article 1454

Any other dispute relating to the constitution of an arbitral tribunal shall be resolved, if the parties cannot agree, by the person responsible for administering the arbitration or, where there is no such person, by the judge acting in support of the arbitration.

*** Article 1455

If an arbitration agreement is manifestly void or manifestly not applicable, the judge acting in support of the arbitration shall declare that no appointment need be made.

*** Article 1456

The constitution of an arbitral tribunal shall be complete upon the arbitrators' acceptance of their mandate. As of that date, the tribunal is seized of the dispute. Before accepting a mandate, an arbitrator shall disclose any circumstance that may affect his or her independence or impartiality. He or she also shall disclose promptly any such circumstance that may arise after accepting the mandate. If the parties cannot agree on the removal of an arbitrator, the issue shall be resolved by the person responsible for administering the arbitration or, where there is no such person, by the judge acting in support of the arbitration to whom application must be made within one month following the disclosure or the discovery of the fact at issue.

*** Article 1457

Arbitrators shall carry out their mandate until it is completed, unless they are legally incapacitated or there is a legitimate reason for them to refuse to act or to resign.

If there is disagreement as to the materiality of the reason invoked, the matter shall be resolved by the person responsible for administering the arbitration or, where there is no such person, by the judge acting in support of the arbitration to whom application must be made within one month following such incapacity, refusal to act or resignation.

*** Article 1458

An arbitrator may only be removed with the unanimous consent of the parties. Where there is no unanimous consent, the provisions of the final paragraph of Article 1456 shall apply.

Article 1459

The judge acting in support of the arbitration shall be the President of a *Tribunal de grande instance*.

However, the President of a *Tribunal de commerce* shall have jurisdiction to rule on applications made on the basis of Articles 1451 through 1454 if there is an express provision to that effect in the arbitration agreement. In that case, he or she may apply Article 1455.

The arbitration agreement shall determine which court has territorial jurisdiction, failing which, jurisdiction shall lie with the court of the place where the seat of the arbitral tribunal has been set. Where the arbitration agreement is silent, territorial jurisdiction shall lie with the court of the place where the party or one of the parties resisting the application resides or, if that party does not reside in France, with the court of the place where the applicant resides.

*** Article 1460

Application to the judge acting in support of the arbitration shall be made either by a party or by the arbitral tribunal or one of its members.

Such application shall be made, heard and decided as for expedited proceedings (*référé*).

The judge acting in support of the arbitration shall rule by way of an order against which no recourse can be had. However, such order may be appealed where the judge holds that no appointment need be made for one of the reasons stated in Article 1455.

Article 1461

Subject to the provisions of Article 1456, paragraph 1, any stipulation contrary to the rules set forth in the present chapter shall be deemed not written.

Chapter III – The Arbitral Proceedings

*** Article 1462

A dispute shall be submitted to the arbitral tribunal either jointly by the parties or by the most diligent party.

Article 1463

If an arbitration agreement does not specify a time limit, the duration of the arbitral tribunal's mandate shall be limited to six months as of the date on which the tribunal is seized of the dispute.

*** The statutory or contractual time limit may be extended by agreement between the parties or, where there is no such agreement, by the judge acting in support of the arbitration.

Article 1464

Unless otherwise agreed by the parties, the arbitral tribunal shall define the procedure to be followed in the arbitration. It is under no obligation to abide by the rules governing court proceedings.

However, the fundamental principles governing court proceedings set forth in Articles 4, 10, Article 11, paragraph 1, Article 12, paragraphs 2 and 3, Articles 13 through 21, 23 and 23-1 shall apply.

*** Both parties and arbitrators shall act diligently and in good faith in the conduct of the proceedings.

Subject to legal requirements, and unless otherwise agreed by the parties, arbitral proceedings shall be confidential.

*** Article 1465

The arbitral tribunal has exclusive jurisdiction to rule on objections to its jurisdiction.

*** Article 1466

A party which, knowingly and without a legitimate reason, fails to object to an irregularity before the arbitral tribunal in a timely manner shall be deemed to have waived its right to avail itself of such irregularity.

*** Article 1467

The arbitral tribunal shall take all necessary steps concerning evidentiary and procedural matters, unless the parties authorise it to delegate such tasks to one of its members.

The arbitral tribunal may call upon any person to provide testimony. Witnesses shall not be sworn in.

If a party is in possession of an item of evidence, the arbitral tribunal may enjoin that party to produce it, determine the manner in which it is to be produced and, if necessary, attach penalties to such injunction.

*** Article 1468

The arbitral tribunal may order upon the parties any conservatory or provisional measures that it deems appropriate, set conditions for such measures and, if necessary, attach penalties to such order. However, only courts may order conservatory attachments and judicial security.

The arbitral tribunal has the power to amend or add to any provisional or conservatory measure that it has granted.

*** Article 1469

If one of the parties to arbitral proceedings intends to rely on an official (*acte authentique*) or private (*acte sous seing privé*) deed to which it was not a party, or on evidence held by a third party, it may, upon leave of the arbitral tribunal, have that third party summoned before the President of the *Tribunal de grande instance* for the purpose of obtaining a copy thereof (*expédition*) or the production of the deed or item of evidence.

Articles 42 through 48 shall determine which *Tribunal de grande instance* has territorial jurisdiction in this regard.

Application shall be made, heard and decided as for expedited proceedings (*référé*).

If the president considers the application well-founded, he or she shall order that the relevant original, copy or extract of the deed or item of evidence be issued or produced, under such conditions and guarantees as he or she determines, and, if necessary, attach penalties to such order.

Such order is not readily enforceable.

It may be appealed within fifteen days following service (*signification*) of the order.

*** Article 1470

Unless otherwise stipulated, the arbitral tribunal shall have the power to rule on a request for verification of handwriting or claim of forgery in accordance with Articles 287 through 294 and Article 299.

Where an incidental claim of forgery of official documents is raised, Article 313 shall apply.

Article 1471

Abatement of proceedings shall be governed by Articles 369 through 372.

*** Article 1472

Where necessary, the arbitral tribunal may stay the proceedings. The proceedings shall be stayed for the period of time set forth in the stay order or until such time as the event prescribed in the order has occurred.

The arbitral tribunal may, as the circumstances require, lift or shorten the stay.

Article 1473

Unless otherwise stipulated, arbitral proceedings shall also be stayed in the event of the death, legal incapacity, refusal to act, resignation, challenge or removal of an arbitrator, and until such time as a substitute arbitrator has accepted his or her mandate.

The substitute arbitrator shall be appointed in accordance with the procedure agreed upon by the parties or, failing that, in accordance with the procedure followed for the appointment of the original arbitrator.

Article 1474

An abatement or stay of the proceedings shall not put an end to the arbitral tribunal's mandate.

The arbitral tribunal may ask the parties to report any steps taken towards resuming the proceedings or putting an end to the situation having caused the abatement or stay. If the parties fail to take action, the tribunal may terminate the proceedings.

Article 1475

The arbitral proceedings shall resume at the stage reached before the abatement or stay, once the underlying causes for such abatement or stay cease to exist. When the proceedings resume, and by way of an exception to Article 1463, the arbitral tribunal may extend the duration of the proceedings for a period not exceeding six months.

Article 1476

The arbitral tribunal shall set the date on which the award is to be rendered.

During the course of the deliberations, no claim may be made, no argument raised, nor evidence produced, except at the request of the arbitral tribunal.

Article 1477

Arbitral proceedings shall come to an end upon expiration of the time limit set for the arbitration.

Chapter IV – The Arbitral Award

Article 1478

The arbitral tribunal shall decide the dispute in accordance with the law, unless the parties have empowered it to rule as *amiable compositeur*.

*** Article 1479

The arbitral tribunal's deliberations shall be confidential.

Article 1480

The arbitral award shall be made by majority decision.

It shall be signed by all the arbitrators.

If a minority among them refuses to sign, the award shall so state and shall have the same effect as if it had been signed by all the arbitrators.

*** Article 1481

The arbitral award shall state:

(1) the full names of the parties, as well as their domicile or corporate headquarters;

(2) if applicable, the names of the counsel or other persons who represented or assisted the parties;

(3) the names of the arbitrators who made it;

(4) the date on which it was made;

(5) the place where the award was made.

*** Article 1482

The arbitral award shall succinctly set forth the respective claims and arguments of the parties.

The award shall state the reasons upon which it is based.

Article 1483

An arbitral award which fails to comply with the provisions of Article 1480, the provisions of Article 1481 regarding the names of the arbitrators and the date of the award, and those contained in Article 1482 regarding the reasons for the award, shall be void.

However, no omission or inaccuracy in the particulars required for the award to be valid shall render the award void if it can be established, through the case record or any other means, that it does, in fact, comply with the relevant legal requirements.

Article 1484

*** As soon as it is made, an arbitral award shall be *res judicat*a with regard to the claims adjudicated in that award.

*** The award may be declared provisionally enforceable.

The award shall be notified by service (*signification*) unless the parties agree otherwise.

Article 1485

*** Once an award is made, the arbitral tribunal shall no longer be vested with the power to rule on the claims adjudicated in that award.

*** However, on application of a party, the arbitral tribunal may interpret the award, rectify clerical errors and omissions, or make an additional award where it failed to rule on a claim. The arbitral tribunal shall rule after having heard the parties or having given them the opportunity to be heard.

If the arbitral tribunal cannot be reconvened and if the parties cannot agree on the constitution of a new tribunal, this power shall vest in the court which would have had jurisdiction had there been no arbitration.

*** Article 1486

Applications under Article 1485, paragraph 2, shall be filed within three months of notification of the award.

Unless otherwise agreed, the decision amending the award or the additional award shall be made within three months of application to the arbitral tribunal. This time limit may be extended in accordance with Article 1463, paragraph 2.

The decision amending the award or the additional award shall be notified in the same manner as the initial award.

Chapter V – Exequatur

Article 1487

An arbitral award may only be enforced by virtue of an enforcement order (*exequatur*) issued by the *Tribunal de grande instance* of the place where the award was made.

Exequatur proceedings shall not be adversarial.

Application for *exequatur* shall be filed by the most diligent party with the Court Registrar, together with the original award and arbitration agreement, or duly authenticated copies of such documents.

The enforcement order shall be affixed to the original or, if the original is not produced, to a duly authenticated copy of the arbitral award, as per the previous paragraph.

Article 1488

No enforcement order may be granted where an award is manifestly contrary to public policy.

An order denying enforcement shall state the reasons upon which it is based.

Chapter VI – Recourse

Section 1 – Appeal

Article 1489

An arbitral award shall not be subject to appeal, unless otherwise agreed by the parties.

Article 1490

An appeal may seek to obtain either the reversal or the setting aside of an award.

The court shall rule in accordance with the law or as *amiable compositeur*, within the limits of the arbitral tribunal's mandate.

Section 2 – Actions To Set Aside

Article 1491

An action to set aside an award may be brought except where the parties have agreed that the award may be appealed.

Any provision to the contrary shall be deemed not written.

Article 1492

An award may only be set aside where:

(1) the arbitral tribunal wrongly upheld or declined jurisdiction; or

(2) the arbitral tribunal was not properly constituted; or

(3) the arbitral tribunal ruled without complying with the mandate conferred upon it; or

(4) due process was violated; or

(5) the award is contrary to public policy; or

(6) the award failed to state the reasons upon which it is based, the date on which it was made, the names or signatures of the arbitrator(s) having made the award; or where the award was not made by majority decision.

Article 1493

When a court sets aside an arbitral award, it shall rule on the merits within the limits of the arbitrator's mandate, unless otherwise agreed by the parties.

Section 3 – Appeals And Actions To Set Aside – Common Provisions

Article 1494

Appeals and actions to set aside shall be brought before the Court of Appeal of the place where the award was made.

Such recourse can be had as soon as the award is rendered. If no application is made within one month following notification of the award, recourse shall no longer be admissible.

Article 1495

Appeals and actions to set aside shall be brought, heard and decided in accordance with the rules applicable to adversarial proceedings set forth in Articles 900 through 930-1.

Article 1496

Unless an arbitral award is provisionally enforceable, enforcement shall be stayed until expiration of the time limit set for appeals or actions to set aside, or upon the filing of an appeal or action to set aside during this period.

Article 1497

The first president ruling in expedited proceedings (*référé*) or, once the matter is referred to him or her, the judge assigned to the case (*conseiller de la mise en état*) may:

(1) if the award is provisionally enforceable and where enforcement may lead to manifestly excessive consequences, stay or set conditions for enforcement of the award; or

(2) if the award is not provisionally enforceable, order that the award or any part thereof be provisionally enforceable.

Article 1498

If an award is provisionally enforceable or if it has been made provisionally enforceable as per Article 1497(2), the first president or, once the matter is referred to him or her, the judge assigned to the case may grant enforcement (*exequatur*) of the arbitral award.

A decision denying an appeal or an application to set aside an award shall be deemed an enforcement order of the arbitral award or the parts thereof that were not overturned by the court.

Section 4 – Recourse Against Orders Granting Or Denying Enforcement

Article 1499

No recourse may be had against an order granting enforcement of an award.

However, an appeal or an action to set aside an award shall be deemed to constitute recourse against the order of the judge having ruled on enforcement or shall bring an end to said judge's jurisdiction, as regards the parts of the award which are challenged.

Article 1500

An order denying enforcement may be appealed within one month following service (*signification*) thereof.

If it is appealed, and if one of the parties so requests, the Court of Appeal shall rule on an appeal or application to set aside the award, provided that the time limit for such appeal or application has not expired.

Section 5 – Other Means Of Recourse

Article 1501

Third parties may challenge an arbitral award by petitioning the court which would have had jurisdiction had there been no arbitration, subject to the provisions of Article 588, paragraph 1.

Article 1502

*** Application for revision of an arbitral award may be made in the circumstances provided in Article 595 for court judgments,[3] and under the conditions set forth in Articles 594, 596, 597 and 601 through 603.

*** Application shall be made to the arbitral tribunal.

However, if the arbitral tribunal cannot be reconvened, application shall be made to the Court of Appeal which would have had jurisdiction to hear other forms of recourse against the award.

*** Article 1503

No *opposition*[4] may be filed against an arbitral award, nor may the Cour de Cassation be petitioned to quash the award.

[3] Article 595 provides as follows:
An application for revision of a judgment may be made only where:
1. it comes to light, after the judgment is handed down, that it was obtained fraudulently by the party in whose favour it was rendered;
2. decisive evidence that had been withheld by another party is recovered after the judgment was handed down;
3. the judgment is based on documents that have since been proven or have been held by a court to be false;
4. the judgment is based on affidavits, testimonies or oaths that have been held by a court to be false.

In all four cases, an application for revision shall be admissible only where the applicant was not able, through no fault of his or her own, to raise such objection before the judgment became *res judicata*.

[4] *Opposition* is a form of recourse under French law, available when a judgment is rendered by default because a defendant was not properly notified of a hearing. The defendant can then "oppose" the judgment.

TITLE II – INTERNATIONAL ARBITRATION

Article 1504

An arbitration is international when international trade interests are at stake.

Article 1505

In international arbitration, and unless otherwise stipulated, the judge acting in support of the arbitration shall be the President of the *Tribunal de grande instance* of Paris when:

(1) the arbitration takes place in France; or

(2) the parties have agreed that French procedural law shall apply to the arbitration; or

(3) the parties have expressly granted jurisdiction to French courts over disputes relating to the arbitral procedure; or

(4) one of the parties is exposed to a risk of a denial of justice.

Article 1506

Unless the parties have agreed otherwise, and subject to the provisions of the present Title, the following Articles shall apply to international arbitration:

(1) 1446, 1447, 1448 (paragraphs 1 and 2) and 1449, regarding the arbitration agreement;

(2) 1452 through 1458 and 1460 regarding the constitution of the arbitral tribunal and the procedure governing application to the judge acting in support of the arbitration;

(3) 1462, 1463 (paragraph 2), 1464 (paragraph 3), 1465 through 1470 and 1472 regarding arbitral proceedings;

(4) 1479, 1481, 1482, 1484 (paragraphs 1 and 2), 1485 (paragraphs 1 and 2) and 1486 regarding arbitral awards;

(5) 1502 (paragraphs 1 and 2) and 1503 regarding means of recourse other than appeals or actions to set aside.

CHAPTER I – INTERNATIONAL ARBITRATION AGREEMENTS

Article 1507

An arbitration agreement shall not be subject to any requirements as to its form.

Article 1508

An arbitration agreement may designate the arbitrator(s) or provide for the procedure for their appointment, directly or by reference to arbitration rules or to procedural rules.

Chapter II – Arbitral Proceedings And Awards

Article 1509

An arbitration agreement may define the procedure to be followed in the arbitral proceedings, directly or by reference to arbitration rules or to procedural rules. Unless the arbitration agreement provides otherwise, the arbitral tribunal shall define the procedure as required, either directly or by reference to arbitration rules or to procedural rules.

Article 1510

Irrespective of the procedure adopted, the arbitral tribunal shall ensure that the parties are treated equally and shall uphold the principle of due process.

Article 1511

The arbitral tribunal shall decide the dispute in accordance with the rules of law chosen by the parties or, where no such choice has been made, in accordance with the rules of law it considers appropriate.

In either case, the arbitral tribunal shall take trade usages into account.

Article 1512

The arbitral tribunal shall rule as *amiable compositeur* if the parties have empowered it to do so.

Article 1513

Unless the arbitration agreement provides otherwise, the award shall be made by majority decision. It shall be signed by all the arbitrators.

However, if a minority among them refuses to sign, the others shall so state in the award.

If there is no majority, the chairman of the arbitral tribunal shall rule alone.

Should the other arbitrators refuse to sign, the chairman shall so state in the award, which only he or she shall sign.

An award made under the circumstances described in either of the two preceding paragraphs shall have the same effect as if it had been signed by all the arbitrators or made by majority decision.

Chapter III – Recognition And Enforcement Of Arbitral Awards Made Abroad Or In International Arbitration

Article 1514

An arbitral award shall be recognised or enforced in France if the party relying on it can prove its existence and if such recognition or enforcement is not manifestly contrary to international public policy.

Article 1515

The existence of an arbitral award shall be proven by producing the original award, together with the arbitration agreement, or duly authenticated copies of such documents.

If such documents are in a language other than French, the party applying form recognition or enforcement shall produce a translation. The applicant may be requested to provide a translation by a translator whose name appears on a list of court experts or a translator accredited by the administrative or judicial authorities of another Member State of the European Union, a Contracting Party to the European Economic Area Agreement or the Swiss Confederation.

Article 1516

An arbitral award may only be enforced by virtue of an enforcement order (*exequatur*) issued by the *Tribunal de grande instance* of the place where the award was made or by the *Tribunal de grande instance* of Paris if the award was made abroad.

Exequatur proceedings shall not be adversarial.

Application for *exequatur* shall be filed by the most diligent party with the Court Registrar, together with the original award and arbitration agreement, or duly authenticated copies of such documents.

Article 1517

The enforcement order shall be affixed to the original or, if the original is not produced, to a duly authenticated copy of the arbitral award, as per the final paragraph of Article 1516.

Where an arbitral award is in a language other than French, the enforcement order shall also be affixed to the translation produced as per Article 1515.

An order denying enforcement of an arbitral award shall state the reasons upon which it is based.

Chapter IV – Recourse

Section 1 – Awards Made In France

Article 1518

The only means of recourse against an award made in France in an international arbitration is an action to set aside.

Article 1519

An action to set aside shall be brought before the Court of Appeal of the place where the award was made.

Such recourse can be had as soon as the award is rendered. If no application is made within one month following notification of the award, recourse shall no longer be admissible.

The award shall be notified by service (*signification*), unless otherwise agreed by the parties.

Article 1520

An award may only be set aside where:

(1) the arbitral tribunal wrongly upheld or declined jurisdiction; or

(2) the arbitral tribunal was not properly constituted; or

(3) the arbitral tribunal ruled without complying with the mandate conferred upon it; or

(4) due process was violated; or

(5) recognition or enforcement of the award is contrary to international public policy.

Article 1521

The first president or, once the matter is referred to him or her, the judge assigned to the case (*conseiller de la mise en état*) may grant enforcement (*exequatur*) of the award.

Article 1522

By way of a specific agreement the parties may, at any time, expressly waive their right to bring an action to set aside.

Where such right has been waived, the parties nonetheless retain their right to appeal an enforcement order on one of the grounds set forth in Article 1520.

Such appeal shall be brought within one month following notification of the award bearing the enforcement order. The award bearing the enforcement order shall be notified by service (*signification*), unless otherwise agreed by the parties.

Article 1523

An order denying recognition or enforcement of an international arbitral award made in France may be appealed.

The appeal shall be brought within one month following service (*signification*) of the order.

If the order is appealed, and if one of the parties so requests, the Court of Appeal shall rule on an action to set aside unless the parties have waived the right to bring such action or the time limit to bring such action has expired.

Article 1524

No recourse may be had against an order granting enforcement of an award, except as provided in Article 1522, paragraph 2.

However, an action to set aside an award shall be deemed to constitute recourse against the order of the judge having ruled on enforcement or shall bring an end to said judge's jurisdiction, as regards the parts of the award which are challenged.

Section 2 – Awards Made Abroad

Article 1525

An order granting or denying recognition or enforcement of an arbitral award made abroad may be appealed.

The appeal shall be brought within one month following service (*signification*) of the order.

However, the parties may agree on other means of notification when an appeal is brought against an award bearing an enforcement order.

The Court of Appeal may only deny recognition or enforcement of an arbitral award on the grounds listed in Article 1520.

Section 3 – Awards Made In France And Abroad – Common Provisions

Article 1526

Neither an action to set aside an award nor an appeal against an enforcement order shall suspend enforcement of an award.

However, the first president ruling in expedited proceedings (*référé*) or, once the matter is referred to him or her, the judge assigned to the matter (*conseiller de la mise en état*), may stay or set conditions for enforcement of an award where enforcement could severely prejudice the rights of one of the parties.

Article 1527

Appeals against orders granting or denying enforcement and actions to set aside awards shall be brought, heard and decided in accordance with the rules applicable to adversarial proceedings set forth in Articles 900 through 930-1.

A decision denying an appeal or application to set aside an award shall be deemed an enforcement order of the arbitral award or of the parts of the award that were not overturned by the court.

Article 3 – The provisions of the present decree shall come into force on the first day of the fourth month following the date of publication, subject to the following provisions:

(1) The provisions of Articles 1442 through 1445, 1489 and 1505, paragraphs 2 and 3 of the Code of Civil Procedure shall apply where the arbitration agreement was concluded after the date mentioned in the first paragraph of the present article;

(2) The provisions of Articles 1456 through 1458, 1486, 1502, 1513 and 1522 of the same Code shall apply where the arbitral tribunal was constituted after the date mentioned in the first paragraph of the present article;

(3) The provisions of Article 1526 of the same Code shall apply to arbitral awards made after the date mentioned in the first paragraph of the present article.

Article 4 – The present decree shall apply in Wallis and Futuna.

Article 5 – The Keeper of the Seals, Minister of Justice and Civil Liberties and the Minister of the Interior (*Ministre de l'intérieur, de l'outre-mer, des collectivités territoriales et de l'immigration*), are responsible, in their respective capacities, for the enforcement of the present decree, which will be published in the official gazette (*Journal Officiel*) of the French Republic.

Paris, 13 January 2011

Prime Minister

François Fillon

Keeper of the Seals, Minister of Justice and Civil Liberties
Michel Mercier

Minister of the Interior

Brice Hortefeux

APPENDIX 7

EXCERPT FROM THE SWISS PRIVATE INTERNATIONAL LAW ACT

Translated by Drs. Marc Blessing, Robert Briner, and Pierre A. Karrer

TWELFTH CHAPTER: INTERNATIONAL ARBITRATION

I. FIELD OF APPLICATION; SEAT OF THE ARBITRAL TRIBUNAL

Article 176

1 The provisions of this chapter shall apply to all arbitrations if the seat of the arbitral tribunal is in Switzerland and if, at the time of the conclusion of the arbitration agreement, at least one of the parties had neither its domicile nor its habitual residence in Switzerland.

2 The provisions in this chapter shall not apply where the parties have agreed in writing that the provisions of this chapter are excluded and that the cantonal provisions on arbitration should apply exclusively.

3 The seat of the arbitral tribunal shall be determined by the parties, or the arbitral institution designated by them, or, failing both, by the arbitrators.

II. ARBITRABILITY

Article 177

1 Any dispute of financial interest may be the subject of an arbitration.

2 A state, or an enterprise held by, or an organization controlled by a state, which is party to an arbitration agreement, cannot invoke its own law in order to contest its capacity to arbitrate or the arbitrability of a dispute covered by the arbitration agreement.

III. ARBITRATION AGREEMENT

Article 178

1 The arbitration agreement must be made in writing, by telegram, telex, telecopier or any other means of communication which permits it to be evidenced by a text.

2 Furthermore, an arbitration agreement is valid if it conforms either to the law chosen by the parties, or to the law governing the subject-matter of the dispute, in particular the main contract, or to Swiss law.

3 The arbitration agreement cannot be contested on the grounds that the main contract is not valid or that the arbitration agreement concerns a dispute which had not as yet arisen.

IV. Arbitrators

1. Constitution of the Arbitral tribunal

Article 179

1 The arbitrators shall be appointed, removed or replaced in accordance with the agreement of the parties.

2 In the absence of such agreement, the judge where the tribunal has its seat may be seized with the question; he shall apply, by analogy, the provisions of cantonal law on appointment, removal or replacement of arbitrators.

3 If a judge has been designated as the authority for appointing an arbitrator, he shall make the appointment unless a summary examination shows that no arbitration agreement exists between the parties.

2. Challenge of an arbitrator

Article 180

1 An arbitrator may be challenged:

a) if he does not meet the qualifications agreed upon by the parties;

b) if a ground for challenge exists under the rules of arbitration agreed upon by the parties;

c) if circumstances exist that give rise to justifiable doubts as to his independence.

2 No party may challenge an arbitrator nominated by it, or whom it was instrumental in appointing, except on a ground which came to that party's attention after such appointment. The ground for challenge must be notified to the arbitral tribunal and the other party without delay.

3 To the extent that the parties have not made provisions for this challenge procedure, the judge at the seat of the Arbitral tribunal shall make the final decision.

V. Lis Pendens

Article 181

1 The arbitral proceedings shall be pending from the time when one of the parties seizes with a claim either the arbitrator or arbitrators designated in the arbitration agreement or, in the absence of such designation in the arbitration agreement, from the time when one of the parties initiates the procedure for the appointment of the Arbitral tribunal.

VI. Procedure

1. Principle

Article 182

1 The parties may, directly or by reference to rules of arbitration, determine the arbitral procedure; they may also submit the arbitral procedure to a procedural law of their choice.

2 If the parties have not determined the procedure, the Arbitral tribunal shall determine it to the extent necessary, either directly or by reference to a statute or to rules of arbitration.

3 Regardless of the procedure chosen, the Arbitral tribunal shall ensure equal treatment of the parties and the right of both parties to be heard in adversarial proceedings.

2. Provisional and conservatory measures

Article 183

1 Unless the parties have otherwise agreed, the Arbitral tribunal may, on motion of one party, order provisional or conservatory measures.

2 If the party concerned does not voluntarily comply with these measures, the Arbitral tribunal may request the assistance of the state judge, the judge shall apply his own law.

3 The Arbitral tribunal or the state judge may make the granting of provisional or conservatory measures subject to appropriate sureties.

3. Taking of evidence

Article 184

1 The Arbitral tribunal shall itself conduct the taking of evidence.

2 If the assistance of state judiciary authorities is necessary for the taking of evidence, the Arbitral tribunal or a party with the consent of the Arbitral tribunal, may request the assistance of the state judge at the seat of the Arbitral tribunal; the judge shall apply his own law.

4. Other judicial assistance

Article 185

For any further judicial assistance the state judge at the seat of the Arbitral tribunal shall have jurisdiction.

VII. JURISDICTION

Article 186

1 The arbitral tribunal shall itself decide on its jurisdiction.

1bis It shall decide on its jurisdiction notwithstanding an action on the same matter between the same parties already pending before a State Court or another arbitral tribunal, unless there are serious reasons to stay the proceedings.

2 A plea of lack of jurisdiction must be raised prior to any defence on the merits.

3 The Arbitral tribunal shall, as a rule, decide on its jurisdiction by preliminary award.

VIII. Decision on the merits

1. Applicable law

Article 187

1 The Arbitral tribunal shall decide the case according to the rules of law chosen by the parties or, in the absence thereof, according to the rules of law with which the case has the closest connection.

2 The parties may authorize the Arbitral tribunal to decide ex aequo et bono.

2. Partial award

Article 188

Unless the parties otherwise agree, the Arbitral tribunal may render partial awards.

3. Arbitral award

Article 189

1 The arbitral award shall be rendered in conformity with the rules of procedure and in the form agreed upon by the parties.

2 In the absence of such an agreement, the arbitral award shall be made by a majority, or, in the absence of a majority, by the chairman alone. The award shall be in writing, supported by reasons, dated and signed. The signature of the chairman is sufficient.

IX. Finality, Action for annulment

1. Principle

Article 190

1 The award is final from its notification.

2 The award may only be annulled:

a) if the sole arbitrator was not properly appointed or if the Arbitral tribunal was not properly constituted;

b) if the Arbitral tribunal wrongly accepted or declined jurisdiction;

c) if the Arbitral tribunal's decision went beyond the claims submitted to it, or failed to decide one of the items of the claim;

d) if the principle of equal treatment of the parties or the right of the parties to be heard was violated;

e) if the award is incompatible with public policy.

3 Preliminary awards can be annulled on the grounds of the above paras 2(a) and 2(b) only; the time limit runs from the notification of the preliminary award.

2. Judicial authority to set aside

Article 191

The sole judicial authority to set aside is the Swiss Federal Supreme Court. The procedure follows Art. 77 of the Swiss Federal Statute on the Swiss Federal Supreme Court of June 17, 2005.

X. Waiver of annulment

Article 192

1 If none of the parties have their domicile, their habitual residence, or a business establishment in Switzerland, they may, by an express statement in the arbitration agreement or by a subsequent written agreement, waive fully the action for annulment or they may limit it to one or several of the grounds listed in Art. 190(2).

2 If the parties have waived fully the action for annulment against the awards and if the awards are to be enforced in Switzerland, the New York Convention of June 10, 1958 on the Recognition and Enforcement of Foreign Arbitral Awards applies by analogy.

XI. Deposit and Certificate of enforceability

Article 193

1 Each party may at its own expense deposit a copy of the award with the Swiss court at the seat of the Arbitral tribunal.

2 On request of a party, the court shall certify the enforceability of the award.

3 On request of a party, the Arbitral tribunal shall certify that the award has been rendered pursuant to the provisions of this Statute; such certificate has the same effect as the deposit of the award.

XII. Foreign arbitral awards

Article 194

The recognition and enforcement of a foreign arbitral award is governed by the New York Convention of June 10, 1958 on the Recognition and Enforcement of Foreign Arbitral Awards.

APPENDIX 8

EXCERPT FROM THE US FEDERAL ARBITRATION ACT

TITLE 9—ARBITRATION

CHAPTER 1—GENERAL PROVISIONS

Sec. 1. "Maritime transactions" and "commerce" defined; exceptions to operation of title

"Maritime transactions", as herein defined, means charter parties, bills of lading of water carriers, agreements relating to wharfage, supplies furnished vessels or repairs to vessels, collisions, or any other matters in foreign commerce which, if the subject of controversy, would be embraced within admiralty jurisdiction; "commerce", as herein defined, means commerce among the several States or with foreign nations, or in any Territory of the United States or in the District of Columbia, or between any such Territory and another, or between any such Territory and any State or foreign nation, or between the District of Columbia and any State or Territory or foreign nation, but nothing herein contained shall apply to contracts of employment of seamen, railroad employees, or any other class of workers engaged in foreign or interstate commerce.

Sec. 2. Validity, irrevocability, and enforcement of agreements to arbitrate

A written provision in any maritime transaction or a contract evidencing a transaction involving commerce to settle by arbitration a controversy thereafter arising out of such contract or transaction, or the refusal to perform the whole or any part thereof, or an agreement in writing to submit to arbitration an existing controversy arising out of such a contract, transaction, or refusal, shall be valid, irrevocable, and enforceable, save upon such grounds as exist at law or in equity for the revocation of any contract.

Sec. 3. Stay of proceedings where issue therein referable to arbitration

If any suit or proceeding be brought in any of the courts of the United States upon any issue referable to arbitration under an agreement in writing for such arbitration, the court in which such suit is pending, upon being satisfied that the issue involved in such suit or proceeding is referable to arbitration under such an agreement, shall on application of one of the parties stay the trial of the action until such arbitration has been had in accordance with the terms of the agreement, providing the applicant for the stay is not in default in proceeding with such arbitration.

Sec. 4. Failure to arbitrate under agreement; petition to United States court having jurisdiction for order to compel arbitration; notice and service thereof; hearing and determination

A party aggrieved by the alleged failure, neglect, or refusal of another to arbitrate under a written agreement for arbitration may petition any United States district court which, save for such agreement, would have jurisdiction under title 28, in a civil action or in admiralty of the subject matter of a suit arising out of the controversy between the parties, for an order directing that such arbitration proceed in the manner provided for in such agreement. Five days' notice in writing of such application shall be served upon the party in default. Service thereof shall be made in the manner provided by the Federal Rules of Civil Procedure. The court shall hear the parties, and upon being satisfied that the making of the agreement for arbitration or the failure to comply therewith is not in issue, the court shall make an order directing the parties to proceed to arbitration in accordance with the terms of the agreement. The hearing and proceedings, under such agreement, shall be within the district in which the petition for an order directing such arbitration is filed. If the making of the arbitration agreement or the failure, neglect, or refusal to perform the same be in issue, the court shall proceed summarily to the trial thereof. If no jury trial be demanded by the party alleged to be in default, or if the matter in dispute is within admiralty jurisdiction, the court shall hear and determine such issue. Where such an issue is raised, the party alleged to be in default may, except in cases of admiralty, on or before the return day of the notice of application, demand a jury trial of such issue, and upon such demand the court shall make an order referring the issue or issues to a jury in the manner provided by the Federal Rules of Civil Procedure, or may specially call a jury for that purpose. If the jury find that no agreement in writing for arbitration was made or that there is no default in proceeding thereunder, the proceeding shall be dismissed. If the jury find that an agreement for arbitration was made in writing and that there is a default in proceeding thereunder, the court shall make an order summarily directing the parties to proceed with the arbitration in accordance with the terms thereof.

Sec. 5. Appointment of arbitrators or umpire

If in the agreement provision be made for a method of naming or appointing an arbitrator or arbitrators or an umpire, such method shall be followed; but if no method be provided therein, or if a method be provided and any party thereto shall fail to avail himself of such method, or if for any other reason there shall be a lapse in the naming of an arbitrator or arbitrators or umpire, or in filling a vacancy, then upon the application of either party to the controversy the court shall designate and appoint an arbitrator or arbitrators or umpire, as the case may require, who shall act under the said agreement with the same force and effect as if he or they had been specifically named therein; and unless otherwise provided in the agreement the arbitration shall be by a single arbitrator.

Sec. 6. Application heard as motion

Any application to the court hereunder shall be made and heard in the manner provided by law for the making and hearing of motions, except as otherwise herein expressly provided.

Sec. 7. Witnesses before arbitrators; fees; compelling attendance

The arbitrators selected either as prescribed in this title or otherwise, or a majority of them, may summon in writing any person to attend before them or any of them as a witness and in a proper case to bring with him or them any book, record, document, or paper which may be deemed material as evidence in the case. The fees for such attendance shall be the same as the fees of witnesses before masters of the United States courts. Said summons shall issue in the name of the arbitrator or arbitrators, or a majority of them, and shall be signed by the arbitrators, or a majority of them, and shall be directed to the said person and shall be served in the same manner as subpoenas to appear and testify before the court; if any person or persons so summoned to testify shall refuse or neglect to obey said summons, upon petition the United States district court for the district in which such arbitrators, or a majority of them, are sitting may compel the attendance of such person or persons before said arbitrator or arbitrators, or punish said person or persons for contempt in the same manner provided by law for securing the attendance of witnesses or their punishment for neglect or refusal to attend in the courts of the United States.

Sec. 8. Proceedings begun by libel in admiralty and seizure of vessel or property

If the basis of jurisdiction be a cause of action otherwise justiciable in admiralty, then, notwithstanding anything herein to the contrary, the party claiming to be aggrieved may begin his proceeding hereunder by libel and seizure of the vessel or other property of the other party according to the usual course of admiralty proceedings, and the court shall then have jurisdiction to direct the parties to proceed with the arbitration and shall retain jurisdiction to enter its decree upon the award.

Sec. 9. Award of arbitrators; confirmation; jurisdiction; procedure

If the parties in their agreement have agreed that a judgment of the court shall be entered upon the award made pursuant to the arbitration, and shall specify the court, then at any time within one year after the award is made any party to the arbitration may apply to the court so specified for an order confirming the award, and thereupon the court must grant such an order unless the award is vacated, modified, or corrected as prescribed in sections 10 and 11 of this title. If no court is specified in the agreement of the parties, then such application may be made to the United States court in and for the district within which such award was made. Notice of the application shall be served upon the adverse party, and thereupon the court shall have jurisdiction of such party as though he had appeared generally in the proceeding. If the adverse party is a resident of the district within which the award was made, such service shall be made upon the adverse party or his attorney as prescribed by law for service of notice of motion in an action in the same court. If the adverse party shall be a nonresident, then the notice of the application shall be served by the marshal of any district within which the adverse party may be found in like manner as other process of the court.

Sec. 10. Same; vacation; grounds; rehearing

(a) In any of the following cases the United States court in and for the district wherein the award was made may make an order vacating the award upon the application of any party to the arbitration—

(1) where the award was procured by corruption, fraud, or undue means;

(2) where there was evident partiality or corruption in the arbitrators, or either of them;

(3) where the arbitrators were guilty of misconduct in refusing to postpone the hearing, upon sufficient cause shown, or in refusing to hear evidence pertinent and material to the controversy; or of any other misbehavior by which the rights of any party have been prejudiced; or

(4) where the arbitrators exceeded their powers, or so imperfectly executed them that a mutual, final, and definite award upon the subject matter submitted was not made.

(b) If an award is vacated and the time within which the agreement required the award to be made has not expired, the court may, in its discretion, direct a rehearing by the arbitrators.

(c) The United States district court for the district wherein an award was made that was issued pursuant to section 580 of title 5 may make an order vacating the award upon the application of a person, other than a party to the arbitration, who is adversely affected or aggrieved by the award, if the use of arbitration or the award is clearly inconsistent with the factors set forth in section 572 of title 5.

Sec. 11. Same; modification or correction; grounds; order

In either of the following cases the United States court in and for the district wherein the award was made may make an order modifying or correcting the award upon the application of any party to the arbitration—

(a) Where there was an evident material miscalculation of figures or an evident material mistake in the description of any person, thing, or property referred to in the award.

(b) Where the arbitrators have awarded upon a matter not submitted to them, unless it is a matter not affecting the merits of the decision upon the matter submitted.

(c) Where the award is imperfect in matter of form not affecting the merits of the controversy. The order may modify and correct the award, so as to effect the intent thereof and promote justice between the parties.

Sec. 12. Notice of motions to vacate or modify; service; stay of proceedings

Notice of a motion to vacate, modify, or correct an award must be served upon the adverse party or his attorney within three months after the award is filed or delivered. If the adverse party is a resident of the district within which the award was made, such service shall be made upon the adverse party or his attorney as prescribed by law for service of notice of motion in an action in the same court. If the adverse party shall be a nonresident then the notice of the application shall be served by the marshal of any district within which the adverse party may be found in like manner as other process of the court. For the purposes of the motion any judge who might make an order to stay the proceedings in an action brought in the same court may make an order, to be served with the notice of motion, staying the proceedings of the adverse party to enforce the award.

Sec. 13. Papers filed with order on motions; judgment; docketing; force and effect; enforcement

The party moving for an order confirming, modifying, or correcting an award shall, at the time such order is filed with the clerk for the entry of judgment thereon, also file the following papers with the clerk:

(a) The agreement; the selection or appointment, if any, of an additional arbitrator or umpire; and each written extension of the time, if any, within which to make the award.

(b) The award.

(c) Each notice, affidavit, or other paper used upon an application to confirm, modify, or correct the award, and a copy of each order of the court upon such an application. The judgment shall be docketed as if it was rendered in an action. The judgment so entered shall have the same force and effect, in all respects, as, and be subject to all the provisions of law relating to, a judgment in an action; and it may be enforced as if it had been rendered in an action in the court in which it is entered.

Sec. 14. Contracts not affected

This title shall not apply to contracts made prior to January 1, 1926.

Sec. 15. Inapplicability of the Act of State doctrine

Enforcement of arbitral agreements, confirmation of arbitral awards, and execution upon judgments based on orders confirming such awards shall not be refused on the basis of the Act of State doctrine.

Sec. 16. Appeals

(a) An appeal may be taken from—

(1) an order—

(A) refusing a stay of any action under section 3 of this title,

(B) denying a petition under section 4 of this title to order arbitration to proceed,

(C) denying an application under section 206 of this title to compel arbitration,

(D) confirming or denying confirmation of an award or partial award, or

(E) modifying, correcting, or vacating an award;

(2) an interlocutory order granting, continuing, or modifying an injunction against an arbitration that is subject to this title; or

(3) a final decision with respect to an arbitration that is subject to this title.

(b) Except as otherwise provided in section 1292 (b) of title 28, an appeal may not be taken from an interlocutory order—

(1) granting a stay of any action under section 3 of this title;

(2) directing arbitration to proceed under section 4 of this title;

(3) compelling arbitration under section 206 of this title; or

(4) refusing to enjoin an arbitration that is subject to this title.

Chapter 2—Convention On The Recognition And Enforcement Of Foreign Arbitral Awards

Sec.

201. Enforcement of Convention.

202. Agreement or award falling under the Convention.

203. Jurisdiction; amount in controversy.

204. Venue.

205. Removal of cases from State courts.

206. Order to compel arbitration; appointment of arbitrators.

207. Award of arbitrators; confirmation; jurisdiction; proceeding.

208. Chapter 1; residual application.

Sec. 201. Enforcement of Convention

The Convention on the Recognition and Enforcement of Foreign Arbitral Awards of June 10, 1958, shall be enforced in United States courts in accordance with this chapter.

Sec. 202. Agreement or award falling under the Convention

An arbitration agreement or arbitral award arising out of a legal relationship, whether contractual or not, which is considered as commercial, including a transaction, contract, or agreement described in section 2 of this title, falls under the Convention. An agreement or award arising out of such a relationship which is entirely between citizens of the United States shall be deemed not to fall under the Convention unless that relationship involves property located abroad, envisages performance or enforcement abroad, or has some other reasonable relation with one or more foreign states. For the purpose of this section a corporation is a citizen of the United States if it is incorporated or has its principal place of business in the United States.

Sec. 203. Jurisdiction; amount in controversy

An action or proceeding falling under the Convention shall be deemed to arise under the laws and treaties of the United States. The district courts of the United States (including the courts enumerated in section 460 of title 28) shall have original jurisdiction over such an action or proceeding, regardless of the amount in controversy.

Sec. 204. Venue

An action or proceeding over which the district courts have jurisdiction pursuant to section 203 of this title may be brought in any such court in which save for the arbitration agreement an action or proceeding with respect to the controversy between the parties could be brought, or in such court for the district and division which embraces the place designated in the agreement as the place of arbitration if such place is within the United States.

Sec. 205. Removal of cases from State courts

Where the subject matter of an action or proceeding pending in a State court relates to an arbitration agreement or award falling under the Convention, the defendant or the defendants may, at any time before the trial thereof, remove such action or proceeding to the district court of the United States for the district and division embracing the place where the action or proceeding is pending. The procedure for removal of causes otherwise provided by law shall apply, except that the ground for removal provided in this section need not appear on the face of the complaint but may be shown in the petition for removal. For the purposes of Chapter 1 of this title any action or proceeding removed under this section shall be deemed to have been brought in the district court to which it is removed.

Sec. 206. Order to compel arbitration; appointment of arbitrators

A court having jurisdiction under this chapter may direct that arbitration be held in accordance with the agreement at any place therein provided for, whether that place is within or without the United States. Such court may also appoint arbitrators in accordance with the provisions of the agreement.

Sec. 207. Award of arbitrators; confirmation; jurisdiction; proceeding

Within three years after an arbitral award falling under the Convention is made, any party to the arbitration may apply to any court having jurisdiction under this chapter for an order confirming the award as against any other party to the arbitration. The court shall confirm the award unless it finds one of the grounds for refusal or deferral of recognition or enforcement of the award specified in the said Convention.

Sec. 208. Chapter 1; residual application

Chapter 1 applies to actions and proceedings brought under this chapter to the extent that chapter is not in conflict with this chapter or the Convention as ratified by the United States.

APPENDIX 9

EXCERPT FROM THE ENGLISH ARBITRATION ACT 1996

(CHAPTER 23)

PART I

ARBITRATION PURSUANT TO AN ARBITRATION AGREEMENT

Introductory

1. General principles

The provisions of this Part are founded on the following principles, and shall be construed accordingly—

(a) the object of arbitration is to obtain the fair resolution of disputes by an impartial tribunal without unnecessary delay or expense;

(b) the parties should be free to agree how their disputes are resolved, subject only to such safeguards as are necessary in the public interest;

(c) in matters governed by this Part the court should not intervene except as provided by this Part.

2. Scope of application of provisions

(1) The provisions of this Part apply where the seat of the arbitration is in England and Wales or Northern Ireland.

(2) The following sections apply even if the seat of the arbitration is outside England and Wales or Northern Ireland or no seat has been designated or determined—

(a) sections 9 to 11 (stay of legal proceedings, etc.), and

(b) section 66 (enforcement of arbitral awards).

(3) The powers conferred by the following sections apply even if the seat of the arbitration is outside England and Wales or Northern Ireland or no seat has been designated or determined—

(a) section 43 (securing the attendance of witnesses), and

(b) section 44 (court powers exercisable in support of arbitral proceedings);

but the court may refuse to exercise any such power if, in the opinion of the court, the fact that the seat of the arbitration is outside England and Wales or Northern Ireland, or that when designated or determined the seat is likely to be outside England and Wales or Northern Ireland, makes it inappropriate to do so.

(4) The court may exercise a power conferred by any provision of this Part not mentioned in subsection (2) or (3) for the purpose of supporting the arbitral process where—

(a) no seat of the arbitration has been designated or determined, and

(b) by reason of a connection with England and Wales or Northern Ireland the court is satisfied that it is appropriate to do so.

(5) Section 7 (separability of arbitration agreement) and section 8 (death of a party) apply where the law applicable to the arbitration agreement is the law of England and Wales or Northern Ireland even if the seat of the arbitration is outside England and Wales or Northern Ireland or has not been designated or determined.

3. The seat of the arbitration

In this Part "the seat of the arbitration" means the juridical seat of the arbitration designated—

(a) by the parties to the arbitration agreement, or
(b) by any arbitral or other institution or person vested by the parties with powers in that regard, or
(c) by the arbitral tribunal if so authorised by the parties,

or determined, in the absence of any such designation, having regard to the parties' agreement and all the relevant circumstances.

4. Mandatory and non-mandatory provisions

(1) The mandatory provisions of this Part are listed in Schedule 1 and have effect notwithstanding any agreement to the contrary.

(2) The other provisions of this Part (the "non-mandatory provisions") allow the parties to make their own arrangements by agreement but provide rules which apply in the absence of such agreement.

(3) The parties may make such arrangements by agreeing to the application of institutional rules or providing any other means by which a matter may be decided.

(4) It is immaterial whether or not the law applicable to the parties' agreement is the law of England and Wales or, as the case may be, Northern Ireland.

(5) The choice of a law other than the law of England and Wales or Northern Ireland as the applicable law in respect of a matter provided for by a non-mandatory provision of this Part is equivalent to an agreement making provision about that matter.

For this purpose an applicable law determined in accordance with the parties' agreement, or which is objectively determined in the absence of any express or implied choice, shall be treated as chosen by the parties.

5. Agreements to be in writing

(1) The provisions of this Part apply only where the arbitration agreement is in writing, and any other agreement between the parties as to any matter is effective for the purposes of this Part only if in writing.

The expressions "agreement", "agree" and "agreed" shall be construed accordingly.

(2) There is an agreement in writing—

(a) if the agreement is made in writing (whether or not it is signed by the parties),
(b) if the agreement is made by exchange of communications in writing, or
(c) if the agreement is evidenced in writing.

(3) Where parties agree otherwise than in writing by reference to terms which are in writing, they make an agreement in writing.

(4) An agreement is evidenced in writing if an agreement made otherwise than in writing is recorded by one of the parties, or by a third party, with the authority of the parties to the agreement.

(5) An exchange of written submissions in arbitral or legal proceedings in which the existence of an agreement otherwise than in writing is alleged by one party against another party and not denied by the other party in his response constitutes as between those parties an agreement in writing to the effect alleged.

(6) References in this Part to anything being written or in writing include its being recorded by any means.

The arbitration agreement

6. Definition of arbitration agreement

(1) In this Part an "arbitration agreement" means an agreement to submit to arbitration present or future disputes (whether they are contractual or not).

(2) The reference in an agreement to a written form of arbitration clause or to a document containing an arbitration clause constitutes an arbitration agreement if the reference is such as to make that clause part of the agreement.

7. Separability of arbitration agreement

Unless otherwise agreed by the parties, an arbitration agreement which forms or was intended to form part of another agreement (whether or not in writing) shall not be regarded as invalid, non-existent or ineffective because that other agreement is invalid, or did not come into existence or has become ineffective, and it shall for that purpose be treated as a distinct agreement.

8. Whether agreement discharged by death of a party

(1) Unless otherwise agreed by the parties, an arbitration agreement is not discharged by the death of a party and may be enforced by or against the personal representatives of that party.

(2) Subsection (1) does not affect the operation of any enactment or rule of law by virtue of which a substantive right or obligation is extinguished by death.

Stay of legal proceedings

9. Stay of legal proceedings

(1) A party to an arbitration agreement against whom legal proceedings are brought (whether by way of claim or counterclaim) in respect of a matter which under the agreement is to be referred to arbitration may (upon notice to the other parties to the proceedings) apply to the court in which the proceedings have been brought to stay the proceedings so far as they concern that matter.

(2) An application may be made notwithstanding that the matter is to be referred to arbitration only after the exhaustion of other dispute resolution procedures.

(3) An application may not be made by a person before taking the appropriate procedural step (if any) to acknowledge the legal proceedings against him or after he has taken any step in those proceedings to answer the substantive claim.

(4) On an application under this section the court shall grant a stay unless satisfied that the arbitration agreement is null and void, inoperative, or incapable of being performed.

(5) If the court refuses to stay the legal proceedings, any provision that an award is a condition precedent to the bringing of legal proceedings in respect of any matter is of no effect in relation to those proceedings.

10. Reference of interpleader issue to arbitration

(1) Where in legal proceedings relief by way of interpleader is granted and any issue between the claimants is one in respect of which there is an arbitration agreement between them, the court granting the relief shall direct that the issue be determined in accordance with the agreement unless the circumstances are such that proceedings brought by a claimant in respect of the matter would not be stayed.

(2) Where subsection (1) applies but the court does not direct that the issue be determined in accordance with the arbitration agreement, any provision that an award is a condition precedent to the bringing of legal proceedings in respect of any matter shall not affect the determination of that issue by the court.

11. Retention of security where admiralty proceedings Stayed

(1) Where Admiralty proceedings are stayed on the ground that the dispute in question should be submitted to arbitration, the court granting the stay may, if in those proceedings property has been arrested or bail or other security has been given to prevent or obtain release from arrest—

- (a) order that the property arrested be retained as security for the satisfaction of any award given in the arbitration in respect of that dispute, or
- (b) order that the stay of those proceedings be conditional on the provision of equivalent security for the satisfaction of any such award.

(2) Subject to any provision made by rules of court and to any necessary modifications, the same law and practice shall apply in relation to property retained in pursuance of an order as would apply if it were held for the purposes of proceedings in the court making the order.

Commencement of arbitral proceedings

12. Power of court to extend time for beginning arbitral proceedings, etc.

(1) Where an arbitration agreement to refer future disputes to arbitration provides that a claim shall be barred, or the claimant's right extinguished, unless the claimant takes within a time fixed by the agreement some step—

- (a) to begin arbitral proceedings, or

(b) to begin other dispute resolution procedures which must be exhausted before arbitral proceedings can be begun,

the court may by order extend the time for taking that step.

(2) Any party to the arbitration agreement may apply for such an order (upon notice to the other parties), but only after a claim has arisen and after exhausting any available arbitral process for obtaining an extension of time.

(3) The court shall make an order only if satisfied—

(a) that the circumstances are such as were outside the reasonable contemplation of the parties when they agreed the provision in question, and that it would be just to extend the time, or
(b) that the conduct of one party makes it unjust to hold the other party to the strict terms of the provision in question.

(4) The court may extend the time for such period and on such terms as it thinks fit, and may do so whether or not the time previously fixed (by agreement or by a previous order) has expired.

(5) An order under this section does not affect the operation of the Limitation Acts (see section 13).

(6) The leave of the court is required for any appeal from a decision of the court under this section.

13. Application of limitation Acts

(1) The Limitation Acts apply to arbitral proceedings as they apply to legal proceedings.

(2) The court may order that in computing the time prescribed by the Limitation Acts for the commencement of proceedings (including arbitral proceedings) in respect of a dispute which was the subject matter—

(a) of an award which the court orders to be set aside or declares to be of no effect, or
(b) of the affected part of an award which the court orders to be set aside in part, or declares to be in part of no effect,

the period between the commencement of the arbitration and the date of the order referred to in paragraph (a) or (b) shall be excluded.

(3) In determining for the purposes of the Limitation Acts when a cause of action accrued, any provision that an award is a condition precedent to the bringing of legal proceedings in respect of a matter to which an arbitration agreement applies shall be disregarded.

(4) In this Part "the Limitation Acts" means—

(a) in England and Wales, the Limitation Act 1980, the [1984 c.16.] Foreign Limitation Periods Act 1984 and any other enactment (whenever passed) relating to the limitation of actions
(b) in Northern Ireland, the Limitation (Northern Ireland) Order 1989, the Foreign Limitation Periods (Northern Ireland) Order 1985 and any other enactment (whenever passed) relating to the limitation of actions.

14. Commencement of arbitral proceedings

(1) The parties are free to agree when arbitral proceedings are to be regarded as commenced for the purposes of this Part and for the purposes of the Limitation Acts.

(2) If there is no such agreement the following provisions apply.

(3) Where the arbitrator is named or designated in the arbitration agreement, arbitral proceedings are commenced in respect of a matter when one party serves on the other party or parties a notice in writing requiring him or them to submit that matter to the person so named or designated.

(4) Where the arbitrator or arbitrators are to be appointed by the parties, arbitral proceedings are commenced in respect of a matter when one party serves on the other party or parties notice in writing requiring him or them to appoint an arbitrator or to agree to the appointment of an arbitrator in respect of that matter.

(5) Where the arbitrator or arbitrators are to be appointed by a person other than a party to the proceedings, arbitral proceedings are commenced in respect of a matter when one party gives notice in writing to that person requesting him to make the appointment in respect of that matter.

The arbitral tribunal

15. The arbitral tribunal

(1) The parties are free to agree on the number of arbitrators to form the tribunal and whether there is to be a chairman or umpire.

(2) Unless otherwise agreed by the parties, an agreement that the number of arbitrators shall be two or any other even number shall be understood as requiring the appointment of an additional arbitrator as chairman of the tribunal.

(3) If there is no agreement as to the number of arbitrators, the tribunal shall consist of a sole arbitrator.

16. Procedure for appointment of arbitrators

(1) The parties are free to agree on the procedure for appointing the arbitrator or arbitrators, including the procedure for appointing any chairman or umpire.

(2) If or to the extent that there is no such agreement, the following provisions apply.

(3) If the tribunal is to consist of a sole arbitrator, the parties shall jointly appoint the arbitrator not later than 28 days after service of a request in writing by either party to do so.

(4) If the tribunal is to consist of two arbitrators, each party shall appoint one arbitrator not later than 14 days after service of a request in writing by either party to do so.

(5) If the tribunal is to consist of three arbitrators—

- (a) each party shall appoint one arbitrator not later than 14 days after service of a request in writing by either party to do so, and
- (b) the two so appointed shall forthwith appoint a third arbitrator as the chairman of the tribunal.

(6) If the tribunal is to consist of two arbitrators and an umpire—

(a) each party shall appoint one arbitrator not later than 14 days after service of a request in writing by either party to do so, and
(b) the two so appointed may appoint an umpire at any time after they themselves are appointed and shall do so before any substantive hearing or forthwith if they cannot agree on a matter relating to the arbitration.

(7) In any other case (in particular, if there are more than two parties) section 18 applies as in the case of a failure of the agreed appointment procedure.

17. Power in case of default to appoint sole arbitrator

(1) Unless the parties otherwise agree, where each of two parties to an arbitration agreement is to appoint an arbitrator and one party ("the party in default") refuses to do so, or fails to do so within the time specified, the other party, having duly appointed his arbitrator, may give notice in writing to the party in default that he proposes to appoint his arbitrator to act as sole arbitrator.

(2) If the party in default does not within 7 clear days of that notice being given—

(a) make the required appointment, and
(b) notify the other party that he has done so,

the other party may appoint his arbitrator as sole arbitrator whose award shall be binding on both parties as if he had been so appointed by agreement.

(3) Where a sole arbitrator has been appointed under subsection (2), the party in default may (upon notice to the appointing party) apply to the court which may set aside the appointment.

(4) The leave of the court is required for any appeal from a decision of the court under this section.

18. Failure of appointment procedure

(1) The parties are free to agree what is to happen in the event of a failure of the procedure for the appointment of the arbitral tribunal.

There is no failure if an appointment is duly made under section 17 (power in case of default to appoint sole arbitrator), unless that appointment is set aside.

(2) If or to the extent that there is no such agreement any party to the arbitration agreement may (upon notice to the other parties) apply to the court to exercise its powers under this section.

(3) Those powers are—

(a) to give directions as to the making of any necessary appointments;

(b) to direct that the tribunal shall be constituted by such appointments (or any one or more of them) as have been made;

(c) to revoke any appointments already made;

(d) to make any necessary appointments itself.

(4) An appointment made by the court under this section has effect as if made with the agreement of the parties.

(5) The leave of the court is required for any appeal from a decision of the court under this section.

19. Court to have regard to agreed qualifications

In deciding whether to exercise, and in considering how to exercise, any of its powers under section 16 (procedure for appointment of arbitrators) or section 18 (failure of appointment procedure), the court shall have due regard to any agreement of the parties as to the qualifications required of the arbitrators.

20. Chairman

(1) Where the parties have agreed that there is to be a chairman, they are free to agree what the functions of the chairman are to be in relation to the making of decisions, orders and awards.

(2) If or to the extent that there is no such agreement, the following provisions apply.

(3) Decisions, orders and awards shall be made by all or a majority of the arbitrators (including the chairman).

(4) The view of the chairman shall prevail in relation to a decision, order or award in respect of which there is neither unanimity nor a majority under subsection (3).

21. Umpire

(1) Where the parties have agreed that there is to be an umpire, they are free to agree what the functions of the umpire are to be, and in particular—

- (a) whether he is to attend the proceedings, and
- (b) when he is to replace the other arbitrators as the tribunal with power to make decisions, orders and awards.

(2) If or to the extent that there is no such agreement, the following provisions apply.

(3) The umpire shall attend the proceedings and be supplied with the same documents and other materials as are supplied to the other arbitrators.

(4) Decisions, orders and awards shall be made by the other arbitrators unless and until they cannot agree on a matter relating to the arbitration.

In that event they shall forthwith give notice in writing to the parties and the umpire, whereupon the umpire shall replace them as the tribunal with power to make decisions, orders and awards as if he were sole arbitrator.

(5) If the arbitrators cannot agree but fail to give notice of that fact, or if any of them fails to join in the giving of notice, any party to the arbitral proceedings may (upon notice to the other parties and to the tribunal) apply to the court which may order that the umpire shall replace the other arbitrators as the tribunal with power to make decisions, orders and awards as if he were sole arbitrator.

(6) The leave of the court is required for any appeal from a decision of the court under this section.

22. Decision-making where no chairman or umpire

(1) Where the parties agree that there shall be two or more arbitrators with no chairman or umpire, the parties are free to agree how the tribunal is to make decisions, orders and awards.

(2) If there is no such agreement, decisions, orders and awards shall be made by all or a majority of the arbitrators.

23. Revocation of arbitrator's authority

(1) The parties are free to agree in what circumstances the authority of an arbitrator may be revoked.

(2) If or to the extent that there is no such agreement the following provisions apply.

(3) The authority of an arbitrator may not be revoked except—

- (a) by the parties acting jointly, or
- (b) by an arbitral or other institution or person vested by the parties with powers in that regard.

(4) Revocation of the authority of an arbitrator by the parties acting jointly must be agreed in writing unless the parties also agree (whether or not in writing) to terminate the arbitration agreement.

(5) Nothing in this section affects the power of the court—

- (a) to revoke an appointment under section 18 (powers exercisable in case of failure of appointment procedure), or
- (b) to remove an arbitrator on the grounds specified in section 24.

24. Power of court to remove arbitrator

(1) A party to arbitral proceedings may (upon notice to the other parties, to the arbitrator concerned and to any other arbitrator) apply to the court to remove an arbitrator on any of the following grounds—

- (a) that circumstances exist that give rise to justifiable doubts as to his impartiality;
- (b) that he does not possess the qualifications required by the arbitration agreement;
- (c) that he is physically or mentally incapable of conducting the proceedings or there are justifiable doubts as to his capacity to do so;
- (d) that he has refused or failed—
  - (i) properly to conduct the proceedings, or
  - (ii) to use all reasonable despatch in conducting the proceedings or making an award,

and that substantial injustice has been or will be caused to the applicant.

(2) If there is an arbitral or other institution or person vested by the parties with power to remove an arbitrator, the court shall not exercise its power of removal unless satisfied that the applicant has first exhausted any available recourse to that institution or person.

(3) The arbitral tribunal may continue the arbitral proceedings and make an award while an application to the court under this section is pending.

(4) Where the court removes an arbitrator, it may make such order as it thinks fit with respect to his entitlement (if any) to fees or expenses, or the repayment of any fees or expenses already paid.

(5) The arbitrator concerned is entitled to appear and be heard by the court before it makes any order under this section.

(6) The leave of the court is required for any appeal from a decision of the court under this section.

25. Resignation of arbitrator

(1) The parties are free to agree with an arbitrator as to the consequences of his resignation as regards—

(a) his entitlement (if any) to fees or expenses, and
(b) any liability thereby incurred by him.

(2) If or to the extent that there is no such agreement the following provisions apply.

(3) An arbitrator who resigns his appointment may (upon notice to the parties) apply to the court—

(a) to grant him relief from any liability thereby incurred by him, and
(b) to make such order as it thinks fit with respect to his entitlement (if any) to fees or expenses or the repayment of any fees or expenses already paid.

(4) If the court is satisfied that in all the circumstances it was reasonable for the arbitrator to resign, it may grant such relief as is mentioned in subsection (3)(a) on such terms as it thinks fit.

(5) The leave of the court is required for any appeal from a decision of the court under this section.

26. Death of arbitrator or person appointing him

(1) The authority of an arbitrator is personal and ceases on his death.

(2) Unless otherwise agreed by the parties, the death of the person by whom an arbitrator was appointed does not revoke the arbitrator's authority.

27. Filling of vacancy, etc.

(1) Where an arbitrator ceases to hold office, the parties are free to agree—

(a) whether and if so how the vacancy is to be filled,
(b) whether and if so to what extent the previous proceedings should stand, and
(c) what effect (if any) his ceasing to hold office has on any appointment made by him (alone or jointly).

(2) If or to the extent that there is no such agreement, the following provisions apply.

(3) The provisions of sections 16 (procedure for appointment of arbitrators) and 18 (failure of appointment procedure) apply in relation to the filling of the vacancy as in relation to an original appointment.

(4) The tribunal (when reconstituted) shall determine whether and if so to what extent the previous proceedings should stand.

This does not affect any right of a party to challenge those proceedings on any ground which had arisen before the arbitrator ceased to hold office.

(5) His ceasing to hold office does not affect any appointment by him (alone or jointly) of another arbitrator, in particular any appointment of a chairman or umpire.

28. Joint and several liability of parties to arbitrators for fees and expenses

(1) The parties are jointly and severally liable to pay to the arbitrators such reasonable fees and expenses (if any) as are appropriate in the circumstances.

(2) Any party may apply to the court (upon notice to the other parties and to the arbitrators) which may order that the amount of the arbitrators' fees and expenses shall be considered and adjusted by such means and upon such terms as it may direct.

(3) If the application is made after any amount has been paid to the arbitrators by way of fees or expenses, the court may order the repayment of such amount (if any) as is shown to be excessive, but shall not do so unless it is shown that it is reasonable in the circumstances to order repayment.

(4) The above provisions have effect subject to any order of the court under section 24(4) or 25(3)(b) (order as to entitlement to fees or expenses in case of removal or resignation of arbitrator).

(5) Nothing in this section affects any liability of a party to any other party to pay all or any of the costs of the arbitration (see sections 59 to 65) or any contractual right of an arbitrator to payment of his fees and expenses.

(6) In this section references to arbitrators include an arbitrator who has ceased to act and an umpire who has not replaced the other arbitrators.

29. Immunity of arbitrator

(1) An arbitrator is not liable for anything done or omitted in the discharge or purported discharge of his functions as arbitrator unless the act or omission is shown to have been in bad faith.

(2) Subsection (1) applies to an employee or agent of an arbitrator as it applies to the arbitrator himself.

(3) This section does not affect any liability incurred by an arbitrator by reason of his resigning (but see section 25).

Jurisdiction of the arbitral tribunal

30. Competence of tribunal to rule on its own jurisdiction

(1) Unless otherwise agreed by the parties, the arbitral tribunal may rule on its own substantive jurisdiction, that is, as to—

(a) whether there is a valid arbitration agreement,
(b) whether the tribunal is properly constituted, and

(c) what matters have been submitted to arbitration in accordance with the arbitration agreement.

(2) Any such ruling may be challenged by any available arbitral process of appeal or review or in accordance with the provisions of this Part.

31. Objection to substantive jurisdiction of tribunal

(1) An objection that the arbitral tribunal lacks substantive jurisdiction at the outset of the proceedings must be raised by a party not later than the time he takes the first step in the proceedings to contest the merits of any matter in relation to which he challenges the tribunal's jurisdiction.

A party is not precluded from raising such an objection by the fact that he has appointed or participated in the appointment of an arbitrator.

(2) Any objection during the course of the arbitral proceedings that the arbitral tribunal is exceeding its substantive jurisdiction must be made as soon as possible after the matter alleged to be beyond its jurisdiction is raised.

(3) The arbitral tribunal may admit an objection later than the time specified in subsection (1) or (2) if it considers the delay justified.

(4) Where an objection is duly taken to the tribunal's substantive jurisdiction and the tribunal has power to rule on its own jurisdiction, it may—

(a) rule on the matter in an award as to jurisdiction, or
(b) deal with the objection in its award on the merits.

If the parties agree which of these courses the tribunal should take, the tribunal shall proceed accordingly.

(5) The tribunal may in any case, and shall if the parties so agree, stay proceedings whilst an application is made to the court under section 32 (determination of preliminary point of jurisdiction).

32. Determination of preliminary point of jurisdiction

(1) The court may, on the application of a party to arbitral proceedings (upon notice to the other parties), determine any question as to the substantive jurisdiction of the tribunal.

A party may lose the right to object (see section 73).

(2) An application under this section shall not be considered unless—

(a) it is made with the agreement in writing of all the other parties to the proceedings, or
(b) it is made with the permission of the tribunal and the court is satisfied—
   (i) that the determination of the question is likely to produce substantial savings in costs,
   (ii) that the application was made without delay, and
   (iii) that there is good reason why the matter should be decided by the court.

(3) An application under this section, unless made with the agreement of all the other parties to the proceedings, shall state the grounds on which it is said that the matter should be decided by the court.

(4) Unless otherwise agreed by the parties, the arbitral tribunal may continue the arbitral proceedings and make an award while an application to the court under this section is pending.

(5) Unless the court gives leave, no appeal lies from a decision of the court whether the conditions specified in subsection (2) are met.

(6) The decision of the court on the question of jurisdiction shall be treated as a judgment of the court for the purposes of an appeal.

But no appeal lies without the leave of the court which shall not be given unless the court considers that the question involves a point of law which is one of general importance or is one which for some other special reason should be considered by the Court of Appeal.

The arbitral proceedings

33. General duty of the tribunal

(1) The tribunal shall—

(a) act fairly and impartially as between the parties, giving each party a reasonable opportunity of putting his case and dealing with that of his opponent, and
(b) adopt procedures suitable to the circumstances of the particular case, avoiding unnecessary delay or expense, so as to provide a fair means for the resolution of the matters falling to be determined.

(2) The tribunal shall comply with that general duty in conducting the arbitral proceedings, in its decisions on matters of procedure and evidence and in the exercise of all other powers conferred on it.

34. Procedural and evidential matters

(1) It shall be for the tribunal to decide all procedural and evidential matters, subject to the right of the parties to agree any matter.

(2) Procedural and evidential matters include—

(a) when and where any part of the proceedings is to be held;
(b) the language or languages to be used in the proceedings and whether translations of any relevant documents are to be supplied;
(c) whether any and if so what form of written statements of claim and defence are to be used, when these should be supplied and the extent to which such statements can be later amended;
(d) whether any and if so which documents or classes of documents should be disclosed between and produced by the parties and at what stage;
(e) whether any and if so what questions should be put to and answered by the respective parties and when and in what form this should be done;
(f) whether to apply strict rules of evidence (or any other rules) as to the admissibility, relevance or weight of any material (oral, written or other) sought to be tendered on any matters of fact or opinion, and the time, manner and form in which such material should be exchanged and presented;
(g) whether and to what extent the tribunal should itself take the initiative in ascertaining the facts and the law;

(h) whether and to what extent there should be oral or written evidence or submissions.

(3) The tribunal may fix the time within which any directions given by it are to be complied with, and may if it thinks fit extend the time so fixed (whether or not it has expired).

35. Consolidation of proceedings and concurrent hearings

(1) The parties are free to agree—

(a) that the arbitral proceedings shall be consolidated with other arbitral proceedings, or
(b) that concurrent hearings shall be held,

on such terms as may be agreed.

(2) Unless the parties agree to confer such power on the tribunal, the tribunal has no power to order consolidation of proceedings or concurrent hearings.

36. Legal or other representation

Unless otherwise agreed by the parties, a party to arbitral proceedings may be represented in the proceedings by a lawyer or other person chosen by him.

37. Power to appoint experts, legal advisers or assessors

(1) Unless otherwise agreed by the parties—

(a) the tribunal may—
  (i) appoint experts or legal advisers to report to it and the parties, or
  (ii) appoint assessors to assist it on technical matters,

and may allow any such expert, legal adviser or assessor to attend the proceedings; and

(b) the parties shall be given a reasonable opportunity to comment on any information, opinion or advice offered by any such person.

(2) The fees and expenses of an expert, legal adviser or assessor appointed by the tribunal for which the arbitrators are liable are expenses of the arbitrators for the purposes of this Part.

38. General powers exercisable by the tribunal

(1) The parties are free to agree on the powers exercisable by the arbitral tribunal for the purposes of and in relation to the proceedings.

(2) Unless otherwise agreed by the parties the tribunal has the following powers.

(3) The tribunal may order a claimant to provide security for the costs of the arbitration.

This power shall not be exercised on the ground that the claimant is—

(a) an individual ordinarily resident outside the United Kingdom, or
(b) a corporation or association incorporated or formed under the law of a country outside the United Kingdom, or whose central management and control is exercised outside the United Kingdom.

(4) The tribunal may give directions in relation to any property which is the subject of the proceedings or as to which any question arises in the proceedings, and which is owned by or is in the possession of a party to the proceedings—

- (a) for the inspection, photographing, preservation, custody or detention of the property by the tribunal, an expert or a party, or
- (b) ordering that samples be taken from, or any observation be made of or experiment conducted upon, the property.

(5) The tribunal may direct that a party or witness shall be examined on oath or affirmation, and may for that purpose administer any necessary oath or take any necessary affirmation.

(6) The tribunal may give directions to a party for the preservation for the purposes of the proceedings of any evidence in his custody or control.

39. Power to make provisional awards

(1) The parties are free to agree that the tribunal shall have power to order on a provisional basis any relief which it would have power to grant in a final award.

(2) This includes, for instance, making—

- (a) a provisional order for the payment of money or the disposition of property as between the parties, or
- (b) an order to make an interim payment on account of the costs of the arbitration.

(3) Any such order shall be subject to the tribunal's final adjudication; and the tribunal's final award, on the merits or as to costs, shall take account of any such order.

(4) Unless the parties agree to confer such power on the tribunal, the tribunal has no such power.

This does not affect its powers under section 47 (awards on different issues, etc.).

40. General duty of parties

(1) The parties shall do all things necessary for the proper and expeditious conduct of the arbitral proceedings.

(2) This includes—

- (a) complying without delay with any determination of the tribunal as to procedural or evidential matters, or with any order or directions of the tribunal, and
- (b) where appropriate, taking without delay any necessary steps to obtain a decision of the court on a preliminary question of jurisdiction or law (see sections 32 and 45).

41. Powers of tribunal in case of party's default

(1) The parties are free to agree on the powers of the tribunal in case of a party's failure to do something necessary for the proper and expeditious conduct of the arbitration.

(2) Unless otherwise agreed by the parties, the following provisions apply.

(3) If the tribunal is satisfied that there has been inordinate and inexcusable delay on the part of the claimant in pursuing his claim and that the delay—

(a) gives rise, or is likely to give rise, to a substantial risk that it is not possible to have a fair resolution of the issues in that claim, or
(b) has caused, or is likely to cause, serious prejudice to the respondent,

the tribunal may make an award dismissing the claim.

(4) If without showing sufficient cause a party—

(a) fails to attend or be represented at an oral hearing of which due notice was given, or
(b) where matters are to be dealt with in writing, fails after due notice to submit written evidence or make written submissions,

the tribunal may continue the proceedings in the absence of that party or, as the case may be, without any written evidence or submissions on his behalf, and may make an award on the basis of the evidence before it.

(5) If without showing sufficient cause a party fails to comply with any order or directions of the tribunal, the tribunal may make a peremptory order to the same effect, prescribing such time for compliance with it as the tribunal considers appropriate.

(6) If a claimant fails to comply with a peremptory order of the tribunal to provide security for costs, the tribunal may make an award dismissing his claim.

(7) If a party fails to comply with any other kind of peremptory order, then, without prejudice to section 42 (enforcement by court of tribunal's peremptory orders), the tribunal may do any of the following—

(a) direct that the party in default shall not be entitled to rely upon any allegation or material which was the subject matter of the order;
(b) draw such adverse inferences from the act of non-compliance as the circumstances justify;
(c) proceed to an award on the basis of such materials as have been properly provided to it;
(d) make such order as it thinks fit as to the payment of costs of the arbitration incurred in consequence of the non-compliance.

Powers of court in relation to arbitral proceedings

42. Enforcement of peremptory orders of tribunal

(1) Unless otherwise agreed by the parties, the court may make an order requiring a party to comply with a peremptory order made by the tribunal.

(2) An application for an order under this section may be made—

(a) by the tribunal (upon notice to the parties),
(b) by a party to the arbitral proceedings with the permission of the tribunal (and upon notice to the other parties), or
(c) where the parties have agreed that the powers of the court under this section shall be available.

(3) The court shall not act unless it is satisfied that the applicant has exhausted any available arbitral process in respect of failure to comply with the tribunal's order.

(4) No order shall be made under this section unless the court is satisfied that the person to whom the tribunal's order was directed has failed to comply with it within the time prescribed in the order or, if no time was prescribed, within a reasonable time.

(5) The leave of the court is required for any appeal from a decision of the court under this section.

43. Securing the attendance of witnesses

(1) A party to arbitral proceedings may use the same court procedures as are available in relation to legal proceedings to secure the attendance before the tribunal of a witness in order to give oral testimony or to produce documents or other material evidence.

(2) This may only be done with the permission of the tribunal or the agreement of the other parties.

(3) The court procedures may only be used if—

- (a) the witness is in the United Kingdom, and
- (b) the arbitral proceedings are being conducted in England and Wales or, as the case may be, Northern Ireland.

(4) A person shall not be compelled by virtue of this section to produce any document or other material evidence which he could not be compelled to produce in legal proceedings.

44. Court powers exercisable in support of arbitral proceedings

(1) Unless otherwise agreed by the parties, the court has for the purposes of and in relation to arbitral proceedings the same power of making orders about the matters listed below as it has for the purposes of and in relation to legal proceedings.

(2) Those matters are—

- (a) the taking of the evidence of witnesses;
- (b) the preservation of evidence;
- (c) making orders relating to property which is the subject of the proceedings or as to which any question arises in the proceedings—
  - (i) for the inspection, photographing, preservation, custody or detention of the property, or
  - (ii) ordering that samples be taken from, or any observation be made of or experiment conducted upon, the property;

and for that purpose authorising any person to enter any premises in the possession or control of a party to the arbitration;

- (d) the sale of any goods the subject of the proceedings;
- (e) the granting of an interim injunction or the appointment of a receiver.

(3) If the case is one of urgency, the court may, on the application of a party or proposed party to the arbitral proceedings, make such orders as it thinks necessary for the purpose of preserving evidence or assets.

(4) If the case is not one of urgency, the court shall act only on the application of a party to the arbitral proceedings (upon notice to the other parties and to the tribunal) made with the permission of the tribunal or the agreement in writing of the other parties.

(5) In any case the court shall act only if or to the extent that the arbitral tribunal, and any arbitral or other institution or person vested by the parties with power in that regard, has no power or is unable for the time being to act effectively.

(6) If the court so orders, an order made by it under this section shall cease to have effect in whole or in part on the order of the tribunal or of any such arbitral or other institution or person having power to act in relation to the subject-matter of the order.

(7) The leave of the court is required for any appeal from a decision of the court under this section.

45. Determination of preliminary point of law

(1) Unless otherwise agreed by the parties, the court may on the application of a party to arbitral proceedings (upon notice to the other parties) determine any question of law arising in the course of the proceedings which the court is satisfied substantially affects the rights of one or more of the parties.

An agreement to dispense with reasons for the tribunal's award shall be considered an agreement to exclude the court's jurisdiction under this section.

(2) An application under this section shall not be considered unless—

- (a) it is made with the agreement of all the other parties to the proceedings, or
- (b) it is made with the permission of the tribunal and the court is satisfied—
  - (i) that the determination of the question is likely to produce substantial savings in costs, and
  - (ii) that the application was made without delay.

(3) The application shall identify the question of law to be determined and, unless made with the agreement of all the other parties to the proceedings, shall state the grounds on which it is said that the question should be decided by the court.

(4) Unless otherwise agreed by the parties, the arbitral tribunal may continue the arbitral proceedings and make an award while an application to the court under this section is pending.

(5) Unless the court gives leave, no appeal lies from a decision of the court whether the conditions specified in subsection (2) are met.

(6) The decision of the court on the question of law shall be treated as a judgment of the court for the purposes of an appeal.

But no appeal lies without the leave of the court which shall not be given unless the court considers that the question is one of general importance, or is one which for some other special reason should be considered by the Court of Appeal.

The award

46. Rules applicable to substance of dispute

(1) The arbitral tribunal shall decide the dispute—

(a) in accordance with the law chosen by the parties as applicable to the substance of the dispute, or
(b) if the parties so agree, in accordance with such other considerations as are agreed by them or determined by the tribunal.

(2) For this purpose the choice of the laws of a country shall be understood to refer to the substantive laws of that country and not its conflict of laws rules.

(3) If or to the extent that there is no such choice or agreement, the tribunal shall apply the law determined by the conflict of laws rules which it considers applicable.

47. Awards on different issues, etc.

(1) Unless otherwise agreed by the parties, the tribunal may make more than one award at different times on different aspects of the matters to be determined.

(2) The tribunal may, in particular, make an award relating—

(a) to an issue affecting the whole claim, or
(b) to a part only of the claims or cross-claims submitted to it for decision.

(3) If the tribunal does so, it shall specify in its award the issue, or the claim or part of a claim, which is the subject matter of the award.

48. Remedies

(1) The parties are free to agree on the powers exercisable by the arbitral tribunal as regards remedies.

(2) Unless otherwise agreed by the parties, the tribunal has the following powers.

(3) The tribunal may make a declaration as to any matter to be determined in the proceedings.

(4) The tribunal may order the payment of a sum of money, in any currency.

(5) The tribunal has the same powers as the court—

(a) to order a party to do or refrain from doing anything;
(b) to order specific performance of a contract (other than a contract relating to land);
(c) to order the rectification, setting aside or cancellation of a deed or other document.

49. Interest

(1) The parties are free to agree on the powers of the tribunal as regards the award of interest.

(2) Unless otherwise agreed by the parties the following provisions apply.

(3) The tribunal may award simple or compound interest from such dates, at such rates and with such rests as it considers meets the justice of the case—

(a) on the whole or part of any amount awarded by the tribunal, in respect of any period up to the date of the award;

(b) on the whole or part of any amount claimed in the arbitration and outstanding at the commencement of the arbitral proceedings but paid before the award was made, in respect of any period up to the date of payment.

(4) The tribunal may award simple or compound interest from the date of the award (or any later date) until payment, at such rates and with such rests as it considers meets the justice of the case, on the outstanding amount of any award (including any award of interest under subsection (3) and any award as to costs).

(5) References in this section to an amount awarded by the tribunal include an amount payable in consequence of a declaratory award by the tribunal.

(6) The above provisions do not affect any other power of the tribunal to award interest.

50. Extension of time for making award

(1) Where the time for making an award is limited by or in pursuance of the arbitration agreement, then, unless otherwise agreed by the parties, the court may in accordance with the following provisions by order extend that time.

(2) An application for an order under this section may be made—

(a) by the tribunal (upon notice to the parties), or
(b) by any party to the proceedings (upon notice to the tribunal and the other parties),

but only after exhausting any available arbitral process for obtaining an extension of time.

(3) The court shall only make an order if satisfied that a substantial injustice would otherwise be done.

(4) The court may extend the time for such period and on such terms as it thinks fit, and may do so whether or not the time previously fixed (by or under the agreement or by a previous order) has expired.

(5) The leave of the court is required for any appeal from a decision of the court under this section.

51. Settlement

(1) If during arbitral proceedings the parties settle the dispute, the following provisions apply unless otherwise agreed by the parties.

(2) The tribunal shall terminate the substantive proceedings and, if so requested by the parties and not objected to by the tribunal, shall record the settlement in the form of an agreed award.

(3) An agreed award shall state that it is an award of the tribunal and shall have the same status and effect as any other award on the merits of the case.

(4) The following provisions of this Part relating to awards (sections 52 to 58) apply to an agreed award.

(5) Unless the parties have also settled the matter of the payment of the costs of the arbitration, the provisions of this Part relating to costs (sections 59 to 65) continue to apply.

52. Form of award

(1) The parties are free to agree on the form of an award.

(2) If or to the extent that there is no such agreement, the following provisions apply.

(3) The award shall be in writing signed by all the arbitrators or all those assenting to the award.

(4) The award shall contain the reasons for the award unless it is an agreed award or the parties have agreed to dispense with reasons.

(5) The award shall state the seat of the arbitration and the date when the award is made.

53. Place where award treated as made

Unless otherwise agreed by the parties, where the seat of the arbitration is in England and Wales or Northern Ireland, any award in the proceedings shall be treated as made there, regardless of where it was signed, despatched or delivered to any of the parties.

54. Date of award

(1) Unless otherwise agreed by the parties, the tribunal may decide what is to be taken to be the date on which the award was made.

(2) In the absence of any such decision, the date of the award shall be taken to be the date on which it is signed by the arbitrator or, where more than one arbitrator signs the award, by the last of them.

55. Notification of award

(1) The parties are free to agree on the requirements as to notification of the award to the parties.

(2) If there is no such agreement, the award shall be notified to the parties by service on them of copies of the award, which shall be done without delay after the award is made.

(3) Nothing in this section affects section 56 (power to withhold award in case of non-payment).

56. Power to withhold award in case of non-payment

(1) The tribunal may refuse to deliver an award to the parties except upon full payment of the fees and expenses of the arbitrators.

(2) If the tribunal refuses on that ground to deliver an award, a party to the arbitral proceedings may (upon notice to the other parties and the tribunal) apply to the court, which may order that—

- (a) the tribunal shall deliver the award on the payment into court by the applicant of the fees and expenses demanded, or such lesser amount as the court may specify,
- (b) the amount of the fees and expenses properly payable shall be determined by such means and upon such terms as the court may direct, and
- (c) out of the money paid into court there shall be paid out such fees and expenses as may be found to be properly payable and the balance of the money (if any) shall be paid out to the applicant.

(3) For this purpose the amount of fees and expenses properly payable is the amount the applicant is liable to pay under section 28 or any agreement relating to the payment of the arbitrators.

(4) No application to the court may be made where there is any available arbitral process for appeal or review of the amount of the fees or expenses demanded.

(5) References in this section to arbitrators include an arbitrator who has ceased to act and an umpire who has not replaced the other arbitrators.

(6) The above provisions of this section also apply in relation to any arbitral or other institution or person vested by the parties with powers in relation to the delivery of the tribunal's award.

As they so apply, the references to the fees and expenses of the arbitrators shall be construed as including the fees and expenses of that institution or person.

(7) The leave of the court is required for any appeal from a decision of the court under this section.

(8) Nothing in this section shall be construed as excluding an application under section 28 where payment has been made to the arbitrators in order to obtain the award.

57. Correction of award or additional award

(1) The parties are free to agree on the powers of the tribunal to correct an award or make an additional award.

(2) If or to the extent there is no such agreement, the following provisions apply.

(3) The tribunal may on its own initiative or on the application of a party—

- (a) correct an award so as to remove any clerical mistake or error arising from an accidental slip or omission or clarify or remove any ambiguity in the award, or
- (b) make an additional award in respect of any claim (including a claim for interest or costs) which was presented to the tribunal but was not dealt with in the award.

These powers shall not be exercised without first affording the other parties a reasonable opportunity to make representations to the tribunal.

(4) Any application for the exercise of those powers must be made within 28 days of the date of the award or such longer period as the parties may agree.

(5) Any correction of an award shall be made within 28 days of the date the application was received by the tribunal or, where the correction is made by the tribunal on its own initiative, within 28 days of the date of the award or, in either case, such longer period as the parties may agree.

(6) Any additional award shall be made within 56 days of the date of the original award or such longer period as the parties may agree.

(7) Any correction of an award shall form part of the award.

58. Effect of award

(1) Unless otherwise agreed by the parties, an award made by the tribunal pursuant to an arbitration agreement is final and binding both on the parties and on any persons claiming through or under them.

(2) This does not affect the right of a person to challenge the award by any available arbitral process of appeal or review or in accordance with the provisions of this Part.

Costs of the arbitration

59. Costs of the arbitration

(1) References in this Part to the costs of the arbitration are to—

(a) the arbitrators' fees and expenses,
(b) the fees and expenses of any arbitral institution concerned, and
(c) the legal or other costs of the parties.

(2) Any such reference includes the costs of or incidental to any proceedings to determine the amount of the recoverable costs of the arbitration (see section 63).

60. Agreement to pay costs in any event

An agreement which has the effect that a party is to pay the whole or part of the costs of the arbitration in any event is only valid if made after the dispute in question has arisen.

61. Award of costs

(1) The tribunal may make an award allocating the costs of the arbitration as between the parties, subject to any agreement of the parties.

(2) Unless the parties otherwise agree, the tribunal shall award costs on the general principle that costs should follow the event except where it appears to the tribunal that in the circumstances this is not appropriate in relation to the whole or part of the costs.

62. Effect of agreement or award about costs

Unless the parties otherwise agree, any obligation under an agreement between them as to how the costs of the arbitration are to be borne, or under an award allocating the costs of the arbitration, extends only to such costs as are recoverable.

63. The recoverable costs of the arbitration

(1) The parties are free to agree what costs of the arbitration are recoverable.

(2) If or to the extent there is no such agreement, the following provisions apply.

(3) The tribunal may determine by award the recoverable costs of the arbitration on such basis as it thinks fit.

If it does so, it shall specify—

(a) the basis on which it has acted, and
(b) the items of recoverable costs and the amount referable to each.

(4) If the tribunal does not determine the recoverable costs of the arbitration, any party to the arbitral proceedings may apply to the court (upon notice to the other parties) which may—

(a) determine the recoverable costs of the arbitration on such basis as it thinks fit, or
(b) order that they shall be determined by such means and upon such terms as it may specify.

(5) Unless the tribunal or the court determines otherwise—

(a) the recoverable costs of the arbitration shall be determined on the basis that there shall be allowed a reasonable amount in respect of all costs reasonably incurred, and
(b) any doubt as to whether costs were reasonably incurred or were reasonable in amount shall be resolved in favour of the paying party.

(6) The above provisions have effect subject to section 64 (recoverable fees and expenses of arbitrators).

(7) Nothing in this section affects any right of the arbitrators, any expert, legal adviser or assessor appointed by the tribunal, or any arbitral institution, to payment of their fees and expenses.

64. Recoverable fees and expenses of arbitrators

(1) Unless otherwise agreed by the parties, the recoverable costs of the arbitration shall include in respect of the fees and expenses of the arbitrators only such reasonable fees and expenses as are appropriate in the circumstances.

(2) If there is any question as to what reasonable fees and expenses are appropriate in the circumstances, and the matter is not already before the court on an application under section 63(4), the court may on the application of any party (upon notice to the other parties)—

(a) determine the matter, or
(b) order that it be determined by such means and upon such terms as the court may specify.

(3) Subsection (1) has effect subject to any order of the court under section 24(4) or 25(3)(b) (order as to entitlement to fees or expenses in case of removal or resignation of arbitrator).

(4) Nothing in this section affects any right of the arbitrator to payment of his fees and expenses.

65. Power to limit recoverable costs

(1) Unless otherwise agreed by the parties, the tribunal may direct that the recoverable costs of the arbitration, or of any part of the arbitral proceedings, shall be limited to a specified amount.

(2) Any direction may be made or varied at any stage, but this must be done sufficiently in advance of the incurring of costs to which it relates, or the taking of any steps in the proceedings which may be affected by it, for the limit to be taken into account.

Powers of the court in relation to award

66. Enforcement of the award

(1) An award made by the tribunal pursuant to an arbitration agreement may, by leave of the court, be enforced in the same manner as a judgment or order of the court to the same effect.

(2) Where leave is so given, judgment may be entered in terms of the award.

(3) Leave to enforce an award shall not be given where, or to the extent that, the person against whom it is sought to be enforced shows that the tribunal lacked substantive jurisdiction to make the award.

The right to raise such an objection may have been lost (see section 73).

(4) Nothing in this section affects the recognition or enforcement of an award under any other enactment or rule of law, in particular under Part II of the [1950 c.27] Arbitration Act 1950 (enforcement of awards under Geneva Convention) or the provisions of Part III of this Act relating to the recognition and enforcement of awards under the New York Convention or by an action on the award.

67. Challenging the award: substantive jurisdiction

(1) A party to arbitral proceedings may (upon notice to the other parties and to the tribunal) apply to the court—

- (a) challenging any award of the arbitral tribunal as to its substantive jurisdiction; or
- (b) for an order declaring an award made by the tribunal on the merits to be of no effect, in whole or in part, because the tribunal did not have substantive jurisdiction.

A party may lose the right to object (see section 73) and the right to apply is subject to the restrictions in section 70(2) and (3).

(2) The arbitral tribunal may continue the arbitral proceedings and make a further award while an application to the court under this section is pending in relation to an award as to jurisdiction.

(3) On an application under this section challenging an award of the arbitral tribunal as to its substantive jurisdiction, the court may by order—

- (a) confirm the award,
- (b) vary the award, or
- (c) set aside the award in whole or in part.

(4) The leave of the court is required for any appeal from a decision of the court under this section.

68. Challenging the award: serious irregularity

(1) A party to arbitral proceedings may (upon notice to the other parties and to the tribunal) apply to the court challenging an award in the proceedings on the ground of serious irregularity affecting the tribunal, the proceedings or the award.

A party may lose the right to object (see section 73) and the right to apply is subject to the restrictions in section 70(2) and (3).

(2) Serious irregularity means an irregularity of one or more of the following kinds which the court considers has caused or will cause substantial injustice to the applicant—

(a) failure by the tribunal to comply with section 33 (general duty of tribunal);
(b) the tribunal exceeding its powers (otherwise than by exceeding its substantive jurisdiction: see section 67);
(c) failure by the tribunal to conduct the proceedings in accordance with the procedure agreed by the parties;
(d) failure by the tribunal to deal with all the issues that were put to it;
(e) any arbitral or other institution or person vested by the parties with powers in relation to the proceedings or the award exceeding its powers;
(f) uncertainty or ambiguity as to the effect of the award;
(g) the award being obtained by fraud or the award or the way in which it was procured being contrary to public policy;
(h) failure to comply with the requirements as to the form of the award; or
(i) any irregularity in the conduct of the proceedings or in the award which is admitted by the tribunal or by any arbitral or other institution or person vested by the parties with powers in relation to the proceedings or the award.

(3) If there is shown to be serious irregularity affecting the tribunal, the proceedings or the award, the court may—

(a) remit the award to the tribunal, in whole or in part, for reconsideration,
(b) set the award aside in whole or in part, or
(c) declare the award to be of no effect, in whole or in part.

The court shall not exercise its power to set aside or to declare an award to be of no effect, in whole or in part, unless it is satisfied that it would be inappropriate to remit the matters in question to the tribunal for reconsideration.

(4) The leave of the court is required for any appeal from a decision of the court under this section.

69. Appeal on point of law

(1) Unless otherwise agreed by the parties, a party to arbitral proceedings may (upon notice to the other parties and to the tribunal) appeal to the court on a question of law arising out of an award made in the proceedings.

An agreement to dispense with reasons for the tribunal's award shall be considered an agreement to exclude the court's jurisdiction under this section.

(2) An appeal shall not be brought under this section except—

(a) with the agreement of all the other parties to the proceedings, or
(b) with the leave of the court.

The right to appeal is also subject to the restrictions in section 70(2) and (3).

(3) Leave to appeal shall be given only if the court is satisfied—

(a) that the determination of the question will substantially affect the rights of one or more of the parties,

(b) that the question is one which the tribunal was asked to determine,
(c) that, on the basis of the findings of fact in the award—
  (i) the decision of the tribunal on the question is obviously wrong, or
  (ii) the question is one of general public importance and the decision of the tribunal is at least open to serious doubt, and
(d) that, despite the agreement of the parties to resolve the matter by arbitration, it is just and proper in all the circumstances for the court to determine the question.

(4) An application for leave to appeal under this section shall identify the question of law to be determined and state the grounds on which it is alleged that leave to appeal should be granted.

(5) The court shall determine an application for leave to appeal under this section without a hearing unless it appears to the court that a hearing is required.

(6) The leave of the court is required for any appeal from a decision of the court under this section to grant or refuse leave to appeal.

(7) On an appeal under this section the court may be order—

(a) confirm the award,
(b) vary the award,
(c) remit the award to the tribunal, in whole or in part, for reconsideration in the light of the court's determination, or
(d) set aside the award in whole or in part.

The court shall not exercise its power to set aside an award, in whole or in part, unless it is satisfied that it would be inappropriate to remit the matters in question to the tribunal for reconsideration.

(8) The decision of the court on an appeal under this section shall be treated as a judgment of the court for the purposes of a further appeal.

But no such appeal lies without the leave of the court which shall not be given unless the court considers that the question is one of general importance or is one which for some other special reason should be considered by the Court of Appeal.

70. Challenge or appeal: supplementary provisions

(1) The following provisions apply to an application or appeal under section 67, 68 or 69.

(2) An application or appeal may not be brought if the applicant or appellant has not first exhausted—

(a) any available arbitral process of appeal or review, and
(b) any available recourse under section 57 (correction of award or additional award).

(3) Any application or appeal must be brought within 28 days of the date of the award or, if there has been any arbitral process of appeal or review, of the date when the applicant or appellant was notified of the result of that process.

(4) If on an application or appeal it appears to the court that the award—

(a) does not contain the tribunal's reasons, or
(b) does not set out the tribunal's reasons in sufficient detail to enable the court properly to consider the application or appeal,

the court may order the tribunal to state the reasons for its award in sufficient detail for that purpose.

(5) Where the court makes an order under subsection (4), it may make such further order as it thinks fit with respect to any additional costs of the arbitration resulting from its order.

(6) The court may order the applicant or appellant to provide security for the costs of the application or appeal, and may direct that the application or appeal be dismissed if the order is not complied with.

The power to order security for costs shall not be exercised on the ground that the applicant or appellant is—

- (a) an individual ordinarily resident outside the United Kingdom, or
- (b) a corporation or association incorporated or formed under the law of a country outside the United Kingdom, or whose central management and control is exercised outside the United Kingdom.

(7) The court may order that any money payable under the award shall be brought into court or otherwise secured pending the determination of the application or appeal, and may direct that the application or appeal be dismissed if the order is not complied with.

(8) The court may grant leave to appeal subject to conditions to the same or similar effect as an order under subsection (6) or (7).

This does not affect the general discretion of the court to grant leave subject to conditions.

71. Challenge or appeal: effect of order of court

(1) The following provisions have effect where the court makes an order under section 67, 68 or 69 with respect to an award.

(2) Where the award is varied, the variation has effect as part of the tribunal's award.

(3) Where the award is remitted to the tribunal, in whole or in part, for reconsideration, the tribunal shall make a fresh award in respect of the matters remitted within three months of the date of the order for remission or such longer or shorter period as the court may direct.

(4) Where the award is set aside or declared to be of no effect, in whole or in part, the court may also order that any provision that an award is a condition precedent to the bringing of legal proceedings in respect of a matter to which the arbitration agreement applies, is of no effect as regards the subject matter of the award or, as the case may be, the relevant part of the award.

Miscellaneous

72. Saving for rights of person who takes no part in proceedings

(1) A person alleged to be a party to arbitral proceedings but who takes no part in the proceedings may question—

- (a) whether there is a valid arbitration agreement,
- (b) whether the tribunal is properly constituted, or
- (c) what matters have been submitted to arbitration in accordance with the arbitration agreement,

by proceedings in the court for a declaration or injunction or other appropriate relief.

(2) He also has the same right as a party to the arbitral proceedings to challenge an award—

(a) by an application under section 67 on the ground of lack of substantive jurisdiction in relation to him, or
(b) by an application under section 68 on the ground of serious irregularity (within the meaning of that section) affecting him;

and section 70(2) (duty to exhaust arbitral procedures) does not apply in his case.

73. Loss of right to object

(1) If a party to arbitral proceedings takes part, or continues to take part, in the proceedings without making, either forthwith or within such time as is allowed by the arbitration agreement or the tribunal or by any provision of this Part, any objection—

(a) that the tribunal lacks substantive jurisdiction,
(b) that the proceedings have been improperly conducted,
(c) that there has been a failure to comply with the arbitration agreement or with any provision of this Part, or
(d) that there has been any other irregularity affecting the tribunal or the proceedings,

he may not raise that objection later, before the tribunal or the court, unless he shows that, at the time he took part or continued to take part in the proceedings, he did not know and could not with reasonable diligence have discovered the grounds for the objection.

(2) Where the arbitral tribunal rules that it has substantive jurisdiction and a party to arbitral proceedings who could have questioned that ruling—

(a) by any available arbitral process of appeal or review, or
(b) by challenging the award,

does not do so, or does not do so within the time allowed by the arbitration agreement or any provision of this Part, he may not object later to the tribunal's substantive jurisdiction on any ground which was the subject of that ruling.

74. Immunity of arbitral institutions, etc.

(1) An arbitral or other institution or person designated or requested by the parties to appoint or nominate an arbitrator is not liable for anything done or omitted in the discharge or purported discharge of that function unless the act or omission is shown to have been in bad faith.

(2) An arbitral or other institution or person by whom an arbitrator is appointed or nominated is not liable, by reason of having appointed or nominated him, for anything done or omitted by the arbitrator (or his employees or agents) in the discharge or purported discharge of his functions as arbitrator.

(3) The above provisions apply to an employee or agent of an arbitral or other institution or person as they apply to the institution or person himself.

75. Charge to secure payment of solicitors' costs

The powers of the court to make declarations and orders under section 73 of the [1974 c.47.] Solicitors Act 1974 or Article 71H of the [S.I. 1976/582 (N.I. 12)] Solicitors (Northern Ireland) Order 1976 (power to charge property recovered in the proceedings with the payment of solicitors' costs) may be exercised in relation to arbitral proceedings as if those proceedings were proceedings in the court.

Supplementary

76. Service of notices, etc.

(1) The parties are free to agree on the manner of service of any notice or other document required or authorised to be given or served in pursuance of the arbitration agreement or for the purposes of the arbitral proceedings.

(2) If or to the extent that there is no such agreement the following provisions apply.

(3) A notice or other document may be served on a person by any effective means.

(4) If a notice or other document is addressed, pre-paid and delivered by post—

- (a) to the addressee's last known principal residence or, if he is or has been carrying on a trade, profession or business, his last known principal business address, or
- (b) where the addressee is a body corporate, to the body's registered or principal office,

it shall be treated as effectively served.

(5) This section does not apply to the service of documents for the purposes of legal proceedings, for which provision is made by rules of court.

(6) References in this Part to a notice or other document include any form of communication in writing and references to giving or serving a notice or other document shall be construed accordingly.

77. Powers of court in relation to service of documents

(1) This section applies where service of a document on a person in the manner agreed by the parties, or in accordance with provisions of section 76 having effect in default of agreement, is not reasonably practicable.

(2) Unless otherwise agreed by the parties, the court may make such order as it thinks fit—

- (a) for service in such manner as the court may direct, or
- (b) dispensing with service of the document.

(3) Any party to the arbitration agreement may apply for an order, but only after exhausting any available arbitral process for resolving the matter.

(4) The leave of the court is required for any appeal from a decision of the court under this section.

78. Reckoning periods of time

(1) The parties are free to agree on the method of reckoning periods of time for the purposes of any provision agreed by them or any provision of this Part having effect in default of such agreement.

(2) If or to the extent there is no such agreement, periods of time shall be reckoned in accordance with the following provisions.

(3) Where the act is required to be done within a specified period after or from a specified date, the period begins immediately after that date.

(4) Where the act is required to be done a specified number of clear days after a specified date, at least that number of days must intervene between the day on which the act is done and that date.

(5) Where the period is a period of seven days or less which would include a Saturday, Sunday or a public holiday in the place where anything which has to be done within the period falls to be done, that day shall be excluded.

In relation to England and Wales or Northern Ireland, a "public holiday" means Christmas Day, Good Friday or a day which under the [1971 c.80.] Banking and Financial Dealings Act 1971 is a bank holiday.

79. Power of court to extend time limits relating to arbitral proceedings

(1) Unless the parties otherwise agree, the court may by order extend any time limit agreed by them in relation to any matter relating to the arbitral proceedings or specified in any provision of this Part having effect in default of such agreement.

This section does not apply to a time limit to which section 12 applies (power of court to extend time for beginning arbitral proceedings, etc.).

(2) An application for an order may be made—

- (a) by any party to the arbitral proceedings (upon notice to the other parties and to the tribunal), or
- (b) by the arbitral tribunal (upon notice to the parties).

(3) The court shall not exercise its power to extend a time limit unless it is satisfied—

- (a) that any available recourse to the tribunal, or to any arbitral or other institution or person vested by the parties with power in that regard, has first been exhausted, and
- (b) that a substantial injustice would otherwise be done.

(4) The court's power under this section may be exercised whether or not the time has already expired.

(5) An order under this section may be made on such terms as the court thinks fit.

(6) The leave of the court is required for any appeal from a decision of the court under this section.

80. Notice and other requirements in connection with legal proceedings

(1) References in this Part to an application, appeal or other step in relation to legal proceedings being taken "upon notice" to the other parties to the arbitral proceedings, or to the tribunal, are to such notice of the originating process as is required by rules of court and do not impose any separate requirement.

(2) Rules of court shall be made—

(a) requiring such notice to be given as indicated by any provision of this Part, and
(b) as to the manner, form and content of any such notice.

(3) Subject to any provision made by rules of court, a requirement to give notice to the tribunal of legal proceedings shall be construed—

(a) if there is more than one arbitrator, as a requirement to give notice to each of them; and
(b) if the tribunal is not fully constituted, as a requirement to give notice to any arbitrator who has been appointed.

(4) References in this Part to making an application or appeal to the court within a specified period are to the issue within that period of the appropriate originating process in accordance with rules of court.

(5) Where any provision of this Part requires an application or appeal to he made to the court within a specified time, the rules of court relating to the reckoning of periods, the extending or abridging of periods, and the consequences of not taking a step within the period prescribed by the rules, apply in relation to that requirement.

(6) Provision may be made by rules of court amending the provisions of this Part—

(a) with respect to the time within which any application or appeal to the court must be made,
(b) so as to keep any provision made by this Part in relation to arbitral proceedings in step with the corresponding provision of rules of court applying in relation to proceedings in the court, or
(c) so as to keep any provision made by this Part in relation to legal proceedings in step with the corresponding provision of rules of court applying generally in relation to proceedings in the court.

(7) Nothing in this section affects the generality of the power to make rules of court.

81. Saving for certain matters governed by common law

(1) Nothing in this Part shall be construed as excluding the operation of any rule of law consistent with the provisions of this Part, in particular, any rule of law as to—

(a) matters which are not capable of settlement by arbitration
(b) the effect of an oral arbitration agreement; or
(c) the refusal of recognition or enforcement of an arbitral award on grounds of public policy.

(2) Nothing in this Act shall be construed as reviving any jurisdiction of the court to set aside or remit an award on the ground of errors of fact or law on the face of the award.

82. Minor definitions

(1) In this Part—

"arbitrator", unless the context otherwise requires, includes an umpire;
"available arbitral process", in relation to any matter, includes any process of appeal to or review by an arbitral or other institution or person vested by the parties with powers in relation to that matter;
"claimant", unless the context otherwise requires, includes a counterclaimant, and related expressions shall be construed accordingly;
"dispute" includes any difference;
"enactment" includes an enactment contained in Northern Ireland legislation;
"legal proceedings" means civil proceedings in the High Court or a county court;
"peremptory order" means an order made under section 41(5) or made in exercise of any corresponding power conferred by the parties;
"premises" includes land, buildings, moveable structures, vehicles, vessels, aircraft and hovercraft;
"question of law" means—

(a) for a court in England and Wales, a question of the law of England and Wales, and
(b) for a court in Northern Ireland, a question of the law of Northern Ireland;

"substantive jurisdiction", in relation to an arbitral tribunal, refers to the matters specified in section 30(1)(a) to (c), and references to the tribunal exceeding its substantive jurisdiction shall be construed accordingly.

(2) References in this Part to a party to an arbitration agreement include any person claiming under or through a party to the agreement.

[. . .]

PART III

RECOGNITION AND ENFORCEMENT OF CERTAIN FOREIGN AWARDS

Enforcement Of Geneva Convention Awards

99. Continuation of Part II of the Arbitration Act 1950

Part II of the [1950 c.27] Arbitration Act 1950 (enforcement of certain foreign awards) continues to apply in relation to foreign awards within the meaning of that Part which are not also New York Convention awards.

Recognition and Enforcement of New York Convention awards

100. New York Convention awards

(1) In this Part a "New York Convention award" means an award made, in pursuance of an arbitration agreement, in the territory of a state (other than the United Kingdom) which is a party to the New York Convention.

(2) For the purposes of subsection (1) and of the provisions of this Part relating to such awards—

(a) "arbitration agreement" means an arbitration agreement in writing, and
(b) an award shall be treated as made at the seat of the arbitration, regardless of where it was signed, despatched or delivered to any of the parties.

In this subsection "agreement in writing" and "seat of the arbitration" have the same meaning as in Part I.

(3) If Her Majesty by Order in Council declares that a state specified in the Order is a party to the New York Convention, or is a party in respect of any territory so specified, the Order shall, while in force, be conclusive evidence of that fact.

(4) In this section "the New York Convention" means the Convention on the Recognition and Enforcement of Foreign Arbitral Awards adopted by the United Nations Conference on International Commercial Arbitration on 10th June 1958.

101. Recognition and enforcement of awards

(1) A New York Convention award shall be recognised as binding on the persons as between whom it was made, and may accordingly be relied on by those persons by way of defence, set-off or otherwise in any legal proceedings in England and Wales or Northern Ireland.

(2) A New York Convention award may, by leave of the court, be enforced in the same manner as a judgment or order of the court to the same effect.

As to the meaning of "the court" see section 105.

(3) Where leave is so given, judgment may be entered in terms of the award.

102. Evidence to be produced by party seeking recognition or enforcement

(1) A party seeking the recognition or enforcement of a New York Convention award must produce—

(a) the duly authenticated original award or a duly certified copy of it, and
(b) the original arbitration agreement or a duly certified copy of it.

(2) If the award or agreement is in a foreign language the party must also produce a translation of it certified by an official or sworn translator or by a diplomatic or consular agent.

103. Refusal of recognition or enforcement

(1) Recognition or enforcement of a New York Convention award shall not be refused except in the following cases.

(2) Recognition or enforcement of the award may be refused if the person against whom it is invoked proves—

(a) that a party to the arbitration agreement was (under the law applicable to him) under some incapacity;
(b) that the arbitration agreement was not valid under the law to which the parties subjected it or, failing any indication thereon, under the law of the country where the award was made;
(c) that he was not given proper notice of the appointment of the arbitrator or of the arbitration proceedings or was otherwise unable to present his case;

(d) that the award deals with a difference not contemplated by or not falling within the terms of the submission to arbitration or contains decisions on matters beyond the scope of the submission to arbitration (but see subsection (4));
(e) that the composition of the arbitral tribunal or the arbitral procedure was not in accordance with the agreement of the parties or, failing such agreement, with the law of the country in which the arbitration took place;
(f) that the award has not yet become binding on the parties, or has been set aside or suspended by a competent authority of the country in which, or under the law of which, it was made.

(3) Recognition or enforcement of the award may also be refused if the award is in respect of a matter which is not capable of settlement by arbitration, or if it would be contrary to public policy to recognise or enforce the award.

(4) An award which contains decisions on matters not submitted to arbitration may be recognised or enforced to the extent that it contains decisions on matters submitted to arbitration which can be separated from those on matters not so submitted.

(5) Where an application for the setting aside or suspension of the award has been made to such a competent authority as is mentioned in subsection (2)(f), the court before which the award is sought to be relied upon may, if it considers it proper, adjourn the decision on the recognition or enforcement of the award.

It may also on the application of the party claiming recognition or enforcement of the award order the other party to give suitable security.

104. Saving for other bases of recognition or enforcement

Nothing in the preceding provisions of this Part affects any right to rely upon or enforce a New York Convention award at common law or under section 66.

[…]

SCHEDULES

SCHEDULE 1

MANDATORY PROVISIONS OF PART I

sections 9 to 11 (stay of legal proceedings);
section 12 (power of court to extend agreed time limits);
section 13 (application of Limitation Acts);
section 24 (power of court to remove arbitrator);
section 26(1) (effect of death of arbitrator);
section 28 (liability of parties for fees and expenses of arbitrators);
section 29 (immunity of arbitrator);
section 31 (objection to substantive jurisdiction of tribunal);
section 32 (determination of preliminary point of jurisdiction);
section 33 (general duty of tribunal);
section 37(2) (items to be treated as expenses of arbitrators);
section 40 (general duty of parties);
section 43 (securing the attendance of witnesses);

section 56 (power to withhold award in case of non-payment);
section 60 (effectiveness of agreement for payment of costs in any event); section 66 (enforcement of award);
sections 67 and 68 (challenging the award: substantive jurisdiction and serious irregularity), and sections 70 and 71 (supplementary provisions; effect of order of court) so far as relating to those sections;
section 72 (saving for rights of person who takes no part in proceedings);
section 73 (loss of right to object);
section 74 (immunity of arbitral institutions, etc.);
section 75 (charge to secure payment of solicitors' costs).

[...]

Appendix 10

IBA Rules On The Taking Of Evidence In International Arbitration

Adopted by a resolution of the IBA Council 29 May 2010 International Bar Association

International Bar Association
10th Floor, 1 Stephen Street
London W1T 1AT
United Kingdom
Tel: +44 (0)20 7691 6868
Fax: +44 (0)20 7691 6544

www.ibanet.org

ISBN: 978 0 948711 54X

The Rules

Preamble

1. These IBA Rules on the Taking of Evidence in International Arbitration are intended to provide an efficient, economical and fair process for the taking of evidence in international arbitrations, particularly those between Parties from different legal traditions. They are designed to supplement the legal provisions and the institutional, ad hoc or other rules that apply to the conduct of the arbitration.

2. Parties and Arbitral Tribunals may adopt the IBA Rules of Evidence, in whole or in part, to govern arbitration proceedings, or they may vary them or use them as guidelines in developing their own procedures. The Rules are not intended to limit the flexibility that is inherent in, and an advantage of, international arbitration, and Parties and Arbitral Tribunals are free to adapt them to the particular circumstances of each arbitration.

3. The taking of evidence shall be conducted on the principles that each Party shall act in good faith and be entitled to know, reasonably in advance of any Evidentiary Hearing or any fact or merits determination, the evidence on which the other Parties rely.

Definitions

In the IBA Rules of Evidence:

> *'Arbitral Tribunal'* means a sole arbitrator or a panel of arbitrators;
>
> *'Claimant'* means the Party or Parties who commenced the arbitration and any Party who, through joinder or otherwise, becomes aligned with such Party or Parties;
>
> *'Document'* means a writing, communication, picture, drawing, program or data of any kind, whether recorded or maintained on paper or by electronic, audio, visual or any other means;
>
> *'Evidentiary Hearing'* means any hearing, whether or not held on consecutive days, at which the Arbitral Tribunal, whether in person, by teleconference, videoconference or other method, receives oral or other evidence;
>
> *'Expert Report'* means a written statement by a Tribunal-Appointed Expert or a Party-Appointed Expert;
>
> *'General Rules'* mean the institutional, ad hoc or other rules that apply to the conduct of the arbitration;
>
> *'IBA Rules of Evidence'* or *'Rules'* means these IBA Rules on the Taking of Evidence in International Arbitration, as they may be revised or amended from time to time;
>
> *'Party'* means a party to the arbitration;
>
> *'Party-Appointed Expert'* means a person or organisation appointed by a Party in order to report on specific issues determined by the Party;
>
> *'Request to Produce'* means a written request by a Party that another Party produce Documents;
>
> *'Respondent'* means the Party or Parties against whom the Claimant made its claim, and any Party who, through joinder or otherwise, becomes aligned with such Party or Parties, and includes a Respondent making a counterclaim;
>
> *'Tribunal-Appointed Expert'* means a person or organisation appointed by the Arbitral Tribunal in order to report to it on specific issues determined by the Arbitral Tribunal; and
>
> *'Witness Statement'* means a written statement of testimony by a witness of fact.

Article 1 Scope of Application

1. Whenever the Parties have agreed or the Arbitral Tribunal has determined to apply the IBA Rules of Evidence, the Rules shall govern the taking of evidence, except to the extent that any specific provision of them may be found to be in conflict with any mandatory provision of law determined to be applicable to the case by the Parties or by the Arbitral Tribunal.

2. Where the Parties have agreed to apply the IBA Rules of Evidence, they shall be deemed to have agreed, in the absence of a contrary indication, to the version as current on the date of such agreement.

3. In case of conflict between any provisions of the IBA Rules of Evidence and the General Rules, the Arbitral Tribunal shall apply the IBA Rules of Evidence in the manner that it determines best in order to accomplish the purposes of both the General Rules and the IBA Rules of Evidence, unless the Parties agree to the contrary.

4. In the event of any dispute regarding the meaning of the IBA Rules of Evidence, the Arbitral Tribunal shall interpret them according to their purpose and in the manner most appropriate for the particular arbitration.

5. Insofar as the IBA Rules of Evidence and the General Rules are silent on any matter concerning the taking of evidence and the Parties have not agreed otherwise, the Arbitral Tribunal shall conduct the taking of evidence as it deems appropriate, in accordance with the general principles of the IBA Rules of Evidence.

Article 2 Consultation on Evidentiary Issues

1. The Arbitral Tribunal shall consult the Parties at the earliest appropriate time in the proceedings and invite them to consult each other with a view to agreeing on an efficient, economical and fair process for the taking of evidence.

2. The consultation on evidentiary issues may address the scope, timing and manner of the taking of evidence, including:

   (a) the preparation and submission of Witness Statements and Expert Reports;

   (b) the taking of oral testimony at any Evidentiary Hearing;

   (c) the requirements, procedure and format applicable to the production of Documents;

   (d) the level of confidentiality protection to be afforded to evidence in the arbitration; and

   (e) the promotion of efficiency, economy and conservation of resources in connection with the taking of evidence.

3. The Arbitral Tribunal is encouraged to identify to the Parties, as soon as it considers it to be appropriate, any issues:

   (a) that the Arbitral Tribunal may regard as relevant to the case and material to its outcome; and/or

   (b) for which a preliminary determination may be appropriate.

Article 3 Documents

1. Within the time ordered by the Arbitral Tribunal, each Party shall submit to the Arbitral Tribunal and to the other Parties all Documents available to it on which it relies, including public Documents and those in the public domain, except for any Documents that have already been submitted by another Party.

2. Within the time ordered by the Arbitral Tribunal, any Party may submit to the Arbitral Tribunal and to the other Parties a Request to Produce.

3. A Request to Produce shall contain:

(a) (*i*) a description of each requested Document sufficient to identify it, or

(*ii*) a description in sufficient detail (including subject matter) of a narrow and specific requested category of Documents that are reasonably believed to exist; in the case of Documents maintained in electronic form, the requesting Party may, or the Arbitral Tribunal may order that it shall be required to, identify specific files, search terms, individuals or other means of searching for such Documents in an efficient and economical manner;

(b) a statement as to how the Documents requested are relevant to the case and material to its outcome; and

(c) (*i*) a statement that the Documents requested are not in the possession, custody or control of the requesting Party or a statement of the reasons why it would be unreasonably burdensome for the requesting Party to produce such Documents, and

(*ii*) a statement of the reasons why the requesting Party assumes the Documents requested are in the possession, custody or control of another Party.

4. Within the time ordered by the Arbitral Tribunal, the Party to whom the Request to Produce is addressed shall produce to the other Parties and, if the Arbitral Tribunal so orders, to it, all the Documents requested in its possession, custody or control as to which it makes no objection.

5. If the Party to whom the Request to Produce is addressed has an objection to some or all of the Documents requested, it shall state the objection in writing to the Arbitral Tribunal and the other Parties within the time ordered by the Arbitral Tribunal. The reasons for such objection shall be any of those set forth in Article 9.2 or a failure to satisfy any of the requirements of Article 3.3.

6. Upon receipt of any such objection, the Arbitral Tribunal may invite the relevant Parties to consult with each other with a view to resolving the objection.

7. Either Party may, within the time ordered by the Arbitral Tribunal, request the Arbitral Tribunal to rule on the objection. The Arbitral Tribunal shall then, in consultation with the Parties and in timely fashion, consider the Request to Produce and the objection. The Arbitral Tribunal may order the Party to whom such Request is addressed to produce any requested Document in its possession, custody or control as to which the Arbitral Tribunal determines that (*i*) the issues that the requesting Party wishes to prove are relevant to the case and material to its outcome; (*ii*) none of the reasons for objection set forth in Article 9.2 applies; and (*iii*) the requirements of Article 3.3 have been satisfied. Any such Document shall be produced to the other Parties and, if the Arbitral Tribunal so orders, to it.

8. In exceptional circumstances, if the propriety of an objection can be determined only by review of the Document, the Arbitral Tribunal may determine that it should not review the Document. In that event, the Arbitral Tribunal may, after consultation with the Parties, appoint an independent and impartial expert, bound to confidentiality, to review any such Document and to report on the objection. To the extent that the objection is upheld by the Arbitral Tribunal, the expert shall not disclose to the Arbitral Tribunal and to the other Parties the contents of the Document reviewed.

9. If a Party wishes to obtain the production of Documents from a person or organisation who is not a Party to the arbitration and from whom the Party cannot obtain the Documents on its own, the Party may, within the time ordered by the Arbitral Tribunal, ask it to take whatever steps are legally available to obtain the requested Documents, or seek leave from the Arbitral Tribunal to take such steps itself. The Party shall submit such request to the Arbitral Tribunal and to the other Parties in writing, and the request shall contain the particulars set forth in Article 3.3, as applicable. The Arbitral Tribunal shall decide on this request and shall take, authorize the requesting Party to take, or order any other Party to take, such steps as the Arbitral Tribunal considers appropriate if, in its discretion, it determines that (*i*) the Documents would be relevant to the case and material to its outcome, (*ii*) the requirements of Article 3.3, as applicable, have been satisfied and (*iii*) none of the reasons for objection set forth in Article 9.2 applies.

10. At any time before the arbitration is concluded, the Arbitral Tribunal may (*i*) request any Party to produce Documents, (*ii*) request any Party to use its best efforts to take or (*iii*) itself take, any step that it considers appropriate to obtain Documents from any person or organisation. A Party to whom such a request for Documents is addressed may object to the request for any of the reasons set forth in Article 9.2. In such cases, Article 3.4 to Article 3.8 shall apply correspondingly.

11. Within the time ordered by the Arbitral Tribunal, the Parties may submit to the Arbitral Tribunal and to the other Parties any additional Documents on which they intend to rely or which they believe have become relevant to the case and material to its outcome as a consequence of the issues raised in Documents, Witness Statements or Expert Reports submitted or produced, or in other submissions of the Parties.

12. With respect to the form of submission or production of Documents:

    (a) copies of Documents shall conform to the originals and, at the request of the Arbitral Tribunal, any original shall be presented for inspection;

    (b) Documents that a Party maintains in electronic form shall be submitted or produced in the form most convenient or economical to it that is reasonably usable by the recipients, unless the Parties agree otherwise or, in the absence of such agreement, the Arbitral Tribunal decides otherwise;

    (c) a Party is not obligated to produce multiple copies of Documents which are essentially identical unless the Arbitral Tribunal decides otherwise; and

    (d) translations of Documents shall be submitted together with the originals and marked as translations with the original language identified.

13. Any Document submitted or produced by a Party or non-Party in the arbitration and not otherwise in the public domain shall be kept confidential by the Arbitral Tribunal and the other Parties, and shall be used only in connection with the arbitration. This requirement shall apply except and to the extent that disclosure may be required of a Party to fulfil a legal duty, protect or pursue a legal right, or enforce or challenge an award in bona fide legal proceedings before a state court or other judicial authority. The Arbitral Tribunal may issue orders to set forth the terms of this confidentiality. This requirement shall be without prejudice to all other obligations of confidentiality in the arbitration.

14. If the arbitration is organised into separate issues or phases (such as jurisdiction, preliminary determinations, liability or damages), the Arbitral Tribunal may, after consultation with the Parties, schedule the submission of Documents and Requests to Produce separately for each issue or phase.

Article 4 Witnesses of Fact

1. Within the time ordered by the Arbitral Tribunal, each Party shall identify the witnesses on whose testimony it intends to rely and the subject matter of that testimony.

2. Any person may present evidence as a witness, including a Party or a Party's officer, employee or other representative.

3. It shall not be improper for a Party, its officers, employees, legal advisors or other representatives to interview its witnesses or potential witnesses and to discuss their prospective testimony with them.

4. The Arbitral Tribunal may order each Party to submit within a specified time to the Arbitral Tribunal and to the other Parties Witness Statements by each witness on whose testimony it intends to rely, except for those witnesses whose testimony is sought pursuant to Articles 4.9 or 4.10. If Evidentiary Hearings are organised into separate issues or phases (such as jurisdiction, preliminary determinations, liability or damages), the Arbitral Tribunal or the Parties by agreement may schedule the submission of Witness Statements separately for each issue or phase.

5. Each Witness Statement shall contain:

   (a) the full name and address of the witness, a statement regarding his or her present and past relationship (if any) with any of the Parties, and a description of his or her background, qualifications, training and experience, if such a description may be relevant to the dispute or to the contents of the statement;

   (b) a full and detailed description of the facts, and the source of the witness's information as to those facts, sufficient to serve as that witness's evidence in the matter in dispute. Documents on which the witness relies that have not already been submitted shall be provided;

   (c) a statement as to the language in which the Witness Statement was originally prepared and the language in which the witness anticipates giving testimony at the Evidentiary Hearing;

   (d) an affirmation of the truth of the Witness Statement; and

   (e) the signature of the witness and its date and place.

6. If Witness Statements are submitted, any Party may, within the time ordered by the Arbitral Tribunal, submit to the Arbitral Tribunal and to the other Parties revised or additional Witness Statements, including statements from persons not previously named as witnesses, so long as any such revisions or additions respond only to matters contained in another Party's Witness Statements, Expert Reports or other submissions that have not been previously presented in the arbitration.

7. If a witness whose appearance has been requested pursuant to Article 8.1 fails without a valid reason to appear for testimony at an Evidentiary Hearing, the Arbitral Tribunal shall disregard any Witness Statement related to that Evidentiary Hearing by that witness unless, in exceptional circumstances, the Arbitral Tribunal decides otherwise.

8. If the appearance of a witness has not been requested pursuant to Article 8.1, none of the other Parties shall be deemed to have agreed to the correctness of the content of the Witness Statement.

9. If a Party wishes to present evidence from a person who will not appear voluntarily at its request, the Party may, within the time ordered by the Arbitral Tribunal, ask it to take whatever steps are legally available to obtain the testimony of that person, or seek leave from the Arbitral Tribunal to take such steps itself. In the case of a request to the Arbitral Tribunal, the Party shall identify the intended witness, shall describe the subjects on which the witness's testimony is sought and shall state why such subjects are relevant to the case and material to its outcome. The Arbitral Tribunal shall decide on this request and shall take, authorize the requesting Party to take or order any other Party to take, such steps as the Arbitral Tribunal considers appropriate if, in its discretion, it determines that the testimony of that witness would be relevant to the case and material to its outcome.

10. At any time before the arbitration is concluded, the Arbitral Tribunal may order any Party to provide for, or to use its best efforts to provide for, the appearance for testimony at an Evidentiary Hearing of any person, including one whose testimony has not yet been offered. A Party to whom such a request is addressed may object for any of the reasons set forth in Article 9.2.

Article 5 Party-Appointed Experts

1. A Party may rely on a Party-Appointed Expert as a means of evidence on specific issues. Within the time ordered by the Arbitral Tribunal, (i) each Party shall identify any Party-Appointed Expert on whose testimony it intends to rely and the subject-matter of such testimony; and (ii) the Party-Appointed Expert shall submit an Expert Report.

2. The Expert Report shall contain:

   (a) the full name and address of the Party-Appointed Expert, a statement regarding his or her present and past relationship (if any) with any of the Parties, their legal advisors and the Arbitral Tribunal, and a description of his or her background, qualifications, training and experience;

   (b) a description of the instructions pursuant to which he or she is providing his or her opinions and conclusions;

   (c) a statement of his or her independence from the Parties, their legal advisors and the Arbitral Tribunal;

   (d) a statement of the facts on which he or she is basing his or her expert opinions and conclusions;

   (e) his or her expert opinions and conclusions, including a description of the methods, evidence and information used in arriving at the conclusions. Documents on which the Party-Appointed Expert relies that have not already been submitted shall be provided;

(f) if the Expert Report has been translated, a statement as to the language in which it was originally prepared, and the language in which the Party-Appointed Expert anticipates giving testimony at the Evidentiary Hearing;

(g) an affirmation of his or her genuine belief in the opinions expressed in the Expert Report;

(h) the signature of the Party-Appointed Expert and its date and place; and

(i) if the Expert Report has been signed by more than one person, an attribution of the entirety or specific parts of the Expert Report to each author.

3. If Expert Reports are submitted, any Party may, within the time ordered by the Arbitral Tribunal, submit to the Arbitral Tribunal and to the other Parties revised or additional Expert Reports, including reports or statements from persons not previously identified as Party-Appointed Experts, so long as any such revisions or additions respond only to matters contained in another Party's Witness Statements, Expert Reports or other submissions that have not been previously presented in the arbitration.

4. The Arbitral Tribunal in its discretion may order that any Party-Appointed Experts who will submit or who have submitted Expert Reports on the same or related issues meet and confer on such issues. At such meeting, the Party-Appointed Experts shall attempt to reach agreement on the issues within the scope of their Expert Reports, and they shall record in writing any such issues on which they reach agreement, any remaining areas of disagreement and the reasons therefore.

5. If a Party-Appointed Expert whose appearance has been requested pursuant to Article 8.1 fails without a valid reason to appear for testimony at an Evidentiary Hearing, the Arbitral Tribunal shall disregard any Expert Report by that Party-Appointed Expert related to that Evidentiary Hearing unless, in exceptional circumstances, the Arbitral Tribunal decides otherwise.

6. If the appearance of a Party-Appointed Expert has not been requested pursuant to Article 8.1, none of the other Parties shall be deemed to have agreed to the correctness of the content of the Expert Report.

Article 6 Tribunal-Appointed Experts

1. The Arbitral Tribunal, after consulting with the Parties, may appoint one or more independent Tribunal-Appointed Experts to report to it on specific issues designated by the Arbitral Tribunal. The Arbitral Tribunal shall establish the terms of reference for any Tribunal-Appointed Expert Report after consulting with the Parties. A copy of the final terms of reference shall be sent by the Arbitral Tribunal to the Parties.

2. The Tribunal-Appointed Expert shall, before accepting appointment, submit to the Arbitral Tribunal and to the Parties a description of his or her qualifications and a statement of his or her independence from the Parties, their legal advisors and the Arbitral Tribunal. Within the time ordered by the Arbitral Tribunal, the Parties shall inform the Arbitral Tribunal whether they have any objections as to the Tribunal-Appointed Expert's qualifications and independence. The Arbitral Tribunal shall decide promptly whether to accept any such objection. After the appointment of a Tribunal-Appointed Expert, a Party may object to the expert's

qualifications or independence only if the objection is for reasons of which the Party becomes aware after the appointment has been made. The Arbitral Tribunal shall decide promptly what, if any, action to take.

3. Subject to the provisions of Article 9.2, the Tribunal-Appointed Expert may request a Party to provide any information or to provide access to any Documents, goods, samples, property, machinery, systems, processes or site for inspection, to the extent relevant to the case and material to its outcome. The authority of a Tribunal-Appointed Expert to request such information or access shall be the same as the authority of the Arbitral Tribunal. The Parties and their representatives shall have the right to receive any such information and to attend any such inspection. Any disagreement between a Tribunal-Appointed Expert and a Party as to the relevance, materiality or appropriateness of such a request shall be decided by the Arbitral Tribunal, in the manner provided in Articles 3.5 through 3.8. The Tribunal-Appointed Expert shall record in the Expert Report any non-compliance by a Party with an appropriate request or decision by the Arbitral Tribunal and shall describe its effects on the determination of the specific issue.

4. The Tribunal-Appointed Expert shall report in writing to the Arbitral Tribunal in an Expert Report. The Expert Report shall contain:

   (a) the full name and address of the Tribunal-Appointed Expert, and a description of his or her background, qualifications, training and experience;

   (b) a statement of the facts on which he or she is basing his or her expert opinions and conclusions;

   (c) his or her expert opinions and conclusions, including a description of the methods, evidence and information used in arriving at the conclusions. Documents on which the Tribunal-Appointed Expert relies that have not already been submitted shall be provided;

   (d) if the Expert Report has been translated, a statement as to the language in which it was originally prepared, and the language in which the Tribunal-Appointed Expert anticipates giving testimony at the Evidentiary Hearing;

   (e) an affirmation of his or her genuine belief in the opinions expressed in the Expert Report;

   (f) the signature of the Tribunal-Appointed Expert and its date and place; and

   (g) if the Expert Report has been signed by more than one person, an attribution of the entirety or specific parts of the Expert Report to each author.

5. The Arbitral Tribunal shall send a copy of such Expert Report to the Parties. The Parties may examine any information, Documents, goods, samples, property, machinery, systems, processes or site for inspection that the Tribunal-Appointed Expert has examined and any correspondence between the Arbitral Tribunal and the Tribunal-Appointed Expert. Within the time ordered by the Arbitral Tribunal, any Party shall have the opportunity to respond to the Expert Report in a submission by the Party or through a Witness Statement or an Expert Report by a Party-Appointed Expert. The Arbitral Tribunal shall send the submission, Witness Statement or Expert Report to the Tribunal-Appointed Expert and to the other Parties.

6. At the request of a Party or of the Arbitral Tribunal, the Tribunal-Appointed Expert shall be present at an Evidentiary Hearing. The Arbitral Tribunal may question the Tribunal-Appointed Expert, and he or she may be questioned by the Parties or by any Party-Appointed Expert on issues raised in his or her Expert Report, the Parties' submissions or Witness Statement or the Expert Reports made by the Party-Appointed Experts pursuant to Article 6.5.

7. Any Expert Report made by a Tribunal-Appointed Expert and its conclusions shall be assessed by the Arbitral Tribunal with due regard to all circumstances of the case.

8. The fees and expenses of a Tribunal-Appointed Expert, to be funded in a manner determined by the Arbitral Tribunal, shall form part of the costs of the arbitration.

Article 7 Inspection

Subject to the provisions of Article 9.2, the Arbitral Tribunal may, at the request of a Party or on its own motion, inspect or require the inspection by a Tribunal-Appointed Expert or a Party-Appointed Expert of any site, property, machinery or any other goods, samples, systems, processes or Documents, as it deems appropriate. The Arbitral Tribunal shall, in consultation with the Parties, determine the timing and arrangement for the inspection. The Parties and their representatives shall have the right to attend any such inspection.

Article 8 Evidentiary Hearing

1. Within the time ordered by the Arbitral Tribunal, each Party shall inform the Arbitral Tribunal and the other Parties of the witnesses whose appearance it requests. Each witness (which term includes, for the purposes of this Article, witnesses of fact and any experts) shall, subject to Article 8.2, appear for testimony at the Evidentiary Hearing if such person's appearance has been requested by any Party or by the Arbitral Tribunal. Each witness shall appear in person unless the Arbitral Tribunal allows the use of videoconference or similar technology with respect to a particular witness.

2. The Arbitral Tribunal shall at all times have complete control over the Evidentiary Hearing. The Arbitral Tribunal may limit or exclude any question to, answer by or appearance of a witness, if it considers such question, answer or appearance to be irrelevant, immaterial, unreasonably burdensome, duplicative or otherwise covered by a reason for objection set forth in Article 9.2. Questions to a witness during direct and re-direct testimony may not be unreasonably leading.

3. With respect to oral testimony at an Evidentiary Hearing:

   (a) the Claimant shall ordinarily first present the testimony of its witnesses, followed by the Respondent presenting the testimony of its witnesses;

   (b) following direct testimony, any other Party may question such witness, in an order to be determined by the Arbitral Tribunal. The Party who initially presented the witness shall subsequently have the opportunity to ask additional questions on the matters raised in the other Parties' questioning;

   (c) thereafter, the Claimant shall ordinarily first present the testimony of its Party-Appointed Experts, followed by the Respondent presenting the testimony of its Party-Appointed Experts. The Party who initially presented the Party-Appointed Expert shall subsequently have the opportunity to ask additional questions on the matters raised in the other Parties' questioning;

(d) the Arbitral Tribunal may question a Tribunal-Appointed Expert, and he or she may be questioned by the Parties or by any Party-Appointed Expert, on issues raised in the Tribunal-Appointed Expert Report, in the Parties' submissions or in the Expert Reports made by the Party-Appointed Experts;

(e) if the arbitration is organised into separate issues or phases (such as jurisdiction, preliminary determinations, liability and damages), the Parties may agree or the Arbitral Tribunal may order the scheduling of testimony separately for each issue or phase;

(f) the Arbitral Tribunal, upon request of a Party or on its own motion, may vary this order of proceeding, including the arrangement of testimony by particular issues or in such a manner that witnesses be questioned at the same time and in confrontation with each other (witness conferencing);

(g) the Arbitral Tribunal may ask questions to a witness at any time.

4. A witness of fact providing testimony shall first affirm, in a manner determined appropriate by the Arbitral Tribunal, that he or she commits to tell the truth or, in the case of an expert witness, his or her genuine belief in the opinions to be expressed at the Evidentiary Hearing. If the witness has submitted a Witness Statement or an Expert Report, the witness shall confirm it. The Parties may agree or the Arbitral Tribunal may order that the Witness Statement or Expert Report shall serve as that witness's direct testimony.

5. Subject to the provisions of Article 9.2, the Arbitral Tribunal may request any person to give oral or written evidence on any issue that the Arbitral Tribunal considers to be relevant to the case and material to its outcome. Any witness called and questioned by the Arbitral Tribunal may also be questioned by the Parties.

Article 9 Admissibility and Assessment of Evidence

1. The Arbitral Tribunal shall determine the admissibility, relevance, materiality and weight of evidence.

2. The Arbitral Tribunal shall, at the request of a Party or on its own motion, exclude from evidence or production any Document, statement, oral testimony or inspection for any of the following reasons:

(a) lack of sufficient relevance to the case or materiality to its outcome;

(b) legal impediment or privilege under the legal or ethical rules determined by the Arbitral Tribunal to be applicable;

(c) unreasonable burden to produce the requested evidence;

(d) loss or destruction of the Document that has been shown with reasonable likelihood to have occurred;

(e) grounds of commercial or technical confidentiality that the Arbitral Tribunal determines to be compelling;

(f) grounds of special political or institutional sensitivity (including evidence that has been classified as secret by a government or a public international institution) that the Arbitral Tribunal determines to be compelling; or

(g) considerations of procedural economy, proportionality, fairness or equality of the Parties that the Arbitral Tribunal determines to be compelling.

3. In considering issues of legal impediment or privilege under Article 9.2(b), and insofar as permitted by any mandatory legal or ethical rules that are determined by it to be applicable, the Arbitral Tribunal may take into account:

(a) any need to protect the confidentiality of a Document created or statement or oral communication made in connection with and for the purpose of providing or obtaining legal advice;

(b) any need to protect the confidentiality of a Document created or statement or oral communication made in connection with and for the purpose of settlement negotiations;

(c) the expectations of the Parties and their advisors at the time the legal impediment or privilege is said to have arisen;

(d) any possible waiver of any applicable legal impediment or privilege by virtue of consent, earlier disclosure, affirmative use of the Document, statement, oral communication or advice contained therein, or otherwise; and

(e) the need to maintain fairness and equality as between the Parties, particularly if they are subject to different legal or ethical rules.

4. The Arbitral Tribunal may, where appropriate, make necessary arrangements to permit evidence to be presented or considered subject to suitable confidentiality protection.

5. If a Party fails without satisfactory explanation to produce any Document requested in a Request to Produce to which it has not objected in due time or fails to produce any Document ordered to be produced by the Arbitral Tribunal, the Arbitral Tribunal may infer that such document would be adverse to the interests of that Party.

6. If a Party fails without satisfactory explanation to make available any other relevant evidence, including testimony, sought by one Party to which the Party to whom the request was addressed has not objected in due time or fails to make available any evidence, including testimony, ordered by the Arbitral Tribunal to be produced, the Arbitral Tribunal may infer that such evidence would be adverse to the interests of that Party.

7. If the Arbitral Tribunal determines that a Party has failed to conduct itself in good faith in the taking of evidence, the Arbitral Tribunal may, in addition to any other measures available under these Rules, take such failure into account in its assignment of the costs of the arbitration, including costs arising out of or in connection with the taking of evidence.

Appendix 11

IBA GUIDELINES ON CONFLICT OF INTEREST IN INTERNATIONAL ARBITRATION

Approved on 22 May 2004 by the Council of the International Bar Association

Introduction

1. Problems of conflicts of interest increasingly challenge international arbitration. Arbitrators are often unsure about what facts need to be disclosed, and they may make different choices about disclosures than other arbitrators in the same situation. The growth of international business and the manner in which it is conducted, including interlocking corporate relationships and larger international law firms, have caused more disclosures and have created more difficult conflict of interest issues to determine. Reluctant parties have more opportunities to use challenges of arbitrators to delay arbitrations or to deny the opposing party the arbitrator of its choice. Disclosure of any relationship, no matter how minor or serious, has too often led to objections, challenge and withdrawal or removal of the arbitrator.

2. Thus, parties, arbitrators, institutions and courts face complex decisions about what to disclose and what standards to apply. In addition, institutions and courts face difficult decisions if an objection or a challenge is made after a disclosure. There is a tension between, on the one hand, the parties' right to disclosure of situations that may reasonably call into question an arbitrator's impartiality or independence and their right to a fair hearing and, on the other hand, the parties' right to select arbitrators of their choosing. Even though laws and arbitration rules provide some standards, there is a lack of detail in their guidance and of uniformity in their application. As a result, quite often members of the international arbitration community apply different standards in making decisions concerning disclosure, objections and challenges.

3. It is in the interest of everyone in the international arbitration community that international arbitration proceedings not be hindered by these growing conflicts of interest issues. The Committee on Arbitration and ADR of the International Bar Association appointed a Working Group of 19 experts[1] in international arbitration from 14 countries to study, with the intent of helping this decision-making process, national laws, judicial decisions, arbitration rules and practical considerations and applications regarding impartiality and independence and disclosure in international arbitration. The Working Group has determined that existing standards lack sufficient clarity and uniformity in their application. It has therefore prepared these Guidelines, which set forth some General Standards and

[1] The members of the Working Group are: (1) Henri Alvarez, Canada; (2) John Beechey, England; (3) Jim Carter, United States; (4) Emmanuel Gaillard, France; (5) Emilio Gonzales de Castilla, Mexico; (6) Bernard Hanotiau, Belgium; (7) Michael Hwang, Singapore; (8) Albert Jan van den Berg, Belgium; (9) Doug Jones, Australia; (10) Gabrielle Kaufmann-Kohler, Switzerland; (11) Arthur Marriott, England; (12) Tore Wiwen Nilsson, Sweden; (13) Hilmar Raeschke-Kessler, Germany; (14) David W. Rivkin, United States; (15) Klaus Sachs, Germany; (16) Nathalie Voser, Switzerland (Rapporteur); (17) David Williams, New Zealand; (18) Des Williams, South Africa; (19) Otto de Witt Wijnen, The Netherlands (Chair).

Explanatory Notes on the Standards. Moreover, the Working Group believes that greater consistency and fewer unnecessary challenges and arbitrator withdrawals and removals could be achieved by providing lists of specific situations that, in the view of the Working Group, do or do not warrant disclosure or disqualification of an arbitrator. Such lists—designated Red, Orange and Green (the "Application Lists")—appear at the end of these Guidelines.[2]

4. The Guidelines reflect the Working Group's understanding of the best current international practice firmly rooted in the principles expressed in the General Standards. The Working Group has based the General Standards and the Application Lists upon statutes and case law in jurisdictions and upon the judgment and experience of members of the Working Group and others involved in international commercial arbitration. The Working Group has attempted to balance the various interests of parties, representatives, arbitrators and arbitration institutions, all of whom have a responsibility for ensuring the integrity, reputation and efficiency of international commercial arbitration. In particular, the Working Group has sought and considered the views of many leading arbitration institutions, as well as corporate counsel and other persons involved in international arbitration. The Working Group also published drafts of the Guidelines and sought comments at two annual meetings of the International Bar Association and other meetings of arbitrators. While the comments received by the Working Group varied, and included some points of criticisms, the arbitration community generally supported and encouraged these efforts to help reduce the growing problems of conflicts of interests. The Working Group has studied all the comments received and has adopted many of the proposals that it has received. The Working Group is very grateful indeed for the serious considerations given to its proposals by so many institutions and individuals all over the globe and for the comments and proposals received.

5. Originally, the Working Group developed the Guidelines for international commercial arbitration. However, in the light of comments received, it realized that the Guidelines should equally apply to other types of arbitration, such as investment arbitrations (insofar as these may not be considered as commercial arbitrations).[3]

6. These Guidelines are not legal provisions and do not override any applicable national law or arbitral rules chosen by the parties. However, the Working Group hopes that these Guidelines will find general acceptance within the international arbitration community (as was the case with the IBA Rules on the Taking of Evidence in International Commercial Arbitration) and that they thus will help parties, practitioners, arbitrators, institutions and the courts in their decision-making process on these very important questions of impartiality, independence, disclosure, objections and challenges made in that connection. The Working Group trusts that the Guidelines will be applied with robust common sense and without pedantic and unduly formalistic interpretation. The Working Group is also publishing a Background and History, which describes the studies made by the Working Group and may be helpful in interpreting the Guidelines.

7. The IBA and the Working Group view these Guidelines as a beginning, rather than an end, of the process. The Application Lists cover many of the varied situations that

[2] Detailed Background Information to the Guidelines has been published in *Business Law International* at BLI Vol.5 No.3, September 2004, pp.433–458 and is available at the IBA website *ww.ibanet.org*.

[3] Similarly, the Working Group is of the opinion that these Guidelines should apply by analogy to civil servants and government officers who are appointed as arbitrators by States or State entities that are parties to arbitration proceedings.

commonly arise in practice, but they do not purport to be comprehensive, nor could they be. Nevertheless, the Working Group is confident that the Application Lists provide better concrete guidance than the General Standards (and certainly more than existing standards). The IBA and the Working Group seek comments on the actual use of the Guidelines, and they plan to supplement, revise and refine the Guidelines based on that practical experience.

8. In 1987, the IBA published Rules of Ethics for International Arbitrators. Those Rules cover more topics than these Guidelines, and they remain in effect as to subjects that are not discussed in the Guidelines. The Guidelines supersede the Rules of Ethics as to the matters treated here.

Part I: General Standards Regarding Impartiality, Independence And Disclosure

(1) General Principle

Every arbitrator shall be impartial and independent of the parties at the time of accepting an appointment to serve and shall remain so during the entire arbitration proceeding until the final award has been rendered or the proceeding has otherwise finally terminated.

Explanation to General Standard I:

The Working Group is guided by the fundamental principle in international arbitration that each arbitrator must be impartial and independent of the parties at the time he or she accepts an appointment to act as arbitrator and must remain so during the entire course of the arbitration proceedings. The Working Group considered whether this obligation should extend even during the period that the award may be challenged but has decided against this. The Working Group takes the view that the arbitrator's duty ends when the Arbitral Tribunal has rendered the final award or the proceedings have otherwise been finally terminated (e.g., because of a settlement). If, after setting aside or other proceedings, the dispute is referred back to the same arbitrator, a fresh round of disclosure may be necessary.

(2) Conflicts of Interest

(a) *An arbitrator shall decline to accept an appointment or, if the arbitration has already been commenced, refuse to continue to act as an arbitrator if he or she has any doubts as to his or her ability to be impartial or independent.*

(b) *The same principle applies if facts or circumstances exist, or have arisen since the appointment, that, from a reasonable third person's point of view having knowledge of the relevant facts, give rise to justifiable doubts as to the arbitrator's impartiality or independence, unless the parties have accepted the arbitrator in accordance with the requirements set out in General Standard (4).*

(c) *Doubts are justifiable if a reasonable and informed third party would reach the conclusion that there was a likelihood that the arbitrator may be influenced by factors other than the merits of the case as presented by the parties in reaching his or her decision.*

(d) *Justifiable doubts necessarily exist as to the arbitrator's impartiality or independence if there is an identity between a party and the arbitrator, if the arbitrator is a legal representative of a legal entity that is a party in the arbitration, or if the arbitrator has a significant financial or personal interest in the matter at stake.*

Explanation to General Standard 2:

(a) It is the main ethical guiding principle of every arbitrator that actual bias from the arbitrator's own point of view must lead to that arbitrator declining his or her appointment. This standard should apply regardless of the stage of the proceedings. This principle is so self-evident that many national laws do not explicitly say so. See e.g. Article 12, UNCITRAL Model Law. The Working Group, however, has included it in the General Standards because explicit expression in these Guidelines helps to avoid confusion and to create confidence in procedures before arbitral tribunals. In addition, the Working Group believes that the broad standard of "any doubts as to an ability to be impartial and independent" should lead to the arbitrator declining the appointment.

(b) In order for standards to be applied as consistently as possible, the Working Group believes that the test for disqualification should be an objective one. The Working Group uses the wording "impartiality or independence" derived from the broadly adopted Article 12 of the UNCITRAL Model Law, and the use of an appearance test, based on justifiable doubts as to the impartiality or independence of the arbitrator, as provided in Article 12(2) of the UNCITRAL Model Law, to be applied objectively (a "reasonable third person test"). As described in the Explanation to General Standard 3(d), this standard should apply regardless of the stage of the proceedings.

(c) Most laws and rules that apply the standard of justifiable doubts do not further define that standard. The Working Group believes that this General Standard provides some context for making this determination.

(d) The Working Group supports the view that no one is allowed to be his or her own judge; i.e., there cannot be identity between an arbitrator and a party. The Working Group believes that this situation cannot be waived by the parties. The same principle should apply to persons who are legal representatives of a legal entity that is a party in the arbitration, like board members, or who have a significant economic interest in the matter at stake. Because of the importance of this principle, this non-waivable situation is made a General Standard, and examples are provided in the non-waivable Red List.

The General Standard purposely uses the terms "identity" and "legal representatives." In the light of comments received, the Working Group considered whether these terms should be extended or further defined, but decided against doing so. It realizes that there are situations in which an employee of a party or a civil servant can be in a position similar, if not identical, to the position of an official legal representative. The Working Group decided that it should suffice to state the principle.

(3) Disclosure by the Arbitrator

(a) *If facts or circumstances exist that may, in the eyes of the parties, give rise to doubts as to the arbitrator's impartiality or independence, the arbitrator shall disclose such facts or circumstances to the parties, the arbitration institution or other appointing authority (if any, and if so required by the applicable institutional rules) and to the co-arbitrators, if any, prior to accepting his or her appointment or, if thereafter, as soon as he or she learns about them.*

(b) *It follows from General Standards 1 and 2(a) that an arbitrator who has made a disclosure considers himself or herself to be impartial and independent of the parties despite the disclosed facts and therefore capable of performing his or her duties as arbitrator. Otherwise, he or she would have declined the nomination or appointment at the outset or resigned.*

(c) *Any doubt as to whether an arbitrator should disclose certain facts or circumstances should be resolved in favour of disclosure.*

(d) *When considering whether or not facts or circumstances exist that should be disclosed, the arbitrator shall not take into account whether the arbitration proceeding is at the beginning or at a later stage.*

Explanation to General Standard 3:

(a) General Standard 2(b) above sets out an objective test for disqualification of an arbitrator. However, because of varying considerations with respect to disclosure, the proper standard for disclosure may be different. A purely objective test for disclosure exists in the majority of the jurisdictions analyzed and in the UNCITRAL Model Law. Nevertheless, the Working Group recognizes that the parties have an interest in being fully informed about any circumstances that may be relevant in their view. Because of the strongly held views of many arbitration institutions (as reflected in their rules and as stated to the Working Group) that the disclosure test should reflect the perspectives of the parties, the Working Group in principle accepted, after much debate, a subjective approach for disclosure. The Working Group has adapted the language of Article 7(2) of the ICC Rules for this standard.

However, the Working Group believes that this principle should not be applied without limitations. Because some situations should never lead to disqualification under the objective test, such situations need not be disclosed, regardless of the parties' perspective. These limitations to the subjective test are reflected in the Green List, which lists some situations in which disclosure is not required.

Similarly, the Working Group emphasizes that the two tests (objective test for disqualification and subjective test for disclosure) are clearly distinct from each other, and that a disclosure shall not automatically lead to disqualification, as reflected in General Standard 3(b).

In determining what facts should be disclosed, an arbitrator should take into account all circumstances known to him or her, including to the extent known the culture and the customs of the country of which the parties are domiciled or nationals.

(b) Disclosure is not an admission of a conflict of interest. An arbitrator who has made a disclosure to the parties considers himself or herself to be impartial and independent of the parties, despite the disclosed facts, or else he or she would have declined the nomination or resigned. An arbitrator making disclosure thus feels capable of performing his or her duties. It is the purpose of disclosure to allow the parties to judge whether or not they agree with the evaluation of the arbitrator and, if they so wish, to explore the situation further. The Working

Group hopes that the promulgation of this General Standard will eliminate the misunderstanding that disclosure demonstrates doubts sufficient to disqualify the arbitrator. Instead, any challenge should be successful only if an objective test, as set forth above, is met.

(c) Unnecessary disclosure sometimes raises an incorrect implication in the minds of the parties that the disclosed circumstances would affect his or her impartiality or independence. Excessive disclosures thus unnecessarily undermine the parties' confidence in the process. Nevertheless, after some debate, the Working Group believes it important to provide expressly in the General Standards that in case of doubt the arbitrator should disclose. If the arbitrator feels that he or she should disclose but that professional secrecy rules or other rules of practice prevent such disclosure, he or she should not accept the appointment or should resign.

(d) The Working Group has concluded that disclosure or disqualification (as set out in General Standard 2) should not depend on the particular stage of the arbitration. In order to determine whether the arbitrator should disclose, decline the appointment or refuse to continue to act or whether a challenge by a party should be successful, the facts and circumstances alone are relevant and not the current stage of the procedure or the consequences of the withdrawal. As a practical matter, institutions make a distinction between the commencement of an arbitration proceeding and a later stage. Also, courts tend to apply different standards. Nevertheless, the Working Group believes it important to clarify that no distinction should be made regarding the stage of the arbitral procedure. While there are practical concerns if an arbitrator must withdraw after an arbitration has commenced, a distinction based on the stage of arbitration would be inconsistent with the General Standards.

(4) Waiver by the Parties

(a) *If, within 30 days after the receipt of any disclosure by the arbitrator or after a party learns of facts or circumstances that could constitute a potential conflict of interest for an arbitrator, a party does not raise an express objection with regard to that arbitrator, subject to paragraphs (b) and (c) of this General Standard, the party is deemed to have waived any potential conflict of interest by the arbitrator based on such facts or circumstances and may not raise any objection to such facts or circumstances at a later stage.*

(b) *However, if facts or circumstances exist as described in General Standard 2(d), any waiver by a party or any agreement by the parties to have such a person serve as arbitrator shall be regarded as invalid.*

(c) *A person should not serve as an arbitrator when a conflict of interest, such as those exemplified in the waivable Red List, exists. Nevertheless, such a person may accept appointment as arbitrator or continue to act as an arbitrator, if the following conditions are met:*

(i) *All parties, all arbitrators and the arbitration institution or other appointing authority (if any) must have full knowledge of the conflict of interest; and*

(ii) *All parties must expressly agree that such person may serve as arbitrator despite the conflict of interest.*

(d) *An arbitrator may assist the parties in reaching a settlement of the dispute at any stage of the proceedings. However, before doing so, the arbitrator should receive an express agreement by the parties that acting in such a manner shall not disqualify the arbitrator from continuing to serve as arbitrator. Such express agreement shall be considered to be an effective waiver of any potential conflict of interest that may arise from the arbitrator's participation in such process or from information that the arbitrator may learn in the process. If the assistance by the arbitrator does not lead to final settlement of the case, the parties remain bound by their waiver. However, consistent with General Standard 2(a) and notwithstanding such agreement, the arbitrator shall resign if, as a consequence of his or her involvement in the settlement process, the arbitrator develops doubts as to his or her ability to remain impartial or independent in the future course of the arbitration proceedings.*

Explanation to General Standard 4:

(a) The Working Group suggests a requirement of an explicit objection by the parties within a certain time limit. In the view of the Working Group, this time limit should also apply to a party who refuses to be involved.

(b) This General Standard is included to make General Standard 4(a) consistent with the non-waivable provisions of General Standard 2(d). Examples of such circumstances are described in the non-waivable Red List.

(c) In a serious conflict of interest, such as those that are described by way of example in the waivable Red List, the parties may nevertheless wish to use such a person as an arbitrator. Here, party autonomy and the desire to have only impartial and independent arbitrators must be balanced. The Working Group believes persons with such a serious conflict of interests may serve as arbitrators only if the parties make fully informed, explicit waivers.

(d) The concept of the Arbitral Tribunal assisting the parties in reaching a settlement of their dispute in the course of the arbitration proceedings is well established in some jurisdictions but not in others. Informed consent by the parties to such a process prior to its beginning should be regarded as effective waiver of a potential conflict of interest. Express consent is generally sufficient, as opposed to a consent made in writing which in certain jurisdictions requires signature. In practice, the requirement of an express waiver allows such consent to be made in the minutes or transcript of a hearing. In addition, in order to avoid parties using an arbitrator as mediator as a means of disqualifying the arbitrator, the General Standard makes clear that the waiver should remain effective if the mediation is unsuccessful. Thus, parties assume the risk of what the arbitrator may learn in the settlement process. In giving their express consent, the parties should realize the consequences of the arbitrator assisting the parties in a settlement process and agree on regulating this special position further where appropriate.

(5) Scope

These Guidelines apply equally to tribunal chairs, sole arbitrators and party-appointed arbitrators. These Guidelines do not apply to non-neutral arbitrators, who do not have an obligation to be independent and impartial, as may be permitted by some arbitration rules or national laws.

Explanation to General Standard 5:

Because each member of an Arbitral Tribunal has an obligation to be impartial and independent, the General Standards should not distinguish among sole arbitrators, party-appointed arbitrators and tribunal chairs. With regard to secretaries of Arbitral Tribunals, the Working Group takes the view that it is the responsibility of the arbitrator to ensure that the secretary is and remains impartial and independent.

Some arbitration rules and domestic laws permit party-appointed arbitrators to be non-neutral. When an arbitrator is serving in such a role, these Guidelines should not apply to him or her, since their purpose is to protect impartiality and independence.

(6) Relationships

(a) *When considering the relevance of facts or circumstances to determine whether a potential conflict of interest exists or whether disclosure should be made, the activities of an arbitrator's law firm, if any, should be reasonably considered in each individual case. Therefore, the fact that the activities of the arbitrator's firm involve one of the parties shall not automatically constitute a source of such conflict or a reason for disclosure.*

(b) *Similarly, if one of the parties is a legal entity which is a member of a group with which the arbitrator's firm has an involvement, such facts or circumstances should be reasonably considered in each individual case. Therefore, this fact alone shall not automatically constitute a source of a conflict of interest or a reason for disclosure.*

(c) *If one of the parties is a legal entity, the managers, directors and members of a supervisory board of such legal entity and any person having a similar controlling influence on the legal entity shall be considered to be the equivalent of the legal entity.*

Explanation to General Standard 6:

(a) The growing size of law firms should be taken into account as part of today's reality in international arbitration. There is a need to balance the interests of a party to use the arbitrator of its choice and the importance of maintaining confidence in the impartiality and independence of international arbitration. In the opinion of the Working Group, the arbitrator must in principle be considered as identical to his or her law firm, but nevertheless the activities of the arbitrator's firm should not automatically constitute a conflict of interest. The relevance of such activities, such as the nature, timing and scope of the work by the law firm, should be reasonably considered in each individual case. The Working Group uses the term "involvement" rather than "acting for" because a law firm's relevant connections with a party may include activities other than representation on a legal matter.

(b) When a party to an arbitration is a member of a group of companies, special questions regarding conflict of interest arise. As in the prior paragraph, the Working Group believes that because individual corporate structure arrangements vary so widely an automatic rule is not appropriate. Instead, the particular circumstances of an affiliation with another entity within the same group of companies should be reasonably considered in each individual case.

(c) The party in international arbitration is usually a legal entity. Therefore, this General Standard clarifies which individuals should be considered effectively to be that party.

(7) Duty of Arbitrator and Parties

(a) *A party shall inform an arbitrator, the Arbitral Tribunal, the other parties and the arbitration institution or other appointing authority (if any) about any direct or indirect relationship between it (or another company of the same group of companies) and the arbitrator. The party shall do so on its own initiative before the beginning of the proceeding or as soon as it becomes aware of such relationship.*

(b) *In order to comply with General Standard 7(a), a party shall provide any information already available to it and shall perform a reasonable search of publicly available information.*

(c) *An arbitrator is under a duty to make reasonable enquiries to investigate any potential conflict of interest, as well as any facts or circumstances that may cause his or her impartiality or independence to be questioned. Failure to disclose a potential conflict is not excused by lack of knowledge if the arbitrator makes no reasonable attempt to investigate.*

Explanation to General Standard 7:

To reduce the risk of abuse by unmeritorious challenge of an arbitrator's impartiality or independence, it is necessary that the parties disclose any relevant relationship with the arbitrator. In addition, any party or potential party to an arbitration is, at the outset, required to make a reasonable effort to ascertain and to disclose publicly available information that, applying the general standard, might affect the arbitrator's impartiality and independence. It is the arbitrator or putative arbitrator's obligation to make similar enquiries and to disclose any information that may cause his or her impartiality or independence to be called into question.

PART II: PRACTICAL APPLICATION OF THE GENERAL STANDARDS

1. The Working Group believes that if the Guidelines are to have an important practical influence, they should reflect situations that are likely to occur in today's arbitration practice. The Guidelines should provide specific guidance to arbitrators, parties, institutions and courts as to what situations do or do not constitute conflicts of interest or should be disclosed.

For this purpose, the members of the Working Group analyzed their respective case law and categorized situations that can occur in the following Application Lists. These lists obviously cannot contain every situation, but they provide guidance in many circumstances, and the Working Group has sought to make them as comprehensive as possible. In all cases, the General Standards should control.

2. The Red List consists of two parts: "a non-waivable Red List" (see General Standards 2(c) and 4(b)) and "a waivable Red List" (see General Standard 4(c)). These lists are a non-exhaustive enumeration of specific situations which, depending on the facts of a given case, give rise to justifiable doubts as to the arbitrator's impartiality and independence; i.e., in these circumstances an objective conflict of interest exists from the point of view of a

reasonable third person having knowledge of the relevant facts (see General Standard 2(b)). The non-waivable Red List includes situations deriving from the overriding principle that no person can be his or her own judge. Therefore, disclosure of such a situation cannot cure the conflict. The waivable Red List encompasses situations that are serious but not as severe. Because of their seriousness, unlike circumstances described in the Orange List, these situations should be considered waivable only if and when the parties, being aware of the conflict of interest situation, nevertheless expressly state their willingness to have such a person act as arbitrator, as set forth in General Standard 4(c).

3. The Orange List is a non-exhaustive enumeration of specific situations which (depending on the facts of a given case) in the eyes of the parties may give rise to justifiable doubts as to the arbitrator's impartiality or independence. The Orange List thus reflects situations that would fall under General Standard 3(a), so that the arbitrator has a duty to disclose such situations. In all these situations, the parties are deemed to have accepted the arbitrator if, after disclosure, no timely objection is made. (General Standard 4(a)).

4. It should be stressed that, as stated above, such disclosure should not automatically result in a disqualification of the arbitrator; no presumption regarding disqualification should arise from a disclosure. The purpose of the disclosure is to inform the parties of a situation that they may wish to explore further in order to determine whether objectively—i.e., from a reasonable third person's point of view having knowledge of the relevant facts—there is a justifiable doubt as to the arbitrator's impartiality or independence. If the conclusion is that there is no justifiable doubt, the arbitrator can act. He or she can also act if there is no timely objection by the parties or, in situations covered by the waivable Red List, a specific acceptance by the parties in accordance with General Standard 4(c). Of course, if a party challenges the appointment of the arbitrator, he or she can nevertheless act if the authority that has to rule on the challenge decides that the challenge does not meet the objective test for disqualification.

5. In addition, a later challenge based on the fact that an arbitrator did not disclose such facts or circumstances should not result automatically in either non-appointment, later disqualification or a successful challenge to any award. In the view of the Working Group, non-disclosure cannot make an arbitrator partial or lacking independence; only the facts or circumstances that he or she did not disclose can do so.

6. The Green List contains a non-exhaustive enumeration of specific situations where no appearance of, and no actual, conflict of interest exists from the relevant objective point of view. Thus, the arbitrator has no duty to disclose situations falling within the Green List. In the opinion of the Working Group, as already expressed in the Explanation to General Standard 3(a), there should be a limit to disclosure, based on reasonableness; in some situations, an objective test should prevail over the purely subjective test of "the eyes of the parties."

7. Situations falling outside the time limit used in some of the Orange List situations should generally be considered as falling in the Green List, even though they are not specifically stated. An arbitrator may nevertheless wish to make disclosure if, under the General Standards, he or she believes it to be appropriate. While there has been much debate with respect to the time limits used in the Lists, the Working Group has concluded that the limits indicated are appropriate and provide guidance where none exists now. For example, the three-year period in Orange List 3.1 may be too long in certain circumstances and too short in others, but the Working Group believes that the period is an appropriate general criterion, subject to the special circumstances of any case.

8. The borderline between the situations indicated is often thin. It can be debated whether a certain situation should be on one List of instead of another. Also, the Lists contain, for various situations, open norms like "significant". The Working Group has extensively and repeatedly discussed both of these issues, in the light of comments received. It believes that the decisions reflected in the Lists reflect international principles to the best extent possible and that further definition of the norms, which should be interpreted reasonably in light of the facts and circumstances in each case, would be counter-productive.

9. There has been much debate as to whether there should be a Green List at all and also, with respect to the Red List, whether the situations on the Non-Waivable Red List should be waivable in light of party autonomy. With respect to the first question, the Working Group has maintained its decision that the subjective test for disclosure should not be the absolute criterion but that some objective thresholds should be added. With respect to the second question, the conclusion of the Working Group was that party autonomy, in this respect, has its limits.

1. Non-Waivable Red List

1.1. There is an identity between a party and the arbitrator, or the arbitrator is a legal representative of an entity that is a party in the arbitration.

1.2. The arbitrator is a manager, director or member of the supervisory board, or has a similar controlling influence in one of the parties.

1.3. The arbitrator has a significant financial interest in one of the parties or the outcome of the case.

1.4. The arbitrator regularly advises the appointing party or an affiliate of the appointing party, and the arbitrator or his or her firm derives a significant financial income therefrom.

2. Waivable Red List

2.1. Relationship of the arbitrator to the dispute

2.1.1 The arbitrator has given legal advice or provided an expert opinion on the dispute to a party or an affiliate of one of the parties.

2.1.2 The arbitrator has previous involvement in the case.

2.2. Arbitrator's direct or indirect interest in the dispute

2.2.1 The arbitrator holds shares, either directly or indirectly, in one of the parties or an affiliate of one of the parties that is privately held.

2.2.2 A close family member[4] of the arbitrator has a significant financial interest in the outcome of the dispute.

2.2.3 The arbitrator or a close family member of the arbitrator has a close relationship with a third party who may be liable to recourse on the part of the unsuccessful party in the dispute.

2.3. Arbitrator's relationship with the parties or counsel

[4] Throughout the Application Lists, the term "close family member" refers to a spouse, sibling, child, parent or life partner.

2.3.1 The arbitrator currently represents or advises one of the parties or an affiliate of one of the parties.

2.3.2 The arbitrator currently represents the lawyer or law firm acting as counsel for one of the parties.

2.3.3 The arbitrator is a lawyer in the same law firm as the counsel to one of the parties.

2.3.4 The arbitrator is a manager, director or member of the supervisory board, or has a similar controlling influence, in an affiliate[5] of one of the parties if the affiliate is directly involved in the matters in dispute in the arbitration.

2.3.5 The arbitrator's law firm had a previous but terminated involvement in the case without the arbitrator being involved himself or herself.

2.3.6 The arbitrator's law firm currently has a significant commercial relationship with one of the parties or an affiliate of one of the parties.

2.3.7 The arbitrator regularly advises the appointing party or an affiliate of the appointing party, but neither the arbitrator nor his or her firm derives a significant financial income therefrom.

2.3.8 The arbitrator has a close family relationship with one of the parties or with a manager, director or member of the supervisory board or any person having a similar controlling influence in one of the parties or an affiliate of one of the parties or with a counsel representing a party.

2.3.9 A close family member of the arbitrator has a significant financial interest in one of the parties or an affiliate of one of the parties.

3. Orange List

3.1. Previous services for one of the parties or other involvement in the case

3.1.1 The arbitrator has within the past three years served as counsel for one of the parties or an affiliate of one of the parties or has previously advised or been consulted by the party or an affiliate of the party making the appointment in an unrelated matter, but the arbitrator and the party or the affiliate of the party have no ongoing relationship.

3.1.2 The arbitrator has within the past three years served as counsel against one of the parties or an affiliate of one of the parties in an unrelated matter.

3.1.3 The arbitrator has within the past three years been appointed as arbitrator on two or more occasions by one of the parties or an affiliate of one of the parties.[6]

3.1.4 The arbitrator's law firm has within the past three years acted for one of the parties or an affiliate of one of the parties in an unrelated matter without the involvement of the arbitrator.

3.1.5 The arbitrator currently serves, or has served within the past three years, as arbitrator in another arbitration on a related issue involving one of the parties or an affiliate of one of the parties.

[5] Throughout the Application Lists, the term "affiliate" encompasses all companies in one group of companies including the parent company.

[6] It may be the practice in certain specific kinds of arbitration, such as maritime or commodities arbitration, to draw arbitrators from a small, specialized pool. If in such fields it is the custom and practice for parties frequently to appoint the same arbitrator in different cases, no disclosure of this fact is required where all parties in the arbitration should be familiar with such custom and practice.

3.2. Current services for one of the parties

3.2.1 The arbitrator's law firm is currently rendering services to one of the parties or to an affiliate of one of the parties without creating a significant commercial relationship and without the involvement of the arbitrator.

3.2.2 A law firm that shares revenues or fees with the arbitrator's law firm renders services to one of the parties or an affiliate of one of the parties before the arbitral tribunal.

3.2.3 The arbitrator or his or her firm represents a party or an affiliate to the arbitration on a regular basis but is not involved in the current dispute.

3.3. Relationship between an arbitrator and another arbitrator or counsel.

3.3.1 The arbitrator and another arbitrator are lawyers in the same law firm.

3.3.2 The arbitrator and another arbitrator or the counsel for one of the parties are members of the same barristers' chambers.[7]

3.3.3 The arbitrator was within the past three years a partner of, or otherwise affiliated with, another arbitrator or any of the counsel in the same arbitration.

3.3.4 A lawyer in the arbitrator's law firm is an arbitrator in another dispute involving the same party or parties or an affiliate of one of the parties.

3.3.5 A close family member of the arbitrator is a partner or employee of the law firm representing one of the parties, but is not assisting with the dispute.

3.3.6 A close personal friendship exists between an arbitrator and a counsel of one party, as demonstrated by the fact that the arbitrator and the counsel regularly spend considerable time together unrelated to professional work commitments or the activities of professional associations or social organizations.

3.3.7 The arbitrator has within the past three years received more than three appointments by the same counsel or the same law firm.

3.4. Relationship between arbitrator and party and others involved in the arbitration

3.4.1 The arbitrator's law firm is currently acting adverse to one of the parties or an affiliate of one of the parties.

3.4.2 The arbitrator had been associated within the past three years with a party or an affiliate of one of the parties in a professional capacity, such as a former employee or partner.

3.4.3 A close personal friendship exists between an arbitrator and a manager or director or a member of the supervisory board or any person having a similar controlling influence in one of the parties or an affiliate of one of the parties or a witness or expert, as demonstrated by the fact that the arbitrator and such director, manager, other person, witness or expert regularly spend considerable time together unrelated to professional work commitments or the activities of professional associations or social organizations.

3.4.4 If the arbitrator is a former judge, he or she has within the past three years heard a significant case involving one of the parties.

[7] Issues concerning special considerations involving barristers in England are discussed in the Background Information issued by the Working Group.

3.5. Other circumstances

3.5.1 The arbitrator holds shares, either directly or indirectly, which by reason of number or denomination constitute a material holding in one of the parties or an affiliate of one of the parties that is publicly listed.
3.5.2 The arbitrator has publicly advocated a specific position regarding the case that is being arbitrated, whether in a published paper or speech or otherwise.
3.5.3 The arbitrator holds one position in an arbitration institution with appointing authority over the dispute.
3.5.4 The arbitrator is a manager, director or member of the supervisory board, or has a similar controlling influence, in an affiliate of one of the parties, where the affiliate is not directly involved in the matters in dispute in the arbitration.

4. Green List

4.1. Previously expressed legal opinions

4.1.1 The arbitrator has previously published a general opinion (such as in a law review article or public lecture) concerning an issue which also arises in the arbitration (but this opinion is not focused on the case that is being arbitrated).

4.2. Previous services against one party

4.2.1 The arbitrator's law firm has acted against one of the parties or an affiliate of one of the parties in an unrelated matter without the involvement of the arbitrator.

4.3. Current services for one of the parties

4.3.1 A firm in association or in alliance with the arbitrator's law firm, but which does not share fees or other revenues with the arbitrator's law firm, renders services to one of the parties or an affiliate of one of the parties in an unrelated matter.

4.4. Contacts with another arbitrator or with counsel for one of the parties

4.4.1 The arbitrator has a relationship with another arbitrator or with the counsel for one of the parties through membership in the same professional association or social organization.
4.4.2 The arbitrator and counsel for one of the parties or another arbitrator have previously served together as arbitrators or as co- counsel.

4.5. Contacts between the arbitrator and one of the parties

4.5.1 The arbitrator has had an initial contact with the appointing party or an affiliate of the appointing party (or the respective counsels) prior to appointment, if this contact is limited to the arbitrator's availability and qualifications to serve or to the names of possible candidates for a chairperson and did not address the merits or procedural aspects of the dispute.
4.5.2 The arbitrator holds an insignificant amount of shares in one of the parties or an affiliate of one of the parties, which is publicly listed.

4.5.3 The arbitrator and a manager, director or member of the supervisory board, or any person having a similar controlling influence, in one of the parties or an affiliate of one of the parties, have worked together as joint experts or in another professional capacity, including as arbitrators in the same case.

APPENDIX 12

IBA GUIDELINES ON PARTY REPRESENTATION IN INTERNATIONAL ARBITRATION

Adopted by a resolution of the IBA Council on 25 May 2013 by the International Bar Association

Preamble

The IBA Arbitration Committee established the Task Force on Counsel Conduct in International Arbitration (the 'Task Force') in 2008.

The mandate of the Task Force was to focus on issues of counsel conduct and party representation in international arbitration that are subject to, or informed by, diverse and potentially conflicting rules and norms. As an initial inquiry, the Task Force undertook to determine whether such differing norms and practises may undermine the fundamental fairness and integrity of international arbitral proceedings and whether international guidelines on party representation in international arbitration may assist parties, counsel and arbitrators. In 2010, the Task Force commissioned a survey (the 'Survey') in order to examine these issues. Respondents to the Survey expressed support for the development of international guidelines for party representation.

The Task Force proposed draft guidelines to the IBA Arbitration Committee's Officers in October 2012. The Committee then reviewed the draft guidelines and consulted with experienced arbitration practitioners, arbitrators and arbitral institutions. The draft guidelines were then submitted to all members of the IBA Arbitration Committee for consideration.

Unlike in domestic judicial settings, in which counsel are familiar with, and subject, to a single set of professional conduct rules, party representatives in international arbitration may be subject to diverse and potentially conflicting bodies of domestic rules and norms. The range of rules and norms applicable to the representation of parties in international arbitration may include those of the party representative's home jurisdiction, the arbitral seat, and the place where hearings physically take place. The Survey revealed a high degree of uncertainty among respondents regarding what rules govern party representation in international arbitration. The potential for confusion may be aggravated when individual counsel working collectively, either within a firm or through a co-counsel relationship, are themselves admitted to practise in multiple jurisdictions that have conflicting rules and norms.

In addition to the potential for uncertainty, rules and norms developed for domestic judicial litigation may be ill-adapted to international arbitral proceedings. Indeed, specialised practises and procedures have been developed in international arbitration to accommodate the legal and cultural differences among participants and the complex, multinational nature of the disputes. Domestic professional conduct rules and norms, by contrast, are developed to apply in specific legal cultures consistent with established national procedures.

The IBA Guidelines on Party Representation in International Arbitration (the 'Guidelines') are inspired by the principle that party representatives should act with integrity and honesty and should not engage in activities designed to produce unnecessary delay or expense, including tactics aimed at obstructing the arbitration proceedings.

As with the International Principles on Conduct for the Legal Profession, adopted by the IBA on 28 May 2011, the Guidelines are not intended to displace otherwise applicable mandatory laws, professional or disciplinary rules, or agreed arbitration rules that may be relevant or applicable to matters of party representation. They are also not intended to vest arbitral tribunals with powers otherwise reserved to bars or other professional bodies.

The use of the term guidelines rather than rules is intended to highlight their contractual nature. The parties may thus adopt the Guidelines or a portion thereof by agreement. Arbitral tribunals may also apply the Guidelines in their discretion, subject to any applicable mandatory rules, if they determine that they have the authority to do so.

The Guidelines are not intended to limit the flexibility that is inherent in, and a considerable advantage of, international arbitration, and parties and arbitral tribunals may adapt them to the particular circumstances of each arbitration.

Definitions

In the IBA Guidelines on Party Representation in International Arbitration:

'*Arbitral Tribunal*' or '*Tribunal*' means a sole Arbitrator or a panel of Arbitrators in the arbitration;
'*Arbitrator*' means an arbitrator in the arbitration;
'*Document*' means a writing, communication, picture, drawing, program or data of any kind, whether recorded or maintained on paper or by electronic, audio, visual or any other means;
'*Domestic Bar*' or '*Bar*' means the national or local authority or authorities responsible for the regulation of the professional conduct of lawyers;
'*Evidence*' means documentary evidence and written and oral testimony.
'*Ex Parte Communications*' means oral or written communications between a Party Representative and an Arbitrator or prospective Arbitrator without the presence or knowledge of the opposing Party or Parties;
'*Expert*' means a person or organisation appearing before an Arbitral Tribunal to provide expert analysis and opinion on specific issues determined by a Party or by the Arbitral Tribunal;
'*Expert Report*' means a written statement by an Expert;
'*Guidelines*' mean these IBA Guidelines on Party Representation in International Arbitration, as they may be revised or amended from time to time;
'*Knowingly*' means with actual knowledge of the fact in question;
'*Misconduct*' means a breach of the present Guidelines or any other conduct that the Arbitral Tribunal determines to be contrary to the duties of a Party Representative;
'*Party*' means a party to the arbitration;
'*Party-Nominated Arbitrator*' means an Arbitrator who is nominated or appointed by one or more Parties;
'*Party Representative*' or '*Representative*' means any person, including a Party's employee, who appears in an arbitration on behalf of a Party and makes submissions, arguments or representations to the Arbitral Tribunal on behalf of

such Party, other than in the capacity as a Witness or Expert, and whether or not legally qualified or admitted to a Domestic Bar;
'*Presiding Arbitrator*' means an arbitrator who is either a sole Arbitrator or the chairperson of the Arbitral Tribunal;
'*Request to Produce*' means a written request by a Party that another Party produce Documents;
'*Witness*' means a person appearing before an Arbitral Tribunal to provide testimony of fact;
'*Witness Statement*' means a written statement by a Witness recording testimony.

Application of Guidelines

1. The Guidelines shall apply where and to the extent that the Parties have so agreed, or the Arbitral Tribunal, after consultation with the Parties, wishes to rely upon them after having determined that it has the authority to rule on matters of Party representation to ensure the integrity and fairness of the arbitral proceedings.

2. In the event of any dispute regarding the meaning of the Guidelines, the Arbitral Tribunal should interpret them in accordance with their overall purpose and in the manner most appropriate for the particular arbitration.

3. The Guidelines are not intended to displace otherwise applicable mandatory laws, professional or disciplinary rules, or agreed arbitration rules, in matters of Party representation. The Guidelines are also not intended to derogate from the arbitration agreement or to undermine either a Party representative's primary duty of loyalty to the party whom he or she represents or a Party representative's paramount obligation to present such party's case to the Arbitral Tribunal.

Comments to Guidelines 1–3

As explained in the Preamble, the Parties and Arbitral Tribunals may benefit from guidance in matters of Party Representation, in particular in order to address instances where differing norms and expectations may threaten the integrity and fairness of the arbitral proceedings.

By virtue of these Guidelines, Arbitral Tribunals need not, in dealing with such issues, and subject to applicable mandatory laws, be limited by a choice-of-law rule or private international law analysis to choosing among national or domestic professional conduct rules. Instead, these Guidelines offer an approach designed to account for the multi-faceted nature of international arbitral proceedings.

These Guidelines shall apply where and to the extent that the Parties have so agreed. Parties may adopt these Guidelines, in whole or in part, in their arbitration agreement or at any time subsequently.

An Arbitral Tribunal may also apply, or draw inspiration from, the Guidelines, after having determined that it has the authority to rule on matters of Party representation in order to ensure the integrity and fairness of the arbitral proceedings. Before making such determination, the Arbitral Tribunal should give the Parties an opportunity to express their views.

These Guidelines do not state whether Arbitral Tribunals have the authority to rule on matters of Party representation and to apply the Guidelines in the absence of an agreement by the Parties to that effect. The Guidelines neither recognise nor exclude the existence of such authority. It remains for the Tribunal to make a determination as to whether it has the authority to rule on matters of Party representation and to apply the Guidelines.

A Party Representative, acting within the authority granted to it, acts on behalf of the Party whom he or she represents. It follows therefore that an obligation or duty bearing on a Party Representative is an obligation or duty of the represented Party, who may ultimately bear the consequences of the misconduct of its Representative.

Party Representation

4. Party Representatives should identify themselves to the other Party or Parties and the Arbitral Tribunal at the earliest opportunity. A Party should promptly inform the Arbitral Tribunal and the other Party or Parties of any change in such representation.

5. Once the Arbitral Tribunal has been constituted, a person should not accept representation of a Party in the arbitration when a relationship exists between the person and an Arbitrator that would create a conflict of interest, unless none of the Parties objects after proper disclosure.

6. The Arbitral Tribunal may, in case of breach of Guideline 5, take measures appropriate to safeguard the integrity of the proceedings, including the exclusion of the new Party Representative from participating in all or part of the arbitral proceedings.

Comments to Guidelines 4–6

Changes in Party representation in the course of the arbitration may, because of conflicts of interest between a newly-appointed Party Representative and one or more of the Arbitrators, threaten the integrity of the proceedings. In such case, the Arbitral Tribunal may, if compelling circumstances so justify, and where it has found that it has the requisite authority, consider excluding the new Representative from participating in all or part of the arbitral proceedings. In assessing whether any such conflict of interest exists, the Arbitral Tribunal may rely on the IBA Guidelines on Conflicts of Interest in International Arbitration.

Before resorting to such measure, it is important that the Arbitral Tribunal give the Parties an opportunity to express their views about the existence of a conflict, the extent of the Tribunal's authority to act in relation to such conflict, and the consequences of the measure that the Tribunal is contemplating.

Communications with Arbitrators

7. Unless agreed otherwise by the Parties, and subject to the exceptions below, a Party Representative should not engage in any Ex Parte Communications with an Arbitrator concerning the arbitration.

8. It is not improper for a Party Representative to have Ex Parte Communications in the following circumstances:

- *(a) A Party Representative may communicate with a prospective Party-Nominated Arbitrator to determine his or her expertise, experience, ability, availability, willingness and the existence of potential conflicts of interest.*
- *(b) A Party Representative may communicate with a prospective or appointed Party-Nominated Arbitrator for the purpose of the selection of the Presiding Arbitrator.*

(c) *A Party Representative may, if the Parties are in agreement that such a communication is permissible, communicate with a prospective Presiding Arbitrator to determine his or her expertise, experience, ability, availability, willingness and the existence of potential conflicts of interest.*

(d) *While communications with a prospective Party-Nominated Arbitrator or Presiding Arbitrator may include a general description of the dispute, a Party Representative should not seek the views of the prospective Party-Nominated Arbitrator or Presiding Arbitrator on the substance of the dispute.*

Comments to Guidelines 7–8

Guidelines 7–8 deal with communications between a Party Representative and an Arbitrator or potential Arbitrator concerning the arbitration.

The Guidelines seek to reflect best international practises and, as such, may depart from potentially diverging domestic arbitration practises that are more restrictive or, to the contrary, permit broader Ex Parte Communications.

Ex Parte Communications, as defined in these Guidelines, may occur only in defined circumstances, and a Party Representative should otherwise refrain from any such communication. The Guidelines do not seek to define when the relevant period begins or ends. Any communication that takes place in the context of, or in relation to, the constitution of the Arbitral Tribunal is covered.

Ex Parte Communications with a prospective Arbitrator (Party-Nominated or Presiding Arbitrator) should be limited to providing a general description of the dispute and obtaining information regarding the suitability of the potential Arbitrator, as described in further detail below. A Party Representative should not take the opportunity to seek the prospective Arbitrator's views on the substance of the dispute.

The following discussion topics are appropriate in pre-appointment communications in order to assess the prospective Arbitrator's expertise, experience, ability, availability, willingness and the existence of potential conflicts of interest: (a) the prospective Arbitrator's publications, including books, articles and conference papers or engagements; (b) any activities of the prospective Arbitrator and his or her law firm or organisation within which he or she operates, that may raise justifiable doubts as to the prospective Arbitrator's independence or impartiality; (c) a description of the general nature of the dispute; (d) the terms of the arbitration agreement, and in particular any agreement as to the seat, language, applicable law and rules of the arbitration; (e) the identities of the Parties, Party Representatives, Witnesses, Experts and interested parties; and (f) the anticipated timetable and general conduct of the proceedings.

Applications to the Arbitral Tribunal without the presence or knowledge of the opposing Party or Parties may be permitted in certain circumstances, if the parties so agreed, or as permitted by applicable law. Such may be the case, in particular, for interim measures.

Finally, a Party Representative may communicate with the Arbitral Tribunal if the other Party or Parties fail to participate in a hearing or proceedings and are not represented.

Submissions to the Arbitral Tribunal

9. A Party Representative should not make any knowingly false submission of fact to the Arbitral Tribunal.

10. In the event that a Party Representative learns that he or she previously made a false submission of fact to the Arbitral Tribunal, the Party Representative should, subject to countervailing considerations of confidentiality and privilege, promptly correct such submission.

11. A Party Representative should not submit Witness or Expert evidence that he or she knows to be false. If a Witness or Expert intends to present or presents evidence that a Party Representative knows or later discovers to be false, such Party Representative should promptly advise the Party whom he or she represents of the necessity of taking remedial measures and of the consequences of failing to do so. Depending upon the circumstances, and subject to countervailing considerations of confidentiality and privilege, the Party Representative should promptly take remedial measures, which may include one or more of the following:

(a) advise the Witness or Expert to testify truthfully;

(b) take reasonable steps to deter the Witness or Expert from submitting false evidence;

(c) urge the Witness or Expert to correct or withdraw the false evidence;

(d) correct or withdraw the false evidence;

(e) withdraw as Party Representative if the circumstances so warrant.

Comments to Guidelines 9–11

Guidelines 9–11 concern the responsibility of a Party Representative when making submissions and tendering evidence to the Arbitral Tribunal. This principle is sometimes referred to as the duty of candour or honesty owed to the Tribunal.

The Guidelines identify two aspects of the responsibility of a Party Representative: the first relates to submissions of fact made by a Party Representative (Guidelines 9 and 10), and the second concerns the evidence given by a Witness or Expert (Guideline 11).

With respect to submissions to the Arbitral Tribunal, these Guidelines contain two limitations to the principles set out for Party Representatives. First, Guidelines 9 and 10 are restricted to false submissions of fact. Secondly, the Party Representative must have actual knowledge of the false nature of the submission, which may be inferred from the circumstances.

Under Guideline 10, a Party Representative should promptly correct any false submissions of fact previously made to the Tribunal, unless prevented from doing so by countervailing considerations of confidentiality and privilege. Such principle also applies, in case of a change in representation, to a newly-appointed Party Representative who becomes aware that his or her predecessor made a false submission.

With respect to legal submissions to the Tribunal, a Party Representative may argue any construction of a law, a contract, a treaty or any authority that he or she believes is reasonable.

Guideline 11 addresses the presentation of evidence to the Tribunal that a Party Representative knows to be false. A Party Representative should not offer knowingly false evidence or testimony. A Party Representative therefore should not assist a Witness or Expert or seek to influence a Witness or Expert to give false evidence to the Tribunal in oral testimony or written Witness Statements or Expert Reports.

The considerations outlined for Guidelines 9 and 10 apply equally to Guideline 11. Guideline 11 is more specific in terms of the remedial measures that a Party Representative may take in the event that the Witness or Expert intends to present or presents evidence that the Party Representative knows or later discovers to be false. The list of remedial measures provided in Guideline 11 is not exhaustive. Such remedial measures may extend to the Party Representative's withdrawal from the case, if the circumstances so warrant. Guideline 11 acknowledges, by using the term 'may', that certain remedial measures, such as correcting or withdrawing false Witness or Expert evidence may not be compatible with the ethical rules bearing on counsel in some jurisdictions.

Information Exchange and Disclosure

12. When the arbitral proceedings involve or are likely to involve Document production, a Party Representative should inform the client of the need to preserve, so far as reasonably possible, Documents, including electronic Documents that would otherwise be deleted in accordance with a Document retention policy or in the ordinary course of business, which are potentially relevant to the arbitration.

13. A Party Representative should not make any Request to Produce, or any objection to a Request to Produce, for an improper purpose, such as to harass or cause unnecessary delay.

14. A Party Representative should explain to the Party whom he or she represents the necessity of producing, and potential consequences of failing to produce, any Document that the Party or Parties have undertaken, or been ordered, to produce.

15. A Party Representative should advise the Party whom he or she represents to take, and assist such Party in taking, reasonable steps to ensure that: (i) a reasonable search is made for Documents that a Party has undertaken, or been ordered, to produce and (ii) all non-privileged, responsive Documents are produced.

16. A Party Representative should not suppress or conceal, or advise a Party to suppress or conceal, Documents that have been requested by another Party or that the Party whom he or she represents has undertaken, or been ordered, to produce.

17. If, during the course of an arbitration, a Party Representative becomes aware of the existence of a Document that should have been produced, but was not produced, such Party Representative should advise the Party whom he or she represents of the necessity of producing the Document and the consequences of failing to do so.

Comments to Guidelines 12–17

The IBA addressed the scope of Document production in the IBA Rules on the Taking of Evidence in International Arbitration (*see* Articles 3 and 9). Guidelines 12–17 concern the conduct of Party Representatives in connection with Document production.

Party Representatives often are unsure whether and to what extent their respective domestic standards of professional conduct apply to the process of preserving, collecting and producing documents in international arbitration. It is common for Party Representatives in the same arbitration proceeding to apply different standards. For example, one Party Representative may consider him- or her-self obligated to ensure that the Party whom he or she represents undertakes a reasonable search for, and produces, all responsive, non-privileged Documents, while another Party Representative may view Document production as the sole responsibility of the Party whom he or she represents. In these circumstances, the disparity in access to information or evidence may undermine the integrity and fairness of the arbitral proceedings.

The Guidelines are intended to address these difficulties by suggesting standards of conduct in international arbitration. They may not be necessary in cases where Party Representatives share similar expectations with respect to their role in relation to Document production or in cases where Document production is not done or is minimal.

The Guidelines are intended to foster the taking of objectively reasonable steps to preserve, search for and produce Documents that a Party has an obligation to disclose.

Under Guidelines 12–17, a Party Representative should, under the given circumstances, advise the Party whom he or she represents to: (i) identify those persons within the Party's control who might possess Documents potentially relevant to the arbitration, including electronic Documents; (ii) notify such persons of the need to preserve and not destroy any such Documents; and (iii) suspend or otherwise make arrangements to override any Document retention or other policies/practises whereby potentially relevant Documents might be destroyed in the ordinary course of business.

Under Guidelines 12–17, a Party Representative should, under the given circumstances, advise the Party whom he or she represents to, and assist such Party to (i) put in place a reasonable and proportionate system for collecting and reviewing Documents within the possession of persons within the Party's control in order to identify Documents that are relevant to the arbitration or that have been requested by another Party; and (ii) ensure that the Party Representative is provided with copies of, or access to, all such Documents.

While Article 3 of the IBA Rules on the Taking of Evidence in International Arbitration requires the production of Documents relevant to the case and material to its outcome, Guideline 12 refers only to potentially relevant Documents because its purpose is different: when a Party Representative advises the Party whom he or she represents to preserve evidence, such Party Representative is typically not at that stage in a position to assess materiality, and the test for preserving and collecting Documents therefore should be potential relevance to the case at hand.

Finally, a Party Representative should not make a Request to Produce, or object to a Request to Produce, when such request or objection is only aimed at harassing, obtaining documents for purposes extraneous to the arbitration, or causing unnecessary delay (Guideline 13).

Witnesses and Experts

18. Before seeking any information from a potential Witness or Expert, a Party Representative should identify himself or herself, as well as the Party he or she represents, and the reason for which the information is sought.

19. A Party Representative should make any potential Witness aware that he or she has the right to inform or instruct his or her own counsel about the contact and to discontinue the communication with the Party Representative.

20. A Party Representative may assist Witnesses in the preparation of Witness Statements and Experts in the preparation of Expert Reports.

21. A Party Representative should seek to ensure that a Witness Statement reflects the Witness's own account of relevant facts, events and circumstances.

22. A Party Representative should seek to ensure that an Expert Report reflects the Expert's own analysis and opinion.

23. A Party Representative should not invite or encourage a Witness to give false evidence.

24. A Party Representative may, consistent with the principle that the evidence given should reflect the Witness's own account of relevant facts, events or circumstances, or the Expert's own analysis or opinion, meet or interact with Witnesses and Experts in order to discuss and prepare their prospective testimony.

25. A Party Representative may pay, offer to pay, or acquiesce in the payment of:

(a) expenses reasonably incurred by a Witness or Expert in preparing to testify or testifying at a hearing;

(b) reasonable compensation for the loss of time incurred by a Witness in testifying and preparing to testify; and

(c) reasonable fees for the professional services of a Party-appointed Expert.

Comments to Guidelines 18–25

Guidelines 18–25 are concerned with interactions between Party Representatives and Witnesses and Experts. The interaction between Party Representatives and Witnesses is also addressed in Guidelines 9–11 concerning Submissions to the Arbitral Tribunal.

Many international arbitration practitioners desire more transparent and predictable standards of conduct with respect to relations with Witnesses and Experts in order to promote the principle of equal treatment among Parties. Disparate practises among jurisdictions may create inequality and threaten the integrity of the arbitral proceedings.

The Guidelines are intended to reflect best international arbitration practise with respect to the preparation of Witness and Expert testimony.

When a Party Representative contacts a potential Witness, he or she should disclose his or her identity and the reason for the contact before seeking any information from the potential Witness (Guideline 18). A Party Representative should also make the potential Witness aware of his or her right to inform or instruct counsel about this contact and involve such counsel in any further communication (Guideline 19).

Domestic professional conduct norms in some jurisdictions require higher standards with respect to contacts with potential Witnesses who are known to be represented by counsel. For example, some common law jurisdictions maintain a prohibition against contact by counsel with any potential Witness whom counsel knows to be represented in respect of the particular arbitration.

If a Party Representative determines that he or she is subject to a higher standard than the standard prescribed in these Guidelines, he or she may address the situation with the other Party and/or the Arbitral Tribunal.

As provided by Guideline 20, a Party Representative may assist in the preparation of Witness Statements and Expert Reports, but should seek to ensure that a Witness Statement reflects the Witness's own account of relevant facts, events and circumstances (Guideline 21), and that any Expert Report reflects the Expert's own views, analysis and conclusions (Guideline 22).

A Party Representative should not invite or encourage a Witness to give false evidence (Guideline 23).

As part of the preparation of testimony for the arbitration, a Party Representative may meet with Witnesses and Experts (or potential Witnesses and Experts) to discuss their prospective testimony. A Party Representative may also help a Witness in preparing his or her own Witness Statement or Expert Report. Further, a Party Representative may assist a Witness in preparing for their testimony in direct and cross-examination, including through practise questions and answers (Guideline 24). This preparation may include a review of the procedures through which testimony will be elicited and preparation of both direct testimony and cross-examination. Such contacts should however not alter the genuineness of the Witness or Expert evidence, which should always reflect the Witness's own account of relevant facts, events or circumstances, or the Expert's own analysis or opinion.

Finally, Party Representatives may pay, offer to pay or acquiesce in the payment of reasonable compensation to a Witness for his or her time and a reasonable fee for the professional services of an Expert (Guideline 25).

Remedies for Misconduct

26. If the Arbitral Tribunal, after giving the Parties notice and a reasonable opportunity to be heard, finds that a Party Representative has committed Misconduct, the Arbitral Tribunal, as appropriate, may:

- *(a) admonish the Party Representative;*
- *(b) draw appropriate inferences in assessing the evidence relied upon, or the legal arguments advanced by, the Party Representative;*
- *(c) consider the Party Representative's Misconduct in apportioning the costs of the arbitration, indicating, if appropriate, how and in what amount the Party Representative's Misconduct leads the Tribunal to a different apportionment of costs;*
- *(d) take any other appropriate measure in order to preserve the fairness and integrity of the proceedings.*

27. In addressing issues of Misconduct, the Arbitral Tribunal should take into account:

- *(a) the need to preserve the integrity and fairness of the arbitral proceedings and the enforceability of the award;*
- *(b) the potential impact of a ruling regarding Misconduct on the rights of the Parties;*
- *(c) the nature and gravity of the Misconduct, including the extent to which the misconduct affects the conduct of the proceedings;*
- *(d) the good faith of the Party Representative;*
- *(e) relevant considerations of privilege and confidentiality; and*
- *(f) the extent to which the Party represented by the Party Representative knew of, condoned, directed, or participated in, the Misconduct.*

Comments to Guidelines 26–27

Guidelines 26–27 articulate potential remedies to address Misconduct by a Party Representative.

Their purpose is to preserve or restore the fairness and integrity of the arbitration.

The Arbitral Tribunal should seek to apply the most proportionate remedy or combination of remedies in light of the nature and gravity of the Misconduct, the good faith of the Party Representative and the Party whom he or she represents, the impact of the remedy on the Parties' rights, and the need to preserve the integrity, effectiveness and fairness of the arbitration and the enforceability of the award.

Guideline 27 sets forth a list of factors that is neither exhaustive nor binding, but instead reflects an overarching balancing exercise to be conducted in addressing matters of Misconduct by a Party Representative in order to ensure that the arbitration proceed in a fair and appropriate manner.

Before imposing any remedy in respect of alleged Misconduct, it is important that the Arbitral Tribunal gives the Parties and the impugned Representative the right to be heard in relation to the allegations made.

APPENDIX 13

INTERNATIONAL LAW ASSOCIATION RECOMMENDATION OF JUNE 2006

RESOLUTION No. 1/2006

INTERNATIONAL COMMERCIAL ARBITRATION

The 72th Conference of the International Law Association held in Toronto, Canada, 4–8 June 2006:

HAVING CONSIDERED the Final Report on Res Judicata and Arbitration as well as the Report on Lis Pendens and Arbitration by the Committee on International Commercial Arbitration;

RECOGNISING the need for efficiency in conducting arbitral proceedings, the need for finality of arbitral awards and the role of party autonomy regarding arbitral proceedings;

THANKS the Chairman, the Rapporteur and the Members of the Committee for their work done in developing an understanding of the topic and its role;

ADOPTS the Recommendations annexed to this Resolution;

COMMENDS the Recommendations to arbitral tribunals, with a view to facilitate uniformity and consistency in the interpretation and application of provisions and principles concerning parallel proceedings and the conclusive and preclusive effects of prior arbitral awards:

REQUESTS the Committee and others to encourage the application of the Recommendations within the arbitral community; and

RECOMMENDS that the Executive Council renews the mandate of the Committee for a period of four years and to study and report on the topic of *iura novit curia* and issues related to the determination of the content of the applicable law in international commercial arbitration.

RECOMMENDATIONS ON LIS PENDENS AND RES JUDICATA AND ARBITRATION

ANNEX 1

INTERNATIONAL LAW ASSOCIATION RECOMMENDATIONS ON LIS PENDENS AND ARBITRATION

RECOMMENDATIONS

1. An arbitral tribunal that considers itself to be *prima facie* competent pursuant to the relevant arbitration agreement should, consistent with the principle of *competence-competence*, proceed with the arbitration ("Current Arbitration") and determine its own jurisdiction, regardless of any other proceedings pending before a national court or another arbitral tribunal in which the parties and one or more of the issues are the same or substantially the same as the ones before the arbitral tribunal in the Current Arbitration ("Parallel Proceedings"). Having determined that it has jurisdiction, the arbitral tribunal should proceed with the arbitration, subject to any successful setting aside application.

2. Nevertheless, in the interest of avoiding conflicting decisions, preventing costly duplication of proceedings or protecting parties from oppressive tactics, an arbitral tribunal requested by a party to decline jurisdiction or to stay the arbitration on the basis that there are Parallel Proceedings should decide in accordance with the principles set out in paragraphs 3., 4. and 5. below.

3. Where the Parallel Proceedings are pending before a court of the jurisdiction of the place of the arbitration, in deciding whether to proceed with the Current Arbitration, the arbitral tribunal should be mindful of the law of that jurisdiction, particularly having regard to the possibility of setting aside of the award in the event of conflict between the award and the decision of the court.

4. Where the Parallel Proceedings are pending before a court of a jurisdiction other than the jurisdiction of the place of the arbitration, consistent with the principles of *competence-competence*, the tribunal should proceed with the Current Arbitration and determine its own jurisdiction, unless the party initiating the arbitration has effectively waived its rights under the arbitration agreement or save in other exceptional circumstances.

5. Where the Parallel Proceedings have been commenced before the Current Arbitration and are pending before another arbitral tribunal, the arbitral tribunal should decline jurisdiction or stay the Current Arbitration, in whole or in part, and on such conditions as it sees fit, for such duration as it sees fit (such as until a relevant determination in the Parallel Proceedings), provided that it is not precluded from doing so under the applicable law and provided that it appears that:

   5.1 the arbitral tribunal in the Parallel Proceedings has jurisdiction to resolve the issues in the Current Arbitration; and

   5.2 there will be no material prejudice to the party opposing the request because of *(i)* an inadequacy of relief available in the Parallel Proceedings; *(ii)* a lack of due process in the Parallel Proceedings;

(iii) a risk of annulment or non-recognition or non-enforcement of an award that has been or may be rendered in the Parallel Proceedings; or *(iv)* some other compelling reason.

6. Also, as a matter of sound case management, or to avoid conflicting decisions, to prevent costly duplication of proceedings or to protect a party from oppressive tactics, an arbitral tribunal requested by a party to stay temporarily the Current Arbitration, on such conditions as it sees fit, until the outcome, or partial or interim outcome, of any other pending proceedings (whether court, arbitration or supra-national proceedings), or any active dispute settlement process, may grant the request, whether or not the other proceedings or settlement process are between the same parties, relate to the same subject matter, or raise one or more of the same issues as the Current Arbitration, provided that the arbitral tribunal in the Current Arbitration is:

   6.1 not precluded from doing so under the applicable law;
   6.2 satisfied that the outcome of the other pending proceedings or settlement process is material to the outcome of the Current Arbitration; and
   6.3 satisfied that there will be no material prejudice to the party opposing the stay.

7. The effects of Parallel Proceedings need not be raised on its own motion by an arbitral tribunal. If not waived, such effects should be raised as soon as possible by a party.

ANNEX 2

INTERNATIONAL LAW ASSOCIATION RECOMMENDATIONS ON RES JUDICATA AND ARBITRATION

RECOMMENDATIONS

1. To promote efficiency and finality of international commercial arbitration, arbitral awards should have conclusive and preclusive effects in further arbitral proceedings.
2. The conclusive and preclusive effects of arbitral awards in further arbitral proceedings set forth below need not necessarily be governed by national law and may be governed by transnational rules applicable to international commercial arbitration.
3. An arbitral award has conclusive and preclusive effects in further arbitral proceedings if:

   3.1 it has become final and binding in the country of origin and there is no impediment to recognition in the country of the place of the subsequent arbitration;
   3.2 it has decided on or disposed of a claim for relief which is sought or is being reargued in the further arbitration proceedings;
   3.3 it is based upon a cause of action which is invoked in the further arbitration proceedings or which forms the basis for the subsequent arbitral proceedings; and
   3.4 it has been rendered between the same parties.

4. An arbitral award has conclusive and preclusive effects in the further arbitral proceedings as to:

    4.1 determinations and relief contained in its dispositive part as well as in all reasoning necessary thereto;
    4.2 issues of fact or law which have actually been arbitrated and determined by it, provided any such determination was essential or fundamental to the dispositive part of the arbitral award.

5. An arbitral award has preclusive effects in the further arbitral proceedings as to a claim, cause of action or issue of fact or law, which could have been raised, but was not, in the proceedings resulting in that award, provided that the raising of any such new claim, cause of action or new issue of fact or law amounts to procedural unfairness or abuse.

6. The conclusive effects of an arbitral award can be invoked in further arbitration proceedings at any time permitted under the applicable procedure.

7. The preclusive effects of an arbitral award need not be raised on its own motion by an arbitral tribunal. If not waived, such preclusive effects should be raised as soon as possible by a party.

APPENDIX 14

RESOLUTION No. 6/2008

ILA RECOMMENDATIONS ON ASCERTAINING THE CONTENTS OF APPLICABLE LAW

The 73rd Conference of the International Law Association held in Rio de Janeiro, Brazil, 17–21August 2008:

HAVING CONSIDERED the Report on Ascertaining the Contents of the Applicable Law in International Commercial Arbitration by the Committee on International Commercial Arbitration;

RECOGNISING the need for guidance and the development of best practices for parties, counsel and arbitrators in relation to ascertaining the contents of the applicable law in international commercial arbitration;

ADOPTS the Recommendations annexed to this Resolution;

COMMENDS the Recommendations to arbitral tribunals, with a view to facilitating uniformity and consistency in ascertaining the contents of the applicable law in international commercial arbitration;

REQUESTS the Committee and others to encourage the application of the Recommendations within the arbitral community; and

RECOMMENDS that the Executive Council renews the mandate of the Committee for a period of four years to study and report on the topic of confidentiality in international commercial arbitration.

ANNEX

INTERNATIONAL LAW ASSOCIATION RECOMMENDATIONS ON ASCERTAINING THE CONTENTS OF THE APPLICABLE LAW IN INTERNATIONAL COMMERCIAL ARBITRATION

General considerations

1. At any time in the proceedings that a question requiring the application of a rule of law (including a question of jurisdiction, procedure, merits or conflicts of laws) arises, arbitrators should identify the potentially applicable laws and rules and ascertain their contents insofar as it is necessary to do so to decide the dispute.

2. In ascertaining the contents of applicable law and rules, arbitrators should respect due process and public policy, proceed in a manner that is fair to the parties, deliver an award within the submission to arbitration and avoid bias or appearance of bias.

Acquiring information

3. When it appears to the arbitrators that the contents of applicable law might significantly affect the outcome of the case, arbitrators should promptly raise that topic with the parties and establish appropriate procedures as to how the contents of the law will be ascertained (in submissions with materials attached, through experts, witnesses or otherwise).

4. Arbitrators attempting to ascertain the contents of applicable law should bear in mind that the rules governing the ascertainment of the contents of law by national courts are not necessarily suitable for arbitration, given the fundamental differences between international arbitration and litigation before national courts. In particular, arbitrators should not rely on unexpressed presumptions as to the contents of the applicable law, including any presumption that it is the same as the law best known to the tribunal or to any of its members, or even that is the same as the law of the seat of the arbitration.

Interaction with parties

5. Arbitrators should primarily receive information about the contents of the applicable law from the parties.

6. In general, and subject to Recommendation 13, arbitrators should not introduce legal issues – propositions of law that may bear on the outcome of the dispute – that the parties have not raised.

7. Arbitrators are not confined to the parties' submissions about the contents of applicable law. Subject to Recommendation 8, arbitrators may question the parties about legal issues the parties have raised and about their submissions and evidence on the contents of the applicable law, may review sources not invoked by the parties relating to those legal issues and may, in a transparent manner rely, on their own knowledge as to the applicable law as it relates to those legal issues.

8. Before reaching their conclusions and rendering a decision or an award, arbitrators should give parties a reasonable opportunity to be heard on legal issues that may be relevant to the disposition of the case. They should not give decisions that might reasonably be expected to surprise the parties, or any of them, or that are based on legal issues not raised by or with the parties.

Making use of information about law's content

9. In ascertaining the contents of a potentially applicable law or rule, arbitrators may consider and give appropriate weight to any reliable source, including statutes, case law, submissions of the parties' advocates, opinions and cross-examination of experts, scholarly writings and the like.

10. If arbitrators intend to rely on sources not invoked by the parties, they should bring those sources to the attention of the parties and invite their comments, at least if those sources go meaningfully beyond the sources the parties have already invoked and might significantly affect the outcome of the case. Arbitrators may rely on such additional sources without further notice to the parties if those sources merely corroborate or reinforce other sources already addressed by the parties.

11. If in the course of deliberations arbitrators consider that further information about the contents of applicable law is necessary to the disposition of the case, they should consider reopening the proceedings to enable the parties to make further submissions on the open legal issues, but only to the extent necessary to address the open legal issues and taking into account considerations of relevance, time and cost.

12. In applying the rules of the applicable law, arbitrators should give due regard to available information about the application of the rules in the jurisdiction from which the rules emanate.

Special circumstances

13. In disputes implicating rules of public policy or other rules from which the parties may not derogate, arbitrators may be justified in taking measures appropriate to determine the applicability and contents of such rules, including by making independent research, raising with the parties new issues (whether legal or factual), and giving appropriate instructions or ordering appropriate measures insofar as they consider this necessary to abide by those rules or to protect against challenges to the award.

14. In applying the foregoing Recommendations, arbitrators may take account of the nature of the proceedings, in particular regarding default and expedited interim relief proceedings, and may take a more active role than might otherwise be the case in questioning legal submissions.

15. If after diligent effort consistent with these Recommendations the contents of the applicable law cannot be ascertained, arbitrators may apply whatever law or rules they consider appropriate on a reasoned basis, after giving the parties notice and a reasonable opportunity to be heard.

Rio de Janeiro, 21 August 2008

SELECTED BIBLIOGRAPHY

The list contains books and articles which have been referred as a general matter to in Part I of the Handbook.

Abedian H., "Judicial Review of Arbitral Awards in International Arbitration – A Case for an Efficient System of Judicial Review" (2011) J Int'l Arb No. 6, p.553.

Aboukrat G., "A propos du statut de l'arbitre et de celui de la magistrature: quelle place pour le droit français?" in *Les Cahiers de l'Arbitrage Volume I* (Gazette du Palais, 2002), p.121.

Adeline S., "L'édification de la notion d'estoppel par la Cour de cassation (France) – Société Merial c. Société Klocke Verpackungs-Service GMBH" (2010) ASA Bull., p.406.

Affolder N., "Awarding Compound Interest in International Arbitration" (2001) Am Rev Int'l Arb Vol.12, p.45

Aksen G., "The Tribunal's Appointment" in *The Leading Arbitrators' Guide to International Arbitration* 2nd edition (Juris Publishing/Staempfli Publishers, 2008), p.31.

Ancel P., "Note under Cass Com, January 14, 2004, *Prodim v Logidis*" (2004) Rev Arb No.3, p.591.

Annacker C. & Greig R.T., "State Immunity and Arbitration" (2004) ICC ICArb Bull Vol.15 No.2, p.70.

Arfazadeh H.

— "Considérations pragmatiques sur la compétence respective de l'arbitre et du juge en matière de corruption" (2001) ASA Bull Vol.19 No.4, p.672.

— *Ordre public et arbitrage international à l'épreuve de la mondialisation* (Bruylant, LGDJ, Schulthess, 2006), 2nd ed.

Arnaldez J.-J., Derains Y. & Hascher D.

— *Collection of ICC Arbitral Awards 1996–2000, Vol.IV* (ICC Publishing/ Kluwer, 2003).

— *Collection of ICC Arbitral Awards 1991–1995, Vol.III* (ICC Publishing/ Kluwer, 1997).

Arroyo M.

— "*Lis Pendens* in International Arbitration – The Newly Adopted Swiss Approach" SIAR 2007:1, p.19.

— "Dealing with Dissenting Opinions in the Award: Some Options for the Tribunal," (2008) ASA Bulletin No.3, p.437.

Art J. Y., "Challenge of Arbitrators: Is an Institutional Decision Final?" (1986) Arb Int Vol.2 No.3, p.261.

Aubert G., "L'arbitrage en droit du travail" (2000) ASA Bull Vol.18 No.1, p.2.

Audit B., "Le contrat de partenariat ou l'essor de l'arbitrage en matière administrative" (2004) Rev Arb No.3, p.541.

Bachand F., "Must An ICC Tribunal Comply with an Anti-Suit Injunction Issued by the Courts of the Seats of Arbitration–Comment on the Salini Costruttori S.p.a. v Ethiopia" (2005) Mealey's IAR Vol.20 No. 3, p.47.

Bagner H., "Arbitrator Impartiality: Appearance Is Everything" (2006) Mealey's IAR Vol.21 No.6, p.26.

Baizeau D., "Waiving the Right to Challenge an Award Rendered in Switzerland: Caveats and Drafting Considerations for Foreign Parties", Int ALR 3/2005, p.69.

Bamford S. & Maidment B., " 'All join in' or not? How well does international arbitration cater for disputes involving multiple parties or related claims?" (2009) ASA Bull. 27/1, p.3.

Baron P.M. & Liniger S., "A Second Look at Arbitrability, Approaches in the United States, Switzerland and Germany" (2006) Arb Int Vol.19 No.1, p.27.

P. Bärtsch and A. M. Petti, "The Arbitration Agreement" in *International Arbitration in Switzerland: A Handbook for Practitioners*, 2nd edition (Kluwer 2013), p.25.

Baude-Texidor Ch., "Les intérêts moratoires postérieurs à la sentence devant l'arbitre et devant le juge" (2005) Gazette du Palais, May 27 and 28, 2005, p.2.

Bennett S., *Arbitration: Essential concepts* (ALM Publishing, 2002).

Bensaude D.

— "Thalès Air Defence BV v. GIE Euromissile: Defining the Limits of Scrutiny of Awards Based on Alleged Violations of European Competition Law" (2005) J Int'l Arb Vol.22 No.3, p.239.

— "SA Otor Participations v S.A.R.L. Carlyle (Luxembourg) Holdings 1: Interim Awards on Provisional Measures in International Arbitration" (2005) J Int'l Arb Vol.22 No.4, p.357.

Berger B., "Notification and Deposit, Publication, Confidentiality and Preservation of the File" in Pierre Tercier (ed.) *Post-Award Issues*, ASA. Spec. Suppl. No 38 (2011).

Berger K.P., "Pre-Arbitral Referees: Arbitrators, Quasi-Arbitrators, Hybrids or Creatures of Contract Law?" in *Liber Amicorum in honour of Robert Briner* (ICC Publishing, 2005), p.73.

Bernardini P.

— "International Arbitration and A-National Rules of Law" (2004) ICC ICArb Bull Vol.15 No.2, p.58.

— "The Powers of the Arbitrator" (1993) ICC ICArb Bull, Special Supplement, p.21.

— "International Arbitration: How to Make it More Effective", in Liber Amicorum Serge Lazareff (2011), pp.71–80.

Bernini G., "The civil law approach to discovery: a comparative overview of the taking of evidence in the anglo-american and continental arbitration systems" in *The Leading Arbitrators' Guide in International Arbitration*, 2nd edition (Juris Publishing/Staempfli Publishers, 2008), p.265.

Bertrand E., "Sur le bon usage des sentences d'accord parties" (2006) ASA Bull Vol.24 No.1, p.13.

Besson S.

— *Arbitrage international et mesures provisoires–Etude de droit comparé* (Schulthess, 1998).

— "Le Recours contre la Sentence Arbitrale Internationale selon la nouvelle LTF (Aspects procéduraux)" (2007) ASA Bull Vol.25 No.1, p.2.

Bishop D. & Reed L., "Practical Guidelines for Interviewing, Selecting and Challenging Party-Appointed Arbitrators in International Commercial Arbitration" (1998) Arb Int Vol.14 No.4, p.395.

Blanke G., "Defining the Limits of Scrutiny of Awards Based on Alleged Violations of European Competition Law–A Réplique to Denis Bensaude's Thalès Air Defence BV v. GIE Euromissile" (2006) J Int'l Arb Vol.23 No.3, p.249.

Blessing M.

— "The Law Applicable to the Arbitration Clause and Arbitrability" (1999) ICCA Congress Series No.9, p.168.

— "Choice of Substantive Law in International Arbitration" (1997) J Int'l Arb Vol.14 No.2, p.39.

— "The ICC Arbitral Procedure Under the 1998 ICC Rules–What Has Changed?" (1997) ICC ICArb Bull Vol.8 No.2, p.16.

Bond S.

— "The Nature of Conservatory and Provisional Measures", in Conservatory and Provisional Measures, 1993 ICArb Bull, Special Supplement, pp. 8–16.

— "Case Management by Arbitrators: Experiences and Suggestions" in *Liber Amicorum in honour of Robert Briner* (ICC Publishing, 2005), p.115.

de Boisséson M. & Duprey P., "L'arbitrabilité subjective en matière de droit des sociétés" in *Les Cahiers de l'Arbitrage Volume II* (Gazette du Palais, 2004), p.121.

Born G.

— *International Commercial Arbitration* (Kluwer Law International 2009).

— *International Commercial Arbitration–Commentary and Materials*, 2nd edition (Transnational Publishers/ Kluwer, 2011).

— *International Arbitration: Law and Practice* (Kluwer Law International 2012).

Bowman Rutledge P., Kent R. & Hennel C., "Arbitration in the United States" in *Practitioner's Handbook on International Arbitration*, 2nd edition (Oxford University Press, 2009), p.877.

Bredin J.-D.

— "Retour au délibéré arbitral" in *Liber Amicorum Claude Reymond* (Litec, 2004), p.43.

— "Le secret du délibéré arbitral" in *Etudes offertes à Pierres Bellet* (Litec, 1991), p.71.

Briner R.

— "Article 177" in *International Arbitration in Switzerland–An Introduction to and a Commentary on Articles 176–194 of the Swiss Private International Law Statute* (Helbing & Lichtenhahn/Kluwer, 2000), p.317.

— "The Role of the Chairman" in *The Leading Arbitrators Guide to International Arbitration*, 2nd edition (Juris Publishing/Staempfli Publishers, 2008), p.49.

— "The Evaluation of Evidence: Some Observations Based on the Practice of the Iran-United States Claims Tribunal" in *Liber Amicorum Thomas Bär and Robert Karrer* (1997), p.41.

Brower C.N., "Awarding Interest–Ex Officio or Only If Requested, At What Rate, As of When, Compound or Not?" in *ASA Special Series No. 29* (September 2007).

Brower C.N. & Sharpe J.K.

— "Awards of Compound Interest in International Arbitration: The Aminoil Non-Precedent" in *Liber Amicorum in honour of Robert Briner* (ICC Publishing, 2005), p.155.

— "Determining the extent of discovery and dealing with request for discovery: perspectives from the common law" in *The Leading Arbitrators' Guide in International Arbitration*, 2nd edition (Juris Publishing/Staempfli Publishers, 2008), p.303.

Brown-Berset D. & Lévy L., "Faillite et arbitrage" (1998) ASA Bull Vol.16 No.4, p.664.

Bruna S., "Control of time-limits by the International Court of Arbitration" (1996) ICC ICArb Bull Vol.7 No.2, p.72.

Bühler M.W.

— "Note–Sentence Partielle du 1er juin 2004 dans l'affaire CCI No 12491/KGA/EC–Non-payment of the advance on costs by the respondent party–is there really a remedy?" (2006) ASA Bull Vol.24 No.2, p.290.

— "Awarding Costs in International Commercial Arbitration: an Overview" (2004) ASA Bull Vol.22 No.2, p.249.

— "Cross-claims in international arbitrations: a common law perspective", paper delivered at the 22nd Symposium of Arbitrators held in Paris at the ICC on March 26, 2007.

— "Costs in arbitration. Some further considerations" in *Liber Amicorum in honour of Robert Briner* (ICC Publishing, 2005), p.179.

Bühler M.W. & Conybeare Williams H., "New York Law: Awards of Attorney's Fees in International Arbitration" (2005) Mealey's IAR Vol.20 No. 5, p.36.

Bühler M.W. & Dorgan C., "Witness Testimony Pursuant to the 1999 IBA Rules of Evidence in International Commercial Arbitration–Novel or Tested Standards?" (2000) J Int'l Arb Vol.17 No.1, p.3.

Bühler M.W. & Jarvin S.

— "L'amiable compositeur peut-il laisser la question du droit applicable au fond indéterminée?" in *Mélanges dédié à François Knoepfler, Droit international privé, droit de l'arbitrage et droit comparé* (Helbing & Lichtenhan, 2005).

— "The Arbitration Rules of the International Chamber of Commerce" in *Practitioner's Handbook on International Arbitration*, 2nd edition (Oxford University Press, 2009), p.1133.

Cachard O., "Le contrôle de la nullité ou de l'inapplicabilité manifeste de la clause compromissoire" (2006) Rev Arb No.4, p.893.

Cadiet L., "La renonciation à se prévaloir des irrégularités de la procédure arbitrale" (1996) Rev Arb No.1, p.3.

Caher, "§7502(c) of the US Civil Practice Laws and Rules authorizing New York courts to grant provisional measures in international arbitration", NewYork Law Journal, October 12, 2005.

Callé A.E.B.

— "Note under Cass Civ 1re, July 11, 2006, Société National Broadcasting v Bernadaux", Juris-data No.2006/0334549, (2006) JCP (G) 2006. II.10182.

— "Note under Paris, June 2, 2005, Bacque et autres v Société Carlyle Luxembourg Holding" (2005) Rev Arb No.4, p.1015.

Calvo Goller K., *The 2012 ICC Rules of Arbitration – An Accelerated Procedure and Substantial Changes*, Journal of International Arbitration , Vol. 29, Issue 3 (2012), pp. 323–344.

Caprasse O., "The setting up of the arbitral tribunal in multi-party arbitration" (2006) RDAI/IBLJ No.2, p.197.

Cárdenas E. & Rivkin D.W., "A Growing Challenge for Ethics in International Arbitration" in *Liber Amicorum in honour of Robert Briner* (ICC Publishing, 2005), p.191.

Carlevaris A., "La qualification des décisions des tribunaux arbitraux dans le Règlement d'arbitrage CCI et dans la jurisprudence française" in *Les Cahiers de l'Arbitrage Volume I* (Gazette du Palais, 2002), p.153.

Caron D.D., "The World of Intellectual Property and the Decision to Arbitrate" (2003) Arb Int Vol.19 No.4, p.441.

Carter J.H., "Emerging Issues in International Arbitration. A Kiss for Arbitration Costs Allocation" (2012) Am Rev Int'l Arb Vol. 23, p.475.

Castineira E., "The Emergency Arbitrator in the 2012 ICC Rules of Arbitration" (2012) Les Cahiers de l'Arbitrage No. 2012/1, p.65.

Castineira E. & Petsche M., "The Language of the Arbitration: Reflections on the Selection of Arbitrators and Procedural Efficiency" (2006) ICC ICArb Bull Vol.1 No.1, p.33.

Cavalieros Ph., "La confidentialité de l'arbitrage" (2005) Les Cahiers de l'Arbitrage No.2005/3, p.6, Gazette du Palais 14–15 décembre 2005.

Clarke A., "International Arbitration: Current Corporate Concerns" (2009) ICC ICArb Bull. Vol. 20 No. 2, p.9.

Clay Th.

— "Panorama–Arbitrage et modes alternatifs de règlement des litiges" (2008) Dalloz No.3, p.180.

— "Le secrétaire arbitral" (2005) Rev Arb No.4, p.931.

— *L'arbitre* (Dalloz, 2001), p.231.

Cordero Moss G., "Is the Arbitral Tribunal Bound by the Parties' Factual and Legal Pleadings?" SIAR 2006:3, p.1.

Courtois-Champenois E., "L'arbitrage des litiges en droit du travail: à la redécouverte d'une institution française en disgrâce. Etude comparative des droit français et américain" (2003) Rev Arb No.2, p.349.

Craig L.W., Park W.W. & Paulsson J., *International Chamber of Commerce Arbitration*, 3rd edition (Oceana/ICC Publishing, 2000).

Craig L. & Jaeger L., "The 2012 ICC Rules: Important changes and issues for future resolution" (2012) Les Cahiers de l'Arbitrage (1), p.15 (30).

Cremades B.

— "The Arbitral Award" in *The Leading Arbitrators' Guide to International Arbitration*, 2nd edition (Juris Publishing/Staempfli Publishers, 2008), p.483.

Croze H. & Reinhard Y., "Procédures collectives et arbitrage: Conseils pratiques aux parties et aux arbitres" (2005) JCP Entreprises et Affaires No.14, p.612.

Daly B.W., "Correction and Interpretation of Arbitral Awards under the ICC Rules of Arbitration" (2002) ICC ICArb Bull Vol.13 No.1, p.61.

Darwazeh N. & Zeman K., "Joint Nominations in Multiparty Arbitration: The Exercise of the ICC Court's Discretionary Power to Appoint the Entire Arbitral Tribunal Post-Dutco" (2012) ICC ICArb Bull Vol.23 No.1, pp.29–35.

Dasser F., "International Arbitration and Setting Aside Proceedings in Switzerland: A Statistical Analysis" (2007) ASA Bull Vol.25 No.3, p.444.

Degos L.

— "La CNUDCI abandonne l'exigence d'écrit pour la convention d'arbitrage" (2007) Les Cahiers de l'Arbitrage No.2007/1, p.5.

— "Decision by the French Cour de Cassation, First Civil Chamber rendered on 6 December 2005 in Case 1660 FS-P+B", SIAR 2006:1, p.149.

Delaume G., "Reflections on the Effectiveness of International Arbitral Awards" (1995) J Int'l Arb Vol.12 No.1, at pp.5–8.

Delelis Ph., "Partenariats public-private" in *JurisClasseur Administratif* (LexisNexis, 2005) Fasc. 670.

Delvolvé J.-L., Rouche J. & Pointon G. H., *French Arbitration Law and Practice* (Kluwer, 2003).

Derains Y.,

— "Amendments to the claims and new claims: where to draw the line?" in *Arbitral Procedure at the Dawn of the Millennium* (Bruylant, 2005), p.65.

— "La pratique du délibéré arbitral" in *Liber Amicorum in honour of Robert Briner* (ICC Publishing, 2005), p.221.

— "Le témoin en matière d'arbitrage international" in *Mélanges en l'Honneur de François Knoepfler* (Helbing & Lichtenhahn, 2005), p.227.

— "La pratique de l'administration de la preuve dans l'arbitrage commercial international" (2004) Rev Arb No.4, p.781.

— "L'arbitre et l'octroi de mesures provisoires ex parte" in *Les Cahiers de l'Arbitrage Volume II* (Gazette du Palais, 2003), p.45.

— "Evidence and Confidentiality" (2009) ICC ICArb Bull., Spec. Supp., *Confidentiality in Arbitration*, pp. 61, 67–68.

— "Les nouveaux principles de procédure: confidentialité, célérité, loyauté" in T. Clay (ed.) *Le nouveau droit français de 1' arbitrage* (Lextenso 2011), pp.91–104.

Derains Y. & Schwartz E.A., *A Guide to the ICC Rules*, 2nd edition (Kluwer Law International, 2005).

Dimolitsa A.

— "*Quid* encore de la confidentialité" in *Mélanges en l'Honneur de François Knoepfler* (Helbing & Lichtenhahn, 2005), p.249.

— "Giving Evidence: Some reflections on oral evidence vs documentary evidence and on the obligations and rights of the witnesses" in *Arbitration and Oral Evidence*, ICC Dossier 2004, publication No.689, p.11.

Dolmans M. & Grierson J., "Arbitration and the Modernization of EC Antitrust Law: New Opportunities and New Responsibilities" (2003) ICC ICArb Bull Vol.14 No.2, p.37.

Donovan D. F.

— "Introduction to the Sixteenth Annual Workshop of the Institute for Transnational Arbitration" (2007) Arb Int Vol.23 No.2, p.163, at pp.250–251.

— "Powers of the arbitrators to issue procedural orders, including interim measures of protection, and the obligations of parties to abide by such orders" (1999) ICC ICArb Bull Vol.10 No.1, p.57.

Dupeyré R., "Note – Département de commercialization du pétrole – Petroleum Marketing Department (Syrtol) v. SARL Babanapht, Cour d'appel de Paris (Pôle 1 – Ch. 1), 3 February 2011", (2011) Rev Arb No.2, p.472.

Dwyer J. & Greene P., Chapter 37: "Interim Measures in Antitrust Matters before Arbitrators" in Gordon Blanke and Phillip Landolt (eds), *EU and US Antitrust Arbitration: A Handbook for Practitioners* (Kluwer Law International, 2011), pp. 1417–1439.

Eastwood G., "A Real Danger of Confusion? The English Law Relating to Bias in Arbitrators" (2001) Arb Int Vol.17 No.3, p.287.

Eisemann F., "La clause d'arbitrage pathologique" in *Arbitrage commercial–Essais in memoriam Eugenio Minoli*, Colloria di Studi sull'Arbitrator (AIA, 1974), p.129.

Elder T.E., "The Case Against Arbitral Awards of Specific Performance in Transnational Commercial Disputes" (1997) Arb Int Vol.13 No.1, p.1.

Elsing S.H. & Towsend J.M., "Bridging the Common-Law Civil Divide in Arbitration" (2002) Arb Int Vol.1 No.1, p.59.

Epstein, "Arbitrator Independence and Bias: The view of a Corporate In-House Counsel" (2007) ICArb, Special Supplement on Independence of Arbitrators, p.55.

Escobar K., "The Relative Merits of Oral Argument and Post-Hearing Briefs" in Albert Jan van den Berg (ed), *Arbitration Advocacy in Changing Times*, ICCA Congress Series, 2010 Rio Volume 15 (Kluwer Law International, 2011), pp.221, 226.

Fadlallah I., "Payment of the Advance on Costs in ICC Arbitration: The Parties' Reciprocal Obligations" (2003) ICC ICArb Bull Vol.14 No.1, p.53.

Farhad A., "Provisional Enforcement of International Arbitral Awards Made in France–The Dilatory Effect of the French Set Aside Application" (2006) J Int'l Arb Vol.23 No.2, p.115.

Favre-Bulle X., "Les conséquences du non-paiement de la provision pour frais de l'arbitrage par une partie–Un tribunal arbitral peut-il condamner un défendeur au paiement de sa part de l'avance de frais?" (2001) ASA Bull Vol.19 No.2, p.227.

Fellas J.

— "Using Section 1782 In International Arbitration" (2007) Mealey's IAR Vol.22 No.2, p.39.

— "Anti-Suit Injunctions in Aid of Arbitration" (2005) Mealey's IAR Vol.20 No.4, p.25.

Figueroa Valdés J.E., "The Principle Of Kompetenz-Kompetenz In International Commercial Arbitration" (2007) Mealey's IAR Vol.22 No.5, p.29.

Fortier Y.

— "The Tribunal s deliberation" in *The Leading Arbitrators' Guide to International Arbitration*, 2nd edition (Juris Publishing/Staempfli Publishers, 2008), p.477.

— "The New *Lex Mercatoria*, or, Back To The Future" (2001) Arb Int Vol.17 No.2, p.121.

Fouchard Ph.

— "Arbitrage et Faillite" (1998) Rev Arb No.3, p.471.

— "La portée internationale de l'annulation de la sentence arbitrale dans son pays d'origine" (1997) Rev Arb No.3, p.329.

— "Final Report on the Status of the Arbitrator" (1996) ICC ICArb Bull Vol.7 No.1, p.27.

— "Le statut de l'arbitre dans la jurisprudence française" (1996) Rev Arb No.3, p.325.

— "Les institutions permanentes d'arbitrage devant le juge étatique (à propos d'une jurisprudence récente)" (1987) Rev Arb No.3, p.225.

Fouchard Ph., Gaillard E. & Goldman B., *On International Commercial Arbitration* (Kluwer, 1999).

Friedland P. D., "The Swiss Supreme Court Sets Aside an ICC Award" (1996) J Int'l Arb Vol.13 No.1, p.111.

de C. Fróes C. H., "Correction and Interpretation of Arbitral Awards" in *Liber Amicorum in honour of Robert Briner* (ICC Publishing, 2005), p.285.

Gabriel P., "Chemin du droit et droit chemin–Libres propos sur l'arbitrage commercial international" in *Liber Amicorum in honour of Robert Briner* (ICC Publishing, 2005), p.297.

Gaffney J.P., "*Ex Parte* Measures In International Arbitration" (2002) Mealey's IAR Vol.17 No. 11, p.39.

Gaillard E.

— "La jurisprudence de la Cour de cassation en matière d'arbitrage international" (2007) Rev Arb No.4, p.697.

— *Anti-Suit Injunctions in International Arbitration* (IAI series No.2, 2005).

— "La reconnaissance, en droit suisse, de la seconde moitié du principe d'effet négatif de la compétence-compétence" in *Liber Amicorum in honour of Robert Briner* (ICC Publishing, 2005), p.311.

— *La jurisprudence du CIRDI* Volume 2 (Pedone, 2010).

— "Il est interdit d'interdire: réflexion sur l'utilisation des anti-suit injunctions dans l'arbitrage commercial international" (2004) Rev Arb No.1, p.47.

— "Anti-suit injunctions et reconnaissance des sentences annulées au siège: une évolution remarquable de la jurisprudence américaine" (2003) JDI No.4, p.1107.

— "The Consolidation of Arbitral Proceedings and Court Proceedings", (2003) ICC ICArb Bull, Special Supplement, p.35.

— "Convention d'arbitrage et immunités de juridiction et d'exécution des Etats et des organisations internationales" (2000) ASA Bull Vol.18 No.3, p.471.

— "L'effet négatif de la compétence-compétence" in *Etudes de Procédure et d'Arbitrage en l'honneur de Jean-François Poudret* (Lausanne, 1999), p.387.

— "The Enforcement of Awards set Aside in the Country of Origins" (1999) ICSID Review No.14, p.16.

— "L'exécution des sentences annulées dans leur pays d'origine" (1998) JDI, p.645.

— "La distinction des principes généraux du droit et des usages du commerce international" in *Etudes offertes à Pierre Bellet* (Litec, 1991), p.203.

— "L'interdiction de se contredire au détriment d'autrui comme principe général du droit du commerce international" (1985) Rev Arb No.2, p.241.

— "Arbitration in France" *in Practitioner's Handbook on International Arbitration*, 2nd edition (Oxford University Press, 2009), p.423.

Gaillard E. & Pinsolle P., "The ICC Pre-Arbitral Referee: First Practical Experiences" (2004) Arb Int Vol. 20 No. XX, p.13.

Garaud J.-Y. & de Tafin O., "The ICC Rules for a Pre-Arbitral Referee Procedure" (2005) ICC ICArb Bull. Vol.16 No.1, p.33.

Gee S., "The Autonomy of Arbitrators, and Fraud Unravels All" (2006) Arb Int Vol.22 No.3, p.337.

Geisinger E. & Lévy L., "*Lis Alibi Pendens* in International Commercial Arbitration" (2003) ICC ICArb Bull, Special Supplement, p.53.

Gélinas P.-A., "Evidence through witnesses" in *Arbitration and Oral Evidence*, ICC Dossier 2004, publication No.689, p.29.

Genton P., "An Efficient Dispute Management Tool: The Dispute Board and the ICC DB Rules" in *ADR in Business–Practice and Issues across Countries and Cultures* edited by Goldsmith, Ingen-Housz & Pointon (Kluwer 2006), Chapter 5, p.93.

Gill J., "The Role of the Arbitrator in bringing about a Settlement–An English Perspective", in Best Practices in International Arbitration, *ASA Special Series No.26*, July 2006, p.155.

Gonzales F., "The Treatment of Tort in ICC Arbitral Awards" (2002) ICC ICArb Bull Vol.13 No.2, p.39.

Goode R., "The Role of the *Lex Loci Arbitri* in International Commercial Arbitration" (2001) Arb Int Vol.17 No.1, p.19.

Gotanda J., "Compound Interest in International Disputes" (2004), *http://oucl.iuscompa.org*

Greenberg S., "Arbitral Award Scrutiny under Scrutiny: An Assessment," in: Habegger P., Hochstrasser D. et al. (eds), Arbitral Institutions under Scrutiny (2013), ASA Special Series No. 40, p. 89.

Greenberg S. & Lautenschlager, F., "Adverse Inferences in International Arbitral Practice", in Kröll S.M., Mistelis L.A. et al. (eds), *International Arbitration and International Commercial Law: Synergy, Convergence and Evolution* (Kluwer Law International, 2011), pp.179–205.

Greenberg S. & Mange F., "Institutional and Ad Hoc Perspectives on the Temporal Conflict of Arbitral Rules," (2010) J Int'l Arb Vol. 27 No. 2, p.XX.

Greenberg R. & Feris A., "Consolidation, Joinder, Cross-Claims, Multiparty and Multicontract Arbitrations, Recent ICC Experience" in Hanotiau B. & Schwartz E.A. (eds), Multiparty Arbitration, Dossier VII, ICC Institute of World Business Law, (2010) ICC Publication No. 701 161.

Griffith G. & Pintos Lopez R., "Renegotiating Arbitrators' Terms of Remuneration" (2002) J Int'l Arb Vol.19 No.6, p.581.

Grigera-Naón H.

— "Les contrats d'Etat: quelques réflexions–Les états dans le contentieux économique international, I. Le contentieux arbitral" (2003) Rev Arb No.3, p.667.

Hafter P., "The Provisions on the Discovery of Internal Documents in the IBA Rules of 1999" in *Liber Amicorum in honour of Robert Briner* (ICC Publishing, 2005), p.347.

Haller, H., "Protection of Business Secrets by way of protective orders" (2013) SchiedsVZ no 3, p.135.

Hamilton & Maestre de Robles, "Madrid Update: Confidentiality in Arbitration, An Issue for Personal Privacy" (2009) 24–5 Mealey's Int'l Arb Rep, p.18.

Hammoud L. & Secomb M., "Interest in ICC Arbitral Awards: Introduction and Commentary" (2004) ICC ICArb Bull Vol.15 No.1, p.53.

Hanotiau B.

— *Complex Arbitrations–Multiparty, Multicontract, Multi-Issues and Class Actions* (Kluwer, 2005).

— "Panorama de jurisprudence belge–Décision de la Cour Suprême de Belgique, 15 octobre 2004, No.C020216N" Les Cahiers de l'Arbitrage No.2005:1, p.46.

— "L'arbitrage et les groupes de sociétés" in *Les Cahiers de l'Arbitrage Volume II* (Gazette du Palais, 2004), p.111.

— "Problems raised by complex arbitrations involving multiple contracts-parties-issues–An analysis" (2001) J Int'l Arb Vol.18 No.3, p.253.

— "A New Development in Complex Multiparty-Multicontract Proceedings: Classwide arbitration" (2004) Arb Int Vol.20 No.1, p.39.

— "L'arbitrabilité des litiges de propriété intellectuelle: une analyse comparative" (2003) ASA Bull Vol.21 No.1, p.3.

— "Problems Raised by Complex Arbitrations Involving Multiple Contracts-Parties-Issues-An Analysis" (2001) J Int'l Arb Vol.18 No.3, p.253.

Heitzmann P., "The Contrat de Partenariat: A New Form of French Public Private Partnership" (2006) ICRL Vol.23 Part 1, p.2.

Heitzmann P. & Grierson J., "SNF v Cytec Industrie: National Courts within the EC Apply Different Standards to Review International Awards Allegedly Contrary to Article 81 EC" SIAR 2007:2, p.39.

Henry M.

— "The Group of Companies Doctrine Applied to Arbitration Involving a State" (2006) RDAI/IBLJ No.3, p.297.

Hirsch L., "Contractual Exclusion of Annulment Actions Against International Arbitral Awards Made in Switzerland" (2006) SIAR 2006:2, p.43.

Houte van, H. & McAsey, B., The liability of arbitrators and arbitral institutions, in: Habegger, Hochstasser et al. (eds), Arbitral Institutions under Scrutiny, (2013) ASA Special Series No.40, p.133.

Horvath G.J., "Guerilla Tactics in Arbitration, an Ethical Battle: Is There a Need for a Universal Code of Ethics", in Klausegger C., Klein P., et al, *Austrian Yearbook on International Arbitration*, Vol. 2011 pp.297–313.

van Houtte H.

— "The Delivery of the Awards–Ten Pitfalls" ASA Special Series No.29, September 2007, p.76.

— "The Delivery of Awards to the Parties" (2005) Arb Int Vol.21 No.2, p.177.

— "Ten Reasons Against a Proposal for Ex Parte Interim Measures of Protection in Arbitration" (2004) Arb Int Vol.20 No.1, p.85.

— "The Vienna Sales Convention in ICC Arbitral Practice" (2000) ICC ICArb Bull Vol.11 No.2, p.22.

Howell D., "English Court Of Appeal Decision Supports The Position That Proper Law Of The Arbitration Agreement May Be Law Of The Seat Of Arbitration Where Arbitration Clause Contains No Express Governing Law" Mealey's IAR January 2008 Vol.23 No.1, p.27.

Hunter M.

— "Final Report on Dissenting and Separate Opinions" (1990) ICC ICArb Bull Vol.2 No.1, p.32.

— "Final Report on Interim and Partial Awards" (1990) ICC ICArb Bull Vol.1 No.2, p.26.

IBA Working Party, "Commentary on the New IBA Rules of Evidence in International Commercial Arbitration" (Jan. 2000) IBA Intl Bus Lawyer, p.14.

International Chamber of Commerce (ICC)

— ICC ICArb Bull, Special Supplement (2007), *Independence of Arbitrators*.

— *ICC Arbitration Commission Report on Techniques for Controlling Time and Costs in Arbitration* (ICC Publication No.861 E, 2012).

— *Global Reflections on International Law, Commerce and Dispute Resolution–Liber Amicorum in honour of Robert Briner* (ICC Publication No.693, 2005).

— ICC ICArb Bull, Special Supplement (2005), *UNIDROIT Principles: New Developments and Applications*.

— *Arbitration and Oral Evidence* (ICC Publication No.689, 2005).

— *Arbitration–Money Laundering, Corruption and Fraud* (ICC Publication No.651, 2003).

ICC Institute of World Business Law 22nd Annual Symposium of Arbitrators, Paris, March 26, 2007 co-hosted by the School of International Arbitration–Queen Mary University of London, "Claims, Counterclaims, Cross-Claims and Set-off Claims".

ICCA's Guide to the Interpretation of the 1958 New York Convention: A Handbook for Judges, (International Council for Commercial Arbitration 2011).

Jacquet, "Qualification et conséquences des mesures provisoires prises par un tribunal arbitral" (2005) JCP G No.22, 1er juin 2005, p.1027.

Jacobs M., "Requirement Of Writing And Of Signatures Under the UNCITRAL Model Law And the New York Convention" (2006) Mealey's IAR Vol.21 No.11, p.46.

Jaeger, L., "The administration and assessment of testimonial evidence" (2013) *Les Cahiers de l'Arbitrage*, Vol.1, p.71.

Jarrosson Ch.

— "La mise en cause en cause de la responsabilité de la CCI devant le juge français, note sous Tribunal de grande instance de Paris 1re Ch., 10 octobre 2007" (2007) Rev Arb No.4, p.847.

— "L'expertise juridique" in *Liber amicorum Claude Reymond* (Litec, 2004), p.127.

— "Observations on Poiré v Tripier" (2003) Arb Int Vol.19 No.3, p.363.

Jarvin S.

— "La renonciation à la convention d'arbitrage" in *Liber Amicorum Mitrovic* (2007).

— "Irregularity in the composition of the Arbitral Tribunal and the Procedure" in *Enforcement of Arbitration Agreements and International Arbitral Awards: The New York Convention 1958 in Practice* edited by E. Gaillard and D. di Pietro (Cameron, 2007).

Jarvin S. & Derains Y., *Collection of ICC Arbitral Awards 1974–1985, Vol.I* (ICC Publishing/Kluwer, 1990).

Jarvin S., Derains Y. & Arnaldez J.-J., *Collection of ICC Arbitral Awards 1986–1990, Vol.II* (ICC Publishing/Kluwer, 1994).

Jarvin S. & Dorgan C., "Are Foreign Parties Still Welcome in Stockholm?–The Svea Court's Decision in Titan Corporation v. Alcatel CIT S.A. Raises Doubts" (2005) Mealey's IAR Vol.20 No. 7, p.42.

Jarvin S. & Magnusson A., *International Arbitration Court Decisions*, 2nd edition (JurisNet, 2008).

Jimenez Figueres D.

— "Multi-Tiered Dispute Resolution Clauses in ICC Arbitration" (2003) ICC ICArb Bull Vol.14 No.1, p.71.

Jolivet E.

— "Access to information and Awards" (2006) Arb Int Vol.22 No.2, p.265.

— "Chronique de jurisprudence arbitrale de la Chambre de commerce internationale (CCI): l'incompétence de l'arbitre" (2006) Les Cahiers de l'Arbitrage 2006/1, p.38.

— "L'intérêt de recourir à une institution d'arbitrage. L'exemple de la Cour internationale d'arbitrage de la CCI" in *Liber Amicorum in honour of Robert Briner* (ICC Publishing, 2005), p.413.

— "Chronique de jurisprudence arbitrale de la Chambre de commerce internationale: Quelques exemples du traitement du droit communautaire dans l'arbitrage CCI" in *Les Cahiers de l'Arbitrage Volume II* (Gazette du Palais, 2004), p.247.

— "Chronique de jurisprudence arbitrale de la Chambre de commerce internationale (CCI): Quelques exemples du traitement du droit communautaire dans l'arbitrage CCI" (2003) Cahiers de l'Arbitrage 2e partie, p.3.

— "Chronique de jurisprudence arbitrale de la Chambre de commerce internationale: Arbitrage CCI et procédure ADR" in *Les Cahiers de l'Arbitrage Volume I* (Gazette du Palais, 2002), p.261.

— "La jurisprudence arbitrale de la CCI et la *lex mercatoria*" (2001) Gazette du Palais–recueil mai-juin 2001, p.563.

Jolles A., "Consequences of Multitier Arbitration Clauses: Issues of Enforcement" (2006) Arbitration Vol.72 No.4, p.329.

Kantor, "New Amendments to ICSID's Arbitration Rules", SIAR 2006:1, p.213.

Karali M. & Ballantyne J., *"Arbitration in England" in Practitioner's Handbook on International Arbitration*, 2nd edition (Oxford University Press, 2009), p.351.

Karrer P.A. & Desax M., "Security for Costs in International Arbitration; Why, When and What if . . ." in *Liber Amicorum Karl-Heinz Böckstiegel* (Cologne, 2001), p.339.

Karrer P.A. & Straub P.A., "Arbitration in Switzerland" in *Practitioner's Handbook on International Arbitration*, 2nd edition (Oxford University Press, 2009), p.815.

Kaufmann-Kohler G.

— "The Arbitrator and the Law: Does He/She Know It? Apply It? How? And a Few More Questions" (2005) Arb Int Vol.21 No.4, p.631.

— " *Iura Novit Arbiter*–Est-ce bien raisonnable? Réfléxions sur le statut du droit de fond devant l'arbitre international" in *De Lege Ferenda–Réflexions sur le droit désirable en l'honneur du Professeur Alain Hirsch* (Editions Slatkine, 2004), p.71.

— "Discovery in International Arbitration: How Much is Too Much?" (Jan/ Feb 2004) SchiedvsVZ, p.13.

— "Qui contrôle l'arbitrage? Autonomie des parties, pouvoirs des arbitres et principes d'efficacité" in *Liber Amicorum Claude Reymond* (Litec, 2004), p.153.

Kaufmann-Kohler G. & Rigozzi A., *Arbitrage international–Droit et pratique à la lumière de la LDIP*, 2nd edition (Schulthess, 2010).

Kiffer L., "Amiable Composition and ICC Arbitration" (2007) ICC Bull ICArb Vol.18 No.1, p.51.

King D.B. & Bosman L., "Rethinking Discovery in International Arbitration: Beyond the Common Law/ Civil Law Divide" (2001) ICC ICArb Bull Vol.12 No.1, p.24.

Kirby J.

— "The ICC Court: A Behind-the-Scenes Look" (2005) ICC ICArb Bull Vol.16 No.2, p.9.

— "Insigma Technology Co. Ltd. V. Alstom Technology Ltd.: SIAC Can Administer Cases under the ICC Rules?!?" (2009) Arb Int Vol. 25 No.3, p.319.

Kleinheisterkamp J., *International Commercial Arbitration in Latin America* (Oceana Publication, Inc, 2005).

Knutson R.D.A., "The Interpretation of Arbitration Awards. When is a Final Award not Final?" (1994) J Int'l Arb Vol.11 No.2, p.99.

Koch C., "Standards and Procedures for Disqualifying Arbitrators" (2003) J Int'l Arb Vol.20 No.4, p.325.

Kreindler R.

— "Final Rulings on Costs: Loser Pays All?" in ASA Special Series No.26, July 2006, p.4.

— "Aspects of Illegality in the Formation and Performance of Contracts" (2003) ICCA Congress Series No.11, p.209.

Kurkela, Levin, Liebscher & Sommer, "Certain Procedural Issues in Arbitrating Competition Cases" (2007) J Int'l Arb Vol.24 No.2, p.189.

Lalive P.

— Dérives Arbitrales (I), (2005) ASA Bull. Vol. 23 No. 4, p.587.

— Dérives Arbitrales (II), (2006) ASA Bull. Vol. 24 No. 1, p.XX.

Lalive P., Poudret J.-F. & Reymond C., *Le droit de l'arbitrage interne et international en Suisse* (Payot Lausanne, 1989).

Lamèthe D., "Les langues de l'arbitrage international: liberté raisonnée de choix ou contraintes réglementées? D'autres intérêts économiques sont en jeu: ils sont culturels, moraux et sociaux et ils doivent être préservés. C'est au juriste de dire comment (Philippe Fouchard)" (2007) JDI No.4, p.1174.

Landoldt Ph., "The IBA Guidelines on Conflicts of Interest in International Arbitration: An Overview" (2005) J Int'l Arb Vol.22 No.5, p.409.

Lawson D., "Impartiality and Independence of International Arbitrators–Commentary on the 2004 IBA Guidelines on Conflicts of Interest in International Arbitration" (2005) ASA Bull Vol.23 No.1, p.22.

Lazareff S.

— "Terms of Reference" (2006) ICC ICArb Bull Vol.17 No.1, p.21.

— " L'arbitre singe ou comment assassiner l'arbitrage" in *Liber Amicorum in honour of Robert Briner* (ICC Publishing, 2005), p.477.

— "De l'amour du juge", Les Cahiers de l'arbitrage 2005/1 p.3 and Gazette du Palais, Special Arbitrage, October 21–22, 2005, p.3.

— "Aux frontières de l'arbitrage et de l'ADR: La Sentence d'Accord Parties" in *Les Cahiers de l'Arbitrage Volume I* (Gazette du Palais, 2002), p.8.

Lazareff S. & Le Gall J.-P., "L'assujettissement des arbitres à la TVA sous l'empire de l'article 259 du code général des impôts" (2006) Rev Arb No.2, p.543.

Leben Ch., "L'évolution de la notion de contrat d'Etat–Les états dans le contentieux économique international, I. Le contentieux arbitral" (2003) Rev Arb No.3, p.629.

Leboulanger Ph.

— "Principe de collégialité et délibéré arbitral" in *Mélanges en l'Honneur de François Knoepfler* (Helbing & Lichtenhahn, 2005), p.259.

— "Some Issues in ICC Awards relating to State Contracts" (2004) ICC ICArb Bull Vol.15 No.2, p.93.

Lévy L.

— "Insolvency in Arbitration (Swiss Law)" (2005) IntALR No.1, p.23.

— "Witness Statements" in *De Lege Ferenda–Réflexions sur le droit désirable en l'honneur du Professeur Alain Hirsch* (Slatkine, 2004), p.95.

Lévy L. & Schlaepfer V., "La suspension d'instance dans l'arbitrage international" in *Les Cahiers de l'Arbitrage Volume I* (Gazette du Palais, 2002), p.132.

Lew J.D.M.

— "Commentary on Interim and Conservatory Measures in ICC Arbitration Cases" (2000) ICC ICArb Bull Vol.11 No.1, p.23.

Lew J.D.M., Mistelis L.A. & Kröll S., *Comparative International Commercial Arbitration* (Kluwer, 2003).

Liber Amicorum Dobrosav Mitrovic (Belgrade, 2007).

Liber Amicorum in honour of Robert Briner, Global Reflections on International Law, Commerce and Dispute Resolution (ICC Publishing, 2005).

Liber Amicorum Claude Reymond, Autour de l'arbitrage (Litec, 2004).

Liber Amicorum Karl-Heinz Böckstiegel, Law of International Business and Dispute Settlement in the 21st Century (Cologne, 2001).

Liber Amicorum Michel Gaudet, Improving International Arbitration–The need for speed and trust (ICC, 1999).

Liber Amicorum Thomas Bär and Robert Karrer (1997).

Liber Amicorum Pieter Sanders, The art of Arbitration: essays on International arbitration (Kluwer, 1982).

Liebscher C., "Arbitration and EC Competition Law–The New Competition Regulation: Back to Square One?" (2003) IntlALR Vol.6 No.3, p.84.

Lindsey D., Hosking J. & Lahlou Y., "Application of US Discovery Law To Arbitration Upheld On Appeal" (2007) Mealey's Vol.22 No.5, p.26.

Lionnet K., "Once Again: Is Discovery of Documents Appropriate in International Arbitration?" in *Liber Amicorum in honour of Robert Briner* (ICC Publishing, 2005), p.491.

Lloyd H., Darmon M., Ancel J.-P., Dervaird, Liebscher Ch. & Verbist H., "Drafting Awards in ICC Arbitration" (2005) ICC ICArb Bull Vol.16 No.2, p.12.

Loquin E.

— "Chroniques–Tribunaux de commerce et arbitrage" (2006) RTD com No.4, p.760.

— "Les obligations de confidentialité dans l'arbitrage" (2006) Rev Arb No.2, p.324.

Lörcher G., "Enforceability of Agreed Awards in Foreign Jurisdictions" (2001) Arb Int Vol.17 No.3, p.275.

Lowenfeld A., "The Party appointed Arbitrator: Further Reflections" in *The Leading Arbitrators' Guide to International Arbitration*, 2nd edition (Juris Publishing/Staempfli Publishers, 2008), p.41.

Mackie K., "The Future for ADR Clauses After Cable & Wireless v. IBM" (2003) Arb Int Vol.19 No.3, p.345.

Madsen F. & Eriksson P., "Deliberations of the Arbitral Tribunal–Analysis of Reasoned Awards from a Swedish Perspective" (2006) SIAR 2006:2, p.1.

Maleville L., "Pathologies des clauses compromissoires, 'Pathological' arbitration clauses" (2000) RDAI/IBLJ No.1, p.61.

Malinvaud C., "Modification de la loi modèle CNUDCI sur les mesures intérimaires: un texte de compromis sur les mesures ex parte", Les Cahiers de l'Arbitrage 2007/1, p.12.

E. Marcareno, "An In-house Counsel Perspective on the Promotion of International Commercial Arbitration" 2013 Eur Int'l Arb R, Vol.1-2, p.145.

von Mehren A.T., "The Eco Swiss and International Arbitration" (2003) Arb Int Vol.19 No.4, p.465.

Mélanges dédiés à François Knoepfler, Droit international privé, droit de l'arbitrage et droit comparé (Helbing & Lichtenhan, 2005).

Meyer B., "Formalism in Arbitration – Good or Evil?" in Wirth, Rouvinez, Knoll (eds) *The Search for "Truth" in Arbitration. Is Finding the Truth What the Dispute is About?*(2011).

Meyerson B. & Townsend J. M., "Revised Code of Ethics for Commercial Arbitrators Explained" (2004) Dispute Resolution Journal Vol.59, p.10.

Ming W., "The Strange Case of Wang Shengchang" (2007) J Int'l Arb Vol.24 No.1, p.63.

Minjauw H., "The Relationship Between the Belgian 1961 Act on the Termination of Exclusive Distributions Agreements and Arbitration" (2007) RDAI/IBLJ No.1, p.3.

Mistelis L., "International Arbitration–Corporate Attitudes and Practices–12 Perceptions Tested: Myths, Data and Analysis–Research Report" (2004) Am Rev Int'l Arb Vol.15 No.3-4, p.525.

Moreau B., "Les effets de la nullité de la sentence arbitrale" in *Etudes offertes à Pierre Bellet* (Litec, 1991), p.403.

Mourre A.

— "Arbitration and Criminal Law: Reflections on the Duties of the Arbitrator" (2006) Arb Int Vol.22 No.1, p.95.

— "L'impact de la réforme de la clause compromissoire sur les litiges relatifs aux sociétés" in *Les Cahiers de l'Arbitrage Volume II* (Gazette du Palais, 2004), p.125.

— "Les rapports de l'arbitrage et du droit communautaire après l'arrêt Eco Swiss de la Cour de Justice des Communautés Européennes" in *Les Cahiers de l'Arbitrage Volume I* (Gazette du Palais, 2002), p.77.

— Mourre A. & Radicati di Brozolo L., "Towards Finality of Arbitral Awards: Two Steps Forward and One Step Back" (2006) J Int'l Arb Vol.23 No.2, p.171.

Müller Ch.

— "La confidentialité en arbitrage commercial international: un trompe-l'oeil? On est souvent satisfait d'être trompé par soi-même" (2005) ASA Bull Vol.23 No.2, p.216.

— *International Arbitration–A Guide to the Complete Swiss Case Law (Unreported and Reported)* (Thomson/Schulthess, 2004).

Mustill, The Rt Hon Lord Justice M., "The *New Lex Mercatoria*: The First Twenty-Five Years" (1988) Arb Int Vol.4 No.2, p.86.

Nater-Bass G., "Consent Awards–How to Draft Them" in ASA Special Series No.29, September 2007, p.36.

Newman L. & Klieman R., *Take the Witness: The Experts Speak on Cross-Examination* (Jurispublishing Inc, 2006), p.55.

Newmark C. & Hill R., "Can a Mediated Settlement Become an Enforceable Arbitration Award?" (2000) Arb Int Vol.16 No.1, p.81.

Nicholas G. & Partasides C., "LCIA Court Decisions on Challenge to Arbitrators: A Proposal to Publish" (2007) Arb Int Vol.23 No.1, p.1.

Noussia K., "Antisuit Injunctions and Arbitration Proceedings: What Does the Future Hold?" (2009) J Int'l Arb, p.311.

O'Malley N., "An annotated commentary on the 2010 revised IBA Rules of Evidence for International Arbitration" (2010) Int'l Const Law R, p.463.

Oetiker C.

— "Witnesses before the International Arbitral Tribunal" (2007) ASA Bull Vol.25 No.2, p.253.

— "The Principle of Lis Pendens in International Arbitration: The Swiss Decision in Fomento v. Colon" (2002) Arb Int Vol.18 No.2, p.137.

Orrego Vicuña F., "The binding nature of procedural orders in international arbitration" (1999) ICC ICArb Bull Vol.10 No.1, p.38.

Ortcheidt J., "Un nouvel exemple de l'effacement du droit commun des contrats en ce qui concerne les conventions d'arbitrage international" (2007) JCP (E) No.1602, p.23.

Paillusseau J., "L'arbitre responsable du délai d'arbitrage" (2006) JCP I 129, p.666.

Park W.

— "The Nature of Arbitral Authority: A Comment on Lesotho Highlands" (2005) Arb Int Vol.21 No.4, p.483.

— "Irony in Intellectual Property Arbitration" (2003) Arb Int Vol.19 No.4, p.451.

— "The Arbitrator's Jurisdiction to Determine Jurisdiction" (2007) ICCA Congress Series No.13, p.55.

Partasides C., "The Fourth Arbitrator? The Role of Secretaries to Tribunals in International Arbitration" (2002) Arb Int Vol.18 No.2, p.147.

Patocchi P.M., "Deciding on the Costs of the Arbitration–Selected Topics" in ASA Special Series No.29, September 2007, p.49.

Patocchi P. M. & Frey-Brentano H., "The Provisional Timetable in International Arbitration" in

Liber Amicorum in honour of Robert Briner (ICC Publishing, 2005), p.575.

Patocchi P. M. & Geisinger E., *IPRG Internationales Privatrecht* (Zurich, 2000).

Paulsson J.

— "United States Court of Appeals for the District of Columbia Circuit, May 25, 2007, Termorio S.A. E.S.P. and LeaseCo Group LLC v Electranta S.P. et al, No.06–7058" (2007) Rev Arb No.3, p.553.

— "Arbitration-Friendliness: Promises of Principles and Realities of Practice" (2007) Arb Int Vol.23 No.3, p.477.

— "The Timely Arbitrator: Reflections on the Böckstiegel Method" (2006) Arb Int Vol.22 No.1, p.19.

— "Enforcing Arbitral Awards Notwithstanding a Local Standard Annulment (LSA)" (1998) ICC Bull. Vol.9 No.1, p.14.

— "Arbitration Without Privity" (1995) ICSID Rev Vol.10, p.232.

— "The Unwelcome Atavism of Ken Ren: The House of Lords shows is Meddle" (1994) ASA Bull, Vol. 12, No.3/4, p.439.

— "May a State Invoke its Internal Law to Repudiate Consent to International Commercial Arbitration? Reflections On the Benteler v. Belgium Preliminary Award" (1986) Arb Int Vol.2 No.2, p.90.

— "Arbitration Unbound" (1981) Int'l Comp Law Quart, p.358.

Paulsson J. & Rawding N., "The Trouble with Confidentiality" (1995) Arb Int Vol.11 No.3, p.303.

Peter W., "Witness 'Conferencing' " (2002) Arb Int Vol.18 No.1, p.47.

Peters P., "Presiding Arbitrator, Deciding Arbitrator: Decision-Making in Arbitral Tribunals," Austrian Yearbook on International Arbitration 2011, p.129.

Phull C., "U.S. Anti-suit Injunctions in Support of International Arbitration: Five Questions American Courts Ask" (2011) J Int'l Arb, p.21.

Philippe M.

— "Les pouvoirs de l'arbitre et de la Cour d'arbitrage de la CCI relatifs à leur compétence" (2006) Rev Arb No.3, p.591.

— "Difficultés procédurales causées par les clauses compromissoires paritaires et les tribunaux arbitraux tronqués" Gazette du Palais 2005, p.21.

— "ICC NetCase: At The Forefront of IT In Arbitration", http://www.iccwbo.org/court

Pietrowski R., "Evidence in International Arbitration" (2006) Arb Int Vol.22 No.3, p.373.

Pinsolle Ph., "Les applications du principe de l'interdiction de se contredire au détriment d'autrui en droit du commerce international" in *L'interdiction de se contredire au détriment d'autrui*, colloque du CEDAG, Economica 2001, at p.37.

Pinsolle Ph. & Kreindler R., "Les limites du rôle de la volonté des parties dans la conduite de l'instance arbitrale" (2003) Rev Arb No.1, p.41.

Poudret J.-F.

— "Les recours au tribunal fédéral suisse en matière d'arbitrage international (Commentaire de l'art. 77 LTF)" (2007) ASA Bull Vol.25 No.4, p.669.

— "Exception d'arbitrage et litispendance en droit suisse–Comment départager le juge et l'arbitre?" (2007) ASA Bull Vol.25 No.2, p.230.

— "Les mesures provisionnelles et l'arbitrage. Aperçu comparatif des pouvoirs respectifs de l'arbitre et du juge" in *Mélanges en l'Honneur de François Knoepfler* (Helbing & Lichtenhahn, 2005), p.235.

— "Le tribunal fédéral suisse opte pour le régime de la litispendence entre le juge et l'arbitre: Note–Tribunal fédéral suisse, 14 mai 2001" (2001) Rev Arb No.4, p.835.

Poudret J.-F. & Besson S., *Comparative Law of International Arbitration*, 2nd edition (Thomson/Sweet & Maxwell, 2007).

Pryles M., "Confidentiality" in *The Leading Arbitrators' Guide in International Arbitration*, 2nd edition (Juris Publishing/Staempfli Publishers, 2008), p.501.

von Quitzow C.M., "The Benetton Judgment and its Practical Implications on Arbitration" SAR 2000:1, p.23.

Queen Mary University School of International Arbitration and White & Case, 2010 International Arbitration Survey: Choices in International Arbitration.

Queen Mary University School of International Arbitration and PricewaterhouseCoopers, Corporate Choices in International Arbitration: Industry Perspectives (2013).

Racine J.-B.

— "Réflexions sur l'autonomie de l'arbitrage commercial international (II.–L'arbitrage, Deuxième Séance)" (2005) Rev Arb No.2, p.305.

— "Paris, June 20, 2002, Odartech v W Management" in *Les Cahiers de l'Arbitrage–Volume II* (Gazette du Palais, 2004), p.357; (2002) Rev Arb No.4, p.973.

Radicati di Brozolo L.

— "Note–Tribunal Fédéral Suisse, 8 mars 2006" (2006) Rev Arb No.3, p.769.

— "L'ordre public et l'overkill du Tribunal Fédéral suisse" (2006) Rev Arb No.3, p.763.

— "L'illicéité qui crève les yeux: critère de contrôle des sentences au regard de l'ordre public international (à propos de l'arrêt Thalès de la Cour d'appel de Paris)" (2005) Rev Arb. No.3, p.529.

Rau A. S.

— "Provisional Relief in Arbitration: How Things Stand in the United States" (2005) J Int'l Arb Vol.22 No.1, p.1.

Raviv A., "No More Excuses: Towards a Workable System of Dispositive Motions in International Arbitration" (2012) Arb. Int'l Vol. 28 No.3, p.487.

Redfern A., Hunter M. with Blackaby N. & Partasides C., *Law and Practice of International Commercial Arbitration*, 4th edition (Thomson/Sweet&Maxwell, 2004).

Reed L., Paulsson J. & Blackaby N., *Guide to ICSID Arbitration*, 2nd edition (Kluwer, 2010).

Rees P., "Dissenting Opinions: Can they Fulfill a Beneficial Role?" (2009) Arb Int'l No. 3, p.329.

Reiner A. & Ascauer C., Chapter II: ICC Rules, in: Schütze R.A. (ed), *Institutional Arbitration, Article-by-Article Commentary* (Munich 2013), pp. 25–201.

Robine E., "The Liability of Arbitrators and Arbitral Institutions in International Arbitrations under French Law" (1989) Arb Int Vol.5 No.4, p.323.

Rosell J. & Prager H., "International Arbitration and Bankruptcy: United States, France and the ICC" (2001) J Int'l Arb Vol.18 No.4, p.417.

Rosher P., "Legal privilege et confidentialité des communications avocat-client en matière d'arbitrage international–Vers une possible harmonisation?", Les Cahiers de l'Arbitrage No.2007/3, p.21.

Roth M. & Reith C., "Emergency Rules" (2012) Yearbook on International Arbitration Vol.II, pp.65–74.

Roth M., "Interim Measures" (2012) Yearbook on International Arbitration Vol. III, pp. 2–13.

Rouche J., "Le paiement par le défendeur de sa part de provision sur les frais d'arbitrage: simple faculté ou obligation contractuelle?" (2002) Rev Arb No.4, p.841.

Sanders P., "The Terms of Reference in ICC Arbitration" in *Liber Amicorum in honour of Robert Briner* (ICC Publishing, 2005), p.693.

Sayed A., "La question de la corruption dans l'arbitrage commercial international: Inventaire des solutions" (2001) ASA Bull Vol.19 No.4, p.653.

Scalbert H. & Marville L., "Les clauses compromissoires pathologiques" (1988) Rev Arb No.1, p.117.

Schäfer E.

— "Arbitration of Intellectual Property Law Disputes in Germany" in *Arbitration in Germany: The Model Law in Practice* edited by K.-H. Böckstiegel, S. Kröll and P. Nacimiento (Kluwer, 2007), p.953.

— "IT in Arbitation: The Work of the ICC Task Force" (2004) ICC ICArb Bull, Special Supplement, p.59.

— "Videoconferencing in Arbitration" (2003) ICC ICArb Bull Vol.14 No.1, p.35.

Scherer M.

— "Jurisprudence–Introduction to Case Law Section–Advance on the costs of the arbitration" (2003) ASA Bull Vol.21 No.4, p.749.

— "Circumstantial Evidence in Corruption Cases Before International Arbitral Tribunals" (2002) 5:2 Int A L Rev 29.

— "International Arbitration and Corruption–Synopsis of Selected Arbitral Awards" (2001) ASA Bull Vol.19 No.4, p.710.

— "Editors Note: When Should an Arbitral Tribunal Sitting in Switzerland Confronted with Parallel Litigation Abroad Stay the Arbitration?" (2001) ASA Bull Vol.19 No.3, p.451.

Schlosser, "Generalizable Approaches to Agreements with Experts and Witness Acting in Arbitration and International Litigation" in *Liber Amicorum in honour of Robert Briner* (ICC Publishing, 2005), p.775.

Schreuer C., *The ICSID Convention: A commentary*, 2nd edition (Cambridge UP, 2009).

Schwab/Walter, *Schiedsgerichtsbarkeit*, 6th edition (Munich, 2005).

Schwartz E.A.

— " 'New Claims' in ICC Arbitration: Navigating Article 19 of the ICC Rules" (2006) ICC ICArb Bull Vol.17 No.2, p.55.

— "Do International Arbitrators Have a Duty to Obey the Orders of Courts at the Place of the Arbitration? Reflections on the Role of the Lex Loci Arbitri in the Light of a Recent ICC Award" in *Liber Amicorum in honour of Robert Briner* (ICC Publishing, 2005), p.795.

Schwebel S.M., "The authority of truncated international arbitral tribunals" in *International Arbitration: three salient problems* (Grotius Publications Ltd, 1987).

Secomb M., "Awards and Orders Dealing with the Advance on Costs in ICC Arbitration: Theoritical Questions and Practical Problems" (2003) ICC ICArb Bull Vol.14 No.1, p.59.

Senkovic P. & Lastenouse P., "International Arbitration And Antitrust Law: Eco Swiss Judgment Revisited By the Paris Court of Appeal" (2005) Mealey's IAR Vol.20 No. 2, p.1.

Seppälä Ch., "Obtaining The Right International Arbitral Tribunal: A Practitioner's View" (2007) Mealey's IAR Vol.22 No.10, p.36.

Seraglini Ch., "Brèves remarques sur les Recommandations de l'Association du droit international sur la *litispendance* et l'autorité de la chose jugée en arbitrage" (2006) Rev Arb No.4, p.909.

Sfeir-Slim M., "L'application de la règle 'le criminel tient le civil en l'état' en matière d'arbitrage" in *Mélanges en hommage à Méliné Topakian, Le Droit en Mouvement* (Bruylant, Presse de l'Université Saint Joseph, 2005).

Sheppard A., "Interim ILA Report on Public Policy as a Bar to Enforcement of International Arbitral Awards" (2003) Arb Int Vol.19 No.2, p.217.

Sheppard B., Jr

— "US Discovery Can Be Obtained For Use in Foreign BIT Arbitration Proceedings" (2007) ASA Bull Vol.25 No.2, p.402.

— "The Moth, the Light and the United States Severability Doctrine–The Decision of the Supreme Court in Buckeye Check Cashing, Inc v Cardegna" (2006) J Int'l Arb Vol.23 No.5, p.479.

— "A New Era of Arbitrator Ethics for the United States: The 2004 Revision to the AAA/ABA Code of Ethics for Arbitrators in Commercial Disputes" (2005) Arb Int Vol.21 No.1, p.91.

Silva-Romero E.

— "The Dialectic of International Arbitration Involving State Parties, Observations on the Applicable Law in State Contract Arbitration" (2004) ICC ICArb Bull Vol.15 No.2, p.79.

— "ICC Arbitration and State Contracts" (2002) ICC ICArb Bull Vol.13 No.1, p.34.

Simont L., "Arbitrage et droit de la concurrence: quelques réflexions d'un arbitre" (1998) RDAI/IBLJ nos 4/5, p.547.

Slim H., "Les contrats d'état et les spécificités des systèmes juridiques dualistes– Les états dans le contentieux économique international, I. Le contentieux arbitral" (2003) Rev Arb No.3, p.691.

Smeureanu I., *Confidentiality in International Commercial Arbitration* (Kluwer Law International, 2011).

Smit R. H.

— "Dissenting Opinions in Arbitration" (2004) ICC ICArb Bull Vol.15 No.1, p.37.

— "Mitsubishi: It is Not What it Seems To Be" (1987) J Int'l Arb Vol.4 No.3, p.7.

— "Mandatory ICC Arbitration Rules" in *Liber Amicorum in honour of Robert Briner* (ICC Publishing, 2005), p.845.

Smit R. H. & Turner A., "Enforcement by US Court of International Arbitration Interim Orders and Awards under the New York Convention, Publicis Communication v True North Communications Inc", SAR 2001:1, p.47.

Smith R.H. & Freeman P., "Anti-Suit Injunctions in Europe: Another Advantage of Arbitration" (2005) Mealey's IAR Vol.20 No. 3, p.45.

Söderlund C., "Lis Pendens, Res Judicata and the Issues of Parallel Judicial Proceedings" (2005) J Intl Arb Vol.22 No.4, p.301.

Sono, "The Limitation Convention: The Forerunner to Establish UNCITRAL Credibility" (September 2003), *http://www.cisg.law.pace.edu*

Steyn, "England: The Independence and/or Impartiality of Arbitrators in International Commercial Arbitration" (2007) ICArb, Special Supplement on Independence of Arbitrators, p.91.

Sutton D., Gill J. & Gearing M., *Russell on Arbitration*, 23rd edition (Thomson/ Sweet & Maxwell, 2007).

Svenson Th., "New Norwegian Arbitration Act–Draft statute", SAR 2003:1 p.47.

Tallerico Th. & Behrendt J., "The Use of Bifurcation and Direct Testimony Witness Statements in International Commercial Arbitration Proceedings" (2003) J Int Arb Vol.20 No.3, p.295.

Tan D., "Enforcing Arbitration Agreements With Antisuit Injunctions" (2006) Mealey's IAR Vol.21 No.7, p.39.

Tattevin G., "NIOC v. Israel: 'The End' . . . Or Is It?", SIAR 2005:2, p. 221.

Taylor T. & Baruti R., "Reopening The Case After The Hearing–To What Extent And Under What Circumstances Should It Be Allowed" in *ASA Special Series No.29*, September 2007, p.8.

Tchakoua J.-M., "The Status of the Arbitral Award by Consent: The limits of a Useful Ruse" (2002) RDAI/IBLJ No.7, p.775.

Tchanz P.-Y.

— "The Award–How To Structure It, How Detailed? Orders and Reasons, Adding Insult To Injury", in ASA Special Series No. 29, September 2007, p.25.

— "Switzerland: Confidentiality of Swiss Supreme Court Review of Arbitral Awards", Mondaq Business Briefing, September 28, 2006.

Tercier P.

— "Dissenting Opinions and Majority Decision", in ASA Special Series No. 29, September 2007.

— "Emerging trends in ICC arbitration and the Institution's vision for the future" in Global Arbitration Review 2007, at p.2.

Train F.-X., "Denial of Justice in International Arbitration: How the French 'Juge d'appui' Extends Its Jurisdiction", SIAR 2005:2, p.230.

Truong C.Q.C., *Les différends liés à la rupture des contrats internationaux de distribution dans les sentences arbitrales CCI* (Litec, 2002).

Tweeddale A. & K., *Arbitration of Commercial Disputes–International and English Law and Practice* (Oxford University Press, 2007).

Ulmer N., "Swiss Arbitration Update: First Amendments Of International Arbitration Law" (2006) Mealey's IAR Vol.21 No.12, p.35.

UNIDROIT Principles of International Commercial Contracts, 2nd edition (UNIDROIT 2004).

Veit, "Note–Procedural Order No.14 of November 27, 2002–Security for Costs in International Arbitration–Some Comments to Procedural Order No 14 of November 27, 2002", (2005) ASA Bull Vol.23 No.1, p.116.

Verbist H.

— "Arbitrability of Exclusive Distributorship Agreements in Belgium: *Lex Fori* (and *Lex Contractus*" (2005) J Int'l Arb Vol. 22 No.5, p.427.

Vogt, "Article 181" in *International Arbitration in Switzerland–An Introduction to and a Commentary on Articles 176–194 of the Swiss Private International Law Statute* (Helbing & Lichtenhahn/Kluwer, 2000), p.182.

Voser N.

— "Interim Relief in International Arbitration: The Tendency Towards a More Business-Oriented Approach" (2007) Dispute Resolution International Vol.1 No.2, p.171.

— "Overview of the Most Important Changes in the Revised ICC Arbitration Rules" (2011) ASA Bull. 29/4, pp.783–795.

— Emergency Arbitrator, ICC Bull [XX]

— "Overview of the Most Important Changes in the Revised ICC Arbitration Rules" (2011) ASA Bull. Vol. 29 No. 4, p.783.

Voser N. & Mueller A., "Appointment of Experts by the Arbitral Tribunal: the Civil Law Perspective" (2006) Business Law International Vol.7 No.1, p.73.

Waincymer J., "Procedure and Evidence in International Arbitration" (Kluwer Law International, 2012)

Waincymer J., "International Arbitration and the Duty to Know the Law" (2011) J Int'l Arb Vol.28 No.3, pp.201, 236.

Weber-Stecher, U., "Principles of good governance and organisation of arbitral institutions" Habegger, Hochstrasser et al. (eds), *Arbitral Institutions under Scrutiny* (2013) ASA Special Series No 40, p.37.

Webster Th.

— "Party Control in International Arbitration" (2003) Arb Int Vol.19 No.2, p.119.

— "Terms of Reference and French Annulment Proceedings" (2003) J Int'l Arb Vol.20 No.6, p.561.

— "Selection of Arbitrators in a Nutshell" (2002) J Int'l Arb Vol.19 No.3, p.261.

— "Obtaining Documents from Adverse Parties in International Arbitration" (2001) Arb Int Vol.17 No.1, p.41.

— "Obtaining Evidence from Third Parties in International Arbitration" (2001) Arb Int Vol.17 No.2, p.143.

— "Review of Substantive Reasoning of International Arbitral Awards by National Courts: Ensuring One-Step Adjudication' (2006) Arb Int Vol.22 No.3, p.431.

— "Evolving Principles in Enforcing Awards Subject to Annulment Proceedings' (2005) J Int'l Arb Vol.23 No.3, pp.201–226.

— "Handbook of UNCITRAL Arbitration" (Sweet & Maxwell, 2010).

— "Handbook of Investment Arbitration: Commentary, Precedents and Models for ICSID Arbitration" (Sweet & Maxwell, 2012).

Weiler T., *NAFTA Investment Law and Arbitration: Past Issues, Current Practice, Future Prospects* (Transnational Publisher, Inc, 2004).

Wenger W.

— "The Role of the Arbitrator in bringing about a Settlement–A Swiss Perspective" in ASA Special Series No.26, July 2006, p.139.

— "Article 178" in *International Arbitration in Switzerland–An Introduction to and a Commentary on Articles 176–194 of the Swiss Private International Law Statute* (Helbing & Lichtenhahn/Kluwer, 2000), p.327.

Werner J.

— "Who controls speed? A few reflections on the relationship between parties and arbitrators in ICC arbitration" in *Liber Amicorum Michel Gaudet, Improving International Arbitration–The need for speed and trust* (ICC, 1999), p.99.

—"The Arbitrator as Master of Time", in Liber Amicorum Serge Lazareff (2011), pp. 595–597.

Wessel J. & Eyre P., "US Discovery in Aid of Foreign or International Proceedings: the Rise of 28 USC, s.1782", The Journal of the Dispute Resolution Section of the International Bar Association June 2007 Vol.1 No.1, p.23.

Wetter J.G., "Issues of Corruption before International Arbitral Tribunals: The Authentic Text and True Meaning of Judge Gunnar Lagergren's 1963 Award in ICC Case no 1110" (1994) Arb Int Vol.10 No.3, p.277.

Whitesell A. M.

— "Independence in ICC Arbitration–ICC Court Practice concerning the Appointment, Confirmation, Challenge and Replacement of Arbitrators" (2007) ICC ICArb, Special Supplement on Independence of Arbitrators, p.7.

— "The 1998 ICC Rules of Arbitration Today" in *Liber Amicorum in honour of Robert Briner* (ICC Publishing, 2005), p.919.

Whitesell A.-M. & Silva Romero E., "Multiparty and Multicontract Arbitration: Recent ICC Experience" (2003) ICC ICArb Bull, Special Supplement, p.7.

Wilske S. & Stock M., "Rule 3.3.7 of the IBA Guidelines on Conflicts of Interest in International Arbitration–The Enlargement of the Usual Shortlist?" (2005) ASA Bull Vol.23 No.1, p.45.

Wilske S. & Mackay N., "The Myth of the 'Manifest Disregard of the Law' Doctrine: Is this Challenge to the Finality of Arbitral Awards Confined to U.S. Domestic Arbitrations or Should International Arbitration Practitioners be Concerned?" (2006) ASA Bull Vol.24 No.2, p.216.

Wirth M., "Article 189" in *International Arbitration in Switzerland, An Introduction to and a Commentary on Article 176-194 of the Swiss Private International Law Statute* (Helbing & Lichtenhahn/Kluwer, 2000), p.558.

Wirth M., Rouvinez C. & Knoll J., "The Search for the Truth in Arbitration – Is Finding the Truth What Dispute Resolution is About?" ASA Special Series No. 35 (2011), pp.135–145.

Witt Wijnen O.L.O., Voser N. & Rao N., "Background Information on the IBA Guidelines on Conflicts of Interest in International Arbitration" (2004) Business Law International Vol.5 No.3, p.433.

Wolrich P.M.

— "Techniques for Controlling Time and Costs in Arbitration" (2007) ICC ICArb Bull Vol.18 No.1, p.23.

— "ICC Expertise–The New, Revised ICC Rules for Expertise: A Presentation and Commentary" (2002) ICC ICArb Bull Vol.13 No.2, p.11.

Yesilirmak A., "Interim and Conservatory Measures in ICC Arbitral Practice" (2000) ICC ICArb Bull Vol.11 No.1, p.31.

Zuberbühler T., Müller Ch. & Habbeger Ph., *Swiss Rules of International Arbitration–Commentary* (Kluwer/Schulthess, 2005).

INDEX